W9-AQI-797

The Safe Hiring Manual

The Complete Guide to Employment Screening Background Checks for Employers, Recruiters, and Job Seekers

3rd Edition

By Lester S. Rosen

Facts
ON DEMAND
PRESS

©2017 by BRB Publications, Inc.
Facts on Demand Press
PO Box 27869
Tempe, AZ 85285
800-929-3811

www.brbpublications.com

The Safe Hiring Manual

The Complete Guide to Employment Screening Background Checks for Employers, Recruiters, and Job Seekers

Third Edition

©2017

Written by Lester S. Rosen
Edited by Thomas Ahearn and Michael Sankey
Cover Design by Robin Fox & Associates

BRB Publications, Inc.
PO Box 27869 • Tempe, AZ 85285 • 800.929.3811
ISBN: 978-1-889150-63-5-8

Cataloging-in-Publication Data
(*Provided by Quality Books, Inc.*)

Rosen, Lester S., author.
 The safe hiring manual : the complete guide to
employment screening background checks for employers,
recruiters, and job seekers / by Lester S. Rosen. -- 3rd
edition.
  pages cm
  Includes index.
  ISBN 978-1-889150-63-5

  1. Employee screening. 2. Employee selection.
I. Title.

 HF5549.5.E429R67 2017   658.3'112
                QBI16-90008

From the Author

Educational Purposes Only – Not Legal Advice

The material in this book is presented for educational and informational purposes only and is not offered or intended as legal advice in any manner whatsoever. The materials should not be treated as a substitute for independent advice of counsel.

All policies and actions with legal consequences should be reviewed by your legal counsel. Specific factual situations should also be discussed with your legal counsel. Where sample language is offered, it is only intended to illustrate a potential issue. A sample policy cannot address all specific concerns of a particular company and should not be relied on as legal advice.

For Both Private and Public Employers

This book was written primarily for private employers. However, public employers may also find the information useful as well. However, public employers should keep in mind that some of the legal restrictions placed on private employers may not apply to a public employer. For example, public employers may be allowed by law to consider criminal matters that a private employer could not.

Regarding Updates and Changes to the Content

Updates to this book and important new information can be found online at www.esrcheck.com/The-Safe-Hiring-Manual/Updates.

There is no charge for this service.

Praise for *The Safe Hiring Manual*

"*The Safe Hiring Manual* is **the source** and its author, Les Rosen, is **the authority** on background screening applicants, whether employees or volunteers...Given the complexity of federal and state laws that regulate background screening, you need to be very careful in threading the legal needle. That's why we rely on Les and that's why you need the Safe Hiring Manual, the most comprehensive and up-to-date book on background screening."

Ralph Yanello | Attorney-at-Law

" . . .an extraordinarily detailed and complete book on how HR Depts. can be used to help protect a company from criminal acts and civil liability. . . . Security professionals will benefit from this book in several ways. First, it is an invaluable resource on protecting an organization from a bad hire and it can help security depts. make the case for better screening to senior management. Second, it shows how organizations that ignore due diligence in hiring are leaving themselves exposed to liability. Third, anyone auditing the hiring process, will learn what is legal, what is not, and what is considered best practice."

Security Management
Sept. 2005 (about the First Edition)

"The update of *The Safe Hiring Manual* is very timely because the practice of conducting background checks is facing many challenges with the EEOC's focus on credit checks, education verifications and issuance of their New Guidance on use of Criminal Background Checks as well as many special interest groups advocating for previously incarcerated persons rights. From 'Ban the Box' to expanded expungement of criminal records rights employers are facing an affront on getting information they believe will help them provide a safe workplace, reduce theft, embezzlement, fraud , identify theft, other crimes and to assess overall employee trustworthiness. In this edition of his landmark book Les Rosen provides an insightful mosaic of information that provides clear guidance and every person involved in hiring people needs to read this book."

W. Barry Nixon, SPHR
Executive Director
National Institute for Prevention of Workplace Violence, Inc.

"Hiring employees has never been riskier than it is today. Employers must comply with a myriad of employment and other laws in order to stay compliant and out of court. Once again, Les Rosen, one of the preeminent experts in background searches and accompanying laws hits it out the park with the only book you will ever need to guide you on safe hiring practices. Packed with practical advice in an easy to read format, this book provides you policies, forms, tips to help you understand the data you collect and guidance along the way to make sure you are legally compliant with all avenues of your background checks. Your lawyers will thank you for getting this book!"

Allison West, Attorney-at-Law, SPHR
Trainer/Speaker/Investigator/ HR Consultant
Employment Practices Specialists

"… a comprehensive reference for the critically-important area of applicant/employee background checking/verification in this era of privacy protection and legal liability for bad hiring decisions. The chapters on using proper applications and employment history, by themselves, more than justify purchasing this book and using it to guide during every hiring decision."

Craig Pratt, SPHR
Human Resource Consultant
Craig Pratt and Associates

"The Safe Hiring Manual is a great volume for your professional reference collection, and an even better giveaway for your clients. How often are you trying to explain the legal and diligence searches that are possible for pre-employments? Or the fall-out that occurs when they don't do a background check. The timeliness of this work is seen in the coverage of topics such as FCRA, International background checks, drug checks, identity theft and terrorist searches."

Cynthia Hetherington
www.hetheringtongroup.com/publishing.shtml
Hetherington Information Services, LLC

"The Safe Hiring Manual is the 'bible' of background checks. This should be the textbook for anyone in the background screening industry and everyone involved with the human resource function at any company, large or small. First published in 2004 and revised in 2012, the changing world of background checks is due for Les Rosen's incomparable update. Read it through and then keep it as the ultimate reference guide."

Bruce Berg
President, Berg Consulting Group.
Consulting only to the screening industry.

"The breadth and depth of this new book (like the first two versions) impresses. Employment screening is complex; the FCRA, the DPPA, EEOC, 50 states, international applicants—*The Safe Hiring Manual* helps guide users through these complexities. I would not think about starting or managing a background screening firm without having *The Safe Hiring Manual*. There is no other resource that comes close. Were I the HR Manager or the head of Security of an employer, the book would be dog-eared".

Derek Hinton
President, CRAZoom, Inc.
www.CRAZoom.com

"If you are in charge of talent acquisition or in the business of hiring, this is a must read! The book gives you easy access to set up secure hiring practices and reinforces the importance of checking out candidates, before it is too late. Do your due diligence and read this book - before you hire your next candidate."

Brenda Gilchrist, SPHR
The HR Matrix, LLC

Table of Contents

Acknowledgments

First and foremost, this third edition of the Safe Hiring Manual is dedicated to my wife Donna for her unending support and everything that she does, and my daughter Alex.

This book, in particular, owes a large debt of gratitude to two extremely talented and dedicated individuals: Michael Sankey, CEO of BRB Publications, and Thomas Ahearn, News Editor at Employment Screening Resources (ESR). The book would not have been possible without their professionalism, commitment, and contributions.

My gratitude also extends to a number of people who contributed directly to this edition or previous editions of the Safe Hiring Manual and to my understanding of the area. They include (in alphabetical order): Kerstin Bagus, Tim Baxter, Robert R. Belair, Bruce Berg, Craig Bertschi, Wendy Bliss, Ron S. Brand, Frank A. S. Campbell, Diane Clark, Arthur J. Cohen, Eyal Ben Cohen, Kevin L. Coy, Jim Crockett (ESR Executive Vice President), Dennis DeMay, Pamela Q. Devata, Rod M. Fliegel, Beth Givens, Phillip Gordon, Bruce Guerra (ESR Director of Operations), Barry A. Hartstein, Andy Hellman, Larry D. Henry, Derek Hinton, Stephen J. Hirschfeld, Lewis Maltby, Jennifer L. Mora, W. Barry Nixon, Barbara de Oddone, Kristin L. Oliveira, Scott M. Paler, Kendra Paul, Elaine S. Rosen, Dr. John Schinnerer, Chuck Salvia, and Courtney Stieber. I would also like to acknowledge and thank three people that made invaluable contributions to previous editions of the Safe Hiring Manual and whose work carries over into this edition: Greg Pryor, Esther Lynn Dobrin, and Heather M. Garcia.

To everyone at Employment Screening Resources (ESR), I thank you for your dedication and professionalism. A number of team members at ESR also participated in reviewing chapters, and I would like to acknowledge and thank the following people (in alphabetical order): Alexander Alvarez, Shawnee Baker, Andrew Church, John Cummings, Zavien Fisher, Kelly Funk-Rivera, Adam Herndon, Andre Lapeere, and Heidi Winterble.

A special thanks is extended to Brad Landin, President of ESR, for his review of many of the legal compliance chapters, and for the input of Dawn Standerwick, Vice President of Strategic Growth at ESR and the 2016-17 Chairperson of the National Association of Professional Background Screeners (NAPBS).

In a larger sense, I would like to thank all of the employers, human resources professionals, security and risk management professionals, and members of the screening industry that I have spent time with over the years who have contributed to my understanding of the subject of safe hiring. Especially critical have been the active members and board members past and present of the NAPBS who have raised the degree of professionalism in the screening industry that has created an environment where a book such as this can make a contribution.

Finally, this book is also dedicated to the memory of Carl R. Ernst, a legendary visionary and early pioneer in the area of Public Records and the application of the Fair Credit Reporting Act (FCRA) to background checks.

You have all made this book possible.

Les Rosen
January 2017
Novato, CA

Introduction to *The Safe Hiring Manual*

Who Benefits from this Book?

The Safe Hiring Manual benefits anyone who hires or wants to be hired. More broadly, this book applies to any type of work engagement, including employees, volunteers, independent contractors, temporary workers, contingent workers, and workers in the new so-called *gig economy*.

This book is written for employers who desire to hire the highest quality applicants and to maintain a safe and profitable workplace for everyone's benefit. It is also written to help job applicants understand the processes employers must endure to avoid the legal and financial nightmare of even one bad hiring decision. After all, job applicants do not wish to work in an environment with co-workers who represent a safety risk or who are not qualified or honest.

Human Resources and Security professionals will find these pages contain the needed tools and best practices to obtain and use the needed accurate and actionable information vital to the hiring process. Recruiters and staffing vendors, as well as volunteer, youth, and faith-based organizations, will also gain knowledge and benefit. As you will learn, it is not enough for an organization to merely obtain relevant and accurate information on applicants. The critical point is that the information is obtained, protected, and used legally. The whole area of hiring—and background checks in particular—is heavily controlled by legislation, governmental regulation, and litigation.

This book is a blueprint to help employers identify candidates who may pose a risk to the employer, co-workers, or the public and how to protect a workplace from hiring a person with an unsuitable criminal record, false credentials, or a person intent on harming this country. The critical topic, where information is harder to come by, is how to determine who NOT to hire, and why. No employer wants to hire someone who is unqualified, unsafe, dangerous, or dishonest. This book is a guide on how to avoid a bad hire and create an environment for safe hiring.

What is *Safe Hiring*?

The tools, skills, knowledge, and resources aimed at keeping an unqualified person from the workplace falls under the general term **safe hiring**. Putting everything together in a comprehensive program to exercise due diligence in hiring is referred to as a **Safe Hiring Program or SHP.** A number of themes recur throughout this book:

- From the employer's point of view, one consistent theme is the old adage, "an ounce of prevention is worth a pound of cure." When an employer fails to exercise due diligence in hiring, and just one bad hire slips through, the results can be disastrous. Since the events of 9/11, safe hiring and employment screening have become a greater factor of American life. Just as everyone who goes into an airport is screened to ensure everyone's safety, safe hiring and pre-employment screening protect employers, employees, and the general public alike.

- Another critical theme is that due diligence and safe hiring are not signs that Big Brother has arrived or that privacy and civil liberties are being sacrificed for the sake of security for a few. An essential theme in this book is, as Americans, we need to balance our needs for security in the workplace with fundamental American notions of privacy, fairness, and giving people a second chance. Balance! To quote Benjamin Franklin: "They that can give up essential liberty to obtain a little temporary safety deserve neither liberty nor safety."

- We will look at privacy considerations as well as the proper use of information in a legal and non-discriminatory fashion. A Safe Hiring Program is conducted with the consent of job applicants. You will also learn about criminal records—specifically that a criminal record may not be used automatically to deny employment without a job-related justification to do so. As a society, we want ex-offenders to have jobs in order to become law abiding and tax paying citizens. However, not every ex-offender is a good fit for every job. Chapter 23 contains advice for ex-offenders on how to deal with a past criminal record during the job-hunting process.

Employers have long recognized that many employee problems are caused by problem employees. The goal of this book is to help an employer to not hire a problem employee in the first place. By using this book, you will gain new tools, skills, knowledge, and resources that can be used to implement the very best Safe Hiring Program.

Don't Fall Victim to the *Parade of Horribles*

The process of matching the right person to the right job is a subject that affects nearly everyone – employers, employees, job applicants, and professionals in human resources, security, staffing, and recruiting, as well as the general public – when visiting a business or when a service person enters a home.

The term **Parade of Horribles** is used to describe the negative, undesirable, and unpleasant consequences that can occur if a person fails to do something they should do, or does something they should not. In the world of safe hiring, the Parade of Horribles is the economic and legal fallout that can occur from just one bad hire, as described below.

The following true stories concern **bad hires**—employees who did not undergo proper background screening and who were too unfit, unqualified, and dangerous for their jobs—that caused financial loss, severe damage, and death. These stories also show negative outcomes which may have been prevented with proper pre-employment background checks:

- A carpet-cleaning firm in California hired new employees using the *warm body theory*. If the firm needed to hire someone quick and the applicant claimed relevant experience and looked good to the hiring manager, then no background checking was performed. In 1998, a newly hired employee was immediately sent into homes to clean carpets. Within a month, a horrible event occurred—the new employee committed a brutal murder. The victim was a woman who was having her carpets cleaned. As the facts came out, it became apparent this employee's past employment claims were false. He had been convicted of a violent crime and had been in prison for the past ten years. If the employer had just taken two minutes to pick up the phone and call the supposed past employment references, then the employer would have immediately discovered the applicant's fraudulent past employment claims. Had the employer done a simple background check, it would have raised red flags. A brief phone call or a simple record check would have saved a life. The victim's husband sued the company. The case went to trial, and a jury awarded the victim's family $9.38 million in 2002. After an appeal by the company, the parties eventually settled out of court for an undisclosed amount. (*'How to Avoid Hiring Mishaps'* https://sm.asisonline.org/Pages/how-avoid-hiring-mishaps-005529.aspx.)
- In 2001, a woman was raped and beaten to death in her suburban Florida home, which her killer then set on fire with the intent of destroying any evidence. Six months before her violent death, the victim had contracted with a major department store to have the air ducts in her home cleaned. Unknown to her, both men sent on the service call had criminal records. One of the men, a twice-convicted sex offender on parole, returned to the home six months later to rape and kill her. The tragedy inspired the victim's sister to start 'Sue Weaver C.A.U.S.E. – Consumer Awareness of Unsafe Service Employment' to honor her murdered sister. C.A.U.S.E.'s national awareness campaign educates consumers, employers, and legislators on the necessity of proper annual criminal background checks on workers entering homes or working with vulnerable populations. The Sue Weaver C.A.U.S.E. website is at www.sueweavercause.org.
- A proper *integrity* background check for a C-level executive could have saved investors $340 million they invested in a start-up firm that went bankrupt due to a dysfunctional CEO who was only minimally

background checked. The firm that was developing 'pay by touch' machines for biometric payment at checkout lost $137 million on $600,000 in revenues in 2007 after the CEO engaged in drug abuse, partying, and other excesses, such as instructing his staff to give jobs and shares of stock to women he met. Smart investors, including two billionaires and venture capitalists, were among the people hoodwinked into investing millions of dollars. A nationally known wealth management investment firm continued to ensnare investors, including NFL players, even after the firm was in trouble and even though it did not do a background check. There was plenty in the CEO's past which would have demonstrated that no sensible person would have invested in this endeavor. The *San Francisco Chronicle* uncovered civil judgments and other run-ins that would have been big red flags for rational investors. *(How 'visionary' raised - and lost - a fortune 12/7/2008 at www.sfgate.com/cgi-bin/article.cgi?f=/c/a/2008/12/06/MNIK147QU3.DTL)*

Bad Hires Are a Worldwide Problem

The majority of employers in each of the ten largest world economies have experienced a *bad hire* – when an employee was not a good fit for a job or did not perform the job well – that negatively impacted their business with a significant loss in revenue and productivity. These facts are from a May 2013 survey from CareerBuilder that shows how hiring the wrong person can have serious implications for companies. This global survey, conducted online by Harris Interactive©, included more than 6,000 hiring managers and human resource professionals in countries with the largest gross domestic product (GDP) and produced the following results:

- **Percentage of reported bad hires:** Russia (88%); Brazil (87%); China (87%), India (84%); United States (66%); Italy (66%); United Kingdom (62%); Japan (59%); Germany (58%); and France (53%).
- **Costs of bad hires:** 27 percent of U.S. employers reported a single bad hire cost more than $50,000. In the U.K., 27 percent of companies said a bad hire cost more than 50,000 British pounds. In Indian, 29 percent reported a bad hire cost more than 2 million Indian rupees, and 48 percent of employers in China reported costs exceeding 300,000 CNY.

The impacts of a bad hire include a variety of negative effects such as lost productivity and revenue, negative effects on employee morale and client relations, fewer sales, and the costs to recruit and train another worker. See: www.careerbuilder.com/share/aboutus/pressreleasesdetail.aspx?sd=5%2F8%2F2013&id=pr757&ed=12%2F31%2F2013

So Why Should Employers Use a Safe Hiring Program? — It's Necessary!

How ridiculous is the following?

On a busy downtown street, you look for a person walking by who appears to be reasonable—based on whatever criteria you wish to use for reasonable. You have a five-minute conversation with this person who proceeds to tell you all about him/her. Since this person appears to be sound and reasonable, you say to him/her: "Here are the keys to my house. Come over and walk inside anytime, day or night—my house is your house."

Obviously, no one would hand a total stranger the keys to his or her personal residence. But compare the example above with the current system in place in America for hiring a great many workers:

A worker sends in a resume, which is merely a marketing device whereby an applicant tells an employer only what the applicant chooses to reveal. The applicant comes in for an interview and talks about himself or herself. The interviewer makes a judgment about the person based on whatever criteria the interviewer is using. If the judgment is positive, a hiring decision is made within a short period of time.

Consider the fact that once a worker is hired, this person literally has the keys to your economic house. This person now has access to your clients, co-workers, money, assets, reputation, and even potentially, your very existence as a business. If you make a bad hiring decision, the results can be devastating. At the root of the problem is the fact that one of the most utilized hiring tools in America is simply the use of *gut instinct*.

Ironically, some employers spend more time agonizing over which phone system or copier to buy than who to hire. Yet, if an employer makes a bad purchasing decision the damages a very limited, but with even a single bad hiring decision they may face the dreaded *Parade of Horribles*.

Essential Reasons Why Employers Need a Safe Hiring Program

Ask any labor lawyer, human resource manager, or security professional whether an employer should engage in a Safe Hiring Program using pre-employment background screening. Their response: it is an absolute necessity. The exercise of due diligence is a must in today's environment, and proper due diligence includes verifications, background checks—a complete pre-employment screening.

1. The Economic Fallout from a Bad Hire

With the recent upheaval in the U.S. economy, hiring the right person for the job has become even more crucial for both employers and employees alike. For almost every firm in the United States, the direct cost associated with labor is either the first or second largest line item in a budget. This includes revenues spent for pay, benefits, recruiting, and training. If firms add the cost of managing employees, the figure is even greater. It has been estimated by CFO Research Services that companies spend about 36 percent of their revenues on "human capital." That figure has been even higher in some industries, such as financial services or the pharmaceutical industry. Yet many employers spend more time and effort choosing a copier or deciding between competing brands of laptops than they do in selecting employees.

2. Replacement Costs and Damage Control

The direct economic cost of replacing a single bad hiring decision can be very expensive. Staffing industry sources estimate the cost of a single bad hire can range from twice the yearly salary to a much higher amount, depending upon the position. The time, money, and energy spent recruiting, hiring, and training is wasted, not to mention the amount of time lost from the date a bad hire is identified to when a suitable replacement is trained and in place.

An employer must also consider costs that are hard to quantify, such as loss of productivity, knowledge, know-how, and workflow disruption. With a 10% turnover rate, a firm will spend a substantial amount of its revenue on employee replacements.

Even more difficult to measure are other intangible costs that should also be taken into consideration when calculating the long-term fallout from a bad hiring decision:

- Lost customers or business that can cause damage to a firm's credibility.
- Damage to employee morale and retention of good employees.
- Brand destruction.
- Damage to corporate culture.
- Litigation.

Firms spend millions of dollars to brand their products or services. One bad hire can create irrevocable brand destruction. A fast food worker can contaminate food, or a hotel worker can assault a guest. With just one highly publicized incident, millions of dollars spent building brand identification is lost.

Termination lawsuits, harassment claims, negligent hiring lawsuits, and customer dissatisfaction all undermine a company's finances and reputation. The financial costs to defend these suits can be staggering, and the damage these suits can cause to relationships with customers and employees may cause the business to fail.

3. Litigation and Attorneys' Fees for Bad Hires

If the matter turns into litigation, then the legal fees stemming from a single incident can easily soar into six-figures, and jury awards can be astounding. Employers have a duty of due diligence in hiring, and if their hiring practices cause harm to co-workers or members of the public, an employer can be sued for *negligent hiring*. Employers can be sued for *negligent retention* when they fail to terminate, discipline, or properly supervise an employee after learning that employee is dangerous or unfit. Even the bad employee may sue, claiming wrongful termination.

According to a very detailed legal article on negligent hiring lawsuits:

> "One of the fastest growing areas of tort litigation involves the imposition of liability upon third parties for intentional or criminal acts committed by one person against another." *29 Am Jur Trials, Sec. 1*

This in-depth article was written for the purpose of assisting lawyers who are either suing or defending employers in negligent hiring lawsuits. The fact that how-to books are written expressly for lawyers about negligent hiring cases should be a wake-up call to employers. Safe Hiring is a priority for employers who want to stay out of court.

An example of just how dramatic jury verdicts can be was demonstrated by the 1998 Massachusetts case of *Ward, et al. v. Trusted Health Resources, Inc.* A health care facility failed to check the background of ex-felon Jesse Rogers. The facility had hired Rogers to care for a 32-year-old quadriplegic with cerebral palsy and his 77-year-old grandmother. Weeks after he was removed from the assignment due to failure to consistently show up for work, Rogers murdered both the patient and the grandmother formerly in his care. A jury awarded a $26.5 million dollar verdict.

Believe it or not, the Ward case is not the highest amount awarded in a negligent hiring case. In 2001, a New Jersey jury awarded $40 million in damages to the estate of a home health care patient stabbed to death in her own home by an employee of a home health care provider. This health care provider had not performed a background check even though the attacker has told his employer he had a criminal record. If a background check had been performed, the employer would have also uncovered the soon-to-be murderer's history of mental problems.

Negligent hiring cases are not limited to healthcare. Firms from all industries have been subject to lawsuits and claims of negligent hiring stemming from not only acts of violence but also workplace theft and embezzlement. A firm can be sued for hiring employees who steal confidential information for the purpose of fraud or identity theft, or for hiring a person who harasses his or her co-workers.

These jury verdicts and settlements underscore the legal duty of employers to exercise due diligence in hiring.

Once litigation starts, HR and security managers will find that in addition to their normal duties they now have a second, nearly full-time job—dealing with the discovery process, the learning curve accompanying the litigation process, and managing the ensuing organizational fallout.

4. Workers with Criminal Records and Workplace Violence

Unless a firm engages in due diligence in hiring, **it is a statistical certainty that the firm will eventually hire someone with an unsuitable criminal record**. As we learn later, there must be a special emphasis on the word "unsuitable," since the use of criminal records in hiring is a hot topic. Industry statistics show that as many as ten percent of the applicants who are screened have criminal records. Of course, not all ten percent would necessarily be dangerous or disqualified from being hired. Some of the criminal matters can be for minor acts, or the record may have already been disclosed to the employer. Rules concerning the proper use of criminal records in hiring—including U.S. Equal Employment Opportunity Commission (EEOC) guidance on arrest and conviction records and Ban-the-Box laws that help ex-offenders get a fair chance at employment—are discussed later in this book.

The impact of violence in the American workplace is staggering. The Occupational Safety and Health Administration (OSHA) defines workplace violence as "any act or threat of physical violence, harassment, intimidation, or other threatening and disruptive behavior that occurs at the work site." Workplace violence can range from threats and verbal abuse to physical assaults and homicide. Nearly 2 million American workers report being victims of workplace each year, and many more cases go unreported. More information is available at www.osha.gov/SLTC/workplaceviolence/index.html.

Workplace violence experts have concluded it is difficult to predict ahead of time who will be violent. However, experts have found there is an important common denominator when it comes to workplace violence—a history of past violence. Given the reluctance that many employers have in giving a reference that may reveal past violence, a criminal background check is often the most recommended method to help avoid workplace violence in the future.

5. Effects of Resume Fraud

Industry statistics kept by individual screening firms clearly demonstrate that resume fraud is as high as 40%. In other words, in 2 of every 5 resumes an employer receives, there are material misstatements or omissions that go beyond the acceptable bounds of puffing up a resume. These resumes venture into the world of fantasy, make-believe, and deception. Applicants have the right to put their best foot forward in resumes, but when they are untruthful, there is a problem.

An example of resume fraud can be as simple as claiming to have worked at a job for a longer period as is accurate. There can be outright distortions such as an overstatement of title or inaccurate claims of promotion, e.g. claiming to be a supervisor when the position is really a file clerk. In more extreme instances, some applicants go so far as to entirely make up jobs, degrees, and credentials. There have been high-profile examples of false credentials in resumes, including:

- Scott Thompson, former CEO of Yahoo!, falsely claimed a Bachelor's degree in accounting and computer science from Stonehill College but his degree was in accounting only.
- Ram Kumar, Research Director of Institutional Shareholder Services, falsely claimed a law degree.
- Kenneth Lonchar, former CFO of Veritas, falsely claimed an MBA from Stanford.
- Ron Zarrella, CEO of Bausch & Lomb, falsely claimed an MBA from New York University.
- Bryan Mitchell, Chairman of MCG Capital, falsely claimed a BA in economics from Syracuse University.

The resume fraud issue has also surfaced in the sports world. George O'Leary lost his job as football coach at a major university because he claimed he had an advanced degree that he did not have.

6. Potential Shareholder Suits, Corporate Fraud and Honesty Issues, and Sarbanes-Oxley

It is only a matter of time before publicly-traded firms are the subjects of shareholder lawsuits for loss of value as a result of negligent hiring. A California-based software firm failed to perform a simple background check on its CFO. When it was revealed that the CFO did not, in fact, have an MBA as he claimed, the stock's value plummeted fifteen percent, and a major analyst lowered the rating on the firm's stock from "out-perform" to "neutral." How can a publicly-traded company not justify spending a few minutes and a few dollars in order to make sure there was a qualified, truthful person running their finances?

In the recent business climate, corporate honesty and integrity are also critical issues. Spectacular corporate and financial fraud cases in the past such as those involving Tyco, Enron, and WorldCom have placed emphasis on honesty as a critical element of corporate life. Under the Sarbanes-Oxley Act, publicly-held corporations are now held to a standard of exercising proper control over their financials, which means knowing whom they are hiring. Without a Safe Hiring Program, a firm is at increased risk of finding itself the main subject of the next negative headline.

7. Employee Theft and Fraud

Another reason why employers need to be very concerned about who they hire is employee theft and fraud. Consider these startling facts and figures from the *2016 Report to the Nations on Occupational Fraud and Abuse* from the Association of Certified Fraud Examiners (ACFE):

- The typical organization *loses 5% of annual revenues* to fraud.
- The median loss from a single case of occupational fraud was *$150,000*.
- Occupational fraud caused a total loss of more than *$6.3 BILLION worldwide*.

- More than 23% of occupational fraud cases resulted in *a loss of at least $1 MILLION.*

The ACFE 2016 Report to the Nations, which provides an analysis of 2,410 cases of occupational fraud that occurred in 114 countries throughout the world, is available at www.acfe.com/rttn2016.aspx.

Another reason for concern is embezzlement. As discussed in detail in a later chapter, embezzlers are typically difficult to spot once hired. They often come disguised as the perfect employee. In order to obtain a position of trust, this employee often makes himself or herself indispensable and highly regarded. In order to prevent the embezzlement from being discovered, the embezzler must typically go through extraordinary steps to prevent anyone from finding out what he or she is doing. If an embezzler was to take a vacation or miss a day of work, an employer might discover something amiss.

The bottom line is the best strategy to keep embezzlers, liars, and cheats out of your workplace is safe hiring!

8. The Cost of Firing and the Importance of Documentation

If a firm determines it must terminate an individual, the firm may risk litigation for wrongful termination regardless of the reason for the termination. There will be attorney fees. This explains why some employers have a fear of firing. Consider the following scenario experienced by many firms:

> First, an employer takes steps to avoid the necessity of firing the person. The employer may move the person into a different position, trying to find a position where the employee will do the least harm, or perhaps the employer will place the employee on a 90-day improvement plan. When the employer finally realizes that the employee is not going to work out, the employee is let go. Afterward, the HR or legal department discovers the firm did not sufficiently document the reasons for termination. The next week the former employee files a lawsuit for wrongful termination.

Once a firm recognizes an employee will be terminated, it must begin the process of documenting the reasons. Merely saying, "It just didn't work out," is usually not a sound basis for termination. If the employee happens to be a member of a protected classification under anti-discrimination laws, it is even more critical to be able to document a bona fide business reason for the termination. As a result, it is necessary to take appropriate steps to avoid hiring a problem employee in the first place.

Safe Hiring Includes Following the Right Processes and Legal Compliance

Another critical theme that runs throughout this book is that safe hiring is extremely impacted by legal compliance issues because it involves such a fundamental aspect of society—getting a job. Hiring in general and background checks, in particular, are increasingly subject to legislation, government regulation, and litigation on the national, state, and local levels. For example, the ensuing chapters will cover:

1. **Legislation:** Laws passed regulating the use of credit reports, social media passwords, past salary history, Ban-the-Box and other second chance measures, offshoring data, and a number of other topics.

2. **Regulation:** The Equal Employment Opportunity Commission (EEOC) in its April 2012 Guidance on the use of criminal records has changed the way Americans hire. In addition, two federal agencies that regulate the Fair Credit Reporting Act (FCRA) have been active in the area of background checks: The Federal Trade Commission (FTC) and the Consumer Financial Protection Board (CFPB).

3. **Litigation:** The explosion of lawsuits, particularly class action lawsuits, based upon violations of the FCRA, the federal law that regulates background checks, as well as lawsuits under state law versions of the FCRA, and lawsuits from the EEOC, among others.

The walk-a-way point is that employers who do not engage in due diligence face near-certain legal and financial issues, but on the other hand, the due diligence performed must be conducted properly in accordance with a host of legal considerations. It must be done but done correctly. Background screening is no longer just about pulling data or having technology. The key is legal compliance.

Due Diligence Tells Employers Who NOT to Hire Rather than Who to Hire

This book is not about how to identify, recruit, hire, or retain the best qualified candidates. There are numerous outstanding resources to help employers do this. Rather, the processes in this book assume an employer is looking for the best hire and wants to ensure there is no reason NOT to hire. For example, a background check typically occurs at the end of the hiring process after a finalist has (or finalists have) been identified and an employer is about to make an offer. However, many of the processes in this book help an employer exercise due diligence earlier in the selection process, so while the employer is whittling down a large pool of applicants, dishonest or unsafe applicants may be eliminated from the final pool.

Author Tip

Safe Hiring is NO Laughing Matter

A cartoon on the author's wall shows a terminated employee being escorted out of the building with his box of personal items. As he is leaving, the escort says: "Don't worry. If it is any conciliation, we are also going to fire the idiot who hired you." Unfortunately, a bad hiring decision can also have negative career repercussions for the hiring manager. The HR or security manager can come under fire even if not involved in the hiring decision. One of the goals of this book is to supply the tools so you will not be that 'idiot.'

What Can Employers Do?

Given the enormous price tag of a bad hiring decision, it is no surprise that employers of all sizes are looking to various tools in the hope of boosting the effectiveness of the hiring process. However, the good news is that employers do not need to live through this Parade of Horribles. There is something employers can do—**institute a Safe Hiring Program**.

You Need To Know

Two-Thirds of Organizations Conduct Criminal Background Checks

A 2012 survey from the Society for Human Resource Management (SHRM) found more than two-thirds of organizations surveyed—69 percent—conducted criminal background checks on all of their job candidates. Key findings of the survey include:

- 62 percent of organizations conducting criminal background checks initiated them after a contingent job offer while 32 percent conducted them after an interview.

- 52 percent of organizations conducting criminal checks on candidates to reduce legal liability for negligent hiring while 49 percent conducted them to ensure a safe work environment for employees.

- 69 percent of organizations conducted criminal checks on job candidates for positions with fiduciary and financial responsibilities while 66 percent conducted them on job candidates who would have access to highly confidential employee information.

More information about this SHRM survey on background checks is available at www.shrm.org/Research/SurveyFindings/Articles/Pages/CriminalBackgroundCheck.aspx.

CHAPTER 1

Establishing a Safe Hiring Program

A fact of business life is **employee problems are often caused by problem employees**. Each new hire represents an enormous investment and potential risk to an employer. Ironically, many employers spend more time, energy, and money shopping for a new piece of office equipment than they do on a new hire. Also, as shown in the *Introduction*, bad hires are a worldwide problem.

Why Safe Hiring is Such a Challenge

Every employer assumes a large invisible burden when hiring workers. That burden is the obligation—the duty—to exercise reasonable care for the safety of others. The legal description of the duty of care is called **due diligence.** The employer's duty to exercise due diligence means the employer must consider if a potential new employee represents a risk to others in view of the nature of the job. The duty also extends to supervision, training, and retention once hired. Sadly, there are many employers who either do nothing or very little about due diligence during the hiring process.

Employers of all sizes know that just one bad hire can create a legal and financial nightmare. Employers need to take reasonable efforts to avoid allowing a *bad hire*—someone who is too unfit, dishonest, unqualified, disruptive, or dangerous for the job—from even entering the workforce in the first place. If a bad hire manages to get through the front door in the first place, employers can be held liable for negligent supervision or negligent retention.

Although everyone agrees that safe hiring and due diligence are missions critical for any business, there are numerous challenges facing employers who wish to establish safe hiring practices in their workplace. Here is a quick look at some of the issues facing employers:

1. There Are No Magical Tools That Find an Honest Person

In the wake of the financial meltdown and home mortgage crisis, and what appears to many to be a general deterioration of corporate ethics and morality, more emphasis is now placed on the age-old question asked by Greek philosopher Diogenes: *How do you find an honest person?*

Part of the challenge in safe hiring is that by definition, employers are seeking an elusive quality. Ultimately, the ability to find an honest person depends on the correct use of a number of overlapping tools. These include: 1) a number of objective fact-finding tools such as pre-employment screening and reference checks, 2) tools used to convince applicants to be self-revealing (applications and interviews), 3) a variety of assessment tools that are now available to employers, and 4) to a subjective extent, instinct and intuition. However, reliance only on instinct and intuition can be dangerous. Consider this fact—every dishonest person ever hired was sized up by someone and deemed a good fit for the job.

2. It is Almost Impossible to Spot Deception at Interviews

Even if Diogenes had found an honest person, there is a body of modern evidence that suggests it is difficult for anyone, from ancient philosophers to modern day employers, to use an interview to determine who is really who. Employers have a distinct challenge when it comes to spotting those attempting to deceive. Industry statistics suggest that as many as 40% of all job applicants falsify information about their credentials. There is also scientific evident to suggest that even if the honest person appeared for an interview, it might be difficult, if not nearly impossible, for an average employer or Human Resources professional to even detect who is honest or dishonest. There is now a body of scientific evidence to suggest the human beings are not nearly as good as they think they are in determining who is honest or dishonest, so trying to spot the dishonest applicants at interviews is difficult if not impossible. (See Chapter 3 for more information on this subject.)

3. Compliance with Hiring Laws

Certainly, all citizens have a reasonable expectation of privacy and a right to be treated fairly; yet, at the same time, an employer has the right to make diligent and reasonable job-related inquiries into a person's background so that the company, its employees, and the public are not placed at risk. Employers need to know if there are facts about an applicant that are either job related or run contrary to a "business necessity," such as creating an unacceptable risk factor. Laws associated with hiring and the employment screening processes have sought to achieve a balance between privacy and fairness on the one hand, and due diligence and business necessity on the other. Since laws can and do vary from one state to another, multi-state employers are faced with a difficult task of staying up-to-date with all the legal obstacles to keep the hiring process within specified legal boundaries.

4. There is No Instant Database That Gives All the Answers

Unfortunately, there is no magic database in existence for employers to use. There is no national credentials database where an employer can instantly confirm an applicant's past employment or education. There is no public record database where an employer can instantly find out if the applicant has a criminal record, a problematic driving record, or a job-related civil lawsuit. It would be helpful if there was a magic website called *www.ShouldIHireThisPersonOrNot.com,* where an employer received an instant answer, but that just does not exist and is unlikely to do so in the foreseeable future.

Some employers have been given the legal authority to obtain government criminal records when filling positions involving security or access to groups at risk. In many states, for positions involving access to vulnerable patients or children, screeners for hospitals and school districts can submit applicants' fingerprints to be checked by the FBI or state authorities. However, as discussed in later chapters, even that database does not have all the answers for employers.

5. The Effects of Corporate Culture and Other Impediments

At some firms, efforts at safe hiring may be impeded by the simple fact that it has not been done historically. Some employers are still reluctant to engage in background screening out of a concern that an applicant may find it insulting. There is, even more, reluctance to perform screening for higher-level positions, especially positions with a "C" in the title, such as CEO or CFO. The higher a person is in the organization, the more harm that person can potentially do to that organization. Internationally, the idea of background checks is just not part of the cultural norm in many countries.

The Anatomy of a Safe Hiring Program (SHP)

The best way for employers to make one of the most critical decisions in their business is to institute a **Safe Hiring Program (SHP)**. The definition of a Safe Hiring Program is: *A series of policies, practices, and procedures designed to minimize the probability of hiring dangerous, questionable, or unqualified candidates, while at the same time helping to identify those candidates who are capable, trustworthy, and best suited to the job requirements.*

A Safe Hiring Program should consist of **Four SHP Core Competencies** that encompass specific, customized steps for employers to use when facing the inherent challenges during the hiring process. See the flowchart to follow.

Components of the Four Core Competencies of a Safe Hiring Program (SHP)

---

1. Organizational Infrastructure
Organizational commitment to a Safe Hiring Program including the development of training policy and procedures. Use of the S.A.F.E System (see below) sets in place the critical Policies, Practices, and Procedures necessary for a Safe Hiring Program.

↓

---

2. Initial Screening Practices

Implementation of the A.I.R. Process (Application, Interview, & References - Chapter 3) which begins with the first job announcement or advertisement. The Sorting and Weeding Stages include intake of resumes and CVs; verification of candidate-provided statements and information; and notification of candidates regarding status (which may include conditional selection contingent on a background check).

↓

3. In-Depth Screening Practices

After making a decision on who to hire, this stage is part of an employer's due diligence to determine if there is any reason NOT to hire the person. Further research and review of candidate's statements and past. These practices include a criminal record check and other tools described throughout this book.

↓

4. Post-Hire Practices

Continued commitment to maintaining a safe workplace.

You Need To Know

The Compliance Issue

For the Four Core Competencies to be lawful, each one must be in compliance with federal and state laws. Important criminal records issues for employers include Ban-the-Box laws as well as compliance with federal and state discrimination laws.

Compliance with federal and state laws is emphasized throughout this book with in-depth facts and advice on best practices. Each Legal Compliance Chapter contains detailed information per the subject.

A Safe Hiring Program Must Be an Integral Part of a Business

A Safe Hiring Program must be part of the fabric of how a firm operates its businesses. The SHP:

- Dictates the types of precautions to be taken, and sets limits for eligibility for employment.
- Incorporates screening and selection procedures, clearly stating qualifiers and disqualifiers.
- Utilizes a series of overlapping tools, recognizing that no one tool is perfect.
- Recognizes that due diligence requires multiple approaches.

Moreover, a Safe Hiring Program:

- Maps out the events in the hiring process.
- Dictates policy in order to ensure all candidates are treated equally and fairly.
- Establishes legally defensible practices for dealing with undesirable or potentially problematic applicants.
- Is comprised of practices supported by documented procedures.
- Must show compliance with federal and state laws.

All relevant departments and personnel must be familiar with—and committed to—their company's Safe Hiring Program. Only then will a Safe Hiring Program show **due diligence**.

The above sounds well and good, but how does one start?

The first step is deciding to incorporate the elements of the S.A.F.E. System and the AIR Process into an overall Safe Hiring Program and to implement these elements. In this way, large organizations can ensure that hiring managers within different divisions, and even different physical locations, follow the same procedures.

The second step is to work with a reputable pre-employment screening agency to guide and ensure that your screening practices and legal compliance practices will stand up in court.

About the Pre-Employment Screening Process

A key term presented throughout this book is *pre-employment screening* or as it is sometimes called *employment screening*. This process is also referred to as *background checks*. The background screening occurs towards the END of the hiring cycle, at the point where the employer has used in-house processes to narrow down the applicant field to decide who they tentatively want to hire. A background check is an additional due diligence tool to assist an employer in determining if there is a reason NOT to hire a finalist for a position. Background checks are not used to identify candidates to hire, but to confirm there is no reason not to hire.

Pre-employment screening is but one critical part of the total approach to a Safe Hiring Program. The background screen occurs when an employer or an outside professional firm assembles information such as criminal records, credit reports, or credentials verifications on an applicant. Many employers mistakenly believe that safe hiring is a process that is typically outsourced to a screening firm or investigator. This is likely the result of many employers who think that in order to show due diligence, they merely need to pay others to perform background checks and criminal record searches. These employers erroneously view pre-employment screening as a process that begins after a hiring manager selects an applicant and submits the name to the company's security or human resources department, or they choose to outsource the process by calling an employment screening firm to do the background report or the screening.

In fact, safe hiring begins with the employer's internal hiring process well before the background check. An employer who engages in safe hiring program should find that a background check seldom reveals information that is inconsistent, negative or derogatory. A company that has solid hiring practices will normally have eliminated problem candidates before they even reach the point of having a background check. In fact, the Safe Hiring process occurs even before recruiting for a position starts. As seen in later chapters, a well-written job description is a central tool in hiring the right person.

Four Benefits of a Safe Hiring Program

A Safe Hiring Program will help employers substantially minimize risk to their businesses. The Program requires taking appropriate steps toward the development of policies and countermeasures before the hiring process begins. Properly implemented, a Safe Hiring Program helps employers in four key ways.

1. Provides Deterrence

Making it clear that screening is part of the hiring process can deter potentially problematic applicants and discourage applicants with something to hide. An applicant with a serious criminal history that is inconsistent with the needs of the job or falsified information on his or her resume is less likely to apply at a firm that announces pre-employment background checks are part of the hiring process. Do not become the employer of choice for people with problems when simply having a screening program can deter those problem applicants. However, as discussed in Chapter 10, an employer should be mindful of the proper and non-discriminatory use of criminal records.

2. Encourages Honesty

The goal of a safe hiring program is not to find "perfect" candidates. Many job-seekers with blemished records may still be well-suited for employment. Few employers enjoy the luxury of choosing only from a pool of perfect candidates. However, employers need to be fully informed when making hiring decisions. Having a Safe Hiring Program encourages applicants to be especially forthcoming in their interviews. Making it clear that background checks are part of the hiring process is strong motivation for applicants to be open, honest, and truthful.

3. Yields More Factual Information

Although intuition can play an important role in hiring, basing a decision on solid information is more reliable and safer. Effective screening obtains factual information about candidates to supplement interview impressions. It is also a valuable tool for judging the accuracy of a candidate's resume. Facts limit uncertainty in the hiring process. As the old saying goes, an employer can "trust, but verify."

4. Promotes Due Diligence

Implementing a Safe Hiring Program helps employers practice due diligence in their hiring. Having an SHP is a powerful defense in the event of a negligent hiring lawsuit, and understanding how due diligence is associated with liability for negligent hiring is critical for any employer. If a bad hire results in a legal action, then an employer must show that it utilized appropriate measures of due diligence.

Firms that do not perform due diligence are sitting ducks for litigation, including attorneys' fees and big damage awards. Employers who implement and follow a Safe Hiring Program show due diligence measures that are a powerful legal protection. Fortunately for these employers, the cost of exercising due diligence through a SHP is very modest. Even if there is a cost involved, employers need to measure the risk of hiring blind with the considerable and near certain risk of litigation and attorney fees stemming from a single bad hiring decision. As another old saying goes, it is a matter of "paying now or paying later."

In addition, a SHP protects employers when bad hires slip through. Despite an employer's best efforts, there is always the possibility someone will be hired which may result in a lawsuit. Employers who can demonstrate to a jury that due diligence was maintained as part of a SHP will have a powerful defense against a lawsuit.

Introduction to Due Diligence and Negligent Hiring

Question: What is a term that can be used to describe an employer who fails to exercise due diligence in the hiring process?

Answer: The term is **defendant,** who is the party who is sued for damages in a civil lawsuit for failure to perform a legal duty.

When an employer fails to exercise due diligence and a person is harmed by an employee, that employer can be sued. The name of the legal action is called **negligent hiring**, sometimes referred to as **the negligent hiring doctrine**. Under the doctrine of *co-employment*, liability for the acts of a worker may not even be limited to just employees. An independent contractor or a worker sent from a staffing vendor can also potentially land a business in hot water.

Negligent hiring is the flip side of due diligence. If an employer hires someone who they knew—or in the exercise of reasonable care *should have known*—was dangerous, dishonest, unfit, or unqualified for the position, and it was reasonably foreseeable that some sort of injury could happen to someone as a result, then the employer can be sued for negligent hiring. This is called *the knew or reasonably should have known standard*.

Obviously, most employers will not hire someone they know for a fact is dangerous or unfit for a job. It is the *should have known* part that gets employers into difficulties. As a general rule, employers should assume that a jury may find that if an employer COULD have known the applicant was unsafe, dangerous, unfit, or dishonest, the employer SHOULD have known. For many jurors, *could have known* is the same as *should have known*.

The threat of being sued for negligent hiring is far from theoretical. As discussed in the Introduction, lawsuits for negligent hiring are a significant concern for employers. Business can be hit with multi-million dollar jury verdicts and settlements as well as enormous attorneys' fees, and the odds seem to be against an employer.

Author Tip ▷ ### Negligent Hiring—How Big of a Threat?

The argument has been made that the threat of negligent hiring lawsuits has been overblown since the reported cases do not show a great many such decisions. However, that argument may miss the point. First, a great many negligent hiring lawsuits end up getting settled out of court, and therefore would not be the subject of a reported jury verdict or appeals court decision. Often times in litigation, the risks are too high and the parties have an incentive to settle. Secondly, even if they do not occur frequently, just the threat that the lawsuits can be brought presents a significant risk-management consideration for employers. Even if an employer eventually wins the lawsuit, it comes at a great cost which can include attorney's fees and damage to reputation. However, as seen below, experts in the area caution employers against overreacting to negligent hiring concerns to the point of unfair exclusion of applicants with criminal records.

Negligent Hiring a Legitimate Concern but Fear of Liability Can Be Overstated

By Lewis Maltby, President, National Workrights Institute

Negligent hiring liability is a legitimate concern, but employers don't need to turn down every applicant with a criminal record. Negligent hiring cases are relatively uncommon; most employers have never seen one. Almost all negligent hiring awards involve employees whose prior offenses were crimes of violence. Unless a job involves access to customers' or clients' valuable property, hiring an applicant with a property crime conviction poses little risk. D.U.I. or drug convictions create little risk of liability unless the job involves operating a motor vehicle or controlled substances.

Employers who try to escape this risk entirely by refusing to hire anyone with a criminal record are likely to face liability under Title VII because of the discriminatory impact of such a policy. In addition, when almost a third of job seekers have a record, refusing to consider them will cause employers to lose valuable employees.

Employers' best course is to conduct a record check, but disqualify the applicant only when hiring them would create a predictable risk that outweighs the positive aspects of their background and experience.

Lewis Maltby is president of the National Workrights Institute, a 501(c)(3) research and advocacy organization specializing in employment issues. He is the author of "Can They Do That?: Retaking Our Fundamental Rights in the Workplace." The National Workrights Institute website is at http://workrights.us/.

Keep in mind that if a negligent hiring case is brought, the plaintiff's attorney is likely working on a contingency fee basis, which means the attorney representing the injured party only gets paid if the plaintiff prevails through a settlement or trial and receives a percentage of the award of damages. Consequently, the plaintiff's attorney has an incentive to only take serious cases with substantial monetary damages. That means the case will likely be about a serious injury or occurrence. In the most extreme case, the victim may not even be in court if he or she was killed as a result of some alleged failure on the part of the employer. In that case, the victim's family is normally the plaintiff in what is called a *wrongful death case.*

In addition, the reality is that cases brought against employers are generally not decided by a jury of *peers* in the sense that it is unlikely that there will be 12 business owners, private investigators, or human resources professionals on the jury. The jury is likely to be composed primarily of men and women who have been employees, and anyone with any HR experience will likely be "thanked and excused" during the jury selection process. As a result, an employer will face a jury that may well believe that the employer had the resources, opportunity, staffing, and duty to conduct proper due diligence. Certainly, the victim of whatever crime or act that gave rise to the lawsuit had no opportunity to exercise due diligence.

In other words, if an employer is sued, that employer will have some explaining to do. In addition, an employer may find that an inordinate amount of time is required when involved in a lawsuit. Not only may there be numerous requests for all sorts of documents, but hours may be spent in preparing employees for depositions or court appearances.

See The Addendum ⟩ **More Information about Negligent Hiring and Case Law Examples**

Negligent hiring is a complex topic. The Addendum contains more information about negligent hiring, including:

- How parties prove negligent hiring.
- What is meant by *Standard of Care* for employers.
- The essential elements of a negligent hiring claim.
- Successful and unsuccessful defenses to claims of negligent hiring.
- How to avoid negligent hiring.

What the Safe Hiring Program Does NOT Do

Although it is important to understand the benefits of a Safe Hiring Program, it is also important to be clear about what the SHP does not do. While a properly implemented program can considerably minimize the risk of hiring a problem employee, it does not guarantee that every person with an undisclosed criminal record or false credential will be identified.

The world's experts on background screening and pre-employment investigations are probably the FBI and the CIA. They spend millions on pre-hiring investigations and have access to much more information than a private employer. Yet, from time to time, newspapers report stories about bad hires by the FBI and the CIA. If the world's experts do not have a 100% success rate with millions of dollars to spend and full access to governmental databases, what chance do private employers have? That is another reason why it is critical to document that an employer has exercised due diligence. Even if a bad hire somehow gets through the door, the employer can still show that it took reasonable steps to prevent that from happening.

As the term suggests, background screening is a large-scale process that operates on a cost/benefit basis. Employers look to confirm known information (such as past employment or education) or do quick and cost-effective checks of readily available public documents, such as criminal records.

However, background screening for employment purposes is not meant to be a full investigation, where investigators develop leads and intensely focus on individuals. Rather, private investigators focus on one person (as opposed to a group) and do in-depth examinations (as opposed to using diagnostic tools) where the information is either hidden or not readily apparent. Thus, investigations are typically much more expensive than background screenings.

By its very nature, background screening is not foolproof. Given that screening is relatively inexpensive, employers cannot expect a failsafe process. However, screening is extremely effective in keeping the workplace safe, productive, and reasonably trouble-free. Moreover, screening demonstrates due diligence which is important in the case of litigation.

The Return on Investment (ROI) of a Screening Program

Employers justify the costs associated with employment screening with the clear Return on Investment, or ROI, that these programs bring to the workplace.

Two costs are associated with a screening program. First, is the cost of the in-house time and effort needed to pursue a Safe Hiring Program; second, the cost of any outsourced services such as background checks. These costs will be covered in greater detail in a later section. In the meantime, let us assume as a general rule, the cost of a background screening is likely less than the cost of an employee's salary on just his or her first day on the job. Of course, the depth of screening, and therefore the costs, will vary depending upon the job position. Screening for a janitorial position, for example, will likely cost less than that for an executive. Since executives are more highly paid, however, the cost of a screening as a percentage of salary is still less than their first-day salary.

Two Approaches to Calculating ROI

Because the purpose of background screening is to prevent harm, it is often difficult to quantify the ROI of events that did not happen. A firm hit with even a single incident of workplace violence or related legal action immediately recognizes the advantages of a Safe Hiring Program.

Method One: Making a Judgment as to the Value of Avoiding the Parade of Horribles

Assume an average background check performed by a third party firm is $50, and a firm submits 100 names to a screening firm during a twelve month period. Keep in mind that most employers only screen finalists, not all who apply. The third-party costs of this service would be $5000.

If a firm can avoid just one problem employee as a result of a background check, the $5000 cost of the screening program was more than worth it. Just one bad hire can exceed the cost of an applicant's yearly salary. Given industry statistics that suggest up to 40% of all applicants contain potential issues, it is likely that a background check would save an employer a great deal of time, money, and grief in terms of a bad hire. Given the negative impact that even one bad hire can cause, it would appear to be a very small price to pay.

Method Two: Calculation of Benefit from Lack of Turnover

The benefits of a Safe Hiring Program can also be measured by estimating the average costs associated with a single employee turnover. An easy way to consider these costs is by building a *turnover calculator* that breaks down all the costs associated with having and filling a vacancy on an item-by-item basis. When the expenses involved are broken down to basics, it is easy to see how such costs can add up to a sizeable figure.

Turnover Cost Calculator Form

An example of a *Turnover Cost Calculator Form* appears in the Addendum.

Responses to 10 Commonly Expressed Concerns of Employers

Even with all of the advantages of a Safe Hiring Program, many employers have questions and concerns about implementing safe hiring and background checks. Here are the ten most common concerns that employers express regarding safe hiring or a screening program.

1. Is a Safe Hiring Program Legal?

Employers have an absolute right to select the most-qualified candidate for a job. The only limitations on employers are those that employers should already understand and abide by in all of their workplace policies. For example, employers must ensure that all selection procedures and tools are non-discriminatory, are based upon factors that are valid predictors of job performance, and do not invade privacy rights or other laws. A Safe Hiring Program easily falls within these limitations. If a firm utilizes a pre-employment screening agency, a federal law called the Fair Credit Reporting Act (FCRA) balances the right of an employer to know who they hire with the applicant's rights of disclosure and privacy. Under this law, the employer first obtains the applicant's written consent to be screened. In the event negative information is found, the applicant must be given the opportunity to correct the record. Employers should set up a consistent policy so similarly situated applicants are treated the same. A qualified screening company will assist an employer with legal compliance issues. The FCRA is examined in detail in Chapter 5.

2. Does Safe Hiring Invade Privacy?

No. Employers can obtain information regarding what an applicant has done in his or her public life. For example, checking court records for criminal convictions or calling past employers or schools does not invade a zone of personal privacy. Employers are looking only at information that is a valid and non-discriminatory predictor of future job performance. As a general rule, employers will not ask for any information that they could not obtain in face-to-face interviews. Employers should also take steps to maintain confidentiality within their organization, such as isolating personnel reports from those of a more general nature. Most background firms offer internet systems with secured websites to maintain privacy. These new systems also mean that employers do not need to collect Personally Identifiable Information (PII) such as the applicant's date of birth or Social Security number (SSN). Those are collected securely online by the screening firm. Although social media searches and credit reports can approach a zone of privacy, employers and screening firms can take steps to protect job applicants. In addition, employers and screening firms can follow best practices to keep PII safe and secure.

3. Is Safe Hiring Cost-Effective?

In a Safe Hiring Program, the cost to select one new employee will typically be less than the cost of that new employee on his or her first day on the job. That is pocket change compared to the damage that one bad hire can cause. In addition, if an employer utilizes an outside agency, the service is typically used only to screen an applicant if an employer has extended a conditional job offer or the applicant is a candidate for an offer. Employers certainly do not screen all applicants but only finalists. It is ironic that some firms will spend hours shopping for a computer bargain; yet, at the same time, try to save money by not adequately checking out a job applicant, which represents an enormous investment. As emphasized in this book, problem employees usually cause employee problems, and money is well spent to avoid problems in the first place.

4. Does Safe Hiring Discourage Good Applicants?

Employers who engage in a safe hiring program do not find that good applicants are deterred. Job applicants have a desire to work with qualified and safe co-workers in a profitable environment. A good candidate understands background screening is a sound business practice that is commonplace in today's business environment and is not an invasion of privacy or an intrusion. A good background firm is keenly aware of the importance of employer branding, which includes making the applicant's experience as seamless and intuitive as possible. Background checks are now seamlessly interwoven into Applicant Tracking Systems and mobile devices. See later chapters on the applicant experience.

5. Does Background Screening Delay Hiring?

No. Background screening is normally done in 48 to 72 hours. Most of the necessary information is obtained from court records or by contacting previous employers or schools. Occasionally there can be delays beyond anyone's control, such as previous employers who will not return calls, schools that are closed for vacation, or a court clerk who needs to retrieve a record from archive storage.

In addition, with advances in technology, the process has speeded up considerably. Gone are the days of filling out or faxing paper forms or even filling out data online. Advanced screening firms are able to initiate a background check just with an applicant's name and email, where the applicant gets an email alert with all of the necessary legal consents and disclosures and online forms to fill out that provides for an electronic signature.

Furthermore, an organization that is careful in its hiring practices should find a lower rate of negative hits during background checks. As discussed in later chapters, there are a number of steps a firm should take to ensure safe hiring well before a name is submitted to a background screening company. These techniques include making it clear that your firm does background checks in order to weed out bad applicants, knowing the red flags to look for in an application, and asking questions in interviews that will help filter out problem candidates.

6. Does Safe Hiring have to be Outsourced to be Effective?

Not at all. In fact, the most effective safe hiring tools are completed in house and cost nothing. A company that takes the time to thoroughly develop an application process, an interview process, and a reference checking process receives a great deal of protection. Many employers do outsource part of the task, such as criminal record checks, because of the specialized skills, knowledge, and resources that are involved. Typically these tasks, although vital, are not part of an employer's core expertise and can be performed by a third party more quickly and efficiently allowing the employer to focus on those tasks that keep its business productive and profitable.

7. If a Company Outsources the SHP, Is It Difficult to Implement?

Even for an overburdened HR, security, or risk management department already handling numerous tasks, outsourcing background screening can be done quickly and effectively. A qualified pre-employment screening firm can set up the entire program and provide all the necessary forms and training in a short time. Many firms have internet-based systems that speed up the flow of information and allow employers to track the progress of each applicant in real time. As technology improves, background checks can be seamlessly integrated into an employer's Applicant Tracking System (ATS) or other online tools.

8. How is a Background Check Service Provider Selected if All or Part of the SHP is Outsourced?

Employers should apply the same criteria they would use in selecting any other providers of critical professional services. Employers should look for a professional partner and not just an information vendor selling data at the lowest price. For example, if an employer were choosing a law firm for legal representation, it would not merely select the cheapest—the employer would clearly want to know it is selecting a firm that is competent, experienced, and knowledgeable, as well as reputable and reasonably priced. The same criteria should also apply to critical HR services. A background screening firm should have an understanding of the legal implications of background checks, particularly the federal Fair Credit Reporting Act. A list of screening firms that have voluntarily agreed to an industry code of ethics by joining the National Association of Professional Background Screeners (NAPBS) is available at www.napbs.com. Employers can also choose to select a background screening firm that has formally achieved accreditation from the NAPBS Background Screening Credentialing Council (BSCC) for successfully completing the requirements of the Background Screening Agency Accreditation Program (BSAAP). An even higher level of security that some background screening firms choose to achieve is to undergo a yearly audit for SSAE 16 SOC 2® Type 2 compliance which confirms a firm meets high standards set by the American Institute of Certified Public Accountants (AICPA) for protecting the security, confidentiality, and privacy of the systems and consumer information used to process background checks. How to select a background screening firm is discussed in more detail later in this book.

9. Does a Company Risk Being Sued by an Applicant?

Unfortunately, anyone can go to the courthouse and sue anybody. As a practical manner, background screening—as with anything related to employment—has become a matter of legal compliance. Employers need to always be concerned about governmental regulation, legislation, and litigation. However, on a risk/management basis, the advantages of performing pre-employment screening clearly outweigh the possibility that an applicant may sue. It is an absolute certainty that, without screening, an employer becomes the employer of choice for everyone with a problem, and will unwittingly hire unsuitable applicants with false credentials. An employer can be protected by following certain basic guidelines in a fair and legal screening program.

10. Is It Worth the Time and Energy to Even Think About Safe Hiring, Given Everything Else an Employer Has To Do?

Since the fundamental rule in running a business of any size is that employee problems stem from problem employees—it is time and money well spent to avoid hiring a problem in the first place. If there is an incident of embezzlement, theft of trade secrets, workplace violence, or litigation due to a bad hire, a firm would want to have paid almost anything to have avoided the bad hire in the first place. Use of a legally sound screening program can protect against the vast majority of employee issues.

Both employers and applicants have learned that pre-employment screening is an absolute necessity in today's business world. More importantly, we have learned that due diligence in hiring is a way to keep businesses safe and profitable in difficult economic times.

Getting Started on a Safe Hiring Program

Having reviewed the advantages of a Safe Hiring Program, the next logical question is: how to get started? The key is to implement the first Core Component, which is:

> *An organizational commitment to a Safe Hiring Program, including the development of training policy and procedures. Use of the S.A.F.E System sets in place the critical Policies, Practices, and Procedures necessary for a Safe Hiring Program.*

The first step is deciding to incorporate the elements of the S.A.F.E. System and the AIR Process into an overall Safe Hiring Program and to implement the elements of the program. In this way, large organizations ensure that hiring managers within different divisions, and even different physical locations, follow the same procedures. Small and Medium Businesses (SMB) can ensure they are utilizing Policies, Practice, and Procedures to hire the best and avoid bad hires. The second step is to work with a reputable pre-employment screening agency for guidance and to ensure that your screening practices and legal compliance practices are legal. That will be discussed in more detail later in the book.

The Elements of the S.A.F.E. System

As stated previously, having an organizational commitment and structure is the creative driving force behind a Safe Hiring Program. The Organizational Structure depends on the *S.A.F.E. System*. S.A.F.E. stands for:

S—Set-up a safe hiring program consisting of documented policies, practices, and procedures.
A—Acclimate and train all people with safe hiring responsibilities including hiring managers.
F—Facilitate and implement the safe hiring program.
E—Evaluate and audit the safe hiring program.

By evaluating and auditing the Safe Hiring Program, organizations can make sure the people responsible understand that their compensation and advancement is judged in part by the attention they pay to the hiring process. Organizations typically accomplish those things that are measured, audited, and rewarded. Let us take a look at each element:

S = Set-up a Program of Policies and Procedures to be Used throughout the Organization

This is done in four steps:

1. **Establish Authority**—For any program to succeed, someone in the organization must have both the responsibility and the authority to carry out the program. Unless someone is firmly accountable and holding others accountable, it is hard to succeed.

2. **Clarify Policies** — Have internal policies and procedures in place. A sample policy memorandum is contained in this chapter.

3. **Perform the First Elements for Safe Hiring**—The critical elements are the Application, Interview, and Reference Checking Process, also called the ***AIR (Application, Interview & Reference Checking) Process***. These are done within an organization and are a matter of training and commitment. Typically it is not a line item in the budget.

4. **Conduct Criminal checks**—Once an applicant has gone through the AIR Process, a criminal check program can then be conducted along with other due diligence checks.

A = Acclimate/Train All Persons with Safe Hiring Responsibilities, Especially Hiring Managers

It is recommended that each hiring manager go through training on the AIR (Applicant, Interview & References) process. The program would reinforce the importance of safe hiring and pre-employment screening, demonstrate how to implement the AIR Process, and convey to hiring managers why it personally matters to them that due diligence is demonstrated in the hiring process. It is critical that all training be documented, to eliminate potential charges, in the event of a lawsuit, that training was inadequate.

F = Facilitate/Implement the Program

Each hiring manager should be provided with a Safe Hiring checklist that goes into every applicant file. This checklist makes it easier for hiring managers to follow the program since it creates a routine and provides a clear audit trail. The elements on the checklist may vary for each employer. (A sample checklist is attached at the end of this chapter.)

E = Evaluate and Audit the Program

As a general rule, members of an organization accomplish those things that are clearly measured, audited, and rewarded. As a result, a Safe Hiring Program will be most effective if hiring managers clearly understand they will be audited periodically on how well they implement and follow the system. If regional and division managers routinely ask to see a number of files in order to ensure the Safe Hiring checklists are in the file, then the hiring managers will quickly understand this is something they must do. Compliance with the system must be part of a hiring manager's evaluation for purposes of salary and promotion. In turn, the regional managers must be held accountable by their supervisors who make sure they are checking. The audit trail must go to the top. Only then will every member of the company understand that safe hiring is, in fact, a priority.

You Need To Know ▷

Defining Key Terms: Policy, Practice, and Procedure

Public records and screening expert Carl R. Ernst describes Policies, Practice, and Procedures:

Policy: A policy is a general statement of a principle according to which a company performs business functions. A company does not need to maintain policies in order to operate. However, practices and procedures that exist without the underpinnings of a consistent policy are continually in jeopardy of being changed for the wrong reasons, with unintended legal consequences.

Practice: A practice is a general statement of the way the company implements a policy. Good practices support policy. To implement the policy statement example above, your company could establish a practice of validating the existence and currency of the registered entity on the public record.

Procedure: A procedure documents an established practice. Use of forms is one of the useful ways procedures are documented. For a company that has a practice of checking past court records for criminal records, the procedures would be the documentation on how it is done, as well as the documents showing it was done.

Policies, practices, and procedures that are not in writing are worthless. To the extent that policies, practices, and procedures are documented in writing, it is possible to independently verify from the procedure whether employees are conforming to the practice, and therefore to the policy. This kind of documentation makes it easy to perform reliable audits. However, if policies and practices are not documented in writing, the only documentation available are the results of actions of employees documented in paper output, such as copies of filings, search requests and search reports, and vendor invoices. In addition, it is also worthless having policies, practices, and procedures unless an employer can also demonstrate with documentation that there was training, implementation, and auditing to ensure that programs were followed.

Sample Documents of a Safe Hiring Program Using the S.A.F.E. System

The Addendum contains sample internal policy and procedure documents from a fictitious firm that cover the basics of their Safe Hiring Program and provide a hands-on example of how a S.A.F.E. System is implemented.

The Importance of Documentation

Of course, it is not sufficient to merely talk about safe hiring. Unless there are written employer policies, practices, and procedures, it is difficult to understand how an employer can have any sort of effective and credible program. It does not help in a court case, for example, if an HR Director testifies that safe hiring was a topic discussed at a lunch meeting. That is more accurately described as an "oral tradition" and is not likely to provide a credible defense if an employer is ever sued or its hiring practices challenged.

Documentation Provides a Number of Advantages to an Employer

1. The process of committing the program to a written company document requires an employer to think through the policies and the practical implementation.

2. Documentation leads to accountability so that everyone knows what has to be done, who has to do it, and how to measure success.

3. It creates a common understanding, purpose, or goal throughout the organization.

4. It enables an organization to provide effective training.

Author Tip — Don't Ignore Your Safe Hiring Process

Just having a written policy that sits on a shelf is useless. In fact, it can even be counterproductive in a court case if the evidence shows an employer had a safe hiring process but ignored it.

In addition, employers must actively audit and measure compliance with the documentation, and perform periodic reviews.

Sample Written Documentation of Polices and Procedures

Attached in the Addendum are a series of sample policies and procedures intended to provide employers with a starting point in drafting their own documentation. Keeping in mind that there is no one size fits all documentation, the attached material provides a starting point. The reader is cautioned to confer with his or her legal counsel as well.

Stages of Hiring

A key part of understanding how to develop any type of pre-hiring assessment, including background checks, is to understand that hiring is a process consisting of separate stages—each potentially requiring specific Safe Hiring practices. In some instances, employer activities and inquiries can be conducted only after certain pre-requites have been met. The stages and available tools for the hiring process can roughly be divided as follows:

1. Pre-Hire Stage: At this stage, the employer first determines if a hire is needed. An employer can explore other options such as a temporary worker or independent contractor to determine if a Full-Time Employee (FTE) is even necessary. If there is a position to be filled, employers should prepare a job description that will help with both the recruiting and the hiring decision. There is more on job descriptions later in this book.

2. Sourcing Stage: This is the process of gathering potential applicants through a variety of means that can include inbound applications from job boards, websites and social media, newspapers, or outbound efforts, such as recruiters seeking passive candidates. Care must be taken to utilize methods that are non-discriminatory and do not invade privacy.

3. Preliminary Screening Stage: To narrow down the applicant pool, there is a preliminary screening based primarily upon the applicants' self-stated qualifications which are included in applicants' resumes, applications, or newer tools such as video websites. This is sometimes called "progressive screening," where an employer may look for keywords or certain Knowledge, Skills, and Experience (KSA) related to the position. An employer could even perform telephone screens on candidates who on paper appear to qualify in order to further narrow down the list of potential candidates an employer may wish to interview in person. Some employers may utilize a "social media" review at this stage, a tool that will be explored in-depth later in this book.

4. Assessment Stage: This can include the interviewing process to further narrow down the field of candidates, as well as numerous other assessment tools, ranging from objective testing, references from past employers or supervisors, or various other testing methods.

5. Decision Process Stage: Here, the employer has narrowed the pool to one, two, or possibly three finalists and is moving toward a conditional job offer based upon an internal decision-making process.

6. Background Checking Stage: At this point, either a conditional job offer has been made or is contemplated, and the employer needs to exercise due diligence, typically through a background screening firm, to determine if there is any reason to NOT hire the candidate. The emphasis of a background screening firm at this point is a factual verification of details such as job titles and dates.

7. The Post Offer/Pre-Hire Stage: At this stage, employers are able, for the first time, to address such areas as pre-employment physicals, if they so choose.

8. The Post Hire/On-Boarding Stage: This is where an employer, for example, can complete the 'Employment Eligibility Verification, Form I-9' process (which is discussed more in depth in Chapter 16).

Many tasks discussed in this book are performed in stages 2 through 5 with the AIR Process. As discussed later, certain tasks, including a workers compensation records inquiry or the Form I-9 procedures, can only be performed post-offer.

The important point about background checks is that they do not tell employers who to hire. There are a number of tools that help employers seek and identify the best and most qualified applicants. Background checks are a due diligence task aimed at raising potential Red Flags that may be relevant to reasons NOT to hire someone.

Putting It All Together – Taking the Safe Hiring Audit

The balance of this chapter is a Safe Hiring Audit. This audit enables an employer to judge the effectiveness of its current Safe Hiring Program and how well the program would stand-up in court if the employer is required to explain to a jury what precautions were taken in case of a lawsuit for negligent hiring . The purpose is to understand what the company's current hiring practices are now before reviewing additional chapters of the book. Everything in the Audit is covered in *The Safe Hiring Manual*.

Author Tip ⟩ | **The Safe Hiring Audit is for Educational Purposes Only**

A reader should be careful not to create a document that could be construed as a company policy analysis and used against your organization in legal matters. If your organization decides to conduct a formal audit, a recommended practice could be to have an attorney involved in the audit so the audit would potentially be protected by attorney work product or attorney-client privilege.

The Safe Hiring Audit

The Audit consists of 25 questions dealing with safe hiring practices. For each of the 25 questions, test takers should score their organizations on a 0-4 point scale. Thus a score of 100 would be a perfect score. Which is not likely. The following is the suggested scoring table:

- **0** = Your organization does nothing for safe hiring and is out of compliance (an F on a report card).
- **1** = Your organization takes a few steps for safe hiring but falls far short of what is needed (D).
- **2** = Your organization take several measures for safe hiring but improvements are needed (C).
- **3** = Your organization takes strong measures for safe hiring but does not have all documentation (B).
- **4** = Your organization could be a model for safe hiring and all documentation is verified as legal (A).

Each question includes some "Best Practice" guides to help test takers calculate their scores.

1. **Does your organization have written policies, practices, and procedures for safe hiring? SCORE: _____**

   Best Practice:

   How would you rate your company's written policies as far as demonstrating a commitment to safe hiring, such as found in your employee manuals or operations manuals?

   How accurately are specific practices documented?

   How well will written forms and procedures stand up to an audit?

   Do your written policies also cover the need for data protection and confidentiality as well as the need to limit the use of information to hiring and selection purposes?

   Case in Point:

   Although a firm has an "understanding" between managers to hire safe and qualified workers, the hiring procedure is done on the basis of "oral tradition." This would be a "0" – not compliant.

2.   **Are all hiring policies and practices reviewed for legal compliance? SCORE: _____**

   Best Practice:

   Are there consequences/penalties if the hiring manager, HR personnel, etc. fail to implement or follow the plan?

   Procedures:

   Can employer document that anyone not following procedures is adversely impacted?

3.   **Are the safe hiring policies, practices, and procedures regularly reviewed and updated internally for compliance? SCORE: _____**

   Best Practice:

   Review your Policies, Practices, and Procedures for legal compliance:

   Federal Fair Credit Reporting Act (FCRA) followed if third party firms involved.

   In compliance with EEOC and state equivalent rules, especially the EEOC Guidance on criminal records issued April 25, 2012, as well as applicable ban-the-box rules.

   ADA and state ADA rules followed.

   Specific state laws obeyed (i.e., California regulates both third-party screening AND internal employer investigations through the Investigative Consumer Reporting Agencies Act).

   Privacy Protection and Defamation-avoidance procedures in place.

4.   **Are the organization's policies and procedures on safe hiring communicated effectively to the workforce and managers? SCORE: _____**

   Best Practice:

   Are the company's policies and procedures on safe hiring communicated effectively to the workforce and managers?

   Procedures:

   Can you document how frequently policies and procedures are communicated?

   If you are in a deposition, how can you document communication of your policies?

   If so, what are the details? Hint—written documentation detailing dates and times works best.

5.   **Is there documented organizational responsibility for safe hiring with consequences of not following program spelled out? SCORE: _____**

   Best Practice:

   Is there a position specifically responsible for safe hiring practices?

   Are safe hiring responsibilities in someone's job description?

   If safe hiring is decentralized in hiring departments, are there documented procedures in place across the organization, including training and audit of performance?

6.   **Are tools and training in place to ensure hiring managers follow a Safe Hiring Program? SCORE: _____**

   Best Practice:

   Is there training for hiring managers, HR, etc.?

   Procedures:

   How is the training conducted?

   What is the frequency of training?

   How is training success monitored and measured?

   Is an identifiable person responsible to analyze, implement, and evaluate the training program?

How is compliance documented?

<u>Case in Point:</u>

A school district had great policies, but managers failed to follow practice guidelines, which permitted a teacher with a questionable history to be hired. Also, the managers failed to document the results of background checking done on the teacher.

7. **Is a procedure in place to audit all the safe hiring practices? SCORE: _____**

<u>Best Practice:</u>

Is there a documented audit procedure to ensure safe hiring practices are followed?

…i.e. can you prove someone was auditing your procedures periodically to see if they were followed?

<u>Procedures:</u>

How is the completed audit information maintained?

How frequently does auditing occur?

Who conducts the audit process?

Does the audit trail go to the TOP; i.e. local managers checked by regional managers, etc.

8. **Is the Fair Credit Reporting Act (FCRA) followed if third-party firms are involved in screening? SCORE: _____**

<u>Best Practice:</u>

Make sure screening services are in compliance with FCRA.

<u>Procedures:</u>

Obtain applicant's written release/disclosure on a stand-alone document.

Pre-adverse action copy of report and statement of rights so applicant can object if information is inaccurate or incomplete.

Second letter sent to the applicant if the decision is made final.

The employer must also certify law will be followed, i.e. not discriminate, use for employment purposes only.

If forms provided by screening firm, review for legal compliance.

Be aware many states have their own rules on screening.

9. **Are there procedures to place applicants on notice that your organization engages in "Best Practices" for hiring? SCORE: _____**

<u>Best Practice:</u>

Is there a notice in the job announcement, bulletin, classified advertisement, internet site, etc. that you perform background checks?

<u>Reason:</u>

Discourages applicants with something to hide and encourages applicants to be truthful.

<u>Procedures:</u>

Is there a notice on the application form that a prospective candidate receives?

Do applicants sign a release for a background check?

Do your notices take into account applicable federal, state or local ban-the-box laws?

10. **Does your firm use an application form (either paper or electronic)? SCORE: _____**

<u>Best Practice:</u>

Utilize application forms, not resumes.

Reasons:

Resumes are often not complete or clear.

To the applicant, a resume is a marketing tool.

Applications ensure uniformity.

Also, requires the applicant to provide all necessary information, prevents employer having impermissible info, and gives places where applicants sign certain statements.

If no application process, is there a supplemental form with necessary language?

11. Does the application form have all necessary and correct language? SCORE: _____

Best Practice:

Depending on how an employer chooses to implement the April 25, 2012, EEOC Guidance on criminal records, does your firm address the issue of when it asks about past criminal history? For example, does your firm provide an advisement that an appropriate inquiry will be made at an appropriate time in the hiring process?

Does the application contain a statement that fraudulent statements or material omissions are grounds to terminate the hiring process, or employment, no matter when discovered?

12. Are completed applications reviewed for potential "red flags" including employment gaps? SCORE: _____

Procedures:

Review applications for potential "red flags" from applicant such as:

Does not sign application

Does not sign release

Leaves criminal questions blank (This depends on how an employer implements the 2012 EEOC Guidance on criminal records and ban-the-box rules.)

Applicant self-reports offense

Fails to identify past employers

Fails to identify past supervisors

Fails to explain why left past jobs

Excessive cross-outs and changes

Unexplained employment gaps

Explanations for employment gaps or leaving past jobs do not make sense

13. Are the six critical questions used in a structured interview? SCORE: _____

Best Practice:

Since they have signed consent and believe you are doing checks, job applicants have a powerful incentive to be Truthful.

1. "Our firm has a standard policy of conducting background checks on all hires before an offer is made or finalized. You have already signed a release form. Do you have any concerns about that?"

(Good applicants will shrug this question off.)

2. "We also check for criminal convictions for all finalists. Do you have any concerns about that?"

(Make sure question reflects updated EEOC Guidance for the use of arrest and conviction records and what employer may legally ask in your state.)

3. "When we talk to your past employers, what do you think they will say?"

(This tells applicants past employers will be contacted and provides an incentive to be accurate.)

4. "Will your past employers tell us that there were any issues with tardiness, meeting job requirements, etc.?"

(Questions must be on job-related issues only.)

5. "Can you tell me about any unexplained gaps in your employment history?"

(Where gaps in the employment history are not explained, it is critical to ask this question.)

6. "Is everything in the application and everything you told us in the hiring process true, correct, and complete?"

(This critical final question sends a clear message to applicants that the employer takes the process seriously,

And they need to be completely open, honest, and truthful.)

14. Are interviewers trained in legal compliance? SCORE: _____

Best Practice:

Train all interviewers to:

Question all applicants in a similar fashion.

Not ask illegal questions, i.e., questions that are discriminatory or prohibited by law.

Respond when an applicant volunteers impermissible information.

Not to make statements to an applicant such as promises about the job.

Not mark or make notes on a resume.

Procedure:

Document the interviewer's training and audit results.

15. Does the firm check past employment, education credentials, and references? SCORE: _____

Best Practice:

Critical to find out where the applicant lived, worked, and went to school in the past seven years to get an idea of where to look for criminal records.

Verify employment to determine where a person has worked even if you only get dates and job title.

Verify academic credentials to avoid embarrassing situations later (See Yahoo CEO who had to leave company and cases of doctors practicing without licenses.)

Reasons:

Biggest mistake employer can make is not contact past employers—this is just as critical as criminal checks.

Looking for unexplained gaps.

To target locations to search for criminal records.

If able to verify person gainfully employed during the last five-to-ten years, there is less likelihood of having spent time in custody for a serious offense.

Just attempting/documenting demonstrates due diligence.

Check academic records to see if the degree is from "diploma mill" (fake college).

16. Does the firm look for "employment gaps"? SCORE: _____

Best Practice:

Critical to verify employment to determine where a person has been even if you only get dates and job title.

Looking for unexplained gaps.

Procedures:

Document that the interviewer reviewed the application for gaps and asked the applicant.

If able to verify person gainfully employed for last five-to-ten years, then less likely to have spent time in custody for a serious offense.

17. Is the firm conducting an appropriate search for criminal records? SCORE: _____

Best Practice:

Understand EEOC rules for the use of criminal records based upon business necessity:

The nature and gravity of the offense

The amount of time that has passed since the conviction or completion of sentence

The nature of the job being held or sought

(Also be aware of updated EEOC guidance for criminal records as of April 2012.)

Special rules considering arrests only.

Did the applicant lie in the application?

Criminal information was verified and the information is current, belongs to the applicant, the employer has an understanding of information, and there is no prohibition on the information's use.

18. Does the firm understand the appropriate uses and the limitations on criminal record databases? SCORE: _____

Best Practice:

Use criminal databases only as a secondary tool in connection with county court level criminal searches since databases may contain inaccurate and incomplete information.

Verify possible criminal "hits" from databases with a county court level search since databases may contain "false positives."

19. Are the firm's policy and procedures for the use of negative criminal information legal and compliant with federal and state laws? SCORE: _____

Best Practice:

Policies—are there written guidelines to follow?

Second chance rules—are you aware of the proper rules to handle expungements, deferred adjudication of other forms of judicial set aside preventing an employer from considering a criminal record?

Documentation—are all procedures and decisions documented to file?

Individualized review—flat policy can be discriminatory.

Uniformity—are similarly situated applicants treated the same?

Legal compliance—if third party utilized under the FCRA, have a procedure to ensure pre-adverse action and post-adverse letters?

Individualized Assessment—if a criminal record is revealed or located does your firm engage in the "Individualized Assessment" practices recommended by the EEOC?

20. Does the firm use other screening tools and, if so, is the information used in accordance with safe hiring guidelines? SCORE: _____

Best Practice:

Take these additional steps as necessary if related to job:

Criminal record checks.

Civil records if relevant.

Social Security trace.

Education and past employment credentials.

Credit report (if appropriate and if policies are in place to ensure that use of credit information is recent, relevant, and fair).

Driving record.

21. Are the mechanics of your screening program documented? SCORE: _____

Best Practice:

Document all procedures.

The process to send requests to screening company, track progress, receive reports, maintain privacy, and restrict results to only authorized persons.

Track the stages in the hiring process for screening.

(Typically only the finalists are subject to screening.)

The degree of screening for each position.

(Not every position needs to be screened at the same level.)

Uniform screening procedures – similarly situated applicants treated in the same non-discriminatory manner.

Storage and retention of reports separately from personnel files.

22. If screening is outsourced to a third-party firm, can the employer demonstrate Due Diligence and show procedures are in compliance with the FCRA? SCORE: _____

Best Practice:

If background check failed due to screening firm, then the employer may be liable if it failed to exercise due diligence in selection of the screening firm.

Factors:

Expertise/knowledge of the service provider

Legal compliance—FCRA and state law compliance

Personal service and consulting—providing professional consulting services

Training/consulting services available

References

Pricing of secured internet order/reporting options.

Accreditation through the National Association of Professional Background Screeners (NAPBS®). See: www.napbs.com.

Privacy practices documented by a process such SOC (as Service Organization Control) 2® compliance. See: www.esrcheck.com/SOC-2/.

23. Are procedures in place if a person with negative information is hired? SCORE: _____

Best Practice:

The firm has examined the type of support, supervision, and structure needed to improve the chances of success within the organization.

The firm has considered the nature of the job and the circumstances of the past offense to take appropriate measures to protect the firm, co-workers, and the public from harm.

The firm has documented decision-making factors.

24. **Are procedures in place if employment is offered before a background check is completed? SCORE: _____**

Best Practice:

If employment begins before completion of a background check, is there a written statement that employment is conditioned upon receiving a report that is satisfactory to the employer?

Does policy eliminate a possible debate over what is an acceptable background report?

Issue:

May need to escort the person off premises if a background check is negative.

25. **Does the organization have written policies, practices, and procedures for screening employees post-hire? SCORE: _____**

Best Practice:

Safe hiring also extends to retention, supervision, and promotion.

Procedures:

Are supervisors periodically trained and educated regarding the employer's liability for negligent retention, supervision, or promotion?

Are supervisors trained to recognize, report, and deal appropriately with workplace misconduct?

Are there procedures to investigate workplace misconduct?

Is there a mechanism for workers or managers to report and record workplace misconduct?

Is it part of written job descriptions for supervisors to record, report, and address workplace misconduct and part of performance appraisal?

Does firm audit and review entire Safe Hiring Program each year?

YOUR SAFE HIRING AUDIT TOTAL SCORE: _____

Conclusion – How Do Your Safe Hiring Practices Measure Up?

After taking the Audit and assessing your practices, you should begin a program of improving those areas where there is potential litigation exposure. If there are areas where your firm needs improvement, utilize the resources in this book.

If your overall score is less than 75 points:

> **You may have to do some work to improve your safe hiring program.**

If your score is above 75 points:

> **Good job but there still may be some room for improvement.**

See The Addendum

More Sample Written Documentation

Sample documentation for a Safe Hiring Program including Policies, Practices and Procedures and sample material for including in an Employee Handbook can be found in the Addendum to this book.

CHAPTER 2

Discrimination and Privacy

A primary tenet that forms a foundation of a Safe Hiring Program (SHP) is **legal compliance**—a critical area of concern for employers, human resources professionals, hiring managers, recruiters, and employment (and tenant) screening companies. There are several chapters in this book devoted to this issue.

This chapter introduces critical **discrimination and privacy compliance issues**, primarily associated with Phase Two of a Safe Hiring Program (SHP)—the initial Screening Practices by an employer—which is examined in the next two chapters. This includes the **Application, Interview, and Reference Checks (AIR)** process steps that carry their own sets of legal implications, many of which are influenced by the laws covered in this chapter. Matching your hiring procedures to these compliance factors is paramount to avoiding any practice that may even suggest an invasion of privacy or a discriminatory practice. Discrimination issues in the context of criminal records are covered in more detail in Chapter 10.

Discrimination and Privacy – An Overview

The important concepts of legal limits and privacy/confidentiality will be revisited throughout this book and are intertwined with a Safe Hiring Program.

Legal limits are what an employer can and cannot find out about applicants as well as how employers handle and maintain confidential and sensitive information. The primary laws that affect this issue are equal employment opportunity laws on the federal, state, and sometimes even the local level. The basic rule is that an employer can ask an applicant either directly on an application or interview—or find out indirectly through a past employment reference check—information that is:

- A valid predictor of job performance.

- Not barred specifically by an equal employment law, such as questions concerning race, ethnicity, religion, age, sex, or other prohibited criteria.

- Not prohibited due to a disparate impact even though neutral on its face, such as the use of arrest records or criminal history.

- Not prohibited by a specific statute, such as the prohibition on lie-detector machines.

- Not prohibited due to illegal procedures, such as failure to follow the federal Fair Credit Reporting Act (FCRA).

The role of privacy rights and confidentiality is also a key point in a Safe Hiring Program. An employer who follows the FCRA should generally not run afoul of privacy rights.

About Discrimination Laws and Employers

Federal and state anti-discrimination laws make it clear that decisions based on prohibited criteria are illegal. These criteria include race, color, national origin, religion, ancestry, medical condition, age, marital status, sex, or exercise of family care or medical leaves. These are prohibited criteria because they are not valid predictors of job performance or bona fide occupational qualifications (BFOQ). In the past, prohibited criteria have been found to cause unfair treatment and discrimination. This type of discrimination is called **disparate treatment.** A person is being pre-judged based upon membership in a group or status instead of what he or she can accomplish as an individual. The word *prejudice* simply means to pre-judge a person based upon the color of the person's skin, country of origin, sex or some other criteria that have nothing to do with job performance or the abilities of the particular individual applying for employment.

The situation becomes complicated because information that appears neutral on its face can be utilized in a discriminatory way. This is called **disparate impact** and occurs when employer selection processes that appear fair on the surface actually result in a screening out of identifiable groups from employment.

For example, credit reports and criminal records are perfectly legal for employers to obtain provided the methods used comply with various state and federal rules. However, the use of credit reports or criminal records can have a discriminatory impact if they are used in such a way that statistically results in a disparate impact upon certain groups. The generally accepted limitations to the use of these records are discussed in later chapters.

Employers need to have a basic understanding of the legal statutes, cases, and regulations on both the federal and state levels that affect how any employer can legally collect and utilize personal information about job applicants in order to make hiring decisions.

> **You Need To Know** ⟩

Census Bureau Agrees to Pay $15 Million to Settle Lawsuit for Discrimination in Background Checks

In April 2016, the United States Census Bureau agreed to pay $15 million to settle a lawsuit claiming that the criminal background checks performed when hiring workers for the 2010 census racially discriminated against African-American and Hispanic job applicants with arrest records.

The settlement agreement ends a lawsuit filed in April of 2010 that claimed job applicants for the 2010 Census with an arrest record for any offense in their lives faced an arbitrary barrier to employment since the Census Bureau required these job applicants to produce "official court documentation" of the disposition of their arrests within 30 days to remain eligible for work.

The Census Discrimination Lawsuit website states the requirement from the Census Bureau for "official court documentation" caused 93 percent of the job applicants with an arrest record of almost any arrest—approximately 700,000 people—to be excluded from being hired for Census jobs. As a result, this requirement operated as a "no arrest or conviction history allowed" policy.

The website also states the Census Bureau background checks excluded people "with old and minor convictions for non-criminal offenses, misdemeanors, and other crimes that do not involve violence or dishonesty, which are irrelevant according to Census' own policy for work in the field or at a desk job." More information about the case is available at www.censusdiscriminationlawsuit.com.

The Settlement Agreement and Release for the case of *Gonzalez et al v. Pritzker*, filed on April 19, 2016, in the U.S. District Court, Southern District of New York, No. 10-

03105, is available on the Census Discrimination Lawsuit website at www.censusdiscriminationlawsuit.com/sites/default/files/documents/census-settlement-agreement.pdf.

Important Federal Discrimination Laws Affecting a Safe Hiring Program

Nine significant federal laws that prohibit discrimination in employment are listed below. The **U.S. Equal Employment Opportunity Commission (EEOC)** enforces many of these laws at the federal level. The EEOC also provides oversight and coordination of all federal equal employment opportunity regulations, practices, and policies.

The Number of Employees Matters

You will see in the following list of nine laws that many federal laws only affect employers above a certain size. For example, the Civil Rights Act and the Americans with Disabilities Act cover employers with fifteen or more employees based upon the number of employees during each working day of twenty or more calendar weeks of the current or preceding calendar year. However, the Age Discrimination Act utilizes twenty employees as the threshold.

As a practical matter, even small employers who believe they fall below the federal limits are well advised to take these federal laws into consideration. First, it can be complicated to determine how many employees a small firm has for purposes of determining if the law applies. All employees including part-time and temporary workers may be counted. An employer may not count "independent contractors," but the possibility exists that the independent contractors may be counted if, in fact, they are misclassified and are really engaged in an employment-type relationship regardless of how the employer chooses to compensate them. If an employer has two or more separate businesses, there are circumstances where the businesses can be counted as one for the purpose of determining the employee count.

The rules about counting employees to determine if a firm is large enough to meet the threshold for application of federal civil rights laws can also be very complex. In addition, there are states where state laws can be in effect even if a federal law technically does not apply. More importantly, if small employers engage in any conduct that would have been a violation of federal law if they were larger, an aggrieved applicant or employee may still be able to go to court stating an alternative cause of action such as intentional infliction of emotional distress.

Age Discrimination in Employment Act of 1967 (Amended 1975)

Who it Affects:　　Employers of 20 or more persons.

Overview:　　Prohibits discriminating against persons who are 40 years of age or older. There are certain apprenticeship programs, retirement or benefit systems exempted. Many states also have age laws, some of which have no age limitation or are subject to employers with fewer than 20 employees.

Copy of Act:　　www.eeoc.gov/laws/statutes/adea.cfm

Americans with Disabilities Act (ADA)

Who it Affects:　　Employers with 15 or more employees.

Overview:　　Prohibits employment discrimination against qualified individuals with disabilities in the private sector and in state and local governments. This federal law has broad implications for hiring and background screenings. An employer may not use or obtain any information that violates the rights afforded under this law. The most obvious impact of the law relates to medical records, disabilities, and workers' compensation records. Employment screening firms may access and provide workers' compensation records, but only under the strict procedures mandated by the Americans with Disabilities Act.

Copy of Act　　www.eeoc.gov/laws/statutes/ada.cfm

Civil Rights Act of 1964 (Title VII), as amended by Equal Employment Opportunity Act of 1972

Who it Affects:
- All private employers of 15 or more persons.
- All educational institutions, both public and private.
- State and local governments.
- Public and private employment agencies.
- Labor unions with 15 or more members.
- Joint labor-management committees for apprenticeship and training.

Overview: Title VII prohibits employment discrimination based on race, color, religion, sex, or national origin. It also prohibits practices caused by statistically determined adverse impact, as well as intentional, unequal treatment. The Civil Rights Act of 1991 (Pub. L. 102-166) (CRA) and the Lily Ledbetter Fair Pay Act of 2009 (Pub. L. 111-2) amend several sections of Title VII.

For More Info: www.eeoc.gov/laws/statutes/titlevii.cfm

Civil Rights Act of 1991

Who it Affects: All employers Affected by the Civil Rights Act of 1964 (see above).

Overview: Provides (among other things) monetary damages in cases of intentional employment discrimination

For More Info: www.eeoc.gov/laws/statutes/cra-1991.cfm

Equal Protection Clause of the 14th Amendment

Who it Affects: All persons within the United States.

Overview: The Equal Protection Clause of the 14th amendment of the U.S. Constitution prohibits states from denying any person within its jurisdiction the equal protection of the laws - meaning laws of a state must treat an individual in the same manner as others in similar conditions and circumstances.

For More Info: https://www.law.cornell.edu/constitution/amendmentxiv

Executive Order 11246

Who it Affects: Federal contractors and federally–assisted construction contractors and subcontractors, who do over $10,000 in Government business in one year.

Overview: Prohibits discrimination in employment decisions on the basis of race, color, religion, sex, sexual orientation, gender identity or national origin. The Executive Order also requires Government contractors to take affirmative action to ensure that equal opportunity is provided in all aspects of their employment. Additionally, Executive Order 11246 prohibits federal contractors and subcontractors from, under certain circumstances, taking adverse employment actions against applicants and employees for asking about, discussing, or sharing information about their pay or the pay of their co-workers.

For More Info: www.dol.gov/ofccp/regs/compliance/ca_11246.htm

Equal Pay Act of 1963

Who it Affects: All employers in the U.S. Subject to the Fair Labor Standards Act.

Overview: Requires equal pay for men and women performing work substantially similar in skill, effort, responsibility, and working conditions unless wage differentials are due to bona fide systems of seniority, merit, output, or some business factor other than sex.

For More Info: www.eeoc.gov/laws/statutes/epa.cfm

Genetic Information Nondiscrimination Act of 2008 (GINA)

Who it Affects:	Covers employers with 15 or more employees, including state and local governments.
Overview:	GINA makes it illegal to discriminate against employees or applicants because of genetic information with respect to health insurance and employment.
For More Info:	www.eeoc.gov/laws/statutes/gina.cfm

Rehabilitation Act of 1973

Who it Affects:	Employers receiving federal funds.
Overview:	Prohibits discrimination on the basis of disability in programs run by federal agencies; programs that receive federal financial assistance; in federal employment; and in the employment practices of federal contractors.
For More Info:	www.eeoc.gov/laws/statutes/rehab.cfm

Title IX, Education Amendments Act of 1972

Who it Affects:	In addition to traditional educational institutions such as colleges, universities, and elementary and secondary schools, Title IX also applies to any education or training program operated by a recipient of federal financial assistance.
Overview:	Prohibits discrimination on the basis of sex in any federally funded education program or activity. The principal objective of Title IX is to avoid the use of federal money to support sex discrimination in education programs and to provide individual citizens effective protection against those practices.
For More Info:	www.justice.gov/crt/overview-title-ix-education-amendments-1972-20-usc-1681-et-seq

EEOC Guidelines about Discrimination and Disclosure of Criminal Records

On April 25, 2012, the EEOC issued its **Enforcement Guidance on the Consideration of Arrest and Conviction Records in Employment Decisions under Title VII of the Civil Rights Act of 1964.** The guidance has a significant impact on how and when criminal records are considered for employment. The EEOC was clearly concerned with the ability of applicants with criminal records to obtain employment. The updated EEOC Guidance is available at www.eeoc.gov/laws/guidance/arrest_conviction.cfm.

Under Title VII of the Civil Rights Act of 1964, the use of arrest and conviction records to deny employment can be unlawful and discriminatory when it is not relevant for the job since it can limit the employment opportunities of applicants or workers based on their race or ethnicity. The EEOC guidance and policy statements on the use of arrest and conviction records in employment clearly indicate that any use of a blanket "no hire" policy that excludes job applicants with criminal records is unlawful under Title VII of the Civil Rights Act of 1964 since it discriminates against minority groups with higher rates of criminal convictions.

 More Information about the EEOC Guidance

A full analysis of the EEOC Guidance is available in Chapter 10. The full text of the "Enforcement Guidance on the Consideration of Arrest and Conviction Records in Employment Decisions Under Title VII of the Civil Rights Act of 1964" is available in the Addendum and online at www.eeoc.gov/laws/guidance/arrest_conviction.cfm.

Legal Reference and Case Law Examples

The Addendum contains legal reference and case law examples in several areas related to background checks and employment screening.

EEOC Report Reveals Focus on Systemic Discrimination

The EEOC's *Fiscal Year 2015 Performance and Accountability Report (PAR)* on activities designed to meet the priorities outlined in the EEOC Strategic Enforcement Plan (SEP) for Fiscal Years 2012-2016, showed the EEOC continues to focus on alleged **systemic discrimination** where employment practices broadly affect an employer, industry, or wide geographic area.

In the fiscal year 2015, the EEOC completed 268 investigations of alleged systemic discrimination that obtained more than $33.5 million in remedies for victims of alleged systemic discrimination. The EEOC also reported that its administrative enforcement program obtained $356.6 million from claim resolutions, an increase of over $60 million from the $296.1 million collected during the fiscal year 2014. The EEOC also resolved 155 merits lawsuits in the federal district courts for a total recovery of $65.3 million, an increase of $42.8 million over the $22.5 million collected during the fiscal year 2014.

In addition, the EEOC resolved 92,641 discrimination charges while receiving 89,385 new private sector bias charges during the fiscal year 2015. Both figures show increases from the fiscal year 2014 when the EEOC received 88,778 new charges while resolving 87,442 charges of discrimination. The EEOC PAR for FY 2015 is available at www.eeoc.gov/eeoc/plan/upload/2015par.pdf.

This SEP objective of combating employment discrimination through strategic law enforcement reflects the EEOC's primary mission of preventing unlawful employment discrimination through the use of administrative and litigation enforcement with regard to private employers, labor organizations, employment agencies, and state and local government employers

EEOC and the E-RACE Initiative

In an effort to identify and implement new strategies to strengthen its enforcement of Title VII of the Civil Rights Act of 1964 and advance the statutory right to a workplace free of race and color discrimination, the EEOC instituted the **E-RACE (Eradicating Racism And Colorism from Employment) Initiative**.

The E-RACE Initiative is designed to improve EEOC's efforts to ensure workplaces are free of race and color discrimination. Specifically, the EEOC identifies issues, criteria, and barriers that contribute to race and color discrimination, explore strategies to improve the administrative processing and the litigation of race and color discrimination claims, and enhance public awareness of race and color discrimination in employment. The EEOC developed a set of detailed E-RACE goals and objectives to be achieved within a five-year timeframe from FY 2008 to FY 2013. Even though that specific time period has passed, the EEOC continues to follow the E-RACE initiative. An understanding of the E-RACE Initiative is helpful for employers and human resource professionals to understand the underlying mission of the EEOC when it comes to enforcing anti-discriminating laws.

E-RACE Goals

The five main goals of E-RACE are to:

- Improve data collection and data analysis in order to identify, track, investigate, and prosecute allegations of discrimination.
- Improve quality and consistency in EEOC's Charge Processing and Litigation Program and improve federal sector systems.
- Develop strategies, legal theories, and training modules to address emerging issues of race and color discrimination.
- Enhance visibility of EEOC's enforcement efforts in eradicating race and color discrimination.
- Engage the public, employers, and stakeholders to promote voluntary compliance to eradicate race and color discrimination.

The EEOC also combines the objectives of E-RACE with existing EEOC initiatives to increase its outreach to human resource professionals and employer groups to address race and color discrimination in the workplace. For more information on E-RACE, visit: www.eeoc.gov/eeoc/initiatives/e-race/goals.cfm.

Legal Reference and Case Law Examples

The Addendum contains an article entitled, *"From Griggs to SEPTA: The EEOC's Focus on Employment Screening"* by Rod M. Fliegel and Jennifer L. Mora, Attorneys At Law, Littler Mendelson, P.C., that examines activity at the EEOC over the past few years in which the EEOC's "systemic discrimination" unit has been investigating employer policies and/or practices that screen job applicants for employment based on criminal or credit records.

White House Report on Big Data Reveals Opportunities and Challenges with Employment Discrimination

In May 2016, the White House released *'Big Data: A Report on Algorithmic Systems, Opportunity, and Civil Rights'* which revealed that "Big Data"—defined as information so high in volume, velocity, and variety that it requires new forms of processing for decision making—can uncover or even reduce employment discrimination but also risk enabling and automating potentially discriminatory hiring practices.

With regard to employment discrimination, the report found that since traditional hiring practices may unnecessarily filter out applicants with skills that match the job opening, companies looking to hire "turned to new ways of rating applicants, using Big Data analytical tools to automatically sort and identify the preferred candidates to move forward in a hiring process" through using algorithms and large data sets.

However, the report also found that Big Data technology was still controlled by humans and thus potentially discriminatory. Yet even as recruiting and hiring managers look to make greater use of algorithmic systems and automation, the inclination remains for individuals to hire someone similar to themselves, an unconscious phenomenon often referred to as "like me" bias, which can impede diversity.

As a result, this "like me" phenomenon in humans can make well-intentioned Big Data technology fail: Algorithmic systems can be designed to help prevent this bias and increase diversity in the hiring process. Yet despite these goals, because they are built by humans and rely on imperfect data, these algorithmic systems may also be based on flawed judgments and assumptions that perpetuate bias as well.

Big Data systems can help combat bias in traditional hiring practices that can lead to discrimination by making "fairness, ethics, and opportunity" a core part of the original design: Beyond hiring decisions, properly deployed advanced algorithmic systems present the possibility of tackling age-old employment discrimination challenges, such as the wage gap or occupational segregation.

Companies have begun to filter their applicant pools for job openings using various human resources analytics platforms. It is critical to the fairness of American workplaces that all companies continue to promote fairness and ethical approaches with the use of data tools and ensure against the perpetuation of biases that could disfavor certain groups. See:

www.whitehouse.gov/sites/default/files/microsites/ostp/2016_0504_data_discrimination.pdf.

Americans with Disabilities Act (ADA)

Background Screening and ADA

The **Americans with Disabilities Act (ADA)** is a federal law that regulates the hiring of Americans with disabilities and has broad implications. In terms of background screenings, an employer may not use or obtain any information that violates the rights afforded under this law. The most obvious impact of the law relates to medical records, disabilities, and workers' compensation records. Employment screening firms may access and provide workers' compensation records, but only under the strict procedures mandated by the Americans with Disabilities Act.

The ADA can potentially have an impact on the timing of a background check. In *Leonel v. American Airlines*, 400 F.3d 702 (9th Cir. 2005), the plaintiffs were seeking jobs with a major airline. They were issued conditional offers of employment contingent upon passing both their background checks and medical examination. Their blood was drawn prior to the background checks being completed. According to the case, the airline then discovered a medical condition and rescinded the job offers on the basis that the applicants did not disclose the medical condition during the medical exams.

The plaintiffs sued for a violation of both the federal Americans with Disability Act and the California Fair Employment and Housing Act (FEHA), the California law governing employment discrimination. The plaintiffs alleged that, under federal law and California law, there must first be a "real" job offer on the table before a medical test can be performed. Since the background check was not yet completed before the medical information was obtained, the plaintiffs argued that the employer had not met federal and state standards and had conducted a medical test before there was a job offer.

The court accepted the argument ruling that in order to conduct a **post-offer** medical exam, the employer must have first evaluated all relevant and available non-medical information. When the employer still has non-medical information to evaluate, such as a background check, it is premature to request a medical exam because there has not yet been a **job offer**. The rule has two benefits for job applicants. First, it allows job applicants to determine if they were rejected for medical reasons or for some non-medical reason obtained in the background report. Secondly, it safeguards the applicants from having to reveal personal medical information prematurely. If the applicants are not offered jobs, then they are not put into a position of providing personal medical information for no reason.

Due to these benefits, the Leonel test has begun to be used beyond California and the federal 9th Circuit. In 2008, the 4th Circuit used the Leonel test in determining whether the timing was appropriate for requesting a medical exam. *Malone v. Greenville County*, 2008 U.S. Dist. LEXIS 86520 (D.S.C. Aug. 11, 2008). In 2014, a Massachusetts Superior Court also adopted the test. *Boston Police Dep't v. Kavaleski*, 2014 Mass. Super. LEXIS 133 (Mass. Super. Ct. Aug. 14, 2014).

One occasion where the ADA (and similar state laws) may raise a concern is for criminal convictions involving drugs or alcohol. Under the ADA, an employer cannot discriminate on the basis that an applicant is an alcoholic or a former drug user. However, the ADA and similar state laws do not protect a person who is currently using drugs or abusing alcohol. Where a person is otherwise qualified for a position, and the background screening reveals a drug or alcohol conviction, an employer should carefully review the totality of the circumstances involved before denying employment on that basis. Certainly, the current use of illegal drugs is not protected. The decision may also depend upon the position in question. For driving positions, for example, an employer may certainly evaluate driving-related convictions more seriously.

Discrimination Laws at the State and Local Levels

To add to the complexity for employers, a number of states and local jurisdictions have their own rules governing discrimination. The federal Equal Employment Opportunity Commission (EEOC) website indicates over 100 state and local fair employment practice agencies, or FEPA's. Most states have their own Civil Rights Acts as well as an agency within state government that enforces these state laws. State laws can vary from the federal rules in terms of the size of the employer covered and what constitutes a violation. Even local jurisdictions and cities can regulate employers. For example, the City and County of San Francisco have the San Francisco Human Rights Commission which can investigate and mediate complaints of discrimination for employees of any San Francisco employer, regardless of size.

Here is where it gets even more complicated for employers—they are generally subject to the most stringent discrimination laws in their jurisdictions. For example, even though the Federal Civil Rights Act limits jurisdiction to employers with fifteen or more employees, a California employer is subject to the California Fair Employment and Housing Act (FEHA) that has jurisdiction starting at five employees. Other states apply the discrimination laws to all employers.

Examples of State Discrimination Laws

New Jersey became the first state to enact a law to prohibit discrimination against job applicants who are unemployed: New Jersey Statutes, Title 34, Chap. 8B, § § 1-2-C.34B-1 to 34:8B-2 (A.3359/S.2388, approved March 29, 2011). See www.njleg.state.nj.us/2010/Bills/PL11/40_.PDF.

The District of Columbia enacted The Unemployed Anti-Discrimination Act of 2012 which made it unlawful for all employers and employment agencies in the District to consider the unemployed status of an applicant for employment and hiring decisions. See http://dcclims1.dccouncil.us/images/00001/20120308112351.pdf.

Another example is California Assembly Bill No. 1450 (AB 1450) that fines CA employers and employment agencies who refuse to consider jobless applicants for job openings. (Enrolled September 11, 2012) See https://leginfo.legislature.ca.gov/faces/billNavClient.xhtml?bill_id=201120120AB1450.

Yet another example is Massachusetts Senate Bill S.2119, An Act to Establish Pay Equity that will prevent wage discrimination on the basis of gender and also prohibit employers from requiring applicants to provide their salary history before receiving a job offer. S.2119 takes effect July 1, 2018. See https://malegislature.gov/Bills/189/Senate/S2119.

Resources to Find State Laws

Most states provide websites for the agency that enforces civil rights and fair employment practices law. For example, see the site for the state of Michigan at www.michigan.gov/mdcr/.

For an excellent list of statutes and state agency websites, see the website offered by Cornell University Law School at www.law.cornell.edu/wex/table_labor.

You Need To Know >

EEOC Fact Sheet Helps Small Business Owners Prevent Discrimination

In March 2016, the Equal Employment Opportunity Commission (EEOC) issued a one-page fact sheet entitled *Preventing Discrimination is Good Business* to help small business owners understand their responsibilities under the federal employment anti-discrimination laws. The fact sheet provides a brief and user-friendly overview of the legal obligations of small business owners under the anti-discrimination laws.

The EEOC fact sheet is available in the following languages: Amharic, Arabic, Bengali, Burmese, Chinese, English, French (Canadian), French (European), German, Greek, Haitian Creole, Hindi, Hmong, Japanese, Karen, Khmer, Korean, Laotian, Marshallese, Nepali, Polish, Punjabi, Russian, Somali, Spanish, Tagalog, Thai, Ukrainian, Urdu, and Vietnamese at www.eeoc.gov/eeoc/publications/.

Video Interviewing and Discrimination Risk

An example of how hiring tools can be impacted by discrimination laws is the area of **Video Interviewing** which is becoming a widely accepted hiring technique that allows remote interviews and bypasses the traditional model of in-person interviews. Video interviewing is gaining widespread acceptance for hiring and Talent Acquisition (TA) in the 21st century. Still, some employers—particularly Fortune 500 companies and federal contractors—have expressed concern over potential discrimination issues. However, the advantages of video interviewing far outweigh unsubstantiated risks and concerns about potential discrimination issues with the **Equal Employment Opportunity Commission (EEOC)** and the **Office of Federal Contract Compliance Programs (OFCCP)**. Despite their possible initial fears toward video interviewing, employers need to be better educated and equipped for conversations about how they can enjoy the many operational and strategic benefits of video interviewing while eliminating exposure to discrimination laws and remaining in compliance.

What Is Video Interviewing?

Video interviews allow employers and job candidates to connect face-to-face using online video technology removing geography as a consideration. Video interviewing helps employers prescreen and schedule the onrush of applicants more efficiently while job candidates avoid traffic jams, missed flights, or taking a day off of work to interview. Instead, businesses and job candidates engage and learn more about each other "face-to-face" through a video interviewing technology platform.

According to a study by the Aberdeen Group, best-in-class companies are 61% more likely to use video tools for interviewing candidates as compared to all others. Why? Video interviewing not only saves time and money during the interview process by avoiding travel costs and scheduling tasks, but it also expands the hiring company's reach into larger, more diverse applicant pools. Video interviews are easily shared among hiring decision makers as many companies hire by consensus to make certain their hiring decisions are sound. As a result of these conveniences, employers are using video interviewing technology in increasing numbers to address needed efficiencies in the hiring process and heightened competition for scarce skill sets. See: www.aberdeen.com/research/9323/rr-video-talent-acquisition/content.aspx.

What is NOT Video Interviewing?

Frequently, people mistake or confuse video interviews with two other actions that do not provide the safeguards such as consistency and record retention that exist when working with a video interviewing platform designed for hiring:

- Receiving unsolicited video resumes from candidates.
- Interviewing someone using a chat or conference calling tool that allows you to see each other.

Video resumes are when candidates supplement their resume with unsolicited video clips or video cover letters of themselves to employers. These can leave the employer confused as to how to manage, where to store, or how to acknowledge. Just like scheduled face-to-face interviews are "employer driven" and part of a defined workflow, video interviewing is also employer driven and strategically placed into a defined workflow.

Using Skype or a similar chat or conferencing tool to see someone while conducting an interview is not the same as video interviewing using a platform designed for hiring or talent acquisition. The true benefits of video interviewing are only achieved when using a platform designed for the rigors of hiring.

Risk of Discrimination Claims with Video Interviewing

Despite the advantages of video interviewing, some employers still worry about exposure to discrimination claims when video interviewing candidates. Mainly the issue stems from a concern that a pre-recorded or on-demand video interview would allow the hiring team to view the job candidate early in the hiring cycle. The fear is that companies are more exposed to potential discrimination claims because hiring managers and recruiters can see candidates' race, color, sex, age, national origin, or other protected characteristics early in the process. The concern is that a company can be exposed to claims of "failure to hire" based upon the unlawful consideration of criteria that is discriminatory. The problem with this fear is that it is based on a fundamental misunderstanding of the video interviewing process. The fact is that a video interview used correctly presents no greater legal challenge or risk than the traditional in-person interview.

To understand why employers may have concerns with issues of discrimination and video interviews, it is important to understand discrimination law and hiring. The U.S. Equal Employment Opportunity Commission (EEOC) enforces Title VII of the Civil Rights Act of 1964 which prohibits employment discrimination based on race, color, religion, sex, or national origin. The EEOC is responsible for enforcing federal laws that make it illegal to discriminate against a job applicant or an employee because of race, color, religion, sex (including pregnancy), national origin, age (40 or older), disability, or genetic information. In addition, it is illegal to discriminate against people who complain about discrimination, file a charge of discrimination, or participate in an employment discrimination investigation or lawsuit. The EEOC has the authority to investigate charges of discrimination against employers who are covered by the law. Most employers with at least 15 employees are covered by EEOC laws that apply to all types of work situations, including hiring, firing, promotions, harassment, training, wages, and benefits. If the EEOC finds discrimination has occurred, the agency tries to settle the charge or file a lawsuit to protect the rights of individuals and the interests of the public. For more information about the EEOC and Title VII, visit www.eeoc.gov/laws/statutes/titlevii.cfm.

Another area of potential concern is the Department of Labor's Office of Federal Contract Compliance Programs (OFCCP) which enforces Executive Order (E.O.) 11246 that prohibits employment discrimination by most government contractors and imposes affirmative action obligations. E.O. 11246 includes significant recordkeeping requirements relevant to affirmative action. The purpose of the OFCCP is to enforce, for the benefit of job seekers and wage earners, the contractual promise of affirmative action and equal employment opportunity required of those who do business with the Federal government. In carrying out its responsibilities, the OFCCP uses enforcement procedures on federal contractors and subcontractors that include: technical assistance, compliance evaluations and complaint investigations, and conciliation agreements from those federal contractors and subcontractors in violation of regulatory requirements. The ultimate sanction for violations is debarment and the loss of a company's federal contracts. Other forms of relief to victims of discrimination may also be available, including back pay for lost wages. For more information about the OFCCP, visit www.dol.gov/ofccp/.

EEOC and Video Interviewing

In 2004, in view of the increasing use of video interviewing, the EEOC was asked directly about the use of video resumes in the hiring process. The EEOC explained that Title VII of the Civil Rights Act of 1964 and Title I of the Americans with Disabilities Act (ADA) covered the questions regarding record-keeping when viewing video resumes. Under Title VII, it is not illegal for employers to learn the gender, race, or ethnicity of a candidate prior to the interview. Therefore, viewing a video resume or a one-way video interview before interviewing a candidate in-person is legal under this statute. See www.eeoc.gov/eeoc/foia/letters/2004/titlevii_ada_recordkeeping_video.html.

In 2010, EEOC was again asked about discrimination laws as they applied to the video interview. Again, EEOC cited Title VII when explaining why it saw no problem with usage of the video interview: "The EEO laws do not expressly prohibit the use of specific technologies or methods for selecting employees, and therefore do not prohibit the use of video resumes." While the letter is about the use of video resumes, Title VII would play out similarly for one-way video interviews. Live video interviews should not leave employer any more exposed to discrimination laws than an in-person meeting since employer and candidate meet in real-time. The following quote is from an informal discussion letter dated September 21, 2010, regarding video resumes written by EEOC Office of Legal Counsel staff members in response to an inquiry from a member of the public:

> *For example, if a Title VII covered entity identifies an applicant's religion from viewing her religious garb in a video resume and rejects her application for employment on that basis, the covered entity has engaged in unlawful employment discrimination in violation of Title VII. However, biased treatment is not always conscious. The EEO laws prohibit "not only decisions driven by . . . animosity, but also decisions infected by stereotyped thinking." Because viewing a video may trigger unconscious bias, especially if opportunities for face-to-face conversation are absent, covered entities should implement proactive measures, or best practices, to minimize this risk. For example, before using video resumes and other video screening devices, a covered entity could proactively formulate and communicate to selection officials how the video resumes can help assess specific qualifications and skills that are necessary for success in the position. Additionally, a covered entity could require that several people assess each video resume in relation to the stated job requirements. Source: www.eeoc.gov/eeoc/foia/letters/2010/ada_gina_titlevii_video_resumes.html*

How Video Interviewing Can Protect Against Discrimination

Video interviewing provides users the ability to monitor and track all screening and interviewing activity to prevent discrimination in their organization. Video interviewing ensures that recruiters and hiring managers will be held accountable for any discriminatory behavior while providing companies with recorded proof of their compliance with discrimination laws. Video interviewing provides users with a fair and equal process with the following benefits:

- **Transparency:** Everything that happens during the video interview is on the screen for everyone to see: employers, recruiters, and hiring managers, candidates, EEOC, and OFCCP. In other words, "what you see is what you get."
- **Consistency:** Employers may create a single recording of the same interview questions and ask those questions in the same way from the same interviewer to every candidate interviewed. Everyone receives the same consistent experience.
- **Non-Discriminatory**: Video interviewing using pre-prepared and/or pre-recorded standardized questions for candidates prevents small talk, flattery, jokes, and off-subject discussions that may create unwanted opportunities for discrimination.
- **Record Retention:** Using video interviewing in the hiring processes can strengthen compliance with the OFCCP since contractors and sub-contractors are required to store interviewing and applicant data for up to two years. Video interviewing software can perform that task easily.

However, no matter how well video interviewing can help with compliance, organizational leaders still need to establish the right values in their workforces to truly ensure compliance with discrimination laws.

Video Interviewing Can Actually Improve Compliance

Fear of discrimination litigation is not a reason to avoid video interviewing; it may actually be one of many reasons to gravitate toward it. Well-designed video interviewing platforms can become part of the solution by improving compliance and reducing the risk of discrimination.

When used properly, video interviewing becomes an important technology for hiring effectiveness overall and aids in ensuring that no discrimination laws are broken. Setting standard practices that focus on skills, knowledge, and qualifications for a particular job can help employers avoid discrimination in the hiring process.

The obvious advantages of video interviewing far outweigh speculative risks and concerns about exposure to potential discrimination issues with the EEOC and the OFCCP. Based upon current law there is no reason to suspect that employers realistically face such a risk.

Author Tip ⟩ **Whitepaper on Video Interviewing & Discrimination**

Employment Screening Resources (ESR) has released a whitepaper sponsored by leading video interviewing solution provider Montage (www.montagetalent.com) titled **"Video Interviewing & Discrimination – What Talent Acquisition Leaders Need to Know,"** to show how employers can leverage video interviewing technology to improve their hiring process and the quality of their hires and, at the same time, stay in legal compliance. The complimentary whitepaper is available at www.esrcheck.com/Whitepapers/Video-Interviewing-and-Discrimination/.

About the Right to Privacy

The *Right to Privacy* from unwarranted governmental intrusion is guaranteed to every American citizen by the United States Constitution. Although the federal constitutional protections do not extend to private employers dealing with job applicants and employees, most states have passed privacy legislation that recognizes a right to privacy to employees of private employers. Many states have passed privacy laws that cover specific situations, such as states that do not allow consideration or regulation by an employer of various forms of "off-duty" conduct.

In recent years, many states have taken measures to prevent the misuse of Personally Identifiable Information (PII) in order to fight the rising tide of identity theft. The federal government has also taken measures. The main federal protections are contained in Gramm-Leach-Bliley Act (GLBA) and Health Insurance Portability and Accountability Act of 1996 (HIPAA). The federal Fair Credit Reporting Act (FCRA) was amended in 2003 to also provide additional measures to protect against identity theft.

There is also a common law right to privacy in many states in regard to employment matters. A common law right means a legal right created by precedents set by court cases, instead of laws created by a legislative body. Common law rights include:

- The right to avoid public disclosure of private information.

- The right to be protected from false or misleading statements being made in public.

- Unreasonable intrusion into private affairs, either physically (such as a polygraph test) or otherwise invading an area of personal privacy.

- Infliction of emotional distress by outrageous conduct.

Given all the complexities of privacy law, and the fact that privacy is also a cultural concept that can change from society to society, the same can be said about privacy as well. Privacy can be an issue in many different contexts and situations. However, this section is focused only on the issue of privacy and hiring.

NASA Case Limits Privacy Rights of Workers in Employment Background Checks

In a case pitting individual privacy rights of citizens against national security concerns of a country, the U.S. Supreme Court unanimously overturned a ruling limiting government inquiries about contract workers at a National Aeronautics and Space Administration (NASA) laboratory and ruled the federal government can ask employees about their drug treatment, medical conditions, or other personal matters during background checks, and that the questions did not violate the constitutional privacy rights of employees. The case—*NASA v. Nelson, 131 S.Ct. 746 (2011)*—concerned contract workers who challenged the extensive background checks required at NASA's Jet Propulsion Laboratory (JPL) in Pasadena, CA, as overly intrusive. The Supreme Court ruling overturned a federal appeals court ruling that said the government went too far in asking contract workers questions about drug treatment and suitability for employment, and gave the government broad latitude to ask personal questions during backgrounds checks of contractors at government facilities. Federal employees have undergone standard background checks since 1953, and the government began background checks of contract employees in 2005 as part of the policies developed after the terrorist attacks of September 11, 2001. Supreme Court Justice Samuel Alito wrote for the court stating that, "The challenged portions of the forms consist of reasonable inquiries in an employment background check." However, the Court did not announce broad rules or a test for interpreting what questions were permissible, and according to some legal observers, future litigation is still possible. The Court did cite several factors that made these inquiries permissible:

- Citizen employees (and citizen contractors) of the government fall under the hand of the government more than citizens not working for the Government.

- The questions are reasonable and sufficiently employment-related.

- Private employers, as well as the government, have long used background checks.

Information gathered in background checks would be confidential due to the federal Privacy Act on dissemination of employee and contractor information.

The U.S. Supreme Court recognized the value of background checks in the NASA privacy case. The Government has an interest in conducting basic employment background checks. Reasonable investigations of applicants and employees aid the Government in ensuring the security of its facilities and in employing a competent, reliable workforce. In the context of the case, it appears the same rule applies to private employers since the Court cited how private employers do similar searches.

The case *NASA v. Nelson - 131 S.Ct. 746 (2011)* is available at http://supreme.justia.com/cases/federal/us/562/09-530/.

As recently as 2015, lower courts have followed the Supreme Court's holding in NASA—supporting the ability of the government to reasonably seek and collect personal information where distribution is not an issue. See *Lavender v. Koenig, 2015 U.S. Dist. LEXIS 34141.*

Hill v. National Collegiate Athletic Association

California has led the nation in issues involving employee privacy. A leading case is *Hill v. National Collegiate Athletic Association, 7 Cal.4th 1 (1994)*. The *Hill* case provides an excellent framework to analyze privacy claims. In the *Hill* case, the issue was whether a college athletic association could require student athletes to sign consent forms for drug testing. The California Supreme Court ruled that the drug testing requirement was an invasion of privacy because drug testing required an intrusion into bodily integrity. The court further held that the benefits did not outweigh the intrusion of rights, there were less intrusive means to accomplish the goal, and the NCAA failed to show that the particular program it proposed furthered the intended goal. In its discussion, the Court in *Hill* discussed various privacy rights and wrote that, *A 'reasonable' expectation of privacy is an objective entitlement founded on broadly based and widely accepted community norms.*

Privacy claims are typically a balancing test with different competing interests being examined and weighed. In analyzing an invasion of privacy claim in an employment context, courts will first look to see if the employer invaded an employee's or applicant's protected privacy rights. If the employer's action did intrude upon privacy rights, then the court will examine:

- Did the employer's action further a legitimate and socially beneficial aim?

- If so, did the purposes to be achieved outweigh any resulting invasion of privacy?

- Was there a less intrusive alternative that could have accomplished the same aim without invading privacy?

Hill is widely considered a landmark case in California. The California Supreme Court has repeatedly affirmed *Hill's* method of analyzing constitutional privacy claims in cases such as *Hernandez v. Hillsides, Inc., 47 Cal. 4th 272 (Cal. 2009)*. California cases have used the test as recently as June 21, 2016. In re *M.H., 2016 Cal. App. LEXIS 592 (Cal. App. 4th Dist. June 21, 2016*.)

There are other privacy matters that are not a matter of balance but have been made illegal directly by statute. For example, in 1988, the U.S. Congress enacted the Employee Polygraph Protection Act (29 U.S.C. §§ 2001-2009). This act severely limits the ability of most private employers from using a polygraph or lie detector test for job applicants or current employees who are being investigated. Although there are some narrow exceptions, as a practical matter, this law ended the use of lie detectors.

In a United States Supreme Court case concerning pornography, Justice Brennan famously wrote that hard-core pornography was hard to define, but that "I know it when I see it." *Jacobellis v. Ohio, 378 U.S. 184 1964.*

Privacy Issues Employers Face

Employers have a legal duty to respect the privacy of applicants and employees in a variety of areas, such as what information an employer can obtain; how to protect the data; who can see the data; and the rights of applicants and employees to discover what data has been obtained. Maintaining privacy has become a critical concern in recent years after all the news about the large-scale theft of data from firms who store large amounts of personal and identifiable data. Workplace privacy is broad subject spanning a range of issues, from electronic monitoring of email, searches of personal belongings, and physical surveillance, to regulating workplace behavior and dress codes, off-the-job conduct, and the protection and dissemination of confidential information. For purposes of this book, the concern is focused on gathering, utilizing, and protecting information necessary for hiring and retention decisions.

There is no reason why a well-designed Safe Hiring Program should violate any statute or common law right to privacy. The processes outlined in this book are NOT intended to pry into an applicant's private life, turn employers into *big brothers*, or turn hiring managers or HR professionals into the *hiring police*. In fact, the type of job-related information that an employer obtains is about how a person has conducted themselves in their public lives—an area of their life that is visible to the public. For example, where a person has worked or attended school is generally not a confidential matter. Anyone who is interested could see where the applicant was working or studying. Those activities are done in the open. In addition, if a person has a criminal record, that too is a matter of public record. A Safe Hiring Program does not invade those areas that society generally keeps private and confidential. The one tool that comes closest to challenging a reasonable expectation of privacy would be credit reports, which are discussed in a later chapter.

In addition, all of the Safe Hiring techniques recommended in this book are done with an applicant's expressed consent. A conscientious employer will require each applicant to consent to and authorize in writing a background screening. If pre-employment background screening is outsourced to a background screening firm pursuant to the Fair Credit Reporting Act (FCRA), then by federal law there must be written authorization and disclosure (an exception is for truck drivers, and even then, there still must be authorization).

Of course, just because information may not be private does not mean it is not confidential. If an employer locates a criminal record, efforts must be made to limit that information to only those in the company with a need-to-know for purposes of making a hiring decision.

Safeguarding Personally Identifiable Information (PII)

Personally Identifiable Information (PII) such as a Social Security number is confidential and must be safeguarded. The term "personally identifiable information" generally refers to information which can be used to identify, distinguish or trace an individual's identity either directly or when used in conjunction with other information about a person. The right to privacy extends to how information obtained in a Safe Hiring Program is stored in order to protect against unauthorized viewing or theft. Another consideration is computer security when applicant data is transmitted or stored over a network. Maintaining confidentiality and security is a critical employment screening task.

As mentioned throughout this book, employers who engage in a Safe Hiring Program provide safeguards and assurances to ensure the information will be kept confidential and used for legal purposes. Honest candidates understand that background screening is a sound business practice that helps all concerned. Job applicants want to work with qualified and safe co-workers in a profitable, professional environment.

The following are examples of PII:

- Full name.
- Birthday.
- Birthplace.
- Social Security number.
- Vehicle registration plate.
- Driver's license number.
- Credit card number.
- National identification number.
- IP (Internet Protocol) address.
- Face, fingerprints, or handwriting.
- Digital identity.
- Genetic information.

Author Tip **Privacy Issues Are Also Addressed in the Following Chapters:**

- Privacy issues related to defamation are covered in Chapter 4 on The Reference Checking Process.
- International privacy and data protection are addressed in Chapter 17 on International Background Checks.
- The employer's duty to protect confidential information, including employee files, is covered in Chapter 22.
- The duty of a pre-employment screening firm to protect the confidentiality of data is addressed in Chapter 5 on the Fair Credit Reporting Act (FCRA) and in Chapter 7 on Implementing the Employment Screening Process.
- Privacy and drug testing are addressed in Chapter 15 on Drug Testing.

- Privacy and the Internet and social media sites are covered in Chapter 14 dealing with social media background checks and Web 2.0.
- Privacy and data brokers are covered in Chapter 22.

Privacy Considerations When Screening In-house or Outsourcing

In conducting pre-employment screenings, an employer essentially has two choices. The employer can either conduct the screening in-house or outsource to a third party.

One advantage of outsourcing background screening is that screening companies must abide by the Fair Credit Reporting Act (FCRA), which is often termed the *gold standard* of privacy. Under the FCRA, all background screening is done with the applicant's written authorization as well as a disclosure of rights. There are limits to what may be obtained and for what reasons, and who can access the information. There are also rules about maximum accuracy and re-investigation. By following the FCRA, employers have less concern that an applicant can allege a violation of privacy since everything is done pursuant to federal law at the onset. How the FCRA protects privacy is specifically discussed in a later chapter.

However, if an employer performs in-house applicant screening, then the employer no longer has the protection of the FCRA. In this situation, the employer's actions are governed by privacy law considerations. As a result, the employer needs to have an in-depth understanding of the privacy law framework within their jurisdiction or at the location where the job is being performed.

Author Tip〉 **Advice to Employers Doing Screening In-House**

An employer who does in-house screening or investigations must be aware of the tightrope the employer must walk when balancing the need to discover information about job applicants and employees with their need for privacy rights. Of course, it is not unlawful for an employer to conduct its own background checks. However, considering the promulgation of the many laws intended to preserve individual rights to privacy, employers can be at risk when performing screening in-house. To minimize risk, firms performing their own screening should act as though the FCRA applied.

Privacy and the Trend of Offshoring Data by Background Check Firms

Within the background screening industry, it is a well-known fact that some background screening firms are **offshoring PII** in bulk on a daily basis to offices in countries like India or the Philippines to process background checks. Offshore workers may call U.S. employers to perform employment checks, do data entry, or check U.S. Court websites for criminal records. Depending on the screening firm used, job applicants and employers may not even realize there is a measurable likelihood that their PII will end up outside the U.S. and its territories—and beyond U.S. privacy laws—in a foreign call center or data processing location.

Unfortunately, all U.S. privacy protections as a practical matter cease to exist once PII leaves the shores of the United States. Although some countries have extremely strong data and privacy protection laws, such as the European Union (EU) states, many places where information is sent off-shore for processing may have very little, if any, protection.

These countries are selected because they offer a way to cut costs. In addition to a lack of privacy laws or enforcement in some countries, American job applicants, as a practical matter, have no ability to enforce any privacy rights overseas. In many countries, there is little practical or cost-effective access to courts, and it is extremely difficult for an American consumer to contact a foreign police department to lodge a complaint or to obtain assistance. The lack of any meaningful protection once U.S. data is sent off-shore is a major gap in the effort to combat identity theft and to protect privacy. In some countries, for example, private data can be purchased very cheaply.

Of course, data theft can also occur in the U.S. However, in the U.S., there are legal protections, resources, and recourse mechanisms to help victims of identity theft. Once the data goes offshore, that protection dissipates rapidly. Firms that engage in offshoring may well engage in practices to protect PII and keep it confidential. However, that does not mitigate the fact that sending PII overseas for processing carries inherent risks. Although there has been some activity at the state and federal levels of implementing new acts or amending current ones regarding off-shoring, there are no current federal laws that explicitly prevent companies from offshoring personal information. However, before selecting a background screening firm, an employer needs to have a full understanding of how data is protected once it leaves the U.S., and what duty is owed to job applicants in terms of notification that their data is going abroad.

California Senate Bill 909 (SB 909)

On September 29, 2010, Governor Arnold Schwarzenegger signed into law **California Senate Bill 909 (SB 909)**, which became the first law in the nation that addresses the issue of Personally Identifiable Information (PII) of consumers who are the subjects of background checks being sent offshore.

SB 909 required specific disclosures and modifications to be included on Consumer Reporting Agencies' privacy policy made to consumers before their personal information such as Social Security Numbers (SSN) is sent offshore, overseas, and outside of the United States. To view a complete copy of California SB 909, visit www.leginfo.ca.gov/pub/09-10/bill/sen/sb_0901-0950/sb_909_bill_20100929_chaptered.pdf.

More information about California SB 909

More information about California SB 909 is presented in the Addendum - Privacy Case Law and Recent Events.

Concerned CRAs

There are also a number of screening firms that have taken a stand against offshoring PII to cheaper offshore labor centers. Concerned CRAs is a group of some 200 Consumer Reporting Agencies (CRAs) dedicated to consumer protection. The group has endorsed a set of standards that opposes offshoring PII of U.S. citizens outside the country to be processed beyond U.S. privacy laws. See: www.concernedcras.com.

According to the Concerned CRA's website:

> Some employment background screening firms send individuals' sensitive personal information (i.e. social security numbers and financial account information) offshore to be processed. We believe that sending such information off-shore places both applicants and employers at risk and should be avoided whenever possible. Alternatively, when personal information is sent to other countries, applicants and employers should be made aware of this practice in advance.

The bottom line: Privacy is a critical part of the employment process and employers need to clearly understand where PII concerning their applicants is going.

Although there are economic advantages for a screening firm to offshore, a Consumer Reporting Agency (CRA) that chooses to display the No Off-Shoring Seal subscribes to the belief that risking a consumer's personal and identifiable information to make more money is not justified by the risk to the consumer and the employer.

Company to Pay $3.1 Million for Illegally Offshoring Personal Data

In March of 2016, a New York-based company that had been awarded a contract by the state to digitize files holding fingerprint records and personal information collected from 22 million people, agreed to pay $3.1 million in penalties and fees for unlawfully outsourcing and "offshoring" the work overseas to India.

The *New York Times* reported that the company was awarded a $3.45 million contract from New York State that required employees responsible for scanning State Division of Criminal Justice Services records that included fingerprints, Social Security numbers (SSNs), and dates of birth to pass background checks.

However, the company instead outsourced and offshored more than a third of the contract to an Indian company for $82,000 which processed records and risked the privacy of over 16 million people. Under the agreement, the company admitted to violating the New York False Claims Act.

The Times article can be found at www.nytimes.com/2016/03/24/nyregion/new-york-state-contractor-is-said-to-threaten-privacy-of-millions-with-outsourcing.html.

Complimentary Whitepaper on Offshoring

A complimentary whitepaper titled *The Dangers of Offshoring Personally Identifiable Information (PII) Outside of United States* reveals how offshoring PII used in domestic background checks can place PII at considerable risk to compromised privacy, quality, and accuracy. For more information, visit www.esrcheck.com/Whitepapers/Dangers-of-Offshoring-PII/index.php.

Protecting Privacy and the Use of Home Operators

Another employment issue related to off-shoring is using home workers to perform certain employment and education verifications. The concern for employers is that their applicants' personal data could be sent to home operators working from kitchen tables and even dorm rooms across America. The following are key issues that must be addressed when using home operators during the employment screening process:

- **Privacy:** A screening firm would be directly responsible for making private information viewable and printable on people's home computers.
- **Professionalism:** A screening firm would have difficulty accurately claiming that at-home researchers are "professionals" when they are unsupervised, unregulated, and acting as cheap substitutes for what is supposed to be a professional service. How does the sound of barking dogs, crying babies and television sets in the background strike those asked to provide verifications?
- **FCRA Defensibility:** A screening firm would have difficulty defending the practice of using at-home researchers against a claim under FCRA section 607(b) concerning reasonable procedures for accuracy.
- **IC Classification:** A screening firm cannot classify individuals as Independent Contractors (IC) when they work only for you when you tell them exactly how to do their job, and when they are providing the same core services provided by your in-house staff.

- **Training/QC:** A screening firm cannot train and discuss production issues in real time. It is also difficult for at-home researchers to learn from each other when everyone is working in isolation. Furthermore, since everyone works alone, it is harder to enforce quality rules across the entire organization.
- **Supervision:** Unsupervised at-home researchers are very difficult to supervise. In addition, since they are paid by the completed verification, they may be more tempted to fake orders since there is no one supervising them in real-time.
- **Reliability:** A screening firm would be dependent entirely on the researchers' priorities, which may not be your own. They may put a hair appointment ahead of the employer's forty new verifications that have to be called today. The employer wants workload balancing to be under their control and not secondary to at-home researchers' personal schedules.
- **Hidden Costs:** There are hidden costs to managing and maintaining multiple remote researchers as opposed to a central pool of talent. Take, for instance, the time lost to the unreliable performance of at-home researchers' internet connections, home computers, and printers.
- **Due Diligence:** A screening firm and employer could face significant legal exposure if the at-home researcher's performance falls below a professional standard of care due to lack of training and supervision.
- **Disclosure:** Would the employer want to disclose to their applicants that the sensitive data and professional service they've entrusted their employer with was being performed by unsupervised home workers?

A professional background screening company should provide critical employment and education verifications in a professionally supervised call center dedicated to the highest level of customer service, privacy, and accuracy.

International Data and Privacy Protection

Another critical privacy element is **international privacy and data protection**. Numerous countries have privacy and data protection rules. The rules from the European Union (EU) have received the most attention in recent years. In 2016, the EU and the United States formally adopted the new **EU-U.S. Privacy Shield** framework to create stronger protection for transatlantic data flows between the European Union and the United States, to protect the fundamental rights of people in the EU with personal data being transferred to the U.S., and to bring legal clarity to businesses relying on transatlantic data transfers. The practical aspects of international privacy and data protection for not only the EU but also for many other parts of the world is revisited in Chapter 17 in the context of international background checks.

CHAPTER 3

The Application and Interview Process

Part 1 – The Application

In a Safe Hiring Program, the application process starts before applications are printed or given out. It really starts when the job is first created.

Application Process Starts BEFORE Application Is Filled Out

First, an employer needs to create a **job description**. This is important for a number of reasons. Having a job description that clearly defines the essential function of the job and core competence not only helps identify and select the right candidate during recruitment, but also provides legal protection against claims of discrimination or compliance with the Americans with Disabilities Act (ADA). It is essential to have a job description in the event a criminal record is disclosed or discovered. This helps ensure an employer's decision making is consistent with the requirements of the federal Equal Employment Opportunity Commission (EEOC), as explained earlier. A well-designed job description also helps lessen the risks of discrimination complaints and lawsuits for employers who utilize social media resources for recruiting and selection.

A job description should clearly indicate the levels of education and experience required of candidates as well as the experience, training, and technical skills necessary to be successful in the job. It may also include "soft skills" such as the ability to work in a team or show leadership. Those who do not have the required knowledge, skills or abilities (sometimes referred to as KSA), may be discouraged from applying in the first place. If a candidate misleads an employer about their qualifications, then the fact the requirements were clearly set forth in the job description will assist the employer in the event there is a rejection or termination. An employer can always take the position that dishonesty on an application is grounds for termination. However, the employer's position is buttressed when it is clear from a well-written job description there were certain requirements for the position, the job description was provided by the applicant, and the applicant misled the employer about his or her qualifications by making false statements or material omissions.

The job duties of a person in a management or supervisor position are also a critical consideration. Does part of the written job description indicate a manager's duty to "record, report, and address issues of workplace misconduct such as acts of workplace violence, or harassment, or drug abuse?" Placing these duties in the written job description of supervisors serves to re-enforce their role in workplace safety.

Numerous resources and websites, as well as commercially available software, can assist an employer in preparing job descriptions. A link to free job descriptions, as well as other legal resources for employers who conduct background checks, are available on the *Legal Compliance* web page on the Employment Screening Resources (ESR) Resource Center at www.esrcheck.com/Resource-Center/Legal-Compliance/.

How Applicants Fill Out Applications and How Employers Receive Them

Although many employers still accept resumes, an entire industry has developed around the process of helping employers identify, recruit, hire, manage, develop, and retain the talent needed to meet their needs. An essential element in this process is an Applicant Tracking System (ATS), which is essentially an electronic means to handle recruitment and application for employment. There is a wide range of solutions and solution providers available, working with both small and medium businesses to enterprise solutions. An ATS firm will generally also sort and score resumes by keywords and other criteria in accordance with the job and descriptions and requirements.

By working with an ATS, an employer, for example, can have a branded employment page where opportunities can be searched and applications submitted. The ATS industry offers numerous tools and methods for employers to handle the entire recruiting, hiring and onboarding process. ATS providers are constantly devilling new ways to improve the speed and quality of hires and employers have numerous options to choose from. More information about background checks and ATS solutions are discussed in a later chapter.

Author Tip ▷ **Many Employers Look for Alternatives Before Hiring FTE**

Many employers will first examine alternatives before even deciding to hire a full-time employee (FTE). For example, an employer may look to see if they can promote from within the organization, recall someone who has been laid off, transfer someone from another department, or if work can be reshuffled or done more efficiently. In some cases, temporary workers from a staffing vendor can fill the void, or even an independent contractor if the need is more project based. Some employers may use a Professional Employer Organization, or PEO, to help find workers and the PEO can act as the actual employer of record which includes handling payroll and benefits. However, obtaining workers through a staffing vendor does not alleviate an employer's due diligence obligations. See Chapter 18 for a more detailed discussion on issues related to using staffing vendors to supply a workforce.

If the employer decides to increase their FTE count, then the employer may also want to look at their current team and identify those individuals who are outstanding performers and try to determine what knowledge, skills, and abilities they have, in addition to other less tangible traits and soft skills that make them so successful. In other words, if the employer has outstanding workers they would like to literally "clone" because they are such outstanding performers, an employer needs to understand not only what makes them outstanding, but what attracts and keeps them engaged in doing that job at their company. If an employer can understand these things, it increases the chances of identifying, recruiting, attracting, and retaining key performers.

Inform the Applicant about the Background Check

As part of any recruitment effort, the employer is well-advised to place applicants on notice that the firm practices safe hiring with background checks. The goal is to get maximum advantage from safe hiring by discouraging applicants to hide something when applying. Employers can place a phrase in the job announcement, bulletin, classified advertisement, or internet site that indicates the firm requires background checks.

On the one hand, there is the likely effect that applicants with something to hide will go down the block to employers that do not exercise due diligence. Let a competitor be the employer of choice for people with problems. Announcing a company background check policy does not keep good applicants from employers any more than security checkpoints at airports stop people from flying. However, keep in mind that when it comes to criminal records, employers are well advised to follow a policy of Ban-the-Box, which means that questions about any criminal records should not be asked too early in the process. Otherwise, such questions tend to act as an early knockout punch and may chill or deter otherwise qualified applicants from applying at your company. Any language about criminal record checks in a job announcement should be reviewed by legal counsel to ensure it does not violate a Ban-the-Box law in your jurisdiction or deter ex-offenders from applying. Similarly, any job announcement or posting must also be consistent with state and federal discrimination laws. An employer must be careful to avoid language that implies certain protected groups would be at a disadvantage. For example, an announcement that indicates an employer is a *very young company*, or they are looking for a *recent graduate* can be construed as code words showing intent to engage in age discrimination. See page 54 and also Chapter 10 for a more detailed discussion of Ban-the-Box.

Using the Application Form as a Hiring Tool

Although it seems obvious, a critical aspect of the application process is to use a proper job application form. Consider it a best practice. It does not matter if the application process is done through the traditional paper form, an online email application through an employer's website, an employment portal powered by an Applicant Tracking System or Human Resources Information System (HRIS), or through a job board or some other type of internet type system.

A professionally reviewed job application should allow the employer to legally obtain the necessary information to begin the hiring process. Applications ensure uniformity and that all needed information is obtained. It is much easier for an employer to prescreen candidates using a standardized application. An employer trying to screen a large number of applications can more easily compare applicants. Also, applications protect employers from having impermissible information a resume may contain. The application provides employers with a place for applicants to sign (either physically or electronically) necessary statements that are part of the hiring process.

As a rule of thumb, employers should avoid using or even accepting resumes. First, resumes are not always complete or clear. They are far from uniform which creates practical issues in trying to locate the right candidate for the job. Applicants also often feel compelled to add all sorts of personal information to a resume that have little bearing on the job. Even worse, resumes may reveal information an employer did not request or even want that may reveal that an applicant is a member of protected class. For example, the resume may reveal membership in groups or organizations that tend to show the person's race, ethnicity, or national origin. To add to the complication, in some circumstances accepting unsolicited resumes can create substantial record keeping and record retention headaches for employers. Some employers refuse to accept unsolicited resumes and will direct anyone interest in employment to their job portal. Federal contractors, who must deal with the Office of Federal Contract Compliance Programs (OFCCP), need to be concerned with numerous issues created by the so-called *Internet applicant rule*. If an employer insists upon using resumes, then the employer is well-advised to always use a standardized application form as well at some point in the process. At a minimum, anyone invited for an interview should be required to fill out a standard application form.

Author Tip ▷ **What Constitutes an Applicant and the *Internet Applicant* Rule?**

The Internet Applicant rule addresses recordkeeping by Federal contractors and subcontractors about the Internet hiring process and the solicitation of race, gender, and ethnicity of "Internet Applicants" who satisfies all four of the following criteria:

- The individual submitted an expression of interest in employment through the Internet or related electronic data technologies;
- The contractor considered the individual for employment in a particular position;
- The individual's expression of interest indicated that the individual possesses the basic qualifications for the position; and
- The individual, at no point in the contractor's selection process prior to receiving an offer of employment from the contractor, removed himself or herself from further consideration or otherwise indicated that he/she was no longer interested in the position.

See: www.dol.gov/ofccp/regs/compliance/faqs/iappfaqs.htm.

Asking about Past Criminal Matters – Ban-the-Box, the EEOC, and State Specific Laws

In any discussion of an employment application, an employer should keep in mind both ban-the-box laws that are being passed in many states and local jurisdictions and the EEOC's Enforcement Guidance on the Consideration of Arrest and Conviction Records in Employment Decisions under Title VII of the Civil Rights Act of 1964. The Guidance impacts how and when criminal records are considered, including questions on the application form about past criminal matters. How his guidance affects applications is discussed later in this chapter. Chapter 10 has an in-depth review of how this guidance affects the entire hiring and employment screening process. The full text of the EEOC Guidance is available at www.eeoc.gov/laws/guidance/arrest_conviction.cfm.

Assuming that employers follow ban-the-box as a best practice, employers may not even ask about criminal records in the initial application. In addition, when the employer does ask about a criminal record, there are numerous states that have specific rules concerning when, how, and what can be asked on an applicant about past criminal records. More information about state law rules is found in Chapter 6.

However, it is a best practice for employers at some point in the hiring process to understand if a person has a relevant criminal matter that is either job related or creates a business necessity for the employer to consider the risk that may be involved. As discussed in Chapter 10, an employer is well advised to delay that inquiry as late as possible in the hiring process and not to ask questions related to criminal matters on the initial applications. However, it is also true that negative information honestly disclosed and explained at an appropriate point in the hiring process may very well have no effect, especially if the applicant otherwise has an excellent and verified work history. However, when an applicant has failed to honestly disclose negative information, then the employer's concern turns to the lack of honesty involved. If the applicant is dishonest and negative information is first revealed by a background check, then the failure to hire may be justified. That is why it is important to have well thought out language in the application.

You Need To Know

How and When to Ask a Candidate about any Past Criminal Matters

One suggested best practice is to use a supplemental form at or after the interview or post-offer asking about a criminal record. Asking post-offer is the most conservative approach. However, the criminal question must be carefully drafted to take into account state law and the EEOC Guidance on criminal records. In Chapter 6, which covers state laws for screening, various types of restrictions on asking about criminal records are explored. Some of the restrictions relate to timing, such as Ban-the-Box. Laws that require the question be delayed until at or after an interview or job offer. However, numerous states have also imposed restrictions on the extent of the questions or asking about certain types of offenses that have been expunged. In preparing an application form, it is important to carefully review appropriate state laws to ensure that any supplemental application form asking about criminal matters be carefully crafted in accordance with not only the EEOC Guidance but with numerous states laws as well. To add to the complexity, there are city and counties within states that have their own rules as well.

Author Tip

All Applications Should Have This Language:

"The information provided by the applicant is true and correct, and any misstatements or omission of material facts in the application or the hiring process may result in discontinuing of the hiring process or termination of employment, no matter when discovered."

This allows the employer greater flexibility in dealing with dishonest applicants. As discussed elsewhere in this book, there is scientific evidence that demonstrates what employers already know—if applicants are dishonest in the way they get a job, there is a likelihood they will be dishonest once in that job.

In addition, employers may be able to utilize a "falsification" defense in the event that an employment related legal action occurs post-hire. Although state laws differ, finding out that an employee engaged in material falsification during the hiring process may provide a defense in a later employment claim on the basis that the employee would not even have been employed but for the falsification. Even though some states limit that defense, it is still valuable to ensure that all applicants are clearly on the record as understanding that material falsifications are grounds to terminate employment even if discovered post-hire.

Ten Critical Items Every Application Needs

It is much easier for an employer to prescreen candidates using a standardized application. An employer trying to screen a large number of resumes can more easily compare applicants. Ten critical things need to be addressed in every application as part of a Safe Hiring Program:

1. The application needs to clearly state that "there will be a background check" or "a background check will be performed." A well-worded application form discourages applicants with something to hide and encourages applicants to be open and honest. (See the discussion about the added complexities per the EEOC Guidance on criminal records.)

2. An application should state that "untruthfulness or material omissions are grounds to terminate the hiring process or employment, **no matter when discovered**." This is critical when an applicant is not truthful about a criminal conviction or some other important item of information in their application, especially if it is discovered after the person has been hired and onboarded.

3. As a best practice—and consistent with numerous federal, state, and local policies, regulations, or laws—employers should NOT ask about past criminal conduct in an initial application form or process. Such questions should be delayed until at or after the interview. If an employer, for whatever reason, has decided not to follow a Ban-the-Box policy and delay any criminal questions, the questions concerning criminal records on the form should contain some very specific language. The employer should clarify that a criminal conviction will not result in automatic rejection of an applicant and that the employer will take into account the nature and gravity of the crime, the age of the crime, and nature of the job. However, employers have found that there is really no practical reason to inquire about the existence of a criminal record in the application stage. The one time an employer may be arguably justified in having such language is where there is an absolute legal bar to hiring individuals with certain criminal records. Even then, if the prohibition on hiring is based upon a state law, there are still possible EEOC considerations since federal law pre-empts state law. Again, see Chapter 10 on the EEOC and Title VII for a more detailed discussion of these matters. A related issue is how an employer should handle the question of criminal background checks in any job announcement. Unless there is a legal requirement for the job related to a criminal record, employers should be very cautious in making any reference to a criminal record in a job announcement. Statements concerning a criminal record can have the same impact on deterring or chilling ex-offenders from applying as having a criminal question on the application. Such an approach can carry risk for an employer and, as discussed in the ban-the-box section of Chapter 10, may not end up saving an employer any time and may, in fact, create a source of potential legal liability.

4. The application form can ask the applicant to consent to "pre-employment background screening including verifying educational and professional credentials, past employment, and court records." Such a release may discourage an applicant with something to hide or encourage an applicant to be forthcoming in an interview. However, if an employer uses an outside service to perform a pre-employment screening, the Federal Fair Credit Reporting Act (FCRA) requires there must be a consent and disclosure form separate from the application. In other words, release language in the application itself may not be legally sufficient for a third party background check. See more information in Chapter 5 on the FCRA.

5. The consent portion on any release form used for a background check can indicate the release is "valid for future screening for retention, promotion, or reassignment (unless revoked in writing)." This is sometimes referred to legally as an "Evergreen" clause, meaning it stays active in the future for some reasonable period of time. This is helpful, for example, when an employer needs to conduct a post-employment investigation into allegations of sexual harassment or other workplace problems. Even though the Fair and Accurate Credit Transaction Act (FACT Act) of 2003 gives employers more flexibility to conduct investigations where there is suspicion of workplace misconduct or wrongdoing, such a clause provides an employer additional grounds. An employer may also want to check on information brought to its attention after the hiring occurred that may suggest dishonesty on the consumer's part or the existence of a criminal record, even though there is no current misconduct. There is a lack of clear authority as to how long an "Evergreen" consent would remain valid for future screening. To minimize risks, it would be a better practice for an employer to obtain a new consent if there is a need for a supplemental background check if that is possible under the circumstances. If a consent is longer than six months, an employer may well want to check with legal counsel before relying on an "old" consent.

6. The application form should ask for ALL employment for the past 5-10 years. This is critical. A standardized application form makes it easier to spot unexplained gaps in employment. This is an important step in the hiring process and a critical part of exercising due diligence. Even if an employer hires a background screening company to perform a pre-employment criminal check, records can be missed because there is no national criminal record resource available for use by private employers. Criminal checks must be done in each county where the applicant has lived, worked, or attended school. If a person has an uninterrupted job history, an employer may have more confidence that the applicant has not been in serious trouble over the years. See Chapter 4 on past employment verifications for a more detailed discussion as to why past employment checks are just as important, if not more important in some circumstances, then a criminal check.

7. The form should ask about addresses for the last seven to ten years. This helps in determining the scope of any criminal record search. As discussed in the chapters on criminal records, private employers generally do not have access to an "official" criminal record, and criminal searches are based upon locations where a person has been in the past.

8. The form should allow the applicant to indicate whether the current employer may be contacted for a reference.

9. The application should ask: "Please list all degrees or educational accomplishments that you wish to be considered by the employer in the employment decision." It puts job applicants on notice that any degree they list may be considered. This is helpful in situations where applicants are dishonest about their educational accomplishments but the degree may not be a job requirement. The dishonesty becomes the critical factor in that situation.

10. Finally, an employer can cover other standard matters. Examples include: the organization's *at will policy*; the employer is a *non-discriminatory employer*; or the employer uses mandatory arbitration in disputes.

Critical Areas and Questions Applications Must Avoid

The Federal and state laws examined in the last chapter prohibit any non-job related inquiry, either verbal or through the use of an application form, which directly or indirectly limits a person's employment opportunities because of race, color, religion, national origin, ancestry, medical condition, disability (including AIDS), marital status, sex (including pregnancy), age (40+), exercise of family care leave, or leave for an employee's own serious health condition. There are other areas that an employer may go into, but with limits, such as criminal records.

Employers want to avoid application questions and interview questions that directly identify a person as a member of a protected group. However, even questions that appear neutral on their face can be illegal if the question results in a disproportionate screening of members of a protected group or is not a valid predictor of job performance. Examples include application questions about arrests, which will be discussed in detail in later chapters on criminal investigations and criminal records.

As a rule of thumb, an employer cannot ask anything in an application that an employer cannot ask in a face-to-face personal interview. Later in this chapter in the section on interviews, there is an in-depth chart listing questions that are prohibited. **These same rules apply to applications.**

Applications and Compliance with Title VII of the Civil Rights Act and ADA

The **Title VII of the Civil Rights Act** and the **Americans with Disabilities Act (ADA)** are probably the two most well-known laws that apply to discriminatory hiring practices. These laws prohibit any non-job-related inquiry, either verbal or through the use of an application form, which directly or indirectly limits a person's employment opportunities because of race, color, religion, national origin, ancestry, medical condition, disability (including AIDS), marital status, sex (including pregnancy), age (40+), exercise of family care leave or leave for an employee's own serious health condition.

These laws generally prohibit any type of questions of applicants which:

- Identify a person on a basis covered by the Act; or,
- Results in the disproportionate screening out of members of a protected group; or,
- Are not a valid predictor (not a job-related inquiry) of potential successful job performance.

The case *Griggs v. Duke Power Co., 401 U.S. 424 (1971)* was a groundbreaking United States Supreme Court case concerning the disparate impact theory of employment discrimination.

> ### Griggs v. Duke Power Co.
>
> The Court ruled that the company's employment requirements did not relate to the applicants' ability to perform the job, and had the impact of discriminating against African-American employees, even though the company had not intended it to do so. In the 1950s, Duke Power's Dan River plant had a policy that African-Americans were allowed to work only in its Labor department, which constituted the lowest-paying positions in the company. In 1955, the company added the requirement of a high school diploma for its higher paid jobs. After the passage of the Civil Rights Act the company removed its racial restriction, but retained the high school diploma requirement, and added the requirement of an IQ test as well as the diploma. African American applicants, less likely to hold a high school diploma and averaging lower scores on the IQ tests, were selected at a much lower rate for these positions compared to White candidates. It was found that White people who had been working at the firm for some time, but met neither of the requirements, performed their jobs as well as those that did meet the requirements.
>
> The Supreme Court ruled that under Title VII of the Civil Rights Act, if such tests disparately impact ethnic minority groups, businesses must demonstrate such tests are "reasonably related" to the job for which the test is required. As such, Title VII of the Civil Rights Act prohibits employment tests (when used as a decisive factor in employment decisions) that are not a "reasonable measure of job performance," regardless of the absence of actual intent to discriminate. Since the aptitude tests involved and the high school diploma requirement were broad-based and not directly related to the jobs performed, Duke Power's employee transfer procedure was found by the Court to be in violation of the Act.

How to Avoid Previous Names and Marital Status Discrimination

One of the areas where the discrimination laws have an effect on safe hiring is the use of previous names in a criminal search. The issue arises because past names are a necessary identifying piece of information. For example, when searching for criminal records, researchers base the search on the last name. However, if an applicant at one time was known by a different name, a complete criminal search must be conducted under BOTH names. The most typical situation is in the case of a woman who has married and changed her name.

The problem is that by referring to a name as a maiden name, an applicant potentially is being identified on the basis of their marital status or sex, which can be a violation of federal and state discrimination laws. In California, for example, asking for an applicant's maiden name has been specifically labeled as an unacceptable question by the California Department of Fair Employment and Housing, the California agency charged with enforcing the California civil rights laws. Consequently, a previous name search should not be referred to as a "maiden name" search, since that clearly indicates that an employer is obtaining information on marital status, which is a prohibited basis upon which to make an employment decision. That is why any application or consent for background screening should always include the phrase "previous name" instead of "maiden name."

Is this an example of a distinction without a difference or political correctness going too far? No. Marital status has been a traditional basis for a woman to be the subject of discrimination. The fact is that whether a man or woman is married is simply not a valid basis to predict job performance. However, the reality has been that a woman applicant who is married may be the subject of discrimination based on a belief that she may leave the job to have a family. By phrasing it as a "previous name," the same information is obtained for purposes of a background check, but the application information is facially neutral. In addition, a female applicant is not discouraged from applying based on an apprehension that by asking for a "maiden name" there is a likelihood of discrimination.

How to Avoid Age Discrimination

Most authorities agree that any information tending to reveal age should not be requested on an application form or during an oral interview. Asking for date of birth during the selection process could violate the federal **Age Discrimination in Employment Act** as well as various state civil rights laws.

Using Date of Birth Information on the Job Application

Asking for date of birth tends to deter older applicants from applying. If the application material contains date of birth information, the inference is that a firm may be methodically denying consideration of older workers. Many states have rules which prohibit an employer, either directly or through an agent, from seeking or receiving information that reveals date of birth and age before an offer is made. For example, the California Pre-employment Inquiry Guidelines by the California Department of Fair Employment and Housing lists specific age questions that cannot be asked.

Special problems are faced when an applicant's date of birth is not available. When researching court records, the date of birth is probably the most important factor needed to identify an individual since many court records do not contain Social Security numbers. In fact, in some jurisdictions, a criminal search cannot be conducted without a date of birth. It is also needed in many states in order to obtain a driving record. Thus the date of birth is a key piece of identifying data on DMV records.

Under the federal **Age Discrimination Act of 1967**, there is not an absolute prohibition against asking for date of birth or age. That is a common misconception among employers. In fact, the EEOC has specifically ruled that asking for date of birth or age is not automatically a violation of the act. However, the EEOC ruling indicated that any such request would be closely scrutinized to ensure that the request has a permissible purpose. The EEOC also indicated that the reason for asking for date of birth should be clearly disclosed so older applicants are not deterred from applying (See 29 Code of

Federal Regulations §1625.4 – 1625.5). The following information is provided by the EEOC website at https://www.eeoc.gov//eeoc/publications/age.cfm:

"Pre-Employment Inquiries

The ADEA (Age Discrimination in Employment Act) does not specifically prohibit an employer from asking an applicant's age or date of birth. However, because such inquiries may deter older workers from applying for employment or may otherwise indicate possible intent to discriminate based on age, requests for age information will be closely scrutinized to make sure that the inquiry was made for a lawful purpose, rather than for a purpose prohibited by the ADEA. If the information is needed for a lawful purpose, it can be obtained after the employee is hired."

If a firm does screening in-house, then the firm may consider performing all screening and obtaining information **post-offer**. This provides maximum protection since there can be no inference that age played a role in the decision to hire or not hire.

Use of Date of Birth Information by the Employment Screening Company

What if an employer outsources background screening to a private firm? The screening firm will normally need the date of birth to perform the service because it is a key identifier. There are several options.

First, with advancing technology, many screening firms are able to offer a paperless system, where the applicant fills out the forms online, including sensitive information such as date of birth. That way, an employer or Applicant Tracking System (ATS) is not obtaining or storing dates of birth. If working with a screening firm that does not have advanced technology, an employer can consider outsourcing to a screening firm only post-offer. If a conditional offer of employment is made that depends upon a background screening report, then asking for the date of birth post-offer is probably safe. The downside, however, is that it is an administrative burden for most employers to coordinate the process of giving offers, followed by collecting the date of birth, and finally transmitting it to a screening firm. Most employers have a practice of requiring all applicants to fill out a consent form for the background screening firm at the same time the original application is filled out, and the screening firm's forms will typically need the date of birth information.

Another possible route is to only request the date of birth information on the screening firm's form and not on any employer form. Furthermore, the applicant release forms should not be made available to the person or persons with hiring authority in order to avoid any suggestion that age information was used in any step of the hiring process. Most employment screening companies recommend that employers keep the screening forms and reports separate from the employee's personnel file or application papers.

To additionally protect the employer, the form used for the screening company can have such additional language as:

- The information requested on the screening firm's form is for screening and verification of information only and has no role in the selection process.
- All federal and state rights are respected in the employer's screening process.
- The year of birth is optional on the form (although this can lead to delays).
- The information is used for identification only and without such information the screening process may be delayed.

Another best practice is for an employer to require a screening firm to takes steps to remove all references to age and date of birth in its reports so that employers will not receive age information. This is a common screening industry practice, where a date of birth or Social Security number is truncated so that the year will appear as XXXX and only the month and day is in the report in order to assist in identification but protect against identity theft

Discrimination against Unemployed Job Applicants

With the recent economic downturn, discrimination against unemployed job applicants has made the headlines recently. News stories indicate employers and staffing agencies have publicly advertised jobs in fields ranging from electronic engineers to restaurant and grocery managers to mortgage underwriters with the explicit restriction that only currently employed candidates will be considered. Some employers may use current employment as a signal of quality job performance, but such a correlation is decidedly weak. A blanket reliance on current employment serves as a poor proxy for successful job performance. In addition, there had been proposals for legislation to prevent employers from discriminating on the basis of past unemployment. This is an area HR professionals should monitor.

Another area to monitor is asking about past salary history. There have been proposals to prevent employers from asking about past salary and also prohibit employers from requiring applicants to provide their salary history before receiving a job offer as a way to prevent wage discrimination on the basis of gender (See Chapter 2.)

Review the Application as a Whole

A key walk-a-way point is there is no one tool tells an employer the entire story. An employer needs to review and cross-reference all the information they have. An employer needs to not only review each individual part of the application, but to also ask the question: does it make sense as a whole? For example, do past addresses seem to correlate to locations of past employers? Are there unexplained employment gaps? Do dates of graduation from a school or the date a license or certification was obtained make sense in terms of employment history and past addresses?

Author Tip	**The Application Form Can be a Trigger to a Lawsuit**
	Whenever there is an issue of a bad hire, the first step most attorneys or experts take is to carefully examine the initial application form. In those situations, it is quite common to discover issues in the application that clearly suggest this was a problem just waiting to happen. The importance of a careful review of the application cannot be stressed enough. Failure to carefully review an application is one of the leading causes of hires that do not work out.

Ten Sure Signs of a Lawsuit Waiting to Happen

After going through the process of preparing an effective application and utilizing it instead of a resume, many employers make the fatal mistake of not reading the application carefully. This is a major mistake. Employee lawsuits often catch employers by surprise. Another way employers are bitten by their applications happens when, upon closer examination, the employee's application shows that the employer could have reasonably predicted they were hiring a lawsuit just waiting to happen. Per the 2012 EEOC Guidance, a recommended best practice is to NOT ask about criminal records on an application. If an employer adopts that practice, that could impact the suggestions below.

By looking for the following **ten danger signals**, an employer can avoid hiring a problem employee in the first place:

1. **Applicant does not sign the application**. An applicant with something to hide may purposely not sign the application form so the applicant cannot later be accused of falsification.
2. **Applicant does not sign consent for background screening.** When a firm uses an outside agency to perform screening, federal law requires a separate disclosure and signed consent from the applicant. A background consent form protects employers in two ways: 1) it discourages applicants with something to hide and 2) encourages candid interviews. If a candidate fails to sign the consent, it is not a good sign.

3. **Applicant leaves criminal questions blank**. If the application asks about past criminal convictions, an applicant with a past problem may simply skip the questions about criminal records. The timing of when and how to ask about past convictions under the 2012 EEOC Guidance is covered in Chapter 10. Most jurisdictions only permit questions about convictions and pending cases. A criminal record can be either a felony or a misdemeanor; employers make a big mistake if they only ask about felonies since misdemeanors can be extremely serious too. Although employment may not be denied automatically because of a criminal conviction, an employer may consider the nature and gravity of the offense, the nature of the job, and the age of the offense when evaluating whether there is a sound business reason not to employ someone with a criminal record. If an applicant lies about a criminal record, then the false application may be the reason to deny employment.

4. **Applicant self-reports a criminal violation**. Just because an applicant self-reports an offense does not eliminate the possibility other offenses exist, or the applicant may report it in a misleading way to lessen its seriousness. An employer is well-advised to check it out.

Author Tip → ## Honest Criminal Syndrome

The first four points are sometimes referred to as the *honest criminal syndrome*.

A person may have had a criminal record in the past and does not want to be dishonest about it. On the other hand, the person may not want to be fully revealing either. That is why it is so critical to look at the application's criminal question carefully to ensure it is filled out. Self-reported offenses should be looked at extra carefully. For example, an applicant self-reported that he stole some beer from a store. He neglected to mention it was stolen at the point of a gun, which is robbery, a much more serious offense. Another applicant reported he was stopped by police when he was younger, and some recreational drugs he had were found under the car seat. A review of the court records revealed it was actually two pounds of cocaine—which is a lot of recreation.

Again, keep in mind that the EEOC Guidance on criminal records may cause employers to modify when and how they ask these questions.

---

5. **Applicant fails to explain gaps in employment history**. There can be many reasons for a gap in employment. For example, an applicant may have been ill, gone back to school, or had difficulty finding a new job. However, if an applicant cannot account for the past seven to ten years, that can be a red flag. It could potentially mean he or she was in custody for a criminal offense. It is also important to know where a person has been because of the way criminal records are maintained in the United States. Contrary to popular belief, there is not a national criminal database available to most employers. Searches must be conducted at each relevant courthouse, and there are over 10,000 courthouses in the U.S. However, if an employer knows where an applicant has been, it increases the accuracy of a criminal search and decreases the possibility that an applicant has served time for a serious offense. If there is an unexplained gap, an employer may not know where to search and can miss a criminal record. The importance of looking for unexplained employment gaps will be reviewed in more detail in subsequent chapters.

6. **Explanations for employment gaps or reasons for leaving past jobs do not make sense**. If there were employment gaps reported by the applicant, do the reasons for the gaps make sense? A careful review of this section of the application is needed and anything that does not make sense must be cleared up in the interview.

7. **Applicant fails to give sufficient information to identify a past employer for reference checks**. This is another sign of possible trouble. Verifying past employment is a critical and important tool for safe hiring. Some employers make a costly mistake of not checking past employment because past employers historically tend not to give detailed information. However, even if a reference check only reveals dates of employment and job titles,

this critical information eliminates employment gaps. In addition, documenting the fact an effort was made will demonstrate due diligence.

8. **Applicant fails to explain the reason for leaving past jobs**. Past job performance can be an important predictor of future success.

9. **Applicant fails to indicate or cannot recall the name of a former supervisor**. Another red flag. Past supervisors are important in order to conduct past employment checks.

10. **Excessive cross-outs and changes.** This can be an indication an applicant is making it up as he/she goes along.

These ten danger signs all assume that an employer is using an application form, not a resume.

Review the Form with the Applicant

One way to avoid making these mistakes is to go through the application with the job seeker, checking to be certain the applicant filled out the forms completely. Rehash the question with the applicant if he or she has shown questionable answers. The process is intended to both ensure accuracy and to determine with certainty that the applicant stands behind what he or she has stated on the application form.

> **Author Tip** > **Case in Point**
>
> The author testified as an expert witness in a case where a school district hired a teacher who had been convicted in another state of a felony charge—sex with a minor. The offense made the person ineligible to teach. On the employment application where it asked if the applicant had ever been convicted of a crime, the applicant put a slash mark in between the Yes and the No. The school district has a policy of reviewing the application with the applicant to clarify what the applicant meant. A school district employee asked the applicant which box he meant to check, and the applicant then clearly indicated "Yes." Unfortunately, after being on notice there was a criminal offense in the applicant's background, the school district failed to follow through and investigate the offense. After the applicant had been hired, he was accused of inappropriate behavior with female students at the school. Under legal scrutiny, the failure to follow through after being put on notice of a past crime was found to be negligent hiring.

Where to Find a Good Application Form

There is a definite trend towards employers utilizing Applicant Tracking Systems (ATS) to create an employment portal to receive application forms. Employers need to ensure that the ATS from is legally compliant. However, if an employer is still using paper forms, or putting their own application form online, sample application forms are available from a number of sources:

- The local or state Chamber of Commerce may have forms available.
- A firm's business or labor attorney will normally have a new employee package available with an application form.
- Human resources consultants and HR organizations may have forms.
- Office supply stores sell basic business forms including application forms.
- Books about running a business are available from local bookstores and may have sample forms.
- There are firms that specialize in selling employment related forms and products on the Internet.

Many firms design their own employment forms to reflect the particular needs of their firm or industry.

One word of caution: Many states have unique rules regarding what can and cannot be on an application. Some of these rules concern what an employer may ask about past criminal convictions. It is beyond the scope of this book to review the requirements for all fifty states; however, an employer is well-advised to consult with a labor attorney for every state they hire within to review the legality of their application forms.

Cup of Coffee with that Criminal Conviction? Starbucks Case Underscores Importance of Well-Crafted Employment Application

A California appellate court case, *Starbucks Corporation v. Lord*, addressed the issue of how applicants are asked about criminal records on an application form. A class action was filed against Starbucks Corporation on behalf of 135,000 unsuccessful job applicants on the basis that the Starbuck *application contains an 'illegal question' about prior marijuana convictions that are more than two years old.* The lawsuit was claiming $200 per applicant, which meant Starbucks was facing a potential exposure of $26 million dollars.

On the application form Starbucks asked, "Have you ever been convicted of a crime in the last seven (7) years?" It then states, "If Yes, list convictions that are a matter of public record (arrests are not convictions). A conviction will not necessarily disqualify you for employment."

On the reverse side of the application, just before the signature line, Starbucks clarified the criminal question with a disclaimer that reflects protections afforded job applicants under California Labor Code sections 432.7 and 432.8:

CALIFORNIA APPLICANTS ONLY: Applicants may omit any conviction for the possession of marijuana (except for convictions for the possession of marijuana on school grounds or possession of concentrated cannabis) that are more than two (2) years old, and any information concerning a referral to, and participation in, any pre-trial or post-trial diversion program.

The disclaimer, however, was the very last sentence in a 346-word paragraph that went into other areas, including employment being at will, release of information, misrepresentations in the application, and even disclaimers about Maryland and Massachusetts.

The plaintiffs were concerned that since the disclaimer was physically separated from the question about past crimes and was essentially buried in the fine print, those applicants either would overlook the disclaimer, or would not want to go back and cross out their previous responses, or ask for a clear copy.

The Court agreed there was an issue of whether the *one-size-fits-all* style of applications used was ambiguous or not. However, the court also found that two of the plaintiffs in the case were not harmed by any ambiguity since they both testified they understood the question and had no drug history anyway. Because there was no one suing who had actually been harmed, the Court ruled in Starbuck's favor.

The Court discussed how allowing these kinds of suits by plaintiffs who were not actually harmed would potentially "create a whole new category of employment-professional job seekers, whose quest is to voluntarily find (and fill out) job applications which they know to be defective solely for the purpose of pursuing litigation. This is not the law in California." Even though the employer prevailed, it was only because the plaintiffs were not, in fact, real applicants. This type of case should cause every employer to review their application form with their attorney or HR section for legal compliance.

Part 2 – The Interview Process

The Importance of Interviews

Interviews must be conducted in a manner that not only assures the employer of finding the best candidate for the position but also is legal, and does not put the employer in harm's way. This chapter examines the job interview as an integral part of a Safe Hiring Program.

The interview is the first opportunity for an employer to meet face-to-face either in person or through video interview software with applicants who may literally and figuratively hold the keys to future business success in their hands. During the interview process, an employer practicing safe hiring must take steps to protect the workforce and ensure the best and most qualified candidates are hired.

Within a Safe Hiring Program, an interview can accomplish three goals:

1. **Convey critical information to the applicant in order to discourage bad applicants and to encourage honesty**. Applicants need to understand clearly the firm has a Safe Hiring Program. Use the interview to convey the message to all applicants. Since at the same time an employer is recruiting qualified employees who will adopt the firm's values and become loyal and hardworking, the safe hiring process cannot be accomplished in an overbearing fashion. Think of the interview as an opportunity to reinforce the message already communicated in company application forms and job announcements—your firm practices safe hiring!

2. **Allow for the transfer of information from the applicant to the employer**. The interview is a time when an employer has an opportunity to fill in any gaps. Also, the employer has a chance to ask the additional penetrating questions if the candidate seems to have attempted to conceal or lie about unfavorable information.

3. **Permit an assessment of the candidate**. Even though a Safe Hiring Program is based on the premise that instinct and intuition alone are not enough, the interview still provides the employer an opportunity to assess the knowledge, skills, and abilities of the applicant in person. Of course, good candidates can come across poorly, and bad candidates can come across well. The assessment is just one of many overlapping tools used in the calculus of a hiring decision.

However, the fact is that interviews are not nearly as effective as commonly believed in weeding out potential hires who are dishonest, unqualified, unfit, or unsuitable for employment. The sad truth is that every bad hire that a firm had to eventually terminate at one time successfully completed an interview. In every case where an employer has made a bad hiring decision, someone at the hiring firm walked away from the interview thinking the applicant would be a good hire. That is why an interview is just one part of a safe hiring program and must be utilized in conjunction with an entire safe hiring program. As the saying goes: "Trust, but verify." Given these goals, how does an organization ensure that positive results happen? This section examines the needed tools.

Going from Application Process to Interview – Progressive Screening

Before getting into the details of effective interviewing, it's important to first examine how an employer goes from potentially hundreds of applicants to the finalists that are called in for an actual interview? Most employers, hiring managers, Human Resources (HR) professionals, or recruiters have experienced the fact that the majority of applications received for an open position may not have any knowledge, skills, of experience that suggest they are in any way qualified for the job. Some HR veterans estimate that up to 70% of applications some employers receive have qualifications or experience that bear little if any resemblance to what is needed to be successful on the job.

Employers need to go through a process of whittling down a large applicant pool in order to identify those applicants that should be invited for an actual interview. Keep in mind that background checks are done on finalists, so a background check does not help an employer reduce the stack of written or virtual applications.

Employers generally engage in a process that can be called **Progressive Screening.** In this context, progressive screening refers to an employer reviewing and evaluating numerous applications in order to identify those that may be of further interest based upon locating the characteristics, or attributes the employer is seeking for that position. "Progressive" refers to the fact that an employer may go through several rounds of screening, each time either adding attributes to the list, or eliminating applications that seem to be less compelling than others.

For example, an employer, either by a review of resume or use of an automated online tools, may begin by looking for keywords or relevant past experience. Since the remaining stack may well be too large to handle efficiently, an employer may go through a second round of screening and apply criteria such as having a certain number of years of experience. As the field is narrowed down, the employer may then do an additional round of reviews and eliminate applications that are not as strong as others. Some employers may use software tools to look for keywords as well.

The subject of narrowing down a large pile of applicants is the subject of numerous books and articles and is only covered here because it's important to understand the concept of progressive screening as it relates to safe hiring.

It should be noted that sometimes the term progressive screening can refer to a related process where an employer asks a background screening firm to first conduct an initial screen, such as a social security trace. The screening firm does not perform the entire background report unless the applicant passed the first round. The employer does not have to spend additional money if a person does not pass the first round. However, many employers have found that the time and effort to perform this additional intermediate step delays the screening process and does not justify an occasional cost savings.

Preliminary Telephone Screen

Another helpful hiring tool is a preliminary telephone screen used after an employer has reviewed and narrowed down a possible list of candidates. A telephone screen will help narrow down the list even further and save an employer valuable time. Call each potential candidate asking the same list of questions based on the job description. If the candidate appears to meet the initial criteria, then an interview can be immediately scheduled. If a message is left and the applicant does not call back, then that applicant can be eliminated from consideration.

Sample Telephone Screen Script

A sample telephone screen script is found in the Addendum.

New Industry of Video Interviewing

A whole new industry has developed the past few years around video interviewing. A video interview should be the functional equivalent of doing an in person interview without having to have the applicant come to the office, or an interviewing team all having to be in the same physical location. Video interviews allow employers and job candidates to connect face-to-face using online video technology removing geography as a consideration. In some instances, video interviews often can be used to provide candidates the opportunity to answer a specific set of questions formulated by the employer. A video interview should be not confused with unsolicited video from job applicants putting their resume in video form.

All the rules used for an in-person interview should apply to video interviewing as well. A well thought out video interviewing process involves a great deal more than just using video conferencing tools. Software designed for video interviewing will contain a host of additional function and features specifically designed to facilitate an employer's hiring process.

In addition, when used correctly, a professional video interviewing platform can actual assist an employer in EEOC compliance Video interviewing provides users the ability to monitor and track all screening and interviewing activity to try to prevent discrimination in their organization. Video interviewing ensures recruiters and hiring managers will be held accountable for any discriminatory behavior while providing companies with recorded proof of their compliance with discrimination laws.

A whitepaper published by the author in conjunction with video interview firm Montage, **"Video Interviewing & Discrimination: What Talent Acquisition Leaders Need to Know,"** discusses some of the following benefits:

- **Transparency:** Everything that happens during the video interview is on the screen for everyone to see: employers, recruiters, and hiring managers, candidates, EEOC, and OFCCP. In other words, "what you see is what you get."

- **Consistency:** Employers may create a single recording of the same interview questions and ask those questions in the same way from the same interviewer to every candidate interviewed. Everyone receives the same consistent experience.

- **Non-Discriminatory:** Video interviewing using pre-prepared and/or pre-recorded standardized questions for candidates prevents small talk, flattery, jokes, and off-subject discussions that may create unwanted opportunities for discrimination.

- **Record Retention:** Using video interviewing in the hiring processes can strengthen compliance with the OFCCP since contractors and sub-contractors are required to store interviewing and applicant data for up to two years. Video interviewing software can perform that task easily.

The complimentary whitepaper on video interviewing can be downloaded at www.esrcheck.com/Whitepapers/Video-Interviewing-and-Discrimination/.

Author Tip

Hire the Best – NOT the Best Available

Do not fall into the trap of thinking you are looking for the best applicant in the bunch! If you have a written job description and you have an idea of what a star performer looks like, and that person is not in the batch of applications you are working with, it is not a good idea to just settle for the best of the bunch of who happened to apply. It may be time to go back out to the market. But first, the employer should make sure that the job description and job postings and advertisements were aligned with the employer's needs. Maybe you did not describe the job correctly, or really define the attributes of who you are looking for? If you are not getting the right people to apply, then perhaps you were not sending the right message.

Advantages of a Structured Interview

An interview is typically accomplished using a written set of questions selected ahead of time by the employer and provided to the hiring managers conducting the interviews. There are literally thousands of potential interview questions that can be asked. Questions can also depend upon the particular industry, the needs of the firm, and the position being filled. An employer needs to review all potential questions and select a set of questions that would be the most useful for selecting the best employees. That does not mean that everyone is always asked the exact same questions. Different positions may require that certain portions of an interview require customized questions. This can be done by a supplemental question set that is position-specific. However, the interview should assure all similarly situated candidates have the same question set.

A structured interview is defined as an interview format used across an organization. Structured interview questions are usually pre-printed on forms. The advantages for an employer using a structured interview are significant.

- First, it ensures uniformity in the interview process and protects against claims of discrimination or disparate treatment.
- Second, it helps to keep hiring managers on track by using legally defensible questions. By giving interviewers a script to follow, it helps an employer's efforts at training interviewers not to ask prohibited questions. A discussion and chart of permissible and impermissible questions is presented later in this chapter.
- Third, and most critical from the aspect of a Safe Hiring Program, the structured interview ensures the employer that certain essential "integrity questions" are asked of all candidates. Some of these questions are covered below.

At the same time, the process does not mean the interviewers are simply clerical robots, going through the motions and recording responses in a rote fashion. Penetrating follow-up questions and keen observations of the applicants are still critical to make sure all required areas are covered.

Behavior-Based Questions Should be Used

An essential part of a Safe Hiring Program is to question applicants carefully about their knowledge, skills, abilities, and experience. Part of the interview is designed to determine if the applicant will be a good fit, taking into account the work environment and the team the person will work with.

Interview techniques where the applicant is merely told to "tell me about yourself" have not proved altogether effective. In order to obtain more insight employers may ask hypothetical questions such as "what would you do if…" The *if* could be anything ranging from working with difficult people to completing assignments under deadlines. However, that still does not tell an employer about how the person actually did in the past.

Behavior-based interviewing is one of the newest and most effective methods for establishing if a person is a good fit for both the job and the organization. In a behavior-based interview, a person is asked to accurately describe real situations they have encountered and what they did to resolve the issue or problem. The method is based on the concept that the most accurate predictor of how a candidate will perform in the future is how he or she performed in the past in a similar situation. The question could be about a time when a person faced a typical workforce problem. This type of interview question may typically start with the phrase, "Tell me about a time when…"

There are numerous books, resources, and websites that offer suggestions on behavior-based interview questions. Here are sample questions to demonstrate the format:

- Tell me about a time when you had to coordinate several different people to achieve a goal. What were the challenges involved, and how did you overcome them?
- Tell me about the most difficult business related decisions you have had to make in the past six months. Describe the situation and what made it difficult. How did you resolve it?
- Give me an example of when you had to work with someone who was very difficult to get along with, and how you handled that situation.

Interviews - Spotting Liars is Not that Easy

There are lists of so-called tell-tale signs that a person is lying. For example, employers might observe if a person is avoiding eye contact, fidgeting, or hesitating before answering. Some people may think that if a person is smiling, they are telling the truth. Unfortunately, it can be a costly mistake for an interviewer to think lying can always be detected by such visual clues (tells) or by relying upon one's own instinct or intuition. Some of the so-called visual clues can simply be a sign of nervousness about the interview or stress and not an intent to lie. Studies have shown for example that smiling may not be associated with either lying or telling the truth. In fact, accomplished liars are more dangerous because they can disguise themselves as truthful and sincere. An experienced liar will often show no obvious signs.

A number of scientific studies have demonstrated that most people are actually poor judges of when they are being told the truth and when they are being deceived. Paul Ekman, a retired psychology professor in the Department of Psychiatry at the University of California Medical School in San Francisco, is the author of thirteen books, including Telling Lies (W.W. Norton, 2001). Based upon extensive testing, Ekman concluded that without training, a person could only detect who was lying at 50% of the time. According to Dr. Ekman: "Most liars can fool most people most of the time." This is probably particularly true in a job interview environment.

Researchers Identify True Clues to Lying

Below is text from an article in the *New York Times* summarizing this area of study.

"One of the consistent findings of the new research, which is being conducted by psychologists at several universities, is that people think they are better detectors of lies than they really are. Dozens of studies have found that people's accuracy at detecting lies usually exceeds chance by very little. While guessing alone would give a rate of 50 percent accuracy, in the recent studies the best rate of accuracy for any group has never exceeded 60 percent, and is most often near chance.

This is true even for those in professions where lie detection is at a premium. In a study done at Cornell University, for example, customs inspectors proved no better than college students at guessing which people were trying to smuggle contraband. Likewise, a study at Auburn University in Alabama found that police detectives were no more successful in judging people lying about a mock crime than were students.

Another study found that a group of seasoned Federal law enforcement officers from the Secret Service and the Criminal Investigation Divisions of the armed forces were no more accurate in detecting deceit than were newly recruited officers who had just joined those agencies. The one difference between the groups, though, was that the seasoned officers, who averaged seven years of service, felt more confident of their ability to detect lying, even though they were no more accurate. Studies such as these have revealed that people are poor at detecting lies in large part because they base their judgment on the wrong clues. For example, in the study of customs inspectors, people were most often thought to be telling lies if they did such things as hesitating before answering questions, avoided meeting the eyes of their questioner or shifted their posture. None of these signs, though, were actually more common among those who lied than among those who did not."

Source: www.nytimes.com/1985/02/12/science/reseachers-identify-true-clues-to-lying.html?pagewanted=all

Another researcher at the same school as Paul Ekman, Dr. Maureen O'Sullivan, tested 13,000 people for the ability to detect deception. Using three different tests, only 31 subjects—nicknamed *wizards*—could usually tell whether a person was lying about an opinion, how someone is feeling, or about a crime. More information about these studies is available at www.paulekman.com.

This advice is exactly in line with the author has been suggesting to employers for many years—trust but verify. Industry statistics suggest that as many as 30% of all job applicants falsify information about their credentials. Trying to rely on interviews gives limited protection. Some interviewees tell lies they have ingrained in their life story. They have created identities and legends of their own and, when they tell their stories, they are not fabricating on the spot. They put the story on their resumes and talk about it and tell their friends about it. It becomes part of their personalities and personal histories because they have told it so often. It becomes second nature as they retell it again and again.

An employment interviewer may be subject to a psychological phenomenon called the *halo effect*, where an interviewer's overall impression of an applicant may cause the interviewer to falsely assume that either good things or bad things about the applicant in general. A *likable* person, for example, may rate very well in an interview, even if in fact they are a con artist or potential embezzler. A person who does not come across as well may get less favorable ratings even though they may be the better candidate. An interviewer's own perception may also cloud their judgment, such as the HR professional who does not want to think ill of an applicant or conversely suspects a person is lying but ignores their instinct. See: https://en.wikipedia.org/wiki/Halo_effect.

That does not mean some liars cannot be detected at interview. The studies cited above make it clear that the clues are much more subtle and difficult to detect than most people realize. It does not mean that during an interrogation that is part of an investigation that trained law enforcement or fraud investigators do not possess a number of techniques to arrive at the truth. However, a job interview is generally not going to be similar to an investigative interrogation. Hiring managers and HR professionals can increase their odds of detecting fabricators at interviews through training. John E. Reid and Associates, for example, offers a one-day course specifically designed around interviewing of applicants. Information on John E. Reid and Associates one-day course specifically on interviewing applicants is at www.reid.com/training-interview-dates.html.

Employers, HR, and Security professionals should remember that as valuable as instinct may be, it does not substitute for factual verification of an applicant's credentials through background checks and other safe hiring techniques.

Open-Ended Questions and Follow-Up Questions

A proven technique of an integrity interview is the use of open-ended and follow-up questions. A key to using this technique is for the interview not to rely upon information given beforehand.

Let us say the interviewer starts with questions about a person's job history. If the interviewer does not have a resume or application, every question is *open-ended*, meaning the interviewee supplies all the information and no part of the answer is suggested by the question. This is the opposite of a *leading question* where the question itself suggests an answer.

For example, if an interviewer says, "I see you left Acme Industries due to a lay-off." That is a leading question. It suggests the answer, allowing the applicant to merely expand on that theme. An example of an open-ended question is "How long was your employment with Acme?" or "Why did that employment end?"

It is critical to ask follow-up questions when the answers do not make sense. If an applicant says something illogical, the interviewer should not hesitate to ask the applicant to review the answer. Sometimes it helps to ask the same question in a different way. For example, ask the applicant to describe in detail what occurred leading up to or after the event. If the applicant is making something up, that may be obvious. If an applicant gives a non-answer or an answer that is too fast and too pat, then a follow-up question would be helpful. For example, if an applicant says, "We already covered that," the interviewer, simply says, "I must have missed it. Can we review that again?"

As a practical matter, company managers and HR professionals are not expected to give every applicant the third degree. However, interviewers should be trained so they are not so glued to the questioning process that they do not pay attention to how the answers are given.

Six Questions That Should Be Asked In Every Interview

An effective way to empower interviewers is to include some key standard questions. Asking standard questions has several advantages. They allow for a consistent process so that all applicants are subjected to the same questions. Standard questions create a more comfortable environment for the interviewers. They do not have the pressure of having to remember every question they asked because the questions are written out for them. If the questions on safe hiring issues feel uncomfortable, then the interviewer can simply indicate that these questions are asked of everyone and they are required due to standard company policy.

Below are six suggested, critical interview questions every employer or hiring manager should be trained to ask. Of course, an employer would not want to get the interview off on the wrong foot with questions aimed at past criminal conduct or negative employment experiences. One of the goals of an interview is to help foster a talking environment where a potential employee understands and accepts the goals and direction of the organization. However, every interview does have a housekeeping portion where standard questions are asked. That would be a good time for the following six questions.

1. *Our firm has a standard policy of conducting background checks on all hires before an offer is made or finalized. You have already signed a release form. Do you have any concerns about that?*

    This is a general question about screening. Since the applicant has signed a release form, there is a powerful incentive to be honest and reveal any issues.

2. *We also check for criminal convictions for all finalists. Do you have any concerns about that?*

    This question goes from the general to the specific. Be sure to ask the question in a form that is legally permissible in your state and under the EEOC Guidance of 2012. It is important NOT to ask a question that is so broadly worded that it may lead to an applicant revealing more information than allowed by law. Again, make sure the applicant understands that he or she has signed a release and this process is standard company policy (See Chapter 10 for more information on the EEOC Guidance).

3. *When we talk to your past employers, what do you think they will say?*

    Note the questions begins: "When we contact your past employers…" Thus the applicant is given notice past employers will be contacted. This general question again provides a powerful incentive to be very accurate.

4. *Will your past employers tell us that there were any issues with tardiness, meeting job requirements, etc.?*

    This question goes again to a specific area. Ask detailed questions about matters that are expressly relevant to the job opening.

5. *Can you tell me about any unexplained gaps in your employment history?*

    If there are any unexplained employment gaps, it is imperative to ask about them.

6. *Is everything in the application and everything you told us in the interview true, correct, and complete?*

    This is the critical final question. It sends a clear message to an applicant that the employer takes the process seriously and that the applicant needs to be completely open, honest, and truthful. An interview can add an advisement that if there is anything the applicant wants to change on the application, now is the time to do it.

Since applicants have signed consent forms and believe the firm is doing background checks, applicants have a powerful incentive to be truthful. These questions are the equivalent of a New Age lie detector test. Employers can no longer administer actual lie detector tests and probably would not want to even if they could. However, these questions serve a valuable function by providing a strong motivation for applicants to be self-revealing. It also takes advantage of the natural human trait to want to have some control over what others say about you. If an applicant believes a future employer may hear negative information from a past employer, the applicant may want to be able to set the record straight before the future employer has the chance to hear negative information from someone else.

Good applicants will shrug the questions off, and applicants with something to hide may reveal vital information. Applicants with something to hide may react in a number of different ways. Some applicants may tough it out during the first question. However, the questions are designed to go from the general to the specific. By the second question, an applicant may well begin to express concerns or react in some way that raises a red flag. An applicant may object to the questions by asking if the questions invade their privacy rights. If an applicant raises such an objection, then simply indicate that these are standard job-related questions asked of all applicants.

Why Checking Employment Gaps Is So Important

An employer related the following story.

The applicant was just perfect for the computer job. He had all of the right qualifications. During the interview, the interviewer asked the usual questions. While taking a last look at the resume, the interviewer happened to notice a two-year gap in the employment and education history. Out of curiosity, the interviewer asked about the gap.

The applicant explained that he had decided to go back to go school and retrain so he could join the computer age. The interviewer was merely curious about the classes because he wanted to find some good classes for other employees. Where was it? Oh, it was a state-sponsored job-retraining program. Where was the program based?

With just a few questions it finally came out. The so-called computer school where the courses were taken was actually classes offered at a state prison. Of course, the applicant did have a perfect attendance record.

This story illustrates two key points:

1. Look at the resume or application for unexplained gaps.
2. Use the interview to ask the applicant about any gaps.

Actually, the criminal record by itself would not have disqualified the computer technician. The real problem was that the job in question required a person to go inside state prisons to fix computers—and prisons may not care to have former inmates come back in a professional capacity.

The important of verifying past embayment and spotting employment gaps will be revisited in the Chapters on criminal records and past employment verification. The process starts however with a careful examination of the application and looking for unexplained gaps in employment.

Questions Not to Ask and Why: Pre-Employment Inquiry Guidelines Chart

As mentioned at the outset of this chapter, a true Safe Hiring Program means the application, interview, and reference checking process must be conducted in a legal manner. If certain questions are asked, or if questions are asked in a certain way, an employer may be exposed to a variety of discrimination charges and lawsuits. The EEOC has extensive materials on pre-employment inquiries that can be discriminatory. See: www.eeoc.gov/laws/types/index.cfm.

Mr. Rod M. Fliegel, an attorney and shareholder with Littler Mendelson, P.C., has extensive experience defending national and local employers in state, federal, and administrative litigation, including high-stakes class actions. He also has special compliance and litigation expertise concerning the intersection of the federal and state background check laws.

Mr. Fliegel has graciously supplied us with the following **Pre-Employment Inquiry Guidelines Chart** that he authored with Phillip Gordon and Jennifer L. Mora, Attorneys At Law, Littler Mendelson, P.C. This chart, which is an excerpt from the *Littler on Background Screening & Privacy Rights in Hiring* publication, is an excellent guide to use for protecting a Safe Hiring Program's application and interview processes.

Mr. Fliegel also notes that the relationship between a screening firm and the employer is an **agency relationship** with legal ramifications. Both parties must be aware of this. Simply put, when an employer outsources aspects of its hiring process to a screening firm, such as pre-employment background or reference checks, the employer is trusting the screening firm to act on its behalf and in compliance with all applicable federal, state, and local legal constraints.

Take for the sake of example pre-employment disability-related inquiries. The EEOC's *Technical Assistance Manual (TAM): Title I of the ADA* (https://askjan.org/links/ADAtam1.html) expressly states: "If an employer uses an outside firm to conduct background checks, the employer should assure that this firm complies with the ADA's prohibitions on pre-employment inquiries. Such a firm is an agent of the employer. The employer is responsible for actions of its agents and may not do anything through a contractual relationship that it may not itself do directly."

A number of states have their own published guidelines as well. For example, the *Pre-Employment Inquiry Guidelines Chart* below is adapted from "Employment Inquiries," California Department of Fair Employment & Housing, www.dfeh.ca.gov/res/docs/publications/dfeh-161.pdf.

Here is the *Pre-Employment Inquiry Guidelines Chart* attributed to Phillip Gordon, Rod M. Fliegel, and Jennifer L. Mora, Attorneys At Law, Littler Mendelson, P.C.

§ 3.1 PERMISSIBLE INTERVIEW QUESTIONS

There are limits to what an interviewer can ask prospective or current employees when making hiring, retention, promotion or other important employment decisions. The following is a list of areas of inquiry that employers should keep in mind when interviewing prospective employees or conducting reference checks or background investigations.

Topic:	You May Ask:	You Should Not Ask:
ADDRESS/ RESIDENCE	"Can you be reached at this address? If not, would you care to leave another?" "Can you be reached at these telephone numbers? If not, would you care to leave another?"	"Do you own your home or rent?" "Do you live with your spouse?" "With whom do you live?"
AGE	Only questions that verify non-minor status; *i.e.*, "Are you over 18?" "If hired can you show proof of age?" "If under 18, can you after employment submit a work permit?"	"How old are you?" "What is your date of birth?" "What is your age?" "When were you born?" Dates of attendance or completion of elementary or high school. Any questions that imply a preference for persons under 40 years of age.
AIDS/HIV	"Are you able to perform the essential functions of the job applied for either with or without a reasonable accommodation? Yes or No?"	Any question that is likely to illicit information regarding whether an applicant (or current employee) has AIDS/ HIV.

ARRESTS & CONVICTIONS	Employers should check applicable state and local laws, including any ban-the-box laws, with respect to restrictions on the timing and substance of inquiries about arrests and convictions. In some jurisdictions, the following broad inquiry will be permissible: "Have you ever been convicted of a criminal offense? Do not include convictions that were sealed, eradicated or expunged, or convictions that resulted in referral to a diversion program. (Note: Convictions will not necessarily disqualify an applicant from employment. Factors such as the age and time of the offense, the seriousness and nature of the violation, and rehabilitation will be considered when making any employment decisions)."	Any question regarding an arrest that did not result in a conviction including in some jurisdictions even about pending charges in court. Any question regarding criminal records that have been sealed, eradicated or expunged, or otherwise judicially dismissed by a court. Any question about proceedings against an applicant as a juvenile.
CITIZENSHIP/ BIRTHPLACE	"Are you authorized to work in the U.S.? If hired, you will be required to submit verification of your legal right to work in the United States." BUT ask this of all applicants, not only persons appearing to the interviewer to speak a primary language other than English or be foreign-born.	"Are you a United States citizen?" "Where were you born?" Or any questions regarding birthplace or citizenship status of applicant, applicant's spouse, parents or other relatives.
COLOR OR RACE	Statement that photograph may be required after employment.	Any questions concerning race or color of skin, eyes, hair, etc. Should not require applicant to affix a photograph to application nor should applicant be given the option of attaching a photograph.
COURT RECORDS (see also "Arrests & Convictions," above)	"Has a court, jury or government agency ever made a finding you committed unlawful harassment or discrimination?"	"Have you ever filed for bankruptcy?" "Have you ever sued or filed claims or complaints against your employer?" "Have you ever been a plaintiff in a lawsuit?"

PHYSICAL OR MENTAL CONDITION, DISABILITY	"Can you, with or without reasonable accommodation, perform the essential duties of the job(s) for which you are applying (see attached job description)?" "Are you currently able to perform the essential duties of the job(s) for which you are applying?" If the disability is obvious, or disclosed, you may ask about accommodations. Statement by employer that offer may be contingent on applicant's passing a job-related physical examination.	"Do you have any physical disabilities or handicaps?" Questions regarding applicant's general medical condition, state of health, or illnesses. "Are you disabled?" An employer MAY NOT make any medical inquiry or conduct any medical examination prior to making a conditional offer of employment. "Have you ever filed for or received workers' compensation?" What medical problems the applicant may have. The amount of sick time or medical leave taken at last job. Questions that may reveal an applicant's family medical history or other genetic information.
DRUG USE	Current use of illegal drugs. Recent use of illegal drugs.	Questions about past addictions. Questions about use of prescription drugs or frequency of alcohol use.
EDUCATION	"Are you presently enrolled or do you intend to enroll in school?" "What subjects did you excel in at school?" "Did you participate in extracurricular activities?" "What did you select as your major?" "Did you work an outside job while attending school? Doing what? What did you like/ dislike about your part-time job during school?" "Are you interested in continuing your education? Why? When? Where?" "Did your education prepare you for the job you are seeking with us? In what ways?"	"Who paid for your educational expenses while you were in school?" "Did you go to school on a scholarship?" "Do you still owe on student loans taken out during school?" "When did you graduate from high school?"

EXPERIENCE, SKILLS & ACTIVITIES	"Do you have any special skills or knowledge?" "Are your skills recent?" "When did you last use a computer (or any other specific program, machine or skill)?" "Do you enjoy being active in community affairs?" "Are there any activities which have provided you with experience, training, or skills which you feel would be helpful to a position with us?" "How will your involvement in [activity] affect your work here?"	"Does your physical condition make you less skilled?"
FAMILY	"Do you have any commitments that would prevent you from working regular hours?" "Can you work overtime, if needed?" "Are you now or do you expect to be engaged in any other business or employment? If 'yes,' what kind of business or employment is it? How much time does it require?"	"How many children do you have?" "Who takes care of your children while you are working?" "Do your children go to day care?" "What does your husband (or wife) think about your working outside the home?" "What does your husband (or wife) do?" "What is your husband's (or wife's) salary?" Name of spouse or children of applicant. Is your spouse the same gender as you?
MARITAL STATUS	"Please state the name(s) of any relatives already employed by this company or a competitor." "Whom should we contact in case of an emergency?"	"Is it Mrs. or Miss?" "Are you single? Married? Divorced? Separated? Engaged? Widowed?" "Do you have a domestic partner?" "What is your maiden name?" Identity of applicant's spouse.
MILITARY SERVICE	"Have you served in the U.S. military?" "Did your military service and training provide you with skills you could put to use in this job?"	"Have you served in the army of a foreign country?" "What type of discharge did you receive from the U.S. military service?" "Can you provide discharge papers?"
NAME	"Have you ever used another name?" or, "Is any additional information relative to change of name, use of an assumed name, or nickname necessary to enable a check on your work and educational record? If yes, please explain."	"What is your maiden name?"

NATIONAL ORIGIN	To comply with the Federal Immigration Reform and Control Act of 1986, you may ask: "Are you prevented from being employed in the United States because of your visa or immigration status?"	"What is your national origin?" "Where were you born?" "What is the origin of your name?" "What is your native language?" "What country are your ancestors from?" "Do you read, write, or speak Korean (or another foreign language)?" (unless based on job requirements) How applicant acquired the ability to read, write or speak a foreign language. Or any other questions as to nationality, lineage, ancestry, national origin, descent or parentage of applicant, applicant's parents or spouse.
NOTICE IN CASE OF EMERGENCY	Name and address of *person* to be notified in case of accident or emergency.	Name and address of *relative* to be notified in case of accident or emergency.
ORGANIZATIONS	About any organization memberships, excluding any organization of which the name or character indicates the race, color, creed, sex, marital status, religion, national origin, or ancestry of its members: "Do you enjoy being active in community affairs?"	For a list of all organizations, clubs, societies, and lodges to which the applicant belongs.
PHOTOGRAPHS	For a photograph after hiring for identification purposes.	Any applicant to submit a photograph whether mandatory or optional before hiring.
PREGNANCY	"How long do you plan to stay on the job?" "Are you currently able to perform the essential duties of the job(s) for which you are applying?"	"Are you pregnant?" "When was your most recent pregnancy terminated?" "Do you plan to become pregnant?" Any questions about medical history concerning pregnancy and related matters.

PRIOR EMPLOYMENT	"How did you overcome problems you faced there?" "Which problems frustrated you the most?" "Of the jobs indicated on your application, which did you enjoy the most, and why?" "What were your reasons for leaving your last job?" "Have you ever been discharged from any position? If so, for what reason?" "Can you meet the attendance requirements of the job?"	"How many sick days did you take at your old job?" "Did you file any claims against your former employer?" "Have you sustained any work-related injury?"
REFERENCES	"By whom were you referred for a position here?" Names of persons willing to provide professional and/or character references for applicant.	Questions put to applicant's former employers or acquaintances that the employer would be prohibited from asking the applicant, such as questions that elicit information specifying the applicant's race, color, religion, national origin, disability, age or sex.
RELIGION OR CREED	Statement by employer of regular days, hours or shifts to be worked. "Are you available to work on weekends?" (if there is a legitimate business reason for this question)	"What is your religion?" "What church do you go to?" "What are your religious holidays?" "Does your religion prevent you from working weekends or holidays?"
SEXUAL ORIENTATION		"Are you a gay/lesbian/bisexual?" "What is your view regarding same-sex marriage?" "Do you have a domestic partner?"

What if an Applicant Offers Impermissible Information?

In response to an interview question, job applicants may offer information that an employer clearly does not want to know or even have in its possession. For example, in asking about employment gaps, an applicant may mention that they took time off to care for a sick child or deal with a medical condition. That raises the specter that the employer is now aware of potentially discriminatory information that cannot be used or considered for a hiring decision under state or federal civil rights rules or the Americans with Disabilities Act (ADA). Although the answer may sound innocuous, the employer now has information as to an illness or medical condition, marital status, or other matters.

In that case, employers may want to put down their pen, pencil, or computer tablet to make it clear that the information is not being recorded. The employer may then wish to state that such information is not relevant to the job and then inform the applicant, for example: "So the period of unemployment was for personal reasons, is that correct?" If an applicant volunteers information the interviewer did not ask for that touches on protected areas, the interviewer may want to state clearly that the question was not about that, and to repeat the last question or go on to the next question. Under no circumstances should an employer ever ask any type of follow-up question after an applicant makes a statement that potentially leads into protected areas. Of course, an employer should never ask a question that is likely to elicit protected information. If the matter of a disability does come up or is volunteered, an employer may ask: "Are you able to perform the essential functions of the job applied for either with or without a reasonable accommodation? Yes or No?" If a physical condition is apparent from viewing the applicant or volunteered, an employer may ask about accommodation. It is important not to keep, make, or retain any notes or make a notation on a resume or interview form of anything that is not strictly a valid and non-discriminatory predictor of job performance.

Author Tip ⟩ **Make Sure Everyone Knows What Areas are Off Limits During Interviews**

Although Human Resources professionals are generally well aware of the need to avoid sensitive areas protected by law during interviews, problems can arise when interviews are conducted by hiring managers or team members who may not entirely understand those areas that are off limits. It is critical that anyone involved in conducting interviews have training on those areas that are prohibited, and how to avoid getting into subjects that lead to the disclosure of protected information.

Looking for Red Flag Behavior

A savvy interviewer will be able to spot "red flags" that indicate further questions may be needed. Many of these tip-offs are non-verbal in nature. Of course, a perfectly honest and capable candidate may exhibit these red flags, while a practiced liar may not exhibit any at all. Therefore, this standard list of non-verbal clues is certainly not to be used as a basis for a hiring decision but could be used as a basis to ask more questions. The list below is by no means complete since many additional behaviors could be added. Keep in mind that, scientific studies have shown that interviewers, even trained law enforcement professionals, can have difficulty detecting who is lying. However, the following list may be helpful:

- Answering your question with a question or repeating your question.
- Answers do not make sense or are inconsistent.
- Becoming inappropriately defensive.
- Breaking eye contact.
- Clearing throat, stuttering, voice changing pitch, speed, or volume.
- Hesitation before answering.
- Inability to remember dates and details.
- Loss of previous cooperative behavior.
- Making excuses before asked.
- Nervous hand movements such as wringing or tightly gripping hands, repeated fluttering, brushing off lint, or moving documents.
- Non-responsive answers such as answering a question other than the question asked.
- Not remembering something when the applicant has remembered other events in detail.
- Protesting too much that they made the choice to leave a company.
- Shifting body position or defensive body language such as crossing arms, shrugging shoulders.

Summing It Up – An Interesting Story

Below is an interesting story by Dr. Marty Nemko. Dr. Nemko is co-author of *Cool Careers for Dummies*. He is a career and small business counselor in Oakland, California. His writings can be found at www.martynemko.com.

How it Works – A Story by Dr. Marty Nemko

Chester the Molester is looking through the Chronicle's employment ads. He finds an ad that sounds good—assistant manager of Pooh's Corner Children's Bookstore. On the bottom of the ad he reads, "We conduct background checks." He thinks, "Whoops, better look elsewhere."

Then Chester figures, "Ah, what the heck. They probably don't really do background checks."

So he applies, sending that resume and cover letter he so cleverly concocted. For example, "2000-2002: state-sponsored education program." Translation: Two years in San Quentin.

"I mean, I did learn a lot there!" he rationalizes. His cover letter and resume make Chester sound like a cross between T. Berry Brazelton and Maria from The Sound of Music.

The ruse works and Chester gets a call from Happy Chappy. They want him to come in for an interview! In his Mr. Rogers get-up, Chester saunters in, but he is in for a surprise. The receptionist says, "Before your interview, would you complete this application form and sign at the bottom authorizing the background screening?" He replies, "Sure, no problem," but he is thinking, "Uh-oh."

Chester shows for the interview, handing the application to the interviewer, Sally Savvy. Most of the questions are those standard simulations. Chester is so slick at BS'ing questions such as "What would you do if a child throws a tantrum?" Then Sally asks, "Before offering you the position, we would do a background check. Any objection to that?" Chester's heart starts to race, but he forces himself to look calm. "Not at all," he lies.

Sally continues: "As part of that check, we look to see if you have a criminal record. I notice on the application form, you didn't answer the question, 'In the past seven years, have you been convicted of a crime?' " Chester responds, "Oh, I forgot. I'll answer it now." He writes "No." His heart pounds through his chest wall.

Sally is relentless: "Oh, and of course, we contact your previous employers. Is there anything negative they're likely to say about you?" Beads of sweat form above his upper lip, like Richard Nixon in the 1960 presidential debate. "Well, uh, no." Chester manages to keep his voice calm sounding but he cannot control his eyes and forehead. The perceptive Sally knows he is nervous.

"Oh, and one more question. Because this job will require you to handle customers' money,

we will be conducting a credit check. Do you have any objections?" This is the last straw—Chester's debts greatly exceed the job's salary. Now he cannot even control his voice.

"Be my guest," he squeaks.

The interview ends and Chester thinks, "I don't want this stupid job anyway." Sally thinks, "There's something wrong with this guy." Even if she had planned to offer him the position, she would have first done a background check. That would likely have revealed Chester's criminal record and that his previous employer fired him for inappropriately touching children.

The Integrity Interview – A Special In-Depth Due Diligence Interview

For organizations that hire for positions that are high-risk, safety-sensitive, involve access to cash or assets, or deal with a vulnerable population, a special type of in-depth interview called **Integrity Interview** is another available tool. Some retailers also use this more intense interviewing technique to fight internal employee theft. This type of interview was more fully developed after the use of polygraphs, or lie detectors were made unlawful by federal law under the Employee

Polygraph Protection Act (EPPA) of 1988. Prior to that law, some employers would do an in-depth interview as part of a polygraph test.

This type of interview can differ from the standard interview conducted in-house by the employer or human resources. The idea behind an "Integrity Interview" involves more in-depth and probing questions typically by an outside professional. The applicant is told that if there are any corrections or additions they wish to make to their application or information given during their initial interview, now is the time to set the record is straight. The basic message is that information honestly disclosed during the Integrity Interview is much less harmful than the employer later discovering an applicant fudged on the truth. The applicant may believe that the interviewing firm will check out the information given and therefore there is an even stronger incentive to answers each question honestly and completely. The thrust of the Integrity Interview is to give an applicant a strong incentive to be truthful but without the polygraph machine.

This interviewer typically reviews the applicant's full employment history, including details about every job, the name of the supervisors, any difficulty or discipline related to the job, and any gaps between previous employment periods. The interviewer may also go into topics such as drug abuse, gambling, theft from past employers, and similar topics that are typically not the subject of a standard employment interview.

In the case of a large firm, the interview could be completed by another person within the organization such as personnel in security or loss prevention departments. However, the advantage of having a third party is that it adds to the applicant's incentive to be honest and some employers would rather have these types of pointed interviews be conducted outside of the organization.

The core concept is that an applicant is in a situation where they are likely to make the mental calculation that it is best not to hide anything. There is no one methodology for conducting such interviews. An employer has the option of following up the Integrity Interview by additional research or investigation by the third party firm that did the interview. In the alternative, the interview may simply be compared to the information on the employment application.

Integrity questions seek to explore:

- Is all information given during the hiring process true and complete?
- Does the applicant really have the knowledge, skills, abilities, and experience claimed?
- Is the applicant really who he says he is, or she is?
- Has the applicant left any material out of the application process?
- Has the applicant misstated any qualifications in the application process?
- Is there any reason to think the applicant's moral rudder is not set straight?
- In other words, is the applicant an honest person?

A good interviewer creates a comfortable and professional environment but also stresses the need for complete honesty. Consider the following specific questions:

> *It is not unusual to exaggerate in an application or resume. However, we need complete and accurate information concerning certain areas.*

> *Is there anything in your employment application that you want to change or correct? This is the time.*

> *If we checked with your former employers, would any of them report that you were asked to leave?*

If the interviewer wished to cover potential security issues such as criminal records or drug and alcohol use, then this question could be asked:

> *If we were to check court records, would we find any civil cases involving inappropriate behavior at your place of employment?*

Additional Integrity Questions

Below are additional questions that can be used during an in-depth integrity interview:

- Tell me every job you have had in the past 10 years, including start and end date, salary, job title when started and ended, and supervisor, including names, addresses, and telephone numbers.
- Are there any falsifications on your application?
- Did you leave any jobs off your application?
- How will your previous employers describe your attendance? …Excellent? …O.K.? …Poor?
- How many days have you missed in the last year?
- How many verbal/written reprimands for your attendance did you receive in the past 2 years?
- How many tardiness days were recorded in your personnel file in the last year / job? Why?
- How many disciplinary actions in the past 3 years?
- Where have you been suspended? Why?
- Where have you been fired or asked to resign? Why?
- Will any of your previous employers say they let you go or fired you?
- Where will you receive your best evaluation? The worst evaluation?
- Where have you suspected or had knowledge of co-workers or supervisors stealing?
- What have you taken?
- What will be found when your criminal record is checked? (Note: convictions will not necessarily disqualify any applicant from employment.)
- What does your current driving record show in the way of violations?
- Can you describe your best work related qualities?
- What is the worst thing any former employer will say about you?
- Whom do you know at the place of employment you are applying at?
- When was the last time you were in possession of illegal drugs?
- Currently, or within the past six months, what is your use of any controlled substance? …Marijuana? …Cocaine? …Speed? …PCP? …LSD? …Hashish? …Other?
- What is your current use of alcohol?
- Has the use of alcohol ever interfered with your work?
- To what extent do you gamble? Has gambling ever been a problem for you?
- Have you ever been the subject of, or a witness in, any type of investigation at work?

Free Interview Generator Guide Creates Standardized Questions for Human Resources and Hiring Managers

Employment Screening Resources (ESR) has created a free web-based Interview Generator Guide to help employers build printed interview forms for any position. The tool allows employers to select from generic interview questions or to create their own questions and then create a printed form that can be saved or modified. The tool also gives employers the flexibility of adding their own question to different sections of the interview guide.

The free tool solves several issues for employers. It helps employers and HR professionals produce a printed structured interview guide and focus on developing relevant questions for each position. Printed interview forms also help employers ensure that interviewers are asking the right questions every time, in the right way. It helps to ensure that all applicants for a position are treated fairly and uniformly. Using a *structured interview* guide helps employers ask permissible questions in a consistent fashion for all applicants for a position. An employer should only choose those questions that are valid predictors of job performance for a particular position. The tool can be found at www.esrcheck.com/Resource-Center/Interview-Generator/.

CHAPTER 4

The Reference Checking Process

Introduction

Before reading further, it is important to understand the distinction between certain terms:

1. **A Past Employment Verification** refers to verifying **factual or quantitative data** such as start date, end date, job title and salary if available. A verification is typically given by the human resources department or even through third party services, although in smaller firms the owner or bookkeeper may be the best source.

2. **A Reference Check** of past employment means obtaining **qualitative** information about the person's performance such as how well the person did or where improvements are needed or if the person would be rehired. A reference, by comparison, is typically given by someone who actually knew the applicant, such as a former supervisor.

3. **A Personal Reference** comes from someone familiar with the applicant in a context other than employment.

The first part of this chapter examines the importance and use of the verification as part of a Safe Hiring Program, and the legal and practical issue in obtaining employment verifications and references. The chapter also examines what to do when you are asked to provide a reference.

Verification Checks are Critical

Since what is past can often be prologue, an employer has a vested interested in finding out how the applicant performed in past positions. Many human resources professionals believe that how a person has performed in the past is the single best indicator of how they will perform for you at your business. It is always possible that a person's past performance may have been hampered by factors beyond their control, such as a dysfunctional team, lack of clear goals, or resources or a supervisor that micromanaged or mismanaged. However, a new perspective employer still needs to try to obtain as much information as possible about past performance.

 Trust But Verify Because Past Employment is a Critical Leading Edge Indicator of Future Performance

At the height of the Cold War, during negotiations with the Soviet Bloc on weapons reductions, a popular phrase was "Trust, but Verify." Good advice, especially today!

Value of Past Employment Verifications Even if You Cannot Get the 'Good Stuff'

Even if all an employer receives when contacting past employers is "name, rank, and serial number," it can be argued that verifying past employment is one of the most critical components an employer can undertake in the hiring process. In fact, there are times when a past employment verification is just as important if not more important than a criminal record check. Ideally, these checks provide specifics about past job performance that could be used as likely predictors of future success. Unfortunately, some employers make the costly error of not bothering to call past employers because they know many organizations have policies against giving out detailed information about current or former employees. Employers might assume the effort is worthless because all they will get is "name, rank, and serial number," if anything at all. However, here is the critical point:

Even if all you get is verification of dates of employment and job titles, past employer phone calls are still vital for safe hiring.

Why is this so important? There are actually five essential reasons why a Safe Hiring Program requires calling past employers regardless of whether the past employer limits the information to start date, end date, and job title.

1. Eliminates Unexplained Employment Gaps

If you do not know where a person has been, then you are hiring a stranger. If you hire a stranger, then you have a substantial risk of being the victim of the legal and economic fallout of a bad hire.

As explained in the previous chapter, if there are unexplained employment gaps in an application or resume, the employer cannot eliminate the possibility that the person's "absence" from the workforce was involuntary, such as in being incarcerated for a criminal offense. By eliminating any gap in employment over the past five to ten years, it lessens the possibility the applicant spent time in custody for a significant criminal offense.

The issue is not whether a person has gaps in his or her employment, but whether any gaps are unexplained. Not everyone has an uninterrupted employment history where they leave one job on a Friday and start the new one the following Monday. Employment gaps can have very reasonable explanations, such as time off to go to school, for a sabbatical, or for personal and family reasons. Sometimes it can take a person time to find a new job. Gaps can indicate negative things too, such as a prison or jail stay.

2. Indicates Where to Search for Criminal Records

As reviewed in more detail in Chapter 9 on criminal records, there is no national database of criminal records that private employers can legally access. Criminal record searches must be conducted at each relevant courthouse, and there are over 10,000 courthouses covering some 3,500+ county, state, and federal jurisdictions, plus another 5,000 courts at the town and city level. However, when an employer knows where an applicant has been, then *the knowing where to look* increases the accuracy of a criminal search. If an employer does not know where to search, they can easily miss a court where an applicant had a significant criminal act, and thereby inadvertently hire a person with a serious criminal record.

3. Allows an Employer to Hire Based Upon Facts, Not Just Instinct

The pitfalls of using the warm body theory of hiring have been demonstrated in earlier chapters. Although the use of instinct is part of the hiring process, there is simply no substitute for factual verifications. Given the statistics that up to one-third of all resumes contain material falsehoods, the need to verify statements in a resume or application is critical. Just knowing with certainty that the applicant did, in fact, have the jobs and positions claimed goes a long way towards a solid hiring decision.

4. Allows an Employer to Demonstrate Due Diligence

Here is the critical point—if something goes wrong, an employer needs to be able to convince a jury that the **employer made reasonable efforts**, given the situation, to engage in safe hiring. Documentation for each person hired shows that an employer made reasonable steps by contacting past employers to confirm job information and to ask questions. This is powerful evidence an employer was not negligent. As stated before, an employer is not expected to be 100% successful in their hiring. No one is. Any employer is simply expected to act in good faith and to take diligent efforts to hire safe and qualified people. This cannot be done without demonstrating that the employer made the effort, which means documenting that he or she picked up the phone and tried.

What constitutes a reasonable effort? Taking reasonable care means attempting to obtain employer references and documenting those attempts. To a degree, the level of reasonable inquiry depends upon the nature of the job and the risk to third parties. A higher standard of care may be required for hiring an executive than a food service worker. Regardless, every employer has a legal obligation to exercise appropriate care in the selection and retention of employees. The law does not require that an employer be successful in obtaining references. It is clear that an employer must at least try.

5. Potential Employer May Receive Valuable Information

Many employers assume when they call a past employer they will get a "No comment," or "We do not give references." However, there is a significant percentage of time when both a verification and a reference is possible. Sometimes this occurs when a firm has not been strongly counseled by their employment attorney not to give a reference, such a smaller employers who may not have been trained by a lawyer not to give references. Also, the previous employer may feel morally obliged to give references. Successful reference calls can also occur when the person calling has excellent communication skills, is professional, and is able to start some dialogue. There are many HR and security professionals who have developed the ability to obtain references, even from the most reluctant sources. Techniques on how to obtain references are given later in this chapter.

Another Reason to Verify Past Employment – Resumes or Past Claims Are Not Always Accurate

A resume is essentially a marketing tool for an applicant. An applicant picks and chooses whatever information he or she wants to share. Many job hunters use a resume writing service. While there is nothing wrong with using a service to prepare a professional looking resume, the service typically will attempt to enhance the applicant's experience. The service's goal is to get the applicant to the interview stage.

Employers, however, need facts in order to make hiring decisions and there can be inherent dangers when using a resume within a Safe Hiring Program. In fact, some firms astutely reject resumes and return them to applicants. Job seekers are told they must fill out the company-approved application only and are increasingly told to use the employer's online job portal, often powered by an Applicant Tracking System (ATS), as the exclusive means of applying for employment.

Resumes May Have Information an Employer Should Not Have

For some reason, job applicants often feel compelled to reveal things about themselves that an employer does not need or legally should not know. Resumes often reveal volunteer affiliations, hobbies, interests, or memberships in groups that reveal such prohibited information as race, religion, ethnicity, sexual orientation, or age. For example, a resume may reveal a person does volunteer time with a church or belongs to a group that is clearly associated with a particular race or nationality. The problem is the federal Equal Employment Opportunity Commission (EEOC) and equivalent sets of individual state's rules prohibit an employer from obtaining or using such information. Having this information in the form of a resume in the employer's file is not a good practice in the event the employer is ever the subject of civil litigation or a government investigation into their hiring practices. By using an application form, an applicant cannot volunteer irrelevant information an employer should not possess.

Resumes May Not Have Information an Employer Needs

Resumes may not give an employer all the information needed to make an informed hiring decision. Perhaps there are previous jobs an applicant would rather not mention or the applicant has hidden significant employment gaps. Also, job applicants typically do not self-reveal their criminal records in a resume, when this fact is significant to the job.

Spotting Six of the Biggest Job Applicant Lies

Although statistics vary widely, there is widespread agreement that a substantial number of resumes and applications belong in the fiction section of the bookstore. The rate of fraud can be as high as 40% and higher according to different sources. Applicants certainly have the right to put their best foot forward, and puffing their qualifications is an American tradition. But when puffing crosses the line into fabrication, an employer needs to be concerned. When you hire an applicant who uses lies and fabrication to get hired, the issue is that the same type of dishonesty will continue once they have the job. Below are six of the most common fabrications claimed by job applicants.

1. Claiming a Degree not Earned

Yes, believe it or not, applicants will make up a degree. Sometimes, they actually went to the school but never graduated. Some applicants may have had just a few credits to go and decided to award themselves the degree anyway. On some occasions, an applicant will claim a degree from a school they did not even attend. The best practice for an employer is to state clearly on the application form that the applicant should list any school they want the employer to consider. In that way, if an applicant lies, the employer can act on the lack of truthfulness regardless of whether the educational requirement is part of the job requirements.

2. Claiming a Diploma Mill or Fake Degree

A related issue to claiming an unearned degree is declaring a fake degree that can be purchased online from a Diploma Mill. Today one may obtain a degree simply by going online and using a credit card. There are even websites that will print out very convincing, fake degrees from nearly any school in America. In fact, the author obtained a degree for his dog in Business Administration from the University of Arizona—and the dog had been dead for ten years. A transcript was even obtained and the dog got a "B" in English! Some sites will even provide a phone number so an employer can call and verify the fake degree. Some of the degree mills even have fake accreditation agencies with names similar to real accreditation bodies, in order to give a fake accreditation for a fake school.

3. Previous Job Title

Applicants can easily give their career an artificial boost by "promoting" themselves to a supervisor position, even if they never managed anyone.

4. Claiming Knowledge, Skills, Abilities, or Experience They Do Not Possess

Employers normally hire based on a job description that will describe the knowledge, skills, and abilities (KSA) needed for a job as well as the experience required. These are exactly the areas, however, where employers often find a candidate has fibbed.

5. Dates of Employment

Another concern for employers is applicants who cover up dates of employment in order to hide employment gaps. For some applicants, it may be a seemingly innocent attempt to hide the fact that it has taken awhile to get a new job. In other cases, the date fabrication can be more sinister, such as a person that spent time in custody for a crime who may be trying to hide that fact.

One caveat—there can be times when the applicant is honestly mistaken about employment dates due to having started a position as a temporary worker on a staffing firm's payroll. An applicant may have worked at a past employer for five years, but the first year was officially an employee of a staffing vendor. In the applicant's mind, they were there for five years. However, the official records for the company may only show employment for four years.

6. Previous Compensation

A related issue is past salary. Applicants have been known to exaggerate compensation in order to have a better starting point when negotiating the salary for the new job. However, for many employers past salary is a sensitive area and some HR professionals will ask for a written release first.

> **You Need To Know**
>
> ### CareerBuilder Survey Finds 58% of Employers Caught Lies on Resume
>
> A 2014 survey from CareerBuilder found 58 percent of hiring managers said they had caught a lie on a resume. The nationwide survey, which was conducted online by Harris Poll on behalf of CareerBuilder from May 13 to June 6, 2014, included a representative sample of 2,188 hiring managers and human resource professionals across industries and company sizes. According to employers, the most common lies they catch on resumes relate to:
>
> - Embellished skill set – 57 percent
> - Embellished responsibilities – 55 percent
> - Dates of employment – 42 percent
> - Job title – 34 percent
> - Academic degree – 33 percent
> - Companies worked for – 26 percent
> - Accolades/awards – 18 percent
>
> The survey also found that employers in the following industries caught resume lies more frequently than average:
>
> - Financial Services – 73 percent
> - Leisure and Hospitality – 71 percent
> - Information Technology – 63 percent
> - Health Care (More than 50 employees) – 63 percent
> - Retail – 59 percent
>
> The survey found that employers in the following industries catch resume lies more frequently than average:
>
> - Financial Services – 73 percent
> - Leisure and Hospitality – 71 percent
> - Information Technology – 63 percent
> - Health Care (More than 50 employees) – 63 percent
> - Retail – 59 percent
>
> Source: www.careerbuilder.com/share/aboutus/pressreleasesdetail.aspx?sd=8%2F7%2F2014&id=pr837&ed=12%2F31%2F2014.

How Far Back Should Reference Checks Go?

How many years back should one go when checking previous employers? The answer can depend upon the applicant's relevant work history, the sensitivity of the position, and the availability of information. Some applicants may only have had one employer in the past ten years. Others may have had a large number. If a person is an hourly worker, then it is possible the person has held numerous past jobs. A young worker may not have a work history to check.

As a general guideline, employers should go back a minimum of five years, although seven to ten is much better. If the employer is in an industry where there is a great deal of turnover, then it may not be practical to go back even five years, if the five-year span represents a large number of previous employers. Employers should utilize a **rule of reason**, but also keep in mind that an employer should be internally consistent so that all similarly situated applicants are treated in a similar fashion. If an employer goes back five years for an administrative assistant, then all candidates who have reached the stage where references are conducted should also have their references checked going back five years.

Use Questions that are 100% Legal

Remember the same standards that apply to reference checking also apply to interview questions—all questions must be specifically job-related and non-discriminatory. Never ask any question of a reference you would not ask the candidate face-to-face or put on an application. Focus on skills and accomplishments as well as performance issues that apply specifically to your job opening, such as the ability to meet deadlines or to work well with others on a team project.

See the previous chapter for a list of questions that can and cannot be asked of an applicant in an interview. Again, these questions are also applicable when interviewing a past employer.

Procedures to Implement Quality Reference Checking

Operating a successful, in-house system of reference checking is certainly doable for employers. Here is a step-by-step process an employer can use for obtaining past references as part of a Safe Hiring Program (SHP).

1. **Set up a physical system to make and track calls, and monitor your progress by using a Past Employment Worksheet.**

Effective reference checking requires a system; otherwise, it is nearly impossible to track who has been called, the status of each call, and who else needs to be called.

This is especially true in a large company environment. In a typical large company reference-checking situation, a checker may be given a number of applicants to check references. Assume HR is given five applicants to check. Also assume that each applicant has on the average three past employers, making a total of 15 needed calls. The chances are that the percentage of successful first-time calls will be limited. A successful call means getting through to the right person and getting as much information as the person can give you. The reality is most calls will result in an "incomplete," meaning that a call back is needed. Perhaps the caller had to leave a message on a voicemail, the phone number did not work or is busy, or the past employer needs "a release" from the applicant. All of these situations require that HR note the outcome and schedule a follow-up. As the HR person is calling on the third candidate, past employers may be calling back in response to earlier messages. Sometimes a round or two of "phone-tag" is involved. Obviously, a tracking system is a necessity. Here are suggestions to make the workflow easier:

- Have a prepared Past Employment Worksheet ready to go for each candidate. For each applicant, the reference checker needs to fill out the name and contact information for each past employer as well as any standard reference questions. A sample Past Employer Worksheet is found in the Appendix.
- Use the Past Employer Worksheet to track all phone calls, including who was called and the results. The information is worth its weight in gold should an employer ever be called upon to demonstrate due diligence in court. Even if the reference attempt was unsuccessful, a completed worksheet showing each call—including the date, time, phone number, person called, and the result—is the best possible proof that an employer exercised due diligence.
- In advance, it is helpful to place the essential information reported by the applicant on the Past Employment Worksheet. Now, during a call, the reference checker can write down what the past employer reports, providing an easy-to-read side-by-side comparison.
- If specific job-related questions are being asked relevant to the Knowledge, Skill, and Abilities (KSA) related to a particular position, then make sure those questions are ready. This may mean having the application easily accessible for a quick reference.

- Using a Past Employer Worksheet also ensures you are asking the same questions for similarly situated candidates. A critical function of a reference-checking program is to treat all candidates fairly. Treat similarly situated candidates the same way!

2. Independently confirm the existence and phone number for the past employer.

It may not happen very often, but many HR and Security Professionals have heard of situations where an applicant set-up a fake reference on a resume by providing a friend's telephone number, with the friend standing by to answer, posing as a past employer. When the prospective employer makes the phone call, the friend gives a glowing and professorial reference. Or, an applicant bent on a fake reference can use other alternatives such as setting up a voicemail service, leaving a message indicating the voice mailbox belongs to a supposed reference, and later have a friend return the call posing as a past supervisor. Cases are reported of applicants attempting to act as their own reference. With cell phones, call forwarding and internet phone services, such trickery is now easier than ever.

To avoid the possibility of a fake reference, it is recommended that a verifier independently establish the past employer is a legitimate company and to locate a valid phone number by use of an internet service or local phone book. The best way to determine if a company is legitimate is to check with the local Secretary of State office to confirm the business is legally formed and authorized to do business. If the business is a sole proprietorship and is not listed with the secretary of state, then a professional screening firm may use other due diligence techniques.

There are also a number of websites where phone numbers can be found very quickly. They typically have the same data that dialing *411 information* would have, except the internet services are free. Any legitimate firm will have a listed phone number. The chance of an applicant going to the trouble of creating a legal entity just to get a listed phone number is, well, not likely.

There may be times when a firm is not listed. That can happen if the firm has moved, merged, changed names, or gone out of business. In that situation, the new employer may well have to talk further with the applicant to find someone who can verify their past employment.

An employer or screening firm can go even further and verify the legitimacy of the past employer by looking up the employer on a secretary of state website's search of validly registered business entities, or do an online search of Fictitious Business Names sites. An employer can even use one of the commercial services, such as Dunn and Bradstreet, Hoovers, or Manta to name a few.

Of course, a verifier must also use good judgment. If the phone is not answered in a professional manner, or there are the sounds of traffic and children in the background, then something may not be right.

Finally, if there is any suspicion of a set-up or fake reference, it may be necessary to verify if the person giving the reference was, in fact, employed by the past employer. That may even require, in some situations, calling HR or payroll to make sure the person the verifier is talking with was in fact employed there.

Author Tip

Trusted Source

This is part of what the author refers to as the **trusted source** based on independent third-party verification. This approach is described in more detail in Chapter 22. The key point is that in order to combat identity fraud, it is critical to verify information about a person independent of the information an applicant provides. It is critical to not simply assume the applicant's statements about the existence of or contact information of a past employer is correct.

---

3. How to be careful when contacting an applicant's current employer.

A recurring issue in any past employment check is sensitivity about contacting the current employer. A current employer should NOT be contacted unless the applicant specifically gives permission.

The reason is there are some employers who, upon learning a current employee is looking to leave, will immediately take steps to terminate the employee. This is especially true for positions of greater responsibility where the applicant may have access to customer lists or trade secrets. In some industries, within minutes of learning an employee is actively looking for a new position, the current employer will have the Security Department box up the employee's personal items, confiscate all computers and disks, turn off all access to any computer systems, de-activate the parking permit and building access code, and have the person physically escorted off premises with a last paycheck.

If such a hasty departure is caused by a phone call by the prospective new employer, and the job offer does not come through, then the applicant can be left without a job and free to contemplate whether they should visit a lawyer. In order to avoid this, here is a simple two-step program:

- On the application, in large letters, make sure there is a box someplace asking an applicant "May we contact your current employer?"
- Do NOT call the current employer unless the applicant has clearly marked the "Yes" Box. If the applicant failed to check either box, then do not call until that is clarified. Anything other than a clear indication of YES can create problems.

If the employer still needs to verify current employment, there are three options for doing so:

- Ask the applicant for the name of a past supervisor or co-worker who is no longer working with the applicant at the current place of employment. Again, if there is any question about the authenticity of the supplied name, the employer can call and verify the ex-employee did in fact work at the current workplace.
- Ask the applicant to bring in W-2's for each year of work, or at least the full past year.
- Wait until after the employee is hired before calling the past employer; providing the new hire is subject to a written offer letter clearly stating "continued employment is conditional upon a background screening report that is satisfactory to the employer." Once the new employee is working, there can be a final phone call. By making current employment part of the written offer letter, an applicant has a powerful incentive to be accurate about the current employment situation, since any false or misleading statements or omissions will have serious consequences. It is important to include the phrase "satisfactory to the employer" in order to avoid a debate with an applicant/new hire about what is or is not a good screening report.

Although more complicated and time consuming, there are services where a consumer's past tax information can be obtained. However, that is typically not practical for an employment check.

4. Use *Soft Sell Techniques* if you hit a roadblock.

If a verifier faces resistance to a reference, the best approach is usually a soft sale. Here are some techniques that may help convince a past employer to give the information you need:

- Do not start right off asking for an employment reference. That can immediately make an employer defensive and create a barrier to effective communication.
- Explain the purpose and try to convince the past employer to be of assistance. How? By finding common ground. For example, explain that your applicant cannot be employed without some additional information, or that getting some information would be a great benefit.
- Start with a non-controversial request, such as start date, end date, or job title.
- Before asking reference questions, segue into the subject with non-controversial questions such as "What was the nature of that job?" If you are told the person's job title was "project manager," then ask the past employer what that job entails. It is then a short trip to ask "How did the applicant perform the job?"

- If your state has a statute that protects an employer who gives an employment reference, then you may explain that to a reference.
- Offer to send a release. A release gives a past employer a great comfort level. It demonstrates the new employer, in fact, has a valid business reason for requesting the information, and the past employer has permission to give it. Keep in mind, however, a release is not a blank check for the past employer to say anything they want. Even with a release, the past employer must be careful to limit the information to those items that are job-related and factual.

5. How to handle the *Eligible for Rehire* question.

If nothing else works, a firm can at least be asked if the previous employer would rehire the applicant, or whether the applicant is eligible for rehire. This has become a standard reference question. Even firms with a "name, rank, and serial number" policy are sometimes comfortable with answering this question. In reality, the past employer is being asked the ultimate question, which is "Knowing what you know about the person...", and assuming you are also a highly trained, competent and motivated HR manager, "...would you want the person back?"

However, there are several problems with the Eligible for Rehire question. First, if a firm, in fact, has a no reference policy, then they are technically violating their policy if they answer. They are essentially giving a qualitative evaluation of the person. If they answer *no*, that potentially could be a form of defamation.

Second, a real issue with the question is that the answer can be meaningless. Suppose a past employer is called and asked about Eligibility for Rehire, and the past employer says *yes*, what does that mean? It could mean that technically the person is eligible to be rehired because there is no notation on the personnel file that indicates there is a prohibition against accepting that application. However, in truth and in fact, that past employer would never consider rehiring the person, but just won't say so.

Conversely, a *no* answer could mean the particular employer has a policy against rehiring anyone who left, even though the applicant was the best worker they could ever hope for.

The most helpful wording of the question is the following: "Knowing what you know about Mr. Smith, if you were in a position to rehire him for the same job he left, would you want him back?"

In order to interpret that answer, the verifier must understand the assumptions being made. They are assuming that the person who is giving the answer has a similar interest to the new employer and is capable of making a meaningful judgment. In other words, in order to give the answer meaning, the verifier has to make assumptions about the knowledge and judgment of the person giving the information.

If an HR professional giving the information is someone who the verifier happens to know and the verifier has respect for the experience and judgment of this HR professional, then the answer is extremely valuable. If the verifier is talking to a stranger, then it is really a judgment call as to the value of the information. It really comes down to the old rule–information from a trusted source is the best information.

Author Tip | **When You are Told NOT to Answer Reference Questions**

If your organization has been instructed not to answer reference questions but to verify information only, then the "rehire question" is really a reference question. In fact, "Would you rehire?" is the ultimate reference question since Employer 1 is asking Employer 2's ultimate judgment about whether a new employer should hire their former employee.

---

6. Send a faxed request or email—it is harder to ignore than voicemail.

Often times a verifier cannot get through to a live person and must leave a voicemail. As everyone knows in this busy world, it is easy to ignore voicemail. By the time the verifier leaves the third voicemail, it becomes less likely the past employer intends to respond. Assuming the verifier has verified that the reference person is not away, on leave, on vacation, and it is the right person, the verifier needs to find a way to get through.

Short of physically going over to the past employer's office and demanding time (not very practical, of course) the next best thing is to send a fax request or email. For some reasons, a piece of paper or an email demands attention—people feel they need to do something with a piece of paper or email, but they can ignore a voicemail. A fax or email to a former employer can also include the information to be verified, along with a return fax number or email, of course.

If all else fails, a faxed request at least shows a due diligence effort to get the information. The fax to the past employer should be maintained in the file as proof of the efforts made.

Another technique is to mail a written request. This technique is only effective for verification of factual information. How much meaning should be put on past employers answers to faxed, emailed, or mailed reference questions? That is difficult to say.

Author Tip ⟩ **Devil Is In the Details**

There is a trend for screening firms to send emails to past employers with a request to fill out information through an online response or portal. Although it may seem efficient at first glance, the **devil is in the details.**

First, a competent screening firm will follow the rule of independently verifying that the former company is legitimate and the email is to the right person. That is a necessary fraud prevention tool. Merely sending an email to an email address suggested by the applicant creates an opportunity for fraud. Secondly, privacy considerations are paramount. Whoever receives the email should be the only person able to log in with their full email. Under no circumstances should anyone at the previous place of employment be able to log in just under the employer's domain name and see what others have written. That would clearly be an invasion of privacy.

---

7. Use other sources such as former co-workers or supplied references.

Depending on the importance of the position and the time and resources available, the verifier may attempt to talk with a professional reference the applicant has supplied. This is known as a **supplied reference**.

One technique is to ask a supplied reference for another person who may know the applicant. This is known as talking with a **developed reference**. A developed reference is a source of information the verifier has developed on his or her own, without input from the candidate.

Talking to a developed reference can be a very valuable source of information. The verifier can get information from someone who was not told in advance he or she would be contacted, which increases the probability of a truly spontaneous and non-rehearsed conversation leading to additional insights about the candidate. Because it is a time consuming and labor intensive process, it is typically used for just very key positions.

8. Use professional networking when possible.

HR professionals can sometimes engage in **professional networking** to obtain reference information. Sometimes just reading between the lines can be of assistance. A previous employer may be unwilling to give specific information but may be willing to convey a sense about or opinion about the applicant or communicate in some other "unofficial" manner.

It should be noted, however, that in reality there is no such thing as an off the record comment. Should a matter ever go to litigation and a deposition is taken, an HR manager or employer would have a legal obligation to reveal all the details of a conversation if directly asked. Unlike a doctor/patient or spouse to spouse conversation, for example, where the law creates a privilege so that such a conversation can remain a secret, there is no such protection when HR professionals communicate with each other about applicants.

There is, however, an ethical issue to consider. If an HR or security professional knows that a colleague works at a firm that has a strict policy against giving references, then a request for information is really asking another professional to violate a firm's policy. The fact that such a conversation may be "off the record" may not help.

9. Procedures to use if the former employer is out of business, bankrupt, moved, merged, or cannot be located.

For a number of reasons, a previous employer may not be available for a past employment check. First, a verifier may have trouble obtaining contact information if a previous employer has merged, been acquired, or is no longer in business and no one can locate the personnel records. There can also be occasions where the past employment was an independent contractor assignment for a sole proprietorship and no one can be located to verify it.

In these types of situations, a verifier has two options. One is to contact the applicant to locate a former co-worker or supervisor; however, that requires the verifier to confirm the credibility of the former employee, since there would be no way to verify the source of information from the former employer. The second option is to contact the applicant and request a copy of the W-2 (if the applicant was on the payroll) or a 1099 (if the applicant was a contractor). To help confirm employment, an employer can look at secondary sources that may include using a search engine to see if there is a record of the applicant at a previous firm.

A verifier can also run into difficulties if given insufficient information about the past employer. It is critical to require any applicant to completely identify the past employer by name, city, and state in order to facilitate a telephone call. Using an applicant-supplied phone number can be a source of difficulty; not only must the verifier be alert to the possibility of a *fake or set-up reference*, but often, the phone number an applicant recalls was the number for a division or branch, not the number needed for that firm's past employment verifications. The employer or screening firm still needs to independently verify the existence of the past employer and develop a phone number independent of the applicant.

10. If a past employer says there is no record, then a verifier needs to go one step further.

What if a past employer tells a verifier there is no record of an applicant having worked there? Before jumping to the conclusion the applicant has lied, a verifier should dig deeper. There can be reasonable explanations for apparent discrepancies. An applicant may have worked at the previous company as a temporary worker, under contract, or was actually employed by a third-party employer organization.

Some companies utilize the services of a Professional Employer Organization (PEO) or other types of staffing vendors to act as the employer of record although the work is performed at the company workplace under the company's direction and control. In these situations, the previous company's records will show that no such person worked there, though their facility was the physical location where the applicant worked. Since the applicant physically worked at the firm's premises, the applicant may well report that business as the employer. The applicant may not be certain or recall the details of who actually issued the check.

It is also important to ask the employer to double-check their records under the applicant's Social Security number and any other names the applicant may have used.

11. Be prepared to send a written release or authorization if needed.

Some employers will want to see a written release or authorization before giving out information. This practice is seen as protection against defamation and a good privacy practice before releasing more sensitive information such as past salary.

However, keep in mind that this release is not a consent for a past employer to say anything they want. As discussed below, there must still be a factual basis for any past employment reference information provided.

A Case in Point

An applicant reported a two-year employment history. However, a telephone call to the past employer showed the applicant only worked there for a year and a half. On the surface, it looked like the applicant lied about the time period of employment. Since honesty and integrity are integral to any employment relationship, the employer was about to terminate the hiring process and rescind the offer. However, the employer could not believe that such a good prospect actually lied. The employer took the extra step of asking the applicant about the apparent discrepancy. Upon further investigation, it turned out the applicant started off working for the past employer as an unpaid intern for six months, then was hired full-time. From the applicant's point of view, he had worked there for two years—employment records for the company reflected only a year and a half. If the employer had not gone the extra step, then all of the time, energy, and expense of recruiting the prospect would have been wasted. On the other hand, if the person had lied, the extra time spent confirming the facts would also have protected the employer in the event of any adverse legal action.

---

12. What if negative information is found by the screening firm?

If a screening firm is performing the past employment check, it is covered by the Federal Fair Credit Reporting Act (FCRA) which is covered more extensively in Chapter 5.

If the screening firm is asking reference (or qualitative questions), that is a special type of consumer report called an Investigative Consumer Report or ICR. What should a screening firm do if it gets negative information that would likely be adverse to the applicant, such as the applicant stole money, or did a very poor job?

In that case, before reporting adverse information from the reference check, FCRA section 606, the background firm must have followed reasonable procedures to obtain confirmation of the information, from an additional source that has independent and direct knowledge of the information or determine that the person interviewed is the best possible source of the information.

That is another reason why background firms are generally NOT used for reference questions, but as explained below, are best used to verify factual matters and leave the reference checking to the hiring manager or HR.

13. If more information is needed, should a screening firm be utilized to contact the applicant directly?

Some employers or recruiters want background firms to contact an applicant directly if there is a need to obtain additional information or to clarify information from an applicant in order to complete a reference check or some other credential. This can happen for example if there is an incomplete employment verification because the past employer has moved, merged, or gone out of business or will not call back. If the recruiter still needs a verification, then someone needs to contact the applicant and ask for things such as W-2's, or names of past supervisors.

There are some recruiters who ask their background screening firm to do this, even though it is the recruiter that has the most knowledge about the applicant and has direct contact.   If this has ever crossed your mind as an employer or recruiter, you might want to reconsider.

It is generally not a recommended practice to have a background firms get in the middle of the special relationship between the Recruiter and the Applicant. It creates confusion, causes delays, and brings a background screening firm into discussions with the applicant who may not even realize that a third party is involved. Background checks actually go much faster where the recruiter exclusively manages the direct applicant relationship and obtains additional information when needed.

Recruiters who review all applications for completeness, legibility, and accuracy with the candidates before sending the applications to a screening firm will find their report is completed much faster. If an employer is using an Applicant Tracking System and more information is needed, the ideal scenario is for the recruiter to obtain the additional information.

There are a number of complications that arise if the screening firm attempts to contact the applicant.

1. The applicant does not know the background screening firm, and is naturally reluctant to supply a Social Security Number or date of birth to a stranger over the phone, or send pay stubs to someone they do not know. That typically means the applicant will normally call the recruiter anyway to find out what the situation is all about, which, of course, delays the screening process further.

2. The background firm often has to engage in phone tag, requiring back and forth before the screening firm can connect with the applicant. Since the applicant has no relationship with the screening firm, an applicant does not always even realize it is important to call back, especially if the applicant is looking at several different job offers. On the other hand, if a recruiter is in hot pursuit of an applicant, or the applicant is focused on getting the job, it is likely that the recruiter will have a great deal less difficulty getting in touch with him/her to obtain the additional information or clarification.

3. The third issue is tracking. The screening firm needs to track the status of the additional calls to the applicants and to deal with multiple applicants instead of a single point of contact. Recruiters presumably already have an ATS or some other system to keep tabs on the progress of each job and each finalist (since typically only a finalist is getting screened).

4. The last and most important issue is when a screening firm calls the applicant, an applicant may now believe that the screening firm is somehow involved in the hiring decision. There have been applicants who have wanted to continue selling themselves to a background firm's clerical employee, whose only mission was to obtain some missing information and who knows nothing about the job. Or, if the applicant somehow feels that background employee did not give them the attention he or she deserved, the applicant may be left with a negative impression of the potential employer or complain about the contact.

For these reasons, many background firms typically prefer not to contact the applicant on behalf of the Recruiter or Employer. If an employer wants the screening firm to provide this service, the employer should be prepared to pay a premium since the background firm is performing additional work that normally the employer would perform.

Who Should Make the Past Employment Calls?

There are three different groups who can do past employment checks:

1. The actual hiring managers
2. Human Resources
3. An outsourced third party, such as a background firm

Here are the pros and cons of each group.

Hiring Manager

Advantages: The manager knows the job and knows what talents and skills are needed. Also, the hiring manager is the person who has to live with the decision. For sensitive or critical positions, the manager may want to receive input directly from previous employers. Even if the previous employer has a *no comment* policy, there may still be an advantage in talking personally to the previous employer and attempting to glean what information is available *between the lines*.

Disadvantages: There is much less control over the process in terms of whether the hiring manager is asking legal questions or treating candidates in a similar fashion. Many hiring managers may be tempted to make fewer calls and settle for just one completed call before making a decision. Hiring managers may not be as concerned about the need to establish a full employment history or look for employment gaps. Although these drawbacks can be lessened with written procedures, training, and auditing of hiring files, they are still sources of concern.

Human Resources

Advantages: Any reference check done by human resources more likely will be done thoroughly, properly, and legally with proper documentation and consistency.

Disadvantages: The human resources department may not know the job requirements nearly as well as the hiring manager. In addition, even for a firm with a fully staffed Human Resources department, employment reference checking is a time consuming task. The difficulty with performing employment reference checks in-house is not the time the actual interview takes; it is the constant interruptions of returned phone calls throughout the day, tracking the progress of each candidate, and making repeated attempts when there is not a callback. It can also take time to locate former employers and phone numbers as well.

Background Checking Firm

Advantages: By outsourcing, a firm knows that nothing will fall through the cracks since a background screening firm can methodically contact all past employers. In addition, the fees charged by screening firms are typically very modest compared to the time and energy that HR would need to spend in-house.

Disadvantages: A verifier employed by a screening firm typically knows little about the employer or the job. Screening firms often do employment checks in high volume and are unlikely to have the personnel trained to ask in-depth, pertinent questions or do follow-up questions. Given the prices charged by screening firms, the verifiers performing the calls are not seasoned HR professionals but rather have skills that are closer to the needs of call centers. A screening firm is best utilized only for verification calls, and not for reference checks.

Author Tip > **Using Automated Third Party Verification Services**

Some employers utilize outsourced third party services to handle past employment verification calls. The third party service will download all employment information so that verifiers, such as employers or screening firms, call the third party service instead of the employer directly. This saves the employer time and money since they do not need to respond to phone calls, faxes, or emails. The verification is typically completed by the verifier online or through an interface. Examples are uConfirm or The Work Number, a part of Equifax. If there is concern about the accuracy of data about an individual applicant, these sites provide an email address for questions. One drawback is that the information is typically limited to dates, title, and possibly salary, and there is no one to talk to in order to locate additional information.

Who Makes the Call? – Conclusion

The answer is to recognize the difference between *reference checks used to determine if a person should be offered the position* in the first place and *due diligence verification checks of past employment* utilized to ensure an employer has confirmed dates and details of past employment and subjected all finalists to the same process.

In order to make sure nothing falls through the cracks, HR or a background screening firm may be called upon to do a verification check, just to make sure all the bases have been covered. The worst that can happen is some former employer may be called twice—once by the hiring manager and again by HR or a background screening firm.

Many organizations encourage the hiring manager to make whatever employment checks are needed to help decide if the person is a good fit—to form an opinion as to whether or not to make a job offer in the first place. Of course, employers are well advised to make sure a hiring manager is trained so that only legal and permissible questions are asked.

Author Tip ⟩ **Trend of Using Screening Firms Only at the End of Hiring Process**

The trend for employers is to use a screening firm at the end of the hiring process to perform factual verifications only. By the time an employer has decided to spend time and money on a background check, the decision has already been made that the applicant is a good fit for the job. Having a screening firm ask reference questions is very unlikely to help employers make the right decision. On the other hand, the screening industry has a great deal of experience in making the verification calls needed to substantiate the details of the applicant's employment history.

Other Effective Reference Techniques

The Appendix provides a list of sample reference questions. Some suggestions made by experts include:

- Use of questions showing behavior – e.g. "Can you give me a specific example of how he (or she) was a great team player?"
- Ask a targeted question – e.g. "The candidate states he (or she) implemented a sales training program. Can you tell me about their contribution?"
- Read the candidate's resume to the past employer and ask for a reaction to the resume content.
- Use open-ended questions to inspire narrative answers.

Human Resources consultant and expert on hiring and reference questions Wendy Bliss gives the following tips on effective reference techniques. More information on this topic is available in her book *Legal, Effective References: How to Give and Get them*, published by the Society for Human Resource Management in 2001.

Mission Possible: 10 Tips for Effective Telephone Reference Checks

By Wendy Bliss, J.D., SPHR, Author of *Legal, Effective References*

www.wendybliss.com

Due to the popularity of the "name, rank and serial number" approach to reference requests, it is often challenging to uncover useful, in-depth information about job applicants during telephone reference checks. However, it is by no means impossible! With practice and persistence, you can greatly increase the quantity and quality of information obtained in conversations with reference sources. On your next reference-checking mission, use the following tips:

1. **Create a powerful script.** Do not "wing it" when calling references. Develop a written outline that includes questions and comments that will enable you to: 1) establish rapport with reference contacts; 2) minimize potential opposition to your inquiries; 3) obtain relevant, detailed information about the applicant; and 4) follow up with the source as needed. Tips 2 through 9 below provide techniques for accomplishing each of these objectives. To build skill and consistency, use your reference check script for every reference check.

2. **Open the door for effective communication in the first sixty seconds.** When contacting a reference, your initial goal is to make a positive connection and set the stage for a candid conversation. Identify yourself by name and position. Share general information about your company and the specific opening there for which the applicant is being considered. Let the reference contact know that you have the applicant's permission to call, assuming that is the case. (If the applicant has not given your organization prior written consent to do so, it is inadvisable to conduct any reference checks.) After sharing this introductory information, making a complimentary statement about the source, such as "Betty made favorable comments about your guidance and supervision during her interviews with us," may predispose the source to sharing full and frank feedback with you.

3. **Avoid the "R" word.** The mere mention of the word "reference," particularly in the initial stage of a reference check call, may arouse worries about defamation and other legal claims in the mind of the person you have contacted. So, you should set the stage for cooperation. Explain the purpose for the call and the potential benefits of sharing candid information by taking a future focus. For instance, stating that "An important reason for my call is to gain information that will help our company most effectively supervise Richard in the event we hire him" emphasizes the developmental benefit of answering your questions fully.

4. **Ask the right questions, in the right order.** After establishing rapport with the source, climb the ladder of reference inquiries to gain a thorough understanding of the applicant's employment history, qualifications, job performance, and past problems on the job. Start by asking the most innocuous and easily answered questions first, including confirmation of dates of employment, positions held and salary history. Next, move up the ladder of inquiry to gather information about the applicant's job duties, performance, work habits, and his or her suitability for the open position at your company. Finally, inquire about the most sensitive topics including reasons for leaving, and incidents of misconduct or dangerous behaviors. This three-tiered approach to questioning—saving the toughest topics for last—usually leads to at least partial cooperation from reference sources.

5. **Ask open-ended questions, and give prompters.** Questions about the applicant that begin with the words "what," "how," or "why" invite detailed responses. Other phrases that encourage full and specific disclosure begin with phrases such as "Give me an example of the applicant's ability to . . .,"or "Describe a time when the applicant . . ." Follow up questions or statements such as "Can you elaborate on that?" or "That's interesting. Please tell me more about that," to prompt the source to give more details.

6. **Listen carefully for vocal clues.** Many reference sources who are reluctant to share negative information will tip off reference checkers to potential problems with the applicant through a variety of signals. Is the source's tone of voice guarded? Does he or she sound cautious or reluctant to answer even basic fact verification questions? Reference checkers should also be on the alert for unusually long pauses, throat-clearing, or "umms" and "ahs" that may indicate hesitancy to give information candidly, particularly if these occur in response to a sensitive question.

7. **Dig deep when you get shallow responses.** When a reference source gives a vague answer, carefully rehearsed, or inconsistent, probe for more useful information. In such situations, politely ask for more details with remarks such as "I am not sure I understood what you meant when you said . . . Can you clarify that for me?" Another technique that may help you discover the truth when you are being stonewalled is to ask very direct questions that require a "yes" or "no" response. For example, ask "Was Pat fired?" or "Was Chris ever disciplined for poor performance or misconduct while employed at your company?" These pinpointed questions probe non-answers about an applicant's reasons for leaving a prior job, or provide clues about his or her performance and conduct with the previous employer.

8. **Be prepared for reluctant references.** While the above techniques will increase your overall success in obtaining useful information during reference checks, you will undoubtedly still encounter stiff resistance from some reference sources. When this occurs, offer to fax the source a copy of the reference authorization form signed by the applicant. This will be particularly helpful if your reference authorization form includes a waiver of liability that protects anyone who provides a reference about the applicant. You can also explain that the applicant will not be hired without satisfactory information about the applicant's performance in past jobs, which is an effective way to encourage sources having positive information about the applicant to go ahead and do the right thing. Additionally, you can inquire as to whether the source's unwillingness to share information about the applicant is an indication of problems with the applicant. If all else fails, contact a different source at the same organization – such as a higher level manager, another supervisor, or even a colleague – who worked directly with the applicant. It is very possible that a different source in the same organization will be willing to give you the information you seek.

9. **When closing a call, leave the door open to get more information.** At the end of your reference check discussions, thank the source for his or her time. Ask for permission to contact the source again if you have additional questions. Finally, ask if the source knows of any other people inside or outside the source's organization who would have knowledge of the applicant's background, job performance or other matters relevant to the applicant's suitability to work at your organization.

10. **Use good form in documenting calls.** All telephone reference check attempts and calls should be documented using a standardized form. This form can be developed internally, or can be obtained from books on reference checking such as my book *Legal Effective References: How to Give and Get Them*.

Legal Effective References: How to Give and Get Them by Wendy Bliss can be purchased online from the Society for Human Resource Management at www.shrm.org/shrmstore. © Wendy Bliss (2001). All rights reserved

Using Automated Reference Checks

Online automated reference checks and assessment tools are fairly new pre-hire resources. An example is the services offered by Checkster (www.Checkster.com), a company founded by a veteran in the talent management sector. Job candidates select references, such as former supervisors and co-workers, who then receive an email assessment request to fill out and return by email. This self-service eliminates time spent making phone calls and waiting for and tracking responses. The questionnaire itself is a scientifically designed assessment instrument designed to give a fresh look at the applicant and contains a number of state-of-the-art validation tools. The results are communicated back to a recruiter or hiring manager in a graphical and intuitive report. Although there are others competing in the same space, Checkster clearly has thought through and designed the process from both the assessment and talent management point of view.

The employer obtains a quick, candid assessment because the person giving the reference is advised that the actual scores are confidential. The email evaluations provide a scientific assessment of what is "under the candidate's hood" – thus increasing the employer's odds of making a job offer to the best candidate.

However, the question has arisen from some hiring managers: *Can services like Checkster replace the type of employment verifications performed by background firms?* The short answer is that Checkster type services are designed to be used earlier in the process than background checks to tell an employer who to consider. A background check is used at the point where a decision is being made to help an employer determine if there is any reason NOT to hire the person and to verify the applicant's factual history.

Traditional background checks and Checkster type services do complement each other, but they serve different purposes. Although services from firms such as Checkster are extremely valuable, they are different tools for different functions.

Automated reference checks occur in the talent sourcing and selection stages to help eliminate some preliminary candidates from consideration and to focus in on candidates who should be finalists. By comparison, background checks occur AFTER a tentative decision has been reached. In other words, automated type services are used to decide who to focus on out of a pool of candidates, while a background check seeks to assist an employer in exercising due diligence by examining if there is any reason NOT to hire someone that an employer has potentially targeted for employment. Thus there is a fundamental difference between an email-based reference service and the role of a background firm.

A huge advantage for an employer utilizing traditional background checking techniques is in the event of a lawsuit for negligent hiring the employer has a powerful argument in front of a jury that they exercised due diligence. The whole idea behind due diligence as a legal defense is independent factual verification. For example, background firms do not take the applicant's word for whether the past employer even existed. A background screening firm will typically independently verify that the past employer existed as well as verify the phone number is real, independent of what the applicant contends. Even if past references are contacted for evaluation purposes by email, the task of verifying the truthfulness and accuracy of the employment history still requires a screening firm to independently obtain information from past employers, one of the most important and powerful due diligence tools in the employment process.

There is also the possibility of a fake or set-up reference or an applicant creating a fake identity and having the bogus ones verified. Automated reference checking services take steps to minimize the possibility of fraud through analysis of the results. However, in the final analysis, there is no substitute for the hand work of manual background checks. By manually verifying the existence of past employers, and verifying dates of employment to reveal gaps in employment, an employer is taking the final due diligence steps needed for making a hiring decision final.

There are also potential FCRA complications that may prevent a background check firm from offering this type of service. These services encourage responses by telling reference sources that all replies are aggregated and that applicants will not know which particular person gave which score. However, if the use of these tools triggers the FCRA, then such promises of anonymity could not be kept since the FCRA requires transparency and individual scoring would likely need to be revealed at some point.

The bottom-line conclusion is risk management. Although these email assessment tools are an excellent means of providing an in-depth assessment of a candidate during the decision-making stage, the traditional background check complements them for the final candidates and provides the demonstrable due diligence that can be used as a legal defense if there is a negligent hiring lawsuit.

Author Tip ⟩ **Why Not Just Use LinkedIn, Facebook & Social Media Sites or Similar Sites?**

Although business connection sites such as LinkedIn and social media sites are extremely valuable for many purposes, they have limitations if using them to verify an applicant's past employment history. The main problem with LinkedIn is that anyone can say anything they want, and there is no mechanism for anyone to correct or comment on any errors or outright falsehoods. Social media sites are addressed in more detail in Chapters 12 and 14.

The Reason Why Employers Won't Give References

Even though everyone agrees that past employment checking is an essential part of the hiring process, many employers, on the advice of legal counsel, have a *no comment policy,* allowing only verification of basic information such as start and end dates and job title. Some companies will not even release salary information—salaries coming under the heading of competitive intelligence, thus protected—even when presented with a signed release.

Why won't employers give references? Quite simply it is **the fear of being sued.**

Employers who give negative references are concerned about being sued for defamation. When the defamation is in oral form (over the phone), it is called slander. When in written form (such as a negative letter of recommendation) it is called libel.

For example, what if an applicant had a history with previous employers that showed he was often late, did not get along with others, was not productive, did not meet goals, or was disciplined for inappropriate workplace conduct? These are all critical items of information a new employer would want and need to know.

Yet, few former employers are willing to convey this information. Labor lawyers repeatedly instruct employers NOT to give out anything but "name, rank, and serial number."

If there is no question that misconduct occurred, such as a criminal conviction, then the former employer is probably on safer grounds. However, in situations where the former employee can dispute the accusation, an employer may be concerned about a lawsuit. Suppose a former employee was accused of harassment, and an internal company investigation indicated the harassment did occur. If the company reveals this about the applicant to the new employer, the previous employer could still face a lawsuit. An internal company investigation does not carry weight of law, thus it may form the basis for a defamation lawsuit.

To make matters even worse, employers can be sued, believe it or not, by giving a POSITIVE reference. This can happen where the employer gave a good reference letter but withheld negative information for fear of being sued for defamation. If the resulting recommendation created a false impression, and as the result of the misrepresentation it is foreseeable that someone can be injured, the past employer can be sued. And why not? They lied. Below is a true life example.

Liability for a False Positive Reference – the School District Case

In a 1997 California case, the State Supreme Court ruled that a school district could be liable for damages when it gave a very positive job recommendation and left out important negative information. A school administrator was accused of inappropriate sexual misconduct towards a 13-year-old girl. The named victim not only sued the administrator, but also sued former schools that gave him favorable employment recommendations even though the former schools were aware of similar allegations of sexual misconduct at previous schools. The favorable recommendations included statements such as:

- He had "genuine concern" for students and had "outstanding rapport" with everyone.
- "I wouldn't hesitate to recommend (him) for any position."
- He was "an upbeat, enthusiastic administrator who related well to the students."
- He was "in a large part" responsible for making the school "a safe, orderly and clean environment for students and staff."

The Court ruled that a former employer providing a recommendation owes a duty to protect employers and third parties, and cannot misrepresent the qualifications and character of an ex-employee where there is a substantial risk of physical injury. In other words, an employer could not portray a former employee in a false light by only giving the good and not the bad. Having written a letter that they knew would be used to gain employment at other schools where there were potential victims, the schools had an obligation tell the whole truth. See *Randi W vs. Muroc Joint Unified School District*, (14 Cal.4th 1066)(1997)

So, here is the situation. If a past employer gives a negative reference, the past employer can potentially be sued for defamation by the applicant. If the employer gives a positive reference, a victim of misconduct can potentially sue the past employer for giving a false reference if negative information is left out.

The law arguably places employers who give recommendations in a Catch-22. If an employer fails to disclose an accusation because of insufficient credible evidence, then the employer risks being sued by third party victims. However, if the employer does mention an accusation, the ex-employee can arguably sue for defamation by the former employee.

The argument is made that the threat of defamation lawsuits is exaggerated since there are few reported cases. However, most cases get settled so the number of appellate cases is not a good yardstick. In addition, even if something is statistically unlikely, it does not mean that an employer wants to take unnecessary risks.

A hesitation to give references exists despite protection given under many state laws. At least forty states have some sort of employer immunity statute. These statutes are designed to promote good faith communication of job related information between employers. For example, California Civil Code Section 47(c) was amended in 1994 to add a section to protect employers from defamation lawsuits when giving an employment reference to another employer. The code states:

> *This subdivision applies to and includes a communication concerning the job performance or qualifications of an applicant for employment, based upon credible evidence, made without malice, by a current or former employer of the applicant, to and upon request of the prospective employer.*

What does this mean in plain English? Essentially it means that if a new prospective employer contacts a former employer, the former employer has a "qualified privilege" to give information, as long as the information is:

1. Job related;
2. Based upon credible evidence; and
3. Made without malice.

Unfortunately, it is difficult to gauge whether these laws have actually encouraged employers to free up the flow of necessary information. For the most part, these laws merely put into a statute what has already been the case law, or "common law," in most jurisdictions—that good faith communication between interested parties has some protection. However, even with this protection, many legal sources argue that the risk of a defamation claim outweighs any benefit to an employer from giving reference information. For one thing, applicants can still sue for defamation if they contend the reference was given in bad faith. Further, what constitutes *credible evidence* or what is *job related* can be open to interpretation.

One more consideration must be added to the mix. Generally, an employer has no obligation to say anything at all. If a firm was considering the application of Jack the Ripper and called up a past employer, that past employer can legally say "No comment." In other words, past employers have no duty to warn. The exception, of course, may be if the employer only gives the "good stuff" and leaves out the bad, as in the California School case above.

If employers had a duty to warn, it would potentially put an impossible task on employers. Why? Because employers could be placed in the untenable position of being sued every time one of their ex-employees gets a new job. It would create an incredible burden if every time an employer was called up for a reference, they had to choose between being sued by the applicant for defamation or being sued by the new employer or a victim for failure to warn or for giving a negligent reference.

A Tale of Two References – One Makes You Liable for Damages and the Other Does Not

In a 2008 federal appeals case, *Kadlec Medical vs. Lakeview, 527 F.3d 412 (5th Cir. 2008)*, two past medical employers gave past employment information for the same anesthesiologist. After the anesthesiologist had moved on to yet another hospital, he botched a routine 15 minute procedure, leaving a patient in a permanent vegetative state allegedly due to the anesthesiologist's own addiction to drugs.

The new hospital and its insurance company settled with the victim and in turn sued the previous two medical organizations for misrepresentations in the past employment information given to the new hospital.

The allegation was based upon misrepresentations since the new hospital claimed it hired the anesthesiologist because the defendants did not give accurate information by withholding information about misconduct and drug use.

The first defendant was a medical group that was fully aware that the anesthesiologist had a drug abuse issue. After giving the anesthesiologist a second chance, he continued to misuse drugs. The anesthesiologist was terminated for that reason.' However, the first defendant gave the anesthesiologist a glowing recommendation. The court noted that:

> ...if an employer makes a misleading statement in a referral letter about the performance of its former employees, the former employer may be liable for its statements if the facts and circumstances warrant. Here, defendants (medical group) were recommending an anesthesiologist, who had the lives of patients in his hands every day. Policy considerations dictate that the defendants had a duty to avoid misrepresentations in their referral letters if they mislead plaintiffs into thinking that (the anesthesiologist) was an excellent anesthesiologist, where they had information that he was a drug addict.

The situation with the second defendant, the hospital, however, was more complicated. The hospital knew that the anesthesiologist was a potential danger, but yet chose to say nothing, hiding behind a claim that they were too busy to provide more details.

The Court noted that it found no Louisiana case, or cases outside of Louisiana, that imposed a requirement that a past employer reveal negative past information, absent a situation where the past employer made some sort of affirmative misrepresentation. In other words, the first hospital did not have a legal duty to voluntarily step up and give negative information, as long as it limited its report to just factual employment data such as dates and job title. The court noted:

> And although the (hospital) might have had an ethical obligation to disclose their knowledge of (the anesthesiologist's) drug problems, they were also rightly concerned about a possible defamation claim if they communicated negative information about (the anesthesiologist).

The Court noted that if such an obligation were imposed upon employers, there would not only be privacy concerns, but it would create a burden if employers had to investigate each time if negative matters about a past employee were the type that had to be disclosed. As a result, the employer that gave a glowing recommendation where it was obviously not true could be liable. The employer that kept its mouth shut was not liable, even though it knew the truth and kept it to itself. The bottom line: if an employer limits itself to just dates of employment and job title, it has no obligation to warn of future dangerousness, provided the employer did not falsely mislead the new employer.

That is why so many employers choose to not say anything either way and limit verifications to dates of employment and job title. A practice has developed essentially that if you do not have something good to say, then don't say anything at all. Another interesting aspect to this story is that some 40 states have laws that give employers some variation of immunity for statements about past employers that are made in good faith in response to a request from a potential new employer, and are factual and non-malicious. Even with this protection, labor lawyers still often caution employers to stick to the facts only (name and dates of employment) since it can still be murky as to what is factual.

A Conclusion about Past Employer References

Because of these complications, and the fact that an employer has no obligation to give a reference, many lawyers advise the "no comment" policy. That is the reason why many employers will only give "name, rank, and serial number."

Unfortunately, if everyone followed this policy, then all companies would be placed in jeopardy because it becomes very difficult to know whom you are hiring.

Suggestions on How to Deal with Requests for References

Employers concerned about obtaining references will undoubtedly find themselves in the position of being asked for references. Employers and Human Resource professionals have responded in various ways, as we have outlined. So what are the best ways to handle incoming calls for reference checks?

Guidelines to Consider When Responding to Requests for Reference Information

1. A firm should have a written policy and procedure for giving references.
2. All information should go through a central source. This gives a firm consistency and reduces the chances that a manager may give out information that is contrary to company policy. As a practical matter, many organizations understand that even though there may be such a policy, there is, in reality, a practice of individual managers giving information. When that is the case, an alternative policy is to allow managers to do so under a strict program with procedures, training, and consequences for failing to follow procedures.
3. Clearly document who is requesting the information, for what purpose, and exactly what is provided. Former employees have been known to have friends or paid "reference checkers" contact previous employers.
4. Clearly document who in the company is giving the information because this can be important in order to trace who-exactly-said-what in a reference check. Keep in mind that staff members may leave a company and, without a written record, an employer may not be able to defend their reference actions.
5. If the information requested goes beyond dates and job title, a company may ask for a copy of a written release. This also provides some protection against defamation lawsuits.
6. If an ex-employee has a pending claim against the employer such as a worker's compensation claim or has filed a discrimination charge or lawsuit against the company, then the past employer needs to be very careful about what information is given. No information should be given beyond job dates and job title without contacting your legal department. That is because an employer needs to be very concerned about allegations of retaliation against an ex-employee for filing a claim.

If the employer intends to give negative information, the following may be helpful:

1. Remember that employees most often seek the advice of an attorney when they are surprised, or feel that they have been fundamentally disrespected or demeaned as a human being. Imagine an applicant's surprise when he or she hears for the first time from some new potential employer they are getting a negative reference from a past employer. If negative references may be an issue, what the past employer that intends to say should be handled and documented at the time the employee leaves during the exit interview so there are no surprises.
2. Disclose only factual information. Make sure everything has been documented. For example, if the former employee was convicted of a crime, a past employer can simply report the public record. A past employer's performance evaluations can be a good source of information. The employee has already seen the performance evaluations and in most cases signed them.
3. Avoid conclusions and give facts instead. For example, avoid saying a former employee "had a bad attitude." Instead, convey facts showing a failure to get along with team members. Let the facts speak for themselves.
4. Include favorable facts about the employee. That demonstrates an employer is even-handed.
5. Make sure the personnel file is factually correct. That is something HR may do when an employee leaves.

> ## Author Tip

Private Reference Checking Services for Job Applicants

There is another reason to be very careful about giving references. There are a number of firms that offer private reference checking services on behalf of job applicants who want to find out if a past employer is giving a negative reference. In fact, there is one firm that hires court reporters to call past employers on behalf of job applicants. The court reporters transcribe the conversation exactly as it occurs. In many states a tape recording would be illegal, but a court always accepts a court reporter's transcript as accurate. The court reporter calls a past employer and tells them they are doing an employment reference. They just don't happen to mention that it is on behalf of the past employee fishing for material for a defamation lawsuit.

Believe It Or Not—Website Sells Job Applicants Fake Credentials to Get Real Jobs

The website of a company that calls itself a *"Reference Answering Service"* – www.careerexcuse.com – promises to help *"disadvantaged job applicants"* with gaps in their resumes, bad job references, and too many part-time jobs. The company website even proudly boasts that they are *"the Internet's only site committed to the development of truly customized, fake job references!"*

The company acts as their current or past employer and having reference providers give great (but fake) job references for people who sign up for the service. The company can create powerful (but false) resumes with faked professional references that they claim pass through online job screening portals to employers.

They offer subscriptions for both Entry Level Blue Collar positions and Tech/Management White Collar positions. These subscriptions contain live reference providers with company emails, local company numbers in requested areas, professionally located company addresses in requested cities and states, and multi-page company websites. Of course, these subscriptions are not free.

While it is true some job seekers will stop at nothing to land a job, providing false past employment reference information is not the best way for a prospective employee to begin a business relationship with a potential employer. When job seekers offer false past employment information to employers, they may end up being hired for jobs they are too unfit, unqualified, dishonest, or dangerous to complete. Meanwhile, honest job seekers are overlooked for being more truthful with their references.

CHAPTER 5

The Fair Credit Reporting Act (FCRA)

A Basic Understanding of the FCRA

No discussion of background checks can occur without first having a clear understanding of a federal law called the **Fair Credit Reporting Act (FCRA)** that is the underlying national law that controls employment screening in the United States. It also controls information obtained for credit and insurance as well. When an employer uses a third party to conduct a background check, that is the federal law the employer must understand and follow. The FCRA regulates the collection, dissemination, and use of consumer information used for employment purposes. The FCRA fundamentally controls information on applicants that is assembled, evaluated, or disseminated by certain third parties and used for employment purposes.

Some employers are confused by the word *Credit* in the name of the law and mistakenly assume that the FCRA only applies to actual credit reports. In fact, the FCRA establishes specific requirements and rules for a pre-employment background report, called a **Consumer Report**, which is usually much broader in scope than just a credit report.

A Consumer Report can include a wide variety of information concerning job applicants, such as criminal and civil records, driving records, civil lawsuits, reference checks, past employment, education, and any other information obtained by a **Consumer Reporting Agency (CRA)**.

When initially passed in 1970, the FCRA was meant primarily to promote confidentiality, privacy, accuracy, and relevancy regarding information gathered about consumers. The law was extensively amended in 1996 with changes effective September 30, 1997. That amendment substantially overhauled the use of consumer reports for employment purposes by providing greater protection to consumers. Other important amendments were made in 1998, and additional amendments were passed in 2003. The full text of the FCRA is available at www.ftc.gov/enforcement/rules/rulemaking-regulatory-reform-proceedings/fair-credit-reporting-act.

FCRA Table of Contents

The Addendum contains the Table of Contents for the Fair Credit Reporting Act (FCRA).

Who Regulates the FCRA?

Since its inception in 1970, the FCRA was enforced by the **Federal Trade Commission (FTC)**—www.ftc.gov—an independent agency of the United States government focused on the promotion of consumer protection and the elimination and prevention of anticompetitive business practices. The FTC was responsible for prescribing the three essential forms mandated by the FCRA to be used in certain situations during the background screening process: "A Summary of Your Rights Under the Fair Credit Reporting Act," "NOTICE TO USERS OF CONSUMER REPORTS: OBLIGATIONS OF USERS UNDER THE FCRA," and "NOTICE TO FURNISHERS OF INFORMATION: OBLIGATIONS OF FURNISHERS UNDER THE FCRA."

However in 2012, the **Consumer Financial Protection Bureau (CFPB)**—www.consumerfinance.gov—that was created as part of the **Dodd–Frank Wall Street Reform and Consumer Protection Act** ruled that these three essential FCRA-mandated forms used for employment background checks were to be modified to reflect that consumers could obtain information about their rights under the FCRA from the CFPB instead of the FTC beginning on January 1, 2013:

- **A Summary of Your Rights Under the Fair Credit Reporting Act** – The FCRA mandates that a background screening firm must provide this notice to an employer and employers, in turn, must provide the notice to applicants in different situations (This notice is available in English and Spanish at www.consumerfinance.gov/learnmore/).
- **NOTICE TO USERS OF CONSUMER REPORTS: OBLIGATIONS OF USERS UNDER THE FCRA** - The FCRA also mandates that a background screening firm (known as a Consumer Reporting Agency or "CRA") must provide each user of its services the "Notice to Users of Consumer Reports of their Obligations under the FCRA."
- **NOTICE TO FURNISHERS OF INFORMATION: OBLIGATIONS OF FURNISHERS UNDER THE FCRA** - This notice is aimed at certain furnishers of information to CRAs and must be provided in prescribed situations such as a re-investigation where the consumer disputes the report or in a situation involving identity theft.

FCRA-Mandated Forms for Background Screening

Three FCRA-mandated forms for background screening are reprinted in the Addendum: *"A Summary of Your Rights Under the Fair Credit Reporting Act," "NOTICE TO USERS OF CONSUMER REPORTS: OBLIGATIONS OF USERS UNDER THE FCRA,"* and *"NOTICE TO FURNISHERS OF INFORMATION: OBLIGATIONS OF FURNISHERS UNDER THE FCRA."*

The CFPB has rulemaking and enforcement powers over the FCRA but does not have supervisory power over background screening firms. Congress specifically exempted background screening firms from being supervised by the CFPB since a background check report is not a financial product. Since background check firms are still supervised by the FTC under the new law, it remains to be seen exactly how much the CFPB will attempt to extend their jurisdiction to backgrounds checks as well as the exact nature of the relationship between the two agencies.

A joint amicus brief filed by the CFPB and FTC in 2015 advocating for the seven-year reporting period for non-conviction records found in the FCRA to begin on date of the charge or filing and not on the date of the last action in the case described the CFPB, FTC, and FCRA in the following manner:

- The CFPB is a federal agency charged under the Dodd-Frank Act with regulating **"the offering and provision of consumer financial products and services under Federal consumer financial law."**
- The FTC is **"the federal agency with primary responsibility for the protection of consumers from unfair and deceptive trade practices, including through enforcement of the FCRA, 15 USC § 1681(a)."**
- The FCRA – as amended by the Dodd-Frank Act – authorizes the CFPB to **"prescribe regulations as may be necessary or appropriate to administer and carry out objectives"** of the FCRA to ensure consumer privacy.

The CFPB is an active enforcer of the FCRA. In October of 2015, the CFPB ordered two of the nation's largest employment background check firms to pay a total of $13 million—$10.5 million in relief to harmed consumers and a $2.5 million civil penalty—for allegedly failing to take proper steps to ensure the information they reported about job applicants was accurate.

The CFPB – the federal agency responsible for consumer protection in the financial sector – claimed that the firms violated the FCRA by failing to employ reasonable procedures to assure the maximum possible accuracy of information contained in reports provided to potential employers of consumers. The Dodd-Frank Wall Street Reform and Consumer Protection Act authorized the creation of the CFPB which has the authority to take action against institutions or individuals engaging in unfair, deceptive, or abusive acts or practices or violating federal consumer financial laws.

The FTC is also active in the FCRA area since the emergence of the CFPB. In March of 2014, the U.S. Equal Employment Opportunity Commission (EEOC)—www.eeoc.gov—and FTC released a joint publication titled *Background Checks: What Employers Need to Know* to explain how compliance with the FCRA and anti-discrimination laws intersect when employers use employment background checks. The publication is available online at http://business.ftc.gov/documents/0487-background-checks-what-employers-need-know.

In November of 2014, the FTC has issued a follow-up guide called *Background Checks – Tips For Job Applicants and Employees* that expanded on the March 2014 joint publication of the EEOC and FTC. The new guide further specifies the rights of applicants and employees under the federal Fair Credit Reporting Act (FCRA) and anti-discrimination laws when employers run background checks. This guide is available at www.consumer.ftc.gov/articles/pdf-0044-background-checks.pdf.

In May of 2016, the FTC has released new guidance for companies in the business of compiling background information for employment purposes called *What Employment Background Screening Companies Need to Know About the Fair Credit Reporting Act (FCRA)* in order to help these companies understand when their work defines them as a Consumer Reporting Agency (CRA) under the FCRA. The FTC guidance is available at www.ftc.gov/tips-advice/business-center/guidance/what-employment-background-screening-companies-need-know-about.

This change in FCRA enforcement from the FTC to a combination of the CFPB and FTC underscores the fact that background screening is a complex professional endeavor that is increasingly subject to regulation, litigation, and legislation on both the state and federal level. Employers need to carefully select a background screening firm that has an understanding of these regulatory complexities, especially given the increase in class action lawsuits and governmental investigations.

Author Tip

How will Trump Administration affect CFPB?

Following the 2016 Presidential election that will bring in a new administration that has expressed concerns about government regulation, it remains to be seen what will happen to the CFPB, in general, and its role in employment screening, in particular. This is a trend to watch in 2017 and beyond.

Important Term Definitions Found in the FCRA

What is a Consumer Report? (FCRA Section 603(d))

A consumer report, prepared by a Consumer Reporting Agency, consists of any written, oral, or other communication of any information pertaining to the applicant's or employee's credit worthiness, credit standing, credit capacity, character, general reputation, personal characteristics, or mode of living, if this information is used or expected to be used or collected for employment purposes.

What is an Investigative Consumer Report? (FCRA Section 603(e))

An Investigate Consumer Report is a special type of consumer report when the information is gathered through personal interviews (by phone calls or in person) of neighbors, friends, or associates of the employee or applicant reported on, or from other personal acquaintances or persons who may have knowledge about information bearing on the applicant's or employee's credit worthiness, credit standing, credit capacity, character, general reputation, personal characteristics, or mode of living, if this information is used or expected to be used or collected for employment purposes.

The Investigative Consumer Report includes reference checks with former employers about job performance. However, a report would NOT be an Investigative Consumer Report if it were simply a verification of former employment limited to only factual matters such as the date started, the date ended, salary, or job title. Once a reference checker asks about eligibility for rehire and job performance, then the report then becomes an Investigative Consumer Report. Per FCRA Section 606(d)(4), if the information is adverse to the consumer's interest, the CRA must either obtain confirmation of the information from an additional source with independent knowledge or ensure the person interviews is the best possible source of information. In addition, there are some special requirements for notice that a consumer must receive certain time periods including a right to receive information as to the "nature and scope" of the search.

What is a Consumer Reporting Agency (CRA)? (FCRA Section 603(f))

A Consumer Reporting Agency, or CRA, is any person or entity which, for monetary fees, dues, or on a cooperative nonprofit basis, regularly engages in whole or in part in the practice of assembling or evaluating consumer information or other information on consumers for the purposes of furnishing reports to third parties. It includes private investigators that *regularly* engage in pre-employment inquiries.

What is Meant by Employment Purposes? (FCRA Section 603(h))

A report is prepared for employment purposes when the report is used for the purpose of evaluating an applicant or employee for employment, reassignment, or retention. Under the FCRA, a Consumer Report for employment purposes is considered a Permissible Purpose.

What is Meant by Adverse Action? (FCRA Section 603(k))

Adverse action in relationship to employment means a denial of employment or any other decision for employment purposes that adversely affects any current or prospective employee.

You Need To Know ⟩

An Important Area NOT Covered by the FCRA

What if a business needs to investigate another business before entering into an economic relationship, such as investing, joint venturing, licensing agreements, merger or acquisition, a vendor check, or just to check out trade credit? A business may simply want to check out a competitor. The research may involve criminal or civil records, judgments, liens or bankruptcies, or even a business credit report such as a Dun and Bradstreet report. (To learn more about Dun and Bradstreet reports, visit www.dnb.com/us/.) None of these investigations are covered by the FCRA, even if done by a third party. This is because the investigation is not focused on an individual and the FCRA only protects individuals.

What if a business wanted information about the people behind the other business? Any business relationship ultimately depends upon the integrity of the people involved. All the agreements and lawyers in the world cannot protect you or your business if the people you are dealing with lack integrity. Even in that scenario, a firm or a third party working on their behalf may check public records and even call schools and employers as long as the purpose is NOT employment. Here are three important considerations:

1. Even if the investigation is for business due diligence, under no circumstances can the business or their agent pull a personal credit report on any individual involved without consent. A personal credit report is ALWAYS covered by the FCRA, and can only be pulled for FCRA approved purposes with the applicant's express written consent.

2. If the economic transaction really amounts to starting an employment relationship, such as the acquisition of another corporation where the principal is going to work for the acquiring company, this could trigger the need for full FCRA compliance.

3. There may be other laws that apply as well. In some states, the investigation can only be conducted by a state licensed private investigator.

The Four Groups Affected by the FCRA

The FCRA addresses the rights and obligations of four groups. The descriptions below focus on these groups as they relate to employment.

1. **Consumer Reporting Agencies (CRAs)**. Again, these are third parties such as background screening firms or private investigators that provide Consumer Reports.

2. **Users of Consumer Information**. These are primarily employers hiring a CRA to prepare Consumer Reports.

3. **Furnishers of Consumer Information**. Furnishers can include credit card companies that report payment histories to the three national credit collecting agencies, also past employers and schools—anyone who answers telephone calls from Consumer Reporting Agencies.

4. **Consumers**. The FCRA provides the consumers (applicants) with a host of rights in the process. These various rights are discussed in more detail throughout this book.

Here is an important fact to keep in mind: The FCRA kicks in when a pre-employment background pre-screening is conducted by the Consumer Reporting Agency. Therefore, if an employer works with a professional pre-employment background firm, which is a CRA, the employer should select the firm based in part on the background firm's knowledge of the FCRA. A competent background firm should know how to fully comply with legal requirements of the FCRA, including the preparation of all documents and forms needed for a fully compliant screening program. Although a CRA cannot offer or give legal advice, the CRA should have an in-depth understanding of how the FCRA operates.

In addition, a competent background screening firm always operates as though a consumer is also their customer as well. Even though it is the employer that contracts with a screening firm and pays for a report, a background screening firm must also protect the interest of consumers and has the same interest in providing accurate reports and following legal procedures as consumers do. This is discussed in more detail in Chapter 7 under selecting a background screening firm.

Employers risk legal liability if the procedures utilized to check on applicants infringe on legally protected areas of privacy. By following the FCRA, an applicant's privacy rights are protected. For this reason, many legal experts advise employers to engage the services of an outside screening firm. See Chapter 7 for a discussion on the pros and cons of outsourcing.

Author Tip

Does FCRA Apply to Private Investigators?

Any private investigator (PI) who regularly does pre-employment screening is also a CRA and absolutely subject to the rules and regulations of the FCRA. There is no exact definition of the term *regularly*, but any investigator who does more than one background screen for employment purposes must assume the FCRA applies. Any PI who *regularly* does pre-employment screening is also a CRA and absolutely subject to the rules and regulations of the FCRA.

> Some private investigators have incorrectly assumed that the FCRA does not apply to them because they have a state license. Basically, there is no P.I. exception to the FCRA. A Private Investigator has the exact same duties and obligations under the FCRA as a Consumer Reporting Agency.

Understanding the FCRA Numbering System

Part of the complication of dealing with the FCRA has to do with the numbering system. Technically, federal laws are published in the United States Codes and are divided into *Titles*, meaning general subject matter. The FCRA is found at 15 U.S.C. 1681. The 15 stands for the title of the code, which deals with commerce and trade laws. The U.S.C. means United States Code and 1681 refers to the section where the law starts. However, it is much more complicated than that because there have been amendments over the years that have impacted the FCRA. Some of these amendments have been contained in other laws that have been passed by Congress. As a public service, the Federal Trade Commission (FTC) has compiled a working version of the FCRA that incorporates all of the amendments found in various laws and has created a workable version that is commonly used by background screening firms and human resources. It is found at www.consumer.ftc.gov/sites/default/files/articles/pdf/pdf-0111-fair-credit-reporting-act.pdf.

The FTC version for convenience sake has renumbered the FCRA starting with section 601. However, officially, when cited in court cases, the proper citation is the actual United States Code. For example, FCRA section 607 dealing with compliance is actually 15 U.S.C. § 1681e. A convenient conversion chart prepared by the Consumer Financial Protection Bureau (CFBP) in an official document is provided at the end of this chapter.

Bad News and Good News about FCRA

There is bad news and good news about the FCRA. The bad news is that the FCRA is a very complex and convoluted law that makes little sense if an employer sits down and tries to read it. Anyone wanting to read the law can go to the website for the Federal Trade Commission (FTC), the federal agency charged with enforcement of the law. Web links to review the law are available at the end of this chapter.

The good news is that there are only four basic steps an employer needs to know about the FCRA in order to begin a background screening program through an employment screening firm. These steps are explained in detail in the next section of this chapter. When engaging the services of a CRA, both the employer and the CRA must understand how critical it is to follow the FCRA. Failure to do so can result in substantial legal exposures, including fines, damages, punitive damages, and attorney's fees.

Below is a brief summary of the substantial penalties involved for NOT following the FCRA.

FCRA Sec.	Type of Non-Compliance	Maximum Possible Penalties
616	Willful failure to comply with FCRA—applies to both employer and CRA	Attorney's fees / Punitive damages / $1,000 nominal damages even if no actual damages- This section is used in class action lawsuits where the attorney for the class action does not seek to prove each individual's damages but will allege the $1,000 nominal damages per class member, in addition to seeking punitive damages and attorney's fees.
617	Negligent noncompliance—applies to both employer & CRA	Actual damages/attorney's fees (no punitive damages or nominal damages)

619	Obtaining a report under false pretense—applies to both employer and CRA	Fine and two years prison
620	Unauthorized disclosure of consumer information by CRA officer or employee	Fine and two years prison
621	Administrative enforcement against CRAs engaged in a pattern of violations	Civil penalties of $2,500 per violation.

The FCRA in Four Easy Steps

When engaging the services of a Consumer Reporting Agency (CRA), **both the employer and the CRA must follow certain steps to maintain compliance with the FCRA**. Failure to do so can result in substantial legal exposures, including fines, damages, punitive damages, and attorneys' fees.

To utilize the services of a Consumer Reporting Agency, employers do not need to know all of the ins and outs of the FCRA. What is necessary for any employer is to understand the basic FCRA requirements in order to make sure that any supplier of hiring-related services is in compliance. Here are the four primary steps an employer needs to understand in order to make sure their program is in compliance.

> **You Need To Know**
>
> ## Knowledge of State Laws is Also Critical
>
> A number of states have additional requirements on CRAs and employers. Requirements may be very similar to FCRA, but some states have a number of their own special requirements as well. For example, a number of states have very specific rules when it comes to adverse action notices and re-investigations of a report if a consumer disagrees with the results. Each individual state can be an adventure. Many states also have special rules about particular types of searches, such as criminal records, credit reports, or social media that are discussed in later chapters. The general topic of state rules for background screening is addressed in Chapter 6.
>
> The point is that an employer needs to take into account both federal and state rules. In addition, individual counties and cities are now passing ban-the-box laws which add a whole new layer of complexity to legal compliance.

Step 1 – Employer Certification

The FCRA created a unique self-policing system. Prior to receiving a **Consumer Report**—which is another term for a background check report—an employer must first certify to the Consumer Reporting Agency in writing that the employer will follow all the steps set forth in the FCRA. The employer certifies it will do the following:

- Use the information for employment purposes only, which is a permissible purpose under the FCRA.
- Not use the information in violation of any federal or state equal opportunity law.
- Obtain all the necessary disclosures and consents as required by the FCRA (steps 2 and 3 below).
- Give the appropriate notices in the event an adverse action is taken against an applicant based in whole or in part on the contents of the Consumer Report (see step 3 below).
- Give the additional information required by law if an Investigative Consumer Report is needed.

These requirements are explained further in a document prepared by the Federal Trade Commission titled 'NOTICE TO USERS OF CONSUMER REPORTS: OBLIGATIONS OF USERS UNDER THE FCRA.' The FCRA requires a

Consumer Reporting Agency to provide a copy of this document to every employer who requests a background check report. A copy of this notice is reprinted in the Appendix.

Best Practice Note

A CRA may either require an employer to sign an FCRA certification document or may include the required FCRA certification language in an agreement that also contains business terms. A CRA and an employer can certainly negotiate business terms, but the fundamental requirements of the FCRA are not open to discussion for one simple reason—it is the law! In addition, some states impose additional specific requirements regarding the employer certification of how an employer will utilize background reports. One such example is California.

The screening industry operates on the basis that receiving a one-time prospective certification from an employer acts as a blanket certification for all screenings. However, at least one lawsuit has challenged this practice. An employer should ask its CRA how to handle the certification requirement. With new technology, a CRA can, in fact, obtain an employer certification before each background check.

Step 2 – Written Release and Disclosure

Before obtaining a consumer report from a Consumer Reporting Agency, the employer must obtain the applicant's written consent and also provide that applicant with **a clear and conspicuous written disclosure** that a background report may be requested. The disclosure must be provided **in a separate, stand-alone document** in order to prevent it from being buried in an employment application. The 1998 amendment to the FCRA clarified that the disclosure and the consent might be in the same document. However, the FTC, which enforces the FCRA along with the CFPB, cautions that this form should not contain excessive verbiage or information that may distract or confuse a consumer.

A Standalone Document is Critical

The requirement that the release and disclosure be in a separate and standalone document is critical. Otherwise if just part of the application, a consumer may not understand or even realize a consumer report is being prepared. Some labor attorneys recommend the background check forms not even be stapled to any other documents. The release and disclosure can also be provided electronically so an applicant can fill out and sign with an electronic signature. Where the release and disclosure forms are online, it is also critical that it be structured in such a way that it meets the *standalone* requirement.

A special procedure is necessary when the employer requests a Consumer Reporting Agency to obtain employment references. When the Consumer Reporting Agency is merely verifying factual matters such as the dates of employment, job title, or salary, this special procedure is not necessary. However, as mentioned previously, when the Consumer Reporting Agency asks for information on topics such as job performance, that falls into a special category of consumer report called an **Investigative Consumer Report**. When an Investigative Consumer Report is used, there are some special procedures to follow:

- There must be a disclosure to the applicant where it is "clearly and accurately disclosed" that "an investigative consumer report" is being requested, along with certain specified language such as the report will include information concerning "character, general reputation, personal characteristics, and mode of living, whichever are applicable." Unless it is contained in the initial disclosure, the consumer must receive this additional disclosure within three days after the request is made.
- The disclosure must tell the applicant they have a right to request additional information about the nature and scope of the investigation.
- If the applicant makes a written request for more information, then the employer has five days to respond with additional information and must provide a copy of a document prepared by the CFPB called *A Summary of Your Rights Under the Fair Credit Reporting Act* provided by the CRA. This form can also be provided to applicants who are subject to a "consumer report" that does not contain employment references.

As a practical matter, a Consumer Reporting Agency should handle all of these requirements for an employer as part of their services. Still, an employer should be aware there are legal issues involved in preparing a proper form whether it's a paper form or an online form. Not only is there required information that must be conveyed to applicants, but also wrong language or excessive language can put an employer at risk. There is also the issue of asking for date of birth, as discussed in the previous chapter.

Another concern is if a release or disclosure form contains a release of liability meant to protect the employer, the furnisher of information sources, or the screening firm. A release can potentially be contrary to public policy by requiring an applicant to give up rights. A release can also violate the rule against excessive verbiage on a form, which could detract from a consumer's clear understanding of the documents signed. In response to this issue, some firms use separate release forms and disclosure forms, while only placing the release language on the release form. A good idea for firms who utilize release of liability language in a form is to consider adding the phrase, "to the extent permitted by law" after the release language.

The consent portion of an authorization form used for a background check should indicate the release is "valid for future screening for retention, promotion, or reassignment (unless revoked in writing)."

In 1998, Congress passed one exception to the FCRA rules concerning these various notices. The trucking industry has an exception allowing for telephonic or electronic communications from commercial drivers. The reason is that commercial drivers may be hired over the phone from truck stops, and there is not an opportunity to obtain a written release or give certain notices.

Author Tip ▷ **Where Does an Employer Obtain Forms?**

To perform a background check legally under the FCRA (or per state law), the employer will need forms such as those discussed above. While there are no industry-accepted or official standardized forms in use, forms are available from a variety of sources. Many law firms provide forms to their business clients or will review forms provided by a background screening firm. Nearly every background screening firm will provide forms. In fact, part of the selection process of a screening firm is to determine the firm's ability to provide legally compliant forms. However, it is important to note that a CRA cannot provide legal advice.

Step 3 – Pre-Adverse Notice

When an employer receives a Consumer Report and intends not to hire the applicant based on the report, the applicant then has certain rights. If the "adverse action" is <u>intended</u> as a result of a Consumer Report, then the applicant is entitled to certain documents per FCRA Section 604. **Before** taking the adverse action, the employer must provide the following information to the applicant:

- A copy of the consumer report.
- The document "A Summary of Your Rights Under the Fair Credit Reporting Act." This document is usually provided by the screening service.

The purpose of the notice is to give an applicant the opportunity to see the report with the information being used against them. If the applicant feels the report is inaccurate or incomplete, the applicant then has the opportunity to contact the Consumer Reporting Agency to dispute or explain what is in the report. Otherwise, applicants could be denied employment without knowing they were the victims of inaccurate or incomplete data.

In effect, the pre-adverse action and post-adverse action processes act as a release valve to help guard against any mistakes having an adverse impact on applicants due to incomplete or inaccurate records. Although no statistics are available, it appears that in the majority of cases when an employer receives a background report that results in a job offer not being made or being rescinded, the applicant has little to complain about. If an applicant is caught making a material falsehood, or a falsehood by omission, most employers would not want to hire a dishonest person.

However, there can be times when an applicant is truly the victim of some sort of error. For example:

1. An applicant was the victim of identity theft and discovers through a background check for the first time that someone committed a crime using his or her identity

2. An applicant failed to make the final payment on a traffic ticket and did not realize there was a warrant for arrest issued for a failure to appear. This is easily resolved by the applicant going to court and taking care of the matter.

3. An applicant had a discrepancy in the employment dates. The applicant indicated they had worked for the past employer for 3 years, but the employer's records only show two years. In fact, the consumer was assigned there by a staffing company their first year, and the staffing company paid the salary. So from the consumer's point of view, they had been on the job three years, but from the payroll department's vantage point, they only show the consumer as being on salary for two years.

4. A consumer had gone back to court and had a criminal matter judicially set aside. However, the court clerk did not update the files, so when the background firm checked for court reports, it still showed that the criminal record was current.

5. A court retriever just plain misreads the date of birth and reported a criminal record belonging to someone else with the same name and does not see it is a different date of birth. As with any endeavor involving human beings, mistakes can happen. The adverse action notice procedure gives the applicant an opportunity to have the mistake corrected sooner than later.

6. A consumer has a "computer twin" meaning someone else with the exact same name and exact date of birth has a criminal record. Although not very common, this has happened, and there have been instances where a consumer first found out about this unfortunate coincidence as a result of a background report. The good news is that if it happens once, the consumer is now on notice that it may happen again, and can avoid delays and misunderstanding by alerting a potential future employer that if they are a finalist, there is someone with their name and date of birth who has a record so that future screening can go much more smoothly.

7. A consumer had earned two degrees, but the school's computer system was only capable of reporting one degree. At that point, the applicant is on notice that every time there is a background check, the school will only report one of the two degrees.

Below is a sample Pre-Adverse Notice letter under federal law. Keep in mind that the form and its contents can and do vary widely in a number of states with their own FCRA type rules.

Pre-Adverse Notice Sample Letter

[DATE]
[COMPANY NAME]
[ADDRESS1]
[ADDRESS2]
[CITY][STATE][ZIP]

RE: PRE-ADVERSE ACTION NOTICE

Dear [FIRST NAME] [LAST NAME],

We are required to inform you that you may be denied the position you are seeking with our organization based in whole or in part on information received in a background investigation report from the following consumer reporting agency:

Employment Screening Resources ("ESR")

7110 Redwood Blvd, Suite C

Novato, CA 94945

888-999-4474

We attached a copy of the report provided to us, as well as a copy of "A Summary of Your Rights Under the Fair Credit Reporting Act" prepared by a governmental agency.

1. If you want to dispute any inaccurate or incomplete information in the report, please contact ESR directly without delay (see contact information above).

2. If you want to explain any items in the report that will help us make a final decision, please contact the person below without delay.

Sincerely,

[COMPANY NAME]
[USER FIRST NAME][USER LAST NAME]

Enclosures:

Copy of your background investigation report

A Summary of Your Rights Under the Fair Credit Reporting Act

An additional form can also be sent with the pre-adverse action letter if an employer plans on instituting a procedure for an **Individualized Assessment.** This follows a best practice recommendation by the U.S. Equal Employment Opportunity Commission (EEOC) in their updated Enforcement Guidance on the Consideration of Arrest and Conviction Records in Employment Decisions Under Title VII of the Civil Rights Act of 1964 issued on April 25, 2012. See: www.eeoc.gov/laws/guidance/arrest_conviction.cfm.

According to the EEOC, an "Individualized assessment generally means that an employer informs the individual that he may be excluded because of past criminal conduct; provides an opportunity for the individual to demonstrate that the exclusion does not properly apply to him; and considers whether the individual's additional information shows that the policy as applied is not job-related and consistent with business necessity."

An applicant may show that either the background check report is incorrect or incomplete or the background check report is true and complete but there are reasons the criminal record is not disqualifying. If the consumer has a complaint about the accuracy of the background check, the consumer needs to contact the screening firm. If a consumer concedes the background report is accurate but still believes he or she should be considered, then the consumer needs to talk to the employer.

In addition to the pre-adverse action letter, a second letter should be sent advising the applicant that they may request an individualized assessment. It is a better practice to send two separate letters rather than combining the two, in order to demonstrate compliance with both the FCRA and the EEOC Guidance. This is discussed in more detail in Chapter 10.

Below is a sample *Individualized Assessment* notice.

Sample Individualized Assessment Notice

[DATE]
[COMPANY NAME]
[ADDRESS1]
[ADDRESS2]
[CITY][STATE][ZIP]

REQUEST FOR INFORMATION REQUIRED FOR

INDIVIDUALIZED ASSESSMENT OF CRIMINAL RECORD HISTORY

Dear [FIRST NAME][LAST NAME],

This notice provides you with required information that is unrelated to any other communication you may have received regarding your application.

IF NO CRIMINAL HISTORY is found in your background check report (a copy was attached to the Pre-Adverse Action Notice sent to you today by separate email), you may disregard this notice and take no further action.

IF A CRIMINAL HISTORY is found in your background check report; you should immediately review the attached "Individual Assessment Factors" with respect to your criminal record(s) history. If you want to provide an explanation relating to one or more of identified factors, please send an email as soon as possible to the person listed below addressing the specific areas of additional information outlined in the attachment.

If you provide a timely response, we will consider the information and contact you directly if we need anything else or want to speak to you.

Sincerely,

[COMPANY NAME]
[USER FIRST NAME][USER LAST NAME]

Enclosure:

Individual Assessment Factors

The Individual Assessment Factors can be found in the Appendix. It should be noted these factors are a floor, not a ceiling, and an applicant should be allowed to bring up anything he or she believes is relevant.

Of course, if the applicant fails to respond to the letter about an "Individualized Assessment," an employer does not need to take any further action. If the applicant fails to respond to the pre-adverse action letter, the next step is the post adverse action notice.

Step 4 – Notice must be given to Applicant after Adverse Action

If, after sending out the documents required in Step 3, the employer intends to make a final decision not to hire, the employer must take one more step. The employer must send the applicant a Notice of Adverse Action informing the job applicant that the employer has made a final decision and must provide a copy of the form "Summary of Your Rights under the Fair Credit Reporting Act."

Many employers find it difficult to believe that Congress intended an applicant be notified twice, both before an adverse action and after. The law clearly requires two notices. This is also the interpretation of the Federal Trade Commission staff. The purpose is to give job applicants the maximum opportunity to correct any incomplete or inaccurate reports that could affect their chances of employment. Here is a sample of a letter that can be used to comply with federal law, keeping in mind that some states may have their own requirements. As with the pre-adverse action notice, the form and its contents can and do vary widely in a number of states with their own FCRA type rules.

Sample of Notice of Post-Adverse Action Letter

[DATE]
[COMPANY NAME]
[ADDRESS1]
[ADDRESS2]
[CITY][STATE][ZIP]

Dear [FIRST NAME][LAST NAME],

We are required to inform you that you are no longer being considered for the position you were seeking with our organization. This decision was based in whole or in part on information in a background check report obtained from the following consumer reporting agency:

Employment Screening Resources ("ESR")

7110 Redwood Blvd, Suite C

Novato, CA 94945

888-999-4474

Employment Screening Resources had no role in the decision regarding your employment and cannot explain to you why the decision was made.

Pursuant to the Fair Credit Reporting Act, you have the following rights:

1. You may obtain an additional free copy of your report within sixty days of receipt of this notice by contacting Employment Screening Resources (see contact information above).

2. You may dispute any information contained in the report directly with Employment Screening Resources (see contact information above).

Sincerely,

[COMPANY NAME]

[USER FIRST NAME][USER LAST NAME]

Enclosures:

Copy of your background investigation report

A Summary of Your Rights Under the Fair Credit Reporting Act

See FCRA section 615 for more information on notice of adverse action. Attached in the Appendix is a copy of "A Summary of Your Rights Under the Fair Credit Reporting Act" that should be given to a job applicant any time an employer sends either a pre-adverse action or a post-adverse action letter.

FAQs about Adverse Action Letters

1. **Question:** *Should the employer still send the adverse action notices (both pre and post notices) to the rejected job candidate, even though the rejected candidate's background report played no part in the hiring decision?*

   Answer: Although a background screening firms cannot give legal advice, it can give a very lawyer-like answer, which is: It depends.

   Suppose an employer has two finalists for one position. The employer submits both names for background checks, and both candidates have clear background reports. The firm then decides to offer the job to one candidate over the other, purely based on the belief that one candidate was a better fit than the other, with nothing to do with the background reports. Even assuming the screening report is 100% not related to the decision, and it was entirely a fit issue, then theoretically an employer can bypass adverse action. Technically, adverse action notices are required only where a background report played a role, in whole or in part, in the employment decision. The idea is to give an applicant a meaningful opportunity to review, reflect, and act upon a report if the applicant feels it is incorrect or incomplete in any fashion.

   Even if the background report played just a minimal part in the final decision, the adverse action notices would be required. However, if the employer merely decided to screen both finalists and found nothing in the screening report that impacted the final decision, then strictly speaking the adverse action notices would not be required.

   Of course, as with most things involving employment decisions and background checks, nothing is ever quite that cut and dried. Here are some possible complications:

   - The first issue is proof. The rejected applicant may claim that the fit argument was a pretext. This is especially risky if the candidate not hired is a member of a protected class and argues failure to hire due to discrimination. Invariably, the attorney for the plaintiff that chooses to sue would probably add on a cause of action for failure to follow the FCRA by not giving the rejected applicant a chance to correct a report. Plaintiff lawyers have become very sophisticated in their understanding of the FCRA, and employers and screening firms that violate it can well be targets of litigation.

   - In addition, the subject of what is adverse can be tricky. Even if there is nothing derogatory on the face of the report, the rejected applicant can still claim that the report gave the wrong impression. For example, a job title may have been reported that was different than what the applicant used. Another example would be a credit report if it was run as part of the background check. If the credit report came back and there was nothing derogatory, such as late payments, there still could be information that was incorrect. For example, some employers look to see how much debt an applicant is in and compare their monthly obligations to their salary. If the reported debt information was incorrect, the applicant could argue he/she was placed in a false light without a chance to correct it.

   - Another problem is the consistent administration of the adverse action rules. If an employer starts picking and choosing when to send or not send notices, an error can be made in other cases since it can be a judgment call to a certain extent as to whether there was anything negative that influenced the decision. Some employers choose to send the notice to any rejected applicant that was the subject of a background report and not hired to ensure full compliance. After all, employers usually only submit background check requests generally on finalists so the situation may not come up that often.

The bottom line is always about risk management. Providing adverse action notices are a quick clerical task that takes little time. Many employers decide to follow a consistent policy of always sending out adverse action notices, even if not strictly required so nothing falls through the cracks, and they don't need to justify anything later. If for some reason, the lack of notices becomes an issue in an employment-related litigation, it may be hard to convince a jury that, in fact, the report was 100% irrelevant to the decision.

If there is a particular case where an employer does not want to send out the adverse action notices, then the employer may want to prepare a memo to file clarifying that it was a fit issue only, and the screening report was not involved even one iota.

2. **Question:** *How long an employer must wait between the two letters in order to deny employment based upon information contained in a Consumer Report?*

   Answer: The Fair Credit Reporting Act is silent on this point. However, many legal authorities advise that an employer should wait a reasonable period of time before making the final decision and sending the second and final letter. An opinion letter from the Federal Trade Commission (FTC), seemed to agree that a minimum period of five (5) business days would appear to be reasonable although that is not binding in courts. See: www.ftc.gov/os/statutes/fcra/weisberg.shtm. However, an employer may consider a longer period just to be on the safe side. This period should be the time that would be needed for an applicant to meaningfully review and consider the report and make known to the employer or the Consumer Reporting Agency any inaccurate or incomplete information in the Consumer Report. It is critical the applicant has an appropriate opportunity to review, reflect, and react before the employer takes the official adverse action. However, there is another wrinkle to the time period an employer should wait.. States, counties, and cities implementing ban-the-box laws can impose local requirements, such as the City of Philadelphia, Pennsylvania that instituted a 10-day requirement.

3. **Question:** *What if the information in the consumer report used against an applicant is not even negative on its face. Do the adverse action rules still apply?*

   Answer: Yes. For example, an applicant may have a perfect payment record on his or her credit report, but an employer may be concerned that the debt level is too high compared to the salary. The applicant still is entitled to a notice of pre-adverse action, because it is possible that the credit report is wrong about the applicant's outstanding debts. In a situation where the employer would have made an adverse decision anyway, regardless of the background report, following the adverse action procedures is still the best practice for legal protection.

4. **Question:** *If we send out a notice of pre-adverse action, how long do we need to keep the job open?*

   Answer: After the first notice is given, an employer may either wait until there has been a response or re-investigation or fill the position with another applicant. An employer, in fact, could proceed to hire the next person. The FCRA does not require an employer to hold the job open.

   In the real world, this issue has not presented nearly as many issues as employers and consumers first thought. When the whole concept of pre- and post-adverse action notices were introduced in 1996, employers were concerned about whether and how long they needed to keep a job open On one hand, an applicant had the right to receive both letters and even to ask for a re-investigation, which could take up to 45 days. If it turns out that the report was incomplete or incomplete, a person may be unfairly denied a job. On the other hand, employers could not operate a business by keeping the position open for that long.

   There are some second chance and workers' rights groups that argue that an employer should be required to keep the job open if a consumer files a request for a re-investigation since it would be unfair to lose a job if it turns out the background report had any inaccurate information. The counter argument is that in the real world, the number of instances when keeping a job open would help the consumer are statistically rare, compared to the economic burden such a policy would have on businesses.

As a practical matter, allowing employers to make the decision as to how long to keep the job open has worked very well. By the time an applicant is the subject of a Consumer Report, an employer has spent time, money, and effort in recruiting and hiring that person. Employers do not spend money and time on a background report unless they seriously want to employ a candidate. An employer may well be vested in the applicant and, at a minimum, a Human Resources department will want to know if and how an unqualified applicant got through the process to the background check stage. Therefore, it is often in the employer's best interest to give an applicant an opportunity to explain any adverse information before denying a job offer. If there was an error in the public records, giving the applicant the opportunity to explain or correct it could be to the employer's advantage. In the event that it requires a re-investigation to clear up a matter, many employers will then out of fairness make an effort to provide that applicant the next available opening.

Most employers find as a practical matter that this provision of law does NOT impose hardship or burden upon an employer. Even though, in rare situations, an employer may have questions on how to proceed, the clear advantages of a pre-employment screening program far outweigh any complications that can theoretically arise from the adverse action rules.

5. **Question:** *What if a background check is not completed before employment starts and then after employment, the background check forms the basis to terminate the new employee. Do we still have adverse action obligations?*

   Answer: Yes. A special problem arises when an employer brings a worker on the premises before the background check is complete, only to later find the background report uncovers negative information that may have disqualified the person. An employer may be tempted to simply call the person in, hand them the report, a final paycheck, and both letters at the same time. However, this does not give the applicant a reasonable time to review, reflect, and respond to the report. If the background report was incomplete or incorrect, there is not a meaningful opportunity for the applicant to exercise their rights under the FCRA. The best procedure is to follow the FCRA by providing the worker with their report, a statement of rights, the first letter and an opportunity to offer any response. The second letter should be delayed until a reasonable time has passed for an applicant to respond. Although it is administratively more difficult than giving two letters at once, two letters at once may violate an applicant's rights. An employer may choose to put the person on leave pending the outcome, but both letters are needed. (See Chapter 7 for additional considerations involved in bringing an applicant onboard before the background check is completed.)

6. **Question:** *What if the person is already employed, and the employer performs some additional check, such as a criminal check or credit report. Do we still need an adverse action period?*

   Answer: Details are everything if taking adverse action on a current employee due to a background check.

   A 2010 federal district court case demonstrates the importance of handling the adverse action process correctly when terminating an existing employee due to an unsatisfactory background check.

   In the case decided on February 26, 2010 by the U.S. District Court for the Southern District of Ohio, *Burghy v Dayton Racquet Club, Inc.*, 695 F.Supp.2d 689 (S.D.Ohio 2010), an employer ran a credit check on all employees in the accounting department, including the plaintiff who had been working in the current location for seven years. For reasons not disclosed in the case, the employer decided to terminate the plaintiff due to the result of the credit report.

   According to the plaintiff, a meeting was called on January 16, 2008, where she was told she would never work for the employer again and to go home. Shortly thereafter, she received a copy of the report as well as a letter stating that the information in the report may or may not affect employment. On January 23, 2008, she received a second letter indicating she was terminated.

   The plaintiff sued on the basis that the FCRA requires that an employer provide a consumer with a copy of any consumer report and a statement of their rights BEFORE an adverse decision is made about employment. The plaintiff argued that she was both given the report and terminated all on the same day, so she did not receive a pre-adverse action notice.

The employer disputed the account and argued that the first meeting did not constitute a termination; it only indicated an intention to terminate. In addition, the plaintiff was still paid for another week after the second letter, and there was some discussion about trying to get her job back.

The court ruled that since there was a disputed issue of fact, it was up to the jury to decide what happened, and the employer's motion to dismiss was denied. In other words, if the jury accepted the plaintiff's version of the facts, then the jury could find an FCRA violation.

This case illustrates the important point for employers **about terminating current employees.** As discussed in the preceding pages, under the FCRA, when an employer receives a Consumer Report and decides not to hire the applicant based upon the report in any way, the applicant has certain rights. Before taking the adverse action, the employer must provide certain information to the applicant. A second letter is required if the decision is to be made final.

In this case, where the consumer was already on the job, employers need to be much more careful. To avoid any misunderstandings, an employer should make it absolutely clear in writing (and with witnesses) that the first letter is NOT a final decision, and the consumer has the opportunity to review the report and make his or her objections known. The difficulty, in this case, was that the employer allegedly made it clear that the termination was final in the first meeting. Of course, the problem with an existing employee, especially one in a sensitive position such as accounting, is that an employer may not want them on premises if it turns out the decision becomes final.

In this case, the employer did send the plaintiff home with salary being paid but allegedly made the mistake of making the termination final immediately as opposed to the required waiting period.

This case again underscores the fact that employment screening is a highly regulated area of employment law that requires specialized skills and knowledge.

7.   **Question:** *Who has the responsibility to send out the notices of pre-adverse and post-adverse action?*

Answer: Under the FCRA, it is the employer who has the ultimate legal responsibility to ensure that notices of pre and post adverse action are sent out. However, it is a duty that can be delegated to a background screening firm. It is sometimes referred to as a "delegable duty." Obviously, a screening firm does not make hiring decisions, so the employer must advise the screening firm if a first notice is to be sent out. The background firm also had no way of knowing if an applicant has contacted the employer and cleared up any issues or if the second letter is needed. Therefore, there must be a mechanism for the CRA to know if a second letter is needed. With advances in technology, more sophisticated screening firms have solved the issue by providing an automated adverse action process into their software, where the employer can press a button and the notices are generated. The new online systems used by advanced screening firms usually contain a provision where the consumer agrees they can be contacted by email for all notices, and the notices can go by email. If the employer decides a second letter is warranted to make the decision final, the online system can also accomplish that with a mouse click. A sophisticated screening firm that emphasizes legal compliance will take steps to ensure that the letter also complies with applicable state laws as well, which means that an employer may be required to select a reason for the adverse action based upon state law. See Chapter 6 for special rules about state laws and adverse action notices.

8.   **Question:** *If an employer sends an adverse action notice and a notice of Individualized Assessment, can it be combined in the same document?*

Answer: Although there is currently no law directly on point, some authorities take the position that there should be separate letters. Even though the two letters are closely related, they are required by different laws and address different rights. By sending two separate letters, there is an argument that consumers will not be confused about their rights. In addition, the notice of Individualized Assessment may come into play before a background report is ever done. As explained more fully in the chapter on the legal use of criminal records in Chapter 10, a consumer may reveal a criminal record at or after an interview resulting in an employer disqualifying the person before the background check ever occurred. In that case, the consumer should still be given to a Notice of Individualized Assessment. In order to make sure nothing falls through the cracks, having the letters separate two letters may provide greater protection.

Other Important FCRA Provisions

In addition to the four steps for FCRA compliance mentioned earlier, it is important for employers and Human Resources professionals to understand that the FCRA highly regulates the activates of Consumer Reporting Agencies (CRAs). Understanding that these numerous obligations exist can also become important when an employer selects a CRA to assist with background investigations. If a background screening firm does not thoroughly understand and comply with the FCRA, it potentially creates a litigation risk for the employer as well.

- **A CRA must follow reasonable procedures concerning identity and proper use of information per FCRA 607(a).** Per the requirements of the FCRA, every consumer reporting agency shall maintain reasonable procedures designed to avoid violations of section 605 (relating to what may be reported) and to limit the furnishing of consumer reports to the purposes listed under section 604. These procedures require that prospective users of the information identify themselves, certify the purposes for which the information is sought, and certify that the information will be used for no other purpose. Every consumer reporting agency is required to make a reasonable effort to verify the identity of a new prospective user and for the uses certified by a prospective user prior to furnishing the user a consumer report. No consumer reporting agency may furnish a consumer report to any entity if it has reasonable grounds for believing that the consumer report will not be used for a purpose listed in section 604. *Lesson—A CRA must know the client and the limitations on what can be reported. These rules are of particular importance in view of well-publicized incidents in 2005 of the theft of data from firms where criminals posed as legitimate users and were able to set-up accounts in order to steal personal information, using it to commit crimes.*
- **CRA must take measures to ensure accuracy of report (FCRA 607(b)).** Whenever a consumer reporting agency prepares a consumer report, it shall follow reasonable procedures to assure maximum possible accuracy of the information concerning the individual about whom the report relates. *Lesson—The CRA should have written procedures that are followed and enforced to ensure maximum accuracy.*
- **CRA must provide the employer with the form entitled "Notice to Users of Consumer Reports: Obligations of Users under the FCRA."** See FCRA Section 607(d). A copy of the notice is in the Appendix.
- **CRA must provide employer with the form entitled "Summary of Your Rights Under the Fair Credit Reporting Act" with every report.** See FCRA 604(b)(1)(B). A copy of the summary is in the Appendix.
- **A CRA may only include certain items of information in a consumer report.** FCRA Section 605 specifically limits certain information:
  - Bankruptcy cases older than 10 years, from the date of entry of the order for relief or the date of adjudication, as the case may be. See Chapter 20 for limitations on bankruptcy as related to employment.
  - Civil suits, civil judgments, and records of arrest older than seven years from the date of entry. Due to the 1998 FCRA amendment, this section now only refers to a seven-year limitation on arrests, but not criminal convictions. There are no limits under the federal FCRA for reporting criminal convictions although there are some state limits.
  - Paid tax liens older than seven years from the date of payment.
  - Accounts placed for collection or charged to profit and loss which are older than seven years.

o Any other adverse item of information, other than records of convictions of crimes, which are older than seven years. Note that criminal convictions are excluded from the limitations, which leaves a seven-year limitation on using arrests without dispositions.

The FCRA, however, provides that these exceptions do not apply to an individual whose annual salary is reasonably expected to equal $75,000 a year or more.

- Communication with employers about arrests. In a federal case, it was alleged that a national employment screening firm uncovered information that the applicant had an arrest record over seven years ago. There were no convictions, only arrests. The federal Fair Credit Reporting Act (FCRA) prohibits the reporting of an arrest older than seven years old unless the applicant is reasonably expected to make a salary of over $75,000 per year. In order to determine if the arrests were reportable, the screening firm sent a communication to the prospective employer indicating there was a criminal history over seven years old but was not a conviction, and it could only be reported if the applicant was going to make over the $75,000 yearly limit. The employer was told that if they wished to receive this information, they must confirm to the screening firm if the applicant met the salary threshold. The job applicant filed a lawsuit in the United States District Court for the Eastern District of Pennsylvania alleging damages for the practice of disclosing the existence of outdated arrest records. The basis of the lawsuit was that the manner in which the background firm asked about salary amounted to a notification that an applicant has an arrest record. The screening firm, among other arguments, suggested merely reporting the existence of old arrest records did not violate the FCRA since the background firm did not provide disclosure of the actual records. The court denied the screening firm's motion to dismiss and allowed the lawsuit to proceed. The Court ruled that even if the FCRA was ambiguous on what constitutes reporting an arrest record, the FCRA was clear that the general prohibition against reporting items of adverse information over seven years old was violated. By informing the employer there was such information in the process of establishing the applicant's salary, the screening firm ended up reporting something adverse that may have been prohibited.

- Rules concerning accuracy in reporting adverse public records. If a CRA reports items of information as matters of public record that are likely to have an adverse effect on a consumer's ability to obtain employment, the CRA must maintain "strict procedures" designed to ensure whenever such public record information is reported, it is complete and up to date. For purposes of this duty, items of public record relating to arrests, indictments, convictions, suits, tax liens, and outstanding judgments shall be considered up to date if the public record status of the item is current at the time it is reported. This means the best way to ensure that information is accurate is to look at the public record, such as the actual courthouse documents for a criminal record, and not rely solely upon assembled databases. See FCRA Section 613(a)(2). The duty to accurately report a criminal matter under FCRA section 613 is typically satisfied by a CRA sending a researcher directly to the courthouse to pull public record to ensure it is accurate, up to date, and to also look for identifiers. See FCRA section 613(a)(2). In most courthouses, the docket sheet or clerk's minute orders will have the requisite information. See Chapter 9 on criminal record for more information on how criminal records are searched and how accuracy is maintained and identifiers located

- However, the FCRA does provide an alternative procedure under FCRA section 613(a)(1). Instead of going to the courthouse, a CRA can notify the consumer that public record information is being reported by the consumer reporting agency along with the name and address of the person to whom such information is being reported (See FCRA Section 613(a)(1)). However, there is the question , arguably, in some states: is this alternative procedure advisable? Reputable background firms follow the California, rule, which requires a background check firm to only report a criminal conviction or other matters of public record for employment purposes if "it is complete and up to date," which is defined as checking the status at the time the matter is reported (See

California Civil Code section 1786.28(b)). That means double-checking the current status of the case, usually by means of checking the current court docket. That would tell a screening firm, for example, if a consumer received an expungement, or if the case is too old to report. Double-checking a database "hit" at the courthouse certainly affords employees, applicants, and background firms the most protection and the highest degree of accuracy. The duty to deal with adverse information in a public record can have an important impact when using criminal record databases.

Practice Notes about the Section 613 Letter

FCRA section 613 allows for a *letter option* which means a CRA does not need to go to the courthouse to reconfirm the accuracy of the information. However, FCRA section 607(b) discusses "reasonable procedures for maximum possible accuracy." The practical impact is that sending a letter does not absolve a CRA from the duty to ensure that its data sources are reliable. The issue of databases and accuracy comes into play again in Chapter 9 concerning criminal records. The bottom line is that under the FCRA, just sending a letter does not mean the CRA has done their duty if they know, or should know, that the databases it uses has old, inaccurate, or incomplete information.

However, here is where it gets more complicated. Some screening firms have started sending out 613 letters even though the screening follows strict procedures to ensure accuracy. That is partly in response to the consent decree mentioned earlier entered by the CFPB against two large screening firms.

Part of the problem is that there is an open question as to how "reasonable procedures for maximum possible accuracy" differs from "strict procedures." A good screening firm will verify the criminal data from the court docket. As explained in Chapters 8 and 9 on criminal records, the vast majority of a "criminal" file is not a public record and is not available to the screening firm or the employer. Generally, there is not much more a screening firm can do then examine the court docket, the charging document and if available, sentencing information.

Attorney Larry Henry, with Rhodes Hieronymus, is a national expert on the FCRA. He notes that based upon a 2016 New York federal case, the strict procedures section of 613 refers to a CRA's obligation to make certain that the criminal information is up to date. In other words, a CRA always has the underlying duty to maintain reasonable procedures, but above and beyond that, if a criminal record is found, then the CRA must either send a 613 letter or make certain the criminal information is current. However, sending the letter seems to relieve the CRA of making certain that the information is up to date, but the CRA must still use reasonable procedures.

What does this all mean? Given the uncertainty on the subject, the one thing that is clear is that by sending a 613 letter when adverse information is found, both the consumer and the screening firm have more protection. That is another reason why screening firms are starting to send out 613 letters even though they utilize what they consider to be **strict procedures**. Although it may cause additional work and consumers sometimes get confused by such a letter, the process adds an extra layer of protection to everyone by giving consumers clear notice that something potentially negative is being reported about them.

However, the best practice when a criminal matter is reported may be for the CRA to ensure the information provided is up to date no matter what and not rely on the letter option.

- **Re-investigation rule.** When a CRA prepares an investigative consumer report, no adverse information in the consumer report (other than information which is a matter of public record) may be included in a subsequent consumer report unless such adverse information has been verified during the process of making such subsequent consumer report, or the adverse information was received within the three-month period preceding the date the subsequent report is furnished. See FCRA Section 614. This only applies to matters that are adverse on its face. Employment or education verification is not adverse on its face, even if it becomes adverse in the context of the application, such as the information shows an applicant lied about job history.
- **Disclosure rules.** Upon request, a CRA must disclose to a consumer what is in the consumer's file, identify sources, identify everyone who procured a report for employment for the past two years, and comply with various rules, e.g. provide trained personnel who can explain to a consumer any information in the report. See FCRA Sections 609 and 610.
- **Duty to investigate.** If an applicant contests what is in the report, the CRA has an obligation to investigate and determine accuracy within 30 days (or up to 45 days in some instances), and to take appropriate actions. The CRA must give notice to the report furnisher within five days. Various other duties are dependent upon results of re-investigation. See FCRA Sections 611 and 612. The CRA must carefully follow a series of rules in terms of various notices and responses and have an FCRA compliance procedure in place.
- **Identity theft information.** FCRA Section 605A (g) sets out the duty of a CRA to give certain information to consumers if a consumer reports a suspicion that they have or are about to become a victim of identity theft including information on how to file an alert.

About the 2003 FCRA Amendment: Fair and Accurate Credit Transactions (FACT) Act or FACTA

On December 4, 2003, President George W. Bush signed into law H.R. 2622, known as the **Fair and Accurate Credit Transactions (FACT) Act or FACTA**. This amended the Fair Credit Reporting Act. This wide-ranging law dealt with a number of topics such as identity theft, increased consumer access to their credit report, pre-emption of certain state financial laws by the federal law, and increased the accuracy of credit reports. The new law allows consumers to receive a fee credit report once a year from a **Nationwide Specialty Consumer Reporting Agency (NSCRA),** which includes not only credit bureaus but other types of national firms collecting data on consumers (See Chapter 11 for more details on what constitutes a NSCRA). This is sometimes referred to as a **FACT Act Disclosure.** The law also provides for fraud alerts to be placed in credit reports and the ability to block credit reports in certain situations.

For purposes of employment, these are some of the critical components of FACT:

- **Truncation of Social Security Number.** FCRA Section 609 was amended to allow consumers to request that the first five digits of his or her Social Security Number be deleted from any disclosure to the consumer. The purpose is to help combat identity theft since identity theft often occurs at the consumer's mailbox.
- **Statute of limitations.** FCRA Section 618 sets the period of time someone may sue for a violation of the FCRA. The statute of limitations has been extended from two years from the date of violation, to two years from the date of the discovery of the violation by the consumer, and up to five years from the date of the actual violation. Consumer reporting agencies should plan on keeping records for at least six years to allow time for the statutory period plus the normal delay time experienced in receiving notice of a lawsuit.

Consumer reporting agencies should plan on keeping records for at least six years to allow time for the statutory period plus the normal delay time experienced in receiving notice of a lawsuit.

- **Investigation of current employees.** Under FCRA Section 604, employers now have the ability to conduct third party investigations of current employees without disclosure or having to first get written authorization.

Fixing a Flaw—Investigation of Current Employees

This was probably the most critical issue the FACT amendment addressed for employers. A little history is in order here: When the 1997 amendments to the FCRA were first enacted, many security professionals, as well as labor attorneys and human resource professionals, had widely interpreted the notice and disclosure requirements as applying only to pre-employment hiring and not post-hire workplace investigations.

However, in 1999, attorney Judi Vail sent a letter to the FTC (the federal agency that enforces the FCRA) asking whether the FCRA applied to investigations of sexual harassment claims against current employees. The FTC staff had a practice from 1997 to 2001 of issuing staff opinion letters in response to inquiries. In what was commonly referred to as the Vail letter, the FTC flatly stated that investigation of current employees by third parties who regularly conduct such investigations are covered by the same FCRA rules used for pre-employment screening.

There are many situations when a firm may wish to use a third party to investigate a current employee. If there are allegations of sexual harassment, employers have a duty to conduct a thorough, prompt, and fair investigation, and this is often done by hiring an outside professional. If there is suspicion of misconduct, such as theft, drug dealing, or other criminal conduct, then the expertise of an outside investigator may also be required.

However, when investigative secrecy is required, it is difficult to conduct an effective third-party investigation under FCRA ground rules as interpreted by the Vail letter. As soon as the target is tipped off, it is very easy to destroy evidence, influence witnesses, or attempt to derail the investigation.

Another problem was securing witness cooperation. The FCRA provides a mechanism for the object of the inquiry to obtain a copy of the report, thereby revealing information sources. The result is that witnesses cannot be promised anonymity, discouraging witnesses from assisting an investigation.

Before the FACT amendment, to comply with the FCRA, a third-party investigator had to obtain written authorization from the subject of the report. The employee also had to receive a stand-alone disclosure that a consumer report is being prepared.

A number of court cases whittled away at the Vail letter. Finally, the issue was put to rest by the FACT legislation. The FCRA was amended so that an employer would not need to obtain a written release and authorization in order to conduct investigation of current employees, where the investigation involved one of the following:

- Suspected misconduct relating to employment.
- Compliance with federal, state, or local laws and regulations.
- The rules of a self-regulating organization.
- Any preexisting written policies of the employer.

Author Tip > **Future Consents**

In order to protect the right to conduct future investigations when necessary, employers may consider adding the following language to their authorization forms: "This authorization and release will remain valid for future preparation of a consumer report or investigative consumer report for purposes of retention, promotion, or reassignment unless revoked in writing." This is sometimes legally referred to as an "Evergreen" clause meaning it stays active in the future (although most likely not forever since that would not be reasonable to assume a consumer would consent forever). Because of the special notice requirements needed for an Investigative Consumer Report (ICR), such a clause would likely be best suited to public record check, such as a future criminal check.

Limitations Still Exist on Investigating Current Employees for Wrongdoing or Misconduct Even with FACT Act

First, the investigation cannot be made for the purpose of investigating a consumer's credit worthiness, credit standing, or credit capacity. A credit report is always covered by the FCRA. Second, the matter cannot be reported to an outside person or entity except for certain governmental agents and agencies.

Finally, there is still a procedure in place that must be followed if there are any adverse actions because of the investigation, such as termination or discipline. After taking any adverse action that was based in any part on the report, the employer must provide the consumer with a summary of the nature and substance of the investigation. However, there are limits on providing the source of information.

Employment Screening Lawsuits Increase as Attorneys and Consumers Become Familiar with FCRA

A number of cases, including class action lawsuits, are being brought against employers and screening firms for alleged violations of the FCRA. It is anticipated that this trend towards lawsuits will continue. The lesson here is while employers need to be diligent in their hiring, at the same time they need to ensure they are following the FCRA rules that regulate the collection, dissemination, and use of consumer information, including consumer credit information. This means it is even more critical for employers to review policies and procedures to ensure accuracy and legal compliance given how heavily background checks are regulated.

One source of lawsuits occurs when certain vendor database searches produce inaccurate and incomplete information used for background checks. These databases should only be used for secondary research and not as the primary, sole source of information. Inexpensive and instant vendor database searches with unreliable results can miss criminal records and give both employers and consumers a false sense of security. As discussed later in this book, background checks based solely upon vendor databases have substantial issues in terms of timeliness, completeness, and accuracy.

Part of the reason FCRA class action lawsuits make a tempting target is that the damages being sought can be enormous. Under the FCRA, an allegation of a "willful" violation in a class action lawsuit can results in damages in the amount of **$100 to $1,000 for every consumer impacted**. For an employer that handles a large volume, that adds up quickly. In addition, class action lawsuits commonly ask for attorney's fees and court costs, which can be substantial.

The big reason that class action lawsuits are very appealing is due to a United States Supreme Court case decided in June 2007, *Safeco Ins. Co. of America v. Burr*, 127 S.Ct.2201 (2007) that substantially increased the risk of punitive damages under the FCRA by ruling that a reckless disregard of the FCRA could be sufficient to show *willful* non-compliance. The net effect is it is now easier to sue an employer or a background screening firm for punitive damages.

More About U. S. Supreme Court Case on *Willfulness* Under the FCRA Based on Conduct that is *Objectively Unreasonable*

The Safeco case dealt with the use of credit reports to set insurance rates and the obligation of insurers to send out adverse action notices to consumers whose rates were affected by their credit reports.

In that case, the U.S. Supreme Court broadened the definition of "willful" under the FCRA to also include "reckless conduct." Since under FCRA section 616 (15 U.S.C. 1681n) punitive damages are only allowed if there was "willful" non-compliance, this decision caused a serious impact on employers and consumer reporting agencies.

The Court dealt with a split among lower federal courts on the interpretation of what the FCRA meant by "willfulness." Some federal courts had ruled that a willful violation of the FCRA meant a business had to have actual knowledge their conduct was in violation of the FCRA. However, in this case, the Supreme Court ruled that a reckless disregard can be an action entailing an unjustifiably high risk of harm that is either known or *so obvious that it should be known*. Consequently, if an employer or Consumer Reporting Agency (CRA) had an interpretation of its duties under the FCRA that was **objectively unreasonable**, then the CRA faced potential exposure for punitive damages.

The net effect is that it is now somewhat easier to sue an employer or screening firm for punitive damages and for statutory damages of up to $1,000 per background report for willful non-compliance. If a lawsuit is filed against screening firms or employers for FCRA violations, a request for punitive damages on a recklessness theory is now more likely. There is also an increased possibility of class action lawsuits based upon FCRA violations because of the loosened willfulness definition to include recklessness. As a practical matter, lawyers bringing lawsuits against employers or screening firms will try to allege, among other things, punitive damages.

The bottom line is a screening firm or employer is now held to a higher standard of compliance. Where the line will be drawn between mere negligence and recklessness in any particular case is always a difficult proposition. However, just because a screening firm or employer believes it is acting lawfully or is unaware it is acting unlawfully, it is NOT protected from an allegation of willful violation of the FCRA with exposure to punitive damages. Since insurance coverage for a defendant typically does not cover punitive damages, a plaintiff in such a legal action generally has greater leverage. This issue again underscores the critical nature of legal compliance associated with background checks.

The Explosion of FCRA Lawsuits for Technical Violations of the FCRA

With the explosion of legal action involving the FCRA against employers who conduct background checks on job applicants as well as background firms, businesses need to be aware of the traps and pitfalls to avoid during the hiring process. FCRA lawsuits against employers, especially class actions, have become very common. Ironically, these class action lawsuits often could have been easily avoided. More often than not, employers are sued for violating FCRA 101 – simple rules and procedures that are clearly set out in the law.

Most claims of FCRA violations involve aspects of the employer's screening process that could be easily remedied to comply with the FCRA, such as reviewing forms used for background checks. In other instances, the employer simply needed to send the applicant certain information required under the FCRA or some other very simple FCRA compliance practice to avoid a lawsuit. To avoid multi-million dollar settlements, employers should review their practices and procedures to avoid litigation under the FCRA.

In 2015 alone, companies such as Food Lion, Home Depot, Chuck E. Cheese, and Whole Foods paid FCRA lawsuit settlements ranging from $803,000 to $3 million. In 2016, Wells Fargo agreed to a settlement of $12 million to resolve an FCRA lawsuit. In addition, FCRA lawsuits have been filed or are pending against other well-known businesses.

Author Tip ⟩ **Updates on FCRA Lawsuits**
To stay current with many of the lawsuits filed against employers and screening firms under the FCRA, visit the **ESR News Blog** at www.esrcheck.com/wordpress/.

To be clear, the mere fact a lawsuit is filed and allegations are made by no means proves the validity of the claims, and filing of the lawsuit is merely the first step in the legal process. Even if a case is settled by agreement between the parties that is not proof of any wrongdoing since lawsuits are often settled by both sides in order to hedge against litigation costs and the risks inherent in any lawsuit, and the settlement typically contains a clause that the defendant denies any wrongdoing. However, this uptick in lawsuits underscores the need for employers to carefully review background checking programs and to work with accredited background screening firms that can provide information to assist in compliance with the federal FCRA and various other federal and state laws concerning background checks.

You Need To Know

Statistics Show Rise of FCRA Lawsuits

Lawsuits involving the federal Fair Credit Reporting Act (FCRA) increased by nearly 35 percent in June 2016 over May 2016, according to the Debt Collection Litigation and Consumer Financial Protection Board (CFPB) Complaint Statistics Report from WebRecon LLC. The Debt Collection Litigation and CFPB Complaint Statistics Report for June 2016 revealed that 409 FCRA lawsuits were filed from June 1, 2016, to June 30, 2016, while 304 FCRA lawsuits were filed from May 1, 2016, to May 31, 2016, a robust gain of 34.5 percent. The report from WebRecon LLC also found that FCRA court filings were up a strong 33.7 percent over the same period in June 2015, as 304 FCRA lawsuits were filed from June 1, 2015, to June 31, 2015, compared to the 409 FCRA lawsuits filed in June 2016. The complete report is available at http://webrecon.com/back-on-track-debt-collection-litigation-cfpb-complaint-stats-june-2016/.

Common Ways Prospective or Current Employees Sue Employers under the FCRA

In response to the rising trend of FCRA class action lawsuits, Attorney Lester Rosen wrote a whitepaper entitled **"Common Ways Prospective or Current Employees Sue Employers Under the FCRA"** that explains how FCRA lawsuits are often filed over alleged technical violations when employers fail to dot the "i's" and cross the "t's" in the screening process. The following is a listing of nine areas where employers should review their practices and procedures to avoid litigation under the FCRA. It should be noted that this list does NOT represent all of the different claims that have been brought against employers or could potentially be brought. It is only intended to illustrate some of the most prevalent problems for employers. With a recent U.S. Supreme Court ruling in the Spokeo case (discussed below), it is possible that cases that were hyper-technical where no one was actually harmed may diminish, but employers still need to be careful to follow the FCRA.

1. **Employer failed to obtain written authorization from the job applicant to obtain the consumer report or provide a required disclosure to the consumer:** A basic and fundamental rule of any effort by an employer to conduct a background check through a background screening firm is that it must be done with the applicant's consent and with legally required notices to applicants. When it comes to hiring, background checks cannot be done in secret. The FCRA requires that the prospective employer receives written authorization from the prospective employee before conducting a background check.

2. **Employer's failure to provide plaintiff with a document consisting solely of the stand-alone disclosure:** This is by far the most common claim seen in lawsuits brought against employers. The FCRA, in Section 604(b)(2) (15 U.S.C. §1681b(b)(2)), requires that the employer disclose to the job applicant that a background check may be obtained in a disclosure that must be made in writing and "in a document that consists solely of the disclosure."

3. **Release authorization contained language purporting to release the employer and anyone providing information from liability:** Closely related are claims Plaintiffs have recently filed in several cases where they allege that the employer has included a liability release in its application or employment forms. These cases not only argue that such a release is contrary to the "standalone form" rule cited above, but that the very notion of a release violates the FCRA.

4. **Failure to comply with *pre-adverse action* requirements or allow sufficient time for a consumer to respond:** Another common lawsuit centers around claims that an employer failed to follow the required procedures where a consumer report results in an adverse action against the applicant. An employer risks litigation when it fails to provide the job applicant with a copy of the consumer report and a "pre-adverse action notice, as well as a summary of the prospective employee's rights under the FCRA." This claim is sometimes accompanied with alleged violations of analogous state credit reporting laws.

5. **Failure to provide applicant with a post-adverse action notice:** Section 615 of the FCRA requires employers to provide the applicant with a post-adverse action notice after the employer takes adverse action. In this post-adverse notice, the employer must inform the applicant that adverse action has been taken based on information contained in a consumer report. The notice must also include the name, address, and phone number of the consumer reporting agency that provided the consumer report, a statement that the consumer reporting agency did not decide to take the adverse action and cannot provide the consumer with specific reasons for the adverse action, a notice that the applicant has the right to obtain a free copy of his report from the consumer reporting agency within 60 days, and the applicant has the right to dispute the accuracy of any information in the report.

Author Tip

Some States Have Unique FCRA Requirements

As discussed in Chapter 6, it is not enough to simply send out the standard federal FCRA language for the Adverse Action notice. A number of states have some very unique and particularized requirements that must be followed as well. Employers are well advised to work with a screening firm that not only understands each state law but has also incorporated appropriate compliance measures into their software.

6. **Failure to update forms:** Although it is easily preventable, some applicants sue their employers simply because the employer has not updated their forms pursuant to the FCRA. One major company settled a class action lawsuit for $3 million dollars on that claim alone. In that case, the plaintiff alleged that he had been offered employment pending the results of his background check. He soon received a copy of his background report along with an outdated statement of his rights under the FCRA. This statement was a copy of the version the FTC released in 1997, rather than the updated form the FTC later released in 2005. The 1997 form listed inaccurate contact information for the FTC and the Federal Reserve and also omitted important rules such as the fact that consumers have the right to dispute incomplete and wrong information on their consumer report.

7. **Employee screening policy disqualifies applicants based on criminal history that is unrelated to the job:** Employers can also be sued for subjecting their job applicants to an overly broad and unduly harsh criminal background check. In one such case, nine African-American men alleged that criminal background check policy of the Washington Metropolitan Area Transit Authority (WMATA) disproportionately barred qualified African-Americans workers from WMATA jobs because the WMATA screening policy is based on criminal history that is unrelated to the job or occurred so long ago that it is irrelevant to any sort of determination about the applicant's character. The plaintiffs claimed that such results violate their civil rights.

8. **Failure to follow state law:** Closely related to FCRA are claims that an employer failed to follow state laws. Numerous states have their own rules and procedures governing the process of obtaining background checks and how information can be used. Although many state laws closely follow the FCRA, there are some states with their own special and unique requirements above and beyond the FCRA, creating potential compliance concerns for firms that operate in more than one state. In one California case involving retail theft databases, the claim was made that the FCRA was violated because dismissed cases were being reported that under California law that were prohibited under a state civil rights law. The FCRA, in turn, requires that an employer not utilize a background

report in violation of any state or federal civil rights law. Therefore the use of a dismissed criminal record violated the FCRA.

9. **Lawsuit for actions of staffing firm:** Where employers rely upon the services of third party staff vendors, it is also important to ensure that all FCRA processes are being followed by the vendor. In one case, major national online retailer Amazon was sued along with a staffing firm on the basis that the staffing firm did not comply with the FCRA. The case raises important considerations when it comes to employers that work with staffing vendors. In the lawsuit, even though it was the staffing firm that allegedly failed to provide the required notice process, the case is also aimed at the company where the applicant would be placed and would likely be working under the direction and control of that company. It underscores the need for employers to work carefully with staffing providers to ensure that the FCRA requirements are being followed. The dangers of FCRA lawsuits against employers for the actions of their staffing vendors may have increased with the recent decision by the National Labor Relations Board (NLRB) in a case where the definition of "joint" employer was arguably expanded by holding that the ability of an employer to exercise control over a worker can create joint employment. This line of reasoning can potentially open up more employer liability for acts of staffing vendors. (More information about staffing firms is covered in Chapter 18.)

The complimentary whitepaper "Common Ways Prospective or Current Employees Sue Employers under the FCRA" is available at www.esrcheck.com/Whitepapers/Ways-Employees-Sue-Employers-Under-FCRA/.

Statistics Show Increasing Trend in Employer Facing Lawsuits

In 2015, Attorney Les Rosen, CEO of Employment Screening Resources (ESR) and author of this book, wrote a comprehensive whitepaper titled, "Common Ways Prospective or Current Employees Sue Employers under the FCRA." Rosen described the current circumstances surrounding employer facing background screening lawsuits and made many important points, a few of which are bulleted below:

- Litigation against employers surrounding checks is increasing at a dramatic rate.
- More often than not employer facing lawsuits are based on violations of simple rules and procedures, not complicated employment law matters.
- Fair Credit Reporting Act (FCRA) lawsuits, including class actions, can be brought based on failure to comply with innocuous administrative details within the FCRA even when no one is harmed in any way.

In June of 2016, Brad Landin, president of ESR, looked at and analyzed this increasing trend in employer facing lawsuits using data used derived from readily available public information consisting of a sufficient enough sample to adequately identify the trends. The research was not undertaken or intended to be an exhaustive and comprehensive study of every court case. Rather, the study was intended to demonstrate trends in both numbers of cases, the type of claims, and the amounts awarded.

This is what was found. Since 2011, class action lawsuits against employers have increased dramatically and have resulted in judgments or settlements totaling at least $92,520,000. Improper disclosure was the leading cause of action with $18.6 million in judgments or settlements, followed by: a combination of improper disclosure and adverse action ($14.5 million); use of credit reports ($8.75 million); improper use of information ($7.75 million); and a combination of disclosure, authorization, and adverse action ($5.9 million).

In addition to class action lawsuits, the number of single plaintiff lawsuits has also increased dramatically, rising from just 3 in 2006 to 45 in 2015. Through June of 2016, 30 lawsuits have been filed. Virtually all of these lawsuits settle before trial, so there are no meaningful numbers surrounding awards. Although many of these suits target background check companies, it is very common to name the employer as well. Even if there is no real cause of action against the employer and they ultimately get dropped, it is still an expensive and time-consuming proposition.

Since the study most likely did not include every case brought, the actual numbers are likely to be larger. The takeaway is for employers to be aware of these risks and to align themselves with a background screening company with little or no litigation history that educates and assists its clients on how to stay compliant.

U.S Supreme Court Rules there are Limits to How Technical the Violations Can Be and that Some Harm is Needed

A major change in this area did occur in May 2016 when the United States Supreme Court revisited the FCRA on the issue of what level of harm is needed in order to bring a class action lawsuit for a technical violation of the FCRA.

The case of *Spokeo, Inc. v. Robins* involved a Virginia man named Thomas Robins who filed a class action lawsuit against Spokeo, an online "people search engine" that sells publicly available information about individuals, for alleged violations of the Fair Credit Reporting Act (FCRA). The class action lawsuit claimed Spokeo violated the FCRA by publishing inaccurate information about the age, education, marital status, and professional experience of Robins. The issue was whether or not a plaintiff had the legal right, or "standing," to bring a class action lawsuit for a technical violation of the FCRA if that individual suffered no actual concrete harm from the violation. There was no evidence that anyone actually used the information or that the plaintiff suffered any adverse impact in the real world. Nevertheless, the incorrect information was available. Under the FCRA, consumers may claim damages from $100 to $1000 if a company publishes inaccurate information about them under the willful non-compliance standard.

On May 16, 2016, the Supreme Court of the United States (SCOTUS) ruled in the case of *Spokeo, Inc. v. Robins* (Docket No. 13-1339) that consumers must prove "concrete injury" in class action lawsuits for alleged "bare" violations of a federal statute. The SCOTUS ruling sent the case back to the Ninth Circuit Court of Appeals stating its Article III standing analysis in a February 4, 2014, decision to reverse a dismissal of the case was incomplete because the Ninth Circuit "failed to consider both aspects of the Article III injury-in-fact requirement."

In a 6-2 decision in the opinion delivered by Justice Samuel Alito – with Justices John Roberts, Anthony Kennedy, Clarence Thomas, Stephen Breyer, and Elena Kagan joining Alito, and Justices Ruth Bader Ginsburg and Sonia Sotomayor dissenting – the Court stated that "Article III standing requires a concrete injury even in the context of a statutory violation. For that reason, Robins could not, for example, allege a bare procedural violation, divorced from any concrete harm, and satisfy the injury-in-fact requirement of Article III."

In explaining that there must be three elements to an Article III standing analysis, the Court stated: (a) A plaintiff invoking federal jurisdiction bears the burden of establishing the "irreducible constitutional minimum" of standing by demonstrating (1) an injury in fact, (2) fairly traceable to the challenged conduct of the defendant, and (3) likely to be redressed by a favorable judicial decision. The injury-in-fact requirement requires a plaintiff to show an injury is "concrete and particularized" and "actual or imminent, not conjectural or hypothetical."

The Court ruled that the injury to Robins needed to be "concrete" and the Ninth Circuit had not analyzed if the alleged violations of FCRA had created a "degree of risk sufficient to meet the concreteness requirement." Although an injury can be intangible, there still must be a risk of harm above and beyond a technical violation. The Court also noted that because the Ninth Circuit failed to fully appreciate the distinction between concreteness and particularization, its standing analysis was incomplete.

The SCOTUS opinion notes that while the Court "takes no position on the correctness of the Ninth Circuit's ultimate conclusion," that the Plaintiff "cannot satisfy the demands of Article III by alleging a bare procedural violation." The opinion also states that: "Robins cannot satisfy the demands of Article III by alleging a bare procedural violation. A violation of one of the FCRA's procedural requirements may result in no harm." The SCOTUS opinion in the case of *Spokeo, Inc. v. Robins* is at www.esrcheck.com/file/SCOTUS-Spokeo-v-Robins-Opinion.pdf.

More information about the case is at www.scotusblog.com/case-files/cases/spokeo-inc-v-robins/.

Source:
www.esrcheck.com/wordpress/2016/05/16/supreme-court-rules-in-spokeo-case-on-whether-consumers-must-prove-concrete-injury-in-class-action-lawsuits/.

Author Tip | **Employers and CRAs Need to Remain Vigilant in Legal Compliance**

Although the Spokeo case is still not finished since the Supreme Court sent it back to the Ninth Circuit to take a closer look at whether the plaintiff had sufficient damages to sue, the one lesson that everyone can agree upon is that the need for employers and CRAs to remain vigilant in their legal compliance efforts. A number of attorneys feel that although the Spokeo decision may dampen claims that are purely technical in nature where it is unlikely that any consumer can be hurt in the real world, there can still be litigation on matters that could lead to harm. Attorneys bringing class action lawsuits will need to demonstrate some sort of harm under the Spokeo standard.

In addition, lawsuits previously brought in federal courts may still find a home in state courts under state CRA laws (see Chapter 6 on state laws). Since numerous states have their own unique version of the federal FCRA, that could open a brand new areas of litigation as plaintiff's attorney examine state laws under a microscope. It also means that employers and screening firms now need to ensure that they are in compliance in each state where they do business, in addition to following federal law.

The bottom line is that the need for legal compliance is not going way anytime soon and although the Spokeo case may rein in cases based entirely on a technical failure to dot an 'i' or cross a 't,' background screening remains a process that requires a great deal of legal compliance expertise.

Not All Bad News for Employers

Despite the growth of lawsuits agent smokers, it is not all bad news. Some courts have ruled in favor of employers especially in cases involving highly technical violations of the FCRA. Here are some examples:

Judge Dismisses FCRA Lawsuit Against Time Warner Citing the Supreme Court Spokeo Ruling

In August 2016, a Wisconsin federal judge dismissed a class action lawsuit against Time Warner Cable, Inc. brought by that plaintiff over alleged violations of the federal Fair Credit Reporting Act (FCRA) by finding the plaintiff could not show he suffered "concrete harm" from the background check process in a decision that cited a ruling in the case of Spokeo v. Robins by the Supreme Court of the United States.

In granting the defendant's Motion to Dismiss, U.S. District Judge Pamela Pepper found that since the plaintiff, who claimed Time Warner violated the FCRA during a background check for employment, "has not alleged a concrete harm resulting from the defendant's alleged violation," he "does not have standing, and the court must dismiss the case.

Judge Pepper wrote: *In Spokeo, the Court emphasized the distinction between concreteness and particularization. The latter is "necessary to establish injury in fact, but it is not sufficient. . . . We have made it clear time and again that an injury in fact must be both concrete and particularized." A concrete injury must be "'de facto'; that is, it must actually exist.*

The named plaintiff alleges that he applied for employment with the defendant, and that in the course of considering his application, the defendant obtained a consumer report on him "without first providing [him] a clear and conspicuous written disclosure, in a document consisting solely of the disclosure, that a consumer report may be obtained for employment purposes."

He alleges that this failure to disclose violated §1681(b)(2)(A)(i) of the Fair Credit Reporting Act. Id. While the complaint alleges, in several places, that the defendant's action violated the Fair Credit Reporting Act, it makes no mention of any concrete harm the plaintiff (or any putative class members) suffered as a result of the alleged violation.

The plaintiff has not alleged that he did not get the job he applied for as a result of the consumer report the defendant obtained. He has not alleged that the defendant released the information in the report to other people, causing him embarrassment or damaging his credit. He has not alleged that the defendant used the consumer report against him in any way.

In fact, in his October 7, 2015 deposition, when defense counsel asked him if he was aware of anything that might entitle him to actual damages, the plaintiff responded, "I do not know of any actual damages that I am claiming nor do I believe I've ever actually claimed actual damages against [the defendant] nor do I intend to." In short, he has not alleged a concrete harm.

The full text of the Decision and Order granting the defendant's Motion to Dismiss in *Groshek v. Time Warner Cable, Inc.*, Case No. 15-C-157, dated August 9, 2016, in the United States District Court, Eastern District of Wisconsin, is available at www.esrcheck.com/file/Groshek-v-Time-Warner-Cable-Opinion.pdf.

On May 16, 2016, the Supreme Court ruled in the Spokeo case that consumers must prove "concrete injury" in class action lawsuits for alleged "bare" violations of a federal statute, sending the case back to the Ninth Circuit Court of Appeals stating its Article III standing analysis in a February 2014 decision to reverse a dismissal of the case was incomplete. The ruling is available at www.esrcheck.com/file/SCOTUS-Spokeo-v-Robins-Opinion.pdf.

Judge Dismisses FCRA Class Action Lawsuit Against Lyft Citing Supreme Court Spokeo Decision

In October 2016, a California federal court judge dismissed a class action lawsuit filed against Lyft, Inc. over alleged violations of the federal Fair Credit Reporting Act (FCRA) during the transportation network company's background check process citing the Supreme Court decision in *Spokeo, Inc. v. Robbins* that held plaintiffs must show concrete injury when alleging FCRA violations.

The plaintiff in the lawsuit – Michael Nokchan, a Lyft driver in California – claimed Lyft failed to comply with the FCRA and state laws because the document he signed to give Lyft consent for a background check did not provide disclosures in a separate "stand-alone" document and that he was also not notified his right to receive a summary of his legal rights under the FCRA.

In the Order Granting Motion to Dismiss, Chief Magistrate Judge Joseph C. Spero agreed with Lyft's assertion that Nokchan lacked standing under Article III of the U.S. Constitution, citing the Supreme Court decision in Spokeo, Inc. v. Robins in May of 2016, which found consumers must prove "concrete injury" in class action lawsuits for alleged "bare" violations of a federal statute.

Judge Spero wrote in the Order: *Under Spokeo, a plaintiff who seeks to assert a claim under the FCRA is required to allege facts showing a concrete injury. While procedural violations that have resulted in real harm – or even a risk of real harm – may be sufficient to meet this requirement, Plaintiff in this case has alleged no such injury.*

Judge Spero also wrote that the plaintiff "has not alleged he suffered any real harm as a result of the fact that he did not receive required disclosures in a separate document or that he did not receive a summary of his rights under the FCRA." The plaintiff also has not claimed "he was confused about his rights" or "that he was harmed by the background check in any way."

Judge Spero continued: *Rather, based on the allegations in the complaint, Nokchan was hired by Lyft after he successfully completed its background investigation and he continues to work for Lyft. Under these circumstances, the Court can find no real harm, or a threat of such harm, that gives Nokchan standing under Article III to pursue his claims in federal court.*

The Court concluded that – under Spokeo – the plaintiff failed to establish he met Article III's injury-in-fact requirement. The Order Granting Motion to Dismiss in *Nokchan, v. Lyft, Inc.*, Case No. 15-cv-03008-JCS, United States District Court Northern District of California, is at www.esrcheck.com/file/Nokchan-v-Lyft_Order-Granting-Motion-to-Dismiss.pdf.

You Need To Know ⟩ ## Plaintiff in Dismissed Lawsuit against Time Warner Previously Won $230,000 in FCRA Settlements against Employers

The lead plaintiff in the dismissed case *Groshek v. Time Warner Cable, Inc.* is a fine example of the explosion of FCRA class action lawsuits since he previously won at least $230,000 in settlements from employers for alleged violations of the FCRA before this latest setback in the wake of the Supreme Court ruling in the Spokeo case.

According to a report from the *Milwaukee Journal Sentinel*, the Green Bay, Wisconsin job seeker applied for 562 jobs over an 18 month period in an effort to catch companies in alleged FCRA violations, threatened to sue at least 46 companies that performed background checks on him for alleged FCRA violations, and received settlements from approximately 20 of these companies.

The Journal Sentinel reports that the job seeker "believed the FCRA required a separate, single-page disclosure of a company's intent to obtain consumer credit reports." He found some companies included the disclosure in other documents and some companies included it in an online application program."

The Journal Sentinel also reports that the job seeker "taught himself to spot when companies fail to properly make that disclosure, burying it in fine print or several pages of forms" and also "admitted during a deposition that he has applied for hundreds of jobs, hoping to initiate the background check process that could lead to an FCRA violation."

However, as noted above, the ruling by the Supreme Court in the Spokeo case may have limited his ability – as well as others – to sue employers for technical violations of the FCRA. See: www.jsonline.com/news/wisconsin/professional-plaintiff-uses-credit-law-to-threaten-companies-win-230000-in-settlements-b99748699z1-384400481.html.

Judge Dismisses FCRA Class Action Lawsuit against Target

In May 2016, a federal judge in Minnesota has dismissed a class action lawsuit against Target Corp. by ruling the discount retailer did not willfully violate the federal Fair Credit Reporting Act (FCRA) that regulates background checks for employment in the U.S., according to a report from Top Class Actions.

The lead plaintiff Thomas Just claimed in a lawsuit filed in November of 2015 that Target violated the FCRA by including "extraneous" information on the required notification and authorization used to let job applicants know that employers will run background checks on them.

In December of 2015, Target asked the court to dismiss the FCRA lawsuit by claiming its notice and authorization did not include language that would distract or confuse job applicants but only worked to clarify and enhance the understanding of the notice by job applicants.

According to its motion to dismiss the class action, Target claimed the FCRA itself includes qualifications that indicate that including additional and supplementary language in a notice and authorization is not a "willful" violation of the statute.

U.S. District Judge Donovan W. Frank dismissed the case, noting in his order that: "Even if the court assumes, for the sake of argument, that Target violated the FCRA, it cannot conclude that [the plaintiff] plausibly alleges that such violation was willful."

Additionally, Top Class Actions reports that Judge Frank cited the "less than clear text" of the FCRA regulation as well as the "dearth of guidance" from higher courts and the Federal Trade Commission (FTC) – which help to enforce the FCRA – as being both at issue in this class action lawsuit.

The lawsuit is *Thomas J. Just v. Target Corp.*, Case No. 0:15-cv-04117, in the U.S. District Court for the District of Minnesota.

Source: https://topclassactions.com/lawsuit-settlements/lawsuit-news/335388-judge-tosses-target-employment-background-check-class-action/.

Ways Consumer Reporting Agencies are Sued Under the FCRA and Why This is Important for Employers to Know

Up until this point, we have discussed how employers can be sued under the FCRA. However, equally as important to employers is to work with screening firms that are FCRA compliant as well. A lawsuit against a screening firm for violations of the FCRA can create unnecessary complications for employers that can cause an employer being named in the lawsuit. Even if the lawsuit does not result in the employer being named, most employers do not want their applicants having to deal with a background screening process that results in litigation.

The text below is taken from a whitepaper *Common Ways Consumer Reporting Agencies are Sued Under the FCRA* that was written by the author Lester Rosen.

1. **Using a loose matching system:** Section 607(b) of the FCRA requires that CRAs "follow reasonable procedures to assure maximum possible accuracy of the individual about whom the reports relates" when preparing a consumer report. While there are no explicit guidelines in the FCRA for what constitutes "reasonable procedures," it can be helpful to look at previous lawsuits under this statute to get a clear picture about the procedures that would likely not meet this standard due to their inability to produce accurate reports. Several different specific allegations have been made against CRAs under section 607(b). A common type of claim under section 607(b) is when a CRA employed a loose matching system that reported incorrect information about a prospective employee and did not meet the "reasonable procedure" threshold.

2. **Reporting withdrawn, expunged, or incorrect charges:** Another type of claim common under section 607(b) that deals with accuracy under the FCRA is made against firms who report withdrawn or incorrect charges. This can happen when a firm reports charges that were once attributable to a Plaintiff but were subsequently withdrawn, removed, expunged, or adjudication was withheld from the individual's record. For example, in one case that was recently settled, Defendant was sued for reporting crimes that were dismissed. Also, one of the most common mistakes related to incorrect charges is when firms report a crime as a felony instead of a misdemeanor. This false information can preclude an employee from securing a job because the prospective employer will view this as the employee blatantly lying on his or her application by stating they had committed no felonies or create the impression the offense was more serious than it really was. These are exactly the unfortunate situations for potential employees that section 607(b) seeks to prevent and that can lead to legal problems for CRAs and employers if not strictly followed.

3. **Providing repetitive information:** Another area of trouble for CRAs that has been the focus of lawsuits is when firms intentionally or inadvertently provide criminal reports about a prospective employee that contain repetitive information. For example, one complaint claimed that a report made by the Defendant included undisputed charges but the charges were repeated 13 times each throughout the report, therefore making it appear that Plaintiff has more of a criminal record than is true.

4. **Reporting a violation that is non-criminal under state law:** Under section 607(b), background check firms can get sued for failing to state that a charge in a report is non-criminal under state law. Charges such as disorderly conduct may appear on an individual's background check. However, a violation of disorderly conduct is not a criminal offense in some states such as New York. Listing this violation as a criminal report can be misleading and cause an employer to believe that the prospective employee lied on their application when stating that they have not been convicted of any crimes, therefore unjustly minimizing their chances of being hired. This same claim was alleged in one recent case that was settled.

5. **Failing to provide a contemporaneous notice to the prospective employee in addition to failing to ensure the information in a report is up to date:** Section 613 of the FCRA governs situations where CRAs report matters of public record information that are likely to have an adverse effect on the consumer's ability to obtain employment. Section 613 gives two alternatives in terms of the accuracy requirement. First, a CRA can report such public record information if the CRA notifies the consumer the information is being reported along with the name and address of the person to whom such information is being reported "at the time such public record information is reported to the user of such consumer report." This is sometimes referred to as the "contemporaneously notice" or "the letter notice" option. The second option is that the CRA must "maintain strict procedures designed to insure that whenever public record information which is likely to have an adverse effect on a consumer's ability to employment is reported it is complete and up to date." Most complaints against CRAs under section 613 allege that the firm did not comply with either requirement.

6. **Selling instant searches without providing contemporaneous notice or using bad data:** Even assuming the information provided in the report may be correct, failing to file a contemporaneous notice to the individual is a violation of the firm's obligation under section 613 of the FCRA and can lead to lawsuits if the CRA utilized an instant database. Allegations of incorrect data or failing to provide contemporaneous notice is common for firms that provide immediate electronic reports to prospective employers at the click of a button, which makes it difficult to provide accurate information and to provide notice to the prospective employee at the same time. The use of the word "instant" in relationship to a criminal search should automatically raise a red flag.

7. **Failing to conduct a timely re-investigation:** Section 611 of the FCRA requires a CRA to conduct a reasonable reinvestigation if consumers dispute the contents of their report to determine whether the disputed information is inaccurate and record the current status of the disputed information, or delete the item from the file before the end of the 30-day period beginning on the date on which the firm receives a notice of dispute from the consumer. Several firms have been sued for simply not performing a reinvestigation at all.

8. **Failing to conduct an adequate investigation of a consumer dispute, and/or limiting what a consumer can communicate to the CRA about their dispute:** A bank employee was terminated after a background check revealed a criminal conviction. The employee disputed the findings, eventually leading to a federal lawsuit alleging various theories of liability based upon allegations of inaccurate records and for an inadequate investigation of the consumer's dispute. The Court ruled the case could proceed on the basis that the CRA did not obtain and review the actual court records to examine the consumer's claim. The FCRA sets forth a detailed set of rules and procedures where a consumer disputes the results of a consumer report. Among other rules, FCRA, Section 611(a)(1), requires that a CRA shall "conduct a reasonable reinvestigation to determine whether the disputed information is inaccurate and record the current status of the disputed information, or delete the item from the file...." FCRA Section 611(a)(4) states that where there is a consumer dispute a CRA shall "review and consider all relevant information submitted by the consumer . . . with respect to such disputed information." This Court opinion reinforces that the best practice concerning a dispute as to the accuracy of a criminal record is for a background firm to obtain the court record and to examine the underlying records for accuracy and completeness.

9. **Reporting arrests that antedate the seven-year statutory requirement if the exception to the rule is not known to be met:** Section 605 requires CRAs to refrain from reporting adverse items of information like arrest records that antedate the consumer report they produce by more than seven years, unless the salary threshold requirement of $75,000 is met for the job for which the consumer credit report is being furnished. Firms can be sued by not ensuring this salary threshold is met before reporting arrest records over seven years old and thus, must check whether the salary threshold is met if they are reporting arrests older than seven years. For example, in one class action case that was settled before trial, an individual sued a CRA for intentionally and willfully violating section 605 in reports for thousands of consumers by producing reports with form paragraphs that state that an applicant has an arrest on their criminal history which is over seven years old before determining whether the applicant's job would meet the salary threshold requirement exemption for revealing this adverse information.

10. **Not obtaining certification from the employer of their compliance with the FCRA:** Section 604 of the FCRA requires a clear disclosure to the prospective employee that a consumer report may be obtained for employment purposes and that the consumer has authorized this procurement in writing before a consumer report may be procured. In practice, this authorization is acquired by the prospective employer and CRAs can get sued for not making sure this requirement has been met before conducting the consumer report. For example, in a case that was settled, a prospective employee sued the CRA for conducting a background check before obtaining a certification from the employer that they had complied with the FCRA, thus violating the FCRA requirement that this authorization be made before conducting a consumer report.

11. **Failing to provide consumers with a summary of their rights:** Section 604 also requires the person who procures the consumer report to provide the consumer notice and a summary of the consumer's rights under section 615(a)(3) concurrently or prior to furnishing the report. For example, in a case filed last year, a firm was sued for not providing Plaintiff with a copy of the report and a written description of her rights before furnishing the report.

12. **Reporting criminal records contrary to a state equal employment law can result in allegation of FCRA violations:** CRAs can find themselves in violation the FCRA by failing to adhere to state criminal laws in certain circumstances. For example, New York codifies the many provisions of the FCRA into state law through the New York Fair Credit Reporting Act. Thus, in many cases, the CRA has been forced to respond to allegations of violating state law as well as federal law for reporting non-criminal offenses and not providing notice, for example. In addition, CRAs can violate the FCRA by making an inquiry that violates a state law equal employment law. The FCRA specifically prohibits an employer from using a consumer report in violation of any Federal or state equal employment opportunity law or regulations.

13. **Failing to tell employers that the FCRA applies:** CRAs must also notify their employer-clients of the obligation employers have under the FCRA. In a recent case, an online data provider settled for $800,000 after facing allegations that it was selling background screening information without telling the users of its reports about their

obligations under the FCRA, including the requirement to notify consumers if the user took an adverse action against the consumer based on information contained in the consumer report.

14. **Prohibiting an employer from disclosing the contents of the report to the consumer:** CRAs have also been sued for employing policies that effectively prevent consumers from receiving the consumer report that was the basis, in whole or in part, on the adverse action taken against the consumer. In one case, a CRA maintained a policy of prohibiting users of their reports from disclosing the contents of the report to the consumer as well as directing consumers to obtain their reports from other CRAs instead of proving the information to them directly. A plaintiff affected by these policies and unable to access the report alleged that the combination of these policies violated §607(c) of the FCRA by prohibiting the user of the reports from disclosing the contents of the report to the consumer.

15. **Providing legally defective forms to an employer:** Even the forms a CRA uses when processing a background check can be legally suspect. In a recent case, a plaintiff alleged that she applied for a job and signed forms provided by a CRA that did not comply with the FCRA for several reasons. First, the form contained a waiver of liability for claims against the CRA and the employer. Also, the CRA violated the rule that the authorization form be a standalone form that is clear and conspicuous in its meaning because it had extraneous language asking about past criminal matters. Finally, the form also indicated the record report would go back ten years which in some instances according to the complaint can violate the FCRA.

16. **Not properly training employees on the requirements of the FCRA:** Some cases filed against CRAs involve an employee of the CRA providing incorrect information to the prospective applicant due to their lack of training under the FCRA. One case involved a CRA employee incorrectly telling the disputing individual that the firm would not perform a reinvestigation but that the individual must prove their case by seeking out their own criminal court records. This is in direct violation of section 611 of the FCRA. These errors display the need to properly train employees on the correct procedures to take when an individual disputes his or her report and what they should do in situations where FCRA requirements may arise.

17. **Failure to clearly and accurately disclose all consumer information in the CRA's file upon consumer's request:** Section 609 of the FCRA requires that during normal business hours, when a consumer provides proper identification and wants to know what is in his file, the credit report agency must disclose all the information in the consumer's file – including the sources of information. This disclosure must "clearly and accurately" disclose all information at the time of the request. In one case, the plaintiff claimed that the accurate disclosure of information in the file was insufficient. Rather, in order to be "clear," the disclosure must be made in a manner sufficient to allow consumers to compare disclosed information from their file against their own personal information to determine the accuracy of the information in the file.

Author Tip | **No Strict Liability Standard When CRA Makes Mistake Under FCRA.**

If a CRA provides a report with inaccurate information, this does not mean the CRA is automatically liable in a lawsuit. In other words, there is not a strict liability standard when a mistake is made under the FCRA. The real question is whether the CRA used *reasonable procedures*. Making a mistake does not automatically mean the procedures were not reasonable.

To sue a CRA for a mistake, a consumer must show that 1.) Inaccurate information was in a consumer report, 2.) It was caused by the CRA's failure to follow reasonable procedures for maximum possible accuracy, 3.) The consumer was injured, and 4.) The injury was caused by the inaccurate report.

Basically, courts look at the process the CRA used and what the CRA knew or reasonably should have known Some courts have held that if a CRA accurately reported what is in the court's file, then as a matter of law there is no liability (assuming it was not on notice or should have known that there was a problem). Otherwise, a CRA would have to do a full analysis of every court docket just in case the court makes a mistake. Other courts have determined that it is up to a jury to take into account all of the facts to determine if the CRA acted in a reasonable fashion.

However, the main point is that a CRA has a duty to take reasonable steps to get it right so that the employer has the facts and the consumer is treated fairly. As one federal court put it, a CRA "traffics in the reputation of ordinary people" and needs to "to train its employees to understand the legal significance of the documents they rely upon." (*Dennis v. BEH-1 and Experian Information Solutions*, Ninth Cir. 2007).

As shown by the above list of potential areas of litigation, it is critical for a Consumer Reporting Agency to spend a great deal of time and effort focused clearly on legal compliance. In reviewing these lawsuits, it is obvious that an employer needs to engage the services of a screening firm that utilizes best practices to avoid these potential litigation landmines. One way to help employers select firms that are sensitive to these issues is to look for background screening firms accredited by the National Association of Professional Background Screeners (NAPBS). The whitepaper "Common Ways Consumer Reporting Agencies are sued Under the FCRA" is available at www.esrcheck.com/Whitepapers/Ways-CRAs-Sued-Under-FCRA/index.php.

Class Action Lawsuits

Many of the types of cases mentioned above are brought as *Class Action* lawsuits. That means that instead of just one person bringing a lawsuit for themselves, a lawsuit is brought on behalf of everyone that allegedly suffered the same harm. Theoretically, it does away with needs for numerous individual lawsuits. Instead of each person who sues proving their own damages, an award for damages as well as attorney's fees, costs, and potentially even punitive damages, Damages are awarded group wide. Since this is such an important legal tool, the following column is provided by an expert on class action lawsuits in the area of FCRA litigation.

Class Actions Under the Fair Credit Reporting Act

By Craig Bertschi, McRae Bertschi, LLC

July 2016

Among the many challenges facing the background screening industry today, one of the most significant is class action lawsuits. Since 2010, there has been an increase in the number of class action lawsuits filed against background screening companies asserting claims under the Fair Credit Reporting Act ("FCRA"). Some of these suits have produced eight figure settlements and commensurate awards of attorneys fees. These settlements have naturally incentivized plaintiffs and their counsel to bring claims for violations of the FCRA.

What is a class action lawsuit?

Although most people have heard of class action lawsuits, through the media or perhaps as a result of receiving a "class notice" in the mail, few people have more than a rudimentary understanding of class action litigation. A class action is a lawsuit by proxy in which a single plaintiff or group of plaintiffs brings a lawsuit on their own behalf and on behalf of all other people who have suffered the same harm, e.g. smokers, people exposed to asbestos, purchasers of a particular model of car with defective brakes, etc. For a case to proceed as a class action, it is essential that the claims of the members of the class be similar, based on the same facts and legal theories and not dependent upon individualized proof. If the plaintiffs bringing the suit can convince a judge to "certify" a class, which means to allow the case to proceed as a class action, then the plaintiffs serve as "class representatives" and litigate the case on behalf of themselves and everyone in the class. The absent class members do not actively participate in the litigation; however, they do share in the proceeds of any judgment or settlement obtained in the case. In the past, "coupon settlements" or other settlements resulting in nominal compensation for absent class members has resulted in public skepticism and justified criticism of these suits, particularly when the attorneys fees awards have been disproportionately large.

Class actions under the FCRA

Claims for violations of the FCRA are particularly appropriate for class action treatment. This is true for many reasons.

First, background screeners and their clients, typically employers, tend to follow standardized procedures with respect to the creation and use of consumer reports. The same disclosure and authorization forms are given to all job applicants. Employers' pre- and post-adverse action procedures are usually set forth in a written policy that is followed each time a consumer report with negative or disqualifying information is obtained. And, background screeners generally follow standard procedures when compiling consumer reports, responding to consumer requests for disclosures and otherwise complying with their obligations under the FCRA. Because of this uniformity, there are often no (or few) individualized issues of fact and litigating the case as a class action is, therefore, appropriate. See Federal Rule of Civil Procedure 23(b)(3).

Second, the FCRA allows for the recovery of "statutory" damages if a plaintiff can prove a willful violation of the statute. Under the FCRA, the damages that a plaintiff can recover depends upon whether the defendant has negligently or willfully violated some provision to the statute. For plaintiffs alleging a negligent violation under the statute, the only damages recoverable are "actual damages," which requires the plaintiff to prove that he actually suffered some injury as a result of the defendant's violation of the statute. 15 U.S.C. § 1681o. However, if the plaintiff is able to demonstrate that the defendant willfully violated the FCRA, then the plaintiff is entitled to recover statutory damages ranging from $100 to $1000 per violation. 15 U.S.C. § 1681n. In the context of a class action, plaintiffs will often allege that the defendant has willfully violated the FCRA so they do not have to present evidence on the actual damages suffered by each individual member of the class. As the reasoning goes, individualized proof of damages is unnecessary if a willful violation is proven.

Third, the FCRA does not contain a cap on the amount of damages that can be recovered by a plaintiff in a class action lawsuit. Other consumer protection statutes, like the Truth and Lending Act and the Fair Debt Collection Practices Act contain statutory damages caps. For example, under the Truth and Lending Act, plaintiffs can recover a maximum of $500 or 1% of a defendant's net worth, whichever is less. The same is true under the Fair Debt Collection Practices Act. The Fair Credit Reporting Act does not contain a similar limitation on damages, which significantly raises the stakes for defendants in FCRA class action litigation.

Fourth, the Fair Credit Reporting Act expressly authorizes counsel for a prevailing plaintiff to recover attorneys' fees. 15 U.S.C. § 1681n and 1681o. In class actions, courts typically award attorneys fees ranging from 20 to 33% of the size of the amount paid by the defendant in settlement of a case. Thus, in the case of one of the larger, eight-figure settlements, attorneys' fees could be millions of dollars. Even in smaller cases, class counsel could recover hundreds of thousands of dollars in attorneys' fees.

In the last ten years, the United States Supreme Court has issued two decisions that directly affect FCRA class actions.

In *Spokeo, Inc. v. Robbins*, 578 U.S. ___ (2016), the Supreme Court considered the issue of "standing," and, more precisely, whether the plaintiff had sufficiently pled that he suffered a "concrete" injury as a result of the defendant's alleged violation of the FCRA. The Court's decision in Spokeo will likely raise more questions than it answers; however, it is clear from the case that a "bare procedural violation" of the FCRA that does not result in concrete harm to the plaintiff is insufficient to confer standing. In employment cases under the FCRA, the concrete injury requirement should be easily met, with the plaintiff alleging the loss of a job or employment opportunity.

In *Safeco Ins. Co. of America v. Burr*, 551 U.S. 47 (2007), the Supreme Court addressed the issue of what constitutes a willful violation of the FCRA. In its decision, the Court held that while the plaintiff is not required to prove that the defendant had a subjective intent to violate the FCRA, he must nevertheless prove that the defendant either knew or should have known that its actions violated the FCRA. Put differently, the plaintiff must demonstrate that the defendant's interpretation of its obligations under the Statute and corresponding actions were "objectively unreasonable." Safeco Ins. Co. of America v. Burr, 551 U.S. 47 (2007). This is a high standard and has been found to preclude a finding of willfulness when the plaintiff asserts novel claims under the FCRA.

Conclusion

In summary, FCRA lawsuits, when brought as class actions, pose significant risks for background screeners and their clients. Background screening companies are well advised to insure that their procedures comply with the FCRA in order to minimize the risk that they become the next defendant in one of these suits.

Does FCRA Apply to Employers Performing Background Checks In-House?

Employers with an in-house security department may decide to avoid the requirements of the FCRA by conducting their own investigations. On its face, the FCRA only applies to third parties and not in-house resources. With that in mind, many employers believe that if internal security or Human Resources perform the background checks, the FCRA mandates are not applicable.

In-house checks can go from large firms with its own security department to an HR Manager or a hiring manager jumping on the internet and looking at so-called background check sites (Note: Firms may also be tempted to look at social media sites which also carries FCRA implications. However, that is addressed in Chapter 14 on Social Media Background Checks).

Unfortunately, these employers may still find their actions inadvertently trigger the FCRA compliance rules resulting in numerous legal complications.

For example, suppose an in-house security department hires a court retrieval service or an investigator merely to go to a courthouse to pull criminal records. According to an opinion letter by the FTC legal staff (see the Slyter letter dated June 12, 1998, available at www.ftc.gov/policy/advisory-opinions/advisory-opinion-slyter-06-12-98), some court researching firms and private investigators can, in fact, be Consumer Reporting Agencies. If an employer happens to select a court researcher to obtain records who happens to qualify as a Consumer Reporting Agency, then what the employer thought was an in-house report suddenly turns into a Consumer Report. At this point, even though the investigation started out as an internal security procedure, hiring a consumer reporting agency can mean that all FCRA rules apply. This includes the need for written consent and disclosure and adverse action letters. Starting an in-house investigation without FCRA consent turns into an FCRA covered investigation.

Similarly, an employer who directly accesses an online database to obtain information about an applicant may also invoke the FCRA. In general, there are two types of databases an employer may access. If an employer accesses a public records database maintained by courts or other public entities, then the employer is not going through a third party, and the FCRA is probably not invoked (although additionally there may be state laws that apply). However, if an employer utilizes a commercial database service, such as an *online background check* that compiles public records, then the employer is performing a background check covered by the FCRA and the FCRA rules apply. An example is an online criminal record service that compiles millions of criminal records from public sources. The FCRA comes into play in this situation because an employer is accessing information assembled by third parties that bears upon an individual's character, general reputation personal characteristics, or mode of living as defined in the FCRA. In addition, some online commercial databases do not permit their data to be used for any FCRA-covered purpose, such as employment. These databases require a user to agree that the information can only be used as a source of *lead-generation* to conduct further investigation, such as going to the courthouse to confirm a criminal conviction.

The best advice for private employers who do in-house screening is: **Act as though the FCRA applies!**

Conducting Internal Background Checks

A policy least likely to trigger the FCRA is for an internal security department to only obtain records that any member of the general public can obtain and only to use their own internal employees to obtain the records. An example of the latter is a company sending its own employees to a courthouse to obtain criminal records.

Additionally, if the employer operates per the FCRA, the applicant would have the right to first review the report before any decision is finalized and to clarify any mistakes. If corporate security does not follow the FCRA, and the applicant is erroneously denied employment without a pre-adverse action letter and the opportunity to be heard, then the employer could be held liable for illegal employment practices if the rejected applicant pursues legal recourse.

When considering whether to conduct internal investigations, companies must also consider pertinent state laws. There are two sets of laws any employer must consider. The first set is the myriad of labor laws that apply to all information obtained by employers, regardless of who obtains it. Examples are the discrimination rules discussed in Chapter 2. The second set of laws to consider is state FCRA-type laws. If an employer accidentally triggers the federal FCRA, the employer may be sued under state law as well.

In addition, there is a new trend aimed at applying FCRA-type protections to applicants who are screened in-house. Many privacy advocates consider the fact that internal investigations are not regulated as a loophole in the FCRA. Here is the issue: Suppose an employer utilizes a screening firm and operates under the FCRA. If negative information is found, the applicant has a right to receive an adverse action letter and has the opportunity to review and respond before the action is made final. However, if an employer conducts the investigation, the employer does not have to follow the FCRA procedures – including the adverse action sections – since the FCRA only applies to outside agencies. An employer can simply deny employment and never tell the applicant. But there have been documented cases of employers getting the information wrong or there were errors in the public records, and the applicant never knew why they did not get the job.

Author Tip | **Beware Of Online Websites That Will Get You The Dirt On Anyone!**

Most internet search engines will reveal a number of websites offering to sell all sorts of data about anyone, and *do-it-yourself background checks* are a popular subject for spam email. Some of these sites advertise they have billions of records on Americans— all it takes is a credit card and supposedly anyone can find out anything about anyone.

Putting aside the significant privacy issues, there is one important piece of advice for employers: Do not use these sites for employment unless you really know what you are doing. Since the use of these sites is likely to fall under the FCRA if used for employment, an employer needs to proceed with caution. A clue is these sites either do not even mention the FCRA or mention it only briefly in passing.

In a Safe Hiring Program, an employer needs to work one-to-one with a professional with an understanding of the FCRA. These do-it-yourself sites typically have no one to talk with who can give employers the professional assistance needed. An additional problem with these sites is employers may not know the source, accuracy, or integrity of the data. If an employer does an online criminal search, an employer may be getting a questionable database search subject to limitations and issues. Conclusion—online websites may be helpful for limited purposes, but employers need to proceed with extreme caution when using them.

The Story of Mr. Lewis

In a lawsuit filed by Scott Lewis in the Southern District of Ohio, Mr. Lewis alleged he suddenly lost his current job and had severe difficulty getting a new job. He could not figure out why suddenly no one wanted to talk to him. He reported on one occasion he called the employer back after believing he had a good interview and was told he was an unsavory character and if he contacted the employer again the employer would contact the police.

According to the case allegations:

> "Plaintiff states that, after months of searching for employment with no success, he engaged a private investigator to determine the reason for his repeated rejections. The investigator conducted a criminal background check on Plaintiff, which, according to Lewis, produced a record consisting of various felony convictions, including a 1996 murder conviction, all of which properly belong to Timothy Lockhart. Plaintiff contends that whomever entered Mr. Lockhart's arrest data entered the last four digits of his telephone number as the last four digits of his social security number. This error resulted in Mr. Lockhart's information being entered under Plaintiff's social security number. Thus, any third party who did a search using Plaintiff's social security number would retrieve Mr. Lockhart's criminal history."

> —*Lewis v. Ohio Professional Electronic Network LLC, 190 F.Supp.2d 1049, 1054 (S.D.Ohio 2002).*

The problem, according to Mr. Lewis, was private employers accessed a private database in Ohio and obtained information about applicants. If the information was erroneous, as it was in this situation, the applicant would never know because private employers had no FCRA duty to give the applicant a copy of the report or a chance to explain. Essentially, a person could be blackballed and never know it.

Partly in response to the facts in the Lewis matter, California passed the nation's first law that attempted to regulate in-house employer investigations. Effective in 2002, the law required that information about public records obtained by an employer, even without the use of an outside agency, must be provided to an applicant, unless that applicant waived the right. California employers are required to follow a series of steps when they do an in-house investigation that gives FCRA type protection, including adverse action notices if the public record is obtained and used adversely. *Cal. Civ. Code § 1786.53*.

U.S. Government Steps Up Oversight of Background Checks as Well

It is not only private consumers bringing legal actions under the FCRA against employers and screening firms, but agencies of the United States government are also stepping up their oversight. The primary agencies are the Federal Trade Commission (FTC) and the Consumer Financial Protection Board (CFPB). As explained above, the have a joint and overlapping jurisdiction over background checks. Here are several samples where the two agencies have been concerned about actions by employers and screening firms.

CFPB Orders Background Check Firms to Pay $13 Million for Alleged Inaccurate Reports

In October 2015, the Consumer Financial Protection Bureau (CFPB) entered into a consent order where two of the nation's largest employment background check firms agreed to correct their practices, provide $10.5 million in relief to harmed consumers, and pay a $2.5 million civil penalty for allegedly failing to take steps to ensure the information they reported about job applicants was accurate. The screening firms neither admitted nor denied the allegations in the order.

The CFPB – a federal agency responsible for consumer protection in the financial sector – claims that the firms violated the Fair Credit Reporting Act (FCRA) by failing to employ reasonable procedures to assure the maximum possible accuracy of information contained in reports provided to potential employers of consumers. Under the terms of the CFPB consent order, the two screening firms are required to:

- Provide $10.5 million in relief to harmed consumers.
- Revise their compliance procedures.
- Retain an independent consultant.
- Develop a comprehensive audit program.
- Pay a civil monetary penalty of $2.5 million.

The CFPB claims the serious inaccuracies reported by the background check firm and its affiliate potentially affected the eligibility of consumers for employment and caused them reputational harm. The two firms collectively generate and sell more than 10 million consumer reports about job applicants each year to prospective employers that include criminal history records along with other types of data. Screening firms across the U.S. carefully analyzed the order to determine how it impacted their practices.

The Dodd-Frank Wall Street Reform and Consumer Protection Act authorized the creation of the CFPB which has the authority to take action against institutions or individuals engaging in unfair, deceptive, or abusive acts or practices or violating federal consumer financial laws.

The CFPB consent order is at http://files.consumerfinance.gov/f/201510_cfpb_consent-order_general-information-service-inc.pdf. A CFPB news about the fines is at website www.consumerfinance.gov/newsroom/cfpb-takes-action-against-two-of-the-largest-employment-background-screening-report-providers-for-serious-inaccuracies/.

FTC Fines Data Broker $800,000 Dollars to Settle Charges of Violating FCRA

In the first Federal Trade Commission (FTC) case to address the sale of Internet and social media data in the employment screening context, Spokeo, Inc.—a data broker that compiles and sells detailed information profiles on millions of consumers—agreed in June 2012 to pay a $800,000 fine to settle FTC charges that the company marketed profiles to companies in the human resources, background screening, and recruiting industries without taking steps to protect consumers required under the Fair Credit Reporting Act (FCRA).

The FTC charged that Spokeo operated as a Consumer Reporting Agency (CRA) and violated the FCRA by:

- Failing to make sure the information it sold would be used only for legally permissible purposes;
- Failing to ensure the information was accurate; and
- Failing to tell users of its consumer reports about their obligation under the FCRA, including the requirement to notify consumers if the user took an adverse action against the consumer based on information contained in the consumer report.

In addition to imposing the $800,000 civil penalty, the FTC's settlement order with Spokeo—which is available at www.ftc.gov/os/caselist/1023163/120612spokeoorder.pdf—bars the company from future violations of the FCRA.

According to the FTC:

> "Spokeo collects personal information about consumers from hundreds of online and offline data sources, including social networks. It merges the data to create detailed personal profiles of consumers. The profiles contain such information as name, address, age range, and email address. They also might include hobbies, ethnicity, religion, participation on social networking sites, and photos."

The FTC alleged that:

> "Spokeo marketed the profiles on a subscription basis to human resources professionals, job recruiters, and others as an employment screening tool. The company encouraged recruiters to "Explore Beyond the Resume." It ran online advertisements with taglines to attract employers, and created a special portion of the Spokeo website for recruiters. It created and posted endorsements of its services, representing those endorsements as those of consumers or other businesses."

More information about *The United States of America (For the Federal Trade Commission), Plaintiff, v. Spokeo, Inc., Defendant (United States District Court for the Central District of California) Case No. CV12-05001 FTC File No. 1023163* is available at www.ftc.gov/os/caselist/1023163/index.shtm.

Source: www.ftc.gov/opa/2012/06/spokeo.shtm.

You Need To Know ⟩ **Background Screening Company to Pay $2.6 Million Penalty to Settle FTC Charges of Multiple FCRA Violations**

In August 2012, a leading employment background screening firm that provides consumer reports to employers, without admitting any wrongdoing, agreed to pay a $2.6 million penalty to settle Federal Trade Commission (FTC) charges that it violated the Fair Credit Reporting Act (FCRA) multiple times. The case represented the first time the FTC charged an employment background screening company with violating the FCRA.

The FTC charged the company violated the FCRA as required by law by failing to use reasonable procedures to assure the maximum possible accuracy of the information it provided, failing to give consumers copies of their reports, and failing to reinvestigate consumer disputes. In addition to the $2.6 million civil penalty, the settlement also prohibits the company from continuing its alleged illegal practices. See: www.ftc.gov/opa/2012/08/hireright.shtm.

FTC Warns Background Check Mobile Apps May Violate FCRA

In February 2012, the Federal Trade Commission warned marketers of six background check mobile applications ("apps") they may be violating the FCRA. The FTC sent letters to three background check app marketers warning that they must comply with the FCRA if the background check reports they provide are being used for employment, housing, and credit purposes.

The FTC named the three background check mobile app marketers that received the warning letters and also provided links to copies of the warning letters. According to the letters, the FTC has made no determination whether the companies are violating the FCRA but encourages them to review their background check apps and their policies and procedures. A portion of the letters read:

> "At least one of your company's mobile applications involves background screening reports that include criminal histories. Employers are likely to use such criminal histories when screening job applicants. If you have reason to believe that your [background] reports are being used for employment or other FCRA purposes, you and your customers who are using your reports for such purposes must comply with the FCRA."

Under the FCRA, operations that assemble or evaluate such information to provide to third parties qualify as CRAs. Background check mobile apps marketers may qualify as CRAs under the Act since they assemble or evaluate similar information to provide to third parties. As CRAs, they must:

- Take reasonable steps to ensure the user of each report has a "permissible purpose" to use the report;
- Take reasonable steps to ensure the maximum possible accuracy of the information conveyed in its reports; and
- Provide users of its reports with information about their obligations under the FCRA, such as their obligation to provide notice to employees and applicants of any adverse action taken on the basis of a consumer report.

The press release 'FTC Warns Marketers That Mobile Apps May Violate Fair Credit Reporting Act' is available at: www.ftc.gov/news-events/press-releases/2012/02/ftc-warns-marketers-mobile-apps-may-violate-fair-credit-reporting.

White Paper Analysis of Background Check Mobile Phone Apps

A 2011 white paper –**Background Check Mobile Phone Apps and Instant Background Check Web Sites: Fast and Easy, But Are They Accurate?** – also noted the same issues about FCRA compliance that the FTC warned of regarding background screening apps that allow users to perform instant background checks on anyone at any time from their mobile phones by searching publicly available records. Co-authored by Lester Rosen and Kerstin Bagus, the white paper examined the accuracy of background screening mobile apps and found that while these apps may be fast, cheap, and easy to use, the information they provide may not be entirely accurate. According to the authors, the instant background screening information "can lead to hasty and dangerous conclusions" in the hands of average users, including:

- **Reporting inaccurate information**. Since these apps typically return raw data not fully verified or confirmed with the original record source, they can include "false positives" with outdated results such as a conviction history that does not exist. Even worse, they can show "false negatives" with no criminal history when one actually does exist.
- **Returning information for the wrong person with the same name**. Since these services do not generally require identifiers such as dates of birth, they can return results that match the name entered, but do not necessarily match that exact person—an issue often referred to as "common names."
- **Creating a false sense of security**. Safety issues can quickly arise when a "clear" background check result is naively interpreted as a promise that the person being searched has no criminal record.
- **Privacy issues for the person being checked.** Since the average person is not knowledgeable about the proper usage of public records, there are no privacy controls in place for the individual being searched.
- **Reputational injuries.** The reputation of the individual being searched may be harmed if the information is not correct.
- **Misuse of information for employment or tenant purposes.** Employers and landlords who use results from these sites can find themselves in a legal and financial nightmare due to intense legal regulation surrounding the use of information for employment purposes from the FCRA as well as numerous state laws. While some of these services say that the data should not be used for employment or tenant screening or any FCRA purpose, these warnings are often buried in fine print. There are even sites that do not even mention the FCRA.

This complimentary white paper 'Background Check Mobile Phone Apps and Instant Background Check Web Sites: Fast and Easy, But Are They Accurate?' is available at: www.esrcheck.com/Whitepapers/Background-Check-Mobile-Phone-Apps/index.php.

Where to Find More Information on the FCRA

A list of resources follows with more information about the FCRA and how it impacts employers can background screening firms. However, there are several important FTC documents that are very relevant and should be mentioned.

In July 2011, the Federal Trade Commission issued a staff report that compiled and updated the agency's guidance on the FCRA. The report, *Forty Years of Experience with the Fair Credit Reporting Act: An FTC Staff Report and Summary of Interpretations,* provides a brief overview of the FTC's role in enforcing and interpreting the FCRA. The report also includes a section-by-section summary of the agency's interpretations of the Act and also withdraws the agency's 1990 Commentary on the FCRA, which has become partially obsolete since it was issued 21 years ago.

The 1990 Commentary that the FTC withdrew was comprised of a series of FTC statements about how it would enforce the various provisions of the FCRA. Since 1990, the FRCA has been updated several times, most significantly by the Consumer Credit Reporting Reform Act of 1996 and as mentioned previously, the Fair and Accurate Credit Transactions Act of 2003, also known as the FACT Act. Both updates expanded the provisions of the FCRA. The new staff report deletes several FTC interpretations in the 1990 Commentary that have since been repealed, amended, or have become obsolete or outdated. The report also adds several interpretations reflecting changes that Congress has made to the FCRA over the years, rules issued by the FTC and other agencies under the FACT Act, statements in numerous staff opinion letters, and the staff's experience from enforcement actions.

The section-by-section Staff Summary in the report contains the FTC staff's interpretations of the FCRA and includes many interpretations from the *Statement of General Policy or Interpretations* that the Commission published in May 1990. It includes informal guidance the staff has provided to the public in the ensuing years and their experience in enforcing the FCRA. In some cases, the Staff Summary – which should be used in conjunction with the text of the FCRA – includes a partial summary of the statute, rather than the full text, as a preamble to discussion of issues pertaining to various sections and subsections. These summary statements of the law should not be used as a substitute for the statutory text. The report is available at www.ftc.gov/reports/40-years-experience-fair-credit-reporting-act-ftc-staff-report-summary-interpretations.

Other Sources of Information about the FCRA

- Fair Credit Reporting Act (FCRA) home page on the Federal Trade Commission (FTC) website:
  - www.ftc.gov/enforcement/rules/rulemaking-regulatory-reform-proceedings/fair-credit-reporting-act
- Fair Credit Reporting Act 15 USC § 1681 et seq (Text of Rule):
  - www.consumer.ftc.gov/sites/default/files/articles/pdf/pdf-0111-fair-credit-reporting-act.pdf
- "What Employment Background Screening Companies Need to Know About the Fair Credit Reporting Act." The FTC created new guidance in May 2016 for businesses aimed at giving employment background screening companies information on how to comply with the FCRA.
  - www.ftc.gov/tips-advice/business-center/guidance/what-employment-background-screening-companies-need-know-about
- "Background Checks: What Employers Need to Know." A February 2014 joint publication of the EEOC and the FTC on how the FCRA and the mandate to comply with anti-discrimination laws intersect when employers use background checks in personnel decisions.

- o www.ftc.gov/tips-advice/business-center/guidance/background-checks-what-employers-need-know
- "Using Consumer Reports: What Employers Need to Know." The FTC Guidance from January 2012 for when employers use consumer reports to make hiring, promotion, reassignment, and retention decisions to let them know the FCRA requires them to take important compliance steps to keep their company within the law.
  - o www.ftc.gov/tips-advice/business-center/guidance/using-consumer-reports-what-employers-need-know
- "Forty Years of Experience with the Fair Credit Reporting Act: An FTC Staff Report and Summary of Interpretations. " The FTC issued a staff report in July 2011 that compiles and updates the agency's guidance on the FCRA, the 1970 law designed to protect the privacy of credit report information and ensure that the information supplied by credit reporting agencies (CRAs) is as accurate as possible.
  - o www.ftc.gov/reports/40-years-experience-fair-credit-reporting-act-ftc-staff-report-summary-interpretations
- Information on the Fair and Accurate Credit Transaction Act (FACTA) Act of 2003
  - o www.congress.gov/bill/108th-congress/house-bill/02622
- Hayes Advisory Opinion Letter (08-05-98) regarding Section 604(b)(2) of the FCRA.
  - o www.ftc.gov/policy/advisory-opinions/advisory-opinion-james-08-05-98
- "A Summary of Your Rights Under the Fair Credit Reporting Act"
  - o www.esrcheck.com/file/CFPB-Summary-of-Rights-Under-FCRA-2015.pdf
- "Un resumen de sus derechos en virtud de la Ley de Informe Justo de Crédito"
  - o www.esrcheck.com/file/CFPB-Summary-of-Rights-Under-FCRA-Spanish-2015.pdf
- "NOTICE TO USERS OF CONSUMER REPORTS: OBLIGATIONS OF USERS UNDER THE FCRA"
  - o www.esrcheck.com/file/CFPB_Obligations-of-Users-Under-FCRA.pdf
- "NOTICE TO FURNISHERS OF INFORMATION: OBLIGATIONS OF FURNISHERS UNDER THE FCRA"
  - o www.esrcheck.com/file/CFPB_Obligations-of-Furnishers-Under-FCRA.pdf
- Copies of FCRA required documents are also found in the Appendix.

Source: www.esrcheck.com/Resource-Center/Legal-Compliance/

Citations for FCRA sections in the U.S. Code, 15 U.S.C. § 1681 et seq from www.esrcheck.com/file/CFPB_Obligations-of-Users-Under-FCRA.pdf:

Section 602 15 U.S.C. 1681
Section 615 15 U.S.C. 1681m
Section 603 15 U.S.C. 1681a
Section 616 15 U.S.C. 1681n
Section 604 15 U.S.C. 1681b
Section 617 15 U.S.C. 1681o
Section 605 15 U.S.C. 1681c
Section 618 15 U.S.C. 1681p
Section 605A 15 U.S.C. 1681cA
Section 619 15 U.S.C. 1681q
Section 605B 15 U.S.C. 1681cB
Section 620 15 U.S.C. 1681r
Section 606 15 U.S.C. 1681d

Section 621 15 U.S.C. 1681s

Section 607 15 U.S.C. 1681e

Section 622 15 U.S.C. 1681s-1

Section 608 15 U.S.C. 1681f

Section 623 15 U.S.C. 1681s-2

Section 609 15 U.S.C. 1681g

Section 624 15 U.S.C. 1681t

Section 610 15 U.S.C. 1681h

Section 625 15 U.S.C. 1681u

Section 611 15 U.S.C. 1681i

Section 626 15 U.S.C. 1681v

Section 612 15 U.S.C. 1681j

Section 627 15 U.S.C. 1681w

Section 613 15 U.S.C. 1681k

Section 628 15 U.S.C. 1681x

Section 614 15 U.S.C. 1681l

Section 629 15 U.S.C. 1681y

CHAPTER 6

State Laws Affecting Employment Screening

Introduction

In addition to the Federal Fair Credit Reporting Act (FCRA), a large number of states have their own rules and laws for regulating the background checks performed by Consumer Reporting Agencies (CRAs). The importance of employers working with employment screening firms who are fully familiar with the applicable state laws is obvious. This chapter will review important state laws regarding background checks performed for employment purposes. These laws deal with many aspects of background checks including:

- State type FCRA rules that are often unique and different than the Federal FCRA.
- State criminal laws such as expungements, deferred adjudications, or other judicial set asides that can impact if a criminal matter can be reported.
- Ban-the-Box laws delaying questions about criminal history until at or after an interview or contingent job offer.
- Other restrictions on what and when an employer can ask job applicants about their criminal history.
- Restrictions on credit reports and social checks of job applicants.
- A seven-year rule restriction for criminal searches in some states.
- Mechanisms that vary state by state to relieve offenders of the collateral consequence of their convictions, including various protections that can assist ex-offenders in the job market.
- State laws that provide immunity to a varying degree for employers that perform background checks and hire someone with a criminal record after making a determination that the records are not job related or do not impose undue risk.

To add to the complexity is the trend among cities and counties to add additional legal requirements. For example, the cities of New York and Philadelphia have passed laws concerning the use of credit reports. Numerous cities and counties have their own version of Ban-the-Box. The City and County of San Francisco has, in fact, passed a version of ban-the-box, that makes that jurisdiction unique nationwide. (See Chapter 10 for more information on ban-the-box.)

This chapter is NOT intended to be a complete guide to state and local laws. That is a complex topic that is subject to change without notice. The purpose is to help readers understand that this is a critical area that requires attention, and there are resources available to comply with and track ever changing state laws. In addition, a competent CRA should be able to assist employers in complying with state requirements.

Where it gets even more complicated is that some of these rules apply to background firms and other rules may apply just to employers. For example, there may be a situation where it is perfectly legal for a screening firm to report an item such as a criminal matter but not legal for the employer to consider it or use it.

To add to the complexity there is the question of when to apply each state's rules if more than one state is involved in an employment decision. For example, a person may be applying to work in Ohio, although they currently live in Florida and their criminal record is in California. Firms that operates in more than one state also need to understand how to comply with varied and sometimes competing state rules in trying to run a program in multiple states or even nationally.

These complexities demonstrate once again that background screening takes place in a very complex and ever changing legal environment.

State Laws Controlling Employers vs. State Laws Controlling CRAs on Performing and Using Background Checks

In reviewing the impact of state laws, there are two distinct set of rules to examine:

- State rules that impact what a background firm can do: These are primarily rules under the state equivalent of the FCRA.
- State rules that impact what an employer can do: Examples would be rules limiting the use of criminal records in employment decisions, ban-the-box, or laws on social media or credit reports.

Here is where it gets tricky: There may be situations for example where a CRA can legally report a criminal matter under the FCRA, but a specific state rule limits the employer's use of that same information. For example, under the FCRA a CRA under some circumstances may report an arrest not resulting in a conviction. However, the employer may be under some separate state limitation that prohibits utilizing the arrest in any way or even knowing about it.

In addition, each state is an adventure. Each state can have its own FCRA type laws as well as laws on such topics as the use of criminal records in employment, social media, or credit reports.

Author Tip ⟩ **A Basic Rule about State Background Screening Laws**

Here is a basic rule that a competent background screening firm will follow: Do not provide an employer with information that an employer cannot use under the law of their state. That does not mean that a CRA is offering or giving legal advice. However, it does mean that a CRA should understand generally accepted industry practice on what employers can and cannot consider in making an employment decision. A competent CRA will take steps NOT to provide information that an employer clearly cannot use or consider.

The bottom line is that in order to ensure full legal compliance, employers must:

1. Follow the federal rules under the FCRA.
2. Follow state rules that impact both what their background firm is doing as well as what employers can do.
3. Understand that the rules of other states can even apply if the employer is hiring across state lines, in multiple states or hiring applicants who have lived in states with different rules.
4. Be aware of county and city laws that also apply.

The remainder of this chapter will explore some of these complexities.

Author Tip ⟩ **How Does an Employer or Background Screening Firm Possibly Keep Up to Date on All 50 States?**

One answer is CRAHelpDesk.com, a resource for consumer reporting agencies and hiring managers.

The State Rules Register product at this site explains in detail the states' laws as well as restrictions placed over and above the FCRA that affect Consumer Reporting Agencies (CRAs) and hiring managers.

See www.crahelpdesk.com/home.aspx

State Screening Rules that Impact a CRA

The primary types of state laws impacting Consumer Reporting Agency (CRAs) directly are state equivalent FCRA laws.

You Need To Know ⟩ **A Number of States have Stricter Background Check Rules than FCRA**

At least twenty states arguably have stricter state FCRA rules. The states include Arizona, California, Colorado, Georgia, Kansas, Kentucky, Louisiana, Maine, Maryland, Massachusetts, Minnesota, Montana, New Jersey, New Hampshire, New Mexico, New York, Oklahoma, Rhode Island, Texas, and Washington. Of course, state laws affecting background screening can change at any time.

Special State, County, and City Laws Apply to Adverse Action Notices

Where it gets even more complicated is dealing with special procedures needed for pre-adverse action and post-adverse action process beyond the federal FCRA based upon special laws on the state level. To add to the complexities, there are even individual counties and cities with their own rules. Some states have their own rules about adverse action.

For **pre-adverse action notices**, employers and screening firms need to know, for example, that there are some states, counties, or cities that may require in addition to the FCRA rules such as:

* Employer must include the items from the report that are the basis for adverse action. e.g. criminal record(s), civil record(s), education verification(s), sex offender search(es), etc.
* Requiring the notice to identify the specific reasons for pre-adverse action, in some cases on a special additional form that must be completed and sent with the pre-adverse action notice.
* The form must provide the person and his or her phone number to contact at the employer regarding inaccuracies, as well as the number of days a consumer has to contact the employer or the number of waiting days before the next notice goes out.

For **post-adverse action notices**, there can be similar complications on the state, county, and city level. They can include:

* Requiring the employer to identify the specific type of adverse action being taken, such as they are unable to offer employment, terminating employment, unable to offer promotion, or unable to offer reassignment.
* Employers must in some cases identify the specific items from the report that are the basis for adverse action. These can include criminal record(s), civil record(s), education verification(s), sex offender search(es), and sometimes the specific reason as well.
* Additional special language is required when a credit report is part of the background check report, whether or not adverse action was linked to the credit report.

Subtle FCRA and State Law Difference

Differences between the FCRA and state laws can be very subtle. Here are just a few examples:

* In **New Jersey**, a CRA must not only notify a consumer within five days that a dispute is considered frivolous (which is similar to FCRA 611) but must also state reasons why. *NJSA §56:11-36.*
  See: http://law.justia.com/codes/new-jersey/2009/title-56/56-11/56-11-36/.
* In **New York**, if an item of information is corrected or can no longer be verified, an agency must mail a corrected copy of the consumer's report to the consumer at no charge. A mailing is not required under FCRA § 611. *N.Y. Gen. Bus. Law § 380-f.*
  See: http://law.justia.com/codes/new-york/2010/gbs/article-25/380-f/.

- In **Massachusetts**, the final adverse action letter must be in minimum 10 point type, sent within 10 days, with specified language. *Mass. Gen. Laws ch. 93, §62.*
  See: https://malegislature.gov/Laws/GeneralLaws/PartI/TitleXV/Chapter93/Section62.

- In **Texas**, a CRA must mail a corrected copy to everyone who requested a consumer report in the past six months. The statute also requires "the agency shall provide notice of the dispute to each person who provided any information related to the dispute." *Tex. Bus. & Com. Code Ann. §20.06.*
  See: www.statutes.legis.state.tx.us/Docs/BC/htm/BC.20.htm.

- **California**, **Minnesota**, and **Oklahoma** have a "check the box" requirement where an applicant can check a box and is entitled to a copy of the report. *Cal. Civ. Code § 1785.20.5; Minn. Stat. § 13C.02; Okla. Stat. Ann. Tit. 24, § 148.* In addition, California has two other possible boxes to check—one for credit reports and one for employers who do their own background reports. See the section "Only in California" in later in this chapter.
  See: www.leginfo.ca.gov/cgi-bin/displaycode?section=civ&group=01001-02000&file=1785.20-1785.22, www.revisor.mn.gov/statutes/?id=13C.02 & http://law.justia.com/codes/oklahoma/2006/os24.html.

Additional Examples of Different State Rules for Background Checks

The following list of states and state rules are not intended to be a comprehensive or definitive statement of current state laws. These examples are only illustrations of some of the differences found in some states. Of course, this list is subject to change without notice due to legislative, judicial, or administrative actions in a state. The reader should NOT assume that became their state is not listed there is not a relevant law, nor assume that if their state is on the list there is a law that is currently in effect.

Type of Restriction	Sample States Affected
Special rules concerning the notice and initial disclosure.	CA, MA, MN, NY & OK.
Rules for notice of Investigative Consumer Report (ICR) to consumers.	CA, ME, MA, MN, NJ & NY.
Rules for the Nature and Scope letter that is given to a consumer if they request more information about an ICR.	ME & NY.
Special rules for pre-adverse action and post-adverse action letters.	GA, KS, LA, ME, MD, MA, MN, MT, NH, RI & WA.
Right of applicant to know if report is requested.	ME & NY.
Disclosures to consumer by agency.	AZ, CA, CO, GA, ME, MD, NJ & RI.
Disputed accuracy rules.	AZ, CO, MA, ME, MD, NJ, NY, RI & TX.
Rules on timing of notice for Investigative Consumer Report (ICR)	CA, ME, MA, MN, NJ & NY.
States that prohibit the CRA from utilizing arrests not resulting in convictions. This is a separate set of rules where the CRA itself is under a state mandate (as opposed to employers being under the mandate).	KY, NM & NY.
States that limit the use of arrest records not resulting in a conviction by employers.	AK, CA, CO, CT, GA, HI, ID, IL, KY, MA, ME, MI, MN, MS, MT, NV, NY, OH, OR, PA, RI, TX, UT, VA, WA, WV & WI.
States that have a seven-year limitation on reporting	CA, CO, DE, DC, HI, KS, ME, MD, MA, MT, NH, NM,

Type of Restriction	Sample States Affected
criminal convictions and impose that state law directly on a Consumer Reporting Agency. Even though the federal FCRA was amended in 1998 to do away with the seven-year limitation on reporting criminal convictions, some states still have a version of a seven-year limitation law.	NY, TX & WA.

> **You Need To Know**

Nevada Removed its Seven-Year Reporting Restriction for Convictions

In June 2015, Nevada Governor Brian Sandoval signed **Senate Bill 409 (S.B. 409)** which "...removes the prohibition against disclosing a record of conviction of a crime which is more than 7 years old, meaning that there is no limitation of time for which such a record may be disclosed."

According to S.B. 409, existing Nevada state and federal law prohibits a credit reporting agency from disclosing in the credit report of a person information related to a bankruptcy filing that is more than 10 years old and certain other negative credit information that is more than 7 years old. However, existing federal law provides certain exceptions to the preceding federal prohibition, including an exception for a credit report prepared in connection with the employment of an individual whose salary will be greater than $75,000.

Sections 1 and 2 of Nevada S.B. 409 create a similar exception in Nevada state law for a credit report prepared for a gaming licensee in connection with a person who is seeking employment with the licensee or employment in a position connected directly with the licensee's operations. Section 2 of Nevada S.B. 409 also removes the prohibition against disclosing a record of conviction of a crime which is more than 7 years old, meaning that in Nevada there is no limitation of time for which such a record may be disclosed.

The text of Nevada SB 409 is available at www.esrcheck.com/file/Nevada-SB409-Enrolled.pdf.

States That Restrict the Reporting of Records Based on Time Periods

Another type of state rule that impacts a CRA is reporting of criminal records in states where there is a seven-year rule. According to Derek Hinton and Larry Henry *(from The Criminal Records Manual 3rd Edition*, published in 2008 by Facts on Demand Press):

"There is a big difference in a state law that restricts the use of a criminal record by employers and a state law that restricts what a vendor, i.e., consumer reporting agency, CRA, can report. Several states restrict what a vendor can report, i.e., they have different limitations than the federal FCRA based on time periods. However, there are many exceptions and many of the states are changing their laws to mirror the federal guidelines.

States that still restricted vendor reporting of criminal conviction information to seven years are California, Colorado, Kansas, Maryland, Massachusetts, Montana, New Hampshire, New Mexico, New York, Texas, and Washington.

However, Kansas, Maryland, Massachusetts, New Hampshire, and Washington waive the time limit if the applicant is reasonably expected to make $20,000 or more annually. In New York, the exception is $25,000. In Colorado and Texas, the figure is $75,000. Further, since Colorado and Texas enacted their FCRA analog statutes after September 30, 1996, they are arguably preempted by the FCRA 15 U.S.C. §1681t(b)(1)(E). California removed its $75,000 salary cap after September 30, 1996, and as such, at least that portion of the law is arguably preempted.

Author Tip ▷ **Is California Seven Year Rule Pre-Empted by FCRA?**

Not only is there an argument that the California seven year rule is pre-empted by the FCRA, but there are also cases that have declared the California statute regulating background checks and the seven-year rule to be unconstitutional. Another case found that the California law was constitutional. That case has been appealed at the California Supreme Court and the decision is pending as of the time of publication of this book. As a practical matter, employers and background screening firms are generally following the current California statute including the seven-year rule until the Courts clarify the matter.

These facts leave employers with two immediate problems:

1. First, it is harder to create a workable national rule when some states have their own state-imposed limitation. To avoid complex issues in determining applicable state law, as a matter of practical convenience some screening firms simply adopt the seven-year rule nationwide. This has some logic since cases older than seven years could potentially be stale under EEOC standards. However, it can also lead to serious cases not being reported in states with no seven-year rule. Conversely for states with a seven-year rule, a CRA that is aware that an applicant has a serious but old criminal conviction by law must keep it under wraps and sit on potentially important information.

2. The second problem is the question: "When does the seven years begin?" The general rule is the seven years begins to run from the date the consumer is free of physical custody, regardless of whether the person was on parole or probation. However, if the consumer violated probation or parole and went back into custody even for one day, the clock would arguably start to run all over again. See the 'When Does the Seven Year Limit Begin?' section below.

The following examples are some further complexities associated with the seven-year rule imposed by states:

- It is arguable that some of these seven-year restrictions are not enforceable because they are "pre-empted" by the FCRA, meaning that the federal rules override the state limitations. However, that depends upon a complicated analysis of both federal and state law, as described later in this chapter. State laws cannot be ignored, especially if a state court has yet to acknowledge that a state rule has been pre-empted. Texas is a good example of that. On the other hand, if an analysis of the FCRA clearly shows a state law is pre-empted, an employer clearly cannot violate the FCRA either.

- The lack of a national rule when it comes to the seven-year rule also creates potential confusion when more than one state is involved. This confusion can occur if the applicant, the employer, the screening firm, or the job location is physically located in different states, and one of them has a seven-year rule.

- The seven-year rule applies to what a background screening firm can report. This rule does not apply to employers who do their own criminal checks in-house.

- However, even an employer who does their own search in-house must still be aware if they utilize records older than seven years, they need to consider the EEOC implications. See Chapter 10 for a discussion of how the EEOC affects the use of older criminal records.

- If an employer does their own search to avoid the seven-year rule, the employer must be careful to use the same time period for all similarly situated applicants so no applicant can claim disparate treatment.
- An employer who does their own search in-house must be cautious about utilizing any outside researchers since that can trigger the application of the FCRA or state law versions of the FCRA. See the section 'Conducting Internal Investigations' on how an internal investigation can inadvertently trigger the FCRA.

You Need To Know

State Laws on Background Screening Can Conflict with Each Other

To make matters more complicated, state laws can even conflict with each other when it comes to background screening. Many states have a version of a Pre-Employment Inquiry Guidelines Chart (See the discussion in Chapter 3). Often time these are part of a state's administrative code. Among other things, these guidelines often impact what an employer can ask about criminal records pre-employment including application questions as well as interview and reference questions.

Employment Screening Resources (ESR) president and chief compliance officer (COO) Brad Landin noted the following conflict between the Washington state version of the FCRA and the Washington Pre-Employment Guidelines:

- The state of Washington, for example, covers the use of conviction records in employment in both the Washington Administrative Code (WAC), executive branch agency regulations, and The Revised Code of Washington (RCW), the compilation of all permanent laws now in force.

- Under the WAC 162-12-140 convictions discovered through inquiries made to applicants, persons other than the applicant and third parties such as a consumer reporting agency may be considered in the hiring decision process if such convictions (or release from prison) occurred within the last ten years. However, under RCW 19.182.040 a consumer reporting agency cannot report conviction records that, from the date of disposition, release, or parole, antedate the report by more than seven years. For a consumer reporting agency, the winner in this conflict is the seven year limit in the RCW.

- States should and do have processes in place to identify and hopefully eliminate these types of conflicts, but as with this instance, they are not foolproof. The takeaway is to always rely on the advice of competent employment law counsel and to use the services of a background screening provider that not only follows the law but is aware of and knows how to deal with these types of conflicts.

So When Does the Seven Year Limit Begin?

An ongoing question for employers, screening firms, and criminal record search firms is "When do the seven years begin?" The Federal Trade Commission published commentaries to the FCRA which are contained in the Code of Federal Regulations. The FTC commentaries are intended to be interpretations of the law and clarify how the FTC will construe the FCRA in light of congressional intent as reflected in the statute and legislative history. According to page 514 of the commentary, the reporting time period is calculated as follows:

The seven-year reporting period runs from the date of disposition, release or parole, as applicable. For example, if charges are dismissed at or before trial, or the consumer is acquitted, the date of such dismissal or acquittal is the date of disposition. If the consumer is convicted of a crime and sentenced to confinement, the date of release or placement on parole controls. (Confinement, whether continuing or resulting from revocation of parole, may be reported until seven years after the confinement is terminated.) The sentencing date controls for a convicted consumer whose sentence does not include confinement. The fact that information concerning the arrest, indictment, or conviction of crime is obtained by the reporting agency at a later date from a more recent source such as a newspaper or interview does not serve to extend this reporting period.

(Source: Section 605(a)(5) of the FDIC Laws and Regulations www.fdic.gov/regulations/laws/rules/6500-2750.html.)

(NOTE: The FTC is rescinding its Statements of General Policy or Interpretations Under the Fair Credit Reporting Act. Recent legislation transferred authority to issue interpretive guidance under the FCRA to the Consumer Financial Protection Bureau (CFPB) effective Date: July 26, 2011.)

The logical conclusion is the FCRA intends the seven years to start when a person is out of custody, even though he or she may still be on parole or probation.

However, nothing is as easy as it may seem. The difficulty is a court record will only indicate the date the sentence was imposed by the court and the length of the sentence. It is not always possible to tell from the docket or court record when the confinement actually ended since the release date from custody is often NOT contained in a public file. The date is actually contained in files maintained by the county jail or probation office for a county sentence or by the state Department of Corrections for a state prison sentence. Information from these offices is not easily accessible without a subpoena or perhaps a Freedom of Information Act (FOIA) request.

When a person is sentenced, the Court will indicate any credit the person will receive for time already served, such as time in custody awaiting trial if the person was not able to make bail. That would be part of the public record. With that information, a background firm may have a slightly better idea of when the person got out custody, but still, without knowing how much the sentence was reduced in jail or prison for *good time* or for some other factor, the actual get out of jail date is not a public record. In addition, a person may be released from physical custody when their sentence is coming to an end and placed in a half-way or re-entry house. However, in that situation, a person is still typically considered to be in custody and not released.

Also, criminal record reporting is not based on simply counting back seven years. Assume a screening firm did a background check in California in 2012. California has a seven-year rule. Suppose the court docket shows the applicant was convicted of a serious crime in 2003, which is beyond the seven years, but received a 3-year prison sentence so that according to the sentence, the applicant would have likely been in custody during a portion of the past seven years. Under the FCRA, the criminal conviction is reportable because there is no limit on reporting convictions (although the EEOC rules may apply*). Is it reportable in a state such as California that has a seven-year reporting limit?* Based on the sentence imposed, the consumer's sentence would have apparently gone into the seven-year period and is reportable. However, since custody information is generally not public record, in some situations, the date of release is both unknown and unattainable to an employer or CRA.

The background check firm is in a Catch-22 situation. If a background check agency did not report that, and the applicant was hired and re-offended on the job or harmed the public, the background check agency would have exposure to fault. If the background check firm reports it, there is a possibility the person was out of custody early and did not go within the seven years. Most CRAs, if they are concerned about the issues involved with legal compliance, will take the position that a determination must be made on the publicly available information, and assumptions cannot be made either way about early releases.

What happens if the person was released and was out of custody for seven years but was still on parole or probation? If the person was arrested for violation of parole or probation and spent any time in jail because of that fact, the better view is the seven-year clock is reset and starts over again. The reason? The person was in custody for the offense with the seven years due to a parole or probation violation.

This demonstrates that even in states with a seven-year limit, a CRA must go back further than seven years since a case is still reportable that is older than seven years if a person was incarcerated during the past seven years due to the case. And a CRA cannot assume an older case is not reportable without further research since a case older than seven years is brought back into the seven years rule if a person is jailed for having violated probation or parole within the seven year period. The seven years starts over again.

The lesson—a screening firm or court researcher should not limit their research to the past seven years since reportable older cases can be missed.

Author Tip **San Francisco Ban-the-Box Ordinance Re-Defines Seven Year Rule**

San Francisco, California passed a ban-the-box Ordinance that re-defined the seven-year rule. The San Francisco Fair Chance Ordinance (FCO) that took effect on August 13, 2014, requires San Francisco City and County employers with 20 or more workers to follow strict rules about inquiring into and using the criminal record history of job applicants and employees.

The FCO prohibits affected employers in the City and County of San Francisco from considering a conviction older than seven (7) years. Why is this critical?

The San Francisco FCO defines the seven year period as starting from the date of sentencing. The other 57 counties in California operate on a rule that a person needs to be custody free for seven years before a conviction becomes too old for a background check firm to report legally. The FCO look-back period is seven years even if a person has been in custody during those seven years. A San Francisco employer would not be able to legally consider the criminal record of a person convicted seven years and one day ago for a serious offense that was just released from custody.

While there are strong arguments to give non-violent offenders protection before the seven years have elapsed, the original San Francisco law made no exception for offenders just released for violent crimes or sex offenses applying for jobs where there may be a bonafide reason to disallow workers with certain serious convictions that could potentially put vulnerable groups such as youth, the aged, infirmed, or challenged at great risk.

An Amendment to the Fair Chance Ordinance was passed on December 9, 2014, that allows employers "...to consider convictions more than seven years old when hiring for positions involving the supervision or care of minors, dependent adults, or seniors." A Legislative Digest Summary of the Amendment to the FCO is available here.

However, a person convicted of a violent sexual offense such as rape whose date of sentencing was over seven years ago could apply to work in a women's shelter the day after being released from prison. Under the FCO, an employer could not inquire about, discover, or use the offense to protect that particular population at risk.

Ironically for San Francisco, an example of a real-life violent offender who would have benefitted from the same FCO seven-year rule is a person whose name is infamous in the city. Dan White was a former San Francisco Supervisor who shot and killed San Francisco Mayor George Moscone and Supervisor Harvey Milk on November 27, 1978. He was convicted on two counts of voluntary manslaughter on May 21, 1979, and sentenced on July 3, 1979. He served five years of his seven-year sentence and was paroled on January 7, 1984. If the San Francisco Fair Chance Ordinance had been in effect at the time, two years after being released from prison White could have applied for a job in San Francisco and it would have been unlawful for a compliant, covered San Francisco employer to consider the fact that he killed a mayor and supervisor. (NOTE: White committed suicide on October 21, 1985, less than two years after his release from prison.)

This will be discussed in more detail in the ban-the-box sections in the chapters on criminal records.

Legal Limitations on Questions Employers Can Ask Applicants about Criminal Records

When an employer asks an applicant about any criminal record, it is critical to understand state laws that restrict such questions. It is now widely considered to be a best practice to ban-the-box, meaning that a question about a criminal record should be delayed until at or after the interview, or in some jurisdictions, after a conditional job offer. An employer may consider a supplemental application for on the subject of criminal records to be used later in the hiring process. (Also see more information about the application process in Chapter 3.)

Regardless of timing, employers need to understand there are numerous state restrictions on such questions, as well as laws imposed by various cities and counties. The following chart is offered for educational purposes only to help employers understand the type and nature of various restrictions. This is not provided or intended for the purpose of a comprehensive or current listing of all state and local requirements. States may change their rules, or rules can be impacted by court cases or even state administrative agency decisions.

An employer should confer with their legal counsel to determine the exact wording on a form asking about past criminal records in their jurisdiction. Employers that hire in more than one location in particular need to be very careful that their application process accurately reflects the rules for all jurisdictions where they hire. In Chapter 10, we review a case where two national retailers failed to tailor their application form for the ban-the-box laws for the City of Buffalo, New York resulting in a substantial fine.

Restrictions On Employer	Restrictions on Private Employers	Restrictions on Public Employers, Vendors, and/or Contractors*
Timing Restrictions: Where an employer may only ask about an applicant's criminal record at certain points in the hiring process, such as Ban-the-Box restrictions.	AZ (Tucson, Pima County), CA, CO, CT, DC, GA, HI, IL, MD, MA, MI (Ann Arbor, Detroit, East Lansing, Genesee County, Kalamazoo, Muskegon County), MN, MO, NE, NJ, NM, NY, OH, OK, OR, PA (Philadelphia), RI, TN, VT, VA, WA (Seattle), WI, TX (Austin).	CA, CO, CT, DE, GA, HI, LA, MD, NM, MN, NE, RI, NJ, VA, VT.
Arrest Restrictions: Where an employer is restricted from asking about arrests that did not result in a conviction	CA, NY, WA, IA, MA, MI, RI.	CA, CT, MN, RI.
Sealed and Expunged Record Restrictions: Where an employer is restricted from asking about criminal records that have been sealed or expunged.	CA, OH, OK, NC, NY, VA, CT, IL, IN, NH, CN, GA, MA.	CA, CO, MN, NC (Durham County).

Conviction Restrictions: Where an employer is restricted from asking about criminal records that resulted in a conviction and have not been sealed.	PA.	TX (Austin).
Crime Specific Restrictions: Where an employer is restricted from asking about criminal records pertaining to certain enumerated crimes (i.e. Marijuana related arrests or convictions).	CA, GA, NV, CN, MA, NY, OH.	CA, MN.
Old Offense Restrictions (7 Year Rules): Where an employer is restricted from asking about criminal records past a certain age, usually 5 or 7 years old.	CA, CO, DE, DC, HI, KS, ME, MD, MA, MT, NH, NM, NY, PA (Philadelphia), TX, WA.	CA, DE, HI.
Relationship to Position: Conviction used in hiring decision must bear a relationship to position sought.	DC, GA, KS, PA, WA (Seattle).	CO, CT, DE, HI, IL, MN, NC (Durham, Spring Lake), VA.

Chart of City or County Ban-the-Box Restrictions

Since these rules a not statewide, employers need to pay special attention to each location where they offer employment in order to ensure compliance with local law.

Restrictions on Private Employers	Restrictions on Public Employers, Vendors, and/or Contractors*
AZ (Tucson, Pima County), CA (Alameda County, Los Angeles, San Francisco, IL (Chicago), MA (Boston, Cambridge, Worcester), MD (Baltimore, Montgomery County, Prince George's County), MI (Ann Arbor, Detroit, East Lansing, Genesee County, Kalamazoo, Muskegon County), NJ (Newark), NY (Buffalo, Rochester, New York City), MO (Columbia), OR (Portland), PA (Philadelphia), TN (Memphis), WA (Seattle), WI (Madison), TX (Austin).	AL (Birmingham), AR (Pulaski County), AZ (Pima County, Glendale, Phoenix, Tucson), CA (San Francisco, Sacramento, Alameda County, East Palo Alto, Berkeley, Santa Clara County), CT (Norwich, New Haven, Hartford, Bridgeport), DE (Wilmington, New Castle County), GA (Columbus, Macon-Bibb County, Atlanta, Fulton County, Albany, Cherokee County), IN (Indianapolis), KS (Wichita, Topeka, Kansas City, Wyandotte County), KY(Louisville), , NC (Carrboro, Charlotte, Cumberland County, Durham City, Durham County, Spring Lake), NY (Ithaca, Tomkins County, Dutchess County), FL (Gainsville, Miami-Dade County, Daytona Beach, Orlando, Tallahassee, Pompano Beach, Clearwater, Broward County, Jacksonville, Sarasota, Tampa, Fort Myers, St. Petersburg), KS (Johnson County, Kansas City), MA (Boston, Cambridge, Worcester), MD (Baltimore), MI (Kalamazoo, Detroit, East Lansing, Ann Arbor, Genesee County), MN (St. Paul, Minneapolis), MO (Kansas City, St. Louis), NC (Charlotte, Buncombe County, Wake County, Mecklenburg County, Durham County, Carrboro), NY (Kingston, Newburgh, Ulster County, Syracuse, Yonkers, Woodstock), OH (Newark, Alliance, Warren, Youngstown, Massillon, Cincinnati, Hamilton County, Dayton, Franklin County, Cuyahoga County, Summit County, Canton, Akron, Lucas County), OR (Multnomah County), PA (Reading, Allentown, Allegheny County, Lancaster, Bethlehem, Pittsburg), RI (Providence), TN (Chattanooga, Nashville, Memphis, Hamilton County), TX (Dallas County, Travis County), VA (Prince William County, Arlington County, Roanoke, Fairfax County, Fredericksburg, Harrisonburg, Danville, Alexandria, Charlottesville, Richmond, Staunton, Blacksburg, Montgomery County, Newport News, Portsmouth, Norfolk, Petersburg, Virginia Beach), LA (Baton Rouge, New Orleans), WA (Pierce County, Spokane), WA (Tacoma), WI (Madison, Dane County).

*Some restrictions on public employers apply only to the city or county, while some apply to private vendors and contractors working for the city or county as well.

New York City Fair Chance Act Notice Published by NYC Commission on Human Rights

A good example of a local ban-the-box law is New York City. Effective October 27, 2015, the Fair Chance Act (FCA) amended the New York City Human Rights Law (NYCHRL) to prohibit most employers in the city from inquiring about the criminal history of job applicants until after a conditional offer of employment is extended. To help city employers comply with the FCA, the NYC Commission on Human Rights (NYCCHR) published a "Fair Chance Act Notice" that employers can use to perform an analysis of applicants under Article 23-A of the New York Correction Law.

The FCA prohibits employers in the city from conducting criminal background checks or inquiring about arrest or conviction records, inquiring about the criminal history on employment applications or during interviews, or advertising or soliciting job offers with requirements regarding the arrest or conviction history of job applicants until a conditional offer of employment is extended to applicants.

After a conditional offer of employment is extended to an applicant, the FCA allows employers in New York City to conduct criminal background checks provided they comply with certain procedures before taking adverse action: 1) provide a copy of the report to the applicant, 2) perform an analysis of the applicant using the "Fair Chance Act Notice" and provide a written copy of the analysis to the applicant, and 3) hold the position open at least three (3) business days to allow the applicant time to respond.

The FCA does not apply to New York City employers following state, federal, or local laws that require criminal background checks for employment or bar employment based on criminal history. Individuals pursuing FCA claims may seek remedies available under the NYCHRL. More information about the FCA is available in a Fact Sheet at www.nyc.gov/html/cchr/downloads/pdf/Fair%20Chance_1Page-Employee.pdf. The FCA notice is available at www.nyc.gov/html/cchr/downloads/pdf/FairChance_Form23-A_distributed.pdf.

Updated Philadelphia Ban the Box Ordinance Took Effect March 14, 2016

Another example of a ban-the-box law is in Philadelphia, Pennsylvania where an update to the ban-the-box legislation— Bill No. 150815 – An Ordinance Amending Chapter 9-3500 of The Philadelphia Code entitled "Fair Criminal Records Screening Standards"—took effect on March 14, 2016, to help strengthen anti-discrimination protections for ex-offenders seeking employment in the City.

The ban-the-box law prohibits all private employers and city agencies in Philadelphia from inquiring about criminal history on job applications and performing background checks before a conditional offer of employment. If a criminal conviction is found in a background check, the employer must consider the nature of the crime, the time passed since the offense, and the duties of the job. Key provisions of the updated ban-the-box ordinance include:

- Employers may conduct a criminal background check only after a conditional offer of employment has been made.
- The ban-the-box ordinance is applicable to all employers, public and private, with one or more employees.
- Employers must consider guidelines when determining whether to disqualify an applicant on the basis of his or her criminal record.
- An employer can only examine a criminal record going back seven years, excluding periods of incarceration.
- Employers must notify the applicant in writing if they are rejected and provide the applicant with a copy of the criminal history report. Applicants have 10 business days following the rejection to provide evidence of an inaccuracy or to provide an explanation.
- Applicants have 300 calendar days to file a complaint with the Philadelphia Commission on Human Relations.

A copy of the Philadelphia ban-the-box ordinance is available at www.esrcheck.com/file/Fair-Criminal-Screening-Standards-Ordinance-Amended.pdf.

Author Tip	Additional Information on Ban-the-Box

For more information about ban-the-box rules and regulations, employers may refer to the ban-the-box page maintained by Employment Screening Resources (ESR) at www.esrcheck.com/Ban-the-Box/ and resources maintained by the National Employment Law Project (NELP) at http://nelp.org/publication/ban-the-box-fair-chance-hiring-state-and-local-guide/.

State Screening Laws that Primarily Impact an Employer

The following are some of the types of state laws that employers must understand and follow. Areas of concerns include:

1. Ban-the-Box.
2. Credit reports.
3. Expungement and judicial set asides.
4. Employer immunity.

1. Ban-the-Box Laws for Criminal History Questions at State Level

The ban-the-box movement that seeks to remove the box from job applications that applicants must check if they answer "Yes" to the question asking if they have past criminal records is rapidly spreading across the United States. The following states currently have some form of ban-the-box legislation. Here is a summary of states with ban-the-box types laws, and there are numerous cities and counties with the own version. More information on ban-the-box is found in the chapters on criminal records. Some of these states only instituted ban-the-box for public employment while others apply to private employers as well.

State	Ban-the-Box Law(s)	Public/Private Employers
California	California Assembly Bill 218 (AB 218) - 2013	Public Employers Only
Colorado	Colorado House Bill 1263 (HB 1263) - 2012	Public Employers Only
Connecticut	Connecticut House Bill 5207 (HB 5207) 2010 & Substitute House Bill No. 5237 Public Act No. 16-83 2 of 7 - 2016	Public and Private Employers
Delaware	Delaware House Bill 167 (HB 167) - 2014	Public Employers Only
District of Columbia	Fair Criminal Record Screening Act, (Bill 20-642) - 2012	Public Employers Only
Georgia	Executive Order from Georgia Governor Nathan Deal - 2015 & 2016	Public Employers Only
Hawaii	Hawaii House Bill 3528 (HRS § 378-2.5) - 1998	Public and Private Employers
Illinois	Illinois HB 5701 "Job Opportunities for Qualified Applicants Act" - 2013 & 2014	Public and Private Employers

State	Ban-the-Box Law(s)	Public/Private Employers
Louisiana	Louisiana House Bill No. 266 (HB 266) - 2016	Public Employers Only
Maryland	Maryland Senate Bill 4 (SB 4) = 2013	Public Employers Only
Massachusetts	Massachusetts Senate Bill 2583 & (Chapter 256 of the Acts of 2010) - 2010	Public and Private Employers
Minnesota	Minnesota Senate File 523 (SF 523) & Minn. Statute § 364 et seq. - 2009 & 2013	Public and Private Employers
Missouri	Missouri Executive Order 16-04 - 2016	Public Employers Only
Nebraska	Nebraska Legislative Bill 907 (LB 907) - 2014	Public Employers Only
New Jersey	New Jersey S2124 "The Opportunity to Compete Act" - 2014	Public and Private Employers
New Mexico	New Mexico Senate Bill 254 & N.M. Statute § 28-2-3 - 2010	Public Employers Only
Ohio	Ohio House Bill 56 (HB 56) - 2015	Public Employers Only
Oklahoma	Executive Order 2016-03 from Oklahoma Governor Mary Fallin - 2016	Public Employers Only
Oregon	Oregon House Bill (HB) 3025 - 2015	Public and Private Employers
Rhode Island	Rhode Island Senate Bill 357 (SB 357) - 2013	Public and Private Employers
Tennessee	Tennessee Senate Bill 2440 (SB 2440) - 2016	Public Employers Only
Vermont	Vermont Executive Order No. 03-15 & H.261 - 2015 & 2016	Public and Private Employers
Virginia	Virginia Executive Order Number Forty One - 2015	Public Employers Only
Wisconsin	Wisconsin Assembly Bill 373 (AB 373) - 2015	Public Employers Only

2. Limits on Credit Report Checks by Employers at State Level

A number of U.S. states have either passed laws regulating credit reports used by employers for employment purposes. At the end of this chapter is a more detailed summary of the states that provide additional rights when it comes to credit reports, along with a reference to two cities that also provide such protection: New York and

Philadelphia. Here is a summary of the states that have restricted the use of credit histories of applicants and employees by employers. Additional details on credit reports are outlined in Chapter 11.

State	Credit Report Check Law(s)
California	California Assembly Bill 22 (AB 22) - 2011
Colorado	The "Employment Opportunity Act" (SB13-018) - 2013
Connecticut	Connecticut Senate Bill No. 361 (S.B. 361) - 2011
Delaware	Delaware House Bill No. 167 (H.B. 167) - 2014
Hawaii	House Bill 31 SD1 CD1 - 2009
Illinois	The "Employee Credit Privacy Act" (Illinois House Bill 4658) - 2010
Maryland	The "Job Applicant Fairness Act" (Maryland House Bill 87) - 2011
Nevada	Senate Bill 127 (SB 127) - 2013
Oregon	Oregon Senate Bill (SB) 1045 - 2010
Vermont	Vermont Act No. 154 (S. 95) - 2011
Washington	Law amending the Revised Code of Washington (RCW) - 2007

Author Tip

More Details on State Limitations on Credit Report Use by Employers

Currently, eleven states – California, Colorado, Connecticut, Delaware, Hawaii, Illinois, Maryland, Nevada, Oregon, Vermont, and Washington – have laws regulating the use of employment credit reports of job applicants and employees. A more detailed summary of these laws restricting the use of credit histories of applicants and employees is available in Chapter 11.

3. Expungement and Judicial Set Asides

Another critical area concerns state laws that in a number of different ways reduce offenses or provide a judicial set aside and relief from the burdensome collateral consequences of a criminal conviction. A criminal conviction can carry a number of significant penalties or disabilities impacting voting, obtaining or maintaining certain professional licenses, limitation on certain professions, holding office, serving on a jury, receipt of public benefits, immigration status, or firearm ownership. However, one of the biggest concerns is the ability to become employed. An excellent summary of various collateral consequences state by state and how to obtain a judicial set aside is maintained by The Collateral Consequences Resource Center at http://ccresourcecenter.org/resources-2/state-specific-resources/. This resource has a state by state summary of the types of penalties and disability brought on by a criminal record and the mechanisms in each state to set aside or reduce the impact of a criminal conviction.

4. Employer Immunity Statutes

Recidivism is a problem exacerbated by the daunting job prospects ex-offenders face when they leave incarceration. To solve this problem, there is a growing trend among states to offer degrees of immunity from negligent hiring lawsuits to employers who hire ex-offenders.

States have different methods to accomplish this goal. Most states offer some sort of liability protection to an employer where the employee's record has been expunged or sealed, by making the records inadmissible, or by granting the employer immunity. As an example, Alabama and Minnesota both do this. However, there tend to be three basic categories of methods that states use when going above and beyond simple expungement:

- Granting a certificate to an employee that grants the employer protection,
- Requiring the employer to undertake some sort of affirmative action, and/or
- A variety of evidentiary restrictions on the use of employee's criminal records.

The next section examines three states with unique state laws affecting employers and employment screening.

States Laws that Create Employer Immunity

The Addendum contains a summary of some states laws that create employer immunity. Negligent hiring is a complex topic.

A Focus on Three Sample States

The following is an example of three states—**California**, **New York**, and **Massachusetts**—that provide employers and Human Resources professionals insight into the complexities of state laws and the need for vigilance regarding legal compliance. Later in this chapter, there is a 50 state list that highlights states that have their own complex issues. A qualified screening firm should be able to guide an employer in all fifty states.

Only in California: Compliance with a Whole Different Set of Rules than the Rest of the Country

You have heard it said before many times in both positive and negative ways: California is different. This fact rings true regarding background checks. California has unique rules for background checks that go beyond the other 49 states and the FCRA. California employers must follow these rules to the letter since applicants can sue for up to $10,000 for any violation arguably regardless of damages!

To add to the confusion, there are courts that have ruled that the entire California statutory scheme for background checks is unconstitutionally vague. That is an issue as of the publication of this book that is still being litigated in courts. California also has a seven-year rule on criminal records, and there is a strong argument that the FCRA has pre-empted the California rule. The following discussion is based upon the laws currently on the book, but it can change at any time as court decisions are rendered. The walk-a-way point? It's complicated!

California even added more critical screening rules effective January 1, 2012. Senate Bill 909 (SB 909) and Assembly Bill 22 (AB 22) changed how employers conduct background checks in the state. SB 909 relates to the off-shoring of Personally Identifiable Information (PII) of consumers who are the subjects of background checks outside of the United States and beyond the protection of U.S. privacy laws. AB 22 regulates the use of credit report checks of job applicants and current employees by employers for employment purposes.

SB 909 requires a consumer must be notified before the background check as part of a disclosure, and of the Web address where that consumer "may find information about the investigative reporting agency's privacy practices, including whether the consumer's personal information will be sent outside the United States or its territories." SB 909 also requires background check firms to conspicuously post on its primary Web site a statement in their privacy policy entitled

Personal Information Disclosure: United States or Overseas that indicates whether the personal information will be transferred to third parties outside the U.S. In the event consumers are harmed by a background check firm negligently sending data outside of the U.S., SB 909 provides for damages to consumers.

AB 22 prohibits employers or prospective employers – with the exception of certain financial institutions – from obtaining a consumer credit report for employment purposes unless the position of the person for whom the report is sought is specified under the law. In addition, AB 22 requires the written notice informing the person for whom a consumer credit report is sought for employment purposes to also inform that person of the specific reason for obtaining the report. More information about credit reports is available in Chapter 11.

In addition to the new laws SB 909 and AB 22, California has many existing rules for background checks in the state. Employers must understand the California Investigative Consumer Reporting Agencies (ICRA) Act, CA Labor Code, and the Regulations for the California Department for Fair Employment and Housing Act (FEHA).

Employers face substantial civil exposure up to $10,000 for failure to follow the special rules for background checks that include the following:

- Special CA check the box rule for a free report (similar to MN and OK). *Cal. Civ. Code § 1785.20.5*
- Second checkbox if the employer obtains public records directly.
- Special CA rules for the Consent and Disclosure including name, address, and phone of CRA and right to obtain additional information.
- Special language on the first page of each report about accuracy.
- Consent before each ICR.
- Special additional statements of California specific rights on the authorization form.
- Special rule for employer certification; employer needs to certify additional matters above and beyond FCRA certifications.
- Spanish Language Form if the applicant requests more information.
- Seven-year limit on criminal records (unless governmental requirement), but the math is tricky.
- California is a "No Arrest" state (but a pending case can be reported).
- Limitation on reporting diversion programs or arrest (with an exception for certain hospitals).
- Placing the background firm's privacy policy on the forms.

One significant difference between California and the rest of the states is the limitation on the use of criminal records that have not been verified at the courthouse. Under the federal FCRA, a Consumer Reporting Agency (CRA) has two choices. Upon locating a criminal record, a CRA can either send a letter notice to the applicant at the same time the criminal record is reported to the employer, or it can "maintain strict procedures designed to insure that whenever public record information which is likely to have an adverse effect on a consumer's ability to obtain employment is reported it is complete and up to date." This most often comes up in a situation where a screening firm utilizes a database.

- California law has a prohibition on the letter notice to an applicant. California instead requires that:
    "b) A consumer reporting agency which furnishes a consumer report for employment purposes and which for that purpose compiles, collects, assembles, evaluates, reports, transmits, transfers, or communicates items of information on consumers which are matters of public record and are likely to have an adverse effect on a consumer's ability to obtain employment shall, in addition, maintain strict procedures designed to insure that whenever public record information which is likely to have an adverse effect on a consumer's ability to obtain employment is reported it is complete and up to date. For purposes of this paragraph, items of public record relating to arrests, indictments, convictions, suits, tax liens, and outstanding judgments shall be considered up to date if the current public record status of the item at the time of the report is reported." *(CA Civil Code Section 1786.28(b))*

- California also placed limits on "do-it-yourself" background checks by employers. If an employer does their own investigation of an applicant or current employee without using the services of a background screening provider and collects public records such as criminal records, there are new rules that are in effect. Any information must be turned over to the applicant/employee within seven days unless the employer suspects misconduct or wrongdoing, in which case supplying the information may only be delayed. In addition, an employer who uses this procedure must provide a form to all applicants/employees with a checkbox that, if checked, permits a person to waive the right to receive the copy of any public record. If the investigation results in an adverse action, there are additional employer requirements as well. This procedure is only in effect if an employer does its own investigation.

Author Tip **California Terminology is Also Different**

California uses different terminology than the FCRA. For example, in California all background checks are called **Investigative Consumer Reports (ICR)**, as opposed to the FCRA language that uses the terms "Consumer Reports" and "Investigative Consumer Reports."

See The Addendum **Article about "Only in California" Rules for Screening**

The Addendum contains the article "California Background Checks: Different from the Rest of the United States" by Attorney Lester Rosen.

Megan's Law and Registered Sexual Offenders – Another Only in California Twist

The use of the California Sexual Registration listing, commonly known as Megan's Law, is widespread among employers. However, there is a little known provision in California that may actually limit an employer's legal use of that information in some situations.

Megan's Law is a Federal Act (HR 2137) first passed in 1996. Originally, information on sex offenders that register under California Penal Code Section 290 was only available by personally visiting police stations and sheriff's offices or by calling a 900 number.

The website at www.meganslaw.ca.gov was established by the California Department of Justice pursuant to a 2004 California law for the purpose of allowing "the public for the first time to use their personal computers to view information on sex offenders required to register with local law enforcement under California's Megan's Law."

The California version of Megan's law contains a provision which prohibits the information to be used in regards to insurance, loans, credit, employment, education, housing, or accommodation or benefits or privileges provided by any business. California Penal Code Section 290.4(d) (2).

However, there is an exception. According to California law, a person is authorized to use information disclosed pursuant to this section only to protect a person at risk. California Penal Code Section 290.4(d) (1).

The problem for employers who want to use this information is there is no legal definition for the term *a person at risk*. Neither the California Penal code, the legislative history of the section, or the Megan's Law website defines a person at risk. Until a court provides a definition, employers are well advised to apply a common-sense approach by looking at risk factors associated with the nature of the job. For example, there is a widespread industry agreement that vulnerable individuals, such as the young, the aged, the infirmed, or the physically or mentally disabled, are at risk. In addition, people inside their own home are likely to be at greater risk, since it is harder to obtain help, so home workers may be considered a population segment that works with people at risk. Another category is workers who operate under some sort of badge or color of authority or who wear a uniform. In this situation, a person may let their guard down. Until a court makes a clear decision, employers should make an effort to determine if there is a good faith belief it is reasonably foreseeable that a member of a group at risk could be negatively impacted if a sexual offender was hired.

Of course, if the underlying criminal record is discovered and otherwise meets the many complicated rules governing the reporting and use of criminal records in California, then the at risk analysis may not be needed, and the employer can handle it like any other criminal record.

There are two other challenges for California employers using the Megan's law website:

1. First, it is possible that a person may be registered as a sex offender, but the crime is beyond the 7 year California reporting provisions that restrict what a Consumer Reporting Agency can report. Although not yet tested in the Courts, the industry standard is for a screening firm to report the listing, on the basis that the background firm is reporting on the offender's current status as a registered sexual offender.
2. The other issue is that there are large numbers of sex offenders that either do not register or abscond from the jurisdiction.

New York: State Rules Include Additional Language for Criminal Background Checks to Give Ex-Offenders a Second Chance

In New York, *Article 23-*A *Licensure and Employment of Persons Previously Convicted of One or More Criminal Offenses,* which became effective September 2008, gives employers some additional protections against lawsuits for negligent hiring if they can show an applicant with a criminal record was hired after good faith consideration of the rules affecting the use of criminal convictions. Article 23-A states an employer is required to consider and balance various factors where an applicant has a criminal record (unless, of course, there is a statute that prohibits the employment of a person with certain convictions). The factors enumerated in section 753 of Article 23-A include such things as:

- The duties of the job.
- The relationship between the criminal offense and the job.
- How long ago the conviction occurred.
- The applicant's age at the time of the crime.
- How serious the offense was.
- Information produced regarding the applicant's rehabilitation and good conduct.

Effective February 1, 2009, three additional laws went into effect in the State of New York also designed to give ex-offenders a second chance of entering the workforce. These laws affect both employers and background firms. When passing some of these laws, the New York legislature cited a 2007 study that found New York employees were largely not familiar with New York laws on utilizing past convictions or that a criminal record poses a significant barrier to employment. These three laws required the following effective February 1, 2009:

1. **Provide a copy of Article 23-A:** An employer must provide a copy of Article 23-A to all job applicants undergoing a background check. An employer may want to provide that notice at the same time the applicant signs a consent form and receives a disclosure form. A technical reading of the statute may suggest such a requirement is limited only to a situation where an employer is requesting a special type of background report called an 'Investigative Consumer Report' where information is obtained through interviews. However, the legislature in New York, based upon the legislative history, clearly intended this to apply to all consumer reports. As a best practice, employers should consider providing this notice regardless of the type of background report being conducted.
2. **Posting a copy of Article 23-A:** An employer must also post a copy of Article 23-A in 'a place accessible to his or her employees and in a visually conspicuous manner.' Employers can simply download the copy of

23-A linked in this article. The required notice was included in commercial labor posters that come out in 2009 for the state of New York.

3. **Provide an additional copy of Article 23-A if a criminal record is found:** When a background report on an applicant contains information on a criminal conviction, the employer must again provide a copy of Article 23-A to the applicant.

As part of the legislative approach, New York employers that follow Article 23-A now have increased protection from lawsuits for negligent hiring. This protection applies where an employer hires someone that has a conviction history but the employer has made a reasonable and good faith determination that, due to the factors in Article 23-A, the applicant should still be hired. In that situation, there is a 'rebuttable presumption' that evidence of the employee's past criminal record cannot be admitted into evidence and be used against the employer. A 'rebuttable presumption' is an assumption of fact accepted by the court until disproved by the other side. For example, evidence of the employee's past criminal record can only be used in a negligent hiring case if the plaintiff can overcome the presumption by showing there was not a reasonable and good faith determination by the employer under article 23-A. This new protection can potentially provide employers that do hire applicants with a criminal record protection from a lawsuit as long as the employer can document the employer discovered the criminal record and then applied the criteria in Article 23-A in a reasonable and good faith manner. Article 23-A is available at www.labor.ny.gov/formsdocs/wp/correction-law-article-23a.pdf.

Massachusetts: The Criminal Offender Record Information (CORI) Reform Law

In August 2010, Massachusetts Governor Patrick signed into law Chapter 256 of the Acts of 2010 – known as "CORI Reform." This law changed who has authorized access to CORI and how CORI could be accessed. While most of the new provisions went into effect on May 4, 2012, the CORI Reform law did prohibit employers from asking about criminal offender record information – which includes criminal charges, arrests, and incarceration – on "initial" written job applications effective November 4, 2010.

In May 2012, the Massachusetts Department of Criminal Justice Information Services (DCJIS) launched a new Criminal Offender Record Information (CORI) request service online called 'iCORI' to allow individuals and organizations to request and obtain Massachusetts criminal offender record information over the Internet. For more information about iCORI, one of the main provisions of the new CORI Reform law that took effect on May 4, 2012, visit the DCJIS web page at www.mass.gov/eopss/agencies/dcjis. The new CORI regulations are available at www.mass.gov/eopss/crime-prev-personal-sfty/bkgd-check/cori/cori-regulations.html.

Since May 4, 2012, employers, volunteer organizations, landlords, and individuals can request, pay for, and receive CORI online using the iCORI online service. Employers have "Standard Access" to CORI data on any criminal charges pending as of the date of the request; felony or misdemeanor convictions; convictions that have not been sealed; and any murder, manslaughter, and sex offenses. Certain employers who must comply with statutory, regulatory, or accreditation requirements regarding employees' criminal records have "Required Access" to CORI for additional adult CORI information dating back to an individuals' 17th birthday. All users and organizations are required to register.

CORI Reforms that Took Effect November 4, 2010:

- **No Inquiry about Criminal History on Job Application (Ban-the-Box):** Bans questions about criminal history from initial written job application, unless conviction information is required for a particular job by federal or state law. (§101)

CORI Reforms that Took Effect May 4, 2012:

- **Access to CORI by Non-Statutorily Authorized Requestors:** Employers, landlords, and professional licensing authorities will have access to CORI (subject to content and time limits mentioned above) on the internet. (§21)
- **Conducting CORI Screening:** CORI checks are permitted only after a CORI Acknowledgement Form has been completed, and The CORI subject has signed an authorization from.

- **Verify a Subject's Identity:** If a criminal record is received from the DCJIS, the information is to be closely compared with the information on the CORI Acknowledgement Form and any other identifying information provided by the applicant to ensure the record belongs to the applicant. Also, if the information in the CORI record provided does not exactly match the identification information provided by the applicant, a determination is to be made by an individual authorized to make such determinations based on a comparison of the CORI record and documents provided by the applicant.

- **Provide Criminal Record before Asking Questions Related to them and in the Event of likely Adverse Decision:** An employer (or other decision-maker), must provide a copy of any criminal record information in the employer's possession before questioning an applicant about his/her record. (§19) Also, when an adverse decision is made based on a criminal record, the employer (or other decision-maker) must give the applicant a copy of the record the decision is based on. (§19)

- **Adverse Decisions Based on CORI:**
  o Where adverse action is contemplated based on the results of a criminal history background check (regardless of source), the applicant will be notified immediately.
  o The source(s) of the criminal history will also be revealed.
  o Subject must have an opportunity to dispute the accuracy of the CORI record.
  o Subjects shall be provided a copy of DCJIS' Information Concerning the Process for Correcting a Criminal Record. See: www.mass.gov/eopss/docs/chsb/cori-process-correcting-criminal-record.pdf.

- **Procedure to Correct Inaccurate Record:** CORI subjects have a right to inspect and obtain a copy of their own records. (§35) Also, the department of criminal justice information services will publish guidelines on how to correct inaccurate information and may work with other agencies to help individuals fix inaccurate records. (§35)

- **Limitations on Conviction Dissemination:**
  o Prohibits dissemination of convictions after a specified waiting period that begins after release from incarceration or custody. (§21) (10 years for felonies; 5 years for misdemeanors; Violations of domestic abuse orders will be treated as felonies.)
  o Prior records will remain available for as long as last conviction is still available to be disseminated. (§21)
  o Permanent access to convictions for murder, manslaughter, sex offenses. (§21)

- **Limitations on Non-Conviction Dissemination:**
  o Non-conviction (not guilty, dismissed cases) will not be disseminated to most requestors. (§21)
  o Pending cases will be disseminated. (§21)
  o CWOFs will be treated as pending cases until they are dismissed, after which they will be treated as non-convictions. (§21)
  o Only entities with specific statutory access can receive non-convictions.

- **Employer Negligent Hiring/Liability Protection:**
  o Employers that make decisions within 90 days of obtaining CORI from the state will not be held liable for negligent/discriminatory hiring practices by reason of reliance on the CORI. (§21)
  o No protection for employers using info from private companies.

- **Department of Criminal Justice Information Services (DCJIS) Model CORI Policy:** A 'DCJIS Model CORI Policy' available at www.mass.gov/eopss/docs/chsb/dcjis-model-cori-policy-may-2012.pdf shows the practices and procedures to be followed when Criminal Offender Record Information (CORI) and other criminal history checks may be part of a general background check for employment, volunteer work, licensing purposes.

- **Criminal Offender Record Information (CORI) Acknowledgment Form:** The 'CORI Acknowledgment Form,' which is required of organizations using a Consumer Reporting Agency (CRA) for CORI criminal background checks, is available at www.mass.gov/eopss/docs/chsb/fillable-cori-acknowledgment-form-organizations-using-a-cra.pdf.

- **Information Concerning the Process in Correcting a Criminal Record:** Must be provided to subjects of background checks where adverse decisions are made on CORI. www.mass.gov/eopss/docs/chsb/cori-process-correcting-criminal-record.pdf.

Other Special State Laws

The issue of special state laws will also come into play in other areas examined as subject matter in additional chapters within this publication. For example, there are specific state rules affecting:

- E-verify requirements.
- Drug testing.
- Sex offender registration rules.
- Limitation on obtaining a consumer social media password or viewing password protected sites.

These issues are discussed in the appropriate chapters through this book.

50 State Background Screening Law on Employers Comparison Guide

The chart below compares the many varied types of laws affecting background screening by employers that were passed in each of the 50 United States and the District of Columbia (DC).

Column Definitions:

- **Ban-the-Box** - States that have local or statewide regulations on when employers can ask an applicant about the applicant's criminal history
- **State FCRA** - States that have their own comprehensive legislation covering the same subject matter as the Fair Credit Reporting Act.
- **Seven Year Limit** - States that regulate the use of criminal records of a certain age in consumer reports. This age is usually 7 years, although some states have special rules that cover records 5 or 10 years old, and can apply to government jobs, government contractors, or even private employers.
- **Credit Report Rules** - States that regulate the use of credit reports by employers and/or CRAs.
- **Social Media Rules** - States that protect an applicant's social media information from employers, often by prohibiting employers from requesting an applicant's social media login information.
- **Special Criminal Rules** - States that have special laws regarding the reporting of criminal records, beyond the FCRA. These usually regulate what a CRA can report, an employer can consider, or a consumer can expunge.
- **Employer Immunity Protections** - States that offer degrees of immunity from negligent hiring lawsuits to employers who hire ex-offenders.

Answer Keys

- **Y** - This state regulates this area.
- **G** - The regulations in this city or county only apply to government, government vendor, and/or government contractor jobs.
- **C** - There is a city in this state that regulates this area.
- **CO** - There is a county in this state that regulates this are.

State	Ban-the-Box	State FCRA	Seven Year Limit	Credit Report Rules	Social Media Rules	Special Criminal Rules	Employer Immunity Protections
AL	Y-G-C					Y	
AK						Y	
AZ	Y-G-C	Y				Y	

State	Ban-the-Box	State FCRA	Seven Year Limit	Credit Report Rules	Social Media Rules	Special Criminal Rules	Employer Immunity Protections
AR				Y	Y	Y	
CA	Y	Y	Y[1]	Y	Y	Y	
CO	Y	Y	Y[1]	Y	Y	Y	Y
CT	Y			Y	Y	Y	Y
DE	Y		Y[2]	Y		Y	
DC	Y		Y			Y	Y
FL	Y-G-C-CO					Y	Y
GA	Y	Y		Y		Y	Y
HI	Y		Y[3]	Y		Y	
ID						Y	
IL	Y			Y	Y	Y	Y
IN	Y-G-C-CO					Y	
IA						Y	
KS	Y-G-C	Y	Y			Y	
KY	Y-G-C	Y				Y	
LA	Y-G-C	Y			Y	Y	Y
ME		Y				Y	
MD	Y	Y	Y	Y	Y	Y	
MA	Y	Y	Y[4]			Y	Y
MI	Y-G-C-CO				Y	Y	Y
MN	Y	Y			Y	Y	Y
MS						Y	
MO	Y					Y	
MT		Y	Y		Y	Y	
NE	Y	Y				Y	
NV		Y		Y	Y	Y	
NH		Y	Y		Y	Y	
NJ	Y	Y			Y	Y	
NM	Y	Y	Y		Y	Y	
NY	Y	Y	Y			Y	Y
NC	Y-G-C					Y	
ND						Y	
OH	Y					Y	Y
OK	Y	Y			Y	Y	
OR	Y			Y	Y	Y	
PA	Y-C-CO					Y	
RI	Y	Y		Y	Y	Y	
SC		Y				Y	
SD						Y	

State	Ban-the-Box	State FCRA	Seven Year Limit	Credit Report Rules	Social Media Rules	Special Criminal Rules	Employer Immunity Protections
TN	Y				Y	Y	Y
TX	Y-C-CO	Y	Y[1]			Y	Y
UT					Y	Y	
VT	Y	Y		Y		Y	
VA	Y				Y	Y	
WA	Y-C-CO	Y	Y	Y	Y	Y	
WV						Y	
WI	Y				Y	Y	
WY						Y	

[1] Colorado and Texas have seven (7) year rules in their statues but it is widely accepted that they are pre-empted by the Fair Credit Reporting Act (FCRA). California's seven-year rule is also likely pre-empted.

[2] Delaware seven-year limit applies to Government contractors and public Government employees only.

[3] Hawaii seven-year limit applies to public employers only.

[4] Massachusetts seven-year limit limited to MA Criminal Offender Record Information (CORI).

Background Checks in All Fifty States – Which State Law Applies?

A recurring issue for larger employers with facilities in multiple states is 50-state legal compliance. As seen above, the rules for pre-employment background screening have become Balkanized, meaning many states have their own rules and regulations. This is similar to the early days of the railroads—one state had one type of rail, and the next state had a different rail, so at state borders things usually came to a halt. Compliance does become challenging for large employers trying to exercise due diligence across state lines, but challenging is not the same as impossible. Compliance just requires a little more work.

FACT Act, Preemption & National Standards

As mentioned previously, in late 2003 President Bush signed the Fair and Accurate Credit Transaction (FACT) Act. The primary thrust of FACT was to extend the FCRA federal pre-emption of conflicting state laws in the area of consumer credit. Congress and the financial industry were concerned that the FCRA allowed states to begin passing their own laws in 2004, undermining a uniform national credit reporting system. The FACT Act prevented that. The FACT Act also increased identity theft protection, provided for free yearly credit reports, and changed the rules concerning investigation of current employees.

Although the FACT Act established that the FCRA takes priority over state laws in areas involving credit reporting, the inter-relationship between federal and state law is still complicated regarding employment issues.

FCRA section 625 (as amended in the 2003 FACT Act) provides that, in certain areas, state laws that exist prior to September 30, 1996, could prevail over the FCRA. Any state limit in effect on reporting criminal convictions prior to that date would be valid, although, under federal FCRA rules, there is no limit on how far back a background firm can go on reporting a criminal conviction.

For example, California had a seven year limit in place prior to September 30, 1996, that did not allow criminal records to be reported beyond seven years unless the applicant made over $30,000 a year. That was changed in 1998 to $75,000 a year, and, in 2002, California changed that limit to place a prohibition on reporting any convictions older than seven years regardless of salary *(See Cal. Civ. Code § 1786.18)*. The California law contains an exception if the investigative consumer report is to be used by an employer who is explicitly required by a governmental regulatory agency to check for criminal convictions older than seven years when the employer is reviewing a consumer's qualification for employment *(See Cal. Civ. Code § 1786(b)(2))*. An argument can be made that by changing the law, any California limitation is now null and void and is pre-empted since the current law was not passed prior to September 30, 1996, and California now falls under the federal rules, which have no limit on reporting convictions. To date, no one has stepped forward as a guinea pig to test this theory. Similarly, Texas has a statute with a $75,000 limit that was effective September 1, 1997, that arguably has no force and effect under the FCRA *(See Tex. Bus. & Com. Code Ann. § 20.05)*. In addition, many authorities argue that the Colorado and Texas seven-year rule has also been pre-empted by the federal FCRA.

The Forms Issue

A major issue for multi-state employers is which form to use. A 50-state form would be a challenge due to the number of states with their own rules. If a form is written to accommodate all of the various state rules, it may be so long and convoluted that one could argue such a form would be improper as it violates the FCRA mandate "a clear and conspicuous disclosure has been made in writing to the consumer at any time before the report is procured or caused to be procured, in a document that consists solely of the disclosure..." *(See FCRA § 604(b)(2)(A))*. Opinion letters issued by the Federal Trade Commission warn employers that a form may be improper if it is "encumbered by any other information… [in order] to prevent consumer from being distracted by other information side-by-side with the disclosure." (See the FTC Leathers letter at www.ftc.gov/os/statutes/fcra/leathers.shtm.)

The biggest source of complexity comes from the use of disclosure forms that include "investigative consumer report" language to enable employers to go beyond factual matters such as dates of employment and job title and to gather quantitative reference information, such as job performance. Since a number of states have complex rules that cover that, a 50-state form would present particularly difficult. If an employer is just seeking public records, there are not as many exceptions to cover. In addition, there are a number of states with their own rules when it comes to forms needed for adverse action. That adds another layer of complexity that must be taken into account. Added to the mix, as noted below, are special disclosures needed in some states for credit reports.

Multi-state employers should work with CRA's that understand each of the separate state rules discussed above. This understanding should include not only forms but also the different rights afforded to applicants at different stages of the process, as outlined in the previous sections.

A new solution is to use online processes to ensure the proper disclosures are used in the appropriate circumstances. An applicant can be asked to fill in a form online and also indicate the state where they live and the state where the job is to be performed. Software can then automatically display the appropriate state-specific disclosures or language through a software solution. If the software provides an automated adverse action process, there must be the ability to comply with a number of state specific rules as well. See an example at www.esrcheck.com/ESR-Assured-Compliance.php.

Which State Law(s) to Follow

In order to give applicants all of their rights under state law, the next issue is which state's laws apply.

Assume that a California resident is applying for a job in Ohio with a firm that is owned by a company in New York, and a California screening firm does the background check. Both California and New York have a seven-year restriction on criminal records, but Ohio does not. Even though the applicant would likely move to Ohio if he gets the job, at the time of the search he is still a California resident. If the candidate has a criminal record in California older than seven years, can it be reported for a job in Ohio by a California screening firm? Can the candidate sue in California or New York for reporting a conviction that was too old under California and New York law even though it would be permissible under the laws of Ohio?

Author Tip | **Rule of Thumb for Deciding which State's Screening Laws to Follow**

The employer should first consider the law of the state where the employment is to occur. However, an employer or screening firm needs to understand where a consumer can possibly sue them and consider the laws of that state. For example, an applicant may conceivably sue a prospective employer or screening firm based upon the state where they are living at the time of the background check. If the laws are contradictory, then a choice must be made as to the state that would most likely have jurisdiction over a lawsuit.

There are several issues to also consider when deciding which state's laws to follow:

- The first issue is **which claims can be brought in what court**. This is sometimes referred to as "subject matter jurisdiction." This can be a complex issue since there are two court systems in the U.S.—federal courts and state courts. A legal action for violations of the FCRA may be brought in federal court since FCRA § 618 provides for federal jurisdiction. However, a consumer cannot bring claims in a federal FCRA lawsuit in the nature of defamation, invasion of privacy, or negligence since those are pre-empted by FCRA section FCRA 610(e) except as to information furnished with malice or willful intent to injure. However, there are state claims that can be litigated in federal court, such as violation of a state's civil rights statutes. To get around federal limitations on certain claims, a plaintiff may attempt to bring an action solely under state law in state court. An employer or screening firm sued in state court under state law may argue the claim is still pre-empted under federal law and ask for removal to federal court. However, one federal district court in the Eastern District of Kentucky ruled in 2006 that FCRA Section 610(e) does NOT prevent a consumer from suing for a state court claim for defamation because FCRA Section 610(e) only provides immunity for disclosures required under law but does not give immunity where a consumer report is inaccurate. *Poore v. Sterling Testing Systems, Inc., 410 F.Supp.2d. 557 (E.D.Ky.2006)*. This can have important implications for background screening firms.
- The second issue is **venue**. Venue means a place where an act or injury occurred. It is the proper place, or forum, for the lawsuit.
- The third issue is **jurisdiction**. Jurisdiction means the ability of the court to exercise power over a business or a person. Just because the applicant may have been injured in Ohio does not automatically mean an Ohio court has any power over the New York employer or the California-based CRA. For the applicant to go into an Ohio court and to file a lawsuit, the Ohio court must have personal jurisdiction over the parties. *(NOTE: This is different from choice of law or Conflict of Law. In general terms, Conflict of Law means which law a court should apply in a lawsuit where the case has a relationship to more than one state. Factors include the place where the injury occurred, place where the conduct occurred that caused injury, the domicile of the parties, and where the relationship between the parties is centered. Jurisdiction refers to the power of the court to even exercise control over the parties to the lawsuit in the first place.)*

New York Case Gives Potential Guidance on Issue of Which State Law Applies for Reporting Criminal Records: The IMPACT Rule

An ongoing issue for employers and background screening firms is the question of which law applies when a criminal record found in one state impacts an employment decision in another state. Since state reporting laws can vary widely, employers and screening firms are sometimes left without clear guidance whether a criminal record can be reported or utilized because it is not clear which state law to apply.

A case from New York – *Hoffman v. Parade Publications,15 N.Y.3d 285 (2010).* – provides some potential guidance on the issue of which state law applies for reporting criminal records. In this case, a New York-based publisher made the decision to close down their offices in Atlanta and to terminate the Atlanta employee. The terminated employee serviced accounts in ten states in the south and southeast but did NOT service any accounts in New York. The terminated employee brought a legal action in state court in New York City on the basis of age discrimination in violation of both New York City and State of New York civil rights laws. The publisher defended on the basis there was not subject matter jurisdiction because the plaintiff did not live in New York and, other than attending corporate meetings in New York, had no connection to New York.

The trial court agreed and dismissed the case on the basis that there was no impact in New York even though the decision was made there. The Appellate court disagreed and ruled that making the decision in New York was sufficient to invoke New York law, even for an out of state resident. New York's highest court, in a split 4-3 decision, reversed again holding there had to be an "impact" in New York to apply New York laws to an out of state plaintiff. In other words, a person from out of state could not utilize the courts of New York to pursue a claim of a violation of rights just because the decision was made in New York if there was no impact within the state. The Court noted any other rule could result in inconsistent and arbitrary results. On the other hand, a requirement that there be an impact in the state is relatively simple to follow and leads to predictable rules.

Although the case does not address background screening and criminal records directly, the logic of the case is very instructive in situations where multiple states may be involved. By following an impact rule, screening firms and employers are able to implement predictable rules that do not depend upon the happenstance of which state a person committed a crime or where the person now lives but instead focuses the impact on where the employment incurs.

This case by no means settles the debate, but it does demonstrate the advantages to a logical approach to the multiple state issues. However, there can still be complicated scenarios depending upon where the job is to be performed, where the consumer is living when the background check was performed, and even possibly the location of the screening firm (which in this case was California).

The bottom line is professional background screening is far from merely being a data retrieval service but is a professional endeavor that is highly regulated and requires a knowledgeable safe hiring partner.

NOTE: The impact test of Hoffman specifically applies to nonresidents pleading discrimination which occurred outside of New York. What's more, the impact test is even more limited than that—only to be applied to discrimination cases under the New York City and State Human Rights Laws. The test is not to be used in any other scenario. Clark v Allen & Overy LLP, 35 Misc. 3d 1229(A) (N.Y. Sup. Ct. 2012). Harte v. Woods Hole Oceanographic Inst., 495 Fed. Appx. 171 (2d Cir. N.Y. 2012). Magnuson v. Newman, 2013 U.S. Dist. LEXIS 158893 (S.D.N.Y. Nov. 6, 2013). A recent case which applied impact test in very similar circumstances to Hoffman, finding that the plaintiff showed insufficient impact is Vangas v. Montefiore Med. Ctr., 823 F.3d 174 (2d Cir. N.Y. 2016) where Vangas' connections to New York were tangential and mostly involved speaking with patients in New York on the phone.

Long Arm Statute

The topic of jurisdiction fills numerous law books. One of the key concepts is called a Long Arm Statute which allows a state to have a long reach when it comes to exercising personal jurisdiction over people and businesses. States can assume broad jurisdiction based on such concepts as minimum contacts or systemic and continuous activity in a state. Another basis for a state court to obtain jurisdiction is when a business intends to conduct business in that state.

For employers, the issue is generally very simple—the firm can generally be sued in any state where it does business, which is very broadly defined. Similar rules apply to screening firms. A screening firm can be sued in any state where it does business. Legal cases suggest if a screening firm has an interactive website where the screening firm conducts background checks, then that firm is doing business in all fifty states for purposes of personal jurisdiction. Additionally, the screening firm can likely be sued in any state where it solicits business or has clients.

Understanding where a lawsuit can be brought is the key to choosing which state laws to apply. In the example above, the issue is whether a California court would likely exercise jurisdiction in a lawsuit against a California screening firm and a New York employer when the criminal record was appropriate to report under Ohio law but not under California law.

What does all this mean? As a general rule, firms that hire in more than one state should first consider the law of the state where the employment occurs. However, the employer should also consider if other states may be likely to allow a consumer to sue for a violation of their state law. This can include the state where the consumer resides, the state where the employer is located, or the state where the consumer reporting agency has its place of business.

The result, of course, is employers and screening firms are occasionally left to take their best "guess" about which laws to apply since there is not a clear national rule. In addition, employers can find themselves in the position of having to apply different rules to different applicants. Until Congress pre-empts the area with a clear national rule, this will remain a confusing area for employers.

News about State Laws Affecting Background Checks

The ESR News Blog contains updates about state laws affecting background checks at www.esrcheck.com/wordpress/tag/state-laws/.

CHAPTER 7

Implementing the Pre-Employment Screening Process

Introduction

The third core component of a Safe Hiring Program is *In-Depth Screening Practices.* As outlined in Chapter 1, this third phase comes after setting up an organizational infrastructure (Step 1) and the Initial Screening Processes (Step 2). This phase is also known as pre-employment screening or employment screening or background check. To lessen any confusion, this process is referred to interchangeably as *pre-employment screening* or *background screening* throughout this chapter.

When the third phase is reached, the employer has already engaged in recruiting and has gone through a progressive screening process to focus on the candidates who are potential finalists. The employer has made a tentative candidate selection. The employer may, in fact, be ready to issue a job offer or may have already made a conditional job offer contingent on a successful completion of a background check.

The employer is now at the stage where they need to determine if there is any reason NOT to hire the applicant. In other words, this is the stage in the hiring process here the employer performs the due diligence necessary to ensure the employer is about to make the right decision

The Point When Pre-Employment Screening Process Occurs

Quite simply, pre-employment screening occurs at the point of the process where an employer has a candidate in mind and the employer has made, or is about to make, a job offer. The process of researching and assessing further information on candidate's statements and past will begin to take place. The pre-employment screening process is meant to reasonably discover if an applicant is truly qualified for the particular job by looking at factors such as:

1. Do they have the past employment experience, credentials or credentials claimed or;

2. Are there other factors such as an unsuitable criminal record that may pose an unacceptable risk to the employer, other employees, the public, or those using the employer's services?

As with the other core portions of a Safe Hiring Program, the practices used in the screening process must be documented using procedures that methodically assemble standardized types of information concerning applicants. The approach and methods a firm takes to implement these pre-employment screening practices are very much integral to the success of a firm's Safe Hiring Program.

Below is a formal definition of pre-employment screening:

> *Pre-employment screening is an assessment of an applicants for employment by means of methodically assembling standardized types of information concerning qualifications and behavior that, when obtained and applied in a legal fashion, is considered relevant to the potential job in order to reasonably detect those applicants that are either not qualified, not honest or have risk factors that need further consideration.*

Occasionally, an employer may have two finalists and will perform a pre-employment screening on more than one finalist to help whittle it down, but that is less common. However, once the finalist is selected, there are steps an employer needs to take before an applicant is onboarded as an employee.

By now you probably are fully aware of why pre-employment screening is a necessary process for employers, the advantages are covered in earlier chapters. Performing background screenings is certainly not a guarantee that every bad applicant will be discovered. For the prices charged by screening firms, employers cannot expect an in-depth and exhaustive FBI-type investigation. However, just engaging in a prescreening program demonstrates due diligence and provides an employer with a great deal of legal protection.

It is also important to understand that a prescreening program is aimed at how a person has performed in the public aspect of their lives. Items such as criminal records or previous job performance reflect how a person behaved towards others or discharged his/her obligations or responsibilities. Screening is NOT an invasion of privacy, a sign of mistrust, or an act of Big Brother.

About the Term Background Check and the Difference between a Screening and an Investigation

The phrase *background check* is now common in today's business vocabulary. There are numerous news stories about the need for background checks or efforts made by various organizations, such as churches, charities, or businesses to obtain background checks. However, there is one significant problem: There is simply no one specific definition as to what constitutes a background check.

When the phrase *background check* is used, the meaning can vary from a one county criminal check all the way to an in-depth FBI-type investigation that costs thousands of dollars. Employers and consumers can be misled into making certain assumptions about a person because they have been the subject of a background check. The biggest assumption is the person must be safe or qualified because they passed a background check.

Unfortunately, nothing may be further from the truth. Employers, consumers, and online daters should not be lulled into a false sense of security just because some site has performed a background check unless you know exactly what was checked, how it was checked, when and by who.

The same confusion applies when trying into interchange a *pre-employment screening* with *a background investigation*. It is important to note that a background screen is NOT the same thing as an in-depth investigation of each applicant. The term investigation refers to a more focused look at each candidate and can include seeking to develop information unknown to the investigator. For example, in an investigation, the investigator may not know the past employers and schools and may have to locate that information. In a background screening, the employer is seeking to verify the past employment and school information given. In addition, an investigator may look for all property and assets owned by a subject, and this detailed of an approach is normally not appropriate for pre-employment screening.

Screening is not going to detect every potential problem of an applicant, and neither may an investigation.

Given that a pre-employment screening is performed on a number of potential hires and that cost considerations are always present, even the best screening program can result in a bad apple getting through. However, reasonable steps are taken to try to limit and discourage bad hires and to demonstrate due diligence.

Employment Screening Versus Investigation – Not the Same Thing

There is a difference between screening and investigations. They are two separate endeavors. **Screening** is done with the applicant's consent on a large scale using information supplied by the applicant. A screening firm uses standardized techniques to either confirm supplied information such as employment or education, or find public records such as criminal matters. Screening firms will use court runners to find public records, but the work is done primarily in an office or call center utilizing advanced technology.

Investigation, on the other hand, is seeking to discover information that is not readily apparent. Many professional investigators do not consider making routine phone calls from a call center environment to past employers or assembling computerized information to be a professional investigation, A professional Private Investigator (PI) may provide a wide range of services, including preparing criminal or civil cases, locating missing people or assets, locating and interviewing witnesses, conducting due diligence of businesses, surveillance, undercover investigations, investigating fraud or theft, and numerous additional tasks.

Think of screening as working with what you see. Investigation is digging for what is not seen.

The difference is analogous to the difference between giving cholesterol tests to a large number of consumers to measure a medical risk versus doing an exploratory surgical procedure one patient at a time. Obviously, an exploratory procedure is much more reliable, but it is also intrusive, time consuming, and expensive. On the other hand, a cholesterol test may not catch a more serious condition.

Regardless of whether the firm used is a background screening firm or a Private Investigator, for purposes of employment screening, anyone who does background checks is considered a **Consumer Reporting Agency (CRA)** under the federal Fair Credit Reporting Act (FCRA). The bottom-line is that there is no FCRA exception for a private investigator doing employment background checks. They are held to the same rules as any other CRA. Even the Transportation Security Agency (TSA), a branch of the federal government, must abide by the FCRA. The FCRA clearly states in section 603(f) that:

> *The term "consumer reporting agency" means any person which, for monetary fees, dues, or on a cooperative nonprofit basis, regularly engages in whole or in part in the practice of assembling or evaluating consumer credit information or other information on consumers for the purpose of furnishing consumer reports to third parties, and which uses any means or facility of interstate commerce for the purpose of preparing or furnishing consumer reports.*

That means that a PI who regularly engages in background checks must follow the FCRA and their status as a licensed investigator has no bearing on their FCRA obligations. Of course, an investigator may argue that the first background check he or she performs does not fall under the FCRA because it is not done on a regular basis, but if a PI holds himself or herself out as a performer of background checks, then that is a risky argument.

The best advice for a Private Investigator performing employment background checks is to always keep in mind that for any assignment involving an employment background check, they are considered a background screening firm and have all of the same obligations and duties of any other CRA.

State Licensing Requirements

A number of states have statutes to license private investigators (PIs). Whether screening firms also need to have a PI license is unclear in many states. State statutes that regulate private investigators normally exempt those other entities that regularly examine public records, otherwise anyone who utilizes public records—from real estate agents to genealogists—would be in violation of state PI laws. Some confusion has been caused by the fact that the FCRA labels certain screening activity as an Investigative Consumer Report. This applies when a Consumer Reporting Agency calls a past employer and asks about past job performance. Because the word Investigative is used, the argument has been made that when a screening firm does an Investigative Consumer Report, a PI license is necessary. On the other hand, many pre-employment screening firms do not possess PI licenses because they do not consider their work to be investigative. The best advice is that an employer should determine if, in their state, a private investigator license is required for employment screening firms.

The Basics of Screening

The acronym SCREEN summarizes the core concepts behind background checks. These basics of screening is expanded upon in future chapters throughout *The Safe Hiring Manual*.

S **Sources** – Sources of information are public information (e.g. criminal records) and private records, such as verification of credentials. The key point is that a background check covers those areas of a person's life conducted in the public sphere.

C **Consent** – Consent must be in writing under Fair Credit Reporting Act (FCRA) and state laws.

R **Rationale** – Pre-employment screening discourages applicants with something to hide, encourages honesty, demonstrates due diligence, and helps to hire based on facts and not just instinct.

E **Even-handed** – Similarly situated people must be treated similarly.

E **Effectiveness** – No single tool can be relied upon but need series of overlapping tools.

N **Not** – Background screening is not an FBI check or Big Brother watching, but a valuable due diligence employment tool.

Author Tip > **No Single Item Tells the Whole Story**

Of particular importance is the fact that no one single item of information all by itself tells the whole story. From the point of view of an employer, it may be helpful if the employer can go to a website, put in the person's name and last four digits of the social security number, and get a thumbs up or thumbs down. Of course, the real world does not work that way. Data is not gathered neatly in one place, and even if it was, there would be large privacy concerns. An employer needs to establish the big picture by utilizing many sources of information. Background screening firms also do not simply push a button and get results. As can be seen throughout *The Safe Hiring Manual*, each type of search has many moving and complicated parts, all with substantial legal considerations.

Background Screening: In-House or Outsource?

The majority of this chapter assumes the employer will work with a pre-employment screening company. Certainly, there are numerous tasks an employer could certainly perform in-house, such verifying professional licenses or contacting past employers. Employers doing the initial reference phone calls in-house before performing the background screen can provide an advantage.

However, when certain screening tasks must be performed, most employers find it more efficient to outsource even if they have sufficient staffing to do it themselves. Most employers do not clean their own office windows or build their own office furniture just because they can. Deciding who will do screening tasks – in-house or outsource – comes down to economics and a focus on core competency."

Below are seven points to consider when an employer is deciding what part of the screening program should be performed in-house and what should be outsourced to a professional screening firm.

1. Is outsourcing a better use of time and energy?

Human resources and security departments realize there are only so many functions an in-house department can provide. Many firms find it an inefficient use of their time and energy to attempt to perform services that a third-party specialist can provide efficiently and cost-effectively. As a result, many firms outsource their screening tasks to professional pre-employment screening firms, and this allows HR and security departments to devote more time and resources to the function of managing people and delivery of vital HR services to employees.

2. Does the employer have the required expertise to perform background screening in-house?

Pre-employment screening requires highly specialized knowledge and resources required. To do prescreening in-house, an employer would have to learn how to perform all the screening tasks plus become extremely knowledgeable about the many complicated state and federal laws governing what information they can and cannot access. In addition, an employer would need software to manage the process effectively and to locate and understand various information sources. For an employer to attempt to perform many of the tasks involved in pre-employment screening may not be practical.

3. Is outsourcing more cost-effective than in-house processing?

Consider the cost of devoting staff time and resources to the physical management of the process, including computers and implementing a software solution to manage and track all applicants being screened including each applicant's current status. A typical report from a screening firm should cost less than the first day's salary paid to the new employee. This is called the *Less than One Day's Pay Rule*. Considering the cost of a bad hire, this is a very minimal investment. Of course, firms may do more in-depth screening for higher paying positions. However, even if the position is paid more, the Less than One Day's Pay Rule usually holds true.

For larger employers, deep discounts from screening vendors are often available with volume. Even with such discounts, some employers look at the total spent on screening as a line item on the budget and are concerned with the total amount. However, even for large firms hiring thousands of employees, screening costs are still likely to be less than the cost of just one lawsuit.

The true cost calculations should also include soft costs and associated overhead costs. For example, an employer may feel it is less costly to do educational verifications in-house than to pay a screening firm. This logic fails to take into account all the associated costs including training, supervision, the infrastructure costs; the administrative cost of maintaining employees; the cost of other tasks not being done; and all of the other costs associated with employees. One reality is verification phone calls are typically not completed on the first attempt; chances are an employer makes four calls but only one will get through. Leave a message? Quite often those verification targets call back up to 48 hours later. During the day, the employer will be continually interrupted with return calls. In the end, the true cost of an in-house verification process is usually much higher than most employers' first estimates.

4. Can the employer effectively manage the outsource process in terms of quality and performance levels?

There must be appropriate and prioritized controls in place. If outsourcing to a third party provider firm that utilizes an internet software tracking system, then employers have a high degree of control over timeliness and quality since these systems usually allow the employer to privately monitor in real-time the exact status of all reports. Will an employer have an in-house system with the same performance benefits? Perhaps, but it may be costly to set up.

5. Are there legal advantages to outsourcing?

The fifth consideration is legal compliance. By outsourcing screening tasks, employers enjoy the protection of the Fair Credit Reporting Act (FCRA). As explained in Chapter 5, this federal law governs the activities of screening companies and third party agencies in a way to provide both employers and job applicants with significant legal protection.

When an employer performs these services in-house, care must be taken to not unduly invade an applicant's privacy. Employers that do perform any screening in-house are well advised to conduct the program under the rules of the FCRA, which includes:

- A disclosure to the applicant that a screening is being conducted,
- Obtaining a written consent, and
- Giving an applicant an opportunity to correct any information before it is used as a basis not to hire.

There are additional special circumstances employers need to be aware of. In states where there is a seven-year limitation on a background screening firm reporting criminal information, an employer who does their own criminal investigation is not subject to the limitation.

6. In-house screening may hit the FCRA Trip Wire?

As explained in Chapter 5, even a firm that believes it is doing their pre-employment screening in-house can easily hit the FCRA trip wire, and turn what the employer thought was a non-FCRA background check into a background check covered by the FCRA. If that happens, an employer could easily find themselves a target of lawsuits or an investigation by governmental agencies. The notion that in-house searches can potentially avoid having to comply with FCRA may not work to an employer's advantage.

7. Are there organizational advantages to outsourcing?

As a matter of corporate culture, many organizations do not want new applicants to feel as though other company employees are conducting an investigation into their background. By outsourcing the task to an independent third party, there is a greater sense of privacy. Job applicants understand that background screening is a necessary business practice, but many feel relieved if others in the same organization are not doing the investigation. In addition, why should an applicant's first contact with the HR Department be a background screening? That is a potential negative. Human resource managers have found there is a substantial advantage to advising applicants that a professional outside agency conducts the screening.

The Benefits of Performing In-House or Using a Management Fee Model with a Pre-Employment Screening Firm

For organizations that do substantial hiring, there can be advantages to performing the task of screening in-house as long as the employer understands that they are essentially getting into the background screening business. That means they need all the knowledge, training, resources, and staffing a third party firm would also have. Another alternative for larger employers is using a management fee model. In this approach, the employer retains a screening firm or screening industry expert as a management consultant. For a fixed percentage fee, the screening firm helps set-up procedures, provides software, and negotiates prices with information provider sources. This gives the large enterprise employers the same economic advantages enjoyed by an outside screening firm. Instead of the employer paying the screening firm for data, the employer pays for information services at a wholesale level. Of course, the employer pays all overhead and labor when using its own employees and facilities. The big advantage for the employer is the total control over the process and the fact there is complete transparency in the pricing model. With a standard vendor relationship, the employer has no idea as to the mark-up of data or the profit level. The employer has no control over what profit margin the screening firm is taking or how much the screening firm is spending on qualified labor. Conversely, under the management fee model, the employer has direct control over all costs and is only paying for expertise. Under this model for reasons previously stated, an employer should still adhere to the FCRA.

When deciding if performing screening in-house or using a management fee model is right for them, employers should consider the following factors:

- The employer's hiring volume is so large there is significant cost savings by setting up its own screening program.
- Safe hiring is such an integral part of its business that having internal control is a crucial business need.

- The firm operates in a number of states and jurisdictions, so a centralized office can contend with each jurisdiction, helping the firm to meet national screening and hiring standards.

What a Screening Firm Does NOT Do!

It is equally important to understand what a screening firm does not do:

1. A screening firm does NOT make employment decisions or render any opinions whatsoever. A screening firm provides information in a heavily regulated legal environment. The screening firm generally has limited if any contact with the applicant and has no involvement in writing the job description, recruiting or interviewing.
2. A screening firm does NOT provide legal advice
3. A screening firm does not invade an applicant's privacy since a background report is looking at what a person has done in their public life.
4. A screening firm is not profiteering off public data or endangering privacy. As discussed in more detail in Chapter 9 on Criminal Records, some court clerks are sabotaging efforts of employers to hire by hindering access to public records under the mistaken and uninformed belief that consumer privacy may be compromised or a background firm is making a profit off public records. Nothing can be further from the truth. Screening firms go to great lengths to protect privacy and perform a valuable service that otherwise employers may have to perform themselves.

The Compliance Issues Screening Companies Face

The Fair Credit Reporting Act (FCRA), which is the gold standard in the U.S. for privacy and consumer protection, controls the operations of background screening firms. Screening firms only obtain information on "consumers" who have given their full written authorization and have received an extensive written disclosure. Background reports are governed by detailed procedures designed to provide accuracy, transparency, and accountability.

Rules for the screening industry also include an extensive procedure to give consumers notice of any adverse information and recourse in the event a consumer considers any information contained in a consumer report to be inaccurate or incomplete. Consumers have a right to obtain reports and to have anything re-investigated that they disagree with. Furthermore, consumers are protected by the rules of the Equal Employment Opportunities Commission (EEOC) as well as numerous state laws on issues such as credit reports, ban-the-box, social media among others, which are discussed elsewhere in the book.

 Author Tip | **Don't Know Anything about Screening Firms or the Screening Industry?**
The last half of this chapter introduces the background screening industry and how to choose a competent background screening firm.

The Core Tools Used in a Pre-Employment Screen

Below is a list of the most common elements used in a pre-employment screen. There are more, and some of these elements may be optional in your Safe Hiring Program.

- Civil Lawsuits, Judgments, Liens
- Credit Report
- Criminal History
- Education and Credentials Verifications
- International searches
- Merchant Databases
- Motor Vehicle Report (driving record)

- Past Employment References
- Security Clearances
- Social Security Number Trace
- Workers' Compensation Records

Each of these elements is discussed in detail in later chapters including suggestions regarding proper procedures, documentation, and related legal compliance issues.

Importance of Consistency and Scope

A critical concept in nearly every area of pre-employment screening, as well as HR in general, is the notion that similarly situated people should be treated in a similar fashion. Proper pre-employment screening does not mean all applicants must be screened exactly the same. What it does mean is that all applicants who are finalists for a particular job opening should receive the same level of scrutiny. A firm may choose to screen in more detail candidates for a vice president's position than those applying to be on the maintenance crew. However, all vice presidential applicants should be screened in the same way while all maintenance worker candidates should be screened like all other maintenance worker candidates. The difference level of scrutiny is a reflection of the risk associated with each position.

The degree of scrutiny for any particular category of jobs is based upon risk and job requirements. It is determined by a number of factors, such as access to money or assets, the level of authority over others the position carries, access to the public or groups at risk, or the level of supervision. Also, employers should take into account the difficulty faced in replacing the new hire if he or she does not work out or the damage that could be done to the organization's productivity if an incompetent person is hired in that position. Once an employer has determined how intensively the position should be researched, then all finalists for this job level should receive consistent treatment.

The Background Screen – The Employer's Step-by-Step Process

This section addresses background checks from the employer's point of view. It outlines how to manage the mechanics of pre-employment screening, including procedures considered to be best practices. Again, this section also assumes the employer is working with a pre-employment screening company, also termed a Consumer Reporting Agency (CRA).

1. How to start the screening process with a CRA

Initially, an employer needs to sign a Certification Form with the CRA. This is required under the Fair Credit Reporting Act (FCRA) as explained earlier. Certification means the employer will utilize the information provided according to the law. The CRA and employer typically will also have an agreement in place setting out the business terms, which may or may not be part of the certification form as discussed later in this chapter. A typical certification form covers the following legally required topics:

- The employer understands the information can be used for employment purposes only,
- That all information must remain confidential,
- That information will not be used to discriminate unlawfully, and
- The employer will follow the rules contained in the FCRA for the use of consumer reports.

Under the FCRA, a CRA is required to provide two documents to an employer:

- The first document is the "Notice to Users of Consumer Reports: Obligations of Users under the FCRA."
- The second document is "A Summary of Your Rights under the Fair Credit Reporting Act" for job applicants.

California has Special Requirements for Screening

California has additional special certification rules to follow contained in the California Investigative Consumers Reporting Agencies Act (ICRAA) - Civil Code section 1786 et.

seq. Any background firm or employer doing business in California, hiring in California, or using the consumer report in connection with a California resident or California employment location must be familiar with and follow special California requirements.

2. The forms an applicant needs to receive and/or sign

It is critical that employers utilize forms that are legally compliant under both federal law and state law.

Disclosure Form

Since September 30, 1997, the FCRA requires the use of a separate Disclosure Form for any background check report whether or not it involves a credit report. Previously, release forms could be contained in the back of employment applications or be part of another document. The amended FCRA requires an employer to:

"…make a clear and conspicuous written disclosure to the consumer before the report is obtained, in a document that consists solely of the disclosure, that a consumer report may be obtained."

Although a CRA may provide an employer with forms, it is still the employer's responsibility to ensure the forms are legal in their state.

Release and Authorization Form

The Release Form serves several purposes. First, it is the release of information so a CRA may obtain background information under the FCRA. Second, it is the place where the job applicant provides the necessary identifying information to the CRA to obtain public records. Third, this release may be needed when a former employer or school requests a release before the information is given. Also, it can be used to reassure a job applicant that all of his rights are protected, and that screening is a sound business practice that is not to be taken personally. Whether or not it can be combined with the disclosure form depends upon how much information an employer wants to have in their release form. Too much information can violate the rule that the disclosure cannot have excess verbiage that distracts from the plain meaning of the disclosure.

The Release and Authorization typically does ask for the date of birth. The correct date of birth will be needed for positive identification. If an employer does not want to have a date of birth on the release form, then arrangements need to be made with a CRA to obtain it separately. The employer needs to be aware that without date of birth, there are likely to be delays. See the Chapter 5 for additional issues surrounding these forms and the exception for truck drivers enacted by Congress in 1998. The form can be printed or the information provided electronically through an email to the applicant or by integration with an Applicant Tracking System.

There is currently no nationally accepted set of disclosure and release forms for employment screening. However, a competent screening firm can provide all the necessary forms for pre-employment screening. If an employer is using paper forms and the employer's attorney or legal department already has forms, use those forms—assuming they are fully complying with the requirements of the FCRA as well as applicable state rules. If a screening firm is using online forms, then it is critical to ensure the forms comply with the FCRA. Recall from Chapter 5 on the FCRA that class action lawsuits over forms have become very common.

There are two special issues to consider involving these forms:

1. The disclosures may not have excessive language that detracts from a clear understanding of the form; and
2. Whether a form may request that an applicant waive his rights to sue the employer or CRA.

Per the FTC staff, an applicant cannot be required to waive his rights under the FCRA (See staff letter to Richard Hauxwell, January 12, 1998, at www.ftc.gov/policy/advisory-opinions/advisory-opinion-hauxwell-06-12-98). However, a form may ask that an applicant waives his or her rights to the extent permitted by law. It is not clear that such waiver language gives a screening firm or the employer a great deal of protection against state torts such as defamation or invasion of privacy. Even if there is such a waiver, there is a problem of putting it on the disclosure form. For those reasons, some employers and CRAs will use two separate forms.

- First, the release form that contains the identifying information along with the waiver language, if utilized.
- Second, the disclosure form contains only the required language.

3. Transmitting the Consent and Screening Request to the CRA

The process of transmitting the request to the CRA depends on the workflow between the employer and the CRA as well as any software being used.

You Need To Know

The Technology Used Impacts the Screening Process

The level of technology used by the CRA will guide the process. For example, for many years employers would either mail in or fax a screening request as well as the release documents to the screening firm. As technology developed, screening firm developed online systems where an employer could enter the data themselves plus view online the progress of the screening as well as reports. That has given way to newer systems where an employer causes an email to be sent to an applicant, and the applicant fills out the information online and provides an electronic signature. Even more advanced are systems where the background screening process is built into an Applicant Tracking System (ATS) and a request for the applicant to fill out an online form can be generated by the push of a button. For the Gig economy where a software provider acts as a clearinghouse for on-demand labor, the same logic can be built directly into a website.

Regardless of the technology being used, background screening remains a professional service and not just an automated data vending service. The technology merely enhances the workflow but does not replace professional knowledge, legal compliance and the need for customer service where the employer or consumer has a question or concern. In other words, advanced technology is really just a starting point.

If the employer is faxing an order to a CRA instead of self-entry of the order into the CRA's software, then an **Employee Order Form** is typically sent with each order. The form tells the CRA what is being requested, who requested it, and sending instructions. The CRA can customize the form for each employer so paperwork is minimized. The customized form will reflect the type of screening program the employer requires and the employer's name, contact person, and contact information. To ensure accuracy and to avoid delays, the employer needs to confirm that the applicant's name, Social Security number, driver's license number, and any other data needed to fulfill the order has been provided and is legible. Any information that is incorrect or not clear will cause a delay or result in inaccurate information returned. If a screening firm is given a name that is spelled wrong or a driver's license number or Social Security number is not legible, say, a 3 looks like an 8, the result may be either bad data or data that is delayed. If the applicant has not given the names of past employers or provided the city and state, a delay may ensue. The applicant's telephone number may be requested so the CRA may contact an applicant directly to clarify anything that is not clear on the form, however, having a screening firm contact the applicant is not always a good practice—an applicant may get concerned or confused, especially if the screening firm is calling to obtain the applicant's Social Security number or other confidential data.

If an employer utilizes an online system to enter screening orders, the employer first needs to carefully review the application materials before placing the order online. For any material that is illegible or incomplete, the employer can contact the applicant to clarify. This not only saves time and avoids data errors, but also speeds up the screening process considerably since the screening begins as soon as the employer transmits the order electronically. If the order is faxed to the background firm, the order can be delayed pending the background firm entering the order into its computer system or by having to contact the employer to clear up any uncertainties.

Of course, all of these issues are moot with new technology that allows an applicant to receive an email and to self-enter their own data. Depending on the software, an applicant will be promoted to enter needed information based upon the services the employer is requesting, so that an applicant cannot hit the continue button unless all information has been provided. If a screening firm is only doing a criminal check, the software system should know not to ask about past employment for example.

Even more advanced technology allows employers to initiate a background check seamlessly from their Applicant Tracking System (ATS) with the click of the mouse. That can generate an email to the applicant prompting them to go online, fill out the required forms, and provide a mouse signature. In addition, real-time report status, as well as a link to the final report, can be transmitted back to the employer's ATS so all processes are performed on the ATS site. By the use of a single sign-on, an employer never needs to leave the ATS site to review progress or see the finished background report.

To the extent the employer has already collected past employment or education data from the applicant as part of the process, this data can also be seamlessly passed to the background screening firm. Thus when the applicant goes online to enter their data, some data can be pre-populated.

Even when electronic methods are used, there may still be an occasion when a physical piece of paper must be handled. This occurs when a past employer, school, or DMV requires a written release form from the requestor. The screening company may need to contact the employer to obtain a physical copy of the release form. However, technologically advanced firms can provide an online solution where the applicant not only provides an electronic signature but can use the mouse to create a wet signature that should generally satisfy past employers and schools.

The technology to facilitate such communications and efficiencies between system and employer is made possible with widespread advances and uses of **Application Program Interface or API**. That allows, for example, a screening firm to communicate seamlessly with an **Applicant Tracking System (ATS).** There have also been advances in using a standard suite of software specifications that enables the automation of human resources-related data exchanges between software systems. One such standard is **HR-XML**—the human resources version of a language used to write software that facilitates communication. More firms are now using other forms of web services such as **RESTful JASON API** to facilitate communication between firms and systems.

Author Tip ▷ **Don't be Fooled by Marketing Buzz about "Disruptive" HR Technologies**

Employers and Human Resources (HR) professionals will be bombarded with meaningless marketing buzz offering new HR technology that promises to disrupt stodgy old industries and radically change outdated business models. Unfortunately, these new claims end up being largely without substance.

It's popular for start-ups worldwide to claim they are disrupting stodgy old dormant industries and are radically changing outdated old business models, including Human Resources processes such as pre-employment background checks. However, it is important to really understand if an HR disrupter is really just an outstanding marketer who has convinced investors that they have done something new instead of just taking old processes and repackaging them with a pretty new bow.

In the HR space, there are firms that have done the equivalent of taking a number two pencil and claiming they have re-invented and disrupted a dormant industry by putting the eraser on the other end. Much of this buzz is being generated in the so-called "Gig" or "on-demand" economy. The problem with applying this part-time economy approach in HR technology – especially in the background check process – is that background checks are closer to rocket science in terms of its sheer complexity than simply data retrieval and distribution. Background check laws are constantly subject to legislation, regulation, and litigation.

Although HR processes like background checks may be attractive to the technology sector since it appears on the surface to simply involve slicing and dicing data, in fact, it is all about domain expertise, accuracy, and legal compliance.

There is nothing all that new about this technology but some 'tech' firms claim they are revolutionizing the background check process when they are in fact doing the same thing numerous other firms have done for a number of years. Many firms have long utilized proprietary technology that includes an Application Program Interfaces (API), including a Representation State Transfer (RESTful) API, to connect with partners and employers. In fact, that is relatively old hat in the background screening industry.

You Need To Know

Nature of Employer and Workforce when Screening

The choice of how to obtain an applicant's consent and information and how to transfer the information to the CRA may also depend upon the nature of the employer and the workforce. For example, some employers hire from an applicant pool where applicants may have easy access to computers, laptops, tablets, or smartphones. On the other hand, an employer that is hiring hourly workers may need solutions that do not require that applicants be "wired," meaning an applicant may need to use paper forms, a kiosk, or other innovative approaches.

---

4. Place the necessary language needed in the employment application form

In addition to the forms supplied by a CRA, an employer should also have recommended sections in their own employment application forms. The application, either paper or online, can re-enforce that any lack of truthfulness and honesty in the application process can be grounds to terminate the hiring process or employment *no matter when discovered.* Employers may also place information about the nature of the employment relationship, such as *at will*, and can also set out its anti-discrimination and diversity policies. Due to Ban-the-Box, having questions about a past criminal matter on the initial form is not considered a best practice. States have their own requirement and an employer should consult legal counsel on these issues.

5. Avoid screening some finalists but not others.

Another important consideration in administering a screening program is that once a decision is made to screen for a particular opening, all finalists being considered for that opening should be screened. Selective screenings could raise an inference of discriminatory practice, particularly if the subject is a member of a legally protected group. Furthermore, all individuals who are screened should also be evaluated using the same criteria—for each position, the screening level must be the same for all candidates.

An employer may certainly have different screening requirements for different positions. A maintenance worker does not have to be screened at the same level as a bookkeeper. If there are different screening standards for different positions, an employer should be able to articulate a rational basis as to why some positions are screened differently than others. That typically revolves around the risk associated with the position. However, all maintenance workers should be screened the same way, and all bookkeepers screened the same way. For any particular opening, all candidates must be treated the same.

6. Determine what job positions should be screened and what data should be requested

The level of pre-employment screening a firm should utilize is normally determined by the extent of the risk involved if a firm makes a bad hire. There are two primary reasons a company would perform pre-employment screening:

- To exercise due diligence in the hiring process, primarily for the protection of co-workers, innocent third parties, and the public; and
- To protect the company from the legal and financial harm stemming from a bad hire.

Decision Based Upon Due Diligence Considerations

The law requires an employer exercise reasonable care when selecting new employees. Unless a firm is regulated by a state or federal law or by accepted industry standards, there is generally no single accepted industry standard as to what level of care is required in pre-employment screening. Whether a firm meets a standard of reasonableness would, under judgment, likely be determined based upon the totality of all the circumstances and the testimony of expert witnesses.

For employers that do not have a minimum statutory obligation, the depth of screening to some extent is a moving target. Of course, an employer can wait to get sued and then a jury will tell them if they exercised sufficient due diligence or not, but that is not likely to be considered a rational approach. Nor can an employer simply look at what other firms are doing, and just copy them. There is a difference between an industry practice and exercising a standard of care. More about negligent hiring is in the Addendum for Chapter 1.

Given the relatively modest cost of pre-employment screening compared to the harm that can be caused by a bad hire, it is likely that a jury would hold an employer to a high standard if some harm occurred. It would be difficult to defend a company against a charge of negligent hiring when the victim's attorney can argue that if the company had spent just another $20.00 on screening, some terrible crime would not have occurred, or a problem or loss could have been avoided.

Decision Based Upon Protecting the Company

Any company needs to protect its own economic and legal interests, and companies with shareholders, in fact, have a duty to take reasonable steps to protect assets.

Employers should consider various levels of background screening that increase in depth as the risk for a bad hire also increases. Certainly, an employer is not held to the standard of an FBI level check for each hire. However, given the relatively modest cost of screening compared to the protection afforded, a firm should probably error on the side of more screening than less.

One approach that will be discussed in more detail in the chapter on criminal records and discrimination is to look at whether any criteria is either job related or if the criteria is related to a business necessity, which generally means a review of risk factors. An employer, of course, cannot consider factors that are discriminatory and prohibited by law (See Chapter 2).

Employers can consider the following factors among others:

1. What are the essential functions and duties of the job?
2. Does the position have access to money or assets?
3. Does the position carry significant authority or fiduciary responsibility?
4. Does the position have access to members of the public or co-workers so that any propensity to violence would cause harm?
5. Does the position require the worker to go into someone's home?
6. Does the person work with a vulnerable group such as children, elderly, infirmed or people with disabilities?
7. Would the position be difficult to replace in terms of recruitment, hiring, and training?

8. Would a falsification of skills, experience, or background put the firm at risk or lower the firm's productivity?

9. Would a bad hire expose the firm to litigation or financial claims from the applicant, co-workers, customers, or the public?

10. What degree of supervision is the worker under?

11. Is the person full-time, part-time, seasonal, temporary, or a volunteer?

Using the above factors, an employer can create a risk matrix for each position. The employer needs to consider the risk inherent in the position and the amount of supervision the position needs.

7. The point when the applicant signs the forms

How and when the consent and disclosure forms are signed depends again on the Technogym being used by the employer and CRA.

If an employer is still using paper forms, there are two approaches employers can take.

1. An employer can have all applicants sign paper screening forms as part of the initial application process. There are some advantages to that approach. By having background forms in the standard application packet, it discourages applicants with something to hide. Some employers find it much easier to administer the screening program if the candidate's necessary forms have already been signed.

2. The alternative approach is to have the finalist only sign the consent forms. Some firms wait until an offer has been made first, although there is not a requirement that here be a formal job offer first. Firms use this approach if they feel a background screening may interfere with effective recruiting, although in this day and age, most job applicants understand that pre-employment screening is a standard business practice and is not a reflection upon them personally. This approach requires the HR, Security Department, or the hiring manager give the finalist the forms at a second interview. Of course, this can present administrative difficulties. Even if forms are not filled out as part of the initial application, it is suggested the applicants still be informed there will be a pre-employment background screening as a standard part of the hiring process.

Technology provides an option by allowing the applicant to fill out the forms at the point in the process where an employer believes a background screening would be appropriate. That happens where an employer initiates a background screening with a finalist through the software being used. That way, an employer is not requesting or collecting a date of birth or Social Security number prematurely.

The use of technology can also allow employers to comply with individual state laws. For example, in 2009, Utah passed The Employment Selection Procedures Act. The law prohibits an employer with more than 15 employees from collecting an applicant's social security number, date of birth or driver's license number before a job offer or before the time when a background check is requested. The idea appears to be to limit the flow of personal data before or unless it is needed and to destroy it if no longer needed. For employers using paper applications, it creates an administrative burden since the employer needs to add another step to get the data required for a background check if an applicant moves forward in the hiring process. However, electronic hiring procedures, such as the Applicant Generated Report (AGR) system solves this issue since an applicant is only asked to provide confidential data only if the employer decides to perform a background check and the information only goes to the screening firm. See: http://le.utah.gov/~2009S1/bills/hbillenr/hb1002.htm.

Author Tip ▷ **Do We Need to Wait for a Contingent Job Offer First?**

Some employers are concerned about asking for a consent to the background check before a formal continent job offer is made. This has become more of an issue with the increase in jurisdictions that have enacted ban-the-box laws where questions about a criminal record must be delayed.

The most conservative approach is to wait until there has been a conditional job offer. That offers employers the most protection. However, as a practical matter, many employers feel that a formal offer letter is not needed and is not a condition precedent to requesting a consent to a background screening. Obviously, an employer will only spend time and money checking a candidate of serious interest. Employers utilize different processes and procedures in their hiring, and for some employers, going through a formalized offer letter before the background check is not practical. Sometimes during the hiring process, the employer may want the background check report completed before making the formal offer in case a matter comes up that would result in the employer not wanting to hire the candidate. In addition, an employer may be evaluating more than one finalist. It is difficult to envision how a candidate is harmed if the employer has not yet formally issued an offer letter. Unless an employer is subject to a particular state or local law, an employer generally has no requirement to extend an official offer letter first. With the use of electronic systems, some of these concerns are handled by the fact that an employer can wait until the offer stage to initiate a check electronically. For employers that rely upon a paper process, waiting until the offer stage to get a signed consent adds another step to the process. Employers that have a concern with this issue should, of course, consult their attorney

8. The Decision of which applicants should be screened and when?

Because of time and expenses involved, firms do not typically request screening on the entire applicant pool. Employers typically utilize pre-employment screening toward the end of the selection process—after the field has been narrowed down. After all, employment screening is designed generally help an employer decide who NOT to hire. Screening normally occurs after a company has decided that an applicant is a good prospect and wants to verify their hiring assessment is correct.

There are two directions that firms typically take. The more common approach is to have a CRA perform its screening function on a finalist or after a conditional job offer has been tendered. The purpose of pre-screening at that point is to demonstrate due diligence and to eliminate uncertainties about an applicant.

Alternatively, a firm will ask a CRA to screen the two or three finalists, then use the results in the selection process. The advantage is that a firm can make a selection with more facts. The disadvantages are:

- Multiple screens cost more; and
- Adds two to four days to the selection process.

Some employers use a system referred to as **progressive screening**, where the employer may ask the screening firm to run a preliminary screen that may utilize a Social Security trace. (Note: The same term is sometimes applied to the process of employers reviewing and narrowing down a batch of applications. However, in this context it refers to the use of incremental screening tools).

If the preliminary screening is satisfactory, the employer may request a more detail check. The problem with progressive screening is that any cost savings in eliminating an applicant early before doing a full background check may be lost due to the increased administrative time and cost of monitoring such a process plus potential delays involved with the employer having to review the initial screen and then order additional research. Even if requested to review the preliminary results, a screening firm can only apply the employer's criteria, and cannot make judgments on the employer's behalf. If a screening firm or employer eliminates a candidate with an automated scoring or adjudication process then this can run contrary to the EEOC rules concerning individualized consideration. For these reasons, an employer may find it more efficient and cost-effective to avoid progressive screening on the basis that whatever cost saving can occur on occasion are offset by the greater cost and risk involved in a progressive screening program.

Using pre-employment reports to choose among finalists can also arguably impact EEOC considerations when EEOC-sensitive reports such as criminal history or credit reports are used. An argument can be made that **the initial selection should be based upon the applicant's job qualifications and job fit only**; a pre-employment report is used only to eliminate an applicant with a **job-related criminal history, falsified credentials, or if negative history** is uncovered.

Author Tip ▷ **Employment Screening and ADA**

Under a federal case from the Ninth Circuit, the timing of the background screening may also impact **Americans with Disabilities Act (ADA)**. If a background report is necessary before a person becomes a finalist, then a firm may need to complete the background check before obtaining medical information or performing pre-employment physicals. The idea is that medical information should only be requested after there has been a real job offer, which means all relevant non-medical information has been evaluated. This enables an applicant to determine if there was a medical basis to a rejection, and to maintain medical privacy until later in the hiring process. See *Leonel v. American Airlines*, 400 F.3d 702 (9th Cir. 2005). Read about the ADA in Chapter 2.

In addition, if any part of the selection process involves consideration of the pre-employment background report, then the adverse action rules apply. This means the applicant has the right to receive a copy of the report and the FCRA-compliant statement of his or her rights. Even if the information relied upon was not negative, the rejected applicant still has rights under the FCRA.

For these reasons, pre-employment screening reports are most often utilized at the very end of the selection procedure, after the company has selected a finalist.

Setting the Different Background Screening Levels

The following are some suggested background screening levels for job candidates:

Sample Screening Level	Sample Recommended Searches
Basic Screening: For entry-level employees, retail, or manufacturing positions, or positions where the employer has internally checked references. Basic Screening is the very least background screening an employer should conduct to maintain due diligence.	A full seven-year onsite criminal records check for felonies and misdemeanors, credit report or Social Security and identity check, and driver's license check. The number of counties searched depends upon the risk factors listed above. For maximum protection, an employer may consider doing ALL counties where a person lived, worked, or studied.
Standard Screening: For more responsible positions and permanent hires.	The Basic Screening plus verification of the last three employers and references (if available), and highest post high school education
Extended Screening: For positions involving increased responsibility or supervision of others.	The Basic and Standard Screenings plus checking superior court civil cases for litigation matters that may be job related.
The Integrity Check: For any type of position involving significant responsibility, access to cash or assets, or	Includes everything previously mentioned plus searches of federal court for criminal and civil cases, employment history verifications, college degrees and professional

access to sensitive data or a company's proprietary materials. Especially good for C-Level positions such as CEO & CFO.	licenses checks, and for superior court civil lawsuits in the last two counties of residence.

Author Tip > ### Packages and a la Carte

Many screening firms will bundle a number of services into a package, and provide a package price. Many employers will have two or three packages that are related to the risk factors discussed above. However, employers need to be careful when analyzing "package pricing." Some firms may offer a seven-year criminal search but limit the number of counties. Most packages do not include third-party fees that are charged by courts, schools or some employment services such as "The Work Number For Everyone." Some firms may markup the third party fees and others do not. It can be tricky to compare package pricing between vendors and as the old saying goes, "the devil is in the details." Comparing packages between vendors is often like comparing apples and oranges because of all the possible variations.

In addition, some vendors may offer an "a la carte" menu of services where employers can select their services, or do a combination of packages and a la carte if they want to go deeper. The obvious problem? Consistency between applicants. The use of packages allows employers to ensure they are treating all applicants in the same general category in a similar fashion based upon the position and risk involved.

---

9. When conditional hiring is based upon receipt of the background check report

An employer can make an offer of employment or begin the employment relationship contingent upon the receipt of an acceptable background report. This may occur when an employer has a difficult position to fill and does not want to chance losing a good candidate. It is recommended that the offer letter contains the following language:

> "This offer of employment is conditioned upon the employer's receipt of a pre-employment background screening investigation **that is acceptable to the employer at the employer's sole discretion**."

The suggested language specifies that the report must meet the employer's satisfaction so there can be no debate on what constitutes a satisfactory report.

10. How long should the employer expect a report to take?

A 72 hour turnaround time for a background report is a general industry standard. It is sometimes expressed as three working days, but that does not take into account the fact that the day the report is received is often not counted, depending upon the information needed, time zones where the information is located, and the time of the day the request is submitted. For example, if a West Coast employer submits a request on a Monday at 4:00 pm P.S.T., and it includes a request for information from courts, schools, or employers on the East Coast, it is already 7:00 on the East Coast. That means that courts, schools, and business are closed. That is why it is more accurate to express completion in terms of hours.

In addition, turnaround time can also depend upon the screening firm's technology. Advanced technology allows a screening firm to automatically fill some request, such as driving records or Social Security trace reports. Even those requests that need manual fulfillment, a sophisticated system immediately puts the request in a queue with no time being lost for data processing.

There can be delays beyond the 72 hours in situations where a CRA has no control. For example, it can take longer than three days if there is a potential name match in a criminal case and the court clerk must obtain records from storage. In addition, schools may be closed during summer or holidays, or employers may not call back or may have merged, moved, or closed. If a form is unreadable, that can delay a report. Some reports take longer than three days as a matter of course, such as international background checks. Sources of potential delay are discussed in the following chapters on criminal record, employment, education and international background checks. However, most firms will have the ability to inform employers about potential delays and the estimated time for completion.

Employers should also understand that the turnaround time for the entire report is only as fast as the slowest order to complete. For example, an employer may order ten searches and nine of them can be done quickly. However, if there is a delay for the tenth search for reasons that are out of the background screening firm's control, then the entire report can be delayed. Any search involving an international request will probably be subject to delays as well.

11. How are reports received by the employer?

Screening firms using state-of-the-art software systems can make reports available to their clients in real time over the Internet with appropriate security. Also, Internet retrieval allows employers to have real-time access to the exact status of the report at any time in order to monitor progress or answer questions from hiring managers. If a criminal search is delayed, an online system can advise the employer about the delay and the estimated time to obtain the information. For a screening firm using older technology, reports can also be faxed or emailed to the employer. A CRA will generally require the fax machine be private and secured. A faxed report should have a cover sheet to warn the unauthorized against seeing confidential information.

 Copies of Background Check Reports in CA, OK & MN

When a California, Oklahoma, or Minnesota applicant requests to receive a copy of his or her credit report, the CRA must provide a copy to the applicant at the same time the employer receives the report.

---

12. What should an employer do with the completed report and who sees it.

Because the report contains sensitive and confidential information, all efforts must be made to keep the contents private and only available to decision-makers directly involved in the hiring process. The screening report itself, along with the Release and Authorization forms signed by the applicant, should be maintained separately from the employee's personnel file. They should be kept in a relatively secured area, in the same fashion that medical files or sensitive employee matters are kept. These reports should not be made available to supervisors or managers other than those in the hiring approval process. For example, during periodic performance appraisals, an employer would not want a supervisor to have access to a non-performance-related confidential background report.

For screening firms with advanced software systems, there is, in fact, no need to physically download the report since it is available online. The screening firm should be instructed to keep the report in case it may be needed later. However, an employer needs to be assured of Internet security, and the employer needs to maintain a system of strong password protections. It is important that authorized users do not share passwords with those not authorized, nor reveal the password in any manner. Some screening firms require the user to change passwords every thirty days as a security measure.

Typically, reports are returned to either the Human Resource or Security Department. Reports are reviewed for any negative information. If the report is clear, then the hiring manager is notified and the hiring proceeds. If there is a red flag or derogatory information, then the information itself is shared with the appropriate decision-makers. The physical report, however, normally stays with HR or Security. This protects against confidential information wrongfully being made known generally within the company.

13. How the employer reviews, analyzes, and utilizes the report information.

How such information is utilized of course is the crux of the issue for employers. Later chapters outline the specific types of information employers see on the background screening reports and specific issues are discussed. The basic rule is that employers should only be collecting and viewing non-discriminatory information that is job related and a valid predictor of job performance. However, there are several areas of concern that employers should always consider:

- **Honesty:** If the background check reveals dishonesty on the part of the applicant that is a matter the employer must consider. A lack of honesty is normally a bar to employment. If an applicant is dishonest in the manner they obtain a job, there is a strong likelihood they will demonstrate dishonesty once in the job.

  Dishonesty can either be a material lie or a material omission where the applicant deceived an employer by intentionally omitting material information. A falsehood or material omission is not necessarily a failure to admit matters that are potentially adverse on their face, such as a criminal matter. Many employers find it equally troublesome if an applicant lies about the date of employment, or gives false dates in such a way to hide a significant past employer out of concern that the past employer may respond negatively to a reference call.

  When analyzing dishonesty, the two important issues that surface are materiality and willfulness.

  o **Materiality** means that the lie or omission was about something relevant and important, as opposed to a minor manner where an applicant may have simply glossed over something that did not seem relevant, such as a temporary job years ago.

  o **Willfulness** means that the applicant was not confused or, misinformed or forgetful, but made a conscious decision to mislead the employer. For example, an applicant may check a box on an employment application to indicate he has NO criminal record, and it is discovered that the applicant has a failure to appear in court to handle a traffic ticket. Or, an applicant fails to report a misdemeanor conviction and when confronted informs HR that the lawyer told her that the matter was all taken care of and she no does need to admit to anyone. At that point, the employer needs to determine whether there was an intentional act of dishonesty or the applicant may have assumed that the employer was not interested in traffic matters or the applicant did not, in fact, know there was a warrant for his arrest. A related issue is whether the application form was clear or was the question murky and confusing. Unfortunately, there is no surefire test for an employer or human resources professional to ascertain if an applicant was willfully dishonest. It depends upon the totality of the circumstances and how the decision maker accesses the creditability of the applicant.

- **Lack of Credentials:** The background report may show the applicant did not possess the job prerequisites and therefore does not qualify for the position (which may also potentially act of dishonestly).
- **Disbarment or Disqualification:** A background checks may show that an applicant is on disbarment or sanctions list that eliminates them from consideration.
- **Past Conduct Inconsistent with Business Needs:** It is often observed that past conduct is the most reliable indication of future conduct, and that it is unlikely that an applicant will perform better for you than they did in the past. Of course, that is a gross generalization and certainly is not true for everyone. Job applicants should not be forever saddled with their past or an assumption that people do not change. For example, an applicant may not have performed well in the past, but it could have been due to being a member of a dysfunctional team, led by a micromanager, where the team had no clear goals, agenda or resources.
- **Inability to perform the essential functions of the job:** An employer may find information showing the person is not qualified or cannot do the job.
- **Other Risk:** An employer may find information that there are other risks, such as past conduct that would create an unsafe working environment.

14. When a CRA finds information that an employer is not supposed to have.

Competent CRAs should carefully monitor their reports to ensure that no information is given to an employer that violates the various rules concerning limitations on what employers can and cannot use in making employment decisions. However, this is a tricky area. A CRA is not acting as an attorney and cannot make legal decisions. On the other hand, there are clear industry accepted practices about what an employer can and cannot have. Firms with expertise and technology can build into software a great deal of intelligence in order to have the information needed to analyze a criminal record, for example, to determine if its reportable under generally accepted industry standards.

Some CRA's take the position they are primarily data conduits to the employer, and it is the employer's obligation to not utilize any information an employer should not have. An employer should carefully consider this issue in selecting a service provider.

An employer may not be clear how their screening firm operates on this issue and not realize if a screening firm does not do any filtering. The employer should clarify how their screening firm operates in order to avoid using information an employer is not supposed to possess.

15. How long forms signed by applicants and applicant records should be kept

Record keeping requirements for employers can vary in accordance with the type of document in question. However, it is generally advisable for an employer to maintain all paperwork concerning the formation of the employment relationship for a period of at least three years from the termination of any relationship. That means if a person is hired, the report and all related screening documentation should be kept during the entire employment relationship and for three years after termination. If an applicant is screened and an employment relationship does not occur, then the reports and documents should be maintained for three years from the date of the report. The three-year period should cover any statute of limitations in the event of a claim or lawsuit as well as a period of time a state may allow to serve the legal action.

However, the 2003 FCRA amendment changed the applicable statute of limitations for claims under the FCRA to up to five years for **records concerning pre-employment screening by a CRA**. An employer and consumer reporting agency should maintain records concerning pre-employment screening by a CRA for at least six years following a screening, based on the five-year statute, and an extra year to reflect the amount of time states generally allow to serve a lawsuit. Employers utilizing a CRA with an advanced Internet system may have the ability to archive the reports indefinitely.

There are two reasons why an employer should also maintain the background screening authorization forms and disclosure forms as well as any other forms related to ordering a screening report for the same period of time.

1. First, they may be needed to prove that the employer had consent for a screening report and a permissible purpose under the FCRA.

2. Second, if a screening firm is audited by a data provider (such as a state motor vehicle department), the applicant's consent may be needed by both the background firm and the employer to demonstrate that the request for information was legal.

If a background firm is still accepting faxes or having the employer do data entry, there should be a requirement that employers that all applications and FCRA releases will be maintained by the employer and provided to the CRA if necessary for an audit.

One issue is that the domestic U.S. practice can potentially be in conflict with privacy and data protection approaches used by other countries. A common privacy standard is for a party that possesses Personal and Identifiable Information (PII) should destroy it when no longer needed. Whether this apparent conflict is important is an issue that privacy professionals and screeners should be following.

16. What the employer does if a decision is made not to hire an applicant

If an employer decides to take any type of adverse action regarding an application for employment, based in any way upon information contained in a screening report, the provisions of the FCRA come into play. At that point, it is the employer's responsibility to first provide the applicant with a copy of the report and a statement of the consumer's rights. If the applicant does not contest the report or does contest it and the decision stands, then the employer must send a second notice to the applicant under Section 615 of the FCRA notifying the applicant of a number of specific rights. This is set forth in more detail in Chapter 5 on the FCRA.

Under the federal FCRA, an employer does NOT need to specify exactly why an applicant was rejected. The procedures set forth in the FCRA only require the applicant have an opportunity to review the background report prior to an adverse action being taken and be given a statement of his or her rights.

> **You Need To Know** > **Some States DO Require an Employer to Give More Information about an Adverse Action**
>
> Be aware that although the federal FCRA does not require the employer to specify the part of the report that led to an adverse action, a number of states do have some sort of requirement about more specific employer disclosures.

Some CRAs will provide all the necessary notices to the applicant. Under the rules of the FCRA, although it is the employer's responsibility to provide the pre-adverse and post-adverse action notices, that duty can be delegated to an agent such as a screening firm. If the applicant disagrees with any of the information contained in the report, then the applicant communicates directly to the CRA. The CRA has a duty under the FCRA to re-investigate within 30 days—up to 45 days under certain circumstances. The employer, however, has no obligation to keep the position open during the re-investigation period.

In addition, under the 2012 EEOC Guidance on criminal records, employers should also consider conducting an Individualized Assessment.

> **Extension of 30-Day Period to Reinvestigate Disputed Information**
>
> *From 15 USC § 1681i - Procedure in case of disputed accuracy*
>
> **(a) Reinvestigations of disputed information**
>
> **(1) Reinvestigation required**
>
> **(A) In general**
>
> Subject to subsection (f) of this section, if the completeness or accuracy of any item of information contained in a consumer's file at a consumer reporting agency is disputed by the consumer and the consumer notifies the agency directly, or indirectly through a reseller, of such dispute, the agency shall, free of charge, conduct a reasonable reinvestigation to determine whether the disputed information is inaccurate and record the current status of the disputed information, or delete the item from the file in accordance with paragraph (5), before the end of the 30-day period beginning on the date on which the agency receives the notice of the dispute from the consumer or reseller.
>
> **(B) Extension of period to reinvestigate**
>
> Except as provided in subparagraph (C), the 30-day period described in subparagraph (A) may be extended for not more than 15 additional days if the consumer reporting agency receives information from the consumer during that 30-day period that is relevant to the reinvestigation.
>
> **(C) Limitations on extension of period to reinvestigate**

> Subparagraph (B) shall not apply to any reinvestigation in which, during the 30-day period described in subparagraph (A), the information that is the subject of the reinvestigation is found to be inaccurate or incomplete or the consumer reporting agency determines that the information cannot be verified.

17. Steps if an employer rejects an applicant as a result of a screening report.

When an employer follows the procedures in the FCRA, and also makes all hiring decisions utilizing legal and job related reasons, the chances of a lawsuit from a rejected applicant are minimized. However, no employer can ever make itself immune from a lawsuit. Anyone with enough money to cover the court's filing fee can go to the court and file a lawsuit. The real issue is whether the benefits from a pre-employment screening program outweigh the risks.

If an employer intends to take adverse action based upon a background report, an applicant must first be provided with a copy of the report and a statement of his or her rights. Because of this procedure, an applicant will have the chance to correct anything in a report that is incorrect or inaccurate. If the information is inaccurate, the applicant will have the opportunity to object and to offer a correction. At that point, the employer can proceed with the hire. Under the previous system where applicants did not have to be told their reports contained negative or derogatory information, employers ran a greater risk of making hiring decisions based upon incorrect information.

18. Conduct pre-employment screening without interfering with recruitment or employee morale

In performing pre-employment screening, it is important not to damage the bond of trust an employer seeks to develop with potential and current employees. The employer does not want to make bad hiring decisions, but also cannot afford to use a process that alienates its applicants or interferes with recruiting or a positive onboarding experience. Furthermore, obnoxious background procedures can discourage good applicants. In other words, an employer does not want to diminish their employer branding in a way to hamper recruiting top talent or by making the employer a seemingly less desirable place to work. Some background investigators start with the proposition that all applicants are potential criminals until they prove otherwise—applicants may not want to work for a firm that treats them that way.

The solution is to make it clear to applicants that pre-employment screening is a sound business practice benefiting not only the company but all employees as well. No one wants to work with an unqualified person who obtained the job under false pretext or with a co-worker with an undisclosed criminal record. Once an applicant understands the process is not a reflection on him or her but is actually for their benefit as well, they will understand this is a good thing for a company to do.

Furthermore, the applicant should be assured all procedures used will respect his or her rights to privacy, all information is kept strictly confidential and is used only for employment purposes, and all legal rights are respected. Furthermore, the scope of the investigation should be clearly job-related. Finally, the screening process itself must be easy and intuitive, especially for firms that are recruiting Millennials who are used to doing everything online. Ideally, the screening process should be able to be performed on mobile devices such as phones or tablets. More information about the employment screening process and employer branding is discussed in Chapter 20.

How Pre-Employment Screening Companies Perform Their Tasks

Although there is no standard industry terminology, two separate terms can be used—PROFILE and ORDER. The term PROFILE in this section refers to all information about an applicant. The term ORDER means a particular search, such as a search in Santa Clara County, California, for a criminal record, or contacting the University of Kansas to verify a former student's past education. *One profile may contain a number of orders.* Other screening firms may use different terminology but the concept is the same.

When assembling and evaluating data on applicants, background firms fundamentally perform tasks in five areas. How it is accomplished of course depends upon the business processes and technology that a firm uses. Nothing happens of course until the CRA first receives the request from the employer in one of the forms discussed above in the section on Transmitting the Screening Request to the CRA.

> ### You Need To Know > ### Vetting an Employer Before Providing Reports
>
> As previously mentioned in Chapter 5 on the FCRA, a background firm has an obligation to vet a new employer before providing background checks. This requirement is to ensure that the employer is a legitimate business and is using the information for employment purposes.
>
> A background firm may take steps such as checking with a Secretary of State office to ensure the employer is a legal entity, verifying a website, using Google maps to confirm a postal address, or verifying the phone number belongs to the company among other measures. If a sole practitioner is requesting a background report, a background screening firm will still need identifying information. Where an employer is requesting credit report, credit bureaus rules require a screening firm go even further and vetting must include a physical onsite inspection of the business premises.

1. Engage in Various Workflows to Fulfill the Requests

Once a request for a screening is put into progress, each order must be routed to the proper source in order to obtain the information. For firms with a software system, the orders are normally routed automatically to the proper source. For background firms without a software system, some delays can occur.

The following is a brief description of some of the workflows involved:

- **Criminal records from local or state courts**

  When a screening firm receives an order for a criminal search, the order is normally transmitted to the researcher who specializes in that specific court. Available to background firms is an entire industry—a virtual subculture—of court researchers covering every court in America, typically providing a turnaround time within 48 hours for record search requests. In most cases, court researchers work for multiple background firms. Again, employers may find that their report requests are subject to delay if they use screening firms that do not utilize web-enabling software.

  As spelled out in more detail in Chapter 9 on obtaining criminal records, many firms have developed screen scraping and automated searches that allow them to search court criminal records by computer without the need for a live person. However, there are a number of ways such an approach can lead to records either being missed, reported inaccurately or reported when they should not be reported at all.

  As mentioned previously, background firms must sometimes deal with county or state court officials who do not understand background checks and try to impede the efforts of a screening firm to get information on the misguided premise they are "protecting an applicant." Nothing can be further from the truth.

  Another important issue is determining who is in charge of reporting criminal hits to employers. Employers need to be certain that any criminal hit is reviewed by a knowledgeable member of the screening firm's staff. The complicated legal and factual determinations of what is and is not reportable should not be made by court researchers who are from all walks of life, including PIs, genealogists, and abstractors who have gone into the public record retrieval business. They are typically not lawyers, paralegals, or HR professionals. Their expertise is in looking for names and understanding court record indices. They are generally not experienced in the immensely complicated and highly regulated legal ramifications to the end users.

- **Driving records, credit reports, and Social Security number (SSN) trace reports**

  For the most part, background firms use online access to obtain these reports in a matter of moments and can quickly pass results electronically to their clients by using a seamless business to business interface.

  Although there are a few states where driving records cannot be obtained instantly, the majority of states do have instant access. Credit reports, if ordered online, offer immediate results. (However, see Chapter 11 for detailed discussions on the challenges involved in obtaining and using credit reports). A Social Security trace can be immediate also, although it may entail additional time and workflow if an employer is using the trace to determine where to search for criminal records. Some background screening firm's offer enhanced software features that will automatically place orders for these specialty reports.

- **Credentials verification – employment, education, and licenses**

  When an employer requests a Credentials Verification, the background firm must typically route the request to the specific company employee, department, or vendor handling these requests. These searches are subject to delays out of the control of a screening firm, such as schools that are closed for vacation or holidays, or employers that will not call back, or have moved, merged, or gone bankrupt. These are disused in more details in the chapters on employment and education verification. Again, a firm with software systems is in a better position to track and manage the process. Firms without software systems must manually handle papers and files which can take longer.

2. Track the Status of All Orders and Manage Handling Delays

While the orders are being processed in various workflows, a screening firm must be able to track in real time the status of each order and keep the employer informed. Background firms with online systems give employers an advantage—the employer goes online to see the exact progress of each order and the likely time of completion. If there is a delay, then the employer is told exactly what is causing the delay.

Background screening firms not using an online system to manage the workflow generally use a paper-based system where all work is monitored manually. A physical file is maintained for each applicant. The screening firm must wait to receive back information on each order and then enter the results into a written report to present to the employer. Each manual step adds time to the overall process and increases the possibility of clerical errors. The use of technology allows a screening firm to track all progress electronically, saving valuable time in the process.

It is important to understand that, for certain searches, there may be delays beyond the control of anyone. Hiring famous detective Sam Spade would not get results any sooner. Sources of delays can be:

- Where courthouses require that the researcher gives the county clerk a list of names to search and the county clerk, in turn, gives the researcher an estimated turnaround time. When there is a possible "hit," then the clerk needs to pull the file. No one has control over how long a court clerk takes to provide information. Court delays can be caused by the courthouse being closed for a holiday.
- The date of birth is required to obtain or verify some information and has not been provided.
- On employment verifications, an employer may not return calls despite repeated attempts, or a past employer cannot be located, has no records, has moved, or is no longer in business. After three attempts it is unlikely an employer will respond.
- On education verification, school record checks can be delayed where the school is closed or on break, verification can only be done by mail, or advanced fee prepayment is required.

The critical issue for employers is they need real-time updates and status reports on any source of delays. They need to know the report is being worked on and when the information is expected back.

3. Assemble Orders into an Applicant Profile

From the screening firm's point of view, each aspect of the order must be monitored and usually completed within 72 hours. From the point of view of the employer, individual orders are not as relevant as obtaining the entire profile as soon as possible so a hiring decision can be made.

The profiling function requires a screening firm to reassemble each order into a comprehensive report. Firms with more advanced software are able to assemble each of the components into a report automatically and quickly. If assembling reports becomes a manual process, then expect some lag time.

4. Provide the Profile Report to the Employer

How fast and how efficiently the employer receives the entire applicant profile is what separates the good screening companies from the not so good. Firms with sophisticated software programs that automatically send updates and final reports may provide a time advantage, but the real issue of concern to employers is—does the screening firm review what is being sent or does the screener's software merely send raw data automatically to the employer? Firms that tend to be essentially data vendors simply dispense completed reports without review or "flags" that point out potential areas of concern.

5. Handling Data Exceptions

Background screening is often referred to as an *exceptions business* meaning that if everything comes back on time with no problem, it is a procedure that occurs seamlessly in the background. A large number of consumer reports come back *clear*. *Clear* in this context means there is no potentially derogatory, negative, or contradictory information located, and no criminal records located. It is when a report is delayed or there is an issue (i.e. something contradictory or negative) that an employer may become concerned.

When there is a *hit*, the employer may need assistance. A *hit* means the screening firm has located information potentially derogatory or adverse. This information may be derogatory on its face alone, such as a criminal record. There can be other instances when information only becomes derogatory when it is compared to other data. For example, if the screening firm reports the applicant was employed for a two-year period, this information alone is not derogatory. If the applicant falsely claims he or she was at the job for four years, then the report data could be adverse. The employer may need guidance on how to follow the FCRA or how to handle the situation. Although a screening firm cannot give legal advice, a screening firm should be able to give generally industry accepted advice on how to approach issues.

It is important for an employer to clearly understand how their screening firm operates regarding data exceptions. First, an employer needs to be certain screening firm offers customer service and expert assistance to guide them through any exception. Secondly, an employer needs to be concerned with whether their screening firm operates as a data vendor or a professional service. Some firms operate solely on the data vendor approach, giving employers whatever information they find without regard to the limitations of federal and state laws, or without making any attempt at flagging potential discrepancies or providing any assistance regarding the use of the information. Other firms, though, follow a service model that has a policy of not providing employers with information they cannot legally possess.

Even though a screening firm cannot give legal advice, an employer may at least expect general industry guidance and some advice on the issues to consider. If the employer decides not to hire the applicant, then the employer may need assistance with the adverse action procedures.

Does a Background Screening Firm Need a SOC 2® Type 2 Report?

Independent auditors may conduct a Service Organization Control (SOC) 2® examination of a background screening company's operations for a six-month testing period and issued a SOC 2® Type 2 report stating that management has maintained effective controls over the security, confidentiality, and privacy of its employee screening system and related data.

This annual, comprehensive, and independent examination ensures that a company meets the current high standards set by the American Institute of Certified Public Accountants (AICPA) to protect customer and third-party information. NDB Accountants & Consultants LLP (NDB), a nationally recognized CPA firm specializing in regulatory compliance and consulting services, performs the examination and issues the report.

Having a SOC 2® Type 2 report to review is becoming increasingly important to a background screening company's existing and potential customers seeking assurance about the effectiveness of controls related to the security, confidentiality, and privacy of the systems and information used by the firm to process the background check orders of customers. Financial institutions require it, and publicly traded as well as larger private companies are frequently asking for a SOC 2® report before selecting an outsourced service organization for screening.

The SOC 2® Type 2 examination of controls at a background screening firm is conducted using stringent criteria established by the AICPA. These internationally recognized standards address technological advances and associated risks including cloud services not covered in the now retired SAS 70 standards. The following principles and related criteria used in ESR's SOC 2® examination were developed by the AICPA and the Canadian Institute of Chartered Accountants (CICA) for use by practitioners in the performance of trust services engagements:

- Security: The system is protected against unauthorized access (both physical and logical).
- Confidentiality: Information designated as confidential is protected as committed or agreed.
- Privacy: Personal information is collected, used, retained, disclosed, and destroyed in conformity with the commitments in the entity's privacy notice and with criteria set forth in Generally Accepted Privacy Principles (GAPP) issued by the AICPA and CICA.

For more information about SOC 2 reports, visit the American Institute of Certified Public Accountants (AICPA) website at www.aicpa.org/InterestAreas/FRC/AssuranceAdvisoryServices/Pages/ServiceOrganization%27sManagement.aspx.

Introduction to the Background Screening Industry

With the advances in technology spurring widespread data availability, the pre-employment background screening industry has grown substantially in the past 30 years. The size of the employment background screening industry is currently estimated to be anywhere between two to five billion dollars.

Although there is no exact count of the number of firms that provide employment screening services, industry observers estimate there are literally thousands of firms involved in some level of background screening. Firms range from large, publicly held companies to retired police officers and other one-person services. Using an Internet search engine to look up the keyword "employment screening" or "background checks" will take an employer to literally thousands of web pages. Of course, many firms are in adjacent industries, such as security, human resources, drug or psychological testing, or payroll, and offer screening as a secondary service.

You need to know:

There are Different Types of CRAs

As mentioned, a background screening firm is considered to be a CRA – Consumer Reporting Agency. However, there are different types of CRAs.

First, a traditional **background screening firm** is typically NOT a data broker (although it is possible a firm may do both). A professional background screening firm will typically acquire data for a one-time use only, and does not maintain a database of consumer data that is used again in the future.

A **data broker**, on the other hand, aggregates large amounts of data on Americans for resale and other use. There are numerous websites where consumers are told they can do a background check on anyone, many of which do not even mention the FCRA rule, or if it is mentioned, is buried in the fine print. Data brokers are sometimes erroneously lumped in with professional screening firms in discussions about the background screening industry. In fact, the FTC has proposed in March of 2012 that the practices of data brokers be regulated. See: www.ftc.gov/os/2012/03/120326privacyreport.pdf.

Another type of CRA can be a **Nationwide Specialty Consumer Reporting Agency (NSCRA)**. FCRA Section 603(w) defines the term NSCRA as a:

"...consumer reporting agency that compiles and maintains files on consumers on a nationwide basis relating to:

- Medical records or payments;
- Residential or tenant history;
- Check writing history;
- Employment history; or
- Insurance claims."

A CRA may "re-sell" data it acquires from an NSCRA, such as employment history information where the data has been compiled in a database for purposes of resale, but that does not make a CRA an NSCRA. A CRA that resells data is also referred to as a "reseller," since a CRA obtains data from a number of sources.

For example under the FACT Act of 2003 that amended the FCRA, consumers were given the right to obtain a free copy of his or her consumer file from a National Specialty Consumer Reporting Agency once during a 12 month period. (FCRA Section 612) Many CRAs who are NOT a National Specialty Consumer Reporting Agency have also offered such a choice purely as a convenience to consumers, even though they are not an NSCRA and are not required to offer such a disclosure.

More Information about the Background Screening Industry

The Addendum contains more information about the past, present, and possible future of the background screening industry.

How to Choose a Pre-Employment Background Screening Firm

There are numerous screening firms and there can be large differences between firms. The most important point is that background screening is a legally regulated professional service and not just a matter of sending data to an employer.

An employer should apply the same criteria that it would use in selecting any other provider of critical professional services. For example, if an employer were choosing a law firm for legal representation, it would not simply choose the cheapest law firm. Although cost is always a consideration, the employer would clearly want to know it is selecting a law firm that is competent, experienced and knowledgeable, reputable and reasonably priced. Above all, an employer would want to know that it is dealing with a firm with integrity. The same criteria should be used for selecting any provider of a professional service. A screening service must have the proven ability and knowledge to provide this professional service. A review of the company's Web site and materials as well as contacting the firm's current clients for a professional reference should be helpful in establishing the firm's qualifications.

More Information about Selecting a Screening Firm and RFPs

The Addendum contains the article **"Selecting a Background Screening Firm"** by Attorney Lester Rosen as well as a sample **Request for Proposal (RFP)**.

Author Tip ⟩ **Screening Firms Work for Consumers Just as Much as Employers and Considers the Consumer to Also be their Client**

Even though a screening firm may be hired and paid by an employer, a good screening firm takes the position that they work for BOTH the consumer and the employer.

As a Consumer Reporting Agency, a screening firm has a duty to protect the interests and legal rights of BOTH consumers and employers. A CRA, for example, has duties and obligations to consumers, such as a duty of accuracy, to prevent certain information from going into a report, and to prevent reports being obtained by unauthorized parties or for unauthorized reasons.

In addition, a CRA has an absolute duty to re-investigate a background report if an applicant feels there is anything about it that is incomplete or incorrect. In fact, a good CRA is just as concerned about a report being accurate as a consumer would be. A good screening firm, for example, will go out of their way to help job applicants understand the process, answer their questions, and to make it very easy to launch a re-investigation.

Although a CRA may take some reasonable steps to ensure the identity of a consumer to guard against identity theft, a CRA will not place any undue barriers in a consumer's path in requesting a reinvestigation, and will accommodate the consumer by communicating in any manner that works best for the consumer, including phone, email, U..S Mail, personal visit to the CRA's office or fax.

If fact, screening firms are well advised to have their best customer service staff members provide assistance to Consumers. Not only are consumer clients of a background screening firm, but great customer service may diffuse a situation where an upset consumer either does not understand the process or genuinely has a question or concern that a good CRA wants to make sure gets resolved properly.

45 Questions Employers Should Ask Their Current Background Screening Partner

The following 45 questions will help employers identify quality background screening firms and avoid companies offering a "knock-off service" where the employer is not receiving the professional services they deserve. Employers need to be aware of the difference between firms that are mere data vendors versus firms that offer professional services as a Safe Hiring Partner (SHP). By asking the following questions, employers will know they have selected a background screening firm that meets the highest industry standards.

45 Questions Employers Should Ask Their Current Background Screening Partner

1. Are you a member of the background screening trade association - National Association of Professional Background Screeners (NAPBS®) and does your firm actively participate and support professionalism in the screening industry?

2. Is your background screening firm accredited by the National Association of Professional Background Screeners (NAPBS®) Background Screening Credentialing Council (BSCC) as successfully proving compliance with the Background Screening Agency Accreditation Program (BSAAP)? If not, why not?

3. Does your background screening firm have legal staff and help desk with expertise on pre-employment screening and the Fair Credit Reporting Act (FCRA) and equivalent state laws?

4. Do you perform yearly (Service Organization Control) SOC 2® (SSAE 16) Audits to confirm the company meets high standards set by the American Institute of Certified Public Accountants (AICPA) for protecting the security, confidentiality, and privacy of customer information used for background checks?

5. Do you provide written documentation, whitepapers and online resources on safe hiring, due diligence, and legal compliance issues?

6. Does your background screening firm carry errors and omissions insurance coverage of at least $2,000,000?

7. Has the firm never been the subject of a lawsuit for violations of the Fair Credit Reporting Act or equivalent state laws?

8. Does your background screening require its public record researcher's to carry errors and omissions insurance?

9. Does your background screening firm have a highly automated completely paperless online system and processes that require no special software and provides CPI compliant security and data privacy protection?

10. Does your background screening firm have real-time compliance built into the system assuring that all forms, notices, disclosures and consent documents are always up to date for use in all 50 states?

11. Is all work done in the USA to protect privacy and control quality—i.e., nothing sent offshore to India or other "cheaper places" that puts applicants personally identifiable information and quality control at risk from "offshoring"?

12. Is all information about your applicants available on the web 24/7, including real-time status complete with notes?

13. Does your background screening system track the real-time status of every search so that nothing falls through the cracks?

14. Can your background screening firm archive all records so an employer can maintain paperless systems?

15. Does your background screening firm operate on a platform that is HR-XML compliant that integrates seamlessly into HRIS and ATS systems?

16. Can your background screening firm provide control features so an employer can set up multiple sub-accounts, so that the Administrator can view all accounts, but each sub-account can only view their own reports?

17. Are all employment and education checks conducted by well trained personnel in a controlled, call center environment with nothing being sent to cheaper at-home workers where data privacy and the quality of work is at risk?

18. Are all employees with your background screening firm subject to an intensive training when they are hired, and attend documented ongoing training?

19. For employment verifications, are anti-fraud procedures in place, such as verifications of all past employer phone numbers instead of relying upon an applicant supplied number?

20. For Education verifications, are steps taken to verify if a college or university is accredited and to watch out for Diploma Mills?

21. Do you have a policy of NO Set-up fees and no minimum usage? (Credit report access requires a credit bureau mandated on-site inspection that is subject to a third party fee.)

22. Do you offer 24/7 online ordering that gives an employer total control over the ordering process and speeds up turnaround time?

23. Do you offer report delivery options and are your background screening reports easy to read, with important information summarized at the top for ease of use?

24. Are criminal searches conducted using primary sources using the most accurate means, with no reliance on third party databases?

25. Where third party databases are used as a supplement to a primary source criminal records check, are results verified at the source before being reported?

26. Do you search for both felonies and misdemeanors when available?

27. When a criminal hit is reported, does a knowledgeable person in your background screening firm report the findings (as opposed to having the information entered by some unknown court researcher)?

28. When there is a felony or high-level misdemeanor criminal record found, are you proactive in calling the client to advise them there is a potential problem?

29. Does your background screening firm take measures to ensure that ALL legal and relevant criminal records are searched, as opposed to just going back "seven" years, which can leave an employer exposed?

30. Do you accurately describe the pros and cons of criminal databases, and ensure clients are informed that databases are research tools only and are subject to false negatives and false positives?

31. Do you provide clients with all necessary FCRA and state-specific forms and compliant procedures?

32. Do you notify your clients of changes in the FCRA and other applicable laws?

33. Is a member of your background screening firm a nationally recognized subject matter expert and speaker on safe hiring, use of criminal records and the FCRA?

34. Does the President of your background screening firm have an open door policy for any customer issues or questions?

35. Is your average turnaround time 72 hours less?

36. If there is a delay for reasons that are out of your control, do you notify us online with in-depth notes and the ETA?

37. Does your background screening firm have large clients with nationally recognized names?

38. Do you partner with leading websites and HR service providers?

39. Regarding customer service, will there be customer service professionals familiar with our needs instead of being serviced by a call center?

40. Does your background screening firm provide no-cost training programs and webinars?

41. Do you offer ordering options such as customized packages or individual searches and competitive pricing?

42. Do you provide a guide or interactive US map showing the significant rules for all 50 states when it comes to screening?

43. Has your background screening firm published books, whitepapers or other material on background checks and safe hiring?

44. Does your background screening firm have extensive international capabilities?

45. Does your firm adhere to the "EU-U.S. Privacy Shield Framework" that replaced most of the "Safe Harbor" data transfer agreement to perform screenings of job applicants from the EU (European Union)?

Source: www.esrcheck.com/Resource-Center/Select-Screening-Firm/

Author Tip ⟩ **Screening is an Exceptions and Compliance Business**

Although a great deal of the screening process can be automated through technology, at the end of the day, technology does not solve two big issues. First, as we have seen repeatedly, screening has become a legal compliance business. Furthermore, screening is often called an "exception" business. The vast majority of background checks come back on time and clear. However, where there is an exception such as a delay in getting data, or negative or inconsistent information is found, then that becomes an exception from the normal process, and employers need the background firm to be there to help them. For example, if an employer is trying to complete a background screen in order to onboard a new hire, some hiring manager will be calling the HR department to find out why the hire is not completed. HR, in turn, needs to be able to call the screening firm to find out more if the information on the screening firm's website is insufficient. Or if potentially adverse information is found, the employer needs to figure out what to do next. Although technology may help these processes, an employer is hiring professionals to assist with their screening, they are not hiring software.

Language that Should Go in a Background Screening Contract

Because of the FCRA employer certification requirement, there must be a written agreement between the background firm and the employer. An agreement between an employer and CRA contains several areas. First, there are the legally required employer FCRA certifications. There may also be required state certifications as well such as the language required by California.

Next, the agreement usually will often lay out other duties, such as an employer's duty to keep matters confidential and passwords secured (in order to ensure only those with a permissible see the reports), the duty to only utilize the report for employment screening purposes and the duty to follow all laws and regulations. An agreement will review the duties of the CRA, such as the duties to use best efforts for accuracy, to follow the FCRA and all applicable laws and regulations, and to re-investigate any disputed information. Other advisements typically include advising the employer that a CA does not give legal advice, and reminding the employer of their duty to provide adverse action notices.

There is not widely accepted national standard industry form. Some employment law firms have prepared summaries of the minimum FCRA requirements that must be in a background screening employer certification. The National Association of Professional Background Screeners (NAPBS®) Background Screening Agency Accreditation Program (BSAAP) uses certain clauses that are considered best practices to add at http://pubs.napbs.com/pub.cfm?id=D57EDE10-A720-5C5D-BBCE-21CBC45A276C. These include:

- 3.1 Client Legal Responsibilities" – CRA shall have procedures in place to inform client of client's legal responsibilities when using consumer reports for employment purposes. CRA shall advise client to consult their legal counsel regarding their specific legal responsibilities. These legal responsibilities include:
    - o Having permissible purpose,
    - o Disclosing to consumer,
    - o Obtaining consumer authorization,
    - o Following prescribed adverse action procedures,
    - o Complying with all applicable state and federal law, and
    - o Obtaining, retaining, using, and destroying data in a confidential manner.
- 3.4 Adverse Action – CRA shall advise client that there are legal requirements imposed by the federal FCRA and, in some instances, state consumer reporting laws, regarding taking adverse action against a consumer based on a consumer report. CRA shall advise client that they should consult their legal counsel prior to taking adverse action.
- 3.6 Understanding Consumer Reports – CRA shall communicate to client that they are not acting as legal counsel and cannot provide legal advice. CRA shall communicate to client the importance of working with counsel to develop an employment screening program specific to their needs. CRA shall also communicate to client the necessity to work with counsel to ensure that client's policies and procedures related to the use of CRA-provided information are in compliance with applicable state and federal laws.
- A CRA shall provide information to client regarding (1) the sensitive nature of consumer reports, (2) the need to protect such information and (3) the consumer report retention and destruction practices as outlined in the federal FCRA and the DPPA (Drivers Privacy Protection Act).

Agreements will also cover business terms with many provisions reflecting the same language appearing in any agreement with a service provider. However, there are some unique matters that often arise in background screening agreements.

Mistakes and Guarantees

An issue that often surfaces is the degree of a screening firm's liability in the event of a mistake. Screening firms will typically have language that protects them or their vendors, suppliers, officers and employees from liability from ordinary negligence. That is because a screening firm does not make or maintain the data on the record's being reported. If a court clerk or a past employer conveys incorrect information, and the background firm has used reasonable procedures, then any error is not the fault of the screening firm. (Of course, an employer may argue a screening firm should be responsible for its own negligence.) A screening contract will also typically include a clause that in no event shall either party be liable to the other party for any special, incidental, consequential or punitive damages arising out of this agreement. This is because the screening firm is only playing one role in the entire hiring process. The screening firm typically does not have contact with the applicant and is not involved in the interview or other processes. For the services charged, a screening firm cannot in effect provide any guarantee or insurance that the applicant will work out. In addition, a screening firm has no way to positively identify an applicant and cannot be responsible for identification.

Some employers require a turnaround time guarantee, sometimes as part of a Service Level Agreement (SLA). However, a screening firm can only guarantee their own work. If a court clerk delays results, or a school is closed for vacation, or an employer refuses to return a phone call, there is little a screening firm can do about it.

Some of larger screening firms may request a guaranteed contract period in exchange for price concessions. Employers need to judge this carefully. Screening is a professional knowledge based service in a complex legal environment. Normally, professional services are not subject to a contract period. If the service is not satisfactory, an employer may want the option to make adjustments.

Author Tip **Beware of Red Flag Web Sites**

There are a number of online sites offering all sorts of data on consumers including pre-employment background checks. If the site does not prominently mention the FCRA or require a **written agreement** that contains the above material, DO NOT use the site for employment background checks. Background checks are subject to intense legal regulation, legislation, and litigation. An employer that uses a do-it-yourself online service without the proper compliance is putting their organization at extreme risk. For an example of this risk, read the section 'FTC Fines Data Broker $800,000 Dollars to Settle Charges of Violating FCRA' in Chapt

Introduction to the National Association of Professional Background Screeners (NAPBS)

One of the most interesting developments in the pre-employment screening industry was the emergence of the first industry non-profit trade association in 2003. Called the **National Association of Professional Background Screeners**, or **NAPBS**, the new association attracted nearly 500 of the nation's leading pre-employment screening companies. The NAPBS Association currently represents over 750 member companies engaged in background screening across the United States (See: www.napbs.com/about-us/about-napbs/).The association's website is found at www.napbs.com.

Per the current website, the mission of NAPBS is "to advance excellence in the screening profession" with a vision "to be the trusted global authority for the screening profession." According to the NAPBS 'About Screening' page (www.napbs.com/resources/about-screening/), the background screening profession serves several critical functions, including:

- *Protecting the rights of consumers;*
- *Promoting safe homes and workplaces;*
- *Helping employers and property managers comply with state and federal screening regulations;*
- *Helping public and private employers make informed placement decisions; and*
- *Providing risk mitigation tools for employers and property managers.*

With our common goal of safe communities in which we live, work and play, screening companies and the NAPBS will continue to work together to advance excellence in the screening profession. Promoting an awareness of the importance of screening to organizations, government entities, legislators, and consumers will always be one of our primary goals.

Author Tip **Make Sure Your Screening Provider is an NAPBS Member**

It is highly recommended that any employer who engages the services of a background screening firm ensure that the firm is a member of NAPBS. Although membership does not guarantee any particular level of knowledge or service, it is a valuable indicator that the firm has a commitment to the industry organization that is promoting professional standards and has promulgated a code of conduct.

See The Addendum **More Information about NAPBS**

The Addendum contains more information about the National Association of Professional Background Screeners (NAPBS) including a brief history of the NAPBS and its accreditation program.

Why Choose an NAPBS Accredited Background Screening Firm?

The National Association of Professional Background Screeners (NAPBS®) has maintained that there is a strong need for a singular, cohesive industry standard and thus created the **Background Screening Agency Accreditation Program (BSAAP)**. Governed by a strict professional standard of specified requirements and measurements, the BSAAP is a widely recognized seal of achievement that recognizes a background screening organization's commitment to excellence, accountability, high professional standards and continued institutional improvement.

The NAPBS Background Screening Credentialing Council (BSCC) oversees the application process and is the governing accreditation body that validates the background screening organizations seeking accreditation meet or exceed a measurable standard of competence. To become accredited, background screening organization's must pass a rigorous onsite audit, conducted by an independent auditing firm, of its policies and procedures as they relate to six critical areas:

- Consumer protection
- Legal compliance
- Client education
- Product standards
- Service standards
- General business practices

Accreditation is a significant professional achievement, which is why there is a growing trend among employers to only choosing to work with accredited screening firms. Of course, accretion is not a guarantee that a particular screening firm would be the right choice for an employer. In fact, there are accredited firms who have been sued, and there are non-accredited firms that may do an excellent job. However, by choosing an accredited screening firm, an employer has greater confidence that the firm meets the prescribed professional standards and has taken the time and effort to review its operation in depth and undergo an accreditation process.

See The Addendum

The 58 Clauses of the BSAPP

A list of the 58 individual clauses of the **Background Screening Agency Accreditation Program (BSAAP)** that an NAPBS Accredited Consumer Reporting Agency (CRA) must comply with is contained in the Addendum. There are other certifications a screening firm can seek that are arguably even more stringent than Accreditation, such as a Service Organization Control (SOC) 2® examination surrounding data and privacy protecting. However, NAPBS accreditation provides a significant yardstick for professionalism in background screening.

Conclusion

In the early days of the background screening industry, screening firms had to sell the very idea of background checks to employers who were not used to safe hiring practices. Fast forward to current times and the majority of employers do, in fact, perform background checks. Nearly seven out of ten organizations—69 percent—conduct criminal background checks on all of their job candidates, according to a 2012 survey from the Society for Human Resource Management (SHRM). A current issue for most employers is not whether to perform background checks, but which screening firm to utilize and the extent of the checks. And it's not just large employers either that perform checks—an increasing number of small and medium firms are also performing background checks as well. That is why selecting a competent and professional background screening firm is a critical matter to employers wanting a safe and profitable workplace.

CHAPTER 8

A Criminal Record Primer

Introduction to Criminal Records, Employment, and Collateral Consequences

The next three chapters will review one of the most critical hot button issues in hiring and background checks—the topic of criminal records and employment. Employers have a keen interest in knowing who they are hiring, and the existence of a past criminal record, especially if it's recent, relevant, and serious, can be of great importance. On the other hand, there is also the need to ensure that criminal records are accurate and used fairly, and do not result in the unfair exclusion of people seeking a second chance, or exclusion from the workforce as a result of discrimination.

- **Chapter 8** will introduce the general topic of crime and courts, punishment and the collateral consequences of a criminal conviction.
- **Chapter 9** will discuss criminal records—who creates and maintains them and how to find them, as well as issue surround accuracy of records.
- **Chapter 10** will discuss the fair and relevant use of criminal records in hiring and related issues such as ban-the-box and the U.S. Equal Employment Opportunity Commission (EEOC) Guidance on the use of criminal records.

Why Criminal Records are Inherently a Hot Button Issue

When news stories are run about criminal records and employment, they generally fall in one of two categories. Some news stories focus on crime victims who could have been helped if only there was a background check or the check was more robust. Conversely, news stories may focus on how background checks made it more difficult for someone— possibly even a member of a protected group—to get a job. The stories may involve a person with an old record being used or being unfairly labeled a criminal because he or she had a similar to name to someone who was actually a criminal. Stories may appear on the same day that claim employers or screening firms either do too little or too much background screening, all depending upon who was perceived as the victim.

These articles could leave employers wondering how much background checking is too much and how much is too little. These types of stories appearing from major news organizations but with vastly different angles underscore the point that background checks occur at the intersection of two fundamental American values: security and giving people a second chance.

On the one hand, background checks can promote safety, security, and honesty while lessening the chance for workplace violence or the hiring of unqualified workers with fake credentials. On the other hand, employers using background checks should be concerned with issues of fairness and privacy while combating discrimination, as well as the need to give ex-offenders a second chance so that they can become law abiding tax paying citizens. Without giving ex-offenders a second chance, we will build more jails and prisons and less schools and hospitals as a society.

There are a Massive Number of Criminal Records in the United States

Criminal records are also important because of the large number of Americans that are impacted. A 2011 study called *'65 Million Need Not Apply'* by the National Employment Law Project (NELP) estimated 64.6 million people in the U.S.— representing 27.8 percent or more than one in four adults—had a criminal record on file (although that includes arrests that did not result in a conviction). NELP, a research and advocacy group for low-wage and unemployed workers, has since revised that number up to approximately 70 million U.S. adults. The NELP study can be found at www.nelp.org/content/uploads/2015/03/65_Million_Need_Not_Apply.pdf.

However, as discussed below, it is also important to differentiate between records of arrests and those records that actual result in a criminal conviction. In his book, The Eternal Criminal Record by Professor James B. Jacobs (Harvard University Press 2015) provides an overview on the proliferation of criminal records in America for criminal justice and law enforcement use and their secondary uses in ways not intended or even foreseen by policy makers. The book clarified that a criminal record is different than having a criminal conviction, since "a criminal record is created for every arrest, regardless of the ultimate disposition." The author notes that an estimated twenty million Americans, about 8.6 percent of the total adult U.S. population, have recorded felony convictions. The remaining people with convictions are misdemeanors. Although the author indicates that there are criminal records on 25% of the population, the math indicates that a large percentage of those criminal records are arrests only, which many states prohibit employers from using.

It is estimated that the United States has the highest number of individuals in custody in the world. According to widely cited and verified statistics in an article in a July 2015 article in *The Washington Post*, the U.S. only has 5 percent of the world's population but is home to 25 percent of the world's prison population. Even using the more reliable way to compare incarceration practices between countries – the prison population rate – the United States had the highest prison population rate in the world at 716 per 100,000 people. The Washington Post article can be viewed at www.washingtonpost.com/news/fact-checker/wp/2015/07/07/yes-u-s-locks-people-up-at-a-higher-rate-than-any-other-country/.

The Department of Justice (DOJ) collects numerous statistics on criminal records. These statistics can be found on the U.S. Department of Justice (DOJ) Office of Justice Programs (OJP) Bureau of Justice Statistics (BJS) web page located at http://bjs.ojp.usdoj.gov/index.cfm. The mission of the BJS is to collect, analyze, publish, and disseminate information on crime, criminal offenders, victims of crime, and the operation of justice systems at all levels of government to ensure justice is both efficient and evenhanded.

According to the BJS webpage, the total correctional population includes all persons incarcerated, either in prison, jail, or supervised in the community (probation or parole). The basic count for the correctional population is updated annually. The BJS report *Correctional Population in the United States, 2014 (NCJ 249513)* presents statistics on persons supervised by adult correctional systems in the United States at year end 2014, including offenders supervised in the community on probation or parole and those incarcerated in state or federal prison or local jail. The report describes the size and change in the total correctional population during 2014.

Key highlights of the report include:

- Adult correctional systems supervised an estimated 6,851,000 persons at year end 2014.
- About 1 in 36 adults (or 2.8% of adults in the United States) were under some form of correctional supervision at year end 2014.
- The incarcerated population (up 1,900) slightly increased during 2014.
- Seven jurisdictions accounted for almost half (48%) of the U.S. correctional population at year end 2014.

For more information about this report, visit: www.bjs.gov/content/pub/pdf/cpus14.pdf.

The BJS report *Probation and Parole in the United States, 2014 (NCJ 249057)* presents data on adult offenders under community supervision while on probation or parole in 2014. The report presents trends over time for the overall community supervision population and describes changes in the probation and parole populations

Key highlights of the report include:

- At year end 2014, an estimated 4,708,100 adults were under community supervision.
- Approximately 1 in 52 adults in the United States were under community supervision at year end 2014.
- The adult parole population increased by about 1,600 offenders (up 0.2%) between year end 2013 and 2014, to an estimated 856,900 offenders at year end 2014.

- The incarceration rate among parolees at risk of violating their conditions of supervision remained stable at about 9% in 2013 and 2014.

For more information about this report, visit: www.bjs.gov/index.cfm?ty=pbdetail&iid=5415.

For these reasons, understanding criminal records is critically important for employers and human resource professionals. The solution for employers is reaching the right balance in their background check program when it comes to criminal records and to ensure the records are used in ways that are accurate, relevant, and fair. These three chapters are intended to help employers understand the issues surrounding the use of criminal records.

Why Criminal Records are Important Indicators for Employers

For an employer, the importance of a criminal offense is not necessarily the mere fact a person committed a crime in the past. The importance can come down to a matter of character. The conduct and behavior leading to the criminal offense may demonstrate a character trait that does not bode well in terms of future workplace conduct. For example, "Thou shall not steal" is not a difficult concept. It's ingrained in our culture, as well as many other cultures. If a person decides to steal or commit an act of dishonesty, the employer's real fear is that the person revealed their true character—a willingness to take from others even though they know it is wrong.

In the book *"The Eternal Criminal Record"* by Professor James B. Jacobs, it is noted that "It is not irrational for businesses, not-for-profits, volunteer organizations, and individuals to commission criminal background checks on those with whom they do business or employ. It is desirable to enter business and social relationships with more information rather than less." The book goes on to state that, "In general, we would prefer to hire and associate with people whose biographies indicate honesty, reliability, and self-control." See: www.hup.harvard.edu/catalog.php?isbn=9780674368262.

Of course, nothing is that simple. What if the past conviction was a theft which was minor in nature, such as a youthful indiscretion of a small amount? Or what if it was driven by a need for food due to hunger? Or the offense was in the past and the applicant has done well since? Should that offense really bar someone from gainful employment for life?

There are also numerous stories of individuals with past criminal records having the doors of opportunity slammed in their face due to past behavior that no longer reflects who they are, what he or she can do, or what they have done to turn their lives around. Without the opportunity for employment, ex-offenders trying to turn their lives around and support themselves or their families are at a big disadvantage.

Employers, of course, did not create the economic and social environment surrounding these various issues, but since the ability to obtain a job is so critical, much of the burden of helping solve these issues end up falling on employers making employment decisions. As a result, no employer can ignore the need to fully understand the appropriate uses and limitations of past criminal records when used for employment.

Repeat Offenders, Recidivism, and Rehabilitation

In employment law, the fundamental basis of many negligent hiring lawsuits is the assumption that a person with proven dangerous propensities in the past may well exhibit those in the future. Statistics seem to bear out that employers and non-profit organizations, in fact, have a need to exercise due diligence.

 Recidivism Defined

According to the Bureau of Justice Statistics (BJS), **recidivism** is measured by criminal acts that resulted in the rearrest, reconviction, or return to prison with or without a new sentence during a three-year period following the prisoner's release. Statistics on recidivism published by the BJS are contained in the Addendum to Chapter 10 titled *"Studies Cited by EEOC Concerning Recidivism and Statistics."*

There are numerous statics gathered by the DOJ suggesting that ex-offenders re-offend fairly often, especially with a relatively short time period following their release. A number of statics are cited in the Addendum to Chapter 10.

- About two-thirds (67.8%) of released prisoners were arrested for a new crime within 3 years, and three-quarters (76.6%) were arrested within 5 years.

- Within 5 years of release, 82.1% of property offenders were arrested for a new crime, compared to 76.9% of drug offenders, 73.6% of public order offenders, and 71.3% of violent offenders.

- Released prisoners who were incarcerated for a violent, property or drug crime were more likely than other released inmates to be arrested for a similar type of crime. Regardless of the incarceration offense, the majority (58 percent) of released prisoners were arrested for a public order offense within five years of release. An estimated 39 percent of released prisoners were arrested within five years for a drug offense, 38 percent for a property offense and 29 percent for a violent offense.

However, there are counterbalancing considerations. First, it is unknowns how much these recidivism statistics are impacted by factors such as lack of rehabilitation while incarcerated, lack of reentry programs, the inability to obtain employment, or other factors that may doom a high percentage of ex-offenders to failure. The failure to assist ex-offenders as well, as the prejudice against them in the job market, may well make recidivism a self-fulling prophecy.

Furthermore, there is a substantial body of literature that suggests that over time, the importance of a past criminal record as a predictor of future behavior fades to the point where a person with a criminal record is no more likely to re-offend than a person without a criminal record. According to the EEOC Guidance on criminal records issued in 2012 (discussed in Chapter 10), the age of a criminal conviction is a critical consideration in determining the relevancy of a criminal record to a hiring decision. Numerous studies show that over time, a criminal record has little if any importance in predicting future behavior. There is substantial evidence to suggest that over time, it is no more likely that an ex-offender will commit a crime than a person with no prior conviction. The EEOC cited a number of these studies that are summarized in the Addendum to Chapter 10.

Screening industry statistics also strongly suggest that without doing a screen for criminal records, there is a statistical certainty an employer will eventually hire a person with a criminal record that that raises safe hiring issues. Screening firms report a criminal hit rate up to ten percent, whether disclosed by the applicant or non-disclosed. Keep in mind this hit ratio represents applicants who signed a background screening form telling them that background checks would be conducted.

Of course, all statistics need to be examined carefully. The hit rate statistic may include lesser offenses that are not disqualifying or offenses the applicant may have revealed. However, a ten percent hit rate is still an astounding number. The hit rate statistic is not that surprising in view of government studies concerning the rate of criminal convictions and incarceration in America.

Recidivism Statistics May Understate the Extent of Problem

There is another argument that, if anything, recidivism statistics may understate the extent of the problem, These statistics just represent when an ex-offender is caught Since not all crimes are solved, there is a significant chance that ex-offenders may have committed other offenses before being arrested OR that ex-offenders may commit crimes and are never re-arrested or convicted These are likely difficult numbers to come by but based on known statistics as to the number of unsolved crimes, it is not reasonable to assume that the problem is likely worse than it appears from the government statistics. However, there are also studies on recidivism showing that after a period of time, the chance of an ex-offender re-offending is no greater than a non-offender. So there are two sides to this coin.

Courts and the Relevancy of Repeat Offenders

A good example of how knowledge of past criminal conduct impacts decision making is demonstrated by the rules used by courts to determine if past criminal conduct should be admissible in a ceramal prosecution.

If a person is charged for example with the offense of driving under the influence of alcohol, and the person has been convicted in the past of the same offense, chances are the jury will never be told about the first conviction. Why is that information kept from the jury? Is it because evidence of prior bad conduct is not relevant?

Actually, prior criminal behavior is often kept from juries because experience demonstrates it is **too relevant**. Courts all across the U.S. have recognized the basic principle that evidence of a prior criminal conviction is so powerful that it can potentially overwhelm the jury's decision-making process — that human beings jump to the conclusion the accused did it again regardless of the evidence of the actual crime in the new case. Courts recognize part of the human make-up is to assume what a person has done in the past is what they will do in the future. For that reason, in criminal cases, evidence of past misconduct is admitted under very limited circumstances, for instance. However, a prosecutor may not introduce evidence of prior criminal behavior just to show the defendant is a bad person; if he did it before, then he did it again.

There are specific situations where a prosecutor can argue that evidence of a past crime is admissible. However, because the evidence is considered so prejudicial against a defendant, there must be a justification to introduce the past bad acts. The probative value of the past criminal conduct must exceed the prejudicial impact in the case.

Reasons to introduce the evidence of past crimes is limited to the following types of situations:

- The past crime proves some element of the new case, such as a unique method or *modus operandi* of committing a crime that provides proof of identity, motive, or means;

- The defendant testifies and the past act is used to impeach the defendant's credibility or to contradict the claim of defendant while testifying;

- The defense presents evidence of good character, and the past acts are used to impact the character witness under cross-examination;

- The past crime is an element of the new crime, such as a charge of a felon in possession of a gun, so that the past felony is part of the new offense;

- The past crime is considered by the jury as part of the penalty such as in a death penalty case.

The walk-a-way point is that evidence of past criminal conduct is so powerful, that the use of past crimes should be carefully monitored to ensure its use is relevant and fair.

When Mandatory Criminal Record Checks are Required

In some regulated industries, state or federal law mandates criminal record checks. This is not a matter of criminal propensities or statistics — it is the law.

All states have regulations requiring criminal background checks for jobs that involve contact with populations who are vulnerable or at risk. This may include teachers, childcare workers, health care professionals, and workers who care for the elderly or populations at risk. Another example is a professional licensing board. Per state law, these boards are state agencies that oversee the certification of certain professions. Those applicants subject to such regulations are normally aware of the criminal record check requirements through licensing procedures or industry contacts. Typical professions requiring a criminal record background check include private investigators, security guards, security brokers, insurance agents, bail bondsmen, jockeys, casino workers, and so forth.

Mandatory criminal record checks are typically done with a fingerprint check of state and federal criminal records. Usually, the checks are arranged for the employer directly through the specific state licensing agency rather than using the services of a professional background screening company.

There are also federal rules for certain industries. For example, the Federal Aviation Administration (FAA) has rules for mandatory background checks for workers employed by airport operators as well as employees having unescorted access to restricted areas. Similarly, the banking industry has certain mandatory background checks.

Given the news stories surrounding negligent hiring or child abductions and child abuse in volunteer and community organizations, new laws are proposed in nearly every state every year. These laws seek to expand the number of occupations that are subject to mandatory checks. For example, in Pennsylvania, in response to the horrific murder of a guest by a hotel worker with a criminal record, a grassroots effort is under way to require hotels to conduct background checks on all employees (See www.nanslaw.org). The clear trend is towards the government getting into the background checking business by making criminal record checks mandatory. However, as discussed later, the EEOC has indicated that state licensing laws that deny opportunity based upon criminal records are still subject to Title VII and can be discriminatory. (See Chapter 10.)

Crime and Punishment – The Abridged Version

The following is a brief introduction to the criminal justice system for employers, human resource professionals, and security professionals who utilize criminal records. The purpose is to assist the user in understanding a potential criminal record when making an employment decision. Keep in mind that, in addition to federal law, each state and U.S. territory has its own laws. Consequently, our Abridged Version is intended as a general introduction to criminal law and procedures only; users need to take additional steps to understand the appropriate rules and procedures in any relevant jurisdictions.

A **crime** is an act or omission that is prosecuted in a criminal court by a government prosecutor and can be punished by confinement, fine, restitution, and/or a forfeiture of certain civil rights. Legislative bodies such as state legislature or the U.S. Congress decide what acts or omissions are against the law. Such prohibited criminal acts are published by a legislative body as part of a "code." For example, in California, criminal acts are published primarily in the California Penal Code. However, criminal acts can be defined in other codes as well—certain drug offenses are contained in the California Health and Safety Code. Federal crimes are defined in the United States Codes.

When a person is charged with a crime, the plaintiff is the prosecuting attorney who brings the criminal case in the name of The People or the government. In a civil case, a private party brings a tort action for monetary damages. (A **tort**, in common law jurisdictions, is a civil wrong that unfairly causes someone else to suffer loss or harm resulting in legal liability for the person who commits the act. See: https://en.wikipedia.org/wiki/Tort)

> ### Here is an Example
>
> Assume Jack D. Ripper assaults Stewart Victim with a knife in California. Jack is caught and arrested shortly afterward. If Jack is prosecuted for the crime in state court, the case is called *The People of the State of California vs. Jack D. Ripper*. If Stewart Victim sued Jack for damages in civil court, then that would be a TORT case. That case would be titled *S. Victim vs. Jack D. Ripper*.

A criminal case can be brought in either a federal court or a state court. When a criminal case is brought in a **state court**, a District Attorney or County Prosecutor prosecutes the case. Every county has its own state court at the county level. In some circumstances, a city or municipal attorney may bring lesser charges based on local law or county or municipal ordinance in a city court. When charges are brought in **federal court**, a Federal Assistant U.S. Attorney (AUSA), who is part of the United States Justice Department, prosecutes it.

Some sort of **accusation** initiates a criminal charge. The accusation is typically brought by a prosecuting authority against the person arrested, either pursuant to an arrest warrant or a warrantless arrest by a law enforcement agent who had probable cause to believe a crime had been committed. In the case of a misdemeanor arrest, there is generally a requirement that it be committed in the presence of a law enforcement officer, but there are certain exceptions.

Depending on the jurisdiction, the accusation is commenced with some sort of **charging** document. The charging document may be known by such terms as a complaint, information, or indictment. For serious charges, called felonies, there is typically a *probable cause* determination before a trial in which there is a judicial determination that there is sufficient evidence for a trial to go forward. The standard of proof is just that it is more likely than not that a crime occurred and the defendant committed the crime. This is a much lower standard than proof beyond a reasonable doubt, which is needed in order to achieve a conviction. In some jurisdictions, the probable cause determination is accomplished by some sort of hearing before a magistrate or judge, sometimes referred to as a preliminary or probable cause hearing. In other jurisdictions, and typically in federal courts, there is a procedure for a **grand jury indictment**.

State courts generally have three levels—the trial courts, an intermediate appellate court, and the highest appellate court. Furthermore, in many states, trial courts are further divided into a lower court, which typically hears misdemeanor and preliminary criminal matters such as probable cause hearings, and felony trial courts. Certain states also have higher and lower civil courts, divided by a monetary limit. Other states have unified the trial court system so there is no upper and lower trial court.

Federal courts also have three levels. The federal courts where trials are heard are called a **Federal District Court**. There are 94 Federal District Courts. Each state has at least one district court. Larger states will have up to four district courts. For example, New York State has four district courts—Eastern District, Northern District, Southern District, and Western District. Furthermore, district courts can have various divisions. The Southern District of New York, for example, has divisions in New York City and White Plains. The New York City Federal District Court only covers Bronx and Manhattan boroughs. Other boroughs are under the jurisdiction of the Eastern Division which includes Queens, Kings, Richmond boroughs, and the two Long Island counties.

The federal courts also have intermediate appellate courts called United States Circuit Courts. The U.S. Circuit Courts are divided into thirteen circuits. For example, the Ninth Circuit hears appeals from the nine western-most states and two territories, Guam, and the Marianas Islands.

The highest court in the land is the United States Supreme Court, with nine members nominated by the President for a lifetime term, approved by the United States Senate, and headed by the Chief Justice of the United States.

State Courts

If a person is convicted of a crime in **STATE** court, several things can happen:

- **Sentenced to State Prison**. A state prison is an institution that is administered by the state, as opposed to a local county jail. In other words, a state prison will accept a prisoner from any county in the state. Sometimes the prison is referred to as the Big House, such as San Quentin Prison in California, or Sing-Sing in New York. Depending on your generation, think James Cagney in *White Heat* or Tim Robbins in *The Shawshank Redemption.*
- **Sentenced to County Jail**. A county jail is run by the local sheriff and accepts prisoners from the local county. Every county, parish, or borough in the U.S. has a local jail.
- **Fined.** A person convicted of a crime can have a fine imposed.

There are two other important terms to consider—**Probation and Parole**.

- **Probation:** Probation means in exchange for not giving a defendant his or her full jail sentence, a judge has imposed terms and conditions of behavior on a convicted criminal defendant. Probation occurs on the county level at a state court. Assume for example a defendant is convicted of a drug crime that carries a potential sentence of one year in the county jail. Instead of sentencing the defendant to jail for the entire year, the judge can impose just 90 days and hold the rest of the sentence in abeyance as long as the defendant obeys the terms of his or her probation. Typical terms of probation may include:
  - o Violate no law or ordinance.
  - o Participate in a drug rehabilitation program.

- o Pay a fine.
- o Pay restitution, if applicable.
- o Perform community service.
- o Do no change residence or move from the county without prior approval of the probation department.
- o Submit to search and seizure upon request by a police officer without a warrant or probable cause of your person, vehicle or home.
- o Do not possess any item connected to the crime. For example, in a drug case, a person will have a term and condition to not possess drugs or drug paraphernalia.
- o Do not possess weapons, firearms, or dangerous animals.
- o Stay away from certain people or places (associated with the case).
- o Submit to testing of breath or urine for controlled substances or alcohol use if the probationer has a history of substance abuse or if there is a reasonable suspicion that the probationer has illegally used controlled substances.
- o If physically able, find and maintain gainful full-time employment, approved schooling, or a full-time combination of both.

If a defendant violates the probation by not adhering to the terms or conditions, then the defendant can be sentenced to jail for the remainder of the sentence. In other words, when a defendant is on probation, the unused jail time is like a reverse bank account being held in reserve. If he or she misbehaves, then the judge can impose more jail time.

- **Parole:** When a person is sentenced to prison, he is placed on parole when released. That is an important difference when compared to probation. If a person violates his parole, then he can be sent back to state prison.

A parole officer is employed by the state, while the local county government employs a probation officer. As a practical matter, parole is out of the hands of the county judge or prosecutor and is instead handled by the state.

The actual sentence a defendant receives in state court depends upon a number of factors. There may be minimum or maximum penalties set forth by statute. For certain crimes, a defendant is not eligible for probation and MUST go to state prison. This can occur where the crime is serious, such as certain sex offenses or an offense using a weapon, or where by statute the person is classified as a repeat offender, such as a third strike in a three-strike case.

If a defendant is eligible for probation, a court will look at mitigating and aggravating factors of the crime and factors about the defendant to determine if probation is appropriate. If a person is sentenced to prison and a court has some sentencing discretion in terms of the length of sentence, the court again looks at mitigating and aggravating facts about the offender and the offense. A mitigating factor may be for example a lack of a record, the young age of a defendant, or the defendant's minor role in the offense. Examples of aggravating factors are:

- o The defendant has a history of committing offenses,
- o Committed an offense while on parole or probation,
- o The offense was particularly violent.

Urban Myth: A Current License Means a Person has NO Criminal Record

A popular urban myth is that members of regulated and licensed professions, such as doctors, lawyers, CPA's, nurses or teachers do not need a background check because some governmental agency is in charge of ensuring that individuals that commit crimes or misconduct will not have a license to practice their profession. Unfortunately, nothing can be further from the truth.

Licensing is conducted by numerous state occupational licensing boards in the 50 states and territories. The system for a licensing board to discover a criminal conviction is far from perfect. It is entirely possible for an applicant with a criminal action that would otherwise forbid licensing to be licensed by the state agency, per the following:

1. Conviction data may not be sent to a licensing board immediately or at all. In addition, there can be a substantial lag time between the alleged criminal act, the arrest, and the conviction.

2. Even if the criminal conviction is discovered by the licensing board, the disciplinary process takes time. Unless the licensing board takes action to issue an immediate suspension, the licensee may be able to continue to practice while the administrative procedures drag on.

3. While the disciplinary action is pending, a licensee may simply move to another state and apply for a license, covering up the proceedings in the first state. In other words, a licensee may try to *beat the discipline* before the new state finds out about it.

4. Even if a person is suspended in one state, an employer cannot assume that all state licensing boards share information with each other. As we discovered post 9/11, we do not live in a world where the government routinely collects and shares data with other governmental entities.

5. There can even be situations where a person commits a crime that does not result in losing a license but is still important for an employer to know about. In fact, in some licensed occupations, a person may even get a private reprimand meaning that a check with the appropriate licensing board may not reveal anything.

The bottom line: Employers that hire a member of a licensed or regulated occupation cannot assume that they are immune from liability simply because a person appears to have a current license. Since it is possible for a criminal conviction or act of misconduct to fall through the cracks, an employer still has a duty to exercise due diligence by its own independent background check.

For a listing of the numerous state agencies that license occupations including and those that offer free search capabilities, visit www.brbpublications.com and click on the Free Public Record Searches tab.

Federal Courts Are a Separate System

As previously mentioned, there are two entirely separate court systems in the United States – federal courts and state courts. A search of one system does not include a search of the other system, and each system operates under its own set of rules and has its own courthouses, clerk's offices, indexes, and judges.

Federal District Courts are the trial courts that oversee criminal law cases and therefore these court records can be a critical search resource for employers.

Based on the fact that the overwhelming number of prosecutions are located in state courts, many feel that federal searches have a relatively low rate of return. The decision to include a federal search, especially when hiring for a lower paid position, should take into account two other factors:

1. **The Nature of Federal Prosecutions**. The old saying, "Don't make a federal case out of it" has some relevance to the type of cases employers might find in federal court. By definition, federal courts are the places where violations of federal law are prosecuted. Although there has been a trend in congress in recent years toward federalizing more offenses that have traditionally been associated with state courts, federal crimes still tend to be slanted toward more serious cases, such as large drug cases, financial fraud, bank robbery, kidnappings, and interstate crimes. The majority of criminal cases in federal court are for immigration violations. According to *Federal Justice Statistics, 2011–2012* from the U.S. Department of Justice Office of Justice Programs, the number of federal arrests in 2012 was 172,248. Illegal immigration (50%) was the most common arrest offense in 2012, followed by drug (15%) and supervision (13%) violations. See: http://www.bjs.gov/content/pub/pdf/fjs1112.pdf.

2. **Federal Sentencing Procedures**. In federal courts, defendants are sentenced according to procedures set forth in the U.S. Sentencing Guidelines. This procedure has produced very long sentences, especially for drug offenders and those who commit acts of violence or crimes with weapons. In 2001, the average federal prison sentence was 57 months, with the highest sentences going to defendants convicted of violent felonies (91 months), weapons felonies (87 months), and drug felonies (74 months).

In many instances, the tip-off to a federal violation is not a court record search, but a large unexplained gap in the employment history. This underscores a key point made previously—that a past employment check can be just as critical as a criminal record check.

Because of the nature of federal crimes and sentences, many employers have seen less relevance in doing federal searches. Another reason for the lack of enthusiasm for federal record searches is the fact that a federal offense by definition can occur anywhere in the U.S. Thus, it is harder to select which jurisdictions to search unless an employer uses the Public Access to Court Electronic Records (PACER) system described below.

Federal Bureau of Prisons

Persons convicted in federal court and sentenced to prison fall under the authority of the Federal Bureau of Prisons (BOP). The BOP operates a federal prison system throughout the United States. Think of such institutions such as the old Alcatraz Federal Prison that housed such famous federal prisoners as the Birdman of Alcatraz and Al Capone, or the well-known Leavenworth Federal Penitentiary in Kansas, also known as *Club Fed* (the popular name for the low security federal institutions where Watergate Conspiracy participants and white collar criminals like Martha Stewart have spent time).

The BOP is solely responsible for calculating federal terms of imprisonment and makes inmates serve approximately 87.5% of their sentence. The remaining portion can be spent on parole, supervised by the U.S. Probation office. Federal defendants not sent to prison are supervised by the U.S. Probation office and subject to probation terms and conditions. For more information about BOP Time Computation, visit www.fd.org/docs/select-topics---bop/fed_bop_merchant.pdf.

Similar to state systems, a federal defendant can also be sentenced to a federal version of probation. This may include *local time* on a supervised program under the direction of a federal probation officer.

The maximum and minimum sentences for federal crimes are set forth in the code section defining the crime. The factors that go into a sentence—and that serve to mitigate or aggravate a sentence—are found in the Federal Sentencing Guidelines. For more information, visit https://en.wikipedia.org/wiki/United_States_Federal_Sentencing_Guidelines.

Bureau of Justice Statistics

The **Prisoners in 2014** report from the U.S Department of Justice (DOJ) Office of Justice Programs – Bureau of Justice Statistics (BJS) presents final counts of prisoners under the jurisdiction of state and federal correctional authorities as of December 31, 2014, collected by the National Prisoner Statistics (NPS) program. The report presents prison capacity for each state and the Federal Bureau of Prisons (BOP), examines the use of private prisons by state and the BOP from 1999 to 2014, and describes the offense and demographic characteristics of year-end federal and state prison populations.

According to the *Prisoners in 2014* report, **the United States held an estimated total of 1,561,525 prisoners in state and federal correctional facilities at the end of 2014**. The vast majority of prisoners were held under the jurisdiction of state correctional authorities as of December 31, 2014—1,350,958 or 87%—while the number of prisoners held under the jurisdiction of federal correctional authorities was only 13% at 210,567. Likewise, an overwhelming amount of the prisoners in state and federal correctional facilities at the end of 2014 were male—1,448,564 or 93%—while only 7% were female at 112,961.

Other highlights of the report include:

- The number of prisoners held by state and federal correctional authorities on December 31, 2014 (1,561,500) decreased by 15,400 (down 1%) from year end 2013.
- The federal prison population decreased by 5,300 inmates (down 2.5%) from 2013 to 2014, the second consecutive year of decline.
- The number of women in prison who were sentenced to more than 1 year increased by 1,900 offenders (up 2%) in 2014 from 104,300 in 2013 to 106,200 in 2014.
- The imprisonment rate declined from 621 prisoners per 100,000 U.S. residents age 18 or older in 2013 to 612 per 100,000 in 2014.
- In 2014, 6% of all black males ages 30 to 39 were in prison, compared to 2% of Hispanic and 1% of white males in the same age group.
- Violent offenders made up 54% of the state male prison population at year-end 2013, the most recent year for which data was available.
- Half of males (50%) and more than half of females (59%) in federal prison were serving time for drug offenses on September 30, 2014.

See the Prisoners in 2014 report from the Bureau of Justice Statistics (BJS) at www.bjs.gov/content/pub/pdf/p14.pdf.

Classifying Crimes by Seriousness

Criminal acts can be classified into three distinct categories based on the potential sentence:

Felony

A Felony is a serious offense that is punishable by a sentence to a state or federal prison. Note the use of the word punishable, as opposed to actually punished. The distinction is important because a person can be convicted of a felony but may not go to prison. How does that work? Depending upon the state and the crime, there are certain felonies wherein a judge can give a defendant felony probation. This typically occurs with a relatively less-serious felony committed by a relatively less serious offender. An example may be a first-time felony drug offender convicted of a less serious drug offense such as possession of a small amount of drugs for sale. If a defendant receives felony probation, the court can still sentence him/her to custody but in the local county jail. If the defendant violates his/her probation, the court then has the option of sending the defendant to state prison. That obviously creates a great deal of incentive for a felony defendant to not violate probation.

Misdemeanor

A Misdemeanor is a less serious offense that is only punishable by local jail time at the county level. Typically a misdemeanor may be punishable by up to one year in the county jail in the custody of the local county sheriff and a fine up to $1,000. A court can also impose terms and conditions of probation such as discussed above. However, there are drawbacks to assuming that a misdemeanor is less serious in all cases than a felony. As noted below, misdemeanors can be extremely serious.

Infraction

An Infraction is a public offense punishable only by a fine. This is typically a traffic violation such as an illegal left turn, speeding, or seat belt not fastened.

Two Reasons Misdemeanors Can Be Serious Matter

There are two reasons that a misdemeanor can still be a very serious matter, even though it carries the possibility of a lower sentence than a felony:

Wobbler or Hybrid Crime

Criminal laws become even more complicated because there are a number of offenses that can be charged as EITHER a felony or a misdemeanor. For example, grand theft is typically a felony that involves a larger amount of money stolen than a petty theft. However, in many states, a District Attorney can choose to charge such an offense as a misdemeanor instead of a felony. In some states, a judge can also reduce a felony to a misdemeanor if the offense is a wobbler. This decision can be based upon a number of factors, including mitigating information about the accused, the alleged crime, the behavior, or the harm. For example, a person who has no record and faced some degree of provocation commits assault with the intent to commit great bodily injury could be charged with a misdemeanor offense instead of a felony.

> **Author Tip** ▶ **Hybrid Crimes**
>
> For a number of real world reasons, the eventual status of a hybrid crime can have little or nothing to do with the seriousness of the crime but instead relate to a number of unpredictable variables in the criminal justice system. Very serious conduct may end up as a misdemeanor because of court overcrowding resulting in plea bargains, critical evidence being excluded pursuant to a motion to suppress, a critical witness may be reluctant to testify, unskilled attorneys can impact the outcome, or a jury may reach a compromise verdict. The only time that an employer can assume with some level of confidence that a misdemeanor is a less serious offense is when the crime charged can only be charged as a misdemeanor offense, which means that the legislature has made a determination that in all cases, the highest punishment can only be at a misdemeanor level.

Plea Bargaining

To add to the complication, in many states a defendant may be able to plea bargain a felony to a misdemeanor. This can happen for any number of reasons, including overcrowded court calendars, witness problems for the District Attorney, a prosecutor who is just not inclined to prosecute the case to a jury, or some equitable facts about the crime or the defendant that convinces a District Attorney to plea bargain. The importance of understanding the role of pleas escalated with the 2012 EEOC Guidance on the use of criminal records. The problem is that the eventual disposition in terms of either being a felony or misdemeanor may have nothing to do with the seriousness of the underlying conduct.

> **You Need To Know** ▶ **Dispositions**
>
> One word that appears in this chapter frequently is **disposition**, which means the final outcome in a criminal case. For example, if a case is dismissed, the defendant pleads guilty, or a judge or jury finds the defendant guilty, that is the disposition of the case. The word can also be used more broadly to include the terms and conditions of a sentence if the person is found guilty. An example of disposition may be that a "defendant was found guilty, given three years informal probation the terms and conditions of which are to serve 10 days in the county jail with 3 days credit for time served, perform 50 hours of community service, and during the three-year probation period break no law or ordinance, and not use or possess alcohol or a controlled substance." Sometimes criminal lawyers will use the shorthand term **dispo**, such as "what was the dispo in that case?" The end of this chapter has a glossary of terms associated with criminal proceedings and files.

Understanding that misdemeanors can, in fact, reflect very serious conduct becomes important in the context of evaluating criminal matters pursuant to the EEOC updated Enforcement Guidance on the Consideration of Arrest and Conviction Records in Employment Decisions Under Title VII of the Civil Rights Act of 1964 issued April 25, 2012. The EEOC Guidance (covered in detail in Chapter 10), the EEOC provides:

Careful consideration of the nature and gravity of the offense or conduct is the first step in determining whether a specific crime may be relevant to concerns about risks in a particular position. The nature of the offense or conduct may be assessed with reference to the harm caused by the crime (e.g., theft causes property loss). The legal elements of a crime also may be instructive. For example, a conviction for felony theft may involve deception, threat, or intimidation. 115 With respect to the gravity of the crime, offenses identified as misdemeanors may be less severe than those identified as felonies.

It is noteworthy that the EEOC does recognize that misdemeanors may be less serious than felonies. The table below indicates how state court offenses are carried out.

State Court Offenses Table

	Sentence	**Supervisor**
Felony	State prison or local jail time or felony probation.	If sentenced to prison – placed upon parole upon release from state prison and supervised by a parole officer. If given probation – supervised by local probation office.
Misdemeanor	Up to one year in a local county jail.	If probation – supervised by a local probation officer who works for the county where the sentence is imposed.
Infraction	A fine only.	No custody or supervision.

Classifying Crimes by Types

Another way to classify criminal behavior is by the type of crime. Although there is no one accepted standard, a typical breakdown of types of crimes is shown below:

Crimes against the Person

A crime that is committed using direct harm or force against the victim is a crime against the person. These crimes are typically the most serious and include acts such as murder, robbery, child molestation, kidnapping, or rape. Because of the seriousness or potential harm, these offenses are typically felonies. However, there are a number of offenses that can be wobbler/hybrid so that they can be either a felony or misdemeanor. For example, assault crimes can vary widely in their seriousness and can be either a felony or misdemeanor depending upon factors such as the nature of the offender, the degree of harm, and the details surrounding the offenses. Some authorities place sex offenses in a separate category.

Crimes against Property

A crime committed by damaging, destroying, or intruding on the property of another is a crime against the property victim. An example can be arson, vandalism, burglary, or trespassing. Some property crimes also carry with them elements of crimes against the person or theft. For example, a burglary committed for the purposes of harming someone inside of a house can be both a crime against property and a person. A burglary committed with the intent to steal from inside the house carries an element of theft. Many property crimes that only involve a threat to property, and do not involve a threat of harm or an element of theft, can be misdemeanors. Other offenses such as arson are typically classified as felonies because of the large potential dangers involved.

Theft and Fraud Crimes

Theft is the taking of another person's property without that person's permission or consent with the intent to deprive the rightful owner of it. **Fraud** is an intentional deception made for personal gain or to damage another individual. A related offense is embezzlement which is the act of dishonestly appropriating assets by one or more individuals to whom such assets have been entrusted. There are a great many such crimes, all revolving around dishonesty. These crimes are categorized as a felony or misdemeanor depending upon factors such as the value of the stolen property, the sophistication involved, the method used, and the history of the offender. A related offense is robbery, which is the taking of money or goods in the possession of another, from his or her person or immediate presence, by force or intimidation. Robbery involves elements of both theft and a crime against persons and is typically a felony. Armed robbery means a weapon was used. The difference between petty theft and grand theft is the amount taken. However, some jurisdictions provide that a person with a previous petty theft can be charged with a felony if there is a second petty theft. Robbery, which is the taking of property from another using force, is classified as a felony.

Crimes against the Public Order, Health, and Morals

There are crimes based upon acts that have been determined by a legislature to be needed to preserve public order, health, and morals. Some examples include disorderly conduct, vagrancy, public lewdness, and prostitution. Crimes against public order are generally considered misdemeanors. However, if a child is involved, crimes in the category may be considered more serious and could be a felony level offense. This is a broad catch-all category that can include traffic-related offenses, as well as violations of health or licensing ordinances. A Failure to Appear (FTA) in court after an arrest including a traffic ticket may be another example.

Substance Related Crimes

Crimes relating to substances can include simple possession of drugs for personal use, possession for purposes of sale, the sale or transportations of drugs, or the manufacturing of drugs. Driving under the influence can also be included. Again, the criteria for the punishment of such crimes as a felony, misdemeanor, or infracting depends upon the crime and the alleged criminal.

National Incident-Based Reporting System (NIBRS)

Another way of breaking down crimes is by reference to the reporting structure of the **National Incident-Based Reporting System (NIBRS)**. This is a mechanism for law enforcement reporting of criminal incidents to the FBI. (See www.icpsr.umich.edu/icpsrweb/NACJD/NIBRS/ for details on how this system was developed.)

NIBRS is broken down into Category A and B offenses as follows:

Group A Offenses

1. Arson
2. Assault (Aggravated, Simple, Intimidation)
3. Bribery
4. Burglary/Breaking and Entering
5. Counterfeiting/Forgery
6. Destruction/Damage/Vandalism of Property
7. Drug/Narcotic Offenses (including drug equipment violations)
8. Embezzlement
9. Extortion/Blackmail
10. Fraud (false pretenses/swindle/confidence game, credit card and ATM fraud, impersonation, welfare, and wire fraud)
11. Gambling (betting, wagering, operating/promoting/assisting gambling, gambling equipment violations, sports tampering)

12. Homicide (murder and non-negligent manslaughter, negligent manslaughter, justifiable homicide)
13. Kidnapping/Abduction
14. Larceny (pocket picking, purse snatching, shoplifting, theft and all other larceny)
15. Motor Vehicle Theft
16. Pornography/Obscene Material
17. Prostitution Offenses (prostitution, assisting or promoting prostitution)
18. Robbery
19. Sex Offenses, Forcible (forcible rape, forcible sodomy, sexual assault with an object, forcible fondling)
20. Sex Offenses, Non-forcible (incest, statutory rape)
21. Stolen Property Offenses/Fence
22. Weapon Law Violations

Group B Offenses

1. Bad Checks
2. Curfew/Loitering/Vagrancy Violations
3. Disorderly Conduct
4. Driving Under the Influence
5. Drunkenness
6. Family Offenses, Nonviolent
7. Liquor Law Violations
8. Peeping Tom
9. Runaway
10. Trespass of Real Property
11. All Other Offenses

Criminal Sanctions and Collateral Consequence

This section introduces the reader to a critical part of understanding the use and significance of criminal punishment by employers, Human Resources, Hiring Managers, recruiters, and others for hiring decisions—**the punishment and sanctions imposed by the criminal justice system**. This concept will be revisited in Chapter 10 concerning the fair and legal use of criminal records. There are voluminous resources on the whole area of criminal sanctions including the collateral consequences to a person that has been labeled a criminal.

However, the purpose of this section is just to introduce core concepts for those involved in making employment decisions. There are five general purposes for criminal sanctions:

1. **Punishment.** When a person violates the rules of society, imprisonment is used for pure punishment and revenge. Also, monetary fines can be imposed.
2. **Deterrence of others**. By punishing an offender, there is a possibility that others will be deterred from committing criminal offenses because they can see that such behavior results in certain punishment.
3. **Deterrence of the criminal in the future**. There is also an element of personal deterrence. If a person learns that criminal activity will result in punishment, then he or she may be less likely to commit a crime in the future.
4. **Rehabilitation.** Part of any sentencing scheme can be the goal of using punishment to effect rehabilitation. With the goal of dissuading future criminal conduct, the rehabilitation can be either by means of personal deterrence as noted above or by using some program intended to actively assist an offender to resolve problems that create

criminal behavior, such as a mandatory drug program or educational program (See section on typical terms and conditions of probation above).

5. **Protecting society.** Another use of punishment is to simply warehouse offenders so they cannot harm society.

Author Tip **Restorative Justice**

A concept that employers and HR professionals may hear more about in the future is **Restorative Justice.** This is essentially a community-based alternative approach to a traditional law and order approach where society looks at who was hurt, why the offense occurred, and how the community including the victim and the offender can work together to achieve a better outcome than labeling someone a criminal and putting them through the criminal justice system. To some degree, drug court programs and other jail alternative programs share this approach. Some major retailers are attempting to use a restorative justice approach for example to combat internal employee theft. It is particularly useful for young offenders, first-time offenders, or less serious criminal matters.

Collateral Consequences of a Criminal Conviction

As discussed above, criminal sentencing can include incarceration, monetary fines, as well as terms and conditions of probation. However, of utmost concern to consumers who have been convicted of a criminal offense are the **Collateral Consequences** of a criminal conviction.

There are two types of collateral consequences that are relevant:

1. First, there are *statutory consequences* found in laws that can flow from a criminal conviction. These can include limitations or prohibitions on obtaining certain types of professional licenses, practicing certain occupations, serving on a jury, voting, possession of firearms, and obtaining certain public benefits, among others. A state by state listing of such consequences can be found at http://ccresourcecenter.org/resources-2/state-specific-resources/.

2. Second, there are also well documented unofficial but real *collateral consequences* of a criminal conviction – the stigma of a criminal conviction. It has been likened to being branded in terms of a person's ability to obtain a job and housing. Numerous academic studies have proven conclusively that a criminal conviction carries numerous implications in a person's ability to obtain employment. This will be discussed in more detail in Chapter 10 on the use of criminal records.

Author Tip **ABA Website Identifies Collateral Consequences of Convictions**

The **American Bar Association (ABA)** maintains a state by state website that exhaustively identifies the collateral consequences of a criminal conviction (See: www.abacollateralconsequences.org/).

You Need To Know **Study Finds People with Criminal Records Face Disadvantages**

An academic study **"Indefinite Punishment and the Criminal Record: Stigma Reports among Expungement-Seekers in Illinois"** published in Criminology, 2016 from Simone Ispa-Landa of Northwestern University and Charles E. Loeffler of the University of Pennsylvania explores how individuals with criminal records face disadvantages in terms of employment, housing, and higher education. Ispa-Landa and

Loeffler interviewed 53 men and women living in Chicago and the surrounding area who sought to have their criminal backgrounds expunged and found the following:

- One out of three American adults have been involved with the criminal justice system and have a record, even if they were not found guilty of any crime.

- Those with criminal records can no longer easily conceal their contact with the justice system due to the ease and immediacy of internet searches. Since the 1990s, criminal justice agencies have been posting their databases online. Private companies purchase and aggregate the databases and then sell them at low-cost to employers, landlords, and others. Therefore, the decentralized release of this personal background information exacerbates the challenge of trying to remove out-of-date or inaccurate information that could potentially impact an individual's upward mobility.

- Almost half—49 percent—of black males are arrested by age 23, compared with 38 percent of white males. Black males with criminal backgrounds are judged more harshly by employers than their white counterparts.

- Most states—45 of them—and the District of Columbia allow criminal records to be expunged or sealed, although some states have more restrictions than others.

- Of the study participants, 89 percent reported ongoing criminal stigmatization. Those with extensive arrest histories and those with minor ones shared experiences of being blocked from jobs, housing, college programs and financial aid because of their criminal backgrounds. "Blocked opportunities were a pervasive theme in their accounts, and this was true whether their criminal record histories were extensive or minor."

There are numerous studies that similarly document the challenges facing an ex-offender seeking employment. This particular study is available online at http://onlinelibrary.wiley.com/doi/10.1111/1745-9125.12108/abstract.

Status of Individuals in the Criminal Justice System

Another critical way to analyze an applicant's involvement in the criminal justice system is to review their current status. A person's status, as we will see in Chapter 10, can impact an employer's analysis of how to deal with the applicant. It can also impact what a background screening firm is allowed to report in the first place, or what an employer is allowed to utilize. The primary status categories are:

1. Arrested only.
2. Case pending.
3. Convicted but no longer on parole or probation.
4. Convicted but currently in custody or on parole or probation.
5. Conviction expunged, pardoned, or judicially set aside.

An arrest is an action by a police officer in taking a person into custody on suspicion of having committed a criminal violation. An arrest does not always result in a person being taken to jail. An arrest can also be a citation to appear in court. (See Chapter 10 on the limitations of using an arrest under EEOC guidelines, and Chapter 6 concerning state laws that also limit the consideration of an arrest.)

There are many reasons an arrest may not turn into a conviction, including:

- A prosecuting attorney may determine there is insufficient evidence to file the charges, and a criminal charge is never filed in the courthouse.
- In some jurisdictions, arrestees for certain offenses are taken before a magistrate for a probable cause determination or a grand jury. At that point in the system, charges may not be filed or are dropped.
- In some instances, even after the charges are filed, a District Attorney may end up dropping the charges for any number of reasons, such as insufficiency of the evidence or inability to obtain witnesses.
- In some cases, the criminal charges may be dismissed by a court based upon motions brought by the defendant, alleging such things as illegal search and seizure or some other deficiency.
- Finally, a person could be found not guilty as a result of a court trial or jury trial, meaning the underlying facts of the arrest were insufficient for a determination of guilt.

In each of the first four instances, the end result was never a judicial determination on the guilt or innocence to the person arrested. Therefore, the arrest itself is only an opinion of the police officer and not facts of any conduct or behaviors. As the United States Supreme Court has ruled, "[t]he mere fact that a [person] has been arrested has very little, if any, probative value in showing that he has engaged in misconduct." *Schware v. Board of Bar Examiners, 353 US 232, 241 (1957).*

A conviction occurs where there has been a factual adjudication of guilt. That can be done by a jury trial where 12 jurors make a finding of guilt beyond a reasonable doubt (NOTE: typically there are 12 jurors, but certain courts allow less). Or, a person can be found guilty by a judge in a court trial, where a judge makes the decision if the defendant waives the right to a jury trial. Guilt can also be judicially established where a defendant admits his or her guilt. This can occur when a defendant pleads guilty to the criminal charge. It can also occur if a defendant pleads no contest. In criminal courts, a no contest is the same as a guilty plea but gives a defendant some protection in the event of a civil lawsuit.

If a person has been convicted, it is also important to determine their current status in term of custody, probation or parole. If the case is entirely behind the applicant, meaning the person is out of custody and beyond probation or parole, the case is likely to be older and is a factor that should be considered under the EEOC Guidance concerning criminal records discussed in Chapter 10.

A **pending matter** is where an arrest is still pending in court because the prosecuting attorney has filed a charge, but no facts have yet been adjudicated, and there is no disposition. This is a gray area status since the case has not either been terminated in favor of the defendant, but there has also been no factual adjudication by either a jury, a court trial, or a guilty plea. In California, for example, Labor Code Section 432.7 appears to allow consideration of a pending case. Since an essential function of any job is to show up, an unresolved criminal matter presents an issue for an employer since there is no certainty about the outcome. Of course, the more minor the charge, the less likely it is that a person will have substantial jail sentence. The 2012 EEOC Guidance mentioned previously does not appear to address this issue when discussing arrests.

Delayed Adjudication/First Offender Programs/Expungements/Pardons: Numerous states have case disposition rules that are somewhere between an arrest and a conviction, or programs that act as a judicial set aside where an offender can legally state they have not been convicted of a crime. These can occur in a number of situations.

For example, some states have a disposition called a *Diversion Program*. This occurs when a first offender for a relatively less serious offense is literally diverted from the criminal justice system and allowed to escape the criminal charge if he or she participates in and successfully completes certain court assigned tasks such as a counseling program or volunteer service. One of the most famous diversion case participants is O.J. Simpson. Prior to the death of his wife, Simpson was charged with domestic violence and allowed to participate in a domestic violence diversion program.

States also have diversion programs for such offenses as petty theft or drug use. If there is a violation of the terms of the program or a new arrest, then the court may terminate the diversion and reinstate charges, and the criminal case begins again. A variation of the diversion program is a *delayed entry of judgment program*. In that program, the defendant actually enters a guilty plea to the offense. However, the court delays entry of the judgment in order to allow the defendant to participate in a prescribed program, which may include a course of counseling and volunteer work. Upon the successful completion of the court's requirements without having any additional violations, the criminal matter is dismissed. In some jurisdictions, there are special drug courts where defendants are given the opportunity to by-pass criminal drug charges if they participate in one or more various programs.

Many jurisdictions have first offender programs where a court will discharge the defendant and set aside the conviction upon completion of various conditions, as though the arrest and/or conviction had never occurred. The primary condition is often that the defendant must not get arrested again or must stay away from a particular person. This is often used as a means of dealing with less serious misdemeanor offenses.

Post-Offender Programs: Many states also have various provisions to seal, expunge, or somehow erase a criminal conviction after it occurs. Some states have procedures by which an offender can receive some sort of state pardon or a governor's pardon. There are procedures to have criminal records legally sealed, expunged, or judicially erased in some other fashion.

California, for example, has a provision called Penal Code section 1203.4, under which a misdemeanor offender who successfully completes probation can move to have his conviction set aside and to be relieved of all penalties and dualities. Under California law, an employer may not consider the offense when making an employment decision. Nor may an employer ask an applicant for employment to disclose information concerning participation in any pretrial or posttrial diversion program, under California Labor Code 432.7.

Another type of program is called **deferred adjudication**. Texas, for example, has a system whereby a person enters a guilty plea, and a judge may defer the adjudication of guilt pending completion of a probation period. Upon completion of the deferred adjudication, the individual may request that the case be set aside. *Tex. Code Crim. Proc. art. 42.12* provides further that the dismissal and discharge under this section may not be deemed a conviction for the purposes of disqualifications or disabilities imposed by law for conviction of an offense. For additional state court procedures affecting the status of criminal convictions, see Chapter 9.

Urban Myth: Courts Destroy Criminal Records That are Set Aside or Expunged

An Urban Myth that may surprise job applicants is that once a judge vacates, expunges, sets aside, defers the adjudication or otherwise judicially erases a criminal record in some fashion, the record will disappear and can never be found. With limited exceptions, the general rule is *government does not destroy records*. In the typical scenario, even if the judge orders a set aside, the consumer's name can still be found by searching the court indexes and the case can still be viewed as a public record. Therefore, often the only way a background firm knows there has been a judicial set aside is to examine the court file where all court orders should be noted.

Of course, each state is different, but as a general rule, unless an applicant has been advised by an attorney that the criminal case will be sealed and physically not available anywhere, applicants need to understand that even a criminal case that they thought was erased may still show up.

Even in those situations where the court has ordered the case sealed, the damage may already be done since the record of the case may already reside in a commercial database. If a background firm locates the case in a commercial database, then the background firm has certain obligations under the federal Fair Credit Reporting Act and similar state laws. A background screening firm is required to either notify the applicant that a criminal record is being provided or must pull and examine the actual court file to ensure accuracy. For employers who want to avoid finding out about criminal records that have been judicially set aside, the best practice is to make sure to work with a screening firm that automatically pulls the court file whenever there is a database match. This will ensure sure the criminal record is complete, accurate, up to date, applies to your applicant and is reportable.

Keep in mind that usually these post-conviction processes do not result in a record being physically removed from the court's computer system. Once a unit of government creates a record, it is unlikely that anyone will physically destroy or delete it. It is unlikely a clerk's office will have access to a "case delete" button. Which means in most instances the record still exists. Even if a judge orders a record to be physically sealed, there is normally going to be some sort of record of the case somewhere in the public domain—the case number and the defendant's name will remain in some computerized index, which is available to a court researcher. In those instances, the court record and the court public index will normally include documentation that there has been some sort of judicial or executive action to lessen the offense through some post-judgment procedure. If a screening firm comes across such a record, a competent screening firm should have a procedure in place to not report such a conviction. However, if an employer does his own search of the court records and comes across such a record, the employer is asked to wipe their own memory clean.

Another new wrinkle is dealing with cases involving Drug courts. Drug courts use a post-conviction procedure where a court closely monitors and supervises a defendant with a personal drug abuse problem or who is accused of a drug-related crime. The court gives a defendant the opportunity to participate in a program, and upon successful completion, the defendant is relieved from criminal sanctions.

> **You Need To Know**

Un-Ringing the Bell

In TV land, a lawyer makes an inflammatory statement in front of a jury, knowing it is inadmissible, prompting the other side to noisily object. The judge admonishes the jury to disregard the last comment. Of course, the jury heard it, and the offending lawyer continues as though he scored some sort of victory. The TV viewer is wondering how a jury is supposed to un-remember something they just heard. Sometimes this is referred to as **un-ringing the bell** in court. Once a bell has rung, it is hard to take it back. Another analogy is—how do you get a jury to not remember the word *elephant* after *elephant* is mentioned?

This happens much more on TV than in real life. In real life, judges take a dim view of lawyers who try to insert inadmissible evidence or arguments before a jury. In fact, judges have a great deal of latitude in making lawyers who do that sort of unauthorized dramatics regret having done so.

Employers can find themselves in a similar position. If they come across a record they cannot use or consider, how do they ignore it? If the record was located by in-house security or the HR Department, then the record should not be passed on to a hiring manager or a person with hiring authority. That, of course, assumes HR or internal security has received the proper training to recognize an impermissible record and that there are policies and procedures in place.

The Anatomy of a Criminal Case and Criminal Justice Records

The following is a high-level summary of the life of a criminal case. For those that watch episodes of *Law and Order* or anyone of 1000's of other television shows and movies on criminal trials, this may seem redundant. However, a summary is important to give employers an understanding of all the various agencies that may produce criminal record information as a case progresses through the system, from the police investigation, all the way through trial, sentencing, incarceration, appeal and post-conviction relief. As discussed in Chapter 9, it turns out that only a very small percentage of the documentation generated by a criminal case is actually available to employers.

It is based upon what generally happens in state courts where the majority of criminal matters are prosecuted. Since each state has its own rules, and even individual counties in states can have their own procedures, this chart is meant as a general representation only. This is not intended as a complete list of every step in a case or of all possible documents produced by the criminal justice apparatus but is intended as a general guide. Depending upon the jurisdiction, certain information may be public in some courts or may be reflected in the court's docket, which is a record of all proceedings in a case. There may be instances where a record can be obtained either through a Freedom of Information Act (FOIA) type request or some other process that is not practical for employers to use in terms of the hiring time frame.

Event	Documentation and Public (P) or Not Public (NP)
Police Investigation of the Crime	Police reports including witness statements, crime scene evidence and all documentation by police (NP) Police Search Warrants affidavits and Warrants (NP)
Arrest	Arrest Warrants (NP)
Initial Incarceration	Mug shots(NP) Incarceration intake and custody records (NP) Fingerprints (NP)
Review by Prosecution	Prosecution notes, interviews or other internal work products generated by the prosecution office (NP)
Charging Document	An indictment, accusation, complaint, information or similar term. (P)
Pre-Trial Procedures	Court Dockets or Minute Orders (P) Bail hearing/Motions Pre-Trial motions by prosecution and defense (motions to suppress evidence, and numerous other matters that can be the subject of pre-trail motions by either side possibly including exhibits and memorandums of authorities that may discuss the case (depends on document and court)
Trial	Court Reporter transcript of proceedings (See note below)
Sentencing	Probation Report (NP) Sentencing memorandums by the Prosecution and/or defendant (Depends on Court)
Appeal	Briefing by parties (Depending upon Court and state, can likely be located) Court decision (in some situations can be obtained by taking additional time and effort unless it's a published Appels decision)
Serving Sentence	Records maintained by custodial institutions (NP)
Violation of Probation from a Sentence in County Jail	Typically brought as a court proceeding (P)

Event	Documentation and Public (P) or Not Public (NP)
Violation of Parole	Typically an internal record (NP)
Expungement, Pardon, or Other Set Aside	Court Record (P)

Notes:

Court reporter transcripts: Most court proceedings will have a Court Reporter (sometimes called a court stenographer) who transcribes all words spoken during court proceeding using a stenograph machine, shorthand or some sort of voice recording system. However, these are typically not turned into written transcripts unless there is an appeal or a specific request by a party to the case for some specific legal need. As a practical matter, they are not available for a pre-employment screening report.

Entry of Guilty Plea and Probation Report: If the defendant entered a guilty plea, the file would contain a waiver of rights as well as information on the sentencing. A court file may contain the written arguments by both the prosecutor and defense attorney about the appropriate sentence and there may even be letters written to the judge by the victim, or friends or family members of the defendant. If the defendant pleads guilty or is found guilty after a trial, there may be a pre-sentencing report and recommendation prepared by a probation officer. It can include a treasure trove of information including a summary of the offense, the victim's statement, the defendant's statement, the defendant's personal history including any drug or alcohol issues, the defendant's criminal history and the probation office analysis of the appropriate sentence. In most jurisdictions, none of that is available to employers.

Docket: The Court file contains substantial additional information. Every court maintains an ongoing record of all proceedings in the case by the court clerk. It is sometimes known as a Docket or Clerk's Minute Order (coming from the concept of keeping minutes of official proceedings) or Registry of Actions. For convenience, this book refers to this document as a Docket.

The Docket will show for example all court appearances by the defendant and the attorneys for the prosecution and defense, including a summary of what occurred as well as any court orders. In many instances, the Court issues rulings and orders orally from the bench and the Clerk's minutes reflect all such orders. The court file may contain numerous other documents, Attorneys for the prosecution and defense can file various motions concerning matters in the case. For example, a defendant has the opportunity to file various motions, such as a motion to suppress evidence or a statement, or to request some other legal remedy, such as a dismissal of charges.

Other information: Sometimes a review of the Court file may result in various documents in public section that can at times shed more light on the case. However, for the most part, the public is restricted to the charging document, the docket, and potentially sentencing material.

Federal Courts: More information about the underlying offense and the defendant may be available, in some cases, on the federal online PACER system (discussed in Chapter 9). For example, if the Assistant U.S Attorney (AUSA) or the defense attorney filed a sentencing memorandum, that would likely be available on PACER and may include details about the case or the defendant.

More information about criminal dockets is in Chapter 9 under the topic "County Courthouse Searches."

Glossary of Criminal Terms

The following glossary of common criminal terms may be helpful. Some of the definitions were provided by Derek Hinton and attorney Larry Henry, authors of *The Criminal Records Manual 3rd Edition* (Facts on Demand Press):

abstract of record: a complete history in short, abbreviated form of the case as found in the record.

acquittal: a term used in cases where a criminal defendant goes forward to trial, with the jury or judge finding the defendant not guilty of a certain crime or crimes.

administrative license suspension (ALS): a law enforcement officer may seize the driver's license of an individual believed to be driving under the influence if the person's test results show an alcohol concentration higher than the legal limit or the presence of drugs or other intoxicating substances. That individual has seven days after receiving the notice of suspension to petition the court to challenge the suspension.

Alford plea: a plea entered by a defendant while maintaining his/her innocence in order to gain the benefit of a plea agreement.

alternative dispute resolution (ADR): a process by which an independent party is asked to review the issues in dispute between two other parties in hopes of bringing the dispute to a resolution before the court is required to conduct a formal hearing or trial. This process may occur prior to the filing of the civil action or may occur after the case is filed. A judge may choose to refer a case for alternative dispute resolution.

amicus curiae: a friend of the court; one who interposes and volunteers information or argument upon some matter of law.

arraignment: the defendant is advised of the charge against him or her and the rights he or she has. Bail is set. If the charge is a misdemeanor the defendant enters a plea in the Magistrate's Division. If the charge is a felony, the defendant appears first in the Magistrate's Division, but the defendant cannot enter a plea—the defendant determines whether he or she desires a preliminary hearing. If the defendant is bound over on a felony to answer the charge in district court, the defendant enters a plea in the District Court.

arrest of judgment: the act of staying the effect of a judgment already entered.

arrest warrant: is a warrant that authorizes law enforcement to arrest an individual.

attachment: a remedy by which a plaintiff is enabled to acquire possession of property or effects of a defendant for satisfaction of judgment which a plaintiff may obtain in the future.

bail bond: an obligation signed by the accused, with sureties, to secure his presence in court. If the defendant fails to appear, the bondsman has a period of time to deliver the defendant to the court. If this is not done, the bond is forfeited.

bail bond forfeiture: the process in which the court requires the surety to pay over the amount of bail

bail bond exoneration: a process by which the bond money paid to the court to ensure an individual's appearance in court is returned to that individual, typically when the case is concluded.

bailiff: a court attendant whose duties are to keep order in the courtroom and to have custody of the jury.

banc-(bangk) bench: the place where a court permanently or regularly sits. A "sitting en banc" is a hearing with all the judges of a court, as distinguished from the sitting of a single judge.

bench warrant: process issued by the court itself, or "from the bench," for the attachment or arrest of a person.

binding instruction: one in which a jury is told if they find certain conditions to be true, they must find for the plaintiff, or defendant, as the case may be.

burden of proof: the necessity or duty of affirmatively proving a fact or facts in dispute.

caption: the caption of a pleading, or other papers connected with a case in court, is the heading or introductory clause which shows the names of the parties, name of the court, number of the case, etc.

certiorari-(ser'shi-o-ra'ri): an original writ commanding judges or officers of inferior courts to certify or to return records of proceedings in a cause for judicial review. Proceedings for a writ of certiorari are not applicable in the Idaho judicial system, except as the United States Supreme Court may grant certiorari on a case decided by the Idaho Supreme Court.

change of venue: the removal of a case begun in one county or district to another, typically done for the convenience of the parties, or when the news coverage of the circumstances associated with a case make it difficult to find a jury that can put aside what they have heard about the case and judge it fairly on the evidence presented in court.

Child Protective Act: (commonly referred to as CPA) the statutory law dealing with the protection of neglected or abused children.

common law: the body of law arising from decisions made by the courts. Also called "case law."

concurrent sentence: sentences for more than one crime in which the time of each is to be served at the same time, rather than successively

consecutive sentence: a sentence, additional to others, imposed at the same time for another offense, one sentence to begin at the expiration of another.

contempt of court: any act calculated to embarrass, hinder, or obstruct a court in the administration of justice, or calculated to lessen its authority or dignity. Contempt is of two kinds: direct and indirect. Direct contempt are those committed in the immediate presence of the court; indirect contempt is the term chiefly used with reference to failure or refusal to obey a lawful order outside the presence of the Court.

corroborating evidence: evidence supplementary to that already given and tending to strengthen or confirm it.

count: In a criminal action, the distinct allegation in an indictment or information that the defendant committed a crime.

counterclaim: a claim presented by a defendant against the plaintiff.

de novo (de no'vo): anew, afresh. A "trial de novo" is the retrial of a case.

declaratory judgment: one which declares the rights of the parties or expresses the opinion of the court on a question of law, without ordering anything to be done.

default: a "default" in an action of law occurs when a party omits to plead within the time allowed or fails to appear at the trial.

default judgment: the court may enter judgment against a defendant in a civil case in his/her absence or in the event they have failed to complete the filing of required documents within a specified time.

deferred adjudication: a form of plea deal available in various jurisdictions, where a defendant pleads "guilty" or "No Contest" to criminal charges in exchange for meeting certain requirements laid out by the court within an allotted period of time also ordered by the court. Upon completion of the requirements, which may include probation, treatment, community service, or some form of community supervision, the defendant may avoid a formal conviction on their record or have their case dismissed. In some cases, an order of non-disclosure can be obtained, and sometimes a record can be expunged.

directed verdict: an instruction by the judge to the jury to return a specific verdict.

discovery: a process whereby one party to an action may be informed as to facts known by other parties or witnesses. In Idaho, the usual modes of discovery are depositions, interrogatories, requests for production of documents, and requests for admission.

dismissal: the dropping of charges by the district attorney before a jury or judge renders a verdict.

disposition: the final outcome in a criminal case.

District Attorney: also known as the Prosecutor or DA, is a government attorney responsible for overseeing the prosecution of an accused in a criminal court of law.

dockets: in a criminal case refer to the court case calendar or schedule of cases to be heard at a given time.

domicile: that place where a person has his true and permanent home. A person may have several residences, but only one domicile.

en banc: on the bench; all judges of the court sitting together to hear a cause.

enjoin: to require a person, by writ of injunction from a court to perform, or to abstain from or stop some act.

equitable action: an action which may be brought for the purpose of restraining the threatened infliction of wrongs or injuries, and the prevention of threatened illegal action.

estoppel (es-top'el): a person's own act, or acceptance of facts, which preclude that person from later making claims to the contrary.

et al.: an abbreviation for et alli, meaning "and others."

et seq.: an abbreviation of et sequentes, or et sequentia, meaning "and the following"

ex parte (ex par'te): by or for one party; done for, in behalf of, or on the application of, one party only.

ex post facto (ex post fak'to): after the fact; an act or fact occurring after some previous act or fact, but which relates back thereto. In criminal law, an ex post facto law is one that imposes or increases punishment for an act that was committed before the law was passed, such a law is forbidden by the U.S. and Idaho Constitutions.

fugitive warrant: a judge in one state may issue a warrant for the arrest of an individual being held in custody in another state. The fugitive may then be returned to the state where he is charged through the process of extradition.

Grand Jury: In some Felony cases, a Grand Jury typically consisting of twelve to twenty-three members is used to establish probable cause to proceed with the criminal case.

guardian ad litem (ad li'tum): a person appointed by a court to look after the interests of a child or incompetent whose property or rights are involved in litigation.

Guilty by plea or verdict: in criminal law, a defendant admits the conduct before trial, is said to be guilty. Guilt can also be established by means of a jury or court trial.

habeas corpus (ha'be-as kor' pus): "you have the body." The name given a variety of writs whose object is to bring a person before a court or judge. In most common usage, it is directed to the official or person detaining another, commanding him to produce the body of the prisoner or person detained so the court may determine if such person has been denied liberty without due process of law.

harmless error: in appellate practice, an error committed by a lower court during a trial, but not prejudicial to the rights of the party or the outcome of the case and for which the court will not reverse the judgment.

hearsay: evidence of a statement made out of court and offered to prove the truth of the statement, e.g., "I didn't see the accident myself, but my friend told me the light was red." It should be noted that the law on hearsay is one of the more complicated areas of the law of evidence with many qualifications and exceptions.

hung jury: in a criminal trial, a hopelessly deadlocked jury in which neither side is able to prevail.

impeachment of witness: an attack on the credibility of a witness by the testimony of other witnesses or evidence.

in camera (in kam'e-ra): in chambers; in private.

indeterminate sentence: an indefinite sentence of "not to exceed" so many years, the exact term to be served being afterwards determined by parole authorities within the maximum limits set by the court or by statute.

indictment: an accusation in writing found and presented by a grand jury, charging that a person has committed a crime.

information: an accusation for a felony criminal offense which is presented by a prosecuting attorney instead of a grand jury.

Infraction: a minor offense that is not criminal in nature but rather is a civil public offense punishable by a fine only. Examples of infractions include: speeding or failure to fasten a safety belt.

injunction: a mandatory or prohibitive writ issued by a court.

instruction: a direction given by the judge to the jury concerning the law of the case.

interlocutory: provisional; temporary; not final; refers to orders and decrees of a court.

interrogatories: written questions propounded by one party and served on an adversary, who must provide written answers under oath.

jurisdiction: the power of a court to hear and determine a given class of cases; the power to act over a particular defendant. Referred to as subject matter jurisdiction (jurisdiction over the subject of the case) or personal jurisdiction (jurisdiction over the parties).

jury, grand: a jury of inquiry whose duty is to receive complaints and accusations in criminal cases, hear the evidence and return an indictment when they are satisfied that there is a probable cause that a crime was committed and the defendant committed it.

jury, petit: the ordinary jury of twelve (or fewer) persons for the trial of a civil or criminal case. So called to distinguish it from the grand jury.

Lesser included crime: generally means an alternative to the charged crime at trial where the jury is given a lesser but related charge, in case the jury feels the defendant is not guilty of the charged crime, but is guilty of a related yet less serious crime.

mandamus: the name of a writ which issues from a court commanding the performance of a particular act.

manslaughter: the unlawful killing of another without malice; may be either voluntary, upon a sudden impulse, or involuntary in the commission of some unlawful act.

misdemeanor: offenses less than felonies; generally those punishable by a fine or imprisonment in a county jail, rather than in the state prison.

mistrial: an erroneous or invalid trial, a trial which cannot stand in law because of lack of jurisdiction, wrong drawing of jurors, deadlocked jury or failure of some other fundamental requisite

moot: unsettled; undecided. A moot point is one not settled by judicial decisions.

no bill: this phrase, endorsed by a grand jury on the indictment, is equivalent to "not found" or "not a true bill." It means that in the opinion of the jury, evidence was insufficient to warrant the return of a formal charge.

No contest: a type of plea in a criminal case that is the same as a guilty plea, for all purposes, including applying for jobs and background checks. The no-contest plea is utilized in criminal cases to avoid civil litigation (being sued) as a result of the criminal plea.

NOLLE PROSEQUI: An entry made on the record, by which the prosecutor or plaintiff declares that he will proceed no further.

of counsel: a phrase commonly applied to counsel employed to assist in the preparation or management of the case, or its presentation on appeal, but who is not the principal attorney of record.

order to show cause hearing: a hearing in which a person is ordered to court to show cause why they did not comply with the order of the court.

peremptory challenge: the challenge which the parties may use to reject a certain number of prospective jurors without assigning any reason.

petition: in the context of juvenile case processing, the petition is the formal document filed with the court outlining the charges against the juvenile.

pleading: the process by which the parties in a suit or action alternately present written statements of their contentions, to narrow the field of controversy.

post-conviction relief: a court hearing in which a defendant convicted of a crime petitions the court set to aside the conviction or modify or reduce the sentence imposed by court.

power of attorney: an instrument authorizing another to act as one's agent or attorney.

prejudicial error: synonymous with "reversible error"; an error which warrants the appellate court to reverse the judgment before it.

preliminary hearing: a hearing held in the Magistrate's Division on a felony charge to determine if the defendant should be bound over to the District Court to stand trial. If the magistrate determines that there is probable cause to believe that an offense has been committed and that the defendant committed the offense, the case is then presented to the District Court.

pretrial hearing: a court hearing that occurs before trial in which the judge sits down with the parties to the matter to review issues associated with the case. A hearing that attempts to ensure that all proceedings and documents have been completed and efforts to resolve the matter have been exhausted.

preponderance of evidence: greater weight of evidence, or evidence which is more credible and convincing to the mind, not the greater number of witnesses.

probable cause: The amount of information needed to justify the issuance of an arrest warrant or search warrant, or to allow an officer to make an arrest without a warrant, or to permit a defendant to be bound over to the district court on a felony charge at a preliminary hearing. It is defined as facts and circumstances sufficient to allow a prudent person to believe that a person committed a crime, or that contraband or evidence of a crime is present at a particular location.

probable cause hearing: a hearing to determine if there is sufficient evidence to warrant the filing of a charge or to bind a defendant over for trial.

probation: a sentence whereby a defendant is permitted to avoid serving the full sentence under specified conditions.

probation violation: a person who has been found guilty or has admitted to committing a crime is often placed on probation by a judge. Typically, there are conditions attached to probation that if not fulfilled or violated by the defendant, may result in probation being revoked.

pro se: representing himself or herself

proximate cause: a cause which, in natural or probable sequence, produced the damage complained of. It need not be the only cause. It is sufficient if it concurs with some other cause acting at the same time, which in combination with it, causes damage.

Public Defender's Office: lawyers employed specifically to represent indigent clients in criminal court.

punitive damages: are damages in excess of those required to compensate the plaintiff for the wrong done which are imposed to punish the defendant because of the particularly wanton or willful character or his or her wrongdoing.

quash: to vacate; to annul or void

reasonable doubt: an accused person is entitled to acquittal if, in the minds of the jury, his guilt has not been proved beyond a "reasonable doubt"; that state of the minds of jurors in which they cannot say they feel an abiding conviction as to the truth of the charge.

remanded: ordered back to custody, or sent back; e.g., a defendant being remanded to the custody of the sheriff or an appeal being remanded to the lower court.

retained jurisdiction: a judge, after sentencing an individual to a correctional institution may retain jurisdiction over that individual, which typically lasts 180 days. At the end of that time, the prisoner is returned to the court where his/her progress is evaluated to determine whether the prisoner should be placed on probation or required to serve out the sentence originally imposed.

sequestration: holding a jury separate and apart from outside contact.

small claims: known as the "peoples' court," the small claims court handles disputes between people that involve monetary amounts of less than $5,000. No jury trials are available in small claims nor are attorneys allowed to represent parties in small claims court.

stare decisis (sta're de-si'sis): the doctrine that when a court has once laid down a principle of law as applicable to a certain set of facts, it will adhere to that same principle and apply it to future cases where the facts are substantially the same.

statute of limitations: the statutory provisions limiting the amount of time within which a claim must be filed.

stay: a stopping or arresting of a judicial proceeding by order of the court.

stipulation: an agreement by the opposing parties or attorney pertaining to the proceedings that is binding on the parties to the stipulation.

subpoena: a notice or process served upon a witness to compel the witness to appear and give testimony before a court or agency authorized to issue subpoenas.

subpoena duces tecum: a notice or process by which the court commands a witness to produce certain documents or records.

summons: a court document used to require a person's appearance in Court.

tort: an injury or wrong committed, either with or without force, to the person or property of another.

trial de novo (de no'vo): a new trial or retrial held in a higher court in which the whole case is heard as if no trial had been held in a lower court.

under advisement: if during the course of a hearing, a question is posed that requires the judge to give more thought or do further research before making a decision, the judge takes the matter under advisement to review the matter and to render a decision.

venire-(ve-ni're): technically, a writ summoning persons to court to act as jurors; popularly used as meaning the body of names thus summoned.

venue-(ven'u): the particular county, city or geographical area in which a court with jurisdiction may hear and determine a case.

voir dire-(vwor der): to speak the truth - the process by which potential jurors are questioned to determine if they may serve on a jury.

waiver of speedy trial: State law requires that a defendant be tried within a specified period of time. The U.S. and Idaho Constitutions also provide every defendant with the right to a speedy trial. A defendant may waive that right to allow the proceeding to continue beyond the speedy trial deadline.

with prejudice: The dismissal of an action that prevents further proceedings on the same claim.

withheld judgment: A criminal disposition in which a judge does not impose a judgment of conviction but grants probation and imposes other conditions deemed appropriate. If the defendant successfully completes the conditions as outlined by the judge, the judge will then dismiss the case, resulting in the defendant having a clean record.

without prejudice: a dismissal "without prejudice" allows a new suit to be brought on the same cause of action.

writ: an order issued from a court requiring the performance of a specified act, or giving authority and commission to have it done.

CHAPTER 9

Where and How Employers Legally Obtain Accurate and Relevant Criminal Records

Introduction

The previous chapter dealt with some of the basics of criminal law and criminal procedure for employers and human resource professionals. It also discussed the fact that the U.S. is literally flooded with criminal records.

This chapter examines the next step in dealing with criminal records—the *where and how* to properly access relevant criminal records as part of an employer's Safe Hiring Program. This step involves knowing where to obtain criminal records that are accurate and actionable and well pertain to the job applicant that is the subject of the background check.

In the next chapter, the subject of relevancy will be visited again in the context of whether or not a criminal record is relevant to the job decision or should even be used, as well as Ban-the-Box and discrimination laws that impact the use of criminal records. However, that step cannot occur until after the employer has actionable and accurate information.

Six Core Concepts of Obtaining Criminal Records

There are six core concepts central to the content in this chapter.

1. Employers Need *Actionable and Accurate* Criminal Records to Make Intelligent and Lawful Decisions
2. Criminal Records Come from a Variety of Sources that were Not Intended for Employment Use
3. Not All Criminal Records are Public and Available to Employers
4. There is No Central Location for All U.S. Criminal Records—Not even the FBI Database is Perfect
5. There is No Such Thing as a National Criminal Database or an Instant Nationwide Search
6. Accuracy and Relevancy Presents Challenges

Each of these core concepts is examined in detail, followed by an examination of each record search method.

Core Concept #1—Employers Need *Actionable and Accurate* Criminal Records to Make Intelligent and Lawful Decisions

For many employers and screening firms, the emphasis often associated with criminal record access is on speed and price. In reality, however, what employers need most is **accurate** and **actionable** information to make intelligent hiring decisions.

Accurate data means that information is complete and up to date as of the time it is reported. The data can include, for example, the courthouse where the data was obtained, the code section violated, the conviction date, and the sentencing. Having accurate data also means that there are sufficient identifiers located in the criminal records to relate the records to the job applicant.

Under the FCRA, a screening firm always has an obligation to ensure that it is following "…reasonable procedures to assure maximum possible accuracy of the information concerning the individual about whom the report relates." FCRA Section 607b).

There are additional obligations under FCRA Section 613 where a background screening firm reports a criminal case. There is either a letter notice option or the obligation to "…maintain strict procedures designed to insure that whenever public record information which is likely to have an adverse effect on a consumer's ability to obtain employment is reported it is complete and up to date."

Actionable data means that the case data is usable. This means the case was not subject to an expungement or some other judicial set aside, or its use is not prohibited by applicable law. Most states have laws that provide protection against certain minor offenses or crimes that have been judicially set aside under a state procedure. Perhaps there is a state law prohibiting use if a criminal matter was only an arrest that did not result in a conviction, or there may be a state law that prohibits the reporting of an arrest only. To know if a criminal matter is reportable, a screening firm needs an understanding of the laws of all 50 states and the District of Columbia (DC), as covered in Chapter 6.

Author Tip ⟩ **An Arrest is Not Always a Conviction**

It is extremely critical to keep in mind the difference between a criminal record that is an *arrest* as opposed to one that is a *conviction*. The conviction rate is much less than the arrest rate. Although technically a "criminal record" is created for every arrest, no matter how minor, that does not mean the person was convicted.

Employers have a need for accurate and actionable information to ensure they are hiring safe, fit, and qualified team members. Just one bad hire can lead to a legal and financial nightmare. Employers have a duty to exercise due diligence in hiring, and hiring someone that is dishonest, unfit, or too risky for the position can lead to a lawsuit for negligent hiring if someone is hurt and the employer should have known there was a risk. Without the proper information, an employer cannot make good hiring decisions that protect their workplace, their customers, and the public.

Core Concept #2—Criminal Records Come from a Variety of Sources that were Not Intended for Employment Use

As used in casual conversation, the term **criminal record** usually means that someone has a criminal history. But it's much more complicated than that for employers. The term criminal record generally deals with documents or electronic computer files. However, to complicate the issue, there is no single record or a particular single piece of paper. Records concerning interactions between individuals and the authorities can be generated by any number of agencies, such as police, sheriff or other law enforcement agencies as well as courts, prosecution offices, custodial institutions, and probation departments. (See the chart in Chapter 8 concerning the various agencies that can create criminal records as a criminal case proceeds through the criminal justice system).

It is important to keep in mind the various custodial institutions and agencies of government at the local, state, and federal level that create, utilize, process, and maintain criminal records do so only for the use of the criminal justice system. The use of such records by employers or the need for screening firms to obtain the record is of zero concern to the machinery of criminal justice. For example, as discussed below, federal criminal records do not contain identifiers which makes them extremely difficult for employers to use and State court criminal record searches can also be difficult.

In addition, not every interaction between law enforcement and a person suspected of criminal activity creates what is usually thought of as a criminal record. A person may have been stopped and questioned on the street (sometimes called a *stop and frisk*), resulting in a police officer creating an internal police contact card. A person may only have been arrested but not charged with a criminal offense. Theoretically, a speeding ticket could be classified as a criminal record.

However, we do not usually think of a person with a speeding conviction as a criminal. On the other hand, a great deal of crime goes unsolved, so people who, in fact, committed criminal acts may not have ever been charged. There may be a police report relating to the crime, but no information associated with the perpetrator.

What this Core Concept means for employers is as a practical matter that finding, obtaining, and utilizing criminal records is not an easy task. The records are not readily available or easy to find and use.

Core Concept #3—Not All Criminal Records are Public and Available to Employers

In Chapter 8, a chart showed the life of a criminal case along with all of the various agencies and entities that create criminal justice records. It demonstrated an important point that employers need to know and understand—that the documentation available for an employment background report is a very small and limited subset of all the material in the possession of the criminal justice system. Although numerous records can be created by law enforcement, prosecution offices, courts, probation offices or custodial institutions, a very small subset is available to an employer or a background firm.

To obtain the most information about a past criminal case, a researcher would, of course, want to see the actual police report as well as the probation report, affidavits for search warrants and arrest warrants, and similar documents that provide all of the nitty gritty details of the case. However, none of these are public records and therefore cannot be obtained during the typical employment background screening.

Despite a wide variety of records produced in a criminal matter, what an employer can obtain through an employment screening firms is limited to public records only.

An often used definition of a Public Record is a record required by law to be made and kept by public officials in the course and scope of their duties that is filed and maintained in a public office and open to public inspection. In other words, anyone can walk in off the street and look.

Generally speaking, as described in more detail later in this chapter, a researcher can obtain the charging document, the court docket showing what occurred at each court date, and information about the sentence imposed if the person was found or plead guilty.

Still, reviewing just that information may be helpful since a great deal of information can be gleaned from the public documents. The information that is generally available in the public records will reveal the dates and nature of the offense, and the disposition (convicted, acquitted, dismissed, a judicial set aside granted, or some other result). It will show if the case was finally resolved as a felony or misdemeanor and will give the sentencing details. Typically, the charging document would state the basis of the charges and may reveal the nature of the victim or additional case details. The ultimate disposition of the case can be critical. The court may state certain terms and conditions in the sentencing that may shed light on the case. If the defendant was convicted of assault, and the court orders the defendant to attend a drug program, that may indicate drugs were involved. Somewhere in a court file some form of identification can usually be found, such as the defendant's date of birth and in some cases a driver's license number. (A Social Security number is not made public on court files.)

Depending on the jurisdiction, there may be documents in the file pertaining to some legal process of interest that remains with the public file. For example, there may be a bail application or material related to bail or custody status that may contain identification information. Also, depending on the jurisdiction, some legal papers filed by both either the prosecution or on behalf of the defendant may be available which can reveal some, critical facts of the case.

There is another category of records, however, that may be accessible under legislation that provides a means to obtain governmental records. These are records that, under some open records acts, are public in the sense that the public may request them through a process, but are not maintained in a public office such as the Court Clerk's Office where the public can enter during normal work hours and request them. There is a federal Freedom of Information Act (FOIA) as well as laws in all 50 states that in varying ways and to varying degrees allow requests to be made. For example, for our purposes, a request in some states may be a way to obtain county jail arrests and booking information. These requests would apply to records that although available through a request are not immediately available for public inspections. As a practical matter, the type of records available are of limited value since employment decisions must be made much faster than FOIA type requests can be made.

Core Concept #4—There is No Central Location for All U.S. Criminal Records—Not even the FBI Database is Perfect

Contrary to popular belief, obtaining a criminal record is not as easy as going on a computer and getting a thumbs up or a thumbs down. There are over 12,000 state and federal courthouses in the United States that are spread out over more than 3,100 counties and county equivalents, each with their own records files. **There is simply no national computer database of all criminal records available to private employers. Period. End of story.**

There are private databases that are sometimes incorrectly referred to as a "national database." These are assembled by private companies and are subject to a wide variety of errors. These databases are discussed later in this chapter.

The Federal Bureau of Investigation (FBI) and state law enforcement agencies have access to a national computer database called the **National Crime Information Center (NCIC)**. The NCIC is a computerized index of criminal justice information, such as criminal record history information, fugitives, stolen properties, and missing persons, maintained by the FBI's Criminal Justice Information Services Division in Clarksburg, West Virginia. A summary of the various components of the NCIC database is contained in the excerpt from the **About NCIC** page on the FBI website at www.fbi.gov/services/cjis/ncic.

About NCIC

The Files: The NCIC database currently consists of 21 files. There are seven property files containing records of stolen articles, boats, guns, license plates, parts, securities, and vehicles. There are 14 persons files, including: Supervised Release; National Sex Offender Registry; Foreign Fugitive; Immigration Violator; Missing Person; Protection Order; Unidentified Person; Protective Interest; Gang; Known or Appropriately Suspected Terrorist; Wanted Person; Identity Theft; Violent Person; and National Instant Criminal Background Check System (NICS) Denied Transaction. The system also contains images that can be associated with NCIC records to help agencies identify people and property items. The Interstate Identification Index, which contains automated criminal history record information, is accessible through the same network as NCIC.

How NCIC is Used: Criminal justice agencies enter records into NCIC that are accessible to law enforcement agencies nationwide. For example, a law enforcement officer can search NCIC during a traffic stop to determine if the vehicle in question is stolen or if the driver is wanted by law enforcement. The system responds instantly. However, a positive response from NCIC is not probable cause for an officer to take action. NCIC policy requires the inquiring agency to make contact with the entering agency to verify the information is accurate and up-to-date. Once the record is confirmed, the inquiring agency may take action to arrest a fugitive, return a missing person, charge a subject with violation of a protection order, or recover stolen property.

Cooperation is Key: NCIC has operated under a shared management concept between the FBI and federal, state, local, and tribal criminal justice users since its inception. There are two facets to the shared management concept—policy and functional.

The policy facet provides a means for user input on NCIC policy through the Criminal Justice Information Services (CJIS) Advisory Policy Board. The board enables NCIC users to make recommendations to the FBI Director for policy and operational enhancements to the system. The CJIS

Division actively promotes the use of the system and its benefits through daily interaction with users—whether by phone, video teleconference, or e-mail; attendance at meetings and seminars; and via the advisory process.

The functional facet provides a means for agencies to access NCIC. The FBI provides a host computer and telecommunication lines to a single point of contact in each of the 50 states, the District of Columbia, Puerto Rico, the U.S. Virgin Islands, Guam, and Canada, as well as federal criminal justice agencies. Those jurisdictions, in turn, operate their own computer systems, providing access to nearly all local criminal justice agencies and authorized non-criminal justice agencies nationwide. The entry, modification, and removal of records are the responsibility of the agency that entered them. The CJIS Division serves as the custodian of NCIC records.

Security and Quality Controls: *The head of the CJIS Systems Agency—the criminal justice agency that has overall responsibility for the administration and usage of NCIC within a district, state, territory, or federal agency—appoints a CJIS Systems Officer (CSO) from its agency. The CSO is responsible for monitoring system use, enforcing system discipline and security, and assuring that all users follow operating procedures. NCIC policy establishes a number of security measures to ensure the privacy and integrity of the data. The information passing through the network is encrypted to prevent unauthorized access. Each user of the system is authenticated to ensure proper levels of access for every transaction. To further ascertain and verify the accuracy and integrity of the data, each agency must periodically validate its records. Agencies also must undergo periodic audits to ensure data quality and adherence to all security provisions.*

Recent Accomplishments:

The Court also addressed the fact that there are different approaches to analyzing if a background check firm utilized reasonable procedures in reporting criminal records:

- *Set a new single day record on July 28, 2016, by processing 17,492,427 NCIC transactions;*
- *Implemented the Violent Person File to provide law enforcement officers with a warning if they approach an encountered individual who has the propensity to be violent toward law enforcement;*
- *Implemented the NICS Denied Transaction File which contains records on individuals who have been determined to be prohibited persons according to the Brady Handgun Violence Prevention Act of 1993 and were denied as a result of a NICS background check.*

NCIC Success Story: *Recently, a special agent with the U.S. Forest Service contacted the NCIC staff at the CJIS Division for assistance with off-line searches of purged NCIC records and past transactions in connection with a significant drug trafficking investigation in the Midwest. Several crucial off-line searches connected names of individuals with specific vehicles. This connection assisted in locating and identifying suspects associated with the case, and was invaluable in following the suspects' activities in relation to moving people, money, and products. To date, 20 people have been arrested and convicted, with more subjects identified and additional information regarding the drug trafficking organization uncovered. Approximately $1 million worth of property, illegal drugs, and contraband was seized, including marijuana, cocaine, firearms, vehicles, and cash.*

NCIC Files: *The NCIC database includes 21 files (seven property files and 14 person files):*

- ***Article File:*** *Records on stolen articles and lost public safety, homeland security, and critical infrastructure identification.*

- **Gun File:** *Records on stolen, lost, and recovered weapons and weapons used in the commission of crimes that are designated to expel a projectile by air, carbon dioxide, or explosive action.*

- **Boat File:** *Records on stolen boats.*

- **Securities File:** *Records on serially numbered stolen, embezzled, used for ransom, or counterfeit securities.*

- **Vehicle File:** *Records on stolen vehicles, vehicles involved in the commission of crimes, or vehicles that may be seized based on federally issued court order.*

- **Vehicle and Boat Parts File:** *Records on serially numbered stolen vehicle or boat parts.*

- **License Plate File:** *Records on stolen license plates.*

- **Missing Persons File:** *Records on individuals, including children, who have been reported missing to law enforcement and there is a reasonable concern for their safety.*

- **Foreign Fugitive File:** *Records on persons wanted by another country for a crime that would be a felony if it were committed in the United States.*

- **Identity Theft File:** *Records containing descriptive and other information that law enforcement personnel can use to determine if an individual is a victim of identity theft of if the individual might be using a false identity.*

- **Immigration Violator File:** *Records on criminal aliens whom immigration authorities have deported and aliens with outstanding administrative warrants of removal.*

- **Protection Order File:** *Records on individuals against whom protection orders have been issued.*

- **Supervised Release File:** *Records on individuals on probation, parole, or supervised release or released on their own recognizance or during pre-trial sentencing.*

- **Unidentified Persons File:** *Records on unidentified deceased persons, living persons who are unable to verify their identities, unidentified victims of catastrophes, and recovered body parts. The file cross-references unidentified bodies against records in the Missing Persons File.*

- **Protective Interest:** *Records on individuals who might pose a threat to the physical safety of protectees or their immediate families. Expands on the U.S. Secret Service Protective File, originally created in 1983.*

- **Gang File:** *Records on violent gangs and their members.*

- **Known or Appropriately Suspected Terrorist File:** *Records on known or appropriately suspected terrorists in accordance with HSPD-6.*

- **Wanted Persons File:** *Records on individuals (including juveniles who will be tried as adults) for whom a federal warrant or a felony or misdemeanor warrant is outstanding.*

- **National Sex Offender Registry File:** *Records on individuals who are required to register in a jurisdiction's sex offender registry.*

- **National Instant Criminal Background Check System (NICS) Denied Transaction File:** *Records on individuals who have been determined to be "prohibited persons" according to the Brady Handgun Violence Prevention Act and were denied as a result of a NICS background check. (As of August 2012, records include last six months of denied transactions; in the future, records will include all denials.)*

- ***Violent Person File:*** *Once fully populated with data from our users, this file will contain records of persons with a violent criminal history and persons who have previously threatened law enforcement.*

Source: www.fbi.gov/services/cjis/ncic

However, it is absolutely illegal for most private companies to obtain criminal information from law enforcement computer databases without specific legal authorization. There are three situations where this information is provided to private employers.

1. First, a state may pass legislation authorizing such a check. Examples are school teachers, child care, and water-treatment plant workers.
2. Second, the federal government may require an FBI criminal check. Examples are nuclear plant workers, aviation, or certain other positions in transportation.
3. Third, some types of employers have been given direct access to the FBI, such as banking institutions through the American Banking Association (ABA).

One difficulty for employers—if there is a "hit" on the FBI rap sheet—the report can be very confusing. It can be difficult to determine the nature and current status of the record without going to the courthouse and examining underlying court documents.

In 2006, the U.S. Congress requested the Justice Department to conduct a study on the feasibility of opening up the FBI database to private employers directly. A subsequent report issued by the Justice Department examined a host of issues involved with opening direct employer access for all private employers to the FBI criminal records. As of the printing of this book, there is still no direct employer access to the FBI criminal records to all private employers. Information about the report and the whole issue of the accuracy of the FBI database is addressed in Chapter 18.

You Need To Know

FBI is NOT the "Gold Standard" of Criminal Background Checks

Contrary to Hollywood movies, the FBI simply is NOT the Gold Standard when it comes to criminal background checks. For a number of technical reasons—which are discussed in Chapter 18 as well as articles in the Addendum—the FBI database can have information that is inaccurate or in incomplete. However, as discussed later, the FBI database is extremely useful, especially when combined with searches offered by private screening firms.

The topic of FBI checks is revisited in Chapter 18 when discussing and comparing fingerprint checks versus the type of searches done by private background firms using public records. Additional information on the accuracy of the FBI databases is contained in the Addendum to Chapter 18.

Core Concept #5—There is No Such Thing as a National Criminal Database or an Instant Nationwide Search

Employers can get into trouble when using so-called **national criminal databases**, **incomplete statewide systems**, and **instant searches**.

Using so-called national criminal databases: The so-called "national criminal databases" offered by private screening firms are a source of confusion and potential mistakes. Although these databases are comprised of millions of records sourced from public records information from all 50 states, the depth, breadth, and accuracy varies widely.

Because the information can be so hit and miss, it's a complete misnomer to call it a national criminal search. It's merely a large data dump of publically available court records that can be screen scraped, purchased in bulk, or obtained from some courts. In states that do not provide access to bulk-criminal records data, such as California, these databases are nearly useless.

While such privately assembled databases can be useful to screening firms as an internal research tool, employers need to be aware that these databases are not a "real" standalone background check. When a screening firm is sued for providing inaccurate data, the use of an unconfirmed database record is often the source of the issue. For example, if a consumer obtains an expungement or there has been some other post-disposition change in status, there is little guarantee that private databases will be updated with that information. Employers need to ensure that any criminal provider is taking steps to ensure that impermissible information such as expungements is not being reported. The only way for a screening firm to ensure the information from such a database is accurate and actionable is to check the courthouse file to determine if the information is complete, accurate, and up to date.

Using incomplete statewide systems: Some screening firms may try to save time and money by using statewide databases to avoid the cost and trouble of performing county court searches. However, state websites often have a disclaimer that the database has limitations, is subject to errors, and is not intended for commercial use. A limited number of states have a statewide records system that is the equivalent of courthouse searches, such as those maintained by Washington, Oregon, and New York. A recent article by BRB Publications Inc. noted that some statewide criminal record repositories have inaccuracies that make the completeness, consistency, and accuracy of these records suspect. See https://www.brbpublications.com/documents/crimrepos.pdf.

Instant searches: The words *instant* and *criminal checks* simply do not belong together in the same sentence if one is describing a single or one-time wide ranging search. For example, there are numerous counties in the U.S. where there is no electronic access or the access cannot be considered a real or primary search because the electronic records are not complete and accurate. Per statistics compiled in the *Public Record Research System* by BRB Publications, 25% of criminal record data is not available online. Any screening firm offering instant reports is offering potential litigation risk to both itself and its clients.

An employer is well advised to avoid any screening service that advertises itself as providing instant criminal records. Plus there is a potential violation of the accuracy requirements contained in the FCRA when a screening firm provides database information with instant results. If there is any type of potential match, a professional screening firm will need to go through steps to verify that the record is, in fact, related to the applicant, and that the record is accurate and up to date as well as reportable, meaning there was no expungement and it does not fall under any legal prohibition on reporting. A record that meets all of the above is considered reliable and actionable.

Report on Inaccurate Criminal Records

The Addendum contains a summary of a report by the author titled **21 Shortcuts and Traps that Can Lead to Inaccurate Criminal Records** that includes due diligence questions an employer can ask a screening provider to determine if the employer is receiving good data on which to make decisions. Part of the material covers so-called national criminal databases and instant searches.

Employment Screening Background Checks and Annual Criminal Statistics

Various organizations publish their annual criminal **hit rates** showing how many applicants subject to background screening had criminal records or other discrepancies.

On the one hand, these figures are extremely valuable because they confirm an already compelling case that background checks are critical for any employer that wants to exercise due diligence and protect its workforce and the public. On the other hand, as with all statistics, these yearly reports need to be taken with a grain of salt. First, not all criminal records come as a surprise to employers. Given the number of Americans with some sort of criminal record, many employers are still willing to hire someone for an appropriate position, providing the applicant was not dishonest in the application. In fact, certain industries by nature of their workforce are more likely to draw upon a pool of potential applicants that may tend to have higher levels of past criminal conduct. Examples might be construction or firms that provide employment for entry level workers.

A statistic that would be very interesting but much harder to obtain is how many criminal records were discovered where the applicant was dishonest about past conduct. Of course, that gets complicated by the fact that an applicant may have been genuinely confused about what is or is not reportable on an application. A related issue is that not all criminal records have the same impact. A criminal record for underage drinking is not in the same league as a conviction for armed robbery.

In reviewing these types of statistics, employers also need to keep in mind that not all of the criminal records located are job related. Employers should NOT automatically deny employment to an applicant with a criminal record unless there is a business justification that takes into account the nature and gravity of the crime, the nature of the job and the age of the crime. As noted in this book, the EEOC takes the position that the overuse of criminal records without a business justification can create a disparate impact, and therefore can be discriminatory.

Finally, it is difficult to draw firm conclusions from the statistics without knowing the search methodology. Depending on how the searches were conducted, it is entirely possible in fact that such annual statistics may even understate the number of criminal records applicants had. The most accurate criminal record searches are done by accessing information directly from the county courthouse level, either by physically going the court or by use of the court computer system that is the functional equivalent of going to the courthouse. Databases on the other hand, although much wider in scope, are not nearly as accurate, do not have all courts or jurisdiction, may not be updated, or may not contain sufficient identifiers. To the extent any searching was done by the use of databases, the numbers could potentially be understated.

The bottom line: These statistics are an excellent reminder that employers need to be careful in hiring. However, as with most statistics, there is more to the story.

Core Concept #6—Accuracy and Relevancy Presents Challenges

The sixth core concept relates to the accuracy of the criminal record and the need to ensure the record truly relates to the applicant. This applies to both a background screening firm and any employer that obtains criminal records themselves without going through a background firm. The key concepts to consider here are **false positives** and **false negatives.**

A **false positive** occurs where a person is incorrectly identified as a criminal offender and, in fact, they should not be. For example, an applicant may have received an expungement or some other judicial set aside so they can legally say they have no criminal record. Or the criminal record may belong to someone else, and a job applicant has been labeled a criminal when they are not. Another example is where the criminal record is reported as a more serious offense, such as a felony, and in fact, it was only a misdemeanor. When there is a false positive, the concern is that a person can be denied an employment opportunity unfairly.

A **false negative** is also of grave concern. That occurs where an applicant does, in fact, have a relevant criminal record that should be reported and analyzed, and is missed. This can happen when a screening firm takes shortcuts by using faulty data sources or search methodologies that do not fully protect an employer. One possible result of a false negative is that an applicant is hired for a position where the criminal record created a foreseeable risk and someone is harmed as a proximate cause of a failure to exercise due diligence which can result in a lawsuit against an employer for negligent hiring.

Examples of inaccurate criminal information caused by false positives include:

1. Reporting an offense that did not, in fact, belong to the applicant.
2. Reporting an offense as a felony when, in fact, it was a misdemeanor.
3. Reporting an offense that has been judicially set aside under state law, such as an expungement, pardon, deferred adjudication, or some other provision of law.
4. Misreporting details about the offense, such as the sentence or terms of probation, that makes the offense appear more serious than it really is.
5. Reporting counts that have been dismissed, which has the potential to misrepresent again the seriousness of the matter.
6. Reporting arrests that did not result in convictions in states that do not allow such reporting (and as discussed in Chapter 10, could potentially be a violation of the EEOC Guidance).
7. Reporting convictions that are beyond seven years in states with seven-year limitations.
8. Reporting arrests that are older than seven years in violation of the FCRA.
9. Reporting criminal matters inadvertently by asking questions of employers designed to determine if a matter is reportable by means of a question that reveals a criminal matter.
10. Repetitive references to the same offense, creating a false impression of greater criminality.

Some of these types of errors were documented in a report issued by National Consumer Law Center (NCLC) called *Broken Records: How Errors by Criminal Background Checking Companies Harm Workers and Businesses* found at www.nclc.org/images/pdf/pr-reports/broken-records-report.pdf. Although such errors may exist, the report has been heavily criticized for taking a few incidents out of the millions of background checks conducted in order to create a false impression of widespread inaccuracies. The NCLC report also did not appear to understand the difference between data brokers and a background screening firm. The author of this book issued a detailed response to the NCLC report, see www.esrcheck.com/articles/NCLC-Report-on-Criminal-Background-Checks-Inaccurate.php.

Although the NCLC report received a great deal of publicity, it also came under heavy criticism for being inaccurate, misleading, and lacking objectivity and subject matter knowledge. The report cites a handful of anecdotal stories and some court cases (out of the millions of background checks conducted yearly) where an inaccurate background check had grave consequences on a consumer's ability to get a job. In fact, based upon an objective evaluation of the claims made, given the NCLC could only find an extremely small number of erroneous reports per the millions done, the accuracy rate is actually extremely high. The report also failed to understand the difference between data brokers that aggregate raw data and a Consumer Reporting Agency (CRA) operating under the Fair Credit Reporting Act (FCRA). It also failed to acknowledge the horrendous harm done to victims of crimes when employers could have prevented a situation with a proper background check. It is much easier for applicants to get a job after an erroneous background report then it is for crime victims to get on with their lives after harmed as a result of negligent hiring. To read a detailed discussion by the author regarding the NCLC report, visit: www.esrcheck.com/articles/NCLC-Report-on-Criminal-Background-Checks-Inaccurate.php.

In the event a criminal record is reported, FCRA section 613 is also concerned about accuracy and relevancy. That section provides two options to background firms. One option involves the use of *strict procedures*, and the other is to send the consumer notice at the same time the criminal matter is reported to the employer so the consumer can dispute it. FCRA section 613 states that:

"(A) *In general.* A consumer reporting agency which furnishes a consumer report for employment purposes and which for that purpose compiles and reports items of information on consumers which are matters of public record and are likely to have an adverse effect upon a consumer's ability to obtain employment shall:

(1) at the time such public record information is reported to the user of such consumer report, notify the consumer of the fact that public record information is being reported by the consumer reporting agency, together with the name and address of the person to whom such information is being reported; or

(2) maintain strict procedures designed to insure that whenever public record information which is likely to have an adverse effect on a consumer's ability to obtain employment is reported it is complete and up to date. For

purposes of this paragraph, items of public record relating to arrests, indictments, convictions, suits, tax liens, and outstanding judgments shall be considered up to date if the current public record status of the item at the time of the report is reported."

Congress drove this point home even further in the statement of Congressional findings and statement of purpose contained in section 602:

(b) *Reasonable procedures.* It is the purpose of this title to require that consumer reporting agencies adopt reasonable procedures for meeting the needs of commerce for consumer credit, personnel, insurance, and other information in a manner which is fair and equitable to the consumer, with regard to the confidentiality, accuracy, *relevancy*, and proper utilization of such information in accordance with the requirements of this title. (*Emphasis added.*)

The use of the word *relevancy* in the FCRA further underscores the need for a background check firm to ensure that reasonable steps are taken to only report information relevant to the consumer.

On the other side of the coin, accuracy also means NOT missing relevant criminal information that would assist an employer in making a better hiring decision. Failure to locate criminal records that would be germane to a hiring decision can be equally devastating to innocent victims if an employer hires someone that is dangerous, dishonest, unqualified, or unfit due to the failure of a background screening firm to locate potentially relevant information. As mentioned above, reporting someone as clear, when in fact, there is a relevant criminal record, is known as a false negative.

Key Sources of Criminal Data and How to Access

The remainder of the chapter examines six major sources of criminal records including their worthiness and the pros and cons of using them, and how to best access these sources.

1. County Courthouses
2. Individual County and Statewide Court Online Databases Sites
3. State Record Repositories
4. Other Criminal Record-Related Databases
5. Federal Court Searches
6. Private Sector Commercial Databases

1. County Courthouse Searches

The **access method most often used** is to **physically visit each relevant county courthouse and look up the record**. That is done for two good reasons.

1. First, it is reliable and usually the fastest method. Indexes and records can be viewed immediately.
2. Second, if there is a potential match, the researcher can make arrangements to view the file and look at case details, finding identifiers to be certain it is indeed their person on the spot.

The First Step –Determine Where to Search

Since every county courthouse cannot be searched, the key is to choose which counties are relevant. Here are some guidelines:

- **County of Residence**: At a minimum, employers should search the county of residence or the last place where the applicant spent the most time. Although there are no conclusive studies to prove the point, many criminal justice professionals have observed that the county of residence is the most likely location for a criminal to commit a crime. Many background screening firms have found that employers get the biggest bang for the buck by searching the county of residence – assuming a person has not moved there recently.

- **Last Three Counties**: Some employers have a policy to search the last three counties lived in. Use of three counties is not based upon any court case or official government recommendation; rather, it is based on the experience of screening firms showing that most applicants have lived in an average of two to three counties in a seven-year period.
- **Seven-Year Search**: A much higher degree of protection is a minimum seven-year county search of all places where the applicant lived, worked, or studied based on his or her application. Some states have forms of seven-year limitations. The county names can be determined as a result of verification of past employment and all past addresses provided as part of a Social Security Trace or an Address Information Manager tool that will typically contain more information.
- **Adjacent County or Metro Searches**: An employer can go to an even higher level by also searching metro areas of adjacent counties. This search recognizes the fact that there is nothing to prevent a person with a criminal record from crossing county lines. For example, if an employer wanted to search for criminal records for a person who lived in Boston, the employer would likely check Suffolk County. However, a metro search would include Norfolk, Middlesex, and Essex Counties. Here are several other examples (the first county named is where the city is located):
  - **Atlanta** – Fulton, Clayton, Cobb, Dekalb, Douglas
  - **Baltimore** – City of Baltimore, Anne Arundel, Baltimore, Howard
  - **Chicago** – Cook, Dupage, Kane, Lake, Will
  - **Dallas** – Dallas, Collin, Ellis, Kaufman, Tarrant
  - **Detroit** – Wayne, Macomb, Monroe, Oakland, Washtenaw
  - **San Francisco** – San Francisco, Alameda, Contra Costa, Marin, San Mateo
  - **San Jose** – Santa Clara, Alameda, San Benito, San Mateo, Santa Cruz, Stanislaus

A database of all adjoining counties in the U.S. is available through BRB Publications. The adjoining county data is available as a CD-ROM product and as part of an online subscription service. See www.brbpublications.com.

How to Do a County Courthouse Search

Since the most accurate and least complicated search is at the courthouse, employers should have an understanding of how this type of search is performed at the actual courthouse, in the clerk's records office, by human beings. Keep in mind the methods of access, retrieval, and storage can vary from court to court.

First – Determine Who Performs the Actual Search?

There are actually two venues when answering this question.

1. The employer can either do the search itself or hire someone, usually called a record researcher, to do it for them.
2. At the courthouse, either the court provides a searchable index of records so the public can do their own searching or else the court has a mandatory rule that all searches must be performed by court personnel.

Searches Performed by Researchers. Some courts have public computer terminals that a researcher can view in person; the researcher may have to type in each name, or the researcher views a list of names to see if the applicant's name appears. Some courts index names in other searchable formats such as ledgers, microfiche, or microfilm, although with increased computerization, that is becoming less common.

If the research is being conducted by a background screening firm, the actual court researcher is most likely not a direct employee of the screening firm. Because there are over 10,000 courthouses in 3,144 counties and county equivalents in the U.S., most screening firms do not have employees at each and every courthouse. Instead, there is an entire industry of court researchers that service background firms by providing a search in nearly any county in America within one to three days. Generally, the firms or individuals who specialize in court record searching will only work for ongoing business customers, such as attorneys or screening firms. Researchers are hired to provide all information available, and it is the background firm that has the responsibility under the FCRA to determine if the matter is reportable. See Chapter 10 on the Legal Use of Criminal Records for information on the legal requirements for accuracy in reporting criminal records. A county-by-county list of a select group of researchers who abide by a code of professional conduct is found at the Public Record Retriever Network (PRRN) web page at www.prrn.com.

Searches Performed by Court Personnel. Some courts require that the names to be searched must be handed over to a member of the court clerk staff who then performs the actual search. This is because there is no public terminal or other readily usable index which is made available to the public. Approximately 45% of the courts in the U.S. do not provide a public access terminal.

What to Expect if Employers Do the Screening themselves

If an employer is hiring locally, the employer can go to the local courthouse, talk to the court clerk, learn the system, and search the records. Of course, the court clerk cannot give an employer legal advice, but he or she may be helpful in showing the employer the local record keeping system. Many court clerks' offices have signs indicating they are prohibited by law from giving legal advice. (Free legal advice is often worth exactly what it costs.)

Another issue is the logistics and travel involved. Suppose an employer has an applicant from the next county, or from the other side of the state, or even from another state. Record checking then becomes a very different process. First, the employer needs to locate the courthouse(s) for that county. Since every court is different, the employer then needs to contact the court ahead of time to find out exactly what search procedures they use. The court may require a letter or fax, a consent form, or a fee. Then there is the issue of turnaround time. By the time the request is mailed, processed, and returned, weeks may have passed. If there is a potential match—a hit—then further communication is needed to arrange to get a copy of the file. Courts typically charge a per-page copy fee and usually require any fees to be paid in advance. However, as mentioned earlier many courts will not do a name search of criminal records, ignoring requests sent by mail or telephoned.

That is where the alternative of hiring a record searcher is advantageous. Presumably, an employer does not want to drive everywhere to check records, not to mention the value of the employer's time.

Internet search services are also available, but employers need to be very aware of their pluses and minuses. These types of searches are covered later in this chapter and in Chapter 10.

Start by Doing a Name Search

When a case is filed, a case number is assigned. Use of a case number is the primary indexing method in every court. Therefore, to search specific case file documents, you will need to know – or find – the applicable case number. Be aware that case numbering procedures are not necessarily consistent throughout a state court system. One district may assign numbers by district while another may assign numbers by location (division) within the district, or by judge.

Typically, when a screening firm is searching for a criminal record, it does not have the case number. So how does a criminal screening firm determine if a job applicant has a criminal case? It is done by use of Court Indexes. Unless you know the exact case number, to search for a record or to determine if a record exists the index is one of first items you need to check.

In most jurisdictions, a clerk's office will contain some sort of public access to a register of actions. For most courts, that is now done by means of a computer. The register of actions will list criminal cases by the last name. As outlined below, however, the listing is normally based upon name only, and the presence of a person's name in such a listing does not mean it is the same person applying for the job until the court file is pulled and additional identification information located.

A public record index can be electronic but also can exist on-site on card files, in books, on microfiche, etc. A record index can be organized in a variety of ways – by name, by year, by case or file number, or by name and year. A record index points to a location or file number of the case. The same type of index system exists for other types of public records such as recordings, deeds, and articles of incorporation. A record index can be electronic but also can exist on-site on card files, in books, on microfiche, etc. A record index can be organized in a variety of ways—by name, by year, by case or file number, or by name and year. With increased computerization, these older ways of indexing are less frequent but can still be encountered.

The first step in using the court index involves the researcher looking on an index or docket for the applicant's name, or the absence of it. If the name is not shown, then the search is marked clear. When the name is found, there are additional steps to follow.

The critical point in doing a name search depends upon a human being either entering data in a computer or visually reviewing a list of names. As with any human endeavor, errors are possible. Any human error in data input, or reviewing a list of names, can result in either a false negative or false positive.

Names can also be missed if the applicant used a variation of his or her first name. For example, if looking for Robert Smith a researcher must also look for a Rob Smith or a Bob Smith. If a researcher was looking for a James Evans and the person was arrested under Jim Evans, then the name could be missed. If the applicant is a Junior, a court index may list that at the very end instead of in alphabetical order. If an applicant was arrested under the name Joe Smith, Jr., a search under the "S" category may miss it.

One factor working in a researcher's favor is that by the time the court record had been created, there normally has been some sort of process whereby a law enforcement officer, a jail official, a District Attorney, or Judge will have verified the person's true name. For example, if a consumer is arrested, a police officer will normally look at a consumer's identification in the form of a state issued driver's license or identification card. If a person is booked into custody, a jail may take fingerprints. If a district attorney decided to file a criminal charge, it is usual and customary to run a criminal history and/or driving record to determine the consumer's criminal history for purposes of making a decision on the appropriate charges. As part of the arraignment process, in court, where an accused individual makes an initial court appearance, a Court will typically inquire if the name on the charging document is the defendant's true name. The criminal justice system is very aware that a defendant may have an incentive to play games with their true identity in order to escape more serious charges stemming from past conduct or to avoid having to pay fines or comply with probation terms or conditions. Of course, as discussed in Chapters 11 and 22, the ability to positively identify everyone is not perfect. But court procedures do assist in minimizing name and ID issues with criminal records.

A researcher also faces cultural name complications. In some cultures, a person uses both the maiden name and the family surname. For example, Spanish names are often based on a first name, the mother's maiden name, and the family name. However, if an applicant only goes by the mother's name, a completely different search strategy is needed. If a search is conducted for the name "Juan Garcia Hernandez," and a person was arrested under the name "Juan Garcia," then there is a strong likelihood the record will be missed.

Be Aware of Alias Names

A similar problem exists with former names or aliases, also called AKAs (Also Known As). A common former name issue is when a female applicant has changed her last name as a result of marriage. An employment application or screening form should ask for previous names. It should also ask for the DATE of the name change. For example, if a name change was 20 years ago, and an employer is only searching back seven years, there is no reason to search under the former name.

It is also important to remember that an alias search is considered a separate search. If an applicant now has the name of Susan Jones, and she changed her name three years ago from Susan Barry, then both names should be searched. As far as court records are concerned, Susan Jones and Susan Berry are two entirely separate people. If the court is doing the search, two fees will be involved because two names are searched. The same can hold true if a screening firm conducts the search. There is normally an extra charge for the second name or alias search since the court researcher is looking for two entirely different names in the court records.

Author Tip

Previous Name Search

A second name search should *not* be referred to as a **maiden name** search since that clearly indicates that an employer is obtaining information on marital status, which is a prohibited basis upon which to make an employment decision. The second name search should be referred to as a **previous name search.** More information about this trap and other legal concerns stemming from discrimination laws are reviewed in Chapter 2.

The idiosyncrasies surrounding the name search make it critical for employers to understand that criminal record searching is not perfect and should only be considered as only one of many tools that are part of an overlapping system of checks. The fact that a criminal record can also be missed serves to underscore the importance of getting the applicant to be honest on his or her application and in interviews. Employers who utilize the AIR (Application-Interview-Reference) Process described in Chapters 3 and 4 find there is a much-reduced likelihood of hiring a criminal.

If There Is a Hit, a Researcher Must Pull or Review a Court File to Confirm Identity

If a researcher finds a criminal record in the name of the applicant, does that mean the applicant cannot be employed? The answer is an emphatic NO. The location of a criminal record by a name match is just the start of the process. If there is a hit (a name match), then the researcher or background firm needs to determine if the person located is truly the applicant.

For purposes of employment screening, the relevant public records are the charging documents and the Docket typically maintained by a court clerk. Most of the documents briefly summarized above are NOT public records and therefore are not available to an employer or background firm. The normal documents available are:

1. The charging documents.
2. The court clerk summary of all court proceedings (in some jurisdictions called Clerk's Minute Order, registrar of actions, or a docket sheets).
3. Sentencing information such as a waiver of rights form.

You Need To Know

Some Court Information is Available Online

In some courts, this information may be available online or through a public terminal.

While docket sheets differ somewhat in format from court to court, the basic information contained on a docket sheet is consistent. Docket sheets will contain:

*   Name of court, including location (division) and the judge assigned;
*   Case number and case name;
*   Names of all defendants;
*   Names and addresses of attorneys for the prosecuting and the defendant;
*   Charges against the defendant. Date and summary of all materials and motions filed in a case;
*   Summary of all court appearances and what occurred; and
*   Case outcome (disposition).

A best practice is to utilize all information in the possession of the researcher, employer, or screening firm to determine if the criminal record found reasonably is associated with the subject of the search. A researcher needs to locate an identifier in order to match the court record to the applicant. Examples of commonly used identifiers are:

*   Date of birth.
*   Driver's license number.
*   Social Security number.

Some records may track by race. However, for reasons discussed in Chapter 2 concerning discrimination laws, race is not a helpful criteria category for private employers to use. Another potential source of identification may be physical characteristics, such as height or weight. The issue, however, is that such information may well be missing from the public records. Remember, a researcher is looking only at available public records, and that does not include items that may contain racial or other physical identifiers such as police reports, jail book photos (commonly called "mug shots), and arrest warrants, jail booking records, or similar data.

Where are the identifiers located?

That depends upon the court and the way the records are kept. In some courthouses, identifiers may be part of the index system. An identifier may be in the computerized index, microfiches, or whatever system the court uses to provide a record index. In some courts, there are limitations on identifiers in order to protect privacy. In courts that limit identifiers, criminal case research is made more difficult because a researcher only has a name match.

You Need To Know > ## When There is Only a Name Match

There are times when identifiers are not available from the court. This can happen, for example, if the Court has purged its old files and the case file has been physically destroyed. At that point, the researcher has a name match only without identifiers, so there is a question if that case is associated with the applicant.

If there is a name match on an index without identifiers, then the court researcher must review each possible court file that bears the same name of the applicant, in order to determine if there is an identifier that relates to the name of the subject of the search. At this point, a researcher will typically try to use the court file to match the date of birth. If it is a common name, this can become a very laborious procedure.

The problem with using a name match only and not finding any other identifiers is twofold:

1) If the screening firm fails to report a potential criminal case where there are no identifiers but only a name match, and in fact, it would have led to a red flag being discovered and a workplace problem avoided, then the screening firm can be potentially liable for not providing adequate information. On the other hand, if the name match only leads to a consumer dispute by an applicant that maintains it is not his or her criminal record, the screening firm must under the FCRA do a re-investigation (Section 611) and remove any data it cannot verify. That potentially puts a screening firm in a Catch-22.

2) If a background screening firm does report a result based upon a name match only without identifiers, it is critical for the screening firm to be clear that there are no identifiers. Many screening firms, however, will not report a name match only, out of concern that it does not meet the accuracy requirements of the FCRA. This again underscores that although background checks are a critical due diligence tool, there are times when there are matters beyond the control of a screening firm. That is why it is important to keep in mind that no one tool should be relied upon to conduct due diligence and that overlapping tools and processes are critical.

Author Tip〉 **Issues with Middle Name Logic**

There are some issues with **middle name logic** that may be encountered during a background check. A person may not have a middle name or middle initial OR a person may omit or change the middle name or middle initial on purpose to fool the system and hide their true identity. Middle name logic is a factor to look at but is typically not dispositive.

What data does a researcher look at in the court files?

As mentioned, in order to review the case file to look for identifiers, a court researcher may need to ask court personnel to find—or pull—files. In other counties, the informant is already available online. There are two primary sources that are usually reviewed.

- The charging document specifies the exact law by section that the defendant is charged with, along with other details such as the name and location of the court and the prosecution who brings the case. This document may contain identifiers about the defendant.
- The court docket and/or clerk minutes contain the events that occurred at each court appearance. It is essentially the history of the case. The docket will include such items as the plea entered by the defendant, and in the event the defendant either pleads guilty or is found guilty, it will contain the sentence imposed as well as the exact charges for which the defendant was convicted. This file may also contain identifiers.

In some courts, there are limits to how many files a court clerk can pull. Further delays are possible if the file is placed in storage. Although citizens generally have a right to access public files, the speed at which a court clerk chooses to obtain the files is up to that court clerk. Even when an employer performs background checks in person, there can be delays.

Why Do Some Government Agencies Feel Compelled to Shoot Themselves in the Foot?

In some jurisdictions, court clerks have taken the position that identifiers should be masked or not be made public in order to protect privacy and to guard against identity theft. Some counties have even restricted the access to court records. When this occurs, several things happen. First, employers and job applicants are immediately penalized because background checks take much longer. Any delay in a CRA's ability to complete reports in a timely manner works to the determent of consumers and employers. Consumers want a CRA to have fast access to criminal records. Second, criminals and terrorists are arguably the primary beneficiaries since they have a better chance of avoiding detection. Finally, the courts end up becoming over-burdened because suddenly there is a much increased workload, as employers and researchers have a greater need to pull files to search for identifiers. If a researcher finds a match for common names in the court index, the researcher will need to request and review every file to look at identifiers in an effort to determine if the case belongs to the applicant in question. That substantially increases the workload on county clerks.

Although protecting privacy and combating identity theft are important considerations, courts need to balance privacy versus public access and the public good. Perhaps the best way to achieve the balance is to leave in the date of birth identifier needed to perform an accurate check and mask out the Social Security number. This way, researchers have access to date of birth, which is the primary identifier. Privacy is protected since typically the Social Security number is the tool used for identity theft. Leaving a date of birth on a court record presents a small privacy risk since little harm occurs to an individual if the date of birth is used.

The Researcher Must Confirm Case Details

Assuming the criminal file is examined and identifiers are located, that still does not mean the criminal matter can be used in the consideration of the applicant's employment. There are a number of reasons a criminal record may not be legal to use — there are a number of regulatory considerations to weigh before using a criminal record.

In order to determine if the record may be used, a researcher must obtain details about the case — the nature of the offense, the offense date, future court dates, sentencing, probation terms, and whether the case is a *felony* or a *misdemeanor*.

It Can Be a Big Mistake Not to Look for Misdemeanors – If Permitted

One of the biggest mistakes an employer can make is only to ask about or search for felonies, or the job application only asks about felonies. This practice is partly because in many states there are limitations on asking about misdemeanors. However, in some states, misdemeanors can be very serious.

An employer certainly wants to know if an applicant has been convicted of:

- Resisting arrest
- Battery on a police officer
- Possession of drug paraphernalia
- Illegal gun possession
- Commercial burglary
- Assaulting a child or spouse

In many states, these violations are misdemeanors, not felonies. In some instances, a misdemeanor case can be extremely relevant to a job and even more relevant than a felony. For example, petty theft may be a misdemeanor, but if an applicant was being considered for a bookkeeping position, that would be good information to have. Another example: a driving under the influence can be a misdemeanor but a very relevant one to any position involving driving.

It is not unusual for felony charges to be reduced to a misdemeanor through a plea bargain. When some element of the case may be hard to prove, the felony charge can be reduced to a misdemeanor by plea-bargaining. There may have been mitigating circumstances in either the crime itself or in the life of the perpetrator so that a prosecutor feels a misdemeanor is appropriate under the circumstances. Sometimes one *bad actor* commits a crime against another *bad actor*, leading to one person with a criminal record testifying against another with a criminal record after having bargained for a lesser penalty in exchange for cooperating with authorities. In large jurisdictions with more crimes to prosecute than there are resources, there may be more pressure to plea-bargain cases out of the system.

The Bottom Line: Because a misdemeanor can be the result of behavior that may otherwise have been serious enough to be considered a felony, and is only a misdemeanor due to a plea bargain, employers cannot afford to ignore misdemeanors. But in order to ask about misdemeanors, it is important for the employer to first be aware of the rules in its state.

About Court Access Fees

When court personnel must perform the search on site, there is often an **access fee** or **search fee charged**. This court fee ranges from $1.00 to $27.00. A court may also charge a copy fee for documents and a certification fee if that document needs to be certified. Some courts even charge for each file or case that must be pulled.

Fees are often incurred as well when the record index is searched online. The highest fee for a search, $65.00, is charged by the New York State Office of Court Administration's (OCA) of its statewide Criminal History Record Search (CHRS). Although New York authorities claim that is for an entire statewide search, it is not clear that all relevant courts or all potential offense are covered.

Background firms add these court fees as a surcharge to all searches since the fee represents an actual out-of-pocket cost. Since the fees vary by courts, some background screening firms add the surcharge automatically when an employer orders a search from a particular court. Other screening firms use a pricing platform that may average in the cost of the court fees on the theory that flat fees make accounting easier. Either way, it is a real cost that is eventually passed on to employers. An employer should make sure they understand which billing/fee approach a background firm utilizes.

Be Prepared for Court Delays

A common problem for background screening firms and employers is unavoidable court delays. By now, it is clear that criminal record searches done correctly are not a matter of just sitting at a computer and pushing buttons. Researchers need to do actual work for each and every name for the most accurate record. However, there are occasions that despite the best efforts of a court researcher, a court caused delay frustrates the employer's need to have the search completed in a short time period. Unfortunately, there are some situations where even if an employer hired Sherlock Holmes, the search cannot be completed any faster. For example:

- As mentioned, some counties do not provide access to a public terminal and require that names of applicants be submitted to the court clerk. Since this is probably not the highest court priority, there can be delays.
- If a file needs to be physically examined to find additional identifiers or to verify the details of the case, there can be delays in the court clerk pulling the physical court file. If a court file has been moved to storage, and the court clerk only drives to the storage facility once a week, there is nothing anyone can do to make a court clerk go to the storage facility any faster.
- On occasions, the court is subject to slow-downs due to budget cuts and layoffs. When that occurs, updating or processing criminal records is simply not a priority.
- Some courts are behind in computerizing case files.
- Winter weather, natural disasters, power outages, or similar problems can also adversely impact court researching. In such circumstances, a court may not be able to operate normally, or researchers may be physically prevented from accessing the court.

Looking for Criminal Offenses in Counties with Multiple Courts

The services of background screening firms typically only provide a search of court records from the central courthouse.

While most counties have a central court where all felony records are held, some jurisdictions have multiple lower level courts such as municipal courts or justice of the peace courts. These local courts may not report all convictions to a central court. The good news, however, is that these outlying lower courts often only handle minor cases such as town or municipal infractions. If these cases were more serious, then they would typically be sent to the central court. An example is Aiken County, SC. There is a central Circuit Court where felonies and most misdemeanors are available. There are also five Magistrate Courts with minor case offenses. In this county, it is not practical for employers to go driving all over the country side in case there is a minor record in a remote lower court not reported to that central circuit court.

Therefore, it is not likely employers are missing much if they fail to check the small courts. In addition, these local courts can be difficult to search, have irregular hours of operation, or may be located in remote areas. One plus is that if the offense is driving-related, such as a driving under the influence case, it should be reported to the state motor vehicle department and should show up on a driving record. While there are exceptions, the bottom line is that once again criminal record searches are not perfect and some offenses can still slip through the cracks.

See The Addendum | **Repetition of Single Criminal Incident Can Violate FCRA**

The Addendum contains the article *"Federal Court Rules Unnecessary Repetition of Single Criminal Incident can be Misleading and be the Basis of an Allegation for Punitive Damages Against Background Screening Firm."*

Using Individual County and Statewide Court Online Database Sites

Per statistics from the Public Record Research System maintained by BRB Publications, over 75% of courts holding felony and misdemeanor records offer some type of online access to the docket index. A much, much lower percentage for courts offer online access to case file records. Many of these online sites are managed by a State Administrative Office of Courts (AOC). In fact, at least 32 of these state agencies provide online searching capabilities to the public.

The Benefits

With online access, employers can go to a court website and do name searches to see if their candidate is listed on any index of criminal cases. If the person's name is not on the list, the person can potentially be marked clear. That assumes, of course, the database is complete and up to date.

Some systems offer a statewide search. If the state has a centralized case management system, the chances of there being a comprehensive online search are increased.

The Drawbacks

Unfortunately, there is much more bad news about the online judicial websites:

- Typically, court website searches are only of a record index. If there is an index hit, the site does not give the searcher the full case file information. This means that arrangements must be made to retrieve actual court records. That may require some back-and-forth correspondence with the court, plus fees, release forms, etc., as described earlier.
- The throughput and lag time will often vary. For example, one county may update nightly with cases dating back seven years, while the next county over may take 72 hours to post online plus may only go back three years.
- Online searches can also have limitations when using first names. Some courts will only search the exact name entered and not take into account any variations or "wildcard" first. So, if the employer has a Robert Smith who was charged under the name "Rob Smith" or "Bob Smith," an employer can get a "false negative." This means the person will come back "clear" and, in fact, he or she could have a criminal record. The alternative is to pay to search for each permutation of the first name.
- Identifiers are another issue for online services. Many systems operate on a name only basis, or only show a DOB or address if entered in a docket. If the name does not appear (assuming the correct first name was run), then the person is clear. If a common name was run and gets matches, someone is then required to go to the courthouse and pull files to determine the proper identity. A related problem is that the online court system may require a requester to submit a date of birth and as discussed earlier, there can be a problem for the employer to obtain the DOB. Another problem is that the online index may contain only names with no identifiers.
- Most courts will have a disclaimer that the online data is *as is* and may not be a true reflection of actual court records. There may even be a prohibition against commercial use or using for background screening purposes (see Rhode Island).
- A number of the court online sites are not equivalent to an onsite search at the courthouse (such as in Minnesota). Note there are online vendors selling so-called instant statewide court criminal record searches in states where not all the records are online (such as Arizona).

Remember those TV shows where a professional stunt person would perform, and the announcer would say, "Remember, we are professionals. Do not try this at home." To avoid getting false results, there is an element of training and experience needed when using some databases. Unless a researcher or employer is knowledgeable about these issues described above, the chance that a search will be incomplete will escalate.

Federal Case Illustrates Problems with Using Statewide Court Data

In a case decided by a federal court in Kentucky, the court observed the difficulties with using a statewide court repository of records as the basis of a background check. The opinion also reviewed various difficulties in reporting public records. The court first noted that the statewide criminal records maintained by the Kentucky Administrative Office of the Courts (AOC) does not contain official court records, but is only a statewide repository of official records and clearly indicates in bold type it does not provide an official court report. The court reviewed the difficulties in reading and analyzing the Kentucky AOC records in this case that could lead to a misunderstanding of the actual court records from the county where the offense occurred. See below:

Court Finds No Liability Though Background Check Report Inaccurate Since Employer Already Decided Not to Hire

In a case that touched upon a number of issues affecting background checks, a federal district court held that even though a background check report was erroneous and inaccurate, it had no bearing on the employment decision since a hospital had already decided not to hire a candidate based on their prior knowledge of misconduct and a bad interview.

In a decision from the U.S. District Court for the Western District of Kentucky, the plaintiff applied for a position as an Associate Medical Director. Before the background check report was returned, the hospital discovered that the plaintiff had been involved in criminal activity related to prescription drugs, although not aware of the details. The plaintiff also interviewed very poorly. The decision had already been made to continue the search to fulfill that position before the background check report was returned.

The background check report, based on a review of a statewide repository of county court records maintained by the Kentucky Administrative Office of the Courts (AOC), reported a felony for possession of controlled substance not stored in their original container.

Upon reviewing the background check report, the Plaintiff notified the background check firm that the report was wrong. Within several minutes, the background check firm contacted the county where the offense occurred and attempted to correct the background check report to show the plaintiff only had a misdemeanor conviction (although the details were still not entirely correct).

In ruling on a motion for summary judgment, the Court ruled that even assuming all of the allegations by the plaintiff were correct, the plaintiff failed to state a grounds for relief in that the hospital had already decided NOT to hire before reviewing the inaccurate background check report, and that the incorrect report "merely supported the decision they had already made." The court noted that the background check report was promptly amended, and although it was still not entirely accurate, did indicate the offense was only a misdemeanor.

The opinion also reviewed various difficulties in reporting public records. The Court first noted that the statewide criminal records maintained by the Kentucky AOC does not contain official court records, but is only a statewide repository of official records and that it clearly indicates in bold type that it is not an official court report. The Court reviewed the difficulties in reading and analyzing the Kentucky AOC records in this case that could lead to a misunderstanding of the actual court records from the county where the offense occurred. The Court noted that even after contacting the court clerk in Jefferson County, the background check firm still did not have an entirely accurate report, although it was correct insofar as the ultimate offense was a misdemeanor.

The Court also addressed the fact that there are different approaches to analyzing if a background check firm utilized reasonable procedures in reporting criminal records:

- The Court noted that one approach is that a background check firm is entitled to rely upon whatever is noted in the official court records and is not obligated to go beyond that. To require more would be unduly burdensome and expensive. In addition, if there is an inaccuracy, a consumer is in the better position to note it and can bring it to the attention of the consumer reporting agency (CRA) that can then correct it.

- A second approach is that a background check firm is responsible for looking beyond the notations in a court report to ensure the information is correct.

- A third approach is that a background check firm can report what is in a public record, provided that it believes the source is reputable and there is nothing to suggest that there are problems with the sources of information, or that the information appears implausible or inconsistent.

- A fourth approach is that any allegation of errors are an issue for a jury to decide unless the issue of reasonableness is beyond question or was not the cause of an adverse hiring decision as in this case.

This case was complicated by the fact that the background check firm did NOT utilize the actual county legal records but instead relied upon on a statewide repository, which did not apparently tell the entire story. However, given that any error was not the cause of the plaintiff's failure to get the job under the unique facts of the case, but was only an "additional cumulative justification," the Court did not have to decide if the background check firm used reasonable procedures.

The case potentially creates a defense for background check firms sued for inaccurate reports, where the facts show that a decision has already been made not to hire and therefore the background check report was not a cause of any alleged damages.

In addition, the case also demonstrates potential dangers of using secondary sources of information instead of going to the actual courthouse to view the primary records. Although the court ultimately decided the case on the basis that the background check report did not cause the decision, the court discussion demonstrates once again that background checks are heavily legally regulated. Background check firms need to take precautions to ensure accuracy in reporting criminal records. See:

http://law.justia.com/cases/federal/district-courts/kentucky/kywdce/3:2008cv00272/65643/47.

Here is another example:

A Graphic Illustration of the Need for Caution in Using Court Databases

During the 2003 California recall elections, an individual made allegations of misconduct against one of the candidates. A supporter of an opposing candidate apparently went online to the Los Angeles County court system and ran the name, finding serious criminal records that certainly raised questions about the character of the accused. The problem was, according to news accounts that came out later, the criminal record belonged to someone else. So, defamation lawsuits were contemplated. This is a graphic reminder of the pitfalls of using court indexes without pulling files to look for all possible identifiers *before* making conclusions.

Using the State Criminal Record Repository

All states have a central criminal record repository of records on individuals who have been subject to that state's criminal justice system. The repository content comes from information submitted by state, county, parish, and municipal courts as well as from local law enforcement. Information forwarded to this agency includes notations of arrests and charges, all usually with a set of fingerprints. Afterward, the disposition is later forwarded by the court as well (most of the time).

The Good News

- There is usually no problem with identifiers.
- If fingerprints are being used, this is the place to go.
- Some states have designated these agencies as the "official source."

The Bad News

For employment purposes, accessing state-held records at the official state repository may not be as useful as it might be expected due to a number of reasons including:

- Many statewide systems are only clearinghouses for those counties that choose to deposit records and are not actually the most accurate source of data. There are no guarantees that all counties are up-to-date or even participating.
- There are some counties that have their records online and some states that have online records directly from the state court – but not all.
- Some states do not even have such a resource, such as California.
- In some states offering a criminal records service, especially through a law enforcement agency, there can be substantial time delays.
- Complicating matters, the employer must make sure they utilize the appropriate form and send the required means of fee payment. Often, a release form signed by the applicant and even fingerprints are required. There is a bureaucratic delay as someone in the appropriate state office physically processes and responds to each request. If the request form is not filled out correctly, the request may be sent back.
- If there is a potential hit, then delays can be even longer since someone at the state agency may be required to conduct a physical review of the material to determine if it is eligible for release. Reviewing criminal files quickly may not be a state employee's number one priority.
- If the state is willing to release information, the data in their computer system may be only a summary of the charges or incomplete. Then the employer may need to request and view the actual file to determine what the case is about.

For the reasons discussed above, these sources must be approached with caution and are typically not a primary source of information for employers. First, consider: In the event of a hit during a database search or online search, the physical files still need to be pulled for inspection, and there are a number of traps for the unwary. A case in point is Texas:

> **State Audit Reveals Gaps in Criminal Records Database Affect Background Checks in Texas**
>
> A 2011 state audit in Texas has revealed that gaps in the state's criminal records database may cause criminal background checks used to screen job applicants – including teachers, doctors, nurses and daycare employees – to fail to uncover arrest records. The audit also found that the state's Department of Public Safety (DPS) Computerized Criminal History System is an unreliable source for complete information and that DPS should improve the timeliness and accuracy of its data.

According to the Fort Worth Star-Telegram, while Texas state law requires courts and prosecutors to submit information to the state within 30 days of receiving it, in 2009 prosecutors and courts failed to submit disposition records on about one of every four arrests, a slight improvement from a 2006 audit. In addition, the audit found:

- In November 2010, 1,634 of 21,351 offenders – 7.65 percent – admitted to jail, prison, or probation by the Texas Department of Criminal Justice did not have a corresponding prosecutor and court records in the DPS system.

- County officials cannot submit some records because they lack required arrest incident numbers or state identification numbers (Tarrant County alone had 1,730 probation records that lacked the state identification number).

- Computer problems may cause county officials to receive rejection or error notices when the DPS system does not accept records they submit.

- The Texas Code of Criminal Procedure does not provide DPS with the ability to penalize prosecutor offices and courts for not submitting information.

- Criminal history background checks provided by DPS do not include probation records.

See www.star-telegram.com/2011/09/29/3406283/database-gaps-hinder-texas-criminal.html for the full story from the *Star-Telegram*.

The problem with gaps in criminal database records hindering background checks in Texas is not new. A 2004 investigation by the *Dallas Morning News* concerning inadequacies in the statewide criminal database maintained by the Texas Department of Public Safety, found that the Texas database was used over 3 million times a year but only had 69 percent of the complete criminal history records for 2002.

The Morning News revisited the story in August 2008 and found, essentially, that nothing had changed. For 2006, the database still only had 69% of the state's criminal history. The story noted that only 106 out of Texas' 254 counties reported electronically and even then there appeared to be glitches or communication issues with various state law enforcement agencies. Other problems had to do with keeping trained personnel or officials in smaller jurisdictions that kept forgetting to report the status of a case.

These stories underscore common issues for employers performing background checks where searches of criminal databases can be problematic. Employers need to keep these problems in mind when utilizing criminal databases. The best practice is for all possible criminal hits on databases to be reconfirmed at the county court level to ensure the information is accurate, complete, and up to date.

U.S. Department of Justice Survey

Below is the front portion of an interesting article written by public record expert Michael Sankey. To read the entire article, see https://www.brbpublications.com/documents/crimrepos.pdf.

Shocking Facts from a U.S. Department of Justice Survey

Employers and state occupation licensing boards often depend on states' criminal record repositories as primary resources when performing a criminal record background check. However, these entities may not realize that a search of these record repositories may not be as accurate and complete as assumed, regardless if fingerprints are submitted. There are three key reasons why the completeness, consistency, and accuracy of state criminal record repositories could be suspect—

1. Timeliness of Receiving Arrest and Disposition Data

2. Timeliness of Entering Arrest and Disposition Data into the Repository

3. Inability to Match Dispositions with Existing Arrest Records

The basis for these concerns is supported by documented facts provided by the U.S. Department of Justice (DOJ). Every two years the DOJ's Bureau of Justice Statistics releases an extensive Survey of State Criminal Record Repositories. The latest survey, released December 2015 and based on statistics compiled as of Dec 31, 2014, is an 117-page document with 36 data tables. The survey is available at https://www.ncjrs.gov/pdffiles1/bjs/grants/249799.pdf.

Below are some eye-catching facts taken directly from the current DOJ Survey:

*   8 states report 25% or more of all dispositions received could NOT be linked to the arrest/charge information in the state criminal record database. 14 states don't know how many dispositions they have that cannot be linked. (Table 8a)

*   20 states have over 3 million unprocessed or partially processed court dispositions, ranging from 200 in Michigan and North Dakota to over 1 million in Nevada. (Table 14)

*   11 states report at least a 50-day backlog between the time when a felony case is decided and when the record is entered in that state's criminal history database. 18 states do not know how long the delay is. (Table 14)

Report on Inaccurate Criminal Records

The Addendum contains an article from BRB Publications, Inc. (www.brbpublications.com) entitled **New Facts About the Currency and Accuracy of Criminal Records at State Criminal Record Repositories**.

Searching Other Criminal Record-Related Databases

In addition to the sources already mentioned, there are other search resources available to employers. These include driving records, the local prison system, the Federal Bureau of Prisons (BOP), and sex offender databases.

What each of these searches has in common is that, in theory, the records should have already been found. For example, a search of state and federal prisons should indicate the same record found during a court search. The driving records and sex offender databases are compilations of a particular category of conviction that also would have generated a criminal record in the first place.

Given the limitations inherent in criminal records, checking these "secondary sources" provides an extra layer of protection. However, each of the searches has a drawback.

State Sex Offender Registers

State sex crimes registration requirements became mandatory on May 17, 1996, when a law, popularly now known as Megan's Law, was signed by President Clinton. This law had two primary goals:

*   To require each state and the federal government to register sex predators; and
*   To provide for community notifications.

A more detailed discussion of the uses and limitations of these sex offender searches is provided in Chapter 13.

State Prison Records

A number of states have state prisoner locator services on the Internet. Each state with a locator operates differently. Some sites contain only current prisoners, some contain those on parole, and others contain historical information. Again, as with any database, a researcher needs to fully understand the look-up logic and be prepared to run a number of name variations. There are two excellent resources to find these websites:

- www.corrections.com/links (Go to "Inmate Locator")
- https://brbpublications.com/freesites/freesites.aspx

Many of the state correctional databases are included in proprietary databases compiled by vendors, as described in a later next section.

Federal Prison Locator

The Federal Bureau of Prisons (BOP) has an inmate locator on its website www.BOP.gov. The site contains information about inmates going back to 1982. However, as a research tool, the database has the same drawbacks as most other large databases of names. If an employer already has the inmate's prison number — or another government number, such as the FBI or INS number — then the look-up is easy. However, for a pre-employment inquiry, an employer presumably would not have that number. There may be additional look-up options that allow lookup by other factors such as race, sex, and age usually within two years. Due to rules concerning the use of race as a factor in employment, it is unlikely that any employer will use that search option. In addition, many employers have the same sensitivity about age. This leaves only a name search. Any database that depends upon a name only look-up inherently has problems, plus, when information is entered into a database from numerous sources, there is increased likelihood of discrepancies. As a result, this is another database that requires a researcher to run all sorts of first name variations, including just the first letter of the target's first name.

State Motor Vehicle Records – MVRs

Of course, matters reported on driving records are driving-related only, thus not nearly a complete resource of criminal records. On the plus side, an MVR search is a true statewide search. These records are discussed in detail in Chapter 13.

Searching Federal Court Records

Searching criminal records at the federal court system can be one of the easiest or one of the most frustrating experiences that record searchers may encounter. Although the federal court system offers advanced electronic search capabilities, at times it is practically impossible to properly identify a subject.

Where Pacer is Excellent

The federal courts use a centralized online system called **PACER (Public Access to Court Electronic Records)** that provides record searches for the public for most U.S. courts. According to the PACER website at www.pacer.gov:

Public Access to Court Electronic Records (PACER) is an electronic public access service that allows users to obtain case and docket information online from federal appellate, district, and bankruptcy courts, and the PACER Case Locator. PACER is provided by the Federal Judiciary in keeping with its commitment to providing public access to court information via a centralized service.

The Federal Judiciary has developed a Next Generation (NextGen) Case Management/ Electronic Case Files (CM/ECF) system that will allow you to use the same account for both PACER and electronic filing access.

The PACER Case Locator is a national index for U.S. district, bankruptcy, and appellate courts. A subset of information from each case is transferred to the PACER Case Locator server each night.

The system serves as a locator index for PACER. You may conduct nationwide searches to determine whether or not a party is involved in federal litigation.

Through PACER, a user accesses the U.S. Party/Case Index. This index contains certain information from the court files — case numbers and the names of those involved in the case. For an employer trying to determine if an applicant has a federal criminal record, the system is beneficial since it allows one to search by name.

The PACER Case Locator is a national index for U.S. district, bankruptcy, and appellate courts for conducting nationwide searches to determine whether or not a party is involved in federal litigation. A small subset of information from each case is transferred to the PACER Case Locator each night and the system serves as a locator index for PACER.

In addition, the CM/ECF system is the Federal Judiciary's comprehensive case management system for all bankruptcy, district, and appellate courts that allows courts to accept filings and provide access to filed documents over the Internet. Some of the advantages of CM/ECF include:

- Keeping out-of-pocket expenses low;
- Giving concurrent access to case files by multiple parties;
- Offering expanded search and reporting capabilities;
- Offering the ability to immediately update dockets and make them available to users;
- Offering file pleadings electronically with the court, and
- Downloading documents and printing them directly from the court system.

The PACER website is www.pacer.gov.

Where PACER is Weak

A poor component about PACER is that it typically does not provide enough identifiers to do a proper match. The date of birth or Social Security number of a person indicted for a criminal event is not part of a PACER report. If the applicant has a common name, identification can be very difficult. According to BRB Publication's Public Record Research System, more than 85% of the district courts show only the name on search results. The other 15% show a partial identifier such as the birth year. Even if a federal court document is pulled, identifiers are typically hard to find, unlike the county level courts where there is often a date of birth.

Under the FCRA, a screening firm may not be exercising "reasonable procedures for maximum possible accuracy" by merely reporting a name match only. If the consumer requests a re-investigation, a screening firm may have a difficult time justifying having reported a mere name match in the first place. Often additional documents are needed.

If there is a name match only, then other means must be used to determine if that case relates to a particular applicant. For example, if a person was found guilty of a serious offense, and the court files indicate a substantial prison sentence, but the applicant in question was employed during that time period, then the case was probably not the same person. If a conclusion cannot be reached by comparing information in the court file to information that has been confirmed by the employer, then it may be necessary to do some sleuthing, perhaps with a phone call to the AUSA (an Assistant United States Attorney who acts as the prosecutor in federal court cases) or the criminal defense attorney. Case materials will typically reveal the attorneys for both sides.

Using Private Sector Commercial Databases

Commercial criminal record databases are maintained by data aggregators who combine public sources of bulk data and/or online access to develop their own in-house database products. They collect or buy data from government repositories, compiled from a number of various state repositories, sex offender registries, correctional, and county sources. Many of these vendors use data extraction, which is often referred to as *screen scraping*. More on this concept will follow later in this section.

Before you sign up with each criminal record vendor that catches your eye online, it is well advised to try to narrow your search to the vendor most suitable for your record needs.

As previously mentioned, a tool widely touted online to employers is a national database search of criminal records. A number of vendors advertise they have, or have access to, a *national database of criminal record information*. These services typically talk about having millions of records from all states. Unfortunately, this form of advertising can create an impression in an employer's mind that they are getting the real thing — access to all nation's criminal records. Nothing could be further from the truth.

There are a number of reasons why this database information may not be accurate or complete. It is critical to understand that these multi-state database searches represent **a research tool only, and under no circumstances are they a substitute for a hands-on search at the county level.**

Users of these databases must proceed with caution. Just because a person's name appears in one of these databases, it does not mean the subject is a criminal. On the other hand, if a person's name does not appear, this likewise should not be taken as conclusive that the person is not a criminal. In other words, these databases can result in false negatives or false positives and an over-reliance can cause one to develop a false sense of security.

Database Value and Limitation Issues

These database searches provide **value** because they cover a much larger geographical area than traditional county-level searches. By casting a much wider net, a researcher may pick up information that might be missed. The firms that sell database information can show test names of subjects that were *cleared* by a traditional county search, but criminal records were found in other counties through their searchable databases. In fact, it could be argued that failure to utilize such a database demonstrates a failure to exercise due diligence given the widespread coverage and low price.

But overall, the best use of these databases is as a **secondary or supplemental research tool**, or "lead generator" which tells a researcher where else to look.

The compiled data typically comes from a mix of state repositories, correctional institutions, courts, and any number of other county agencies that are willing to make their data public, or to sell data to private database brokers that accumulate large data dumps of information.

The **limitations** of searching a private database are the inherent issues about completeness, name variations, timeliness, and legal compliance.

Completeness and Accuracy Issues

The various databases that vendors collect may not be the equivalent of a true all-encompassing multi-state database.

- **The databases may not contain complete records from all jurisdictions.**
  Not all state court record systems contain updated records from all counties. The various databases that vendors collect are not the equivalent of a true all-encompassing multi-state database. First, the databases may not contain complete records from all jurisdictions — not all state court record systems contain updated records from all counties. In California, for example, a limited number of counties allow their data to be used, and even those counties do not provide data of birth. Since most firms need to use both name and date of birth to find names, there are very few hits from California.
- **For reporting purposes, the records actually reported may be incomplete or lack sufficient detail about the subject or the offense.**
- If the date of birth was not used in the search, then there would be too many names returned to deal with. New York is another example. These databases only contain New York corrections records of people who have been to prison and can only be obtained by going through an official New York statewide search offered by the New York Office of Court Administration (OCA) for a large fee. So, when Texas is added into the mix as discussed earlier with its problems, then the three of the largest states—California, New York, and Texas—will represent insufficient coverage. In those situations, it is necessary to run a search in just the state in question and then individually review each name match. That can be tedious, especially if a common name is being searched.

- **Some databases contain only felonies or contain only offenses where a state corrections unit is involved.** This inconsistency is directly related to what is available for sale on a bulk basis.
- **The database may not carry subsequent information or other matter that could render the results not reportable, or result in a state law violation concerning criminal records use.** For example, in states that provide for deferred adjudication, once a consumer goes back to court and gets the record corrected, the database firm may still be reporting the old data. There is typically not a mechanism for a data broker to correct any one individual's record. Because of the issues with databases as to completeness and accuracy, another issue is a false sense of security. Databases can have both false positives and false negatives. This is another reason why employers should be very cautionary.

The result is a crazy quilt patchwork of data from various sources and lack of reliability. These databases are more accurately described as "multi-jurisdictional databases."

More about Name and Date of Birth Match Issues

Besides the possibility of lacking identifiers as described above, an electronic search of a vendor's database may not be able to recognize variations in a subject's name, which a person may potentially notice if manually looking at the index. The applicant may have been arrested under a different first name or some variation of first and middle name. A female applicant may have a record under a previous name. Some database vendors have attempted to resolve this problem with a wild card first name search (i.e. instead of Robert, use Rob* so that any variations of ROB will come up).

However, there is an argument that using first name variations can result in "false positives." The idea is that once arrested, jail authorities will use the driver's license or some other identification means to ensure they have the proper person and will use their "official" first name. One screening firm was sued successfully for reporting a case where there was a date of birth match, but the first names were different but related. The screening firm reported a criminal case belonging to a person named Ricky Williams where the applicant was named Richard Williams, and both had the same date of birth. The screening firm made the error twice, so there was a suggestion that the screening firms should have been on notice. The case resulted in a nearly $3.6 million verdict against the screening firm. Read more about this story at www.gainesville.com/news/20161031/man-wins-nearly-36m-verdict-after-background-check-goofs.

The problem remains that there are still too many different first and middle name variations. There is also the chance of name confusion for names where a combination of mother and father's name is used. In addition, some vendors require the use of date of birth in order to prevent too many records from being returned. If an applicant uses a different date of birth, it can cause errors.

The issue comes down to technically how broad or how narrow the database provider sets the search parameters. If a database sets the search parameters on a narrow basis, so it only locates records based upon the exact date of birth and last name, then the number of records located not related to the applicant would be reduced. In other words, there will be less false positives. However, it can also lead to records being missed, either because of name variations or because some states do not provide the date of birth in the records which can lead to false negatives. Conversely, if the parameters are set broadly to avoid missing relevant records, then there is a greater likelihood of finding criminal records relating to the applicant, but at the same time, there are likely to be a number of records that do not belong to the applicant. That can happen for example in a state where no date of birth is provided, and the database is run on a name match only basis.

Timeliness Issues

Records in a vendor's database may be stale to some extent. A good question to ask is, "How often is each database comment updated?" Perhaps the government agency selling the data only offers the data on a monthly basis. Even after a vendor receives new data, there can also be a lag time before the new data is downloaded and viewable in the vendor database. Thus the most current offenses are the ones less likely to appear in a database search.

Legal Compliance Issues

When there is a hit an employer must be concerned about legal compliance. If an employer uses a web-based commercial database, the employer must have an understanding of the proper use of criminal records in that state. If the employer acts on face value results without any additional due diligence research, potentially the applicant could sue the employer if the record was not about them.

If a screening firm locates a criminal hit, then the screening firm has an obligation under the FCRA Section 613 (a)(2) to send researchers to the court to pull the actual court records. This section requires that a background-screening firm must:

> "...maintain strict procedures designed to insure that whenever public record information, which is likely to have an adverse effect on a consumer's ability to obtain employment, is reported, it is complete and up-to-date. For purposes of this paragraph, items of public record relating to arrests, indictments, convictions, suits, tax liens, and outstanding judgments shall be considered up-to-date if the current public record status of the item at the time of the report is reported."

As discussed in Chapter 3, FCRA section 613(a)(1) provides an alternative procedure. Instead of going to the courthouse, a Consumer Reporting Agency (CRA) can notify the consumer that public record information is being reported by the consumer reporting agency and give name and address of the requester. However, some states arguably do not permit this alternative procedure. This is a potential compliance issue for employers who operate in states that do not allow the **notification procedure** to be used instead of the **strict procedure** method of double-checking at the courthouse.

So, unless an industry is controlled by a federal or state regulation, there are no national standards and few state standards for conducting criminal record checks by private employers (beyond FCRA). When there is a lawsuit involving the wrongful use of criminal records, a jury decides whether an employer was negligent or not.

Florida and Texas are examples of states that have passed laws setting criminal records use standards. In Florida, an employer that uses the official Florida online database is presumed not to be negligent, although NOT using official state databases does not result in an employer being presumed to be negligent. Texas now requires criminal record checks on in-home workers (*V.T.C.A., Civil Practice & Remedies Code § 145.002*).

The best approach for an employer is to insist that a CRA always confirm the details of a database search by going to the courthouse to review the actual records. For a detailed discussion about the legal uses of a database, see the November 2002 report called *"National" Criminal History Databases: Issues and Opportunities in Pre-employment Screening* at www.esrcheck.com/file/NationalCriminalHistoryDatabases.pdf. Below is an excerpt from this article, which is older but does remain current. Additional information about the FCRA and databases is covered in Chapters 3 and 10.

"National" Criminal History Databases: Issues and Opportunities in Pre-employment Screening

By Carl R. Ernst and Les Rosen, November 26, 2002

"...7. Conclusions

We have looked at the issues raised by the availability of online, proprietary criminal history databases from the point of view of the vendors that provide them, the CRA/pre-employment screening firms that use them, and the employers who either use them or obtain information through CRA's from them.

We have concluded that such databases are a potentially useful and legal tool for employers and their agents to use, as long as each kind of user understands:

1. The inherent limitations of the information in these databases,

2. The inherent liabilities under FCRA and other federal and state laws for misuse of information garnered from these databases,

3. The necessity of also performing actual searches in actual courts to verify criminal case information unless FCRA 613(a)(1) is invoked, and

4. The necessity of contractual provisions among vendors, CRA's and employer clients to determine how information may be reported.

Whether or not the proprietary criminal history database vendors come to grips with the issues raised in this article, CRA's and employers should use the information obtained from these databases with great care to assure compliance with the letter as well as the spirit of the FCRA.

The entire report is available at www.esrcheck.com/file/NationalCriminalHistoryDatabases.pdf. The paper was cited in several footnotes by the EEOC in the April 25, 2012, Guidance.

Author Tip ▷ **Criminal Database Reports Sold Directly to Employers without Courthouse Verifications puts Entire Screening Industry in a Bad Light**

Under FCRA section 613, it is the **letter notice option** that is a significant cause of inaccurate data. Inaccurate criminal records come primarily from data aggregators that sell data over the Internet directly to businesses. These records are unfiltered by a professional CRA that has an obligation under the FCRA to provide accurate data.

In California, by comparison, a background screening firm can only report a criminal conviction or other matters of public record for employment purposes if **it is complete and up to date**, which is defined as checking the status at the time the matter is reported. See California Civil Code section 1786.28(b).

Some data brokers do have language that attempts to tell employers that such databases are not to be used for employment and are not FCRA compliant. However, these warnings, if even given, are often in the fine print.

Double-checking a database hit at the courthouse certainly affords employees, applicants, and background screening firms the most protection and the highest degree of accuracy. The duty to deal with adverse information in a public record can have an important impact when using criminal record databases.

If the goal is to increase accuracy and to prevent unsubstantiated bulk data from being provided to employer's, the obvious and most immediate remedy is to apply the above mentioned California rule nationally and to prohibit the letter option.

Concerned CRAs and the Use of Databases

Approximately 200 leading Consumer Reporting Agencies (CRAs) have joined Concerned CRAs (www.concernedcras.com) to publically reject the use of databases without taking the steps necessary to ensure accuracy and completeness as required under the FCRA. The Concerned CRAs and their position statements on the responsible use of criminal record databases (as well as bulk data and offshoring) can be found on their website.

According to the "Responsible Use of Criminal Records Database" section on the "Our Positions" page on the Concerned CRAs website:

(S)ome employment background screening firms sell "national criminal records databases" to employers without appropriate safeguards to ensure that the information they are delivering is accurate and up to

date. We believe that criminal records databases are valuable sources of information if they are used in a responsible manner. We are concerned that these practices do not appropriately protect employment applicants from avoidable harm. Likewise, employers are placed at increased risk of litigation and public relations problems when their employment background screening partners employ these practices.

Background screening firms participating in Concerned CRAs have certified that they practices conform to the Concerned CRAs guidelines:

When using criminal records in databases in the context of employment-related screening, exclusive of the screening of volunteers, tenants, and other non-employment relationships:

1. Criminal records databases compiled by non-government entities will only be used as indicators of possible records. Prior to making any report to an employer about a criminal record from a database, the CRA will verify the information directly with the reporting jurisdiction. This ensures that employers make decisions based on accurate and up-to-date information.

2. Current or prospective employer clients will be provided information about the limited nature of criminal records databases and the importance of researching each applicant's criminal history in the jurisdictions in which the applicant currently or previously has lived or worked.

Source: www.concernedcras.com/about-us-3/.

FTC Issues Pertaining to Data Vendors

There are also specific issues with the database vendors being **data brokers**.

While most CRAs do not store personal data of consumers, public record brokers are a separate issue. The FTC has made an effort to rein in data brokers as evidenced by the report detailed below.

FTC Privacy Report Recommends Legislation to Regulate Data Brokers

The FTC final report—'Protecting Consumer Privacy in an Era of Rapid Change: Recommendations For Businesses and Policymakers'—recommended that Congress consider enacting data broker legislation.

In the report, the FTC calls on data brokers to make their operations more transparent by creating a centralized website to identify themselves, and to disclose how they collect and use consumer data. In addition, the website should detail the choices that data brokers provide consumers about their own information. The FTC report notes that data brokers often buy, compile, and sell highly personal information about consumers who are often unaware of their existence and to how their data is used.

To address the invisibility of—and the lack of consumer control over—the collection and use of consumer information by data brokers, the FTC supports legislation that would provide consumers with access to information about them held by data brokers. To further increase transparency, the FTC calls on data brokers that compile data for marketing purposes to explore creating a centralized website where data brokers could:

- Identify themselves to consumers and describe how they collect and use consumer data and

- Detail the access rights and other choices they provide with respect to the consumer data they maintain.

While Congress considers such privacy legislation, the FTC urges individual companies and self-regulatory bodies to accelerate the adoption of the principles contained in the privacy framework if they have not already done so. The FTC will work to encourage consumer privacy protections by focusing on greater transparency whereby companies should disclose details about their collection and use of consumer information and provide consumers access to the data collected about them.

The FTC report recommends companies to develop clear standards regarding privacy and train their employees to follow them. Trade associations and self-regulatory groups also should be more proactive in providing guidance to their members about retention and data destruction policies. Accordingly, the FTC calls on industry groups for data brokers and other sectors – including the online advertising industry, online publishers, mobile participants, and social networks – to do more to provide guidance in this area.

According to the report, data brokers are "companies that collect information, including personal information about consumers, from a wide variety of sources for the purpose of reselling such information to their customers for various purposes, including verifying an individual's identity, differentiating records, marketing products, and preventing financial fraud." However, the FTC also noted that consumers "are often unaware of the existence of these entities, as well as the purposes for which they collect and use data."

The FTC report is at www.ftc.gov/os/2012/03/120326privacyreport.pdf.

Are There Limits to the Use of Private Databases?

Remember the story in Chapter 3 about a data broker who agreed to pay $800,000 to settle Federal Trade Commission (FTC) charges? (See the section "FTC Fines Data Broker $800,000 Dollars to Settle Charges of Violating FCRA.") The company, among other things, allegedly marketed online information to employers and recruiters in violation of the FCRA by failing to tell users of its consumer reports about their obligation under the FCRA, including the requirement to notify consumers if the user took an adverse action against the consumer based on information contained in the consumer report.

Some companies appear to take the position that because of the letter notice opting contained in FCRA section 613 that there are no additional duties to confirm accuracy. After all, the FCRA specifically sets out a letter option.

However, FCRA section 607(b) also set a standard for "reasonable procedures for maximum possible accuracy." Although groups such as Concerned CRA's oppose the use of the letter option, the fact remains it is still part of the law Congress passed. However, FCRA section 607(b) is also the law. A basic rule in reading a statute is that a court should "give effect, if possible, to every clause and word of a statute." See: www.fas.org/sgp/crs/misc/97-589.pdf.

The way the two statutes can be read together is to place upon a CRA the obligation to use reasonable procedures in the selection of the databases that they use. In other words, section 613 is not a blank check to send out any data a data broker or CRA can find. If the CRA or data broker have not tested the database, there can well be a 607(b) violation even if there was a letter notice sent. The situation is complicated since much of the data included in criminal databases came from governmental sources. However, many governmental databases carry a clear disclaimer that errors can exist. This is probably a matter that will eventually be resolved by litigation.

Issues Screening Companies Face When Dealing With Government Officials

It is critical for employers, legislators, the courts, and public officials to understand that background screening is not in the same category as *data miners* and other entities who are *data profiteers*.

Unreasonable restrictions on screening firms have only served to harm employers and taxpaying citizens seeking employment. When a public record-holder deletes dates of birth from files and the public index, they have inadvertently removed the primary identification—the date of birth—used by a screening firm to make a determination if a record belongs to a particular applicant. Although it is understandable that courts would desire to protect Social Security numbers, masking a date of birth does not promote privacy or consumer protection, but only serves to delay employment decisions. This delay can ultimately hurt the very consumer who has signed a consent form and wants the potential employer to have the information. Other government restrictions and impediments that serve to hurt employers and job applicants are lengthy delays in providing access to public records and excessive court fees.

There is a need for public officials to have a better understanding of the following:

- Background checks by a CRA are normally only conducted when a consumer has received (or is about to receive) a job offer and the consumer has authorized the background check in writing. Both the applicant and the employer want the report completed to the extent possible within 72 hours, which is the industry standard.
- Any delay in a CRA's ability to complete reports in a timely manner works to the determent of consumers. Consumers want a CRA to have fast access to criminal records.
- A CRA can only access criminal records with the express written authorization of a job applicant pursuant to the federal Fair Credit Reporting Act (FCRA) and applicable state laws.
- The researchers who go to courthouses across the U.S. for background screening firms do NOT make any decision as to what is or is not reportable. One of the services provided by a CRA is that they filter out any information that is non-reportable with reference to applicable federal and state rules.
- Background screening is an intensely regulated task, subject to not only to the FCRA and state laws but also other laws including civil rights laws and privacy laws. In addition, background screening is subject to regulation by the Federal Trade Commission (FTC) and the Equal Employment Opportunity Commission (EEOC). There is also a substantial body of case law on subjects such as accuracy in reporting criminal records.
- Unless expressly authorized by an act of Congress or a state legislature, a private employer cannot utilize the Federal Bureau of Investigation (FBI) database or state criminal database for a "LiveScan" background check. The vast majority of private employers need to utilize the services of a background screening firm to perform a background check

Some courts and public officials have attempted in recent years to limit screening firms' access to public records in the mistaken belief that such restrictions protect privacy and serve the public good. Nothing could be less accurate.

Web Data Extraction and Robotic Searches

As technology advances, new ways have been found to access court records. Background firms are able to electronically connect to a number of state and county databases through a variety of means. Automated processes with built in intelligence can permit screening firms to access publically available material with automated processes. Some companies have developed "screen scraping" techniques where court information may be gleaned from court websites.

This is not new technology according to an article called *Web Data Extraction (a.k.a. screen scraping) and Online Public Records*, written by John Kloos and appearing in *The Manual to Online Public Records* (Facts on Demand Press):

"...In the public records research marketplace, this technology is often referred to as *Screen Scraping*. In fact, *Screen Scraping* is a term dating to the 1960's when programmers wrote processes to read or "scrape" text from computer terminals so that it could be used by other programs. *Web Data Extraction* is a much more sophisticated technology that incorporates the automated scheduling, extraction, filtering, transformation and transmission of targeted data available via the Internet." To say that a well-deployed *Web Data Extraction* system is performing *Screen Scraping* is like calling a modern refrigerator an ice box.

An example of a relatively simple *Web Data Extraction* application is the free service Google provides for repeatedly searching news articles on a specific topic."

Although this approach sounds good on paper, there are many practical pitfalls for the unwary. Since the key is always accuracy, the critical part is to ensure that the information obtained is the "functional equivalent" of going to the courthouse and accessing a public computer terminal or other means of locating names of defendants.

If employers and background firms use this technology to search records in thousands of counties that in fact do not have data that is complete and up to date, then there is a great deal of risk. Unless a background firm performs proper due diligence so the remote computer search renders the same detail as going to the courthouse, the employer may otherwise find they are not getting the protections they thought they were receiving.

Another issue with such remote computer access is at least one major jurisdiction, Cook County, Illinois (Chicago), does not allow such remote access for commercial use. And its use for commercial purposes may even be unlawful. See www.cookcountyclerkofcourt.org/?section=TERMSPage.

Author Tip ⟩ **A Screening, a Scanning, or a Scamming?**

Some background firms advertise fast turnaround times by accessing data directly from courts through some variation of screen scraping, data extraction or software connection to the court's public site. Here is the issue: all data is not created equally. Unless the background firm has verified that the data they are accessing for each county is the **functional equivalent** of going to the courthouse, then it is difficult to consider that to be a background **screening.**

If the court interface is only getting some data but not all, then employers need to understand that the screening firm is only **scanning** available data and is not getting the best data possible.

If a screening firm reports county searches from a county where the screening firm either knew or reasonably should have known with due diligence that the data is inaccurate or incomplete, but sold it as a true background screen, then it has been suggested that such an approach more resemble a **scamming.** That is another reason why employers need to ask plenty of questions when selecting a screening provider.

Summary of Issues with Private Databases

- Multi-jurisdictional database searches are NOT official FBI database searches. FBI records are only available to certain employers or industries where Congress or a state has granted access. Searches offered by background firms are drawn from government data that is commercially available or has been made public.
- Multi-jurisdictional and statewide database searches are a research tool only and are not a substitute for a hands-on search at the county level under any circumstances (or the functional equivalent of a county level search). The best use is to indicate additional places to search in case a record is found in a jurisdiction that was not searched at the county court level.
- In addition, not all states have a database that is available to employers. In some instances, the databases that are available have limited information. Therefore, the value of these searches may be very limited in some states. That means searches in those states should be conducted by a single state search in order to locate all possible names. An employer should carefully review what information is available in their state and not merely depend upon a database search.
- Databases in each state are compiled from a number of sources. There are a number of reasons that database information may not be accurate or complete. Because of the nature of databases, the appearance of a person's name on a database is not an indication the person is a criminal any more than the absence of a name shows he/she is not a criminal. Any positive match MUST be verified by reviewing the actual court records. Any lack of a match is not the same as a person being "cleared." However, a database is a valuable tool in helping employers cover a wider area and know where to search for more information.

- There are some states that make official state police records or records directly from the court available. However, even these databases have potential drawbacks. The information may not be reportable under state or federal law for various reasons. Information from these sources should be reviewed by a qualified background checking professional.
- The search is based upon matching last name, the date of birth, and the first three letters of the first name in order to eliminate computer matches that are not applicable. Note: In some states, there is no date of birth information or limited date of birth information. The database description will indicate where the records do not contain a date of birth, which means a search of that state will have little or no value.
- All possible hits should be reconfirmed at the county court level to ensure that the information is accurate, complete, and up to date at the time it is reported, per FCRA Section 613. Also keep in mind that a criminal record should not be used to automatically disqualify an applicant without taking into account the EEOC rules as to what is a job-related criminal offense.

The only way that remote computer access represents a best practice is if the information being accessed is the same as going to the courthouse. If it is not the functional equivalent, then an employer is not getting a real background screen. At best, they are getting a scan of what information may be available, but it is not complete or up to date. A scam is where a background firm sells such remote access as the real thing when in fact it is not. Employers selecting a background firm that advertises quick turnaround time by means of electronic courthouse connecting need to make sure they are getting a screen, and not a scam.

Another danger sign? A background firm claims they have some special or exclusive access. All public records are available to the public.

Criminal record vendors and background firms should make clear, and employers need to understand, the exact nature and limitations of any database they access. These private database searches are ancillary and can be very useful, but proceed with caution. In other words, it cannot be assumed that a search of a proprietary criminal database by itself will show if a person is or is not a criminal, but these databases are outstanding secondary or supplemental tools with which to do a much wider search.

Shortcuts that Lead to Inaccurate Criminal Records

A summary of the whitepaper **"Employer Beware! 21 Shortcuts and Traps that Can Lead to Inaccurate Criminal Records"** by Attorney Lester S. Rosen, founder and CEO of Employment Screening Resources® (ESR), is in the Addendum.

Bottom Line

Each of these issues above may not be readily apparent to an employer or Human Resources professional trying to analyze a background screening program or implement a Safe Hiring Program. In fact, there are even more behind the scene details that can cause an employer to have less protection than they thought they were receiving. The bottom line is that an employer needs to choose carefully when selecting a screening provider. An employer cannot ask too many questions to ensure they are getting the real thing when ordering background reports to ensure they are protecting both employers and job applicants.

CHAPTER 10

The Legal and Non-Discriminatory Use of Criminal Records in Safe Hiring

Introduction

An essential element of a Safe Hiring Program is performing a criminal record check. An unsuitable criminal record may be evidence of past behavior that may be inappropriate for a particular job. Previous chapters addressed criminal law, criminal procedure and the issues surrounding the *how to* and *where at* procedures for obtaining accurate and actionable criminal information.

In this chapter, we examine factors related to the most pertinent question—**should past criminal matters even be used as part of the job evaluation process and, if so, how can it be used fairly and legally?**

Topics include:

- Compliance with the 2012 U.S. Equal Employment Opportunity Commission (EEOC) Enforcement Guidance on the use of criminal records by employers.
- Recidivism and rehabilitation.
- The ban-the-box movement—re-entry and giving offenders a second chance.
- The use of arrest information.
- How to incorporate legal and non-discriminatory procedures in a Safe Hiring Program (SHP).
- Evaluation of the relevancy of a criminal record to employment.

The EEOC 2012 Enforcement Guidance on the Consideration of Arrest and Conviction Records in Employment Decisions

Against the backdrop of concerns over the widespread use of background check reports and especially criminal records, the U.S. Equal Employment Opportunity Commission (EEOC) issued its updated *Enforcement Guidance on the Consideration of Arrest and Conviction Records in Employment Decisions Under Title VII of the Civil Rights Act of 1964* on April 25, 2012. Below are four important links regarding this Guidance:

1. The updated EEOC Enforcement Guidance for criminal background checks by employers is available at www.eeoc.gov/laws/guidance/arrest_conviction.cfm.
2. A brief Q&A was also issued at www.eeoc.gov/laws/guidance/qa_arrest_conviction.cfm.
3. Materials for the EEOC public meeting held April 25, 2012, on the use of arrest and conviction records, including testimony and transcripts, are available at www.eeoc.gov/eeoc/meetings/4-25-12/index.cfm.
4. A video of the proceedings of the meeting is available online at www.eeoc.gov/eeoc/meetings/4-25-12/video.cfm.

A Guidance — Not a Law

It should be noted that the 2012 guidelines are internal investigation guidelines for the EEOC and are not official rules or regulations and do not have the force or effect of laws. They were passed by the EEOC by a 4-1 vote without any public preview or comment period. Until the morning of April 25, 2012, no one knew what the guidelines would say. However, the EEOC has the power to investigate complaints based upon the provisions of these guidelines and to issue right to sue letters or to file lawsuits, which means that an employer takes a substantial risk in ignoring them. A court will generally consider the opinion of the EEOC, although a court may disregard and overrule such guidance. An example is in the area of the Americans with Disabilities Act (ADA), see *Sutton v. United Air Lines, 130 F3d 893 (10 Cir. 1997).*

It has been argued that Congress intentionally withheld rulemaking authority from the EEOC when it passed Title VII of the Civil Right Act of 1964, and it only gave the power to issue suitable procedural regulations to carry out the federal law 42 USC § 2000e–12. However, the EEOC has adopted a practice of issuing enforcement "guidance" instead. Such guidance can be issued without public comment, as this one was, because it does not have the force or effect of law. However, a large firm targeted by the EEOC under the new Enforcement Guidance may need to spend substantial time, money, and effort resisting the Guidance in court.

Per the EEOC, the updated Enforcement Guidance "builds on longstanding court decisions and guidance documents that the EEOC issued over 20 years ago" and "focuses on employment discrimination based on race and national origin." The EEOC noted previous guidance but noted that "this Enforcement Guidance will supersede the Commission's previous policy statements on this issue."

> **You Need To Know** > **Are Small Businesses Impacted?**
>
> Title VII only applies to employers who employ 15 or more employees for 20 or more weeks in the current or preceding calendar year (42 U.S.C. § 2000e(b)). However, how employee counts are determined if the threshold is met for the application of federal laws can get complicated. If an employer is close to the 15 employee mark, they should realize the EEOC may look at "independent contractors" to see if they should also be counted as employees, if the relationship more resembles employment. The government can also look at common ownership of separate firms and lump those together if they are sufficiently integrated. See: www.eeoc.gov/policy/docs/threshold.html#2-III-B-1-a-i.

Previous EEOC guidelines include:

- **1987** - EEOC Policy Statement on the Issue of Conviction Records under Title VII of the Civil Rights Act of 1964 , as amended, 42 U.S.C. § 2000e et seq. (1982)(2/4/87):
  - www.eeoc.gov/policy/docs/convict1.html
- **1987** - EEOC Policy Statement on the Use of Statistics in Charges Involving the Exclusion of Individuals with Conviction Records from Employment (7/29/87):
  - www.eeoc.gov/laws/guidance/arrest_conviction.cfm#sdendnote3sym
- **1990** - Policy Guidance on the Consideration of Arrest Records in Employment Decisions under Title VII of the Civil Rights Act of 1964, as amended, 42 U.S.C. §2000e et seq. (1982)(9/7/90):
  - www.eeoc.gov/policy/docs/arrest_records.html

The EEOC guidelines came on the heels of EEOC enforcement actions, the **E-RACE initiative (Eradicating Racism and Colorism in Employment)** and a strategic plan to target systemic violators. The findings were somewhat telegraphed in advance by means of two letters written by EEOC staff counsel. One letter was written to the Peace Corp and was critical of an open ended application form with very broad questions about past convictions and arrests. See: www.eeoc.gov/eeoc/foia/letters/2011/title_vii_criminal_record_peace_corps_application.html. Fair Credit Reporting Act (FCRA) attorneys Rod Fliegel, a Shareholder in Littler Mendelson's San Francisco office, and Jennifer Morazán,

Associate in the Los Angeles office, wrote a review of the letter at www.littler.com/publication-press/publication/eeoc-advisory-guidance-offers-insight-use-arrest-and-conviction-record.)

Also, see www.eeoc.gov/eeoc/foia/letters/2011/titlevii_crimial_history.html.

A number of other factors arguably led to the EEOC's increased focus in this area including:

- In 2011, a case was brought in Philadelphia that clearly focused on the issue of past criminal conduct being used for employment, regarding an applicant with a 40-year-old homicide conviction applying for a job with the public transportation system. (See in El v. Southeastern Pennsylvania Transportation Authority, 479 F.3d 232 (3d. Cir. 2007) (See article in the Addendum for Chapter 2 called, *"From Griggs to SEPTA: The EEOC's Focus on Employment Screening,"* by Rod M. Fliegel and Jennifer L. Mora, Attorneys At Law, Littler Mendelson, P.C.

- The American Bar Association (ABA) became focused on the issue and in 2012, the launched the National Inventory of the Collateral Consequences of Conviction, an interactive database of sanctions and restrictions across the nation. See: www.abacollateralconsequences.org.

- In January 2012, the EEOC fined a national beverage company $3.13 million to resolve a charge of race discrimination involving more than 300 Black Americans under a hiring policy that excluded black applicants from permanent employment. See: www.eeoc.gov/eeoc/newsroom/release/1-11-12a.cf.

- The EEOC held its first major meeting on the topic of criminal records and employment in November 2008, and held a second meeting on July 26, 2011.

- Ban-the-box and the second chance movement also focused attention on the issue of criminal records being a barrier to employment for "protected groups" that are legally protected from discrimination on the basis of a characteristic that can include race, color, religion, national origin, age (40 and over), sex, pregnancy, citizenship, familial status, disability status, veteran status, and genetic information. See: https://en.wikipedia.org/wiki/Protected_class.

- The National Employment Law Project (NELP) issued a report called *"65 million People Need Not Apply - The Case for Reforming Criminal Background Checks for Employment"* documenting the number of people with criminal records in the U.S.

- The increased number of people with contact with the criminal justice system occurred at the same time that there had been an increase in the number of employers performing background checks

The EEOC's stated purpose in issuing the new guidelines was based upon statistics showing a disproportionate impact of criminal records on protected groups, including Blacks and Hispanics. The EEOC cited statistics and studies showing criminal records have a discriminatory impact on Blacks and Hispanics. At the same time, they cited a 2010 Society for Human Resources Management (SHRM) study where 92 percent of responding employers stated that they subjected all or some of their job candidates to criminal background checks. See: www.slideshare.net/shrm/background-check-criminal?from=share_email

According to the EEOC Guidance:

"In the last twenty years, there has been a significant increase in the number of Americans who have had contact with the criminal justice system and, concomitantly, a major increase in the number of people with criminal records in the working-age population. In 1991, only 1.8% of the adult population had served time in prison. After ten years, in 2001, the percentage rose to 2.7% (1 in 37 adults). By the end of 2007, 3.2% of all adults in the United States (1 in every 31) were under some form of correctional control involving probation, parole, prison, or jail. The Department of Justice's Bureau of Justice Statistics (DOJ/BJS) has concluded that, if incarceration rates do not decrease, approximately 6.6% of all persons born in the United States in 2001 will serve time in state or federal prison during their lifetimes."

The EEOC further noted:

> "Arrest and incarceration rates are particularly high for African American and Hispanic men. African Americans and Hispanics are arrested at a rate that is 2 to 3 times their proportion of the general population. Assuming that current incarceration rates remain unchanged, about 1 in 17 White men are expected to serve time in prison during their lifetime; by contrast, this rate climbs to 1 in 6 for Hispanic men; and to 1 in 3 for African American men."

The EEOC also expressed concern about the accuracy of criminal records. The EEOC Guidance indicated: "recent studies have found that a significant number of state and federal criminal record databases include incomplete criminal records."

- A 2011 study by the DOJ/BJS reported that, as of 2010, many state criminal history record repositories still had not recorded the final dispositions for a significant number of arrests.
- A 2006 study by the DOJ/BJS found that only 50% of arrest records in the FBI's III database were associated with a final disposition.

Additionally, the EEOC cited other studies suggesting inaccuracies of criminal records:

- One report found that even if public access to criminal records has been restricted by a court order to seal and/or expunge such records, this does not guarantee that private companies also will purge the information from their systems or that the event will be erased from media archives.
- Another report found that criminal background checks may produce inaccurate results because criminal records may lack unique information or because of "misspellings, clerical errors or intentionally inaccurate identification information provided by search subjects who wish to avoid discovery of their prior criminal activities."

The EEOC was clear to say background checks are not eliminated. They noted some situations where there is a clear nexus between the job and the offense, and in some situations, federal or state laws eliminate certain individuals with certain offenses.

The EEOC then addressed the different considerations for an **arrest** as opposed to a **conviction**. It re-stated its long standing position that: "The fact of an arrest does not establish the criminal conduct has occurred, and an exclusion based on an arrest, in itself, is not job related and consistent with business necessity. However, an employer may make an employment decision based on the conduct underlying an arrest if the conduct makes the individual for the position in question."

The EEOC Guidance noted "in contrast, a conviction record will usually serve as sufficient evidence that a person engaged in particular conduct. In certain circumstances, however, there may be reasons for an employer not to rely on the conviction record alone when making an employment decision."

To protect job applicants from discrimination, the EEOC noted: "As a best practice, and consistent with applicable laws, the Commission recommends that employers not ask about convictions on job applications and that, if and when they make such inquiries, the inquiries be limited to convictions for which exclusion would be **job related** for the position in question and **consistent with business necessity**."

This approach appears to serve two purposes:

1. This is essentially a reaction to suggestions that a criminal record is a lifetime ban on employment. If an applicant is asked to reveal their entire criminal history without regard to relevance as to the offense or the time period involved, there is a concern that large numbers of individuals with criminal records will never be allowed in the workforce.
2. It is a restatement of the ban-the-box approach. The idea is that an applicant is not asked about a criminal record on the initial application in order not to deter or chill otherwise qualified applicants from applying since an applicant with a criminal record may reasonably suspect that his or her chances of proceeding successfully through the employment process would be diminished. In fact, applicants with criminal records may fear that their

application may immediately end up in the trash heap, regardless of their qualifications. The ban-the-box approach is to ensure that all applicants, even those with past criminal records, are initially evaluated based upon their qualifications, and at an appropriate time, an employer can then do a background check including relevant criminal records. If a criminal record is located, the employer is better able to put the criminal matter in context, having first evaluated the applicant as an individual without regard to their status as an ex-offender.

The EEOC drove home the point in a discussion of potential defenses to discrimination that an employer may have in determining disparate impact. Although the Commission would assess the probative value of an employer's applicant data, the guidance quoted a Supreme Court decision that noted an "application process might itself not adequately reflect the actual potential applicant pool since otherwise qualified people might be discouraged from applying" because of an alleged discriminatory policy or practice.

The Disparate Treatment and Disparate Impact Concern

The EEOC Guidance reviewed two types of discrimination.

- **Disparate Treatment:** "A violation may occur when an employer treats criminal history information differently for different applicants or employees, based on their race or national origin (disparate treatment liability)."
- **Disparate Impact:** "An employer's neutral policy (e.g., excluding applications from employment based on certain criminal conduct) may disproportionately impact some individuals protected under Title VII, and may violate the law if not job related and consistent with business necessity." **In other words, "Disparate Impact" means that an employer may not intend or even want to treat people differently, but statistically, the result of a practice that may appear natural on its face is to end up with members of a protected class being at a disadvantage.**

In determining Disparate Impact, the EEOC summarized a three-part test:

1. **Identifying the policy or practice:** The first step in disparate impact analysis is to identify the particular policy or practice that causes the unlawful disparate impact. For criminal conduct exclusions, relevant information includes the text of the policy or practice, associated documentation, and information about how the policy or practice was actually implemented. More specifically, such information also includes which offenses or classes of offenses were reported to the employer (e.g., all felonies, all drug offenses); whether convictions (including sealed and/or expunged convictions), arrests, charges, or other criminal incidents were reported; how far back in time the reports reached (e.g., the last five, ten, or twenty years); and the jobs for which the criminal background screening was conducted. Training or guidance documents used by the employer also are relevant, because they may specify which types of criminal history information to gather for particular jobs, how to gather the data, and how to evaluate the information after it is obtained. The Guidance noted that, in addition, the "Commission will closely consider whether an employer has a reputation in the community for excluding individuals with criminal records."
2. **Determining if there is a Disparate Impact:** Per EEOC, studies that show nationally that African Americans and Hispanics are arrested in numbers that are disproportionate, supports a finding that an employer that uses criminal records to prevent employment will have a disparate impact on groups protected by Title VII that include race, color, religion, sex, and national origin (See: www.eeoc.gov/laws/statutes/titlevii.cfm). During an EEOC investigation, the employer also has an opportunity to show, with relevant evidence, that its employment policy or practice does not cause a disparate impact on the protected group(s). At this point, these cases can become a battle of statistics, as well as evidence of employer practices. For example, an employer may be able to show that within the relevant hiring area, protected groups do not face criminal charges or conviction at a greater rate than the general population.
3. **If Disparate Impact is Established, Employer has the Burden:** After the plaintiff in litigation establishes disparate impact, Title VII shifts the burdens of production and persuasion to the employer to "demonstrate that the challenged practice is job related for the position in question and consistent with business necessity."

Assuming the employer meets the burden, the EEOC or applicant still has one last bite of the apple which is an argument that there was a less discriminatory alternative available that the employer did not adopt. The argument could be that different policies were needed, or perhaps even a longer time was needed for applicants to contest the decision.

Two Circumstances Where Employers Meet EEOC Approved Defense

Assuming a discrimination charge gets to the third part or stage, the key issue for employers is to meet the requirement that the "challenged practice is job related for the position in question and consistent with business necessity." The Guidance describes two circumstances in which the EEOC believes employers will consistently meet the "job related and consistent with business necessity" defense:

1. "The employer validates the criminal conduct exclusion for the position in question in light of the Uniform Guidelines on Employee Selection Procedures (if there is data or analysis about criminal conduct as related to subsequent work performance or behaviors); or

2. The employer develops a targeted screen considering at least the nature of the crime, the time elapsed, and the nature of the job."

The three-part test was issued in the 1987 "EEOC Policy Statement on the Issue of Conviction Records under Title VII of the Civil Rights Act of 1964."

Three part test dates to 1987 based *upon Green v .Missouri Pacific Railroad*, 523 F.2d 1290 (8th Cir. 1975) However, the EEOC added some additional insights to this case:

1. **Nature and Gravity of offense**
   "Careful consideration of the nature and gravity of the offense or conduct is the first step in determining whether a specific crime may be relevant to concerns about risks in a particular position. The nature of the offense or conduct may be assessed with reference to the harm caused by the crime (e.g., theft causes property loss). The legal elements of a crime also may be instructive. For example, a conviction for felony theft may involve deception, threat, or intimidation. With respect to the gravity of the crime, offenses identified as misdemeanors may be less severe than those identified as felonies."

2. **Time since the conviction and/or completion of the sentence**
   "Employer policies typically specify the duration of criminal conduct exclusion. While the Green court did not endorse a specific timeframe for criminal conduct exclusions, it did acknowledge that permanent exclusions from all employment based on any and all offenses were not consistent with the business necessity standard. Subsequently, in El, (plaintiff was rejected for a job as a paratransit driver based on his 40-year old homicide conviction which is discussed in detail in Chapter 2) the court noted that the plaintiff might have survived summary judgment if he had presented evidence that "there is a time at which a former criminal is no longer any more likely to recidivate than the average person . . . Thus, the court recognized that the amount of time that had passed since the plaintiff's criminal conduct occurred was probative of the risk he posed in the position in question. Whether the duration of exclusion will be sufficiently tailored to satisfy the business necessity standard will depend on the particular facts and circumstances of each case. Relevant and available information to make this assessment includes, for example, studies demonstrating how much the risk of recidivism declines over a specified time."

3. **Nature of the job held or sought**
   "Finally, it is important to identify the particular job(s) subject to the exclusion. While a factual inquiry may begin with identifying the job title, it also encompasses the nature of the job's duties (e.g., data entry, lifting boxes), identification of the job's essential functions, the circumstances under which the job is performed (e.g., the level of supervision, oversight, and interaction with co-workers or vulnerable individuals), and the environment in which the job's duties are performed (e.g., out of doors, in a warehouse, in a private home). Linking the criminal conduct to the essential functions of the position in question may assist an employer in demonstrating that its policy or

practice is job related and consistent with business necessity because it "bear[s] a demonstrable relationship to successful performance of the jobs for which it was used."

Author Tip ▷ **What are the Green Factors?**

The term **Green Factors** refers to the three-part test used by employers to determine the "business necessity" for using criminal records through three factors (nature and gravity of the offense, time since the conviction and/or completion of the sentence, and nature of the job held or sought) based upon *Green v .Missouri Pacific Railroad*, 523 F.2d 1290 (8th Cir. 1975).

Individualized Assessment

If an applicant is the subject of a targeted screen using the Green Factors, the EEOC indicated that an individualized assessment is recommended, but not required by law. According to the EEOC:

"The employer's policy then provides an opportunity for an individualized assessment for those people identified by the screen, to determine if the policy as applied is job related and consistent with business necessity. (Although Title VII does not require individualized assessment in all circumstances, the use of a screen that does not include individualized assessment is more likely to violate Title VII)."

The EEOC Guidance described the process as follows:

"Individualized assessment generally means that an employer informs the individual that he may be excluded because of past criminal conduct; provides an opportunity to the individual to demonstrate that the exclusion does not properly apply to him; and considers whether the individual's additional information shows that the policy as applied is not job related and consistent with business necessity.

The individual's showing may include information that he was not correctly identified in the criminal record, or that the record is otherwise inaccurate. Other relevant individualized evidence includes, for example:

- The facts or circumstances surrounding the offense or conduct;
- The number of offenses for which the individual was convicted;
- Age at the time of conviction, or release from prison (whichever is oldest);
- Evidence that the individual performed the same type of work, post-conviction, with the same or a different employer, with no known incidents of criminal conduct;
- The length and consistency of employment history before and after the offense or conduct;
- Rehabilitation efforts, e.g., education/training;
- Employment or character references and any other information regarding fitness for the particular position; and
- Whether the individual is bonded under a federal, state, or local bonding program."

Also per the EEOC:

"If the individual does not respond to the employer's attempt to gather additional information about his background, the employer may make its employment decision without the information. In others words, the employer does not need to chase down applicants who are being rejected. If the applicant has been clearly informed that the procedure is available and declines to take advantage of it, the employer can stop at that point except for the final adverse action letter."

Author Tip ▷

Use the Individualized Assessment Process Now

Any employer not utilizing the Individualized Assessment process should consider its use immediately. It is a very simple process and procedure that potentially affords an employer a great deal of protection. The process is essential a clerical task to start. The employer generates a letter and it is up to the applicant to respond if they choose. Of course, if the applicant does choose to respond, it is incumbent upon the employer to have a procedure in place to seriously consider and evaluate that applicant's information and to document any subsequent employer action. It should also be noted that the eight (8) specific factors noted by the EEOC should probably be considered a floor, and not a ceiling. In other words, an applicant should be allowed to share whatever information he or she believes is relevant, and not be limited to just the categories mentioned in the EEOC Guidance.

You Need To Know ▷

Relationship Between Individualized Assessment Process and FCRA

In Chapter 5, we learned that under the federal Fair Credit Reporting Act (FCRA), there must be a notice of pre-adverse action sent to an applicant if a Consumer Reporting Agency (i.e. a background firm) is used, and the background report forms a basis in whole or in part to take an **adverse action**, which means not hiring, retaining, or promoting an employee.

In many situations, if a background check reveals a disqualifying criminal record, then the applicant would be entitled to both the adverse action process and the individualized assessment process.

So how do the new EEOC rules on **Individualized Assessment** and the FCRA pre-adverse action rules work together? The EEOC Guidance does not address this issue. However, an employer should probably send out a pre-adverse action notice at the same time the employer informs the applicant that they can ask for an Individualized Assessment. See Chapter 3 for information on this topic and sample language which can be used for both the pre-adverse action letter and a notice to the consumer about the Individualized Assessment. A best practice may be to send out two letters—one for adverse action and one for the Individualized Assessment—because they are separate rights under separate laws.

However, keep in mind that there can be times when an Individualized Assessment letter is needed and there has been no background check. How can that happen? If an applicant provides information at or after the interview about a criminal record, an employer may decide at that point to not offer the job after using the Green Factors. There has been no background check, but the applicant should still receive an Individualized Assessment.

State and Local Regulations Affected by the EEOC Guidance

An area of potential concern for employers is that the EEOC has also taken the position that employers subject to state or local regulations, as opposed to federal regulation, concerning background checks are not shielded from a Title VII action just because of the legal requirements since federal law supersedes state and local law. Per the Guidance:

"States and local jurisdictions also have laws and/or regulations that restrict or prohibit the employment of individuals with records of certain criminal conduct. Unlike federal laws or regulations, however, state and local laws or regulations are preempted by Title VII if they "purport[] to require or permit the doing of any act which would be an unlawful employment practice" under Title VII. Therefore, if an employer's exclusionary policy or practice is not job related and consistent with business necessity, the fact that it was adopted to comply with a state or local law or regulation does not shield the employer from Title VII liability."

The Catch-22 for employers is they may follow state or local laws in good faith, and yet still be subject to an EEOC action. If an employer determines it needs to violate state or local laws to comply with Title VII, the employer is potentially subject to legal actions for violation of the state or local law in question. However, most observers believe the EEOC was merely restating existing law, and not intending to place employers in a bind by being put in legal jeopardy by obeying state law.

EEOC's Suggested Best Practices for Employers

The EEOC Guidance concluded with some suggested best practices for employers:

"<u>General</u>

- Eliminate policies or practices that exclude people from employment based on any criminal record.
- Train managers, hiring officials, and decision makers about Title VII and its prohibition on employment discrimination.

<u>Policy</u>

Develop a narrowly tailored written policy and procedure for screening applicants and employees for criminal conduct.

- Identify essential job requirements and the actual circumstances under which the jobs are performed.
- Determine the specific offenses that may demonstrate unfitness for performing such jobs.
  - o Identify the criminal offenses based on all available evidence.
- Determine the duration of exclusions for criminal conduct based on all available evidence.
  - o Include an Individualized Assessment.
- Record the justification for the policy and procedures.
- Note and keep a record of consultations and research considered in crafting the policy and procedures.
- Train managers, hiring officials, and decision makers on how to implement the policy and procedures consistent with Title VII.

<u>Questions about Criminal Records</u>

- When asking questions about criminal records, limit inquiries to records for which exclusion would be job related for the position in question and consistent with business necessity.

<u>Confidentiality</u>

- Keep information about applicants' and employees' criminal records confidential. Only use it for the purpose for which it was intended."

What Does All of this Mean?

- First, the EEOC makes it clear that employers can certainly do background checks. That is not an issue. The issue is the fair and relevant use of criminal records so it does not create a discriminatory disparate impact.
- Second, the EEOC restated its long standing position dealing with automatic disqualification based upon a criminal record, reaffirming a no automatic disqualification rule.

  This is a critical rule when it comes to the use of criminal records: an employer cannot deny employment automatically. An employer needs a business justification not to hire based upon a criminal past. The United

States Supreme Court ruled in *Griggs v. Duke Power CO.*, 401 U.S. 424 (1971), that a plaintiff can allege employment discrimination without a proving a discriminatory intent.

Author Tip **Business Necessity**

As a result of Griggs and ensuing cases, the EEOC has made it clear the automatic use of a criminal record without showing a **business necessity** can have a discriminatory impact by disqualifying a disproportionate number of members of minority groups. The key term is, of course, **business necessity**. Important court cases on the subject were summarized recently in *El v. Southeastern Pennsylvania Transportation Authority*, 479 F.3d 232 (3d. Cir. 2007). See the article *'From Griggs to SEPTA: The EEOC's Increased Focus on Employment Screening'* in the Addendum for Chapter 2.

- Third, the EEOC restated it reaffirmed another long standing position on the use of arrests records. Although the EEOC stated the new guidance superseded previous guidance, the 1990 Policy Guidance on the Consideration of Arrest Records in Employment Decisions went into arrest records in considerably more detail. (See additional discussion below.)
- Fourth, the EEOC is clearly concerned about lifetime disqualification from the job market, as well as the deterrent effect of asking about a criminal record too soon in the process, so that an otherwise qualified applicant does not have a fair chance. A key thrust of the EEOC efforts seem to be concerned that if an applicant reveals a criminal record too early, that an employer may summarily throw out the application and not even give an otherwise potentially qualified person a chance to compete.
- A related concern is that a broad and opened question about a person's entire criminal history can be discriminatory and that employers should only ask about criminal matters that are job related.
- In addition, nothing in the EEOC Guidance or the FCRA prohibits a background firm from turning over everything they find. There is no obligation for a background firm to censor any data that is otherwise not prohibited by any other state or federal laws. However, by the time a background check is ordered by an employer, the applicant is either a finalist or a semi-finalist and has clearly been considered on his or her merits. However, if a background check is returned with a criminal record, the employer clearly should apply the Green Factors and if a decision is made not to hire, the Individualized Assessment.

Author Tip **Systemic Discrimination and Pattern and Practice Investigation**

It is worth noting that if the EEOC responds to a complaint of discrimination, they are typically not looking at just what may have happened to the person making the complaint. The EEOC investigator would be focused on the big picture: *Is there a systemic pattern or practice that has a broad impact or is systemic in the organization?*

Criticism of EEOC Guidance

The rules of the 2012 EEOC Guidance have come under criticism as evidenced below:

- Commissioner Constance S. Barker cast the lone dissenting vote against issuing the Guidance. Her concerns were the Guidance goes beyond the jurisdiction of the EEOC, it will negatively affect business owners, and did not receive sufficient public comment. She felt the new Guidance represented a large shift from the advice being given for 22 years, yet no one from the public actually saw the Guidance until the day of the vote. It has also been suggested that the EEOC was not given authority to make rules and therefore acted in excess of its jurisdiction.

- These are not regulations with the force and effect of law. These are litigation guidance only. Many experts are questioning how much credence to give them. However, if the EEOC makes an employer a test case, then the employer is exposed to a significant legal and financial challenge, even if the EEOC's position loses in court.

- The EEOC is clearly focused on the notion that after a period of time, the impact of a criminal record lessens, and furthermore, over time the likelihood of re-offending is diminished. The Guidance contains citations in various footnotes to studies arguing that the predictive value of criminal records statistically diminish over time. However, the EEOC Guidance is noticeably vague on exactly what the time periods should be. A close examination of the studies shows the scope is extremely limited and certainly not advanced to the point where it can be the basis of social policy. The failure of the EEOC to even suggest time periods and to only cite very limited studies is a major shortcoming in the Guidance.

- On July 14, 2016, the U.S. Court of Appeals for the Fifth Circuit ruled in *Texas v. EEOC* (No. 14-10949, 6/27/16) that Texas may challenge in court the U.S. Equal Employment Opportunity Commission (EEOC) enforcement guidance on the use of criminal background checks by employers. Bloomberg BNA reported the ruling found "a federal district court erred by dismissing the state's lawsuit for lack of subject-matter jurisdiction" and "Texas as a state employer has standing because it is covered by the EEOC's 2012 guidance and must alter its hiring policies or incur significant costs if the guidance were enforced against the state." The decision on the appeal to reverse the dismissal stated: Texas's complaint seeks a declaration that an Enforcement Guidance document from the Equal Employment Opportunity Commission ("EEOC") regarding the hiring of persons with criminal backgrounds violates the Administrative Procedure Act ("APA"), 5 U.S.C. §§ 701–06. The appeals board ruling of June 27, 2016, also stated: *Texas filed suit on November 4, 2013, and filed its amended complaint on March 14, 2014. The amended complaint seeks declaratory and injunctive relief, alleging that the Enforcement Guidance is, in effect, a binding substantive interpretation of Title VII and thus violates the APA.* Bloomberg BNA reports the latest decision in the case of Texas v. EEOC "clears the way for a potential district court ruling on whether the EEOC's guidance exceeds the agency's authority under Title VII of the 1964 Civil Rights Act." The complete Bloomberg BNA report is available at www.bna.com/5th-cir-revives-n57982076255/.

Practice Note: How Would the EEOC or Private Parties Bring Lawsuits or Legal Actions?

The EEOC may itself investigate, mediate, or file lawsuits on behalf of employees where it is alleged there is discrimination. The EEOC's 'Strategic Plan for Fiscal Years 2012-2016' that establishes a framework for achieving the EEOC's mission to "stop and remedy unlawful employment discrimination." See: http://www.eeoc.gov/eeoc/plan/strategic_plan_12to16.cfm.

Furthermore, certain state agencies that enforce state fair employment laws can also enforce Title VII. All states have such agencies with the current exception of Arkansas and Mississippi. See: www.eeocoffice.com. Under Title VII, individuals can bring a private lawsuit. However, the individual must first file a complaint of discrimination with the EEOC within 180 days of learning of the discrimination or the individual may lose the right to file a lawsuit. The idea is that the EEOC or state agency can review the claim to determine if it will take any action in the matter. If the EEOC or state agency does not pursue the matter, that individual can obtain a "right to sue" letter. State agencies may have different time period or procedures. Such a letter does not mean the EEOC endorses the complaint and it is still up to the individual to obtain an attorney.

- The examples given in the EEOC Guidance were not that useful. They utilize extreme examples that may illustrate the points, but the extreme examples are the easy ones—in real life, decisions much more difficult and close calls often need to be made.

- The EEOC Guidance notes a study in a footnote that suggests a LACK of a background check is actually a barrier to employment by members of protected groups. Per the Guidance, "a 2006 study demonstrated that employers who are averse to hiring people with criminal records sometimes presumed, in the absence of evidence to the contrary, that African American men applying for jobs have disqualifying criminal records. Harry J. Holder et al., *Perceived Criminality, Criminal Background Checks, and the Racial Hiring Practices of Employers*, 49 J.L. & ECON. 451 (2006)."

- The EEOC quotes figures showing a dramatic number of individuals that are the subject of the criminal justice system:

    "By the end of 2007, 3.2% of all adults in the United States (1 in every 31) were under some form of correctional control involving probation, parole, prison, or jail. In footnote 8, the EEOC quotes a study that suggests: noting that when all of the individuals who "are probationers, parolees, prisoners or jail inmates are added up, the total is more than 7.3 million adults; this is more than the populations of Chicago, Philadelphia, San Diego, and Dallas combined, and larger than the populations of 38 states and the District of Columbia)."

    The difficulty with the figures cited by the EEOC is they include "probationers." For example, every person convicted of driving under the influence (DUI) would be a person that falls into the statistic quoted by the EEOC since the vast majority of all misdemeanor convictions for DUI result in a period of probation. It is elementary that in state courts, where misdemeanors can be typically be punished by up to one year in jail, a Judge will normally impose just a portion of the sentence, place the person on probation, and leave the remainder of the sentence pending the person's successful completion of probation. A misdemeanor sentence will typically include either formal probation (meaning there is an assigned probation officer) or informal (sometimes called Court probation) where there is no probation officer, but the Court's file says active, and the defendant is placed under Court orders appropriate to the case. A misdemeanor defendant, for example, may be ordered to obey all laws, attend a program, not to possess or consume drugs or alcohol, or other conditions related to the conviction. If the defendant fails to satisfy these conditions, a Court has the option to impose the jail time not previously imposed. This means the statistics cited by the EEOC for the proposition that an alarming number of Americans are involved in the criminal justice system may be inflated because it includes practically all misdemeanor conviction.

- Another expressed concern is the new standards will create brand new industries: Professional litigants consisting of ex-offenders assisted by plaintiffs who can simply apply to any possible employer just to try to set up a lawsuit and seek damages. Also, the Guidance promotes new opportunities for lawyers and experts in statistics, industrial organizations, and related topics to advise employers on how to deal with this complex web of new rules.

- The emphasis on criminal records as the primary cause of ex-offenders not being employed may be misplaced as well. According to professor James B. Jacobs, author of *The Eternal Criminal Record* (Harvard University Press 2015) the impact of employment discrimination based on criminal records "ought not to be exaggerated," since most ex-offenders also suffer one or more additional employment handicaps, such as educational deficiency, mental illness, drug dependency, and little or no legitimate work history.

- Critics have argued that the EEOC Guidance appears to have the impact of nearly conferring upon ex-offenders the status of a protected group, similar to protections given on the basis of race, color, religion, sex, or national origin through Title VII of the Civil rights Act, or other laws that provide protection based on such facts as age or physical disability. With the very complex procedures outlined by the EEOC for consideration of criminal records, it can be argued that ex-offenders may even have more rights than groups protected by Title VII, even though such status was not approved by Congress.

> **Author Tip**
>
> ## What Will the Impact of 2016 Presidential Elections Be?
>
> With the election of Donald J. Trump as the 45th president of the United States, there are numerous questions being raised about the new administration's approach towards a number of policies and regulations that may impact employers. One issue may well be the new administration's attitude about the EEOC and the Criminal Guidance. In addition, there are questions being raised as to the future of the Consumer Financial Protection Bureau. Although it is too early know what will happen, this is certainly an area employers must track beginning in 2017.

Recent EEOC Failed Enforcements

The EEOC has received some setbacks in their enforcement efforts. However, employers are well advised not to read too much into that. In those cases, the issues revolved around technical evidentiary issues of statistical proof. As these types of cases progress, it is reasonable to assume the EEOC litigation approach will be fined tuned. The court cases where the EEOC did not prevail should not be any indication for employers to not take their responsibilities very seriously.

> **You Need To Know**
>
> ## Court Affirms Judgment against EEOC in Freeman Case
>
> On February 20, 2015, the United States Court of Appeals for the Fourth Circuit affirmed a summary judgment in a lawsuit filed by the EEOC alleging that corporate events service provider Freeman conducted criminal background checks that had an unlawful disparate impact on black and male job applicants in violation of Title VII.

In the ruling, the Fourth Circuit Court of Appeals unanimously affirmed the decision by Judge Roger Titus of the U.S. District Court for the District of Maryland to exclude a report from a designated EEOC expert due to the "alarming number of errors and analytical fallacies" and "mind-boggling number of errors and unexplained discrepancies" that made it "impossible to rely on any of his conclusions." Federal Rule of Evidence 702 governs the admissibility of expert evidence and expert testimony is admissible if it "rests on a reliable foundation and is relevant," according to the ruling.

On August 9, 2013, Judge Titus issued a Memorandum Opinion that dismissed a lawsuit brought by the EEOC claiming Freeman "unlawfully relied upon credit and criminal background checks that caused a disparate impact against African-American, Hispanic, and male job applicants." The Judge labeled the EEOC expert reports prepared to support its claims of disparate impact as "based on unreliable data," "rife with analytical error," "distorted," "cherry-picked," and "an egregious example of scientific dishonesty."

However, it could be a costly mistake for employers or screening firms to interpret this decision to mean they can become complacent about EEOC compliance in hiring.

Discrimination cases based on disparate impact necessarily involve statistical arguments, which means there will be a 'battle of the experts. Just because one side loses the expert battle in one or two cases does not mean that employers can assume these laws are no longer important. This is an emerging area of litigation and employers should not assume the same approaches rejected by courts now will be used in the future.

The appeal decision in EEOC vs. Freeman, No.13-2365 is available at www.esrcheck.com/file/EEOC-v-Freeman-Decision.pdf. The Memorandum Opinion is at www.esrcheck.com/file/EEOC-v-Freeman-Memorandum-Opinion.pdf.

A Summary on the Effects of the EEOC Guidance on Employers

As a result of the EEOC Guidance, employers may find that there is the Good, the May Be Good, and the Impossible.

The Good

- First, the Guidance does not prevent employers from performing a mission critical function—obtaining the highest quality of hire possible. A business is often only as good as its workers, and background checks are critical to select honest, safe, and qualified workers. In a Question and Answer page, the EEOC made it clear that the EEOC in no way is impinging upon the ability of an employer to receive background reports. Per the EEOC web page at www.eeoc.gov/laws/guidance/qa_arrest_conviction.cfm:

  > **"2. Does Title VII prohibit employers from obtaining criminal background reports about job applicants or employees?**
  >
  > No. Title VII does not regulate the acquisition of criminal history information. However, another federal law, the Fair Credit Reporting Act, 15 U.S.C. § 1681 et seq. (FCRA), does establish several procedures for employers to follow when they obtain criminal history information from third-party consumer reporting agencies. In addition, some state laws provide protections to individuals related to criminal history inquiries by employers."

- Second, the EEOC Guidance actually gives employers additional guidance regarding the Green Factors that are part of the long standing three-part test. Before for example, the EEOC merely recommended an employer considers the nature of the job. The EEOC has added sensible enhancements to help employers deal with that requirement, such as the job duties, the essential functions of the job, the circumstances, and the environment of the job.

The Probably Good

Two suggestions were made in the EEOC Guidance that explicitly stated they were not required of employers. But these may be practices that employers would find useful.

- First, the EEOC is essentially suggesting that employers adopt a ban-the-box approach. The later in the process an employer waits before asking about a criminal record, the more protections an employer has against allegations of discrimination since the employer can show that they have considered the individual on his or her merits and that they were not "knocked out" early due to their status as an ex-offender. Of course, when the criminal record is considered, it is critical that there be a business justification to not proceed further with the applicant, based on the enhanced "Green" actors.
- Second, the notion of the Individualized Assessment can help employers ensure that any decision about a criminal record has been well documented. Further, it provides a "safety" value against an employer acting too hastily. Although the EEOC recognized that there may be situations where such an assessment is not needed due to the "demonstrably tight nexus" between the job and crime, a better practice may be for the employer to conduct the assessment in all cases, in order to avoid allegations of discrimination based on performing the procedure for some and not others.

The Challenging

There are three aspects to the new Guidance that appear to put employers in a nearly impossible situation:

1. The use of recidivism studies that are in their infancy.
2. Limiting the inquiries about past criminal records to matters relevant to the position.
3. Indicating that employers who follow state hiring requirements may not be protected under federal laws.

1. The use of recidivism studies that are in their infancy.

The EEOC cites studies that criminal past becomes irrelevant over time and even suggests employers consider recidivism studies when applying the Green Factors revolving around the time of the offense. These studies are summarized in the Addendum to Chapter 10, along with recidivism statistics published by the Bureau of Bureau of Justice Statistics (BJS) on recidivism in the U.S., which is an office in the U.S, Department of Justice.

The problem?

First, the EEOC itself notes that these studies ae somewhat limited. The EEOC notes: "Although there may be social science studies that assess whether convictions are linked to future behaviors, traits, or conduct with workplace ramifications, and thereby provide a framework for validating some employment exclusions, such studies are rare at the time of this drafting."

However, when discussing the Green Factors, the EEOC then goes on to suggest: "Whether the duration of exclusion will be sufficiently tailored to satisfy the business necessity standard will depend on the particular facts and circumstances of each case. Relevant and available information to make this assessment includes, for example, studies demonstrating how much the risk of recidivism declines over a specified time."

The problem is that studies relating crime to future conduct are just the reverse side of the question as to the risk of recidivism. The bottom line is that inquiries still revolve around predicting future dangerousness from current offenses. In other words, an employer must determine if a person's past is the prologue for future conduct. If an employer gets it wrong, they have substantial exposure for negligent hiring if a person who is dangerous, unfit, dishonest, or unqualified is employed and causes harm.

The studies cited by the EEOC concerning recidivism, although useful and a good place to start, are in the very early stages of research and are not developed to the point where such studies can form the basis of social policy. The science of judging rehabilitation over time is in its infancy. Even the authors of one of the most often cited studies from Carnegie Mellon University concluded much more study was needed and there are substantial issues still to be addressed. The authors' characterization that the study represents a "significant step forward in area where so little is known empirically" is well-taken. Yet the EEOC has acknowledged these drawbacks but also has suggested that millions of employers consider them. It raises the question as to how small and medium businesses are supposed to deal with detailed scientific and statistical studies and draw any conclusions.

Studies Cited By EEOC

See the Addendum for information concerning the studies cited by the EEOC and an in-depth analysis of the Carnegie Mellon University study *"Redemption in the Presence of Widespread Criminal Background Checks."* Also included are detailed statistics on recidivism prepared by the Bureau of Justice Statistics (BJS) in 2014.

2. Limiting the inquiries about past criminal records to matter relevant to the position.

Another practical issue is the challenge of having employers limit criminal record inquiries to relevant criminal matters as suggested by the EEOC. The EEOC suggested some best practices, such as employers having a policy or limiting inquiries or questions about past criminal acts that are relevant to the job in question. The recommendation by the EEOC is: "When asking questions about criminal records, limit inquiries to records for which exclusion would be job related for the position in question and consistent with business necessity."

The purpose is to apparently prevent a lifetime ban on employment because of an old and potentially irrelevant criminal record. Yet the commission has not provided any examples of such material.

There are hundreds and hundreds of different crimes in each state. There are thousands of different types of jobs. It would be exceedingly burdensome to try to analyze every job in terms of what criminal behavior is impacted, especially for multi-state employers. It is possible to create broad categories such as "crimes against persons" or "crimes against property," but those titles are extremely wide and encompass a large range of conduct and behavior stemming from the insignificant to exceedingly relevant.

In addition, the EEOC Guidance does not take into account the realities of state criminal laws when judging the seriousness of a crime based upon the level of conviction. The Guidance suggests for example that, "With respect to the gravity of the crime, offenses identified as misdemeanors may be less severe than those identified as felonies." As noted in Chapter 9, the mere fact a case is a misdemeanor does not mean it was not serious. The only time an employer can assume with some level of confidence that a misdemeanor is a less serious offense is where the crime charged can only be charged as a misdemeanor offense. This means the legislature has made a determination that in all cases, the highest punishment can only be at a misdemeanor level. Also important is to understand there is no way for an employer to even make an informed judgment as to the nature and gravity of an offense unless the employer obtains some information from the actual court file. If an employer is prevented from asking a broad-based criminal question at some point during the hiring process, an employer cannot exercise due diligence or ensure that it has the information to determine which counties should be searched for criminal records. When a court researcher goes to the courthouse, on behalf of either a background firm or employers, there is no mechanism to only identify "serious crimes." Court indexes do not contain the information needed to make those sorts of judgments. In some counties, court clerks do the actual search, and there are no mechanisms for a court clerk to make any determinations. The bottom line is that a court case must be reviewed first.

Even assuming an employer was to analyze numerous crimes (not to mention federal crimes) in the context of numerous different jobs to determine which crimes may be relevant to a particular job, the next issue is trying to have job applicants review what could well be a very large listing of possible crimes. There are a number of real world drawbacks with following the EEOC suggestion of only asking about relevant crimes. In fact, it can be argued that the section of the EEOC Guidance suggesting employers attempt to limit their inquiries can actually have the unintended real world consequence of working against ex-offenders trying to get jobs. Consider the following:

- Even if only relevant crimes were determined and then listed, the crimes can have a wide range of possible seriousness. This can make it impossible for an employer to only ask about serious crimes that could impact a job decision.
- Even if the crimes are filtered by age with the idea that older crimes are less serious, employers need to determine whether to use the date of occurrence, the date of conviction, or the date of release from custody. Due to the workings of the criminal justice system and based in part on the past record of the offender, it is entirely possible that two offenders that commit the same crime on the same date can have widely different dates of conviction and release.
- Given the complexities of the criminal justice system, job applicants historically have a difficult time recalling the exact details of a criminal disposition. An applicant may not recall exactly what he or she was charged with or the details of the eventual outcome. An applicant may not have understood that terms and conditions of his or her sentence, or their lawyer's instructions in terms of the collateral consequences of a conviction. An applicant could be forced to make difficult legal and factual determinations to ensure they are giving honest answers. More information and resources about collateral consequences are in Chapter 8.
- If the applicant is asked a question that calls for a subjective answer or a judgment call, such as: "Have you ever been convicted of a serious theft crime," then the applicant is put into a position of having to make a very complicated legal and factual judgment of what is serious and what is not.
- If the applicant answers any questions about past criminal conduct inaccurately due to a lack of recollection or understanding of past events, or based upon information they believed was given by their attorney or based upon some subjective response that the employer finds unreasonable, the applicant is placed in a position where it may appear he or she is deceptive and dishonest. For example, any Human Resources professional involved in hiring

has likely heard on at least one occasion an applicant with a criminal record explaining incorrect or false statements about their record by saying they thought their attorney was going to take care of it, or the attorney said not to worry because it will go away. Since an employer is never under an obligation to hire someone who lies during the hiring process, the new EEOC Guidance potentially works against the interest of ex-offenders seeking a second chance. If the applicant claims an incorrect statement about past criminal questions was a mistake or misunderstanding, it puts the employer in the difficult position of trying to determine if the ex-offender made a mistake, genuinely misunderstood, or was being intentionally dishonest and deceitful.

Author Tip | **Law of Unintended Consequences**

The EEOC approach of narrowing the criminal question may set-up ex-offenders for failure, since an ex-offender must try to deal with very specific questions, and many people who go through the criminal justice system really do not recall or understand the exact legal details of their offense, what their lawyer told them, or subtle differences between offenses or offense levels. So, by asking ex-offenders to thread a very difficult needle, any errors or inaccuracies can be perceived as an attempt to fabricate and is a basis not to hire. Essentially, the whole concept that an employer needs to somehow limit the criminal inquiry when made somehow based upon on the job may well end up in the real world being harmful and detrimental to ex-offenders. This is an example of the *law of unintended consequences.*

The EEOC has not provided concrete examples of the types of questions it recommends employers ask when attempting to only ask about relevant criminal matters. Based upon court decisions in the EEOC against Kaplan Higher Education Corporation, where the court ordered the EEOC to produce information about how the EEOC itself uses credit reports in hiring, it would seem that the EEOC will shortly be ordered to turn over its own hiring procedures if the EEOC challenges what private employers are doing. At that point, the EEOC will be able to see firsthand the difficulties involved in implementing its own Guidance.

3. Indicating employers that follow state hiring requirements may not be protected under federal laws.

The EEOC states in the 2012 Guidance:

> "States and local jurisdictions also have laws and/or regulations that restrict or prohibit the employment of individuals with records of certain criminal conduct. Unlike federal laws or regulations, however, state and local laws or regulations are preempted by Title VII if they "purport to require or permit the doing of any act which would be an unlawful employment practice" under Title VII. Therefore, if an employer's exclusionary policy or practice is not job related and consistent with business necessity, the fact that it was adopted to comply with a state or local law or regulation does not shield the employer from Title VII liability."

Thus employers can be potentially put in a "Catch 22" situation if state or local rules require elimination from a job due to certain criminal matters. And then the EEOC threatens to pursue employers for just following the state law. Some labor attorneys are recommending that employers required to follow state rules continue to do so. Presumably, if elected state legislators and the elected governor have passed a law prohibiting individuals with certain criminal records from holding certain jobs or licenses, there must have been a factual bias for the decision. It has been suggested that the EEOC emphasis on state laws is actually aimed at encouraging states to think through such restrictions, as opposed to placing employers in an impossible situation. In addition, it is just a black letter statement of law that in the absence of some specific provision in the statute, federal law preempts state law. Some observers had indicated that the EEOC was merely restating the obvious.

The Bottom Line

Regardless what approach an employer uses, these primary points must be well understood:

- An employer should **<u>NEVER</u>** utilize a technique that creates automatic exclusions based upon a criminal record. Actually, that is not a new issue and was the subject of detailed discussions when the first edition of this book was published in 2004. However, the new Guidance makes that even clearer.

- An employer should clearly not rely on records that are so old they are no longer relevant to the job or business necessity.

- If an adverse decision is made based upon a criminal record, employers must be able to document what was done and why. It is critical to maintain all documents relating to a decision not to hire a particular applicant due to a criminal record. An employer needs to show this decision was a result of a consistent and considered process that was approached fairly and uniformly. Failure to maintain documentation can imply that such decisions were made automatically in a knee-jerk reaction or in an arbitrary or capricious manner.

- The EEOC Guidance suggests appropriate steps need to be taken to protect confidential information about an applicant's criminal record. This includes both the security of data and documents, as well as limited access on a need to know basis within an organization.

- An employer should utilize the enhanced Green Factors to analyze the nature and gravity of the crime, the age of the offense, and the nature of the job.

- An employer should consider the Individual Assessment recommendation in the event the use of the Green Factors suggests a person should not be hired due to a criminal record.

- An employer should consider taking the criminal question out of the initial employment applicant or process. An employer may consider a **Criminal Advisement** stating that a criminal check relevant to the position will be performed at an appropriate time before a person is onboarded. The statement advises applicants the employer will conduct an appropriate background check on anyone prior to the start of employment, including a criminal record check, pursuant to all applicable state and federal laws including all discrimination laws, and that no candidate will be automatically eliminated as a result of a criminal check. Even then, an employer must be careful to ensure such a notice does not amount to a roundabout way of shutting the door to any applicant with a record by deterring or chilling their efforts to apply and by suggesting that any criminal record may disqualify them.

- An employer should have a written policy. However, just having a policy sitting on a shelf gathering dust is meaningless. Make certain all managers are trained on the policy and are following it.

- Even if an employer decides not to have a labor law firm design a compliance program, an employer should consider a review by an attorney or qualified professional such as a Human Resources consultant.

You Need To Know ⟩ **How Hiring Works Under EEOC Guidance on Criminal Records**

A short description of how hiring works under the EEOC Guidance on Criminal Records:

1. Establish a skill set—start with a well written job description that will be used later if a criminal record is discovered in order to determine if a conviction is job related or if there is a business necessity not to hire the applicant.

2. Delay the criminal questions until at or after the interview (which may depend on whether your jurisdiction has a ban-the-box law that dictates timing.

3. When a criminal question is asked, it should be limited in scope so that it does not illicit information that is old or irrelevant to the position.

4. If a criminal record is located, subject it to the three-part Green Factor criteria, (the "targeted" screen). If it turns out not to be relevant, then proceed as though there was no criminal record.

5. If the applicant fails the targeted screen, then before making the decision final, utilize the "Individualized Assessment" process.

Author Tip

Is there a "Safe Harbor" or Guaranteed Path to Compliance?

Although the next section will suggest compliance strategies with the EEOC Guidance, it is important to understand that there is no guaranteed process or procedure that provides a "Safe Harbor" against any possible allegation of the discriminatory use of criminal records. The EEOC cannot legally pre-judge ahead of time if an employer is in compliance. In fact, the Guidance even notes in section VA2 that under applicable law, evidence that the workplace is racially balanced is not always a defense, and that under some circumstances, the EEOC can even take into account whether an employer has a reputation in the community for excluding individuals with criminal records.[1]

The Guidance also notes even if "an employer successfully demonstrates that its policy or practice is job related for the position in question and consistent with business necessity, a Title VII plaintiff may still prevail by demonstrating that there is a less discriminatory 'alternative employment practice' that serves the employer's legitimate goals as effectively as the challenged practice but that the employer refused to adopt."

Suggested EEOC Compliance Tools

Two compliance tools are suggested for understanding the EEOC Guidance — the *Best Practice Standards: The Proper Use of Criminal Records in Hiring* and a joint publication of the EOC and the Federal Trade Commission (FTC) called *Background Checks: What Employers Need to Know.*

1. *Best Practice Standards: The Proper Use of Criminal Records in Hiring*

In May 2013, a group of national civil and workers' rights organizations released a report titled *Best Practice Standards: The Proper Use of Criminal Records in Hiring* that addressed the use of criminal records of job applicants by employers during employment background checks.

The organizations preparing the report included the **Lawyers' Committee for Civil Rights Under Law**, the **National H.I.R.E. Network**, and the **National Workrights Institute**. Background screening industry consultants who helped to

---

[1] An employer's evidence of a racially balanced workforce will not be enough to disprove disparate impact. In *Connecticut v. Teal*, the Supreme Court held that a "bottom line" racial balance in the workforce does not preclude employees from establishing a prima facie case of disparate impact; nor does it provide employers with a defense. The issue is whether the policy or practice deprives a disproportionate number of Title VII-protected individuals of employment opportunities.

Finally, in determining disparate impact, the Commission will assess the probative value of an employer's applicant data. As the Supreme Court stated in *Dothard v. Rawlinson*, an employer's "application process might itself not adequately reflect the actual potential applicant pool since otherwise qualified people might be discouraged from applying" because of an alleged discriminatory policy or practice. Therefore, the Commission will closely consider whether an employer has a reputation in the community for excluding individuals with criminal records. Relevant evidence may come from ex-offender employment programs, individual testimony, employer statements, evidence of employer recruitment practices, or publicly posted notices, among other sources. The Commission will determine the persuasiveness of such evidence on a case-by-case basis.

develop the Best Practice standards included this book's author Attorney Lester S. Rosen as well as Frederick G. Giles, Senior Vice President of CARCO's Research Division, and James C. Owens, CEO and President of CARCO Group, Inc. According to the report:

> *Responsible hiring practices should incorporate the recommendations made by the Equal Employment Opportunity Commission (EEOC), the agency that enforces federal employment discrimination laws, in its 2012 'Enforcement Guidance on the Use of Arrest and Conviction Records in Employment Decisions under Title VII of the Civil Rights Act of 1964.' The Best Practice Standards presented here set out concrete, practical procedures that will help employers make hiring decisions that: Comply with the EEOC Guidance and limit liability under Title VII of the Civil Rights Act and state and local anti-discrimination laws; Comply with the Fair Credit Reporting Act (FCRA); and Minimize the risk of liability from hiring an unfit employee.*

The report includes the following 15 Best Practice Standards that "enable employers to protect their interests and the interests of those they serve, without unduly burdening applicants for past mistakes":

1. CONSIDER ONLY CONVICTIONS AND PENDING PROSECUTIONS: The fact that someone has been charged with a crime should not disqualify them for a job if they were not convicted. If a person is being prosecuted for an offense that is relevant to a job for which they have applied, an employer may consider it.

2. CONSIDER ONLY CONVICTIONS THAT ARE RELEVANT TO THE JOB IN QUESTION: A person who has committed an illegal act in the past may be more likely than the average person to commit a similar act in the future, but they are no more likely to commit other offenses. A person who has been convicted of DUI may put the public at risk in a job that involves driving, but not in other jobs.

3. CONSIDER ONLY CONVICTIONS RECENT ENOUGH TO INDICATE SIGNIFICANT RISK: The risk that someone who has been convicted of a crime will commit another offense decreases over time. Employers should consider the available evidence on recidivism rates before rejecting an applicant.

4. DO NOT ASK ABOUT CRIMINAL RECORDS ON APPLICATION FORMS: Delaying learning about an applicant's criminal record until the interview or later enables the employer to make more informed hiring decisions.

5. USE A QUALIFIED CRA TO CONDUCT RECORD CHECKS: All consumer reporting agencies are not equal. Employers should consider the quality of CRAs' procedures and results and not decide which one to use based solely upon cost.

6. CRAS SHOULD REPORT ONLY CONVICTIONS THAT ARE RELEVANT AND RECENT: Employers should determine in advance the convictions that it considers relevant for specific jobs and the time period during which they are relevant. These determinations should be provided to the CRA with instruction to report only convictions that meet these criteria.

7. REPORT CONVICTIONS ONLY WHEN FULL NAME AND ONE OTHER IDENTIFIER MATCH: In a country of over 300 million people, many people have the same first and last name. A conviction should only be reported to an employer when the full name (including middle name where available) and at least one other identified match.

8. CONFIRM ALL INFORMATION FROM ONLINE DATABASES WITH ORIGINAL SOURCE: Online databases are not always accurate or up-to-date. All information from such databases should be confirmed with the original source.

9. GET CURRENT DISPOSITION OF ALL RELEVANT INFORMATION: All information obtained from any source should be updated to ensure that it is current.

10. PROVIDE APPLICANT THE OPPORTUNITY TO CHALLENGE THE CRA'S REPORT: Whether or not required to do so by FCRA, employers should provide applicants with a prompt and convenient method of challenging information in the CRA's report.

11. ALL CHARGES RELATED TO A SINGLE INCIDENT SHOULD BE REPORTED AS A SINGLE ENTRY: Reporting information relating to a single incident in different sections of a report can create the impression that multiple incidents took place. All information related to a single incident should be reported in a single entry.

12. CONSIDER EVIDENCE OF REHABILITATION: People change over time. Some people with criminal convictions change their lives and become good citizens who can be good employees. Applicants with relevant convictions recent enough to be of concern should not automatically be rejected. Instead, he or she should be given the opportunity to present evidence of rehabilitation which the employer should carefully consider before making a decision.

13. MINIMIZE CONFLICT OF INTEREST BY DECISION MAKERS: Employees making hiring decisions regarding applicants with criminal records are in a difficult situation. If the company hires an applicant with a record who later commits another offense, the employee who hired them may be blamed. Hiring decisions should be made by an employee (or employees) who are in the best position to make an objective decision.

14. TRAIN HUMAN RESOURCES STAFF: Hiring decisions regarding applicants with criminal records require an understanding of the practical steps an employer should take to comply with federal and state law on background checks and to comply with federal, state and local anti-discrimination laws, without exposing the employer to unreasonable risks. Human resources employees should be thoroughly trained on these subjects.

15. HAVE A DIVERSITY PROGRAM: One of the benefits of making sound decisions regarding applicants with criminal records is a more diverse workforce. Having a diversity program helps an employer determine how well it is making such decisions.

A more detailed description of each of the 15 Best Practice Standards—which apply to both employers and Consumer Reporting Agencies (CRAs)—is included in the report. A copy of the report is available at www.esrcheck.com/file/Best-Practice-Standards-Criminal-Records.pdf.

2. *Background Checks: What Employers Need to Know According to the FTC and the EEOC*

In March 2014, a joint publication of the EEOC and the FTC, *Background Checks: What Employers Need to Know,* explained that when employers use an applicant's or employee's background information to make an employment decision, regardless of how they got the information, they must comply with federal laws that protect applicants and employees from discrimination based on race, color, national origin, sex, or religion; disability; genetic information (including family medical history); and age (40 or older). These laws are enforced by the EEOC. Below are excerpts from this report:

Before You Get Background Information

In all cases, make sure that you're treating everyone equally. It's illegal to check the background of applicants and employees when that decision is based on a person's race, national origin, color, sex, religion, disability, genetic information (including family medical history), or age (40 or older). For example, asking only people of a certain race about their financial histories or criminal records is evidence of discrimination.

Except in rare circumstances, don't try to get an applicant's or employee's genetic information, which includes family medical history. Even if you have that information, don't use it to make an employment decision. (For more information about this law, see the EEOC's publications explaining the Genetic Information Nondiscrimination Act, or GINA.) Don't ask any medical questions before a conditional job offer has been made. If the person has already started the job, don't ask medical questions unless you have objective evidence that he or she is unable to do the job or poses a safety risk because of a medical condition.

Using Background Information

Any background information you receive from any source must not be used to discriminate in violation of federal law. This means that you should:

- *Apply the same standards to everyone, regardless of their race, national origin, color, sex, religion, disability, genetic information (including family medical history), or age (40 or older). For example, if you don't reject applicants of one ethnicity with certain financial histories or criminal records, you can't reject applicants of other ethnicities because they have the same or similar financial histories or criminal records.*

- *Take special care when basing employment decisions on background problems that may be more common among people of a certain race, color, national origin, sex, or religion; among people who have a disability; or among people age 40 or older. For example, employers should not use a policy or practice that excludes people with certain criminal records if the policy or practice significantly disadvantages individuals of a particular race, national origin, or another protected characteristic, and does not accurately predict who will be a responsible, reliable, or safe employee. In legal terms, the policy or practice has a "disparate impact" and is not "job related and consistent with business necessity."*

- *Be prepared to make exceptions for problems revealed during a background check that were caused by a disability. For example, if you are inclined not to hire a person because of a problem caused by a disability, you should allow the person to demonstrate his or her ability to do the job - despite the negative background information - unless doing so would cause significant financial or operational difficulty.*

Disposing of Background Information

Any personnel or employment records you make or keep (including all application forms, regardless of whether the applicant was hired, and other records related to hiring) must be preserved for one year after the records were made, or after a personnel action was taken, whichever comes later. (The EEOC extends this requirement to two years for educational institutions and for state and local governments. The Department of Labor also extends this requirement to two years for federal contractors that have at least 150 employees and a government contract of at least $150,000.) If the applicant or employee files a charge of discrimination, you must maintain the records until the case is concluded.

Further Information

To find out more about federal antidiscrimination laws, visit www.eeoc.gov, or call the EEOC toll-free, 800-669-4000 (voice); TTY: 800-669-6820. For specific information on:

- *Pre-employment medical inquiries: see Pre-employment Disability-Related Questions and Medical Examinations at www.eeoc.gov/policy/docs/preemp.html.*
- *Medical inquiries during employment: see Questions and Answers: Enforcement Guidance on Disability-Related Inquiries and Medical Examinations of Employees Under the Americans with Disabilities Act (ADA) at www.eeoc.gov/policy/docs/qanda-inquiries.html.*
- *Genetic inquiries, including inquiries about family medical history: see Background Information for EEOC Final Rule on Title II of the Genetic Information Nondiscrimination Act of 2008 at www.eeoc.gov/laws/regulations/gina-background.cfm.*
- *EEOC recordkeeping requirements: see Summary of Selected Recordkeeping Obligations in 29 C.F.R. Part 1602 at www.eeoc.gov/employers/recordkeeping_obligations.cfm.*
- *Using arrest and conviction records to make employment decisions: see Questions and Answers about EEOC's Enforcement Guidance on the Consideration of Arrest and Conviction Records in Employment Decisions Under Title VII at www.eeoc.gov/laws/guidance/qa_arrest_conviction.cfm.*
- *Whether arrest and conviction records act as an automatic bar to all employment: see Reentry Myth Buster: On Hiring/Criminal Records Guidance at csgjusticecenter.org/wp-content/uploads/2012/11/Reentry_Council_Mythbuster_Employment.pdf.*
- *Background on the EEOC for small businesses: see Get the Facts Series: Small Business Information, www.eeoc.gov/eeoc/publications/smallbusiness.cfm.*

The web page is at www.eeoc.gov/eeoc/publications/background_checks_employers.cfm.

Three Potential EEOC Compliance Approaches for Employers

Employers need an action plan to comply with the EEOC rules. The following are three potential paths employers can consider. Note these steps do NOT constitute legal advice and are offered for educational purposes only.

EEOC Compliance Alternative Number One:

The best protection, but most expensive, is to retain a labor law firm and appropriate statistical experts to review and develop the employer's program by analyzing every job, creating a matrix of related criminal criteria that is defensible, developing appropriate criminal questions for each position, and ensuring that its procedures are in conformity with the Guidance. A labor law firm can also write policies and procedure, do training to meet the guidelines, and can document the processes and facts used to create the policies and any matrix. Part of the reason large organizations should consider this approach is because the EEOC has already announced its plan to further its goals of implementing the E-race Initiative through its Strategic Plan and large employers may well be a target. Another advantage of utilizing the services of a law firm is the employer receives some protection since any communication with the law firm is covered by attorney-client privilege and work product privilege.

EEOC Compliance Alternative Number Two:

For small to medium firms that wish to avoid the time and expenses of having a labor attorney and associated experts prepare an overall program, the following four steps can be taken. In addition, an employer should consider its method for asking applicants questions about past criminal records as explained below.

Step 1:   Use a **Job Class Analysis** to analyze each job class in terms of potential risk. In order to demonstrate an even-handed approach, jobs can be grouped into a classification such as *Laborer, Administrative, Management, Professional*, or *Executive*. There may be additional subcategories such as *Driver* or *Access to Cash or Assets*. An employer can further break down each job category by characteristics of the job. This where an employer considers such things as the job duties, the essential functions of the job, the circumstance under which the job is performed (such as level of supervision), and the environment of the job (such as in a factory or going into a client's home). Taking into account the EEOC factors for judging the nature of the job, an employer can analyze the importance of various job characteristics. This then becomes the basis to analyze the impact on the job of prior criminal behavior. This approach also enables an employer to avoid having a great many different protocols for inquiring about criminal behavior and instead groups jobs by risk factor.

The Job Class Analysis can also include an analysis of other screening tools relevant to the position, such as past employment, education, or special credentials. Of course, if an applicant does not possess the required qualifications, or it turns out that the background check reveals an applicant lied about their credentials, then the employer may well act upon the dishonesty and may never need to even consider any criminal records.

Step 2: Create a **Risk Assessment Matrix** to demonstrate how various frequently encountered criminal matters compare to each job or job groups, taking into account the age and level of the crime. For example, the crime of assault may be further divided into level of offense (such as felony or misdemeanor) and age of offense, such as 3-7 years.   If based on the **Job Analysis Worksheet** and the **Risk Assessment Matrix**, the applicant would not be eliminated, and then the applicant can proceed. If based upon the job and crime and further research is needed, then the applicant goes to step 3 which is a Stage Two Assessment based upon Green Factor analysis.

Employers also need to consider other factors, such as if the time period starts from the date of the criminal act, conviction, or release. In addition, how does an employer handle someone with more than one crime where each crime represents separate acts of behavior? When considering attempted crime, a conspiracy to commit or a charge of aiding and abetting, employers would generally treat it as though the applicant committed the crimes being attempted.

The Risk Assessment Matrix can actually do double duty. It can be used before a background check to determine if a self-admitted offense is relevant, and it can be used after the background check to document how the employer proceeded in the event a criminal matter is found. Keep in mind that a Risk Assessment Matrix is not related to the old "Decision" making matrix where an employer would list various crimes as basically an unacceptable "red light," and essentially use a chart to decide who not to hire. That is discussed in more detail below.

Author Tip

About the Risk Assessment Matrix

At first blush, an employer may be tempted to say that a great deal of work is involved in creating a **Risk Assessment Matrix**. In reality, it is no more difficult than a number of other HR functions, such as creating an employee handbook, reviewing employee classification, or dealing with open enrollment for benefits. Once it's done, then the employer has an essential tool in place that only needs to be reviewed periodically.

It is also important to understand an employer does not go through this process with every single job. Because jobs can be grouped (such as Administrative), an employer can have a Risk Assessment Matrix that covers a number of workers. The key point, however, is that an employer needs to analyze why a particular criminal matter would eliminate someone from employment. The essential thrust of the EEOC Guidance is to eliminate a knee-jerk reaction to a past offense and instead think through what the offense actually means in terms of employment. The process of using the Job Class Analysis and Risk Assessment Matrix to whiteboard out the relationship between jobs and criminal records provides a framework for an employer to develop a plan. This can also be a powerful defense to discrimination allegations to show an employer spent time and effort to make these judgments, and the decisions about criminal records were carefully thought out and considered.

Reasonable minds may differ on the final results, but where an employer can demonstrate the use of such a process in good faith to carefully analyze jobs and crimes, it would presumably be less likely a judge or jury will try to second guess the employer's conclusions as long as they are reasonable.

Step 3: In the event a criminal record is located that potentially has a bearing on employment based upon the first two steps, the employer then goes into a Green Factor analysis. In this step, a *Green Factors Assessment* is used based upon the Green Factors to determine if the applicant is permitted to be considered further. If the assessment shows the applicant should not be eliminated, then the person may continue down the hiring process. If the person is eliminated, Step 4 comes into play.

Step 4: At this state, the applicant has been eliminated based upon the first three steps. However, the applicant would have the opportunity to have an individualized assessment in order to demonstrate a reason to overturn the finding of elimination.

3. EEOC Compliance Alternative Number Three:

Even if an employer takes the position that it is not necessary to utilize a **Job Analysis Worksheet"** and a **Risk Assessment Matrix,** in order to comply with all of the EEOC recommendations, an employer is still well advised to carefully review the new EEOC Guidance and to implement those portions that can give it extra protection. The most helpful suggestions may be:

1. Review and follow the 15 best practice recommendations referred to earlier in this chapter.
2. Extend the traditional Green Factors to include the enhanced considerations suggested by the EEOC.
3. Remove the criminal question from the initial application and replace it with a Criminal Record Check Advisement.
4. Modify any questions about criminal conduct so they is asked later in the process, such as after the interview process, and also place reasonable modifications on the question so it is not broad and open ended.
5. Utilize the individual assessment approach recommended by the EEOC as the final safety valve to ensure that each applicant has been considered fairly and any decision based upon a criminal record has a business justification.
6. Review current policies to ensure that an employer does not have any blanket prohibitions that may run into conflict with an employer's Title VII obligations.
7. Conduct training for anyone involved in making hiring decisions on the issues raised by the EEOC in the new Guidance and an employer's duties under Title VII.
8. Ensure that all information about criminal records for applicants and employees are held confidential and only used for hiring purposes.

Many employers are likely already following some of the EEOC Guidance on an informal basis. For example, when an employer requests a background check that means the applicant is already a finalist or at least a semi-finalist. That also means the employer has gone through time and effort to whittle down the applicant pool and has invested resources in the applicant, not to mention the cost of a background check. If an employer is surprised by an unexpected criminal record, the employer has a vested interest in finding out more about the applicant. In effect, a great many employers already conduct an Individualized Assessment informally. The only change is a more formalized and documented process.

Author Tip ⟩ **Document Each Time Criminal Records Eliminate Job Applicants**

Another critical point is that the employer documents each time a criminal record is the basis for elimination of an applicant from further consideration. The employer can use the data to develop a "Job Analysis Worksheet" and a "Risk Assessment Matrix."

The one point of caution an employer will need to show is there is no disparate treatment or impact between those who are eliminated from consideration per the criminal records. A best practice would be for the in-house reviewer to be trained in discrimination laws.

Three Mistakes to Avoid in Creating Policies to Deal with the EEOC Guidance on Criminal Records

Given all the EEOC, FCRA, and state restrictions, what policy should an employer have regarding the use of criminal records? In Chapter 6, a sample policy template was provided along with an internal memo on procedures. Depending upon how a firm responds to the 2012 EEOC Guidance, an employer may need to adjust the Policy, Practices, and Procedures with a description of the actual practices followed in light of the new Guidance.

In preparing policies, employers make three common mistakes that should be avoided:

1. Having a policy that flatly prohibits employment of an applicant with a criminal record or employment for persons with certain crimes.
2. Having a scoring policy, where a conviction of certain crimes automatically eliminates an applicant.
3. Having no policy for criminal records.

1. Mistake Number One: Having a Policy that Flatly Prohibits Employment of an Applicant with a Criminal Record or Employment for Persons with Certain Crimes

According to the EEOC, a flat "blanket" policy against anyone with a criminal conviction is likely to have an adverse impact on members of a protected class and therefore could be contrary to the rules of the EEOC. The EEOC covers this topic in EEOC Enforcement Guidance No: N-915, "Policy Statement on the Use of Statistics in Charges Involving the Exclusion of Individuals with Conviction Records from Employment," July 29, 1987, at www.eeoc.gov/policy/docs/convict2.html. If challenged, the employer has a duty to present statistical data concerning applicant data flow to demonstrate that a flat policy against hiring anyone with a conviction would not have an adverse impact. However, the EEOC also cautions that such data could also be challenged if the applicant pool artificially limits members of the protected groups from applying in the first place. According to the EEOC notice, "if many Blacks with conviction records did not apply for a particular job because they knew of the employer's policy and they therefore expected to be rejected, then applicant flow data would not be an accurate reflection of the conviction policy's actual effect." Notice N-915 (7/29/87). (NOTE: This exact same language has been stated more recently in EEOC compliance Manual Section 604 "Theories of Discrimination" in the appendices – policy documents – current through August 2009.)

Author Tip ⟩ **Are Flat Polices Against Criminal Offenders Inherently Unfair?**

Some Security and HR professionals have suggested a flat policy against criminal offenders is inherently fairer because an employer is not required to make a distinction between candidates. They suggest further a flat policy is fair because it is applied regardless of the person.

In fact, the opposite is true. A flat policy that judges a person by his or her status or membership in a category (i.e. criminal offender) is inherently prejudicial because it denies individualized consideration. In other words, a person is being pre-judged not based upon who they are, but upon the label attached to them. The root of the word prejudice is to "pre-judge."

Of course, this means that an employer could be placed in a situation where they have two applicants with identical criminal records, but one gets a job offer and the other does not. That can happen because one applicant has engaged in substantial rehabilitation and has great references. In this decision, an employer needs to document why the two individuals are being treated differently. The answer is simple—although they committed the same crime, they are different people with different qualifications.

Unless an employer plans to hire a professional statistician and a team of labor lawyers and demographics experts, the best policy is to not have a flat and automatic prohibition on applicants with criminal records. Employers using criminal background checks for employment purposes should be careful not to have a "blanket policy" that excludes job applicants who are ex-offenders. Employers should follow the EEOC guidelines for conviction records under Title VII of the Civil Rights Act of 1964 that prohibits discrimination in employment based on race, gender, national origin, and other protected categories.

2. Mistake Number Two: Having a Scoring Policy, Where a Conviction of Certain Crimes Automatically Eliminates an Applicant

Another potential mistake employers make is to have a flat prohibition regarding certain crimes. For example, an employer may have a flat and automatic prohibition against hiring someone with certain convictions such as theft, robbery, violence, or drugs.

Some employers go even further and have a scoring system whereby an employer uses the services of a screening firm to automatically eliminate an applicant. Some employers use a *traffic light system*. If the applicant has no criminal record, then he or she is given a *green light*. If the applicant has a disqualifying criminal record, such as a violent crime, the screening company gives the applicant a *red light*. If there is a crime that is not on the employer's automatic elimination list, that person receives a *yellow light or caution light* so that the crime can be reviewed with the employer.

The same EEOC notice mentioned above also addresses this issue. According to the Commission, past decisions were based upon national or regional statistics for crime as a whole. However, if the employer can present more narrow regional or local data on conviction rates for all crime or the specific crime showing that protected groups are not convicted at disproportionably higher rates, then the employer may be able to justify such a policy. In addition, the employer can show that the policies, in fact, did not result in disproportionately higher rates of exclusion. This is a tough sell for an employer.

In view of the legal exposure for discrimination and the potential high cost of defending the process, employers may consider changing the *red light* from automatic disqualification to a policy of "strict scrutiny of the offense" pursuant to the EEOC three-part test. Now the red-flagged person will go through a special process whereby the employer reviews the details of the past offense, the applicant, the job, then reaches an individualized, documented decision.

3. Mistake Number Three: Having No Policy for Criminal Records

Given the complexities of criminal record usage, some employers have asked if they should simply ignore the whole issue in their policy documenting on the theory that saying nothing cannot get them into trouble. The opposite is probably true. As a general rule, it is a best practice for employers to have written policies on important issues. Without a policy, an employer's actions in denying employment may become harder to defend. Having no policy also subjects an employer to claims of a discriminatory practice. In addition, in the event of an investigation by the EEOC or a state office or a lawsuit, the lack of a policy may be seen as evidence that an employer has failed do take appropriate steps to prevent the unfair use of criminal records.

Author Tip > **Screening Firms Act in a "Clerical" Capacity to Carry Out an Employer Policy**

It is worth remembering that if a screening firm performs any process to carry out an employer's policies or compliance with the new EEOC Guidance, the screening firm is only acting in a "clerical" capacity carrying out the employer's policies and instructions and is not making any independent decisions, analysis, or recommendations. However, screening firms should be able to build in a great deal of compliance capacity into their screening software to process the employer's particular policies.

EEOC and Use of Arrest Only Records

In Chapter 8, there was a discussion on the differences between an arrest and a conviction. Essentially, the underlying behavior of an arrest that did not turn into a conviction has not been established by a judicial proceeding. It is critical for employers to understand that an arrest needs to be treated much differently than a conviction. Many states also treat an arrest only different than a conviction (See Chapter 6). Below is a discussion of the EEOC position on arrests.

EEOC Rules on Arrest Records

Under the previous Guidance issued on September 7, 1990, the EEOC went into some detail on how an arrest is to be considered. See: www.eeoc.gov/policy/docs/arrest_records.html. The EEOC Guidance issued April 25, 2012, by its own terms superseded previous Guidance. However, it would appear the 1990 Guidance is still in effect due to comments made by the EEOC in its Question and Answer page where it specifically referred to this 1990 Guidance. (See www.eeoc.gov/laws/guidance/qa_arrest_conviction.cfm.) Regardless, both the 1990 and 2012 guidance make it clear that:

- An employer must look beyond the arrest and determine what actually happened.
- After determining what actually happened, the employer must then determine whether the conduct is relevant to an employment decision.

In the 1990 Guidance on arrests, the EEOC notes the following:

"Conviction records constitute reliable evidence that a person engaged in the conduct alleged since the criminal justice system requires the highest degree of proof ("beyond a reasonable doubt") for a conviction. In contrast, arrests alone are not reliable evidence that a person has actually committed a crime. *Schware v. Board of Bar Examiners*, 353 U.S. 232, 241 (1957) ("[t]he mere fact that a [person] has been arrested has very little, if any, probative value in showing that he has engaged in misconduct"). Thus, the Commission concludes that to justify the use of arrest records, an additional inquiry must be made. Even where the conduct alleged in the arrest record is related to the job at issue, the employer must evaluate whether the arrest record reflects the applicant's conduct. It should, therefore, examine the surrounding circumstances, offer the applicant or employee an opportunity to explain, and, if he or she denies engaging in the conduct, make the follow-up inquiries necessary to evaluate his/her credibility. Since using arrests as a disqualifying criteria can only be justified where it appears that the applicant actually engaged in the conduct for which he\she was arrested and that conduct is job related, the Commission further concludes that an employer will seldom be able to justify making broad general inquiries about an employee's or applicant's arrests."

If an employer locates an arrest, it can be very difficult to determine the underlying conduct. Phone calls to the local police or prosecutor may be required, and they may not be willing to cooperate. According to the 1990 guidance, an employer should not summarily dismiss the applicant's statement about the arrest. In fact, the EEOC notes in the 1990 Guidance that:

"An arrest record does no more than raise a suspicion that an applicant may have engaged in a particular type of conduct. Thus, the investigator must determine whether the applicant is likely to have committed the conduct alleged. This is the most difficult step because it requires the employer either to accept the employee's denial or to attempt to obtain additional information and evaluate his/her credibility. An employer need not conduct an informal "trial" or an extensive investigation to determine an applicant's or employee's guilt or innocence. However, the employer may not perfunctorily "allow the person an opportunity to explain" and ignore the explanation where the person's claims could easily be verified by a phone call, i.e., to a previous employer or a police department. The employer is required to allow the person a meaningful opportunity to explain the circumstances of the arrest(s) and to make a reasonable effort to determine whether the explanation is credible before eliminating him/her from employment opportunities."

Even if the employer is able to establish the underlying conduct, the employer must then go through an analysis to determine if there is a business justification to deny the employment similar to the analysis used for a conviction. However, the EEOC notes that where the position involves security, or "gives the employee easy access to the possessions of others, close scrutiny of an applicant's character and prior conduct is appropriate where an employer is responsible for the safety and/or well-being of other persons."

As a practical matter, employers need to think long and hard before using information from an arrest in the view of clear EEOC rules. Even though the 2012 guidance did not go into as much detail about an arrest as the 1990 Guidance, the better view is to assume the 1990 Guidance is still in force and effect, and the 2012 Guidance is merely supplemental but does not replace the 1990 EEOC position.

In addition, employers should take into account their own state laws on the use of arrests not resulting in convictions. As outlined in Chapter 6, many states have specific laws that restrict the use of an arrest not resulting in a conviction. Most states also have some form of pre-employment inquiry guidelines covering what is proper and improper to put on an application form or to ask at an interview. These typically prohibit an employer from asking about an arrest only. (See Chapter 3 section 'Questions Not to Ask and Why: Pre-Employment Inquiry Guidelines Chart.')

Some Practical and Frequently Asked Questions Concerning the EEOC Criminal Guidance

Below are some FAQs concerning the EEOC Criminal Guidance:

1.   What if an Applicant is Not a Member of a Class Protected by Title VII?

A frequently asked question is: Do the EEOC rules about the use of criminal records apply to applicants who are not members of a protected class?

Although if such a person were to bring a private lawsuit for discrimination, an employer could attempt to defend on the basis of a lack of a legal standing to sue, the short answer is that an employer is well advised to apply these same criminal record rules to all applicants. First, it is risky business for an employer to make assumptions about whether a particular applicant is a member of a protected group just based on factors such as physical appearance or name. More importantly, if a non-covered applicant were to file a complaint with the EEOC or a state enforcement agency, there would be no barrier to investigation if the case suggested a pattern and practice of the discriminatory use of criminal records. The bottom line is that treating applicants differently can create a high risk and the best approach may well be to assume the EEOC rules on criminal records apply to everyone.

2.   What is the Procedure if an Applicant Accurately Self-Reveals a Criminal Record before the background check?

When the applicant accurately tells an employer about a criminal record, and there is no element of dishonesty, then the issue arises as to what an employer can legally do and should do. At that point, an employer needs to be aware of their obligations under both federal and state discrimination laws. The 2012 Criminal Guidance comes into play.

However, if there was no background check, there is not an FCRA issue. If it turns out that the criminal matter is either job related or there is a business necessity that prevents hiring, the applicant should receive an individualized assessment process even though the employer did not do a background check report.

Keep in mind the EEOC has urged employers in its 2012 Guidance to not ask about criminal records in the application. However, at some point in the process, an employer can and should ask properly worded questions about past criminal records.

3.   Do the EEOC rules apply when the applicant lied and did not reveal a criminal record?

Conversely, if the applicant lies about a past criminal record, that can be a serious issue. The act of dishonesty can be either an attempt to completely hide the past criminal conviction or by minimizing what was, in fact, a more serious charge. For example, an applicant may misrepresent a criminal record such as disclosing a petty theft that was, in fact, a robbery.

This discovery may occur in a variety of ways. During the hiring process, an employer may discover the criminal record through a past employer reference check or from the background report. A past criminal record may also come to the employer's attention after the applicant has been hired. For example, a new worker may tell a co-worker about his or her criminal past and the conversation is reported to management.

When the employer does ask the criminal question (at or after the interview or after a conditional job offer), the question regarding criminal issues should be asked in broad language and clearly inform applicants that dishonesty is a basis to deny employment or for termination no matter when discovered. If a background check locates criminal matters that an applicant misrepresented, then the dishonesty can be the grounds to deny employment.

If the question on the application was worded properly, and the employer caught the applicant in a lie, then it is the LIE that forms the basis for the termination of the hiring process. Most employers take the position that dishonesty can always be a basis not to hire.

However, there are some potential wrinkles to be careful about in this process. First, was the application poorly written so that the answer was the literal truth? The person may have committed a serious misdemeanor, but the question was only about felonies. Or, what if the applicant was genuinely confused about his or her criminal past and thought they were answering honestly. Or, what if the criminal matter they lied about has no bearing on the job. These all create additional issues for employers to examine.

One important point—if the matter came to light as a result of a background check, then the applicant is entitled to both the FCRA adverse action process as described in Chapter 5 and the individualized assessment process.

4. What about arrests and convictions that occur after employment?

Employer can discover new criminal matters after employment. An employer may learn about a criminal matter that was missed during the background check. Or a new criminal matter can occur after a person was hired. An employer may hear about an arrest or conviction from the news media, or as a result of investigating absenteeism, or even after being contacted by the local probation office to arrange for an employee's participation in some sort of jail-release program.

First, an employer should review their employee manual on the subject of arrests and convictions occurring post-hire. In Chapter 1, suggested language was offered on employment screening and safe hiring. An employer also needs to review their application form to ensure there was language that covered any material falsehood to avoid a situation where an employee hid information about a criminal offense during the hiring period. (See Chapter 3 on Applications.)

However, employers should assume the EEOC rules also apply to current employees who are already on the job. The rule would apply regardless of where the criminal matter occurred before or after hiring. However, if the criminal matter occurred before hiring and the applicant lied about it, then the dishonesty may be the deciding factor.

5. Should an employer take special steps if they hire a person with a criminal record?

If a firm decides to hire an individual with a criminal record, then it is crucial to document the reasons for the decision and the processes the firm used leading up to the decision that the applicant is reasonably suited for the job. Employers should also note any considerations made as to whether these individuals need special supervision or assistance to help them succeed—and maintain workplace safety.

The Ban-the-Box Movement

The issue of whether employers can use a job application to ask about an applicant's criminal record is becoming more complicated. In an effort to provide fair employment opportunities for ex-convicts, some states, cities, counties, and local governments across the country are joining **the fast growing ban-the-box movement**.

This ban-the-box practice removes the box that job applicants are asked to check regarding the question on the job application which asks about past criminal arrest and conviction. The purpose is to give those applicants with criminal pasts a fair shot at obtaining employment. By removing this question, supporters claim job applicants can be sure that they will not be automatically excluded from consideration for a job because of their past mistakes.

However, ban-the-box does NOT mean there can never be a criminal background check. A ban-the-box approach prevents an early knock-out punch before ex-offenders even have the opportunity to be considered on their individual merits. The concern is that their employment application will be automatically rejected just based upon their status as ex-offenders as opposed to what they can offer an employer. That does not mean that a background check will not be conducted or that an employer cannot exercise appropriate due diligence, but just that it is delayed until later in the process.

At least 150 cities and counties, as well as 24 states, have some form of ban-the-box legislation. The National Employment Law Project (NELP) runs a ban-the-box campaign called *"Ensuring People with Convictions Have a Fair Chance to Work"* that offers both employers and ex-offenders information, resources, and guides that are available online at www.nelp.org/campaign/ensuring-fair-chance-to-work/.

According to NELP, states that currently have passed ban-the-box legislation include: California; Colorado; Connecticut; Delaware; Georgia; Hawaii; Illinois; Louisiana; Maryland; Massachusetts; Minnesota; Missouri; Nebraska; New Jersey; New Mexico; New York; Ohio; Oklahoma; Oregon; Rhode Island; Tennessee; Vermont; Virginia; and Wisconsin.

Some major cities that states that currently have passed ban-the-box legislation include: Atlanta, GA; Austin, TX; Baltimore, MD; Boston, MA; Charlotte, NC; Chicago, IL; Cincinnati, OH; Cleveland, OH; Detroit, MI; Jacksonville, FL; Kansas City, MO; Memphis, TN; Minneapolis, MN; New Orleans, LA; New York, NY; Oakland, CA; Philadelphia, PA; Pittsburgh, PA; San Francisco, CA; Seattle, WA; St. Louis, MO; St. Paul, MN; Tampa, FL; and Washington, DC.

The information above is from the NELP publication "Ban-the-Box: U.S. Cities, Counties, and States Adopt Fair Hiring Policies" available at www.nelp.org/publication/ban-the-box-fair-chance-hiring-state-and-local-guide/.

> **You Need To Know** > ## Ban-the-Box Laws Not Uniform Across Country

Ban-the-box laws are not entirely uniform across the country. Although some organizations have proposed model laws, they can vary by jurisdiction.

A typical ban-the-box law is first focused on the timing of asking about past convictions. Laws may regulate for example that a question cannot be asked until at or after an interview or a job offer. Some laws then go a step further and regulate what an employer can ask about. Some laws even go a step further and will regulate what an employer can consider.

The major drawback with ban-the-box laws at the local level is that a county or city cannot offer an employer any type of statewide immunity against negligent hiring if they follow ban-the-box rules and end up hiring a person with a criminal record who re-offends and subjects the employer to negligent hiring claims. Only a state legislature can provide a solution where employers are given some form of immunity or legal protection if they incorporate ban-the-box and hire individuals with criminal records.

Public vs. Private Law

In reviewing if a ban-the-box rule impacts your place of business, it is important to distinguish between public and private application of the rules. It is important to note that ban-the-box started off as an effort aimed at governmental entities to encourage the hiring of ex-offenders for public positions. A large number of ban-the-box laws are aimed at public employment.

In April 2016, President Barack Obama showed his support of the ban-the-box movement by signing a "Presidential Memorandum for Promoting Rehabilitation and Reintegration of Formerly Incarcerated Individuals" to help the estimated 70 million or more Americans with a record of arrest, criminal adjudication, or conviction reenter society through employment. See: www.whitehouse.gov/the-press-office/2016/04/29/presidential-memorandum-promoting-rehabilitation-and-reintegration.

Some of the ban-the-box laws impacted private employers by also covering any employer that supplied goods and services to a ban-the-box jurisdiction.

Eventually, it morphed into laws that applied to private employers as well, and a number of states and local jurisdictions now extend a ban-the-box approach to private employers. As noted above, the EEOC has recommended, but not required, that private employers utilize a ban-the-box approach nationwide.

The most recent trend is for private employers to voluntarily adopt a ban-the-box approach, especially larger national employers that operate in multiple states.

Practical Reasons to Ban-the-Box

Ban-the-box is close to a tipping point nationwide where it will be widely accepted and recommended that private employers redo their application forms and incorporate the ban-the-box approach even if not required by a state or local law. There are several practical reasons:

1. Every employer and recruiter knows that up to 70% of all applications really have little if any bearing on the job. Asking about criminal records early in the hiring process probably does very little to lighten the load and reduce the amount of applications to review. It only serves as an early knock-out punch before a candidate has the chance to be considered on his or her qualifications, and unnecessarily exposes employers to allegations they are automatically tossing out applications with a criminal record. An employer is better served using good hiring techniques based upon neutral factors to whittle down the applicant pool through progressive screening as described in Chapter 3. The initial pool of applicants can be reviewed based on knowledge, skills, abilities, and experience. At some appropriate time, such as an interview, when an employer has narrowed the field, an appropriate criminal question can be asked. Asking it early does not accomplish that much and unnecessarily exposes an employer to potential allegations of discrimination.

2. An employer may find that a candidate who would have otherwise been eliminated early due to a criminal record is, in fact, a good candidate for the position. This may become even more critical in the future. As "baby boomers" retire, the working population in the U.S. according to some studies is shrinking. If there is a decrease in immigration into the U.S. as a result of the 2016 election, the available labor pool may shrink even further. That means employers may be pressed to look harder and further for potential employees. Cutting out an entire potential workfare of people with past criminal records that may no longer be relevant may deny employers workers they need and result in a **talent shortage.** This can especially impact sectors that rely on seasonal, temporary or on-demand workers.

You Need To Know > **Employers Report Highest Global Talent Shortage Since 2007**

Employers around the world are facing the largest talent shortage since the recession as **40 percent of global employers have experienced difficulties filling jobs**—the highest level since 41 percent in 2007—according to the *2016-2017 Talent Shortage Survey from ManpowerGroup*.

The survey of 42,300 global employers from 43 countries found more employers than ever are turning to training and development of their own workforce to address talent shortage problems. The number of employers using this strategy has more than doubled since 2015, from one in five to over half.

An Infographic for the Talent Shortage Survey shows skilled trade jobs such as electricians, carpenters, and plumbers were the hardest to fill globally for the fifth consecutive year, while Information Technology (IT) roles jumped seven places to be the second hardest jobs to fill.

When asked why it was so hard to fill positions, the survey revealed 24 percent of employers said lack of available applicants or no applicants, 19 percent of employers said lack of hard skills and technical competencies, and 19 percent of employers said lack of experience.

The survey also found that the countries having the most talent shortage problems included Japan (86 percent), Taiwan (73 percent), Romania (72 percent), Hong Kong (69 percent), Turkey (66 percent), Bulgaria (62 percent), Argentina (59 percent), and Greece (59 percent). For more details, visit www.manpowergroup.com/talentshortage.

3. Another reason to ban-the-box is because it is extremely difficult to adjust employment application to reflect all the state, county or city ban-the-box laws. It is very difficult to have a workable national employment application asking about criminal records when there is a crazy quilt map of states, counties and cities all with their own laws that can operate in different ways. A case in point is a recent Buffalo, New York court case involving two major national retailers that failed to adjust their forms for stores subject to local ban-the-fox rules in Buffalo, New York. In January 2016, New York State Attorney General Eric T. Schneiderman has announced settlements totaling $195,000 with two major national retailers – Big Lots Stores and Marshalls – over violations of a ban-the-box law that prohibits employers from inquiring about the criminal history of job applicants on initial employment applications at their Buffalo stores.

In addition to satisfying the requirements of the local ban-the-box ordinance, Big Lots and Marshalls took the additional step of removing such inquiries from applications to their combined 139 stores in New York State. Along with new policies, training, and reporting to the Attorney General's Office, Big Lots agreed to pay a monetary penalty of $100,000, while Marshalls will pay a penalty of $95,000.

The press release from the Attorney General is available at www.ag.ny.gov/press-release/ag-schneiderman-announces-settlements-two-major-national-retailers-over-violations

Are there Disadvantages to Using a Ban-the-Box Approach?

What is the worst that can happen if an employer uses the ban-the-box approach? An employer may end up finding the ideal candidate through progressive screening and interviews. At or after the interview the candidate then reveals a criminal record. Based upon an analysis of the risks involved an employer may not be able to hire that person resulting in some time having been wasted. In reality, the likelihood of that occurring is extremely remote versus a much greater certainty that an employer can face legal and regulatory issues if it asks about criminal questions too soon.

Progressive Application Review

Another way of dealing with ban-the-box is the use of **Progressive Application Review**.

By not having the criminal question on the application, the employer must first look at other factors, such as whether the applicant has the knowledge, skills, and abilities listed to even meet job requirements. For example, does the person's past job history show they have the experience needed? What about degrees or credentials needed?

In addition, even among those that appear on a first screening to be in the running, the employer may then continue to whittle down the applicant pool to the best qualified before starting telephone screening or scheduling interviews. That part of the process is based on facts provided by the applicant. The employer is making decisions based upon a screening for neutral (that is, non-discriminatory) factors. An employer does not need to have the criminal history to engage in an initial screen to determine if the candidate is even in the running. By having a progressive process of first looking at objective factors related directly to job qualifications, the employer does not even get to the issue of criminal records.

If it turns out that a person has the qualifications needed for the job, was invited for an interview, and then a criminal record is discovered that makes the person unsuitable for the job, the employer is in a position to evaluate the criminal record in light of having talked with the candidate. An employer may say that the interview was a waste of time.

However, the employer needs to weigh and balance if an occasional wasted interview is a small price to pay for overall compliance. In other words, having a criminal question at the beginning of the hiring process that serves as an early "knock-out" punch to ex-offenders may be more trouble than it is worth. Why use a question that may invite litigation or investigation when an employer can instead use non-controversial methods to whittle down the applicant pool to qualified workers?

Should an Applicant be made Aware that a Criminal Question May Eventually be Asked?

As part of banning the box, an employer may consider replacing the questions about past criminal conduct with an advisement that a job related criminal check will be needed before the job is finalized. If that, in fact, is part of the procedure, there is nothing in the EEOC Guidance or case law that requires an employer to hide that fact or to create a false impression of the hiring process. If an employer is regulated so that certain criminal convictions eliminates a candidate as a matter of law, that is certainly something an employer needs to know up front, provided it is a **bona fide occupational qualification (BFOQ)**.

By the same token, an employer cannot make such an advisement concerning criminal background checks if it amounts to a backdoor effort to keep out anyone with criminal records and acts to deter or chill ex-offenders from applying in the first place. If used as subterfuge, it would probably not be advisable.

By analogy to other sensitive areas, this appears to be a tried and proven path. For example, it is generally recommended that an employer not ask an applicant about citizenship or place of birth in an application or interview. However, an employer can advise an applicant that as a condition of employment, there will be a verification of the legal right to work in the U. S. Similarity an employer cannot ask about any disability until well into the process. However, a valid pre-employment inquiry is a statement that employment may be conditional upon an employer conducting a physical exam. A third example is the EEOC position on the date of birth. As discussed in Chapter 2, there is actually not a prohibition from asking about age. However, since it may tend to deter older applicants, such a request would be scrutinized closely to determine if it was made for a lawful purpose. (See, for example, sample California guidelines on proper questions at www.dfeh.ca.gov/res/docs/Publications/DFEH-161.pdf)

Sample Criminal Record Advisement

Here is a sample of what such a criminal advisement may contain. However, this is not legal advice, and an employer should review the matter carefully with their legal counsel:

> *If the company determines an applicant is suitable for the position based on a job related evaluation of skills and experience that may also include an interview, prior to final selection and subsequent employment, an applicant will be subject to a background check that is appropriate to the job functions and business necessity. If related criminal records are revealed in the process, the applicant will not be disqualified automatically.*

Top U.S. Employers Move towards Ban-the-Box

A number of high profile U.S. employees have adopted ban-the-box proactively. These include Walmart, Target, Home Depot, Bed Bath & Beyond, and Koch Industries.

In April 2016, several major American corporations including Coca-Cola, Facebook, and Starbucks joined President Barack Obama as the founding members in signing the **"Fair Chance Pledge"** that asks all of the U.S. private sector to ban-the-box on employment applications in order to eliminate barriers to job seekers with a criminal record.

Companies that signed the Fair Chance Pledge to ban-the-box include: American Airlines, Busboys and Poets, The Coca-Cola Company, Facebook, Georgia Pacific, Google, Greystone Bakery, The Hershey Company, The Johns Hopkins Hospital and Health System, Koch Industries, Libra Group, PepsiCo, Prudential, Starbucks, Uber, Under Amour/Plank Industries, Unilever, and Xerox. Businesses may take the Fair Chance Pledge at www.whitehouse.gov/issues/criminal-justice/fair-chance-pledge.

In August 2016, the White House announced a new round of signers of the Fair Chance Business Pledge that included Walmart – the largest private employer in the world with more than 2 million employees – to bring the total number of companies and organizations pledging to ban-the-box and help job candidates with criminal histories to return to the workforce to 185 employers.

The "FACT SHEET: White House Launches the Fair Chance Business Pledge" estimates that approximately 70 million Americans have a criminal record – almost one in three Americans of working age – and the United States accounts for 25 percent of the world's inmates. Roughly 2.2 million Americans are in jail, and more than 600,000 inmates are released from federal and state prisons each year while another 11.4 million individuals cycle through local jails.

In November 2015, President Obama announced an Executive Order to ban-the-box since "advancing policies and programs that enable these men and women to put their lives back on track promotes not only justice and fairness, but also public safety." To learn more about the Fair Chance Business Pledge, visit www.whitehouse.gov/issues/criminal-justice/business-pledge.

The "FACT SHEET: White House Launches the Fair Chance Business Pledge" is available at www.whitehouse.gov/the-press-office/2016/04/11/fact-sheet-white-house-launches-fair-chance-business-pledge.

You Need To Know ▷ **Study Finds Workers with Criminal Records No Worse than Non-Offenders**

Researchers at Northwestern University have released a study entitled **'Criminal Background and Job Performance'** that found employees with criminal records "have an involuntary separation rate that is no higher than that of other employees and a voluntary separation rate that is much lower."

The study—authored by Dylan Minor and Nicola Persico of the Northwestern University Kellogg School of Management, and Deborah M. Weiss or the Northwestern University School of Law—found workers with criminal records to "be no worse, and possibly even better" than workers without criminal records.

The researchers examined the records of over one million applicants to jobs such as customer service and sales representatives collected between 2008 and 2014 and found approximately 264,000 applicants with criminal records who were less likely to get hired for these jobs and more likely to head back to prison.

Statistics from the study show over 650,000 offenders are released from U.S. prisons each year (Carson and Golinelli 2013), over half of released prisoners are re-convicted within three years (Durose, Cooper, and Snyder 2014), and failure to find work can cause recidivism (Uggen and Shannon 2014; Yang 2016).

According to the study: *Job applicants with criminal records are much less likely than others to obtain legitimate employment. Recent audit studies suggest that lower human capital alone does not fully explain this difference, and that employers apply a hiring penalty to job applicants with a criminal record.*

Researchers looked at "why hiring firms impose a hiring penalty and whether their concerns are founded on an accurate view of how ex-offenders behave on the job if hired." Since "little empirical evidence" exists, the study tried to answer these questions by looking at hiring practices and performance outcomes.

Although data indicating workers with criminal records had "a psychological profile different from other employees, with fewer characteristics that are associated with good job performance outcomes," these workers generally performed the same in the workplace as workers who had no criminal record.

However, researchers did find workers with criminal records had "a slightly higher overall rate of discharge for misconduct than do employees without a record, although we find increased misconduct only for sales positions." There was no increased risk for customer service workers.

The study—released in October of 2016—also found that "firms that do not use information about criminal backgrounds seem to compensate by placing more weight on qualifications that are correlated with a criminal record, such as low educational attainment."

The findings "indicate the need for some caution about drafting Ban-the-Box provisions that restrict the use that employers make of a criminal record once it is revealed" and Ban-the-Box requires "a better understanding of the predictive value of a criminal record for misconduct."

The study concluded "those with a criminal record are less likely to quit their job voluntarily, and no more likely to leave it involuntarily," and "workers with a criminal background appear to be no worse, and possibly even better, than workers without such a background."

The study stated: *In terms of policy recommendations, we must stress the need for additional work. At present we have no way of balancing the benefits of the longer tenure of workers with a criminal record against the potential costs of their higher rate of misconduct discharges.*

Source: https://papers.ssrn.com/sol3/papers.cfm?abstract_id=2851951.

Can Ban-the-Box Policies Have Unintended Consequences?

Two studies on ban-the-box (BTB) policies that prevent employers from asking job applicants if they have a criminal record on initial applications claim that these well intentioned laws meant to help ex-offenders re-enter the workforce may have the unintended consequence of causing more harm than good for minority job seekers.

Ban-the-Box, Criminal Records, and Statistical Discrimination: A Field Experiment

In June 2016, the study *Ban-the-Box, Criminal Records, and Statistical Discrimination: A Field Experiment* (University of Michigan Law & Econ Research Paper No. 16-012) co-authored by Amanda Y. Agan, Princeton University Department of Economics, and Sonja B. Starr, University of Michigan Law School, was released. According to the Abstract:

"Ban-the-Box" (BTB) policies restrict employers from asking about applicants' criminal histories on job applications and are often presented as a means of reducing unemployment among black men, who disproportionately have criminal records. However, withholding information about criminal records could risk encouraging statistical discrimination: employers may make assumptions about criminality based on the applicant's race. To investigate this possibility as well as the effects of race and criminal records on employer callback rates, we sent approximately 15,000 fictitious online job applications to employers in New Jersey and New York City, in waves before and after each jurisdiction's adoption of BTB policies. Our causal effect estimates are based on a triple-differences design, which exploits the fact that many businesses' applications did not ask about records even before BTB and were thus unaffected by the law.

Our results confirm that criminal records are a major barrier to employment, but they also support the concern that BTB policies encourage statistical discrimination on the basis of race. Overall, white applicants received 23% more callbacks than similar black applicants (38% more in New Jersey; 6% more in New York City; we also find that the white advantage is much larger in whiter neighborhoods). Employers that ask about criminal records are 62% more likely to call back an applicant if he has no record (45% in New Jersey; 78% in New York City) — an effect that BTB compliance necessarily eliminates. However, we find that the race gap in callbacks grows dramatically at the BTB-affected companies after the policy goes into effect. Before BTB, white applicants to BTB-affected employers received about 7% more callbacks than similar black applicants, but BTB increases this gap to 45%.

The study is available at http://papers.ssrn.com/sol3/papers.cfm?abstract_id=2795795.

Does Ban-the-Box Help or Hurt Low-Skilled Workers? Statistical Discrimination and Employment Outcomes When Criminal Histories are Hidden

In July 2016, the study *Does "Ban-the-Box" Help or Hurt Low-Skilled Workers? Statistical Discrimination and Employment Outcomes When Criminal Histories Are Hidden"* co-authored by Jennifer L. Doleac, University of Virginia Frank Batten School of Leadership and Public Policy, and Benjamin Hansen, University of Oregon Department of Economics, was released. According to the Abstract:

Jurisdictions across the United States have adopted "Ban-the-Box" (BTB) policies preventing employers from conducting criminal background checks until late in the job application process. Their goal is to improve employment outcomes for those with criminal records, with a secondary goal of reducing racial disparities in employment. However, removing information about job applicants' criminal histories could lead employers who don't want to hire ex-offenders to try to guess who the ex-offenders are, and avoid interviewing them. In particular, employers might avoid interviewing young, low-skilled, black and Hispanic men when criminal records are not observable. This would worsen employment outcomes for these already-disadvantaged groups. In this paper, we use variation in the details and timing of state and local BTB policies to test BTB's effects on employment for various demographic groups. We find that BTB policies decrease the probability of being employed by 3.4 percentage points (5.1%) for young, low-skilled black men, and by 2.3 percentage points (2.9%) for young, low-skilled Hispanic men. These findings support the hypothesis that when an applicant's criminal history is unavailable, employers statistically discriminate against demographic groups that are likely to have a criminal record.

The study is available at www.nber.org/papers/w22469.

Other Criticisms of Ban-the-Box

Other criticisms of ban-the-box have been that ban-the-box policies do not actually create new jobs. If an ex-offender gets a job, then someone else does not. In addition, it has also been noted that employers alone cannot solve all of the issues related to employment of people with criminal records. Government programs, re-training, and criminal justice reform, among other things, are needed as well. However, as seen below, proponents of ban-the-box have never suggested that it is a cure-all.

NELP Argues Studies Critical of Ban-the-Box Reach the Wrong Conclusion

In August 2016, the National Employment Law Project (NELP) released a policy brief – *Racial Profiling in Hiring: A Critique of New Ban-the-Box Studies* – critical of two studies that claimed ban-the-box policies meant to help applicants with criminal records find work could do "more harm than good" by unintentionally harming minority job seekers. NELP believes these ban-the-box studies reach "the wrong conclusion."

According to the ban-the-box policy brief from NELP, two recent studies claim that ban-the-box policies enacted around the country detrimentally affect the employment of young men of color who do not have a conviction record. One of the authors has boldly argued that the policy should be abandoned outright because it "does more harm than good."

It is the wrong conclusion. In reviewing these ban-the-box studies, NELP concludes:

- The core problem raised by the studies is not ban-the-box but entrenched racism in the hiring process, which manifests as racial profiling of African Americans as "criminals."
- Ban-the-box is working, both by increasing employment opportunities for people with records and by changing employer attitudes toward hiring people with records.
- When closely scrutinized, the new studies do not support the conclusion that ban-the-box policies are responsible for the depressed hiring of African Americans.
- The studies highlight the need for a more robust policy response to both boost job opportunities for people with records and tackle race discrimination in the hiring process—not a repeal of ban-the-box laws.

NELP concludes that "the studies focus their criticism on the ban-the-box policy—not the racism that the policy exposes." The policy brief about the ban-the-box studies from NELP, a national advocacy organization for employment rights of lower-wage workers, is available for download at www.nelp.org/publication/racial-profiling-in-hiring-a-critique-of-new-ban-the-box-studies/.

Author Tip ▷ **Will Ban-the-Box End Up Hurting Ex-Offenders with Employment History Gaps?**

Will ban-the-box actually hurt ex-offenders by encouraging employers to use uninterrupted past employment history as a safety barometer instead of criminal records? This issue with ban-the–box is being demonstrated by the version of the law passed by the City and County of San Francisco as reviewed in Chapter 6. San Francisco changed the definition of the California seven-year rule and potentially is exposing groups at risk to harm.

This underscores the problem with each city or county having the ability to implement their version of ban-the-box rules. Employers are faced with a bewildering array of different rules when an extreme version of the law is passed like in San Francisco. Employers are faced potentially with too many laws to comply with or laws that endanger their workforce or the public, the challenge for employers is how to avoid risk. As noted earlier, the San Francisco law is so restrictive that a battered women's shelter, for example, may be required to hire a sex-offender newly released from prison.

In reviewing the situation with some San Francisco employers, it is clear they have found a solution that will enable them to comply with the letter of the law as well as protect their organization and clients. However, this solution may negatively affect ex-offenders as well as people with no criminal record. Since a serious barrier has been placed on their ability to obtain or use relevant criminal records, employers appear to be poised to utilize an applicant's employment history as a leading barometer of safety, assuming no employment gaps would mean no prison time.

The idea is that if an applicant has a documented employment history without significant interruptions, then an employer can have some degree of confidence that the person has probably not spent time in custody for a serious criminal matter. The practical result is that a person with a criminal record that created gaps in their employment history would be knocked out early in the process anyway so that the ban-the-box rules become meaningless.

By forcing employers to rely more heavily on employment history, the San Francisco ban-the-box law also potentially ends up punishing individuals with no criminal record but who had difficulties maintaining a consistent employment record during the recent recession.

The bottom line is that by over regulating the use of criminal records when hiring, worker rights and civil rights organizations, although certainly well intended, may arguably make the situation worse for ex-offenders by encouraging employers to rely increasing on a solid and uninterrupted job history as the initial and most critical screening tool.

Read more on this subject at www.esrcheck.com/wordpress/2015/08/13/san-francisco-ban-the-box-ordinance-may-hurt-ex-offenders-the-law-was-meant-to-help/.

You Need To Know

HOPE for Prisoners Program Shows Benefits of Hiring Ex-Offenders

A member of a registered nonprofit organization called **HOPE for Prisoners** that helps ex-offenders "transition out of prison to reenter society successfully" says that workers with past criminal records "work harder than other employees" and "truly value their jobs," according to the article "Should You Hire An Ex-Con?" that is available on the Forbes.com website.

"People who have served their time for a crime have an extensive file on who they are and where they have been. They work harder than other employees, show up to work early, stay later, accept overtime, ask for more work, do more, and truly value their jobs," Arte Nathan, a member of the board of HOPE for Prisoners, told Forbes Contributor Louis Efron, the author of the article.

The article explains how HOPE for Prisoners "facilitates reentry and reintegration services to men, women, and young adults who are exiting various segments of the judicial system" so that "ex-offenders returning to the community can overcome the many barriers to successful living that the incarceration experience can create." Only 6 percent of people involved with the program return to prison.

Operating since 2009, HOPE for Prisoners was formally established as an independent non-profit organization in January 2012 to encourage and impart hope to ex-offenders re-entering society. The complete article is available on the Forbes.com website at www.forbes.com/sites/louisefron/2016/11/17/should-you-hire-an-ex-con/#4c1617225d24.

Summary: Criminal Records and Safe Hiring Checklist

As has been shown, federal and state laws associated with obtaining and using a criminal record are not only overwhelming but also very confusing. What is legal in one state to utilize for employment purposes may not be legal in another state. Employers and professional screening companies must pay strict heed to the Federal Fair Credit Reporting Act (FCRA) and the requirements of the Equal Employment Opportunity Commission (EEOC). Certain portions of these laws can apply depending on "when" the record was discovered.

If negative information is located, is there a company policy in place or procedure to follow? What are the important considerations? Below is a quick checklist guide:

- **Policies** — Are there written guidelines to follow?
- **Documentation** — Are all procedures and decisions documented to file?
- **Review** — Is there a review process, with a particular person in the organization in charge of the process?

- **Uniformity** — Are similarly situated applicants treated the same?
- **Privacy** — Is there a mechanism to ensure that information remains private and secured, and only appropriate decision makers view the information? (e.g., reports with negative information are not sent through office mail to a hiring manager's desk).
- **Legal Compliance FCRA** — If a third party obtains information under the FCRA, is there a procedure to ensure pre-adverse action and post-adverse letters are handled as required by law?
- **Legal Compliance EEOC** — If the negative information is a criminal record, does the firm understand and follow the Equal Employment Opportunity Commission rules concerning the use of criminal records? Under EEOC rules, an employer may not deny employment to an ex-offender unless it is a business necessity, determined by reviewing the following three factors:
  o The nature and gravity of the offense;
  o The nature of the job being held or sought; and
  o The amount of time that has passed since the conviction or completion of sentence.

Author Tip ⟩ **People with Criminal Records Should Still Be Able to Find a Job**

As always, there are two sides to any story. On the one hand, employers have an incentive to conduct background checks because of the overwhelming evidence of the importance of criminal records in anticipating future behavior.

However, as we review criminal records, it is important to keep in mind that no one is suggesting that just because a person has a criminal past, he or she can never be hired. Unless our society wishes to create a permanent criminal class, it is critical for ex-offenders who have paid their debt to society to be able to get a J-O-B. Without a job, ex-offenders can never become tax-paying, law-abiding, productive citizens. Logic and statistics suggest that ex-offenders who are not able to find and keep gainful employment are likely to re-offend. Unless our society wants to spend an inordinate amount of tax money on building prisons, ex-offenders need a chance at a decent career. In fact, the law provides that a criminal record cannot be used to deny a job automatically.

People with criminal records do not have a big scarlet C for criminal emblazoned on their forehead so that they can never rejoin society. There are certain jobs that are just inappropriate for individuals with certain backgrounds. For example, a person with an embezzlement record may not be a good candidate to be a bookkeeper. However, such a person may do perfectly well in other jobs. There is a job for everyone, but not everyone is suitable for every job.

With All of These Rules, Are Criminal Records Still Worth Accessing?

By this time, an employer may well be scratching his or her head wondering if it is worth the trouble to do a criminal records check given all the rules and procedures involved. If the employer makes a mistake, then they risk a lawsuit from a disgruntled applicant accusing them of violating their rights. Or, an employer may be concerned about the EEOC or a state authority becoming involved if an applicant complains of discriminatory practices.

Even with these complications, experts agree that it is incumbent upon employers to check for criminal records. Here is why: The chance of being sued, much less being sued successfully by a person with a serious criminal record, is remote. As long as the employer does not engage in the automatic disqualification of applicants with criminal records and treats every applicant fairly, the chance of a lawsuit is remote.

On the other hand, according to all of the available statistics, there is a statistical certainty that unless a firm exercises due diligence, they will hire a person who is dangerous or unfit for the job. As discussed in the Introduction, "The Parade of Horribles," the legal and financial fallout can be a never-ending nightmare.

To put it another way: *The number of lawsuits from disgruntled applicants with criminal records is minimal. The potential lawsuits or harm from not doing a criminal check is enormous.*

You Need To Know

Who Can They Sue?

Attorneys are often asked by employers, "Can they sue me?" The answer is always "YES." Anyone in the U.S., for a modest filing fee, can sue anyone else for nearly anything they want. The exception is certain people who have abused the system by filing multiple lawsuits of doubtful validity can be declared a "vexatious litigant" and not be allowed to sue without court approval.

Of course, the key term is a "successful" lawsuit. So, there is never a guarantee that a lawsuit will not be filed. The question is: "What risk is there of a successful lawsuit?".

Whether or not to use criminal records ultimately comes down to a risk management decision where an employer has to weigh the cost versus the benefit.

1. **Costs:** Overall costs include the time, money, and effort spent in obtaining the criminal report, as well as the potential, though not very realistic, risks of a lawsuit from a disgruntled applicant.
2. **Benefits:** The benefits can range from merely avoiding an unpleasant situation to avoiding the loss of life and the loss of the business.

On a cost-benefit basis, employers are probably ahead performing some degree of reasonable criminal background checks as long as the information is accurate and actionable (as discussed in Chapter 9) and the employer has policies consistent with the 2012 EEOC Guidance on the use of criminal records.

The Million Dollar Question – How to Judge the Seriousness of a Criminal Conviction

The EEOC Enforcement Guidance on the Use of Arrest and Conviction Records by employers has placed a great deal of emphasis on understanding the criminal offense. The EEOC indicated that one of the tests to initially screen for a criminal record is the nature and gravity of the crime, which can include:

- The harm caused
- The legal elements of the crime
- The classification of the offense (e.g., misdemeanor vs. felony)

The EEOC indicates that if such a screening reveals an offense that may cause an employer not to hire an applicant, a best practice is for the employer to conduct an **individualized assessment** that includes:

- Facts or circumstances surrounding the offense or conduct;
- Number of offenses for which the individual was convicted;
- Age at the time of conviction or release from prison;
- Evidence that the individual performed the same type of work post-conviction without any known incidents of criminal conduct;
- Length and consistency of employment before and after offense;
- Rehabilitation efforts; and

- Whether individual is bonded under a federal, state, or local bonding program

To minimize the risk of violating discrimination laws, it appears that an employer must analyze the offense and the offender. But that is easier said than done. The problem is that public records do not include police reports, search warrant affidavits, arrest warrants and declarations, statements of probable cause, or probation reports – all documents that provide the real details about the offender and the offense. Of course, if there is a trial by judge or jury, transcripts of the trial may be available, but they can be expensive, time consuming, difficult to obtain, and require a great deal of reading. In fact, trial transcripts are not prepared in every case but normally only when there is an appeal.

Some steps an employer can consider are:

1. Review the allegations in the charging documents.
2. Understand the elements of each offense. Most jurisdictions have books of jury instructions used in criminal trials that break down and define each and every element of the charges.
3. In the case of a conviction either by a guilty plea or a trial, the employer can compare the outcome to the original charges. In other words, if the applicant was found guilty to a lesser charge, that may give insight as to the seriousness of the situation. It is always possible that the original charge overstated the situation and the fact that the charge was originally more serious may not always be an indicator of anything.
4. View the court minutes or orders concerning sentencing, which are public. Often the degree of sentencing can shed light as to the seriousness of the offense or offender. For example, if the person only receives probation, that is a much less serious matter than a four month jail sentence.
5. If a defendant was placed on probation, an employer can view the terms and conditions of probation. There can be conditions of probation such as counseling, stay away orders from victims, or specific order prohibiting possession of guns, drugs, alcohol, or other items related to the offense.
6. Determine if there are any orders of restitution.
7. Determine if there are any pardons, expungements, or judicial set asides so that the matter should not be considered at all in the first place.
8. If the criminal matter was a misdemeanor, analyze state law to determine if the charge was a hybrid that could be either a felony or a misdemeanor or if it can only be a misdemeanor, which means the state has determined that it is inherently less serious than a felony.

The problem with all of these methods is it can be like reading tea leaves to attempt to interpret the underlying crimes. Crimes can be reduced to a misdemeanor or counts dismissed for all sorts of reasons having nothing to do with the applicant's conduct. The reduction can relate to problems with a witness or other evidence, motions to suppress evidence, or court congestion leading to a plea bargain. Dispositions can be impacted by a number of other factors, including the quality of the defendant's lawyer, the actions of the Judge or DA, and local practices when it comes to charging, plea bargain, and sentences. The charges brought against a defendant can have a certain degree of arbitrariness depending upon who happened to be the prosecutor, who filed the charge, and what they knew at the time. It can also depend on geography—one county may charge a case one way, and the same conduct three counties over could be charged much differently.

However, under the EEOC guidelines, employers need to go beyond just the name and definitions of the offense and make some good faith effort to determine the seriousness of the underlying conviction.

CHAPTER 11

Credit Reports and Social Security Number Traces

Introduction

The use of credit reports for employment is a hot button issue for many consumers. For employers, a credit report can be a useful screening tool to evaluate a candidate and to exercise due diligence in the hiring process, especially for positions involving access to cash, assets, or significant responsibility. However, job applicants may feel the use of a credit report is discriminatory, unrelated to the ability to perform the job, an invasion of privacy, or a violation of their rights.

Of all the potential tools available to the employer to make safe hiring decisions, a credit report comes closest to invading a perceived zone of privacy since it directly reflects where and how we spend money in our personal lives. A credit report can indicate where you shop and the amount you spend.

There are a number of urban myths about credit reports and employers, such as bad credit scores can cause a consumer to lose job opportunities, or that employers routinely run credit reports on all applicants. When a credit report is ordered for employment purposes, the credit bureaus provide a customized form of the report referred to as an **employment credit report**. And contrary to misstatements sometimes found in news stories, an employment credit report does <u>NOT</u> contain a credit score. This is because there is no evidence of a connection between a credit score and employment. Nor does an employment credit report have any impact on a consumer's credit score. In addition, employers typically only run a credit report on finalists seriously being considered for a job.

Author Tip | **Credit Reports from the Viewpoint of Applicants**

This chapter is focused on credit reports from the point of view of employers. For a discussion of credit reports from the applicant's viewpoint, including a number of rights consumers have regarding credit checks, see Chapter 23.

Facts about the Employment Credit Report

Employers initiate background checks because they are interested in hiring the applicant and are conducting due diligence to make sure there is no reason not to hire. Under the rules of the federal Fair Credit Reporting Act (FCRA), a credit report is only obtained after the applicant has given consent and after a legally required disclosure has been given. Employers should approach credit reports with caution, making sure they are used only for valid business-related reasons and only using information that is fair, recent, and relevant.

What is Contained in an Employment Credit Report?

The type of credit report used for employment purposes typically contains four types of information:

- Identifying data such as name, Social Security Number (SSN), and past addresses.

- Payment and credit data that shows how persons pay their debts such as credit cards and personal loans and indicates if there are car payments, student loans, and mortgage payments. It also shows how much credit a person has been given, how much they currently owe, and whether debts have been paid late, were delinquent, or sent for collection.
- Records of others who have requested the credit report. When used for employment, requesting a credit report does NOT affect a person's credit score.
- Public records are reported such as court judgments, liens, and bankruptcies. Negative information will stay on a report for seven years and bankruptcies for 10 years (there are limitations to using a bankruptcy in an employment decision).

Job applicants have substantial legal protection concerning the use of credit reports for employment. In fact, an employer cannot obtain a credit report without an applicant's written permission and cannot use it to deny a job until the applicant has had the chance to review the report and given the opportunity to object to a report.

What is NOT On an Employment Credit Report?

As mentioned above, a common misperception is that credit scores are used for employment purposes. There is a difference between credit reports used to obtain financing, loans, credit cards and personal credit and the types of reports used for employment purposes. The three major credit bureaus use a special reporting format that leaves out actual credit card account numbers, credit risk scoring, and age. Credit reports used for employment purposes will have a credit history showing, for example, if a person misses payments, but an employment credit report does not contain a credit score. Even though there is research suggesting that credit scores can have a discriminatory impact, credit scores are simply NOT used for employment purposes. That is an urban myth.

Other important differences between a credit report used for employment and a credit report used for credit granting purposes are:

- An employment credit report does NOT contain a person's age or date of birth, in order to prevent age discrimination.
- Although the source and type of credit are listed, such as the store name or loan holder, specific account numbers are not included on a credit report for employment purposes.
- The generation of an employment credit report generally does not have any impact on a credit score. Any time an "Inquiry" is made on a credit report, it must be listed so a consumer knows who is viewing their report. However, an employment inquiry is listed separately from an inquiry that may be made for the purpose of applying for a loan or credit cards. When a credit report is related to a credit transaction, there is the possibility that a consumer's credit score is impacted, since an act to obtain more credit may be relevant to the credit score. However, if the inquiry is for employment purposes, generally speaking, there is no impact on a credit score.

Who Can Obtain an Employment Credit Report?

In order to even have access to an employment credit report, an employer itself must essentially undergo an extensive background check. Credit Bureaus, concerned about the sensitive and confidential nature of credit information, have required background screening firms to undertake an extensive vetting process of any employer requesting a credit report. For example, part of the process includes a physical onsite inspection of the employer's business to ensure the employer requesting the report is a legitimate business and is not on a list of businesses that cannot obtain credit reports from credit bureaus. Employers must also agree to data and privacy protection measures concerning an employment credit report. In turn, a background firm providing this service to employers must also undergo vetting including an onsite inspection to even be able to offer an employment credit report to a qualified business.

The reason? Credit reporting agencies clearly recognize and are extremely concerned about the sensitive and confidential nature of credit report data on consumers, and go to great lengths to ensure the information is handled properly and protected, which includes preventing information from falling into the wrong hands.

How is Credit Information Accumulated?

Credit reports are based upon millions of records being gathered in a variety of methods all over the United States. Records are obtained directly from furnishers of credit such as credit card companies, gas companies, or department stores that issue credit cards. Data is also obtained from court runner services that go to courts regularly across the U.S. to obtain public records including judgments, liens, and bankruptcies. Add to the mixture the fact there are competing credit organizations in the U.S. There are the three major national credit bureaus, as well as local or regional organizations that gather credit data and may be associated with one of these national bureaus.

What Should Employers Take into Account before Using a Credit Report?

Employers should approach the use of credit reports with caution; having policies and procedures in place to ensure the use of credit information is both relevant and fair. An employer should first determine if there is a sound business reason to obtain a credit report. Many employers limit credit reports to management and executive positions, or to positions that have access to cash, assets, company credit cards, or confidential information. Employers are well advised to run credit reports on bookkeepers or others who handle significant amounts of cash.

Unless the information in a credit report is directly job related and a valid predictor of job performance, its use can be considered discriminatory. For example, running a credit report for an entry-level person with low levels of responsibility or little or no access to cash is probably not a good practice. Unnecessary credit reports can discourage applicants from applying, and running mass credit reports on all applicants, regardless of the position, can arguably have the effect of discriminating against certain protected classes. Although an employer may want to run credit reports on prospective cashiers, for example, most employers do a drawer count at night, and if money is missing, an employer will know almost immediately. Strong internal financial controls are often a much better means of protecting against internal theft than running a credit report.

 How to Protect against Embezzlement and Theft

The best protection against embezzlement and theft is probably having a strong policy of internal controls. There are discussed in more detail in Chapter 21.

In addition, employers should avoid making negative hiring decisions on credit report information that is old, relatively minor, or has no relevance to job performance. For example, poor credit caused by paying a child's medical bills may have nothing to do with employment. Or, a consumer may have refinanced a home and, for a brief period, both the old mortgage and the new mortgage may show on the credit report giving a false impression of greater indebtedness.

Another issue can be the "look back" period, meaning the time frame an employer is concerned about. For example, if a consumer was unemployed during the recession and relied upon credit cards to bridge difficult economic times, then looking at credit history during a rough patch may not be very relevant or helpful.

For those reasons, an employer needs to ensure that the information is recent, relevant and accurate. In order to protect a consumer's rights, and guard against error, an employer must carefully follow the requirements of the federal Fair Credit Reporting Act and any applicable specific state rules.

Are There Mistakes in Credit Reports?

Mistakes are always possible. Although credit bureaus make efforts to be accurate, credit reports are based upon millions of pieces of data assembled by human beings and computers.

According to screening expert Dennis L. DeMey, author of *Don't Hire a Crook:*

"Keep in mind that there may be mistakes. Also, different credit bureaus can have different information. One credit bureau may have extensive information on the subject whereas another may have very little. Lenders do not necessarily utilize and/or communicate with every bureau. Consequently, one bureau may be more up-to-date than another in a specific region. In instances where such a search is critical, it is wise to verify using more than one bureau."

How Frequently are Mistakes Made?

Congress directed the Federal Trade Commission (FTC) to conduct a study of credit report accuracy and provide interim reports every two years, starting in 2004 and continuing through 2012, with a final report in 2014. The reports were produced under Section 319 of the Fair and Accurate Credit Transactions Act, or FACT Act. The FTC)study of the U.S. credit reporting industry conducted in 2012 found that:

- One in four consumers identified errors on their credit reports that might affect their credit scores;
- One in five consumers had an error that was corrected by a credit reporting agency (CRA) after it was disputed, on at least one of their three credit reports;
- Four out of five consumers who filed disputes experienced some modification to their credit report;
- Slightly more than one in 10 consumers saw a change in their credit score after the CRAs modified errors on their credit report; and
- Approximately one in 20 consumers had a maximum score change of more than 25 points, and only one in 250 consumers had a maximum score change of more than 100 points.

More information about this study is available at www.ftc.gov/news-events/press-releases/2013/02/ftc-study-five-percent-consumers-had-errors-their-credit-reports.

In 2014, the FTC conducted a follow-up study of credit report accuracy that found most consumers who previously reported an unresolved error on one of their three major credit reports believe that *at least one piece of disputed information on their report is still inaccurate*. The follow-up study – which focused on 121 consumers who had at least one unresolved dispute from the 2012 study and participated in a follow-up survey – found that 37 of the consumers (31 percent) stated that they now accepted the original disputed information on their reports as correct. However, 84 of these consumers (nearly 70 percent) continue to believe that at least some of the disputed information is inaccurate.

This study—the sixth and final study on national credit report accuracy by the FTC—is available at www.ftc.gov/system/files/documents/reports/section-319-fair-accurate-credit-transactions-act-2003-sixth-interim-final-report-federal-trade/150121factareport.pdf.

This possibility of error is a big reason why employers need to move cautiously when it comes to the use and analysis of credit reports.

Editor's Note: **The term *Credit Report* when used with employment issues throughout the balance of this chapter is generally referring to the Employment Credit Report, as describer earlier.**

Why Employers Use Credit Reports in Employment Decisions

Employers seek credit reports on job applicants for a variety of reasons. However, since the well-known three digit credit score format (such as a 685 for example) is not contained in an employment credit report, employers must look to other methods to evaluate an employment credit report. Currently, there is no nationally accepted and validated mathematical model that attempts to "score" the entire credit report for employment purposes. Such a scoring would face substantial challenges to prove it is a valid and non-discriminatory predictor of job performance. Some employers have attempted to devise some sort of protocol to do an initial analysis, such as looking at the debt-to-income ratio, or the number of late payments, but those measurements can be very tricky and there is no validated study to support the use of such measures as a decision making or predictive tool.

As a result, the use of credit reports tends to be judgment calls, where the credit report is utilized in conjunction with all other available information.

Employers may request credit reports to alert them about applicants whose monthly debt payments are too high for the salary involved. The concern is if a person is under financial stress due to a monthly debt that is beyond their salary, then that can be a red flag. One of the common denominators in cases of embezzlement is a perpetrator in debt beyond his or her means or has excessive financial pressure due to personal debt. See the chapter dealing with Fraud, Embezzlement, and Integrity. However, that approach should be examined carefully, taking into account whether the amount are off by errors, or debts are high due to medical bills or other situations out of the applicant's control.

Some employers take the position that a credit report shows whether an applicant is responsible and reliable by looking at the way that applicant handles his or her personal affairs. The logic is that a person who cannot pay their own bills on time or make responsible personal financial decisions may not be the best fit for a job that requires handling the company's funds or making meaningful decisions. There are numerous center arguments however to that approach. Some individuals may well have difficulty in their personal life on a variety of matters, but there is no evidence that carries over into the workforce. Employers seeking only perfect applicants may find that they have a very limited candidate pool.

Credit History Not a Good Predictor of Job Performance Or Turnover

Two Eastern Kentucky University researchers—Industrial and Organizational psychologists Dr. Jerry Palmer and Dr. Laura Koppes—found that credit checks do not have any validity in predicting the job performance of employees.

Their 2004 study examined the credit reports of nearly 200 current and former employees working in financial services to determine if credit ratings were an indicator of how well they performed their jobs and if they stayed at those jobs.

The results of the study showed that credit history was not a good predictor of job performance or turnover: *In fact, one aspect of the study revealed that workers with a higher number of 30-day late payments actually received higher performance ratings.*

Source: www.newswise.com/articles/credit-history-not-a-good-predictor-of-job-performance-or-turnover

---

Employers hiring sales positions may require that a salesperson utilize a personal credit card. A credit report may help to indicate a potential candidate's ability to use a credit card wisely. There have been employers who discovered months into the employment relationship the reason a salesperson was not making their quota was the person was not able to fly or travel since they were unable to get a credit and therefore unable to book hotels, cars or place travel.

Credit reports may also contribute to verifying identity. The top part of a credit report, often referred to as the "credit header," contains personal data about the applicant such as past addresses. However, an employer does not order an entire credit report just to obtain the credit header.

A separate search, called a **Social Security Trace**, provides an employer with information to help confirm identity. A discussion on this important tool for employers follows later in this chapter. More information about identity verification and additional identity tools are covered in Chapter 22.

The Items an Employer Can Look for in a Credit Report

In reviewing a credit report, an employer is typically looking at the following:

- What are the person's total monthly payments? How does it compare to the projected salary and benefits?

- How many negative items are listed, such as late payments, collection actions, defaults, or accounts closed?
- Are there negative public records and are they related to employment? For example, a tax lien may indicate someone has not paid attention to their affairs or is under financial stress. If there is a bankruptcy on the credit report, the employer should approach that with caution and possibly consult with an attorney. It can argued that it is a form of discrimination to deny employment based on an applicant taking advantage of their legal right to start over and get a fresh start through bankruptcy proceedings. (See Chapter 13 for a more detailed look at the use of bankruptcy information in employment.)
- Are there any alerts from the credit agencies? Some bureaus issue fraud alerts based upon a variety of criteria if there is suspicion of fraud or abuse.

You Need To Know >

You Never Know What You Will Find

An interesting story is told by a private investigator who obtained a credit report during an in-depth background investigation. In reviewing the credit report, the investigator looked at the section concerning inquiries. This is the list of entities that previously requested a credit report on the individual. One requestor was the United States Probation Office. A little further research revealed that the U.S. Probation Office requested a credit report because the applicant was in fact on federal probation for a federal crime and had been ordered to pay restitution. This story demonstrates that doing a background investigation sometimes requires more effort than merely buying data. It is important to look at the whole person and to "connect the dots" by looking at a number of factors and performing appropriate follow-ups.

Survey Shows Credit Background Checks <u>Not</u> Used by Over 50 Percent of Organizations

A July 2012 survey from the Society for Human Resource Management (SHRM), "Background Checking — The Use of Credit Background Checks in Hiring Decisions," found that more than half of the responding organizations (53 percent) do not conduct credit background checks on any of their job candidates, a noticeable increase from 40 percent in 2010 and from 39 percent in 2004. Key findings include:

- While 53 percent of organizations did not conduct credit background checks on any job applicants, 34 percent did conduct them for select job candidates, and 13 percent conducted them on all candidates.

- Of the organizations that did conduct credit background checks, 58 percent initiate a credit background check after a contingent job offer while 33 percent initiate them after a job interview. Only 2 percent initiate credit background checks before a job interview.

- As to why organizations conduct credit background checks, 45 percent conduct credit background checks to reduce/prevent theft and embezzlement while 22 percent said it was to reduce legal liability for negligent hiring.

- Of the organizations that conduct credit background checks, 80 percent reported that they had hired a job candidate with a credit report containing information that reflected negatively on his or her financial situation while 64 percent allow job candidates to explain the results of the credit checks before the decision to hire or not to hire is made.

- Of the organizations that conduct credit background checks, 87 percent conduct credit background checks on job candidates applying for positions with financial responsibilities, 42 percent on candidates applying for senior executive positions, and 34 percent for positions with access to highly confidential employee information.

In addition, the survey also found the three most important factors that influence the final decision to hire a particular candidate over another are previous work experience, a good fit with the job and the organization, and specific expertise needed for the job.

The survey "Background Checking — The Use of Credit Background Checks in Hiring Decisions" is available at: www.shrm.org/Research/SurveyFindings/Articles/Pages/CreditBackgroundChecks.aspx.

What are the Legal Limits in Obtaining a Credit Report?

First and foremost, the job applicant must provide written authorization before an employer can request a credit report. Under the federal Fair Credit Reporting Act (FCRA), an applicant has a series of additional rights. If an employer intends not to hire someone based upon information in the credit report, then the applicant must first receive a copy of the report and a statement of rights. The applicant has a right to review the credit report and to dispute any information believed to be inaccurate or incomplete. This right applies even if the employer has additional reasons not to hire the person or if an applicant has excellent credit and even if there are other concerns such as a reported high debt level. For example, an employer may be concerned that an applicant's debt level is higher than what the job pays even though the applicant has a perfect payment record. It may be that the applicant has refinanced their home and the credit report is erroneously showing the old mortgage to be still outstanding. If the employer did not give the applicant their right under the FCRA to review the credit report for errors, then the applicant would have been unfairly eliminated. If a final decision is made, then an applicant is entitled to a second confirming letter. In California and certain other states, job applicants must also be given the opportunity to request a free copy of a report originally obtained by an employer.

Before utilizing negative information found in a credit report, the employer should consider:

- Is the negative information a valid predictor of job performance?
- Is the information current and correct?
- Is there negative information reported outside the applicant's control such as the result of a disputed bill, medical bills, dissolution of marriage, or some other problem?
- Is there any reason not to consider the negative information? (For example, an employer generally should not consider a bankruptcy.)
- Is the employer consistent in the use of negative information? i.e.: have other applicants been hired with the same type of negative information and, if so, is there a rational reason why it was overlooked for others? Is there a company hiring policy or some documentation put in the file to demonstrate that the employer is consistent?
- Has any decision or conclusion been documented?
- Is the applicant being afforded all of his or her legal rights?

The FTC and Use of Credit Reports by Employers

The Federal Trade Commission (FTC) published an article for employers on the proper use of credit reports. Here is an excerpt every employer should read if they use credit reports for employment decisions:

> **"In Practice...**
>
> You advertise vacancies for cashiers and receive 100 applications. You want just credit reports on each applicant because you plan to eliminate those with poor credit histories. What are your obligations?
>
> - You can get credit reports — one type of consumer report — if you notify each applicant in writing that a credit report may be requested and if you receive the applicant's written consent. Before you reject an applicant based on credit report information, you must make a pre-adverse action disclosure that includes a copy of the credit report and the summary of consumer rights under the FCRA. Once you have

rejected an applicant, you must provide an adverse action notice if credit report information affected your decision.

You are considering a number of your long-term employees for a major promotion. You want to check their consumer reports to ensure that only responsible individuals are considered for the position. What are your obligations?

- You cannot get consumer reports unless the employees have been notified that reports may be obtained and each has given their written permission. If the employees gave you written permission in the past, then you need only make sure that the employees receive or have received a 'separate document notice' that 'reports may be obtained during the course of their employment.' No more notice or permission is required. If your employees have not received notice and given you permission, you must notify the employees and get their written permission before you get their reports.

In each case where information in the report influences your decision to deny promotion, you must provide the employee with a pre-adverse action disclosure. The employee also must receive an adverse action notice once you have selected another individual for the job.

A job applicant gives you the okay to get a consumer report. Although the credit history is poor and that's a negative factor, the applicant's lack of relevant experience carries even more weight in your decision not to hire. What's your responsibility?

- In any case where information in a consumer report is a factor in your decision—even if the report information is not a major consideration—you must follow the procedures mandated by the FCRA. In this case, you would be required to provide the applicant a pre-adverse action disclosure before you reject his or her application. When you formally reject the applicant, you would be required to provide an adverse action notice.

The applicants for a sensitive financial position have authorized you to obtain their credit reports. You reject one applicant whose credit report shows a debt load that may be too high for the proposed salary, even though the report shows a good repayment history. You turn down another, whose credit report shows only one credit account, because you want someone who has shown more financial responsibility. Are you obliged to provide any notices to these applicants?

- Both applicants are entitled to a pre-adverse-action disclosure and an adverse action notice. If any information in the credit report influences an adverse decision, then the applicant is entitled to the notices—even when the information isn't negative.

- **Non-compliance**

There are legal consequences for employers who fail to get an applicant's permission before requesting a consumer report, or who fail to provide pre-adverse-action disclosures and adverse action notices to unsuccessful job applicants. The FCRA allows individuals to sue employers for damages in federal court. A person who successfully sues is entitled to recover court costs and reasonable legal fees. The law also allows individuals to seek punitive damages for deliberate violations. In addition, the Federal Trade Commission, other federal agencies, and the states may sue employers for noncompliance and obtain civil penalties."

See the entire article, including a summary of how to comply with the FCRA, at www.bbb.org/us/article/ftc--using-consumer-reports-what-employers-need-to-know-4533.

For the information that the FTC provides for employers, see http://business.ftc.gov/documents/bus08-using-consumer-reports-what-employers-need-know.

The EEOC, Employment Credit Checks, and Discrimination

It use of credit reports for employment decisions results in the unfair exclusions of applicants with poor credit, there may Equal Employment Opportunity Commission (EEOC) implications. Even though a credit report may appear neutral on its face, if its use results in a "disparate impact" upon members of protected groups, a claim can be made that the use of credit reports is, in fact, discriminatory. Even though an employment credit report does not have a credit score, it still has a "credit history" and an argument can be made potentially that even a credit history can be problematic.

The EEOC held a public meeting in October of 2010 on the 'Employer Use of Credit History as a Screening Tool' that explored the growing use of credit histories of job applicants as selection criteria during employment background screening to see if the practice was discriminatory. The EEOC heard testimony from representatives of various groups to help the Commission ensure that the workplace is made free of all barriers to equal opportunity.

As a result of high unemployment forcing more people into the job market, an increasing number of job applicants are exposed to employment background screening tools such as credit checks that could unfairly exclude them from job opportunities. Critics of using credit histories for employment purposes said the practice could have a disparate and discriminatory impact on protected groups, including people of color, women, and the disabled. They can also be inaccurate and are not valid predictors of job performance.

Another concern expressed was that the use of credit histories creates a Catch-22 situation for job applicants during the current period of high unemployment and high foreclosures, both of which have negative impacts on credit. Many job seekers are caught in a situation where they cannot pay their bills because they do not have a job but cannot get a job because of bad credit since they cannot pay their bills.

Representatives from the business community told the EEOC that the use of credit histories is permissible by law, limited in scope, predictive in certain situations of reliability, and credit histories were only utilized by a few companies for every job opening. Some of the testimony tried to clear up common misperceptions about employment credit reports, including the falsehood that these types of credit reports include a credit score. They do not. The statements of October 2010 meeting can be found on the EEOC website at www.eeoc.gov/eeoc/meetings/10-20-10/index.cfm.

In 2008, the EEOC had an initiative called E-RACE (Eradicating Racism and Colorism from Employment.) According to the EEOC, the use of credit, although it appears facially neutral, can have a discriminatory impact. See www.eeoc.gov/eeoc/initiatives/e-race/.

SHRM Tells EEOC Credit Checks Legitimate Background Screening Tool

A November 2010 news story *Credit Checks Are Legitimate Screening Tool* on the Society for Human Resource Management (SHRM) website reported how a representative for SHRM—the world's largest association devoted to human resource management—told the EEOC during the October 2010 public hearing on the use of credit reports for employment purposes that the federal government should not eliminate an employer's use of credit histories to help make decisions about job candidates.

The representative said that "SHRM believes there is a compelling public interest in enabling our nation's employers— whether that employer is in the government or the private sector—to assess the skills, abilities, and work habits of potential hires." In addition, the representative said credit history is one of many factors—including education, experience, and certifications—that employers use "to narrow that applicant pool to those who are most qualified."

The SHRM representative also pointed out Human Resources typically conducts a background check on the job finalist or group of finalists before making a job offer, and that background check might include checking personal references, criminal history, and credit history depending on the employer and the position to be filled. Citing the Fair Credit Reporting Act (FCRA) of 1970 and the Civil Rights Act of 1964, the representative said SHRM believes "employees already have significant federal protection for the misuse of background checks."

The article is available at www.shrm.org/about/news/Pages/LegitimateScreeningTool.aspx.

What Other Credit Reporting Rights do Job Applicants Have?

If job applicants are concerned about their credit reports, then they should first contact all three major credit bureaus and request a copy. Typically, there is a fee not exceeding $8.00, but in some circumstances reports are free. Under new federal law that took effect in 2004, the FACT Act (discussed in Chapter 5), applicants have a right to a free credit report once a year from a "Nationwide Specialty Consumer Reporting Agency" (NSCRA) which includes each of the "Big Three" national credit bureaus: Equifax, Experian, and TransUnion. See: www.annualcreditreport.com/cra/index.jsp. Credit reports, as well as information on costs and procedures to dispute information, can be obtained from the following sources:

- Equifax:
  - Website: www.equifax.com
  - Phone: 888-532-0179
- Experian:
  - Website: www.experian.com
  - Phone: 800-972-0322
- TransUnion:
  - Website: www.transunion.com
  - Phone: 800-888-4213

You Need To Know ⟩ **What Constitutes a Nationwide Specialty Consumer Reporting Agency (NSCRA)?**

According to the federal Fair Credit Reporting Act (FCRA):

*The term **"nationwide specialty consumer reporting agency"** means a consumer reporting agency that compiles and maintains files on consumers on a nationwide basis relating to—*

(1) medical records or payments;

(2) residential or tenant history;

(3) check writing history;

(4) employment history; or

(5) insurance claims.

Source: www.consumer.ftc.gov/sites/default/files/articles/pdf/pdf-0111-fair-credit-reporting-act.pdf.

If there is an error or explanation the applicant cannot resolve with the creditor, then the applicant should write a detailed letter to the three credit bureaus, which have thirty days to investigate and resolve the dispute. If the report is corrected, the applicant may request the agencies to notify anyone who has received the report for employment in the past two years. If the dispute is not resolved to the applicant's satisfaction, the applicant has a right to place a brief statement on his or her credit report. All of these rights are explained in detail on the Federal Trade Commission (FTC) website at www.ftc.gov which oversees the credit industry.

If a job applicant has bad credit and wants to clear it up, there are excellent credit-counseling services available. The National Foundation for Consumer Credit is a non-profit organization that has over 1,400 affiliates throughout the United States who provide this service, see www.nfcc.org. Unfortunately, there also are scam artists who make false or misleading claims; the Federal Trade Commission issues warnings about these scams and provides information for consumers on the FTC website.

According to an interview with SHRM magazine in April 2007 with an EEOC official, unnecessary credit reports can end up being a subtle form of discrimination and are best utilized when there is a legitimate business need. See SHRM article "EEOC Urges Caution on Unnecessary Credit Checks" at www.shrm.org/hr-today/news/hr-news/Pages/cms_020975.aspx.

> **You Need To Know**

Credit Reporting Agencies Pay $6 Million Settlement

In May of 2015, Attorney Generals from 31 states have announced that the three main credit reporting agencies—Equifax, Experian, and TransUnion—agreed to pay a $6 million settlement to their states and change their business practices to benefit consumers.

The investigation into these credit reporting agencies focused on consumer disputes about credit report errors, monitoring and disciplining data furnishers who provide the credit reporting information, accuracy in consumer credit reports, and the marketing of credit monitoring products to consumers who call the credit reporting agencies to dispute information on their credit report.

Under the settlement, the credit reporting agencies agreed to increase monitoring of data furnishers, require more information from furnishers, limit direct-to-consumer marketing, provide more protection for consumers disputing credit reports, limit data added to credit reports, provide more consumer education, and comply with state and federal laws including the Fair Credit Reporting Act (FCRA).

A copy of the settlement is at www.esrcheck.com/file/2015-05-20-CRAs-AVC.pdf.

State Limitations on Credit Report Use by Employers

Currently, eleven states—**California, Colorado, Connecticut, Delaware, Hawaii, Illinois, Maryland, Nevada, Oregon, Vermont, and Washington**—have passed laws regulating the use of employment credit reports of job applicants and current employees that have impacted the way employers conduct background checks. Here is a summary of the state laws that have restricted the use of credit histories of applicants and employees.

California

Signed into law by Governor Jerry Brown in October of 2011, **California Assembly Bill 22 (AB 22)**—which took effect January 1, 2012—amends Section 1785.20.5 of the Civil Code and added Chapter 3.6 (commencing with Section 1024.5) to Part 2 of Division 2 of the Labor Code, relating to employment. AB 22 prohibits most employers and prospective employers in the state—with the exception of certain financial institutions—from obtaining consumer credit reports for employment purposes unless the position of the person for whom the report is sought is one of the following:

- A managerial position;
- A position in the state Department of Justice;
- A sworn peace officer or other law enforcement position;
- A position for which the information contained in the report is required by law to be disclosed or obtained;
- A position that involves regular access to specified personal information for any purpose other than the routine solicitation and processing of credit card applications in a retail establishment;
- A position in which the person is or would be a named signatory on the employer's bank or credit card account, or authorized to transfer money or enter into financial contracts on the employer's behalf;
- A position that involves access to confidential or proprietary information; or
- A position that involves regular access to $10,000 or more of cash.

In addition, AB 22 also requires written notice informing the person for whom a consumer credit report is sought for employment purposes to also inform that person of the specific reason for obtaining the report.

California AB 22: http://leginfo.ca.gov/pub/11-12/bill/asm/ab_0001-0050/ab_22_bill_20110920_enrolled.pdf.

Colorado

The Colorado Employment Opportunity Act (SB13-018) specifies the purposes for which consumer credit information such as consumer credit reports and credit scores can be used by employers or potential employers in making employment-related decisions. Specifically, the "Employment Opportunity Act":

- Prohibits an employer's use of consumer credit information for employment purposes if the information is unrelated to the job;
- Requires an employer to disclose to an employee or applicant for employment (jointly referred to as "employee") when the employer uses the employee's consumer credit information to take adverse action against him or her and the particular credit information upon which the employer relied;
- Authorizes an employee aggrieved by a violation of the above provisions to bring suit for an injunction, damages, or both; and
- Requires the department of labor and employment to enforce the laws related to employer use of consumer credit information.

The Employment Opportunity Act of 2013 defines employment purposes broadly to include "evaluating a person for employment, hiring, promotion, demotion, reassignment, adjustment in compensation level, or retention as an employee." Two types of employers are permitted to use consumer credit information for employment purposes under the law: "banks or financial institutions" and employers "required by law" to conduct credit checks. The remaining employers may only review credit reports for "executive or management personnel" and positions that involve "contracts with defense, intelligence, national security, or space agencies of the federal government." The law took effect July 1, 2013.

The Colorado Employment Opportunity Act: www.coloradocapitolwatch.com/bill/0/SB13-018/2013/1/.

Connecticut

Connecticut Senate Bill No. 361 (S.B. 361) prohibits certain employers from using credit reports in making hiring and employment decisions regarding existing employees or job applicants. The law, which took effect October 1, 2011, applies to all employers in Connecticut with at least one employee.

Exceptions to S.B. 361 are employers that are financial institutions as defined under law, credit reports required to be obtained by employers by law, and credit reports "substantially related to the employee's current or potential job." These "substantially related" reports are allowable if the position:

- Is a managerial position that involves setting the direction or control of a business, division, unit or an agency of a business;
- Involves access to personal or financial information of customers, employees or the employer, other than information customarily provided in a retail transaction;
- Involves a fiduciary responsibility to the employer, as defined under the law;
- Provides an expense account or corporate debit or credit card;
- Provides access to certain confidential or proprietary business information, as defined under the law; or
- Involves access to the employer's nonfinancial assets valued at $2,005 or more, including, but not limited to, museum and library collections and to prescription drugs and other pharmaceuticals.

Connecticut Senate Bill 361 (CT SB 361): www.cga.ct.gov/2011/ACT/PA/2011PA-00223-R00SB-00361-PA.htm.

Delaware

In 2014, **Delaware House Bill No. 167 (H.B. 167)** amended Titles 19 and 20 of the Delaware Code with regard to employment practices. Under H.B. 167, it is an unlawful employment practice for any public employer in Delaware to inquire into or consider the credit history or credit score of an applicant for employment during the initial application process, up to and including the first interview. A public employer may inquire into or consider an applicant's credit history or credit score after it has determined that the applicant is otherwise qualified and has conditionally offered the applicant the position. The requirements of this law shall not apply where a credit check is a requirement of State or federal law for a particular class of services. Delaware House Bill No. 167 is available at http://legis.delaware.gov/.

Hawaii

The Hawaiian legislature—over the Governor's veto—passed a law that took effect on July 1, 2009, that put limits on the use of employment credit history or credit reports unless it "directly related to a bona fide occupational qualification" or falls under another exception. **Hawaii House Bill 31 S.D. 1 C.D. 1** amended the Hawaiian Fair Employment Practices Act by making it an unlawful discriminatory practice for any employer to refuse to hire or employ, continue employment or to bar or discharge from employment, or otherwise to discriminate against any individual in compensation or in the terms, conditions, or privileges of employment of any individual because of the individual's credit history or credit report, unless the information in the individual's credit history or credit report directly relates to a bona fide occupational qualification.

The law also indicated that in terms of hiring in the first place, the employer could only inquire into the credit history or credit report on a prospective employee only after there has been a conditional job offer, and only if the information is directly related to a bona fide occupational qualification. The law makes exceptions for employers that are expressly permitted to inquire into credit history or a credit report by federal or state law, and financial institutions that are insured by a federal agency or to managerial or supervisory employees. The law sets out a specific definition of what constitutes a "Managerial" or "Supervisory" employee.

Hawaii House Bill 31 SD1 CD1: www.capitol.hawaii.gov/session2009/bills/HB31_CD1_.pdf.

Illinois

Illinois House Bill 4658 was signed by Governor Pat Quinn to create the **Employee Credit Privacy Act** which prohibits employers in the state from discriminating based on the credit history of job seekers or employees. The law took effect January 1, 2011, and prohibits employers from inquiring about or using an employee's or prospective employee's credit history as a basis for employment, recruitment, discharge, or compensation. Employers who violate the new law can be subject to civil liability for damages or injunctive relief.

However, under the new law, employers may access credit checks under limited circumstances, including positions that involve:

- Bonding or security per state or federal law;
- Unsupervised access to more than $1,000;
- Signatory power over businesses assets of more than $100;
- Management and control of the business; and
- Access to personal, financial or confidential information, trade secrets, or state or national security information.

Illinois Employee Credit Privacy Act (House Bill 4658): https://legiscan.com/IL/text/HB4658/2009.

Maryland

Maryland's **Job Applicant Fairness Act (House Bill 87),** which took effect October 1, 2011, enacted legislation placing restrictions on credit checks by employers who use the credit report or credit history of job applicants or employees for employment decisions. The Act reads as follows:

"(c) When employer may request or use employee's credit history. --

(1) An employer may request or use an applicant's or employee's credit report or credit history if:

(i) 1. the applicant has received an offer of employment; and 2. the credit report or credit history will be used for a purpose other than a purpose prohibited by subsection (b) of this section; or

(ii) the employer has a bona fide purpose for requesting or using information in the credit report or credit history that is: 1. substantially job-related; and 2. disclosed in writing to the employee or applicant.

(2) For the purposes of this subsection, a position for which an employer has a bona fide purpose that is substantially job-related for requesting or using information in a credit report or credit history includes a position that:

(i) is managerial and involves setting the direction or control of a business, or a department, division, unit, or agency of a business;

(ii) involves access to personal information, as defined in § 14-3501 of the Commercial Law Article, of a customer, employee, or employer, except for personal information customarily provided in a retail transaction;

(iii) involves a fiduciary responsibility to the employer, including the authority to issue payments, collect debts, transfer money, or enter into contracts;

(iv) is provided an expense account or a corporate debit or credit card; or

(v) has access to: 1. information, including a formula, pattern, compilation, program, device, method, technique, or process, that: A. derives independent economic value, actual or potential, from not being generally known to, and not being readily ascertainable by proper means by, other persons who can obtain economic value from the disclosure or use of the information; and B. is the subject of efforts that are reasonable under the circumstances to maintain its secrecy; or 2. other confidential business information"

Along with prohibiting an employer from using the credit report or credit history of an employee or job applicant for employment purposes, the Act specifically prohibits most employers from using credit checks to determine whether to:

- Deny employment to a job applicant;
- Discharge an employee;
- Decide compensation; or
- Evaluate other terms and conditions of employment.

While the Act applies to Maryland employers of any size, some employers are excluded from the Act's prohibitions, including financial institutions and employers required under federal or state law to inquire into the credit history of job applicants or employees. In addition, the Act also allows exceptions for employers to request or use credit history information if the data is related to "a bona fide purpose that is substantially job–related," an exception that generally applies to:

- Jobs such as managerial positions involving handling money or confidential duties;
- Employees with expense accounts or corporate credit cards; and
- Employees with access to confidential business information.

The Act also requires that employers wishing to request or use credit information of job applicants and employees for a bona fide purpose must disclose the intent to do so in writing to the job applicant or employee.

Maryland Job Applicant Fairness Act (H.B. 87): mlis.state.md.us/2011rs/chapters_noln/Ch_29_hb0087T.pdf.

Nevada

When Governor Brian Sandoval signed **Nevada Senate Bill 127 (SB 127)** into law, Nevada became the tenth state in the U.S. to prohibit employers from conditioning employment on a consumer credit report or other credit information with few exceptions. Nevada SB 127 took effect on October 1, 2013.

Senate Bill 127 amends Chapter 613 of the Nevada Revised Statutes (NRS) that covers "Employment Practices" to make it unlawful for any employer in the state to:

- Directly or indirectly, require, request, suggest or cause any employee or prospective employee to submit a consumer credit report or other credit information as a condition of employment;
- Use, accept, refer to or inquire concerning a consumer credit report or other credit information;
- Discharge, discipline, discriminate against in any manner or deny employment or promotion to, or threaten to take any such action against any employee or prospective employee: (a) who refuses, declines or fails to submit a consumer credit report or other credit information; or (b) on the basis of the results of a consumer credit report or other credit information; or
- Discharge, discipline, discriminate against in any manner or deny employment or promotion to, or threaten to take any such action against any employee or prospective employee who has pursuant to the new law: (a) filed any complaint or instituted or caused to be instituted any legal proceeding; (b) testified or may testify in any legal proceeding instituted; or (c) exercised his or her rights, or has exercised on behalf of another person the rights afforded to him or her.

However, Senate Bill 127 does provide for exceptions where an employer may request or consider a consumer credit report or other credit information for employment purposes if:

- The employer is required or authorized, pursuant to state or federal law, to use a consumer credit report or other credit information for that purpose;
- The employer reasonably believes that the employee or prospective employee has engaged in specific activity which may constitute a violation of state or federal law; or
- The information contained in the consumer credit report or other credit information is "job related" or reasonably related to the position for which the employee or prospective employee is being evaluated for employment, promotion, reassignment or retention as an employee.

If an employer violates the law, the Labor Commissioner may impose an administrative penalty against the employer of not more than $9,000 for each violation.

Nevada Senate Bill 127: http://openstates.org/nv/bills/77/SB127/.

Oregon

Oregon prohibited the use of credit history of job applicants for employment decisions per **Oregon Senate Bill 1045 (SB 1045)** which took effect in February 2010. SB 1045 prohibits the use of credit histories of job applicants in making employment-related decisions including hiring, discharge, promotion, and compensation.

However, SB 1045 provides exceptions for financial institutions, public safety offices, and other employment if credit history is job-related and use is disclosed to applicant or employee. The exceptions to the law include the following circumstances:

- Employers that are federally insured banks or credit unions;
- Employers that are required by state or federal law to use individual credit history for employment purposes;
- The employment of a public safety officer, or

- Employers that can demonstrate that the information in a credit report is substantially job-related AND the employer's reasons for the use of such information are disclosed to the employee or prospective employee in writing.

Oregon Senate Bill 1045: https://olis.leg.state.or.us/liz/2010S1/Downloads/MeasureDocument/SB1045/A-Engrossed.

Vermont

Effective July 1, 2012, **Vermont Act No. 154 (S. 95)** prohibits employers in the state, subject to various exceptions, from using or inquiring into credit reports or credit histories of job applicants and employees in the employment context and further prohibits discriminating against individuals based on their credit information.

Enacted into law by Governor Peter Shumlin on May 17, 2012, Vermont Act No. 154 (S. 95) pertains to **credit history** that includes any credit information obtained from any third party, not only information contained in a credit report. The Act sets forth exemptions based on the type of employers at issue and the position or responsibilities of applicants or employees. Employers are exempt and may obtain and use credit information if they meet one or more of these conditions:

- The information is required by state or federal law or regulation.
- The position of employment involves access to confidential financial information.
- The employer is a financial institution or credit union as defined by state law.
- The position of employment is that of a law enforcement officer, emergency medical personnel, or a firefighter as defined by state law.
- The position of employment requires a financial fiduciary responsibility to the employer or a client of the employer, including the authority to issue payments, collect debts, transfer money, or enter into contracts.
- The employer can demonstrate that the information is a valid and reliable predictor of employee performance in the specific position of employment.
- The position of employment involves access to an employer's payroll information.

However, even exempted employers that seek to obtain or act upon the credit information of an applicant or employee are prohibited by the Act from using a credit report or credit history as the sole factor in making any employment decision. In addition, the Act requires employers to first obtain the written consent of the employee or applicant to the disclosure of the credit information and must also disclose in writing its reasons for accessing the report. If an employer intends to take an adverse employment action based on any contents of the credit report, the employer must notify the applicant or employee in writing of its reasons for doing so and also offer the subject an opportunity to contest the accuracy of the credit report or credit history.

Vermont Act No. 154 (S. 95): www.leg.state.vt.us/docs/2012/Acts/ACT154.pdf.

Washington

Washington passed a law in 2007 amending the **Revised Code of Washington (RCW)** that stated employers could not obtain a credit report as part of a background check unless the information was substantially job related and the employer's reasons for the use of such information were disclosed to the consumer in writing.

Under the amended Washington law, employers cannot obtain a credit report as part of a background check unless the information is:

- Substantially job related and the employer's reasons for the use of such information are disclosed to the consumer in writing; or
- Required by law.

Employers in the state of Washington utilizing employment credit reports needed to change their forms, carefully review any job position where a credit report is requested, and communicate to job applicants the reason a credit report is substantially related to a particular job.

RCW Chapter 19.182 - Fair Credit Reporting Act: http://apps.leg.wa.gov/RCW/default.aspx?cite=19.182 & RCW 19.182.020 (Consumer report - Furnishing - Procuring): http://apps.leg.wa.gov/rcw/default.aspx?cite=19.182.020.

Cities with Credit Reporting Laws

Along with the states mentioned above, some U.S. cities have laws that restrict employers from using credit reports in employment decisions. Here are two examples: New York, New York and Philadelphia, Pennsylvania.

New York, NY

The Stop Credit Discrimination in Employment Act (SCDEA), which took effect on September 3, 2015, strictly prohibits most NYC employers from using credit history to decide whether to hire, fire, or promote an individual. The Act amended the New York City Human Rights Law (NYCHRL)—which prohibits discrimination in employment, public accommodations, and housing—by making credit checks an unlawful discriminatory practice for employers and employment agencies.

The New York City Commission on Human Rights (NYCCHR) released enforcement guidance on this law that bans New York City employers with four or more from requesting or using the credit history of applicants and employees when making employment decisions.

As defined by the NYCCHR enforcement guidance, *credit history* includes creditworthiness, credit capacity, payment history, credit accounts, charged-off debts, items in collections, bankruptcies, judgments, liens, credit card debt, child support obligations, student loans, and home foreclosures.

Positions that NYC businesses will still be allowed to ask about credit history, do a credit check, and use credit history in an employment decision include:

- Police and peace officers (not private security guards); and
- Executive-level jobs with power over finances, computer security, or trade secrets.

NYC employers should inform applicants and employees of any exemption and keep a record of the use of exemptions in employment practices for a period of five (5) years from the date an exemption is used to help them respond to NYCCHR requests for information. These exemption logs should include:

- Which exemption is claimed;
- How the applicant/employee fits into the exemption;
- Qualifications of the applicant/employee for the position/promotion;
- Name and contact information of applicant/employee;
- Nature of the credit history information considered and a copy of such information;
- How the credit history information was obtained; and
- How credit history impacted employment action.

Employers who violate the NYCHRL may have to pay lost wages and other damages to the employees affected and may be subject to civil penalties of up to $125,000. A willful violation may be subject to a civil penalty of up to $250,000. Additional information is available at www.nyc.gov/humanrights.

Stop Credit Discrimination in Employment Act, N.Y.C. Admin. Code §§ 8-102(29), 8-107(9)(d), (24); Local Law No. 37 (2015): www.nyc.gov/html/cchr/downloads/pdf/CreditHistory-InterpretiveGuide-LegalGuidance.pdf.

Philadelphia, PA

The Philadelphia (PA) Ordinance No. 160072 that took effect on July 7, 2016, amended Chapter 9-1100 of The Philadelphia Code entitled "Fair Practices Ordinance: Protections Against Unlawful Discrimination," by adding a section that prohibits employers from obtaining or using credit information regarding employees and job applicants in certain circumstances.

Ordinance No. 160072 made it unlawful for employers to use the credit information of Philadelphia job applicants or employees—unless covered by an exception—for employment decisions such as hiring, firing, or promotion. Credit information is defined as any written, oral, or other communication regarding:

- Debt;
- Credit worthiness, standing, capacity, score, or history;
- Payment history;
- Charged-off debts;
- Bank account balances or other information; or
- Bankruptcies, judgments, liens, or other items under collection.

However, Ordinance No. 160072 does not apply in the following exceptions:

- To any law enforcement agency or financial institution;
- To the City of Philadelphia with respect to efforts to obtain information regarding taxes or other debts owed to the City;
- If such information must be obtained pursuant to state or federal law;
- If the job requires an employee to be bonded under City, state, or federal law;
- If the job is supervisory or managerial in nature and involves setting the direction or policies of a business or a division, unit or similar part of a business;
- If the job involves significant financial responsibility to the employer, including the authority;
- If the job involves significant financial responsibility to the employer, including the authority to make payments, transfer money, collect debts, or enter into contracts, but not including handling transactions in a retail setting;
- If the job requires access to financial information pertaining to customers, other employees, or the employer, other than information customarily provided in a retail transaction; or
- If the job requires access to confidential or proprietary information that derives substantial value from secrecy.

Under the law, if an employer relies on credit information to consider adverse employment action with respect to any person, and certain subsections of the law apply, the employer:

- Shall disclose the fact of such reliance to the person in writing and identify and provide the particular information upon which the employer relied; and
- Give the employee or applicant an opportunity to explain the circumstances surrounding the information at issue before taking any such adverse action.

Philadelphia Ordinance No. 160072:
https://phila.legistar.com/LegislationDetail.aspx?ID=2559337&GUID=1197A1DA-37B0-448E-AEF1-52E7DF676C6E&Options=ID%7cText%7c&Search=Fair+Practices+Ordinance.

CFPB Monthly Complaint Report Spotlights Errors on Credit Reports

The Consumer Financial Protection Bureau (CFPB) *Monthly Complaint Report for May 2016* showed consumers continue to complain about incorrect information on their credit reports as well as the difficulty they face in having these errors corrected. The CFPB has handled approximately 143,700 complaints about credit reports since they began accepting credit reporting complaints in October 2012.

According to the CFPB—the first federal agency solely focused on consumer financial protection—consumer reporting companies track the credit history of consumers and other information. Errors in credit reports of consumers can affect their eligibility to take out a mortgage or whether they are eligible for a job. Some of the findings in the CFPB report for complaints about credit reports include:

- Consumers complain about incorrect information on credit reports: Over three-quarters of complaints about credit reports—77 percent—submitted to the CFPB by consumers are related to incorrect information appearing on their reports.
- Consumers report difficulty disputing inaccuracies on their credit reports: Consumers complained about experiencing long delays trying to speak to representatives at the consumer reporting companies that created the credit reports or the companies that furnished the information for the credit reports.
- High-volume complaint companies: Out of all the complaints about credit reports submitted to the CFPB between December 2015 and February 2016, 95 percent involved the three nationwide credit reporting companies – Equifax, Experian, and TransUnion.
- Specialty consumer reporting companies: In addition to complaints against the three nationwide credit reporting companies, consumers submitted more than 2,000 complaints regarding specialty consumer reporting companies that specialize in screening reports.

The report is available at http://files.consumerfinance.gov/f/documents/201605_cfpb_monthly-complaint-report-vol-11.pdf.

Conclusion – Employers Need Clear 'Business Justification' for Credit Report Checks

While credit report checks are one tool available as part of a background check, employers are not encouraged to perform routine credit checks on all candidates since credit checks may contain errors, may not be job related, can feel like an invasion of privacy, or may violate federal and state laws.

A professional background check provider should proceed with extreme caution when using applicant and employee credit histories in the background screening process. Employment credit reports should not be used unless they can articulate a clear "business justification," which normally means that that the job applicants or current employees have or will hold "sensitive" positions in which they may handle money or have access to personal data. In fact, with many states recently passing laws limiting the use of credit checks for employment purposes, employers need to be careful when, to whom, and how they perform credit checks on prospective job applicants.

> **You Need To Know** **Study Finds Bans on Credit Checks by Employers May Lead to More Unemployment for Some Applicants**
>
> A February 2016 study of bans on credit checks by employers meant to help job applicants with bad credit find work revealed that people with mid-to-low credit scores, those under 22 years old, and—most surprisingly—African-Americans, were more likely to be unemployed as a result of these laws.
>
> The study found that banning the use of credit checks in hiring decisions by employers—a rising trend in many states in the past decade—increased employment of residents in the lowest credit score areas with the largest gains occurring in higher-paying jobs and the government sector.
>
> Census tracts with low credit scores (average credit score below 620) saw employment increase by 1.9-3.3% relative to similar Census tracts in states without bans on credit

checks. However, employment declined at around the same rate in mid-to-low credit score Census tracts (average credit score between 630-650).

The study also revealed that employers increased their demands for other signals of the job performance of applicants—such as education and experience—rather than credit checks. As a result, bans on credit checks generated relatively worse outcomes for African-Americans.

To explore the net impact of on minority populations, the study compared labor market outcomes for African-Americas in states with and without bans on credit checks and found the introduction of these bans were associated with a 1 percent increase in the likelihood of being unemployed.

The study "NO MORE CREDIT SCORE" – EMPLOYER CREDIT CHECK BANS AND SIGNAL SUBSTITUTION from Robert Clifford, an economist at the Boston Fed, and Daniel Shoag, an assistant professor at Harvard's Kennedy School is at http://scholar.harvard.edu/files/shoag/files/no_more_credit_score_employer_credit_che ck_bans_and_signal_sub.pdf?m=1448384143.

The Social Security Trace

A standard verification tool used by nearly every pre-employment screening firm is the "Social Security Trace." In cases where an employer does not have a sound business reason to obtain a credit report, obtaining the Social Security Trace can provide information about a person's past addresses and will help to uncover any identity fraud issues. The Social Security Trace is also used as a critical research tool by screening firms to assist in locating jurisdictions to search that may be relevant to the candidate. However, as noted below, there is a growing trend among screening firms not to provide the details of the Social Security Trace since it is primarily a "locator" tool containing information that cannot be easily verified in the screening process.

Author Tip ▷ **What Does a Social Security Trace Have to Do with Credit Checks?**

The Social Security Trace is covered in this chapter because it is related to the credit check and is used widely for purposes of performing criminal searches. However, the topic will be revisited in Chapter 22 under issues about identity, along with other tools that assist in identification such as Consent Based Social Security Number Verification (CBSV), Social Security Number Verification Services (SSNVS), Employment Eligibility Verifications Form I-9 and E-verify.

The Social Security Trace is a *Credit Header*

The Social Security Trace report contains the same information as a credit report about names and addresses associated with a Social Security Number (SSN), but the Social Security Trace does not include any of the financial information. The information is taken from the top portion of a credit report; ergo this report is referred to as a "credit header."

This top portion of a credit report is compiled from identifying information obtained by credit bureaus when individuals apply for credit cards, provide a change of address to a credit card company, or engage in any transaction that is credit-related. For example, anytime a person applies for a credit card, the data (including the person's SSN as well as a name and address) goes into large computer databanks kept by the major credit bureaus. If two years later a person moves and submits a change of address card, then that new data also goes into the computer memory.

The Social Security Trace Helps Verifies Social Security Numbers

A Social Security Trace report will assist an employer in determining if their applicant is in fact associated with the Social Security Number submitted. Depending on the date issued, it can also reveal other data such as state and approximate date of issue. Remember though: not all employers want the date of issue or date of birth due to discrimination problems associated with knowing an applicant's age (as discussed in Chapter 5).

About the Social Security Number and How Numbers are Issued

A **Social Security Number (SSN)** is a nine-digit number issued by the **U.S. Social Security Administration (SSA)**, the federal agency with responsibility to administer various Social Security programs. Until June 24, 2011, this is how the make-up of an SSN worked. The first three digits of the SSN indicate in which state the number was issued. The middle two digits, known as "group numbers," indicate the range of years when this group of SSNs was issued. Thus by using the methodology behind these two sets of numbers, an employer used to be able to determine the state of issue and the approximate year of issue. For example, using the master table one would know the Social Security Number 212-51-xxxx was issued in Maryland in 1997. The 212 is associated with Maryland. The 52 group was issued in 1997. The last four digits belong uniquely to the individual.

Changes to the Issuance of the Social Security Number

As mentioned, until June 24, 2011, one could verify the state and date range when the number was issued as described above. Since that date, all unassigned numbers have been placed a pool and are now assigned randomly. Below is an article, written by Michael Sankey of BRB Publications, which provides an overview of these changes.

> ### SSN Issuance and Randomization
>
> June 24th, 2011 was the last day the Social Security Administration (SSA) assigned a Social Security Number (SSN) based on the numeric order within a state's allocation of the first 5 digits. All unassigned numbers within the numeric sequence have now been placed in a random pool. Effective June 27, the assignment of a new SSN is much like a lottery; a random number is drawn from the unassigned pool of 420 million numbers available for assignment.
>
> For example, the Series of 048-15-xxxx was assigned to CT and was used to issue new SSNs. Effective June 27, all of the possible unassigned numbers within that Series have been assigned to the random pool. Therefore someone in any state or an immigrant coming into the country could be assigned an SSN in the 048-15 series this year or any year in the future. There are 755 Series groups that were in the process of being assigned as of June 2011. There are over 75,000 groups that have had all possible numbers within the group previously assigned.
>
> Previously unassigned areas numbers (the first three digits of the SSN) that are still excluded from assignment in the pool include 000, 666, and 900-999.
>
> For years employers, investigators, and background screening firms have used software with the assigned SSN groups and corresponding state/date range to validate the state and year of issuance an SSN. The fact that the SSA will no longer provide the ability to validate newly issued numbers has upset quite a few businesses and employers. However, these validations will still be useful, although they will diminish in value over time. Most people entering the workforce were assigned an SSN well before June 27, 2011. The primary people entering the workforce with a new randomly assigned SSN will be immigrants.
>
> The Social Security Administration will continue to provide opportunities for direct name based SSN verification. Internet-based verification services include:
>
> The Social Security Number Verification Service (SSNVS) (www.ssa.gov/employer/ssnv.htm) which is free to use for wage reporting purposes.

E-Verify (www.ssa.gov/employer/ssnv.htm)

Consent-Based SSN Verification Service (CBSV) (www.ssa.gov/employer/ssnv.htm)

There are stipulations. For example, the cost for CBSV is $5,000 to sign-up and $5.00 per verification. For questions about the randomization process, email ssn.randomization@ssa.gov or visit www.ssa.gov/employer/randomization.html.

The Social Security Trace Shows Past Addresses

Past addresses are critical because it helps employers determine where to search for criminal records. Since there is no true national criminal database available for private employers, and there are over 10,000 courthouses in America, a social trace can help employers narrow down which courts to search.

In addition, there may be occasions when there are names or addresses incorrectly associated with an SSN. This can occur for a variety of reasons. For example, if a data entry clerk for a credit card company accidentally switched two numbers in a Social Security Number while entering a change of address form, the credit bureau records may link the wrong name and addresses to a Social Security Number. Sometimes, members of the same family may have their credit history intertwined. For example, if a father and son have similar names, the databases can end up "merging" their data, causing confusion. Also, with the increase in identity theft, confusing numbers can also cause confusing results.

What a Social Security Trace is Not

Many employers mistakenly believe these searches are an official review of government records. The Social Security Trace information is NOT being accessed directly from government records and is therefore not an official verification of a Social Security Number. A Trace report may contain supplemental information from the Social Security Administration's list of deceased individuals, but usually the report is created from data found in the databases created by private firms and in credit headers. When a screening firm reports a trace result and indicates the Social Security Number appears to be valid and also indicates a state and date it was issued, that does NOT mean the screening firm actually checked with the Social Security Administration (SSA) and found information about the particular applicant. Rather, the screening firm is advising an employer that based upon information the SSA provides to the public on how to interpret the numbering sequence prior to June 2011, the number appears valid. However, as time passes the information of year and state of issue will only be applicable to numbers assigned prior to 2011, the value of this service will diminish.

In addition, it is critical to understand that a Social Security Trace report is NOT an official registry of current or past addresses. Nor is it an identity or address valuation tool. Current and past addresses will not appear on a trace report if the applicant never used those addresses in any dealings of interest to the major credit bureaus. On occasion, there may be no names or addresses associated with an SSN. This can occur when a person has never applied for credit, is too young to be in the credit bureau records, or is new to this country and have recently obtained a Social Security Number.

An employer should never make a direct hiring decision based upon the absence of an address in a Social Security Trace. Although Trace reports can be helpful for identity purposes and for determining where to search for criminal records, they are not positive proof of identity or the validity of a Social Security Number. However, the information in a trace report can be the basis for further research of an applicant.

Do Only Dangerous and Nefarious People have AKAs?

The author of this book went into a major department store to purchase some items and was told the store had a promotion whereby the author could get a 10% discount on purchases if he signed up that very day. It only required an SSN and driver's license to get an instant credit card and the discount. Seeing no downside, he went ahead and did it.

It turned out that the young employee behind the cash register was not very experienced and managed to misspell the author's first name as "Lesler" instead of Lester. Signing up for a credit card is a "credit event" since the Social Security Number is involved. The usual procedure is for the SSN used in the credit application, along with the name and address associated with the number, to be forwarded by the store to one or more national credit bureaus. Because of the clerical error, the author's name in some reports could read that he has an Also Known As (AKA), in that he sometimes goes by the alternate name of "Lesler." Of course, not only dangerous and nefarious people trying to hide something have "AKAs."

This story shows the margin for error when millions of SSN's are being recorded every day into credit bureau databases and public record databases.

Because of the possibility of human error, a Social Security Trace is used as a helpful tool in a background report but is not considered an "official report." If an applicant is concerned about any such discrepancy, then they can contact all three major credit bureaus to review their files.

Using Social Security Trace To Cross Check Applicants

A Social Security Trace report or verification showing numerous different names can indicate the applicant is using a fraudulent SSN. Clarify this by asking the applicant to contact the Social Security Administration to demonstrate it is genuinely his or her number. In the alternative, if a person's address history starts, for example, just five years ago, and the person is of an age where they would reasonably have a longer address history, an employer can also be concerned. For example, if a consumer was just released from prison, there can be a hole in past address information. Of course, given that the social trace information is gathered and assembled by private firms and is not an official government record, such inferences should be taken with a grain of salt, since it could lead to inaccurate conclusions.

Examples of Social Security Number Trace Macros

Below are examples of *macros* screening firms may use to explain results of a Social Security Trace to employers:

- **Possible Invalid SSN Reported:** The SSN appears to be an invalid number based on criteria the SSA provides to the public on how to interpret the number sequence for numbers issued prior to June 25, 2011. Numbers beginning with 000, 666, and 900-999 will never be assigned.
- **ALL DIFFERENT Names Reported – SSN is Valid:** The SSN appears to be a valid issued number based on criteria the SSA provides to the public on how to interpret the number sequence but for "ALL" Social Security Trace result(s) returned - different name(s) than the applicant provided name are being reported. The applicant provided name is NOT returned in any of the results.
- **No Names Reported – SSN is Valid:** The SSN appears to be a valid issued number based on criteria the SSA provides to the public on how to interpret the number sequence but there appears to be no names and/or addresses associated with this number. This situation of no names and/or addresses associated with this number can occur when a person is very young and has not yet used their SSN for commercial purposes or is new to the country and has just recently been assigned their SSN.
- **SSN Trace is Un-Performable:** No matching records found in the underlying database that is assembled and maintained by non-governmental sources. This not a definitive indicator of the validity of SSN in question.

In each instance, it can also be helpful pass along this information to the employer:

"For additional information on this topic please visit the Social Security Administration website at www.socialsecurity.gov. As an employer, if you are concerned about an SSN not being valid for a particular applicant you can access the Social Security Number Verification Service (SSNVS) at www.socialsecurity.gov/employer/ssnv.htm or call 800-772-1213. Your Employer Identification Number (EIN) is required."

Obtaining a Social Security Trace through a Background Screening Firm

With the applicant's signed release, the Social Security Trace can be obtained directly from major credit bureaus or through pre-employment screening firms. Background screening firms have introduced new searches that enhance the Social Security Trace search with name and address information gathered from a number of additional sources; the information is gathered by private organizations and comes from multiple sources, including billions of public and private records.

Past Address Location Tools Used by Background Screening Firms

A background screening firm will typically use a much more robust past address location tool than merely the Social Security Trace. There are commercial products available for screening firms that enhance the basic trace with literally billions (with a B) of records that come from a variety of sources that might include for example U.S. Postal Service address forwarding information, utility bills, voter registration records, and information from The Social Security Administration death master file.

It's important to ensure that a background firm is using this more comprehensive source of past addresses. Since criminal checks are based upon where a person has lived, more address information obviously can lead to a more comprehensive search. If a screening firm is using only the Social Security trace, then there is a possibility that they are missing counties where a search could be relevant. The Addendum for Chapter 9 contains a summary of a special report on how background firms can take shortcuts in searching for a criminal record, and the use of the proper past address location is a critical consideration.

Should a Background Screening Firm Even Report the Details of a Social Security Trace to an Employer?

A growing trend among screening firms is not to even report to employers the details of the social trace. There are a number of reasons. Since the social trace information is not an official government record and is based on data gathered by private firms from a large number of sources, it is difficult to defend the accuracy of any information in the trace report. Under the FCRA, a screening firm must use "reasonable procedures for maximum possible accuracy." Since the data comes from so many different sources and is assembled by private firms, it is difficult to make the case the information is accurate.

The best use of the trace report is as a **location tool** to assist a screening firm in determining other places to search for possible criminal records. Given that there are over 3,000 courthouses in America and employers cannot search all of them, the social trace provides valuable information as to where to search. However, employers cannot and should not make any hiring decisions based upon past addresses reported, or whether the trace report validates the Social Security Number or not.

In addition, if a screening firm reports that a Social Security Number is valid, an employer must also keep in mind that only means the SSN appears to be a valid issued number based on criteria the SSA provides to the public on how to interpret the number sequence. The Social Security Trace information is NOT being accessed directly from government records, and no one is calling the Social Security Administration. Therefore it is not an official verification of a Social Security Number.

CHAPTER 12

Education and Credentials Verifications

The Need for Verification of Education Credentials

The verification of educational credentials is an important part of an employer's decision making process in hiring. Educational achievement tells an employer a great deal about an applicant's ability, qualifications, and motivation. Many employers feel that educational qualifications are a critical factor in predicting success on the job. For many positions, education is a prerequisite in terms of subject matter knowledge or for obtaining the appropriate license for the position.

Employers are typically concerned with college-level credentials usually referred to as **Post-Secondary** education which can include education stemming from community colleges to advanced degrees from graduate schools. However, employers may also want to verify vocational or trade schools as well.

Author Tip

The Term *Post-Secondary Education*

While the words *college* and *university* are used throughout this chapter, the technical term to use when dealing with issues of legitimate college or university degrees versus diploma mills is **post-secondary education** as described above. This term means college after high school, but generally excludes vocational or trade schools that offer a certificate in a vocation or trade.

However, various surveys that examine resumes and application fraud suggest that as many as 30% of all job applicants falsify information about their educational backgrounds. The falsifications generally run into one of these three categories:

1. Outright fabrications such as making up degrees from legitimate schools the applicant never attended;
2. Reporting that a degree was earned from a school in which the applicant in fact attended but had never completed the course work required of the listed degree. The falsified educational achievements are based upon some semblance of fact, such as claiming degrees from schools that the applicant did attend without obtaining the degree claimed. Typically, a candidate turns their months or weeks of attendance into an AA degree or claims a BA or an advanced degree even if they did not complete the course work or fulfill all graduation requirements.
3. Reporting meaningless degrees of no value from non-accredited schools, many of which are often referred to as **diploma mill or degree mill**. *A degree mill or diploma mill is generally defined as substandard or fraudulent "colleges" that offer potential students degrees with little or no serious work.* Some are simple frauds, a mailbox to which people send money in exchange for paper that purports to be a college degree. Others require some nominal work from the student or a validation of "life experience" but do not require college-level course work that is normally required for a degree. The common denominator is that a degree mill lack accreditation and therefore is not recognized as a legitimate provider of post-secondary education.

> **You Need To Know** — **Educational Credential Issues Can Even Impact the CEO Level of a Major Nationally Known Company**
>
> In May 2012, Yahoo! Inc. announced that recently hired Chief Executive Officer Scott Thompson had left the company soon after it was revealed that there was a discrepancy in his academic credentials included in online biographies and filings with the Securities and Exchange Commission (SEC). Not only did Thompson's record contain incorrect information, but it was also revealed the Chairwoman of the Search Committee who hired him also had a discrepancy in her academic credentials.
>
> Read more at: www.esrcheck.com/wordpress/2012/05/14/yahoo-ceo-leaves-company-after-discrepancy-in-academic-credentials-revealed/.

The above incident of fraud underscores the need to do research on the educational qualifications of candidates. Confirming diplomas, degrees, or certificates, along with dates of attendance, verifies applicants' education, their skills, and is an indication of their ability to do the job. Confirmation also supports their honesty by substantiating claims made on an application. To an employer, the value of diplomas, degrees, or certificates also depends upon the quality of the degree-granting institution. The issue of accreditation is important for employers attempting to determine if a degree translates into knowledge, skills, or experience that will be beneficial to the workplace.

What about Licensed Schools that Are Not Accredited?

Another related issue is that in the U.S., there are schools that are not accredited but may still be licensed by a state agency. One example is trade or vocational schools. If such a school offers a program to teach a trade (i.e. refrigeration repair), then the school is likely licensed by the state but is not offering a degree and is not post-secondary education for purposes of this chapter. More problematic for employers is that there are some schools that have obtained a state license but are not accredited yet offer "academic" degrees. Such a school may still be essentially a "degree mill" offering substandard education or worthless degrees. In some cases, a school may be in the process of applying for accreditation. Another situation arises where a school has lost their accreditation but is still licensed, and was accredited when the applicant graduated. The bottom-line is that being licensed is not the same as being accredited. A license does not necessarily inform an employer about the quality of the school or the value of the degree in terms of skills and education needed for employment. In the case of a licensed but unaccredited school, an employer will need to conduct its own due diligence to determine the value of the degree in terms of the applicant's qualifications and the requirements of the job. All of this underscores the complexities of academic accreditation in the U.S. and the need for employers to exercise caution when evaluating a degree from an unfamiliar school.

The Verification Process

There are four primary pieces of information needed to verify one's education history and qualifications:

1. The school attended does exist.
2. The school is accredited by an approved accrediting body (or in the least is state licensed).
3. The subject attended the school during the time period claimed.
4. A degree was actually granted to the subject as claimed.

Also, if the position involves proof of course attendance, then the subject completed the courses of study for any degree granted and are shown on an official copy of their school transcripts.

Verifying Attendance or Degree Via the School

Traditionally, a verification request is sent by mail, email, or fax to the school's Registrar office. Few accept phone calls to verify prior attendance. Some schools now provide online, interactive request forms. Some schools require a signed release from the student to be included with the request. Verifications are usually free but not always. Confirmations may be faxed back although the school may have to be asked to confirm their results via phone. Requests should include a truncated Date of Birth (DOB), a truncated Social Security Number (SSN), and the name used during attendance. Gender and approximate or exact years of attendance should be mentioned, and always be concise about where verification results should be returned—your address, phone, company name, etc. If you mail a request, be sure to include a SASE.

Author Tip

A Suggestion of What to Include in the Employment Application

One suggestion to help employers is to include the following language on the employment application:

> "Please list all degrees or educational accomplishments that you wish to be considered by the employer in the employment decision."

This statement has the advantage of putting the burden on the applicant to determine if they want to report a degree or educational accomplishment. The applicant is on notice that any degree they report can be used by the employer for the employment decision. If the applicant chooses to report a worthless degree, or a degree not earned, they can hardly complain if an employer uses that to deny employment, even if the degree was not a requirement of the job.

Hard to Find Schools

Keep in mind that even if an employer reviews the accreditation resources, things can still slip through the cracks. Here is why:

1. A school may have changed names.
2. A website may not have been updated.
3. A school may have lost accreditation.
4. A school may be accredited, but since the last accreditation, the quality has fallen.
5. The so-called accreditation was by a non-accredited accreditation agency (See below).

Finding Records from a Closed School

The applicant's resume reads "Attended 'Aakers' Business College in Fargo, ND." But when one seeks to verify the applicant's attendance there, the school is found to be closed. Perhaps the applicant is claiming they attended there but didn't, knowing that verifications there might be hard to come by.

Closed schools within a state are registered through an education-related state agency. The records may be maintained by the agency, or the agency may know who does and have some mechanism in place to help you either 1) identify the current location of the closed school's student records, or 2) the agency may perform the record check for you. This is also true for transcript requests, but, depending on the state, transcripts and student attendance/degree information may not always be found at the same place. Knowing of the difficulty and urgency of your search request, the state agency can usually handle phone requests or is quick to instruct you how to correctly submit your request.

Verifying Attendance or Degree Via the National Student Clearinghouse

Many schools have outsourced verification duties to a non-profit, third-party vendor called **The National Student Clearinghouse (NSC)**—www.nslc.org—that was founded by the higher education community in 1993. This outsourcing ostensibly takes the tasks out of the hands of cost-conscious registrar offices. For a fee, the NSC offers access to a nationwide coverage of enrollment and degree records encompassing over 252 million students and growing. Here are some facts about NSC participants and services from the Clearinghouse Facts page on the NSC website at www.nslc.org/about/clearinghouse_facts.php:

- Our degree verification service, DegreeVerify, represents over 90% of U.S. four-year degrees.
- Over 3,400 institutions participate in our enrollment verification service, EnrollmentVerify, represents over 90% of currently enrolled U.S. college students.
- Hundreds of high school districts and thousands of high schools participate in the Clearinghouse.
- All guarantors and most major student loan lenders and servicers participate in the Clearinghouse.
- Thousands of the nation's largest employers, recruiters and background search firms have contracted with the Clearinghouse to perform secure, online academic verifications.
- The Clearinghouse performs more than 1.2 billion education record transactions annually.
- Over 4 million degrees are confirmed through DegreeVerify each year.
- Nearly 4 million enrollment verifications are performed through EnrollmentVerify each year.
- Transcripts are requested for nearly 3.5 million recipients each year via our Transcript Ordering service.
- Our free Student Self-Service program is used by nearly 2 million students each year."

Acquiring Transcript Copies

If you do need to obtain a copy of a transcript, this data is considered private and can only be obtained with a signed release of the student. Per the Family Educational Rights and Privacy Act (FERPA), the education records of students are not public record unless used as general directory information.

Most schools charge a fee for each transcript copy; fees vary from $1.00 to $20.00 each but usually around $5.00. Often transcript request forms are found online at the school's web page. Credit card payment may be allowed. A number of schools offer Unofficial Transcripts as a cost-saving measure, the benefit being that an unofficial copy can be returned by fax or email. Official copies are usually mailed back.

A number of schools outsource their transcript fulfillment duties to a 3rd party vendor, including NSC.

Closed private institutions such as military or seminary schools are a different story. Their records may have been transferred to another school, a nearby same-denomination school, or simply held by a surviving alumnus.

How to Verify if a School is Accredited

How are employers supposed to avoid diploma mills or worthless degrees? The first line of defense is to see if a school is accredited by a recognized accrediting agency. Sometimes this is referred to as confirming that a school is on a "white" list of accredited and legitimate schools.

Accreditation is a complicated process of peer and self-assessment aimed at improving academic quality and demonstrating the quality of an institution to the public. A legitimate accreditation can give the employer a greater comfort level in the legitimacy and quality of an applicant's degree.

Adding to the challenge of employers detecting education fraud, some diploma mills have even created fake accreditation agencies to vouch for the phony schools falsely. To combat diploma mills in the United States, schools are generally accredited by private organizations that are recognized as legitimate accreditors.

Unlike most of the rest of the world, however, accreditation in the United States is not done directly by the government. In the United States, numerous private organizations can provide accreditation to a school. The recognized U.S. accrediting organizations all have one thing in common—the accrediting agencies are in turn accredited by one of two nationally recognized agencies.

1. The U.S. Department of Education (DOE). According to the Department of Education: "The goal of accreditation is to ensure that education provided by institutions of higher education meets acceptable levels of quality." For an overview, see www.ed.gov/admins/finaid/accred/accreditation.html#Overview.

   The Department of Education limits their accreditation activities to institutions that receive federal money such as financial aid. The DOE has provided an internet listing of organizations that it has accredited to be an accrediting agency. See www.ed.gov/admins/finaid/accred/accreditation_pg4.html.

   The DOE has also created a website with a 'Database of Accredited Postsecondary Institutions and Programs' at http://ope.ed.gov/accreditation/.

2. The Council for Higher Education Accreditation (CHEA) found online at www.chea.org is the other accepted organization that can accredit the accreditors. CHEA is a successor to two previous organizations that also fulfilled this function—the Commission on Recognition of Postsecondary Accreditation (CORPA) and the Council on Postsecondary Accreditation (COPA). At the CHEA website, employers can find not only the names and contact information for each recognized organization but can also do a lookup by the state that gives a link to every school accredited. The Department of Education website states, "CHEA is currently the entity that carries out a recognition function in the private, nongovernmental sector."

   CHEA offers a 'Database of Institutions and Programs Accredited by Recognized United States Accrediting Organizations' at www.chea.org/search/default.asp.

CHEA and the U.S. Department of Education classify accrediting institutions into three types of organizations:

1. **Regional accreditation organizations.** There are six regional associations that accredit public and private schools, colleges, and universities in the United States. In the list at the end of this chapter, eight such organizations are listed. Two have two branches reflecting a division for "colleges and universities" and a division for "other types of institutions." A list with details about these regional accreditations organizations is located at the back of this chapter and also at:
   - www.chea.org/Directories/regional.asp
   - www.ed.gov/admins/finaid/accred/accreditation_pg5.html

2. **Single purpose national accreditation organizations.** These organizations accredit a particular type of school. At the end of the chapter are the names of eleven such national organizations, of which only six are recognized by CHEA. All are recognized by the U.S. Department of Education. The six national accreditation agencies recognized by CHEA are located at:
   - www.chea.org/Directories/index.asp
   - Additional agencies accredited by the U.S. Department of Education are listed at www.ed.gov/admins/finaid/accred/accreditation_pg6.html.

3. **Specialized and professional accrediting organizations.** These academic programs are administratively located in degree or non-degree granting institutions. These bodies range from acupuncture (Accreditation Commission for Acupuncture and Oriental Medicine) to veterinary medicine (American Veterinary Medical Association, Council on Education). For lists, see:
   - www.chea.org/Directories/special.asp
   - www.ed.gov/admins/finaid/accred/accreditation_pg6.html#aom

---

You Need To Know ▷ **Almeda University – A Diploma Mill that is Gone but Not Forgotten**

A diploma mill is a school that issues degrees with substandard or no academic studies and is not accredited – meaning it is not recognized as an accredited degree-granting school by the U.S. Dept. of Education or by other accredited accrediting organizations.

If there is any doubt as to the prevalence of diploma mills, here is a very simple exercise. Go to the LinkedIn website (www.LinkedIn.com) and under advanced search tools search for a well-known diploma mill called **Almeda University** which sold undergraduate and graduate degrees based on "life experiences." See the detailed write-up about Almeda at en.wikipedia.org/wiki/Almeda_University.

While Almeda University is now defunct, its legacy still lives on. As of an August 2016, a search on LinkedIn revealed that 4,297 people in the U.S. report on their LinkedIn profile that they hold a degree from Almeda University. You can sort the results by industry. For example, 137 people from Human Resources tout they have a diploma mill degree from Almeda, as well as 468 from Information Technology, 247 from Hospital & Health Care, 136 from Financial Services, and even 86 from Security and Investigations.

If this article is of interest to you, check out the widespread use of LinkedIn users touting their degrees from these diploma mills as well: Euclid University, Columbia Pacific University, Golden State University, and Standford University (includes six people associated with a major news organization). Makes you wonder who did the background checks on these people when they were hired. (*Information courtesy of BRB Publications.*)

The Use of Fake Diplomas is a Real Problem

Apparently that act of earning a college diploma apparently no longer requires years of hard work, taking tests, paying tuition, or even reading a book. Why bother going through the formalities when all a person needs is a credit card and a web browser in order to buy an authentic looking diploma that mimics real colleges, universities, and even high schools across the U.S.? Go to any search engine and run keywords such as *fake diploma* and anyone can instantly graduate from nearly any school in America with a very handsome and authentic looking diploma suitable for hanging.

The earlier example of the false education credentials presented by the CEO of Yahoo! is not merely an isolated incident. The use of **genuine fake diplomas** is definitely on the rise. The following recent news stories indicate how widespread the problem of diploma mills and education fraud has become both in the U.S. and the world:

- In April 2016, Federal agents arrested twenty-one recruiters and employers from across the United States for allegedly conspiring with more than 1,000 foreign nationals to fraudulently maintain student visas and obtain foreign worker visas through a "pay to stay" scam uncovered by a fake diploma mill created by the government called the University of Northern New Jersey (UNNJ). The defendants were arrested by special agents with U.S. Immigration and Customs Enforcement (ICE), Homeland Security Investigations (HSI) and charged with conspiracy to commit visa fraud, conspiracy to harbor aliens for profit, and other offenses. Through the UNNJ, undercover HSI agents investigated criminal activities associated with the Student and Exchange Visitor Program (SEVP) that included student visa fraud and the harboring of aliens for profit. As a fake diploma mill, the UNNJ was not staffed with instructors or educators, had no curriculum, conducted no actual classes or education activities, and operated solely as a storefront location with small offices staffed by federal agents posing as school administrators. See: www.justice.gov/usao-nj/pr/21-defendants-charged-fraudulently-enabling-hundreds-foreign-nationals-remain-united.
- In February 2016, the Federal Trade Commission (FTC) filed charges against two operators of alleged online high schools that claim to be legitimate but are "little more than diploma mills charging anywhere from $135 to $349 for a worthless certificate." The FTC claimed these two alleged diploma mills misled consumers about their legitimacy and association with recognized high school equivalency programs and the "courses" amounted to untimed and unmonitored multiple-choice tests with a required score of 70 percent. The filings by the FTC

point to numerous cases of consumers who sought to use the diplomas they received from the alleged diploma mills to get jobs, apply for college, and even join the military, only to find out that their diplomas were not recognized. An FTC press release is at www.ftc.gov/news-events/press-releases/2016/02/ftc-brings-two-actions-against-operators-online-high-schools.

Author Tip ▶ **FTC Article about High School Diploma Scams**

The FTC has also published an article with advice on what to watch out for with regard to online high school diploma mills. See: www.consumer.ftc.gov/articles/0539-high-school-diploma-scams.

- In May 2015, the *New York Times* reported that a vast network of alleged diploma mills with hundreds of websites for phony universities and high schools that offered worthless online education degrees with no true accreditation made "tens of millions of dollars" from people worldwide. The Times reported that a software application company based in Pakistan allegedly received money from these diploma mills by using fake accreditation bodies, fabricated news reports, paid actors posing as professors and students in testimonials, and campuses that exist only as photos. Former employees at the company told the Times that some customers knew they were "buying a shady instant degree for money" and students chose "from high school diplomas for about $350 to doctoral degrees for $4,000 and above." See the NY Times article at www.nytimes.com/2015/05/18/world/asia/fake-diplomas-real-cash-pakistani-company-axact-reaps-millions-columbiana-barkley.html.

- In August 2014, Texas Attorney General Greg Abbott resolved the State's enforcement action against a purported diploma mill that falsely claimed to be an accredited educational institution. The final judgment issued by a Harris County state district court required the purported diploma mill to permanently shut down and pay all costs associated with the shutdown. The court-restricted assets of the purported diploma mill should provide more than $1.4 million in compensation to deceived customers. The final judgment is available at www.texasattorneygeneral.gov/files/epress/files/LincolnAcademyFinalJudgment.pdf.

- In May 2014, Pakistan International Airlines (PIA) fired 300 employees for holding fake degrees according to the corporation's rules and regulations. *Dawn Media Group* reported a PIA spokesperson said in a statement that "the national carrier has been vigorously pursuing the issue of credential verifications of its employees" and that the "gigantic task of verification of credentials of around 16,000 employees" was started in October 2013. The spokesperson said that of more than 6,000 degrees that have been received so far 350 fake degrees were uncovered. Out of those 350 fake degrees, 300 employees were terminated while remaining 50 cases await further action. The report from the Dawn Media Group about the firings is available at www.dawn.com/news/1097810.

 Diploma Mills: How to Recognize and Avoid Them

CollegeChoice.net, an independent online publication dedicated to helping students and their families find the right college, offers these statistics from a 2016 infographic about diploma mills that sell degrees without requiring true academic achievement.

"Diploma Mills are Highly Profitable:

- $200 Million – Estimated amount that diploma mills rake in annually.
- 500 – Estimated number of Ph.D. degrees awarded by Diploma Mills monthly.
- 400 – Estimated number of Diploma Mills.

- 300 – Number of websites run by Diploma Mills.
- 98 – Number of fake accreditation agencies operating in U.S. today.

Preying on the Innocent: Why Having a Degree Matters:

- Bachelor Degree holders earn 85% more than those with high school diploma.
- Masters and Ph.D. holders earn 45% more than those having a B.S. or B.A.

Protect Yourself: 10 Warning Signs of Diploma Mills:

- Be wary of aggressive cold calls, spam, using jargon.
- No studies, no exams, no interaction.
- Admission based on having a Visa or MasterCard.
- Degree based on work experience and faxed resume.
- Instant degree within 30 days of application, regardless of status upon entry.
- Promised a degree in exchange for a lump sum.
- Multiple complaints on file.
- Your online "counselor" assures you international online universities can't be accredited in the U.S by CHEA-recognized agencies.
- School's website lists no faculty or lists faculty who have attended schools accredited by bogus agencies.
- The university offers online degrees to U.S. citizens but is located in a foreign country."

Source: *Diploma Mills: How to Recognize & Avoid Them* (April 2016) from CollegeChoice.net at www.collegechoice.net/diploma-mills/.

The rise of diploma mills is further evidenced by **Accredibase**, a recognized global leader in investigating diploma mills.

Report Reveals 48 Percent Increase Worldwide in Diploma Mills in 2010

Although now defunct, Accredibase™ was a recognized global leader in investigating diploma mills. Accredibase ran a proprietary database of diploma and accreditation mills, and had identified approximately 6,000 suspect educational institutions and accreditors. In addition to the 2,810 confirmed diploma mills known to Accredibase, more than 3,000 suspect institutions were under investigation for inclusion in the database.

Accredibase issued its annual Accredibase Report for 2011 with some interesting statistics that are still relevant. The Report revealed an astounding 48 percent increase worldwide in the number of known, fake diploma mills in 2010. According to the Report, the United States was the world's fake college capital and saw a 20 percent increase in known diploma mills with the number rising from 810 to 1,008.

The Report also listed top ten states areas in the U.S. with the highest number of diploma mills – which the report described as "largely online entities whose degrees are worthless due to the lack of valid accreditation and recognition." These states are:

- California – 147 diploma mills.
- Hawaii – 98 diploma mills.
- Washington – 91 diploma mills.

- Florida – 84 diploma mills.
- Texas – 68 diploma mills.
- New York – 55 diploma mills.
- Arizona – 44 diploma mills.
- Louisiana – 42 diploma mills.
- Delaware – 37 diploma mills.
- District of Columbia – 33 diploma mills.

Per the Report, the United Kingdom (U.K.) remained by far Europe's bogus university capital with a 25 percent increase in known diploma mills, with the number rising from 271 to 339, and also accounting for 57 percent of European diploma mills. The number of diploma mills in Europe rose from 454 to 593, an increase of 31 percent.

Source: www.esrcheck.com/file/Verifile-Accredibase_Diploma-Mills.pdf.

How to Spot a Diploma Mill

The problem with these lists of diploma mills is that the mills are moving targets. They can change their names overnight, and new ones can sprout up as easily as a scam artist can put up a new Internet site. There are literally hundreds of websites that offer fake degrees, diplomas, or certificates.

Here are some of the spins used in their advertisements:

1. Here is an opportunity to get ahead.
2. University diplomas.
3. Obtain a prosperous future, money earning power, and the admiration of all.
4. Diplomas from a prestigious university.
5. Based upon your present knowledge and life experience.
6. No required tests, classes, book or interview.
7. Bachelor's, Master's, MBA, and doctorate (Ph.D.) diplomas available in your field of choice.
8. No one is turned down.
9. Confidentiality assured. Call now to receive your diploma within days.

Of course, these schools have no classes, no faculty, no course catalog, and typically a single point of contact such as an email address or P.O. Box, but these schools typically do have really impressive websites with outstanding testimonials and wonderful pictures of campus life. They also provide wonderful looking diplomas, which any good graphic artist and print shop can produce.

Other Warning Signs that Help Identify of Diploma Mills

The second annual Accredibase™ Report for 2011 also identified the following red flag warning signs that may help identify diploma mills:

1. The institution does not have authority to operate or grant degrees from the education authorities where it claims to be based.
2. Degrees are delivered in a short space of time – sometimes a few days.
3. Degrees are granted based entirely on work or life experience.
4. Contact details are limited to email addresses and vague about the institution's location.
5. The institution allows students to choose their own course titles and specify graduation years on the certificate.
6. Sample certificates, transcripts, or verification letters are available on the website.
7. The institution's name is similar to that of a recognized and respected education institution.

8.   The institution's Internet domain names are misleading.

9.   The institution's website is poorly designed, has poor spelling and grammar, or plagiarizes from other institutions.

You Need To Know › Author's Own Dog Received a Fake Degree from a Real College

Getting a college diploma apparently no longer requires years of hard work, taking tests, paying tuition, or even reading a book. Why bother going through the formalities when all a person needs is a credit card and a web browser in order to buy an authentic looking diploma that mimics real colleges, universities, and even high schools across the U.S. Go to any search engine and run keywords such as "fake diploma" and anyone can instantly "graduate" from nearly any school in America with a handsome and authentic looking diploma suitable for hanging.

In fact, the author's own dog – a Border Collie named Gypsy Rose – received a very genuine-looking diploma in business administration in 2005 purportedly issued by the University of Arizona through an online diploma-selling service. (The author picked the University of Arizona only because a family member was attending Arizona State. Since the author is a UCLA alumni, he considered getting his dog a diploma from USC as well, which was also an option.)

Some sites that offer these fake degrees from real schools have disclaimers that they are sold for fun and novelty purposes only. In order to protect them from copyright infringement or other claims, they do not use the actual school seal. However, to an unsuspecting employer who is not otherwise suspicious, these degrees look extremely authentic and be very convincing at first glance.

In 2004, the situation with fake degrees got so out of hand that the United States Department of Education announced the development of a "positive list" of accredited institutions of higher education. This announcement was in response to a series of incidents of federal workers found holding worthless credentials issued by diploma mills. The government became concerned about diploma mills when a senior director in the Department of Homeland Security was placed on administrative leave following an allegation that his degree came from Hamilton University, allegedly a diploma mill that operated out of a refurbished hotel in Evanston, Wyoming. A memo issued April 2004, by the Federal Office of Personnel Management (OPM) reported other abuses including a computer specialist who claimed both a Bachelors and Master's degree in computers obtained only four months apart and a police officer who submitted his resume online to a diploma mill and received a degree based upon life experiences.

Author Tip › Search an Institution or Accrediting Agency Online

One may do a search of an institution or an accrediting agency at the U.S. Department of Education site at http://ope.ed.gov/accreditation/Search.aspx.

Author Tip ⟩ **Be Aware of a Physical Degree Being Presented as Proof**

It is not uncommon for a person who has been spotted with a fake education diploma to offer up the excuse that the school must have made a mistake and then offer to supply the actual diploma. The problem, of course, with fake diplomas from real schools is that no matter how well they were "photoshopped" or copied some tell-tale differences will be obvious. The insignia of the school may not be used because it's copyrighted and the "Deans" who signed the degree are normally made up.

Other Resources for Locating Degree Mills and Bogus Accrediting Agencies

If an employer is unable to locate a school on a "white" list, an employer does have the option of viewing several free listings of known diploma mills or paying for detailed information.

1. States Education Agencies

Several states have shown an interest in ensuring their citizens do not fall victim to fake degrees. Below are a few examples.

- **Hawaii:** Hawaii Department of Commerce and Consumer Affairs (DCCA) - Unaccredited Degree Granting Institutions (UDGI) in Hawaii at http://cca.hawaii.gov/ocp/udgi/.
- **Maine**: Department of Education State of Maine Non-Accredited Colleges & Degree Mills at www.maine.gov/doe/highered/nonaccredited/index.html (has a link to Wikipedia list).
- **Texas:** Texas Higher Education Coordinating Board (THECB) – Institutions Whose Degrees are Illegal to Use in Texas: www.thecb.state.tx.us/?objectid=EF4C3C3B-EB44-4381-6673F760B3946FBB.
- **Michigan:** The Michigan Civil Service Commission previously published a list of schools whose degrees had been found to not satisfy educational requirements indicated on job specifications for state classified positions. The Commission now offers some guidance and refers people to Council on Higher Education Accreditation (CHEA). See: www.michigan.gov/documents/Non-accreditedSchools_78090_7.pdf.

2. The Publication *Degree Mills* by Ezell and Bear

The most recent 2012 edition of *Degree Mills: The Billion-dollar Industry That Has Sold Over A Million Fake Diplomas'* written by Allen Ezell and John Bear shows how much money can be made while running an unaccredited school that awards unearned degrees.

Here is a description from its Amazon.com page:

"When the first edition of Degree Mills was published, fake universities and counterfeit degrees were already a significant problem. Fueled by the Internet, this scam continues to grow—now more than half of all people claiming a new PhD in fact have a fake degree.

In this updated edition, experts Allen Ezell and John Bear go beyond exposing these fraudulent practices to provide detailed recommendations—for government agencies, educational institutions, and individuals—on what can be done to rid us of them. This eye-opening and definitive guide shows how degree mills operate and how to check the validity of anyone's degree—an indispensable reference book."

The following excerpt comes from an article by Mr. Bear, who has written numerous articles on educational issues:

"There are more than 300 unaccredited universities now operating. While a few are genuine start-ups or online ventures, the great majority range from merely dreadful to out-and-out diploma mills—fake schools that will sell people any degree they want at prices from $3,000 to $5,000.

"It is not uncommon for a large fake school to "award" as many as 500 PhDs every month.

"The aggregate income of the bad guys is easily in excess of $200 million a year. Data show that a single phony school can earn between $10 million and $20 million annually.

With the closure of the FBI's diploma mill task force, the indifference of most state law enforcement agencies, the minimal interest of the news media, and the growing ease of using the internet to start and run a fake university, things are rapidly growing worse."

3. List of Unaccredited Institutions of Higher Education from Wikipedia.org

Online encyclopedia Wikipedia.org offers a list of colleges, seminaries, and universities that do not have educational accreditation. It is essentially an unofficial "crowdsourced" list of unaccredited schools, which means there is no official or recognized firm or body that curates the listing. This list is dynamic and may never satisfy particular standards for completeness or be all-encompassing since existing non-accredited colleges and degree mills disappear, and new ones are created, at a rapid rate. Employers relying on the list are doing so at their own risk, and it is only presented here as one additional resource that may potentially be of value.

See: https://en.wikipedia.org/wiki/List_of_unaccredited_institutions_of_higher_education.

4. The White List and Diploma Mill List From BRB Publications

BRB Publications has an inexpensive subscription product which provides not only detailed information about schools but also includes over 900 known diploma mills in its searchable database. The BRB list is not offered or intended as a complete, or updated listing of degree mills but is another potential resource for employers. The data available about each school includes:

1. Degree levels granted.
2. The Accrediting Agency.
3. The state government agency that gives authority to operate in a state.
4. If verifications are performed by the school (and how to obtain) or if a requester must contact the National Student Clearing House.
5. A cross-reference list of over 1,000 schools that have closed or have had name changes.

Author Tip ▷ **The Role of a Background Screening Firm in Finding Diploma Mills**

According to the National Association of Professional Background Screeners (NAPBS) Background Screening Agency Accreditation Program (BSAAP) **Clause 5.3 Diploma Mills**: "When attempting educational verifications from known or suspected diploma mills, a Consumer Reporting Agency (CRA) shall have procedures in place to advise the client of such." The BSAAP requires the CRA to have a written policy, procedure, or other documentation used "to reasonably ensure validity of academic institution and advise client of findings when the institution is a known or suspected "diploma mill."

The difficulty is a Consumer Reporting Agency cannot necessarily offer an opinion that a school is offering worthless degrees. That potentially creates legal liability for the screening firm. On the other hand, there is a duty to put an employer on notice that there is an issue as to the worth of the claimed degree. If a screening firm determines a school is not on any list of known accredited schools, the screening report may note that the firm is unable to verify the school is accredited and put an employer on notice that more research is necessary.

A screening firm is not typically asked to verify things such a "Certificate of Achievement" or some sort of online training or training program where a certificate is awarded rather than a degree from an accredited post-secondary school.

About Distance Learning (Online) Schools

Diploma mills should not be confused with legitimate schools that offer valuable distance-learning programs over the Internet. If an employer is not familiar with a school, the employer should review the school's website to check out the accreditation, curriculum, faculty, and graduation requirements.

The Accrediting Commission of the Distance Education and Training Council (DETC) at www.detc.org is a legitimate, recognized accrediting agency for schools that provide their curriculum via online learning. But there are many agencies that are unrecognized as a legitimate accrediting body for distance learning, as shown below.

Remember, most diploma mills and degree mills are accredited—but by fake or phony agencies that the degree mills themselves own and operate!

Unrecognized and Fake Agencies for Online College Accreditation

Here is a listing of 30-plus distance learning accrediting agencies that claim to oversee a variety of online college and university degree programs from **Get Educated** (www.geteducated.com). **NONE of these accrediting agencies are recognized as college accreditors in the U.S. by the Council on Higher Education Accreditation (CHEA) or the U.S. Department of Education.** Colleges claiming accreditation by these agencies are not accepted as valid providers of online education or degrees and should be approached with great caution:

- Accreditation Council for Distance Education (ACTDE).
- Accreditation Council for Online Academia (ACOHE).
- Accreditation Council of Online Education (ACOE).
- Accreditation Panel for Online Colleges and Universities (APTEC).
- Accrediting Commission International (ACI).
- American Accrediting Association of Theological Institutions.
- American Council of Private Colleges and Universities.
- American Association of Drugless Practitioners (ADP).
- Association of Accredited Bible Schools.
- Association of Distance Learning Programs (ADLP).
- Association of Private Colleges and Universities.
- Association for Online Academic Accreditation.
- Association for Online Excellence.
- Association for Online Academic Excellence.
- Board of Online Universities Accreditation (BOUA).
- Council for Distance Education.
- Council of Online Higher Education.
- Central States Consortium of Colleges & Schools.
- Distance and Online Universities Accreditation Council (DOUAC).
- Distance Learning International Accreditation Association (DEIAA).

- Global Accreditation Bureau (GAB).
- Global Accreditation Commission for Distance Education (GACDE).
- International Commission for Higher Education.
- International Accreditation Agency for Online Universities (IAAOU).
- International Accreditation Association for Online Education (IAAFOE).
- International Accreditation Commission (IAC).
- International Accreditation Commission for Online Universities (IACOU) (Kingston).
- International Accreditation Organization (IAO).
- International Council on Education (ICE).
- International Education Ministry Accreditation Association.
- International Online Education Accrediting Board (IOEAB).
- National Academic Higher Education Agency (NACHE).
- National Academy of Higher Education.
- National Accreditation and Certification Board (NACB).
- National Board of Education (NBOE).
- National College Accreditation Council (NCAC).
- National Commission of Accredited Schools (NCAS).
- National Distance Learning Accreditation Council (NDLAC).
- New Millennium Accrediting Partnership for Educators Worldwide.
- Organization for Online Learning Accreditation (OKOLA).
- Transworld Accrediting Commission Intl. (TAC).
- United Christian College Accreditation Association (UCCAA) (Divine Heart).
- United Nations Council.
- United States Distance Education & Training Council of Nevada*****.
- Universal Accreditation Council (UAC).
- Universal Council for Online Education Accreditation (UCOEA).
- World Association for Online Education (WAOE)******.
- World Association of Universities and Colleges (WAUC).
- World Online Education Accrediting Commission (WOEAC).
- World-Wide Accreditation Commission of Christian Educational Institutions (WWAC).
- Worldwide Higher Education Accreditation Society (WHEAS).

Remember: Most diploma mills and degree mills are accredited – but only by the fake or phony agencies the degree mills owned and operated by themselves!

*IMPORTANT NOTE 1: A similarly titled agency, the Distance Education & Training Council (DETC) of Washington, D.C.—www.detc.org—is a VALID and RECOGNIZED online learning accreditation agency. NOTE: US-DETC is not to be confused with the legitimate DETC or Distance Education and Training Council, based in Washington DC. DETC is recognized by both the Department of Education and CHEA.

** IMPORTANT NOTE 2: WAOE is a real, esteemed professional agency for educators. It is a discussion group of teachers who are experimenting with computer mediated methods of teaching in their own schools, colleges, and universities around the world. WAOE does not condone the use of its name as an accrediting agency by any online college. Any online college using the WAOE name as a college accrediting agency does so without the consent of WAOE and in contradiction to the organization's mission. For more on the WAOE and its valuable mission uniting educators involved in computer-mediated education visit WAOE online at www.waoe.org.

Source: www.geteducated.com/diploma-mills-police/college-degree-mills/204-fake-agencies-for-college-accreditation.

Author Tip

It's a Moving Target

Part of the problem with keeping up with diploma mills and fake accreditation scams is that it can seem like a game of "Whac-A-Mole." As soon as one scam is discovered, another can pop up almost instantly. It does not take much to start a fake school or accreditation agency beyond having a computer. The lesson for employers again is that if you are not familiar with a school, extreme caution is advised. Employers that utilize the services of a professional Consumer Reporting Agency have an advantage since a Consumer Reporting Agency (CRA) can access resources that help distinguish between legitimate schools and degree mills by virtue of the fact that a CRA is looking at whether a school has legitimate accreditation.

Verifying High School Equivalency Diplomas

Searching for high school records can be a difficult task. Of course, this is easily done if the employer is hiring from a local familiar area, provided the employer understands that during summer vacation and school breaks there may not be anyone at school offices to answer the phone. When employers hire from outside their locale, there are practical problems. First, it is not always easy to locate a particular high school. Over the years, schools can close, merge, or be renamed. A high school name can be misspelled or not quite remembered. Most states have a website or an office that provides school lists. If a student received his or her high school degree by testing, such as GED, then there can be delays in obtaining those through the appropriate state or district office.

There are several excellent websites that provide comprehensive lists and data pertaining to high schools as well as junior highs and elementary schools.

The site maintained by Council of Chief State School Officers (CCSSO) at www.ccsso.org provides detailed information on each school including the school's address, telephone number, total students, and also very detailed comparisons on performance matters. At press time the site is undergoing changes and promises to be up shortly, merged with SchoolDataDirect.

Also, check out the subscription site at www.schoolinformation.com. Designed for entities marketing products to schools, this resource is valuable if extensive searching or due diligence is required. Also, a Google search will reveal a number of state lists. Of course, an on-site visit to a school is a good way to view a yearbook to find pictures and activity information about individual students.

High School Equivalency Credentials (GED, HiSET, and TASC)

Not everyone graduates from a high school, but later on, a person may pass a high school equivalency test and receive a credential. This is done by taking one of three equivalency tests – the GED, the HiSET, or the TASC. Prior to 2014, the GED was exclusive option for a high school equivalency. As of late 2015, 40 states still offer the GED Test, 15 offer the

HiSET, and 6 offer the TASC. GED stands for General Educational Development; HiSET stands for High School Equivalency Test, and TASC stands for Test Assessing Secondary Completion. A database of these test recipients is maintained at the state level by the agency that oversees adult education. A record search will verify if someone truly received a certificate for high school education equivalency. Many of these state agencies will verify over the phone the existence of a certificate or give a yes-no answer by fax. Copies of transcripts or diplomas usually require a fee and a signed release. Search requirements include the name of the student at the time of the test and a general idea of the year and test location.

Many state agencies outsource agency the access of official high school equivalency credentials and transcripts to Diploma Sender (https://www.diplomasender.com). BRB's Public Record Research System provides detailed information on each state's office with record searching requirements for theses tests.

Occupational Licensing and Vocational Verifications

Not all vocational or trade schools are accredited by recognized accrediting organizations. Each state has an agency in charge of certifying state-approved educational programs. If there are questions about the legitimacy of a vocational or trade school, then an employer should contact the appropriate authority in their state. There are numerous distance learning programs available on the internet as well. The same verification rules apply. An employer should determine what accreditation or recognition they have and then evaluate the value of the degree. It is the employer's job to evaluate how a degree or coursework from a vocational, trade school, or distance learning program translates into a person's ability to perform a given job. An employer needs to view the school's literature or website to find out about the quality of the facilities and faculty, the course of study required, and other factors that go into determining the value of the education to the job position.

For helpful information on evaluating non-accredited but otherwise licensed schools, see this publication by the Federal Trade Commission (FTC) that summarizes some factors that potential students and employers may find beneficial to review: www.ftc.gov/bcp/edu/pubs/consumer/products/pro13.shtm.

For confirming the status of a license or credential needed to legally practice a profession, there are literally thousands of governmental boards that have control over licenses and professional certification. There are also private organizations that issue certifications.

Examples? Hospitals may need to verify the license status of a doctor, nurse, radiologist, or physical therapist. An employer may want to confirm that a person claiming to be an accountant is, in fact, licensed by the state board that licenses accountants. In order to verify a license an employer needs to require that the applicant provides key information:

1. The name or type of license.
2. The issuing agency.
3. The state AND date of issuance.
4. Current status and date of expiration.
5. License number (if able to).

Nearly every governmental licensing organization can be contacted by telephone. Many agencies have Internet sites where verifications can be done immediately. An extensive listing of agency websites offering a free public search of a licensee or licensee list is at www.brbpublications.com/freeresources/pubrecsitesOccStates.aspx.

Author Tip ⟩ **Is Applicant's License in Good Standing?**

During the verification process, an employer will also want to know if the agency reports any actions against the license or derogatory information about the applicant. That helps to determine if the applicant's license is in good standing.

Confirmation of certifications issued by private organizations. Certificates issued by private organizations are typically difficult to verify. Unless the certification was conducted through an accredited school, such as a community college, it is a substantial challenge to verify it. These can include items such as any kind of "Certificate of Good Work" and a number of different computer and software-related certificates provided by a number of organizations, legitimate or otherwise.

Conclusion – Educational Credentials Checking

When it comes to education credentials—employers beware! If an employer is not familiar with the school, check it out. Do not be fooled by a slick looking website with pretty pictures of a campus and academic scenes and glowing testimonials. The existence of a very academic looking diploma does not mean anything; fake schools are capable of producing some very convincing worthless diplomas. A common sense approach is a valuable tool in evaluating the worth of a degree. Look first to see if it is accredited by a recognized accreditation agency, then take reasonable steps as necessary to confirm the value of the degree such as examining the curriculum, the qualifications and reputation of the faculty members, the facilities, the qualifications of the institution's president, or graduation requirements.

Author Tip | **Educational Moving from "Ivory" Towers to "Wi-Fi" Towers**

Experts say education is moving from "Ivory" towers to "Wi-Fi" towers with new structures and new business models in response to concerns that there is a global skills gap. Many education verification specialists are also noticing that the educational model is shifting from traditional onsite attendance to more diverse and less centralized alternatives. There is a movement from traditional degrees toward specific credentials and certificates. For example, trade associations may now issue certifications. In addition, there is training that is industry specific such as Information Technology (IT) boot camps.

Additional Education Verification Resources

Regional Accrediting Organizations

The following Regional Accrediting Organizations are recognized by both CHEA and DOE:

- **Middle States Commission on Higher Education** – www.msche.org
  - Delaware, the District of Columbia, Maryland, New Jersey, New York, Pennsylvania, Puerto Rico, and the U.S. Virgin Islands, including distance education programs offered at those institutions.
- **New England Association of Schools and Colleges** – www.neasc.org
  - Connecticut, Maine, Massachusetts, New Hampshire, Rhode Island, and Vermont.
- **Higher Learning Commission** –www.northcentralassociation.org/
  - Arizona, Arkansas, Colorado, Illinois, Indiana, Iowa, Kansas, Michigan, Minnesota, Missouri, Nebraska, New Mexico, North Dakota, Ohio, Oklahoma, South Dakota, West Virginia, Wisconsin, and Wyoming.
- **Northwest Commission on Colleges and Universities** – www.nwccu.org
  - Alaska, Idaho, Montana, Nevada, Oregon, Utah, and Washington.
- **Southern Association of Colleges and Schools** – www.sacscoc.org
  - Alabama, Florida, Georgia, Kentucky, Louisiana, Mississippi, North Carolina, South Carolina, Tennessee, Texas, and Virginia.

- **Western Association of Schools and Colleges, Accrediting Commission** – www.acswasc.org
  - California, Hawaii, the United States territories of Guam and American Samoa, the Republic of Palau, the Federated States of Micronesia, the Commonwealth of the Northern Mariana Islands and the Republic of the Marshall Islands.

National Specialized Accrediting Organizations

The following National Accrediting Organizations are recognized by both CHEA and the DOE:

- Accrediting Association of Bible Colleges (AABC) Commission on Accreditation – www.aabc.org
- Accrediting Commission of the Distance Education and Training Council (DETC) –www.detc.org
- Accrediting Council for Independent Colleges and Schools (ACICS) – www.acics.org
- Association of Advanced Rabbinical and Talmudic Schools (AARTS) – 212-363-1991 (Web: N/A)
- Association of Theological Schools in the United States and Canada (ATS) – www.ats.edu
- Transnational Association of Christian Colleges and Schools Accreditation Commission (TRACS) – www.tracs.org

The following National Accrediting Organizations are recognized only by the DOE:

- Accrediting Bureau of Health Education Schools
- Accrediting Commission of Career Schools and Colleges of Technology
- Accrediting Council for Continuing Education and Training
- Council on Occupational Education
- National Accrediting Commission of Cosmetology Arts and Sciences, Inc.

For listings of Specialized and Professional Accrediting Organizations, see:

- www.ed.gov/admins/finaid/accred/accreditation_pg4.html
- www.chea.org/Directories/special.asp

CHAPTER 13

Other Background Screening Tools for Employers

Introduction

As part of a Safe Hiring Program, there are other sources of information an employer may consider. This chapter builds on the approaches and tools already covered to examine additional tools that an employer can consider. We will cover sources of information such as driving records, workers' compensation records, civil court records, judgments, liens, bankruptcies, sex offender registries, security clearances, military records, merchant databases, and the National Wants and Warrants list.

Two important points. First, just because this information is available does not mean an employer is bound to use it. Each type of inquiry needs to be related to the risk involved and carry with it some return on investment for the employer. Not every employer is going to find every tool useful for every applicant. Secondly, each of these tools carries its own legal considerations. No tool should be used without understanding the potential legal restrictions and ramifications.

Driving Records

The employment screening industry often refers to driving records as **MVRs,** meaning **Motor Vehicle Records.** Many employers simply call them driver records and utilize them as a safe hiring tool whether the position applied for involves driving America's highways and byways or not. It is important to note that each state has its own database of drivers' records—there is no national database. That is because each state manages it owns system to issue, monitor and enforces the issuance of driving licenses.

Typical information on an MVR report might include full name, address, Social Security Number, physical description, and date of birth along with conviction and accident history. Also, there is license type, restrictions, and endorsements which can provide useful background data on an individual. However, while there is some consistency, the data appearing on an MVR record may vary from state-to-state. Also, the specific access requirements will vary by state depending on individual state privacy laws and administrative rules. Sometimes the version of the MVR provided to employers by a background screening firm will contain the applicant's name and driving record, but with personal data—date of birth, address, physical characteristics, etc.—removed.

> **You Need To Know**
>
> ### Outcomes of Driving Records Searches
> There are thousands of vehicle code violations among the 50 states. Driving records are flagged when something other than a good standing is returned from the Department of Motor vehicles. Some examples of good standing are Valid, In Force, Eligible, not suspended, Active, Privileges in Good Standing, Licensed (valid DL). There are 6 common outcomes for an "employment" DMV/MVR check.
>
> 1. Valid license without any violations
> 2. Valid license with violations
> 3. License has been suspended, revoked, or expired
> 4. License status "pending."

5. ID card only (in California): no license.

6. No license or ID card.

If the driving record is relevant to the job position, then employers ALWAYS need to review the DMV/MVR record. Remember that for employment purposes, the DMV only provides 3 years' worth of records. Your insurance carrier can pull more extensive records for an applicant.

Consideration When Driving for an Employer

For a person who is driving a company vehicle or is in a driving position for the company, such a check is a necessity. Many employers assume that if they are not a trucking or transportation company, they do not employ drivers. However, in most jurisdictions, *driving for work* is very broadly defined. The question is: When is an employee driving for work? The term driving for work can cover any employee behind the wheel of a vehicle for the employer's benefit. It can go way beyond just driving large commercial rig.

For example, an employee who drives to the office supply store during lunch or between branches of the same firm or attends classes that are paid for by the company, can be considered "driving for work." If an accident occurs in any of those situations, an employer may be sued.

The one time an employer likely has no responsibility for an employee's driving is for an employee who only drives to work and drives home. This is referred to as the "Going and Coming Rule"—a worker driving to work and driving home does not drive for the employer between work and home.

For positions that involve driving, an employer can review the applicant's driving history and verify a license's status. A check of the driving record may also give insight into the applicant's level of responsibility. Just having moving violations may not relate to the ability to perform the job, but if an applicant has a history of failing to appear in court or pay fines, that can be a telling indicator of their level of responsibility.

Statewide driving records databases may be the first place where difficulties with drugs or alcohol are revealed—there may be driving while impaired violations. However, there are restrictions on the use of this information under the federal Americans with Disabilities Act (ADA), plus anti-discrimination law in certain states. The employer must determine whether the information is job-related and should exercise discretion when using it to the detriment of the applicant.

Author Tip > ## More Information about Drug Testing and Driving

The area of drug testing and driving will be revisited in Chapter 15 on drug testing discussing drug tests required of commercial drivers by the U.S. Departmental of Transportation (DOT).

Record Access Restrictions and Signed Releases

The state laws governing the release of motor vehicle data to the public and to employers must comply with the **Driver's Privacy Protection Act (DPPA),** which was signed into law by President Clinton in 1997. States differentiate between requesters who are permissible users (14 permissible uses are designated in DPPA) and those who are casual requesters to determine who may receive a record and/or how much personal information is reported on the record. For example, if a state DMV chooses to sell a record to a casual requester, the record can only contain personal information (address, gender, etc.) unless written consent of the subject is presented.

Does the permissible use designation apply to employers obtaining driving records on applicants? No, unless the employer is hiring a licensed commercial driver such as truckers of 18-wheelers, etc. This means that employers must obtain a signed release from a prospective applicant before access to the record is granted (except for commercial drivers' records).

The Record Ordering Process

This is how the ordering process works.

- Employers usually obtain MVRs through the services of an employment screening firm. A screening firm can typically obtain a driving record in one or two business days. Most states permit the release forms to be on file with the screening company rather than require a paper release submitted with each request.
- Screening companies, in turn, usually utilize the services of an MVR vendor. These vendors obtain and supply records nationwide in a timely manner for a very low service fee. The MVRs are delivered electronically, are uniform in appearance, and are reliable in content. There are a limited number of national and regional driving record vendors. Many of the national vendors limit their clientele to permissible users, such as the insurance industry, but there are vendors who will process requests from employers and background screening companies, providing the employer or company complies with state regulations.

Some states' DMVs offer a notification program for employers who hire a large number of drivers. The employer is notified if a driver has activity or a moving violation. There is typically a modest fee paid to register each driver, then a fee when activity is shown. More information about these programs can be obtained from state DMVs.

Idea! Have Applicants Obtain Their Own Records

Some employers who hire for a position that requires a driver's license require all applicants to bring a certified driving record to the job interview. Applicants must visit their local DMV office and request an official copy of their own license with a certification stamp showing it is authentic. To obtain your own records, there is usually a minimal fee charged by the DMV

There are two reasons that employers engage in this process. First, it makes the application process go more efficiently by eliminating those without a satisfactory driving record.

Second, some employers feel that by requiring an applicant to bring in a certified license, an employer can eliminate from consideration applicants who are unable or unwilling to accomplish that small task. By requiring an applicant to jump through a small hoop, the employer eliminates anyone who is unable or unwilling to complete a simple task.

At least one employer has reported a potential scam in the process. An applicant with a poor driving record found a friend with a clean record. Both the applicant and the friend went to the DMV and got their records. The applicant then took the bottom half off the friend's clean record, added the top part of his record with his name, and then copied the fake record. He then presented what looked like a clean record to the employer. Fortunately, the applicant's ingenuity was not matched by his artistic skills. He created a suspicious document that caused the employer to look deeper and uncover the deception.

Readers interested in extensive, detailed information about state driving records, access restrictions and procedures, and violation codes, may refer to BRB Publications' *The MVR Access and Decoder Digest*. See www.mvrdecoder.com.

Workers' Compensation Records

Employers have become very aware of the high costs of compensation claims. The loss to American businesses from both fraudulent claims and re-injury causes many employers to want to know whether a job applicant has a history of filing workers' compensation claims.

At the same time, the Federal **Americans with Disabilities Act (ADA),** as well as numerous state laws, seek to protect job seekers from discrimination in hiring as a result of filing valid claims The ADA also seeks to prevent the discrimination against workers who, although suffering from a disability, are nevertheless able to perform essential job functions as long as there are reasonable accommodations.

A duality is a legal term that generally means a physical or mental impairment that substantially limits one or more major life activity.

Before the ADA was introduced in 1990, employers had little legal limitations when it came to asking job applicants about their medical history or past workers' compensation claims. Now there are numerous legal restrictions that must be observed closely. The bottom line is that an employer cannot request workers' compensation records in order to have a policy of not hiring anyone who has made a claim. It is discriminatory to penalize a person who has exercised a lawful right and filed a valid claim. Nor can anyone be automatically excluded due to a physical or medical condition.

Employers are well-advised to contact a labor lawyer before seeking to obtain workers' compensation records. A labor law expert can assist an employer in preparing company policies, job descriptions, and forms and procedures necessary to comply with the ADA, such as a conditional job offer and medical review form.

Obtaining and Using Workers' Compensation Records

The following brief summary describes the major points involved in obtaining and using workers' compensation records.

- There are wide variations between the states in the availability of these records. In a few states, the records are not available to the public, period. In some states, there are special requirements before obtaining the records such as a notarized release. The records may be limited to just cases that went to an appeals board.
- Under the ADA, an employer may not inquire about an applicant's medical condition or past workers' compensation claims until a conditional job offer has been extended. A conditional job offer means that a person had been made a bonafide offer of employment, subject to a job-related medical review. That must be fulfilled prior to coming on-site for employment.
- When it comes to matters controlled by the ADA, the job offer must be "real," meaning there are no other conditions left to fulfill. (See additional material on the ADA in Chapter 2.)
- Any questions in a job interview about a disability must be restricted to whether the person can perform the essential job functions with or without reasonable accommodation.
- If a candidate discloses a disability, then there should not be any follow-up. Questioning should be limited to whether that applicant can perform the job.
- Only after a conditional job offer has been extended may an employer inquire about past medical history, require a medical exam, or inquire about workers' compensation claims.
- The better procedure is to have an applicant fill out a written medical review form that reviews their medical condition and workers' compensation claims history and provides consent as well. Firms that utilize medical examinations as part of their procedures should have a written medical review policy.
- The procedure should be administered uniformly. If one worker in a job category is the subject of such an investigation, then all applicants must be treated the same. However, an employer may treat different job categories differently. Not all employees must be sent for a medical exam.
- If a history of filing workers' compensation claims is found, then the offer may only be rescinded under very limited circumstances:
  a. The applicant has usually lied during a medical examination about a workers' compensation history or medical condition;
  b. The applicant has a history of filing false claims;
  c. In the opinion of a medical expert, the past claims demonstrate the applicant is a safety or health threat to himself or others; and
  d. The past claims demonstrate the applicant is unable to perform the essential functions of the job even with a reasonable accommodation.

Some firms contend that a workers' compensation record may also be used to determine the truthfulness of information on a job application on the theory that an applicant may try to hide a past employer where a claim was filed. However, even with this justification, if used, the best practice may be to review the records post-hire only. Also keep in mind in those states that release records, sometimes it can take two to three weeks for the agency to fulfill the order.

Author Tip ⟩ **When to Order Workers Compensation Records**

The most important walk away point about workers compensation records is that under the ADA and similar state laws, they cannot be ordered until there has been a conditional job offer, which means there has been a real offer of employment, and that the workers' compensation record check or other medical procedure are performed as the very last condition of hiring before the start date.

The bottom line is that workers compensation records should be used with great caution if at all. If an employer sees the need for those records, a competent screening firm will advise the employer to first contact their legal counsel to make certain the employer understands the risks and has a process and plan for legal compliance.

Using Civil Court Case Files

Another screening tool available for employers involves using civil court records. A civil case occurs when one party sues another. Unlike a criminal case, which is brought by the government and a defendant can face jail time, a civil case is typically about money. There are some lawsuits that seek remedies other than money, such as a request for an injunction, which is where a party seeks to have another party ordered to do or not do some physical act. Lawsuits brought in family court or probate courts are also considered civil lawsuits. Civil cases can be for torts or contracts.

A contract case is when one party sues another for a violation or enforcement of an agreement. A tort case is when one party sues another for an injury in civil court for actions other than breach of contract. Tort cases can involve both intentional conduct and unintentional conduct. An unintentional tort is typically a negligence action, such as an auto accident. An intentional tort can be such causes of action as assault, intentional infliction of emotional distress, or some intentional wrong. Although the same conduct could also form the basis of a criminal case as well, a criminal case is only brought by the government. Tort cases can involve injury to the person (assault and battery or infliction of emotional distress), injury to property (trespass, theft, conversion), injury to reputation, or some business advantage (slander and liable). (See Chapter 8 for a more detailed discussion on the differences between a civil case and a criminal matter.)

Author Tip ⟩ **A Familiar Illustration of Civil and Criminal Cases**

When O.J. Simpson was prosecuted for murder, the case was brought in the criminal courts by a prosecuting attorney. The case was called "The People vs. Simpson." However, Simpson was also sued in civil court by private attorneys hired by plaintiffs who were the family members of the victims. That case name had the title of the parties to the case: Sharon Ruffo, et al. vs. Simpson.

The fact that Simpson was found not guilty in the criminal case but guilty in the civil court also illustrated the difference between civil and criminal cases. In a criminal case, a prosecutor must convince all twelve jurors unanimously, beyond a reasonable doubt, the defendant is guilty. On the other hand, in a civil case, a plaintiff only needs to prove the case by a preponderance of the evidence, which is a much lesser standard. That standard means that it is more likely than not the plaintiff proved the case. Sometimes it is described as a standard whereby the plaintiff must prove the case by 51%. In civil cases, a plaintiff only needs nine jurors to agree, not all twelve.

The following table illustrates the differences between civil and criminal cases:

Subject	Criminal Case	Civil Case
Who brings the case	A government prosecutor	A private party normally though their attorney
Name of case	People vs. Smith (if state court) or the United States of America vs. Smith (if federal court)	Adams vs. Smith (the names of the parties)
Outcome if Plaintiff successful	Criminal sanctions including imprisonment, fine, and probation terms	Monetary damages. In some lawsuits, the plaintiff may be seeking injunctive relief.
Jurors who must agree with the plaintiff	All twelve-unanimous verdict	Nine jurors out of 12 (Although the number of jurors for a civil matter may differ depending upon the court and jurisdiction)
Standard of proof	Government must overcome the presumption of innocence by proving guilt beyond a reasonable doubt.	Plaintiff only needs to show their side is more convincing by a preponderance of the evidence, so that it is more probable they are right.

How to Obtain Civil Case Records

Obtaining civil records is similar to obtaining criminal records but with many more complications. Similar to criminal records, civil records are located at the county courthouse level in state court. Researchers locate records for civil lawsuits in the same fashion they search for criminal records. However, unlike criminal records, civil records can be more diverse geographically. A criminal case is brought where the crime occurred, which typically although not always means a consumer has some connection to the county. The rules for jurisdictions are broader for civil cases. For example, in a lawsuit for breach of contract, the suit can be brought where the contract was formed or breached. An applicant may not have lived in any of those places. Therefore, the location of civil record searches can take on a needle in a haystack quality. Published appellate cases where the lawsuit was appealed can also be searched. However, published appellate opinions represent an extremely small fraction of all civil cases.

Locating Identifiers

The next big problem is that civil records have very few identifiers. The initial search is by name match only, a similar problem to searching for federal criminal records, as explained previously. For example, if an Adam Smith is prosecuted for a crime in state court, there is likely going to be a date of birth or a driver's license somewhere in the court file. However, if Adam Smith is involved in a civil lawsuit as either a defendant or a plaintiff, identifiers are necessarily present in the file.

In order to determine if a civil record even belongs to the job applicant, it is often necessary to look for clues in the files. In most civil lawsuits, the allegation will contain a description of the party that is related to the reason for the legal action. So, if there is a lawsuit for medical malpractice, and the applicant is not a doctor, it is not likely such a legal action involves your applicant. The complication occurs when a court researcher goes to the courthouse; the researcher normally does not have the knowledge to determine from the lawsuit or other information in the file if the lawsuit pertains to your applicant. The researcher normally must ask the court clerk for a copy of the file. However, civil files can be very large and also very expensive to copy. Before getting surprised with a large bill for court clerk copies, an employer needs to determine how many pages are necessary. Usually, the first five or so pages will set out the identities and relationship of the parties. There may be other means in the court file to identify the parties, such as information on a summons or proof of service of the lawsuit, reference to employment, or data found in exhibits attached to the civil complaint. Getting copies of the file in order to review if it pertains to the consumer and is relevant can be time consuming and expensive.

Another option is to call an attorney involved with the case and ask for help on identification.

Utilizing Civil Records in Employment Decisions

The third issue is to determine if a civil lawsuit has any relevance to the position. Many civil lawsuits are clearly not job related. For example, if an applicant is a plaintiff (the person bringing the action against the defendant) in a personal injury lawsuit, this would not likely have a bearing on job performance (unless the applicant was suing a past employer and had a custom and practice of doing that). A civil search may uncover a case of dissolution of marriage. Often such lawsuits will have a detailed description where the parties are bringing out all the dirty laundry. As interesting as that might be to read from a human-interest point of view, it likely to have little bearing on employment.

Employers are likely looking for lawsuits that have some rational relationship to the job or workplace performance. These lawsuits can be directly job-related, such as a harassment suit by a former employee or character traits that may be involved in workplace behavior, such as lawsuits for violence or dishonest behavior.

Of course, as we have seen over and over again, nothing is as simple as it seems when it comes to public records. Every lawsuit has some sort of caption that indicates the court where it was filed, the parties involved, and the type of lawsuit. However, lawsuits in state or federal courts usually only have a rather cursory description of the nature of the action in the caption. The lawsuit may only be described as a "Suit for Damages." That tells a researcher nothing at all. In order to determine the underlying nature of the litigation, it is again necessary for the court researcher to request that the court clerk copies the first few pages where the essential thrust of the allegations of the lawsuit is usually recounted. The file could indicate, for example, if a person was being sued for harassment in the workplace, whether the defendant was the employer or manager. In addition, there can be civil suits just not made available to the public such as cases involving juveniles.

A fourth issue deals with civil lawsuits for lesser sums of money that may be filed in lower municipal courts or even in small claims court. That can include, for example, legal cases where damages are under $25,000. There are numerous lower and local courts that may hear such cases and the cases may or may not be linked to a central computer or index at the central courthouse and therefore are very difficult to find.

The bottom line: This is another tool that should be approached carefully. If a firm is hiring someone with a "C" in his or her title, such a search may have value. However, for other positions, civil lawsuits may not be a good use of time or resources.

Judgments, Liens, and Bankruptcies

Databases of judgment, liens, and bankruptcy records can be other valuable data resources.

Judgments are typically a final decision in court cases where the judge or jury awards monetary damages against the defendant. Often, the winning party will record the judgment with the county records clerk. Information provider firms have assembled national databases consisting of these judgments. The purpose is to allow employers to know an applicant has been sued. As with civil records, employers must approach this type of information with caution when using the records for employment purposes. First, the employer must make sure the judgment is valid. Next, the employer needs sufficient data to conclude that the judgment pertains to their applicant. Third, the employer must determine if the judgment is relevant to a job. Another problem is that judgment databases can have errors and be missing judgment records. In addition, the great majority of civil lawsuits are settled out-of-court, so there may not be a judgment entered.

Another search that some employers use is a search for **tax liens**. When a person or business owes delinquent, unpaid taxes to a government agency, the agency can record a tax lien that gives the government priority to collect upon the proceeds from the sale of real property. Like judgments, tax liens must be taken with a grain of salt. An employer must determine 1) if that tax lien data applies to the applicant, 2) if the data is accurate, and 3) if used for employment purposes, is it relevant and fair? Tax liens are generally found in the same state database that records Uniform Commercial Code (UCC) filings.

The third category is **bankruptcies**. All bankruptcy cases are heard in a federal court. The information is easily accessible; however, employers should exercise extreme caution in attempting to utilize these records. The argument against using bankruptcy for employment is that if a person went into bankruptcy to re-arrange their life but cannot get a job because of the bankruptcy, then that person could never get ahead. He or she would be placed in a new form of debtors' prison, unable to break the debt cycle.

Federal Court Case on Bankruptcy

The argument has been made that federal bankruptcy law prohibited the use of bankruptcy records for pre-employment because it prevented a person from having a "fresh start." A decision by the United States Court of Appeals for the Third Circuit in 2010 clarified the issue of whether a private employer can legally consider a job applicant's bankruptcy under U.S bankruptcy law in making an employment decision. The Court ruled that Congress intentionally only protected current employees from discrimination under bankruptcy law, and job applicants were not protected. In that case, the plaintiff applied for employment at a retail store, and it appeared he would be hired. However, after a bankruptcy was discovered, the employer refused to hire him due to the bankruptcy. The job applicant filed a lawsuit on the basis that under federal bankruptcy law, a consumer filing bankruptcy was entitled to a fresh start, and an employer could not discriminate against him based upon a bankruptcy.

The Court noted that there were two sections of federal law concerning bankruptcy and employment. Under 11 U.S.C. Section 525(a), Congress specifically stated that a governmental unit could not deny employment based upon a bankruptcy. (Note: U.S.C. stands for United States Codes, where federal laws are found. They are divided into titles, with Title 11 covering bankruptcy).

Congress later added a section 525(b) covering private employers that read:

(b) No private employer may terminate the employment of, or discriminate with respect to employment against, an individual who is or has been a debtor under this title…"

The section concerning private employers did not specify that a private employer could not deny employment due to bankruptcy. The job applicant argued that the term "discriminate with respect to employment" was board enough to protect job applicants as well as current employees. In addition, even though section 525(b) does not refer specifically to job seekers, such an interpretation is consistent with the reasoning of the section which intends to give someone a fresh start and not let the bankruptcy prevent employment. The applicant further argued the omission of the verbiage concerning denial of employment when it came to private employers was just an error in drafting.

The Court disagreed and noted that Congress clearly wrote the law so that the government may not "deny employment," but specifically declined to add the same language to the section concerning private employers. The Court reasoned that if Congress wanted to extend the same protections to consumers seeking jobs with private employers, then Congress could have used the same language used it used in section 525(a) in regards to government employment.

The Court noted that the United States Supreme Court has established a rule of statutory interpretation that "where Congress included particular language in one section of a statute but omits it in another section of the same Act, it is generally presumed that Congress acts intentionally and purposely in the disparate inclusive or exclusion."

In other words, Congress is presumed to know what was in 525(a) and could have used the same language in 525(b) in regards to private employers but chose not to. The Court ruled that where the language is clear, a Court's duty is to enforce a statute according to its language.

However, this case should not be seen as opening the floodgates for widespread use of bankruptcy information. A bankruptcy should still be used with caution. The case was litigated on just the basis that the actions were discriminatory under bankruptcy law. A job applicant could potentially file a claim of discrimination under Title VII if it can be shown that the use of bankruptcy creates a disparate impact on the basis of race, creed, color, nationality, sex, or some other prohibited criteria.

As with all pre-employment screening tools and assessments, bankruptcy should only be used if there is a business justification, meaning essentially that the tool is a valid predictor of job performance and does not have a discriminatory impact. Employers should still approach the use of bankruptcy with caution. A number of states have or are in the process of limiting the use of credit reports for employment due to concerns that it is being used unfairly. Such concerns can also arise if bankruptcies are used unfairly in a way not related to employment or that has the impact of treating members of protected groups unfairly. Employers may want to consider whether a bankruptcy is related to a bona fide occupational qualification BFOQ.

The case can be found at http://caselaw.findlaw.com/us-3rd-circuit/1548259.html.

Sex Offender Databases

The U.S. congress and the states have passed a series of laws to protect victims from sex offenders by requiring the registration and dissemination of information about sex offenders. The various federal laws for sex offenders are summarized on the Office of Justice Programs (OJP) Office of Sex Offender Sentencing, Monitoring, Apprehending, Registering, and Tracking (SMART) website at http://ojp.gov/smart/legislation.htm.

Megan's Law & Adam Walsh Act of 2006

The two most well-known laws are **Megan's Law** and the **Adam Walsh Act of 2006** which included a critical federal program called the Sex Offender Registration and Notification Act or SORNA.

Author Tip **Sex Offender Registration Complicated and Controversial**

The subject of registration of sex offenders and the dissemination/notification of information about registered sex offenders is both complicated and not without controversy. It is not the intention of this section cover the historical developments of these laws on the state and federal level. Nor will the chapter cover some of the current controversies, such as the effectiveness of these laws in preventing sex crimes, recidivism for sex offenders, or civil rights arguments that have been advanced. The purpose of this section is to introduce employers and volunteer organizations to the uses and limitations of sex offender data as it relates to making informed hiring decisions.

The most familiar law for most employers and organizations is called **Megan's law.** It was named after Megan Kanka, a seven-year-old New Jersey girl who in 1994 was lured into a neighbor's home and sexually assaulted and brutally murdered by a two-time convicted sex offender whose previous victims were also young children. Megan's law is both the name of a federal law passed in 1996 and the informal name for state laws that deal with the registration of sex offenders, as well as community notification and dissemination of information about the location of those offenders required to register.

Another important law is the federal *Adam Walsh Child Protection and Safety Act of 2006* which included the **Sex Offender Registration and Notification Act (SORNA)**, which introduced new sex offender registration standards for all 50 states. It also set up the Office of Sex Offender **Sentencing, Monitoring, Apprehending, Registering, and Tracking (SMART)** at http://ojp.gov/smart

According to its website (http://ojp.gov/smart/sorna), SORNA:

- Extends the jurisdictions in which registration is required beyond the 50 states, the District of Columbia, and the principal U.S. territories, to include also federally recognized Indian tribes.
- Incorporates a more comprehensive group of sex offenders and sex offenses for which registration is required.
- Requires registered sex offenders to register and keep their registration current in each jurisdiction in which they reside, work, or go to school.
- Requires sex offenders to provide more extensive registration information.
- Requires sex offenders to make periodic in-person appearances to verify and update their registration information.
- Expands the amount of information available to the public regarding registered sex offenders.
- Makes changes in the required minimum duration of registration for sex offenders.

The website for SORNA contains a map showing the level of compliance by states and entities showing the vast majority of states are not in compliance with SORNA's criteria. Even though some of the delays revolved around issues of how to treat juvenile offenders, there is still a significant amount of work to be done in most states.

More Information about Sex Offender Laws

More information about sex offender laws such as the Sex Offender Registration and Notification Act (SORNA) is available in the Addendum.

National Sex Offender Public Website (NSOPW)

As part of the Adam Walsh legislation, Congress set up the **Dru Sjodin National Sex Offender Public Website (NSOPW)**. According to the website at www.nsopw.gov/en/Home/About:

The Dru Sjodin National Sex Offender Public Website (NSOPW) is an unprecedented public safety resource that provides the public with access to sex offender data nationwide. NSOPW is a partnership between the U.S. Department of Justice and state, territorial, and tribal governments, working together for the safety of adults and children.

First established in 2005 as the National Sex Offender Public Registry (NSOPR), NSOPW was renamed by the Adam Walsh Child Protection and Safety Act of 2006 in honor of 22-year-old college student Dru Sjodin of Grand Forks, North Dakota, a young woman who was kidnapped and murdered by a sex offender who was registered in Minnesota.

NSOPW is the only U.S. government Website that links public state, territorial, and tribal sex offender registries from one national search site. Parents, employers, and other concerned residents can utilize the Website's search tool to identify location information on sex offenders residing, working, and attending school not only in their own neighborhoods but in other nearby states and communities. In addition, the Website provides visitors with information about sexual abuse and how to protect themselves and loved ones from potential victimization.

NSOPW's advanced search tool provides information about sex offenders through a number of search options:

- *Search by name nationally or with an individual Jurisdiction*
- *Search by address (if provided by Jurisdiction)*
- *Search by zip code*
- *Search by county (if provided by Jurisdiction)*

- *Search by city/town (if provided by Jurisdiction)*

NSOPW presents the most up-to-date information as provided by each Jurisdiction. Information is hosted by each Jurisdiction, not by NSOPW or the federal government. The search criteria available for searches are limited to what each individual Jurisdiction may provide.

All of the information provided through the NSOPW Website is maintained by the separate Jurisdictions, and NSOPW uses Web services to search the individual databases of the Jurisdictions in real-time when a search is conducted. This method ensures that NSOPW is returning the most current information. However, a conservative approach would be to verify information found via NSOPW by visiting the providing Jurisdiction's Public Registry Website for further information and/or guidance at www.nsopw.gov/en/Registry.

The NSOPW website also has an FAQ page at www.nsopw.gov/en/Home/FAQ. According to the FAQ page, each jurisdiction has its own rules and criteria in terms of sex offender registration. States categorize sex offenses in three levels, and only the more serious offenders are required to register. The NSOPW website also has a resources page that takes a user to the rules for each jurisdiction at www.nsopw.gov/en/Registry/Allregistries.

At first glance, it would appear that obtaining information about registered sex offenders would be very straight forward process. It would only require going to the National Sex Offender Public Registry (NSOPR), and running the name of the applicant or volunteer. Unfortunately, it is far from that easy for a number of reasons.

The single biggest issue is that the national approach to a unified system of registration and information dissemination has fallen far short of the national goals. The SORNA law envisions a uniform national system to improve uniformity and accuracy.

However, according to a report issued by the General Accounting Office (GAO) in February 2013, the majority of states have fallen well short of the goals set fight the Adam Walsh Act. Per the GOA report, only about 15 starts have submitted packages showing some degree of complaisance with SORNA. Many states have not even begun to address compliance. The GAO report *"SEX OFFENDER REGISTRATION AND NOTIFICATION ACT: Jurisdictions Face Challenges to Implementing the Act, and Stakeholders Report Positive and Negative Effects"* is available at www.gao.gov/assets/660/652032.pdf.

Summary of GAO Report on Sex Offender Registration

A summary of the highlights of the February 2013 General Accounting Office (GAO) report *"SEX OFFENDER REGISTRATION AND NOTIFICATION ACT: Jurisdictions Face Challenges to Implementing the Act, and Stakeholders Report Positive and Negative Effects"* is available in the Addendum.

When searching state sex offender sites, it is important to note each jurisdiction has its own laws that determine the information that can and will be displayed on the public registry Website.

Frequently Asked Questions (FAQs) about Sex Offender Searches

Are sex offender searches subject to accuracy issues?

Yes. In theory, a sex offender registration list through a state list, or done nationally on the National Sex Offender Public Website, includes the entire state. However, there are a number of problems with the accuracy and completeness of the data, similar to the issues described in Chapter 9 for criminal databases. The information is only as good as the data reported from the courts to the states. There can be both **false positives** and **false negatives**. A false positive is where there is a match, but upon further research, it is not the same person as the job candidate. A false negative is where a sex offender is not located, but in fact, the person is a sex offender. That is one reason why searchable websites, including those maintained by states, have disclaimers warning that records can be missed.

What are the reasons for a false negative?

False negatives can occur for a number of reasons.

- There can be an issue related to timing. An offender may be given a grace period to register, and if the registered sex offender applies for a job or volunteer opportunity during the grace period, the registration may not be picked up.
- If the person should have registered but did not, and the state did not track him or her down, then the current information may not be on the list.
- If a sex offender leaves a jurisdiction and goes elsewhere and does not register, the offender will not show up on the appropriate sex offender registry. Essentially, an offender can choose to take a chance and go underground. That person may roam free unless a law enforcement agency happens to encounter them and runs them through a computer that identifies them as a sex offender that did not register. Some jurisdictions are discussing ways to monitor the movements of sex offenders, such as electronic bracelets, which can be an expensive proposition if it works at all. Registering is often done through the "honor system," meaning that an offender is ordered to register initially by the court at sentencing, and then upon any change of address. Of course, if an offender chooses not to register, they are taking the risk that they will be caught. If they are still on probation or parole, that can be a violation. Even if probation or parole has ended, a failure to register can be a crime all by itself, assuming they are stopped by law enforcement and identified as an offender who failed register. A sex offender may want to take that chance.
- A difficulty with these registries is that each state does things its own way, and not all states do it as well as others. Many states have large holes in their databases. It is an immense task requiring substantial resources to track all offenders and a difficult challenge when law enforcement budgets are tight.
- States generally break down the sex offenders into tiers, and where a crime does not involve violence or acts committed on others, registration may not be required. Nearly all states place some limits based on the severity of the offense. **For example, most states divide offenses into three levels and will only require the more serious offenses, such as level 3 only, or levels 2 and 3, to register.** Or, in theory, a person may have committed a number of crimes, including a sex crime, and pursuant to a plea bargain, the sex crime may have been dismissed resulting in the person not being required to report.
- The date the database began can affect a search. In reviewing state databases, it is important to know when the database was started. Many states began their databases after 1997.
- Registration is not necessarily permanent. Depending upon the state, the offense, and the offender, registration requirements can be removed or may have a time limit.
- There can be errors in terms of the name or other details about the offender at the court or county level and how it is transmitted to the state or entered in the database. There can be a misspelling, an alias, a new name, or confusion about middle initials.
- The manner in which records are maintained by the state can also contribute to an error rate. Each state's central repository must collect data from local courts. If a county is late or inaccurate in any detail, then there can be errors.
- Photographic identification can be problematic. In many states, a photo may be provided, but the photo may be of poor quality. For an older offense, the photo may no longer match the person. Such issues may cause a screening firm to fail to identify a registered offender.

These reasons underscore the basic message—sex offender searches, although valuable, are far from perfect and should just be one element in the background screening process.

What are the reasons for false positives?

As in all public records, identifiers are critical before assuming that a criminal record belongs to a particular applicant. With approximately 320 million people packed into 50 states in the U.S., the statistical likelihood of people with the same name and same date of birth is higher than one might imagine. For this reason, an employer should never assume that an applicant is a sex offender without the positive proof of an ID match or pulling the underlying court record. Other name related issues include dealing with a common name, or a name with no middle initial, in making sure that any positive results are accurate before making a determination. For some common last names such as Smith or Jones, identification can be difficult.

Sometimes a screening firm will need to utilize additional measures to determine a subject is a match to someone on a sex offender database such as comparing a confirmed work history to a penal sentence. If it is confirmed that the person was employed while the sex offender was in custody, that can help to eliminate that applicant from being the person on the sex registry.

Additional FAQs about Sex Offender Registration Searches

Are there other data sources in addition to the National Sex Offender Public Registry?

Yes, there are data provider firms that have assembled large national databases composed of data from various state and local sources including sex offender databases. Sex offender data is normally included in the so-called national criminal searches discussed in Chapter 9. These searches include sex offender registration data. The commercial databases may contain information on individuals who have dropped off the state list due to time limits but are still on the commercial list since commercial lists are not routinely updated with subsequent case history. That can lead on occasions to legal concerns as to whether a matter is reportable as being registered.   On the other hand, some of the national database products may not provide a date of birth or other identifiers for all states, so an employer can be stuck with a name match only which would have to be confirmed by going to a more specific state database or pulling a court record. A best practice may be to use the sex offender information on a commercial database as another tool but to rely on the National Sex Offender Public Registry.

Another issue is whether an employer can rely just on the Department of Justice (DOJ) *National Sex Offender Public Website.* According to the DOJ, the national website accesses each state and therefore should negate the need to go directly to the state site. The national database is not an independent database but is a tool to search all states.   If a state site happens to be down during a national search, there should be a warning to that effect. However, there are still some employers who prefer to search relevant state database directly .

How does a sex offender search differ from a criminal search?

Both searches are looking for criminal records, but a sex offender search is limited to violations that require a person to register with a central authority. The state registry is a compilation of records of offenses that are sexual in nature and taken from counties across the state. Of course, a criminal search is looking at all criminal records regardless of nature or gravity regardless of whether registrations are required.

What should an employer do if a sex offender record is located?

The same rules apply as to any criminal records. First, the employer must ensure that they have positive ID so that they know the record belongs to their applicant. Next, the employer needs to determine if the applicant lied about a criminal record by reviewing the application and what was said in the interview. This is where the AIR Process discussed earlier proves so valuable. Third, the employer or volunteer group should pull a copy of the court file from the courthouse to ensure that the information is accurate and up to date and to ascertain the details. Finally, the employer must also consider if, under EEOC rules, there is a "business justification" for disqualifying the applicant based on the criminal conviction. For example, in California it is illegal to use the sex offender information unless there is an identifiable group at risk, meaning that there must be a job-related reason to utilize sex offender data. (See more about California below).

What if the underlying criminal case is too old to be reported or used, but the person is still registered?

That is a matter of some debate, but the better view seems to be that even if the underlying conviction is too old to report as a criminal conviction under applicable state laws, a person's current and up to date status as a registered sees offender is still a public record that is reportable. That is a question however that eventually may be cleared up by court decisions since there could be questions about whether such a practice violates the EEOC Guidance.

Examples of State Limitations on Sex Offender Registration Searches

The following are two state specific examples and limitations of importance: California and Nevada.

California Sex Offender Search Employment Screening Background Check

The use of the California Sex Offender Registration listing, commonly known as Megan's Law, is widespread among employers. However, *there is a little known provision in California that may actually limit an employer's legal use of this information in certain situations.*

The Megan's Law was first passed in 1996. Originally, information on sex offenders that register under California Penal Code Section 290 was only available by personally visiting police stations and sheriff's offices, or by calling a 900 number. The website at www.meganslaw.ca.gov was established by the California Department of Justice pursuant to a 2004 California law for the purpose of allowing the public for the first time to use their personal computers to view information on sex offenders required to register with local law enforcement under California's Megan's Law.

The purpose of Megan's law is summarized on the website:

California's Megan's Law provides the public with certain information on the whereabouts of sex offenders so that members of our local communities may protect themselves and their children. Megan's Law is named after seven-year-old Megan Kanka, a New Jersey girl who was raped and killed by a known child molester who had moved across the street from the family without their knowledge. In the wake of the tragedy, the Kankas sought to have local communities warned.

The California site allows anyone to search the database by a sex offender's specific name, obtain ZIP Code and city/county listings, obtain detailed personal profile information on each registrant, and use a map application to search their neighborhood or anywhere throughout the State to determine the specific location of any of those registrants on whom the law allows us to display a home address.

Megan's law contains a provision which prohibits the information to be used when it comes to insurance, loans, credit, employment, education, housing or accommodation or benefits or privileges provided by any business. California Penal Code Section 290.4(d) (2).

However, there is an exception. According to California law, a person is authorized to use information disclosed pursuant to this section only to protect **a person at risk.** California Penal Code Section 290.4(d) (1).

The problem for employers wishing to use this information is there is no legal definition for the term *a person at risk.* Neither the California Penal code, the legislative history of the section, or the Megan's law website defines a person at risk. Until a court provides a definition, employers are well advised to apply a common-sense approach by looking at risk factors associated with the nature of the job. For example, there is a widespread industry understanding of who are vulnerable individuals at risk, such as the young, the aged, the infirmed, or the physically or mentally disabled. In addition, people inside their own home are likely to be at greater risk, since it is harder to obtain help, so home workers may be considered a population that works with people at risk. Another category is workers that operate under some sort of badge or color of authority or who wears a uniform. In that situation, a person may let their guard down. Until a court makes a clear decision, employers should make an effort to determine if there is a good faith belief that it is reasonably foreseeable that a member of a group at risk could be negatively impacted if a sex offender was hired.

Of course, if the underlying criminal record is discovered and otherwise meets the many complicated rules governing the reporting and use of criminal records in California, then the at risk analysis may not be needed, and the employer can handle it like any other criminal record.

There are two other challenges for California employers using the Megan's law website:

- First, it is possible that a person may be registered as a sex offender, but their crime is beyond the 7 year California reporting provisions that restrict what a Consumer Reporting Agency can report. Although not yet tested in the Courts, the industry standard is for a screening firm to report the listing, on the basis that the background firm is reporting on the offender's current status as a registered sex offender.

- The other issue is that there are large numbers of sex offenders that either do not register, or abscond from the jurisdiction(s), or do not re-register. Some studies suggest a significant number of sex offenders did not have current registration and authorities have lost track of their whereabouts.

A California case also ruled a background screening firm has a constitutional right to report that an applicant has appeared on the Megan's Law website (MLW) as a registered sex offender. See: *Mendoza v. ADP Screening and Selection Services, Inc.*, (2010) 182 Cal.App.4th 1644.

The bottom line: When an employer is hiring an applicant for a position where it is foreseeable that there would be contact with members of groups at risk, then the sex offender database search can be valuable. However, employers should keep in mind that there are limitations that have yet to be fully defined by courts or the legislature, and the databases may not be up-to-date or 100% accurate.

Nevada Sex Offender Website Cannot Be Used for Employment

The Nevada Sex Offender Registry NV Megan's Law website (www.nvsexoffenders.gov) **contains sex offender information that cannot be used by an employer** and the dissemination of the information is a misdemeanor. The website indicates that all information is proprietary and copyrighted. When taken with the key Nevada Revised Statutes (NRS) copied below, it would seem information from the Nevada sex offender cannot be used.

NRS 179B.270 Restrictions on use of information. Except as otherwise authorized pursuant to specific statute, a person shall not use information obtained from the community notification website for any purpose related to any of the following:

- Insurance, including health insurance.
- Loans.
- Credit.
- Employment.
- Education, scholarships or fellowships.
- Housing or accommodations.
- Benefits, privileges or services provided by any business establishment. Embellished skill set – 57 percent

(Added to NRS by 2005, 2867)

NRS 179B.280   Misuse of information: Civil liabilities.   Any person who uses information obtained from the community notification website in violation of the provisions of NRS 179B.250or 179B.270 is liable:

1. In a civil action brought by or on behalf of a person injured by the violation, for damages, attorney's fees and costs incurred as the result of the violation; and

2. In a civil action brought in the name of the State of Nevada by the Attorney General, for a civil penalty not to exceed $25,000 and for the costs of the action, including investigative costs and attorney's fees.

(Added to NRS by 2005, 2868)

NRS 179B.290 Misuse of information: Attorney General may file action for injunctive relief:

1. If there is reasonable cause to believe that a person or group of persons has engaged in or is about to engage in any act or practice, or any pattern of acts or practices, which involves the use of information obtained from the community notification website and which violates any provision of this section, NRS 179B.250, 179B.270 or 179B.280, the Attorney General may file an action for injunctive relief in the appropriate district court to prevent the occurrence or continuance of that act or practice or pattern of acts or practices.

2. An injunction pursuant to this section: (a) May be issued without proof of actual damage sustained by any person; and (b) Does not preclude or affect the availability of any other remedy including, without limitation, the criminal prosecution of a violator or the filing or maintenance of a civil action for damages or a civil penalty pursuant to NRS 179B.280. (Added to NRS by 2005, 2868)

Source: www.leg.state.nv.us/nrs/nrs-179b.html#NRS179BSec270

Overall, a sex offender database search, both nationwide and using state and local websites, is an extremely valuable tool. It is especially valuable when the position involves access to a group-at-risk such as children, the elderly, the infirmed, or the challenged. However, employers and volunteer groups need to understand that these databases are not primary tools but supplemental tools subject to some degree of error and should be utilized with some caution and in conjunction with other safe hiring procedures.

Military Records

Another record that some employers may want to verify is a military service record. With the national focus on the military after the events in Iraq and Afghanistan, it is likely that employers will receive applications from those with military experience. Many employers realize applicants with military service provide critical skills and training which are extremely valuable in the workforce.

The standard way to verify military records is to ask an applicant for a copy of his or her DD-214. This is the common term for the document given to all members of the military who are discharged from the U.S. Navy, Army, Air Force, Marine Corp, or Coast Guard. The "DD" stand for Department of Defense. The short name is "discharge papers."

For employers who want more than a cursory confirmation of military service, the story goes much deeper. There are actually a number of different copies of the DD-214 with different pieces of information. A discharged service person receives copy 1, which has the least information. The copy with the codes that gives the nature of the discharge, i.e. General, Honorable, Dishonorable, etc. – and details of service is actually on copy 4. The codes characterize the service record of a veteran. The codes are known as SPD (Separation Program Designator), SPN (Separation Program Number), and RE (Re-Entry) codes. Other issues with access and use of the DD-214 are listed below.

- For a discharged service person to get copy 4, the person must actually ask for it.
- If a person did not ask for the copy 4 or wants to hide some embarrassing fact, then the person may only present copy 1 to an employer.
- If the employer wants copy 4, and the applicant does not have it, then there can be a problem acquiring and understanding the copy. The employer can have the applicant sign a Form 180 and send it to the National Personnel Records Center (NPRC) in St. Louis, Missouri. However, there can be a substantial wait—with a minimum of 90 days and potentially longer. Some records are no longer available due to a very destructive fire at the St. Louis facility in 1973, although the government has reconstructed some of the records by use of other military documents. For details about obtaining military records, see:
  o www.archives.gov/research_room/obtain_copies/veterans_service_records.html

- o   www.archives.gov/st-louis/archival-programs/archival-research-room.html
- Even after getting a copy 4, there is the issue of translating the military codes. There are websites that provide a complete list of the codes and definitions. However, should civilian employers use these codes for hiring decisions, since the codes were meant for internal military use only? The various codes may represent items that have no foundation, or were the result of clerical errors, or are simply not related to job performance.

When making hiring decisions, employers should be very careful before attempting to draw conclusions from various codes on the DD-214. Using the codes on the DD-214 to infer conduct in order to make hiring decisions could result in claims of discrimination or decisions being made based upon irrelevant or unsubstantiated criteria. The situation can be further complicated if the employers insist that an applicant first obtains a complete DD-214 and then rejects the applicant. That record request could potentially be viewed as evidence of discrimination.

An employer should also exercise caution in using a discharge as a basis for an employment decision. There are four common types of military discharges: honorable, general, undesirable, and dishonorable. Of these, only a dishonorable discharge is given as a result of a factual adjudication equivalent to a criminal trial. In order to avoid potential EEOC claims, an employer should treat a dishonorable discharge in the same fashion as a criminal conviction, taking into account the various factors reviewed in Chapter 10. A general discharge or undesirable discharge may or may not have any bearing on employment and generally should not be the basis for an employment decision.

The best advice may be to use the basic DD-214 to confirm a person was in fact in the military, then ask for the names of references from their military service to obtain job-related information that would be relevant to an employment decision and do a reference check.

A situation could occur where an employer is conducting an investigation post-hire as a result of an allegation of workplace misconduct wrongdoing. Although generally military service information can only be released with the consent of the subject or a next of kin, the Freedom of Information Act (FOIA) does allow a limited release of information to a member of the public that files a request although it is not clear that the timeframe would be helpful in an employment situation. See: www.archives.gov/st-louis/military-personnel/foia-info.html.

Security Clearances

On occasion, an employer may want to verify that an applicant had a security clearance in the past. This can occur when an employer receives an application indicating, as part of past qualifications, the applicant had a security clearance. The employer wants to confirm that the person is being truthful. Or, the new job may require a security clearance and the employer wants to ensure the applicant will be able to qualify for it.

An employer concerned about a security clearance may ask an applicant if they ever had a security clearance, if they had been refused one, and details about the last clearance held, including granting agent, level, date granted, and date expired. Security clearances are generally one of three types: Confidential, Secret and Top Secret. Details about security clearance, including various levels and how they are obtained, are beyond the scope of this book.

Individuals cannot apply for security clearance on their own. It can only be obtained through an authorized employer or a governmental agency. If the current job requires a security clearance, then there is already an established process in place for an employer to obtain the security clearance. Entities who have security clearance needs, such as private employers working for the government, will have an authorized designatee in charge of the process called a Special Security Officer (SSO).

Security clearances stay with the entity and do not travel with the individual. If the individual leaves a position, the person no longer has a clearance. If a person with a security clearance leaves one employer to go to another position that also requires a clearance, then the SSO at each entity may be able to arrange for the appropriate transfers.

If an employer wants to verify the past claims about a security clearance, a suggested procedure is for the employer or screening firm to contact the past employer and request the name and mailing address of the SSO. If a copy of a release is provided, then the SSO may verify that there was some level of clearance but may not go into detail.

Merchant Databases

Some firms offer a product commonly referred to as a merchant database which is typically used by large retailers who hire a large sales staff. These databases are created from data supplied by retail stores which contribute information about employees who have admitted to theft, whether or not a criminal case occurred. The databases may also contain other information such as records from various state criminal databases and Social Security Number information. These searches are relatively inexpensive, which is an advantage for employers. Since retail positions are often filled by lower-paid employees with high turnover rates, there is pressure on retailers to keep background screening as low cost as possible.

The difficulty with using these databases is the underlying reliability of the data. The databases will include information on individuals who were never prosecuted. The information is often based upon a report from a store loss-prevention employee concerning an interrogation where a person admitted they committed the theft in exchange for not being prosecuted. Since the matter did not go to court, there would not be a court file, police report, or any sort of adjudication in any factual matter.

Given the nature of these databases, there are two obvious problems with their use. First, use of such a database may run contrary to the EEOC rules, as explained in Chapter 3. An applicant may be the victim of a negative decision without any underlying factual determination. Considering the EEOC is concerned about the use of arrest records on the basis that an arrest is not a factual determination, unsubstantiated reports of a confession to store personnel are potentially troublesome.

The second issue is whether these databases are in fact FCRA compliant. Under the FCRA, a Consumer Reporting Agency (CRA) must take reasonable procedures to ensure accuracy. If information from a merchant database is a reported confession with no judicial findings, a CRA may have difficulty justifying the negative information unless it independently contacts the person performing the interview to confirm the facts. Otherwise, a person denied a job on the basis of a merchant database could claim a lack of reasonable procedures. The difficulty with relying upon confessions is that there is a large body of research that shows that false confessions are a significant issue in interrogations. Without other evidence such as recovery of stolen items or eyewitness confirmation, relying on confessions of theft as a basis for entry into a merchant theft database can be problematic. For more information, see *"Dangerous Confessions: The Psychology Behind False Confessions"* by Susan Davis, *California Lawyer*, April 2005.

As seen by the lawsuit explained below, one major supplier of this service suspended its merchant database service.

Lawsuit Over Retail Theft Database Settles for $2.38 Million

In August 2014, a Pennsylvania federal judge approved a settlement for $2.38 million in a class action lawsuit that alleged a retail theft database used for background checks wrongfully labeled job seekers as criminals even if they were not convicted of a crime.

U.S. District Judge Jan E. Dubois also had the background check firm involved in the case agree to suspend its retail theft database under terms of the settlement. The company also agreed to set more stringent requirements to protect job seekers if the database is used for employment background checks in the future.

The two lead plaintiffs alleged that the background check firm distributed damaging information from their retail theft database to current and prospective employers without proper safeguards in violation the Fair Credit Reporting Act (FCRA).

According to the lawsuit, one was denied employment based on information contained in the retail theft database while the other claimed she was denied a promotion and later fired based on retail theft database information, but was eventually reinstated.

The two lead plaintiffs also claim they never received the "pre-adverse action notice" required by the FCRA and were denied copies of theft admission statements on which the retail theft database reports are based, TopClassActions.com reports. Neither of the two lead plaintiffs was charged with theft.

Judge Dubois certified two Classes in the settlement. The first Class includes job seekers who received notice that a report contained negative retail theft database information. This Class is not eligible for compensation from the settlement but will be able to file individual lawsuits.

The second Class includes job seekers who never received a copy of the report after submitting a request or initiating a dispute. This Class of 2,916 people is eligible to receive checks for approximately $800 and retain the right to file individual lawsuits for damages.

The case information is *Goode, et al. v. LexisNexis Risk & Information Analytics Group Inc.*, Case No. 2:11-cv-02950, in the U.S. District Court for the Eastern District of PA.

Source: www.topclassactions.com/lawsuit-settlements/lawsuit-news/36229-lexisnexis-settles-esteem-retail-theft-database-class-action-lawsuit/

National Wants and Warrants

Until 2001, there was one portion of the FBI's National Crime Information Center (NCIC) database that was available to employers through pre-employment screening firms. The portion of the database available to employers was known as the National Wants and Warrants. The data contained information on fugitives wanted on federal warrants, also state warrants when a state was willing to extradite an offender back to the issuing state.

By allowing access to this database, law enforcement did not have to rely entirely on the strategy of chance encounter to apprehend wanted individuals. The primary method for apprehending wanted individuals in the United States is this strategy of **chance encounter.** Most warrants sit patiently in the system in the hope that someday the wanted person will come back into the grips of law enforcement on some chance encounter such as a traffic stop. Unfortunately, it is also possible the person will come to the attention of law enforcement for a new crime or that a wanted individual may commit more offenses. Because of budget restrictions and a host of other priorities, limited law enforcement resources are spent looking for individuals who are the subject of an arrest warrant.

Although the NCIC is no longer available through screening firms for private employers, some private firms are able to gather wants and warrants information directly from various local and state jurisdictions and make this data available. However, this data is subject to all the issues discussed in Chapter 10 on the use of criminal records.

Specialty Databases – Government

Another series of tools used by employers and screening firms are specialty databases with various disbarment or sanctions lists. Below is a summary of some of the more frequently utilized databases. The list is by no means exhaustive and is not presented here as an endorsement or recommendation, but used only to illustrate that such additional sources of informant exist.

OIG/GSA Name Search

The OIG/GSA Name Search is vital for most healthcare industries. Together, the OIG (Office of the Inspector General) Excluded List and GSA (General Services Administration) Sanctions Report search the U.S. Department of Health and Human Services and OIG databases for individuals and businesses excluded or sanctioned from participating in Medicare, Medicaid, and other Federally funded programs.

Expanded healthcare searches cover disciplinary actions taken by federal agencies as well as those taken by licensing and certification agencies in all 50 states. This is the most comprehensive search method available. See http://exclusions.oig.hhs.gov.

FACIS® (Fraud and Abuse Control Information Systems)

FACIS® (Fraud and Abuse Control Information Systems) is a database search of records containing adverse actions against individuals and entities sanctioned in the healthcare field. This includes information on disciplinary actions ranging from exclusions and debarments to letters of reprimand and probation. There are three levels, each with same day turnaround in most cases:

- Level 1 searches against the OIG and GSA and other federal agency sources of information.
- Level 2 searches those sources included in Level 1 plus agencies operating in one selected state.
- Level 3 searches all state and federal sources included in the FACIS® database.

A Level 3 search is the most robust search option to conduct a search of disciplinary actions taken by federal agencies as well as those taken by licensing and certification agencies in all 50 states. The FACIS® database contains information from 800+ source agencies and their databases. This information covers all 50 States on individuals who have been the subject of state licensing board and certification agency sanctions including FRA debarment. This information is helpful in assisting healthcare companies to avoid other potential liabilities and risks of employing or contracting with individuals who have been subject to performance of behavior problems elsewhere. It is not possible to obtain a definitive list due to the proprietary nature of the database. However, we are able to confirm or deny inclusion of a source on a specific state and or federal list via request. For high-risk individuals and contractors, or those who are directly involved in patient care such as physicians, nurses, physical therapists, etc., there are 800+ source agencies searched.

SAM and the Excluded Parties List System

The Excluded Parties List System (EPLS) is provided as a public service by General Services Administration (GSA) and includes information regarding entities debarred, suspended, proposed for debarment, excluded or disqualified under the non-procurement common rule, or otherwise declared ineligible from receiving Federal contracts, certain subcontracts, and certain Federal assistance and benefits, pursuant to the provisions of 31 U.S.C. 6101, note, E.O. 12549, E.O. 12689, 48 CFR 9.404, and each agency's codification of the Common Rule for Non-procurement suspension and debarment.

At the end of July 2012, access to the Excluded Parties List System (EPLS) was taken over by a new system. EPLS, along with Federal Agency Registration (FedReg), the Central Contractor Registration (CCR), and the Online Representations and Certifications Application (ORCA), were migrated into the new System for Award Management also known as SAM. For more information, please visit www.SAM.gov.

The Financial Industry Regulatory Authority (FINRA) Search

The Financial Industry Regulatory Authority (FINRA) Search will check the professional background of current and former FINRA registered securities firms and brokers through the Central Registration Depository (CRD®), the securities industry online registration and licensing database, as reported on industry registration/licensing forms which brokers, brokerage firms, and regulators complete. Additionally, this will also check for information about Investment Adviser (IA) firms through the Investment Adviser Registration Depository (IARD®), regulated by, and electronically registered with, the Securities and Exchange Commission (SEC) or state regulators. (NOTE: Central Registration Depository (CRD) or Investment Adviser Registration Depository (IARD) number required to ensure an exact match.)

Financial Institution Sanctions Search (FISS)

The following Federal government databases are searched for enforcement actions and orders against institutions or their affiliated parties:

- Board of Governors of the Federal Reserve System (FRB)
- Federal Deposit Insurance Corporation (FDIC)
- National Credit Union Administration (NCUA)
- Office of the Comptroller of the Currency (OCC)
- Office of Thrift Supervision (OTS)

Securities and Exchange Commission (SEC) Sanctions

Search by company name for SEC documents regarding Enforcement, Litigation, and Regulatory Actions. (NOTE: The Central Index Key (CIK) number if provided will ensure a more accurate search.)

MIB (Medical Information Bureau)

MIB Group, Inc. (formerly The Medical Information Bureau Inc.) is the only insurance consumer reporting agency in North America and operates a database of medical information on some individuals who have previously applied for health insurance, life insurance, disability insurance, critical illness insurance, and long-term care insurance. According to the Federal Trade Commission (FTC), MIB's member companies account for 99 percent of the individual life insurance policies and 80 percent of all health and disability policies issued in the United States and Canada. Under the FCRA, the MIB is categorized as a "nationwide specialty consumer reporting agency" and must provide an annual disclosure of credit reports to all consumers who request their files. See www.mib.com.

The Data Bank

The Data Bank, consisting of the National Practitioner Data Bank (NPDB) and the Healthcare Integrity and Protection Data Bank (HIPDB), is a confidential information clearinghouse created by Congress to improve health care quality, protect the public, and reduce health care fraud and abuse in the United States. See: www.npdb-hipdb.hrsa.gov/

National Practitioner Data Bank (NPDB)

The National Practitioner Data Bank (NPDB) was established by Title IV of Public Law 99-660, the Health Care Quality Improvement Act of 1986, as amended (Title IV). Final regulations governing the NPDB are codified at 45 CFR Part 60. In 1987 Congress passed Public Law 100-93, Section 5 of the Medicare and Medicaid Patient and Program Protection Act of 1987 (Section 1921 of the Social Security Act), authorizing the Government to collect information concerning sanctions taken by state licensing authorities against all health care practitioners and entities. Congress later amended Section 1921 with the Omnibus Budget Reconciliation Act of 1990, Public Law 101-508, to add "any negative action or finding by such authority, organization, or entity regarding the practitioner or entity." Responsibility for NPDB implementation resides with the Bureau of Health Professions, Health Resources and Services Administration, U.S. Department of Health and Human Services (HHS).

Healthcare Integrity and Protection Data Bank (HIPDB)

The Secretary of HHS, acting through the Office of Inspector General (OIG) and the U.S. Attorney General, was directed by the Health Insurance Portability and Accountability Act of 1996, Section 221(a), Public Law 104-191, to create the Healthcare Integrity and Protection Data Bank (HIPDB) to combat fraud and abuse in health insurance and health care delivery. The HIPDB's authorizing statute is more commonly referred to as Section 1128E of the Social Security Act. Final regulations governing the HIPDB are codified at 45 CFR Part 61. The HIPDB is a national data collection program for the reporting and disclosure of certain final adverse actions taken against health care practitioners, providers, and suppliers. The HIPDB collects information regarding licensure and certification actions, exclusions from participation in Federal and State health care programs, health care-related criminal convictions and civil judgments, and other adjudicated actions or decisions as specified in the regulation.

Specialty Databases – Private

DAC Reports

The DAC employment report is a detailed summary of a trucker's work history in the trucking industry. Most trucking companies today participate in sharing this information about truckers. HireRight (DAC Services) has a proprietary database of employer-contributed employment histories of commercial truck drivers. This assists trucking companies in fulfilling their DOT reference check requirements when hiring drivers. In addition, member truck driving schools contribute their students' performance to the database.

RentBureau®

Experian® RentBureau® collects updated rental histories from property management companies nationwide every 24 hours and makes that information available immediately to the multifamily industry. RentBureau provides property management companies and resident screeners a more accurate and complete picture of residents, leading to improved leasing decisions. To learn more, visit www.experian.com/rentbureau/renter-credit.html.

ChexSystems

ChexSystems is an eFunds check verification service and consumer credit reporting agency like Experian, Equifax, and TransUnion. While most credit reporting agencies broker data about how a consumer handles credit relationships, ChexSystems provides data related to how a consumer has handled deposit accounts at banking institutions. See: https://www.consumerdebit.com/consumerinfo/us/en/index.htm.

Terrorist Database Searches and The Patriot Act

The Post 9/11 World and Terrorist Search Procedures for Employers

Prior to the events of September 11, 2001, the topic of how not to hire terrorists was not on the radar of most employers. Although most Americans would have acknowledged—if asked before 9/11—that we live in a dangerous world, the danger had not significantly impacted American life to the extent it has after the attack on the United States.

Certainly, employers with defense and other sensitive government contracts have long been involved in dealing with security clearance. However, outside of security clearances, most employers were not focused on safe hiring from the point of view of keeping the U.S. safe from terrorists' harm. Employers in sensitive industries or sectors involved with the country's basic infrastructure have become concerned, post-9/11, with the potential risk that just one terrorist can have in their workplace. For example, a terrorist act could be aimed not only at airlines, but food and water supplies, transportation of hazardous materials, nuclear and other energy facilities, transportation, and a host of other vital industries.

Part of the problem is identifying who is a terrorist. Terrorists applying for jobs with U.S. employers are going to take measures to hide their true intentions and possibly their true identity. There is not a single accepted definition of the term terrorist. For purposes of American employers, the following definition from the Code of Federal Regulations is helpful. Terrorism is defined as:

> "…the unlawful use of force and violence against persons or property to intimidate or coerce a government, the civilian population, or any segment thereof, in furtherance of political or social objectives." *(See 28 C.F.R. § 0.85(l) which describes one of the general functions of the FBI within the Department of Justice at www.law.cornell.edu/cfr/text/28/0.85)*

The FBI further describes terrorism as either domestic or international, depending on the origin, base, and objectives of the terrorists. For example:

- Domestic terrorism is the unlawful use, or threatened use, of force or violence by a group or individual based and operating entirely within the United States or Puerto Rico without foreign direction committed against persons or property to intimidate or coerce a government, the civilian population, or any segment thereof, in furtherance of political or social objectives.
- International terrorism involves violent acts or acts dangerous to human life that are a violation of the criminal laws of the United States or any state, or that would be a criminal violation if committed within the jurisdiction of the United States or any state. These acts appear to be intended to intimidate or coerce a civilian population, influence the policy of a government by intimidation or coercion, or affect the conduct of a government by assassination or kidnapping. International terrorist acts occur outside the United States or transcend national boundaries in terms of the means by which they are accomplished, the persons they appear intended to coerce or intimidate, or the locale in which the perpetrations operate or seek asylum.

In 2005, the National Counterterrorism Center (NCTC), adopted the definition of **terrorism** that appears in 22 USC § 2656f(d)(2), "premeditated, politically motivated violence perpetrated against noncombatant targets by subnational groups or clandestine agents." (See www.law.cornell.edu/uscode/text/22/2656f).

Although employers currently tend to think of terrorists as being connected to events in the Middle East, the definition can be much broader. Another definition of terrorism from an online dictionary states:

"...the systematic use of terror or unpredictable violence against governments, publics, or individuals to attain a political objective. Terrorism has been used by political organizations with both rightist and leftist objectives, by nationalistic and ethnic groups, by revolutionaries, and by the armies and secret police of governments themselves."

Identifying terrorists and keeping them out of the workspace is a significant task for employers. It would be made easier, of course, if employers could assume the efforts by the federal government to keep terrorists out of the U.S. in the first place were 100% effective. The U.S. government is taking a number of measures to track terrorists in the U.S. and to prevent their entry in the first place. However, given the enormous numbers of people who are in the U.S. illegally, as well as the fact the U.S. has two very long borders—4,121 miles with Canada and 1,940 miles with Mexico—employers cannot simply assume terrorists will not be in the U.S. applying for jobs due to the unruly nature of larger scale databases. See The Bad News section later in this chapter.

Employers, especially those in vulnerable and critical industries, have no real choice but to consider the importance of terrorism in their hiring program.

Terrorist Databases – The Good and the Bad

The Good News

For employers without access to non-public government terrorist data, the most frequently used tool is a list provided by the U.S. Treasury Office of Foreign Assets Control (OFAC). The OFAC publishes a list of individuals and companies owned or controlled by, or acting for or on behalf of, targeted countries. Also listed are individuals, groups, and entities such as terrorists and narcotics traffickers designated under programs that are not country-specific. Collectively, such individuals and companies are called Specially Designated Nationals or SDNs. Their assets are blocked, and U.S. persons are generally prohibited from dealing with them. The OFAC list also has other designations, such as SDGT, standing for Specially Designated Global Terrorist. There are approximately 3,000 names on the list.

According to the OFAC website at https://www.treasury.gov/resource-center/sanctions/Pages/default.aspx.

"Prohibited transactions are trade or financial transactions and other dealings in which U.S. persons may not engage unless authorized by OFAC or expressly exempted by statute. Because each program is based on different foreign policy and national security goals, prohibitions may vary between programs."

There are public information provider firms who specialize in obtaining all the data that is publicly available from organizations that keep terrorist lists and then assemble all the information into a proprietary database. These databases are useful search tools for employers since they contain the OFAC list and many of the public "most wanted lists" issued by various organizations and generally available on websites. Below is a list of elements that could be found in a typical vendor's terrorist database:

OFAC Specially Designated Nationals (SDN) & Blocked Persons	OFAC Sanctioned Countries, including Major Cities & Ports
FBI Most Wanted Terrorists & Seeking Information	FBI Top Ten Most Wanted
Department of State Trade Control (DTC) Debarred Parties	Bank of England Sanctions List
Politically Exposed Persons List	OSFI - Canadian Sanctions List
U.S. Bureau of Industry & Security (formerly BXA)	United Nations Consolidated Sanctions List
Unverified Entities List	Denied Entities List & Denied Persons List
Non-Cooperative Countries and Territories	INTERPOL Most Wanted List
European Union Terrorism List	World Bank Ineligible Firms

As a practical matter, an employer may want to consider at least searching the following databases, which are easily available either online or through information or software providers:

- OFAC List—See https://sanctionssearch.ofac.treas.gov/.
- Denied Persons List—This list supplied by the United States Commerce Department indicate individuals and entities restricted from exporting from the United States. See: www.bis.doc.gov/dpl/default.shtm.
- OSFI List—This list supplied by the Canadian Office of the Superintendent of Financial Institutions contains names of individuals and organizations subject to the Regulations Establishing a List of Entities made under the Criminal Code or the United Nations Suppression of Terrorism regulations. See: www.osfi-bsif.gc.ca/eng/fi-if/amlc-clrpc/atf-fat/Pages/default.aspx.
- EU Terrorist List—www.consilium.europa.eu/en/policies/fight-against-terrorism/terrorist-list/.
- UN Terrorist List— https://www.un.org/sc/suborg/en/sanctions/un-sc-consolidated-list.

Interpol publishes a web page to check international wants and warrants at https://www.interpol.int/notice/search/wanted.

The Not So Good News

It would be an easy procedure for businesses to avoid hiring or dealing with terrorists just by going online and looking up the OFAC list. Unfortunately, searching this list is easier said than done for the following reasons:

- As mentioned, the OFAC data is maintained at https://sanctionssearch.ofac.treas.gov/. Anyone can access it. However, as a practical matter, most private employers find the search difficult and time consuming. As alternatives, there are a number of private firms who provide Patriot Act compliance services that regularly assemble the OFAC data and make it available to employers and businesses through various web-based and computerized solutions that are combined with other data.

- The OFAC search, although valuable, does not include other terrorist search tools from other organizations and governments.
- Positive identification can be difficult. The OFAC search provides as much data as possible, but it is not always sufficient. The names are often of Middle Eastern origin, and the identifiers are not always sufficient to make a determination as to identity. Typically, international terrorists on the OFAC list do not have valid Social Security numbers.

OFAC provides a Frequently Asked Questions webpage and outlines steps to take in the event of a possible match. The FAQ that follows tell financial institutions what to do if there is a hit. The information is very useful for employers.

OFAC Frequently Asked Questions

If you are calling about an account:

Step 1. Is the hit or match against OFAC's SDN list or targeted countries, or is it hitting for some other reason, (i.e., Control List or PEP, CIA, Non-Cooperative Countries and Territories, Canadian Consolidated List (OSFI), World Bank Debarred Parties, or government official of a designated country) or can you not tell what the hit is?

- If it is hitting against **OFAC's SDN list or targeted countries**, continue to Step 2 below.
- If it is hitting for some other reason, you should contact the "keeper" of whichever other list the match is hitting against. For questions about:

    The Denied Persons List and the Entities List, please contact the Bureau of Industry and Security at the U.S. Department of Commerce at 202-482-4811.

    The FBI's Most Wanted List or any other FBI-issued watch list, please contact the Federal Bureau of Investigation. (www.fbi.gov/contact/fo/fo.htm)

    The Debarred Parties List, please contact the Office of Defense Trade Controls at the U.S. Department of State, 202-663-2700.

    The Bank Secrecy Act and the USA PATRIOT Act, please contact the Financial Crimes Enforcement Network (FinCEN), 1-800-949-2732.

- If you are unsure whom to contact, then you should contact your interdict software provider which told you there was a "hit."
- If you can't tell what the "hit" is, you should contact your interdict software provider which told you there was a "hit."

Step 2. Now that you've established that the hit is against OFAC's SDN list or targeted countries, you must evaluate the quality of the hit. Compare the name of your account holder with the name on the SDN list. Is the name of your account holder an individual while the name on the SDN list is a vessel, organization or company (or vice-versa)?

- If yes, you do not have a valid match.*
- If no, please continue to Step 3 below.

Step 3. How much of the SDN's name is matching against the name of your account holder?

Is just one of two or more names matching (i.e., just the last name)?

- If yes, you do not have a valid match.*
- If no, please continue to Step 4 below.

Step 4. Compare the complete SDN entry with all the information you have on the matching name of your account holder. An SDN entry often will have, for example, a full name, address, nationality, passport, tax ID or cedula number, place of birth, date of birth, former names, and aliases. Are you missing a lot of this information for the name of your account holder?

- If yes, go back and get more information and then compare your complete information against the SDN entry.

- If no, please continue to Step 5 below.

Step 5. Are there a number of similarities or exact matches?

- If yes, please call the hotline at 1-800-540-6322.

- If no, then you do not have a valid match.*

* If you have reason to know or believe that processing this transfer or operating this account would violate any of the Regulations, you must call the hotline and explain this knowledge or belief. [08-22-07]

FCRA, EEOC, and Terrorist Searches

All employment screening is conducted under the federal Fair Credit Reporting Act (FCRA), which requires the use of reasonable procedures to assure maximum accuracy. A terrorist search may contain many common names and not provide the sufficient identifiers to determine if a match belongs to an applicant. As indicated in Step 5 above, OFAC also has a hotline to assist employers in the event of a possible match where there are insufficient identifiers on the search results.

In addition, employers need to be aware that a large number of names may be of Middle Eastern origin. Under the FCRA, a background screening may not be used in violation of any state or federal anti-discrimination laws. As a result, it is important that all efforts be made to determine if there is a positive match before taking any adverse action. This can prevent an employer from being the subject of a complaint for discrimination in hiring based upon national origin or ethnicity.

The EEOC issued a press release on this topic following the September 11, 2001, terrorist attacks:

EEOC Chair Urges Workplace Tolerance in Wake of Terrorist Attacks

WASHINGTON - In the wake of this week's tragic events, Cari M. Dominguez, Chair of the U.S. Equal Employment Opportunity Commission (EEOC), called on all employers and employees across the country to promote tolerance and guard against unlawful workplace discrimination based on national origin or religion.

"We should not allow our anger at the terrorists responsible for this week's heinous attacks to be misdirected against innocent individuals because of their religion, ethnicity, or country of origin," Chair Dominguez said. "In the midst of this tragedy, employers should take time to be alert to instances of harassment or intimidation against Arab-American and Muslim employees. Preventing and prohibiting injustices against our fellow workers is one way to fight back, if only symbolically, against the evil forces that assaulted our workplaces Tuesday morning."

EEOC encourages all employers to do the following:

- Reiterate policies against harassment based on religion, ethnicity, and national origin;

- Communicate procedures for addressing workplace discrimination and harassment;

- Urge employees to report any such improper conduct; and

- Provide training and counseling, as appropriate.

Ms. Dominguez exhorted all individuals to heed the words of President Bush, who said yesterday: "We must be mindful that as we seek to win the war [against terrorism] we treat Arab-Americans and Muslims with the respect they deserve."

EEOC enforces Title VII of the Civil Rights Act of 1964, which prohibits discrimination in employment on the basis of race, color, religion, national origin, sex, and retaliation for filing a complaint. For example, Title VII precludes workplace bias based on the following:

- Religion, ethnicity, birthplace, culture, or linguistic characteristics;

- Marriage or association with persons of a national origin or religious group;

- Membership or association with specific ethnic or religious groups;

- Physical, linguistic or cultural traits closely associated with a national origin group, for example, discrimination because of a person's physical features or traditional Arab style of dress; and

- Perception or belief that a person is a member of a particular national origin group, based on the person's speech, mannerisms, or appearance.

"Our laws re-affirm our national values of tolerance and civilized conduct. At this time of trial, these values will strengthen us as a common people," Ms. Dominguez said. "The nation's workplaces are fortified by the enduring ability of Americans of diverse backgrounds, beliefs, and nationalities to work together harmoniously and productively."

The EEOC press release is online at www.eeoc.gov/eeoc/newsroom/release/9-14-01.cfm.

The Bad News

When private employers utilize publicly available lists for terrorist searches, there are four areas of "bad news."

- As discussed in detail in Chapter 9, any criminal record database has inherent limitations. There are *issues as to timeliness, accuracy, and completeness*. There is no way to know how long it takes for a name to be "approved" to be entered onto the list. In addition, the mechanics of a government agency making a decision that a person is a terrorist is not generally public information. Names can fall through the cracks.
- *Terrorists can circumvent the databases*. If a person is a terrorist, then this person probably knows that he or she may be on a government watch list. A terrorist attempting to obtain employment at an American facility will have a fake name, driver's license, Social Security card, or other false identification. As a result, the bad news is that a determined terrorist may figure out a way around a terrorist database search. For a more detailed discussion on the problems associated with identity fraud, see Chapter 22.
- Employers need to understand a terrorist database is subject to a high rate of *false positives and false negatives*. As explained previously, a false positive means someone is incorrectly identified (as a terrorist or criminal). A false negative is when a person who should have been identified as a risk and stopped for further inquiry was not and was allowed through. This can happen for a number of reasons. Terrorist databases may have a number of name variations and spellings that can lead to names being mixed. Since many names on the terrorist lists are from other countries, there is the issue of translating the person's name into an English version. Terrorists may purposely alter spellings of their name. Since the terrorist may have false ID's or foreign ID's, the number that appears may not be a number consistent with the numbering scheme of legitimate ID's—the terrorist's ID would be a false document. On the other end of the spectrum, it is entirely possible to have "computer twins," where two different people have the same names and the same birthday, which means at least one false positive.
- A terrorist database search can potentially create a false sense of security if employers do not fully understand the *inherent limitations in a terrorist database*. As in a criminal database, just because a name is not in the database does not mean the applicant is not a threat. At the same time, just because a person's name is in a

database does not mean it is that person. A database search is only one tool and is most beneficial when used as part of a series of overlapping hiring tools.

Use All the Tools

As with all safe hiring techniques, no one tool is the complete answer. Besides using the terrorist databases and lists such as OFAC as a measure of safety against hiring terrorists, an employer should use the various employment screening procedures suggested in this book.

- A strong AIR (Application /Interview /Reference checking) Process.
- A minimum seven-year criminal check for all jurisdictions where an applicant has lived, worked, or studied. Include both federal and state criminal convictions.
- A national criminal index search as described in Chapter 14.
- A Social Security trace (or an address information manager search) that utilizes a number of databases including credit bureaus' files for a list of all names and addresses associated with a particular Social Security number. This is particularly important to guard against fake identification documents. It is also critical to review the times that addresses were reportedly used in conjunction with the SSN to look for unexplained gaps in a person's whereabouts. (However, as discussed in Chapter 11, the trend for screening firms is not to provide the address information due to accuracy concerns under the federal Fair Credit Reporting Act.)
- Consent Based Social Security Verification (CBSV).
- Verification of employment for the past five to ten years.
- Verify education and any special credentials.
- A driver record search.
- Complete the I-9 process.
- Social media searches as outland in Chapter 14, although that is subject to the limitations noted in the chapter.

The I-9 Process

If a person is made a conditional offer of employment, then it is also critical to make sure the **I-9 process** is completed. This process, by which an employer verifies a person's eligibility to work in the U.S., is done pursuant to rules prepared by the Immigration and Naturalization Service. This also provides an employer a great deal of protection against someone who may be using a fake identity. As part of the I-9 process, the employer can also contact the Social Security Administration and verify the Social Security number. See Chapter 17 on how employers can contact the Social Security Administration after a conditional job offer has been made.

Consent Based Social Security Number Verification Service (CBSV)

With the consent of the Social Security number (SSN) holder, enrolled users may **utilize Consent Based Social Security Number Verification Service (CBSV)** as part of a pre-employment screening program to verify whether the SSN holder's name and Social Security number (SSN) combination match Social Security Administration (SSA) records. CBSV returns a yes or no verification indicating that the submission either matches or does not match our records. If SSA records show that the SSN holder is deceased, CBSV returns a death indicator. CBSV verifications do not verify an individual's identity.

For more information on CBSV, read the CBSV section in Chapter 21 'Dealing with Fraud, Embezzlement, and Integrity,' or visit the CBSV page on the Social Security Administration at www.ssa.gov/cbsv.

Past Employment Verification – The Key to Protecting Vital Industries from Terrorists

Of all the available tools an employer can use, verifying past employment is probably the most critical. For example, this screening tool could have most likely raised a red flag had any of the 9/11 terrorists applied for employment in a critical industry.

Chapter 22 discusses the nature of identity. When determining who a person really is and what history to attach to them, the least meaningful source of information is what the person says about himself. However, as you check public records, the reliability factor increases. Validations from past employment and education checks give the employer more confidence that a person is who he says he is—and has the history he claims.

The problems with spotting a potential terrorist, however, are as follows:

- They are more likely than most to attempt to thwart safe hiring techniques by misrepresenting themselves and attempting to conceal their true identities and purpose.
- They are more likely to be presenting false identification information and documents.
- There is likely to be less info about the terrorist in the normal domestic database searches.
- Terrorist databases can be circumvented.

The government has warned about "sleeper" terrorists, potential terrorists who have fit into American society and are waiting to be told to take some course of action. If a "sleeper" terrorist applies for a job not requiring a security clearance, then he or she may well be a perfectly honest applicant with nothing to indicate a secret mission. If the government with their resources cannot identify them, then employers are at a distinct disadvantage.

As a result, it is arguably more difficult for employers to prevent the hiring of terrorists than someone with an unsuitable criminal record or falsified credentials. Even though there are substantially fewer terrorists likely to apply to a vital infrastructure employer, the harm can be substantial.

The key is past employment calls. By calling to verify past jobs for the past five to ten years, an employer verifies the applicant's general whereabouts and general accuracy of his or her job history.

Author Tip ⟩ **Trusted Source**

Since information from applicants and databases may not be trusted sources, where can employers turn? The ultimate key to verification of identity and history stems from obtaining information from a "trusted source." For more information about the **"trusted source rule"** see Chapter 22.

Where does this trusted source come in? A researcher doing a past employment check has the ability to access a directory assistance, a printed phonebook, or some other source of information that is generally considered reliable and would be extremely difficult to for an outsider to manipulate. By utilizing a telephone listing independently obtained and calling that past employer, it can be confirmed that the past employers exist and the phone number, in fact, belongs to a legitimate firm.

Although it may sound like a slender thread, the possibility of terrorists, such as the 9/11 hijackers, setting up a five-year to ten-year employment history just to weasel their way into a job in a sensitive industry is remote. It is not impossible, but it would require considerable effort.

To avoid such a possibility, employers in sensitive industries may consider the following certain steps. Once the information is obtained, the researcher should then review the confirmed information, matching it to data known about the applicant—developing a pattern for looking for consistencies or inconsistencies. The employer should develop a protocol to cross-check applicants and other screening materials. For example:

- Does the job history match the address and the Social Security trace? The Social Security trace shows address and name associated with an applicant. If an applicant has a long job history, then the dates and locations should correspond to the information on the trace. The dates must be viewed as a whole to see if it is inherently consistent. In other words, the employer needs to see if the dots connect and all the information makes sense.

- A person claiming to have been self-employed for the past five to ten years creates additional challenges, requiring verifications from trusted sources in the information path. The recommended procedure is to contact customers of the applicant's businesses, and verifying the existence directly by phone. Even more important is to develop references. Call the references supplied by the applicant, and ask those supplied references if they know other clients of the self-employed applicant who can confirm if he was in business.

- With enough resources, know how, and planning, it is possible for a would-be terrorist to set-up an elaborate ruse. A person would need to start a company for the purpose of being in the phonebook, and then an accomplice posing as a legitimate reference would have to stand by to deliver a credible reference when the new prospective employer should happen to call. Of course, when calling past employers, a researcher needs to use common sense and be on the alert for conversations that do not sound businesslike and correct.

A suspected terrorist could set up an elaborate ruse to pass the reference check, and this underscores the inherent difficulty faced by private employers. If the government, with all of its resources, did not detect the terrorist in the United States in the first place, then private employers are certainly at a disadvantage. However, employers can place as many barriers as possible in the way of potential terrorists in order to undermine their efforts or to force would-be terrorists to foul up in their intent to hide their identity or true purpose.

Conclusion

The bottom line—American employers must do what they are able to do to protect the United States.

CHAPTER 14

Social Media Background Checks

The Social Media Explosion

No discussion on employment screening background checks these days is complete without an analysis of how the Internet and **social media** is used for uncovering information about job candidates. Recruiters and employers can harvest information from a variety of social networking sites like Facebook, Google+, and Twitter. Applicants may reveal themselves, in numerous other places ranging from blogs and YouTube videos to business connection sites such as LinkedIn and search engines like Google. Many employers have focused with laser-like intensity on using the plentiful amount of information found online.

Much of this has come about due to the advent of the so-called **Web 2.0**. That term refers to the evolution of the web where social interactions and conversations can occur as opposed to Web 1.0 pages that contained information that viewers simply viewed.

Employers and recruiters believe they are effectively able "to look under the hood" and try "to get into an applicant's head" using what appears to be a treasure trove of job applicants' information on the Internet. Unlike traditional hiring tools such as interviews and contacting past employers, Internet searches and social networking sites hold out the promise of revealing the "real" job applicant. Statistics from various surveys and anecdotal evidence confirm there is an increased interest and use of social media to screen candidates.

The main walk away point for this chapter: Although Internet and social media searches can have immense value for recruiting and screening, there are significant legal and practical risks and pitfalls lurking out there for businesses that do not develop a strategy ahead of time. Employers, recruiters, hiring managers, and anyone else involved in talent acquisition should not simply jump on the Internet and start searching, screening, sourcing, or recruiting without first having reviewed the potential issues and danger areas and then come up with a plan to maximize the benefits and minimize the risk.

This chapter attempts to provide an informative introduction for both employers and recruiters using Internet search engines and social networking sites for recruitment and employment screening background checks. The chapter examines the possible legal and practical risks and pitfalls faced when conducting such **social media background check** screening, as well as potential solutions to avoid legal issues. The chapter finally reviews various options employers, recruiters and job seekers may consider when using the Internet for job screening.

In addition to the legal risks, there are also practical reasons to be concerned about the use of social media websites. In the *war for talent*, where attracting applicants and providing a positive experience is crucial, using the Internet and social networking sites has the potential to hurt the employer's brand if not done right. In addition to the legal pitfalls discussed in this chapter, news travels fast on the web, and employers who misuse social networking sites risk alienating otherwise good candidates if the employer's behavior is viewed as intrusive or unfair.

> **Author Tip**
>
> ### Use of Social Media also a Critical Post-Hire Issue
>
> This chapter discusses the use of social media only in the context of employee recruiting and selection. However, employers also need to recognize that the use of social media, along with related privacy issue, are critical issues **post-hire**. A **social media policy** for current employees needs to address issues such as: Who owns the company computer and what right of privacy does an employee have (i.e. can an employer monitor Internet use and emails)? What is acceptable blogging/posting policy for employees? What happens if an employee posts a derogatory comment about the employer or reveals confidential information? If the employers are unionized, how does that affect the social media policy?
>
> Post-hire social media policies are beyond the scope of this book. However, since they are so critical in today's online world, every employer needs one. A starting place for employers to build a social media policy is on the website for the National Labor Relations Board (NLRB) at www.nlrb.gov/news-outreach/fact-sheets/nlrb-and-social-media. The NLRB has been active in this area since online usage policies could potentially violate the right of workers to discuss terms and conditions of employment.

The Basics of Social Media Searches

The following are some of the basic concepts surrounding social media searches that should be understood before getting in the potential risk areas.

1. What are the advantages of social media screening?
2. What is the extent of social media use in the U.S. by consumers?
3. What social media sites are employers reviewing?
4. How many employers are using the Internet and social media in hiring?
5. Are there employers who purposely avoid social media?
6. Is use of social media impacted by the type of employer or position?
7. Is there a difference between using social media for recruiting and screening?
8. What are the practical challenges for locating information?
9. Who is doing the searching?
10. What would cause an employer to view an applicant in a negative matter?
11. Can social media help an applicant get hire?
12. Since social media is new, have courts and laws kept up with the pace of change?

1. What are the advantages of social media screening?

One of the recurring themes in this book is that hiring the right person is mission critical for any employer. The use of Internet searches and social media is another tool available to employers to try to identify a good hire and to avoid a bad hire. It does not replace a background check or other hiring tools, but rather locates information from publicly available online sources that may not otherwise be revealed in the traditional hiring processes or a standard background check.

For example, a review of social media sites may reveal a person's character and behavior. Firms specializing in these searches report that it can be used to identify individuals who have demonstrated bigotry, bullying, or support for organizations that are contrary to an employer's best interest. By locating this information, an employer can hope to avoid a bad hire and all the associated problems. Another use is to uncover discrepancies between an applicant's claimed attributes and what is discovered online. It is an open issue if a failure to utilize these social networking sites when a search could have revealed relevant information could arguably expose an employer to claims of negligent hiring. That is an area of law employers will need to track.

2. What is the extent of social media use in the U.S. by consumers?

"Social media" is defined as forms of electronic communication such as Web sites for social networking and microblogging through which users create online communities to share information, ideas, messages, and other content such as videos. An important trend is that social media is not just for "young" people anymore, defined as the 18-29-year-old age group. Social media is incredibly popular with 78 percent of online adults in the 30-49 age group and 55 percent in the 50-64 age group using social networking sites as of September 2013. (See: Pew Internet Project Social Networking Fact Sheet at www.pewInternet.org/fact-sheets/social-networking-fact-sheet/). The following are some of the most popular social media websites currently (*Statistics from Wikipedia.org):

Social Media Website	Estimated Users*
Facebook (www.facebook.com)	1.79 billion monthly active users as of September 2016
YouTube (www.youtube.com)	More than one billion users as of September 2016
Twitter (http://twitter.com/)	More than 310 million active users as of March 2016
Instagram (www.instagram.com)	Over 300 million active users as of December 2014
Snapchat (www.snapchat.com)	More than 150 million daily active users in 2016
Google+ (http://plus.google.com/)	111 million active users as of April 2015
LinkedIn (www.linkedin.com)	106 million active users as of September 2016

3. What social media sites are employers reviewing?

According to a study released by the Society for Human Resources Management (SHRM) in January of 2016 entitled *'Using Social Media for Talent Acquisition—Recruitment and Screening,'* LinkedIn (96 percent), followed by Facebook (66 percent), and Twitter (53 percent) are most frequently used social media websites for recruiting, and likely the top sites used by employers for screening. Other sites include Google+, YouTube, and sites that are specific to an industry or occupation. Although there are numerous additional sites that can be searched, those are the ones that seem to contain the bulk of information used by employers. The SHRM study is available at www.shrm.org/hr-today/trends-and-forecasting/research-and-surveys/Pages/Social-Media-Recruiting-Screening-2015.aspx.

Research Shows How Many Employers Use the Internet for Screening

Attached in the addendum are various studies on the use of Internet searches and social media released by organizations such as CareerBuilder, Microsoft, and SHRM. The studies provide useful insight into how employers and recruiters utilize these sources of information.

4. How many employers are using the Internet and social media in hiring?

Per the annual CareerBuilder social media recruitment survey released in April 2016 (summarized in the Addendum), some 60 percent of employers are using social media to research job candidates in 2016, up significantly from 52 percent in 2015, 22 percent in 2008, and 11 percent in 2006, when the survey was first conducted. Although other studies have arrived at different figures, it seems indisputable that the trend line is showing an increase in social media use. That should not be surprising considering just how easy it is to jump online and start researching people.

5. Are there employers who purposely avoid social media?

The studies also show by comparison that there are some employees who have intentionally decided NOT to use social media. Per the SHRM survey, the top reasons are:

- Concerns about the legal risks of discovering information about protected characteristics such as age, race, gender, and religious affiliation.
- Concerns about verification with confidence that the information from the social networking website pages of job candidates.
- Concerns that the information found online may not be relevant to a job candidate's work-related potential or performance.
- Concerns over invasion of privacy rights.

As discussed below, these concerns can be well founded although there are solutions to protect employer that will be reviewed.

6. Is use of social media impacted by the type of employer or position?

Yes. As the studies in the addendum show, certain sectors are more likely to use social media than others for certain types of positions. Essentially, the highest users are larger private sector firm hiring for positions that involve higher risk. For example, employers that provide technical, scientific or professional services are more likely to check out social media than hospitality, food service or construction. Other industries with higher usage can include health care, and finance. Given the free and widespread availability of social media and Internet searches, employers of any size in any industry can use it for any position, but the overall trends seem to suggest that its use is related to the risks involved in the position.

7. Is there a difference between using social media for recruiting and screening?

In reviewing your social media and Internet search policy pre-hire, it is critical to understand the difference between using social media for recruiting and for hiring.

The difference between using social media and Internet searches by recruiters as opposed to HR is a matter of timing—where the search occurs in the hiring process. Hiring occurs in a continuum and recruiting is at the beginning end of the timeline.

Recruiters will use social media to find passive candidates. A "passive" candidate is a person not actually searching for a new job, but may be willing to respond to a new opportunity if presented. To find passive candidates, a recruiter needs to source numerous websites to find potential candidates in order to initiate contact. At the recruiting stage, a recruiter obviously does not have consent. However, during the sourcing process a recruiter may well see information about a candidate from various online sources that may reflect a person's membership in a protected group. Online searches may reveal a candidate's, age, race, nationality, ethnicity, sex, marital status and numerous additional prohibited criteria.

If recruiters use social media for sourcing or screening, they should realize that much of the 'new media' available to them is still covered by current employment regulations.

Recruiters may believe that if a passive job candidate not actively looking for work is passed over because of discriminatory criteria revealed on a social network site, the candidate is not harmed since they did not even know they were disregarded and are none the wiser. The problem with that approach is three-fold.

1. First, discrimination and civil rights laws would likely still apply, even in recruiting passive candidates. Discrimination rules apply to the entire hiring process, and a recruiter would be hard pressed to argue there is a "recruiter's exception" to discriminatory practices.
2. Second, there are few secrets in the world. If a firm is using discriminatory criteria, a member of the recruiting team who feels uncomfortable about such a practice may well say something – either publicly on the web or within the organization.

3. Third, it can be argued that discriminatory criteria were being used if it turns out that the entire workforce happens to be homogeneous and does not include members of protected classes. Such a statistical anomaly could suggest a pattern of discrimination.

On the other side of the spectrum are Human Resources departments, hiring manager or others who are making decisions about applicants who are under active consideration in the company's hiring pipeline. These candidates have either applied for a position with the company or have been recruited and are now under active consideration and in the candidate pool.

Candidates in the active pipeline are potentially subject to an Internet and social media check by the potential employer as part of the hiring process.

This important difference between reciters who are operating at the start of the process, and HR and hiring managers who are screening active candidates, will become more important later when discussing optimal strategies for the use of intent searches and social media searches.

8. What are the practical challenges for locating information?

There are several challenges in searching social media and the Internet for applicant selection:

- There are millions of records. Trying to find useful data on the Internet at times can be like looking for a very small needle in several very large haystacks.
- It can be very difficult to determine if an item on the Internet is even associated with your applicant. As discussed later, there can be substantial issues as to identity and authenticity. Unless your applicant uses his or her real name or provides enough information to identify themselves sufficiently, it can be difficult determine what information belongs to which person.
- Applicants can easily go on the Internet anonymously or mask their identity, by such techniques as using an assumed name, enhanced privacy settings, operating on social media sites where access is limited by permission.
- Even if something is found that can be attributed to your applicant, it may have no bearing on the job or even be illegal to use because it is discriminatory.

There are different ways to perform the actual searching. It can be done by live researchers which of course is very expensive, labor intensive and relies heavily on the abilities of the researcher. Another technique is automation based on keywords and phrases. Although such a process falls into the category of NHI (No Human Involved), the problem, of course, is that many things online are only relevant in a certain context. Without knowing the contextual circumstances, the search can either miss or fail to report relevance matters. A person may use the word ISIS, and it may be difficult for a computer program to differentiate between a person who is potentially dangerous, with a person merely discussing a current issue online. Of course, there can be technology to score the context based on other factors, as the type of website, or who else visits it, among other factors. However, in the final analysis, a human being needs to make a decision as to relevancy.

As a result, a search protocol may combine an initial automated search with a human review of the results to analyze relevancy and context.

Of course, questions can arise as the ability of either human or computer software to evaluate what is real or relevant and to give each employer material that may be of relevance to them. These "social network background checks" will search social networking sites mentioned above and elsewhere on the Internet for information about job applicants, including things they may have put online years ago and completely forgotten about.

9. Who is doing the searching?

The searching can be done in-house or outsourced. There are third party firms that provide social media background checks. Firms providing this service may offer to go online for the employer and locate relevant information and also to filter out information employers should not have, such as results that may be potentially discriminatory or not job-related.

The advantage is that a third-party firm undertakes the burden of looking for relevant information and at the same time attempt to relieve employers from the legal liability of viewing materials that are inappropriate for an employer to view.

The Manual to Online Public Records

For more information about the details of using Internet searches and social media, a good reference for in-depth research is *The Manual to Online Public Records - 4th Edition* from BRB Publications, Inc. that is available online at www.brbpublications.com/books/detail/544.aspx?Id=544.

10. What would cause an employer to view an applicant in a negative matter?

Employers have reported some of the following reasons for either not making a job offer or even rescinding one as a result of an Internet search or using social media:

- Provocative or inappropriate photographs, videos, or information.
- Information about candidate drinking or using drugs.
- Discriminatory comments related to race, religion, gender and or other similar matters.
- Candidate bad-mouthed previous company or fellow employee.
- Poor communication skills.
- Demonstration of bad judgment.
- Information that a candidate told a falsehood or made material omission about qualifications or experience.

11. Can social media help an applicant get hired?

Some studies actual show that a social media search can help get a candidate hired. Some of the reasons cited are:

- Candidate's background information supported job qualifications.
- Candidate's site conveyed a professional image.
- Candidate's personality came across as a good fit with company culture.
- Candidate was well-rounded, showed a wide range of interests.
- Candidate had great communication skills

12. Since social media is fairly new, have courts and laws kept up with the pace of change?

One of the biggest issues for employers is the lack of certainty as to the boundaries and scope of the legal use of Internet and social media searches. Part of the difficulty in analyzing the risk of using social media is that the area is so new that courts and legislators have not yet caught up with technology. Neither Congress nor state legislatures (with some excepting mainly dealing with the privacy of consumer's passwords as discussed in more detail later in this chapter) have taken recent action on these issues. There are limited laws or statutes governing the use of social media sites for pre-employment screening such as the Stored Communications Act (SCA), a federal law enacted as part of the Electronic Communications Privacy Act (See: 18 U.S.C. §§ 2701 to 2712). That law deals with voluntary and compelled disclosure of "stored wire and electronic communications and transactional records" that are stored by third-party Internet service providers (ISPs). However, that law was passed in 1986 when computer users were still utilizing dial-up modems.

The courts have also not yet stepped into this area to date. When a new area of law develops, it takes time for legal precedent to be developed. Lawsuits must first be filed, and then litigated with a losing party taking an appeal to a higher court. As courts begin to issue opinions, the legal contours of a new practice begin to take shape. That takes time. Of course, each case is very fact specific, so the outcome of a case may or may not have broad implications.

At the time of publication, there is very little in the way of court cases on point. There are cases involving social networking site that involve current employees or in the area of employment and education. However, there are no court decisions yet on the exact issue of the use of the Internet for applicant recruiting and selection.

Another issue is that human resources and labor law issues are heavily regulated by state laws, so when court cases begin to appear or legislation is enacted, it may turn out to be a patchwork of various state rules.

It's also worth noting that some of the issues in play in this area rely upon the terms of use of various websites. So, if a social media site indicated that the site is for non-commercial use, it can affect the calculus of piracy unless it is shown that such a restriction is just boilerplate and not enforced in any way. Of course, terms of use can change at a moment's notice, adding another level of complexity.

At this point, given there is little in the way of legal precedent or legislative directives, the best that can be done is to take known existing laws and legal principals and extrapolate from them and project forward to determine how and where they may apply to using social networking for recruiting and hiring. However, this is an area that needs to be followed closely as a new court case can be handed down any day that may significantly alter our view of how to proceed in this area.

Author Tip〉 **Whitepaper on Social Media Background Checks**

To help employers avoid legal risk online when using the Internet to recruit and screen jobs applicants, Employment Screening Resources® (ESR) released a complimentary whitepaper *"Ten Potential Dangers When Using Social Media Background Checks"* written by the author Attorney Lester Rosen. The complimentary whitepaper is available at www.esrcheck.com/Whitepapers/Social-Media-Background-Checks/.

Landmines and Traps with Social Media Background Checks

What tends to get overlooked in the rush to use social media for employment screening background checks is a question that needs to be asked: **What are the legal risks for employers using the social media for employment screening?**

Employers that perform these searches in-house may easily find themselves in legal hot water for a number of reasons. Firms that are providing social network background checks as a service also present challenging questions that HR professionals and recruiters will need to deal with.

This section takes an in-depth look at each of the potential risks when using these Internet and social media sites for screening job applicants. At the same time, this chapter also looks at issues from the point of view of recruiters as well.

1. Too Much Information (TMI) – Discrimination Allegations

Employers can find themselves in hot water when utilizing Internet search engines and social networking sites for screening due to allegations of discrimination. This issue is sometimes referred to as Too Much Information or TMI. The problem surfaces once an employer is aware an individual is a member of a protected group. It is difficult to claim the employer can "un-ring" the bell and forget the information. All hiring decisions need to be based upon information that is non-discriminatory and is a valid predictor of job performance. If an employer has obtained actual knowledge of prohibited information, a rejected job applicant may claim that there was a failure to hire based on discriminatory information.

When using the Internet for employment screening, recruiters could be accused of discrimination by disregarding online profiles of job candidates who are members of protected classes based on prohibited criteria. A job candidate may reveal information that reflects race, creed, color, nationality, ancestry, medical condition, disability (including AIDS), marital status, sex (including pregnancy), sexual preference, age (40+), or other facts an employer may not consider under federal law or state law. There may even be photos showing a physical condition that is protected by the Americans with Disabilities Act (ADA) or showing someone wearing garb suggesting their religious affiliation or national origin. These protected aspects of applicants may be revealed by a search of the Internet.

Of course, the analysis is complicated by the fact that the aggrieved job applicants may have placed the information on the web themselves. However, it would be challenging to suggest that a person somehow consented to discrimination by placing material on the web that was then used illegally by employers. Until Courts rule on these issues, employers can only try to apply established legal concepts to their online recruiting efforts.

A related issue is whether a firm is treating all applicants in a similar fashion. If employers are performing Internet searches on a hit or miss basis, with no written policy or standard approach, an applicant that is subject to adverse action because of such a search can potentially claim to be a victim of discrimination. Also problematic is that on social network sites, an employer may view photos, personal data, discussion of personal issues and political beliefs, behavior at parties, and other information that an applicant may not have intended for the world to see. If a site shows that an applicant has a tattoo or a piercing, employers may need to ask themselves whether having a tattoo is a good reason not to hire someone.

The bottom line is once an employer is aware that an individual is a member of a protected group, they may be exposed to *failure to hire lawsuits* based upon discrimination or Equal Employment Opportunity Commission (EEOC) claims.

You Need To Know

Social Media Use in Workplace Raises Employment Discrimination Concerns

A panel of experts told the U.S. Equal Employment Opportunity Commission (EEOC) that the growing use of social media by employers, applicants, and employees in today's workplace may implicate and impact the federal laws prohibiting discrimination in employment that the EEOC enforces at a Social Media Commission meeting convened at EEOC Headquarters in Washington, D.C. on March 12, 2014.

Panelists told the EEOC that the use of social media sites such as LinkedIn and Facebook could help identify good candidates by searching for specific qualifications but the improper use of information obtained from social media sites may be discriminatory since the race, gender, age, and possibly ethnicity of most individuals can be discerned from information on these social media sites.

A panelist speaking on behalf of the Society for Human Resource Management (SHRM) explained that employers use social media for employee engagement, knowledge sharing, marketing, and recruitment and hiring of new employees. A 2013 SHRM member survey found 77 percent of companies surveyed reported that they used social media sites to recruit candidates, up from 34 percent in 2008.

Another panelist said social media should be used in recruitment to cast a wide net for potential candidates. However, employers conducting a social media background check should have either a third party or a designated person in the company who does not make hiring decisions do the background check, and only use publicly available information and not request passwords for social media accounts.

Source: www.eeoc.gov/eeoc/newsroom/release/3-12-14.cfm.

---

2. Too Little Information (TLI)

On the other hand, a failure to utilize all the available resources could theoretically expose employers to lawsuits for negligent hiring if a victim could show that information was easily accessible online that could have prevented a hiring a person that was dishonest, unfit, dangerous, and unqualified, and it was foreseeable that some harm could occur. In other words, employers that do NOT use such websites can potentially be sued for not exercising due diligence. This is a case of Too Little Information (TLI).

For example, if an organization is hiring for a position that involves access to children, and a simple web search may have revealed the applicant belongs to a group or has written blogs that approve of inappropriate relationships with children, the employer could be at risk for a lawsuit by failing to go to a computer and locate the material. If the employee harms a child, and a lawsuit results, the victim's attorney could argue that the employer failed to exercise reasonable care given the fact that children are very vulnerable, and the employer should have known the applicant was inappropriate for the job.

Another related issue to the use of Web 2.0 and TLI is the ease with which less scrupulous job seekers can utilize the Internet to obtain worthless college diplomas from degree mills, as well as totally fabricated job histories. Job seekers use elaborate scams where fake accreditation agencies and live operators "verify" the fake information or elaborate websites are set up to create fake past employers, as discussed Chapter 12 on Education Verifications. This can be a case of Too Little Information (TLI). The result is that employers may be placed in a "Catch-22" situation where they are in trouble if they do use such websites and are also in trouble if they do not. Similar scams exist for fake past employment. See Chapter 4 on past employment scams and Chapter 12 on past education.

You Need To Know > ### The Ideal Job Candidate?

Stories from recruiters and Human Resources show why these sites are so enticing. One recruiter recounts how she had found **"The Ideal Candidate"** for a prestigious consulting firm. Then, just out of curiosity, she ran the applicant's phone number on a search engine, and up popped some rather explicit ads for discreet adult services that the applicant was apparently providing at night. Another recruiter tells the story of finding an applicant's MySpace page, where the intern had demonized his firm, his boss, and his coworkers in considerable detail and by name.

---

3. Credibility, Accuracy, and Authenticity Issues

Another issue is whether the information found on the Internet about job applicants is even credible, accurate, and authentic – in other words, true. How does the employer know it is true or just a matter of some people being silly with their friends? The authenticity issue can be that the person said it, but it was not true, or the applicant was not even the source or subject of the online information.

Employers should keep in mind that the idea behind social network sites are friends talking to friends, and users of these sites have been known to embellish. Employers may have to consider what a person says on their site and if true, whether it would be a valid predictor of job performance or whether it would be employment related at all. After all, people have been known to exaggerate or make things up. They may believe they are just having fun or spoofing their friends.

When using the Internet for employment screening, how do employers know for sure what is "real" on the Internet? How do employers know that the "name" they found is their applicant's name? They don't.

Even trickier is the issue of third party references to a candidate. If a recruiter or employer goes beyond the material that appears to be authored by the applicant and begins relying on blogs or pictures posted by others about the applicant, the employer is entering even more uncertain territories. A third-party statement about an applicant is clearly "hearsay" in nature and is inherently subject to greater scrutiny. When a photograph that is problematic is posted of someone, there is an issue of whether there was permission to post and is it even your applicant.

If a CRA were to utilize third party comments, then another section of the FCRA comes into play. **FCRA section 606(d)(4)** requires extra precautions when a third party provides adverse information. In such a case, a CRA must either take steps to ensure that the source of information was the best source or use reasonable procures to obtain an additional source of information from an additional source with independent direct knowledge. If a search of the Internet shows a criminal record, the CRA must also consider if **FCRA Section 613** applies, which also has special requirements.

4. Computer Twins and Cyber-slamming

With more than 320 million Americans to date, most people have *computer twin*s meaning people with the same names and same or similar dates of birth. That can also create the question of how does a recruiter or employer even know for sure the applicant wrote the item, authorized its posting, or the online item even refers to your candidate?

Employers need to make sure what they see online actually refers to the applicant in question. There are anecdotes on the Internet of false postings under another person's name – a sort of cyber identity theft.

If the anonymous information is posted in a chat room, this may be the new phenomena of *cyber-slamming*, where a person can commit defamation without anyone knowing their real identity. Cyber-slamming is online smearing usually done anonymously and includes derogatory comments on websites or setting up a fake website that does not belong to the supposed owner.

For example, with practically no time or effort and at no cost, anyone can set up a blog masquerading as someone else and say anything they want. Short of filing a lawsuit against the Internet Service Provider (ISP) that hosts the blog, to obtain records showing the unique IP address of the computer, it is nearly impossible to trace down the person who actually posted the item. Even armed with the IP address, it is extremely difficult as a practical matter to then associate that IP address with a specified account or address, which may even require a second lawsuit.

Employers need to be careful that the site they are looking at actually refers to the applicant. In other words, if negative information about a candidate is found on the Internet or a social networking site, how is the employer supposed to verify that the information is accurate, up-to-date, authentic, and if it even belongs to or applies to the candidate in question?

5. Privacy Issues

Another challenge with Internet background checks yet to be fully explored by the courts is privacy. The conventional wisdom is that anything online is fair game because any reasonable person must understand the whole world has access to the Internet. However, contrary to popular opinion, everything online is not necessarily fair game for employers.

As discussed in more detail in Chapter 2, the concept of privacy in the U.S. can be fluid, and our notions of privacy are based on reasonable expectations and generally accepted community norms. Privacy arguments can often be analogous to ping pong games where the argument can go back and forth.

When it comes to social media, the terms of use for many social network sites prohibit commercial use, and many users may literally believe that their social network site is exactly that, a place to freely socialize. The argument would be that it is the community norm, and a generally accepted attitude, that social media sites are off limits to unwelcomed visitors even if the door is left open. After all, burglars can hardly defend themselves on the basis that the front door to the house they stole from was unlocked so they felt they could just walk in.

Even though online users communicate and share photos in a forum which can be public, there is a sense that what goes on in social networking sites like Facebook stays there. It is analogous to the Las Vegas rule – *What happens in Vegas, stays in Vegas.* This argument is buttressed by the fact that to enter some social networking sites, a user must agree to **terms of use** and to get details of another site member, a new user may be required to set up their own account. Also, these types of websites have terms of use that typically do not allow commercial uses, which can include screening candidates. Since a user must jump through some hoops, it can be argued there is an expectation the whole world will not be privy to confidential information.

On the other hand, if users do not adjust the privacy setting so their social network site is not easily available to an Internet search by any member of the public, it may be more difficult to claim that there is a reasonable expectation of privacy. If an applicant fails to utilize the privacy controls provided by the website, this alone undercuts any reasonable belief that what was on the website would remain confidential.

In addition, employers can argue that the routine boilerplate terms of use language where someone simply hits the *I agree* button is not much of a privacy barrier.

One reason the use of social networking sites presents a risk stems from their original purpose. At first, users intended to limit access to friends or members of their own network, arguably creating a reasonable expectation of privacy. It's like a cyber high school, but instead of people seeing friends near lockers during breaks, they can see friends and make contacts all over the world. Younger workers, in particular, may regard invading their social network sites in the same way older workers may regard someone that crashes a private dinner party uninvited – a tasteless act that violates privacy.

The bottom line is that the question of whether an applicant has a reasonable expectation of privacy can depend upon the specific facts of the case being litigated, and the issue is far from settled. Frankly, it could be decided either way.

Example of a Reasonable Expectation of Privacy

Suppose a recruiter or HR professional attended a convention, and after a long day of listening to speakers or walking the trade show, the recruiter has drinks with colleagues from different firms in the hotel lounge. Soon the talk turns to professional subjects, such as how they like their co-workers, their boss, or their company. Of course, at such an informal conversation, no one has signed a non-disclosure agreement and everyone is talking in a public place. Then suppose one of the recruiter's new found acquaintances proceeds to take what the recruiter considered a private exchange of information between professionals and placed the recruiter's more colorful and derogatory comments on a blog for the world to see. Would the recruiter be offended?

Yes. Most reasonable people under such a circumstance would be appalled. Generally accepted standards of normal behavior would dictate that the conversation was meant to be private, even though there was no agreement not to make the information public, and even though the conversation took place in a public place. Many people feel the same about their statements made on Internet social media sites. Not everything online is necessarily fair game.

---

6. Requiring Applicants to Provide Facebook or Other Social Media Passwords

One prime example of a privacy issue that has made news headlines is the practice by some employers of asking job applicants to provide login information such as usernames and passwords for their Facebook page and other social media websites. News stories have appeared concerning background checks in the digital age where prospective businesses, government agencies, and colleges are increasingly curious about the online life of potential workers and students. Back in 2009, Bozeman, Montana received a great deal of negative publicity for a policy of asking for such information. The City asked:

> *Please list any and all current personal or business websites, web pages or memberships on any Internet-based chat rooms, social clubs or forums, to include, but not limited to: Facebook, Google, Yahoo, YouTube.com, MySpace, etc.*

A poll indicated 98 percent of respondents believed the city's policy had amounted to an invasion of privacy, and the City of Bozeman later dropped the requirement.

Although the city said the information was not actually sought until a conditional job offer, overwhelmingly negative reactions to the city's policy raised privacy and free speech concerns for job applicants. A poll indicated 98 percent of respondents believed the city's policy had amounted to an invasion of privacy. The City of Bozeman later dropped the requirement until it conducted a more comprehensive evaluation of the practice. According to a press release:

> *The extent of our request for a candidate's password, user name, or other Internet information appears to have exceeded that which is acceptable to our community. We appreciate the concern many citizens have expressed regarding this practice and apologize for the negative impact this issue is having on the City of Bozeman.*

(Sources: *'Want a job? Give Bozeman your Facebook, Google passwords'* www.cnet.com/news/want-a-job-give-bozeman-your-facebook-google-passwords/ & *'Bozeman to job seekers: We won't seek passwords'* www.cnet.com/news/bozeman-to-job-seekers-we-wont-seek-passwords/).

While it is not uncommon for some employers to review *publically available* Facebook, Twitter, and other social networking websites to learn about job candidates, many users have their social media profiles set to *'private'* which makes them available only to selected people or certain networks and more difficult for employers to view.

Unless an applicant is applying for a position that requires a security clearance or public safety is involved, such as law enforcement, employers need to be very careful in asking applicants for their Facebook or other social media passwords. It is difficult to see how turning over such information is voluntary in the context of a job interview, where the choice is to hand it over or not get the job. If a lawsuit is filed, an applicant can allege an invasion of privacy by intrusion into private and personal information where an applicant had a reasonable expectation of privacy. The employer would then have the burden to demonstrate both that such a request was justified and that a less intrusive means to make the employment decision was not available. That could be a difficult standard for an employer to meet given all of the hiring tools at an employer's disposal.

Several states have gone a step further and have made such a practice illegal. Starting in 2012, a steady number of states have passed such laws.

You Need To Know **State Social Media Privacy Laws**

According to the National Conference of State Legislatures (NCSL):

"Increasing numbers of Americans use social media both on and off the job and at school. Some employees, job applicants, and students have expressed concerns about requests from employers or educational institutions for access to usernames or passwords for personal social media accounts. They consider such requests to be an invasion of employees' privacy, akin to reading a diary or requiring a visit to their home.

Some employers, however, say that access to personal social media accounts of employees is needed to protect the employer's proprietary information or trade secrets, to comply with certain federal financial regulations or to prevent the employer from being exposed to legal liabilities.

State lawmakers began introducing legislation beginning in 2012 to prevent employers from requesting passwords to personal Internet accounts to get or keep a job. Similar legislation prohibits colleges and universities from requiring access to students' social media accounts.

There are some 25 states with some variation of password protection law and a number of states are introducing laws as well."

Source: www.ncsl.org/research/telecommunications-and-information-technology/state-laws-prohibiting-access-to-social-media-usernames-and-passwords.aspx.

Here are three examples of social media privacy laws enacted in states:

- **Maine LD 686, HP 467, 2015, An Act To Promote Privacy in Social Media** protects the social media privacy of employees and job applicants law by prohibiting employers from requiring employees or job applicants to disclose passwords or any other means for accessing their personal social media accounts. The law prohibits an employer from requiring an employee or job applicant to access personal social media accounts or disclose personal social media account information in the presence of the employer, except when the employers reasonably believe that information is relevant to an investigation of alleged employee misconduct or workplace-related violation of laws.

The law took effect October 15, 2015. See: http://legislature.maine.gov/bills/getPDF.asp?paper=HP0467&item=1&snum=127.

- **New Hampshire House Bill 1407, 2014** prohibits employers in the state from requiring employees or job applicants to disclose social media or electronic mail passwords. HB 1407 adds a subdivision titled "Use of Social Media and Electronic Mail" to the New Hampshire Revised Statutes Annotated (RSA). Under HB 1407, no employer shall request or require that an employee or prospective employee disclose login information for accessing any personal social media account or service through an electronic communication device. HR 1407 also does not prohibit an employer from obtaining information about an employee or prospective employee that is in the public domain or conducting an investigation under certain circumstances. The law took effect on September 30, 2014. See: www.gencourt.state.nh.us/legislation/2014/HB1407.html.

- **Rhode Island 2014 Student and Employee Social Media Privacy Acts 2014-S 2095Aaa and 2014-H 7124Aaa** prevents potential employers or school admissions officers from asking applicants to provide login information or to sign into their social media accounts so an interviewer can view their online activities. The 2014 Student and Employee Social Media Privacy Acts will bar employers and colleges from demanding social media materials of job applicants and prospective students. The legislation signed for the Social Media Privacy Acts also provides that no employer or educational institution can require, suggest, or cause an employee, prospective employee, student, or prospective student to disclose the username, password, or any other means for accessing a personal social media account or divulge any personal social media information. The law took effect on July 3, 2014. See: http://webserver.rilin.state.ri.us/BillText14/SenateText14/S2095.pdf   and http://webserver.rilin.state.ri.us/BillText14/HouseText14/H7124A.pdf

---

Can Employers Demand to See Employees' and Applicants' Facebook Pages?

For an in-depth analysis of the issues surrounding privacy and social media passwords, see the article in the Addendum entitled *"Can Employers Demand to See Employees' and Applicants' Facebook Pages?"* by Stephen J. Hirschfeld, Curiale Hirschfeld Kraemer LLP, CEO Employment Law Alliance & Kristin L. Oliveira, Curiale Hirschfeld Kraemer LLP.

---

7. Legal Off Duty Conduct

Yet another issue is legal off-duty conduct. If a social media search reveals legal off-duty conduct, a candidate can claim they were the victims of illegal discrimination. A number of states protect workers engaged in legal off-duty conduct and have prohibitions limiting the use of private behavior for employment decisions. However, employers do have broader discretion if such behavior would damage a company, hurt business interests, or be inconsistent with business needs.

8. Pretexting or Faking

One area where an employer would be flirting with trouble is if information from Facebook or other social media site is obtained by manipulating the sites. This could be done by creating multiple identities or by using *pretexting*, which can include pretending to be someone else or something you are not.

For example, Facebook allows greater access to sites within the user's own network of friends. If an employer were to violate Facebook rules and create fake identities just to join a network belonging to a job applicant, that would likely cross over into the realm of employer behavior that is overly intrusive and invades too deeply into private matters.

Until the courts sort this out, one thing does seem certain: If an employer uses subterfuge, such as creating a fake online identity to penetrate a social network site, the privacy line has probably been crossed.

The FCRA and Use of Social Media Sites

There are third party services and background firms that will assist employers with Internet and social media searches. The argument is made that many employers are already doing such searches informally and may not be following best practices to prevent the potentially unlawful use of these sites. By outsourcing to a third party, an employer is potentially shielding themselves from allegations of discrimination since they are not viewing potentially discriminatory or irrelevant information.

In addition, a third party can develop expertise and economies of scale, and ensure that a fair and consistent methodology is being applied across the board. As a specialist, a third party screening provider may be able to offer searches at a lower cost, faster, and more comprehensive than an employer could do themselves. Providers of this service will typically provide advanced automation to identify keywords and to strike out information that is potentially discriminatory, then have trained researchers manually review negative reports. Employers should realize that background firms using social media information must follow the FCRA rules regulating the collection, dissemination, and use of consumer information. A June 2011 blog on the Federal Trade Commission (FTC) website, *The Fair Credit Reporting Act & Social Media: What Businesses Should Know*, indicated that background checks using information found with online search engines and on social networking sites must follow the same FCRA rules that apply to the more traditional information that FCRA compliant background screening firms and employers have used in the past.

The FTC blog (see business.ftc.gov/blog/2011/06/fair-credit-reporting-act-social-media-what-businesses-should-know) includes the following paragraph to remind users of Internet background checks of their duty to comply with the FCRA:

> *Employment background checks can include information from a variety of sources: credit reports, employment and salary history, criminal records – and these days, even social media. But regardless of the type of information in a report you use when making hiring decisions, the rules are the same. Companies providing reports to employers – and employers using reports – must comply with the Fair Credit Reporting Act.*

Under the FCRA section 603(f), a CRA can be a third-party firm that engages in the "assembling or evaluation" of consumers for employment. When a firm is reviewing the Internet to create a report about a job applicant's online information for purpose of employment, this is clearly a background report (also known as a "consumer report") under the FCRA. This means that these types of services are essentially background checking firms with all of the same legal duties and obligations of any other background check firm. Therefore, such sites need to have full FCRA compliance, including client certifications under FCRA section 604 as well as adverse action notices and numerous other obligations such as re-investigation upon request. Background checking is subject to heavy legal regulation as outlined in Chapter 5.

Although employers may request background screening firms perform this function, there are several matters to consider.

1. A screening firm does not have the same in-depth knowledge the employer has of the details of the position.

2. If a social network background check is done by a background screening firm, the search falls under the federal Fair Credit Reporting Act (FCRA) which requires a background screening firm to maintain reasonable procedures for maximum possible accuracy.

3. If a website is searched by a background screening firm on behalf of an employer, then consent and certain disclosures are mandated under the federal Fair Credit Reporting Act (FCRA).

4. A background screening firm performing the search also falls under the Accuracy and Relevancy requirements of the FCRA.

FCRA Section 607(b) sets forth in no uncertain terms the duty of a CRA to be accurate. The section reads:

> (b) *Accuracy of report*. Whenever a consumer reporting agency prepares a consumer report it shall follow reasonable procedures to assure maximum possible accuracy of the information concerning the individual about whom the report relates.

That section means that the accuracy requirement applies to both the information reported and the duty to ensure it is being reported about the right person. Congress drove this point home even further in the statement of Congressional findings and statement of purpose contained in section 602:

> (b) *Reasonable procedures*. It is the purpose of this title to require that consumer reporting agencies adopt reasonable procedures for meeting the needs of commerce for consumer credit, personnel, insurance, and other information in a manner which is fair and equitable to the consumer, with regard to the confidentiality, accuracy, *relevancy*, and proper utilization of such information in accordance with the requirements of this title. (Emphasis added.)

The use of the word *relevancy* in the FCRA further underscores the need for a background check firm to ensure that reasonable steps are taken to only report information relevant to the consumer.

One important issue is that it is inherently difficult for a background check firm to know is if the information online was authored or authorized by the applicant or even applies to the applicant. However, firms that specialize in these searches develop new technologies that allow them to check and cross check multiple data sources to confirm identity.

Another issue is if a consumer disputes an item on a social networking site was authored by the applicant, the Consumer Reporting Agency would have barriers in the dispute process.

Under FCRA Section 611, any consumer can dispute the accuracy contents of a consumer report. The CRA then has 30 days (and no more than 45 if a consumer provides supplemental information) to either verify the accuracy of the data or, if unable to do so, remove it. If a consumer contends that information from a social networking site was not authored by them, the question arises as to how a CRA can verify that such material belongs to the applicant. Trying to locate what is "real" in the cyber world is very tricky. Although every computer has an "IP" address, as a practical matter it is very difficult to locate the precise location of an actual computer short of issuing a subpoena as part of a lawsuit. Even if the actual computer is found, there can be an additional issue of who was using it if it was at the public location.

As a result, a CRA may end up having to remove the material from the social networking report if there is a dispute because of the difficulty of proving it was the consumer who made the entry.

A strong argument can be made that a CRA that inserts information in a consumer report that it knows, or reasonably should know, cannot withstand a request for re-investigation and would have to be removed, would be a violation of the FCRA's accuracy requirements. In other words, a CRA should not place in a report anything it cannot defend if a request for a re-investigation is made. The argument has been made that because a background screening firm has no way of knowing if the online information is accurate, authentic, or even belongs to the job applicant in question, it is inherently difficult for background screening firms to perform this service consistent with the FCRA.

Conversely, firms that provide this service maintain that their technology and safeguards provide an extremely high degree of accuracy, and that if there is something negative found, the typical situation is that the applicants want to explain the material and not dispute that they wrote it.

The solution? Before outsourcing this task, an employer should ask a provider of social media searches to first explain their FCRA compliance procedures. A qualified provider will understand the FCRA and be able to provide an explanation of how they comply with legal requirements.

Solutions if Using Social Media Background Checks

Solutions social media for background checks affect three groups: Employers, Recruiters, and Job Applicants.

1. Solutions for Employers

The considerations for employers using the Internet are different than recruiters. That is because an applicant and employer have an active relationship, and the employer can choose when and how to review the Internet and social media. Recruiters, by contrast, are sourcing from consumers who may have no idea anyone is even looking at them.

For employers who want to use social network sites to screen a candidate in-house and do not want to use a background screening firm, the safest path is to obtain consent from the candidate first and search social media as late in the hiring process as possible. The most conservative approach, in fact, is only to search once there has been a conditional job offer to that candidate. This procedure helps ensure that impermissible information was not considered before the employer evaluates a candidate using permissible tools such as interviews, job-related employment tests, references from supervisors, and a background check. In other words, it demonstrates that an employer used permissible criteria that were objective and neutral as to protected classes and did not use anything online to discriminate.

At that point, after using permissible screening tools, the reason for employers to search social networking sites would be to ensure there is nothing that would eliminate the person for employment.

This approach is also consistent with the Americans with Disabilities Act of 1990 (the "ADA") and similar state laws. Under the ADA, an employer may only inquire about medically related information once there has been a real job offer. Per the EEOC:

> *A job offer is real if the employer has evaluated all relevant non-medical information which it reasonably could have obtained and analyzed prior to giving the offer. (From www.eeoc.gov/policy/docs/preemp.html)*

By analogy, waiting until there has been a job offer helps to guard against an inference that an employer was using impressible criteria in deciding who was a finalist.

Reasons for an employer eliminating an applicant for employment or withdrawing the job offer would then need to be based upon the use of social networking and Internet searches which showed an applicant engaging in behavior that damages the company, hurts business interests, or is inconsistent with business needs.

Examples of such behavior could include matters such as:

- Disparaging a co-worker or supervisor during past employment;
- Engaging in online harassment;
- Admitting illegal conduct;
- Information showing dishonest behavior;
- Information showing falsehoods in the application or interview process; or
- Information on the web that shows poor judgment or communication skills.

This is not a complete list, but what these factors have in common is that there is a clear nexus between what is found online and the job. In other words, there is a rational and articulable business justification.

One critical approach is to not have a person in-house connected to any hiring decisions review social network sites in order to ensure impermissible background screening information is not given to the decision makers. The person doing the in-house social media review should also have training in the non-discriminatory use of background screening information, knowledge of the job description, and use objective methods that are the same for all candidates for each type of position. That way only permissible information is transmitted to the person that is making the decision. Again, this is best done post-offer but pre-hire and with consent. An employer may be looking for online information concerning job suitability. For example, did the potential employee say derogatory things about past employers or co-workers or demonstrate that he or she is not the best candidate for the job.

To minimize the risks of using the Internet for background checks, employers should consider taking the following steps when using search engines or social network sites for screening:

- If an employer uses social media searches, they should first consult their attorney in order to develop a written policy and fair and non-discriminatory procedures designed to locate information that is a valid predictor of job performance and non-discriminatory. Employers should focus on objective criteria and metrics when possible.
- Employers should have written job descriptions that contain the essential functions of the job, as well as the knowledge, skills, and ability (KSA) required for the job.

- The employer should have ongoing and documented training on how to avoid discriminatory hiring practices.
- Establish standard practices and procedures to show decision were made on objective basis using METRICS.
- Ensure similarly situated people were treated in a similar fashion. In other words, within each job, the search parameters and techniques should be similar.
- As a general rule, the later in the hiring process social media searches are used, the less open an employer may be to suggestions that matters viewed on the Internet were used in a discriminatory fashion. The most conservative approach is not to use the Internet for a social media search until AFTER there has been a conditional job offer to demonstrate that all applicants were considered utilizing legal criteria.
- Employers need to be concerned if information found online is potentially discriminatory to job candidates who are members of protected classes based on prohibited criteria such as race, creed, color, sex (including pregnancy), ancestry, nationality, medical condition, disability, marital status, sexual preference, or age (40+). All of these protected criteria may be revealed by a social media search.
- Employers need to be concerned if information found on the Internet violates state laws concerning legal "off duty" conduct.
- For legal protection, the most conservative approach is to perform a social media search only after consent from the job applicant and a job offer is made contingent upon completion of a background check that is satisfactory to the employer.
- Employers should not use any fake identities or engage in "pretexting" to gain access to information online.
- Whatever an employer's policy is regarding social media searches, it should be written. For employers that recruit at college, there is a trend to require employers to notify students ahead of time as to their policy for searching the Internet for an applicant's online identity.
- Employers should also consider the use of a person in-house not connected to hiring decisions to review social media sites in order to ensure impermissible or discriminatory information is not given to decision makers. The in-house reviewer should also have training in the non-discriminatory use of online information, knowledge of the job description, and use objective methods that are the same for all job candidates for each type of position. That way only permissible information is transmitted to the person making the decision. The person in-house conducting the review is on the other side of an "ethics" wall from any decision maker and helps prevent allegations that impermissible information was used in the hiring process.
- As an additional protection, an employer may consider having the in-house reviewer first contact the applicant with any potential information found online before it is passed along to the decision maker in order to allow the applicant the opportunity to dispute the accuracy or applicability of the information.

2. Solutions for Recruiters

Recruiters in the sourcing stage may want to consider having a clear internal policy and documented training that Internet sourcing is not being used in violation of federal and state discrimination laws and only factors that are valid predictors of job performance will be considered, taking into account the job description, and the Knowledge, Skills, and Abilities (KSA) required for the position. It also helps to have objective and documented methods and metrics on how to source and screen on the Internet.

Recruiters considering using social media in the sourcing stage may want to consider some of the following:

- Ensure each position has a detailed job description written for that specific position that clearly lays out the essential functions of the job and the knowledge, skills, and abilities (KSA) required for the position.
- Have a clear internal policy that Internet sourcing is NOT being used in violation of federal and state discrimination laws and only factors that are a valid predictor of job performance will be considered, taking into account the job description and the KSA required for the job.
- Have documented training on legal recruiting techniques. The training should include clear information on what would constitute a discriminatory practice.
- Establish standard practices and procedures to show decision were made on objective basis using METRICS.

- Ensure similarly situated people were treated in a similar fashion. In other words, within each job, the search parameters and techniques should be similar
- Have a clear procedure that outlines keywords, criteria, and methodology for sourcing, so recruiters can demonstrate that they are searching for objective requirements to be considered as part of the pool. Even better is if the criteria being used can be measured or have a metric attached.
- If someone meets the objective requirements but is not placed in the pool of potential candidates for other reasons, a recruiter may want to note why the exception is being made. For example, if the social networking website demonstrated behavior inconsistent with business interests, that should be noted.

3.   Solutions for Job Applicants

For job applicants, the advice is simple: Don't be the last to know what a web search about you would reveal. If job applicants do not want employers looking at their social networking site, then they should set the privacy parameter to "restricted use only." Savvy applicants can even go on the offense and create an online presence that helps them get a job.

You Need To Know

Social Network Screening by Employers May Make Companies Unattractive to Job Applicants

Employers that implement online screening practices such as social networking searches through social media sites like Facebook may be unattractive or reduce their attractiveness to job applicants and current employees alike, according to research from a study conducted on the effects of social media screening in the workplace presented at the 27th Annual Society for Industrial and Organizational Psychology (SIOP) Conference in San Diego in April 2012.

In the study by North Carolina State University (NCSU) co-authors Will Stoughton, Lori Foster Thompson, and Adam Meade: "175 students applied for a fictitious temporary job they believed to be real and were later informed they were screened. Applicants were less willing to take a job offer after being screened, perceiving the action to reflect on the organization's fairness and treatment of employees based on a post-study questionnaire. They also felt their privacy was invaded."

Stoughton, a doctoral candidate in industrial and organizational psychology at NCSU, said that studies show sixty-five percent of three employers screen job applicants through social networking websites. While organizations may practice social network screening to find the best applicants, the study found that "the social network screening process actually reduces an organization's attractiveness for the applicant and likely the incumbent worker."

Stoughton said while employers typically look on sites like Facebook or Google for pictures of alcohol or drug-related use and remarks about previous employers or co-workers to weed out bad job applicants, screening social networks doesn't always accomplish the intended goal: "By doing this, you assume the applicants that organizations end up choosing are more conscientious, but no studies show that these individuals are any better," he said. "They could actually be eliminating better applicants."

For more information, read the article *Judging a Facebook by Its Cover* on the SIOP website at www.siop.org/article_view.aspx?article=991.

Domestic Terrorist Attacks Put Social Media Background Checks in National Spotlight

Social media background checks that examine online postings by users of popular websites like Facebook and Twitter will be more in the national spotlight in the United States due to domestic terrorist attacks such as the tragic San Bernardino, California workplace shooting. However, social media background checks are easier said than done given the vast scope of the Internet and the billions of pieces of data available. There is so much information available on social media websites and online searches that trying to locate actionable and meaningful data on a particular person is like trying to find a very small needle in a very large haystack or like trying to take a sip of water from a powerful fire hose. It is a significant task.

The use of social media background checks became a hot news topic following a mass shooting at a holiday party in San Bernardino, CA on December 2, 2015. Pakistani-born Tashfeen Malik, along with her husband Syed Rizwan Farook, killed 14 people and injured 22 before both later died in a police shootout. Initially, several news agencies reported there was widespread speculation that the visa background check for Malik allegedly failed to search publicly available social media messages that may have revealed a potential threat. The Federal Bureau of Investigation (FBI) Director later stated that Malik and Farook did not post public messages on social media about supporting jihad.

Regardless, the events created a great deal of interest in utilizing social media as part of performing background checks. In fact, interest in social media background checks has risen steadily in the past few years. However, the call for widespread social media use in background checks does not necessarily take into account the practical and financial realities of scouring the Internet looking for usable data.

First, the scope of data available is overwhelming. Trying to narrow down a search so that it is relevant is difficult, time-consuming, and expensive. There is simply no magic bullet or currently available technology solution that can create easily accessible 'red flags' that are a sign or warning of any impending danger or disaster. For one thing, not everything on the Internet has identifiers. Anyone can easily operate under a pseudonym or false names. Even if a person somehow identified themselves, it is very easy to set privacy settings so that nothing is available on the public Internet, creating a need to utilize legal procedures to go behind piracy settings to compel Internet Service Providers to reveal information.

An additional practical issue is how to even spot a "red flag." There are two common techniques that are used – automation and human review of flagged words or terms. If software is used to find keywords, it can easily result in "false positives," meaning a person or communication has been flagged that is not related to a threat in any way. It is difficult for software to understand the context of a word and to program software to tell the difference between people who are a potential security threat and people who are merely discussing current events on their social media site.

For example, a citizen may use the word 'terrorist' in a blog post in order discuss the evils of terrorism. If that word trips a 'red flag,' people are needed to review and evaluate the social media posting. There is an enormous cost to hire enough human reviewers to go through every possible 'red flag.' Even if a whole army of online researchers is hired to review the social media profiles of visa applicants, the fact still remains that anything subject to human processes still has a certain margin of error. Certainly, if a person goes online and clearly identifies themselves by name or email address and posts threatening terrorist statements in no uncertain terms, that can more easily be flagged. But there is little to suggest that a potential person of interest will make such threats that easy to find.

Bottom Line with Social Media Background Checks: Proceed with Caution

Employers need to be very careful when it comes to harvesting information about job candidates from the web's social media. Employers need to know how to protect themselves against allegations of discrimination and issues with authenticity, accuracy, credibility, and privacy if no further action is taken after the discovery on the Internet that a person is a member of a protected class or when finding negative information. How and when an employer obtains such information is critical.

At this point in the evolution of social networking, there are no published cases yet on point. Lawsuits take time to work their way through the courts until an appellate court is finally called upon to issue an opinion. However, it is all but certain that someday an employer will land in court being sued on allegations of discrimination or a violation of privacy for making use of a social networking site in the hiring process. The bottom line: Before using the Internet to screen candidates, or using third party services, see your labor attorney.

You Need To Know ›

NFL Combine Involves Social Media Background Checks

The use of social media background checks by the National Football League (NFL) is a good illustration of why some employers find this to be an important source of information. The tweets, posts, and snapchats of NFL prospects are just as important as their physical ability on the field at the NFL Scouting Combine due to the rise of social media background checks performed by NFL teams, according to the February 2015 story "Passing a Social Media Background Check Is More Important Than an NFL Prospect's 40 Time" from SportTechie.com.

SportTechie reports that NFL talent evaluators closely monitor prospects online with social media background checks at the NFL Scouting Combine. College football stars will be *grilled—and sometimes, viciously so—on their upbringings, friend groups, relationships, legal troubles, past drug use, and so on*, according to SportTechie. Drill results showing strength and speed are less important these days "and social media is primarily to blame."

SportTechie describes a process called *ghosting* that NFL teams use to highlight potentially problematic players. Some teams may even use phony Facebook profile tests where NFL prospects receive follow requests from attractive women they have never met who claim to be big fans to see how many fall for the bait.

Social media background checks can hurt a prospect's chances before the NFL Draft. SportTechie cites examples including players on two rival college football teams who all slid in the NFL draft after feuding on Facebook and YouTube and a prospect tweeting about a conspiracy theory video who went undrafted.

Source: www.sporttechie.com/2015/02/20/passing-a-social-media-background-check-is-more-important-than-an-nfl-prospects-40-time/.

See The Addendum ›

Senators and Facebook Warn about Dangers of Using Social Media Sites to Screen

AS an indication of how Congress is potentially looking at this area, two U.S. senators have taken a look at the use of social media and employment. In September 2011, Senator Richard Blumenthal (D-Connecticut) and Senator Al Franken (D-Minnesota) sent a letter to a background screening firm that specializes in reviewing and storing social networking data for employment background checks concerning the dangers of using social networking sites. Portions of that letter are contained in the Addendum. A warning from Facebook to employers about asking job applicants for social media passwords is also in the Addendum.

CHAPTER 15

Drug Testing in the U.S.

Introduction

Drug testing in the workplace is fast becoming a fact of life for many employers. Although the drug testing practice was initially adopted by the Fortune 500 companies, pre-employment drug testing is gaining increasing acceptance in all sizes of businesses looking to keep their workplaces safe and their costs down.

According to numbers cited by the U.S. Department of Labor, drug use in the workplace is extremely costly to employers taking into account lost time, absenteeism, accidents and on the job injuries, health care, and workers' compensation claims each year. Sixty-five percent of all accidents on the job are related to drugs or alcohol, and substance abusers utilize 16 times as many health care benefits and are six times more likely to file workers compensation claims then non-abusers.

National Survey on Drug Use and Health

The **Substance Abuse and Mental Health Services Administration (SAMHSA)** conducts the annual *National Survey on Drug Use and Health (NSDUH)* that is the primary source of information on the use of illicit drugs, alcohol, and tobacco among Americans 12 years and older. The term **Illicit drugs** refers to use of illegal drugs that include marijuana according to federal law, hashish, cocaine (including crack), heroin, hallucinogens, inhalants, and prescription-type psychotherapeutics (pain relievers, tranquilizers, stimulants, and sedatives) used non-medically.

Results from the *2013 NSDUH* revealed that an estimated **24.6 million Americans** aged 12 or older were current (past month) illicit drug users, meaning they had used an illicit drug during the month prior to the survey interview. This estimate represents **9.4 percent of the population** aged 12 or older. Other key results included:

- Marijuana was the most commonly used illicit drug in 2013. There were 19.8 million past month users in 2013 (7.5 percent of those aged 12 or older). Marijuana was used by 80.6 percent of current illicit drug users in 2013.
- Daily or almost daily use of marijuana (used on 20 or more days in the past month) increased from 5.1 million persons in 2005 to 2007 to 8.1 million persons in 2013.
- In 2013, there were 1.5 million current cocaine users aged 12 or older, or 0.6 percent of the population.
- Among young adults aged 18 to 25, the rate of current use of illicit drugs in 2013 was 21.5 percent.
- Among adults aged 26 or older, the rate of current illicit drug use in 2013 was 7.3 percent.
- Among adults aged 50 to 64, the rate of current illicit drug use increased from 2.7 percent in 2002 to 6.0 percent in 2013.
- Among unemployed adults aged 18 or older in 2013, 18.2 percent were current illicit drug users, which was higher than the rates of 9.1 percent for those who were employed full time and 13.7 percent for those who were employed part time. However, most illicit drug users were employed.
- Of the 22.4 million current illicit drug users aged 18 or older in 2013, 15.4 million (68.9 percent) were employed either full or part time.

The *2013 NSDUH* supports the idea of workplace drug testing since **of the approximately 22 million illicit drug users aged 18 or older in 2013, roughly 15 million – or nearly 70 percent – were employed full or part time**.

The *2013 National Survey on Drug Use and Health: Summary of National Findings (NSDUH)* is available at www.samhsa.gov/data/sites/default/files/NSDUHresultsPDFWHTML2013/Web/NSDUHresults2013.pdf.

> **You Need To Know**
>
> ### Positive Drug Tests in U.S. Workforce Rise to Highest Level in a Decade
>
> The percentage of employees in the U.S. workforce receiving positive results in workplace drug tests has steadily increased over the last three years to reach the highest level in 10 years, according to an analysis of nearly 11 million workforce drug tests released by Quest Diagnostics. For more information see the section entitled **"Illicit Drug Positivity Rate Increases Sharply in Workplace Testing"** taken from the Quest Diagnostics website near the end of this chapter.

National Institute on Drug Abuse

The **National Institute on Drug Abuse (NIDA)** noted that studies show that when compared with non-substance users, substance using employees are more likely to:

- Change jobs frequently.
- Be late to or absent from work.
- Be less productive.
- Be involved in a workplace accident and potentially harm others.
- File a workers' compensation claim.

Employers who have implemented drug-free workplace programs have important experiences to share:

- Employers with successful drug-free workplace programs report improvements in morale and productivity, and decreases in absenteeism, accidents, downtime, turnover, and theft.
- Employers with long-standing programs report better health status among employees and family members and decreased use of medical benefits by these same groups.
- Some organizations with drug-free workplace programs qualify for incentives, such as decreased costs for workers' compensation and other kinds of insurance.

Source: www.drugabuse.gov/related-topics/drug-testing.

Impact on Workplace from Drug Abuse

Human Resources and Safety professionals consider drug testing an important safety issue in the workplace to lessen the impact from drug abuse in the workplace, including:

Absenteeism	Accidents	Attitude problems
Crime	Decreased Productivity	Tardiness
Theft	Turnover	Violence

Studies Show Drugs in Workplace Cost Employers Billions

The cost of substance abuse is staggering. The 'Trends & Statistics' page on the National Institute on Drug Abuse (NIDA) website estimates the **abuse of tobacco, alcohol, and illicit drugs costs the U.S. more than $700 billion annually** due to problems related to crime, lost work productivity, and health care. Specifically, **illicit drugs cost the nation $193 billion overall**. See: www.drugabuse.gov/related-topics/trends-statistics#costs.

NDIC National Drug Threat Assessment

The *2011 National Drug Threat Assessment* from the U.S Department of Justice (DOJ) National Drug Intelligence Center (NDIC) stated: "The estimated economic cost of illicit drug use to society for 2007 was more than $193 billion. This estimate reflects direct and indirect public costs related to **crime ($61.4 billion), health ($11.4 billion), and lost productivity ($120.3 billion)**." With regard to the impact on productivity by drug abuse:

NDIC estimates that drug abuse costs the nation more than $120 billion per year in lost productivity. Lost productivity generally occurs through the incapacitation of individuals, either by reduced motivation or by confinement in residential treatment programs, hospitals, or prisons. The most significant factor in lost productivity is reduced labor participation, which costs society an estimated $49 billion each year. Loss of productivity as a result of incarceration costs society at least $48 billion annually, and drug-related homicides result in a further loss in productivity of approximately $4 billion.

The NDIC *2011 National Drug Threat Assessment* is at www.justice.gov/archive/ndic/pubs44/44849/44849p.pdf.

SAMHSA Reports Finds Small Businesses Employ More Drug Users but Drug Test Less

Small businesses are the most vulnerable to drug use and particularly disadvantaged by worker substance use and abuse in the workplace, but they also drug test less than larger businesses. With a little less than half of all U.S. workers working for small and medium-sized businesses with fewer than 500 employees (see Chapter 20), drug testing in the workplace is not just an important issue for large businesses. The 2007 report *'Worker Substance Use and Workplace Policies and Programs'* from Substance Abuse and Mental Health Services Administration (SAMHSA) found:

- About nine in ten employed current illicit drug users and almost nine in ten employed heavy drinkers worked for small and medium sized firms.
- About nine in ten full-time workers with alcohol or illicit drug dependence or abuse worked for small and medium size firms.

However, this report from SAMHSA also found smaller firms were generally less likely to drug test for substance use and to have drug test programs in place to combat the problem. The report also noted that individuals who could not adhere to a drug-free workplace policy sought employment at firms that did not have a drug test policy. The cost of one error caused by an impaired employee could devastate a smaller company.

Furthermore, studies have found the impact of employee substance use and abuse is a problem that extends beyond the substance-using employee, as there is evidence that co-worker job performance and attitudes are negatively affected. Workers have reported being put in danger, having been injured, or having had to work harder, to re-do work, or to cover for a co-worker as a result of a fellow employee's drug use.

The SAMHSA report is available at http://adaiclearinghouse.org/downloads/Worker-Substance-Use-and-Workplace-Policies-and-Programs-133.pdf.

Author Tip **Drug Abuse Can Be a Significant Issue for Some Employers**

A number of statistics are cited in this chapter from various sources that suggest widespread drug abuse with a cost to employers that is significant and runs into the billions of dollars. This chapter does not attempt to analyze the accuracy of those numbers or review the methodologies used to arrive at those figures. While some may question the accuracy of these numbers, the walkway point is simply that drug use can be a significant issue for some employers that is worth reviewing.

SHRM Study Finds More than Half of Employers Favor Drug Testing

A study released in 2011 by the Society for Human Resource Management (SHRM) and the Drug and Alcohol Testing Industry Association (DATIA) examining the use of drug testing programs by employers found that **more than half of employers (57 percent) conduct drug tests on all job candidates**.

According to the poll that surveyed 1,058 randomly selected Human Resource professionals, 69 percent of employers who drug test job candidates have done so for seven years or more while 12 percent have used drug tests for five to six years. The study also found that:

- 71 percent of large organizations with 2,500 or more employees required all job applicants to take a pre-employment drug test.
- 62 percent of medium-sized businesses with 500 to 2,499 employees reported that they required drug testing.
- 56 percent of businesses with 100 to 499 employees required pre-employment drug testing.
- 39 percent of small businesses with fewer than 100 employees had a drug-testing policy for job candidates.

In addition, two-thirds of all businesses polled (66 percent) did not conduct drug testing for any of its contract employees, while almost three-quarters (72 percent) of multinational businesses reported that they used the same drug testing policies in operations outside the United States. For more information about the SHRM study, visit www.shrm.org/hr-today/news/hr-news/Pages/drugtestingfavored.aspx. To see the SHRM and DATIA poll, visit www.shrm.org/hr-today/trends-and-forecasting/research-and-surveys/Pages/ldrugtestingefficacy.aspx.

Cost/Benefit of Drug Testing

Pre-employment drug testing programs can be set up with a minimal amount of effort. Firms that operate from a single location can usually turn to a local medical clinic for tests. For firms with multiple locations, or who have applicants from various areas, programs can be set-up through drug testing agencies to allow testing at locations convenient to the job applicant throughout the United States.

Most employers find that a drug-testing program will eliminate people with problems, but not good applicants. Drug tests for small to medium employers generally cost in the $50-$70.00 range and include a collection of the sample, laboratory analysis, services of a Medial Review Officer (MRO), and communications of the results in the manner most convenient to the employer. Compared to the cost of even one employee with a substance abuse problem, most firms find eliminating the problem in the first place is well worth the time and money involved in a drug-testing.

The ABC's of Drug Testing

Do I Need to Test My Employees?

Although drug testing laws vary from state to state—in some cases, from county to county—only a handful of employers are mandated by law to screen their employees for illicit substances. The majority of these employers are in the transportation industry or other regulated industries with significant safety issues, and they know the regulatory requirements for their industry. For the remainder not bound by federal guidelines, the decision as to whether or not to drug test is up to the employer subjected to the type of legal limitations discussed and risk-management calculations below.

Many positions pose considerable risk to property, personnel, or the public. In these instances, drug or alcohol screening is often considered to be a necessary measure for preventing or mitigating potential mishaps.

Mandatory Screening

Employers are legally required to screen employees for drugs and alcohol in certain cases, for example, truck drivers are regulated by the **Department of Transportation (DOT)** and must be tested if they drive a Commercial Motor Vehicle with a gross combination weight rating of over 26,001 pounds, or if the vehicle is designed to transport 16 or more passengers or hazardous materials. Testing requirements exist for workers in other regulated and safety sensitive industries such as aviation, rail, transit, maritime, and pipeline industries.

Another example centers on employers who operate under federal contracts and are subject to mandatory rules for a Drug Free Workplace. That applies to employers who do business with the federal government and have contracts in excess of a set minimum dollar amount.

Recommended Screening

Employers not legally required to test for drugs or alcohol sometimes choose to require the procedure anyway, especially employers with workers in particularly safety-sensitive positions, such as any employee who:

- Works closely with children, the elderly, the ill or the disabled.
- Has extensive, unsupervised contact with the public.
- Is required to operate a vehicle or heavy machinery.
- Works in or has access to private residences and businesses.
- Handles money or valuables.
- Has access to weapons, drugs, or dangerous substances.
- Works in a supervisory position.

 If You Drug Test Do Not Discriminate

If an employer determines that a drug screening program is necessary, then screening should be implemented universally in order to avoid problems with discrimination.

Pre-Employment and Post-Employment Drug Screens

Pre-employment drug screens are the most common tests used by employers. Courts have consistently upheld the legality of requiring a drug test as a condition of being considered for employment. Employers should consult their attorneys concerning any legal issues involved with drug testing in a particular jurisdiction.

Many employers utilize a single drug screen 'on the way in' to satisfy their requirement for demonstrating due diligence. For the most part, this is true. Screening a job applicant once prior to making a hiring decision does demonstrate that efforts have been made to prevent individuals with substance abuse problems from entering the workplace. However, maintaining a screening program that excludes existing employees from testing makes a potentially fatal presumption that employees' lives do not change past the moment of hire. Factors in any employee's life can change at a moment's notice, and bad habits develop quickly. A drug test administered to a new hire on the way in is accurate only up to the moment that specimen was produced.

The decision to screen should be made considering all employees, not just candidates for the job.

How is drug testing conducted?

Most drug testing is done by sending an applicant to a collection site, where a urine sample is obtained and sent to a certified laboratory for analysis. Negative results are normally available within 24 hours. There are instant test kits on the market. These are similar to home pregnancy tests and require the employer to manipulate a urine sample. Although these tests are considered accurate for immediate screening if the result is negative, they are not considered conclusive in the event of a positive result, since that requires laboratory confirmation and retention of a sample for retesting by the subject. In addition, they are not that much less expensive than laboratory tests. More information about testing techniques are reviewed later in this chapter.

Author Tip | **Is a Drug Test Also an IQ test?**

Most employers will insist that a job applicant give the urine sample within a specific period of time to prevent a drug user from waiting until the drugs leave the system. Some drug experts consider a drug test to be an IQ test—taking a test knowing there are drugs in the system is not a good sign. Laboratories and collection sites also have ways to determine if the applicant has attempted to alter the test sample.

What About Consent?

Prior to the hire, express written consent should be obtained for a pre-employment drug test. When doing post-hire screening, the consent is often covered in the form of workplace rules and policies. Therefore, it is imperative for any firm intending to conduct post-accident testing or probable-cause testing to have written policies and procedures in place before attempting to conduct post-hire drug tests. When done through a background firm it is probably covered by the federal Fair Credit Reporting Act (FCRA), as discussed later in this chapter.

Setting Drug Testing Policies and Procedures

A drug-testing program should not be implemented without first establishing policies and procedures. An effective, comprehensive program covering post-hire testing should address such issues as:

- Communicating to the workforce about the need and advantages of a drug testing program – a safe workplace, lower health costs, improve productivity, etc.
- A well-written policy that has been reviewed by legal counsel.
- Proof that all employees have received and are familiar with the policy.
- Confidentiality of medical records.
- The company's stance on workplace drug or alcohol use (i.e., Zero Tolerance).
- The events or times at which testing takes place.
- What constitutes a passed or failed drug test.
- Having a policy on what to do in the event of a positive test, such as allowing the employee to explain or retest the sample.
- Procedures involved if a person is suspected of violating the policy.
- The consequences of a violation of the policy.
- Options for treatment, counseling, and rehabilitation, and other employee assistance.
- Supervisor training in drug testing procedures and policies.
- Using medically approved tests and procedures.
- Keeping all tests confidential and maintained separate from the personnel file.
- Considering use of a Medical Review Officer (MRO) – mandatory for certain types of testing.

Keep in mind that employers of a certain size are subject to the rules and regulations of the Federal Americans with Disabilities Act (ADA) as well as similar state rules. Although the current use and abuse of drugs or alcohol is not considered to be a disability – and therefore not protected by the ADA – post-hire drug testing can be a very complicated legal area. Any employer looking to implement a post-hire screening program should first consult an attorney specializing in labor practices.

Rules for Testing Other than for Pre-employment?

There may be times when an employer is required by legal obligations or employee behavior to conduct drug testing post-hire. The three major categories of testing other than pre-employment are suspicion-less (or random) testing, post-accident testing, and reasonable suspicion testing. Following are some points to consider.

Suspicion-less Testing	• Applies to safety sensitive positions. • Normally government mandated, such as truck drivers, railroad workers, customs workers, security clearance, nuclear workers, jockeys, airline personnel, and gas pipeline workers. • For example, Department of Transportation (DOT) has extensive rules and regulations including contacting past employers, random pools, special rules for testing, and the use of Medical Review Officers (MRO). See: www.transportation.gov/odapc/part40.
Post-accident Testing	• Announce the program in advance as part of company policy. • Offer counseling or treatment without fear of reprisal. • Will test safety sensitive positions. • Tested only after a serious accident. • Less intrusive testing possible, e.g. urine instead of a blood test.
Reasonable Suspicion Testing	• An employer may test if there are observable phenomena such as direct observation of drug use, or physical symptoms, pattern of abnormal conduct or erratic behavior, arrest for drug related offense, or information provided by credible sources. • Best practice is to have a drug policy in place and have supervisors formally trained to recognize signs of drug use. • On the issue of off-duty conduct justifying drug test—does it raise suspicion of on-duty impairment?

What is Tested? – DOT Drug Tests and Non-DOT Drug Tests

For the most part, drug screens are separated into two categories—DOT (Department of Transportation) screens and Non-DOT screens (also called forensic or non-regulated screens). The two screens vary by criteria.

- In DOT screens, a limited panel of drugs can be tested for only in urine or breath testing with federally-mandated cutoff levels at specific times within the employee's time with the company.
- In non-DOT screens, employers are free to select the specimen to be tested—blood, breath, saliva, urine or hair—the panel of substances to be tested against, the cutoff level, and the times or circumstances at which the test may be taken.

Drug Testing for DOT Employers

DOT regulations require that employers test employees for a specific, limited panel of substances, under specific circumstances:

- Pre-employment.
- Random selection.
- Reasonable suspicion/cause.
- Post-accident.
- Return-to-duty.
- Follow-up

Typically a "5 panel" NIDA (National Institute of Drug Abuse) test and DOT tests include:

- Marijuana (THC).
- Cocaine.
- Phencyclidine (PCP).
- Opiates such as codeine, heroin, and morphine.
- Amphetamines, including methamphetamine.

Nearly every testing facility and vendor in the testing industry refers to these five substances as their "basic 5-panel test." When facilities and vendors refer to "panels," they mean the number of substances for which they are screening, i.e. "5-panel" meaning a test for five substances, "10-panel" for ten substances.

Non-DOT drug tests do not satisfy DOT regulations, but the same laws governing privacy and disclosure still apply to these tests. Non-DOT tests can screen for more and different substances than DOT tests, including:

- Barbiturates.
- Benzodiazepines.
- Methadone.
- Propoxyphene.
- Hallucinogens (LSD, psilocybin).
- Designer drugs.

NOTE: Methaqualone (Quaaludes) is no longer considered to be a standard panel. It was last commercially manufactured in 1993, and it is my understanding that the positivity rate for that drug has not been reported by any of the major labs for years. Many drug testing companies advertise the standard non-DOT panel as a 9.

Drug Testing for Non-DOT Employers

While there are all varieties of illicit substances to be found in most major metropolitan areas—and just about anywhere else—most employers screen their applicants for the five most common "street drugs" using the "5 panel" screen. Some employers may replace the PCP screen with a screen for methamphetamines such as Ecstasy.

Many additional tests are available on the market, including tests for prescription medications or "designer" drugs. A typical ten-panel screen may test for THC (marijuana), cocaine, PCP, opiates, methamphetamines (including Ecstasy), methadone, amphetamines, barbiturates, benzodiazepines, and tricyclic antidepressants (TCAs).

However, the standard five-panel screen serves its purpose – it weeds out those applicants found to have those substances in their systems, deters many more potentially problematic candidates from applying, and demonstrates due diligence in the event that an applicant with a substance-abuse problem slips through.

Standard Drug Testing Panels Chart

Presented below is a **Standard Drug Testing Panels Chart** that shows what specific drugs are included for certain standard drug tests.

Drug Name	5 Panel	DOT	9 Panel	10 Panel	Medical Professional
Amphetamine	X	X	X	X	X
Cocaine	X	X	X	X	X
Marijuana	X	X	X	X	X
Phencyclidine	X	X	X	X	X
Opiates	X	X	X	X	X
Ecstasy		X			
Methadone				X	X
Propoxyphene			X	X	X
Barbiturates			X	X	X
Benzodiazepines			X	X	X
Methaqualone (no longer standard)				X	X
Fentanyl					X
Meperidine					X
Oxycodone					X
Tramadol					X

What Happens if there is a Positive Test or Abnormal Test?

Testing labs have extensive procedures to re-confirm a positive test before reporting it. If a sample tests positive in the initial screening procedures, then the sample is subjected to testing by a gas chromatography/mass spectrometry (GC/MS). This is considered the state-of-the-art science for the definitive testing of drugs.

Most drug testing programs also utilize the services of an independent physician called a Medical Review Officer (MRO) to review all test results. In the case of a positive result, the MRO will normally contact the subject to determine if there is a medical explanation for the positive results.

There can also be tests that are "negative' but show an abnormal result, such as a "low creatine level," which can potentially indicate an applicant attempted to dilute the sample by the excessive drinking of water or some other form of alteration. That is also a result that an MRO would likely examine. A specific gravity test can be conducted to measure the concentration of particles in urine, which can indicate an applicant's attempt to mask drugs by drinking excessive fluids.

If the positive test is confirmed, the subject should have the right to pay for a retesting of the sample they gave at a laboratory of their choice. Urine samples for all positive tests are retained for that purpose. Merely taking a new test is not helpful since the drugs may have left the system. Reputable and certified laboratories will stand behind their results and provide expert witnesses, although the chances of a false positive are practically nil.

If a current employee tests positive, then the employer must follow the policies and procedures they have put into place. Some employers will utilize an Employee Assistance Program (EAP), which can arrange for professional assessment and treatment recommendations. All drug-testing results should be maintained on a confidential basis separate from an employee's personnel file.

How Does the Drug Test Work?

As drugs are processed by the user's system, they produce metabolites – substances produced as a byproduct of the user's body metabolizing or "digesting" the drug. While a drug will pass relatively quickly through the user's system, chemical traces of the metabolites produced by the person's body in processing the substance can remain afterward for days or weeks. In general, drug tests do not screen for the drugs themselves, but instead test the user's system for the metabolites that were derived as a result of the drug passing through the user's system. In other words, drug tests don't test for drugs but for what the drugs leave behind.

When looking for evidence of illegal drug use, labs test bodily fluids (usually urine, but sometimes blood or saliva) or hair for traces of drugs or drug metabolites. Alcohol can be detected in blood but is generally tested for in the breath.

Drug Detection

Although each drug and each person are different, most drugs will stay in the system for the purposes of a urine test for about two to four days. As mentioned above, chronic users of certain drugs such as marijuana or PCP may have results detected for up to fourteen days and sometimes much longer. As noted below, hair testing goes back further, and oral fluid testing may be better suited to post-accident since it may detect drug use that is more recent.

The following chart illustrates the average detection window in which traces of drug use can be found in a user's system. While there is some "wiggle room" on either side of the specified time frames, this chart reflects the average retention periods of the average user.

Drug	Detection Window for Urine Test
Marijuana	3 – 15 days
Cocaine	1 – 3 days
Opiates	1 – 2 days
Methadone	2 – 3 days
Phencyclidine	Up to 7 days
Amphetamines	2 – 4 days
Barbiturates	Up to 14 days
Benzodiazepines	Up to 14 days

Due to the limited detection windows of most drugs for a standard urine test, one would think that the savvy drug user would seek to avoid detection by simply cleaning up for a few weeks prior to an anticipated test. This is not always the case. A whole industry has surfaced purveying cheats, gimmicks, and products designed to help users defeat drug screening techniques. It is even possible to purchase clean urine online, with interesting names such as 'Urineluck" or "Urine the Clear."

Laboratories and collection sites have countered this wave of anti-detection innovation with their own methods to determine whether or not the applicant has attempted to alter or replace the test specimen. The table below indicates the most common cheats and the most common countermeasures.

Cheat	Countermeasure
System dilution (drinking excessive water, "flushing" the system)	Specific gravity tests measure the concentration of particles in urine. A significantly reduced result indicates tampering.
Specimen substitution (substituting clean urine from another individual or reconstituted "powdered" urine)	Measuring the specimen's temperature immediately can indicate whether or not the specimen was produced prior to or at the time of testing.
Prosthetic delivery devices	A firsthand witness is required to successfully prove that an individual used a prosthetic device to administer a false specimen. A possible giveaway is the "clunk" sound the device makes when it contacts the specimen cup.
Additives (doping the sample)	Doping the specimen to be tested only results in a polluted specimen, requiring a re-test.
Refuting results	An applicant refuting the results of a drug test is entitled to prove his or her innocence by having the specimen re-tested at the laboratory of choice. However, applicants typically are not allowed to retake a test since that simply gives time to clear out the system.

Cutoff Levels

The amount of a substance detected during the initial screen is important. The Mandatory Guidelines for Federal Workplace Drug Testing Programs published by SAMHSA (the Substance Abuse and Mental Health Services Administration) indicates a specific cutoff level for each drug. This is the set ratio of drug or drug metabolite to volume of liquid in the specimen that must be found in order for the specimen to legitimately qualify for positive detection. This applies to an initial screen and in a confirmatory screen. In urine analysis, cutoff levels are measured in nanograms per milliliter (ng/mL)—that is, billionths of a gram of the substance per thousandth of a liter of urine, more quantitatively translated into millionths of a gram per liter—in any case, not very much is required for a positive result. Employers held to DOT regulations must follow the SAMHSA cutoff levels for the most commonly tested for drugs.

What are the Cutoff Concentrations for Drug Tests?

A laboratory must use the cutoff concentrations displayed in the following table available on the DOT website for initial and confirmatory drug tests. All cutoff concentrations are expressed in nanograms per milliliter (ng/mL). If an initial urine screen shows marijuana metabolites evidenced in the amount of 26 nanograms per milliliter, and the cutoff level for marijuana metabolites is 50 ng/mL, the initial screen would come back negative for the use of marijuana. Basically, the more frequently a substance is used, the higher the volume will be seen in the specimen in ng/mL. In order to suit the company's needs, "acceptable standards" may be established by any private employer. The Federal Workplace standards are not mandatory. The following chart was last updated in September 2016 and is available on the DOT website at www.transportation.gov/odapc/part40/40-87.

Initial Test Analyte	Initial Test Cutoff Concentration	Confirmatory Test Analyte	Confirmatory Test Cutoff Concentration
Marijuana metabolites	50 ng/mL	THCA[1]	15 ng/mL
Cocaine metabolites	150 ng/mL	Benzoylecgonine	100 ng/mL
Opiate metabolites			
Codeine/Morphine[2]	2000 ng/mL	Codeine	2000 ng/mL
		Morphine	2000 ng/mL
6-Acetylmorphine	10 ng/mL	6-Acetylmorphine	10 ng/mL
Phencyclidine	25 ng/mL	Phencyclidine	25 ng/mL
Amphetamines[3]			
AMP/MAMP[4]	500 ng/mL	Amphetamine	250 ng/mL
		Methamphetamine[5]	250 ng/mL
MDMA[6]	500 ng/mL	MDMA	250 ng/mL
		MDA[7]	250 ng/mL
		MDEA[8]	250 ng/mL

[1] Delta-9-tetrahydrocannabinol-9-carboxylic acid (THCA).

[2] Morphine is the target analyte for codeine/morphine testing.

[3] Either a single initial test kit or multiple initial test kits may be used provided the single test kit detects each target analyte independently at the specified cutoff.

[4] Methamphetamine is the target analyte for amphetamine/methamphetamine testing.

[5] To be reported positive for methamphetamine, a specimen must also contain amphetamine at a concentration equal to or greater than 100 ng/mL.

[6] Methylenedioxymethamphetamine (MDMA).

[7] Methylenedioxyamphetamine (MDA).

[8] Methylenedioxyethylamphetamine (MDEA).

(b) On an initial drug test, you must report a result below the cutoff concentration as negative. If the result is at or above the cutoff concentration, you must conduct a confirmation test.

(c) On a confirmation drug test, you must report a result below the cutoff concentration as negative and a result at or above the cutoff concentration as confirmed positive.

(d) You must report quantitative values for morphine or codeine at 15,000 ng/mL or above.

[65 FR 79526, Dec. 19, 2000, as amended at 75 FR 49862, August 16, 2010; 77 FR 26473, May 4, 2012]

Updated: Friday, September 16, 2016

Source: www.transportation.gov/odapc/part40/40-87

NOTE: The detection windows noted are for urine drug tests only. Much of what is covered in this chapter is based on urine screening although oral fluid and hair have increased in popularity. Each type of drug test has its best use case. For example, hair is good for pre-employment while oral fluid is better for post accident/reasonable suspicion since it detects recent usage more quickly in many cases than urine.

DOT Amends Procedures for Transportation Workplace Drug Testing

The U.S. Department of Transportation (DOT) amended procedures for transportation workplace drug and alcohol testing program. This was part of an effort to create consistency with many new requirements established by the U.S. Department of Health and Human Services (HHS). Full details of the final rule 49 CFR Part 40 – which took effect October 1, 2010 – are available at www.transportation.gov/odapc/part40/.

Some of the changes affect the training of and procedures used by Medical Review Officers (MROs). Highlights of these changes include the following:

- DOT began requiring drug testing for Ecstasy (Methylenedioxymethamphetamine or MDMA). The initial screening cut-off concentration for MDMA is 500 ng/ml, and the confirmatory cut-off concentration is 250 ng/ml for MDMA, as well as Methylenedioxyamphetamine (MDA) and Methylenedioxyethylamphetamine (MDEA), drugs that are chemically similar to Ecstasy;
- The drug test cutoff concentrations for cocaine were lowered. The initial screening test cutoff dropped from 300 ng/ml to 150 ng/ml, and the confirmatory test cutoff concentration was lowered from 150 ng/ml to 100 ng/ml;
- The drug test cutoff concentrations for amphetamines were lowered. The initial screening test cutoff was lowered from 1,000 ng/ml to 500 ng/ml, and the confirmatory drug test cutoff concentration from 500 ng/ml to 250 ng/ml; and
- Initial drug testing for 6-acetylmorphine ("6-AM," a unique metabolite of heroin, considered to be definitive proof of heroin use) is now required. Specific rules were added to address the way in which Medical Review Officers ("MROs") analyze and verify confirmed positive drug test results for 6-AM, codeine, and morphine.

Pros and Cons of Testing Methods

The table below gives an excellent description of the pros and cons of the five most common test methods used by employers.

Method	How it Works	Pros	Cons
Urine sample at third party collection site	Applicant is sent to a third party collection site and is given a Chain of Custody (COC), or one is provided at site. Employers can use one of the national firms (including Quest, Lab Corp, etc.), a regional firm, or a local drug-testing lab. The labs should be certified by the **Substance Abuse and Mental Health Services Administration (SAMHSA)**	There are over 20,000 third party collection sites. The test does not require the employer or HR to be involved in the physical collection procedures. Normally, negatives are returned in 24 hours. One firm offers nearly instantaneous results.	Some employers feel it is unduly intrusive to have applicants provide a urine sample. The test window is only 2 to 4 days for some substances such as cocaine, opiates, and amphetamines.
On-site instant kits	The employer collects the urine sample at the job. A "reagent" is introduced into the sample, creating an instant result by some sort of color change.	Instant results. Relatively inexpensive.	If a positive, then the best practice is to send sample or applicant for a test where the results can be analyzed in a lab. Employers should not use a positive as an indication of drug use without further testing. Requires special care for the

			operator who handles body fluids.
Instant oral test onsite by employer	The applicant places receptor in mouth under the tongue (which is basically the size of a Q-tip). The operator then manipulates the device in order to place saliva onto a reagent pad to view any color change.	Like the on-site instant kit, an instant oral kit is very accurate but less intrusive. May be useful for post-accident testing.	If a positive, then the best practice is to send sample or applicant for a test where results can be analyzed in a lab. Employers should not use a positive as an indication of drug use without further testing. Requires special care for the operator who handles body fluids. Not as legally defensible and kits have a shelf life.
Laboratory saliva test	Similar to above but done in a laboratory. Applicant handles entire procedure, from opening sealed applicator to sealing in a bag, to shipping to a lab.	No handling of body fluids by operators. Much less intrusive than a urine sample. Laboratory testing ensures accuracy.	Slow due to delay in mailing to the lab. Not instant. Not DOT approved as of 01/04.
Hair testing	A sample of hair is taken from the crown of hair and mailed to a laboratory. Results come back in 1-3 days with one lab reporting that 90% of results come back in one day.	Extremely accurate and not subject to contamination or efforts to mask the results. Detection goes back 90 days.	Some people find it an invasion of privacy to cut hair. Test needs a sample from the crown of the head, about the size of pencil eraser. Mailing and testing may take slightly longer than other tests and is more expensive. Turnaround time comparable to other types of testing with typical reporting timeframe of 1-3 business days.

Drug Testing Costs

Most small employers should expect to be able to get a standard, run-of-the-mill, 5-panel screen from a third-party vendor for somewhere in the $40.00 to $60.00 range or, for slightly more money, directly from the detection lab where third parties often receive volume discounts. The fee usually includes the handling and processing of the sample as well as monitoring chain-of-custody—tracking the specimen to ensure at no point is it possible for the specimen to be "switched"—and providing medical review services.

The availability of home testing kits—also called quick and dirty tests—from the web is increasing. These products generally cost between $5.00 and $10.00 each, are usually sold by the box, and often allow the employer to "mix and match" the panel of substances for which the applicants will be tested.

These home testing kits, while a little cheaper, do have their drawbacks. First, they are non-DOT compliant, meaning the detection cutoff levels do not have to match those governed by the DOT. Second, the results cannot be confirmed. Positive results cannot be re-tested to confirm the presence of a substance, and negative results cannot be tested for tampering. The biggest drawback to these tests is the employer is required to manipulate the specimen, not to mention also witness the donation process in order to discourage cheating.

Legal Issues and Drug and Alcohol Testing

The most common type of drug testing program is for pre-employment purposes. Courts have consistently upheld the legality of requiring a pre-employment drug test as a condition of employment. It is a best practice to clearly indicate drug testing is a requirement for employment and to do so after a conditional offer of employment.

Although the Americans with Disabilities Act (ADA) and similar state laws provide protection for people who are in rehabilitation for drug or alcohol addition, the ADA does not protect people currently abusing drugs or alcohol.

The following are some leading cases and current legal issues impacting drug and alcohol testing. At the end of the chapter are resources that will assist employers in all 50 states.

The Conflict between California Medical Marijuana, California Recreational Marijuana & Federal Law

The California Compassionate Use Act of 1996 is a California law which allows patients with a valid doctor's recommendation to possess and cultivate marijuana for personal medical use. However, in *Ross v. RagingWire Telecommunications, Inc.* (*2008*) *42 Cal.4th 920*, the California Supreme Court determined that an employee authorized to use marijuana for medical purposes could not state a cause of action for wrongful termination. The Court's opinion emerged from a collision among principles of California law, federal law, and public policy.

In *Ross*, the employee was directed by his physician to use marijuana to treat chronic pain. He was then fired when a pre-employment drug test required of new employees revealed his marijuana use. The employee alleged that the company violated the California Fair Employment and Housing Act (FEHA) by discharging him and failing to make reasonable accommodation for his disability. The court concluded that The Compassionate Use Act did not require California employers to accommodate the use of marijuana and reaffirmed that employers could take illegal drug use into consideration in making employment decisions.

Ross has consistently been upheld by the courts. For instance, in 2016, a federal district court cited *Ross* and granted summary dismissal of a plaintiff's FEHA claims. In *Shepherd v. Kohl's Department Stores*, 2016 U.S. Dist. LEXIS 101279 (E.D. Cal. 2016), the plaintiff was fired for using medical marijuana, but the court upheld *Ross* and concluded that the plaintiff could not state a claim under FEHA.

California Proposition 64

By Jennifer L. Mora, Attorney at Law, Littler Mendelson, P.C.

In November 2016, California residents voted in favor of Proposition 64, which legalized marijuana for individuals over the age of 21. Proposition 64 will not impact the right of a California employer to prohibit marijuana use nor will it require an employer to accommodate such use. The law expressly states in the "Purpose and Intent" section that its intent is to "allow public and private employers to enact and enforce workplace policies pertaining to marijuana." Moreover, the Act states that it will not be construed or interpreted to:

- Restrict the rights and obligations of public and private employers to maintain a drug and alcohol-free workplace;

- Require an employer to permit or accommodate the use, consumption, possession, transfer, display, transportation, sale, or growth of marijuana in the workplace;

- Affect the ability of employers to have policies prohibiting the use of marijuana by employees and prospective employees; or

- Prevent employers from complying with state or federal law.

Marijuana remains a Schedule I drug under the federal Controlled Substances Act. As a result, and consistent *Ross*, employers can continue to rely on federal law and enforce their workplace substance abuse policies. In the meantime, employers may want to consider reviewing and updating their substance abuse policies, including their drug-testing policies, to ensure they are clear as to their expectations of employee marijuana use.

You Need To Know > ### Colorado Supreme Court Rules Employers Can Fire Workers for Medical Marijuana Use

On June 15, 2015, the Colorado Supreme Court in a six to zero decision affirmed a lower court ruling that employers can fire employees for the use of off-duty medical marijuana.

The Plaintiff in *Coats v. Dish Network, LLC*, had a medical marijuana card and consumed marijuana off-duty to control muscle spasms. He challenged Dish Network's company policy after he was fired in 2010 for failing a drug test by claiming his use of marijuana was legal under state law even though it was illegal under federal law.

However, the firing was upheld in both the trial court and the Colorado Court of Appeals. The case questioned whether the use of medical marijuana in compliance with the Colorado Medical Marijuana Amendment was "lawful" under the state's Lawful Off-Duty Activities Statute.

The Colorado Supreme Court decided the term "lawful" referred to activities lawful under both state and federal law. "Therefore, employees who engage in an activity such as medical marijuana use that is permitted by state law but unlawful under federal law are not protected by the statute," Justice Allison H. Eid wrote in the opinion.

A copy of the opinion by the Colorado Supreme Court in the case of *Coats v. Dish Network, LLC* is available at www.esrcheck.com/file/Coats-v-DishNetwork.pdf.

Job Applicants May be Required to Undergo a Pre-Employment Drug Test

In *Loder v. City of Glendale (1997) 14 Cal.4th 846*, the City of Glendale, CA, implemented a drug testing program for all newly hired or promoted city employees. Loder, a taxpayer, sought to enjoin the drug testing program as an invasion of privacy. The court held that, under the California constitution, employers may require and conduct pre-employment testing for illegal drugs and may take illegal drug use into consideration if making employment decisions. The rules of *Loder v. City of Glendale* have been repeatedly upheld, including in *Ross v. RagingWire*, as discussed above.

The California court, however, also found that drug testing of current employees without any individualized suspicion of drug use or other special circumstances would violate the employees' privacy rights. Under *Loder,* current employees enjoy greater privacy protection than applicants. The rationale for the difference is that, with a current employee, an employer "can observe the employee at work, evaluate his or her work product and safety record, and check employment records to determine whether the employee has been excessively absent or late," an opportunity the employer lacks with a job applicant. The applicant also has a reduced expectation of privacy because they must provide information to an employer, and the applicant expects to answer questions about their suitability for a particular job.

A person may continue to be an *applicant* and not considered a *current employee* after several days of working a job. In *Pilkington Barnes Hind v. Superior Court, 66. Cal. App. 4th 28 (1998)*, the court ruled that after several days of working, the applicant had not performed any substantive work, and the employer had insufficient opportunity to observe and determine if he had performance problems that might be related to substance abuse. Therefore the employee, who had delayed submitting to the pre-employment drug testing until after the start of employment, was not allowed to evade the employer's testing requirement on the grounds he was a current employee and immune from such testing.

It is not constitutionally permissible, however, for an employer to require drug testing of an employee who applies for promotion to another position. According to *Loder*, the reasonableness of testing in promotion situations must turn upon the nature and duties of the position in question.

Loder was decided in the context of a governmental employer; however, it has been extended to California private-sector employers as well. *See Kraslawsky v. Upper Deck Co., 56 Cal.App.4th 179 (1997)*.

One Strike Rules

A California employer had a one-strike rule for applicants: fail the drug test, and you're permanently ineligible for hire. An applicant applied for a job as a longshoreman and was rejected because he failed his mandatory drug test. After the rejection, the applicant entered rehab and, while still in the program, re-applied for a position. The employer again rejected him, citing its one-strike rule. The employee sued, claiming the rule violated the Americans with Disabilities Act (ADA) protections for recovering addicts. The Ninth Circuit upheld the one-strike rule, holding that the company's rule was not intended to exclude past addicts but to ensure a safe workforce. It also noted that the rule applied to all candidates, not just addicts, and therefore didn't discriminate based on addiction under the ADA or California's FEHA. As the court stated, the "one-strike rule bars applicants based on conduct, testing positive for illegal drugs, regardless of whether their failed test was attributable to recreational drug use or an addiction." See: *Lopez v. Pacific Maritime Association, __ F.3d __, 2011 WL 711884* (9th Cir. March 2, 2011).

In conclusion: if a company's one-strike drug testing policy is consistently applied to all employees, then it's likely legal under the ADA and California's FEHA.

Suspicionless Random Testing

At the federal level, Department of Transportation (DOT) employers are responsible for conducting random, unannounced drug and alcohol tests. The goal of random testing is to discourage substance use by making testing unpredictable. The selection must be made by a random, scientifically valid method, like selection by a computer, and all employees covered by the rule must have an equal chance of being tested. The total number of random tests required each year varies between agencies.

State law may limit or prohibit random suspicionless testing of employees unless the position warrants such testing, such as in "safety sensitive positions." For example, California has upheld an Irrigation District's random drug testing program for employees who perform safety-sensitive work. See *Smith v. Fresno Irrigation District, 72 Cal.App.4th 147* (1999). In Smith, a ditch tender and maintenance worker employed by the District was terminated after testing positive for illegal substances in a random drug test. The appellate court found that the District had a legitimate interest in protecting its employees from a substantial and real risk of injury. It also noted that the employer had distributed a written substance abuse policy ahead of time, had informational meetings, and encouraged employees to seek assistance before testing began.

The court rejected the idea that only individuals who worked in positions affecting public safety could be subjected to random testing and held it was enough if holding a work position in which an impairment could pose a real threat to the employee or his coworkers. Whether a particular position is safety-sensitive is determined by "the degree, severity, and immediacy of the harm posed" by the drug impaired performance of the duties of the position. Where there is a hazardous work environment or hazards in the work itself, the position is likely to be considered safety-sensitive.

However, it should be noted that the test to determine whether a drug test is constitutional looks to the legitimate interests *as weighed against the employee's privacy interest.* Here the privacy interest was diminished by the 6-month notice of the random drug tests. *Smith v. Fresno Irrigation District* was cited as a definitive authority on California random drug testing has been affirmed as the penultimate test on random drug testing in California – with a caveat as to privacy rights. While notice can waive privacy rights, there must be facts indicating that there is something that has diminished an employee's privacy rights in California, even if their job is safety-sensitive. *Williams v. WinCo Holdings, Inc.*, 2016 U.S. Dist. LEXIS 88285 (E.D. Cal. July 6, 2016).

Recently in Florida, the random testing of state employees was found to be unconstitutional where there was not a compelling enough reason to do so. The Florida rule ordered random drug testing for about 80,000 state employees. The federal court ruling held that there was no evidence of a large-scale problem and no urgent reason to mandate drug tests. See: www.nytimes.com/2012/04/27/us/court-rules-florida-governors-drug-testing-order-unconstitutional.html. A more current case cited in place of this specific case is *AFSCME Council 79 v. Scott*, 717 F.3d 851 (11th Cir. Fla. 2013).

Other states including Connecticut, Delaware, Maine, Massachusetts, Minnesota, New Jersey, New York, Rhode Island, and West Virginia limit random testing to workers in safety-sensitive positions. Vermont prohibits random testing altogether.

There are also local restrictions on random drug testing. Employers in San Francisco and Berkeley, California, for example, must comply with local laws that further restrict drug testing. Under San Francisco's ordinance, any drug testing requires reasonable grounds and a clear and present physical danger to the employee, co-worker, or a member of the public – thereby prohibiting random testing. A useful website for up to date drug policies by state is at www.drugfreeconstruction.org/docs/StatebyState-Substance-Abuse-Testing-Policy.pdf.

Reasonable-Suspicion Testing

Reasonable suspicion testing is used when a trained supervisor or employer has reasonable suspicion to believe that an employee has used a controlled substance. A reasonable suspicion of drug use must generally be based on actual facts and logical inferences, such as:

- Direct observation of drug use,
- Direct observation of physical symptoms of drug use, including slurred speech, agitated or lethargic demeanor, uncoordinated movement, and inappropriate responses to questions,
- A pattern of abnormal conduct,
- Erratic behavior while at work,
- Arrest for drug-related offense,
- A significant deterioration in work performance,
- A report of drug use provided by a reliable and credible source that has been independently corroborated,
- Evidence the employee has tampered with current drug test results,
- Information that the employee has caused or contributed to an accident at work, or
- Evidence the employee has used, possessed, sold, solicited, or transferred drugs while working or at work.

A California executive secretary at a company with a reasonable suspicion drug testing program was observed by her senior manager slumped over her desk. When she did not move, the manager asked her what was wrong and she did not answer. The human resources director then observed that the employee's speech was slurred, her demeanor was lethargic, she was swaying, she was unable to maintain eye contact, and her answers seemed to be controlled and very deliberate. However, neither the senior manager nor the human resources director had received formal training on detecting substance abuse. The employee was also allowed to drive herself to a lab for drug testing. For a California jury, these facts implied that the employer did not truly believe she was impaired at the time and the employee was allowed to proceed with a lawsuit for invasion of privacy and wrongful termination. See *Kraslawsky vs. Upper Deck Company, (1997) 56 Cal.App.4th 179.*

Another case was cited as a proper test in analyzing drug testing privacy concerns. The case dealt with a Kohl's worker who tested positive for his medical marijuana after an injury in the workplace. The plaintiff was found to have no expectation of privacy under Kohl's drug testing policy. The case addressed some interesting state by state rules barring discrimination in hiring based on medical marijuana cardholder status. See: *Shepherd v. Kohl's Department Stores*, 2016 U.S. Dist. LEXIS 101279 (E.D. Cal. 2016).

In conclusion, the best practice is to have a drug testing policy in place and to conduct formal supervisor training on how to recognize the signs of drug use.

Author Tip   **Symptoms of Drug Use**

The Mayo Clinic website has an excellent summary of the symptoms of drug use. Drug addiction symptoms or behaviors include, among others:

- Feeling that you have to use the drug regularly—this can be daily or even several times a day.
- Having intense urges for the drug.
- Over time, needing more of the drug to get the same effect.
- Making certain that you maintain a supply of the drug.
- Spending money on the drug, even though you can't afford it.
- Not meeting obligations and work responsibilities, or cutting back on social or recreational activities because of drug use.
- Doing things to get the drug that you normally wouldn't do, such as stealing.
- Driving or doing other risky activities when you're under the influence of the drug.
- Focusing more and more time and energy on getting and using the drug.
- Failing in your attempts to stop using the drug.
- Experiencing withdrawal symptoms when you attempt to stop taking the drug.

Source:
www.mayoclinic.org/diseases-conditions/drug-addiction/basics/symptoms/con-20020970 m.

Reasonable-Suspicion Testing Enablers and How to Deal with a Co-Worker on Drugs

A supervisor or co-worker may enable a drug abuser to continue down the path of destruction by making it possible or easier for the abuser to continue by allowing the employee to perform below standards without intervention or corrective actions. You can enable a co-worker who is a drug abuser by:

- Covering up for daily work missed or performed poorly.
- Taking over or doing the job yourself.
- Accepting excuses for drug abuse.
- Lending money to help drug habit.
- Downplaying or minimizing drug abuse issues.

Enabling a drug abuser in the workplace can result from a feeling of guilt or responsibility, or fear of legal reprisal. Instead of enabling a drug abuser, a business should:

- Establish a written policy that prohibits using or being under the influence of drugs/alcohol at work and covers reasonable suspicion testing.

- Explain the need for testing (safe workplace, lower health costs, improved productivity, etc.).
- Post a policy and conduct education.
- Use consent forms.
- Train supervisors.
- Have a policy on what to do if positive test (allow the employee to explain or retest sample).
- Use medically approved tests and procedures.
- Consider service of a Medical Review Officer (MRO) (mandatory in certain types of testing).
- Keep all tests confidential and maintain file separate from the personnel file.
- Have an Employee Assistance Plan (EAP) in effect.
- Access Drug Free Workplace material online at http://webapps.dol.gov/elaws/drugfree.htm.

What to do if you suspect a drug problem in the workplace:

- If an employee is performing below par, must be treated just like any other employee that is not performing.
- Critical to have a job description and periodic reviews so can clearly define an employee's duty and expected level of performance.
- If there is an issue, then need to observe and document.
- Need to meet with the employee (with a witness) and clearly outline and document concerns.
- Can prepare a performance improvement plan.
- Can refer to EAP or counseling.
- Can refer to a drug test if there is a reasonable suspicion of drug abuse.

If all else fails with a drug abuser, then an employer can go down the road of discipline or termination.

You Need To Know ❯ **OSHA Electronic Accident Reporting Rule Could Affect Post-Injury Drug Testing by Employers**

On May 12, 2016, the Occupational Safety and Health Administration (OSHA) issued a Final Rule in the Federal Register requiring certain employers to electronically submit injury and illness data to OSHA that they must keep under existing OSHA regulations. The rule also states that "OSHA believes the evidence in the rulemaking record shows that blanket post-injury drug testing policies deter proper reporting."

Under the "Improve Tracking of Workplace Injuries and Illnesses" rule, OSHA will post the data from these submissions on a publicly accessible Web site but will not post any information on the website that could be used to identify individual employees. Commenters also stated policies mandating automatic post-injury drug testing as a form of adverse action that can discourage reporting:

Although drug testing of employees may be a reasonable workplace policy in some situations, it is often perceived as an invasion of privacy, so if an injury or illness is very unlikely to have been caused by employee drug use, or if the method of drug testing does not identify impairment but only use at some time in the recent past, requiring the employee to be drug tested may inappropriately deter reporting.

The rule stated that the U.S. House of Representatives Committee on Education and Labor recognized that "to intimidate workers, employers may require that workers are tested for drugs or alcohol [after every incident or injury], irrespective of any potential role of drug intoxication in the incident" and cited a study where one-third of Las Vegas hotel workers reporting work-related pain underwent drug testing.

While some commenters who believe drug testing of employees is important for a safe workplace were concerned that OSHA planned a ban on drug testing: To the contrary, this final rule does not ban drug testing of employees. However, the final rule does prohibit employers from using drug testing (or the threat of drug testing) as a form of adverse action against employees who report injuries or illnesses.

The OSHA rule suggests: To strike the appropriate balance here, drug testing policies should limit post-incident testing to situations in which employee drug use is likely to have contributed to the incident, and for which the drug test can accurately identify impairment caused by drug use. The rule is available at www.federalregister.gov/articles/2016/05/12/2016-10443/improve-tracking-of-workplace-injuries-and-illnesses.

The ADA Does Not Protect Current Illicit Drug/Alcohol Use

In general, a person with a drug addiction who is currently in a drug rehabilitation program or has successfully completed rehabilitation and has not used drugs illegally for some time is covered by the Americans with Disabilities Act (ADA). The ADA makes it unlawful to discriminate against qualified people with disabilities in employment.

Persons who are currently illegally using drugs, however, are not protected under the ADA. The illegal use of drugs includes the use of illegal drugs and the misuse of prescription drugs that are "controlled substances." An employer may refuse to hire an applicant or discharge or discipline an employee based upon a test result that indicates the illegal use of drugs. An employer has no obligation toward individuals who are currently using illegal drugs, regardless of whether such individuals are addicts or casual users of drugs, and regardless of whether the illegal drug use impacts upon the individuals' behavior or job performance.

Is Drug Testing Covered by the Fair Credit Reporting Act?

The answer is: it depends.

The Fair Credit Reporting Act (FCRA) requires, among other things, that employers provide disclosure and obtain consent before securing a *consumer report*. The definition of consumer report is broad and includes information about an individual's "character, general reputation, personal characteristics, or mode of living." Additionally, to be covered by the FCRA, a report must be prepared by a consumer reporting agency (CRA). See FCRA § 603(d)(1).

Regarding the applicability of the FCRA to drug tests, the Federal Trade Commission (FTC) takes a circumstance specific approach. In a letter from William Haynes dated June 11, 1998 (Haynes – Islinger letter), the FTC states:

> When a drug lab provides the results directly to the employer, the test is not a "consumer report" under the FCRA. When an intermediary does so, a detailed factual analysis is needed to determine the answer. When a CRA provides the test results, it is clearly making a "consumer report" to the employer.

When a Drug Lab Provides Results Directly to Employer it is NOT a Consumer Report

The Haynes-Islinger letter explains that "[d]rug tests do bear on an individual's character, general reputation, personal characteristics, or mode of living," however, FCRA § 603(d)(2)(A)(i) excludes from the definition of consumer report any report "containing information solely as to transactions or experiences between the consumer and the person making the report." Since drug tests constitute reports based on the experience of the laboratory, these reports fall into the exception and are not covered by the FCRA when they are provided directly to the employer by the laboratory.

Likewise, the Fifth Circuit has concluded that drug test reports are included in the general definition of a "consumer report." See *Hodge v. Texaco, Inc., 975 F.2d 1093* (5th Cir. 1992). However, the Fifth Circuit ultimately found that the drug report in question fell within the "transactions or experiences" exclusion of FCRA § 603(d)(2)(A)(i) ("any report containing information solely as to transactions or experiences between the consumer and the person making the report").

The Fifth Circuit held that this exclusion "exempts from coverage any report based on the reporter's first-hand experience of the subject." Therefore, a laboratory's report to the employer fell within this exclusion and the report did not constitute a "consumer report" for purposes of the FCRA.

More recently, the United States District Court Northern District of Texas affirmed that workplace drug test reports are not categorically excluded from coverage in *Martinets v. Corning Cable Systems, 237 F.Supp.2d 717* (N.D. Tex. 2002). Again, however, the court found that following the administration of a breathalyzer test on an employee, the laboratory prepared a report that was based on information that it derived as part of its own analysis of the test, which purported to measure the alcohol level in the employee's system. Since the report was a direct result of a transaction and experience between the employee and the laboratory, the court concluded that the report also fell within the "transactions or experiences" exclusion and did not constitute a "consumer report"

When testing is conducted first hand by a credible facility such as a laboratory that provides testing results directly to an employer rather than relying on another facility's results, the testing facility is not a "consumer reporting agency" and the FCRA does not apply.

When an Intermediary Provides the Results to the Employer

Where an intermediary reports the results of a test done by a lab, the issue of whether the communication is a consumer report requires a detailed review of the facts. The answer depends on whether the intermediary is a Consumer Reporting Agency (CRA). The term *consumer reporting agency* is defined in FCRA § 603(f) as "any person which, for monetary fees, dues, or on a cooperative nonprofit basis, regularly engages in whole or in part in the practice of assembling or evaluating consumer credit information or other information on consumers for the purpose of furnishing consumer reports to third parties, and which uses any means or facility of interstate commerce for the purpose of preparing or furnishing consumer reports." See: www.consumer.ftc.gov/articles/pdf-0111-fair-credit-reporting-act.pdf.

According to the Haynes-Inslinger letter, if an intermediary contributes to, or takes any action that determines the content of the information conveyed to an employer, it is "assembling or evaluating" the information and the intermediary qualifies as a CRA. If, however, the intermediary does nothing more than perform mechanical functions, such as arranging for a laboratory to conduct a drug test, collecting samples, forwarding them to the laboratory, and transmitting the test results to the employer, it probably will not be a CRA making a "consumer report." The letter states, by way of example that:

> *"... an intermediary that retains copies of tests performed by drug labs and regularly sells this information to third parties for a fee is a CRA whose reports of drug test results are "consumer reports" covered by the FCRA....If a drug test is provided by a party that is indisputably a CRA because of the general nature of its business (e.g. a credit bureau or employment screening service), the report would clearly be a "consumer report" because the communication is made by a CRA..."*

When employers conduct background checks using the service of a background firm, the firm is "assembling or evaluating" information for a consumer. In this case, any drug test results included in the reporting services would likely be considered a consumer report and FCRA guidelines must be followed.

In conclusion, if an employer obtains drug testing information directly from a drug testing lab, it is less likely to be considered a "consumer report" and subject to the FCRA. If, however, if an employer obtains drug test results as part of a background firm's reporting services, it is likely that the drug test **will** be considered a "consumer report."

The Hayes – Islinger letter may be found at www.ftc.gov/os/statutes/fcra/islinger.shtm.

<table>
<tr><td>

**You Need
To Know**

</td></tr>
</table>

DOT Approves Electronic Forms for Drug Testing

A Final Rule that took effect on April 13, 2015, amends U.S. Department of Transportation (DOT) regulations to incorporate changes to the Substance Abuse and Mental Health Services Administration's (SAMHSA) chain of custody and control form (CCF) approved by the Office of Management and Budget (OMB).

According to the rule ""Use of Electronic Chain of Custody and Control Form in DOT-Regulated Drug Testing Programs" in the Federal Register, the electronic CCF (eCCF) was approved for use by the OMB and the DOT is bound by statute to follow SAMHSA's chain of custody and control procedures to include use of an OMB-approved CCF. The CCF is the tool by which agencies and participants in the testing process are assured that the specimen collected during drug testing is that of the tested employee. The DOT developed its drug testing program that followed mandatory guidelines set forth by the Department of Health and Human Services (HHS).

The Federal Workplace Drug Testing Program was established in 1986 and the HHS created a comprehensive set of standards for the drug testing program. These HHS standards included chain of custody procedures designed to ensure the integrity and security of specimens from the time the specimen is collected until the time the drug testing results are reported by the laboratory. The HHS first issued its mandatory guidelines on in 1988 and created the uniform CCF used to identify a specimen and to document its handling at the collection site.

In 1991, Congress passed the Omnibus Transportation Employee Testing Act (OTETA), which directed the DOT to continue to incorporate HHS guidelines into their drug testing program. As a result, the DOT requires its regulated entities to use the CCF developed by HHS and approved by OMB that used to be only available in paper form. On May 28, 2014, the OMB approved the use of both a paper CCF and an eCCF under the HHS Mandatory Guidelines. The final rule expands the DOT's definition of the CCF to include the OMB-approved eCCF.

For more information about the rule "Use of Electronic Chain of Custody and Control Form in DOT-Regulated Drug Testing Programs" – which expands the DOT's definition of the CCF to include both paper and electronic form – visit: www.federalregister.gov/articles/2015/04/13/2015-08256/use-of-electronic-chain-of-custody-and-control-form-in-dot-regulated-drug-testing-programs.

Illicit Drug Positivity Rate Increases Sharply in Workplace Testing

Posted on Quest Diagnostics Website on June 9, 2015

The percentage of American workers testing positive for illicit drugs such as marijuana, cocaine, and methamphetamine has increased for the second consecutive year in the general U.S. workforce, according to insights from more than 10 million workplace drug test results released today by Quest Diagnostics, the world's leading provider of diagnostic information services. The analysis suggests a potential reversal in the decades' long decline in the abuse of illicit drugs in the United States workforce.

The Quest Diagnostics Drug Testing Index (DTI) shows that the positivity rate for approximately 6.6 million urine drug tests in the general U.S. workforce increased overall by 9.3 percent, to 4.7 percent in 2014 compared to 4.3 percent in 2013. 2013 was the first year since 2003 in which the overall positivity rate for urine drug tests increased in the general U.S. workforce. In addition, overall positivity for oral fluid and hair drug tests, representing approximately 1.1 million tests, increased between 2013 and 2014 in the general U.S. workforce.

The Quest Diagnostics Drug Testing Index analyzed urine, oral fluid and hair drug tests performed by Quest Diagnostics workplace drug testing laboratories across the United States in 2014. Test results are examined according to three categories of workers: employees with private companies (general U.S. workforce); employees subject to federal drug testing rules, including safety-sensitive employees such as truck drivers, train operators, airline and nuclear power plant workers (federally-mandated, safety-sensitive workforce); and a combination of both groups (combined U.S. workforce). Quest Diagnostics has analyzed annual workplace drug testing data since 1988.

Marijuana continues to be the most commonly detected illicit drug, according to the Quest Diagnostics Drug Testing Index. Marijuana positivity in the general U.S. workforce increased 14.3 percent (2.4% in 2014 vs. 2.1% in 2013). By comparison, marijuana positivity in the same workforce category increased 5 percent between 2012 and 2013. In the safety-sensitive workforce, marijuana positivity increased 6 percent (0.71% vs. 0.67%) between 2013 and 2014, compared to 5.6 percent between 2012 and 2013. The steady increase in the marijuana positivity rate is consistent with findings from other data sources, such as the National Survey of Drug Use and Health (NSDUH).

Quest researchers also analyzed urine drug test data for the U.S. workforce from two states with recreational marijuana-use laws. In Colorado and Washington, the marijuana positivity rate increased 14 percent (2.62% vs. 2.30%) and 16 percent (2.75% vs. 2.38%), respectively, in the general U.S. workforce between 2013 and 2014, roughly parallel to the national average of 14.3 percent. By comparison, the marijuana positivity rate increased 20 percent and 23 percent in Colorado and Washington, respectively, in the general U.S. workforce between 2012 and 2013, compared to the national average of 5 percent.

The Quest Diagnostics Drug Testing Index analysis showed steady increases in workplace positivity for cocaine in the general U.S. workforce over the past two years, reversing a prolonged period of decline. The positivity rate for cocaine in urine tests increased by 9.1 percent (0.24% vs. 0.22%) between 2013 and 2014. Urine drug tests account for the vast majority of cocaine drug tests. The positivity rate also increased in oral fluid and hair specimens, by 30.6 percent and 13.0 percent, respectively, year over year.

Continuing a multi-year upward trend, amphetamines use – specifically the use of methamphetamine – showed an increase across both urine and oral fluid drug tests. General U.S. workforce data in urine drug tests showed a 7.2 percent year-over-year increase in amphetamines positivity in 2014 compared to 2013 (1.04% vs. 0.97%). In the general U.S. workforce, methamphetamine positivity in urine drug tests increased 21.4 percent (0.17% vs. 0.14%); the positivity rate for oral fluid methamphetamine tests increased 37.5 percent (0.33% vs. 0.24%). Across all specimen types, the positivity rate for amphetamines is now at its highest levels on record and the positivity rate for methamphetamine is at its highest level since 2007.

Amphetamines describe the category, or drug class, that includes both prescription amphetamine drugs like Adderall® and methamphetamine, an illicit drug often known for being produced in clandestine labs. They are a class of central nervous system stimulants that cause increased energy and alertness followed by exhaustion as the effects wear off. The positivity rate for 6-acetylmorphine, or 6-AM, a specific marker for heroin, doubled in the general U.S. workforce between 2011 and 2014 (to 0.031% in 2014 vs. 0.015% in 2011).

The strengths of the Quest Diagnostics Drug Testing Index analysis include its large sample size, the longitudinal nature of the monitoring, a testing population that is generally reflective of the U.S.

workforce and the quality of the company's drug testing services to confirm positive results. Limitations include the selection of the testing population, which is reflective only of results from employers that perform drug testing and a lack of exact cross-specimen comparisons due to variations in substances for which employers test. Quest Diagnostics Drug Testing Index reports involve analysis of de-identified results from urine, oral fluid and hair drug tests.

The Quest Diagnostics Drug Testing Index reveals insights into patterns of drug use among the American workforce. Published annually for more than 25 years, the Drug Testing Index examines positivity rates for workplace drugs tested by the company on behalf of employers. Quest Diagnostics publishes these findings as a public service for government, employers, policymakers and the general public.

Source: www.questdiagnostics.com/home/physicians/health-trends/drug-testing.

Recommended Drug Testing Information Resources

This chapter was intended as a brief introduction to employment drug testing. A great deal more information is available from these government or non-profit websites.

- www.samhsa.gov—Sponsored by the Substance Abuse and Mental Health Services Administration (SAMHSA), an agency of the U.S. Department of Health and Human Services.
- www.drugabuse.gov—Sponsored by the U.S. National Institute of Drug Abuse.
- www.transportation.gov—U.S. Department of Transportation site, covering tests mandated by that department, commonly referred to as DOT testing.
- http://store.samhsa.gov/home—The national clearinghouse for drug and substance abuse information, sponsored by SAMHSA.
- www.drugfreeworkplace.org—Sponsored by the Institute for a Drug-Free Workplace.
- www.datia.org—Drug and Alcohol Testing Industry Association.

Take the Drug Testing Quiz

(Correct answers are in italics at the end of the quiz.)

Question #1 – Drug testing is utilized:

- Answer 1: By both Fortune 500 firms as well as small businesses.
- Answer 2: Usually only by larger firms.
- Answer 3: Only by trucking firms and other industries concerned with safety sensitive positions.
- Answer 4: By employers that observe signs on current drug abuse.

Question #2 – When a drug test is utilized before hiring:

- Answer 1: There is no need to ever conduct future drug tests if the applicant is hired.
- Answer 2: An employer does not need a consent.
- Answer 3: A consent is a best practice.
- Answer 4: A negative result should not be considered unless there is a clear nexus between the result and the position that is being applied for.

Question #3 – A legally prescribed drug like Valium:

- Answer 1: Is protected by the Americans with Disabilities Act (ADA) and therefore cannot be tested.

- Answer 2: Can be still be abused and be the basis for an employer to deny employment.

- Answer 3: Does not present any workplace issue since it is a legal drug.

- Answer 4: Cannot be the basis for a post-employment drug test since it is a legal drug.

Question #4 – The Americans with Disabilities Act (ADA) and similar state laws:

- Answer 1: Do not protect people currently using illegal drugs, and does not affect drug testing.

- Answer 2: Makes it illegal to test applicants with certain medical issues.

- Answer 3: Protects applicants from discipline or termination for the use of drugs.

- Answer 4: Only applies to current employees and therefore had no relevance to drug testing issues.

Question #5 – If a job applicant tests positive:

- Answer 1: An employer should have the test rechecked to ensure there is no error in order to avoid legal liability.

- Answer 2: The applicant should be given the opportunity to retake the test.

- Answer 3: The applicant should not be hired and the employer should warn future employers about the dangers of that worker.

- Answer 4: A Medical Review Officers (MRO) may contact the applicant to determine if there is any accepted medical reason for the test.

Question #6 – An Employee Assistance Plan (EAP):

- Answer 1: Is required by law.

- Answer 2: Is considered a good practice and can be helpful in dealing with employees that have drug abuse issues.

- Answer 3: Has no relevance to drug abuse since anyone who fails a drug test should be terminated in order to prevent liability claims.

- Answer 4: Should not be used in drug abuse situations, since that is a self-created problem and not what an EAP was intended for.

Question #7 – An instant on the spot drug test administered by an employer of either urine or saliva:

- Answer 1: Is not advisable sine there had not been a sufficient showing of accuracy for these toes of tests.

- Answer 2: Can be the basis to deny employment if report comes back other than clear.

- Answer 3: Can be used to eliminate a person from having a positive drug test, but still needs to be retested at a laboratory if the result is positive.

- Answer 4: Should not be utilized since drug testing can only be conducted legally in a sanction drug collection site.

Question #8 – Which of the following is NOT an example of "enabling behavior" towards an employee suspected of having a drug abuse issue:

- Answer 1: Reporting your suspicions to the employee's supervisor.

- Answer 2: Covering-up for daily work not being done.

- Answer 3: Accept excuses for failure to perform the task at work.

- Answer 4: Downplaying or minimizing the behavior that appears to be related to drug abuse.

Question #9 – The term "clean urine" when used in connecting with drug testing commonly means:

- Answer 1: Is slang for not being on drugs.

- Answer 2: That the person was literally "clean" and passed the drug test.

- Answer 3: Something drug abusers can purchase in order to try to pass a drug test by substituting the purchased urine for their own urine.

- Answer 4: A chemical used to mask drugs in the system so that a person can pass a drug test.

Question #10 – Generally speaking, the impact of Cocaine on the human body is that:

- Answer 1: It creates hallucinations.

- Answer 2: It is a common painkiller.

- Answer 3: It is a central nervous system drug that causes a depressed effect.

- Answer 4: It produces a rush of euphoria but leads to brain and damage issues and affects mental health.

Answers for the Drug Testing Quiz:

Question #1 – Drug testing is utilized:

Correct Answer 1: By both Fortune 500 firms as well as small businesses.

Question #2 – When a drug test is utilized before hiring:

Correct Answer 3: A consent is a best practice.

Question #3 – A legally prescribed drug like Valium:

Correct Answer 2: Can be still be abused and be the basis for an employer to deny employment.

Question #4 – The Americans with Disabilities Act (ADA) and similar state laws:

Correct Answer 1: Do not protect people currently using illegal drugs, and does not affect drug testing.

Question #5 – If a job applicant tests positive:

Correct Answer 4: A Medical Review Officers (MRO) may contact the applicant to determine if there is any accepted medical reason for the test.

Question #6 – An Employee Assistance Plan (EAP):

Correct Answer 2: Is considered a good practice and can be helpful in dealing with employees that have drug abuse issues.

Question #7 – An instant on the spot drug test administered by an employer of either urine or saliva:

Correct Answer 3: Can be used to eliminate a person from having a positive drug test, but still needs to be retested at a laboratory if the result is positive.

Question #8 – Which of the following is NOT an example of "enabling behavior" towards an employee suspected of having a drug abuse issue:

Correct Answer 1: Reporting your suspicions to the employee's supervisor.

Question #9 – The term "clean urine" when used in connecting with drug testing commonly means:

Correct Answer 3: Something drug abusers can purchase in order to try to pass a drug test by substituting the purchased urine for their own urine.

Question #10 – Generally speaking, the impact of Cocaine on the human body is that:

Correct Answer 4: It produces a rush of euphoria but leads to brain and damage issues and affects mental health.

CHAPTER 16

Key Procedures After-the-Hire

Introduction to After-the-Hire Issues

A Safe Hiring Program does not stop once the employer decides to hire the candidate or the candidate goes on the payroll. Lawsuits for negligent retention have put employers on notice that due diligence extends well beyond the hiring stage. In fact, employers have a continuing obligation during the entire employment relationship to exercise due diligence for protecting co-workers, the public, customers, and investors.

The laws governing employment relationship are complicated, involved, and covered by scores of outstanding books and resources. *The purpose of this chapter is to focus on a number of areas unique to safe hiring and due diligence that should be considered after the applicant has been hired.*

Author Tip　**Initial After Hire Issues**

To be successful even after a hiring decision is made, a Safe Hiring Program must also take into account how the new employee is brought on board. The following topics are not just Human Resources best practices. They also impact ongoing issues related to retention and supervision. Most importantly, these practices protect an employer in the event a candidate who seemed like a good hire turns out to be a potential nightmare. These best practices help an employer set the stage by clearly outlining expectation, and in the event something goes wrong, gives the employer legal protection if termination is eventually required, or an employer becomes the target of a lawsuit for negligent retention or supervision.

The Offer Letter

Making a formal offer letter in writing is generally considered a best practice. The offer letter will verify the basic terms agreed upon by the employer and the applicant—the salary, job title, start date, and benefits.

If the employer makes the offer prior to the completion of the background report, then the offer letter serves another vital purpose: it explains to the applicant that the hiring decision is conditioned upon the employer's receipt of "a background screening report that is satisfactory to the employer." This is important language. First, the offer letter protects the employer in the event the screening is not yet completed. By specifying the background report must be satisfactory to the employer, it limits a future debate over what is or is not an objectively satisfactory report. The idea is to create a subjective standard. This does not give an employer the right to make judgments that are discriminatory, arbitrary, or capricious, but it does give some measure of protection if something is discovered after the offer is made.

Importance of Well-Written Job Description

We have already seen in Chapter 3 that a well-written and detailed job description is normally the basis of any effort to recruit new employees. It is also critical to making an offer letter, as well as onboarding and subsequent performance evaluations. An employer needs to define precisely what the job requires and what reasonable accommodation will help the employee carry out the job. Job descriptions are used to determine the requirements for the position, identifying responsibilities, and setting compensation. While an offer letter will set out the knowledge, skills, and abilities needed to be successful on the job, a well-written job description will specify the essential functions of the job. This is critical in the event an applicant files a claim under the Americans with Disabilities Act (ADA). From a legal perspective, a well-written job description also assists an employer in defending against claims of discrimination. For the purposes of a Safe Hiring Program, the specification of qualifications is critical.

New Employee Orientations

Another critical step for new hires is the new employee orientation. The orientation starts the employment relationship off on the right track by letting new employees know what role they play in the company and how their contributions are important. Typically, the first few days on the job are stressful for any new employee. Experienced managers know that taking the time to go through a well-planned orientation can lessen the anxiety considerably and contribute to a new employee's success. As a practical matter, the new employee orientation also serves as an opportunity to convey necessary information to that employee on such practical matters as the physical layout of the premises and introduction to co-workers, and to a review of employment terms such as compensation and benefits.

From a Safe Hiring Program perspective, the new employee orientation also serves as a valuable opportunity to impress upon new employees the importance the firm places on safety and employees. It is an opportunity to underscore the firm's commitment to a workplace with zero tolerance for drugs, dishonesty, or violence.

Employee Manual

An employee manual is a mission critical item for any organization. A manual spells out the terms and conditions of employment so there is no misunderstanding. From a legal viewpoint, labor lawyers have long taught employers that a manual is one of the most effective defenses an employer has for defending themselves against employment lawsuits. For example, if an employee violates a work rule, an employer has a much better chance of defending discipline or termination if the work rule was in a manual that the employee received and signed. If an employer has a sexual harassment or discrimination policy in their manual, this also gives increased protection.

An employee manual is invaluable as part of as Safe Hiring Program because it sets out policies in several important areas:

- **Workplace Violence** – It is a critical part of any effort to prevent workplace violence to clearly set out a policy that states the employer maintains a safe workplace; that there is a zero-tolerance policy for violence, threats, or intimidation; that all employees are expected to assist in the effort.
- **Drugs** – An employee manual is an essential aspect of any program to deal with employment related drug abuse.
- **Background Screening** – A best practice is to have information about safe hiring and references about screening in the employee manual.
- **"At Will" Basis** – The employment is "at will," which means there is no employment contract and either side can terminate the relationship.
- **Ethics, Confidentiality, and Standards of Behavior** – Employees are clearly put on notice regarding this critical area.
- **Social Media Policy** – As referenced in Chapter 14, an employer needs a post-hire social media policy that covers issues a ranging from acceptable online behavior that impacts the employer to issues such as who owns the company email.

Form I-9 Employment Eligibility Verification Compliance

Introduction to Identity Verification through Form I-9 and E-Verify

As seen in Chapter 11 concerning the social security trace and Chapter 22 on identity there are steps pre-hire during the screening process that employers can take to attempt to confirm identity. However, these steps are somewhat limited since pre-hire, consumers have great expectation of privacy and more protections.

However, once an offer had been made and an employee is undergoing the onboarding process, additional tools are available to employers to confirm identity. In fact, employers are required to utilize the form I-9 process and may soon be mandated to use E-verify. The next portion of this chapter reviews the Form I-9 and E-Verify programs.

The **Immigration Reform and Control Act (IRCA) of 1986** makes it "unlawful for a person or other entity… to hire, or to recruit or refer for a fee, for employment in the United States an alien knowing the alien is an unauthorized alien." Employers violating that prohibition may be subjected to federal civil and criminal sanctions. The IRCA also requires employers to take steps to verify an employee's eligibility for employment. Per federal law, every employer is obligated to utilize a procedure to ensure that a person has a right to work in the U.S.

The form used in this procedure is called the **'Form I-9, Employment Eligibility Verification'** or simply **'Form I-9.'** The completion of the I-9 Form is done after a person is hired and gives the employer another layer of protection against employing a person with a false identity.

The Form I-9 program is under the authority of the **U.S. Citizenship and Immigration Services (USCIS)** – the government agency that oversees lawful immigration to the United States – within the Department of Homeland Security (DHS). That department was formerly known as the Immigration and Naturalization Service (INS).

USCIS Publishes Revised Form I-9 to Use for All New Hires in the United States

On November 14, 2016, the USCIS published a revised version of *'Form I-9, Employment Eligibility Verification'* with changes designed to reduce errors and enhance form completion using a computer. **Employers must use only the new version of the Form I-9 dated 11/14/2016 N by January 22, 2017.** The new Form I-9 is available on the USCIS website at www.uscis.gov/system/files_force/files/form/i-9.pdf.

Among the changes in the new Form I-9, Section 1 asks for "other last names used" rather than "other names used." Other changes in the new Form I-9 include:

- The addition of prompts to ensure information is entered correctly.
- The ability to enter multiple preparers and translators.
- A dedicated area for including additional information rather than having to add it in the margins.
- Embedded instructions for completing each field.
- A supplemental page for the preparer/translator.
- Streamlining the certification for certain foreign nationals.

The new Form I-9 is also easier to complete on a computer. Enhancements include drop-down lists and calendars for filling in dates, on-screen instructions for fields, easy access to the instructions, and an option to clear the form and start over. When employers print completed forms, a quick response (QR) code is automatically generated that can be read by most QR readers.

The instructions for using the new Form I-9 have been separated from the actual Form I-9, in line with other USCIS forms, and include specific instructions for completing each field on the form. The instructions on how to use the new Form I-9 are available at www.uscis.gov/system/files_force/files/form/i-9instr.pdf.

> **You Need To Know**
>
> ### More Information about Form I-9 Available at "I-9 Central"
>
> For more information on Form I-9—including instructions, questions and answers, learning resources, and customer support—visit the **"I-9 Central"** webpage on the USCIS website at www.uscis.gov/i-9-central.

The Form I-9 Process

In the I-9 procedure, the employer is required to physically view documents concerning identity and list eligibility. The Form I-9 process defines and utilizes three classes or lists of documents—A, B, and C.

List A includes documents that confirm both identity and the right to work. For U.S. citizens, the easiest means of proof is a U.S. passport. For individuals who are citizens of other countries, there are various documents they can provide, such as cards issued by the USCIS.

List B includes documents that show identity, such a driver's license or various other government ID cards.

List C documents show an eligibility to work, and can include a certified birth certificate or a card issued by the Social Security Administration.

There are two important rules to keep in mind:

1. Employers must review and verify by examining one document from List A OR examine one document from List B and one from List C.

2. If a person does not have a List A document, then one document from List B and one from List C must be provided.

Below are acceptable documents for each list on the Form I-9 dated 11/14/2016 N available on the USCIS website at www.uscis.gov/system/files_force/files/form/i-9.pdf.

LISTS OF ACCEPTABLE DOCUMENTS

All Documents Must Be UNEXPIRED

Employees may present one selection from List A
or a combination of one selection from List B and one selection from List C.

List A - Documents that Establish Both Identity and Employment Authorization

1. U.S. Passport or U.S. Passport Card
2. Permanent Resident Card or Alien Registration Receipt Card (Form I-551)
3. Foreign passport that contains a temporary I-551 stamp or temporary I-551 printed notation on a machine-readable immigrant visa
4. Employment Authorization Document that contains a photograph (Form I-766)
5. For a nonimmigrant alien authorized to work for a specific employer because of his or her status: a) Foreign passport; and b) Form I-94 or Form I-94A that has the following: (1) The same name as the passport; and (2) An endorsement of the alien's nonimmigrant status as long as that period of endorsement has not yet expired and the proposed employment is not in conflict with any restrictions or limitations identified on the form
6. Passport from the Federated States of Micronesia (FSM) or the Republic of the Marshall Islands (RMI) with Form I-94 or Form I-94A indicating nonimmigrant admission under the Compact of Free Association Between the United States and the FSM or RMI

List B - Documents that Establish Identity

1. Driver's license or ID card issued by a State or outlying possession of the United States provided it contains a photograph or information such as name, date of birth, gender, height, eye color, and address
2. ID card issued by federal, state, or local government agencies or entities, provided it contains a photograph or information such as name, date of birth, gender, height, eye color, and address
3. School ID card with a photograph
4. Voter's registration card
5. U.S. military card or draft record
6. Military dependent's ID card
7. U.S. Coast Guard Merchant Mariner Card
8. Native American tribal document
9. Driver's license issued by a Canadian government authority

Acceptable List B Documents for Persons Under Age 18 Who are

Unable to Present a Document Listed Above:

10. School record or report card
11. Clinic, doctor or hospital record
12. Day-care or nursery school record

List C - Documents that Establish Employment Authorization

1. A Social Security Account Number card, unless the card includes one of the following restrictions: (1) NOT VALID FOR EMPLOYMENT (2) VALID FOR WORK ONLY WITH INS AUTHORIZATION (3) VALID FOR WORK ONLY WITH DHS AUTHORIZATION
2. Certification of Birth Abroad issued by the Department of State (Form FS-545)
3. Certification of Report of Birth issued by the Department of State (Form DS-1350)
4. Original or certified copy of a birth certificate issued by a State, county, municipal authority, or territory of the United States bearing an official seal
5. Native American tribal document
6. U.S. Citizen ID Card (Form I-197)
7. Identification Card for Use of Resident Citizen in the United States (Form I-179)
8. Employment authorization document issued by the Department of Homeland Security

Of course, a determined individual may find a way around this procedure. As reported on the official USCIS website, "Employers are not required to be document experts. In reviewing the genuineness of the documents presented by employees, employers are held to a reasonableness standard."

However, the I-9 verification process is one of the most powerful tools an employer has. At a minimum, it puts up roadblocks that may deter, or detect persons using fraudulent identification.

U.S. Citizenship and Immigration Services (USCIS) I-9 Procedures

The procedures for the I-9 process can be found online at the **I-9 Central** webpage of the USCIS website at www.uscis.gov/i-9-central. Here are some of the many resources available on this page:

- About Form I-9: www.uscis.gov/i-9-central/about-form-i-9
- Complete & Correct Form I-9: www.uscis.gov/i-9-central/complete-and-correct-form-i-9
- Acceptable Documents: www.uscis.gov/i-9-central/acceptable-documents

- Retain & Store Form I-9: www.uscis.gov/i-9-central/retain-and-store-form-i-9
- Employee Rights & Resources: www.uscis.gov/i-9-central/employee-rights-and-resources
- Penalties: www.uscis.gov/i-9-central/penalties
- Customer Support: www.uscis.gov/i-9-central/customer-support
- Learning Resources: www.uscis.gov/i-9-central/learning-resources
- I-9 Central Questions & Answers: www.uscis.gov/i-9-central/questions-and-answers
- Handbook for Employers (Update Coming Soon): www.uscis.gov/sites/default/files/files/form/m-274.pdf

Here is a brief description of the general procedures taken from the USCIS website.

Employee's Responsibility Regarding Form I-9

A new employee must complete Section 1 of a Form I-9 no later than close of business on his/her first day of work. The employee's signature holds him/her responsible for the accuracy of the information provided. The employer is responsible for ensuring that the employee completes Section 1 in full. No documentation from the employer is required to substantiate Section 1 information provided by the employee.

Employer's Responsibility Regarding Form I-9

The employer is responsible ensuring completion of the entire form. No later than close of business on the employee's third day of employment services, the employer must complete section 2 of the Form I-9. The employer must review documentation presented by the employee and record document information of the form. Proper documentation establishes both that the employee is authorized to work in the U.S. and that the employee who presents the employment authorization document is the person to whom it was issued. The employer should supply to the employee the official list of acceptable documents for establishing identity and work eligibility. The employer may accept any List A document, establishing both identity and work eligibility, or combination of a List B document (establishing identity) and List C document (establishing work eligibility), that the employee chooses from the list to present (the documentation presented is not required to substantiate information provided in Section 1). The employer must examine the document(s) and accept them if they reasonably appear to be genuine and to relate to the employee who presents them. Requesting more or different documentation than the minimum necessary to meet this requirement may constitute an unfair immigration-related employment practice. If the documentation presented by an employee does not reasonably appear to be genuine or relate to the employee who presents them, employers must refuse acceptance and ask for other documentation from the list of acceptable documents that meets the requirements. An employer should not continue to employ an employee who cannot present documentation that meets the requirements.

Questions About Genuineness of Documents

Employers are not required to be document experts. In reviewing the genuineness of the documents presented by employees, employers are held to a reasonableness standard. Since no employer which is not participating in one of the employment verification pilots has access to receive confirmation of information contained in a document presented by an employee to demonstrate employment eligibility, it may happen that an employer will accept a document that is not, in fact, genuine – or is genuine but does not belong to the person who presented it. Such an employer will not be held responsible if the document reasonably appeared to be genuine or to relate to the person presenting it. An employer who receives a document that appears not to be genuine may request assistance from the nearest Immigration field office or contact the Office of Business Liaison.

Discovering Unauthorized Employees

It occasionally happens that an employer learns that an employee whose documentation appeared to be in order for Form I-9 purposes is not actually authorized to work. In such case, the employer should question the employee and provide another opportunity for review of proper Form I-9 documentation. If the employee is unable to provide satisfactory documentation, then employment should be discontinued. Alien employees who question the employer's determination may be referred to an Immigration field office for assistance.

Discovering False Documentation

False documentation includes documents that are counterfeit or those that belong to someone other than the employee who presented them. It occasionally happens that an employee who initially presented false documentation to gain employment subsequently obtains proper work authorization and presents documentation of this work authorization. In such a case, U.S. immigration law does not require the employer to terminate the employee's services. However, an employer's personnel policies regarding provision of false information to the employer may apply. The employer should correct the relevant information on the Form I-9.

Photocopies of Documents

There are two separate and unrelated photocopy issues in the employment eligibility verification process. First is whether an employer may accept photocopies of identity or employment eligibility documents to fulfill I-9 requirements. The answer is that only original documents (not necessarily the first document of its kind ever issued to the employee, but an actual document issued by the issuing authority) are satisfactory, with the single exception of a certified photocopy of a birth certificate. Second is whether the employer may or must attach photocopies of documentation submitted to satisfy Form I-9 requirements to the employee's Form I-9. The answer is that this is permissible, but not required. Where this practice is undertaken by an employer, it must be consistently applied to every employee, without regard to citizenship or national origin.

I-9 Audits of Employers

The **U.S. Immigration and Customs Enforcement (ICE),** the principal investigative arm of the U.S. Department of Homeland Security (DHS), performs inspections to determine if employers in the United States are violating employment laws by hiring unauthorized workers. ICE has the authority to issue a Notice of Inspection (NOI) to employers to give notice the agency is conducting inspections for compliance with proper use of the Form I-9s. Businesses undergoing I-9 audits must hand over all Form I-9s for ICE to inspect, and these audits may result in the firing of illegal workers found on a company's payroll and civil and criminal penalties for employers ranging from fines to criminal charges.

You Need To Know

DOJ Significantly Increases Fines for Form I-9 Violations

On June 30, 2016, the U.S. Department of Justice (DOJ) published a Final Rule in the Federal Register that will significantly increase fines for Form I-9 violations that include incorrect Form I-9 paperwork, unlawful employment of unauthorized workers, and unfair immigration-related employment practices.

The "Civil Monetary Penalties Inflation Adjustment" Final Rule – which took effect August 1, 2016 – increases fines for errors on the Employment Eligibility Verification, Form I-9 that newly hired workers must complete to ensure that they are legally eligible to work in the United States in the following way:

- Form I-9 Paperwork Violations: For the first offense, the minimum fine increased from $110 to $216 per Form I-9 violation while the maximum fine increased from $1,100 to $2,156 per Form I-9 violation. Fines for second and third offenses also increased.

- Unlawful Employment of Unauthorized Workers: For the first offense, the minimum fine will increase from $375 to $539 while the maximum fine will increase from $3,200 to $4,313 per worker. Fines for second and third offenses will also increase.

- Unfair Immigration-Related Employment Practices: The minimum penalty will increase from $375 to $445 while the maximum penalty will increase from $3,200 to $3,563 per charge. Repeat offenders will face a new maximum penalty of $21,563.

While Rule takes effect on August 1, 2016, the increase to Form I-9 fines will apply to violations that took place after November 2, 2015. The DOJ Final Rule is available at www.federalregister.gov/articles/2016/06/30/2016-15528/civil-monetary-penalties-inflation-adjustment.

With the significant increases in fines for Form I-9 violations, employers would be wise to conduct an audit of their Form I-9 compliance practices to make certain they are properly completing the Form I-9 process and have appropriate Form I-9 policies and employment eligibility verification procedures.

Author Tip **DOJ & DHS Issue Guidance to Employers on Internal Form I-9 Audits**

In December of 2015, the Department of Justice's (DOJ) Civil Rights Division and the Department of Homeland Security's U.S. Immigration and Customs Enforcement (ICE) issued joint "Guidance for Employers Conducting Internal Employment Eligibility Verification Form I-9 Audits." Under the Immigration and Nationality Act (INA), employers are required to verify the work authorization of their employees using the Form I-9 and are prohibited from knowingly hiring unauthorized workers. Employers seeking to ensure their Form I-9 practices comply with federal law are increasingly conducting internal audits of their Forms I-9. To ensure that these audits are conducted properly and do not discriminate against employees, ICE and OSC have collaborated to issue formal guidance on the topic that is available at www.justice.gov/crt/file/798276/download.

As part of the government's **quiet immigration raid policy** to crackdown on employers of illegal immigrants, ICE has cracked down on Form I-9 compliance and the hiring illegal workers by issuing NOIs to thousands of businesses in recent years to notify the businesses that they must verify the legal work status of their employees. According to a report by the Wall Street Journal (WSJ) about I-9 audits in September 2013, ICE officials told the WSJ that hiring records are inspected "to ensure compliance with U.S. employment laws" and that the U.S. government has audited "at least 10,000 employers suspected of hiring illegal labor" and imposed administrative and criminal fines totaling more than $100 million in the last four years.

The WSJ report is available at http://online.wsj.com/article/SB10001424127887324755104579071331936331534.html. A Sample Audit Notice from ICE is available at http://online.wsj.com/public/resources/documents/ICEAudit091213.PDF.

ICE issues fines to employers for both the hiring of illegal workers and paperwork errors on forms, with fines ranging from $110 to $1,110 per form depending on the violation. Statistics over the past few years show that ICE has been focusing more and more on targeting the employers that hire illegal workers through the use of Form I-9 audits and investigations. Below are stories about some recent I-9 audits that cost businesses plenty.

Form I-9 Audit Results in Nearly $2 Million Fine for Hotel

In September 2014, The U.S. Immigration and Customs Enforcement (ICE) announced that a hotel chain will forfeit nearly $2 million to the Department of Homeland Security (DHS) for hiring unauthorized workers –including illegal aliens – following a Form I-9 audit and a non-prosecution agreement between the company, the U.S. Attorney for the District of Utah, and ICE's Homeland Security Investigations (HSI).

ICE reported that several lower-level employees and mid-level managers at Salt Lake City, UT-based Grand America Hotels and Resorts "conspired to rehire unauthorized workers" during a Form I-9 audit of employee verification forms. After Grand America had been notified that 133 employees were not authorized to work in the United States and issued a warning notice, the company told HSI those employees were terminated. HSI special agents later learned "the conspirators" in the company created temporary employment agencies to rehire 43 of the unauthorized workers under different names using fraudulent identity documents.

ICE reports that along with forfeiting $195,000 to the DHS Grand America is required to take substantial remedial measures expected to cost the company nearly $500,000 to implement that include:

1.   Adopting new policies to comply with immigration law;

2.   Incorporating immigration law compliance clauses into labor service contracts;

3.   Re-training human resources employees on Form I-9 procedures; and

4.   Agreeing to continue to use the E-Verify employment eligibility verification website.

ICE also reports this settlement is a result of a Form I-9 audit of Employment Eligibility Verification forms. Employers are required by the Immigration Reform and Control Act (IRCA) to maintain original Form I-9 forms for all current employees for inspection. In the case of former employees, retention of forms is required for a period of at least three years from the date of hire or for one year after the employee is no longer employed, whichever is longer. The announcement is at www.ice.gov/news/releases/1409/140910saltlakecity.htm.

One way to be prepared for an audit is to utilize solutions that provide an electronic online verification process. A number of private firms offer commercial solutions.

E-Verify Electronic Employment Eligibility Verification

As indicated in the previous news story, in addition to filling out the paper Form I-9 Form, employers can also utilize the Electronic Employment Eligibility Verification Process known as E-Verify. This program run by the federal government allows employers to verify the employment eligibility of prospective employees through the Social Security Administration and the DHS.

E-Verify is an Internet-based system that compares information from an employee's Form I-9 to data from U.S. Department of Homeland Security and Social Security Administration records to confirm employment eligibility. It is operated by the U.S. Citizenship and Immigration Services (USCIS), part of the Department of Homeland Security (DHS), and is the government agency that oversees lawful immigration to the United States. It utilizes both Homeland Security and Social Security Administration (SSA) data.

The program is voluntary except the federal government requires that all federal contractors and subcontractors use E-Verify to verify that their newly hired workers are legally eligible to work in the United States. In addition, a number of U.S. states have enacted laws mandating the use of E-Verify. A table of these states is proved later in this chapter.

In order to participate in the program, an employer must execute a Memorandum of Understanding (MOU). Background screening firms may also act as an employer's authorized 'Designated E-Verify Employer Agent.'

For information on how the E-Verify program operates, visit: www.dhs.gov/e-verify.

There has been much debate as to the accuracy and completeness of the databases used, and if a worker is not verified, then there are a number of steps an employer must go through to complete the process. In early 2007, the federal government significantly increased the penalty on employers who employ workers with fake Social Security numbers.

What Is E-Verify?

According to the United States Citizenship and Immigration Services (USCIS) website: "E-Verify is an Internet-based system that compares information from an employee's Form I-9, Employment Eligibility Verification, to data from U.S. Department of Homeland Security and Social Security Administration records to confirm employment eligibility." Currently, E-Verify is:

- Used nationwide by more than 600,000 employers of all sizes.
- Used at more than 1.9 million hiring sites.
- Joined by about 1,400 new participating companies every week.
- One of the federal government's highest-rated services for customer satisfaction.

See: www.uscis.gov/e-verify/what-e-verify.

E-Verify History and Milestones

A chronological summary of important milestones of the E-Verify Program taken from the *'History and Milestones'* page of the USCIS website is available in the Addendum.

E-Verify For Federal Contractors

The following information is found on the 'For Federal Contractors' pages on the USCIS website:

Executive Order 12989 Amendment

On June 11, 2008, President George W. Bush amended Executive Order 12989 to direct all executive departments and agencies to require contractors to electronically verify employment authorization of employees performing work under qualifying federal contracts. U.S. Department of Homeland Security (DHS) designated E-Verify as the electronic employment eligibility verification system that all federal contractors must use to comply with the amended Executive order 12989.

Employment Eligibility Verification, Federal Acquisition Regulation (FAR)

On November 14, 2008, the Civilian Agency Acquisition Council and the Defense Acquisition Regulations Council published a Federal Acquisition Regulation (FAR) final rule (FAR case 2007-013, Employment Eligibility Verification) that implements amended Executive Order 12989. FAR is a set of rules and regulations used to manage the way the federal government acquires supplies and services for appropriated funds. The FAR final rule, known as the E-Verify federal contractor rule, directs federal agencies to require many federal contractors to use E-Verify to electronically verify the employment eligibility of certain employees. For more information about FAR, visit: http://edocket.access.gpo.gov/2008/E8-26904.htm.

The Federal Contractor Rule and E-Verify

The final rule became effective September 8, 2009, and requires certain federal contractors, through language inserted into their contract, to begin using E-Verify to verify their new and existing employees. See the E-Verify Supplemental Guide for Federal Contractors manual at www.uscis.gov/USCIS/Verification/E-Verify/E-Verify%20from%20Controlled%20Vocabulary/FAR_Supplemental_Guide_REVISED_FINAL.pdf.

E-Verify Federal Contractor List

In accordance with the E-Verify Memorandum of Understanding, U.S. Department of Homeland Security posts the E-Verify Federal Contractors List - a list of contractors who currently use E-Verify on the Federal Acquisition Regulation clause. The list contains the business name (the name which was used during registration with E-Verify, whether the legal name of the business or individual, a trade name or abbreviation), contact address used at registration, workforce size, employee verification (all new hires or entire workforce), and query volume. You can access by going to the Federal Contractors List page. The list may take several minutes to download."

U.S. States with E-Verify Laws

As mentioned, use of E-Verify is voluntary, other than those employers affected by the federal law mandating use for federal contractors and subcontractors in all states. However, a number several U.S. states have enacted laws mandating the use of E-Verify for all public and private employees while others only government employees. One state, California, passed a law mandating NO E-Verify requirement.

The table below using information from NubersUSA.com identifies the states that have laws regarding E-Verify usage that is available at www.numbersusa.com/resource-article/everify-state-map.

U.S. States with E-Verify Laws (as of May 2016)

State	E-Verify Law(s)
Alabama	**HB 56** - Passed in 2011, HB 56 is regarded by many as the nation's toughest immigration enforcement law passed at the state level. HB 56 requires all employers, public and private, to use E-Verify by April 2012 to ensure the workplace eligibility of all new hires. It also requires E-Verify use as a condition of being awarded any government contract, grant or incentive. The penalty for noncompliance with the E-Verify mandate is a suspension or revocation of a business license, or loss of a contract, grant, or incentive.
Arizona	**HB 2779/HB 2745** - Passed in 2007, HB 2779 prohibits employers from knowingly hiring undocumented workers and requires all employers to use E-Verify, effective January 1, 2008. It was followed up in 2008 with HB 2745, which prohibits government contracts to any businesses not using E-Verify, effective May 1, 2008. Penalty is suspension or revocation of a business license or contract cancellation
California	**AB 1236** - In October 2011, Governor Jerry Brown signed into law AB1236, which prohibits municipalities from enacting or maintaining mandatory E-Verify ordinances. The measure voided a number of ordinances already on the books. **AB 622**- As of January 1, 2016, California employers may face civil penalties of up to $10,000 for misusing E-Verify. Most California employers are not required to use E-Verify (see above). However, some California employers, such as those performing work under a federal contract, may be required by federal law to use E-Verify. California's new E-Verify law is primarily aimed at employers who choose to use E-Verify without being required to do so under federal law or as a condition of receiving federal funds. There are three conditions which reflect current DHS rules: • It is unlawful for an employer to use E-Verify to check the employment authorization status of an existing employee (unless required by federal law or as a condition of receiving federal funds). • An employer may use E-Verify to check the employment authorization status of a person who has been offered employment. • If an employer receives a Tentative Nonconfirmation, the employer must (as soon as

	practicable) give the employee any TNC or any notification issued by the SSA or Department of Homeland Security containing information specific to the employee's case.
Colorado	**HB 1343/SB 193** - Passed in 2006, HB 1343 requires prospective state and local government contractors to either use E-Verify or participate in an alternative state program concerning the examination of work documents. It also prohibits state and local government agencies from entering into contracts with employers who knowingly employ illegal aliens. In 2008, SB 193 extended the requirement to existing state contractors and, under the alternative program, established a new requirement to submit for each new hire an affirmation that legal work status was examined. Penalty is contract cancellation and possible debarment.
Florida	**Executive Orders** - Effective January 2011, Executive Order (EO) 11-02 requires E-Verify used by all state agencies and contractors assigned to perform work pursuant to a state agency contract. EO 11-116 clarifies that the E-Verify requirement for state contractors applies to "all contracts for the provision of goods and services to the state in excess of nominal value." Penalties include possible denial of future projects.
Georgia	**SB 529/HB 87** - Passed in 2006, SB 529 requires the phased-in use of E-Verify by public employers, contractors, and subcontractors through July 1, 2009. HB 87, passed in 2011, requires all private businesses with more than 10 employees to use E-Verify as of July 1, 2013. Failure to comply could result in the suspension or denial of a business license, occupational tax certificate, or other document required to operate a business in the state.
Idaho	**Executive Order** - In May 2009, Governor Butch Otter signed EO 2009-10, which led to regulations requiring all state agencies and contractors to use E-Verify. Penalties include contract cancellation.
Illinois	**HB 1774/HB 1743/SB 1133** - HB 1744 barred Illinois companies from enrolling in E-Verify pending the resolution of accuracy and timeliness issues. A court case invalidated the bar and led to the enactment of HB 1743, which allows companies to use E-Verify but creates privacy and antidiscrimination protections for workers when employers violate E-Verify procedures. Illinois also enacted SB 1133, which prohibits the state or localities from requiring employers to use E-Verify.
Indiana	**SB 590** - Passed in 2011, SB 590 requires state and local government agencies and contractors to use E-Verify. The bill also creates a state tax credit incentive for private employers to use E-Verify.
Kansas	**Executive Order** by the Office of the Secretary of State which has used E-Verify -- and has required all contractors with that office to use E-Verify -- since 2011. But the rest of Kansas state government has declined to follow.
Louisiana	**HB 342/HB 646** - Passed in 2011, HB 342 requires all state and local government contractors to use E-Verify. Penalties include contact cancellation and debarment. HB 646 requires public and private employers to either use E-Verify or check and retain acceptable work authorization documents. Those using E-Verify are not subject to civil penalties if an employee is later found to be working unlawfully.
Minnesota	**Executive Order** - In January 2008, Governor Tim Pawlenty issued an executive order requiring E-Verify use by all state agencies and companies seeking a state contract in excess of $50,000. The executive order expired 90 days after Pawlenty left office but a state budget deal subsequently reinstated the state contractor requirement effective July 20, 2011.
Mississippi	**SB 2988** - Passed in 2008, SB 2988 requires public and private employers to participate in E-Verify by July 2011. Penalties include license suspension and contract debarment.
Missouri	**HB 1549** - Passed in 2008, HB 1549 requires all public employers, businesses with a state contract or grant in excess of $5,000 or any business receiving a state-administered or subsidized tax credit, tax abatement or loan to use E-Verify. Penalties include loss of a business

	license or contract.
Nebraska	**LB 403** - Passed in 2009, LB 403 requires state and local governments and contractors to use E-Verify effective October 1, 2009. The bill also includes incentives for private employers to use E-Verify.
North Carolina	**HB 318/SB 1523/HB 36** - Passed in 2015, HB 318 requires all state and local government contractors to use E-Verify. A 2006 bill, SB 1523, requires all state agencies, offices, and universities to use E-Verify by March 1, 2007. Passed in 2011, HB 36 requires all counties, cities and private employers with more than 25 employees to use E-Verify by July 2013. Seasonal workers are not required to be verified through E-Verify. Penalties can include civil fines.
Oklahoma	**HB 1804** - Passed in 2007, HB 1804 requires public employers, contractors, and subcontractors to participate in E-Verify and requires income tax withholding for independent contractors who do not have valid Social Security numbers.
Pennsylvania	**SB 627** - Passed in 2011, SB 627 requires all public works contractors and subcontractors with contracts of $25,000 or greater to use E-Verify by January 1, 2013. Penalties include debarment.
Rhode Island	**Executive Orders** - In March 2008, Governor Carcieri issued an executive order requiring state agencies, grantees, contractors and their subcontractors and vendors to use E-Verify. Shortly after taking office in 2011, Gov. Lincoln Chafee rescinded Gov. Carcieri's executive order.
South Carolina	**HB 4400/SB 20** - Passed in 2008, HB 4400 requires the mandatory use of E-Verify for all public and private employers by July 1, 2010. After a 2011 U.S. Supreme Court decision, SB 20 replaced the law's civil penalties for noncompliance with loss of a business license.
Tennessee	**HB 1378/SB 1965** - Passed in 2011, HB 1378 requires all public and private employers with more than 6 employees to either use E-Verify or check and retain acceptable work authorization documents. On April 21, 2016, the Governor signed into law SB 1965, which requires mandatory E-Verify use for all employers with 50 or more employees effective January 1, 2017.
Texas	**Executive Order/SB 374** - In December 2014, Texas Governor Rick Perry issued RP-80, which requires E-Verify use by state agencies and contractors, at least with respect to those employees assigned to the contract. In 2015 Texas enacted SB 374, which requires state agencies and institutions of higher education to use E-Verify as of September 1, 2015. The law did not require state contractors to enroll but the Attorney General issued a subsequent finding that it does not negate the related requirement under Gov. Perry's executive order.
Utah	**SB 81/SB 251/HB 118** - SB 81, passed in 2008 and made effective on July 1, 2009, requires public employers, public contractors and subcontractors to use E-Verify and makes it illegal to discharge a lawful employee while retaining an unauthorized alien in the same job category. Penalties include debarment for contractors. Passed in 2010, SB 251 required private employers with 15 or more employees to use E-Verify by July 1, 2011. The measure did not provide for non-compliance penalties or enforcement. In 2011, Utah enacted HB 116, which establishes a state guest worker program but also complicates SB 251's requirements by creating Verify Utah, an alternate verification program. Technically, the requirement for private employers with 15 or more employees to use E-Verify still exists, but cannot be considered a hard mandate like in other states since there is no enforcement and the guest worker program, lacking a needed federal waiver, was never established.
Virginia	**HB 737/HB 1859** - Passed in 2010, HB 737 requires all state agencies to use E-Verify by December 1, 2012. Passed in March 2011, HB 1859 (combined with SB 1049) requires all state contractors with at least 50 employees and a contract worth at least $50,000 to use E-Verify. Penalties include debarment for contractors.

The article below details a ruling by the U.S. Supreme Court that upheld Arizona's E-Verify law.

> ## U.S. Supreme Court Ruling Upholds Mandatory Arizona E-Verify Law
>
> In a 5-to-3 decision in May of 2011, the U.S. Supreme Court ruled states can punish employers who violate mandatory E-Verify laws by upholding a 2007 Arizona law that requires employers to enroll in the voluntary federal E-Verify program which checks the legal status of workers by comparing information on their Employment Eligibility Verification Form I-9s against Department of Homeland Security (DHS) and Social Security Administration (SSA) databases.
>
> In the majority opinion for the Court, Chief Justice John Roberts wrote that Arizona enforces its E-Verify employment verification requirement through licensing laws:
>
>> "Arizona's procedures simply implement the sanctions that Congress expressly allowed the States to pursue through licensing laws. Given that Congress specifically preserved such authority for the States, it stands to reason that Congress did not intend to prevent the States from using appropriate tools to exercise that authority... We hold that Arizona's licensing law falls well within the confines of the authority Congress chose to leave to the states and therefore is not expressly preempted."
>
> The U.S. Chamber of Commerce had sued the state of Arizona over a 2007 law that suspends licenses of businesses if they fail to use E-Verify to check the eligibility of all new hires, arguing that immigration enforcement is exclusively the purview of the federal government. Arizona was the first state in the country to pass a mandatory law requiring mandatory use of the E-Verify electronic employment eligibility verification system by employers. Mississippi and South Carolina have also passed mandatory E-Verify laws, while many other states have passed laws requiring E-Verify use by some businesses. The full Supreme Court ruling on the case is available at www.supremecourt.gov/opinions/10pdf/09-115.pdf.

E-Verify Receives High Scores in User Survey

In October 2014, the U.S. Citizenship and Immigration Services (USCIS) released the "Findings of the E-Verify User Survey" of nearly 3,000 randomly sampled E-Verify employers conducted by Westat to assess their satisfaction with the program.

The independent, in-depth E-Verify survey of 2,819 employers randomly chosen from a list of 76,828 eligible employers in the E-Verify Transaction Database also gathered information on opinions and experiences of employers with using the E-Verify program and solicited recommendations for further improvements. Key findings from the E-Verify survey include:

- 97 percent of E-Verify employers surveyed agree that the system is user-friendly.
- 97 percent of E-Verify employers surveyed report using the program for all new hires.
- 93 percent of E-Verify employers surveyed agree that the mandatory tutorial adequately prepared them to use E-Verify.
- 92 percent of E-Verify employers surveyed believe that E-Verify is effective
- 89 percent of E-Verify employers surveyed perceive E-Verify to be highly accurate.

For more information about E-Verify Program Reports, please visit www.uscis.gov/e-verify/about-program/e-verify-program-reports.

Designated E-Verify Employer Agents

Employers may choose to have a Designated E-Verify Employer Agent assist them in maintaining compliance with the Form I-9 and E-Verify process and can help virtually eliminate I-9 form errors, improve the accuracy of their reporting, protect jobs for authorized workers, and help maintain a legal workforce.

USCIS Website and E-Verify Optimized for Mobile Devices

In March 2016, the USCIS announced a series of enhancements to make both the USCIS website and the online E-Verify program easier to use on mobile devices.

Mobile device users visiting http://uscis.gov/ and http://uscis.gov/es will find both websites easier to use because the content now automatically adjusts to fit the screen of a smartphone, tablet, laptop, or desktop computer. The USCIS mobile-responsive design also includes the new digital assistant Emma.

The USCIS enhancements to E-Verify make logging in and viewing cases quick and efficient. Many of these ideas came from customer submissions through the E-Verify Listens website. These ideas include case creation screens that now replicate the order of fields on Form I-9.

According to the USCIS, approximately 30 percent of visitors to the English site and more than 50 percent visiting the Spanish site now use a mobile device. The USCIS announcement is available at www.uscis.gov/news/uscis-website-e-verify-now-optimized-mobile-devices.

Trump Immigration Policy May Include Mandatory E-Verify

The transition from President Barack Obama to President Donald Trump could be a "very significant change of course" that includes changes to U.S. immigration policy such as mandatory use of the E-Verify electronic employment eligibility verification system, according to a Bloomberg BNA report.

Kansas Secretary of State Kris Kobach – who played a significant role in drafting Arizona's strict immigration law S.B. 1070 – told Bloomberg BNA that the Trump transition team for immigration policy on which he serves is already creating a "to do list" of actions the incoming president "may want to do in immigration policy."

That list includes the mandatory use of the E-Verify system – which is currently optional for most U.S. employers – to ensure newly hired employees are authorized to work in the country. Kobach told Bloomberg BNA that since mandatory E-Verify "would require congressional action," the Trump transition team for immigration policy is drafting bills to introduce in Congress.

Kobach also told Bloomberg BNA that mandatory use of the E-Verify system could become law despite recent congressional gridlock on immigration policy since "Democrats who are concerned about stagnant wages that American workers face are likely to favor E-Verify." The complete Bloomberg BNA article is available at www.bna.com/trumps-immigration-list-n57982082673/.

Employment At Will and Probationary Periods

A critical issue for employers is the nature of the employee-employer relationship. Employers typically hire on an **at will** basis, meaning there is no employment contract and either side can terminate the relationship. Of course, nothing is that simple. Employers are normally advised to be very clear in all stages of the recruiting, interviewing, and hiring procedure so that no promises or contracts are made—either expressed or implied—that modify the at-will arrangement. Again, nothing is that smooth. An applicant may argue that, by certain employer's actions or deeds, there is an implied promise of future employment that can only be terminated "for cause" as opposed to "at will."

Examples of instances where an employee may argue they are no longer "at will" are listed below:

- Language in an interview that says "if a person does well, the company will take care of them," or other similar promises of special treatment on the part of the employer.
- Language in the employee manual that creates a probationary period. The implication is that if a person passes the probationary period, they have vested or obtained a more secure status and there must be *good cause* to terminate rather than a right to terminate at will.
- Employee manual language that sets out a series of progressive disciplinary steps where an employee has a chance to improve performance. The implication is if they meet the standards, then the person is no longer at will.
- A listing of actions or omissions that are grounds for discipline or termination. The argument is if one of these enumerated acts or omissions is not committed, then the employer needs cause to terminate.
- When an employee has been with the employer for a period of time and has received promotions, regular pay increases, and good performance reviews, the employee can argue he or she is no longer at will.

Along with appropriate statements in the application, the employee manual is also a critical tool to reinforce the "at will" nature of employment.

It is also necessary to ensure that everyone with hiring responsibilities is trained not to make statements that imply a commitment beyond "at will." There are also other exceptions to the "at will" status, such as civil service employment, collective bargaining agreements, or public policy exceptions to "at will" status.

From the perspective of a Safe Hiring Program, maintaining the "at will" relationship can be vital to an employer in the event issues arise related to workplace violence or misconduct, or it is later discovered the employee made material misstatements or omissions during the hiring process. Even though an employer may have grounds to terminate based upon the misconduct or misrepresentation, the "at will" status will assist the employer's position.

Confidentiality Agreements and Ethics Policy

Another best practice is to obtain a confidentiality and ethics agreement as part of the employment relationship. Some firms place the language in the employee manual. However, having it as a separate document may give additional emphasis. Although the specific language may vary for a particular industry, the essential thrust is to establish that honest and ethical dealings are part of the firm's culture, and an essential element of the duties and responsibilities of every employee. Although some employers may assume that some truths are self-evident and that it goes without saying that honest and ethical behavior is required, saying so serves as a valuable reminder.

Maintaining Employment Screening Records

Record keeping and maintaining personnel files are always an important issue for employers. Files should contain information regarding the employment application, and qualifications for employment, as well as all personnel actions such as compensation, promotions, transfers, demotions, discipline, and terminations.

In reality, an employer maintains multiple files on an employee. In addition to the "official" personnel file, supervisors or managers may maintain files. In addition, there are matters normally kept in a separate and secured file. These files are normally stored in an area only accessible to Human Resources personnel or those who are authorized. These files contain matters that are confidential or sensitive in nature, and widespread publication could constitute an invasion of personal privacy. These files should NOT be accessible by supervisors during performance appraisals.

Confidential matters contained in these files can include:

- Background reports.
- Letter of reference.
- Verification of right to work (Employment Eligibility Verification "Form I-9").
- Workers' compensation claims.
- Medical information.
- Documents concerning employee status as a disabled person, veteran, or other status.
- Defamatory information.
- Information unrelated to the job.

Supervisors may also keep files reflecting such things as notes or memos of discussions for issues or problems that have arisen. These notes may indicate what was discussed, when, and who was present. These notes may be used during performance evaluations.

When it comes to human resources and employment screening, in particular, the mindset of having a physical file is quickly changing.

A screening firm with more sophisticated software alleviates the need to even have a file since everything from the consent process to the screening report can be performed and stored online. There is no reason for an employer to create a physical file. If the employer uses an Applicant Tracking System (ATS) for the application process, and video interviewing software to perform the interview, there is very little if anything that exists on paper.

Employees May Have the Right to Inspect Their Personnel Files

Keep in mind that, in many states, employees have a right to inspect their own personnel file.

Files should be maintained where the employee reports to work. Employers may generally impose reasonable restrictions such as setting up appointments during regular business hours or on the employee's own time, limiting the frequency, or require an employer representative to be present, but the employer cannot set arbitrary time limits. If there is an inspection, then the employer should keep a history of the request and the response.

The right to inspection may not include:

- A record of the investigation of the possible criminal offense.
- Letters of reference, unless steps are taken to safeguard the identity of the authors.
- If a file contains other confidential data, then the identity of persons can be removed, i.e. the employer should protect the privacy of third persons.

An example is California Labor Code Sec. 1198.5(a) that provides that every public and private employee has a right to inspect his or her personnel files except for public safety offenses and certain employees' subject to the Information Practices Act of 1977. The right to inspect includes files with information used to determine employee qualifications, promotion, compensation, termination, or other disciplinary action. Failure to allow inspection is a misdemeanor, punishable by a fine up to $100 and imprisonment for 30 days.

Screening Current Employees

When reviewing background-checking policies, a question often arises about whether current employees should be screened, or whether the background check policy should apply to new applicants only.

The perceived need to screen current employees can occur in several situations:

1. It may be necessitated by a new contract with a customer who requires all workers performing under the contract have a background check.
2. It can also occur when a firm "acquires" another workforce through a merger or acquisition. The acquiring firm is not familiar with the new workforce
3. A firm that has not previously performed background checks decides to start screening new employees and makes the judgment that instead of "grandfathering" in the current workforce, that all existing employees will also be screened. Some organizations make the decision as a matter of fundamental fairness, so everyone is treated the same, or in order to ensure that the entire workforce has been reviewed for due diligence.
4. There can also be situations where an employer is concerned about some type of workplace misconduct or wrongdoing such as theft or harassment.
5. An employer may decide to perform "continuous" screening, by doing yearly checks, as a due diligence measure designed to minimize risk and a tool against potential insider threats.

There are two factors to consider in screening current employees—legal and cultural.

It is perfectly legal to screen current employees as long as all their rights are respected. (Keep in mind if an employer is unionized, there may be special workplace rules.) A current employee is entitled to the same legal rights as a new applicant, and if there is a union involved, perhaps even additional rights. Under the federal Fair Credit Reporting Act (FCRA), if the background check is performed by a third-party service provider, then current employees are entitled to the same rights as new applicants, which includes a disclosure of rights and written consent. Some states have additional rules that employers must be mindful to follow. As previously mentioned in Chapter 3, if an existing employee is screened for allegations of wrongdoing or misconduct, then his or her consent may not be needed under the FACT Act amendment to the FCRA. In addition, the original screening authorization may have included an "Evergreen" clause allowing for future screening for retention purposes, and depending up the exact situation may be of assistance to an employer.

The cultural or practical consideration is whether the employer wants to ask existing employees to consent to a background check. The issue is one of corporate culture—not alienating employees who have been hardworking and loyal by announcing that the employer will now be performing background checks.

Checking current employees can cause all sorts of anxieties. Not only is there uncertainty about who expect, but an employee can feel they ae being mistrusted or their privacy invaded. If a current employee has something minor that occurred in their life such as a misdemeanor offense of disturbing the peace, they may be concerned that they will suddenly lose their job and be escorted off premises. ,

If an employer decides it is necessary to screen current employees, it is recommended that HR first explain screening is "a business necessity for the good of the entire organization" and not directed to any one employee. This is designed to increase employee buy-in. Equally critical is for employees to understand all their rights are being respected, and nothing will occur as a result of a background check until the employee has a full opportunity to discuss any negative findings with the employer. In fact, an existing employee should certainly have all of the same rights a new applicant would have under the EEOC Guidance of 2012 (Chapter 10) when it comes to employers analyzing the relationship between offense and the job, as well as proving an "Individualized Assessment" process. Problems can arise if an employee feels powerless in the process, concerned about an adverse action without an opportunity to be heard. It is crucial to tell all employees they may come to Human Resources to privately discuss the procedure. An employee may start off talking about privacy concerns when, in fact, there is something of concern in the person's background.

Another consideration occurs when an existing employee may not sign a consent form. If employees have a clear understanding of how this policy helps both the employer and the employee, then there is typically good employee participation. However, in a worst case scenario where an employee absolutely refuses to consent, an employer can take the following position – let the employee know that they have the right not to consent. On the other hand, just as the employee has a right not to consent, the next time the employee is up for a pay raise or promotion, the employer equally has the right not to promote or give a raise. This tactic may be considered if a current employee refuses to sign a consent form before the employer takes the more difficult track of termination. As a practical matter, if an employee delays participating in the process, that can be a sign that the employee has some sort of issue, and an HR professional may well take the person aside to have a confidential discussion as to their concerns.

When criminal record checks are conducted on current employees, the best practice is to consider employees who have been working successfully for at least 18 to 24 months to be presumptively fit for the position. One recommendation is that termination would only be considered if a newly discovered conviction or new legal requirement created a "compelling need." In other words, a successful current employee that has demonstrated they can do the job and present little risk may be essentially be given the benefit of the doubt, even if a matter may disqualify a new applicant Keep in mind that one of the important reasons employers need background checks is that they are hiring people they do not know, which request due diligence. Once the employer knows the worker, and the worker has been successful, there should be a decreased need to rely upon checks.

If the conviction record disqualifies the employee for his current position because of a new statute or legal regulation, or because of a new contractual provision affecting the work the company does for an outside organization, the employee should be offered an opportunity to transfer within the company if any transfer position is appropriate for the employee's qualifications and record with the company.

Sample Letter for Screening Current Employees

Dear (Employee),

As you are probably aware, background checks have become more important in today's business environment. In order to demonstrate due diligence and to protect (Company Name), we believe it is prudent to institute a program for a background check for all new hires. However, to be fair, we believe it is also important to ensure that we have background checks on file for all current employees so that everyone at (Company Name) is treated the same way.

First, please rest assured that by performing background checks on current team members, (Company Name) is in no way whatsoever suggesting that there are any concerns about the background of current team members. The purpose is strictly to demonstrate that as an organization, we are committed to due diligence and maintaining a safe and profitable workplace. This process provides our firm with a great deal of legal protection and is for the benefit of everyone.

It is also important to understand that:

1. All aspects of the background checks are confidential and your privacy is assured.

2. We are conducting the checks through a nationally recognized third party, Employment Screening Resources (ESR) at www.ESRcheck.com. They are accredited by the National Association of Professional Background Screeners (NAPBS), a distinction held by less than 2% of all screening firms.

3. ESR has a strong privacy and data protection program and their privacy policy can be reviewed at www.esrcheck.com/Privacy-Policy.

It is also important to understand that in the extremely unlikely event that something should appear on a background report of concern to the employer, nothing will happen until a team member has had every opportunity to review the background check and meet with Human Resources. Also keep in mind that under the federal Fair Credit Reporting Act (FCRA), consumers have a great deal of protection and many rights when it comes to background checks. This company is firmly committed to treating everyone fairly, and if anything of concern appears on the report, you can be assured that the company will carefully analyze a report consistent with current laws and consult with you before any action is taken.

The process will consist of each team member receiving an email invitation from Employment Screening Resources (ESR) to go to a secured web page, where you will be asked to review your rights and provide identifying information and an electronic signature. Again, your privacy and rights are of paramount importance and your data and information are safe. By checking on a box that is provided, you have a right to also get a free copy of your report sent to you electronically as well. Any report sent to you by email will have key information such as date of birth and social security number truncated for your protection as well.

Please contact me if you have any questions or concerns and I will be happy to discuss the matter with you.

Regards,

(Employer)

Court Case: Kelchner v. Sycamore Manor Health Center

In the first court case to address the issue of an employee not consenting, a Federal District Court in Pennsylvania decided that an employer can terminate a current employee who refused to sign a consent for a background check. In *Kelchner v. Sycamore Manor Health Center*, 2004 U.S. Dist. Lexis 2942 (M.D. Pa. 2004), the employer required all employees to sign a consent to a consumer report. A worker with 19 years on the job refused to sign and was terminated. The Court held that the plain language of the statute, as well as Congressional intent, demonstrated that employers had the right to require such a consent and could terminate if an employee refused, just as an employer could refuse to hire an applicant who did not consent in the first place.

Continuous Screening or Re-Screening

A new evolving practice called Continuous Screening, Infinity Screening, or Re-Screening is aimed at running periodic criminal records checks, such as every two weeks, monthly, semi-annually, or annually on employees. These periodic checks have the potential to identify criminal cases that occur after the person was hired. Although the argument is made that the employer would likely be aware of a crime committed by a current worker because the worker did not show up to work, there are many serious offenses where a worker can be bailed out and serve a sentence with work furlough, weekend jail time, volunteer hours, or some other alternative to actual incarceration. Advocates of these ongoing searches suggest they are a way to continue to demonstrate due diligence, protect the workplace and combat insider threats and workplace violence.

While these continuous searches can be considered as a risk-management tool, an employer needs to consider a number of factors:

- False Sense of Security: Remember, employers sometimes use databases that contain errors.
- Consent Issue: Does the employee know he or she will be re-screened?
- What to do if a Record is found: Will the applicant be put on probation or fired?
- EEOC Considerations: Make sure the re-screening is not discriminatory under Title XII.

- Impact on Workforce: Will morale of employees suffer?

Continual Re-Screening on Current Employees Carries Risks

The verdict on whether or not the advantages of periodic background checks of current employees outweigh the disadvantages is: "the jury is still out."

Even though periodic criminal screening of current employees may have some apparent advantages, it is an open question whether it is a cost-effective tool or even if the advantages outweigh the disadvantages. Here are some points to consider:

- There is no empirical evidence that shows that such checks have resulted in any advantage to employers. There are no studies to suggest, on a cost-benefit basis, such checks produce results.
- If such checks are done, the next issue is how. If databases are used, then there is the possibility of both false positives and false negatives since databases available to private employers are not always complete, accurate, or up to date. In large states like California, New York, and Texas, such database searches have very limited value.
- If there is a periodic check, it should be done ideally on the courthouse level in addition to any databases, which increases the cost.
- There is also the consent issue. Under the federal Fair Credit Reporting Act (FCRA), all checks including periodic checks must be done with consent (unless there is a specific investigation for suspicion of misconduct or wrongdoing), Although most consent forms contain "evergreen" language that makes the initial consent valid indefinitely or until revoked (usually in writing), at some point, an employee can either withdraw the consent or claim it has become stale over time. In California, the argument has been made that a new consent is needed each and every time.
- If an employee withdraws consent, the question arises if the employee can be terminated for refusal to consent. It is clear that employers have much more discretion in requiring pre-employment testing, based on the fact that they do not have experience with the applicant. For that reason, courts have granted wider latitude pre-hire. However, once someone is employed, the necessity argument is less convincing since the employer now has a history with the worker. Therefore, it is not clear that an employee can be terminated for a refusal to consent to an ongoing criminal check, absent some explicit employer policy or a strong showing of need. The employer could argue that since employment is "at will," failure to consent to an ongoing background check can constitute grounds for termination. The problem is that as time goes on, the "at will" relationship can become murky depending upon the facts of the employment relationship.
- The issue becomes more complicated if the refusing employee is a member of a protected class. That raises potential discrimination issues.
- Another complication is when the policy is instituted. If a new worker comes onboard when the policy is in place, it is much harder to object if it is clearly outlined in the employee manual. If conversely, the policy is new, current employees will have more difficulty dealing with it, requiring HR to engage in employee education to show how the policy benefits everyone.
- In addition, a firm needs a well laid out policy in an employee manual as to how they will deal with a new criminal record that may be uncovered during a periodic check. At a minimum, any action must be based upon some business justification, taking into account the nature and gravity of the offense, the nature of the job, and how long ago it occurred per the 2012 EEOC Guidance. In addition, the pre-adverse action notice requirements of the federal Fair Credit Reporting Act (FCRA) would come into play as well as the "Individualized Assessment" process outlined by the EEOC.
- There are also the cultural considerations. What type of message does it send the workplace if workers are constantly suspected of criminal activity? What type of workplace stress is created if an otherwise long time and loyal employees feel they are subject to dismissal at any time for a minor offense that may or may not bear upon their suitably as an employee? If the employer is unionized, then union rules can also play a role.
- One possible solution for employers that have determined that continual screening is necessary is to conduct it in a similar fashion to random drug testing done for certain drivers that are controlled the Department of

Transportation. Random pools can be set up and "real" criminal checks done at the courthouse rather than a so-called "national" database that can be subject to false positives and false negatives.

Having noted the disadvantages, the case can well occur where an employer is sued for a failure to check current employees if such a failure to check was the proximate cause of workplace violence or some other harm that arguably could have been prevented.

The bottom line is that this is an issue that will be worked out in a court decision in the coming years. In the meantime, employers contemplating such periodic checks should approach it with caution and seek the advice of their attorney.

You Need To Know

How A Company Ended Up Paying $1.6 Million to Re-Screen Workers

On September 8, 2015, the U.S. District Court for the District of South Carolina entered a consent decree ordering BMW Manufacturing Co., LLC (BMW) to pay $1.6 million as part of the resolution of a lawsuit filed by the U.S. Equal Employment Opportunity Commission (EEOC) that claimed BMW excluded African-American logistics workers from employment at a disproportionate rate when the company's new logistics contractor applied BMW's criminal conviction records guidelines when re-screening incumbent employees.

The EEOC complaint alleged that when BMW switched contractors handling the company's logistics at a production facility, the company required the new contractor to perform a criminal background re-screening on all existing logistics employees who re-applied to continue working in their positions at BMW. At that time, BMW's criminal conviction records guidelines excluded from employment all persons with convictions in certain categories of crime, regardless of how long ago the employee had been convicted or whether the conviction was for a misdemeanor or felony.

After the criminal background checks had been performed, BMW learned that approximately 100 incumbent logistics workers at the facility, including employees who had worked at there for several years, did not pass the re-screening. The EEOC alleged 80 percent of the incumbent workers disqualified from employment as a result of applying BMW's guidelines were black.

Following an investigation, the EEOC filed suit alleging that blacks were disproportionately disqualified from employment as a result of the criminal conviction records guidelines. EEOC sought relief for 56 African-Americans who were discharged. BMW has since voluntarily changed its guidelines.

Source: www.eeoc.gov/eeoc/newsroom/release/9-8-15.cfm

You Need to Know: Issues Related to Screening Re-Hired Former Employees

A frequently asked question is whether there needs to be rescreening for an employee who left and is now coming back. In other words, in a rehire situation, does an employer we need a new background check.

In formulating a policy for rehires and background checks, the first thing to do is to determine if the employer is subject to any law or regulation with specific requirements. If there is no federal or state regulation on the point, then it is a matter of risk management.

An employer should apply a rule of reason in administering their background checking program to re-hires. There is no one "approved" period of time and each employer needs to determine what is reasonable for their industry given the risks involved. A clear "bright-line" approach is one solution. An employer could, for example, adopt a policy that if the gap is less than six months, no background check is needed (except perhaps a criminal check for the county of current residence). If greater than six months, then an employer could simply take the position that in order to be fair to everyone and to treat everyone the same that a rehire must go through the same process as any new hire. Given how inexpensive background check have become, cost is not a serious fact. In fact, it would arguably cost a company more in terms of administrative overhead to have a program where individual decisions need to be made about each rehire. Of course, there is no need to recheck previously checked past employment or education because that does not change. However, criminal checks by definition start to become stale immediately after they are run. Whatever approach you take, it is important to document it clearly including the business justification.

Where it gets more complicated is where the re-hire is a result of the person having been convicted of a crime. For example, a worker with a stellar employment record is convicted of a crime, serves a sentence, gets out of prison, completes his probation, and then reapplies for a laborer/service maintenance position similar to the position he had prior to his conviction.

The process an employer goes through is just as important as the decision reached. The employer should utilize the Equal Employment Opportunity Commission (EEOC) analysis, and document what was found, and the basis for the decision. For example, if the criminal matter is not job related, does not create an undue risk given the position and the past offense, and the decision making process has been documented, an employer would have a basis to consider the person especially if they performed well in the past. It goes back to the three-part EEOC test to determine if the past conduct is related and if there is a business reason not to hire. Also important is to not to automatically reject an applicant with a record without first going through the three-part analysis. If you decide not to hire, then he should be afforded an opportunity to request a further review under the "Individualized Assessment" procedure.

If you decide to hire, you can also determine if there is any assistance you can provide to help the person succeed or if any special supervision.

The worst case for employers in such a situation is that they take a chance and hire an ex-offender and something bad happens resulting in a lawsuit. However, that is why the employer needs to clearly document what was considered in making the hiring decision and why it appeared justified at the time. Although a "Monday morning quarterback" may try to second guess the decision, the key thing is that the process showed due diligence, even if in the end there were bad results. The critical thing is that although not everyone is qualified for every job, there is a job for everyone.

If Re-Screening Results Lead to Possible Termination Issues

What if the screening of a current employee results in a decision to terminate? If the screening reveals the applicant had a criminal conviction not indicated on the application, then an employer could choose to terminate for dishonesty. However, keep in mind that the exact wording of the criminal question on the employment application is critical. If the employer only asked about felonies, then an undisclosed misdemeanor—even a serious misdemeanor—may not be grounds to terminate for dishonesty. An employee may give other reasons why failure to disclose was not an act of dishonesty. An employee may claim that they did not realize it was a conviction or claim they did not understand what the judge or their lawyer told them. Some defendants enter a plea of "nolo" or "no contest." Although that may give a criminal defendant some protection if they are later sued in a civil court, a "nolo" or "no contest" plea has the same effect as pleading guilty.

Suppose the screening of existing employees reveals a criminal record that was not mentioned in the application or interview process. This is potential grounds for termination, providing the employer's application form put an applicant on notice that any material misstatement or omission is grounds for termination no matter when discovered. (See the discussion about application forms in Chapter 7.) The situation becomes difficult when the employee claims he/she did inform the manager of past difficulties, but the manager failed to inform human resources. The solution is to ensure that all pre-hire procedures are followed and documented, and all managers are trained in the hiring procedures.

In addition, if the screening discloses an offense that occurs AFTER employment, the employer may decide to take action. However, the Equal Employment Opportunity Commission (EEOC) rules should apply. The employer must take into account the nature and gravity of the offense, how long ago it occurred, and whether it is job-related in order to determine if there is a business necessity to deny continued employment.

An employer should also document any decision NOT to terminate in case the employer has to defend a decision to terminate some employees with criminal records and not others. If the employer has a written policy that requires employees to inform the employer if a criminal conviction occurs after employment begins, then an employer can take the position that the termination is a result of a violation of a written company policy. As a practical matter, an employer would likely be aware of any serious criminal matter after employment commences, since an employee may not show up to work or need time off for court appearances. If an employee is arrested and not able to come to work, then an employer should examine the employee manual to determine the company's rule for unexcused absences.

If termination is considered, then the employer needs to be mindful of the FCRA requirements for pre-adverse action. In addition, the "Individualized Assessment" rules should also apply. An employee cannot simply be brought into the office and given their final check. The FCRA requires a pre-adverse action notice, giving the employee has a meaningful opportunity to review, reflect, and respond to the consumer report if the employee feels it is inaccurate or incomplete. One method is to meet with the employee, explain that a matter of concern came up in the screening report, and to provide the employee with a copy of the report and a statement of their rights prepared by the FTC, which the screening firm can provide. The employee should also be provided a letter advising that he or she should respond to the employer or the screening firm as soon as possible if there is anything the employee wishes to challenge or explain.

Since the employer notice is pre-adverse action by definition, an employer may consider placing the employee on five days paid administrative leave with instructions to either contact the employer in five days if the employee plans to contest the consumer report or the leave turns into a termination. If the employer does not hear back, then the employee is terminated. See the Termination Procedures section below for special considerations on terminations.

If the applicant notifies the employer of plans to contest the report, then the employer can make a case-by-case judgment to either continue the employment, place the employee on unpaid leave, or terminate pending resolution of the re-investigation with a right to reapply. The FCRA does not require the employer keep a job open or keep an employee on paid leave during the re-investigation period, but only requires a meaningful opportunity to receive notice of the pre-adverse action and deal with the report before the adverse action is taken. If the decision to terminate becomes final, then the employee is entitled to the second FCRA post-adverse action letter. The decision to place on leave can also be affected by the provisions of the employee manual or the existence of union contracts.

Employee Misconduct Issues

Another situation where a background check may be warranted involves workplace misconduct, such as theft, harassment, or threats of violence. Prior to the 2003 amendments to the FCRA, these types of investigations presented substantial legal issues when background checks were conducted by professional third party investigators. For example, if the investigation centered on suspected criminal activities such as theft, drug dealing, or workplace violence, it would be difficult to conduct an undercover investigation and obtain witness identities if consent had to be obtained first. A number of court decisions undercut the FTC's position. The matter was finally laid to rest with the passage of the Fair and

Accurate Credit Transactions Act (FACT) in 2003, with amendments to the FCRA becoming effective in 2004. The amendments allow investigation of current employees to take place without FCRA consents, subject to some requirements, such as if an adverse action was taken that there be disclosure.

Ongoing Training

Ongoing training is also another critical aspect to employers. Training can cover a wide variety of topics; an employer should include issues related to safety and security.

Training should have an emphasis on supervisors, having them trained to recognize, report, and deal appropriately with workplace misconduct. In addition, supervisors must be properly trained and educated regarding the employer's liability for negligent hiring, supervision, retention and, promotion.

Performance Reviews and Ongoing Monitoring

Periodic performance appraisals—as well as ongoing review of performances—are additional mission critical tasks for employers. For purposes of ongoing safe hiring, the concern is whether the firm conducts periodic performance reviews of workers that include issues related to workplace conduct.

It is especially important that supervisors be evaluated on compliance with the duty to record, report, and address workplace misconduct. Supervisors must also understand they are evaluated in part by monitoring workplace misconduct. Without proper documentation, an employer may lack evidence later.

Advantages of Performance Reviews

According to Dennis L. DeMey in his book *Don't Hire a Crook* (©2001 BRB Publications, Tempe, AZ), performance reviews are an excellent way to maintain quality employment. As mentioned earlier, the job description informs the employee of the company's expectations of him or her. The performance review is the follow-up.

Performance reviews give employers the opportunity to examine employee performance and let them know areas where they need to improve. Oftentimes, a performance evaluation is conducted in conjunction with a salary review, then used to determine if a pay increase should be given and, if so, how much.

There are many times when a review may be conducted. Here are a few reasons:

- The employee has reached the end of his or her probationary period.
- The employee is being considered for promotion.
- The employee has exhibited unsatisfactory performance.
- Company policy requires that a review is documented annually.
- The employee has performed exceptionally well.

Performance reviews are yet another means of good communication between employee and employer. Likewise, it is a step that should be documented. By documenting performance reviews, two goals are accomplished:

- The employee has a written copy of areas that need improvement, and therefore may refer back to it; and
- The employer has a document that can be used to illustrate a history of problems, if that is the case.

Responding to Employee Complaints

Employees concerned about violence, dishonesty, or fraud should have the opportunity to lodge complaints. Timely and attentive management of potential problem situations along with appropriate follow-through and documentation are the keys to avoiding legal claims of negligent hiring/supervision.

To accomplish these goals, employers must have a mechanism for employees to report instances of workplace misconduct, such as violence, dishonesty, or fraud. The mechanism should also include the ability to report acts of harassment, discrimination, or other incidents that create a hostile work environment, but without fear of retaliation or reprisals, especially if the subject of the complaint is a supervisor or someone in authority. Under Sarbanes-Oxley, a whistleblower hotline may also be established.

In fact, in the employee policy manual an employer can even require that in the event of harassment or other misconduct, there is a duty to report it to management so the employer can investigate and take remedial action.

Also, the employer must have a mechanism in place to fairly and promptly investigate complaints and to have demonstrated a commitment to take appropriate actions in response to the results of the investigation. Being able to document these procedures is critical should an employer be sued for negligent retention or supervision.

Termination Procedures

Termination of employees presents numerous challenges and consideration for any organization. Numerous legal and human resources materials are available to employers on dealing with termination. The fear of being sued over a termination is always a key consideration. Presumably, by the time the employer has determined that termination is necessary, the employer has fully documented the objective reason why. An employer at this point may have already attempted an Employee Improvement Plan and documented the results. If it is clear that that employee cannot succeed, then it is time to terminate and move on.

However, employers should also consider the possibility of being sued over the failure to terminate. Employers who fail to take action, including termination, where they have actual or constructive knowledge that a current employee is dangerous or unqualified for a position, can risk litigation for negligent retention, negligent supervision, or even negligent promotion.

Method of Termination

The method of termination is very critical, and numerous resources and checklists of how to go about the process exist. The reason an employee seeks the assistance of a lawyer in order to explore bringing legal action is often because, at some fundamental level, the employee feels mistreated or somehow demeaned as an individual. Therefore it is critical that an employee is treated in a fair, impartial, and dignified way in the termination process. At the same time, the employer needs to protect the organization and co-workers. Below are some points to consider:

- When an employee is called in for the meeting with human resources or security about a consumer report or termination, a best practice is to do so at the end of the day to minimize embarrassment to the employee and disruption in the workplace. Many employers prefer to terminate at the beginning of the week rather than a Friday. Thus a terminated employment does not stew while still on the job and the workweek does not end on a sour note.
- A best practice is to have two employer representatives at the meeting so there is no question afterward as to what was said.
- When the employee leaves the meeting, often a manager will accompany the employee to the employee's desk or to the exit in order to avoid disruption and to keep the situation calm.
- Depending upon the potential for violence or disruptions, some firms will have security service available for assistance.
- As part of the termination process, the employer must arrange to block passwords and access to the computer system and to change building entrance codes. If the employee has business material at his desk, such as customer lists or phone numbers, then the material should also be secured by the employer.
- There are wage requirements to meet, such as giving the terminated employee a final paycheck that accounts for all wages, vacations, and any other time that is owed.

- The manner in which a termination occurs, when the person is escorted off premises or to their work areas to retrieve personal items, is also important. Employers have been sued for causing undue embarrassment and emotional distress in the way termination was handled.
- Many employers will take appropriate precautions to ensure that the reasons for the termination remain confidential.
- Consider if an offer of a severance agreement is appropriate. Such an agreement typically provides an employee with severance pay (such as two weeks) in exchange for a waiver of any claims the employee may feel he or she has against the employer. An employer should contact an attorney to determine what rules apply in their state. Some of the critical aspects include a fair payment to the employee ("adequate consideration" in legal terms), adequate time for the employee to consider all options, a very clearly drafted agreement so the employee cannot later claim a lack of understanding to any rights given up, and the ability to rescind the agreement within a certain time period.

Exit Interviews

Exit interviews are an often overlooked opportunity for employers to exercise due diligence in protecting their workplace and third parties—an opportunity to locate potential landmines in an organization. Employees may have more information on what is actually occurring in an organization than managers and supervisors. An employee who is leaving may be willing to tell an employer what is really going on in the organization. For example, employees who have been terminated may be a source of information for acts of misconduct they have witnessed.

If the separation is involuntary, then the employer should still attempt an exit interview. There have been occasions, for example, where terminated employees used the exit interview to talk about how unfair the termination was in light of what others are doing who have not been terminated.

A simple Google Search will lead you to a number of excellent exit interview forms.

Maintaining Documents after Separation

The question arises as to how long records and documents should be maintained after separation. There are a number of state and federal laws that control document retention, and labor attorneys will typically advise employers on how long various documents must be retained. However, for purposes involving safe hiring and background screening, the recommendation is six years. The FCRA was amended in 2003 to lengthen the statute of limitations under the act to five years. In addition, state laws often allow a one-year period to file and serve a lawsuit. As a workable general rule, a six-year retention period should serve employers—the six years run from the termination of employment or, if not hired, from the time the decision was made not to hire the applicant.

If disposing of any information in a consumer report, it is important to follow regulations set out by the FTC pursuant to FCRA Section 628. Paper or electronic reports must be destroyed, pulverized, or erased so it cannot be read or reconstructed. An employer must show due diligence when a shredding firm is hired. See: http://business.ftc.gov/documents/alt152-disposing-consumer-report-information-new-rule-tells-how.

Background Check Data Retention Requirements

Even though the Fair Credit Reporting Act (FCRA) was amended in 2003 to lengthen the statute of limitations under the act to five years, the FCRA actually has no data retention requirement. Employers may keep background check data for as long as needed. California does currently require data retention for two years, but that is under review for constitutionality and may be subject to client contract. To protect against identity theft, employers can destroy background check data after a reasonable period of time. The EU-U.S. Privacy Shield Framework discussed in Chapter 17 on International Background Checks requires employers to destroy background check data from the European Union (EU) when it is not needed any longer. But employers should not destroy such records if there is a request for that information or if they are involved in litigation.

What to Do When Candidates Want to Know Why They Were Not Hired

In a situation where a candidate is persistent in wanting to know why he or she was not hired, HR needs to strike a delicate balance between giving too much or too little information.

If the decision not to hire was based in any way on a background check, then, of course, the FCRA pre-adverse and post-adverse action rules apply, and an employer should engage in an "individualized assessment" (see Chapter 10) if a criminal record was involved. If the persistent applicant did not even get as far as a background check, but still cannot accept "No" for an answer, an employer or HR professional should still be careful how they handle the situation.

There may be a temptation to help the applicant by engaging in a conversation about why he or she was not a good fit or as qualified for the position. It is worth keeping in mind the old adage that no good deed goes unpunished. The unfortunate fact is sometimes job candidates are insistent on knowing why they were not hired in order to gather ammunition to file a lawsuit or discrimination complaint. Since there is never an obligation to engage in a debate with a candidate over hiring, it is not to the advantage of HR to get into a prolonged discussion. Keep in mind that even if the employer is trying to offer some friendly help, an unhappy applicant may not understand or recall what was said and, in a later court proceeding, may have a very different recollection of any conversation.

Conversely, an impersonal dismissal also carries potential consequences. First, it potentially damages an employer's "branding" in terms of recruitment. In addition, a reason disgruntled applicants may visit an attorney to explore whether any legal action is available is that they felt demeaned in some fashion, or they were dismissed as a human being.

See The Addendum

Importance of Reviewing EPLI Policy

A critical tool available to employers is an Employment Practices Liability Insurance (EPLI) policy. However, since not all EPLI coverage is created equal, the Addendum contains the article **"Importance of Reviewing EPLI Policy"** by Attorney Scott M. Paler, Partner, Chair of Labor and Employment Practice Group, DeWitt Ross & Stevens S.C.

Insider and Post-Hire Threats

An "insider threat" is generally defined as a current or former employee, contractor, or other business partner who has or had authorized access to an organization's network, system, or data and intentionally misused that access to negatively affect the confidentiality, integrity, or availability of the organization's information or information systems. The definition of an insider threat can include sabotage, theft, espionage, fraud, and competitive advantage are often carried out through abusing access rights, theft of materials, and mishandling physical devices. Insiders do not always act alone and may not be aware they are aiding a threat actor (i.e. the unintentional insider threat). See: www.us-cert.gov/sites/default/files/publications/Combating%20the%20Insider%20Threat_0.pdf.

One way to combat insider threats is the use of background checks. However, it is a vastly more complicated area and the important point is that although vital, background checks all by themselves will not protect a business from insider threats. The following article about insider threats by Attorney Lester Rosen was posted on SourceSecurity.com in 2016.

Formulating Background Check Strategies to Minimize Insider and Post-Hire Threats

By Attorney Lester Rosen, Founder and CEO, Employment Screening Resources (ESR)

Employers are increasingly concerned about the risks associated with employees, temporary workers, independent contractors, and others who have the ability to wreak havoc on an organization from the inside. This is often referred to as "insider threat."

There are numerous types of insider and post-hire threats that range from embezzlement, theft of trade secrets, workplace violence or active shooters, and everything else in between. Potential insider threats are not just employees but anyone with access to a business office including contractors, vendors, and temporary workers. While there are numerous tools that can be used for preventing insider threats, this article will focus on background checks.

Although pre-employment background checks are often cited as an essential element of an insider threat prevention program, background checks are just one part of an overall strategy. The identification and prevention of insider threats requires an inter-disciplinary approach that can include mental health assessments, psychological testing, physical security, internal controls, continuous evaluation of personnel and risks, supervisor and co-worker training to recognize danger signals, identification of risk factors, sharing and analyzing information between responsible parties, and a culture of safety, reporting, and integrity. Most critically, an organization needs to have a commitment to prevent these threats, and a leadership team and professionals who are able to formulate and implement an overall strategy.

Background Checks - A Critical Part of the Risk-Management Toolkit

Employees are not only a significant investment and large cost, but each hire also represents a large potential risk. Every employer has an obligation to exercise "due diligence" when hiring. Employers, especially in industries with higher risk, need to be able to vouch for the integrity and honesty of their employees. Generally speaking, people with a past history of honesty are much more likely to be honest in the future. Conversely, there is evidence to suggest that if applicants are dishonest in how they obtained a job, they may be dishonest once they have the job. But it is difficult to identify potential "bad hires" just by interviews since some applicants lie so often they come across naturally as if they believe their own story.

Background screening provides a valuable and objective risk-management tool that gives employers additional protection against a bad hire. Employers utilize background checks to minimize the risks associated with workplace violence, lost customers, negligent hiring lawsuits, identity theft and fraud, embezzlement, data breaches, and high turnover. It has been estimated, for example, that the cost of a single bad hire can run from $10,000 to $100,000 given time wasted to recruit, hire, and train and then having to replace the bad hire.

Do Background Checks Eliminate Future Risks?

Part of the problem for employers is that even if a person passes a background check, it is hard for employers to measure with any accuracy how an employee will react in the future to various situations, such as a need for money, a substance abuse or other personal problem, or ability to act in an ethical fashion when under orders to do something that is less than ethical by a superior. Many organizations have found that the key is to supplement pre-employment background checks with ongoing or continuous screening, and an environment of control and physical safety.

Risk Types - Predictable, Unpredictable, and Secret

Even with "good hires," the potential for insider threats always exists. After getting applicants in the front door, a business must be concerned about employees with substantial authority (C-level and above), access to Information Technology (IT) or proprietary information, access to cash and accounting or access to sensitive information such customer lists and operations information. In fact, a new hire is full of risk. "Predictable risks" include employees with access to cash or assets and little internal controls. "Unpredictable risks" occur when employees develop financial issues, gamble, use drugs, or are encouraged or ordered by supervisors to perform acts of questionable honesty. "Secret risks" involve people with political agendas who use jobs to advance goals detrimental to employers.

There are also potential surprises employers can face post-hire. First, employers may obtain newly discovered information concerning an applicant such as discovering a new employee is a registered sex offender or faked an academic or professional credential. The good news is that employers can take steps to minimize surprises by a well thought out pre-employment screening program. The first step is to have in place policies, practices, and procedures to carefully select your employees in the first place through a well thought out pre-employment screening program commensurate with the risk involved.

There are numerous types of insider and post-hire threats that range from embezzlement, theft of trade secrets, workplace violence or active shooters. Experts recommend employers consider "continuous" evaluation that occurs periodically after hiring to deter employees from committing crimes after being hired

Formulating a Wise Pre-Employment Screening Program

Employers should also ensure their application forms make it clear that any material falsehood or omission can result in termination NO MATTER WHEN DISCOVERED and have language in employee manuals that deals with discovered falsehoods or omissions post-hire. Background check releases can have an "Evergreen" clause to allow future screening if needed (although there are limits to what can be done). Employers need to keep in mind that any screening program for new or existing employees should pay careful attention to the requirements of the FCRA as well as numerous applicable state laws.

There are several screening tools for detecting insider threats: Ongoing "continuous" evaluation (CE); Re-enactment (post-mortem) screenings; Credit Reports and asset searches; Social Media Background Checks; and Screening current workers or newly acquired workforce. It is also important for employers to know that internal "in-house" investigations can invoke the FCRA.

Employee Screening After Hiring

Some experts recommend employers consider "continuous" evaluation that occurs periodically after hiring. The argument in favor of such screening is that employees may commit a crime after being hired. It can also be a deterrence of sorts. Employers may also need to screen newly acquired employees if a merger or acquisition occurs. In addition, certain contracts may also require only screened employees.

However, there are legal implications of using information acquired after hiring. Employers should not have a knee jerk reaction and carefully review all the facts and circumstances to give the employee an opportunity to be heard. It is especially important for employers to carefully document actions – especially if the employee has pending employment related claim – and be careful of allegations of retaliation. In addition, many of these tools have drawbacks. For example, the use of social media sites to track threats is hampered by the fact that there is so much information online; it can be challenging to locate, identify, and utilize actionable data about a particular person, especially since a person may hide their activities behind privacy protection or use an anonymous online persona.

Screening Without Proper Internal Controls Is Insufficient

According to the 2012 Association of Certified Fraud Examiners (ACFE) Report to the Nations, most occupational fraudsters are first-time offenders with clean employment and criminal histories. The walk away point is that although pre-employment screening is critical to detect and deter fraud and threats, it is inadequate as a sole line of defense in the absence of proper internal controls that prevent surprises.

Bottom line: Employers must conduct due diligence before AND after hiring an employee. While this requires spending money, and the cost of background checks can be seen as a drag on the bottom line, the average cost of a screening usually equals the salary paid to employees for their first day of work. To paraphrase a well-known 1970's marketing slogan: "You can pay (a little) now, or pay (a lot) later."

Source: http://us.sourcesecurity.com/news/articles/formulating-background-check-strategies-minimising-threats-co-13811-ga.19836.html.

International Background Checks

Introduction

Due to the mobility of workers across international borders in a global economy, it is no longer adequate to conduct these background screening checks solely in the United States. Background screening also must be done internationally since an increasing number of workers have spent time living, working, and attending school abroad.

As a general working definition, an **international background check** generally means obtaining or sourcing information outside of the employer's "home" country. For an employer in the U.S., an international background check can mean obtaining information relevant to a person that is obtained from another country. For example, if a U.S. employer needs information from Poland that would be considered an "international" background check for the U.S. employer.

On the other hand, if a Polish company needed informant on an applicant that lived for a time in the U.S., from the point of view of the Polish company, a background check done in the U.S. constitutes an "international" background check. It's all a matter of your point of view.

However, it may also depend on where the job is to be performed and where the decision is to be made. If the same U.S. firm is opening an office in Poland, it may well turn to a Polish company that does internal Polish checks which would apply the same processes and rules any other Polish company would use. However, a U.S. firm opening that office may be making its decisions in their U.S. headquarters and would consider that to be an international check.

A need for international background screening can occur in several situations:

- **Applicant Born Abroad**: An American company is considering a job applicant who was born abroad and is either coming directly to the U.S. from another country or has not been in the United States long enough for the employer to rely solely upon checking American references and records. It is important employers never identify applicants as "applicants born abroad" since it may be discriminatory under Equal Employment Opportunity Commission (EEOC) regulations.
- **Applicant Spent Time Abroad**: An American company is considering a job applicant who spent relevant time abroad in another country, and the employer wants to obtain data for that time period.
- **Applicant from Other Country will Work in that Country:** An American company is hiring an individual in another country to work in that country. For example, a U.S. company may open an office in India or they are hiring an outside sales representative.

Author Tip

International Background Checks on Foreign Entities and Its Principles and Employees

Multinational firms, financial intuitions, investors, or other businesses may need international background checks on foreign entities, such as business partners, vendors, distributors, or companies where they may be considering an investment. The checks may include not only the business entity, but also principals, employees, investors, or individuals' associated with the entity. Checks on international business entities are outside the scope of this chapter. That can become very complicated. For example, a firm in China can hide its identity and owners by registering in a location such as the British Virgin Islands. Background checks may be helpful for due diligence on associated individuals. However, this chapter is primarily aimed at employment as opposed to business due diligence. Later in the chapter, we also discuss the difference between international employment "screening" and international "investigation." This chapter, however, is focused on pre-employment of individuals being hired, as opposed to business due diligence.

This chapter provides an informative introduction to international background screening, the risks employers conducting such screenings should be aware of, the many ways background screening overseas differs from background screening in the United States, and the solutions that employers may use to help with international background checks.

Author Tip > **A Comment on What this Chapter Covers**

This chapter does not attempt to cover each country in the world. While this chapter is a summary of the entire international arena and not intended as a country by country view, there are several lists worthy of mention. There are 193 members of the United Nations, as of the date of this publication[1]. Some of the entities may be affiliated with another country but have characteristics that set it apart. A list of 249 country-like entities is available at www.iso.org/obp/ui/#search.

Here are the quick learning points about international background checks that will be covered in this chapter:

- Background checks should no longer be limited to just the United States.
- Even though there are difficulties and challenges, an employer should be prepared to conduct international checks in the global economy.
- However, employers need to understand that outside of the U.S., each country is an adventure, and the processes that are taken for granted as part of U.S. background screening often do not apply internationally.
- There are a number of practical issues with international checks an employer should consider such as the extent and type of information available, language, time and calendar differences, turnaround time, and costs.
- There are a growing number of vendors and resources available to provide checks, although the details as to what is available and how it can be accessed in each country are not standardized across the globe and many times may depend upon which sub-contractor is used and how the sub-contractor accesses information.
- The role of international privacy and data protection is of tremendous importance. Unlike the U.S. where the federal Fair Credit Reporting Act (FCRA) is the primary tool for privacy, much of the world approaches privacy through comprehensive laws and regulations, such as in the European Union (EU).
- For U.S. employers, just because an applicant has a visa does not mean that the U.S. government has done a background check.
- International criminal checks are particularly complex around the world, and employers should not assume every country operates similarly to the U.S. Each country can differ in significant ways, and different sources are available in different countries
- Just as educational and credential fraud can be issues in the U.S., they are also critical issues around the world, especially when dealing with foreign education degrees.

---

[1] United Nations website, www.un.org/depts/dhl/unms/whatisms.shtml#states, accessed December 5, 2016.

- The concept of performing background checks is not as widely accepted in many countries around the globe as in the U.S., but there is an increasing awareness of its importance and an ability for professional screeners to access information from nearly every country.
- For multi-national firms operating in a number of countries, international hiring and screening protocols will need to be adjusted to reflect the laws, legal systems, and even the cultural norms of each country where they operate. Employers must blend their global policies with local policies—a process that has been referred to as **Glocalization.**
- Other standard background check elements, such as drug testing, credit reports or driving records, differ country to country.
- Not all international vendors are created equal, and employers must choose screening providers carefully.

Author Tip **International Employment Screening Difficult But Necessary**

Due to the perceived difficulty in performing international employment screening, some employers may be tempted to skip verifying international credentials or performing foreign criminal checks. However, the mere fact that information may be more difficult to obtain from outside of the U.S. does not relieve employers from their due diligence obligation associated with hiring.

Nor can employers simply assume the U.S. government has conducted background checks if the worker was issued a visa. After the events of September 11, 2001, the U.S. has increased checks on foreign visitors and on workers on government "watch lists." However, the government checks are generally not aimed at verifying credentials or checking for criminal records for employment purposes. Employers cannot simply take the position it is harder to exercise due diligence because the research is international.

If an employer hires a worker without verifying his or her international background, and the employer is sued for negligent hiring when it turns out that a due diligence check would have uncovered important facts, what is the defense? If a victim has been hurt or injured, then the employer's testimony will sound very hollow when they did nothing because international screening was too difficult or they did not know how to conduct such a check. Although international searches come with their own unique challenges and obstacles, employers do have a number of options to exercise due diligence.

Over the past several years, there have been significant improvements in the quality and availability of information around the world. As you will see in this chapter, conducting international background checks can now easily be done and should be a part of any comprehensive employment screen.

Background Checks Can No Longer Be Limited to Just the U.S.

The following statistics show how many people in the U.S. were born or have spent time abroad. They can be broken down into four categories: 1.) Foreign Born U.S. residents, 2.) Legal Permanent Residents (LPRs), 3.) Unauthorized Immigrants, and 4.) U.S. Citizens that spend much time abroad. Together, these four categories make up a surprisingly large amount of the current U.S. population:

- **Foreign Born U.S. Population:** The U.S. Census Bureau uses the term *foreign born* to refer to anyone who is not a U.S. citizen at birth. The *'The Foreign-Born Population in the United States: 2010'* report from the U.S.

Census issued in May 2012 that presents data on the foreign born population using the 2010 American Community Survey (ACS) estimated the number of foreign born in the United States to be **nearly 40 million, or 13 percent of the total population in 2010**. The foreign-born population from Latin America was the largest region-of-birth group, accounting for over half (53 percent) of all foreign born. By comparison, 28 percent of the foreign born were born in Asia and 12 percent in Europe. Among the 21.2 million foreign born from Latin America, 11.7 million, or over half (55 percent), were born in Mexico. Over half of the foreign born population lived in just four states in 2010: California, New York, Texas, and Florida. See: www.census.gov/prod/2012pubs/acs-19.pdf.

- **U.S. Legal Permanent Residents (LPRs):** According to the report *'U.S. Legal Permanent Residents: 2011'* (April 2012) from the Office of Immigration Statistics (OIS), a total of **1,062,040 persons became Legal Permanent Residents (LPRs) of the United States in 2011**. The majority of new LPRs (55 percent) already lived in the United States when they were granted lawful permanent residence. The leading countries of birth of new LPRs were Mexico (14 percent), China (8.2 percent), and India (6.5 percent). An LPR or "green card" recipient is defined by immigration law as a person who has been granted lawful permanent residence in the United States. Permanent resident status confers certain rights and responsibilities. LPRs may live and work permanently anywhere in the United States, own property, and attend public schools, colleges, and universities. They may also join certain branches of the Armed Forces and apply to become U.S. citizens if they meet certain eligibility requirements. See: www.dhs.gov/xlibrary/assets/statistics/publications/lpr_fr_2011.pdf.

- **Unauthorized Immigrants:** The Department of Homeland Security (DHS) Office of Immigration Statistics (OIS) report *'Estimates of the Unauthorized Immigrant Population Residing in the United States: January 2011'* (March 2012) provides estimates of the number of unauthorized immigrants residing in the United States as of January 2011. According to the report, **an estimated 11.5 million unauthorized immigrants were living in the United States in January 2011**. Of all unauthorized immigrants living in the United States in 2011, 55 percent entered between 1995 and 2004. Fifty-nine percent of unauthorized immigrants in 2011 were from Mexico. The unauthorized resident population is the remainder or "residual" after estimates of the legally resident foreign-born population – legal permanent residents (LPRs), asylees (individuals who travel to the U.S. and apply for grants of asylum), refugees, and non-immigrants – are subtracted from estimates of the total foreign-born population. See: www.dhs.gov/sites/default/files/publications/ois_ill_pe_2011_0.pdf.

- **U.S. Citizens That Spend Much Time Abroad:** No reliable statistics exist regarding the number of U.S. citizens that spend a considerable amount of time abroad and outside of the United States. However, some information about how many Americans travel abroad each year is available. According to the 'U.S. Citizen Traffic to Overseas Regions, Canada & Mexico 2015' report from International Trade Administration (ITA) National Travel & Tourism Office, a grand total of **73,453,114 U.S. citizens traveled to international regions in 2015**. Suffice to say, while many U.S. citizens have traveled outside the country on vacation, some of them have lived, worked, or attended school in another country for a considerable amount of time. These people would warrant an international background screening by their employers. See: http://travel.trade.gov/view/m-2015-O-001/index.html.

International Screening vs. International Investigation

As discussed in Chapter 7, there is a difference between screening and investigation. In the U.S., there are also two types of international background checks employers may utilize. The first type is an **international employment screening** while the second type is an **international investigation.**

For most U.S. employers, **international employment screening** involves verifications of supplied information by an applicant who has given express written consent to the screening. In a screening, an employer will have already obtained from an applicant the names, addresses, and phone numbers of previous employers or schools. Also, the employer will have obtained a rough list of locations where an applicant has lived, worked, or studied. A typical international background screen will consist of contacting the employers and schools that have been supplied and conducting a criminal check to the extent possible in that country. A screening may also include, if available, a driving record and credit report. If more information is needed, such as the applicant's school identification number or some other data, then the applicant can be asked to supply the needed data. The applicant will help the employer obtain the information since the applicant has signed a consent form and wants to be hired. The overall cost of international background screening, although greater than a typical U.S. screening, is considerably less expensive than an international investigation.

An **international investigation** typically involves a trained and experienced investigator working in the country where the investigation is being conducted. (In contrast, when an employer utilizes a firm to conduct an international screen, there is not necessarily an agent on the ground in the country where the information is being obtained. The background screening may be conducted by phone or email contact with courts, employers, and schools. The person available to assist in the foreign country may be a humble court runner as opposed to an experienced investigator.) Typically, an international investigation is considerably more expensive than background screening since international investigations may involve a different level of qualifications of personnel on the ground in the foreign country—doing in-person interviews or obtaining records—and the cost can be thousands of dollars. If an employer is filling a highly sensitive position or is conducting a due diligence investigation of a potential business partner, then the services of a qualified investigative firm may be needed. When the stakes are high, there is no substitute for having a trained investigator who knows the country, the language, the customs, and laws. If an employment screening firm only conducts background screening and an investigation is required, that employment screening firm can assist the employer in obtaining qualified professional assistance.

A simple way to understand the difference is that screening involves verifying what was provided. The focus is not on uncovering new information, although that may sometimes occur in the process. An investigation is a much deeper review of the individual and more often can uncover new information. Screening produces a simple report confirming or denying the information. Investigations tend to result in a lengthy report.

Why Employers Cannot Assume the U.S. Government Screens Workers from Abroad

Employers may be tempted to rely on the U.S. Government screening conducted for a work visa instead of conducting their own background screening. This may not be appropriate, since the depth and nature of the screening conducted for a visa may not be equal to the parameters of a U.S. background screen needed by an employer.

The primary problem is that criminal background checks for purposes of a visa are conducted by means of a police certificate. Some types of visas require a certificate, and for other types, a state department consular office has the discretion to require a police certificate.

There are essentially two legal ways for individuals to come to the U.S. to work or live[2]:

1. Apply for an immigrant visa.
2. Apply for a non–immigrant visa. (An example of a non-immigrant visa is an H1-B visa. This visa is issued for an initial three-year period to applicants with specialized professional skills to obtain permission to work in the U.S.)

However, employers cannot assume the U.S. government has performed a background check that relieves employers of their due diligence obligation to conduct their own screening. Government efforts are not foolproof nor are they geared toward the same type of due diligence required for employment decisions. After the events of September 11, 2001, the U.S. Government has certainly increased checks on foreign visitors and workers. However, these checks are primarily aimed at keeping terrorists and international fugitives from entering the U.S. or deporting those non-citizens that commit crimes in the U.S. or overstay their visas. The efforts the government makes, although vital, do not substitute for what an

---

[2] Additional information can be found on the US Citizenship & Immigration Services website: www.uscis.gov/.

employer needs to do. The government efforts are not aimed at lesser convictions that may be relevant to job performance or verifications of credentials.

In addition, information obtained for visa purposes may not always be allowed for use in employment decisions. Accessing information for one purpose and using it for another may not be allowed in some countries. Just as we saw in the chapters about the Fair Credit Reporting Act (FCRA) and Driver's Privacy Protection Act (DPPA), the "permissible use" is important when considering the ability to access a search for international background screens. Some sources only allow their data to be used for a non-employment purpose, such as for a visa or adoption purpose.

The Problem with Police Certificates in the Visa Process in Lieu of a Criminal History Search for Employment Purposes

There are a number of difficulties in conducting international background screening when a person applies for either an immigration visa or a non-immigration visa, and there are potential holes in the criminal background check process. Criminal checks are done in different ways, depending on the type of visa. For non-citizens applying for an immigration visa in order to immigrate to the U.S. to live and to receive a "green card," there is a "police certificate[3]" requirement. The applicants must obtain a police certificate from "appropriate police authorities" in their home countries. The applicants must include any prison records. That sounds good in theory, but in practice there are three main problems with police certificates:

1. The first problem is that the time period for issuing police certificates may allow a person with a criminal record to evade detection. Under the State Department rules, the police certificate comes from a country, area, or locality where the alien has resided for six months. However, if a person has frequently moved around inside that country, criminal records can be missed, depending on how the records are kept. Recent offenses may not be reported. If a person has lived in other countries, then the relevant time period is one year, so records can be missed if the person was in the country for a short period of time or left after committing an offense. The consular officer—a State Department officer assigned to a local U.S. Consulate—may require a police certificate from additional jurisdictions regardless of the length of residence in any country if the officer has reason to believe a criminal record exists.

2. The second problem is that police certificates differ all over the world in terms of reliability, timeliness, and completeness. Police certificates are still only as good as the efforts, resources, and abilities of the local law enforcement authorities in each country, so even when a police certificate is available, the completeness of the data can still be an open question. In addition, a number of countries do not even have police certificates available, or police certificates are too difficult to obtain and not available as a practical matter.

You Need To Know > **Police Certificates Around the World**

In January 2016, The Global Immersion Press, a network of leading global HR practitioners from around the world, published Volume 3 of the Global HR Practitioner Handbook that focuses on 'hard' and 'soft' topics that global Human Resources professionals must understand to add value to their organizations.

Volume 3 of the handbook includes a module authored by Lester Rosen entitled: *"Criminal history screening of global job applicants – Hidden dangers employers should know."* The article reviews the potential problems that impact the reliability of Criminal

---

[3] "A police certificate is a certification by the police or other appropriate authorities stating what, if anything, their records show concerning the alien. An applicant for a nonimmigrant visa is required to present a police certificate if the consular officer has reason to believe that a police or criminal record exists, except that no police certificate is required in the case of an alien who is within a class of nonimmigrants classifiable under visa symbols A–1, A–2, C–3, G–1 through G–4, NATO–1 through N ATO–4 or NATO–6." See: www.uscis.gov/ilink/docView/22CFR/HTML/22CFR/0-0-0-1/0-0-0-500/0-0-0-1716.html

Clearance Certificates from an international perspective. It is intended to increase awareness for global HR practitioners of the issues and challenges surrounding obtaining Criminal Clearance Certificates from different countries for employment background check purposes. Leading practices for meeting due diligent standards are proposed.

The handbook is available as an e-book or as separate modules at www.globalimmersionpress.com. The module by Rosen is available at www.globalimmersionpress.com/products/criminal-history-screening-of-global-job-applicants.

The U.S. State Department recognizes these as important issues. The State Department maintains the Visa Reciprocity and Country Document Finder, an international listing by country of issues involved in obtaining necessary visa documents. For more information, visit: http://travel.state.gov/visa/reciprocity/. Visa applicants can visit the website to find out how to obtain police certificates and court records from their own country.

The State Department also recognizes the need to continuously update the availability of each country's criminal records information. The State Department Foreign Affairs Manual and Handbook is available online at https://fam.state.gov/Default.aspx. According to the State Department rules for visas from 2016:

9 FAM 504.4-4(B) (U) Police Certificates

e. (U) Reporting Availability of Police Certificates to the Department: Consular officers should periodically discuss with the host government the availability and quality of police clearance information, as well as the procedures to be followed for visa applicants to obtain clearances both within and outside the country. Posts should provide information concerning the degree of automation and centralization of records, as well as any purge procedures followed by the host country. Posts should also determine how criminal records are indexed in their nation. The use of a unique national identification number as opposed to nonstandard spellings of names is also significant. Posts should provide background to the Departments Immigration and Employment Division (CA/VO/F/IE), as well as draft language for inclusion in the Reciprocity Schedule. Posts should clear information among all Department of State consular operations within their country and with the regional security officers (RSOs) and coordinate with like-minded foreign embassies as appropriate.

A second type of visa application occurs when a person applies for a non-immigration visa. In other words, he or she is not applying to live permanently in the U.S. but to stay temporarily. An example is the H1-B visa. Another potential hole is that an applicant may come to the U.S. on a student visa and then change to an H1-B visa. In that case, it is not clear exactly what is being checked and by whom.

In the situation of a non-immigrant visa, the applicant is asked about a criminal record on the non-immigrant visa form called a DS-156. Pursuant to 22 CFR 41.105(a) (4), a consular officer may request a police certificate if they have reason to believe a criminal record exists. Therefore, the police certificate is only required by the U.S. Consulate office on a per-case review. If an applicant coming to the U.S. decides to lie, and the U.S. Consulate does not have reason to challenge the lie, then a criminal record could exist, and a person with a disqualifying criminal record could obtain a non-immigrant visa.

In addition, for some visas such as the H1-B, an applicant's past employment and education is a critical part of the visa process. However, given the issues worldwide associated with educational and employment credential fraud, this raises the question of how effective credentials verification can be when done for large numbers of applicants from all over the world by the Government. International degree fraud is an ongoing issue. Employers need to take steps to confirm past education and past employment.

The essential lesson is there are statistically a significant number of potential job applicants where the relevant background information will come from outside of the United States. An employer cannot depend upon the visa process as protection. That means U.S. employers should consider what they can and should do internationally in the area of safe hiring and employment screening. More information on U.S. visas can be found at:

- https://travel.state.gov/content/visas/en/immigrate/employment.html, and
- https://travel.state.gov/content/visas/en/fees/reciprocity-by-country.html.

The Rest of the World Is Different than the U.S. and Every Country Can Be an Adventure

Each and every country is different when performing international background screening. Although there are some common approaches around the world, an employer should start with the basic working assumption that each country is an adventure. Techniques, information, and availability of public records that are taken for granted here in the United States are often times not available abroad. Each country has its own laws, customs, and procedures for background screenings.

With respect to the availability of criminal records or other types of background checks outside of the U.S., employers must realize there may be restrictions on availability based on the use of this information for employment purposes. In some countries, access to searches such as criminal or credit history for employment purposes is not allowed at all or may be restricted to very specific positions. In other countries, there may be no reliable method to obtain this information. In some countries, there may be a different way to obtain the information.

Despite Challenges Employers have Numerous Options and Resources to Perform International Due Diligence

By Kerstin Bagus, Director of Global Initiatives, ClearStar

We now live in a globalized world, where good information, with reasonable effort and cost, is available in many countries. Background screening is no different than other aspects of our expanded globalization. Verifying information about a person's employment, education, and sometimes even criminal history is possible in most countries.

A global network of suppliers now supports the process and many background screening companies have international specialists as part of their team.

Increasingly, companies outside of the U.S. are seeing the value of screening, or have regulatory requirements for screening. Multi-national organizations, especially those headquartered in countries with a strong screening culture such as the U.S., Canada, or the United Kingdom, are moving towards standardizing their screening processes globally, which includes implementing a standard set of background checks. Some industries, specifically in financial services, technology, and pharmaceutical, are at the forefront of globalized background checks. Screening globally can be done with local providers, with one or more larger providers, or with a mixture of local and multi-national providers.

Author Tip

Glocalization

There are special challenges for firms with offices and operations around the world when it comes to background checks. The trend is to attempt to standardize the basic screening processes and procedures as much as possible across the entire organization regardless of country. However, due to the differences between countries and because there are so many legal differences, it is simply not possible to have just one process.

The term often used to describe an international HR program that tries to achieve uniformity worldwide while taking into account local differences is **Glocalization,** which is the combination of the words **globalization** and **localization** and is used by international HR experts to describe a process that is deployed globally, but also accommodates local rules and practices.

What is the right balance between standardized global HR practices and a local approach? Per some experts, the balance can be in the area of 80% global and 20% local.

Here are some of the special challenges and practical difficulties employers may face when performing international background screening.

- **Each country is unique with differences in courts and legal systems:** Techniques and information that are taken for granted in the United States are often times not available abroad. Outside of the United States, there may be limited access to records which in the U.S. are considered public and readily accessible. Other information may be restricted from use for employment purposes. Each country has its own laws, customs, and procedures for background screenings and its own legal codes, definition of crimes, and court system. Employers should keep this in mind when searching international courts. International criminal checking requires an understanding of each country's court system, how criminal records are created and maintained, where searches should be conducted, the type of records available, and what the records mean.

- **Privacy and data protection**: This is a crucial issue. Many countries have strict data privacy regulations that require detailed notice to the individual about the purposes of the data collected, information about who will see the personal information, and restrictions on the use of the data. The EU's privacy rules place strict restrictions on transferring personal information out of the EU and impact any data transfers to the U.S. The U.S. Department of Commerce offers a program called **"EU-U.S. Privacy Shield"** to allow for the legal flow of personal information between the U.S. and EU. Many U.S. background screening firms that do international searches have signed up to participate in this voluntary program (See: www.privacyshield.gov).

You Need To Know ▷ **Different Requirements from Countries for International Screening**

International privacy expert Kerstin Bagus points out two examples where court systems and privacy rules can differ by country.

First, the categorization of criminal records will vary from what is seen in the U.S. For example, many countries do not utilize the concept of "felony" and "misdemeanor" levels or crimes, or if they do, the crimes that fall into these categories will be different than those in the U.S. Employers should keep this in mind when searching and processing to international criminal records.

Second, some countries require the subject be advised and may even require explicit consent from the subject, about the transfer of their personal information to another country, including the U.S. For example, the Office of the Privacy Commissioner of Canada (OPC) has issued guidance for processing personal data across borders. The Commissioner indicates the data subject should be notified in clear and understandable language about the processing outside of Canada. Notification should also be provided to indicate the subject's information may be accessible to foreign law enforcement and / or national security agencies. This will allow the data subject to make an informed decision about providing the consent for the processing of their information. See the OPC guidelines for 'Personal information transferred across borders' at www.priv.gc.ca/en/privacy-topics/personal-information-transferred-across-borders/.

- **Lack of Agreed Upon Protocols for Each Country:** With some 249 political entities around the globe, there is still a lack of an agreed upon and universally accepted protocol for obtaining records in every country. There is no official or industry approved definitive listing of exactly what types of information are available in every country or the legitimate sources or uses of such information. There is no international body that regulates the area. As described below, there are numerous international vendors who provide screening services in countries around the world. In the area of international criminal records, there can be different interpretations by vendors as to the availability, type, and legal use that is allowed. A multitude of factors can impact what actually goes into a specific search. These variations can occur between different vendors, from country to country, and sometimes even within a specific country, such as source variations.

 Selecting an International Screening Provider

The article *"Selecting an International Screening Provider"* by Kerstin Bagus, Director of Global Initiatives, ClearStar, and Andy Hellman, Managing Director, International & Strategic Initiatives, ClearStar is available in the Addendum.

- **Name variations:** The issue of name variations when expressing foreign names in the English alphabet is extremely complicated for two reasons. First, many cultures have naming conventions that are entirely different than the U.S. Some cultures may start the name with the family or clan name, where other cultures may utilize the mother's name as an integral part of the naming mechanism. Many cultures do not have the concept of a middle name. The second difficulty has to do with expressing a foreign name in an English format. For the languages that utilize the English alphabet—such as names in Italian, German, and Spanish—the expression of names is somewhat easier, though keeping in mind that Spanish names can have cultural variations. When it comes to expressing names that utilize a different alphabet, there is room for error and confusion. There is no easy way to translate Chinese, Korean, Arabic, or Japanese names into English. The two techniques used to render names in foreign alphabets into English are transliteration and phonetic transcription.
  - Transliteration into English is based upon using a representation of the characters in the original language with English characters so that certain characters in one language always translate into English by use of agreed upon letters. It is analogous to using a codebook. Transliteration means mapping a name from one language into another. An example is Iraq, where the Q is pronounced as English CK.
  - Phonetic transcription – or "transcribing" – is based on taking the sounds of a foreign name and attempting to associate the same sounds to the sounds of the English alphabet. With either method, there can be any number of variations. For example, "Osama bin Laden" can be represented as both "Laden" with an "e" or "Ladan" with an "a." First name variations can be "Usama" or "Osama."
- **Time differences:** Communicating with researchers, past employers, or schools around the world must take into consideration time differences. This can add lag time to the reporting process and can be very inconvenient. For employers attempting to conduct international past employment verification themselves, it may be necessary to have an employee wake up in the middle of the night to complete a call. There can be delays due to time differences when communicating with researchers, past employers, or schools around the world.
- **Means and cost of communications:** Each country will have different means of communication. Although email would be preferable, not all countries have reliable email delivery. Communications can also be done by fax machine. Of course, an employer wants to be careful about simply picking up the phone and dialing

international numbers. Without having an international calling card or an international phone plan, the employer may suddenly receive a very high phone bill. And before any personally identifiable information is processed, the employer should make sure the information will be provided to the appropriate source and adequately protected.

- **Different forms:** Before submitting a request for international background screening, employers should check which forms are needed. For some searches, there may be very specific forms or consent language required. Additional documentation may also be required, such as a copy of the diploma. In India, for example, most education verifications require a copy of the diploma which includes the seat number. In certain countries, employers need forms with the person's name in the language of that country or may need the mother's or father's name. Before submitting an international background check, employers should check to see if a country has any specific form needed to comply with the rules or the situation in that country, or with privacy and data protection laws.

- **Calendar:** Employers should keep in mind each country has its own holidays. Sometimes communications are delayed because of a country's calendar. And on the topic of dates, be aware that many countries list the dates in a format different than we do in the U.S. It is not uncommon to see dates outside of the U.S. listed as DD/MM/YYYY rather than the U.S. method of listing MM/DD/YYYY.

- **Fraud awareness:** International screening carries an inherent risk of fraud, just as it does in the U.S. There is no guarantee that a past employer is a legitimate firm. In addition, just as the U.S. has a significant problem involving phony "degree mills" and fake degrees, there can be similar issues abroad. Although some steps can be taken to mitigate the possibility of fraud, firms that rely upon screening still face a risk. Engaging an investigator or background screening firm who is familiar with the foreign country is likely to provide the best information.

- **Costs:** International background screenings are normally more expensive when compared to background screening in the United States. Outside of the U.S., there are few databases available for background screening use. Searches are usually manually processed. Since an employment screening normally consists of verifying supplied information, the costs can be kept more reasonable. However, even verifying supplied information can be expensive for the reasons indicated earlier. In some countries, a translation fee is involved. In many countries, criminal searches must be conducted in each relevant location where a person has lived, worked, or studied. In many countries, there are search options that are national in scope. Although the system for international criminal checks is not perfect, making an effort allows an employer to demonstrate due diligence. Checking records also discourages applicants with something to hide.

- **Payments:** Fees and other payments are often required to be in local currency. If an investigator is used, many will require some or all of the fees be paid in advance. Employers who do their own background verifications and contract with an international investigator may find they need to have their bank do an international money transfer by wire (perhaps taking two weeks or more) or purchase a money order in the target country.

You Need To Know

Top 20 Foreign Countries for International Screening

A recent list compiled by a leading international screening company shows the Top 20 Foreign Countries for international education verifications and international employment verifications in alphabetical order: Australia, Brazil, Canada, Chile, China, France, Germany, India, Ireland, Israel, Japan, Malaysia, Mexico, Nigeria, Pakistan, Philippines, Russia, Singapore, South Africa, and United Kingdom (U.K.).

Red Zone Countries

Countries where international background checks are problematic are sometimes referred to **as Red Zone countries**. Red Zone countries are those dealing with issues such as war, political unrest, unreliable communications infrastructure, lack of standardized procedures, bureaucracy, dishonesty, corruption, or ambivalence toward America and/or background checks. Red Zone countries have unpredictable turnaround times and many closed businesses and schools. Local assistance and surcharges may be required.

Current Red Zone countries include (list subject to change) but are not necessarily limited to: Afghanistan, Burma/Union of Myanmar, Cameroon, Chad, China, Congo (Democratic Republic of the Congo), Cote D'ivoire (Ivory Coast), Eritrea, Ethiopia, Haiti, Iran, Iraq, Kenya, Kosovo, Liberia, Libya, Nigeria, Papua New Guinea, Rwanda, Saint Kitts & Nevis, Senegal, Sierra Leone, Somalia, Sudan, Syria, Uganda, Zambia, and Zimbabwe.

Basic Components and Challenges of International Background Screening

To exercise due diligence in hiring, employers should – at a minimum – consider screening internationally to match the same screens as they do in the U.S. Primary searches for consideration are:

- Criminal records,
- Employment records,
- Education records,
- Publicly available terrorist lists and international databases, and
- Other methods such as driver's licenses, media searches, and – in some countries – credit reports. Care should be taken to consider the job relatedness of such searches, just as when considering these searches in the United States.

Challenges Specific to International Criminal Checks

The problem of how to obtain international criminal records today is very similar to the situation employers and screening professionals faced in the U.S. in the 1980's. One can imagine how these issues are magnified, given the potential number of countries where a search may occur and all of the different laws, languages, cultures, and access issues, each adding to the puzzle.

Below are specific issues that employers should be cognizant of when dealing with international criminal records:

- **The Criminal Record Sources:** Outside the United States there is less access to public records and the types of information needed for background screening. Each country has its own laws, customs, and procedures for background screenings. Records may be obtained from courts, police agencies, or other government agencies depending upon the location and job involved. Access to criminal history is rarely available to the requestor in a computerized process, as it is in the U.S. In some countries, there is confusion about the availability of searches and the legality of obtaining records. As a rule, employers should analyze any claim that a particular country does not allow criminal background checks. Some countries consider it illegal for the police to provide the criminal record information to a private firm, while a similar criminal record disclosure may be available from courts or criminal records bureaus. Police records are typically broader and may include arrests for which there is no conviction. When the police are prohibited from providing such records, the courts may be an alternative. Or the country may allow access to a criminal conviction database, held by a Ministry, the police, or other government bodies. Employers should distinguish when a complete prohibition on obtaining criminal records exists versus a lack of availability versus limitations in the manner and means of obtaining and utilizing criminal records. (Note: The EU Privacy Laws and the FCRA for the data privacy rules in effect for European Union members are covered in a later section of this chapter.)

- **Employment Restrictions:** Even in cases where criminal records are available, they may be only available for non-employment proposes. The question becomes if a country does not allow the use of criminal records for employment inside the country, should a U.S. firm be accessing the records for use in the U.S. for employment purposes? That is something that each employer will need to decide for themselves, as there are no global rules on this.

- **The State Department List of Countries:** A useful tool to determine what criminal records are generally available in a country is found at the U.S. Department of State website at Travel.State.Gov which has a list called "Visa Reciprocity and Country" at http://travel.state.gov/visa/fees/fees_3272.html. The site advises immigrants and visitors coming to the U.S. on the availability of required visa documents. Although the information on the website is aimed at assisting individual visa applicants, it is useful for employers and screening firms to determine what information is available from what source. If an individual can obtain his or her own records, it may be possible for an employer or screening firm to obtain these records from abroad, with consent. Note, though, that just because a criminal record certificate may be available for visa or adoption purposes, there may be restrictions on availability or use for employment purposes. For each country listed, the website describes the availability of police certificates and court records.

- **Scope of International Searches and Fees:** Typically, searches for criminal records quote per court in a country and not for the entire country. Unless specifically noted, foreign searches are conducted in each locale where an applicant lived or worked. Not every country has a "national" criminal search available to private employers. A criminal check may require multiple searches. For example, if an applicant merely indicated a certain foreign city, a background firm may search the main criminal court in that city, but the main court may cover very little of the actual jurisdiction of the area, and records can be missed. Before ordering an international criminal record, an employer should carefully specify how many areas will be searched since the average price of an international criminal search can exceed $100 per location.

- **Sources of International Criminal Checks:** There can be different possible sources of checks depending on the country. Where it gets complicated is that each source has its advantages and disadvantages, and can often depend on the criminal record provider and their interpretation of what source is legal and appropriate for employment. Sources can include:
  - A national check based upon a national court or police system.
  - Local check based on local courts or police.
  - Database checks if a country has a criminal database.
  - Adverse Media (also known as a Criminality Check) based upon various sources such as media checks.

- **Foreign Identifiers:** In order to identify the person, an employer will need to supply the proper type of identification needed for each country. Identifiers can include:
  - Full name and date of birth.
  - A national ID number, if a country provides one.
  - Mother's maiden name.
  - Father's name.
  - Applicant's name in the primary language of that country.
  - Each state or city where a person has lived. Some countries only maintain criminal records by a single jurisdiction.
  - A legible copy of passport or picture identification card.
  - A copy of a consent for screening signed (click electronic signatures are not accepted)

- **American Rules May Apply Abroad:** Employers obtaining criminal records from foreign countries need to be careful how it is done. The one thing that no American firm wants to do is pay money to a foreign official to obtain criminal records where the rules of the country do not permit such records to be released. Such actions could conceivably be prosecuted in the United States under the federal Foreign Corrupt Practices Act of 1977 (FCPA), 15 U.S.C. §§ 78dd-1, et seq.

- **Turnaround Time:** The response time for a report can vary greatly depending on the country. The average Turnaround Time (TAT) for international criminal searches is often more than 5 business days. In some extreme situations, the time period may be measured in terms of weeks or even months. Courts in certain countries may take longer for the same reasons as in the U.S.—often the court is located in a remote or less populated region.

- **Audit Trail and No Record Found:** In the U.S., when court records are searched and there is no record found, there is often no document provided by the court clerk. Court clerks do not normally confirm a lack of a finding. A "no record" is normally reported by the researcher, indicating they made the appropriate effort and there were no results found. The same is true in doing court searches throughout most of the world. If the criminal record search is at a court and no record is found, there is not likely going to be a document or paper trail that says "No Record." If the criminal record search is conducted via a process of a "Police Certificate" (also known as a Certificate of Criminal Record, Certificate of No Criminal Record, or Behavior Certificate), the "No Record" result may be listed on the Certificate.

International Criminal Record or Criminality Checks

By Kerstin Bagus, Director of Global Initiatives, and Andy Hellman, Managing Director, International & Strategic Initiatives, ClearStar

Criminal record checks are one of the most frequently requested searches. They are also one of the searches with the most variation in how they are done and what is actually searched and returned. The reasons for this are varied, but essentially come down to differences in interpretation of what is 'correct' and what sources a vendor can access. When we say 'correct,' we mean a vendor's interpretation of what information can be legally obtained, how it can be obtained and when it can be used for employment screening. Even within the U.S., where background screening is a well-established industry with a lot of case law, there are still grey areas of compliance. Outside the U.S., especially in countries where background screening is done less frequently, there may not be clear regulations or case law defining exactly what can be done and how it should be done. As a result, vendors are left to interpret the regulations and make their own decision. Because the decision is not always black and white, it is important that you understand the process which a vendor uses in making their decision, and that this process aligns with how your organization would make such decisions.

Beyond this, there are frequently variations in the actual search offered. Here are descriptions of the most common 'criminal offerings,' and the pluses and minuses of each.

National

A national criminal check, as the name implies, is a check at the national level, which generally covers all records within that country. The source conducting the search will determine what to report to the vendor – in some cases this may contain more than just conviction data. It is important to distinguish between a federal level criminal check and a national level criminal check. A federal level check is similar to a check of PACER in the U.S. It searches for federal crimes, but is definitely not a check of all reportable criminal records within that country. Brazil also offers a similar type of search, where records can be searched at the federal level, or at the state level. Some vendors may also offer a hybrid search of both levels.

National level checks are frequently, although not exclusively, seen in Europe/European-based legal systems.

- Advantages: The great advantage of a national criminal check is the ability to confirm with a single search if a candidate does or does not have a reportable criminal record in the country being searched. This can reduce the complexity of the background screening and reduce costs and turnaround time.

- Disadvantages: As with everything, there are downsides to this as well. In some countries, the process can actually be more complex, sometimes requiring fingerprints to confirm any records before they are reported. Canada and South Africa both require the fingerprint process before returning any records.

Local

Local level criminal checks are similar to county or state level checks in the U.S. They are based on some sort of address history (residential, work, etc.) and are only a check of the specific jurisdiction. In some cases, this may be only a court jurisdiction, such as in India, and in others, such as Mexico, it might be a search of an entire state.

- Advantages: Local checks can sometimes be done faster and with less paperwork than national level checks. They do not typically require fingerprints to return detailed results. For example, in Canada both local and national level searches are available. The national level check, usually referred to as a CPIC search, requires fingerprints before reporting a criminal record. The local search, done at the province level, will return results with basic biographic identifiers only. This can make the process much simpler and faster.

- Disadvantages: To conduct a comprehensive screening, multiple local searches may be required. This can raise costs. There is the risk the person will have a record in another jurisdiction. In some countries, the permissibility and process for conducting local level checks can also vary across jurisdictions, which can make the process more complex.

Typically, a country will have either the national or the local level check available, although this is not always the case. Canada is the most common exception but there are others.

Database

In some countries, vendors may offer a third party database check instead of searching the criminal records source directly. In the U.S. this is commonly done through a multi-jurisdictional criminal records file. Outside the U.S. however, it is relatively uncommon for it to be legal to aggregate criminal records into a third party database. There are some countries though where this has been done legally, and can be the only or best option for the search. As with anything involving global screening, what is most important is that you understand exactly what you are purchasing, so that you can determine whether it is appropriate/adds value to your process.

- Advantages: A database search can be faster than a regular criminal records check. It may also be the only option in some countries.

- Disadvantages: Databases may not be completely comprehensive, or up to date.

Adverse Media (also known as a Criminality Check)

This is a search of a database and online sources for adverse mentions of the data subject, most often focused on possible criminal behavior. It is not a true criminal records check, as most media mentions do not have full details available as one would find in a court record. However, in certain countries where criminal record checks are not permissible, vendors may offer these in lieu of a criminal record check. What is important is that this is transparent to the user. An adverse media search should not be portrayed as a criminal record database search.

- <u>Advantages</u>: A database search can be faster than a regular criminal records check. It may also be the only option in some countries.

- <u>Disadvantages</u>: Records will often not have the necessary details to make them reportable. There is also not often a way to ensure that the record is current. This could result in reporting something that is out of date or incorrect.

Sanctions

A sanctions search is sometimes also sold as a criminal records check, as sanctions lists can contain people who have been criminally charged. It is often used in lieu of a regular criminal records check in countries where a criminal record check is not permissible, or the vendor does not have the capability to conduct a check. It is important to note that some countries view a sanctions search to be similar to a criminal record check and thus require processing under the same rules as criminal record checks are processed (and limited). A Sanctions search is a perfectly legitimate background search. Some hiring requirements or business needs require a Sanctions check on specific positions. Sanctions checks are critical in financial services industry screening for key positions. However, it is not a criminal record search. More on the specifics of Sanctions and Watchlists is covered below.

- <u>Advantages</u>: A sanctions search can be faster than a regular criminal records check. It may also be the only option in some countries.

- <u>Disadvantages</u>: Records will often not have the necessary details to make them reportable. There is also not often a way to ensure that the record is current. This could result in reporting something that is out of date or incorrect. These databases are usually focused on terrorism and human trafficking type offenses. They will not contain more 'regular' offenses, such as theft, fraud or non-terrorist violence.

Special Considerations Specific to International Criminal Checks

Below are specific issues that employers should be cognizant of when dealing with international criminal records:

- <u>Criminal History May Not Be Considered Publically Available</u>: A person's criminal history may not be considered a matter of the public record, as it is in the U.S. Many countries consider criminal history to be restricted. This means that: 1) They may be not be considered public information and are not available for any employment purpose; 2) They may be available only for specific positions; and 3) They may be available but only for specific purposes such as for an immigration visa or for adoptions but not for employment purposes. Some countries consider criminal record history to be sensitive data, which requires a special level of handling and approval. The U.S. is quite unique in its view of criminal history being fully available and accessible to the public.

- <u>Spent Records</u>: Some countries treat certain criminal history as being "spent." For a conviction to be spent, the person must have successfully completed their sentence and they have not recidivated within a specified period of time. A spent record may still be retained in the criminal record systems and will be available to entities such as law enforcement. But spent records are not available for general viewing, such as for employment purposes. In some countries, spent records may be available for consideration if the person is working in specific positions, such as those caring for the vulnerable. In many countries, a spent record does not need to be disclosed to a prospective employer, unless there are specific requirements such as working with the vulnerable. As an example: Canada has a process of Record Suspensions, formerly called a "Pardon." Depending upon the level of conviction and the specific crime, some convictions become eligible for a Record Suspension if the individual has completed their sentence and has demonstrated good conduct. A conviction that has met the Record Suspension requirement is kept separate from other non-suspended records and is shielded from view in most instances. If an individual has received a Record Suspension, they do not need to reveal that criminal record on most employment or tenant screening applications. More information about Record Suspension can be found from the Parole Board of Canada Record Suspensions (http://pbc-clcc.gc.ca/prdons/servic-eng.shtml) and the Royal Canadian Mounted Police Record Suspension (formerly called pardon) and Purges (www.rcmp-grc.gc.ca/en/record-suspension-formerly-called-pardon-and-purges).

- Depth of Criminal Records Varies: The depth of criminal records, meaning how far back the record will go, will vary by country. In the U.S., criminal record checks typically go back 7 years. Some checks can go back farther and must be specially ordered. In other countries, the records may only go back a set number of years, such as 5, or they may be available since the individual became an adult. They may be available only as long as that location or database has them. It is not possible to request a 7-year background check in all countries of the world.

- Translation of Court Documents: If there is a possible or confirmed criminal record, it must be translated into English, or the language of the decision maker. Even when the country uses English as the primary language, the legal system will be different and the different legal terms will need to be interpreted to understand the facts of the offense

- Level of Offenses and Non-Convictions: Some criminal record sources will return information beyond convictions, such as arrests or even if the subject is a person of interest. Results may also contain violations or citations, which are not true criminal convictions. Many background screeners filter out non-convictions and non-criminal results. If you are using a third party provider to obtain international criminal records, check with them on how they handle non-conviction and non-criminal results.

International Education Verifications

Verification of an educational degree earned abroad is critical to verify credentials and to avoid fraud. Statistics show that education fraud can run as high as 20 percent. An employer needs to determine if an applicant attended the school claimed and received the degree claimed. The employer also needs to determine if the school is accredited and authentic. The world is awash with phony schools, fake degrees, and worthless diplomas. If the employer is not familiar with a school, research should be conducted. A legitimate school will often have an e-mail address or phone number so that they can be easily contacted to verify a degree.

Manila Information, Please

One international firm reports being asked to verify a high school degree in Manila in the Philippines. The school had a name similar to "Immaculate Heart" in its title. The exact school phone or address was not provided so the firm dutifully researched, found, and contacted the high school. The school indicated the person never attended much less graduated. The applicant insisted she absolutely had graduated and supplied contact information and a copy of the diploma. Upon further investigation, the screening firm learned that there were numerous schools throughout Manila with similar names. The lesson—screening internationally requires very precise information.

Be prepared to pay additional fees. The amount of additional fees (if any) will depend on the institution. Requests for additional fees from a background screening firm may contain the actual fee amount as well as a small administration fee. If there is a wire transfer fee, they will include that amount as well. All amounts are converted and requested in U.S. dollars. There is also the issue of additional fees that some schools charge to provide the verification. Most employers do an excellent job of providing copies of degrees and mark sheets in advance to the background screener once they understand the reasoning behind the request.

Problems with Applicant Provided Documents

This is probably the #1 question international background screening firms are asked: "If the applicant provides the document, why do we need you?" The answer is fraud. In order for legitimate schools to combat fraud, they need documents to cross check and reference. It helps the international background screening firm to identify the school. Here are the main reasons why the end client should not accept a document from the applicant as the definitive verification and why the background screening firms ask for the degree, mark sheets, or additional documentation:

- **Name confirmation:** The degree copy helps to clearly identify the name, in the local language, under which the degree was granted.
- **Record Archiving Systems:** Some schools overseas need the degree/mark sheet/roll number in order to know exactly which of their systems to check. Some schools have two for the most part: the paper trail system or the updated computerized system.
- **Fraud Prevention:** In India alone, this is a multi-million rupee business. Companies go to H1-B visa hopefuls and write their whole resume giving false credentials on the resume. The subject of the scam sometimes was and sometimes wasn't "aware" of the issue. The other side of the fraud was schools back in early 2000 were actually involved in "Fraudulent Degree Rings." People high up in the institutions in Registrar offices were being paid to confirm a degree when none existed. Fast forward to the present, and schools will now sometimes ask for: Copy of Degree, Seat Number, Roll Number, Mark Sheets, Father's Full Name/Mother's Full Name, Place of Birth, and a copy of the applicant's photo. The reason for this is that all or part are used now to deter fraud. If a school receives a copy of the degree and something from that degree is off according to their records, the school will ask for the next document/piece of information and so on until they cross checked them all and are satisfied. Another reason why a background screening company may ask for a copy of the degree is if they have reasonable suspicion that there may be fraud. They will maintain on file copies of previously provided degrees from schools – both confirmed frauds and legitimate. If the background screening company does suspect fraud, they can forward the actual document to the school and obtain their official response as the authenticity in writing for their customers.
- **Location Assistance:** A background screening firm will ask for a copy of the degree from the customer in order to help locate the school. The applicant may advise that he or she attended Leningrad State University, but the degree will show Saint Petersburg State University. They are both the same, but their name changed back and forth then back again. For schools in countries with dramatic government changes (i.e., fall of Communism in Russia), most higher education institutions changed their name to reflect the new government. In Russia, the fall of Communism spurred the change from Leningrad to Saint Petersburg.

Tips on Performing Education Verification of International Schools

The verification process has three parts:

1. **Determine if applicant attended the school claimed and received the degree claimed:** Did the applicant actually attend the listed school and receive the degree claimed? Verification can be done by an employer or by a screening firm. Internet resources offering lists of schools around the world are available. If the applicant presents a diploma or some other document, it should be sent to the issuing school for verification. Typically, schools can be contacted by phone or by email. Of course, challenges to overcome are language and time differences. Despite these handicaps, there is no question that the verification can certainly occur. Before

performing the verification, it is helpful to obtain as much information as possible from an applicant. An employer needs to obtain the applicant's full name used while attending school, the exact spelling in the language utilized by the school, the dates the person attended the school, and any student ID number that was used. A copy of the degree or other documentation may be needed. It is helpful to obtain as much information as possible, such as school website and email.

2. **Determine if the school is accredited and authentic:** While it is important to establish that a school is accredited and authentic, employers should never assume that accreditation automatically equals a real school since there are many fake accrediting bodies and also real schools that are not accredited. Some public schools may lose their accreditation due to mismanagement or be on probation. So the lack of accreditation, while problematic, may or may not be the deciding factor in deciding if a school is real. There is a significant problem with fake schools abroad. Employers in the United States have a difficult time detecting fraudulent degrees in America, let alone on an international scale. To resolve the authenticity issue, there are numerous resources that can assist an employer. For an example of the size of the problem of diploma mills, an online story in the *Khaleej Times* in India on May 13, 2004, proclaimed 'Fake India Degrees Flood Middle East Market.' "India churns out brilliant graduates by the thousands every year. Unfortunately, it also churns out fake degrees by the thousands. Manufacturing fake certificates is a money-minting industry that has never stopped churning business for the people involved in it. The effect of such fakes is being felt globally." Many agents also say it is quite difficult to spot a fake degree nowadays as it resembles an original one in every way—from the texture of the paper to the university stamp. The story noted that not only are people claiming degrees they did not earn, but job applicants are also making up fake schools. As a result, the process of obtaining actual verifications from schools can be time consuming and can cause harm to a real graduate who must take extra steps to prove his or her education credentials are genuine.

3. **Determine the equivalency of a foreign degree in terms U.S. employers can understand:** Understanding the equivalency of a foreign degree in terms U.S. employer can understand is not an easy task. However, there are several agencies offering services that provide an equivalency analysis. For example, for information about degrees issued by foreign medical schools, there is a well-established mechanism to make that determination: the National Committee on Foreign Medical Education and Accreditation (NCFMEA) was established under the Higher Education Amendments of 1992.

International Employment Verifications

International employment verifications have similar challenges as faced by employers in the United States, augmented by all the problems associated with working internationally. To obtain background screening information, employers may need to schedule calls in the middle of the night, locate foreign phone numbers, and overcome language barriers.

To conduct an international verification efficiently, it is important to have the applicant provide as much information as possible. It is not practical for an American firm to attempt to call a foreign country to locate the past employer's phone number. When a better phone number is required, an international screening agency may need permission to contact an applicant directly to ask for better information. A background screening firm will typically need permission to contact the applicant directly in order to obtain any additional necessary information.

There are three essential keys to successful international employment verifications:

- **No Such Thing as Too Much Information:** Obtain as much information as possible from the applicant. Since locating past employers in a foreign country is difficult, the applicant should be asked to provide as much information as possible. Of course, there is always the possibility of a "set-up" or fake reference. Whenever possible, effort should be made to independently verify the existence and authenticity of past employers.

- **Use Local Languages for Verifications:** In order to obtain the best results, employment and educational verifications should be conducted in the primary language of that country. Even though there are international translation services, communicating with employers and schools in their native language improves the chances of completing a verification task.

- **Be Careful when Providing PII:** If utilizing researchers or firms outside of the U.S. to obtain employment (or even education) verification, be very careful about providing any personally identifiable information (PII), such as date of birth, passport number, or similar information. Unless you have vetted the vendor, a good practice is to utilize researchers outside of the U.S. to the extent possible to obtain contact information, and only provide PII directly to the employer or school.

Employers using international background screening for past employment and credentials verifications may also encounter fake experience certificate issues in India and other countries. This whole fake employment system is a growing problem for employers. For example, a number of stories have appeared recently concerning fake CVs in India. C.V. stands for Curriculum Vitae. When people refer to CVs, they are usually talking about a biographical résumé. Some recent articles about the India fake CVs include:

- 'Fake certificate racket busted' (*The Times of India* 9/26/2008): http://timesofindia.indiatimes.com/city/hyderabad/Fake-certificate-racket-busted/articleshow/3529134.cms
- 'Fake CVs Nightmare for Employers' (*Daily News & Analysis* 2/2/2011): www.dnaindia.com/money/report_fake-cvs-proving-to-be-a-real-nightmare-foremployers_1502008-all.
- 'India Inc grapples with rash of fake CVs' (*Hindustan Time*s 7/20/2008): www.hindustantimes.com/storypage/Print.aspx?Id=f56c6187-c09c-4bc5-8638-059e4d8b92df
- 'India Inc hit by lying job seekers' (IndianExpress.com 1/24/2011): www.expressindia.com/latest-news/India-Inc-hit-by-lying-job-seekers/741670/
- 'IT Firms in Pact to Banish Fake CVs' (*Business Standard* 8/24/2009): www.business-standard.com/india/news/it-firms-in-pact-to-banish-fake-cvs/306440/
- 'Over 51K fake degrees issued in state' (*The Times of India* 10/28/2010): http://timesofindia.indiatimes.com/articleshow/6825330.cms?prtpage=1
- 'Private eye on false resume' (*The Telegraph*, Calcutta, India 5/6/2010): www.telegraphindia.com/1100506/jsp/others/print.html

Other Resources and Tips for International Screening Due Diligence

In addition to the screening tools already mentioned, there are other steps an employer can take for performing due diligence when hiring a person who has spent time abroad that include:

- **Domestic Background Checks:** Even though the person's time in the U.S. could be limited, do whatever background checking is possible based upon their time in the U.S. This effort demonstrates due diligence by documenting the fact employers did what they could do.
- **Domestic Personal References:** Even if a person is relatively new to this country, ask for the names of personal references in the U.S. Be sure to document the relationship between the reference and the applicant. Although this is not a perfect solution, as with domestic background checks, an employer demonstrates due diligence by making and documenting an attempt to do a screening.
- **Disclosure of International Background Checks:** If hiring a number of applicants from abroad, then state in the release forms that you will also conduct background investigations in any countries where an applicant has lived in the past seven to ten years. This can at least have the effect of discouraging an applicant with something to hide. However, this should be worded carefully so that an employer does not imply that any hiring decisions are being made based on country of origin or ethnicity.

Country of Origin

In order not to run afoul of Equal Employment Opportunity Commission (EEOC) rules, never refer to a screening in a foreign country as a search of **country of origin** or any other reference that implies that nationality or ethnicity is a consideration. Instead, employers may indicate that **a search abroad** is simply a search in other countries where an applicant has lived or worked.

U.S. Terrorist Watch Search Lists

Other due diligence tools include the various terrorist databases available to the public, such as the Office of Foreign Assets Control ("OFAC") list maintained by the U.S. Department of the Treasury. Such lists are readily available but there are limitations as well, such as working with name matches only when no additional details are available. See Chapter 13.

International Sanctions Search

Below are recommended resources.

- **Global Sanction List (GSL) – Sanctioned Entities:** The Global Sanction List (GSL) contains information from the most important sanction lists from around the world, which are then aggregated and grouped into one category. The GSL offers close to 20,000 profiles of individuals and companies of the highest risk rating. Covered lists include:
  - Bank of England,
  - Bureau of Industry and Security,
  - Department of State,
  - EU Terrorism List,
  - FBI Top Ten Most Wanted,
  - Interpol Most Wanted,
  - OCC Shell Bank List,
  - Office of Foreign Assets Control (OFAC) Sanctions and SDN & Blocked Entities,
  - Treasury PML List,
  - SECO List,
  - UN Consolidated List,
  - WorldBank Debarred Parties List,
  - CBI List, and
  - ICE List.
- **Global Politically Exposed Persons (PEP) List:** PEPs – or "Politically Exposed Persons" – are considered high risk people, and employers require enhanced due diligence when conducting business with Politically Exposed Persons, particularly in Private Banking. Financial institutions that have conducted business with PEPs without following adequate Know Your Customer procedures and enhanced due diligence processes have been hit with heavy fines. Since the events of September 11, 2001, over 100 countries have changed their Anti-Money Laundering laws to fight against corruption. There has also been greater emphasis and cooperation between nations to enforce the Foreign Corrupt Practices Act. While there exists no global definition for a PEP, the Financial Action Task Force (FATF), U.S. Patriot Act, and the European Union (EU) Directive use similar definitions and guidelines in which the term Politically Exposed Person was typically defined by the following:
  - Local legislations like officials in the executive, legislative, administrative, military, or judicial branch of a foreign government (elected or not).
  - A senior official of a major foreign political party.

- A senior executive of a foreign government-owned commercial enterprise.
- An immediate family member – spouse, parents, siblings, children – of such individuals.
- Any individual publicly known to be a close personal or professional associate.
- While the interpretation of these guidelines varies from country to country, and there might be slight variations, the expectations for organizations doing business with Politically Exposed Person are universally similar. The following process is international standard:
  o Identify the "Politically Exposed Persons" amongst clientele.
  o Make sure that funds managed by an organization on behalf of the Politically Exposed Person do not derive from a corrupt source.
- **Global Enforcement List (GEL) – Enforcement Agencies:** The Global Enforcement List, or GEL, consists of information received from regulatory and governmental authorities that list the content of warnings and actions against individuals and companies. The GEL lists narcotic-traffickers, money launderers, fraudsters, human traffickers, fugitives, and other criminals to provide the most comprehensive protection to clients.
- **Global Adverse Media List (GAL) – News Media:** The Global Adverse Media List (GAL) is an extensive proprietary database comprised of the results of public domain news. The GAL has more than 20,000 newspapers and magazines in over 10 languages that are monitored for risk relevant information to provide impressive protection from risk entities.

International Screening Database Information

International screening database information comes from many resources, sources, and media searches. However, all international screening database information needs to be taken with a grain of salt, due to name similarity. Employers also need to make sure not to discriminate as well on the basis of the national origin of job applicants. For foreign countries, employers need to realize that information in some countries is better than in others. Although there may be limited information available from a country such as Afghanistan, for example, it is nowhere near to being complete and up-to-date.

Legal Implications for Employers Doing International Background Checks

It is important to stay within legal guidelines that are applicable in both the U.S. and the foreign country. When obtaining information from an applicant about past employment or education abroad, it is important not to refer to the country as their country of origin. That would likely be a form of discrimination since such a statement can imply that the employer is considering ethnicity or country of origin as a factor of employment. Instead of using the phrase "country of origin," an employer should refer to any screening outside of the U.S. as simply an "international screening." It is also important not to perform any type of check that would be an invasion of privacy or contrary to the laws of either the U.S. or the foreign country. For example, employers who only conduct background checks on a person's history in the U.S. could potentially be discriminatory in their actions towards individuals who have been long time U.S. residents. For example, if an applicant has lived in the U.S. all of his or her life, the criminal search could be for 7 years or for 10 years of history. If the employer only screens U.S. history on an applicant who just immigrated to the U.S., this second person will get a criminal search for a much shorter period of time. In this example, employers are holding U.S. citizens to an inconsistent and potentially higher standard.

Thus, the legal implications of international background screening can be very complex and involve the intersection of U.S. domestic law and the operation of foreign law. Furthermore, international screening and the flow of information across borders is a relativity new and developing area of law.

Below is a discussion of some of the more significant considerations involved. Employers must be aware of how the data is obtained, transmitted, and utilized.

1. **Obtaining Foreign Data:** The essential rule for any employer in the U.S. is that information should be obtained in a manner consistent with the laws of the country where the data originated. If it is not legal in a particular country to obtain a criminal record from the police, then a U.S. employer should not do so either. A U.S. firm could be exposed to liability for obtaining foreign records that would be prohibited in the foreign country if the employer somehow obtained the records by illegal means in the applicant's home country. If a lawsuit arises, an applicant can claim an invasion of privacy or other violation of rights based upon the illegally obtained records. A complaint could be filed in the foreign country, and the U.S. employer could face a lawsuit in the U.S. or the foreign country. A key element in legally obtaining data is, of course, providing the applicant with information about the processing of their data (called a Notice), and obtaining the applicant's written consent. (Note that in some countries, the ability to process personal information on the basis of consent, in the employment context, is not considered valid.) In the context of employment screening, the assumption is made that the applicant has not only consented but wants to assist the employer in obtaining records in order to facilitate the employment decision.

2. **Transmitting Foreign Records:** The concept of data transmittal has to do with data privacy protection rules in effect for many countries. Data that may be obtained legally from a source may become improper to use if privacy rules are not followed.

3. **Utilization of Foreign Records:** Utilization refers to rules that determine if and how a criminal record can be used in an employment decision. The first issue is whether the record was obtained legally. The next issue is whether a U.S. employer may legally consider information obtained from a foreign country for employment, especially in the context of criminal records. If the job and the applicant are both in a foreign country, then it is likely the rule of the foreign country applies. As the old saying goes, "When in Rome, do as the Romans." In this situation, the employer is best advised to consult legal counsel in the host country and follow the rules used in that country for any type of pre-employment screening. If the job and the applicant are in the U.S., then the best practice for the U.S. employer is to apply at the minimum the same rules they would to information obtained in the U.S. This means to follow the EEOC rules concerning the use of criminal data. This also means a screening firm has the same obligations for accuracy and re-verification when it locates a criminal record in the U.S. For example, under FCRA section 607(b), there is an obligation to utilize reasonable procedures to assure maximum possible accuracy. If a record is found, then there is an obligation under FCRA section 613 to either utilize strict procedures to ensure the record is up-to-date or to give the applicant notice. Other specific adverse action notice procedures also apply. However, when obtaining the data, employers should also take into account any privacy and data protection laws that exist in the country where the information is located. If the job is in the U.S. but the applicant is living abroad, and if there is a law in the foreign country that prohibits the use of criminal records in that country, then the employer needs to make a risk-management decision. The U.S. employer needs to exercise due diligence before bringing the worker to the U.S. Failure to exercise due diligence would leave the employer vulnerable in case the applicant committed some sort of harm or if the employer had to defend hiring practices in court. On the other hand, an employer does not want to be in the position of violating a foreign law. An employer may take the position that the use of the criminal record is regulated under U.S. law since the employment is to be performed in the U.S. and that is where the employer stands the greatest chance of being sued. In addition, any criminal record obtained abroad is done so with the express authorization of the applicant under the FCRA. In the interest of enforcing a consistent policy worldwide, an employer may also decide to operate under U.S. rules when considering how to utilize foreign criminal records on applicants who will be working in the U.S. However, this is still an emerging area of law. For example, in the EU it is generally thought that consent is not valid when used in the employment situation. And in some countries consider it totally not valid. The processing takes place under other permissible purposes, but not under consent. Forcing consent would violate the person's rights in these countries. However, even if you are processing information under another permissible purpose, you still have an obligation to provide a Notice.

When conducting background screening conducted on residents of foreign countries, the employer must also be aware of other regulations that may protect that individual's rights, in addition to privacy laws. Some of these will be Human Rights Codes, Labor Laws, or Consumer Protection laws. Know that these regulations, just as the privacy regulations, may be national and/or localized. Just as in the U.S., it is recommended to consult with counsel to make sure your company is following the local requirements. It is also important to consult with counsel knowledgeable about foreign laws.

Privacy and Data Protection in International Background Screening

Because the background screening process involves collecting and transferring personally identifiable data of the applicant, the process will fall under a country's data privacy regulations, among other regulations. As discussed in other chapters of this book, the primary privacy regulation in the U.S. impacting background screening is the FCRA. Additional regulations are GLB and DPPA, as well as state-specific regulations. Outside of the U.S., privacy regulations, when they exist, are often comprehensive, covering an entire country. These privacy regulations will cover how the personal information is obtained, transmitted, and utilized. A U.S. based employer may legally obtain information from a foreign country and use the information in a legal manner, but yet still run afoul of the source country's privacy laws.

Privacy regulations that are most often impacted by U.S. employers are those dealing with the European Union and Canada. Other country's privacy laws have similar elements to the EU, and Canadian laws and requirements are based upon the OECD (Organization for Economic Cooperation and Development) Guidelines. A good resource for understanding these basic principles, as well as for requirements for moving personal data across a country border is the OECD Guidelines on the Protection of Privacy and Transborder Flows of Personal Data web page: www.oecd.org/document/18/0,3343,en_2649_34255_1815186_1_1_1_1,00.html. Remember, there are over 100 countries in the world with privacy regulations either in force or being developed. Since there are 28 EU Member States (See: https://europa.eu/european-union/about-eu/countries_en) until the United Kingdom exits in 2017, this leaves many other countries with their own privacy regulations that need to be adhered to. A useful website called Privacy International outlines privacy rights and status in many countries is found at www.privacyinternational.org/index.shtml.

Introduction to the European Union (EU) Data Protection Directive *(Directive 95/46/EC of the European Parliament and of the Council of 24 October 1995)*

Protection of an individual's personal data is a fundamental right in the EU. The EU rules went into effect in 1998, and they impact the transmissions of "personally identifiable data" (PII) from the EU countries to the U.S. Each EU Member Country is required to have data protection laws which must be equal or more stringent than the EU Data Privacy Directive. The list of countries in the European Union is found at http://europa.eu/. Information about the EU Directive is at http://ec.europa.eu/justice/data-protection/index_en.htm. The EU Data Protection Directive is the baseline for privacy regulations in the EU.

Protection of Personal Data in the European Union (EU)

The EU Data Protection Directive outlines the following basic enforceable rights for individuals who have their personal data is processed:

- The right to be informed that your personal data is being processed in a clear and understandable language;
- The right to have access to your own data;
- The right to rectify any wrong or incomplete information;
- The right, in some cases, to object to the processing on legitimate grounds;

- The right not to be subjected to an automated decision intended to evaluate certain personal aspects relating to you, such as your performance at work, creditworthiness, reliability, and conduct; and

- The right to receive compensation from the data controller for any damage you suffer, etc.

In addition, the organization responsible for processing an individual's personal data (the "data controller") has certain obligations:

- To ensure that your rights are observed (i.e. inform you, give access to your data);

- To ensure that data are collected only for specified, explicit and legitimate purposes, that they are kept accurate and up to date and for no longer than is necessary;

- To ensure that the criteria for making data-processing legitimate are observed, for example, when you give your consent, sign a contract, or have legal obligations, etc.;

- Confidentiality of the processing;

- Security of the processing;

- Notification to the data protection authority, in some cases; and

- To ensure that, when a transfer of data occurs to countries outside the EU, these countries guarantee an adequate level of protection.

Source: 'Protection of Personal Data in the European Union' at http://ec.europa.eu/justice/data-protection/files/eujls08b-1002 - protection of personnal data a4 en.pdf

European Union (EU) Privacy Laws

"EU-U.S. Privacy Shield" Formally Adopted to Replace "Safe Harbor"

On July 12, 2016, the European Commission formally adopted the new EU-U.S. Privacy Shield framework to create stronger protection for transatlantic data flows between the European Union (EU) and the United States (U.S.), protect the fundamental rights of people in the EU with personal data being transferred to the U.S., and bring legal clarity to businesses relying on transatlantic data transfers, according to a press release from the European Commission.

The EU-U.S. Privacy Shield – which replaces the old Safe Harbor framework invalided by a European Court of Justice (ECJ) ruling in October of 2015 – is based on the following principles:

- **Strong obligations on companies handling data:** Under the new arrangement, the U.S. Department of Commerce will conduct regular updates and reviews of participating companies, to ensure that companies follow the rules they submitted themselves to. If companies do not comply in practice, they face sanctions and removal from the list. The tightening of conditions for the onward transfers of data to third parties will guarantee the same level of protection in case of a transfer from a Privacy Shield company.

- **Clear safeguards and transparency obligations on U.S. government access:** The U.S. has given the EU assurance that the access of public authorities for law enforcement and national security is subject to clear limitations, safeguards, and oversight mechanisms. Everyone in the EU will, also for the first time, benefit from redress mechanisms in this area. The U.S. has ruled out indiscriminate mass surveillance on personal data transferred to the US under the EU-U.S. Privacy Shield arrangement. The Office of the Director of National Intelligence further clarified that bulk collection of data could only be used under specific preconditions and needs to be as targeted and focused as possible. It details the safeguards in place for the use of data under such exceptional circumstances. The U.S. Secretary of State has established a redress possibility in the area of national intelligence for Europeans through an Ombudsperson mechanism within the Department of State.

- **Effective protection of individual rights:** Any citizen who considers that their data has been misused under the Privacy Shield scheme will benefit from several accessible and affordable dispute resolution mechanisms. Ideally, the complaint will be resolved by the company itself, or free of charge Alternative Dispute resolution (ADR) solutions will be offered. Individuals can also go to their national Data Protection Authorities, who will work with the Federal Trade Commission to ensure that complaints by EU citizens are investigated and resolved. If a case is not resolved by any of the other means, as a last resort there will be an arbitration Redress possibility in the area of national security for EU citizens' will be handled by an Ombudsperson independent from the US intelligence services.
- **Annual joint review mechanism:** The mechanism will monitor the functioning of the Privacy Shield, including the commitments and assurance as regards access to data for law enforcement and national security purposes. The European Commission and the U.S. Department of Commerce will conduct the review and associate national intelligence experts from the U.S. and European Data Protection Authorities. The Commission will draw on all other sources of information available and will issue a public report to the European Parliament and the Council.

More information about the EU-U.S. Privacy Shield is available on Department of Commerce website at www.commerce.gov/privacyshield. The "Fact Sheet – Overview of the EU-U.S. Privacy Shield Framework For Interested Participants" is at www.commerce.gov/sites/commerce.gov/files/media/files/2016/fact_sheet-_eu-us_privacy_shield_7-16_sc_cmts.pdf. Source: http://europa.eu/rapid/press-release_IP-16-2461_en.htm

---

You Need To Know > ## Why Did the Safe Harbor Data Transfer Agreement End?

The fifteen-year-old international agreement called **"Safe Harbor"** that allowed companies to transfer the digital data of individuals between the EU and U.S. was invalidated by a Court of Justice for the European Union (CJEU) ruling on October 6, 2015. The decision to invalidate Safe Harbor stemmed from the case of *Maximillian Schrems v. Data Protection Commissioner* where an Austrian citizen lodged a privacy complaint about his data being transferred to servers in the U.S. for processing claiming that the U.S. did not offer sufficient protection against government surveillance due to revelations made by defector Edward Snowden. The ruling by the CJEU is available at www.esrcheck.com/file/CJEU-Ruling-Safe-Harbor-Invalid.pdf. The case was not exactly surprising, however. For many years, European data and privacy authorities felt that the U.S. did not offer sufficient privacy protection.

EU-U.S. Privacy Shield Framework for Data Protection Launched August 1, 2016

The EU-U.S. Privacy Shield Framework designed by the U.S. Department of Commerce and European Commission to provide companies on both sides of the Atlantic that transfer personal data from the European Union (EU) to the United States (U.S.) with a mechanism to comply with EU data protection requirements in support of transatlantic commerce launched on August 1, 2016. The EU-U.S. Privacy Shield Framework website is online at www.privacyshield.gov.

The new website provides information to help U.S. organizations self-certify to the Privacy Shield Framework and the Department of Commerce began accepting certifications at PrivacyShield.gov on August 1, 2016. Although the decision to join Privacy Shield is voluntary, the public commitment by an organization to comply with Privacy Shield Principles through self-certification is enforceable under U.S. law by either the U.S. Federal Trade Commission (FTC) or the U.S. Department of Transportation (DOT).

The EU-U.S. Privacy Shield Framework includes seven commonly recognized privacy principles combined with 16 equally binding supplemental principles that explain and augment the first seven principles. The 23 Privacy Shield Principles lay out requirements for the use and treatment of personal data received from the EU by participating organizations as well as access and recourse mechanisms provided to individuals in the EU. The Privacy Shield Framework is at www.privacyshield.gov/EU-US-Framework:

I. Overview

II. Principles

1. Notice
2. Choice
3. Accountability for Onward Transfer
4. Security
5. Data Integrity and Purpose Limitation
6. Access
7. Recourse, Enforcement, and Liability

III. Supplemental Principles

1. Sensitive Data
2. Journalistic Exceptions
3. Secondary Liability
4. Performing Due Diligence and Conducting Audits
5. The Role of the Data Protection Authorities
6. Self-Certification
7. Verification
8. Access
9. Human Resources Data
10. Obligatory Contracts for Onward Transfers
11. Dispute Resolution and Enforcement
12. Choice – Timing of Opt Out
13. Travel Information
14. Pharmaceutical and Medical Products
15. Public Record and Publicly Available Information
16. Access Requests by Public Authorities

Annex I

Introduction

A. Scope
B. Available Remedies
C. Pre-Arbitration Requirements
D. Binding Nature of Decisions
E. Review and Enforcement
F. The Arbitration Panel
G. Arbitration Procedures
H. Costs

The Privacy Shield provides a number of important benefits for participating to U.S.-based organizations, which will be deemed able to provide "adequate" privacy protection, a requirement for the transfer of personal data outside of the European Union. In addition, compliance requirements are clearly laid out and cost-effective, which should particularly benefit small and medium-sized enterprises. Key new requirements for organizations participating in the Privacy Shield Framework are:

Informing individuals about data processing

- A Privacy Shield participant must include in its privacy policy a declaration of the organization's commitment to comply with the Privacy Shield Principles so that the commitment becomes enforceable under U.S. law.

- When a participant's privacy policy is available online, it must include a link to the Department of Commerce's Privacy Shield website and a link to the website or complaint submission form of the independent recourse mechanisms that is available to investigate individual complaints.
- A participant must inform individuals of their rights to access their personal data, the requirement to disclose personal information in response to lawful request by public authorities, which enforcement authority has jurisdiction over the organization's compliance with the Framework, and the organization's liability in cases of onward transfer of data to third parties.

Providing free and accessible dispute resolution

- Individuals may bring a complaint directly to a Privacy Shield participant, and the participant must respond to the individual within 45 days.
- Privacy Shield participants must provide, at no cost to the individual, an independent recourse mechanism by which each individual's complaints and disputes can be investigated and expeditiously resolved.
- If an individual submits a complaint to a data protection authority (DPA) in the EU, the Department of Commerce has committed to receive, review and undertake best efforts to facilitate resolution of the complaint and to respond to the DPA within 90 days.
- Privacy Shield participants must also commit to binding arbitration at the request of the individual to address any complaint that has not been resolved by other recourse and enforcement mechanisms.

Cooperating with the Department of Commerce

- Privacy Shield participants must respond promptly to inquiries and requests by the Department of Commerce for information relating to the Privacy Shield Framework.

Maintaining data integrity and purpose limitation

- Privacy Shield participants must limit personal information to the information relevant for the purposes of processing.
- Privacy Shield participants must comply with the new data retention principle.

Ensuring accountability for data transferred to third parties

To transfer personal information to a third party acting as a controller, a Privacy Shield participant must:

- Comply with the Notice and Choice Principles; and
- Enter into a contract with the third-party controller that provides that such data may only be processed for limited and specified purposes consistent with the consent provided by the individual and that the recipient will provide the same level of protection as the Principles and will notify the organization if it makes a determination that it can no longer meet this obligation. The contract shall provide that when such a determination is made the third party controller ceases processing or takes other reasonable and appropriate steps to remediate.

To transfer personal data to a third party acting as an agent, a Privacy Shield participant must:

- Transfer such data only for limited and specified purposes;
- Ascertain that the agent is obligated to provide at least the same level of privacy protection as is required by the Principles;
- Take reasonable and appropriate steps to ensure that the agent effectively processes the personal information transferred in a manner consistent with the organization's obligations under the Principles;
- Require the agent to notify the organization if it makes a determination that it can no longer meet its obligation to provide the same level of protection as is required by the Principles;
- Upon notice, take reasonable and appropriate steps to stop and remediate unauthorized processing; and
- Provide a summary or a representative copy of the relevant privacy provisions of its contract with that agent to the Department upon request.

Transparency related to enforcement actions

- Privacy Shield participants must make public any relevant Privacy Shield-related sections of any compliance or assessment report submitted to the FTC if the organization becomes subject to an FTC or court order based on non-compliance.

Ensuring commitments are kept as long as data is held

- If an organization leaves the Privacy Shield Framework, it must annually certify its commitment to apply the Principles to information received under the Privacy Shield Framework if it chooses to keep such data or provide "adequate" protection for the information by another authorized means.

To be assured of Privacy Shield benefits, an organization must self-certify annually to the Department of Commerce that it agrees to adhere to the Privacy Shield Principles via www.privacyshield.gov.

Author Tip ▷ **EU-U.S. Privacy Shield Certification**

In August 2016, the first firms that had achieved the Privacy Shield designation were announced by the U.S. Department of Commerce's International Trade Administration (ITA). Employment Screening Resources® (ESR) received notification that ESR's self-certification of adherence to the EU-U.S. Privacy Shield Framework was approved and effective as of that date. To learn more, read www.esrcheck.com/wordpress/2016/08/15/employment-screening-resources-receives-eu-u-s-privacy-shield-certification-from-department-of-commerce/.

See The Addendum ▷ **Article about EU-U.S. Privacy Shield**

For a more detailed analysis of EU-U.S. Privacy Shield framework, please see the article entitled *'EU/US Privacy Shield Program Replaces Safe Harbor as an Additional Data Transfer Mechanism from the EU to the United States'* submitted for this book by attorney Kevin L. Coy, Partner, Arnall Golden Gregory LLP in the Addendum.

Firms that process data on individuals from EU member countries without compliance with the EU rules can be in violation of EU law. This can have a serious impact on international firms or firms that do business in an EU country. American firms under the general jurisdiction of the FTC or DOT have the option of joining the Privacy Shield program offered by the U.S. Department of Commerce as one means to process information from the EU. This is a voluntary program that involves self-certification regarding the mechanisms to protect confidential personal data.

Note that the Privacy Shield principles have different requirements than the individual EU country data privacy requirements. The Privacy Shield requirements are relevant when the organization intends to transfer information from the EU to the U.S. under the Privacy Shield regime. Organizations that are processing data in an EU member country will need to abide by that country's privacy regulations, which contain other requirements.

By way of illustration of the importance of privacy laws, here is additional information about privacy rules in the two neighbors of the United States—**Canada** and **Mexico**.

About Canada's Strict Privacy Laws – PIPEDA

Canada has a complicated system of Federal and Provincial privacy and data protection laws which have an impact on employment screening. The **Personal Information Protection and Electronics Document Act**, or **PIPEDA**, went into effect on January 1, 2004. PIPEDA privacy rules have a much broader application than just employment screening. For employment purposes, the law broadly applies to not only firms involved in a federal undertaking (such as governmental corporations or private firms involved in fields such as telecommunications, aeronautics, banks, communications, or transportation) but has been extended to nearly all employers engaged in commercial activity unless their province has substantially similar privacy protections in place. Currently, British Columbia, Alberta, and Quebec have laws substantially similar to the federal Canadian law. Under PIPEDA, employers can still conduct pre-employment background screening, but only with some stringent privacy controls.

PIPEDA identifies ten principals for privacy, which employers need to understand and take into account in their screening.

- **Accountability:** Employers are responsible for the personal information under their control, and must designate someone who is accountable for compliance with the Act.
- **Identifying purposes:** Employers must specify why they are collecting personal information from employees at or before the time they do so.
- **Consent:** The employee's knowledge and consent are required for the collection, use, or disclosure of personal information.
- **Limiting collection:** Employers may only collect the personal information necessary for the purpose they have identified and must collect it by fair and lawful means.
- **Limiting use, disclosure, and retention:** Unless they have the consent of the employee, or are legally required to do otherwise, employers may use or disclose personal information only for the purposes for which they collected it, and they may retain it only as long as necessary for those purposes.
- **Accuracy:** The employees' personal information must be accurate, complete, and up-to-date.
- **Safeguards:** All personal information must be protected by appropriate security safeguards.
- **Openness:** Employers must make their personal information policies and practices known to their employees.
- **Individual access:** Employees must be able to access personal information about themselves and be able to challenge the accuracy and completeness of it.
- **Challenging compliance:** Employees must be able to present a challenge about the employer's compliance with the Act to the person that the employer has designated as accountable.

Some helpful links for employers to use to better understand PIPEDA and the substantially similar Provincial regulations are:

- Office of the Privacy Commissioner of Canada: www.priv.gc.ca
- Office of the Information and Privacy Commissioner for Alberta: www.oipc.ab.ca
- Office of the Information and Privacy Commissioner for British Columbia (B.C.): www.oipc.bc.ca
- Commission d'accès à l'information du Québec: www.cai.gouv.qc.ca

More information about the Privacy laws can be found at www.privcom.gc.ca/fs-fi/02_05_d_18_e.asp

As with the EU Data Privacy Directive, the Canadian rules are similar to the FCRA. Both rules require notice, applicant consent, accuracy requirements, limitations on use of data, and the ability of consumers to know what is said about them and to contest it.

However, there are some important differences. First, under the Canadian rules as well as the EU, there is a concept of not retaining information longer than needed. Under the FCRA, data is generally retained for six years in order to meet the FCRA statute of limitation requirement, as well as an extra year that a party may have to actually serve the lawsuit. (See the FCRA material at Chapter 3).

The Canadian rules also require a posted privacy policy and the designation of an individual to be in charge of privacy matters. In the U.S., these are best practices but not mandates.

U.S. employers with offices or facilities in Canada need to review their compliance with PIPEDA and the provincial laws not only for employment screening purposes but also for numerous other aspects of their businesses.

Canadian Criminal Records

A search of the Canadian Police Information Centre (CPIC), managed by the Royal Canadian Mounted Police (RCMP), is often conducted. A search of the CPIC requires a special release signed by the applicant. If the results of the CPIC are unclear, meaning a record may exist, then fingerprints are required before any conviction history is provided. Additionally, the employer needs to verify and provide copies of two (2) photo identification documents and sign the special release as well. The typical turnaround time for a CPIC search is three (3) working days or less. However, while the turnaround time for CPIC may be short for cursory results, the actual turnaround time for more detailed results requiring fingerprints is far longer, and employers need to be aware of the situation.

An addition problem with the CPIC search is that it does not cover all offenses. Lesser offenses (summary offenses) are not included. Also, as of this printing, there is a substantial backlog of criminal records not entered into CPIC. According to some knowledgeable firms, the authorities may be as much as two and a half years behind.

Some employers opt for a local search which can be done through the courts. This local search may cover an entire province. No special consent is needed and summary level results are provided.

Transferring Information to a Country Outside of Canada

If a person's personal information will be transferred to another country, especially one where the privacy laws may be less stringent than those in Canada, the individual should be informed of the fact that such a transfer will occur. The individual should also be informed that government officials may have access to the individual's data. This is in response to concerns about laws such as the U.S. Patriot Act. Information about this consent requirement is available from the Office of the Privacy Commissioner of Canada, Guidelines for Processing Personal Data Across Borders, at www.priv.gc.ca/en/privacy-topics/personal-information-transferred-across-borders/.

Additional Resources for Canada

- Guidelines for Online Consent: www.priv.gc.ca/en/privacy-topics/collecting-personal-information/consent/gl_oc_201405/
- Privacy Toolkit: A Guide for Businesses and Organizations: www.priv.gc.ca/en/privacy-topics/privacy-laws-in-canada/the-personal-information-protection-and-electronic-documents-act-pipeda/pipeda-compliance-help/guide_org/
- Office of the Information and Privacy Commissioner of Alberta: Guidelines for Online Consent: www.oipc.ab.ca/media/383662/guidelines_for_online_consent_may2014.pdf
- Office of the Information and Privacy Commissioner of British Columbia: Guidelines for Online Consent: www.oipc.bc.ca/guidance-documents/1638
- A Guide to PIPA for businesses and organizations: www.oipc.bc.ca/guidance-documents/1438

About Mexico's Privacy Legislation

Comprehensive privacy legislation in Mexico was passed in 2010 with the **Federal Law for the Protection of Personal Data in Possession of Private Entities** (*Ley Federal de Protección de Datos Personales en Posesión de Particulares*) ("the Law"). Regulations to the Law (*Reglamento de la Ley Federal de Protección de Datos en Posesión de*

Particulares[4]) (the "Regulations") were passed in 2011.

The following was obtained from the Mexico Data Protection authority, Instituto Nacional de Transparencia, Acceso a la Información y Protección de Datos Personales ("INAI") *Guía para cumplir con los principios y deberes de la Ley Federal de Protección de Datos Personales en Posesión de los Particulares* (Guidance for complying with the principles and duties of the Federal Law on Protection of Personal Data Held by Private Entities).[5]

The Principles of Personal Data Protection for companies or private entities handling personal data:

- **Principle of Lawfulness and Fairness**: Personal data must be processed in a lawful and fair way.
- **Principle of Consent**: Processing requires consent from the individual. The consent should be linked to the specific purposes of processing.
- **Principle of Information**: Prior to processing personal information, data controllers are required to inform the individual on the nature of the processing and the basic information about the processing. This is done through a **Privacy Notice**. The Notice is required even if consent is not required.
- **Principle of Proportionality**: Entities may process personal data only as necessary, appropriate and relevant in relation to the purposes for which they were obtained.
- **Principle of Purpose**: Personal data may only be processed to fulfill the purpose or purposes which have been identified in the Privacy Notice.
- **Principle of Quality**: Personal information must be accurate, complete, relevant and updated. Information should not be retained for longer than necessary.
- **Principle of Responsibility**: Also known as the principle of "accountability," it establishes the obligation for compliance with other principles and that the items in the Privacy Notice are complied with. This principle requires the data controller to ensure the protection of the personal data when transferred to third parties.

ARCO Rights

A key feature of the Mexico privacy regulation is the individual's ARCO Rights. These are similar to Subject Access Rights and subject dispute rights, in other countries.

ARCO Rights are the "data owner's"[6] rights of Access, Rectification, Cancellation, and Objection. ARCO rights are derived from Article 22 of the Law. They indicate that any owner, or his legal representative, may exercise these rights on their personal data.

- **Access:** The right of the data owner to know what personal information is held on them, why it is processed, and the conditions for access.
- **Rectification:** The right of the data owner to request correction of outdated, inaccurate, or incomplete information.
- **Cancellation:** The right of the data owner to request removal of their personal information that is not being used in accordance with the Regulation.
- **Opposition:** The right of the data owner to oppose the use of their personal information for specific purposes.

Privacy Notice Requirement

The Law requires data controllers to provide a "Privacy Notice" to any data owner (individual) prior to the collection, use, and processing of personal data. The Privacy Notice requirement was overhauled with the publication of the *Lineamientos del Aviso de privacidad*[7] ("Privacy Notice Guidelines" or "Guidelines") in the Mexican Official Gazette of the Federation by the Mexican Ministry of Economy. The Guidelines became effective April 2013, and impact data controllers. The Privacy Notice requirement will most likely be the responsibility of the employer.

---

[4] http://dof.gob.mx/nota_detalle.php?codigo=5226005&fecha=21/12/2011

[5] http://inicio.ifai.org.mx/SitePages/Documentos-de-Interes.aspx?a=m10

[6] The data owner is the subject of the data processing – in this case the job applicant.

[7] http://www.dof.gob.mx/nota_detalle.php?codigo=5284966&fecha=17/01/2013

The Privacy Notice Guidelines establish three forms of a Privacy Notice: Comprehensive, Simplified, and Short. The Privacy Notice is a means to make sure data owners are informed about the details of their data processing which will allow them to make an informed choice about the processing of their personal information. This includes information about the way an organization will use their personal data, if any third parties will receive their data, and if data will be transferred nationally or internationally.

A summary of the three versions of the Privacy Notice and their appropriate use is found in INAI's ABCs of Privacy Notice (http://abcavisosprivacidad.ifai.org.mx/).

Additional Mexico Privacy Resources

- **Mexico Data Protection Authority**, Instituto Nacional de Transparencia, Acceso a la Información y Protección de Datos Personales (INAI): http://inicio.ifai.org.mx.
- **Guía práctica para ejercer el derecho a la Protección de Datos Personales** (A practical guide to the protection of personal data): http://inicio.ifai.org.mx/SitePages/Publicaciones.aspx.

Focus on India and Japan

Three additional examples that demonstrate issues involved in international background checks will be uncovered in a closer look at **India** and **Japan**.

India

In India, data protection laws are in place. There are no country-specific releases required, and a general release is acceptable. Criminal record checks can be done through the police or through the courts. In some areas, there are databases available. Education verifications require a copy of the degree and can have extended time service for some universities with out of pocket fee required. Falsified degrees are common, and diploma mills are fairly abundant.

You Need To Know

Resume Fraud in India Shows Need for International Background Screening

Puzzled as to why a large amount of job seekers listed the same previous employer on their CV (Curriculum Vitae) – a type of resume in India – managers of a New Delhi IT company used a background screening firm to discover the "employer" was a fake IT firm falsifying past work experience for the money.

The Philippine Daily Inquirer reported the "owner of a dingy one-room mobile repair shop who was pretending to be an HR manager of a fake IT firm... answered verification calls and described how the candidates had worked for him previously doing data entry."

Job seekers are resorting to forging qualifications, faking experience, and inventing companies to find work in an Indian jobs market where economic growth has plunged to the lowest level in a decade due to low business confidence and high interest rates.

A survey by one of India's leading background check firms found nearly one in five job candidates "fudged" information on their CV and as many as 51 percent submitted fake education documents, the Philippine Daily Inquirer reports. The background screening industry in India – worth approximately $32 million annually according to the Indian Association of Professional Background Screeners – is driven by the outsourcing and IT industry where foreign companies move their back office operations to the country.

The source of this story is an article titled 'Liar for hire? Fake CVs flood Indian job market' that was published in the *Philippine Daily Inquirer* newspaper in January of

2014 and is available at http://business.inquirer.net/159889/liar-for-hire-fake-cvs-flood-indian-job-market.

Although challenging, more employers in the United States are including international background checks in the hiring processes. Due to the perceived difficulty in performing international employment screening, some U.S. employers have not attempted to verify international credentials or perform foreign criminal background checks. However, the mere fact that information may be more difficult to obtain from outside of the U.S. does not relieve U.S. employers from their due diligence obligation, or duty of care, associated with hiring when performing international background screening.

With nearly 250 political entities in the world, each country can be an adventure when it comes to international background checks and U.S. employers cannot assume that screening internationally is the same as domestic processes. U.S. employers face a number of difficulties that include differences in courts, legal systems, name variations, language, time, calendars, and costs.

Japan

Employers may be able to utilize a Japanese Criminality Search (JCS). JSC is a proprietary database containing criminality information sourced from government records, Japanese media, Japanese courts, public records, independent anti-organized crime associations, and privately held information of individuals and companies with known connections to unlawful associations such as organized crime and right-wing organizations. It is important to note that the JCS is a database search and NOT a search at the courthouse. This search requires a signed release that includes the name of the individual in Japanese characters (kanji), date of birth, and address. While it is not possible to legally conduct a comprehensive criminal record check for employment screening in Japan, the JCS is the most comprehensive resource available in the country covering organized crime and criminality information. The Japanese Criminality Search (JCS) can provide comprehensive and actionable information in a cost effective manner. The typical turnaround time for background screening in Japan is three (3) business days.

Recommendations for International Background Screening Programs

Although international background screening can be challenging, it is not impossible. Employers can find themselves in hot water if they assume that international screening is too difficult or expensive and simply bypass the process. While international background screening is challenging, the mere fact that information is more difficult to obtain from outside of the U.S. does not relieve employers from their due diligence obligation associated with hiring.

Under the Fair Credit Reporting Act (FCRA), both employers and background screening firms still have certain obligations regarding international screening. If the task of international screening is outsourced to a screening firm, that firm has an FCRA obligation to take reasonable procedures to ensure accuracy. If there is a negative public record, such as a criminal record "hit," then the firm must make certain the information is correct, up-to-date, and supplied in a way that does not violate any data or privacy protection rules.

Employers should implement an international background screening program that best fits their needs and follows these recommendations:

- Employers should not assume that just because a person has spent time outside of the U.S., that an international check is not possible.
- Employers should perform international background screening in a legally compliant manner.

- Employers should use the broadest criminal search allowed in each country.
- Employers should find verification of, at the very least, the highest education that the applicant attained and the last employment where the applicant worked.
- Employers should use proper consent forms meeting country and search specifics.
- Employers should include international credit reports and driving records when available in some countries and when the information is job related.

The bottom line very simply is that the rest of the world is not like the United States. Processes that are taken for granted here in terms of due diligence may not exist in other countries. The U.S. standards of due diligence before hiring is not shared around the world, such as in time is not always of the essence as it is in the U.S. These are factors employers need to keep in mind in performing international screening.

Additional Resource Links

Below are more links to pages not mentioned previously, but may be helpful:

- The World Factbook of Criminal Justice Systems: www.bjs.gov/content/pub/html/wfcj.cfm
- Holidays and Celebrations Around the World: www.earthcalendar.net/index.php
- The CIA World Fact Book: www.cia.gov/library/publications/the-world-factbook/
- The World Clock - Time Zones: www.timeanddate.com

You Need To Know

Global Immersion Press Publishes Third Volume of Global HR Practitioner Handbook

In January 2016, Global Immersion Press, a network of leading global HR practitioners from around the world, published *Volume 3 of the Global HR Practitioner Handbook*. In the Preface to Volume 3, Editor-in-Chief Lisbeth Claus writes that the role of HR and Global HR practitioners continues to be brought into question as "the world of work evolves at a rapid pace due to globalization, information technology, and the growing influence of millennial workers."

Volume 3 includes a module called 'Criminal history screening of global job applicants – Hidden dangers employers should know,' written by Attorney Lester Rosen that reviews the potential problems that impact the reliability of Criminal Clearance Certificates from an international perspective. It is intended to increase awareness for global HR practitioners of the issues and challenges surrounding obtaining Criminal Clearance Certificates from different countries for employment background check purposes.

The handbook is available as an e-book or as separate modules at www.globalimmersionpress.com. The module by Rosen is available at www.globalimmersionpress.com/products/criminal-history-screening-of-global-job-applicants.

Introduction to International Background Screening

Employment Screening Resources® (ESR) has published a complimentary whitepaper by ESR founder and CEO Attorney Lester Rosen entitled *"Introduction to International Background Screening"* that provides an informative introduction to International background screening, what risks employers conducting such screenings should be aware of, and the many ways background screening overseas differs from background screening in the United States.

The whitepaper is found at <u>www.esrcheck.com/Whitepapers/International-Background-Screening/</u>.

Acknowledgments for this Chapter

The author would like to sincerely thank several people who assisted in reviewing and providing content for this portion of *The Safe Hiring Manual*—

Kerstin Bagus, Director of Global Initiatives, ClearStar, and Andy Hellman, Managing Director, International & Strategic Initiatives, ClearStar, who worked on a large portion of the chapter, as well as Kevin L. Coy, Partner, Arnall Golden Gregory LLP, who submitted an article on the EU-U.S. Privacy Shield. Thank you all.

CHAPTER 18

Screening Essential Non-Employees

Introduction

Up to this point, *The Safe Hiring Manual* has emphasized that when hiring employees, employers are sitting ducks for expensive litigation, workplace violence, negative national publicity, and economic loss if they do not take measures to conduct pre-employment screening and exercise due diligence in hiring.

However, the duty of due diligence also extends to non-employees as well in a number of different potential situations, including for example:

- A temporary worker supplied by a staffing firm for a limited time or project who is on the staffing firm payroll.
- A worker sent on a temp to perm basis where the worker starts as a temporary worker, and after a specified period of time, hours, or a fee, can be converted to employee status.
- A full-time worker on the payroll of PEO or "leased" to a business through a staffing agency where they are on the payroll of the third party vendor.
- A freelancer or independent contractor hired for a period or job that is paid by the employer for services but is not considered an employee.
- A vendor who comes on premises to deliver goods or services.
- A worker in the burgeoning gig economy that focuses on temporary work, or gigs, for companies like on-demand ride-hailing app providers Uber and Lyft or where people run errands for other people such as driving, walking dogs, cleaning rooms, doing laundry, cooking dinner, or shopping for food.
- A Volunteer who is not paid a salary but nevertheless is contributing hours to organizations stemming from youth sports leagues and faith-based groups to afterschool programs or caring for senior citizens and numerous cases in between. Regardless of whether the organization is a profit or non-profit.

Although this chapter will cover a number of seemingly diverse subjects, it is really a variation on just one theme—just because an organization does not give someone a paycheck does not mean they are not responsible for the behavior of others who in some means, degree or fashion is under their direction and control.

This chapter covers eight broad topics:

1. Issues for businesses that use temporary workers and staffing vendors.
2. Issues from the point of view of staffing vendors.
3. Screening and special issues concerning independent contractors.
4. Vendors and workers that come on premises or to homes to provide goods or services.
5. Screening home-based workers or other workers in close contact with vulnerable populations.
6. Volunteers that need to be screened and issues revolving around fingerprints vs. name checks.
7. How to check non-employees? Fingerprints or private background screening firms?
8. The "Gig" economy where technology firms provide a platform for on demand workers and screening is critical.

#1. Issues for Businesses that Use Temporary Workers and Staffing Vendors

Many employers do not realize they potentially face the same exposure from vendors, independent contractors, or temporary employees from staffing vendor that they face with their own employees. An employer's risk management controls often do not take into account the "need to know" about these workers who are not on their payroll but are on their premises and to some degree under their control and direction, with access to computer systems, clients, co-workers, and assets.

Non-employees are typically described as a contingent workforce that is not on the businesses' payroll and do not receive a W-2 form. A contingent worker may be engaged for a particular project or for a specific time period. A contingent worker may be paid by a third party agency, such as a staffing firm, a Professional Employer Organization (PEO), or firms that specialize in managing contingent workers. A contingent worker can also be paid directly by the business if they are a consultant or independent contractor; but instead of being paid with a paycheck resulting in a W-2 at the end of the year, the worker receives a 1099 form and no benefits (vacation, medical, sick pay, etc.).

The Duty of Due Diligence

The law is absolutely clear if a non-employee working on behalf of a business harms a member of the public or a co-worker, the business can be just as liable as if the person were on the business' payroll. All of the rules of due diligence apply with equal force to vendors, temporary workers, or independent contractors. A business can be liable if, in the exercise of reasonable care, the business should have known that a vendor, temporary worker, or independent contractor was dangerous, unqualified, or otherwise unfit for employment. An employer has an absolute obligation to exercise due diligence not only in whom they hire on payroll, but in whom they allow on premises to perform work. (See e.g. a compilation of cases throughout the U.S. annotated in 78 ALR3d 910).

In addition, many employers have found out the hard way that using unscreened workers from a vendor or staffing firm or hired as an independent contractor can also cause damage. When an employer is the victim of theft, embezzlement, or resume fraud, the harm is just as bad regardless of whether the worker is on their payroll or someone else's payroll. No employer would dream of walking down the street and handing the keys to the business to a total stranger, yet many businesses across America essentially do exactly that every day when engaging the services of vendors and temporary workers.

Employers do have challenges in ensuring they have exercised due diligence regarding contingent workers, vendors, and independent contractors. The practical issue is, fortunately, there are a number of cost-effective avenues available. For example, employers can insist on any contract for any service that any time a worker comes on premises, that worker has been the subject of a background screening. This has become a practice gaining widespread acceptance in American businesses. An employer must have a hard and fast rules—if a background check is needed to demonstrate due diligence, no worker supplied by a third party is allowed to work without a background check.

An area where employers can be blindsided is when working with temporary ("temp") or staffing agencies. Employers would not intentionally bring people on the premises with criminal records, unsuitable for a particular job. Yet employers consistently hire temporary workers and independent contractors from staffing agencies with no idea as to the background or qualifications of those hired. Given the sensitive information found on business computer systems, even one bad temp could do substantial damage. Even though workers may be on the payroll of a staffing agency, since the workers perform duties at an employer's place of business, the employer can be liable for harm a worker causes.

The reality is many staffing firms simply do not routinely perform due diligence checks before supplying workers. That reluctance is for two reasons. First, staffing firms are exceptionally cost conscious and given the large volume of workers they handle, the cost of background checks, such as criminal checks, can have a significant impact on their bottom line. Second, staffing firms must work on an extremely tight timeline. Staffing firms need to place workers as soon as possible.

Every hour of delay is lost revenue to a staffing firm. In addition, if a potential new worker is told to wait a day or two for a background check, that worker may go down the street to another staffing firm.

Staffing firms often advertise that they carefully "screen" all applicants but without stating the extent or nature of the screening. A business utilizing staffing services needs to be very specific when asking a staffing firm exactly what screening is done. Unless the staffing firm specifically tells the employer a criminal check is being done, an employer should assume that no criminal check is being conducted. An employer is well advised to require some of the steps suggested in the previous section in order to confirm exactly what is being done in terms of a criminal background check. Issues regarding screening and criteria should be specifically addressed in any contract between a business and the staffing vendor.

A business needs to carefully document what a staffing firm is doing because employers can have a "co-employment relationship" with temporary workers. Co-employment has been defined as a legal relationship in which more than one employer has legal rights and obligations with respect to the same employee or group of employees. Both the Internal Revenue Service and various courts have found that a temporary worker of a supplier working at the customer's work site—even though paid and treated as an employee of the supplier—may still be considered an employee of both the supplier and the customer for legal purposes. The employer sets the specific duties, the duration of the assignment, and the level and types of skills required even though the staffing firm is responsible for recruitment, placement, and pay rates.

You Need To Know >

Summary of Five Essential Points about Working with Staffing Vendors from the Business's Point of View

1. When staffing vendors say they carefully "screen" workers, they are not saying they are doing background screening! Staffing vendors use the word "screen" to mean they screen qualifications against the employer's needs essentially, but it does not mean they do background screening.

2. For a staffing firm or Professional Employer Organization (PEO), regardless of whether the job is temporary or permanent, a background check presents challenges. It not only impacts costs and profit margins in a competitive business, but it can delay placements. Every day of a lost placement is lost revenue, especially if the staffing firm is providing temporary staffing. A staffing vendor may even lose a potential worker due to a delay. It also adds another layer of complication to the staffing process.

3. Unless staffing vendors specifically tell an employer they do background checks and supply the details, an employer needs to assume that a staffing vendor is NOT doing background checks.

4. Do not work with a staffing vendor until there is a clear understanding of exactly who is doing what when it comes to due diligence and background checks. There needs to be a meeting of the minds.

5. There can be jobs where a background check is not necessarily needed to satisfy due diligence, such as part-time, hourly, on demand tasks where the jobs require no experience and are entry level. However, if a background check is deemed unnecessary due to the risk factors involved, make sure that the employer and staffing firm have analyzed the situation and have documented that they have made a deliberate decision based upon known risk factors to not perform background checks.

Employers can take the following to guard against having an issue when accepting a worker from a staffing vendor:

- Determine if the type and nature of the employer's work requires a background check as part of an employer's due diligence obligations.
- Make it clear to all service providers, staffing vendors, and independent contractors that the business has a policy of maintaining a safe and qualified workforce, the company has a background checking policy for its own employees, and the same policies apply to all workers that perform work for the company, regardless of their status as a contingent worker, independent contractor, or vendor
- Subject any non-employee who represents a risk to the same screening and safe hiring practices as would be done with a W-2 employee.
- When using a temporary worker from a staffing firm, require the staffing agency or Professional Employer Organization (PEO) to conduct a background check. As an extra precaution, an employer can request that the FCRA release extend to the employer's workplace. Under the FCRA, as long as the applicant consents to this, it is perfectly acceptable for both the staffing firm and the employer of the workplace to review the background report. However, ensure that there is language in the FCRA release to the effect that the business where the consumer is performing the assignment can review a background report, and that does not create an employment relationship.
- Make sure there is complete clarity in the contract with staffing vendor as who does exactly what, in terms of the background screening process. Some of the details where there needs to be a "meeting of the minds" are discussed in the next section in the section on staffing vendors.
- A vendor must certify there has been a background check that is acceptable under the employer's criteria. If there is a question about the suitability of a particular worker, a business is within its rights to require a review of the background report to ensure that it meets the business policy. Again, as long as there is consent, under the doctrine of "co-employment," a business would have a "permissible purpose" under the FCRA to do such a review without altering the fact that the contingent worker is on the payroll of the third party staffing vendor.
- The staffing vendor must provide the business with the name and identity of the firm performing the background check and a statement that the firm performing the background checks is experienced and suitable for the assignment.
- A best practice is to have the same firm that does the background checks for the business also perform the vendor's background checks. Another best practice is to ensure that any provider of background screening service is a member of and even accredited by the National Association of Profession Background Screeners (NAPBS). See Chapter 11.
- If a staffing vendor does not use the same screening firm the businesses utilizes, extra precautions can be taken. The business can require the vendor to provide the employer with a "Certification of Compliance." This certification should indicate the following:
  - The name, identity, and qualifications of the firm that provided the vendor's background checks.
  - A statement that vendor has advised their background service of the criteria required.
  - Only workers who pass the background check are allowed on your premises.
  - In the event there is something negative in the worker's background, the vendor has thoroughly investigated the issue and has determined the matter does not otherwise disqualify the worker from going onto your premises.
  - In the event there is negative material, then the business may ask to review it as well to determine if the worker meets the business's criteria. The best practice is to require the vendor to have the worker sign a release permitting that process.

Businesses may be concerned if these policies are illegal and will make it more difficult to find vendors and suppliers of services. The answer is a resounding NO to both concerns. An employer has an absolute right to exercise, and even the obligation, to follow the same due diligence in selecting workers and vendors that they would use in selecting their own employees. As long as the screening requirements are fair, non-discriminatory, and validly job-related, there is no legal reason why a business cannot protect itself.

Author Tip

Who is Responsible?

Employers need to be careful to make sure the vendor, staffing firm, or PEO does more than go through the motions. Reports must be ordered, tracked, and documented. The employer must require that the vendor certifies that they have reviewed the screening reports looking for any red flags and they took appropriate steps. Employers and vendors must have an understanding of the employer's requirements, which are often the same as the employer would use for their own workers. Although this may seem obvious, it is worth clarifying who has the responsibility to review background reports and determine eligibility to work.

In this way, staffing vendors and suppliers also demonstrate that safe hiring and due diligence are critical parts of their business as well as their commitment to supplying quality workers. Any vendor not willing to engage in pre-employment screening is not likely to be a good choice anyway. Although there may be a slight increase to the vendor in terms of expenses, a vendor should be willing to pay necessary costs to obtain good workers and to satisfy the needs of the employer-clients.

The bottom line—there is no reason for employers not to require vendors and independent contractors undergo background checks.

You Need To Know

EEOC Guidance on Criminal Records

The Equal Employment Opportunity Commission (EEOC) *"Enforcement Guidance on the Consideration of Arrest and Conviction Records in Employment Decisions Under Title VII of the Civil Rights Act of 1964"* issued April 25, 2012, on the use of criminal records can potentially impact staffing vendors as well. Staffing vendors may want to review Chapter 10 to become familiar with the EOCC Guidance in order to take appropriate measures. The actual EEOC Guidance is available at www.eeoc.gov/laws/guidance/arrest_conviction.cfm.

See The Addendum

Special Issues for Staffing Companies

An article titled *"Special Issues For Staffing Companies"* by Scott Paler, Partner, Chair of Labor and Employment Practice Group, DeWitt Ross & Stevens S.C., is available in the Addendum.

#2. Issues from the Point of View of Staffing Vendors

This section is the flip side of the discussion above and focuses on due diligence and background checks from the point of view of staffing vendors.

It's a sobering thought, but every time staffing professionals or recruiters make a placement, there is the possibility that the new hire can put them out of business.

Why? Because if a dangerous, unqualified, unfit, or dishonest candidate is placed in a job and harm occurs, a staffing vendor faces the possibility of a lawsuit. Perhaps just as important, a bad placement can result in loss of business and damage to a professional reputation that may have been years in the making.

If it gets to the point of a lawsuit, the heart of the staffing professional may sink when those dreaded words echo across the courtroom: "Ladies and Gentleman of the Jury." In a lawsuit, a staffing professional would need to show, for example, whether credentials and education were verified, whether past employment was checked, and whether a criminal background check was done.

A staffing professional accused of negligence in making a placement can be sued by a number of parties, including the business entity that relied upon the professional judgment of the recruiter or staffing firm. Certainly, a co-worker or member of the public who was injured by the bad hire can sue for damages. The worst case scenario would be that the bad hire resulted in the death of a fellow worker, and the victim's family is suing for wrongful death. This is just what happened in a highly publicized case in California. A 28-year-old female winery worker was stabbed to death by a co-worker who was a convicted murderer and had been placed at the winery by a temp agency. The agency did NOT conduct a background check. The jury awarded the family $5.5 million.

If a recruiter is sued, it may well be an uphill battle to win in court. The jury will hear evidence that the staffing vendor recruited, recommended, or placed the offender. In most cases, the staffing professional probably makes representations about the quality of their services. The staffing professional's website and sales literature may suggest that they provide only the best candidates who are carefully screened. However, in the world of recruiting, "screening" really only means that resumes have been reviewed to determine a good fit for the job opening as opposed to "background screening" for criminal records and verification of facts represented on the resume.

The employer, hoping to lay the blame on someone else, will, of course, claim that they relied on the professional abilities of the staffing professional to send them qualified and safe candidates. There would likely be evidence that the recruiting or staffing firm made a fee on the placement. In the end, the attorney for the injured or deceased employee would ask jury members, "Didn't the staffing professional have not only the resources and opportunity, but also the duty to conduct employee screening on the potential employee before approving their introduction into the workplace?"

The bottom line is that due diligence and background checks go to the very integrity of the product being sold by recruiting and staffing professionals – workers who are qualified and fit for the job. If a staffing firm does not exercise due diligence, it is like playing Russian Roulette with each candidate that is sent out. Which one of these candidates will land you in court or on the front page of the newspaper? Staffing and search professionals have traditionally focused on Sourcing and Sales. Staffing professionals can protect their own business, their clients, and the public by shifting their focus from just Sourcing and Sales to Sourcing, Verifying, and Sales.

Of course, there can be situations where a staffing firm may reasonably feel that background checks are not warranted. For example, if a screening firm is hiring for an on-demand, hourly tasks, the facts and circumstances may not create a need for a background check. However, that decision should be fully documented.

What Can Staffing Companies Do?

Staffing vendors and third party recruiters may want to consider the following best practices:

- Ensure there is a complete understanding and a meeting of the minds between you and your client as the following critical issues:
    - Is a background check going to be performed?
    - Who is reasonable for doing it—the staffing firm or the workplace?
    - Who is going to select the background firm?
    - What depth and level of screening will be utilized?
    - Who has the duty to review the reports?
    - What is an acceptable report and what criteria is used?

- o At what point should the staffing firm escalate the report to the client to review?
- o Who is responsible for the authorization and disclosure forms the worker signs?
- o Who is reasonable for pre-adverse and pots-adverse action decisions?
- o Who is responsible for the Individualized assessment process needed for EEOC compliance (See Chapter 10)?

- Carefully consider the cost of doing background checks versus the risk of not performing them. Preventing even one embezzler or violent offender from being sent to a client can be worth the cost in the long run in terms of avoiding litigation, lost clients, and a loss of professional reputation.

- Carefully review any marketing materials, representations on your website, and sales presentation to ensure that clients are accurately informed about your practices. Do not imply that your firm "carefully screens" or only "sends the best" if, in fact, you are not doing adequate background checks.

- Be careful doing in-house criminal record checks. That can trigger application of the FCRA.

- Be careful of using commercial low-cost databases for all of the reason described in Chapter 9. The use of databases may also trigger the FCRA.

- Utilize the Safe Hiring Program outlined in this book and document all steps taken.

- Make sure that your contracts with clients accurately describe what, if any, background checks you will be doing. Consider:
  - o Adequacy of consent issue – the consent form needs to release information to both the staffing firm and employer where the worker may be sent.

Author Tip **Joint Use of Background Report by Both Staffing Vendor and Business**

Where there is going to be a joint use of the report by both staffing vendor and the business where the work is to be performed, it is important for purposes of the Fair Credit Reporting Act (FCRA) to ensure that only individuals with permissible purpose are reviewing a report and that the consumer has consented. Here is an example of language for that issue:

I agree, authorize, and consent to the release and disclosure of any and all information including but not limited to the above to [COMPANY] and to [CRA], and to a related third party entity only where I am being considered for direct or temporary Engagement with or by them. In no event does consideration for Engagement create an employment relationship.

The last sentence is important in order to prevent any confusion about who the consumer is working for and to clarify that by viewing the report, the business where the consumer is actually providing service does not become the employer.

NLRB Joint Employer Standard Could Increase Liability for Acts of Staffing Vendors and Potentially Other Business Entities

The dangers of lawsuits against employers for the actions of their staffing vendors may have increased with the August 27, 2015 decision by the National Labor Relations Board (NLRB) in a case where the definition of a "joint" employer was expanded by holding that the ability of an employer to exercise control over a worker can create joint employment.

In the 3-2 decision involving Browning-Ferris Industries (BFI) of California, the NLRB refined the joint employer standard by finding that BFI was a joint employer with Leadpoint, the company that supplied employees to BFI. In finding that BFI was a joint employer with Leadpoint, the NLRB relied on indirect and direct authority and control BFI possessed over the employment of employees supplied by Leadpoint.

The NLRB held that the previous joint employer standard failed to keep pace with changes in the workplace and economy circumstances that saw more than 2.87 million of U.S. workers employed through temporary agencies as of August 2014. The NLRB found that two or more entities are joint employers of a single workforce if:

1. They are both employers within the meaning of the common law; and
2. They share or codetermine those matters governing the essential terms and conditions of employment.

In evaluating whether an employer possesses sufficient control over employees to qualify as a joint employer, the NLRB will consider whether an employer has exercised control over terms and conditions of employment indirectly through an intermediary or has reserved the authority to do so. A copy of the Browning-Ferris decision is available at www.esrcheck.com/file/NLRB-Browing-Ferris-Decision.pdf.

It is more important than ever that employers understand what their staffing vendors are doing since the new joint employer standard can potentially open up more employer liability for acts of staffing vendors. Where employers rely on the services of third party staffing vendors, it is also important to ensure that all Fair Credit Reporting Act (FCRA) processes are being followed by the vendor. A recent lawsuit filed against both a nationally known business and a staffing firm underscores the need for employers to work carefully with staffing providers to ensure that the FCRA requirements are being followed.

Browning-Ferris Decision Could Have Big Impact on Employers

Some employment lawyers have expressed concern that the decision in the Browning-Ferris matter could have far reaching implications for employers. For example, under the logic of the ruling, it is possible that a franchisor could be responsible for the conduct of the employees of a franchisee. Although commentators note that the decision has not been applied that broadly, it does underscore the need for businesses to carefully monitor the exact relationship between themselves and partners, vendors, and third parties who perform services. Business entities need to ensure that they have appropriate due diligence in place to avoid lawsuits for negligent hiring.

Special Issues for Staffing Companies

See an article in the addendum titled *"Special Issues For Staffing Companies"* by Scott Paler, Partner, Chair of Labor and Employment Practice Group, DeWitt Ross & Stevens S.C.

Another issue involving staffing firms and background checks is whether an employer can escape liability for using an employee from a staffing firm. In some states, under certain circumstances, there may be some additional protection if it's not your employee. But it is not good to rely on such a strategy, and there is still the issue of negligent supervision and the argument the employer was negligent in picking that particular staffing agency.

Calling Past Employers for Reference Checks

One area where an employment agency can assemble and evaluate consumer information is calling past employers for a reference check. Staffing firms very often do not want to outsource calling past employers because it is an opportunity to not only obtain information but also for prospecting for new business as well.

FCRA Section 603(o) provides an exemption for communications that would otherwise be an investigative consumer report when past employment reference check are made by a firm that is regularity engaged in "procuring an opportunity for a natural person to work for the employer." However, to qualify for this exception, an employment agency must engage in additional steps. First, the consumer must consent in writing. (A consumer can give a verbal consent initially, but it must be followed up with a written consent within three days.)

In addition, the FCRA provides that the staffing agency must notify the consumer in writing of their right to have disclosure of what the staffing firm learns. If the consumer makes that request, the staffing firm must respond in five days and provide that nature and substance of the information, except that it does not need to reveal the source. The staffing firm discloses in writing to the consumer who is the subject of the communication, no later than five (5) business days after receiving any request from the consumer for such disclosure, the nature and substance of all information in the consumer's file at the time of the request, except that the sources of any information that is acquired solely for use in making the communication and is actually used for no other purpose, need not be disclosed other than under appropriate discovery procedures in any court of competent jurisdiction in which an action is brought; and any information obtained can only be for the purposes of employment and the staffing firm cannot use the information in violation of any state of federal discrimination law.

As a result, staffing vendors should ensure that have procedures in place to comply with the FCRA rule.

However, if a staffing firm performs any other types of checks, such as accessing criminal records, then the staffing firm would be a Consumer Reporting Agency and have all of the duties and obligations required under the FCRA.

Author Tip > **Don't Just Go Through the Motions with Background Checks**

The most critical point for a staffing firm is to not simply go through the motions when doing a background check. A background screening veteran tells the story of an employer that utilized a temporary worker from a staffing firm following what the employer thought was a successful background check. Six months later, the employer decided to make the worker a permanent employee and conducted their own background check only to discover a very serious criminal conviction that the staffing firm failed to mention. When confronted with the issue, the staffing firms said, "We were told to do a background check, but no one ever told us to read it."

The walk away point—a staffing firm or business cannot simply go through the motions. A well thought out program needs to be in place for everyone's protection.

#3. Screening and Special Issues Concerning Independent Contractors

The law is clear that classifying a worker as an independent contractor does not shield a business from liability if it fails to exercise due diligence in the selection process.

When reviewing issues related to independent contractor's classification, there are two considerations:

1. Is the worker even an independent contractor? Misclassifying a worker as an independent contractor when in fact they should be an employee on payroll creates a large potential liability.
2. Even if a worker is truly an independent contractor under various tests, it is still a best practice to treat them as though the Fair Credit Reporting Act (FCRA) applies.

In addition to #2 above, the Federal Trade Commission (FTC) has suggested that the FCRA applies to a situation where a consumer has an employment-like relationship regardless of the label. FTC staff issued letters of opinion following the 1997 amendment to the FCRA—although the letters do not have the force of law—are considered highly persuasive. In the Mr. Herman L. Allison letter dated February 23, 1998, the FTC staff was asked if the FCRA rules concerning disclosures and releases applied in the case of a certain trucking company who employed independent owner-operators. The truck drivers were not on the payroll as employees, but "owned and operated their own vehicles."

The FTC rejected the position that there was not an employment relationship. The FTC cited a Fourth Circuit Court of Appeals case [*Hoke v. Retail Credit Corporation,* 521 F.2d 1079, 1082 (4th Cir. 1975), *cert. denied,* 423 U.S. 1087 (1976)] that the broad purposes of the FCRA required that "employment" not be strictly defined in traditional terms, but would include independent contractor relationships. As a result, the application of the FCRA does not depend upon whether a worker receives a W-2 tax form as an employee or a 1099 as an independent contractor. The essential factor is the employment-like nature of the relationship. Keep in mind, if an employer has classified a worker as an independent contractor, it is critical to adjust the background screening consent form to take out any reference to employment in order to not change the independent contractor status. An employer can utilize wording referring to an "engagement" instead.

You Need To Know ▶ **Screening Independent Workers is a BIG Issue**

Think the screening of independent workers is an issue that most employers will never face? Think again. The *MBO Partners State of Independence In America 2016* – the longest-running end-to-end survey of the American independent workforce – estimates that **independent workers numbered nearly 40 million in 2016 and are expanding five times faster than general employment workers**. By 2020, the majority of workers will be independent.

The report found the growing independent workforce is fueled by technology, information, and the desire for flexibility. Other key findings include:

- Contractors made up 25 percent of the total U.S. labor force, a number that is expected to rise to 30 percent in 2021.

- 3 million independent workers earned more than $100,000 in 2016, up from 2 million in 2011.

- Six out of 10 independent workers say working independently was their choice completely.

- By 2021, nearly half of the population (48%) will be independent workers or have tried independent work in their lifetime.

To download the *MBO Partners State of Independence In America 2016*, visit www.mbopartners.com/state-of-independence/mbo-partners-state-of-independence-in-america-2016.

Avoiding the Trap of Misclassifying of Workers

There are obvious financial and tax advantages to classifying home workers as independent contractors instead of employees. This situation even exists in the background screening industry, as covered in Chapter 12 concerning the use of at-home operators.

By classifying a worker as an independent contractor, an employer avoids the payroll costs associated with employees, such as paying workers' compensation insurance premiums, unemployment insurance, withholding taxes, or paying the employer share of payroll taxes. An employer can also save money by not paying benefits, such as paid holidays, vacation, health, or retirement. In addition, firms seek to achieve economic savings by having a flexible workforce.

The issue is whether these so-called "independent" workers are really that independent. In reality, an independent contractor may only be providing services to just one firm. An independent contractor, such as an at-home worker, typically does not have business cards, their own insurance, yellow page ads, a business license, or any of the other attributes of a true independent business.

Simply put, the advantages enjoyed by a business in classifying a worker as an independent contractor are disadvantages for the Internal Revenue Services (IRS) and state agencies that administer tax collection programs. The IRS has an interest in businesses putting workers on payroll to better ensure the collection and withholding of payroll taxes. States want employers to pay workers' compensation premiums and unemployment insurance. As a result, the IRS and the states have a big stake in ensuring that businesses do not misclassify a worker as an "independent contractor" when in fact they should be on payroll.

The IRS and state agencies have the authority, which they do exercise, to conduct extensive audits of a business to determine if the classification was correct. If the IRS or state agencies determine that workers should have been classified as employees, then the business can be subject to fines, penalties, back taxes, and lawyer's fees.

How does the independent contractor or at-home worker trigger an employer being the subject of an IRS or state audit? There are a number of ways:

- The worker gets injured and files for workers' compensation benefits. The business claims that the worker was, in fact, an independent contractor. At that point, the claim can trigger an audit of all business practices related to independent contractors. Failure to have workers' compensation in place is unlawful and has extremely serious consequences for businesses.
- An at-home worker decides to resign, files for unemployment insurance benefits, and lists the firm as the last employer. When the state shows no record of employer contributions, an audit may be triggered.
- An at-home worker files a discrimination claim.
- An at-home worker feels they are doing the same work as employees but without the benefits, and they file a claim or even a lawsuit for benefits. This happened to Microsoft, when so-called independent contractors sued because they were doing the same work as employees, but not getting benefits or stock options.

Thus, if the relationship goes sour for any reason, a business is essentially at the mercy of their former worker who can trigger a very expensive audit that can have significant financial repercussions.

The IRS formerly used what was known as the "20 Factor Test" as part of its audit. However, the IRS recently consolidated the twenty factors into eleven main tests and organized them into three main groups. Per the IRS web page at www.irs.gov/businesses/small-businesses-self-employed/independent-contractor-self-employed-or-employee:

> *Facts that provide evidence of the degree of control and independence fall into three categories:*
>
> 1. ***Behavioral:*** *Does the company control or have the right to control what the worker does and how the worker does his or her job?*
>
> 2. ***Financial:*** *Are the business aspects of the worker's job controlled by the payer? (These include things like how worker is paid, whether expenses are reimbursed, who provides tools/supplies, etc.)*
>
> 3. ***Type of Relationship:*** *Are there written contracts or employee type benefits (i.e. pension plan, insurance, vacation pay, etc.)? Will the relationship continue and is the work performed a key aspect of the business?*

A number of jurisdictions, courts, and state agencies often use variations of the IRS test or various other tests. When applying the various tests, there are three things to keep in mind:

1. First, the most important consideration is whether the at-home worker is truly an "independent" person running their own business or just an employee in disguise. The courts focus on the degree of control. For a worker to be classified as an independent contractor, he or she must be both physically and economically autonomous of the employer.

2. The second consideration is that the independent contractor test is not a mechanical application of the rules—some employers make the mistake of reviewing the list as a scorecard and coming to the wrong conclusion. It can be extremely difficult to predict what the IRS or state will conclude in any given situation. The law of proper classification of workers is very complex and normally requires the assistance of a lawyer, Human Resources consultant, or CPA.

3. Finally, it is irrelevant what the parties chose to call themselves. Courts, the IRS, and state agencies are not influenced at all by a written piece of paper that some worker signed alleging they are independent.

What happens if the audit or test results find a business was essentially "cheating" by misclassifying workers as independent contractors instead of employees? The consequences can be substantial. The IRS or state may flag the business for an audit of how it classifies all of its independent contractors. The auditing process can be extremely time consuming and expensive. Some employers have had the experience of government auditors literally setting up shop for extensive periods of time in their offices during the auditing process. If the audit reveals that there were others who were wrongly classified, the financial consequence could be enormous. A firm can potentially face:

- Liability for all federal and state payroll taxes that should have been paid for all misclassified workers.
- Interest, fines, and penalties to the IRS or state. Penalties can be substantial.
- Costs, and attorney's fees, and compensatory and punitive damages if litigation is involved.
- Benefits the workers would have received if classified as employees, including vacation, health, paid holidays and retirement.
- Overtime pay under the Fair Labor Standards Act and comparable state laws if the hours he or she provided to the contracting party in the past exceeded the standard workweek.
- Unemployment claims.
- Extending any stock option plan the worker would have had if they were properly treated as employees.
- Liability and potential penalties for not paying into state workers compensation fund.

The bottom line is that an employer attempting to justify classifying an at-home worker as an independent contractor faces a substantial uphill challenge and considerable risks.

California Rules Uber Driver is Employee Not Contractor

The California Labor Commissioner's Office has ruled that a driver who worked for ride-sharing application technology provider Uber should be classified as an employee and not an independent contractor, according to a story by *The New York Times*.

The Times reports that the Labor Commissioner's Office – also known as the Division of Labor Standards Enforcement (DLSE) – ordered Uber to reimburse a woman who worked as a driver for approximately eight weeks $4,152.20 in expenses and costs. Uber has appealed the decision.

The *Times* also reports the DLSE cited several instances where Uber—which describes itself "as merely an app that connects drivers and passengers"—acted like an employer. As an employer, Uber would be required to reimburse employees for business expenses under California law.

"The ruling could lead to class action lawsuits against Uber in California and other states, the Times reports, although the company stated similar cases about Uber worker classification in at least five other states "resulted in rulings that categorize drivers as contractors."

A copy of the ruling by the California Labor Commissioner's Office is available at www.scribd.com/doc/268911290/Uber-vs-Berwick.

Source: www.nytimes.com/2015/06/18/business/uber-contests-california-labor-ruling-that-says-drivers-should-be-employees.html

More information on the subject of the Gig economy is found at the end of this chapter.

#4. Vendors and Workers that Come on Premises or to Homes to Provide Goods or Services

Firms routinely hire night time janitorial services without appropriate due diligence. The fast food industry routinely hires suppliers and service firms that come into their restaurants to clean or deliver supplies. Without knowing who has the keys to facilities, an employer is giving total strangers unfettered access to his or her business—and is totally exposed to the risk of theft of property, trade secrets, or damages.

Vendors who come on premises represent the same risks and issues. A business may want to know how a vendor conducts due diligence.   Many employers will require a vendor to certify that they have conducted appropriate background checks on their vendors before the vendor can allow an employee to come on premises. A best practice is for the employer to impose some standards and procedures.

Author Tip〉 **Background Check Firms Can Help with Vendor Screening**

A competent background check firm with updated technology can assist businesses in vendor screening. For example, it is possible to require that a vendor directs its workers to a website to perform background checks in accordance with necessary business requirements. The screening firm can then perform the screen with the results sent to the vendor. The business and vendor would need to agree to the process and procedures if there is something negative or derogatory on the report. Of course, the FCRA and EEOC rules would apply to the process. The results can also be tied into a Badging process.

The section above on screening temporary workers may apply to vendor screening as well.

Any business should have some type of **Office and Physical Security Policy** that applies to any individual that comes to the ESR offices, regardless of whether they are a client, visitor, temporary worker, a vendor, landlord or landlord representative, member of the public or any other person or guest.

Vendors that come into a business facility, regardless of who they are or their status should be issued a badge, escorted by a staff member to the appropriate location, and be generally escorted at all times. All records of Badging should be maintained and all badges should be returned to the front desk when the vendor leaves the premises. All badges should have the current date prominently displayed and shall only be valid for the date issued. All regular employees should be mindful that badges are dated they should immediately report out-of-date badges to their supervisor. At the end of the day, the office manager shall ensure that all badges issued on that date have been accounted for.

There are also numerous horror stories about innocent and unsuspecting people who opened their doors to home service providers or workers and became the victims of serious crimes, including murder, right in their own homes. Routinely, many people casually allow workers in their homes to deliver appliances or furniture, act as nannies or caregivers, clean carpets, make home improvements, perform household repairs such as plumbing or electrical, kill pests, and a multitude of other tasks.

The Nine Million Dollar Service Call

According to a news article by the Daytona Beach News-Journal Online, a civil case was settled for nine million dollars when a well-known air conditioner repair firm sent a worker who was a twice convicted sex offender to a home, and he killed the homeowner. According to the June 1, 2004, article, the repairman cleaned the air ducts and then returned six months later and raped and murdered the victim. According to the news study, a criminal background check would have revealed the repairman's criminal past.

The victim's family started an organization called the Sue Weaver CAUSE (Consumer Awareness of Unsafe Service Employment) to raise awareness that not all contractors can be trusted. The case underscores the heightened responsibilities of employers who send workers into people's homes.

C.A.U.S.E. Shows Background Checks Needed To Uncover Unsafe Service Employees Working In Homes

When hired workers enter homes to perform services, do the homeowners who requested the services know to whom they are opening their doors?

Background checks are needed to uncover unsafe employees working in and around homes of other people, and can help people avoid tragedies like the one experienced by Lucia Bone, the founder of 'Sue Weaver CAUSE (Consumer Awareness of Unsafe Service Employment).'

In 2001, Sue Weaver, Lucia Bone's sister, was raped and beaten to death in her Florida home by a worker who had previously entered her home for a job. Six months before her death, Weaver had contracted with a major department store to clean the air ducts in her home. Both workers sent to her house had criminal records. One was a twice-convicted sex offender on parole who returned to the home where he had once worked to commit a crime.

Sadly, Weaver's murder is not an isolated case, since many consumers are robbed, assaulted, and murdered each year by workers with jobs that allow them access into homes. Because of this, Bone started Sue Weaver CAUSE to both honor her sister and to fight for standardized background checks of all in-home service employees. Through consumer awareness and legislation, Bone wants to ensure that big, reputable retail companies and others perform thorough criminal background checks on the contractors and sub-contractors they send into homes.

Since there are currently no federal or state laws requiring companies to do criminal background checks on contractors or sub-contract workers sent into homes, Sue Weaver CAUSE is demanding legislation for CAUSE Certification compliance. When interviewed for the article on HuffingtonPost.com, Bone said the CAUSE Certification would require annual background checks following CAUSE minimum screening standards on all employees, contractors, and subcontractors. Bone added that these standards were determined from survey results from questions asking background screening professionals what minimum screening should be conducted on workers going into homes of elderly mothers, pregnant wives, and people with special needs.

According to Bone, the minimum requirements for CAUSE Certification are:

- Social Security Number (SSN) Address Trace;
- County-Level Criminal Check (Search records for past seven years in counties where applicant lived, worked, or attended school);
- Multi-jurisdictional/"National" Criminal Database, and;
- National/State Sex Offender Registry.

In addition, Bone says consumers "never think about (criminal background checks for in-home service workers)" and automatically assume the company they hire would not send criminals into their homes. She advises consumers to be proactive and not assume companies properly screen workers sent to homes. "Bonded and insured is not a background check."

The Sue Weaver CAUSE website is located at www.sueweavercause.org.

Source: www.huffingtonpost.com/janet-kinosian/could-you-or-a-loved-one_b_559526.html.

If you hire employees to work in peoples' homes, do not skimp on background checks!

#5. Screening Home-Based Workers or Other Workers in Close Contact with Vulnerable Populations

A related issue is workers who are hired to work in the home or to provide personal services, such as caregivers for the infirmed, challenged, or aged, or Nanny's for children. Unfortunately, people are particularly vulnerable in their own homes. Good help is harder to get, and if there are children, senior citizens, or a disabled person at home, the risks are even greater. Yet, no state except Texas currently requires background checks on workers who enter homes. Results are tragic. A Study by the Northwestern University School of Medicine determined many agencies recruit and place unqualified caregivers in homes of the elderly. See www.feinberg.northwestern.edu/news/2012/07/dangerous_caregivers.html.

U.S. Courts have held employers liable for negligence when their workers committed crimes in the home. An employer obviously does not send a worker into the home in order to steal, murder, or sexually assault. Certainly, criminal action was not within the scope and course of the employee's duties. However, employers are held to a higher standard of care in view of the inherent risks involved in sending workers into homes. Employers can be found negligent for not only hiring someone who they should have known was dangerous, unqualified, or unfit, but also for failure to supervise, train, or properly assign workers. If an employer was on notice that a current worker was unsafe, and retained the person anyway, then that employer can be sued for negligent retention. See ALR5th 21 for an article entitled, *Employer's Liability for Assaults, Theft or Similar Intentional Wrong Committed by Employee at Home or Business of Customer.*

You Need To Know ⟩ **Should a Background Firm Check a Babysitter, Nanny, or a Caregiver for an Elderly Parent?**

Background screening firms are sometimes asked to do background checks for sensitive family situations such as when hiring a babysitter, nanny, or perhaps a caregiver for an elderly parent. Since these are high risk positions, often performed in the home without other people present and involving vulnerable populations, due diligence is needed when hiring.

But is hiring a background screening firm the best route for the family to take? First, if a family hires a background screening firm (a Consumer Reporting Agency or "CRA"), then all the compliance issues described in this book are triggered. For example, the hiring procedure must include the same paperwork and compliance items required at both the state and federal level as well the vetting of the "employer" to ensure there is a permissible purpose and the request is legitimate. In other words, the FCRA rules apply regardless of whether you are hiring one person or 1,000 people. There is no "nanny" exception to the FCRA if hiring directly and doing your own background check. That is a reason many people hire for nanny type positions through an agency. A professional agency can handle the background check, and also make sure that all payroll and I-9 processes are done correctly. Although people hiring a nanny may be tempted to hire and pay "under the table," there are a number of reasons that is not a good idea. Another issue is that larger or more sophisticated background firms may not be willing to set up an account for someone who is hiring one nanny a and likely will not place very future requests.

However, the biggest issue is protecting your loved one. A background check by a screening firm for a nanny or caretaker may not provide the protection people think. A screening firm can provide a public records search. Even if the screening firm calls past employers, this check is still not the type of in-depth interview, and investigative process needed to decide if a caregiver should be in close personal contact with a family member or child in a home often unsupervised.

The danger is a family may develop a false sense of security if using a background report meant for employers in a business environment. The point here is even if the screening firm found no negative information on a public records check this is not the same as vetting a caregiver to work inside a home with vulnerable groups.

The best approach for these highly sensitive personal positions may very well be to utilize the services of a licensed private investor. An investigator can conduct in-person and in-depth personal and professional references. Most investigators are experienced interviewers and having a professional interview of a candidate for a sensitive home position is certainly warranted. An investigator can also follow-up on leads. Hiring an investigator may be more expensive, but considering the stakes, this procedure should be used when family safety is involved.

#6. Volunteers that Need to be Screened and Issues Revolving around Fingerprints vs. Name Checks

Unfortunately, in today's world, the fact remains that sex offenders and deviants exploit volunteer, youth, and faith-based organizations to gain access to potential victims. Doing background checks help protect children and the vulnerable from criminals. The good news is over the past few years, there has been a substantial increase in volunteer groups, youth organizations, and churches performing background checks. Checks for criminal records have become standard procedures for organizations like the Little League or Scouts. The increased emphasis on these checks has been fueled by numerous news stories and lawsuits about children being the victim of criminal conduct, especially sexual abuse. The whole issue of exploitation of children received national attention in 2011 with the allegations of sexual abuse inside athletic facilities at Penn State.

There are numerous organizations involved with helping youth. These organizations rely in large part on volunteers in addition to paid staff, who will have extensive contacts with young people in a variety of situations. These can include:

- Faith-based organizations.
- Youth Sports Leagues (Little League, youth soccer, etc.).
- Youth organization's (Boy Scouts and Girl Scouts or Big Brothers and Big Sisters).
- Volunteer groups that work with youth at risk.
- Sporting associations with youth training.
- Camps and other similar organizations designed for children.

Sexual predators may try to utilize the opportunity to volunteer in these groups to gain access to children to commit sexual crimes. Although "stranger abduction" most often makes the news, the most prevalent form of child sexual abuse is actually perpetrated by someone who knows the child. A predator attempts to exploit a position of trust to not only "groom" a child for sexual abuse in a way that manipulates the child into not telling anyone about it, but to also insulate himself or herself from apprehension by ingratiating themselves inside of the organization so that responsible adults have a hard time believing anything like that could happen. The big problem is that an abuser in a youth organization may appear on the surface to be a wonderful asset. To gain access to the child, the abuser must gain the trust of both the organization and the victim and often times the victim's family. The situation is aggravated because parents and children believe that they are in a safe environment designed for children, which can lead to a false sense of security. Many organizations have difficulty believing that such a thing could happen in their group and even when a molester is revealed, organization leaders or other adults may have difficulty believing the child.

A predator intent on grooming a child will pick their victim very carefully. Although there is not one single profile of a potential victim, there are common traits. A predator is looking for vulnerabilities, such as a child who is a loner, has self-esteem or confidence issues, has been abused previously, is emotionally needy, or comes from a family where there is domestic conflict or parental neglect. As the groomer builds trust, he or she (and yes, there are women offenders) will introduce physical contact into the relationship and will push the boundaries towards sexual acts. The groomer will attempt to maintain control over the relationship in a number of ways, including guilt, threats of what will happen if the secret is revealed, or threatening the child with the loss of the relationship.

Author Tip > **Six Stages of *Grooming* for Victims of Sex Offenders**

There are a number of articles and studies available on the internet that review how predators work and the grooming process in detail. According to one well-known expert, Forensic psychiatrist Dr. Michael Welner, **grooming** is a process consisting of six stages where a sex offender draws a victim into a relationship that becomes shrouded in secrecy and leads to sexual molestation. To learn more, read the article *Child Sexual Abuse: 6 Stages of Grooming* at www.oprah.com/oprahshow/Child-Sexual-Abuse-6-Stages-of-Grooming#ixzz21lJ3BOD6.

Of course, the long-term harm to a child that is victimized by sexual abuse is incalculable. In addition, the efforts of organizations that are dedicated to helping children can be undermined by lawsuits, negative publicity, and a crisis of confidence from parents, contributors, and other stakeholders that cannot understand how an organization designed to support children could have left them unprotected.

A common observation by experts in this field is that child molesters are looking for "soft targets," in the form of organizations that have lower barriers to entry, less supervision, and less attention to the problem. A molester may avoid groups that take precautions such as a careful volunteer selection process, establishment of clear rules and boundaries (such as no child is ever alone with an adult), or training volunteers and children to recognize signs of improper behavior.

To assist youth-serving organizations in dealing with this critical issue and to adopt policies and procedures to safeguard children, the **Centers for Disease Control and Prevention (CDC)** has developed a guide that identifies six key components of child sexual abuse prevention for organizations. It also references a number of excellent resources. The publication is *Preventing Child Sexual Abuse Within Youth-serving Organizations: Getting Started on Policies and Procedures* and is at www.cdc.gov/violenceprevention/pdf/PreventingChildSexualAbuse-a.pdf#page=1.

This Guide identifies these six areas where youth organizations need to focus energy:

1. Screening and selecting employees and volunteers.
2. Guidelines on interactions between individuals.

3. Monitoring behavior.
4. Ensuring safe environments.
5. Responding to inappropriate behavior, breaches in policy, and allegations and suspicions of child sexual abuse.
6. Training about child sexual abuse prevention.

You Need To Know

Training A Key Element of Safe Environment Program

Training is a key element of any Safe Environment program by training adults who interact with children, youths, and elders how to recognize, report, and prevent abuse. It is essential for volunteers and organizational leaders as well as employees that work with children. Although everyone has an ethical responsibility to prevent child abuse and protect children, certain professionals are mandatory reporters and are legally required to report child abuse and neglect, and failure to report is a crime in many states. In addition, another key part of a training program is to train children as well on such topics as appropriate boundaries and what to do if they feel something inappropriate is happening.

Underscreening and selecting employees and volunteers, the Guide examines a number of options including education about the organization and its policies, written applications, personal interviews, reference checks, and background checks.

The following text is taken from pages 7 and 8 of the CDC's *Preventing Child Sexual Abuse Within Youth-serving Organizations: Getting Started on Policies and Procedure.*

Criminal Background Checks

Criminal background checks are an important tool in screening and selection. However, they have limitations. Criminal background checks will not identify most sexual offenders because most have not been caught. When this report was published, an efficient, effective, and affordable national background screening system was not available.

- Use background checks as one part of child sexual abuse prevention efforts. Using background checks alone may give your organization a false sense of security.
- Save time and resources by delaying criminal background checks until the end of the screening and selection process. Applicants who do not make it through the written applications, personal interviews, and reference checks will not need a criminal background check.
- Obtain permission from applicants before beginning a criminal background check.
- Determine the type and level of check required for each applicant. Types of checks include name, fingerprint, sex offender registries, and social security number. Checks may be implemented at county, state, and national levels. Records are not always linked or comprehensive, so a thorough search may be needed to address concerns about an applicant. For example, if an applicant has moved frequently, checks in multiple states may be necessary.
- Plan for the time and financial resources needed to conduct background checks.
- Decide which offenses to examine in the background checks and which offenses will disqualify applicants. For child sexual abuse, absolute disqualifiers include violent behavior and child sexual abuse perpetration history. Depending on the risk of the situation or the mission of your organization, drug and driving offenses may also be disqualifiers. Arrest data are not grounds for disqualification; only offenses resulting in convictions may be used.

- Develop procedures to keep the results of criminal background checks confidential. Select a secure storage location and limit access to the files.
- Ensure that your organization's process for conducting criminal background checks is legally sound. Consult county, state, and national laws and regulations, as well as your organization's attorney and insurance company, as needed.

The critical point is that background checks are a powerful tool when used with a number of other approaches to protecting children. But background checks alone will not always guarantee the safety of children. However, just having a background check program shows an organization is not a soft target. Statistics do seem to show that many child predators have never been caught and therefore would not have a criminal record. However, a background check program is a critical part of an overall due diligence program in conjunction with a host of other tools to discover molesters looking for easy opportunities.

AAU Implements Background Check Program for Staff & Volunteers to Ensure Safety of Youth Athletes

In June 2012, the national Amateur Athletic Union (AAU) released a comprehensive report— *'Recommendations to the Amateur Athletic Union from the Youth Protections and Adult/Volunteer Screening Task Forces*—from two independent task forces. This report announced actions to implement steps to protect the wellbeing of hundreds of thousands of young athletes that include requiring that all adults involved in AAU activities—including coaches, staff, and volunteers—undergo detailed background checks.

The report released by the AAU—one of the largest non-profit volunteer sports organizations in the United States—also calls for adopting clear policies and procedures designed to ensure that young athletes are never left alone with individual adults and requiring all AAU volunteers and staff to report any incidents of suspected child abuse to law enforcement and AAU officials. The task forces included nationally recognized experts in child protection and law enforcement and offered 42 recommendations for changes in AAU policies, procedures, and protocols that covered six broad subject areas: culture, protocols, screening, participation, training, and reporting:

- **Culture:** The AAU should establish and foster a culture that clearly and explicitly makes child protection an overarching value and priority. This includes requiring all adult volunteers, staff, parents, and other youth to report questionable behavior.

- **Protocols:** The AAU should adopt clear policies, procedures, and protocols to protect children from abuse and exploitation to the fullest extent possible, including policies to prevent adults from being alone with children and eliminating other opportunities for abuse to occur.

- **Screening:** The AAU should implement significant initial and ongoing screening procedures for all adults who participate in AAU activities to help identify and exclude individuals who may pose a threat to youth participants.

- **Participation:** Anyone who is prohibited from participating in an organization that serves youth or who violates the AAU's child protection policies should be barred from participating in AAU activities, even if they have not been convicted of a crime.

- **Training:** The AAU should educate staff, adult volunteers, parents/guardians, and youth participants on safety protocols, appropriate vs. inappropriate behaviors and other information they need to keep children safe while participating in AAU activities.

- **Reporting:** All AAU volunteers and staff should be considered mandatory reporters and should be expected to report suspected child abuse to appropriate law enforcement authorities and child abuse hotlines, as well as to AAU authorities.

The report is found at http://image.aausports.org/dnn/pdf/TFreportfinal.pdf.

Is this Any Way to Treat a Loyal Volunteer?

Some organizations report that volunteers, especially those who have been volunteering for some time, sometimes find it objectionable that they are suddenly subject to a background check. Having donated countless hours, volunteers can be miffed since in their mind their integrity and honesty is now being questioned. That is why the rollout of a volunteer screening program is so important. Volunteers need to appreciate a background check is for the good of the organization overall and for the protection of the very people the organization is trying to protect. It is certainly no reflection on an individual volunteer. By submitting to the background check, the volunteer is showing support for the organization and its missions and goals. Volunteers need to understand that it is not personal or aimed at them, but is an essential tool for the organization.

Volunteers with No Social Security Number

This is a common issue for many faith-based organizations. A church wants to be able to serve the needs of all parishioners regardless of documentation, but it does present some additional risk management challenges. Since a screening firm such as ESR is accessing public records based upon name searches, the Social Security Number (SSN) is important since it tends to help verify identity and it is a critical database search parameter. However, in the absence of an SSN, a Church can still conduct due diligence, but additional processes may be considered to make up for the lack of an SSN. The essential problem is that a screening firm is not using biometrics so we do not know with certainty who the applicant really is and whether the name provided is the one that is associated with the applicant. This natural raises the possibility that someone can change their name and slip through the cracks. Short of doing a fingerprint check which is a biometric measure associated with the person regardless of the name used, there is no foolproof system. However, an undocumented worker is not likely to want to do a fingerprint check.

Our suggestion is to first try to obtain trustworthy third party sources of identification, such as a utility bill, credit cards, lease, etc., in order to increase the probability that the name we are using for our search is that name actually associated with the volunteer. A church can even go further and obtain references as to how long a person has been in the community under the name being submitted. If a volunteer has been a member of a church community for six years, for example, and has always been known by the name provided, that increases the reliability of the search. If a person is new to a church, that raises an identification issue, and a reference check, such as calling a past church or people who knew the applicant, would be helpful. The key is to establish through trustworthy documentation, reference or knowledge from the local church as to how long the person has been using that name. A church can take the position that they did what could be done reasonably under the circumstances. The key is to document that the church analyzed this issue and made a reasonable policy.

For applicants who apparently do have an SSN but are just hesitant about giving it out die to privacy concerns, an organization can prepare Frequently Asked Questions (FAQs) or statement assuring someone that their SSN is needed for the greater good of the organization and that effective measures are utilized for privacy and data protection. We find that if someone understands that the SSN is needed for valid reasons and it is being protected and safeguarded, people who initially expressed concerns may provide it.

However, there are still a few people that are just not comfortable in providing an SSN under any circumstances. At that point, it becomes similar to undocumented volunteer. The Church can ask for a utility bill, lease, credit card statement (with the account number blocked out) or some sort of alternative ID such as a driver's license so that a judgment can be made that the name being presented is the name that is associated with the actual volunteer. Also, a statement from the local church as to how long the person has lived in the community and has been known under that name is also useful.

> **You Need To Know**

Does Screening a Volunteer Fall Under the FCRA?

One question that arises is whether a screening on a volunteer needs to be conducted under the Fair Credit Reporting Act (FCRA) since the volunteer is not paid. The best practice is to still operate under the FCRA, even for volunteers. There is no requirement under the FCRA that a person is only employed if they are paid in monetary form. Also, as noted earlier, the FTC takes the position that the FCRA is given broad interpretation to protect consumer's rights. Conclusion—an organization should not assume the FCRA does not apply just because a person is a volunteer. That also means that volunteers should receive pre and post adverse action notices.

> **Author Tip**

Whitepaper on Screening Volunteers for Non-Profits

Does your non-profit organization have a convicted criminal or registered sex offender working as a volunteer? What due diligence are you providing for your non-profit organization to ensure a safe workplace for the people your organization serves, co-workers, and the community in general?

A complimentary whitepaper by Attorney Lester S. Rosen shows why performing background checks on volunteers helps protect children, the elderly, and the vulnerable. To download the whitepaper, visit www.esrcheck.com/Whitepapers/Screening-Volunteers-for-Non-Profits/.

#7. How to Check Non-employees? Fingerprints or Private Background Screening Firms?

One of the first questions volunteer organizations ask when considering using background checks is: *What kind of background check should I use?* There are two options: fingerprints—through federal or state authorities—or private background screening firms.

This issue is discussed in this section for one simple reason—volunteer groups often have access to fingerprints from the **Federal Bureau of Investigation (FBI)** and in many cases, their own state law enforcement agencies. Private employers, on the other hand, do not have access to an FBI criminal check UNLESS there is a federal or state law or rule that permits it. A typical private employer does not need to be concerned about the differences between a fingerprint check and a name check unless they are in a regulated industry where fingerprints are required. Also, keep in mind that fingerprint checks do not always mean an FBI check. A state Department of Justice (DOJ) may have a program where fingerprints are run through a state database. The information is limited to that state, although some states do access other states. Adding an FBI check may add to the cost.

Depending on the organization and the mission, volunteer, charitable, youth and faith-based organizations may have access to the FBI's **National Crime Information Center (NCIC)** database. Certain states have legislation permitting organizations to take advantage of state fingerprinting or criminal record programs. On October 9, 1998, President Clinton signed the Volunteers for Children Act into law – Public Law 105-251 – amending the National Child Protection Act of 1993. Organizations and businesses dealing with children, elderly, or the disabled may now use national fingerprint-based criminal history checks to screen out volunteers and employees with relevant criminal records. The use is "permissive," meaning these groups have permission to use fingerprints if they chose, but are not mandatory. Where it gets complicated is that these organizations may have workers where a fingerprint check is mandatory. A church, for example, may have teachers that it is required to fingerprint but also have volunteers that they may fingerprint if they choose but are not required.

The whole issue of background checks using the FBI fingerprint system compared to doing name checks through private firms has heated up considerably in recent years due to a number of factors:

1. FBI background checks are in the news due to the ongoing discussions in the U.S. over background checks and gun purchases.
2. More cities, counties, and states are mandating background checks, and often initially assume they should be run with fingerprinting through the FBI.
3. There has been a great deal of criticism aimed at the FBI database for not having complete disposition information meaning that there is a significant percentage of fingerprint checks where it does not report what happened to the case. As a result, FBI reports may contain cases where there was no prosecution, the case was dismissed, the person found not guilty, or an expungement or some similar judicial set aside occurred.
4. The General Accounting Office (GAO) issued a report in 2015 indicating that although dispositions information has improved, there are 10 states where dispositions were only reported less than 50% of the time
5. Private screening firms as well organizations such as the National Association of Professional Background Screeners (NAPBS), has been educating policy makers on the value of checks provided by private firms.
6. Worker rights groups have expressed concerns about the accuracy of the FBI database because it can affect eligibility for certain licenses and therefore impact employment opportunities. The Employment Law Project (NELP) has issued a Whitepaper in 2013 on the problems with a lack of dispositions and noted that inaccuracies particularly impacted applicants of color who are arrested at disproportionate rates.
7. There has been well published national debates over the role of fingerprinting and Transportation Network Companies (think for example Lyft or Uber) over the issue of whether individuals who provide transposition by using software should be fingerprinted. In 2016, an election centered on that issue in the city of Austin, Texas received considerable attention.

Because this is an issue that is of particular importance to volunteer groups, that issue is discussed here. Even though there are advantages to fingerprints, some organizations, find the use of fingerprints (or sometimes referred to as Livescan) does not meet their needs. Volunteers must either go to a law enforcement office or a printing location to have their prints taken, and there are fees for that. There are the pros and cons for each approach:

Fingerprint Checks:

Pros:

- Much broader and wider search than any other search since utilizing FBI and state Department of Justice databases from all 50 states.
- Information comes from every county in America.
- A person likely cannot fool the system by ID fraud because it is based on a biometric--fingerprints.
- One-stop shopping-one search of the entire country.
- Even if the final disposition is missing, it still puts an organization on notice that a particular court or county should be searched because it may lead to relevant information
- Results can be reviewed by a third party to obtain dispositions if missing and to remove or filter out unreportable matters, or matters that may be contrary to the employer's policies for compliance with the EEOC and the use of criminal records.

Cons:

- FBI/State databases are not perfect and can miss cases or not have final dispositions since the FBI database was developed primarily an arrest database, and both the FBI and state databases must rely upon states, local courts, or law enforcement to report data.

- More expensive since fees imposed for "rolling" fee (including Livescan) when volunteers go to a law enforcement agency or use private services.

- Although improving, substantial gaps can exist in informant about the disposition of the case.

- Reports can be difficult to read or understand.

- If there is a positive result, organizations still need to have records pulled to understand status, nature, and gravity of offense.

- The organization is responsible for tracking the status of all volunteers who need fingerprints and to coordinate periodic checks if needed.

Checks by Private Background Firms:

Pros:

- Less costly.

- Less of an imposition on volunteers; no traveling to printing locations.

- Screening firm can manage the process to ensure all volunteers are getting screened.

- Screening firm can assist on FCRA and legal compliance.

- By combining screening with a training program, training and background check can be conducted in one program, providing an organization with a tool to know who has been screened and when, when rescreening is due, and can also be used to create a list of past findings so a molester cannot go from one location to another.

Cons:

- Certain positions, such as teaching staff, may be required to use fingerprints.

- Name checks are limited to only the jurisdictions searched. If a person committed a crime in a county not searched, the organization may never know abo t it.

- Private background checks are NOT official FBI or state criminal record checks, and in some states are spotty at best. Best practice is to review each state for completeness of database information and to supplement if needed by local jurisdictions searches.

- The data is only as good as the name and identifiers used, and absent some sort of system of ID check, a name check can lead to a false negative if the subject is using a false name or date of birth.

Different Types of Searches Subject to the Same Criticism

Both types of searches – name checks by private screening firms or the FBI fingerprinting check – are subject to the same criticism that the searches can be overly broad and return information that can lead to disparate impact as discussed in Chapter 10 on the Equal Employment Opportunity Commission (EEOC) Guidance. There has been the suggestion repeated in the press that the FBI database can cause discrimination if used and, therefore, name searches are superior. However, such an argument is a complete non-sequitur. Any criminal search, regardless of its source, can potentially unearth information that can create EEOC concerns. It does not matter if the information is unearthed from checking the courts or from the FBI. The critical point is not the source of the data but accuracy and protections around the use of the data. If the complaint is that dispositions are missing from an FBI record, then a competent employer would use the services of a screening firm to fill in the blanks. If the complaint is that the FBI results would go directly to the employer, the solution is simple—an intermediary such as a screening firm or an employee with no responsibility for hiring or selection would first review the results to ensure that there is complete information and to filter out any information that is old or irrelevant. The bottom line is that arguing that FBI searches are somehow discriminatory and therefore name checks are better makes no sense in the real world.

In fact, the issue of direct employer access has been addressed in some detail by the United States Department of Justice (DOJ) in the *2006 Attorney General's Report on Criminal History Background Checks* made to Congress on the expanded use of FBI fingerprints including access by employers. One of the recommendations was that third party firms could act as the go between to ensure applicant rights are observed. According to the report:

"At the same time, we believe that any process allowing such access to traditionally restricted FBI criminal history information must establish conditions for access and use that: (1) protect the privacy rights of the applicant, including requirements for informed consent and the right to challenge the accuracy of the records reported; and (2) respect state and federal laws designed to ensure that criminal history records are not used to unfairly deny employment." (See pages 76-77)

In terms of accuracy, the report also notes that:

"When a private employer or entity can inquire about the existence of a criminal record of an applicant or employee, we believe that it is reasonable to provide the employer a means to check maintained criminal history records to determine whether the response to the question is truthful and complete. There is no one complete source of criminal history information, and users need to access many sources to ensure the search is comprehensive. FBI-maintained criminal history records are not complete and may serve only as a good, but not comprehensive, source of information for those performing employment screening functions. Nevertheless, the FBI-maintained criminal history database is one of the best sources because it is based on positive identification and can provide, at a minimum, nationwide leads to more complete information." (See pages 76-77).

The Attorney General's Report on Criminal History Background Checks (June 2006) is available at www.bjs.gov/content/pub/pdf/ag_bgchecks_report.pdf.

You Need To Know ⟩ **Neither Search is Perfect but there are No Facts to Suggest a Name Search is Superior to an FBI Fingerprint Search**

The argument between which is better—name checks by private firms or biometric fingerprint based checks through the FBI—is really nonsensical for one reason—neither search is perfect. They both have their pros and cons. It is like comparing apples to oranges. The searches are done differently and have their own pros and cons. As the old saying goes, a courthouse name search is "a mile deep and an inch wide" since it is limited to individual courthouses that are searched based upon non-biometric identifiers. On the other hand, an FBI search can be described as "a mile wide but an inch deep" due to accuracy and completeness concerns. As discussed in Chapter 9, both searches have potential sources of errors.

A statement however that a private name check is superior to a biometric FBI fingerprint check cannot be reconciled with the facts behind each type of search. Even if an FBI search is not the Gold Standard, if available to an employer, it clearly has numerous advantages over a name search. On the whole, name checks are extremely valuable if done right, but they do not have the length and breadth of an FBI check nor the biometric information to confirm identity.

For many employers, the topic is irrelevant because they do not have access to an FBI search. However, for an employer or organization with access to the FBI search that wants to maximize protection, the real solution is to do BOTH searches. Choosing one over the other where an employer or organization has access to both means that a critical source of information is potentially being missed. The question becomes how much time, effort and financial resources an organization wants to spend on due diligence and safety.

See The Addendum

The Big Controversy over FBI Fingerprinting vs. Name Checks

More discussion about the pros and cons of Federal Bureau of Investigation (FBI) fingerprinting vs. name checks by professional screening companies – including information and reports from the Government Accountability Office (GAO), the National Association of Professional Background Screeners (NAPBS), the National Employment Law Project (NELP), and the National Recreation and Park Association (NRPA) – can be found in the Addendum.

One figure that is often quoted about the FBI database is that only 50% of the arrests records have dispositions. That figure came from the 2006 report from the Attorney General's Report on Criminal History Background Checks. The author of that DOJ has addressed that statistic in the article below and explains how the FBI database is improving and the valuable of using it.

The Value of FBI Fingerprint Checks for Employment Screening

By Frank A. S. Campbell, CEO, Highland Strategies, LLC

It has been argued that the FBI criminal history database is not an appropriate source of information for employment screening because it is missing disposition information on a substantial number of arrest records. Those making this argument point to the 2006 Attorney General's Report On Criminal History Background Checks, which cited the statistic that "currently, only 50 percent of [the FBI system] arrest records have final dispositions."

However, in the 10 years since the release of the Attorney General's Report, many states have improved the level of completeness of dispositions in their criminal history record systems and the FBI has made process changes to include more complete state level records when issuing a report for civil background checks. These changes include an increased number of states – 20 today as opposed to 8 in 2006 – that are part of the FBI's National Fingerprint File (NFF), which allows automatic retrieval of data from the state level for inclusion in FBI reports, and an adjustment to the purpose code for civil checks allowing 41 states to respond with all their disposition information, regardless of whether they are part of the NFF.

States have been improving the completeness of their records over the last 10 years, particularly for more recent arrests. For example, according to the 2014 survey of the states by the U.S. Department of Justice, Bureau of Justice Statistics, 17 states representing 38% of the National's criminal history information reported that 80% or more arrests within the past 5 years in the criminal history database have final dispositions recorded; and 26 states representing 54% of the individual offenders in the Nation's criminal history records report that 70% or more arrests in the entire criminal history database have final dispositions recorded. Several large states with high numbers of criminal records reported significantly higher rates of completeness (e.g.,

New York (90%), Texas (86%), Florida (71%) and Illinois (69%). As a result, the percentage of FBI records reported with complete disposition data for noncriminal justice checks is likely materially higher today than the 50% statistic cited in 2006. FBI officials also note that 100% complete records is not possible because arrests in criminal felony cases can take more than a year to produce a final disposition.

Moreover, efforts can be and are made to complete information missing from FBI records reported for employment checks as part of the background check process. FBI regulations require agencies to provide individuals a reasonable time to complete or challenge the accuracy of information before officials can deny a license or employment on the basis of the record. In addition, some users, such as the Office of Personnel Management, will affirmatively seek the disposition themselves before delivering the information to the adjudicating official. The State of California now requires its Department of Justice to seek missing arrest dispositions before releasing a record for licensing or employment. And some private users engage Consumer Reporting Agencies to obtain missing information before using the FBI record. In other words, there are process approaches that can fill-in data missing from an FBI record so that employment screens can take advantage of the value offered by the FBI fingerprint check while also being fair to the individual being screened.

And the value add of FBI fingerprint check is substantial. First, the FBI check offers nationwide coverage, with over 70 million unique individuals and records from all 50 states and territories and 3000-plus counties in the United States. The FBI system is the most comprehensive single source of criminal history information in existence. This is especially valuable when doing an employment screen given our mobile society where people move from state to state. In addition, the FBI check provides the positive identification of fingerprints, avoiding the false positives and negatives that result from name-based checks. Several FBI studies confirm that positive identification of fingerprints yields accuracy and integrity in record matching that name-based checks can never equal. In short, fingerprint checks prevent fraud.

Because of the security benefits of its nationwide scope and the positive identification of fingerprints, the FBI check will continue to be a source of criminal history that policymakers will want to require for screening or licensing for jobs and activities where identifying persons with disqualifying criminal histories is especially important to protecting the public. In addition, as recommended by the 2006 Attorney General's Report, the FBI check should eventually be on the menu of choices of information searched for private employment checks, so long as the process for access includes steps to ensure completeness of the records reported to the user.

Frank Campbell is the Founder and CEO of Highland Strategies, LLC, a Washington, D.C.-based security consulting firm. After a private practice career in litigation and white collar defense, Mr. Campbell served from 1994-2008 as an Assistant General Counsel at the Federal Bureau of Investigation and as a Deputy Assistant Attorney General and Senior Counsel in the United States Department of Justice, Office of Legal Policy. Mr. Campbell authored the 2006 Attorney General's Report on Criminal History Background Checks.

The current state of the FBI database was the subject of a government report in 2015:

Recent GAO Report on Criminal History Records

In March 2015, the Government Accountability Office (GAO) – the congressional watchdog investigating how the federal government spends taxpayer dollars – released a report on the use of criminal background checks titled *'Criminal History Records: Additional Actions Could Enhance the Completeness of Records Used For Employment-Related Background Checks (GAO-15-162).'*

Authorized employers use information from Federal Bureau Investigation (FBI) criminal history record checks to assess a person's suitability for employment or to obtain a license. States create criminal records and the FBI facilitates access to these records by other states for nationwide background checks. The GAO was asked to assess efforts to address concerns about incomplete records.

The GAO analyzed laws and regulations used to conduct criminal record checks and assessed the completeness of records; conducted a nationwide survey, which generated responses from 47 states and the District of Columbia; and interviewed officials that manage checks from the FBI and 4 states (California, Florida, Idaho, and Washington) selected based on geographic location and other factors.

The GAO report addressed to what extent:

- States conduct FBI record checks for selected employment sectors and face any challenges;

- States have improved the completeness of records, and remaining challenges that federal agencies can help mitigate; and

- Private companies conduct criminal record checks, the benefits those checks provide to employers, and any related challenges.

The GAO's nationwide survey found most states conducted FBI criminal history record checks for individuals working with vulnerable populations such as children and the elderly. The GAO report found that some states did not conduct FBI record checks because those states lacked a designated agency to review check results. The employment sectors that most used FBI criminal history record checks were:

- Job or license to be a teacher in schools;

- Youth development positions (e.g. Boys and Girls Club);

- Volunteers serving the elderly or individuals with disabilities; and

- National Service Program participants (e.g. AmeriCorps).

The GAO report also found that states improved the completeness of criminal history records used for FBI checks with more records containing both the arrest and final disposition (such as a conviction). Twenty states reported that more than 75 percent of their arrest records had dispositions in 2012, up from 16 states in 2006. However, there are still gaps such as incomplete records that can delay criminal record checks and affect applicants seeking employment.

Although the Department of Justice (DOJ) helped states improve the completeness of records, challenges remain. A Disposition Task Force created by the FBI's Advisory Policy Board in 2009 to address issues regarding disposition reporting has taken actions to better measure the completeness of state records and identify state requirements for reporting disposition information. However, the task force does not have plans with time frames for completing remaining goals. The GAO recommends that the FBI establish plans with time frames for these remaining goals and the DOJ concurred.

The complete report from the GAO is available at www.esrcheck.com/file/GAO-Criminal-History-Records-Report.pdf.

Report Finds Many FBI Criminal Background Checks for Employment Contain Inaccurate Information

In August 2013, the National Employment Law Project (NELP) released a report – 'Wanted: Accurate FBI Background Checks for Employment' – that estimated 1.8 million workers a year are subjected to Federal Bureau of Investigation (FBI) background checks that contained "faulty or incomplete information" and that as many as 600,000 of those workers "may be prejudiced in their job search" because of inaccurate FBI records.

The report from NELP – a national advocacy organization for the employment rights of lower-wage and unemployed workers – spotlights the failure of the FBI "to ensure that its records are accurate and complete." While arrests are recorded, the final disposition of cases often is not, which is a critical defect since NELP estimates that "one-third of felony arrests are ultimately dismissed and charges are frequently reduced." Other key findings of the 51-page report include:

The use of FBI background checks for employment is rapidly increasing. Roughly 17 million FBI background checks were conducted for employment and licensing purposes in 2012, which is six times the number conducted a decade ago.

Despite clear federal mandates that require the background reports to be complete and accurate, 50 percent of the FBI's records fail to include information on the final disposition of the case.

African Americans are especially disadvantaged by the faulty records because people of color are consistently arrested at rates greater than their representation in the general population, and large numbers of those arrests never lead to a conviction.

Read the report at http://nelp.3cdn.net/bd23dee1b42cff073c_8im6va8d2.pdf.

#8. The Gig Economy where Technology Firms Provide a Platform for On Demand Workers and Screening is Critical

According to the U.S. Bureau of Labor Statistics (BLS), the **non-traditional workforce** includes "multiple job holders, contingent and part-time workers, and people in alternative work arrangements." These workers currently represent a substantial portion of the U.S. workforce, and "nearly four out of five employers, in establishments of all sizes and industries, use some form of nontraditional staffing." People in "alternative work arrangements" include independent contractors, employees of contract companies, workers who are on call, and temporary workers. (Source: https://en.wikipedia.org/wiki/Contingent_workforce.)

It is sometimes called the Gig economy, the sharing economy, the Peer to Peer (P2P) economy, or the 1099 economy—from the Internal Revenue Service (IRS) tax form used to report various types of income other than wages, salaries, and tips on the Form W-2—since workers are typically not employed in the traditional sense.

Background Checks and the Gig Economy?

In the Gig economy, a consumer is able to "rent" or share assets owned by someone else. Examples are housing with firms such as Airbnb or transportation with firms such as Uber, Lyft, or Sidecar where car owners share their vehicle with others. Other examples of the sharing economy can include sites that provide access to caregivers and babysitters, home repair workers, housecleaning, delivery of groceries, meals, and dry cleaning, tutors, or a host of other services where providers and customers are brought to together by technology. Advances in technology have enabled such sharing to occur by providing real-time information to both providers and users.

Technology companies take the position that they are enabling the service but not actually providing it. For example, a company that provides technology that allows ride sharing would dispute an argument they are a transportation company. However, a problem with the sharing economy is that even though technology firms provide solutions to enable peer to peer sharing, the public, legislators and regulators are concerned that without background checks, users of these services can be harmed. Even though the technology firms deny they are service providers, safety concerns are still paramount.

Background checks will be an ongoing focus of concern in the "sharing economy" built around the sharing of human and physical resources in such industries as transportation, short-term housing rentals, temporary job assignments, or services on demand. These types of background checks fall outside the traditional employer-employee situations but are nevertheless critical as users of these services are concerned with the integrity of the service providers or renters. However, the standards for what constitutes a background check remain elusive since there is no one definition or generally accepted standard.

You Need To Know

Gig Economy Growing Fast

Research documenting the rise of this growing trend in America indicates the gig economy is much bigger than the employment data suggests. How big?:

- A 2015 American Action Forum Report estimated the gig economy accounted for 30 percent of new jobs and created new income sources for 2.1 million people in the United States between 2010 and 2014. See: http://americanactionforum.org/research/independent-contractors-and-the-emerging-gig-economy.

- According to a report from business and financial management solutions provider Intuit, 7.6 million people will be part of this on-demand economy by 2020, and that slice of the labor market will grow by 18.5 percent per year over the next five years. The Intuit report also revealed a broader trend in the U.S. within the "contingent" or "independent contractor" workforce which has grown "from 17 percent of the U.S. workforce 25 years ago, to 36 percent today, and is expected to reach 43 percent by 2020." See: http://investors.intuit.com/press-releases/press-release-details/2015/Intuit-Forecast-76-Million-People-in-On-Demand-Economy-by-2020/default.aspx.

- A story at Fusion.net revealed that the number of Americans filing a 1099 tax form that gig economy workers must file increased in the 2000s. See: http://fusion.net/story/173244/there-are-probably-way-more-people-in-the-gig-economy-than-we-realize/.

- Another Fusion.net story found increases in the share of 1099 workers in many major U.S. cities and that a recent survey revealed 60 percent of *9 to 5* workers get at least 25 percent of their income from work outside regular jobs. See: http://fusion.net/story/137028/the-hidden-anxieties-of-the-on-demand-start-up-worker/.

Author Tip

DOL and Others Predicted Gig Economy

It is interesting to note that the non-traditional "Gig" Economy used by companies such as Uber discussed in more detail in Chapter 18 was predicted decades ago by the U.S. Department of Labor (DOL) in the 1999 DOL report *Futurework, Trends, and Challenges for Work in the 21st Century*, as well as by other authors and economists.

Of course, not every independent contractor or non-traditional worker prefers that status. Even though a non-traditional job provides greater flexibility, at the same time it does not afford the same benefits or salary that a full-time employee may typically enjoy.

The economic downturn beginning in 2008 caused many people to have to take part time jobs. During the ongoing recovery, employers wary of adding too many full-time employees are also opting to add only temporary help. Still, these part-time workers need to be screened. There have been numerous lawsuits challenging the assumption that a "Gig" worker is not employed, and numerous economists and academics have written about the pros and cons of the "Gig" economy. However, for the purpose of this book, the focus is on background checks.

The non-traditional workforce raises special considerations when practicing safe hiring. Past employment history is harder to pin down when the applicant has had a number of positions.

When hiring a non-traditional worker, employers need to exercise the same safe hiring precautions they would for any other job applicant. If an employer decides to save costs by not attempting to verify every past work assignment in the past five to ten years or search every past county in the past seven years for criminal records, then utilizing the AIR Process (as outlined in previous chapters) is even more important. In determining how much effort, money, and energy to put into background screening non-traditional workers, an employer should consider two factors:

- **Use consistency.** The same level of screening used for similar positions should be used for a position that is to be filled by a non-traditional worker or else the firm may be subject to allegations of disparate treatment of similarly situated people.
- **The duty to hire with due diligence.** This basic rule still applies. An employer is negligent if they hire someone who the employer either knew or should have known, in the exercise of reasonable care, was dangerous, unfit, or not qualified for the position.

You Need To Know

Free Agent Nation and Corporate Me

The role of non-traditional workers was popularized during the internet bubble from 1990 to 2002. One book, **Free Agent Nation: The Future of Working for Yourself** popularized the notion of a "free agent nation" based on the premise that a person is no longer defined by their job or job title. Instead, the new workers really work for themselves. They are their own corporation with their own brands. When they are on someone else's payroll, they are really "consultants," and every job should be an opportunity to increase their value. www.amazon.com/Free-Agent-Nation-Working-Yourself/dp/0446678791).

In the situations where the worker is paid by a third party agency, but the worker is under the direction or control of the business, a situation can arise called "co-employment." Co-employment means there are two different entities (the staffing vendor and the workplace) with control over a worker. Both organizations have legal rights, duties, and risks with respect to the worker. Although the typical situation involves a worker that is on the business worksite, a contingent worker can create liability for remote job assignments.

A vendor, by comparison, is an independent business that provides services to another business. When vendors have direct physical contact with a business (by coming on site), due diligence becomes an issue.

While the lines between employees and independent contractors are getting blurred, the takeaway point is the need to screen regardless of status as an employee or independent contractor.

No National Standard for Background Checks in Sharing Economy

Even though companies that facilitate Peer to Peer activities have a vested interest in assuring consumers that their service is safe, there continues to be no national standard as to what constitutes an appropriate background check in the sharing economy. Each provider is free to establish its own criteria. In fact, one such company which uses an Uber type approach to matching house cleaners to people who need their house cleaned even says in their terms of use:

> "The Company checks the backgrounds of cleaning service providers via third party background check services; however, the Company does not guarantee or warrant, and makes no representations regarding, the reliability, quality or suitability of such cleaning service providers."

This leads to a number of issues. First, there is no agreed on or standard definition of what exactly constitutes a background check. Background checks can range from a cheap and instant database check which is practically worthless in many areas of the United States all the way to an in-depth investigation including interviews with the candidate or past employers, and many variations in between.

In addition, a background check policy is that it may not be nearly as complete as it may seem on the surface. A person could have attended school or worked in some county where they did not live, and therefore a relevant criminal record could be missed. In some jurisdictions, counties are close enough together that an in-depth check may call for a search of an adjacent county to really afford protection. In some states, it is relatively easy and cost-effective to access a broad statewide search that is much more comprehensive and this not addressed. It is also a well-accepted fact that one of the best defenses against a bad hire is to explore unexplained unemployment gaps. Furthermore, there is value to an in-person interview.

Another problem with the sharing economy is that background checks can be easily fooled by a person undergoing the background check by simply submitting a friend's name and information. The process can take place online with no real interview or methods to detect identity fraud, as compared with a traditional employer-employee relationship where, for example, a person is interviewed and needs to show a certain amount of identification as part of the Form I-9 employment eligibility verification onboarding process. It is not hard to set up offices where a person needs to show up in person to be interviewed and show acceptable identification, or contract with a national business to require some sort of in-person identification validation before a going through a background check.

As the sharing economy grows, stories of consumers being harmed by criminal acts of providers can be expected to increase. Given the negative fallout from such publicity to any firm in the Peer to Peer space, it would seem that an effort to create some standardized and generally accepted background screening protocols would be of great benefit to both providers and consumers. There have been efforts in the past by private firms to create a so-called "badge" that is a cyber-equivalent of a "Good housekeeping" seal of approval. However, no one firm has had the clout to create a nationally recognized and accepted due diligence standard. Of course, technology providers can just wait until they are sued and let juries decide on a case by case basis if the firm was negligent or not, but that is generally not a sound way to run a business.

However, the major peer to peer players have the ability to come together and to set standards for background checks. Such a standardized approach to background checks can be accomplished through a non-profit association that would include input from relevant stakeholders including technology firms, consumers, screening professionals, legislators, and regulators. That way, technology firms providing Peer to Peer service in a sharing economy can demonstrate their commitment to safety by adhering to a generally accepted due diligence standard for background checks and participating in their program as a service provider. Background screening firms would have a clear protocol to follow.

Uber and Driver Background Check Court Cases

On demand ride hailing app provider Uber Technologies Inc. has been involved in several court cases regarding background checks of drivers since the company's creation. Here are a few examples in which Uber did not admit any wrongdoing:

- June 2016: Uber agreed to pay $7.5 million to settle a lawsuit that claimed the online transportation network company terminated drivers after obtaining driver background checks about them without their authorization. See: www.reuters.com/article/us-uber-lawsuit-idUSKCN0Z12GS.

- April 2016: Uber agreed pay at least $10 million to settle lawsuits filed by district attorneys in San Francisco and Los Angeles that claimed the company misled passengers about the quality of driver background checks, a figure that could rise to $25 million if Uber does not fully comply with terms of the settlements. San Francisco and Los Angeles prosecutors sued Uber in 2014 for falsely claiming its driver background checks were the most comprehensive available.

  The lawsuit noted that prospective Uber drivers did not undergo fingerprint checks like taxi drivers do but instead underwent background checks that included a name search of other criminal databases and motor vehicle department files.

Employment Screening Resources Commentary on Alleged Shootings by Uber Driver Published on CNN

The shooting deaths of six people in Kalamazoo, Michigan in February 2016 – where the alleged gunman supposedly picked up fares while working as an Uber driver during the killing spree – raises questions about personal safety in the gig economy where strangers use software applications to provide a host of services for others, according to Employment Screening Resources® (ESR) president and chief compliance officer Brad Landin in his opinion piece *Vetting drivers in the Age of Uber* on CNN.com.

Vetting Drivers in the Age of Uber

By Brad Landin

February 23, 2016

Editor's Note: Brad Landin is president and chief compliance officer of Employment Screening Resources, a background check company based in Novato, California. The opinions expressed in this commentary are solely those of the author.

(CNN)—The recent mass shooting in Kalamazoo, Michigan, in which the alleged gunman apparently provided rides as an Uber driver between shootings, has placed public attention squarely on the issue of the background checks performed on Uber drivers.

Jason Brian Dalton – who is facing murder, assault, and firearms charges – apparently had no criminal record, so a background check would not have helped exclude him. Yet, the case raises questions about personal safety in the so-called "gig economy," where total strangers are invited into your life through software applications to provide a host of services, ranging from transportation and housecleaning to babysitting and acting as a personal assistant.

Background checks are a complex issue. Contrary to public belief, there is no comprehensive database or source of information that provides a perfect one-stop background check solution. Even the fingerprint database maintained by the Federal Bureau of Investigation is far from perfect.

Although the FBI check uses biometric matching, the shortcomings of FBI criminal searches have been well documented. In 2006 the U.S. attorney general revealed that roughly 50% of the records are incomplete and fail to provide information on the final outcome of an arrest.

Employers using background screening firms can and do access millions of records through unofficial private sector databases as a source of possible information. However, these databases are incomplete and subject to both false negatives (meaning a criminal record is missed) and false positives (meaning the record is about the wrong person or that, by law, the criminal matter should not have been reported). In our opinion, this type of database should not be relied upon as a standalone search.

With some 3,200 counties in America to scour, these private sector databases are by no means complete, accurate and up to date. For example, there are a number of states that provide no public access to statewide criminal records, which usually leaves only a small number of county records that are included in the private sector databases for an entire state.

Within the screening industry, these databases are primarily used as a research tool that can lead to the discovery of information, which must be properly vetted as being reportable under the Fair Credit Reporting Act and corresponding state laws. The standard screening industry recommendation is to check primary source courthouse records where a person has lived, worked, or studied for at least the past seven years.

A thorough search does not begin and end with a background check. Employers should utilize a series of overlapping tools to exercise proper due diligence. Often, procedures followed before the background check may be the most important: a thorough review of the application, verification of past employment, accounting for gaps in employment and conducting an in-person or video interview before a making a final offer.

In the gig economy, there are so many moving parts that it is hard to know just how much due diligence a company is using. For example, if a service engages someone through an online application without ever meeting him or her, there is the question of whether the person being researched is actually the person who is applying for the job.

In a standard employment situation, the employer – at some point – meets the person and engages in some sort of identity verification. That may not always be the case in the gig economy, where people may sign up through a software application, sight unseen to provide ad hoc services.

Uber has published a detailed description of its screening program here (https://newsroom.uber.com/details-on-safety/).

To a background screening professional, there are some unanswered questions about this program. For example, Uber claims it searches numerous databases and then does a courthouse confirmation to ensure accuracy.

However, the policy does not explain how Uber deals with those counties where databases are unavailable or do not provide actionable information. A solid due diligence approach generally includes searching counties relevant to the applicant, using primary source information. Using only a database is not the functional equivalent of going to each county courthouse related to the applicant, which leaves the question of whether all applicable counties are being properly searched.

Uber states that it has a seven-year search policy. Even assuming seven years is the proper time limit, the issue of how the seven years is calculated can be complex. A driver may have been convicted and gone to prison 12 years ago and been released from custody three years ago.

If the scope is limited to just the past seven years, an older criminal matter can be overlooked, even though it may be reportable and relevant. In California for example, convictions can be reported from the date of conviction, release or parole. However, San Francisco counts exclusively from the date of the offense.

But, again, safety goes beyond just the background check. Third-party gig economy application providers such as Uber, Lyft and others like them can build in safety protocols that can be very effective for their services.

Background checks are complex, and consumers are entitled to know exactly what measure of safety they are getting.

That said, it is critical to understand that no matter how much due diligence is performed, no system is perfect. In the case of the Kalamazoo driver, a criminal check would have apparently come up clear.

Source: www.cnn.com/2016/02/23/opinions/uber-driver-background-check-landin/index.html

---

You Need To Know

EEOC Strategic Enforcement Plan Concerned with Gig Economy

The U.S. Equal Employment Opportunity Commission (EEOC) recently approved an updated Strategic Enforcement Plan (SEP) for Fiscal Years 2017-2021 that recognizes a new area of potential concern with the complex employment relationships in the emerging gig economy.

The EEOC SEP added the gig economy as an 'Emerging and Developing Issues' priority area: *The Commission adds a new priority to address issues related to complex employment relationships and structures in the 21st century workplace, focusing specifically on temporary workers, staffing agencies, independent contractor relationships, and the on-demand economy.*

The EEOC SEP for FY 2017-2021 is at www.eeoc.gov/eeoc/plan/sep-2017.cfm.

CHAPTER 19

Workplace Violence

Introduction

One of the goals of a safe hiring program is to help employers reduce workplace risk. One of the most well-publicized risks is **workplace violence**. The concern is not limited to a murder that occurs in the workplace, although that certainly captures headlines. Workplace violence can include numerous types of behaviors that create a hostile environment, from bullying and threats all the way to drastic physical harm.

For employers, one of the defenses against workplace violence is a safe hiring program that includes background checks. However, the fact remains that background screening all by itself is no guarantee that workplace violence will be prevented. A person can pass a background check or have no indicators of inappropriate behavior in the past and still engage in hostile conduct after being hired. Conversely, a person with an older or less serious criminal record may represent no issue.

However, there are many cases where workplace violence occurred where there was either no background check or an insufficient check. If it turns out that a background check would have potentially revealed a past offense or negative conduct that could have conceivably raised a "Red Flag," the employer may find themselves in hot water. When workplace violence does occur, employers can assume they are at risk for a lawsuit and one of the most critical issues is whether or not the employer engaged in "due diligence" in hiring the perpetrator in the first place.

The bottom line is that although a background check is no guarantee all by itself that an act of workplace violence would have been prevented, any act of workplace violence will result in questions being asked about the adequacy of screening during the hiring process.

What is even more challenging for employers is that the perpetrators of workplace violence are not always even employees. Domestic disputes and dissolution of marriage cases can spill over to the workplace where one partner commits violence against the other at their partner's workplace. Workplace violence can come from former employees, or even irate customers. Recent events in the U.S. have demonstrated that violence can even be politically related or the work of someone with a serious mental problem. However, this chapter is more focused on the work environment.

This is a well-studied area and there are considerable resources available from many experts who have studied these issues in detail. This chapter is not intended as a substitute for those resources. Rather, this chapter draws upon information provided by governmental and private sources to help employers focus on some of the critical issues involved and provide an introduction to the area. The goal is to highlight important facts and resources that can assist employers in understanding and evaluating the risks associated with workplace violence and note some of the additional resources that are available. The chapter introduces general approaches and strategies to try to recognize, prevent, or respond to hostile acts occurring in the workplace that could harm employees, customers, or members of the public.

The bottom line is that employers need an overall approach and strategy to deal with workplace violence. Background checks are just one part of an overall strategy that needs to include a number of other steps.

What is Workplace Violence?

The U.S. Occupational Safety and Health Administration (OSHA) is charged with assuring safe and healthful working conditions for working men and women by setting and enforcing standards and by providing training, outreach, education, and assistance. OSHA defines **workplace violence** as:

> "…any act or threat of physical violence, harassment, intimidation, or other threatening disruptive behavior that occurs at the work site and can range from threats and verbal abuse to physical assaults and even homicide."

Workplace violence is a major concern for all businesses since it can affect and involve employees, clients, customers, and visitors. OSHA estimates nearly **2 million American workers report having been victims of workplace violence each year**. However, many cases of workplace violence – which can strike anywhere and at any time – go unreported. More information is available at www.osha.gov/SLTC/workplaceviolence.

> **You Need To Know**
>
> ## Hundreds of Workers Die of Workplace Homicides Each Year in U.S.
>
> According to the revised 2014 Census of Fatal Occupational Injuries (CFOI), of the 4,821 fatal workplace injuries that occurred in the United States in 2014, 409 were workplace homicides. Among the workplace homicides in which women were the victims, the greatest share of assailants were relatives or domestic partners (32 percent of those homicides). In workplace homicides involving men, robbers were the most common type of assailant (33 percent of those homicides).
>
> Source: www.bls.gov/iif/cfoi_revised14_table.htm/

Who is at Risk of Workplace Violence?

According to OSHA:

Research has identified factors that may increase the risk of violence for some workers at certain worksites. Such factors include exchanging money with the public and working with volatile, unstable people. Working alone or in isolated areas may also contribute to the potential for violence. Providing services and care, and working where alcohol is served may also impact the likelihood of violence. Additionally, time of day and location of work, such as working late at night or in areas with high crime rates, are also risk factors that should be considered when addressing issues of workplace violence. Among those with higher-risk are workers who exchange money with the public, delivery drivers, healthcare professionals, public service workers, customer service agents, law enforcement personnel, and those who work alone or in small groups.

How can Workplace Violence Hazards be Reduced?

Again, according to OSHA:

In most workplaces where risk factors can be identified, the risk of assault can be prevented or minimized if employers take appropriate precautions. One of the best protections employers can offer their workers is to establish a zero-tolerance policy toward workplace violence. This policy should cover all workers, patients, clients, visitors, contractors, and anyone else who may come in contact with company personnel.

By assessing their worksites, employers can identify methods for reducing the likelihood of incidents occurring. OSHA believes that a well-written and implemented workplace violence prevention program, combined with engineering controls, administrative controls and training can reduce the incidence of workplace violence in both the private sector and federal workplaces.

This can be a separate workplace violence prevention program or can be incorporated into an injury and illness prevention program, employee handbook, or manual of standard operating procedures. It is critical to ensure that all workers know the policy and understand that all claims of workplace violence will be investigated and remedied promptly. In addition, OSHA encourages employers to develop additional methods as necessary to protect employees in high risk industries.

How Does Workplace Violence Affect Businesses?

According to the U.S. Department of Labor (DOL):

The cost to organizations is staggering. It is impossible to overstate the costs of workplace violence, because a single incident can have sweeping repercussions. There can be the immediate and profound loss of life or physical or psychological repercussions felt by the victim as well as the victim's family, friends, and co-workers; the loss of productivity and morale that sweeps through an organization after a violent incident; and the public relations impact on an employer when news of violence reaches the media.

Workplace violence affects other areas as well. The adverse impact on organizations and individuals is wide-ranging and can include:

- *Temporary/Permanent Absence of Skilled Employee*
- *Psychological Damage*
- *Property Damage, Theft, and Sabotage*
- *Productivity Impediments*
- *Diversion of Management Resource*
- *Increased Security Costs*
- *Increased Workers' Compensation Costs*
- *Increased Personnel Costs*

There are many theories about the causes of workplace violence. However, caution should be taken when profiling or stereotyping individuals or organizations since the presence of any of the factors related to these theories does not necessarily indicate a violent act will be carried out. Nevertheless, an incident can be the result of any one or a combination of these factors.

Remember – violence or threats of violence in all forms is unacceptable workplace behavior. It will not be tolerated and it will be dealt with appropriately.

More information is available at www.dol.gov/oasam/hrc/policies/dol-workplace-violence-program.htm.

More Workplace Homicides Occur in Private Industry than Government

According to the 2014 Census of Fatal Occupational Injuries (CFOI), private industry accounted for the vast majority of the total of 409 workplace homicides in 2014 – 84 percent – with 342 workplace homicides occurring in private industry as compared to 67 workplace homicides occurring in the government.

Source: www.bls.gov/iif/oshwc/cfoi/cftb0287.pdf.

Workplace Homicide Statistics

According to the revised **2014 Census of Fatal Occupational Injuries (CFOI)** conducted by the U.S. Bureau of Labor Statistics (BLS), of the 4,821 fatal workplace injuries that occurred in the United States in 2010 – the highest annual total since 2008 – **409 deaths were caused by workplace homicides**. Out of those 409 workplace homicides, **307 were due**

to intentional shootings by other persons. Workplace homicides made up 8 percent of fatal occupational injuries in 2014. To learn more, visit www.bls.gov/iif/oshcfoi1.htm#2014.

Workplace Homicides by Selected Characteristics

The 2014 Census of Fatal Occupational Injuries (CFOI) revealed the following selected characteristics of the total of 409 workplace homicides committed in that year:

- **Gender:**
  - 341 of the victims of workplace homicide in 2014 were men.
  - 68 of the victims of workplace homicide in 2014 were women.
- **Age:**
  - 115 of the victims of workplace homicide in 2014 were aged 45 to 54 years.
  - 93 of the victims of workplace homicide in 2014 were aged 35 to 44 years.
  - 83 of the victims of workplace homicide in 2014 were aged 25 to 34 years.
  - 56 of the victims of workplace homicide in 2014 were aged 55 to 64 years.
  - 30 of the victims of workplace homicide in 2014 were aged 65 years and over.
  - 29 of the victims of workplace homicide in 2014 were aged 20 to 24 years.
  - 1 victim of workplace homicide in 2014 was aged 16 to 17 years.
- **Race or Ethnic Origin:**
  - 200 of the victims of workplace homicide in 2014 were white.
  - 88 of the victims of workplace homicide in 2014 were African-American.
  - 71 of the victims of workplace homicide in 2014 were Hispanic or Latino.
  - 44 of the victims of workplace homicide in 2014 were Asian.
- **Employee Status:** 293 of the victims of workplace homicide in 2014 were wage and salary workers while 116 of the victims of workplace homicide in 2014 were self-employed.

Source: www.bls.gov/iif/oshwc/cfoi/work_homicide.pdf

Workplace Homicides by Occupation

Results from the 2014 CFOI regarding fatal occupational injuries resulting from homicides by occupation in the U.S. found that sales related occupations was the most vulnerable position with 107 workplace homicides. Within this category, supervisors of sales workers (58 workplace homicides) and retail sales workers (44 workplace homicides) were the most common victims of workplace homicides.

Fatal Occupational Injuries Resulting from Workplace Homicides by Occupation in U.S. in 2014

Occupation	Workplace Homicides
Sales and Related Occupations	107
Protective Service Occupations	78
Transportation and Material Moving Occupations	63
Management Occupations	31
Office and Administrative Support Occupations	21
Food Preparation and Serving Related Occupations	15
Installation, Maintenance, and Repair Occupations	14
Building and Grounds Maintenance Occupations	13
Construction and Extraction Occupations	13
Personal care and Service Occupations	13

Source: www.bls.gov/iif/oshwc/cfoi/cftb0291.pdf

Workplace Homicides by Industry

Results from the 2014 CFOI regarding fatal occupational injuries resulting from homicides by industry in the U.S. found that the trade, transportation, and utilities industry had the most workplace homicides with a total of 160 such cases. Within this industry, retail trade (106 workplace homicides) and transportation and warehousing (47 workplace homicides) were the industries most susceptible to homicides in the workplace.

Fatal Occupational Injuries Resulting from Workplace Homicides by Industry in U.S. in 2014

Industry	Workplace Homicides
Trade, Transportation, and Utilities	160
Government	67
Leisure and Hospitality	49
Professional and Business Services	40
Other Services Except Public Administration	25
Financial Activities	21
Manufacturing	14
Educational and Health Services	15
Construction	11
Natural Resources and Mining	6

Source: www.bls.gov/iif/oshwc/cfoi/cftb0287.pdf

Local Government More Dangerous than State & Federal Government

The 2014 Census of Fatal Occupational Injuries (CFOI) found that Local government (53 workplace homicides) by far accounted for most of the 67 total workplace homicides in Government, followed by Federal government (7 workplace homicides) and State government (7 workplace homicides).

Source: www.bls.gov/iif/oshwc/cfoi/cftb0287.pdf.

Workplace Homicides by State of Incident

The 2014 CFOI showed that, not surprisingly, the more populated states of the U.S. had the most incidents of workplace homicides led by California (45 workplace homicides) as shown below.

Top Ten States with Most Workplace Homicide Incidents in 2014

State	Workplace Homicides
California	45
Texas	39
Florida	23
New York	21
Illinois	19
Georgia	18
Indiana	18
Michigan	18
Ohio	18
Maryland	16

Source: www.bls.gov/iif/oshwc/cfoi/work_homicide.pdf

Jury Awards Over $1 Million in Lawsuit Involving Workplace Violence

In November of 2016, a jury in Texas awarded more than $1 million in a negligent hiring lawsuit filed against a company on behalf of an employee and war hero who was killed on the job by a co-worker that claimed the company knowingly providing an unsafe workplace for employees.

The Orange Leader reported that on April 1, 2015, Steven Damien Young shot and killed co-worker Jacob Matthew Cadriel with a 38-caliber handgun. Young was arrested and charged with murder. He is currently serving a 45 year sentence.

The negligent hiring lawsuit claimed that Woven Metal Products – who owned the facility where both Young and Cadriel worked – failed to "conduct comprehensive employment background checks and criminal record searches on their employees."

The company was negligent because it "failed listen to numerous workers at the facility who repeatedly told them about the erratic and unstable behavior of Young" and also "failed to provide any training or education on identifying and handling this type of violence behavior in the workplace."

In 2008, Young was "arrested, charged and convicted in Harris County of the offense of carrying an illegal weapon on the jobsite." In 2014, he was "arrested and charged in Harris County with the offense of making a terroristic threat." He was out on bond awaiting trial when he murdered Cadriel.

The jury returned its verdict stating "Woven Metal Products were negligent and that the Woven premises were in an unreasonably dangerous condition and that they failed in their duty to warn Jacob of the highly foreseeable likelihood of harm, which contributed to Mr. Cadriel's death."

According to the report: *Jacob Matthew Cadriel served his country in the U.S. Army from 2004 through 2009, and was active in two tours in Iraq. He was back home in Texas, married to his high school sweetheart, and raising their 5-year-old son, Jacob Matthew Cadriel, Jr., at the time of his death.*

The jury awarded for the estate of Mr. Cadriel his pain and suffering, medical bills, lost earning potential, and his wife's loss of companionship. The story in *The Orange Leader* is available at www.orangeleader.com/2016/11/14/jury-awards-war-hero-over-1-million-dollars-verdict-returned-on-employee-murder-lawsuit/.

More Workplace Violence Statistics

The National Institute for Occupational Safety and Health (NIOSH) offers statistics from several sources that show the magnitude of workplace violence in the United States:

- The Bureau of Labor Statistics' Census of Fatal Occupational Injuries (CFOI) reported 14,770 workplace homicide victims between 1992 and 2012. Averaging over 700 homicides per year, the largest number of homicides in one year (1080) occurred in 1994, while the lowest number (468) occurred in 2011. From 2003 to 2012 over half of the workplace homicides occurred within three occupation classifications: sales and related occupations (28%), protective service occupations (17%), and transportation and material moving occupations (13%).
- The Bureau of Labor Statistics Survey of Occupational Injuries and Illnesses (SOII) reported an estimated 154,460 nonfatal occupational injuries and illnesses involving days away from work during the 2003 to 2012 time period.

The Healthcare and Social Assistance Industry accounted for over two-thirds of these injuries and illnesses each year.

- Data collected by the Consumer Product Safety Commissions' National Electronic Injury Surveillance System (NEISS) that is collected in collaboration with NIOSH (NEISS-Work Supplement) estimated more than 137,000 workers were treated in emergency departments for nonfatal assaults in 2009.
- The Bureau of Justice Statistics' National Crime Victimization Survey (NCVS) estimated the number of nonfatal violent crimes occurring against persons 16 or older while they were at work in 2009 at 572,000.

As an integral part of a broad-based initiative to reduce the incidence of occupational violence in this country, NIOSH conducts, funds, and publishes research on risk factors and prevention strategies related to workplace violence. This site contains information on NIOSH research as well as links to statistical reports, and public and private initiatives to address the problems of workplace violence.

Source: www.cdc.gov/niosh/topics/violence/

DHS Offers Active Shooter Program to Help Stop Workplace Violence

In January 2016, the U.S. Department of Homeland Security (DHS) issued its **"Active Shooter Preparedness Program"** to enhance preparedness for "active shooter" incidents. According to the DHS:

Active shooter incidents, in many cases, have no pattern or method to the selection of victims, which results in an unpredictable and evolving situation. In the midst of the chaos, anyone can play an integral role in mitigating the impacts of an active shooter incident. The Department of Homeland Security (DHS) provides a variety of no-cost resources to the public and private sector to enhance preparedness and response to an active shooter incident. The goal of the Department is to ensure awareness of actions that can be taken before, during, and after an incident.

The DHS program provides training, products, and resources on issues such as "active shooter awareness, incident response, and workplace violence." The DHS has found that "there is no pattern or method to the selection of victims by an active shooter, and these situations are, by their very nature, unpredictable and evolve quickly."

For more information about the program, visit www.dhs.gov/sites/default/files/publications/dhs-active-shooter-preparedness-program-fact-sheet-01-16-508.pdf.

ISC Guide to *Planning and Response to an Active Shooter*

In November 2015, the Interagency Security Committee (ISC) released **"Planning and Response to an Active Shooter: An Interagency Security Committee Policy and Best Practices Guide"** to the public. A version of this document was initially released only to the Federal community in July 2015 to streamline existing ISC policy on active shooter incidents into one cohesive policy and guidance document to enhance preparedness for an active shooter incident at Federal facilities. The guide was then made publicly available as a reference document for the private sector so a wider audience would benefit from the information. Key research findings of the guide include:

- 160 Active Shooter incidents occurred between 2000 and 2013.
- An average of 11.4 incidents occurred annually: an average of 6.4 annually in the first seven years of the study and an average of 16.4 annually in the last seven years.
- Shootings occurred in 40 of 50 states and the District of Columbia.
- The 160 incidents resulted in 1,043 casualties: 486 killed and 557 wounded, not including the shooter.
- In incidents, the median number of people killed was two, the median wounded was two.
- Approximately 60 percent of the incidents ended before police arrived.
- 64 (40 percent) of the incidents ended with the shooter committing suicide.

- In 21 incidents (13.1 percent), the incident ended after unarmed citizens safely and successfully restrained the shooter. Of note, 11 of the incidents involved unarmed principals, teachers, other school staff, and students who confronted shooters to end the threat.
- In 45 of the 160 (28.1 percent) incidents, law enforcement had to engage the shooter to end the threat. In 21 of those 45 (46.7 percent) instances, law enforcement suffered casualties with nine killed and 28 wounded.
- In 64 cases where the duration could be ascertained, 44 (69 percent) ended in less than five minutes with 23 ending in two minutes or less.
- In five incidents (3.8 percent) the shooting ended after armed individuals who were not law enforcement personnel exchanged gunfire with the shooters.
- Active shooter incidents occurred most frequently in areas of commerce (46 percent), followed by educational environments (24 percent), and government properties (ten percent).

The ISC guide indicates that an effective active shooter plan will include the following general:

- Proactive steps that can be taken by facility tenants to identify individuals who may be on a trajectory to commit a violent act.
- A preferred method for reporting active shooter incidents, including informing all those at the facility or who may be entering the facility.
- How to neutralize the threat and achieve life safety objectives.
- Emergency escape procedures and route assignments (e.g., floor plans, safe areas), including where to evacuate and how to evacuate when the primary evacuation routes are unusable.
- Integration with the facility incident commander and the external incident commander.
- Information concerning local area emergency response agencies and hospitals (i.e., name, telephone number, and distance from the location), including internal phone numbers and contacts.
- How operations will be restored.

The guide suggests that after the company or facility-specific policy and procedures—including an active shooter plan—are finalized, training and exercises should occur, with drills and exercises at least annually. The guide is available at www.dhs.gov/sites/default/files/publications/isc-planning-response-active-shooter-guide-non-fouo-nov-2015-508.pdf.

You Need To Know

Active Shooter Defined

The ISC defines an active shooter as an individual or individuals actively engaged in killing or attempting to kill people in a populated area. In most cases, firearms are the weapon of choice during active shooter incidents, but any weapon (such as a knife, etc.) can be used to harm innocent individuals. Typically, there is no pattern or method to the selection of victims. Active shooter situations are dynamic and quickly evolve. Often, the immediate deployment of law enforcement is required to stop the aggressive action of a shooter to mitigate harm to potential victims. However, because active shooter situations are also frequently over prior to the arrival of law enforcement, individuals must be prepared both mentally and physically to deal with an active shooter situation prior to law enforcement arrival.

Source: www.dhs.gov/sites/default/files/publications/isc-planning-response-active-shooter-guide-non-fouo-nov-2015-508.pdf.

Examples of Workplace Violence

The following are deadly examples of homicides in the workplace from the *Workplace Violence* web page on Wikipedia.org. These examples, which is only a small portion of the list available is presented here for illustration purposes only to help employers understand workplace violence is a serious issue that can happen in any workplace. The walkaway point for employers is that these events can happen.

See the entire list at https://en.wikipedia.org/wiki/Workplace_violence#Deadly_examples:

- *On February 26, 2016, 38-year old Cedric Ford who was employed as a painter at Excel Industries in Hesston, Kansas shot and killed three people and injured 14 other people. A co-worker reported that approximately two hours after the two men had clocked in for their shift at work that day, he saw Ford strapped up with his weapon and shooting at people in the factory's parking lot.*

- *On March 20, 2016, a 55-year-old retired state trooper with the Pennsylvania Turnpike system named Clarence Briggs of Newville, Pennsylvania returned to the roads he used to patrol prior to his retirement and attempted an armed robbery at a toll booth. Briggs shot and killed toll booth worker Danny Crouse, 55, and Ron Heist, 72, a security guard before he was shot and killed by the authorities.*

- *On April 8, 2016, workplace violence erupted at Lackland Airforce Base in San Antonio, Texas. At that time, the squadron's commanding officer was shot and killed by an airman who then killed himself. Thereafter, the facility went into lockdown mode. Soon after the shootings, it was reported that the incident was not a case involving terrorism but was workplace violence. The shooter was being escorted to a disciplinary hearing when he committed the murder-suicide.*

- *On May 4, 2016, a man who had been involuntarily terminated two weeks earlier from his position at Knight Transportation in Katy, Texas approximately 20 miles west of Houston returned to his former workplace armed with a shotgun and a pistol. Marion Guy Williams, 65, was reported to have said words to the effect of "You all ruined my life." Williams then shot and killed a 34-year-old supervisor Michael Dawid, injured two other employees and then killed himself.*

Obviously, the above incidents remind employers they should have education and policies on how to help prevent workplace violence, including training on how to recognize and deal with the warning signs of workplace violence.

On-Air Shooting of Journalists Tragic Example of Workplace Violence

The on-air shooting deaths during a live broadcast of two journalists who worked for WDBJ7 in Roanoke, Virginia – news reporter Alison Parker and photographer Adam Ward – by a former colleague who was fired from his job is another tragic example of the widespread prevalence of workplace violence.

WDBJ7 reported that police said Vester Lee Flanagan II, 41, shot and killed Parker, 24, and Ward, 27, while the two WDBJ employees were conducting a live interview on the morning of August 26, 2015. Parker and Ward died at the scene while the woman being interviewed received non-life threatening injuries.

Flanagan – a former employee of WDBJ-TV who used the on-air name of Bryce Williams – fled the scene and was later spotted by law enforcement in a rented car on a highway. After refusing to stop and crashing the vehicle, he was found with a self-inflicted gunshot wound and later died, WDBJ7 reported.

In the aftermath of the horrific event, WDBJ7 released a statement on Vester Flanagan's employment history with the station that serves as a reminder to employers that workplace violence is a legitimate threat to any industry or profession. Below is WDBJ's statement:

Vester Flanagan was employed by WDBJ7 as a reporter between March 2012 and February 2013. Flanagan applied for the position using the air name of Bryce Williams. As part of WDBJ's standard protocol his background check resulted in positive references.

Flanagan's job performance and his interaction with his co-workers led his manager to place Flanagan on a succession of performance improvement plans. Only slight improvement was noted each time.

Flanagan was placed on a final warning in December 2012 for failure to check his facts in a news story and, generally, for poor news judgment.

In January 2013 he accused a photographer of making trouble for him by questioning a decision to go on private property in pursuit of a story. At that point, he raised some concerns with HR of perceived unfairness, which were immediately investigated and found to be without merit.

Shortly after that, he confronted an anchor who was assigned to review one of his scripts.

At that point, management made the determination that he needed to be separated from the company.

On February 1, two news managers and the HR business partner notified Flanagan of the decision to terminate his employment. He reacted angrily, telling them that they would have to call the police because he was going to "make a stink and it was going to be in the headlines."

The HR rep called 911. Employees had been notified to give Flanagan space to clean out his desk. At his desk, Flanagan attempted to reach the corporate CEO, without success. At that point, police arrived and escorted him from the building. On the way out, he handed a wooden cross to the news director and said, "You'll need this." He also made a derogatory comment to Adam Ward as he left.

The only contact between WDBJ7 and Flanagan after that were routine calls to HR about termination benefits.

Shortly thereafter, Flanagan filed a complaint of harassment and discrimination with the Equal Employment Opportunity Commission. WDBJ7 responded that his claims of mistreatment were unfounded and the EEOC denied the claim. He later filed a civil action in local court in Roanoke. That action was dismissed.

In two and half years since the termination, WDBJ7 employees reported seeing Flanagan in public places and there were no confrontations. He was never seen following employees and he did not attempt to enter the offices of WDBJ7.

All claims of mistreatment were investigated by senior management, by the HR representative and legal counsel. All investigations determined that no reasonable person would have taken any of the cited instances as discrimination or harassment.

The statement is available online at www.cbs58.com/story/29896180/wdbj-releases-statement-on-vester-flanagans-employment-history.

What Workers are the Most Susceptible to Workplace Violence?

All workers are not necessarily susceptible to the same degree of a workplace violence incident. Research has identified these factors that may increase the potential risk and likelihood of workplace violence for some workers at certain worksites:

- Exchanging money with the public.
- Working with volatile and unstable people.
- Working alone or in isolated areas.
- Providing services and care.
- Working where alcohol is served.
- Working late at night or in areas with high crime rates.

According to OSHA, among employees with an increased risk of workplace violence are workers who exchange money with the public, delivery drivers, healthcare professionals, public service workers, customer service agents, law enforcement personnel, and those who work alone or in small groups.

The OSHA Workplace Violence website is located at www.osha.gov/SLTC/workplaceviolence/index.html.

What Can Employers Do to Protect Employees from Workplace Violence?

According to an OSHA Fact Sheet on Workplace Violence:

The best protection employers can offer is to establish a zero-tolerance policy toward workplace violence against or by their employees. The employer should establish a workplace violence prevention program or incorporate the information into an existing accident prevention program, employee handbook, or manual of standard operating procedures. It is critical to ensure that all employees know the policy and understand that all claims of workplace violence will be investigated and remedied promptly. In addition, employers can offer additional protections such as the following:

- *Provide safety education for employees so they know what conduct is not acceptable, what to do if they witness or are subjected to workplace violence, and how to protect themselves.*
- *Secure the workplace. Where appropriate to the business, install video surveillance, extra lighting, and alarm systems and minimize access by outsiders through identification badges, electronic keys, and guards.*
- *Provide drop safes to limit the amount of cash on hand. Keep a minimal amount of cash in registers during evenings and late night hours.*
- *Equip field staff with cellular phones and hand-held alarms or noise devices, and require them to prepare a daily work plan and keep a contact person informed of their location throughout the day. Keep employer provided vehicles properly maintained.*
- *Instruct employees not to enter any location where they feel unsafe. Introduce a "buddy system" or provide an escort service or police assistance in potentially dangerous situations or at night.*
- *Develop policies and procedures covering visits by home health-care providers. Address the conduct of home visits, the presence of others in the home during visits, and the worker's right to refuse to provide services in a clearly hazardous situation.*

The OSHA Fact Sheet is at www.osha.gov/OshDoc/data_General_Facts/factsheet-workplace-violence.pdf.

 Workplace Violence Deaths by Co-Workers on the Rise

Although the number of deaths related to workplace violence by co-workers remains relatively small, U.S. Bureau of Labor Statistics (BLS) data shows this type of workplace violence incident is rising nationwide, according to the article **'Active shooters at work on rise'** on the *Houston Chronicle* website.

The *Chronicle* reports that BLS data reveals 61 people were killed by workplace violence at their jobs by a co-worker in 2014, up from 49 people killed in 2011. However, only 15 percent of the workplace violence victims out of the overall 409 workplace homicides in 2014 were killed by co-workers.

Workplace violence specialists suggest that the increase in workplace violence deaths "reflects the growing anxieties among employees as wages stagnate, living costs rise, and on-the-job pressures intensify from companies operating with leaner staffs."

The Federal Bureau of Investigation (FBI) found that the number of "active shooter" incidents did indeed rise, the Houston Chronicle reports, with the average number of such incidents rising from an average of 6.4 each year between 2000 and 2006 to an average of 16.4 each year from 2007 to 2013. According to the FBI, the 160 workplace violence shootings in the 14-year period killed 486 people and wounded 557.

The article is at www.houstonchronicle.com/business/article/Active-shooters-at-work-on-rise-7468247.php.

Report from the National Council on Compensation Insurance, Inc. (NCCI)

A January 2012 report *Violence in the Workplace* by the National Council on Compensation Insurance, Inc. (NCCI) shows that while work-related homicides and injuries due to workplace assaults remain well below levels observed in the mid-1990s, homicides committed by "work associates" (a Bureau of Labor Statistics category of both co-workers and customers) have increased.

In the report, NCCI states that the "reality of workplace violence is markedly different from popular opinion" and that workplace homicides – which account for 11 percent of workplace fatalities in private industry – "are not crimes of passion committed by disgruntled coworkers and spouses, but rather result from robberies." In addition, the majority of workplace assaults are committed by healthcare patients. Key Findings of the report "Violence in the Workplace" include the following:

- Work-related homicides and injuries due to workplace assaults remain well below levels observed in the mid-1990s, consistent with the patterns of declines in rates of homicide and aggravated assaults reported for the country. The rate of workplace homicides fell 59 percent from 1993 to 2009, while the overall rate of homicides fell 47 percent during the same period, according to NCCI.
- Homicides account for 11 percent of workplace fatalities. Homicides due to robberies and similar criminal acts fell markedly over the late 1990s but still make up 69 percent of all homicides.
- Homicides committed by "work associates" – a BLS category made up of both coworkers and customers – have increased to about 21 percent, mostly reflecting an increase to 9 percent in violent acts by customers while the share of workplace homicides due to coworkers has remained steady at about 12 percent. The actual number of such homicides has been in the 50 to 60 range in recent years.
- Health care workers experience remarkably high rates of injuries due to assaults by patients, especially in nursing homes and other long-term care facilities. In fact, 61 percent of all workplace assaults are committed by healthcare patients.

To view the complete report, visit: https://www.ncci.com/Articles/Documents/II_Workplace_Research.pdf.

Survey Finds Half of Emergency Nurses Experienced Workplace Violence

An *Emergency Department Violence Surveillance Study* released in November 2011 by the Emergency Nurses Association (ENA) Institute for Emergency Nursing Research revealed that more than half of the nurses surveyed by ENA – a mean of 54.8 percent – reported experiencing either physical or verbal abuse at work in the past seven days. These findings mean that every week in the U.S., between approximately eight and 13 percent of emergency department nurses are victims of incidents of physical workplace violence.

In addition, the survey found that 15 percent of emergency nurses who reported experiencing physical violence said they sustained a physical injury as a result of the incident and that, in nearly half of the cases (44.9 percent), no action was taken against the perpetrator of workplace violence. Furthermore, almost three out of four emergency nurses (74.4 percent) who were victims of workplace violence reported the hospital gave them no response regarding that workplace violence.

The survey also found emergency nurses working at hospitals with policies regarding workplace violence reported experiencing fewer incidents of physical or verbal violence. For example:

- Hospitals with zero-tolerance reporting policies had an 8.4 percent workplace violence rate.
- Hospitals with a non-zero-tolerance policy had a 12.3 percent workplace violence rate.
- Hospitals with no policy had an 18.1 percent workplace violence rate.

Based on quarterly surveys of a total of 3,211 emergency nurses across the country from May 2009 to February 2010, *The Emergency Department Violence Surveillance Study* also found that:

- Patients and their relatives were the perpetrators of the workplace violence abuse in nearly all incidents of physical violence (97.1 percent) and verbal abuse (91 percent).
- The majority of incidents of physical violence occurred in patients' rooms (80.6 percent).
- The most frequently reported activities that emergency nurses were involved in when they experienced workplace violence were triaging a patient (38.2 percent), restraining or subduing a patient (33.8 percent), and performing an invasive procedure (30.9 percent).
- Male nurses reported higher workplace violence rates than female nurses (15 percent versus 10.3 percent).
- Workplace violence rates were higher in large urban areas (13.4 percent) than in rural areas (8.3 percent).

As a result of the Surveillance Study findings, the ENA has urged OHSA to make its guidelines for preventing workplace violence into mandatory standards that to which all hospital and health care centers must adhere. To read the study, visit www.ena.org/practice-research/research/Documents/ENAEDVSReportNovember2011.pdf.

The Economic Cost of Workplace Violence

Overall, **workplace violence costs employers more than $120 billion a year**, according to estimates by the National Institute for Occupational Safety and Health (NIOSH), the United States federal agency responsible for conducting research and making recommendations for the prevention of work-related injury and illness. NIOSH is part of the Centers for Disease Control and Prevention (CDC) within the U.S. Department of Health and Human Services." See: https://en.wikipedia.org/wiki/National_Institute_for_Occupational_Safety_and_Health.

The cost of workplace violence to America is staggering not only in personal terms but in economic loss as well. The National Institute for the Prevention of Workplace Violence issued a paper *The Financial Impact of Workplace Violence* that includes some historical data on the cost of workplace violence.

- In 1992 the Department of Justice estimated that the cost of workplace violence to employers was approximately $6.2 million dollars.

- In September of 1993, the National Safe Workplace Institute released a study pegging the cost of workplace violence at $4.2 billion annually. They estimated that in 1992, 111,000 violent incidents were committed in work environments resulting in 750 deaths.
- In 1995 the National Council of Compensation Insurance found $126 million in workers' compensation claims for workplace violence.
- A study released by the Workplace Violence Research Institute in April 1995 showed that workplace violence actually resulted in a $36 billion annual loss.
- According to the Bureau of Justice Statistics, about 500,000 victims of violent crime in the workplace lose an estimated 1.8 million workdays each year. This presents an astounding $55 million in lost wages for employees, not including days covered by sick and annual leave and a loss of productivity that has direct consequences for an employer's bottom line.
- The Bureau's statistic further state that domestic violence causes employees to miss over 175,000 days of paid work annually and 66 percent of Fortune 1000 senior executives recently surveyed said that financial performance of their company would benefit from addressing the domestic violence experienced by employees.
- Lawsuits in the area have been impacting cost substantially. The average out-of-court settlement for this type of litigation approaches $500,000.00 and the average jury award of $3 million. A few awards have reached as high as $5.49 million. (Campbell and Karin, Workplace Violence Reporter).
- For six to 18 weeks after an incident happens there is a 50 percent decrease in productivity and a 20 to 40% turnover in employees according to Duane Frederickson, Detective, Minneapolis Police Department.

The Financial Impact of Workplace Violence: www.workplaceviolence911.com/docs/FinancialImpactofWV.pdf.

Another document by the National Institute for the Prevention of Workplace Violence, Inc. is the *2011 Workplace Violence Prevention Fact Sheet* which reflects an increased cost to employers.

- The economic cost of workplace violence nationwide is around $121 billion a year.
- Nonfatal workplace assaults alone result in more than 876,000 lost workdays and $16 million in lost wages.
- The overall impact and cost to a business of reacting after an incident occurs can be staggering versus the cost of focusing on preventing an incident from occurring in the first place. One report indicates that the cost of reacting after a serious incident has occurred is 100 times more costly than taking preventative actions.

The 2011 Workplace Violence Prevention Fact Sheet is available at www.workplaceviolence911.com/. The author sincerely thanks the Executive Director of the National Institute for the Prevention of Workplace Violence, Inc., Mr. Barry Nixon, SPHR, for his permission to reproduce their information herein.

What Causes Workplace Violence?

Acts of workplace violence can come from two sources. First, the acts can be caused by external parties, such as robbery in the workplace by a stranger. In those circumstances, employers have certain duties to maintain a safe and secure workplace. The second source is existing employees. For purposes of this chapter, the concerns over workplace violence center on workplace violence carried out by existing employees.

Types of workplace violence incidents are usually broken down into two categories – **"Opportunity-motivated incidents"** and **"Stress-based incidents"**:

- **Opportunity-motivated incidents** occur when an employee feels that he or she can get away with something. The motivation behind the action can vary from rationalization such as "I earned a little bonus, and besides, the boss won't miss $20 from the till" to desperation, "I'm way behind on my rent, and the landlord's going to evict me." With a rationale like that, you have an employee who is willing to steal money, equipment, or goods from the employer. This type of action is seldom pre-meditated, occurring usually when the employee has unsupervised access to cash or materials.

- **Stress-based incidents** are usually the result of frustration with work-related issues such as problems with management, co-workers, procedures, etc. These problems are often compounded by external stresses, including marital trouble, issues with sick or dependent family members, or substance abuse problems.

Most employees who commit acts of stress-related workplace violence are not typically bad employees. Violent employees, in fact, can be dedicated and devoted individuals who take their jobs seriously. If their job is the central focus of their lives, perhaps they can their job too seriously. Any slight, disrespect, or perceived mistreatment may be magnified beyond proportion. They can react violently to any perceived threat to work or employment. In a nutshell, their jobs are their life. Therefore, employment-related issues are elevated to life and death decisions. As a result, workplace violence often can be caused by the perpetrator's belief that some form of injustice has been inflicted, and the violence is an attempt to regain a perceived loss of control or an attempt to get even for the perceived injustice or unfair treatment. If an employee defines their self-worth by their job, then a perceived mistreatment by the employer can amount to their devaluation as a human being. The resulting stress that leads to violence can be driven by an intense need to defend their self against what they perceive as such personal devaluation. Obviously, violence is not an acceptable response to stress, and employers must take appropriate measures to identify and protect against any employees who turn to violence.

A particularly sensitive area is termination. Losing a job can be a traumatic experience for anyone. For those people whose work is their life, termination can potentially set off a lethal explosion of workplace violence even if the person being terminated has been warned and knows it is coming. As a result, every termination must be handled carefully, taking into account the potential for an outburst. Part of preventing workplace violence is a well thought out termination policy, which can be compiled with assistance from a labor attorney or a human resources consultant. Some additional information about termination is addressed by attorney Ron Brand below.

Defining the Circumstance

Workplace violence can take place anywhere employees are required to carry out a business-related function. The type of incident liable to occur varies by circumstance but generally breaks down in the following manner:

Event or incident	Where it Occurs	Perpetrated by
Anger-related incidents	At the traditional workplace	An outsider with no legitimate
Arguments	(office, job site)	relationship to the victim or
Arson		workplace
Bullying/intimidation	Off-site at a business-related	
Bringing a handgun on premises, and using it to intimidate, threaten or bully	function (conference, trade show, etc.)	A customer or someone who is a recipient of a service provided by the affected victim or
Harassment	At a social event related	workplace.
Murder	to work	
Physical assaults (biting, hitting, kicking, etc.)		A current or former employee who has an employment-related
Pranks	In customer or client homes	relationship with the workplace
Property damage		victim.
Psychological trauma	Away from work but resulting	
Pushing	from work (such as threats made	
Rape	by clients to employees at their	Employee-related outsider who
Robbery	residences)	is a current/former spouse/lover,

Rumors Sabotage Suicide Swearing Theft Vandalism Verbal abuse Written threats		relative, acquaintance, etc. who has a dispute involving an employee of the workplace. Domestic violence can become workplace violence

While the definition at the start of this chapter covers a fair degree of actions, a better interpretation should be used by employers in order to create an effective, defensible policy. For example, a company policy should account for the type of offense, circumstance—where and when an incident occurs, and whether it is considered to be "on-the-job"—and party or parties involved. This includes examining the severity levels of workplace violence.

Three Severity Levels of Workplace Violence Behavior

A case where a cashier is caught stealing from the register must be looked at differently than a case where an employee beats up a co-worker. Therefore, it becomes necessary to add a level of criteria to define the degree of severity of a behavior or action. Most experts on the subject classify workplace violence behaviors into three severity levels.

Level One: Low-level workplace violence acts or behaviors not severe enough to require disciplinary action but which indicate that a problem may exist. This type of problem may not result in any significant damage to person or property but acts as a warning sign that education or intervention may be necessary. Level One behavior is most frequently seen in an employee's attitude. This type of behavior includes:

- Argumentative or confrontational behavior. Consistently moody, caustic, or mean behavior when dealing with co-workers or customers.
- Uncooperative or arrogant behavior. Consistent refusal to cooperate with co-workers or supervisors.
- Inappropriate behavior. Consistent use of profanity, spreading rumors, or comments of an off-color or sexual nature.

Level Two: Moderate level workplace violence actions that may merit Level Two behavior indicates that a problem exists and must be dealt with before it can escalate into more serious behavior. This includes:

- Outbursts or "acting out." Expressing a desire or intent to hurt others, slamming doors, punching walls, vandalism, verbal or written threats, etc.
- Disobedience. Open and intentional disregard of company policies and procedures.
- Non-mutual displays of affection. Persistent romantic overtures that are clearly one-sided and unwelcome, up to and including light sexual harassment.
- Theft

Level Three: Severe acts of workplace violence against person or property that merit Level Three may include:

- Minor physical assault. Hitting, fights, etc.
- Major physical assault. Murder, rape, etc.
- Strong-arm or armed robbery
- Arson or major destruction of property

A person acting inappropriately and violently may encounter a cycle of violence where he or she goes through a progression. As the outbursts increase in intensity, the cycle can occur more quickly, and the outbursts can become more pronounced. It is critical to deal with signs and symptoms of workplace violence as early as possible before it escalates into a heartbreaking statistic.

Preventing Workplace Violence

Unfortunately, there is no cure-all to eliminate the threat of violence. The unpredictable nature of human behavior makes it necessary for employers to keep a close watch on conditions and events in the workplace in order to ensure the safety and security of employees and customers.

This does not mean that employers are powerless to prevent workplace violence – far from it. The Safe Hiring Program (SHP) described in this book includes a range of tools, techniques, and services available to help employers mitigate the risk of hiring or retaining a potentially dangerous employee. The goal is to ensure that hiring managers company-wide follow procedures and pay attention to safe hiring.

Many employers consider background checks and reference checks to be the cornerstone of a Safe Hiring Program, effectively "weeding out" most potentially troublesome employees. By having a policy in place that lets job applicants know the information they provide to the company will be independently verified—and past employers will be contacted and criminal records checks may be conducted to search for any indication of violence in the past—the employer lets the applicant know that the company is serious about preventing problems in the workplace. Those applicants with a history of violent behavior may be considered ineligible for consideration based on past offenses or just simply dissuaded from applying in the first place.

Some employers go so far as to require that employees submit to a psychological profile to be considered eligible for hire. While this practice might indeed identify that an employee may have some obsessive tendencies or a propensity for violent or aggressive behavior, the number of faults with this type of screening immediately outweighs the benefits in all but the most extreme circumstances. For example, a negative hiring decision based on a psychological profile instead of an actual event or offense would be difficult to defend—the report may potentially identify the person as having a 'disability,' thus invoking the ADA which explicitly prohibits not hiring someone unless there is a preponderance of current medical or other evidence indicating the person is a direct threat. In addition, the sheer cost of a psychological profile quickly puts the process beyond most employers' budgets. If psychological assessments are used, they should be only a part of all the factors considered among an array of selection processes determining a person's employability.

For the most part, the elements of a Safe Hiring Program are relatively basic, inexpensive, and easy-to-implement steps that, as a whole, can be instrumental in minimizing the potential for problems in the workplace. The typical elements of such a program include the development of policies, procedures, and guidelines as well as employee training, policy implementation, and process evaluation. Without a program in place, the employer is subject to the Negative Hiring Doctrine.

Workplace Violence and the Negligent Hiring Doctrine

Under the Negligent Hiring Doctrine, the employer is largely liable for any problems that occur in the workplace under the Negligent Hiring Doctrine.

The Negligent Hiring Doctrine dictates that employers can be held liable for damages if they knowingly employ persons known to pose a potential threat to co-workers or the public. The Doctrine even goes so far as to state that if the employer should have known the employee was a threat, the employer is responsible.

That said, the question arises—how can an employer identify a potentially problematic employee?

Here is the problem. There is no magic formula that tells an employer in advance who will and will not be violent. Predicting future violence is a matter of considerable controversy.

However, experts have found some factors that are present in many cases of workplace violence. One important factor is a history of past violence. For that reason, properly done pre-employment background checks are widely regarded as an effective screening procedure. As discussed in previous chapters, contacting past employers to ask about incidents of past violence may be difficult given the reluctance of many past employers to give any information beyond dates of employment and job title. This is why performing a check for past criminal acts is a critical step.

However, there is more to preventing workplace problems than screening at the door before entry into the workplace.

Factors in employees' lives change. A person who checked out in an initial screen may over time develop the traits or behaviors indicative of a potentially violent employee. It is up to the employer to maintain a constant eye on conditions and events in the workplace—to stay aware of employee attitudes and concerns in order to ensure the safety and security of everyone involved.

Setting a Workplace Policy

One critical task is to have a clear workplace violence policy that everyone acknowledges and understands. In this way, employees have a clear understanding the employer has a commitment to a safe workplace and enforces a policy that includes training for supervisors and consequences for failing to follow the policy.

An employer establishing an SHP should also assemble a team responsible and accountable for the process. The team should be comprised of employees and professionals from different functional areas to ensure all possible considerations are taken into account regarding the scope of establishing and implementing the program. The team will be responsible for administering the program, including the development and implementation of policy and practices, communicating the policies to all employees within the organization, and training employees in identifying and responding to problems. When or if a crisis occurs, they serve as the employer's response and intervention team.

Sample Policy - Establishment of Team

Team members can include:

- Human Resources.
- Security.
- Attorney.
- Psychologist or outside expert on violence.

Team members will need to address the following subjects:

1. Policies, Procedure, and Guidelines:

- Establish a detailed, precise definition of workplace violence, citing examples.
- Clearly define the company's response to violence, both actual and threatened.
- Identify and address all potential problem areas, including security elements currently missing and existing methods of dealing with incidents.
- Assess which areas of security should be outsourced to a third-party vendor versus what can be done with the company's existing resources.
- Have a termination policy, including policies on how a person is evaluated and terminated and the physical termination process.

2. Implementation:

- Make appropriate changes to the application/interview/hiring process—background or reference checks, requiring signed applications, etc.
- Communicate all necessary policy and procedural changes to all employees verbally, as a memo, and in the company manual.

3. Employee Training:

- Train employees in recognizing and responding to situations.

- Create an environment where employees are encouraged to report potential workplace violence issues, including a guarantee of confidentiality.
- Train employees in prevention of possible volatile situations.
- Provide an Employment Assistance Program (EAP) to encourage employees with personal problems to seek help.
- For employees who are victims of violence or threats, EAP may assist in obtaining stay away orders from the court or police (such as in stalking or domestic violence cases).

4. Evaluation:

- Periodically audit all employees involved in the hiring process to ensure their adherence to the program.
- Evaluate elements involved in physical security, such as:

    1) Making sure public areas are set up to protect employees and to make them visible. This protects employees from external violence.

    2) Consider physical barriers, controlling the number of entrances, controlling access, protective fencing, and adequate lighting and alarms.

5. Crisis Response:

- Prepare a crisis response plan taking into account issues of physical security and premises evacuation. The crisis teams should include professionals to assess the stress, security expert to implement an immediate response, and HR and legal assistance to assess what action to take.

Recommendations from OSHA

OSHA recommends that the best protection employers can offer is to establish a zero-tolerance policy toward workplace violence against or by their employees. The employer should establish a workplace violence prevention program or incorporate the information into an existing accident prevention program, employee handbook, or manual of standard operating procedures. It is critical to ensure that all employees know the policy and understand that all claims of workplace violence will be investigated and remedied promptly. In addition, employers can offer additional protections that include the following:

- Provide workplace violence education for employees so they know what conduct is not acceptable and what to do if they witness or are subjected to workplace violence.
- Secure the workplace by installing video surveillance cameras, extra lighting, and alarm systems and minimize access by outsiders through identification badges, electronic keys, and guards.
- Limit the amount of cash on hand by keeping a minimal amount of cash in registers during evenings and late night hours.
- Equip staff with cellular phones and hand-held alarms or noise devices if necessary and keep employer provided vehicles properly maintained.
- Conduct background checks on all staff members to help ensure a safe and secure workplace.

Author Tip OSHA Releases Guidelines Preventing Workplace Violence to Healthcare and Social Service Workers

In 2015, the Occupational Safety and Health Administration (OSHA) released an update to its **"Guidelines for Preventing Workplace Violence for Healthcare and Social Service Workers"** that highlights the most effective ways to reduce the risk of violence in various healthcare and social service settings.

The revised guidelines update OSHA's 1996 and 2004 guidelines and incorporate research in the last decade into the causes, risk factors, and preventive measures of workplace violence in healthcare and social service settings. OSHA found that healthcare and social service workers are almost four times as likely to be injured as a result of workplace violence than the average private sector worker.

The updated OSHA guidelines are at www.osha.gov/Publications/osha3148.pdf.

Workplace Violence: An Attorney's Perspective

Preventing and Addressing Workplace Violence in the Workplace – A Lawyer's Perspective

By Ron S. Brand, Esq., Jackson Tidus, A Law Corporation

The tragic headlines of violence in the workplace are, unfortunately, all too common. There are more than 30,000 violent incidents on the job every year. According to various studies, including ones conducted by the National Institute of Occupational Safety and Health and the U.S. Bureau of Labor Statistics, homicide is the third highest work-related cause of death in the United States. This tragedy is compounded by the fact that many incidents of workplace violence are preventable. There are a variety of steps employers can take to significantly reduce the chance of violence occurring in their workplace, and to increase the safety and welfare of their employees.

The first step toward prevention of violence in the workplace is to avoid, from the beginning, hiring a troubled individual who may be prone to acts of violence. A comprehensive safe hiring program, including having a criminal background check completed in accordance with the Fair Credit Report Act and any applicable state laws, will significantly increase the likelihood that a troubled employee will be weeded out.

Second, employers should institute a comprehensive, zero tolerance policy against violence in the workplace. The policy should be contained in an employee handbook or as a stand-alone document signed by the employees. The policy should address threats of violence and fighting, as well as acts of violence. It should prohibit the bringing of weapons to work and announce that searches of employees' lockers, toolboxes, desks, and vehicles may be conducted. Employees who violate this policy should be disciplined, or, when necessary, terminated before things get out of control. Along with instituting a workplace violence policy, employers may want to consider providing workplace violence education for employees so they know what conduct is unacceptable, and what to do if they witness or are subjected to workplace violence.

Third, supervisors and co-workers should be alert for warning signs of a troubled employee who may be prone to acts of violence. Such warning signs include talking about weapons and violence, making threats to supervisors or co-workers, anger management problems, substance abuse, and inappropriate behaviors such as stalking others or the habitual use of racial epithets. The employee's personal life should be taken into account as well; perpetrators of workplace violence tend to be loners, or have severe marital, financial and/or emotional difficulties. Supervisors should be trained on how to appropriately intervene in situations when potential violence enters the workplace.

Fourth, employers should consider sending troubled employees to an employee assistance program (EAP). An EAP is intended to help employees deal with personal problems that might adversely impact their work performance, health, and well-being. While an EAP may provide valuable assistance to a troubled employee, some state laws (like California) prohibit an employer from forcing an employee to get help. Generally speaking, the EAP must remain a voluntary option. It should be noted that the Americans with Disabilities Act permits an employer to require an employee who appears to present a direct threat to the safety and welfare of other employees to undergo a "fitness for duty" mental examination, but this is often an incomplete solution. The better approach is to treat threatening and violent conduct as a disciplinary matter rather than as an issue for therapy.

Fifth, employers should take reasonable steps to secure the workplace. Such steps may include installing video surveillance cameras, extra lighting, and alarm systems, and minimizing access by outsiders through identification badges, electronic keys and, when appropriate, guards.

Sixth, should a troubled employee have to be terminated, some advance preventive planning is essential. Many local police departments offer assistance in threat assessment and will provide uniformed or plainclothes officers as necessary to assist with the termination of a potentially violent employee. A private security consultant may also provide valuable assistance. Prior to the termination meeting, the employee's access to company databases should be barred. Furthermore, the employee's final paycheck should be prepared and arrangements made for the employee to remove all personal effects at the time of termination so that he or she will have no need to return to the workplace. Following a termination of a violent individual, it may be wise to have surveillance done on the ex-employee, or to post security personnel around the workplace for a few days in case the ex-employee should attempt to return with the intent of committing acts of violence.

Restraining orders are available where an employee has exhibited a pattern of threatening or violent conduct, but such orders should be used with caution. An irrational and angry individual with a genuine propensity for violence may well just be further incited by a restraining order. A careful analysis of the likely effect of such an order on the employee and the level of threat the employee poses should be conducted before such an order is obtained. Often, less confrontational methods are preferable.

Should an employer follow these basic steps, the chances of yet another tragic headline of workplace violence will be significantly reduced.

Sample Workplace Violence Policy

By Ron S. Brand, Esq., Jackson Tidus, A Law Corporation.

The Company has a zero tolerance for violent acts or threats of violence against our employees, applicants, customers or vendors.

We do not allow fighting, threatening words or threatening conduct. Weapons of any kind are strictly prohibited and not permitted on Company premises.

No employee should commit or threaten to commit any violent act against a co-worker, applicant, customer or vendor. This includes discussions of the use of dangerous weapons, even in a joking manner.

Any employee who is subjected to or threatened with violence by a co-worker, customer or vendor, or is aware of another individual who has been subjected to or threatened with violence, is to report this information to his/her supervisor or manager as soon as possible.

All threats should be taken seriously. Please bring all threats to the attention of your supervisor or the Human Resources Department so that we can deal with them appropriately.

All threats will be thoroughly investigated, and all complaints which are reported to management will be treated with as much confidentiality as possible.

Employee Acknowledgment of Receipt of Workplace Violence Policy

This will acknowledge that I received a copy of the Workplace Violence Policy and that I will comply with its requirements.

PRINT FULL NAME_____

SIGNED_____

DATE_____

(RETAIN IN EMPLOYEE'S PERSONNEL FILE)

Other Important Resources for Workplace Violence

There are many excellent websites to assist employers in dealing with issues related to workplace violence. Resources listed below lead to voluminous research and materials on preventing workplace violence:

- www.osha.gov/SLTC/workplaceviolence – Workplace violence resources and sites from OSHA.
- www.ccohs.ca/oshanswers/psychosocial/violence.html – The Canadian Centre for Occupational Health and Safety has assembled a list of examples of factors and situations that increase the potential for risk of workplace violence.
- https://archive.opm.gov/employment_and_benefits/worklife/officialdocuments/handbooksguides/workplaceviolence/index.asp – 'Dealing with Workplace Violence: A Guide for Agency Planners' by the Federal Office of Personnel Management (OPM).
- www.atapworldwide.org – Association of Threat Assessment Professionals.
- www.workplaceviolence911.com – The National Institute for Prevention of Workplace Violence.
- www.asisonline.org – American Society for Industrial Security (ASIS).
- www.opm.gov/policy-data-oversight/worklife/reference-materials/workplaceviolence.pdf – The U.S. Office of Personnel Management (OPM) Office of Workforce Relations publication 'Dealing with Workplace Violence: A Guide for Agency Planners' contains the following paragraph under the heading 'Pre-employment Screening':

  Pre-employment screening is an important part of workplace violence prevention. Prior to hiring an employee, the agency should check with its servicing personnel office and legal office, if necessary, to determine what pre-employment screening techniques (such as interview questions, background and reference checks, and drug testing) are appropriate for the position under consideration and are consistent with Federal laws and regulations.

Author Tip **Important Note on Future Workplace Violence Data**

Beginning with the 2015 reference year, final data from the Census of Fatal Occupational Injuries (CFOI) is now released in December – 4 months earlier than in past years. The final 2015 CFOI data is scheduled for release on December 16, 2016. Preliminary releases, which normally appeared in August or September in past years, are no longer be produced.

Source: www.bls.gov/iif/oshcfoi1.htm#2014

CHAPTER 20

Additional Issues and Trends for Employers

Introduction

This chapter examines special issues for employers as well as trends and future developments for safe hiring. It covers a number of areas but the common denominator is a focus on employer needs and challenges currently and in the future. The chapter first examines the needs of small and medium businesses and large employers that hire in more than one state. It then addresses issues surrounding specifics types of hiring, such as hourly workers, and juveniles. The chapter then examines a number of vital trends that could prove critical to employers, hiring managers, HR professions, and recruiters in the future.

Employers Come in All Sizes

Employers come in all sizes: small, medium, large, and very large. All of them need background screening.

The **2014 Statistics of U.S. Businesses (SUSB) Annual Data Tables** released in 2016 by the U.S. Census Bureau provides a breakdown of U.S. employers by number of paid employees. The study also shows the total number of persons employed and the number of firms within a specific size range.

According to SUSB statistics from the Census.gov website in the table below, of the over 5.8 million employer firms with more than 121 million paid employees in 2014, only 19,076 firms – less than one percent – had more than 500 employees.

These statistics underscore the importance of small businesses since the Census numbers show that small businesses make up over 99 percent of all firms and a little less than 50 percent of all paid employees.

Size of Employer Firms with Number of Firms & Paid Employees in 2013*

Size of Firm	Number of Firms	Paid Employees
0-4 employees	3,598,185	5,940,248
5-9 employees	998,953	6,570,776
10-19 employees	608,502	8,176,519
20 to 99 employees	513,179	20,121,588
100 to 499 employees	87,563	17,085,461
500+	19,076	57,894,592

*Source: *Number of Firms, Number of Establishments, Employment, and Annual Payroll by Large Enterprise Employment Sizes for the United States and States, NAICS Sectors: 2014*
https://www.census.gov/data/tables/2014/econ/susb/2014-susb-annual.html

Frequently Asked Questions about Small Business

The Office of Advocacy of the U.S. Small Business Administration (SBA), the voice of small business in government, provides a *'Frequently Asked Questions'* PDF updated in June 2016 at www.sba.gov/sites/default/files/advocacy/SB-FAQ-2016_WEB.pdf. Here are some of the FAQs.

What is a small business?

The Office of Advocacy defines a small business as an independent business having **fewer than 500 employees**. For the industry-level definitions of small business used in government programs and contracting, see www.sba.gov/content/small-business-size-standards.

Per the SUSB statistics above, in 2014 there were a little over 5.8 million small businesses in the U.S.

Author Tip > **Emerging Business**

Sometimes a small business is referred to as a Small/Medium Business or SMB. Firms that specialize in assisting a small business may use the term **emerging business** in recognition of the fact the business may start small but have big plans!

How big is the role of small businesses in the U.S. economy?

Small businesses comprise:

- 99.9% of all firms.
- 99.7% of firms with paid employees.
- 97.7% of exporting firms (297,000 small exporters).
- 33.6% of known export value ($471 billion out of $930 billion).
- 48.0% of private sector employees (57 million out of 118 million employees).
- 41.2% of private-sector payroll

What is the small business percent of net new jobs?

Small businesses accounted for **63.3% of net new jobs** from the third quarter of 1992 until the third quarter of 2013. The small business share of net job change was strongly positive for most of this 21-year time span, except during two recessionary periods.

How can small businesses' share of net new jobs be larger than their share of employment, yet their share of employment remain steady?

As firms grow, they change employment size classes. So as small firms grow, their growth counts toward small firm job gains; but if they pass the 500-employee mark, their employment is classified as large firm employment.

How are small businesses financed?

The most common source of capital to finance business expansion is personal and family savings (21.9% of small firms), followed by business profits and assets (5.7%), business loans from financial institutions (4.5%), and business credit cards from banks (3.3%).

How many small businesses are in the high tech industry?

In 2012, there were 244,243 small employer firms in high-tech industries, representing 98.5% of all employer firms in these industries. The majority of these small firms provide services in either computer systems design or architecture and engineering.

Among small firms, the industries with the highest growth from 2007 to 2012 were pharmaceutical and medicine manufacturing, data processing and hosting service, and computer systems design services. Notably, the number of small firms in pharmaceutical and medicine manufacturing increased 12.4%, compared to an increase 2.0% for large firms.

Note: This publication uses the Level I high-tech industries listed in Hecker's 2005 analysis, with the exception of 5161 and 5181, as no corresponding NAICS codes were available for 2012 data. For the definition of high-tech industries, see www.bls.gov/opub/mlr/2005/07/art6full.

Special Challenges Faced by Small Businesses

Because small businesses operate with fewer employees, a single bad hire arguably has an even greater impact on small employers. Even though small businesses employ over 50% of all employees, and the impact of a bad hire is significant, it is amazing that small businesses do not take meaningful precautions to know exactly whom they are hiring. There are several reasons why small businesses may not perform background checks:

- Safe hiring is focused on problem avoidance in the future. If a firm has not had a bad experience, then efforts at a Safe Hiring Program can seem like a waste of time and money. It is human nature to base future action on past experience; if a business has not had the issue arise, it's not a priority.
- Some small firms have the ability to hire people that are known to the firm. Firms operating in a small community often hire individuals recommended by current employees. Hiring individuals who are known to the firm helps reduce the firm's risk of hiring a bad employee.
- Some firms are so busy growing they simply do not take the time to re-organize their processes as they expand. For a firm to initiate components of a Safe Hiring Program, someone in management must recognize that safe hiring is a core business practice and take the initiative to make it happen.
- As firms get bigger, they hang onto methods that worked well when they were smaller. These methods often include "flying by the seat of the pants" hiring methods. As a firm matures, it should recognize that more methodical procedures are needed.
- Initially, the tasks associated with HR are handled by the owner of a small firm, or possibly the office manager or bookkeeper. As a small business grows larger, it may eventually use a consultant or hire a human resources professional to handle the many tasks necessary to hire and maintain a large workforce. The number of tasks placed on a new HR manager is immense, particularly if HR is a department of one. By the time a firm reaches fifty employees, an HR position probably is a necessity. Prior to that, someone who holds the position of "office manager" and/or "payroll" may handle the HR functions.

Why Safe Hiring is a Challenge for an HR Department of One

When a small business hires an HR professional, as described throughout this book there are a myriad of tasks an HR professional must address about background screening and safe hiring.

- **Compliance.** A new HR practitioner must first ensure that a firm is in legal compliance with a number of federal and state regulations, including I-9 compliance, proper classification of employees into exempt or non-exempt status, leave of absences including maternity and family leaves, ADA, harassment, and numerous other legal issues. Failure to address these issues leaves a firm with tremendous financial and legal exposure.
- **Employee Manual.** Institute a handbook outlining formal practices and procedures.
- **Employee Files.** A new HR practitioner must typically review existing employee files, assuming those exist. Every employee should have a file that includes at least an application form or resume, a W-2 form, performance reviews, and basic employee data such as start date, salary, dates of promotions, and changes in status.
- **Payroll.** An HR practitioner must review how payroll is performed and determine if the best procedure is to do it in-house or outsourced.

- **Benefits.** This is very complicated for an HR department of one! A new HR practitioner needs to review benefit concerns. Typical issues include selection of benefits to offer, cost control, selecting a benefits broker, reviewing enrollment periods, and dealing with employee complaints concerning benefits.
- **New Employee onboarding.** The HR practitioner must perform all the onboarding paperwork necessary to get a person officially started and on the payroll. The onboarding process will also include a new hire checklist with various new hire forms such as I-9 compliance, benefit sign-up, and tax forms.
- **New Employee Orientation.** In a growing firm, an HR practitioner will also need to implement a new employee orientation, including explanations of company policies and benefits.
- **Compensation Review.** When a small firm hires an HR practitioner, the person must review the current compensation system. As a firm grows, a compensation strategy is necessary to make sure a firm is competitive and consistent.
- **Job Descriptions.** Often a small business grows without ever having prepared job descriptions. Descriptions are vital in helping an employer hire employees with the right skill sets, to perform job performance appraisals, and to comply with the ADA by identifying essential job functions.
- **Performance Appraisal System.** Most small businesses do not have a formalized performance appraisal system in place. Appraisals can be a critical factor to determine the proper compensation rate, to implement improvement plans for an employee, or to determine areas where additional training or supervision may be necessary to help an employee succeed.
- **Information Mechanism for Employees.** Another important function of a new HR department is to institute a system for keeping employees informed of such things as changes in benefits, new laws, harassment training, and even the company holiday schedule.
- **Training.** A growing small business may not have sufficient training in place. This includes not only training specific for a job but also training for managers and workers in areas such as sexual harassment control.
- **Recruiting and Hiring.** A new HR practitioner may be asked to help the "employer effort" to recruit, interview, hire, and train new employees.
- **Retention:** Keeping and motivating key performers is another critical HR task. Studies suggest that one of the key elements behind employee satisfaction is their relationship with their supervisor/manager along with other facts such as the opportunity to learn and make positive contributions. Although employers often think salary is the number one factor for employee retention, numerous studies show that non-monetary factors are just as important if not more important.
- **HR Software.** Another task often assigned to a new HR department is to consider automation procedures and software available to help the firm manage the employment aspects of a growing business.
- **Complaints and Problems.** Very often HR is the place employees go if they have a work related complaint or problem. If there are issues between co-workers or allegations of mistreatment by a supervisor, sexual harassment or other problems, HR is often the first to be involved. If an employee has personal issues, the HR department is normally brought in. Since small firms may not have an Employee Assistance Program (EAP), the HR department of one fills that role as well.
- **Other Tasks:** In a small to medium business, it is not unusual for a number of other tasks that do not have a home to be assigned to HR. For example, HR may be assigned the office party, employee recognition, handling employee complaints, and numerous other duties.

Small to Medium Employers (SME) Can Perform Safe Hiring

The good news is that even a small to medium employer can implement a Safe Hiring Program at very low cost. The Application, Interview, and Reference Checking (AIR) Process described earlier in this book costs next to nothing to implement. It only requires a commitment to spend a modest amount of time thinking through the process and a commitment to follow it. A small to medium business that hires negligently would be hard pressed to defend itself on the basis that it is too small to practice safe hiring. That defense has not proven successful. Although a small to medium business may not be expected to perform at the same level as a Fortune 500 firm, the fact is that a Safe Hiring Program can be implemented and utilized at little or no cost. There is no reason why any small business has to hire blindly.

An employer of any size, including a small to medium business, can have a well-designed application, conduct solid interviews, and contact references as described in the AIR Process. It does not take much time and provides a great deal of protection. If a small business wishes to go further and do a criminal check, it can find screening firms that specialize in the needs of small businesses.

You Need To Know ⟩ **Selecting a Screening Firm that Specializes in Small and Medium Employers**

Many screening firms are reluctant to work with a small/medium business. If a screening firm is geared to handle large clients, small/medium clients represent challenges to a background screening firm. Under the Fair Credit Reporting Act (FCRA), the same forms and procedures are needed to provide compliant background checks to a small business as are needed for a Fortune 500 business. There is no small business exception to the FCRA. Screening firms may be concerned that smaller businesses will order infrequently, yet require training and maintenance. In fact, a small business may take up a great amount of resources just because they use the screening system infrequently and need to be trained more often, and may need a high level of customer service to explain the process and the results. The economic fact of the screening industry is that larger clients are more profitable.

This means small businesses should look for a screening firm that expressly is built to fit the needs of a small business. One example is BackgroundPro (www.backgroundpro.com) which is a screening firm designed especially to be the "small business background check solution" for emerging businesses. They also say:

> BackgroundPro is designed for the unique needs of small and emerging businesses. We offer the same service a Fortune 500 company would expect, but with a simple and easy to use system designed for the small business. We provide everything. All you need to do is to decide what level of screening you want, and give us the applicant's name and email. We do the rest.

There are a number of other firms that emphasize small business screening services, and there are larger screening firms that have built a special platform to accommodate the needs of small business clients. The goal is to streamline the process so that a small business can perform checks quickly and easily. Screening firms specializing and working with small and medium business clients can be found by using a search engine with a phrase such as *small business background check*.

Large Employer Issues

On the other side of the employment spectrum are large enterprises. While there is no generally accepted formula for what constitutes middle market and large or enterprise level employers, when an employer reaches a level of 1,000 employees or has multiple locations, a whole new set of concerns and challenges develops. A discussion of some special considerations that large employers face would include the following:

1. Large Employers Face Legal Complexities by Hiring in Multiple States

A major challenge for large employers operating in a number of states is legal compliance. The complexity of compliance surfaces in two significant areas.

- **Use of criminal records by employers.** Many states have their own rules concerning the use of criminal records; some of these rules are reviewed in Chapters 6 concerning state laws. In addition, numerous states, counties, and cities have their own ban-the-box laws. Many states have their own restrictions on questions about past criminal conduct, and limit what can be asked in various ways. These restrictions are typically set forth in a state's rules on discrimination in employment such as state fair employment guidelines. Some states have restrictions enacted by statutes.

- **Other State Rules:** Individual state rules can also affect any aspect of the hiring process including the language on applications, proper interview questions, and the ability of employers to obtain and use screening information on applicants. Operating in multiple states requires knowledge of the rules for each.

- **State FCRA Laws.** As discussed in Chapter 6, there are a number of states with unique laws controlling background screening by third party professional background firms. An employer that intends to hire and screen in multiple state locations must be aware of the applicable laws. Also, employers must utilize the forms and procedures appropriate for each state. In California, using forms and procedures that work in the other 49 states could expose an employer to substantial damage awards in a civil lawsuit. (California has set its own legal requirements. See the article in the Appendix.)

- **Understanding which state law to apply.** Operating in multiple states also creates complicated issues of which laws apply. Assume a firm incorporated in Delaware hires a Connecticut resident for a job in New York, and a screening firm in Atlanta improperly reports a criminal conviction when the applicant went to school in California, and the case was brought into federal court in New York alleging violations of a New York state law that protect employees. This is an actual case. The case was *Obabueki v. International Business Machines Corp.*, 145 F. Supp.2d 371 (S.D.N.Y. 2001). There were follow-up cases as well. A detailed discussion of the facts and legal issues involved are beyond the scope of this book. However, the general principles involved in considering which state's law to apply are summarized in Chapter 5 on the FCRA.

Author Tip ⟩ **50 State Compliance: A New Innovation in Background Screening**

A new innovation is the ability of a software system to incorporate necessary legal forms and state specific requirements on an online application system. Such a system can also automatically be updated any time there is a change in state or federal law. By asking for certain information, the system will know which states are impacted and if specific forms are required.

---

2. Large Employer Issues with Consistency in the Organization Across Multiple Facilities

An issue for large multi-state employers is maintaining consistency within the organization that extends across multirole facilities in different states and cities. Assume, for example, that an employer has a facility in Arizona that is performing in-depth background reports and utilizing the safe hiring techniques reviewed in previous chapters. Also, assume the same firm has a facility in Ohio that is not doing nearly as much to ensure safe hiring. If a person is injured as a result of workplace violence in the less vigilant Ohio facility, then the injured party's attorney could use the practices and procedures at the more vigilant facility against the employer. The argument would be the employer knew how to hire safely but chose not to follow the higher standard in that particular facility. In other words, an employer may be held to the standard in the facility that exercises the greater degree of due diligence. As a result, management must be sensitive to the need to have a consistent company-wide policy when it comes to safe hiring and employment screening.

The same considerations come into play when utilizing negative information. If the Ohio facility hired an applicant with previous criminal records to be employed, then the Arizona facility could be accused of discrimination if a similarly situated person with a similar record is denied employment.

3. Large Employer Issues with Automation, Integration with HRS, and Applicant Tracking

Another consideration for large enterprise level firms is the automation and integration of the pre-employment process with their Human Resources Information Systems, or HRIS. Some firms will manage all of the human resources with some enterprise level application such as PeopleSoft, Oracle, or SAP. Other firms may coordinate background screening with an applicant tracking system, or ATS.

An ATS system is a database that is used to manage applicant information in a firm's hiring process. The software manages the receipt of resumes and applications (including online applications) as well as correspondence and contact between applicants and the firm. The software can track open positions, engage in some sort of matching process, and track the progress of each applicant. There are at least 300 providers of this type service in a market that is estimated by some as exceeding a billion dollars; each ATS software provider touting any number of different bells and whistles. There are ATS software providers meet the needs of small, medium, large, and enterprise employers.

Author Tip ▷ **New Trend in Development**

There are many systems to choose from with many features. Employers need to determine if they will really use all of the whistles and bells. A new trend is to develop an **Applicant Tracking Software (ATS)** that accomplishes an employer's goal without overburdening the business with unneeded complication. For example, see Newton Software at www.newtonsoftware.com.

One advantage of having a direct business-to-business (B2B) connection between an ATS and a screening firm is the time saved by eliminating double data entry—since the applicant's name, Social Society number, and date of birth are already in the employer's computer system, there is no need to visit the background screening firm's website to re-enter the same data manually. With a seamless B2B integration, employers can instantly send the required data electronically to the screening firm, and the data is automatically populated in the screening firm's HRIS or ATS system. The B2B seamless interface can also communicate the types of searches the employer is ordering. While the order is being processed, the employer can receive updates or status reports.

You Need To Know ▷ **One BIG Advantage**

One big advantage of a system described above is the employer does not need to collect a date of birth or social security number. That can be done on the background firm's online system. Nor does the **Applicant Tracking System (ATS) or Human Resources Information System (HRIS)** need to store background reports. The screening firm can also do that.

Although the technology involved in seamless B2B connections was complex and expensive at one time, the general rule that technology becomes less expensive and more readily available certainly applies to background screening processes for large firms. As discussed in Chapter 7, screening firms and an ATS can use a number of integration tools to work together seamlessly. In fact, for more sophisticated integrations, employers and recruiters never need to leave the ATS site, since the screening firm can pass back to the ATS information on the status of the screening report as well as a link to the final report.

Author Tip > ### An ATS Should Not Dictate an Employer's Choice of Screening Firms

On occasion, an ATS may try to steer an employer towards a screening firm that is already an integrated partner with the ATS. This saves the ATS the time and money of integrating with a new screening firm. In some situations, the ATS and screening firm may have some sort of revenue split arrangement. The attempt to steer an employer to a pre-existing partner may be in the best interest of the ATS but may not be in the employer's best interest.

It is highly questionable whether this is a good practice for employers. It is typically not advisable to let one HR provider dictate the use of another professional service like employment screening just because the ATS already has a partnership or has a financial incentive. Each service—employment screening and the ATS—are separate professional endeavors and employers have the right to select the best of breed that suits their needs. The best advice for an employer is to make a professional selection for each service and to ask the two providers to integrate their services. A competent ATS should have the ability and willingness to accommodate the employer's choice of screening firms assuming the screening firm has the technology needed to perform an integration. If the ATS cannot accommodate the employer, or the screening firm does not have sufficient technology, then the employer may need to revisit their vendor selections. However, if an employer selects a screening firm with an API or IT resources, the employer has the absolute right to insist that its ATS provider cooperate with the screening firm to perform an integration. The bottom line is that HR vendors need to meet the needs of employers, and not the other way around. An employer has an absolute right to choose the screening firm that best meets their needs.

---

4. Large Employer Issues with Managing Privacy and Reports across Organizational Lines

With multiple facilities and/or multiple divisions and hiring managers, a large employer needs to be concerned about how privacy and confidentiality are maintained. Unless precautions are taken, reports may be viewed by co-workers, administrative staff, or others who are not involved in the hiring process and do not have a need to review the reports. A screening report contains information confidential in nature that should not be made available to anyone who is not directly involved in the hiring decision. An argument can be made that even a hiring manager should not view a background screening report but should only be advised by Security or Human Resources if there is a problem that needs to be addressed.

Screening firms can set-up accounts that use parent-child relationships so a supervisor can view all reports, but only the appropriate office or person can view the reports that pertain to them. This also allows a screening firm to set up sub-accounts for an organization so that management reports and billing can be provided to the correct branch or office.

Most screening firms offer online systems where an employer can easily manage the permissions process and control who can see the final report, allowing others to enter information or check completion status. There is typically a screen that indicates the status of all current reports and the degree of completion. An online system can also route reports to the right office.

One solution would be a system whereby reports with potentially negative information can go only to one contact person in charge of reviewing the information where there is a potential issue. This also promotes uniformity across an organization as well.

5. Large Employer Issues with Training Hiring Managers across the Organization

Another issue in large organizations is training the various hiring managers to consistently follow the organization's safe hiring procedures. This is especially an issue for organizations that hire for a large number of branches, such as banks, hotels, or sales offices. Consistency and training are important for a number of reasons especially for documenting that a firm, in fact, follows safe hiring procedures, and it also helps protect the firm against allegations of discrimination. It is very important to train all managers to not ask questions that are impermissible and may violate discrimination rules.

The useful tool is the S.A.F.E. Program outlined in Chapter 6, including a Safe Hiring Checklist, which outlines the essential steps in a Safe Hiring Program. The hiring manager fills out the checklist as new hires are finalized. The checklist gives clear directions on what has to be done and enables an organization to audit, measure, and reward hiring managers for following the safe hiring procedures.

6. Large Employers Contracting for Safe Hiring Services Based Primarily on Price

One trend among large firms is to have purchasing or procurement departments involved in the selection of service providers, including background screening services. Some organizations have even taken to awarding contracts based upon online auctions, where the finalists bid against each other in an effort to obtain the lowest possible price.

The difficulty for large employers with this approach is purchasing a professional service on a purely price-driven model leaves the organizations vulnerable in the event the low-cost provider fails to perform adequately. If a firm utilizes the auctions approach, the firm must recognize they are making a calculated risk-management decision that spending the minimum is sufficient. If the low-cost provider fails to perform, and the firm gets sued, then the employer would face a substantial challenge in attempting to prove they exercised due diligence.

The biggest variable factor in screening is the cost of labor. The raw cost of data has a relatively narrow margin. Shortcuts can include using untrained clerical workers to produce screening reports or utilizing incomplete databases for criminal searches. What if court researchers enter criminal information directly into the computer, and there is no review prior to viewing by the employer? The employer sees data not reviewed for accuracy, completeness, or legality by a screening professional. Another way large employers obtain cheap pricing is to utilize a service that offers screening services essentially as a "loss leader" in order to sell other HR products. Firms using auctions to base the decision primarily on price may also attract screening firms that are purely data houses willing to sell at or near cost to increase their volume or willingly take a smaller profit per transaction as long as they can keep their costs down. Again, since the largest item of overhead is trained staff, a large employer who is driving down the price through an auction cannot count on having the level of professional service the task requires.

Firms using the auction method would probably not do so for finding and hiring other professional services such as a corporate attorney or an auditor. When using an auction for screening and safe hiring services, a large employer is essentially relegating safe hiring to a commodity product, ignoring the professional services aspect.

One employer found out the hard way. In *Kay v. First Continental Trading, Inc.*, 976 F.Supp. 772,774 (N.D.Ill. 1997), a federal court ruled an expert witness could give his opinion that a screening firm could not have effectively conducted a proper investigation for the low price it charged the employer. The end result is employers who focus solely on price may find themselves paying more later. As the saying goes, "You get what you pay for."

Special Problems with Entry Level, Hourly, Seasonal, Piecemeal or Temporary Contract Workforces

Industries with large hourly, seasonal, or temporary contract workforces typically include hospitality and tourism, manufacturing, service, retail, food and restaurants, warehouse fulfillment, drug and groceries stores, and call centers. Compounding their hiring problems are multiple locations and large turnovers.

How many hourly workers are there in the United States? According to the U.S. Bureau of Labor Statistics report released in April 2015, **77.2 million workers** age 16 and older in the United States were paid at hourly rates, representing **58.7 percent of all wage and salary workers** in 2014 (Source: www.bls.gov/opub/reports/minimum-wage/archive/characteristics-of-minimum-wage-workers-2014.pdf).

A Monster.com report on "Recruiting Ideas: How to Find Good Hourly Employees" found that:

> *Hourly employees comprise more than 60 % of the US workforce, yet many employers are unsuccessful in their efforts to find qualified candidates in sufficient numbers and fall short of retaining top employees long enough to realize a return on their investment.*

> *That's because the total cost of losing an hourly, frontline employee ranges from 30 % to 150 % of that person's annual earnings. Add to this the fact that non-exempt turnover is approximately three-and-one-half times greater than exempt and it is clear that hourly employee turnover is by far the greater drain on profitability.*

Source: http://hiring.monster.com/hr/hr-best-practices/small-business/hiring-process/find-good-employees.aspx.

Challenges with these Types of Workforces

Some of the challenges of Entry Level, Hourly, Seasonal, Piecemeal or Temporary Contract workforces include:

1. **Due Diligence:** The challenge is greater if the firm is engaged in providing services that have a greater degree of risk to third parties. For example, resorts hiring seasonally have greater exposure since children are present during their peak seasons. If temporary or seasonal employees are involved in higher risk activities in roles as lifeguards, ski instructors, or other similar jobs, then the stakes are higher. A higher degree of due diligence may also be prudent where a worker has an elevated position of authority over others, since supervisors may often be in a position to assert influence over subordinates.

2. **Costs Involved in Background Checks:** A related issue is cost. Employers in this space may not want to spend a great deal of money on this type of workforce. However, if there are risks involved, cutting back on due diligence can be costly if an employer is sued or has workplace problems.

3. **Processing Applications and Background Checks:** Working in this space can be challenging since acquaints may or may not have access to technology. The use of electronic consent forms sent by email or applicant tracking systems may not be a workable solution. As outlined in Chapter 7, there are other solutions that can include paper forms, kiosks or low-tech processes.

4. **Hiring Rushes:** Another issue is that some employers in this category may find that they are doing large ramp-ups so that hiring is done all at one time. This may involve special accommodations or efforts as well to handle the hiring surge.

5. **Lack of Information on Applicants:** Another potential issue is that for entry level applicants, there may be a lack of available data if the worker is young, new to the U.S. or has a limited job history.

6. **Difficulty in Obtaining Information:** Conversely, applicants may have worked at numerous temporary or hourly jobs and contacting past employers can be difficult if the consumer was not at any one employer for a long period of time. Or an applicant may have moved around a great deal so that a criminal history becomes difficult due to the number of jurisdictions where the person has lived. Employers then need to decide what is relevant given the risk and nature of the job and how much information is actually needed.

7. **Workforce with a Higher Rate of Criminal History:** Another difficulty that may be encountered by employers in this area is that the workforce may have a higher percentage of applicants with criminal records. Of course, employers need to be concerned about the safety of the workplace, co-workers, and the public. On the other hand, the reality is that employers need to be prepared to take reasonable chances on people in order to find enough workers for the type of jobs they need filled. In addition, as discussed at length in chapter 10, the EEOC prohibits employers from having a blanket policy of exclusion based upon a criminal record. Employers need to consider various factors about the criminal record, the job, and age of the past offense in order to make reasonable job

related decisions based upon risk and the ability do the job. It does mean however that an employer may need a well thought out program to handle a higher rate of criminal records.

Author Tip ⟩ **The Need for Speed**

Employers in these labor markets may have a "need for speed" for quick fulfillment and may be tempted to rely on "Instant Background Checks." As set forth in Chapter 9, the word "instant" and "background checks" do not belong in the same sentence. See additional information below on why employers should not be tempted by instant checks.

So, how do industries with significant turnover—or with large numbers of hourly, seasonal, temporary or contract workers—protect themselves in a cost-effective and efficient manner? Employers are under pressure to reduce the time and cost per hire by minimizing those costs and delays associated with pre-employment screening. A cost-effective solution is to devise a mechanism that incorporates the elements of the S.A.F.E. Hiring program and the AIR Process described in previous chapters in an assembly line fashion.

In addition, employers and staffing vendors who hire this type of workforce may consider running at least a basic public records search. It can include a Social Security trace and at least one county criminal record check. Also running a multi-state/multi-jurisdictional search can be helpful assuming the background firm verifies any potential criminal matters at the courthouse before reporting them (See Chapter 9 on accurate and actionable criminal records). If any driving is involved, then a driving record should also be run. Of course, if it is a driving position regulated by the Department of Transportation (DOT) or for any other position that is regulated by federal or state rules, then all applicable laws must be followed.

Even though the cost of background checks can add up for large hiring programs, employers should take into account that they are still held to a standard of due diligence when hiring for hourly, temporary, or seasonal employees. An employer must still evaluate the foreseeable risk involved and act reasonably. If sued, an employer might assert the defense that imposing the requirement of doing background checks was too burdensome or costly given the work involved, or that the harm caused was not foreseeable or a proximate cause of any failure by the employer. However, employers are taking a big risk since there is no guarantee that defense will succeed, especially if the employer is sued in a case where substantial harm occurred. Employers need to make a risk-management decision considering that the cost of safe hiring is minor when compared to the possible harm not implementing a Safe Hiring Program and performing some level of due diligence through background checks. As explained in Chapter 5, the cost of litigation and attorney fees alone from one bad new-hire can negate the money saved on cutting corners.

CEOs and CFOs who take the position that safe hiring and pre-employment screening are not important or are too expensive need to carefully review the true economics of their firm and the risk factors involved from a single bad hire.

In addition, there are screening firms and HR service providers that specialize in this space and can come up with solutions for employers that work with labor demographics that are not as "connected" in terms of having access to computers, tablets, or smartphones. See Chapter 7 for additional discussions on the mechanics of screening individuals without computer access.

Special Issues with Millennials

Now that **Millennials have overtaken Baby Boomers as the largest group in the workforce** (See "You Need to Know" below for details), employers need to be sensitive to special issues in hiring and working with Millennials. Much has been written about the generational divide and how Millennials approach employment differently. Studies and practical experience show Millennials are influenced by factors much different than Baby Boomers and are motivated, work, and communicate in much different ways.

In terms of screening, millennials, by virtue of being younger, may have less information to obtain. They will have a more limited work history and less of a credit history (even assuming an employer wants to obtain a credit report as discussed in Chapter 11). Given a high percentage of millennials that have given up on the idea of car ownership in order to use rideshare services, driving records may not yield much information either. In the chapter on social media background checks, we discussed that many millennials consider the use of social media for screening to be an invasion of privacy.

The most critical issue employers find with millennials, however, is that it is the most "wired" generation so far in history. That means the applicant experience is critical. Any software used to accomplish screening must be intuitive, easy to use and very clear or an employer may find it has an issue attracting millennial candidates. More information about the need for clear communication and the applicant experience is below.

> **You Need To Know**

Millennials Surpass Baby Boomers as Largest Generation of Workforce Aged People

Population estimates from the U.S. Census Bureau have found that **"Millennials"** – defined as people aged 18 to 34 in 2015 – now number 75.4 million and have surpassed the 74.9 million Baby Boomers aged 51 to 69 in 2015, according to a Pew Research Center article.

The article also revealed that Millennials would continue to grow as young immigrants enter the U.S. and are projected to peak in 2036 at 81.1 million. Generation X, defined as people aged 35 to 50 in 2015, should pass the Baby Boomers in population by 2028.

Pew Research Center defines the most recent generations in the U.S. as follows:

- **The Millennial Generation (Millennials):** Born 1981 to 1997 – Aged 18 to 34 in 2015.
- **Generation X:** Born 1965 to 1980 – Aged 35 to 50 in 2015.
- **The Baby Boom Generation (Baby Boomers):** Born 1046 to 1964 – Aged 51 to 69 in 2015.
- **The Silent Generation:** Born 1928 to 1945 – Aged 70 to 87 in 2015.
- **The Greatest Generation:** Born before 1928 – Aged 88 to 100 in 2015.

With Millennials surpassing Baby Boomers as the largest generation of workforce aged people in the U.S., employers will have to adjust workplaces and hiring processes to suit the more mobile technology and social media oriented behavior of this generation.

Source: www.pewresearch.org/fact-tank/2016/04/25/millennials-overtake-baby-boomers/

> **You Need To Know**

More about Hiring Juveniles or Others with a "Thin File"

There are certain workers that will have limited information available about them. In other words, their "dossiers" or files may be very thin. That may apply, for example, to young works, especially juveniles, or workers who are new to the United States, or even workers who have left the workforce and are now re-entering.

Hiring young workers or juveniles (a minor below the age of 18 years) presents special problems. Juvenile records are typically not "public records," and criminal records are difficult to acquire unless the juvenile was tried as an adult. In addition, juvenile workers and young workers may not have a significant employment history. Employers, however, can require that they provide at least two letters of recommendation from non-family members or teachers who know them. This procedure helps eliminate those applicants without the initiative to obtain such letters and helps an employer show some due diligence in hiring. Parental consent and state child labor laws are also issues; if an employer is only obtaining public records, verifying past employment information or school attendance, parental consent is probably not required, in the absence of a specific state law. These procedures are not intrusive, and there are FCRA protections. However, if parental consent is available, it does add extra protection.

Using Instant Online Databases for Quick Hiring Decisions

Another trend is the emergence of web pages with the instant background check. These websites offering employers so-called **instant searches** often include the following sample language:

> *Human resource professionals can conduct extensive national pre-employment background checks in real time! Within seconds our system can reveal the following:*

- *Positively identify your candidate.*
- *Validate their SSN's.*
- *Secure all addresses the candidate used for the past 7-15 years.*
- *Reveal their relatives and associates.*
- *Determine if the applicant has been involved in litigation, bankruptcy, or has tax liens.*
- *Confirm property ownership.*
- *Verify the candidate's driver's license information (available in some states).*
- *Scan for any criminal records or sex offender listings.*

Unfortunately, this type of instant search does not provide as much coverage and protection as employers may believe. One reason is because instant databases are supplemental in nature (remember the fact that only 75% of court records are even online). They are best used as a lead generator by screening firms.

Instant results are essentially **data-dumps** based on an automated search through billions of records. Criminal or sexual offender searches are subject to the database problems since a database search is not necessarily complete, up-to-date, or accurate.

Some types of records sold by instant information vendors are not valid predictors of job performance. For example, a search that focuses on finding out if someone has declared bankruptcy could violate a consumer's rights. Consideration of whether a person owns property is not likely to be a valid predictor of job performance and can be discriminatory by creating a disparate impact on certain groups. Obtaining names and addresses of "relatives and associates" could be a violation of discrimination laws and an invasion of privacy.

Employers using information obtained from the instant web background check sites can violate the federal Fair Credit Reporting Act (FCRA) and state and federal discrimination laws, as explained in previous chapters. These instant internet sites can lead an employer to believe that all they need is a credit card to obtain data. The employer must obtain consents, provide authorizations, and abide by the FCRA or face a serious threat of litigation. Many of these internet services are only giving lip service to FCRA requirements, if mentioned at all.

The value and limitations of private databases are examined in detail in Chapter 14. Please refer to that chapter. Below are summaries of two studies and details of a recent court case that may have a great impact on this topic.

Interesting Results from Two Studies

The dangers of using databases are well known and have been documented for a number of years. For example, on April 11, 2004, article in the *Chicago Tribune* featured a story about a University of Maryland Associate Professor of Criminology who ran a test on an online database service. According to the article, Professor Bushway obtained the criminal records of 120 parolees in Virginia and submitted these names to the popular online background check company. According to the article, sixty names came back showing no criminal record. Many other reports were so jumbled that the offenses were tough to pick out. See Chapter 15 for a more detailed explanation of why database searches can miss names.

The same article reported that the *Chicago Tribune* had conducted its own study. The *Tribune* selected an online data service and submitted the names and birthdates of 10 Illinois offenders whose sentences were in the media for crimes ranging from drunken driving and fraud to possession of child pornography. The online statewide search found no criminal records for any of the names. The search flagged only one person as a sex offender but provided little additional useful information.

The source of these articles is http://articles.chicagotribune.com/2004-04-11/news/0404110512_1_background-checks-criminal-records-offenders.

Class Action Settlement Shows Dangers of "Instant" Database Searches

Any firm that sells instant database material directly to employers should follow this case closely since it can have a far ranging impact. See below for an example of a lawsuit against a screening firm settled for millions of dollars concerning instant database searches and also read the section 'FTC Fines Data Broker $800,000 Dollars to Settle Charges of Violating FCRA' in Chapter 3.

$18 Million Dollar Class Action Settlement against Consumer Reporting Agency for Alleged Violations of the Fair Credit Reporting Act with Instant Database Searches

In November of 2013, two units of the same background check company agreed to pay $18 million to settle three proposed class action lawsuits that claimed the company violated the FCRA by failing to take reasonable measures to ensure the accuracy of background check reports provided. The suit alleged the Defendant reported inaccurate criminal data obtained from an "instant" criminal record search without courthouse confirmation and also that there was allegedly no notice to the consumer who was the subject of the search. The suit also alleged that such acts were in violation of the federal Fair Credit Reporting Act (FCRA) that protects consumers from inaccurate or irrelevant information and failed to meet the standard of accuracy and fairness mandated by the FCRA.

Because of the size of the settlement and the importance of the issue, it is educational to review some of the details of the case. The Plaintiff claimed when she applied for a job, the CRA:

- Reported to two different employers that used their "instant" database that the Plaintiff had been arrested and charged with felony offenses in Los Angeles County but failed to report the felony charge had been dismissed and a misdemeanor conviction had been legally expunged;

- Provided her potential employer with outdated, incomplete, and inaccurate information regarding her alleged criminal record;

- Failed to provide timely notice that such information had been reported; and

- Caused Plaintiff to be denied valuable employment opportunities.

Despite the requirements of FCRA, the complaint alleged the CRA:

- Twice failed to notify Plaintiff contemporaneously of the fact that public record information about her was being reported;

- Failed to maintain strict procedures designed to ensure such information was complete and up-to-date; and

- Failed to utilize reasonable procedures to assure maximum possible accuracy of the adverse information it reported to her potential.

The complaint also claimed the CRA failed to ensure accurate and timely reporting of convictions and other consumer information due to a promise of instant results. According to the complaint filed in the Alameda County Superior Court in California:

> *"Some or all of [Defendant's] unlawful conduct is attributable to its promise of "instant" results, which are incompatible with the accuracy requirements imposed on credit reporting agencies by the FCRA. Plaintiff is informed and believes, and on that basis alleges, that rather than conducting an individualized investigation of a consumer's criminal record at the time a background check is requested, [Defendant] responds to its employer clients' requests on the basis of information collected in internal databases. This information does not and by definition it cannot include the most timely and accurate information, as the FCRA requires."*

The complaint noted that individuals with criminal records have difficulties getting employment, and rehabilitation is even more difficult when expunged criminal records are "illegally and incorrectly reported."

The complaint indicated that because of the impact of the CRA's wrongful practices, the Plaintiff is suing on behalf of consumers throughout the country who have been the subject of similar prejudicial, misleading, and inaccurate background check reports prepared by the Defendant. Since the suit alleges that the CRA's non-compliance was willful, the Plaintiff and class members are entitled to statutory damages provided by the FCRA. Under FCRA section 616, the potential penalties for willful noncompliance can be $100 to $1,000 per victim plus attorney's fees and punitive damages.

The case was brought on behalf of JANE ROE, individually and on behalf of all others similarly situated, Alameda County (CA) Superior Court, Case No: RG12625923. The Attorneys for the Plaintiff JANE ROE and the Proposed Class are Nance F. Becker and Christian Schreiber of Chavez & Gertler LLP in Mill Valley, CA; Devin H. Fok of The Law Offices of Devin H. Fok in Alhambra, CA; and Joshua E. Kim of A New Way of Life Reentry Project in Los Angeles, CA.

Keep in mind that a settlement is not an admission of wrongdoing. For more information about the settlement, please visit *https://topclassactions.com/lawsuit-settlements/lawsuit-news/5437-background-check-firms-agree-to-18m-class-action-settlement/*.

A background screening firm has separate obligations under the FCRA when reporting criminal records. First, as a general rule under section 607(b), a background screening firm "shall follow reasonable procedures to assure maximum possible accuracy of the information concerning the individual about whom the report relates."

In addition, if there is a criminal record likely to adversely impact employment, FCRA Section 613 requires that the background screening firm shall:

- At the time such public record information is reported to the user of such consumer report, notify the consumer of the fact that public record information is being reported by the consumer reporting agency, together with the name and address of the person to whom such information is being reported; or

- Maintain strict procedures designed to insure that whenever public record information which is likely to have an adverse effect on a consumer's ability to obtain employment is reported it is complete and up to date. For purposes of this paragraph, items of public record relating to arrests, indictments, convictions, suits, tax liens, and outstanding judgments shall be considered up to date if the current public record status of the item at the time of the report is reported.

The impact is that the background screening firm can send a letter notice if criminal information is reported to an employer. However, even with a letter, use of a database may not meet the general obligation of "reasonable procedures" if the database had stale information that was not updated.

It appears that the single biggest source of allegations of inaccurate records comes from reporting database results directly to the end-user employer without taking steps to ensure the record is complete, accurate, and up-to-date and belongs to the consumer. However, a great many screening firms do not report database hits directly until the information is confirmed.

The fallout from reporting inaccurate criminal database information to an employer potentially creates a risk to the whole screening industry. The tremendous value of databases as a research tool is well recognized, but if CRAs provide incomplete or inaccurate data directly to employers without vetting, it may well eventually cause a legislative over-reaction.

FCRA section 613 does allow the so-called 'letter-notice' option, but that needs to be read in conjunction with FCRA Section 607(b) that mandates "reasonable procedures for maximum possible accuracy." Although the 613 letter option is part of the law, a CRA cannot ignore the general duty to proceed with reasonable procedures, which can mean that using a database that is inherently flawed by a failure to update, can potentially result in an FCRA violation even if a letter notice is sent.

The bottom line is that the 613 letter option does not open the floodgates to allow a CRA to report anything that comes up in a database as long as a letter is sent to the consumer. If a CRA knows or reasonably should know for example, that a database is not updated, and reports it anyways, that could potentially be a violation of 607(b) even if a letter is sent.

In summary, employers need to be very careful about using online instant data brokers. Not only can there be issues with the accuracy, completeness, and applicability of the data, but there are also a number of FCRA, discrimination, and privacy considerations.

Special Issues When Hiring in a Labor Shortage

Although the *Employment Situation Report* for November of 2016 released by the U.S. Department of Labor's Bureau of Labor Statistics found the unemployment rate in the United States had decreased by 0.3 percentage points to 4.6 percent—the lowest since 2007 before the Great Recession—the real story is that there is a worker shortage, especially for jobs requiring higher education or advanced skills.

According to the *2016-2017 Talent Shortage Survey* from ManpowerGroup, employers around the world are facing the largest talent shortage since the Great Recession as 40 percent of global employers have experienced difficulties filling jobs – the highest level since 41 percent in 2007. For more details on talent shortage problems around the world, visit www.manpowergroup.com/talentshortage.

With this shortage now occurring, the pressure on employers and recruiters to fill positions is much greater. Some employers may be concerned that delaying a new hire to wait for a background report could result in a good candidate being hired elsewhere. However, when employers and recruiters become less selective and take a gamble, they can end up with new hires they may wish they could have avoided. During a labor shortage an employer may wish to consider the following guidelines:

- Resist the temptation to hire as fast as possible. Do not dispense with the fundamentals of a Safe Hiring Program. Shortcuts in hiring can come back to haunt the firm, the recruit, and the hiring manager in the future.
- Understand that if a firm makes a bad hire, the "perceived need for speed" will likely not make much of an impact in front of a jury if the employer is sued.

- If time is of the essence, then make sure the no-cost suggestions made in this book about Applicant/Interview/Reference (AIR Process) checking practices are followed. This helps to minimize problematic hires.
- If the situation demands the applicant be hired without delay, then be certain to provide a written offer letter stating the new hire is conditional based upon receipt of a background report that is satisfactory to the employer.
- Implement ban-the-box and make certain that if a candidate is eliminated due to a criminal record, there is a sound job related reason. Otherwise, an employer may be unnecessarily eliminating qualified and needed applicants.

Special Issues with Safe Hiring and Job Boards

Although it is debated how many job seekers actually find employment from online services, there is no question that millions of Americans use the internet to look for job opportunities. Some of the websites most visited by job seekers looking for work online currently include the list below. Indeed, the world's largest job search site as of February 2012, had 60 million monthly unique visitors and one billion job searches. (Source: http://articles.businessinsider.com/2012-02-21/tech/31081848_1_indeed-com-job-mobile-app.)

Popular Online Job Websites

Online Job Website	Web Address
Indeed	www.indeed.com
CareerBuilder	www.careerbuilder.com
Monster.com	www.monster.com
Simply Hired	www.simplyhired.com
LinkedIn	www.linkedin.com
Craigslist	www.craigslist.com

Understanding the Job Board and Recruitment World

There are a number of useful websites that assemble, categorize, and analyze the various job boards, including recruiting and employment-related sites on the internet. Peter Weddles is a veteran of the online job world. He publishes guides to employment websites for recruiters and job seekers. His recruiting guide has data on over 40,000 career-related sites. See www.weddles.com. Another service is offered by CareerXroads, publisher of a yearly book that reviews job and employment-related sites. See www.careerxroads.com. The leading cyberspace resource to follow major developments in the online employment scene, as well as HR Technolgy, is www.hrexaminer.com. This website offers information for the recruiting industry from John Sumser, who is widely considered the leading source of analysis for the electronic recruiting industry.

Verification of Resumes Found on Job Boards

One difficulty with the millions of resumes on job boards is verification. Resumes are not verified by a trusted third party. Although numerous job boards claim they "screen" candidates, the use of the word "screened" in the job board context is typically a process used to perform some sort of preliminary evaluation of candidate qualifications, at least on cyber-paper. The purpose is to eliminate unqualified candidates and guide employers to candidates more likely qualified. The catch is that job board screening tools are based on the premise that what people say about themselves is true.

Author Tip > **Use of Word "Screened" On Job Boards**

Do not be confused by the use of the word **screened** on job boards. Unless the employer knows for a fact the screening included safe hiring steps and verifiable background screening, the employer must take the same steps with job board candidates as they would with any other. Using proper safe hiring steps will also keep you in compliance with equal opportunity laws.

If job boards independently verified facts on resumes, it would be immensely valuable. Employers could hire with a great deal more accuracy and confidence.

Consequently, the value of job boards is only as a tool for employers and job seekers to find each other in the first place. Job boards, from the smallest local niche board to the biggest boards, are still essentially the electronic equivalent of a local supermarket bulletin board or the want ads in the newspaper. Using a job board does not relieve an employer of their safe hiring obligations—employers still have the same legal duty to exercise due diligence regardless of the source of the candidate.

Special Issues with Safe Hiring and Recruiters

Recruiters are a source of applicants for employers. Recruiters are called upon to find highly qualified candidates appropriate for a particular job description. Employers use recruiters to economically and quickly find applicants interested in long-term job situations. Recruiters find applicants from a number of different venues, from job boards to cold calling to networking. Recruiters can be independent or work for a particular employer on an in-house basis.

The fees and reputations of independent recruiters and recruiting firms depend largely on the qualifications of the candidates they present. Although some recruiters may do some past employment checks themselves, the act of recruiters doing pre-employment screening before presenting candidates does not appear to be a widespread practice. When balancing the relatively low cost of a screening report with the fees a recruiter can receive with the negative impact of just one bad candidate, it would seem to be an ideal due diligence service to have recruiters make a practice of screening all candidates.

Under the Fair Credit Reporting Act, there is no barrier to a recruiter obtaining a background report. A recruiter will need to follow the FCRA in terms of obtaining written authorization and providing the candidate with a disclosure of their rights. A screening firm can provide the necessary documents to the recruiter. There are two special considerations:

- In the release form for a background screening, the recruiter should add a provision indicating the candidate also releases the information to an employer who may wish to view the report. This allows the recruiter to share the background report with a potential employer.
- There are restrictions in obtaining credit reports. The recruiter is not the end user of credit reports, and the credit bureaus require the actual end-user be identified and to show a permissible purpose. However, consistent with the FCRA and state law, recruiters can obtain other basic screening tools such as checking past employment or education or searching for criminal records.

In-house recruiters have different issues. Hiring managers will typically assign an in-house recruiter to fill a certain number of job positions. While the Human Resources or security department dictates the safe hiring protocol for the employer—the background screening process that the firm may use—in-house recruiters typically are under pressure to complete the hiring quickly. As discussed in previous chapters, the process used for background screening usually takes up to three days. For large firms, even a one-day delay can have an impact since many employers have a pre-set new employee orientation schedule. If a new hire misses the start date, then the new hire may have to wait a week or more before the next new employee classes begin.

In-house recruiters can help speed up the process in several ways:

- First, if paper forms are still being used, the recruiter must understand the process can be delayed if screening firms are sent incomplete information or forms that are not legible or completely filled out. Screening firms often face difficulty in deciphering an application in order to identify and locate past employers, but having a recruiter review and correct all candidates' applications before sending those applications to a screening firm will help eliminate delays. This is simply a good practice for any employer or recruiter.

- Second, if a recruiter is working with a screening firm that has an online ordering system, the process is considerably faster and with greater accuracy. Even faster is new technology that allows a seamless and paperless integration between an Applicant Tracking System (ATS) and a background screening firm. However, there may be times when additional information is needed from the applicant. This can occur if there is difficulty locating a past employer, or if there is an international check that requires additional forms or information. If past employment cannot be verified, the recruiters may need to contact the applicant and ask for things such as W-2s, or names of past supervisors. It is imperative for a recruiter or HR to work with screening firms to facilitate the process.

- Third, an in-house recruiter needs to communicate with hiring managers so there are not unrealistic expectations. A hiring manager may not understand, for example, that criminal records are searched at each relevant courthouse or that delays can occur if there is a potential match that needs to be verified. Hiring managers must also be advised that employment and education verifications can be delayed for all the reasons discussed in Chapters 4 and 12. If there is a delay in receiving a completed screening report, the recruiter should examine the source of the delay.

Finally, there are times when a recruiter may determine that even though the screening firm has not been successful in obtaining all of the information, enough data is available to make a hiring decision. Typically, delays happen when verifying previous employment, and past employment oldest in time is the most difficult to obtain, though the oldest employment may be the least relevant. If the applicant, for example, worked in a fast food restaurant six years ago after getting out of school, and the fast food place will not call back, then there may be no reason to delay the hiring decision if the screening firm has obtained the most recent and presumably more relevant job verifications.

You Need To Know

Should a Background Firm be Asked to Deal Directly with Applicants?

Some employers or recruiters request that background firms contact an applicant directly if there is a need to obtain additional information or to clarify information from an applicant. There are some recruiters who ask their background firm to perform this service, even though it is the recruiter that has the most knowledge about the applicant and has direct contact. If this has ever crossed your mind as an employer or recruiter, you might want to reconsider.

Screening professionals often recommend against having background firms getting in the middle of the special relationship between the Recruiter and the Applicant. It creates confusion, causes delays, and brings a background screening firm into discussions with the applicant who may not even realize that a third party is involved. Background checks actually go much faster when the recruiter exclusively manages the direct applicant relationship and obtains additional information when needed.

There are a number of complications that arise if the screening firm attempts to contact the applicant:

- The applicant does not know the background firm and is naturally reluctant to supply a Social Security Number or date of birth to a stranger over the phone or send pay stubs to someone they do not know. That typically means the applicant will normally call the recruiter first anyway to find out what the situation is all about, which, of course, delays the screening process further.

- Second, the background firm often has to engage in phone tag, requiring back and forth before the screening firm can connect with the applicant. Since the applicant has no relationship with the screening firm, an applicant does not always realize it is important to call back, especially if the applicant is looking at several different job offers. On the other hand, if a recruiter is in hot pursuit of an applicant, or the applicant is focused on getting the job, it is likely that the recruiter will have a great deal less difficulty getting in touch with him/her to obtain the additional information or clarification.

- The third issue is tracking. The screening firm needs to track the status of the additional calls to the applicants and to deal with multiple applicants instead of a single point of contact. Recruiters presumably already have an ATS or some other system to keep tabs on the progress of each job and each finalist (since typically only a finalist is getting screened).

- The last and most important issue is when a screening firm calls the applicant, that applicant may now believe that the background firm is somehow involved in the hiring decision. There have been applicants who have wanted to continue selling themselves to a background firm's clerical employee, whose only mission was to obtain some missing information and who knows nothing about the job. Or, if the applicant somehow feels that background employee did not give them the attention he or she deserved, the applicant may be left with a negative impression of the potential employer or complain about the contact.

For these reasons, many background firms typically prefer not to get themselves in the middle of the relationship between the recruiter and the applicant.

Author Tip ⟩ **Employment Kiosks Mostly Replaced by Mobile Devices**

The previous edition of "The Safe Hiring Manual" contained a section on employment kiosks – small, mobile, ATM type devices that job seekers used to apply online. Most of these kiosks have been replaced by "smart" mobile devices such as cell phones and pads.

Electronic Signatures and Applicant Consents

A source of frustration for recruiters in the hiring process is obtaining the paperwork necessary for the background check and then entering data into an online screening system. Typically, recruiters struggle to obtain a "wet signature," meaning that they need to have the applicant sign an actual piece of paper containing the background consent and disclosure, and physically get that to the screening firm. If the recruiter utilizes an online background screening system, then the data must be entered in the background firm's system.

However, by using electronic signatures with the latest technology, sophisticated background firms can now offer "paperless" online background checking systems, where the applicant fills out the online information and signs an online consent.

On the state level, 47 states have adopted the **Uniform Electronic Transactions Act (UETA)**. This was a uniform standard formatted by the National Conference of Commissioners on Uniform State Laws (NCCUSL). The goal was to create uniform state rules that address issues related to electronic contracts and electronic agreement. Through these laws, a traditional "wet signature" where the applicant physically signs a piece of paper is replaced by an electronic signature.

To ensure such a process is permissible nationwide, a federal law was enacted on June 30, 2000, that went into effect in October 2000 called the **Electronic Signatures in Global and National Commerce Act (ESIGN)**. Section 101(a) of the act provides that:

> "(a) . . . Notwithstanding any statute, regulation, or other rule of law (other than this title and title II), with respect to any transaction in or affecting interstate or foreign commerce
>
> (1) a signature, contract, or other record relating to such transaction may not be denied legal effect, validity, or enforceability solely because it is in electronic form…"

The practical impact of the two laws is that electronic signatures can be used in all 50 states and the District of Columbia (DC). The subject of which law, ESIGN or UETA, applies to which transaction can get complicated at times. As a general proposition, the federal ESIGN law governs in the absence of a state law or where states have made modifications to UETA that are inconsistent with ESIGN. New York, Illinois, and Washington are the states with their own statutory schemes.

Electronic Signatures and the FTC

The Federal Trade Commission initially took the position that a mouse click was insufficient to meet the standards of the Fair Credit Reporting Act (FCRA) when written consent is required. (See the *Landever letter*, issued October 12, 1999, at www.ftc.gov/policy/advisory-opinions/advisory-opinion-landever-10-12-99.)

FCRA Section 604(b)(2)(A)(ii) specifically requires that:

> "the consumer has authorized in writing (which authorization may be made on the document referred to in clause (i)) the procurement of the report by that person."

The FTC revisited the issue of electronic authorization in the *Zalenski letter* issued May 24, 2001, after the passage of the federal ESIGN law

The FTC concluded that in view of the ESIGN Act, it was possible to use electronic signatures for authorization for a background check. After reviewing the statutes, the FTC stated that:

> Therefore, electronic signatures, contracts, or other records relating to transactions are not unenforceable or invalid solely based on their electronic format. Moreover, with respect to the reach of this provision, under Section 106(13) of the ESIGN Act, the term "transaction" is defined as "an action or set of actions relating to the conduct of business, consumer, or commercial affairs between two or more persons . . ." This broad definition of "transaction" appears to include the scenario described in the letter where a business that needs a consumer report on an individual includes in a contract or application form clear authorization by the individual to obtain his or her consumer report. Thus, under the ESIGN Act, a consumer's electronic authorization may not be denied legal effect solely based on its electronic nature.

The FTC also indicated that whether or not the electronic signature is valid depends on the specific facts of each situation. Specifically:

- The electronic signature must clearly convey the consumer's instructions.

- The FTC stated that as specified by Section 101(e) of the ESIGN Act, that consumer's electronic authorization "must be in a form that can be retained and retrieved in perceivable form." In other words, there must be a clear and reproducible record showing the electronic consent.

To view the *Zalenski letter*, visit: www.ftc.gov/policy/advisory-opinions/advisory-opinion-zalenski-05-24-01.

Best Practices on Electronic Signatures

In legal terms, the concept of authorization or consent means "an agreement to do something" or to "allow something to happen," and made voluntarily with complete knowledge of all relevant facts such as the risks involved or any available alternatives.

Neither ESIGN nor UETA provide any specifically required wording or specifies exact steps or process that automatically validates the electronic signature procedure. However, the laws do provide a framework for the use of electronic signatures and records in government or business transactions. This framework gives employers and screening firm a basis to design legally complaint procedures for electric online signatures. In addition, since some background screening authorizations carry state law requirements, it is arguable that both federal and state rules must be considered.

Based upon a reading of ESIGN and UETA, some of the best practice steps should include provisions such as the following:

- Notice of and agreement to an electronic transaction.
- Paper based alternative made available to those who decline the electronic transaction.
- Method to determine an electronic signature is attributable to a specific person.
- Method to correct errors before signing.
- Method for subject to print or store the electronic record.
- A clear explanation of what is being consented to.
- An option to discontinue the process at each step and before final agreement.
- Clear instructions on how to withdraw consent in the future.

If the electronic signature is done by mouse click, a potential issue is created when a past school or employer requests an actual signed document. A screening firm may have to track down the applicant and ask for a written release. Another option is to provide the past employer or school with sufficient assurances that there was an electronic release. However, an organization is not legally required to accept an electronic signature.

New technology, however, allows a screening firm to capture an actual signature by use of a mouse or other software, making the whole process paperless. If requested, the screening firm can forward an actual although electronically produced signature.

Additional Links

- Information on UETA: http://uniformlaws.org/Act.aspx?title=Electronic%20Transactions%20Act
- Test of ESIGN: www.gpo.gov/fdsys/pkg/PLAW-106publ229/html/PLAW-106publ229.htm

Some Notable Background Check Trends

Here is information on background check trends such as applicant experience and employer branding, ATS integration reviews, screening industry consolidation, *disruptive* HR technology, and Background Check API.

Since employers are concerned with employer branding and the applicant experience, the background check process will focus on making the applicant experience as comfortable as possible as well as assuring applicants that their background checks are accurate, legally compliant, and their privacy rights are protected.

As part of the war for talent, employer branding is critical and that extends to all interactions between potential applicants and the employer including the background check process. That requires a background check process that is easy and intuitive. If an applicant has any difficulties navigating the background check software, live in-person help should be readily available. In addition, consumers need to be made aware that their privacy and legal rights are protected and that a background check firm uses best practices to obtain accurate and timely information. If there is a dispute, the background check firm will provide the applicant top notch customer service and assistance. A good background check firm treats consumers just as they would treat a client because the background check firm has a duty to protect consumers.

Employers need to recognize the importance of the applicant experience during the background check process in relation to their employer brand. To create an ideal applicant experience first requires transparency with background check policies and practices. Since a background check can be an uncomfortable process for applicants, employers should explain what searches will be performed. The background check release form should be easy to read and explain the process while providing contact information if the applicant has questions. Having applicants fill out their own data using an Applicant Generated Report (AGR) system will also give them more control over the background check process.

It is important for applicants to understand their rights during the background check process under the federal Fair Credit Reporting Act (FCRA), which promotes the accuracy, fairness, and privacy of information in a background check report. Information about applicant rights during a background check is in a form titled 'A Summary of Your Rights Under the Fair Credit Reporting Act' from the Consumer Financial Protection Bureau (CFPB). In addition, Employment Screening Resources® (ESR) offers an Applicant Resources page available at www.esrcheck.com/Resource-Center/Applicant-Resources/.

ATS Operators Will Review Integrations with Screening Partners for Legal Risks

Applicant Tracking System (ATS) operators will review ATS integrations with their background screening partners to address emerging legal risks involving areas such as data breaches and litigation over consent forms in previously accepted processes and revise those integrations accordingly.

There are a large number of ATS and background screening choices in the marketplace today. Because of the complexities in both areas, employers and HR professions are getting an understanding that they are better served where the ATS and the screening firm have a tight integration and close relationship as opposed to using systems that just exchange data with anyone and do not account for the many complexities and legal issues involved in hiring. Although plug and play is a useful model in many areas, it may not serve employers well when it comes to regulated and litigated areas like hiring.

An ATS is defined as a software application that enables the electronic handling of recruitment needs that can be implemented or accessed online and is designed for recruitment tracking. An ATS can filter applications automatically using criteria such as keywords, skills, former employers, years of experience, and schools attended. Almost all recruitment agencies and most major corporations with an in-house recruitment function use some form of an ATS to handle job postings, applicants, resumes, and interviews.

There has been a trend towards more sophisticated ATS integration of workflow that includes two way data transfers so that a background check can be ordered and status updates can be returned at the click of a mouse. However, with the dramatic growth of class action lawsuits over alleged violations of the federal Fair Credit Reporting Act (FCRA) and well documented instances of data breaches reported in the news, many ATS operators are beginning to realize that:

- ATS operators do not want to control or have responsibility over the applicant consent forms. Some systems try to have the applicant consent on the platform and that is an unnecessary risk.
- ATS operators do not want to house background screening data due to data breach issues.
- ATS operators do not want to be a party to the background check in order to avoid any possible applicant form reports that are alleged to have errors.
- ATS operators should only facilitate communications between an employer and a background screening firm but stay out of the process as much as possible.

- ATS operators are rethinking who is in charge of the forms used for background checks and who stores the data used for background checks.

For these reasons, it is important for both ATS firms and employers to choose their background screening partners carefully in order to maximize accuracy and legal compliance to and to minimize risk.

Background Check Industry Will Continue to Expand and Consolidate Simultaneously

Judging by the number of background check firms being bought and sold in the past few years and the number of new start-ups entering the background check business, the screening industry will continue to both expand and consolidate simultaneously. It is easy to see why so many people are interested. According to industry estimates, the background screening business is a multi-billion dollar sector that is expected to grow over the next 10-15 years.

With the growing economy and tight competition, larger firms are showing a renewed emphasis on attempting to acquire market share by mergers and acquisitions. At the same time, new entrants with a business or technology background see screening as merely moving around data and figure how hard can that be. There are also firms and investors in the human capital space that see screening as an easy adjunct to what they are already doing. Since there are few barriers to entry and nearly anyone can call themselves a screening firm, new firms will continue to pop-up. However, these late entries into the background check industry may incorrectly assume that they are only data brokers aggregating information instead of needing strict legal compliance with the myriad of background check laws. In addition, many organizations that are considering entering the screening market are surprised at not only the complexity and laws surrounding the process, but also the explosion in class action lawsuits regarding the federal Fair Credit Reporting Act (FCRA) and governmental enforcement from the Consumer Financial Protection Bureau (CFPB) and the U.S. Equal Employment Opportunity Commission (EEOC).

The problem with both the acquisition of firms by larger players and new entrants into the market is that background screening is not about just providing raw data, but is a professional service that is heavily regulated by lawsuits, government regulation and supervision, and new legislation every year. Employers rightfully expect a high level of customer service and accuracy, as well as domain and compliance expertise, from a background check provider.

This trend should be a cause for concern for employers. When an HR service provider is acquired by a larger player, employers may find that over time that they are dealing with new people, technology, and processes and the results can be mixed. Essentially, when an employer's account is bought and sold, there is no guarantee that the services, expertise, compliance, and protection will remain the same. Employers have an obligation to ensure that they are getting the benefit of the services they contracted for.

HR Will Be Bombarded with Marketing Buzz around New "Disruptive Technology"

Employers and Human Resources (HR) professionals will be bombarded with meaningless marketing buzz offering new "disruptive technology" that promises to disrupt stodgy old industries and radically change outdated business models. However, these new techniques may largely be without substance.

It's popular these days for start-ups worldwide to claim they are disrupting dormant industries and are radically changing outdated old business models, including Human Resources processes such as pre-employment background checks. However, it is important to really understand if an HR disrupter is really just an outstanding marketer who has convinced investors that they have done something new instead of just taking old processes and repackaging them with a pretty new bow.

Marketing "buzz" can be real in the sense that perception can trump reality. For example, in the HR space there are firms that have done the equivalent of taking a number two pencil and claiming they have re-invented and disrupted a dormant industry by putting the eraser on the other end. In other words, HR professionals need to be on the alert for HR and background check solutions that come packaged as disruptive but, in fact, do not really accomplish anything new.

Much of this buzz is coming from the so-called "gig economy" that focuses on temporary work, or "gigs," where people run errands for other people such as driving, walking dogs, cleaning rooms, doing laundry, cooking dinner, or shopping for food. As one commenter put it, the gig economy does everything your mom use to do for you when you lived at home. It's not just transportation applications or house sharing services but numerous websites and apps where people advertise their part-time services.

The problem with applying this part-time economy approach in HR technology—especially in the background check process—is that background checks are closer to rocket science in terms of its sheer complexity than simply data retrieval and distribution. Background check laws are constantly subject to legislation, regulation, and litigation. Along with the federal Fair Credit Reporting Act (FCRA), there are laws for all 50 states and Equal Employment Opportunity Commission (EEOC) guidance on using criminal records.

Although HR processes like background checks may be attractive to the technology sector since it appears on the surface to simply involve slicing and dicing data, in fact, it is all about domain expertise, accuracy, and legal compliance is the name of the game in the background check industry nowadays.

There is nothing new about this technology but some tech firms claim they are revolutionizing the background check process when they are in fact doing the same thing numerous firms have done as early as 2008. Many firms have long utilized an API (Application Program Interface), including a Representation State Transfer (RESTful) API, to connect with partners and employers. That is old hat in the background screening industry. It is just technology placed on top of processes that must occur to do professional screening. The real question is how technology promotes legal compliance, accuracy, and streamlines the process.

JSON/Background Check API

A Background Check API (Application Program Interface) uses Representational State Transfer (REST) software architecture to build online background check services that deliver: Performance, Reliability, Scalability, Simplicity, and Visibility.

A Background Check API uses JavaScript Object Notation (JSON) Order Import service that is a simple REST service endpoint created for initiating and querying background check orders. This import service is:

- Based on JSON standards as recommended by Internet Engineering Task Force (IETF),
- A RESTful resource using standard request/response Hypertext Transfer Protocol (HTTP) headers, and
- Secure running over SSL (Secure Sockets Layer).

A Background Check API integration is quick and easy and gives total access to background check products fully compliant with the federal Fair Credit Reporting Act (FCRA). A competent background firm will have the ability to provide an API or wire to one.

Top Ten Background Check Trends

Each year for the past decade, the author has selected the annual **ESR Top Ten Background Check Trends** that feature emerging and influential trends in the screening industry.

Below is a listing of the **Top Ten Background Check Trends for 2017**:

1. Ban the Box Will Become More the Rule than Exception when Background Screening Workers
2. Re-Entry Programs Will Increase as Employers Discover Ex-Offenders Make Good Employees
3. Financial Institutions Will Seek Stronger Security Measures Such as SOC 2 Reports from Screening Partners
4. New Gig Economy Will Force Employers to Strengthen Screening of Growing On Demand Workforce
5. Continuous Screening of Employees Will Gain More Acceptance as Critical Post-Hire Due Diligence Tool
6. HR Technology Advancements Will Continue to Improve Background Screening in the Hiring Process
7. Millennials in Workforce Will Make Employers Change Methods of Background Screening Job Applicants

8. FCRA Lawsuits Will Remain a Potential Threat to Employers After Supreme Court Decision in Spokeo Case
9. Drug Testing in Workplace Will Have to Deal with Growth of State Laws Allowing Use of Marijuana
10. Use of Big Data for Background Checks Will Be Closely Watched for Potential Discrimination Issues

Bonus Trends

11. Global Screening Will Have to Adapt to EU-US Privacy Shield and Worldwide Talent Shortage
12. Trump Administration Will Bring Changes to Employment Eligibility Verification Process Including E-Verify

Here are the Top Ten Background Check Trends for 2016:

1. Government Oversight and Enforcement of Accuracy in Background Check Industry to Increase in 2016
2. FCRA Lawsuits Will Continue to Increase in Target Rich Background Screening Environment in 2016
3. Background Check Industry Will Continue to Both Expand and Consolidate Simultaneously in 2016
4. Employers and Human Resources Will Be Bombarded with Meaningless Marketing Buzz around Supposed Disruptive Technology in 2016
5. Background Screening Firms, Human Resources, and Employers Will Be Focused on Legal Compliance and Accuracy in 2016
6. Domestic Terrorist Attacks Will Put Social Media Background Checks in the National Spotlight in 2016
7. Ban-the-Box Movement May Reach Tipping Point But Could Also Inadvertently Do More Harm than Good in 2016
8. Applicant Tracking Solutions Will Review ATS Integrations with Screening Partners to Address Emerging Legal Risks in 2016
9. Job Opportunities for Ex-Offenders with Criminal Records Should Increase in 2016
10. Privacy Concerns Will Loom Large Between EU and US in Terms of International Background Checks in 2016

Read more at: www.esrcheck.com/wordpress/2016/01/04/employment-screening-resources-releases-top-ten-background-check-trends-for-2016/.

Candidates Presenting Their Own Verified Credentials

A new development is the concept of applicants proving their own credentials. A candidate self-credentialing website permits applicants to purchase a verified screening report.

One of the first websites to offer this service was MyJobHistory.com – now called MyESRcheck.com. Since the site was introduced, similar services have become available. Some job boards also provide such services through partners. The value of such a site is to help employers sort through a sea of resumes and focus on those candidates who are willing to have their qualifications scrutinized.

Even if an employer hires an applicant that has a verification statement from such a website, an employer should still conduct whatever due diligence they normally perform — to take their normal steps to make sure a person is a good fit for the job and organization, including conducting a criminal record check. That ensures that an employer is testing all applicants in a similar manner, and that there is consistency across the organization.

Applicant-supplied criminal checks create a number of potential issues. First, the employer should decide where to conduct the search and how extensive it should be, not an applicant. An applicant with a criminal record may well decide to not request a criminal record check for that specific jurisdiction. Second, a criminal search is only good up until the day it is conducted. When an applicant supplies the criminal search, there is no way to know if the data is still current.

One website attempts to remedy that by only making the search available for ninety days. However, that still does not address the issue of applicants providing their own report, creating the potential for an applicant to hide his or her past. Another website provides a so-called "national database" search. However, for the reasons reviewed in that chapter, such a search is only a secondary research tool and not a true criminal search.

There is one additional note of caution— an employer should not place a condition for employment upon the job seeker to pay for such a report. Such a policy could be construed as discriminatory. In addition, charging an application fee may violate state law. For example, California Labor Code 450 can make it a criminal act to require an application fee.

Looking Toward the Future – Background Screening and the Creation of a Human Capital Database

In the first edition of this book in 2004, the author predicted that the future of hiring may well involve the creation of large human capital databases that have a great deal of information about consumers, as well as employers and work opportunities to essentially enable jsut in time employment. An essential part of such a database would be the verified credentials of each worker. Although such a database did not exist in 2004 and still does not exist today, there are firms that are starting to take on such a task. With the advent of big data and the explosion of information on the internet, firms are beginning to attempt such databases. There is new technology being developed around discovering a consumer's cyber footprint and to use big data mining techniques to develop profiles and estimates as to trustworthiness or certain skills. Of course, not all segments of the workforce necessarily have a social media footprint.

The big idea is that in a world of perfect and available information about both work opportunities and the skills and qualifications of applicants, employers and workers could find each other instantly. There would be a true labor market, where market forces would operate in such a way to instantly match the right person with right job at the right time, with a minimum of delay or transaction costs. There would essentially be a "just in time" system of employment.

From the point of view of a consumer, life would be good if he or she could simply register their unique "profile," and instantly find the perfect match at the right location and compensation. Ideally, a consumer could use their "smart" mobile device anytime to be automatically be matched with the next ideal assignment. The assignment may or not be a traditional employment. It could be some other type of relationship, such as an independent contractor assignment or a consulting assignment.

The ideal situation for an employer would be to visit a website, put in an applicant's name and Social Security number, and instantly get a thumb up or thumbs down—to hire or not to hire. Or in the alternative, a computer application can make the judgment as to fit, and credentials based upon all the known data about an applicant obtained from numerous sources. In this brave new world, is been suggested that applicants can even have a "safety" score similar to a credit score, using algorithms, known information, and data mining to evaluate a consumer's credentials, fit, honesty, and safety.

Of course, background screening is only one part of such a database. Additional applicant information would be needed, including data as to job fit. Verification of credentials and information about a criminal record would certainly be a major component of any such database.

The future of safe hiring may well involve the creation of these large human capital databases, offering the ability to use information intelligently and fairly. However, all sorts of issues arise from building a human capital database, including how to score, model, profile, and predict without discriminating. Equally important is privacy and the ability of a consumer to fairly access, control, and contest what is in the database. There are also issues as to accuracy, especially when it comes to criminal records, and, of course, numerous legal compliance challenges. However, in the long run, there are efforts underway towards creating massive databases to facilitate employment as well as technology to enable the labor market to operate much more efficiently.

CHAPTER 21

Dealing With Fraud, Embezzlement, and Integrity

Screening for Honesty and Morality

Corporate fraud and dishonesty have been major news topics in recent years. The media has focused on a variety of stories ranging from corporations "cooking the books" and being dishonest to investors to the resume fibs of underachieving sports coaches. These stories all have one thing in common—applicants either lied to get their position or committed acts of dishonesty in the job, or employers were lax about hiring or exercising sound controls over unethical behavior.

It does not happen in just small firms either. In September 2016, Wells Fargo, a major national financial institution, fired nearly 5,300 employees over allegations they created over 1.5 million unauthorized checking and savings accounts and 500,000 unauthorized credit cards since 2011 resulting in an estimated $2.6 million in unauthorized fees for the bank. Those actions allegedly caused by an incentive-compensation program for employees to create new accounts resulted in the Consumer Financial Protection Bureau (CFPB) issuing Wells Fargo $100 million in fines, along with $50 million in fines from the City and County of Los Angeles, and $35 million in fines from the Office of Comptroller of the Currency for a combined total of $185 million in fines. See: https://en.wikipedia.org/wiki/Wells_Fargo#Consumer_Financial_Protection_Bureau_fines.

How do firms hire honest employees? How do organizations stay on an ethical course? Unfortunately, honesty, ethics, and morality are not easy traits to screen. There is no magic scanning machine that can read an applicant's soul or heart, or the synapses of the brain, declaring that an honest person is applying. Most often, in the hiring process, a firm is only able to look for manifestations of past or current dishonesty. These can include:

- Casting oneself in a false light by submitting an application that contains material lies or omissions. It is estimated from various sources that up to one out of three applications and resumes contain material falsehoods or omissions, typically involving past education or employment.
- Lying in an interview, as discussed in Chapter 8.
- Having committed a criminal act which demonstrates dishonesty or a willingness to commit fraud or some other act of moral turpitude, or such an act that results in a civil lawsuit.

An additional complication is the very nature of honesty itself. For example, an applicant may be the type of person who tells a socially polite "little white lie," e.g. "that was delicious, but I am full" when the meal did not taste very good. However, no one would suggest this person is dishonest for purposes of employment.

The bigger issue is predicting future behavior. Honesty has multiple dimensions. One issue is "what standards and moral values does a person have and to what level are they ingrained in a person?" The past is often prologue. If a person had been honest in the past or is being honest now, then there is a very good chance he or she will continue to be honest in the future. Will an employer be able to predict what guides a person's moral compass in the future under a variety of temptations? Some situations can be predicted since they are part of the job.

For example, a bookkeeper will have access to assets and money. Can the new hire with no drug abuse history resist sampling the products at the pharmaceutical warehouse? Other situations cannot be predicted. In the future, a person may undergo sudden life changes or stress that may tempt dishonesty, or a supervisor may ask an employee to participate in a questionable act, such as document shredding—an act with an element of coercion or an implicit threat they would lose their job if they do not cooperate. Or, in the case of a situation like Wells Fargo, a culture develops where shortcuts are not only permitted but potentially even encouraged or rewarded. Part of the complication is to discover ahead of time how a person may react when ordered to do something dishonest.

How does an employer know in advance if applicants will be influenced towards dishonesty if put into a situation where they feel an element of coercion if they do not go along or are tempted by greed or succumb to life's pressures? People's ability to resist life stress and act in an honest an ethical fashion may well depend upon their internal level of ethical development. However, that is extremely difficult to test.

Author Tip > **Internal Financial Controls**

Volumes have been written on the topic of internal financial controls as well as corporate ethics. It is not the purpose of this chapter to try to educate employers about the details of financial controls appropriate for their organization. The main points for this chapter are that it is a significant problem and that hiring the right workers is part of an overall strategy to preserve and protect an organization's tangible and intangible assets.

2016 ACFE Report to the Nations on Occupational Fraud and Abuse

The Association of Certified Fraud Examiners (ACFE) has released the *2016 ACFE Report to the Nations on Occupational Fraud and Abuse* that provides an analysis of 2,410 cases of occupational fraud that occurred in 114 countries throughout the world.

The report is based on the results of the 2015 Global Fraud Survey, an online survey opened to 41,788 Certified Fraud Examiners (CFEs) from July 2015 to October 2015. As part of the survey, respondents were asked to provide a detailed narrative of the single largest fraud case they had investigated since January 2014. Additionally, after completing the survey the first time, respondents were provided the option to submit information about a second case that they investigated.

Some key highlights from the *Executive Summary* of the 2016 ACFE Global Fraud Report include:

- *The CFEs who participated in the survey estimated that the typical organization loses 5% of revenues in a given year as a result of fraud.*

- *The total loss caused by the cases in our study exceeded $6.3 billion, with an average loss per case of $2.7 million.*

- *The median loss for all cases in the study was $150,000, with 23.2% of cases causing losses of $1 million or more.*

- *Asset misappropriation was by far the most common form of occupational fraud, occurring in more than 83% of cases, but causing the smallest median loss of $125,000. Financial statement fraud was on the other end of the spectrum, occurring in less than 10% of cases but causing a median loss of $975,000. Corruption cases fell in the middle, with 35.4% of cases and a median loss of $200,000.*

- *Among the various forms of asset misappropriation, billing schemes and check tampering schemes posed the greatest risk based on their relative frequency and median loss.*

- *The longer a fraud lasted, the greater the financial damage it caused. While the median duration of the frauds in our study was 18 months, the losses rose as the duration increased. At the extreme end, those schemes that lasted more than five years caused a median loss of $850,000.*

- *In 94.5% of the cases in our study, the perpetrator took some efforts to conceal the fraud. The most common concealment methods were creating and altering physical documents.*

- *The most common detection method in the study was tips (39.1% of cases), but organizations that had reporting hotlines were much more likely to detect fraud through tips than organizations without hotlines (47.3% compared to 28.2%, respectively).*

- *When fraud was uncovered through active detection methods, such as surveillance and monitoring or account reconciliation, the median loss and median duration of the schemes were lower than when the schemes were detected through passive methods, such as notification by police or by accidental discovery.*

- *In cases detected by tip at organizations with formal fraud reporting mechanisms, telephone hotlines were the most commonly used method (39.5%). However, tips submitted via email (34.1%) and web-based or online form (23.5%) combined to make reporting more common through the Internet than by telephone.*

- *Whistleblowers were most likely to report fraud to their direct supervisors (20.6% of cases) or company executives (18%).*

- *Approximately two-thirds of the cases reported targeted privately held or publicly owned companies. These for-profit organizations suffered the largest median losses among the types of organizations analyzed, at $180,000 and $178,000, respectively.*

- *Of the cases involving a government victim, those that occurred at the federal level reported the highest median loss ($194,000), compared to state or provincial ($100,000) and local entities ($80,000).*

- *The median loss suffered by small organizations (those with fewer than 100 employees) was the same as that incurred by the largest organizations (those with more than 10,000 employees). However, this type of loss is likely to have a much greater impact on smaller organizations.*

- *Organizations of different sizes tend to have different fraud risks. Corruption was more prevalent in larger organizations, while check tampering, skimming, payroll, and cash larceny schemes were twice as common in small organizations as in larger organizations.*

- *The banking and financial services, government and public administration, and manufacturing industries were the most represented sectors in the fraud cases we examined.*

- *Although mining and wholesale trade had the fewest cases of any industry in the study, those industries reported the greatest median losses of $500,000 and $450,000, respectively.*

- *As in previous studies, external audits of the financial statements were the most commonly implemented anti-fraud control; nearly 82% of the organizations in the r study underwent independent audits. Similarly, 81.1% of organizations had a code of conduct in place at the time the fraud occurred.*

- *Small organizations had a significantly lower implementation rate of anti-fraud controls than large organizations. This gap in fraud prevention and detection coverage leaves small organizations extremely susceptible to frauds that can cause significant damage to their limited resources.*

- *While the implementation rates of anti-fraud controls varied by geographical region, several controls— external audits of the financial statements, code of conduct, and management certification of the financial statements—were consistently among the most commonly implemented across organizations in all locations.*

- *The presence of anti-fraud controls was correlated with both lower fraud losses and quicker detection. When comparing organizations that had specific anti-fraud controls in place against organizations lacking those controls, fraud losses were 14.3%–54% lower and frauds were detected 33.3%–50% more quickly where controls were present.*

- *The most prominent organizational weakness that contributed to the frauds in the study was a lack of internal controls, which was cited in 29.3% of cases, followed by an override of existing internal controls, which contributed to just over 20% of cases.*

- *The perpetrator's level of authority was strongly correlated with the size of the fraud. The median loss in a scheme committed by an owner/executive was $703,000. This was more than four times higher than the median loss caused by managers ($173,000) and nearly 11 times higher than the loss caused by employees ($65,000).*

- *More occupational frauds originated in the accounting department (16.6%) than in any other business unit. Of the frauds we analyzed, more than three-fourths were committed by individuals working in seven key departments: accounting, operations, sales, executive/upper management, customer service, purchasing, and finance.*

- *The more individuals involved in an occupational fraud scheme, the higher losses tended to be. The median loss caused by a single perpetrator was $85,000. When two people conspired, the median loss was $150,000; three conspirators caused $220,000 in losses; four caused $294,000; and for schemes with five or more perpetrators, the median loss was $633,000.*

- *Fraud perpetrators tended to display behavioral warning signs when they were engaged in their crimes. The most common red flags were living beyond means, financial difficulties, unusually close association with a vendor or customer, excessive control issues, a general "wheeler-dealer" attitude involving unscrupulous behavior, and recent divorce or family problems. At least one of these red flags was exhibited during the fraud in 78.9% of cases.*

- *Most occupational fraudsters are first-time offenders. Only 5.2% of perpetrators in this study had previously been convicted of a fraud-related offense, and only 8.3% had previously been fired by an employer for fraud-related conduct.*

- *In 40.7% of cases, the victim organizations decided not to refer their fraud cases to law enforcement, with fear of bad publicity being the most-cited reason.*

- *Of the cases in the study, 23.1% resulted in a civil suit, and 80.8% of such completed suits led to either a judgment for the victim or a settlement.*

- *In the study, 8.4% of the victim organizations were fined as a result of the fraud. The proportion of victim organizations fined was highest in the Western Europe (15.6%), Southern Asia (13.6%), and Asia-Pacific (11.7%) regions.*

The ACFE 2016 Global Fraud report is available at www.acfe.com/rttn2016.aspx.

The Staggering Cost of Fraud

According to the 2016 ACFE Report to the Nations on Occupational Fraud and Abuse:

Anti-fraud professionals, business managers, government and regulatory agencies, and the media each have a vested interest in assessing the total amount of money lost to fraud each year. While many studies have attempted to determine the extent of fraud's financial impact, the challenges in arriving at the true total cost of fraud are numerous. It is impossible to know exactly how much fraud goes undetected or unreported, and even calculations based solely on known fraud cases are likely to be underestimated, as many victims downplay or miscalculate the amount of damage.

Nonetheless, attempts to determine the cost of fraud are important, because understanding the size of the problem helps bring attention to its impact, enables organizations to quantify their fraud risk, and helps management make educated decisions about investing in anti-fraud resources and programs.

The ACFE created an infographic called *"The Staggering Cost of Fraud"* that includes the following statistics:

- Fraud cases caused a total loss of **more than $6.3 billion**.
- More than 23% of occupational fraud cases resulted in a loss of **at least $1 million**.
- CFEs estimate the typical organization loses **5% of annual revenue** to fraud.
- The median loss from a single case of occupational fraud was **$150,000**.

Median Losses from Fraud

The ACFE's "The Staggering Cost of Fraud" infographic also includes information about median losses from occupational fraud by region, scheme, job title, and the number of people involved in the fraud.

Median Losses from Fraud by Region 2016

Middle East and North Africa suffered the highest median loss from occupation fraud while Southern Asia had the lowest median loss.

Region	Median Loss
Middle East and North Africa	$275,000
Western Europe	$263,000
Asia-Pacific	$245,000
Eastern Europe & Western/Central Asia	$200,000
Latin America & The Caribbean	$174,000
Canada	$154,000
Sub-Saharan Africa	$143,000
Southern Asia	$100,000

Median Losses from Fraud by Scheme 2016

Off the three major categories of occupational fraud, financial statement fraud caused by far the greatest median loss per scheme.

Scheme	Median Loss
Financial Statement Fraud	$975,000
Corruption	$200,000
Asset Misappropriation	$125,000

Median Losses from Fraud by Job Title 2016

When owners committed fraud, the median damage was more than ten times worse than when employers were the perpetrators.

Job Title	Median Loss
Owner/Executive	$703,000
Manager	$173,000
Employee	$65,000

Median Losses from Fraud by Number of People 2016

The ACFE report found that the more people conspiring in an occupational fraud, the higher the losses tended to be.

Number of People	Median Loss
Five or more	$633,000
Four	$294,000
Three	$220,000
Two	$150,000
One	$65,000

Anti-Fraud Controls Help Reduce Median Losses from Fraud

The AFCE report also found that victim organizations that lacked anti-fraud controls suffered greater median losses from occupational fraud—in fact, twice as much.

- Proactive data monitoring/analysis:
    - $92,000 median loss to occupational fraud when anti-fraud control in place.
    - $200,000 median loss to occupational fraud when anti-fraud control not in place.
- Management review:
    - $100,000 median loss to occupational fraud when anti-fraud control in place.
    - $200,000 median loss to occupational fraud when anti-fraud control not in place.
- Hotline:
    - $100,000 median loss to occupational fraud when anti-fraud control in place.
    - $200,000 median loss to occupational fraud when anti-fraud control not in place.

The ACFE's "Staggering Cost of Fraud" infographic is available at www.acfe.com/rttn2016/docs/Staggering-Cost-of-Fraud-infographic.pdf.

Behavioral "Red Flags" of Perpetrators of Fraud

According to the Association of Certified Fraud Examiners (ACFE) 2016 Report to the Nations on Occupational Fraud and Abuse:

It is very common for people who are engaged in an occupational fraud scheme to display certain behavioral traits or characteristics associated with fraudulent conduct. In 92% of the cases in our study the perpetrator exhibited at least one of these behavioral red flags, and in 57% of cases multiple red flags were observed before the fraud was detected. Understanding how these behavioral clues are linked to fraudulent conduct can help improve the chances of detecting occupational fraud early and minimizing fraud losses.

Here are the most common behavioral red flags for occupational fraud in found in the ACFE study:

- Living Beyond Means – 45.8%
- Financial Difficulties – 30.0%
- Unusually Close Association with Vendor/Customer – 20.1%
- Wheeler-Dealer Attitude – 15.3%
- Control Issues, Unwillingness to Share Duties – 15.3%

- Divorce/Family Problems – 13.4%
- Irritability, Suspiciousness, or Defensiveness – 12.3%
- Addiction Problems – 10.0%
- Complained About Adequate Pay – 9.0%
- No Behavioral Red Flags – 8.8%

Source: www.acfe.com/rttn2016/perpetrators/red-flags.aspx

More Occupational Fraud Statistics

According to statistics from the American Society of Employers:

- Businesses lose 20% of every dollar to employee theft.
- The U.S. Retail Industry loses $53.6 billion a year due to employee theft.

According to statistics from Jack Hayes International, Inc. 2007 Survey:

- In 2007, one in every 28.2 employees in the U.S. was apprehended for theft from their employer.
- In 2007, 82,648 employees were apprehended from 24 large U.S. retail chains, up 17.57% from 2006.

According to the U.S. Chamber of Commerce:

- Estimates that 75% of all employees steal at least once, and half of these employees steal again and again.
- Reports that one of every three business failures are the direct result of employee theft.

According to David J. Lieberman's book *Executive Power: Use the Greatest Collection of Psychological Strategies to Create an Automatic Advantage in Any Business Situation*, (John Wiley & Sons, March 9, 2009):

- Embezzlement costs organizations somewhere between $450 and $600 billion every year.
- More than 50 percent of all business bankruptcies are attributed to employee theft.
- Each year, employee theft will cause 20 percent of existing businesses and 30 percent of new businesses to fail.
- Security industry experts estimate that 30 percent of all employees steal from their employers and another 60 percent would steal, given sufficient motive and opportunity.

According to Lisa Guerin's book, *The Essential Guide to Workplace Investigations: How to Handle Employee Investigations* (Nolo, July 12, 2010):

- Retailers lose more to their own employees than to shoplifters.
- Up to one-third of small business closures and bankruptcies are due to employee theft.
- 66% of employees would steal if they saw others getting away with it and 13% would steal regardless.

The above figures do not take into account the fallout from employee embezzlement, dishonesty, and fraud. The fallout can include the destruction of a firm's reputation, the inability to stay in business, the damage to employee morale, and the time and energy taken from productive projects to deal with dishonesty. For a small business, the personal loss experienced by the owners can be devastating when a trusted employee is discovered to have been an embezzler or thief.

Research Reveals Warning Signs of Intellectual Property Theft Committed by Corporate Insiders

Corporate insider intellectual property (IP) thieves are usually males under 40 holding technical positions, have a new job ready at the time of the theft, and steal information they were authorized to access, according to the findings of a new report "Behavioral Risk Indicators of Malicious Insider Theft of Intellectual Property: Misreading the Writing on the Wall" from leading information security solutions provider Symantec.

Since the Commerce Department estimates the theft of intellectual property costs U.S. businesses more than $250 billion annually, the research paper – authored by experts in the fields of psychological profiling and employee risk management – helps employers learn about insider theft profiles, key risk indicators and factors, and steps to take to defend against intellectual property theft. The report also addresses the high level of organizational anxiety surrounding potential theft of intellectual property by employees and also describes the people and organizational conditions contributing to this risk.

Based on a review of empirical research, the report identifies the following key behaviors and indicators that contribute to intellectual property theft by corporate insiders:

- The majority of insider intellectual property theft is committed by current male employees averaging about 37 years of age in technical positions that include engineers, scientists, managers, and programmers. Many IP thieves had signed IP agreements, indicating that policy without effective enforcement is ineffective.

- Approximately 65 percent of employees who committed insider intellectual property theft had accepted a new job with a competing company or started their own company at the time of the theft. About 20 percent were recruited by an outsider who targeted the data, and 25 percent gave the stolen IP to a foreign company or country. Over 50 percent stole data within a month of leaving.

- Three out of four employees – 75 percent – who committed insider intellectual property theft stole information they were authorized to access since they knew and worked with the data and often felt entitled to it in some way.

- The most common type of intellectual property stolen by corporate insiders was Trade secrets (52 percent of cases), followed by business information and other administrative data (30 percent), source code (20 percent), proprietary software (14 percent), customer information (12 percent), and business plans (6 percent).

The report also revealed that key patterns and common problems preceded inside intellectual property theft. These warning signs contributed to the motivation of corporate insider thieves and included perceived professional setbacks and unmet expectations that fast-tracked insiders into stealing IP. These signals of impending intellectual property theft showed the role of personal psychology and stressful events as indicators of insider risk.

The report features recommendations for employers concerned with intellectual theft risk that include building a team to fully address insider theft, evaluating risk factors, creating effective policies and practices, training and education, and using pre-employment screening to make informed decisions and mitigate the risk of hiring a "problem" employee.

This free report is available at www.symantec.com/about/news/release/article.jsp?prid=20111207_01.

Ten Tools to Encourage Future Honesty

Along with pre-employment screening of new hires, listed below are eight tools firms can use to help foster an environment that promotes and encourages future honesty.

1. **Establish Clear Policies Regarding Conduct**

   According to the U. S. Declaration of Independence, "some truths are self-evident." That may be true, but an employer should still have a clear written policy that theft, dishonesty, or unethical conduct will not be tolerated, no matter when discovered. Those negative behaviors are grounds for discipline, up to and including termination.

2. **Have Adequate Internal Controls and Auditing in Place**

   One of the most critical parts of preventing fraud is having internal controls in place. If the job involves handling of cash or assets or reporting of financial activity in any way, then there are a number of controls that can be put into place. One of the main thrusts behind the Sarbanes-Oxley Act is an environment of control, discussed later in this chapter.

3. **Audit to Ensure the Internal Controls are being Utilized and Reviewed**

   Having controls is useless if supervisors and management are asleep at the wheel, or the controls only exist on paper. As a general rule, an organization only accomplishes those things that are measured, audited, and rewarded. The same applies to controls in an organization to protect against dishonest or unethical behavior.

4. **Immediate and Appropriate Response to Dishonest or Unethical Conduct**

   Employers need to make it clear that dishonest behavior is not tolerated and will be the subject of swift and certain response by the employer.

5. **Continuing Education on Success, Ethics, and Honesty**

   A continuing effort is critical to institutionalize honest and ethical dealing and to remind all members of the team these concepts are essential to the firm's success and an individual's success. This can be accomplished through continuing education, staff meetings, videotapes, and other visible reminders of the firm's position.

6. **Atmosphere and Corporate Culture**

   The development of a corporate culture often starts at the top. If the leaders of an organization demonstrate honest and ethical dealings in both words and deed, then it should flow down throughout the entire organization. As the old saying goes, "the tone is set at the top." Although this is a maxim that is often repeated, it bears attention. The leaders of an organization set examples that create the environment and culture for a firm. It is up to an organization's leaders to set an example that honesty in all aspects of a company's dealings is the best policy. This extends to all corners of the enterprise, from dealing with customers and employees, to vendors and government agencies including the Internal Revenue Service (IRS).

7. **Anonymous Tip Hotline**

   The establishment of such a hotline is one of the provisions of the Sarbanes-Oxley Act. Experts agree that the ability of employees to give anonymous tips without fear of reprisals is a highly-effective, low-cost best practice.

8. **Ethics and Honesty Advisory Hotline**

   When a good employee is faced with a situation that falls into the category of dishonest or unethical conduct, the employee may simply have no one to talk to. Providing a safe haven for discussion—or where an employee can seek advice—is a best practice.

9. **Psychological Testing for Honesty and Ethics**

The use of such tests is an attempt to predict who will act in an honest and ethical fashion in the future. These tests and their effectiveness are discussed later in this chapter.

10. **Have an Active Policy to Monitor and Investigate Insider Threats**

The topic of insider threats is reviewed in more detail in Chapter 16 concerning issues after employment. However, it is not enough to have policies and procedures about theft and dishonestly, or even internal controls. A firm may want to proactively monitor potential insider threats.

You Need To Know

U.S. Retail Workers Lead World in Employee Theft

Employee theft in the United States accounted for 43 percent of lost revenue – **about $18 billion** – while dishonest employees around the world accounted for only approximately 28 percent of inventory losses globally, according to the Global Retail Theft Barometer 2014[TM].

The study is the first and only global research on the cost of "shrink" – comprised of shoplifting, employee theft, supplier fraud, and administrative errors – and provides data to help retailers around the world benchmark performances for merchandise, markets, and geographies.

Overall, the study found that annual shrinkage cost U.S. retailers around $42 billion a year. Shoppers in the U.S. also paid the price for the loss of merchandise, around $403 annually per household. More information is available at www.globalretailtheftbarometer.com.

How to Avoid Hiring an Embezzler

Embezzlement is an equal opportunity crime. It affects employers of all sizes as well as profit and non-profit firms.

At the root of embezzlement is a violation of trust. By definition, **embezzlement** is a crime where a person legally uses or possesses property belonging to the employer, then permanently converts this property to his or her personal use. Embezzlement differs from theft, where the culprit has no right to possession in the first place. Embezzlement is considered more serious and harder to detect.

Embezzlement can range from simply stealing cash from the cash drawer to more elaborate schemes such as writing checks to oneself or to ghost employees, setting up and making payments to fake vendors, paying phony expense reimbursements, or giving oneself a pay increase. Embezzlement typically occurs when there is a combination of motive, opportunity, and means. The opportunity and means portion is usually a result of a lack of proper internal controls. If an embezzler or thief has a co-conspirator, then the act becomes more difficult to guard against.

For purposes of safe hiring, the critical task is to look for a person who may have a motive for theft or a history of past financial misconduct.

How to Spot an Embezzler

When embezzlement occurs, typically one or more of the following situations are true:

- The business did very little, if any, due diligence when hiring the embezzler. The firm did not determine if the applicant may be motivated to steal or had stolen in the past. Not following the rules of Safe Hiring, the employer made the decision based primarily on the interview and subjective impression of the applicant. In a great number of embezzlement cases, even the slightest due diligence could have revealed the danger signals.

Often times, employers merely need to look deeper instead of handing over the keys to someone who had created a favorable impression during their hiring interview.

- The employer typically had very little, if any, internal controls in place. "Internal controls" typically refers to a system of cross checks so that no one person runs the company's finances. To accomplish embezzlement, a criminal needs to control most, if not all, aspects of the firm's financial life: writing the checks, making deposits, reconciling bank statements, and/or opening mail. If any of these functions are interrupted by external controls or cross checks, then the ability of an embezzler to steal is diminished.

- Embezzlers often come disguised as the hard-working "perfect employee." They are perceived as hardworking and loyal. They never seem to take a vacation. They arrive first, leave last, and always volunteer to get the mail. Embezzlers put on their show for two reasons. First, since embezzlement is fundamentally a violation of an employer's trust, embezzlers need to earn that trust in order to have the opportunity to embezzle—employers are more likely to delegate responsibility and access to cash and assets to someone who is considered hardworking and loyal. Second, embezzlers need to control their environment as much as possible to accomplish their embezzlement and to hide their activities from others. Should an embezzler take a day off, then someone else could answer a call from an unpaid vendor, perhaps prompting the replacement to ask why bills are not being paid. Or, if the embezzler does not get to the mail first, letters demanding payment cannot be intercepted. To keep the scheme going, an embezzler needs complete control.

There is no one profile of an embezzler. Embezzlers can be young or old, male or female, well-educated or high school dropouts. Disguised as perfect employees, embezzlers are very difficult to detect. However, there are some common traits:

- An embezzler is completely self-focused on one's own needs, wants, and desires. He or she is not overly concerned with betraying a trust or hurting co-workers—or the employer or company.

- If they are prosecuted, embezzlers are more focused on their own pain caused by the prosecution and being put into an embarrassing position. There is often a mental disconnect between the fact that they violated trust and stole and the position they find themselves in. "In denial" is the popular term.

- The embezzler almost immediately begins to blame the victim; their reasoning may be:
  o   I needed the money more than they did.
  o   I worked hard and they did not treat me right.
  o   I deserved the extra money.
  o   They made me take it—if they had treated me right, it would not have happened.

- Embezzlers often do not want to give up even one cent of their ill-gotten gains. Even if it would keep them out of jail, embezzlers and white collar criminals are so focused on the money they will often try to do anything to not have to pay it back.

- Many times the embezzled money is simply squandered. It is not uncommon for the stolen money to have already been wasted on clothes, travel, or general high living. Once the person is prosecuted or sued, little can be recovered for purposes of victim restitution.

There is always the possibility that the motivating event could be something totally out of the embezzler's control, such as the sudden illness of a family member requiring an expensive operation. However, this is unusual. More often, the motivation for embezzlement is a need to have something the embezzler cannot otherwise afford. Quite often, the signs of this covetous attitude are spotted before the first time the person embezzles.

Also, the motivating factor can be an outgrowth of some personality trait of the embezzler, such as a drug habit or gambling habit. The problems caused by such habits may be discovered during a standard background check. A credit report may show a debt level incompatible with the salary for their position. Perhaps a past employment check reveals the applicant was habitually late to work, which can be associated with a problem employee profile.

As mentioned above, once an employer is a victim, there often is no ability to obtain restitution. An embezzler may have little left in the way of assets. Court proceedings often prove ineffective at returning property. It is not usual for an employer to attempt to resolve the matter by working out an agreement for restitution that calls for the employer not to contact the police. The result, of course, is that an embezzler is free to move on to yet another victim.

Of course, the best defense for an employer is not to hire the embezzler in the first place. To accomplish that, an employer needs to utilize all of the tools in their Safe Hiring Program.

You Need To Know

Holiday Season Hiring Brings Increased Fraud Risk

Thanksgiving week signals the official start of the holiday season. Along with turkey, football, presents, and good cheer, the holiday season brings an increase in seasonal hiring. However, fraud experts interviewed for an article posted on the Insurance Journal website in November 2014 warn that businesses that skip their usual due diligence background checks when hiring in order to quickly add workers for the holiday season face an increased risk of fraud.

In the article, two fraud experts – Bruce Dorris, Vice President and Program Director of the Association of Certified Fraud Examiners (ACFE), and Eric Feldman, Managing Director, Corporate Ethics and Compliance Programs for Affiliated Monitors – offer tips for businesses hiring seasonal workers. Both fraud experts agree that employers must protect themselves with background checks, training, and codes of ethical conduct to reduce fraud. They answered the following questions:

- **How serious is the fraud risk during the U.S. holiday shopping season?** – Dorris says that according to the ACFE 2014 Report to the Nations on Occupational Fraud and Abuse organizations lose an estimated 5 percent of total revenues to fraud. Other ACFE research indicates fraud rises an estimated 20 percent during the holiday season. He adds that "high traffic and increased sales provide an even bigger opportunity" for fraud.

- **Many businesses increase staffing for the holidays. How does this affect their risk of fraud?** – Feldman says that employers often "short-cut" normal hiring procedures during the holiday season due to the pressure to remain fully staffed. He says businesses should follow usual procedures to avoid fraud.

- **Do seasonal employees need fraud training?** – Dorris answers that with increased volume and crowds during the holiday season all employees "should be aware of fraud in the workplace" to be vigilant against fraud, know the warning signs of fraud, and have training in basic fraud awareness.

- **How important is it for companies to conduct background checks (as permitted by law), even for entry-level and temporary positions?** – Feldman explains that the first defense against hiring employees who may commit fraud is with "thorough employee screening" that includes "criminal checks, complete reference checks, and even brief ethics tests." This includes entry-level and temporary holiday positions.

- **The holiday season is hectic and business is usually good – is it okay to "lighten up" on controls such as audits, management review and segregation of duties while things are so busy?** – Feldman warns that the holiday season is not "the time to lighten up on internal controls" since even normally honest employees "can be tempted to engage in unethical behavior" if they see greater opportunities to commit fraud. He adds that s employers should "keep their guards up" through the holiday season.

The article "Fraud Controls Important When Hiring Seasonal Staff, Experts Say" is at www.insurancejournal.com/news/southcentral/2014/11/18/347427.htm.

From the Courts: A Sobering Tale for Employers

A recent state court case in Iowa concerned a local office of a national staffing firm. The firm supplied an employer with a bookkeeper who turned out to have a criminal record for felony fraud and who also misrepresented her educational background. The worker embezzled $138,350.

The employer sued the staffing firm for their losses. The employer based the lawsuit on the fact that the staffing firm represented they would send a qualified candidate. It turned out the candidate had a criminal conviction for felony fraud as well as false educational claims. However, according to the court decision, since the employer did not specify the staffing firm should do a background check, and the staffing firm never claimed that they would perform a check, the employer's claims were dismissed.

Most employers would probably assume that they would not have to specifically request a staffing professional not send someone convicted of felony fraud who also faked educational claims to handle their books. However, staffing firms should not assume, based upon this decision, that the failure to perform background checks is always legally defensible. Even though the staffing firm won this case, it is not clear that all courts would ultimately dispense the same decision. In addition, given the negative publicity and potential harm to reputation, a background check would have been very cheap by comparison. At a minimum, clearly specifying the staffing firm's policy on background checks would also have been a best practice.

The employer in this case also apparently had a lack of internal financial controls. As the court noted, the embezzler had access to signed blank checks, was the sole person to review the general ledger, handled cash, and had complete access to the employer's bank accounts. However, staffing professionals are generally well acquainted with the fact the small businesses often cannot afford the type of internal controls needed to prevent embezzlement, which is another reason that staffing firms need to be careful when they place people in sensitive positions.

The walkway point: Employers need to be very careful about who they put in charge of their money, and at the same time, have good internal controls in place.

Corporate Fraud and Sarbanes-Oxley

When the Sarbanes-Oxley Act was signed into law on July 30, 2002, over 15,000 publicly held companies were given a new set of rules regarding corporate ethics. This far-reaching law radically changed the landscape of corporate governance, controls, audits, and financial disclosures as follows:

- Chief executive officers and chief financial officers must personally attest to the accuracy of earnings reports and other financial statements.
- Curtailment of non-auditing consulting services must be provided by outside auditors.
- Whistle-blowers should receive protections.
- Criminal penalties are increased, including fines and jail terms for misdeeds by executives.
- Investment firms must take steps to improve the objectivity of reports performed by securities analysts.
- A Public Company Accounting Oversight Board was established to oversee the audits of companies that are subject to securities laws.
- The relationship between executives and directors to outside auditors was regulated.

Among the many critical provisions is Section 404 which requires public firms establish and maintain financial controls and processes. Public corporations are also required to conduct periodic evaluations of their current controls. Also under Section 404, merely having financial controls is inadequate—one of the most important provisions of Section 404 is that external auditors must also attest to the effectiveness and adequacy of the controls in the annual report.

Sec. 404. Management Assessment of Internal Controls

"SEC. 404. MANAGEMENT ASSESSMENT OF INTERNAL CONTROLS. (a) RULES REQUIRED.—The Commission shall prescribe rules requiring each annual report required by section 13(a) or 15(d) of the Securities Exchange Act of 1934 (15 U.S.C. 78m or 78o(d)) to contain an internal control report, which shall— (1) state the responsibility of management for establishing and maintaining an adequate internal control structure and procedures for financial reporting; and (2) contain an assessment, as of the end of the most recent fiscal year of the issuer, of the effectiveness of the internal control structure and procedures of the issuer for financial reporting. (b) INTERNAL CONTROL EVALUATION AND REPORTING.—With respect to the internal control assessment required by subsection (a), each registered public accounting firm that prepares or issues the audit report for the issuer shall attest to, and report on, the assessment made by the management of the issuer. An attestation made under this subsection shall be made in accordance with standards for attestation engagements issued or adopted by the Board. Any such attestation shall not be the subject of a separate engagement."

Under the Sarbanes-Oxley Act (also known as SOX), the Securities and Exchange Commission (SEC) issued rules on how Section 404 must be implemented. To ensure honesty and ethical dealings, public companies must have an ongoing effort aimed at instituting and documenting corporate controls. The SEC has published many sources of useful guidance that can help companies perform the management assessment of internal controls under Sarbanes-Oxley Section 404 on the SEC website at www.sec.gov/spotlight/soxcomp.htm.

Other good sources of information from the SEC about SOX are:

- Sarbanes-Oxley Section 404 - A Guide for Small Business: www.sec.gov/info/smallbus/404guide.shtml.
- The SEC's June 2003 Implementing Rules: www.sec.gov/rules/final/33-8238.htm.
- The SEC's June 2007 Interpretive Guidance: www.sec.gov/rules/interp/2007/33-8810.pdf.
- The SEC's Rules Defining Material Weakness and Regarding Voluntary Use of the Interpretive Guidance: www.sec.gov/rules/final/2007/33-8809.pdf.
- The SEC's Rule Defining Significant Deficiency: www.sec.gov/rules/final/2007/33-8829.pdf.
- The SEC Staff's FAQs: www.sec.gov/info/accountants/controlfaq.htm.

In 1992, the Committee of Sponsoring Organizations of the Treadway Commission (COSO) published *Internal Control— Integrated Framework* that was widely accepted as a framework by which management and auditors evaluate internal controls. On December 15, 2014, this framework was superseded by the *2013 Internal Control— Integrated Framework* released by COSO to help businesses design and implement internal control while taking into account that many changes in business and operating environments since the original Framework was issued. The 2013 COSO Framework also broadened the application of internal control in addressing operations and reporting objectives, and clarified the requirements for determining what constitutes effective internal control. The 2013 COSO Framework is available at www.coso.org/ic.htm.

In 2013, COSO—an organization providing thought leadership and guidance on internal control, enterprise risk management, and fraud deterrence—also issued an article entitled *"The 2013 COSO Framework & SOX Compliance: One Approach to an Effective Transition"* authored by J. Stephen McNally, CPA, and aimed at assisting public companies comply with Section 404 of the U.S. Sarbanes-Oxley Act of 2002. The article outlines an example of one approach to transitioning to COSO's 2013 Internal Control—Integrated Framework from the original framework published in 1992. The article is also available at www.coso.org/ic.htm.

Report Helps Build Fraud Resistant Organizations

A report from The Anti-Fraud Collaboration called **"The Fraud-Resistant Organization: Tools, Traits, and Techniques to Deter and Detect Financial Reporting Fraud"** provides information on how financial organizations can become less susceptible to fraud.

The Anti-Fraud Collaboration report focuses on financial reporting fraud at publicly traded companies and defines financial reporting fraud as "a material misrepresentation resulting from an intentional failure to report financial information in accordance with generally accepted accounting principles." The report examines factors that make some financial organizations more susceptible to fraud. The following three themes emerge at these organizations:

- Lack of a strong "tone at the top" and an ethical culture.
- Insufficient skepticism on the part of participants in the financial reporting supply chain.
- Insufficient communication among financial reporting supply chain participants.

The report also includes research on the qualities and techniques of more fraud resistant organizations. The following themes emerge at these organizations:

- A tone at the top that encourages an ethical culture.
- The presence of skepticism.
- The engagement of all participants in the financial reporting supply chain, with all relevant parties understanding and effectively performing their roles with respect to the company's financial reporting.

The Anti-Fraud Collaboration report also addresses challenges with fraud deterrence and detection that multi-national financial companies face in a global economy and markets that include different languages, cultures, and regulatory requirements.

The Anti-Fraud Collaboration was formed by the Center for Audit Quality (CAQ), Financial Executives International (FEI), The Institute of Internal Auditors (The IIA), and the National Association of Corporate Directors (NACD). The four organizations represent members of the financial reporting supply chain that includes external auditors, company financial management, internal auditors, and audit committees. To learn more, visit www.antifraudcollaboration.org.

The 56-page report is available at www.thecaq.org/docs/anti-fraud-collaboration-report/the-fraud-resistant-organization.pdf.

Psychological Testing for Honesty and Integrity

Another useful tool to help find honest employees is psychological testing. An internet search will reveal a great number of firms offering testing that not only measures attitude, skills, and compatibility for a job, but also purports to measure if a person can be reasonably anticipated to act in an honest and ethical fashion. Generally, an honesty test relies upon three different categories of questions. First, it looks for admissions by an applicant of prior acts of dishonesty. Second, it tests an applicant's attitudes toward dishonest behavior. Third, it explores other personal characteristics of a person that may have a bearing on the potential for dishonest behavior. For example, some test vendors believe a person who feels alienated may be more likely to steal.

For Safe Hiring purposes, an honesty test is a written test designed to identify individuals applying for work who have a relatively high propensity to steal money or property on the job or are likely to engage in counterproductive behavior. Chapter 8 describes "Integrity Interviews" where an applicant is asked point-blank questions about his or her past and habits. However, these interviews are conducted by professionally trained interviewers, and results are not scored or evaluated using psychological measurements and are not subject to the validity studies discussed below.

Honesty tests utilize two types of questions. **"Direct questions"** explore a person's own past dishonest acts. An example is "Describe what you have stolen in the past from an employer." Similar questions may explore an applicant's attitude toward theft or dishonesty such as "If you knew someone was stealing, would you report it to your supervisor?" or "Have you associated with employees who you knew stole from their employers?"

The second type is called **"indirect questions."** These indirect questions seek to discern attitudes or behavior that may have a bearing upon dishonesty. Sample questions include "Do you feel lonely even when with others?" or "How often do you make your bed?" or "Do you feel most people steal at least a few small things from their employer?"

Well-designed honesty tests have generally been shown to have a high degree of accuracy. In addition to using the tests as hiring tools, they can help improve a firm's current culture when, for instance, the tests are combined with leadership development training.

Issues Surrounding Honesty Testing

Employers should be aware of certain issues associated with honesty tests.

1. **Honesty is inherently a difficult character trait to nail down, since it can be situational**

    The basic premise behind a personality test is that it can help predict future behavior. The difficulty with predicting future honesty is that honesty may not be a permanent trait but can be situational. It can be argued that everyone has told "little white lies." In some social situations, it would be considered rude not to lie when the truth would be unnecessary and hurtful. A dinner guest may say the soup is fine when in fact they dislike it. That does not mean this person would not be a good candidate for a job. On the other hand, if a person is dishonest about things that are more critical, this could have a bearing on how he or she will behave in the future. Factors that need to be considered when a lie is told are 1) the motive for the lie; 2) who is being lied to; 3) the methodology of the lie; 4) how effective the person is at lying; and perhaps the most critical, 5) the harm done to others by the consequences of telling the lie.

2. **Too similar to a polygraph**

    Employers must be aware if their honesty testing comes too close to polygraph testing. Although legal in most states, most states do prohibit any test "similar to a polygraph," without defining what that means. Per the passage of the Employee Polygraph Protection Act of 1988, the use of polygraphs was barred for most employment-related situations. As a result, the number of firms offering some sort of honesty testing instrument has increased. An employer should consult legal counsel for the current law in the jurisdiction where the new hire will be employed.

3. **Reliability**

    Reliability is simply a way of stating that if the test is repeated a short time later with the same group, the results would be consistent. In other words, a test is reliable if there is "consistency of measurement." If the same test on the same group produced widely different results, then the testing instrument would come under question.

4. **Validity**

    A valid test is one which measures what it is truly stated. In the context of an employment test, validity means the test actually predicts who is going to be honest. However, if the test does not give job-related information, the test is not valid. The firm that prepares and sells the testing must convince the employer that their instrument is a valid predictor of future job honesty. The subject of demonstrating test validity is extremely complex and beyond the scope of this book. However, good advice to follow is that an employer should not use any test unless the developer is able to produce a substantial body of data as to the validity of the test.

5. **EEOC considerations**

Another critical consideration is whether the testing instrument is discriminatory and violates the rules of the Equal Employment Opportunities Commission (EEOC). Even if the test is not discriminatory on its face, an employer needs to be aware that a test can have the effect of being discriminatory by the manner in which it is applied. Recall the discussion about the use of criminal records in Chapters 5 and 11—The EEOC has ruled that the use of criminal records can have an adverse effect on certain protected groups. The short answer for employers is that firms selling the test instrument are responsible to provide the employer with documentation as to the Title VII implications associated with the test.

6. **Americans With Disabilities ACT (ADA)**

A related issue is the Americans with Disabilities Act implications. A test for honesty will rarely contain a reference to a disability. However, the employer should require a vendor to document that vendor is not asking any questions that indirectly require an applicant to reveal or discuss a disability or in some way discourage an applicant with a disability from applying.

7. **Faking or distortion issues**

A major issue with the validity of honesty tests is when applicants try to outsmart the test and give fake answers based upon what they believe the test makers are looking for. Employers should review with testing vendors if psychologists have devised any methods that take such a distortion into account. Perhaps the test taker notices that for every question the best answer is always the third question.

8. **Administration of test**

Any employer using these tests will want its administration to be as quick and easy as possible. Even though there are pencil and paper tests, tests are also available over the internet and by phone. The costs for these tests are also very reasonable, as low as $10 or less per test for an off the shelf instrument. However, the development of a custom instrument is very expensive, such as those based upon modeling a firm's best current employee.

9. **Security of results and privacy**

Of course, it is critical for an employer to ensure all results are confidential and that the privacy of an applicant is maintained. The vendor should demonstrate that their system is properly secured, and all results are returned in a manner that protects privacy and confidentiality.

10. **Analysis and use of results**

Employers must be very careful using off-the-shelf instruments to make a hiring decision based upon a resulting numerical score. Psychological tests for honesty can be very complicated; a cookie cutter analysis can be deceptive. It is important to note certain cut-off points can be set while making sure not to hire any dishonest workers. For example, in order to make sure all of the potential "crooks" are eliminated, it is possible that some good candidates are eliminated along with the bad. The tests can also be prejudiced against an honest person. Perhaps one applicant may honestly admit he or she once took a pen home, but another applicant may consider that too trivial to report.

The lesson here is to very carefully review the instrument and the manner in which it is scored before using it to make any decision. Many experts suggest the results of an honesty test not be the sole deciding factor but rather they be used as just one of the factors. However, there are employers who have found these tests are highly accurate and do place a great deal of faith in them.

11. **Who is tested**

Another aspect of honesty testing is that they are typically used for hiring lower paid, hourly workers. Retail and manufacturing firms that hire unskilled or semi-skilled labor often use these tests; the tests are not typically used to the same degree for "white-collar" positions. However, given the emphasis on corporate honesty and ethics, a firm may want to consider using these tests for its salaried workers and professionals. The use of these tests serves to underscore the importance of honesty as well as possibly protect a firm from a bad hire in the executive offices.

12. **Possible negative consequences of honesty tests**

There are a number of negative consequences employers must consider and address before administering a testing program. These include:

- *False Sense of Security*—These tests could create a false sense of security among employers.
- *Hardship among Honest Workers*—If workers are denied employment based upon a test, there can be an inability to find a job. These tests can limit honest workers in an effort to find employment if they are unfairly tagged as not having passed a test.
- *Invasion of Privacy*—Lawsuits have been filed based upon unfair or intrusive questions appearing on tests. An employer should review all questions carefully to ensure the tests do not offend applicants.
- *The Employer-Employee Relationship*—It is important that applicants do not develop a negative first impression of a company due to a badly worded phrase, test item, or poor overall test. Typically, applicants receive indirect questions better than direct ones. Direct questions have been shown to offend a greater number of honest applicants. The goal of a test is to ultimately increase the odds of identifying those applicants that have more honest tendencies than others.

Do Honesty Tests Really Work?

Yes. Below is an article by Dr. John Schinnerer. The author sincerely thanks Dr. Schinnerer for permitting this article to be included herein.

Elevating Corporate Behavior One Test at a Time

By John Schinnerer, Ph.D., Executive Coach and Founder of Guide to Self, Inc.

Honesty and integrity tests have been used ever since the polygraph, or lie detector, test was outlawed. The question that many people have is, "Do these tests really work?"

The short answer is "Yes, they do work." The proof that they work has been demonstrated by two concepts known as validity and reliability.

Validity is demonstrated when a test measures what it purports to measure, in this case – honesty and integrity. Most validity studies for honesty tests are done with two groups of people – an average group of people and a group of prison inmates. The idea being that prisoners have already demonstrated antisocial behaviors such as theft, assault, and deceit. The results from these two groups are then used to look at the items individually and collectively.

The major yardstick of honesty tests is predictive validity – a test's ability to predict who is more likely to have honest tendencies. The EEOC has set forth validity guidelines as to the usefulness of tests. These guidelines state that a validity of .21 to .35 is likely to be useful while anything above .35 is highly useful. On average, honesty tests have a validity of .41 (Ones, Chockalingan, & Schmidt, 1993) which has a great benefit to those looking to reduce shrinkage, theft of data, or other counterproductive behaviors.

The majority of these tests rely on very similar questions. These questions have been used over and over on different people (and occasionally the same person) over time. Certain questions have been shown to repeatedly and consistently differentiate between individuals with antisocial tendencies and those who tend to obey the rules of society.

This brings us to the second concept, that of reliability. Reliability occurs when a test measures a concept, such as integrity, similarly in the same individual over time. A reliable integrity test should be able to consistently identify a felon as having more antisocial ideas today as well as one year from now.

Assuming we have a test that is reliable and valid, many people ask, "How do these questions work?" There are two main types of items in integrity and honesty tests – direct and indirect. Direct questions ask test-takers about their past behaviors in a direct manner. For example, "How many times in the past six months have you taken office supplies from your employer?" The answer choices for this question include "Zero", "Once or twice", "Three to five times", "Six to ten times", or "More than ten times."

Indirect items get at the same information in a more discrete manner. These items rely on a psychological concept known as projection. Projection is what humans do in an attempt to normalize their own behaviors. The assumption is that an individual will project his or her characteristic mode of responding into the question. These items are more or less disguised as to their true intent, thereby reducing the chances that the test-taker can deliberately create a desirable impression. An example of an indirect item is the following statement, "Borrowing office supplies from your employer is okay if you plan to replace them later." The test-taker is asked to what extent they agree with the statement above on a 1 to 5 scale. The greater the degree to which they agree with the statement, the more likely it is they are engaging in stealing or "borrowing" office items.

Another tool that test creators use is that of repetition. Most honesty tests will include similar items worded in different ways. Honesty is measured by the degree to which individuals remain consistent between these different items. This is one way to minimize our tendency to manage the impressions that other people have of us. To allow for this, most honesty tests are over 150 items in length to allow the test-taker adequate time and space to forget previous items measuring the same behavior (e.g., employee theft) that are worded differently.

While honesty tests have been shown to be valid, they are also situational. In other words, honesty is applied differently in different situations depending on the importance one places on the situation. Situations that are deemed important are more likely to be handled in an honest manner. For this and other reasons, honesty tests should never be used as the sole hiring criteria.

Honesty tests should be used as part of a battery of tests in an attempt to look at the entire applicant, not merely their honesty. Success on the job is comprised of much more than honesty. Success is usually a result of motivation, emotional intelligence, traditional intelligence, knowledge, and honesty.

Sources: Ones, D., Chockalingan, V., & Schmidt, F. "Comprehensive Meta-Analysis of Integrity Test Validities Findings and Implications for Personnel Selection and Theories of Job Performance" from Journal of Applied Psychology , 78.4 (1993): 679 – 703.

John Schinnerer, Ph.D. is Executive Coach and Founder of Guide to Self, Inc., a coaching company founded in the San Francisco Bay Area in 2005. Dr. Schinnerer received his doctorate in educational psychology from U.C. Berkeley. His areas of expertise range from positive psychology to leadership development to anger management. He has consulted with companies such as Pixar, Sutter Health, Kaiser Permanente and UPS. Contact by email at john@guidetoself.com; the website is www.guidetoself.com.

Author Tip

2016 International Fraud Awareness Week

The 2016 Internet Fraud Awareness week (www.fraudweek.com) takes from **November 13-19, 2016** and is a global effort to minimize the impact of fraud by promoting anti-fraud awareness and education. There are some basic steps that any organization can and should take to help combat fraud:

- **Establish and Communicate a Fraud Policy:** Every organization needs a written policy to address fraud—before it happens. A Sample Fraud Policy provided by the ACFE is available on the website.

- **Take the Fraud Prevention Check-Up:** Encourage your company or your clients to take the Fraud Prevention Check-Up available on the website to help identify and manage your fraud risks.

- **Use Anti-Fraud Resources:** Everyone is encouraged to take advantage of the free resources provided on this website to help train your employees and increase awareness of fraud within your organization. Also, add the Fraud Examiners Manual and Small Business Fraud Prevention Manual available on the website to your reference library, and make them readily available to your employees.

- **Sign Up as an Official Supporter:** Show your support for International Fraud Awareness Week by letting the world know what you are doing to help combat fraud. The sign-up form is at http://pages.acfe.com/FraudWeek-2016 FraudWeek-2016-Sign-Up.html.

CHAPTER 22

Identity and Data and Privacy Protection

Introduction

This chapter will cover employer issues that deal with Identity, ID Theft, Data Privacy, and Data Breaches—basically, the problem employers face in finding out if job applicants are who they say they are (or not).

The Problem of 'Who is Really Who'

America is undergoing an identity crisis. Identity theft is one of the fastest growing crimes in the United States.

For employers, however, the difficulties associated with ID theft goes well beyond credit card fraud and other financial losses. Firms can be the victims of ID theft by hiring someone with a false or fraudulent identity, with serious consequences. Employers do need to be concerned about whom they are really hiring since criminals and terrorists have been known to fake their identities.

Since 9/11/2001 there have been a number of initiatives to use modern technology to firmly establish who is who in our society. However, there is still a widespread ability for one person to steal the identity of another—or create a new identity—and masquerade as someone else. Numerous agencies and private firms are working on biometric and cyber identifiers for a variety of reasons. The use of biometric data has become a critical element in Homeland Security efforts, particularly at airports and essential industries and services. There is a national debate over national ID cards, including the privacy and social implications of the government assigning every individual a unique number or identity. Should we collect biometric data and continue building large information databases?

These issues affect the lives of every American and should be the topic of discussion in a free citizenry. Let us review what employers need to know and what to do in our current environment to protect the workplace.

> **You Need To Know**
>
> **Identity Theft Victimized 17.6 Million People in 2014**
>
> An estimated 17.6 million people in the United States—or about 7 percent of U.S. residents age 16 or older—were victims of at least one incident of identity theft in 2014, according to the report *Victims of Identity Theft, 2014* from the Bureau of Justice Statistics (BJS) released in September 2015.
>
> The report from the BJS found that the majority of identity theft victims in 2014 – about 86 percent or 16.4 million people – experienced the unauthorized fraudulent misuse or attempted misuse of an existing account information such as credit card or bank account information.
>
> The report found that identity theft victims may have experienced multiple types of identity theft: 8.6 million identity theft victims experienced the fraudulent use of a credit card; 8.1 million identity theft victims experienced the unauthorized or attempted use of existing bank accounts such as checking or savings accounts; and 1.5 million

identity theft victims experienced other types of existing account theft such as misuse or attempted misuse of an existing telephone, online, or insurance account.

The report defines identity theft as "the attempted or successful misuse of an existing account such as a debit or credit card account, the misuse of personal information to open a new account, or the misuse of personal information for other fraudulent purposes on persons age 16 or older."

The complete report written by BJS Statistician Erika Harrell, Ph.D., is available at www.bjs.gov/content/pub/pdf/vit14.pdf.

Author Tip **Identity Theft a Significant Workplace Issue**

Identity theft is also a significant issue in the workplace. Employers who obtain background reports may wish to consider having a paperless system. Background check reports can be electronically restricted only to those with a need to know and it prevents the possibility of paper reports floating around the office or sitting on desks. Another solution is to require a screening firm to put a security page on the front of each report with only the applicant's name and no identifiable data. Another option is to truncate the Social Security number (SSN) on any printed version of a screening report.

Identity in America

What is a person's identity? Identity has many different meanings. Use of the word by a psychologist would be very different than use by a teenager, a philosopher, a police officer, a scientist, or a privacy advocate. A popular dictionary, gives this definition of identity:

1. The collective aspect of the set of characteristics by which a thing is definitively recognizable or known.
2. The set of behavioral or personal characteristics by which an individual is recognizable as a member of a group.
3. The quality or condition of being the same as something else.
4. The distinct personality of an individual regarded as a persisting entity; individuality.

For our purposes, we are looking at identity in the bureaucratic sense of the word, utilizing the third definition—the quality or condition of being the same as something else.

Real Identity

Society has an interest in keeping everyone straight when it comes to financial transactions between each other, transactions with various levels of government from the IRS all the way down to getting a speeding ticket, and especially employment. This is a person's **real identity**. Putting aside any philosophical implications—and for the purpose of safe hiring—real identity is the process of matching up the past history with the present person you are dealing with.

A key element of a Safe Hiring Program is to know what a person has done in the past. That is not to say that a person is defined solely by the past, or that every past act can be, or legally should be, considered relevant to employment decisions. However, past acts that were performed in the public domain for the world to see are, such as employment or education, are what an employer needs to have. Now the employer needs to verify the public history of the applicant is not only factual but also is the history that belongs to that person. By knowing a person's real identity, an employer can match up the employment history, education, credentials, or past court records. The real identity is also needed for a number of governmental functions affecting labor regulation such as various tax withholdings.

Positive Identity

Employers are less concerned with the concept of *Positive Identity*. Positive identity means that you are the same person that was part of an original transaction so that you have the right to be a part of the new transaction. For example, if you went to a website in the past and signed up for a service, the site would need positive ID that you are the same person coming back for another transaction. It is irrelevant to the website that you may have initially used a different or even a false identity. As far as the website is concerned—provided there is no fraudulent financial transaction—you are you as long as you now know the username and password and, in some cases, the answer to security questions (the name of your first pet, etc.) that the user set up initially, i.e. you have the unique identifier that only you would know.

Consider this—a person creates or steals an identity and is hired by a firm under the false name. If that firm engages in some biometric identification procedures, such as identity badges, then each time the person comes into the workplace, his or her positive identity is confirmed. The employer knows this is the person presenting the badge. However, there is the possibility that the badge was gained because of a false "real" identity in the first place.

Negative Identity

Another type of identity is "Negative Identity." This means that you are NOT a particular someone. For example, when you get on an airplane, an important consideration is that you are not a terrorist or a wanted criminal. However, as a practical matter, the most efficient way of showing you are not someone is to show who you really are.

Correct Identity is Employer's First Concern in Employer/ Employee Relationship

For employers, the primary concern is real identity. The problem is how to accurately track, in a cost-effective manner that does not unduly invade our privacy, the identities of not only 300 million U.S. citizens, but also the people from around the world who apply for jobs here.

Identification Criteria Used by Employers

There are different identification criteria possible, each with their own set of considerations:

Name

A **person's name** is only one part of one's identity. Under English Common Law, people can change their name and be known by anything they want as long as they are not trying to deceive. Not only can people change names, but also they can use all sorts of variations of their first, middle or last names. In some traditional cultures, a woman may, upon marriage, take the family name of the husband. Many cultures have different protocols with names, such as variations of the family name or mother's maiden name. There is also an issue of non-English names, especially in those countries where a non-familiar alphabet is used, and there are numerous English variations of the same name.

Finally, in any large database of people, there is bound to be a great many duplicate names. It is surprising for people who believe their names are unique to go on the internet and find many others across North America with identical matching first and last names. As discussed in Chapter 9, using middle names or initials to establish identity can often be of little or no help.

The bottom line—name identification by itself is practically worthless for the purpose of real identification. It is necessary to have other identifiers as well. As a matter of math and logic, the more identifiers associated with an individual, the more likely a job applicant can be identified as a "real identity."

Date of Birth

Date of birth is probably the next most used identifier. The initial date used for the date of birth comes from the applicant. However, if an applicant gives a different date of birth, a search for criminal records could be thrown off. This creates a significant issue for the accuracy of a courthouse search for public records, especially if the name is common. It is possible to discover a false date of birth using other tools discussed below, but if a wrong date of birth is used initially, it undermines the integrity of the background check and would generally cause an employer and screening firm to have to repeat criminal searches.

Date of birth is subject to regulation due to laws concerning age discrimination, as discussed in Chapter 2. These laws present barriers for employers or screening firms from requesting the date of birth.

Another difficulty, given the sheer size of the American population, is just name and date of birth can result in "computer twins." "Computer twins" are two people with identical names and dates of birth. The problem is created when two different people are possibly identified as the same person.

A further complication, as noted in Chapter 17, is that the American method of stating the date of birth differs from many parts of the world. In the U.S., the traditional pattern is day/month/year while in many regions it is month/day/year.

Social Security Number (SSN)

The nine-digit **Social Security Number (SSN)** is an assigned number developed for the purpose of administering the U.S. Social Security program. As a practical matter, the SSN is treated as a de facto national identification number. It is widely used as a unique identifier and is commonly required for any number of transactions—practically any financial transaction will require the Social Security number.

Until June 2011, issuance of numbers followed a pattern. The first three numbers represented the state of issue. The second set of numbers was related to the date the card was issued. As a result of the changes to the issuance of SSNs, as described in Chapter 11, all numbers are now issued randomly, with no pattern. But it is still possible to tell the state and date of issue from the SSN, if issued prior to June 2011.

Also as discussed in Chapter 11, an employer will typically obtain a Social Security Trace Report, also known as a credit header. The report gives the employer additional information such as other names and addresses associated with the SSN and possibly the date of birth.

There are problems with using the Social Security number as an identifier. The SSN was never intended to act as a national identification number, and when issued, it is not part of a national ID system that systematically records biometrics to uniquely match an SSN to a particular person. For example, there is no fingerprint or other definite biometric measurement that is permanently associated with a particular SSN. On the other hand, government computers can eventually track if a number is being misused. For example, if an identity thief steals a Social Security number and uses it for employment, the government may eventually note another use of the same number for tax withholding purposes.

Motor Vehicle Driver's License

Each state issues its own **driver's license (DL)** that entitles the name on the card to legally operate a motor vehicle. In fact, the driver's license has become a national identification card since it is the only widespread and easily recognized official government card issued with a photo for identification. The DL is used for such purposes as cashing checks, entering the security area in an airport, and anything else that requires a proof of identify. Among the 50 states, there are not necessarily strict security controls over the issuance of the license. There have been instances of criminals using false identity papers to obtain a driver's license under a false name. In addition, a search on Google of a 'fake driver's license' reveals a number of websites that sell books and resources on how to make a fake driver's license and other ID's. A person on the East Coast could potentially create a fake driver's license from a state in the West and hope that a lack of familiarity will allow the document to pass.

Congress passed the REAL ID Act of 2005, Pub.L. 109-13, 119 Stat. 302, enacted May 11, 2005. The law was intended, among other things, to standardize procedures for issuance of state driving licenses and state issued identification cards. However, the bill has proved controversial and many states have not implemented its provisions. Bills have also been introduced to repeal this act as well.

Physical Characteristics

Identifying **physical characteristics** may be reported on a government identity form such as a driver's license. The most common physical features are height, weight, sex, hair, and eye color. When photo identification is used, a physical identifier will also include facial features depicted in a photograph. It can also refer to race, although that is typically not used as an identifier because of concerns over discrimination.

There are two immediate problems with these physical identifiers. First, the identifiers can change. A person's weight or hair color shown on a driver's license tends to become inaccurate as time goes by. Second, there can be a question as to the integrity of the data in the first place. When the data appears on a driver's license, for example, there is an assumption that a government official verified the data, so the data has verified authenticity. However, the situation is different if the document was forged or obtained under false pretense, as discussed below.

Unique Biometric Characteristics

Biometric characteristics are biological measurements. The notion behind biometrics is to provide a basis for personal authentication. Methods of recognizing a person are based upon physical characteristics such as fingerprints, eye scans of the iris, or retinal scans. Other types of measurements being studied are based on the physical features of the face or geometric features of the human hand and voice print. There is also a study of biometrics based on handwriting. A biometric measure relates to a particular individual as opposed to a password or a document that someone carries.

The challenge with a biometric identification is to ensure that the biometric identity is properly associated with the appropriate person when the measurement is first made. Unless the original identification can be trusted, subsequent identifications based upon the biometric have little value. If a criminal, terrorist, or imposter successfully obtains a false biometric identity, then that person essentially has a future "free pass"—unless the error is somehow detected and corrected.

With its U.S.-VISIT program, the United States has introduced biometric measurements at airports and seaports for visitors from certain countries. The biometric measurements include digital imaging of a visitor's face and a digital fingerprint. For more information about biometric measurements, visit the Department of Homeland Security's (DHS) Office of Biometric Identity Program (OBIM) web page at www.dhs.gov/obim.

Other Government-issued Documents

Identification can also be based upon other documents issued by state or local governments. A United States passport can be the basis for identification. Various governmental agencies may also issue identification of workers, for those in law enforcement or public safety identification. Other government issued identities can involve the issuance of "smart cards" that workers performing certain duties may be required to carry. These cards can contain embedded computer chips that allow identity verification and authorization to perform certain tasks or allow access to certain areas.

Past Data Associated with an Applicant

Another means of identification is to compare the applicant to public records contained in large information databases. There are a number of companies with access to literally billions of public records. One company claims that it has information on nearly 98% of the adult population and data entries relating to approximately 205 million individuals in the United States. Of course, access to the most extensive databases will cost money. There are two excellent websites that list links to literally thousands of free searchable public records databases at http://publicrecords.searchsystems.net/ and www.brbpublications.com/freeresources/pubrecsites.aspx.

In addition to the criminal records databases discussed in Chapter 10 and the Social Security Trace information discussed in Chapter 11, there are numerous other records maintained in proprietary databases. Available record types can include:

- Property ownership records
- Bankruptcies, liens, and judgments
- UCC filings

- Ownership of boats or planes
- Professional licenses

Use of Private Documents for Identifying

Another source of identity documents are those issued by private firms. Examples are credit cards and membership cards. These documents are far from ideal identifiers. Applicants with something to hide can attempt to manipulate the drawbacks on these forms of identities and create false identities. Who would want to do that? Individuals who do not want their true names or intentions divulged! These may be people simply wanting privacy, or they may be criminals or even terrorists.

Additional Identifier Tools

Firms are working on additional methods to validate identity. On example is a questionnaire based on a person's credit report with questions that only the person in question would know. For example, a person may be asked: "Which the following banks do you have a mortgage with?" It may list 4 or 5 choices with the last one being "none." There are also firms working on cyber identity fraud tools. For example, a person's computer IP address or some other information is matched to billions of records. Some websites are attempting to provide a service where there is online cyber identity verification, but the issue still remains how the initial identification is accomplished.

Another potential tool in the future may be validation of official government identification documents, used in conjunction with facial recognition software. Work is being done to enable employers to validate if driver licenses, passports, and other official documents are valid based on known attributes of such documents. If the official document contains a photo, facial recognition software may be able to validate if a person is, in fact, the person in the official photo. The process can take place at the employer's facility or potentially be something that can be accomplished remotely by having an applicant take a photo of both the official document and themselves on a mobile device. That of course also assumes the underlying government document was validly obtained and, in fact, belongs to the individual presenting it.

Employer Tools to Avoid Fraudulent Identification in the Workplace

While it may be beyond our purpose here to review the many ways that identity can be stolen or created, employers do need to be aware there are a great many ways a determined criminal or terrorist can steal or create an identity for the purpose of entering the workplace under false pretenses. Identity theft can run from simple and amateurish attempts, such as simply using another name, to attempting to obtain false identification such as a Social Security number or driver's license, all the way to sophisticated schemes involving document forgery and creation of an entirely fictitious person.

It can be a challenge for employers to identify a well-financed and sophisticated scheme to create a false identity. Although not impossible to do, it is still difficult to create a false identity. Employers do have substantial protections by taking some common sense precautions, mainly by conducting a background check.

To help prevent someone with a stolen identity from coming to your workplace, use the following tools. Keep in mind that use of these tools by themselves or even in combination are not guaranteed to protect an employer. Use of these tools goes a substantial way to discouraging applicants with something to hide. These tools demonstrate due diligence in the workplace.

Screening Discourages False Applicants

The best protection for an employer is to not have the issue of a false ID arise in the first place. Perhaps the first and best approach is to make it very clear to all job applicants that your firm does engage in a Safe Hiring Program. All finalists are subject to background checks. As a general rule, criminals and terrorists are looking for soft and easy targets. Why risk exposure at a firm that will perform a background check if they can go down the block to some organization who is not as particular about whom they hire? An applicant with a false identity may not know the extent of the employer's background checks, but an imposter may not be willing to take the risk.

An employer can take the following steps:

- In a job announcement, indicate that the employer does background checks. In looking at the "classified' section in any newspaper, it is common to see employers state that applicants must undergo drug testing and background checks.

- Clearly state that in the application process a screening will occur, and obtain consent for it.

- Utilize the six critical questions outlined in Chapter 3 that demonstrate the employer's commitment to safe hiring.

As the hiring process begins, some employers utilize the Social Security trace tool as an initial identity tool. If the applicant's identity does not check out then the time and effort of a further background check is saved. However, a Social Security trace is only a limited tool, and the entire screening process is helpful to verify identity, along with post-hire procedures discussed later in this chapter and the next.

The Trusted Source Rule – Third Party Verification

When America was made up of small towns, farms, and villages, everyone knew each other. There was no question who was who. This is obviously no longer the case. The best method for knowing what we know is still based on what people we know say, assuming we give those people credibility.

The Google search engine works in a similar manner. It does not matter to Google what a website says about itself as much as what others say about it, in terms of linking to it; the more third party sites that validate a website by linking to it, the higher the rating. It is a form of third party verification. The same rule applies to safe hiring as well. As we have seen throughout this book, what is important is not what an applicant states, but what can be independently verified.

In employment, the old adage "it is not what you know but who you know" reflects the obvious truth—that employers would prefer to hire a known quantity. If an employer actually knows the applicant, the applicant stands a better chance of being hired. The next best thing is to be recommended by a hiring manager or current worker. That is why firms place so much emphasis on employee-based recruiting. These are all variations of the basic premise of this chapter—that employers prefer to use a trusted source of information.

If every business owner could only hire candidates they either knew personally, or were known personally by people they knew, then there would be less time and effort spent managing and dealing with employee problems. To prevent a person with a false identity from entering your workforce, at some point your knowledge of an applicant must be tied to a trusted source. The trusted source may be another HR manager or a security professional you know and trust.

As seen throughout this book, reliance on public data or criminal databases alone is not advisable. A determined criminal, terrorist, or imposter may be able to steal an identity and pass such a test, or a database may give a false negative, meaning the person is erroneously cleared when they should not be. Furthermore, just trusting a person's word for who they are is obviously insufficient.

The key is a trusted source that can independently verify that the person sitting in front of you for an interview is the same person who has the history they claim. This is best done by **past employment verification**. Verifying past employment allows the employer to detect and hopefully eliminate any red flags caused by unexplained employment history gaps, or discover the resume/application is false. Thus the employer breaks the chain of relying upon what people say about themselves, relying upon documents that can easily be forged, or relying on databases that can contain errors.

If an employer is contacting someone they do not know, then the trusted source may turn out to be the telephone book or directory assistance or some similar online service to validate the authenticity of a past employer's telephone number. Having a listed telephone number provides at least some assurance that the past employer is a legitimate business that qualified for a phone number and directory assistance. Past employers can also be Googled or researched from other databases.

If the applicant claims self-employment, then it is more difficult to find an independent verification source. In this case, the approach is to ascertain from the applicant the names of past clients and then verify through directory assistance or some trusted source that the client is for real.

A warning—there are a number of well-meaning attempts being made to create databases, cards, or other schemes to validate identity. The basis of these efforts is some mechanism to perform some sort of **clearance**, then the individual is tied into some sort of biometric measure. However, the so-called clearance appears to be based on simply searching public records and government databases. Any reliance on any database is problematic. The drawbacks are multiplied when a criminal, terrorist, or imposter manages to obtain such a card, then it can be used to help conceal their identity in the future.

So a recommended best practice to validate identity for purposes of employment, safety, or other type of security concern is to include an element of third party verification from a trusted source. Although contacting a trusted source is a manual task, and not nearly as quick or inexpressive as using databases, it is critical if there is to be any confidence in an identity validation or clearance program.

Confirmation of Facts

Confirmation of facts is covered in a number of previous chapters. As the old saying goes, "trust but verify." Using the tools in this book, it is critical to verify facts and to utilize the various screening tools available, including a Social Security trace, past employment checks, verifying education and professional licenses, and a criminal records check.

Look for Internal Consistency or Inconsistency

Another tool that goes hand-in-hand with the trusted source rule is looking to see if there is a pattern of consistency—or applicant congruence. Congruence means "agreement, harmony, conformity, or correspondence."

Employers, hiring managers, human resources professionals or security professionals must ask themselves, "Does the total package make sense?" An employer needs to look at the applicant as a whole and, based upon the application and interview, be sensitive to anything that does not add up or make sense. For example:

- If a person claims to have a degree in computer science, does the person appear to have the appropriate knowledge in their interview?
- Does the employment history make sense for what the person did, where, and for how long?
- Are the educational accomplishments and past employment consistent with the person's knowledge, skills, and abilities?
- Are the job descriptions consistent with the person's knowledge, skills, and abilities?
- Are there unexplained gaps in employment?
- Did the applicant give specifics in the interview when discussing past jobs, knowledge, skills and experience, or did the person only give vague generalities?

In other words, does the person at the interview seem to match the history shown on the application? If something does not add up, consider this a red flag!

Cross-Referencing Accumulated Data

Based upon all the data the employer obtains, the next step is to cross reference the known facts to determine if everything makes sense. For our purposes, cross-referencing is a process of not relying upon just one fact, but on a combination of accumulated facts obtained both from the applicant and other sources. Information from one source is compared to others to determine if the applicant is factual about their claimed identity and history. Keep in mind that use of massive databases for employment purposes does have some legal limitations as discussed in Chapter 15. Another issue is how to effectively utilize large databases containing literally billions of records. A developing technology is data mining of large databases and specialized software to "connect the dots" to see trends and connections.

Again, another valuable tool is the Social Security trace. As described in Chapter 11, the Social Security trace is based upon information obtained by the three major credit bureaus—names and addresses associated with a particular Social Security number. If an employer is working with a screening firm, then the employer may receive data that is also based upon a number of other public record databases. This should help you create a useful address history. It is important to understand that these reports are not an official list of past residences, and there can be errors and variation. However, for purposes of cross-referencing, it is a tool that employers should use. For example, if a person claimed employment as a production supervisor in Chicago from 1998-2002, but the trace report indicated two different addresses in Los Angeles during the same time period, that would be a red flag.

You Need To Know ⟩ **Bad Information = Bad Results**

A background screening firm runs data based on what it receives—if a person sends in false information, the screening firm will get bad results. It is up to the employer to perform an ID check such as Consent Based Social Security Number Verification (CBSV) Service or Employment Eligibility Verifications Form I-9.

Identity Verification from the Social Security Administration

Legal authority for SSN verification is found in the Freedom of Information Act (FOIA), the Privacy Act at 5 U.S.C. § 552a (b), section 1106 of the Social Security Act, codified at 42 U.S.C. § 1306, and SSA regulation at 20 C.F.R. § 401.100.

There are three methods to verify the social security number of an applicant or new employee through official records of the Social Security Administration (SSA):

- Pre-Hire: Consent Based Social Security Number Verification Service (CBSV).

- Post-Hire: Social Security Number Verification Services (SSNVS).

- Post-Hire: E-Verify checks through the U.S. Citizenship and Immigration Services (USCIS), the government agency that oversees lawful immigration to the United States which accesses both the SSN data and the Department of Homeland Security (DHS), and done in conjunction with an I-9 Employment Eligibility Verification Form.

1. Consent Based Social Security Number Verification Service (CBSV)

The **Consent Based SSN Verification System (CBSV)** allows private businesses and government entities to verify that the name and SSN obtained from a customer matches or does not match the data in SSA's records. The information is matched against SSA's Master File of Social Security Numbers (SSNs), using Social Security number, name, date of birth, and gender code (if available)

With the consent of the SSN holder, enrolled users may utilize CBSV to verify whether the SSN holder's name and Social Security Number (SSN) combination match SSA's records. CBSV returns a "yes" or "no" verification indicating that the submission either matches or does not match our records. If records show that the SSN holder is deceased, CBSV returns a death indicator. CBSV verifications do not verify an individual's identity. CBSV is typically used by companies who provide banking and mortgage services, process credit checks, provide background checks, satisfy licensing requirements, etc.

Costs include a $5,000 initial enrollment fee and a per-SSN verification transaction fee of $1.05, paid in advance. Detailed information about CBSV can be found at www.ssa.gov/cbsv/ including a sample User Agreement, Web Service technical documents, and a User Guide.

Author Tip

What CBSV Does and Does Not Do

CBSV is designed to provide only a "yes" or "no" verification if the submitted SSN matched SSA records. CBSV does not verify identity, citizenship, employment eligibility, nor does it interface with the Department of Homeland Security (DHS) verification system. CBSV verifications do not satisfy DHS's I-9 requirements. Also, an employer must have an Employer Identification Number (EIN) to enroll in CBSV.

Information about Consent Based Social Security Number Verification (CBSV)

From Chuck Salvia, COO, IDValidation.com (www.idvalidation.com/)

1. What alternatives are available to Consent Based Social Security Number Verification (CBSV) from the Social Security Administration (SSA)?

All other pre-hire options to CBSV are non-governmental methodologies gathered from a variety of sources. They are called by the generic phrase "SSN Trace" which is comprised of polluted, flawed, and stale data from Credit Headers, Data Algorithms, and Proprietary Databases. These systems cannot be trusted because identity thieves can easily manipulate and bypass them with Synthetic Name Fraud/Synthetic Identity Theft schemes.

2. How CBSV helps employers

There are numerous ways that CBSV protects the vital business interests of businesses

- CBSV can be used for any business purpose including pre- or post-hire to ensure an authorized workforce

- CBSV validates an applicant's identity by matching Name, SSN, DOB, and Death Indicator

- If an applicant fails the pre-hire CBSV check, the employer can save time and money by ending the application process for this candidate

- The applicant's PII are matched direct to official SSA record resources from their Master File/Death index

- Online results are instantaneous which speeds the application process

- CBSV mitigates fraud and ID theft, reduces losses, net charge-offs, bad and negligent hires, unauthorized applicants and workers

- Avoid government fines and penalties by having an authorized workforce because the feds (IRS, ICE, CFPB) have increased their enforcement practices

- CBSV is used for any business purpose including, but not limited to:

    Background / Tenant / Employment / HR Management

    New Accounts / Clients, Customers, Members, Students, Patients, Policyholders, Volunteers, Licenses, Permits, Tax Audit

    Loan originations / Mortgages / Depository accounts

    Security / Fraud and Special Investigative Units / Insurance Adjustment / Forensic Accounting / Claims Adjusting

    Compliance for Customer Identification Programs (CIP), FTC Red Flags Rule, Fannie Mae Loan Quality Initiative (LQI),

Dodd-Frank Protection Act, Know Your Customer (KYC), CFPB, and more

3. Where and how the information is gathered and obtained.

The information is gathered by the federal government, stored in their Master File/Death index, and obtained from these official SSA record resources. With applicant consent on Form SSA-89, the document is submitted to the SSA through an authorized and proprietary portal. Results from the SSA are returned instantaneously.

4. How it compares to other data sources.

As noted earlier, CBSV does not compare to anything else on the market because it is "The Superlative Personal Identifier Validation Methodology". SSN Trace, the closest alternative, is derived from polluted, flawed, and stale data generated from many sources and NOT from the SSA Master File. Errors, missing, and old information make SSN Trace an inferior solution.

Compared to E-Verify

- CBSV is valid pre-hire. E-Verify is NOT valid pre-hire.

- CBSV is valid post-hire on existing workers. E-Verify is NOT valid on existing workers (except federal contractors).

- CBSV is virtually 100% accurate. E-Verify has an 8% error rate allowing unauthorized workers into businesses.

5. Special notes about using it, such as is a wet signature required, special forms needed, how long does it take, any special employer limitations, how complete is the data, etc.

- Per SSA regulations, wet signature of the applicant is required on Form SSA-89 "Authorization for the SSA to Release SSN Verification".

- The data is complete and accurate yielding a "Match/Successful", "No Match/Unsuccessful" or "Deceased" result.

- Employers are not limited or restricted and may use CBSV for any business purpose.

- Office of the U.S. Inspector General (OIG) reveals that CBSV is a deterrent to ID theft and fraud

- Best defense against fraudsters is from official governmental source data

6. What to do if an applicant disagrees with it, etc.

The applicant can review any errors or issues at the closest SSA Field Office. Here is an example of a letter that can be given to an applicant that fails the CBSV matching process.

Dear _____,

Your Form SSA-89 was processed by the Social Security Administration (SSA) and returned a "No Match" Unsuccessful result.

A "No Match" Unsuccessful result can be due to a number of factors (a name change being the most common). You will need to address this in person at your SSA Field Office. Use this link to locate SSA Field Offices by ZIP Code: https://www.ssa.gov/locator/.

The SSA will update your record and your Form SSA-89 Consent Based SSN Verification (CBSV) will need to be re-processed.

This approach provides a robust audit trail in a defense against any claim of discriminatory employment practices, and it also provides exceptional proof of compliance with employer statutory tax/wage reporting requirements which dictate that any person who works is required to have a valid

SSN issued to them. While CBSV does not satisfy I-9 requirements, it provides background evidence that the applicant is legal to work in the US (as long as the HR Dept. has seen the SSN Card to verify "Valid for Work Only" annotation).

Conclusion

If you are not using CBSV:

- You're at greater risk of ID theft incidents.

- Up to 35% of operational losses are fraud related.

- You're in jeopardy of tarnishing your valuable business reputation by allowing preventable fraud.

You Need To Know

Some CBSV Statistics

As ID theft has become a top U.S. crime, CBSV is more important than ever. ID Theft Prevention Expert Denis Kelly says: "If you're not using CBSV, then you are allowing up to 80% of preventable fraud."

- The U.S. Office of the Inspector General (OIG) published a CBSV report in October 2012 stating that "5% of CBSV searches are No Match/Unsuccessful". What does this mean? Individuals with fraudulent intent try to pass their fake ID through the CBSV system and they are caught. So the next question is: What happens at companies that are NOT presenting the CBSV Form SSA-89 as a deterrent?

- A southern California business tried CBSV on 79 new applicants. Ten (10) were No Match/Unsuccessful. That's a whopping 12.7% fraud rate.

- A University in Connecticut vetted 93 contract workers about to gain access to the campus. Guess what? Seventeen (17) were No Match/Unsuccessful. That's a staggering 18% fraud rate. Can you imagine the repercussions if they had not used CBSV and one or more of these fraudsters perpetrated a crime at the University?

From Chuck Salvia, COO, IDValidation.com (www.idvalidation.com/)

CBSV Could have Uncovered Airport Security Supervisor Who Used Dead Man's ID for 20 Years

In May 2012, authorities arrested a longtime New Jersey airport security supervisor known by his co-workers as "Jerry Thomas" on a charge of impersonating someone else to hide his illegal immigrant status. The suspect was carrying the identity of a victim in an unsolved murder case 20 years earlier.

The Port Authority of New York and New Jersey said "Jerry Thomas" had worked at Newark's Liberty International Airport for about 20 years and had passed background checks by using the name Jerry Thomas since 1992, the year Thomas was killed in New York City.

The use of CBSV would have revealed the Social Security number of a deceased person used by a new hire or existing employee who are unauthorized workers.

The identities of nearly 2.5 million deceased Americans were used improperly to apply for credit products and services each year, according to a new study released today from ID Analytics' ID:A Labs. This is the first study to examine the extent of fraudsters improperly using a deceased person's identity to establish credit accounts.

The study compared the names, dates of birth (DOB) and Social Security numbers (SSNs) on 100 million applications during the first three months of 2011 to data in the Social Security Administration's Death Master File (DMF) to find which applications used personally identifiable information (PII) associated with deceased individuals.

The study found:

- Identity Theft of the Dead – Nearly 800,000 deceased Americans' identities are intentionally targeted for misuse on applications for credit products and cell phone services by fraudsters each year.

- Inadvertently Misusing SSNs of the Deceased – In approximately 1.6 million applications annually, an identity manipulator inadvertently used the SSN of a deceased person.

- Identity Theft of the Dying – Several hundred thousand potential misuses of dying people's identities each year.

Sources:

www.foxnews.com/us/2012/05/14/longtime-security-supervisor-arrested-at-nj-airport-for-using-dead-man-id/ and www.prnewswire.com/news-releases/identities-of-nearly-25-million-deceased-americans-misused-each-year-148491305.html

---

You Need To Know

Restriction on Access to the Death Master File

Effective March 26, 2014, the Social Security Administration Death Index, also known as the Death Master File (DMF), has significant restrictions to access on newer records. In a nutshell, unless the requester is certified, they cannot be provided death record information within 3 years of a subject's data of death. However, this ban does not affect death records distributed/sold/in use prior to March 26, 2014. Below are details.

The U.S. National Technical Information Service issued an interim final rule to establish a certification program under which persons may obtain immediate access to the publicly available Death Master File (DMF), pursuant to Section 203 of the Bipartisan Budget Act of 2013 (Act).

The Act prohibits disclosure of DMF information during the three-calendar-year period following an individual's death unless the person requesting the information has been certified under a program established by the Secretary of Commerce. This rule, which set forth temporary requirements to become a certified person, provides penalties for disclosing or using DMF information in a manner not in accordance with the Act. This rule also provides for the charging of fees for the certification program. This rule was effective on March 26, 2014. Comments are accepted and due on this interim final rule on or before 5:00 p.m. Eastern time April 25, 2014. A significant portion of this rule is below:

"Restriction on Access to the Death Master File" Section 203(a) of the Act directs that the Secretary of Commerce (Secretary) shall not disclose to any person information contained on the Death Master File with respect to any deceased individual at any time during the three calendar- year period beginning on the date of the individual's death, unless such person is certified under a program established under the Act. Section 203(b)(1) of the Act directs the Secretary to establish a program to certify persons who are eligible to access the information contained on the Death Master File, and to perform periodic and unscheduled audits of certified persons to determine compliance with the program

Read the details in the Federal Register at www.gpo.gov/fdsys/pkg/FR-2014-03-26/pdf/2014-06701.pdf.

2. Social Security Number Verification Services (SSNVS)

The Social Security Administration's Social Security Number Verification Service SSNVS is an option to include as part of the new employee intake procedures. The service is free, but registration is required. While the service is available to all employers and third-party submitters, it can only be used to verify current or former employees and only for wage reporting (Form W-2) purposes. A background screening firm or employer cannot use this service prior to an offer of employment being made. Employers typically call after a person has been hired as part of the new hire paperwork.

Requesters will be told if the name and DOB match what the SSA has on file. Once registered, employers have two options:

1. Verify up to 10 names and SSNs (per screen) online and receive immediate results. This option is ideal to verify new hires.

2. Upload overnight files of up to 250,000 names and SSNs and usually receive results the next government business day. This option is ideal if you want to verify an entire payroll database or if you hire a large number of workers at a time.

The registration process takes approximately 14 days. During that time, the SSA will provide verifications over the telephone. For more information, visit www.ssa.gov/employer/ssnv.htm.

The Social Security Administration has also posted a Legal Use Policy - Don't Discriminate or Misuse SSNVS, which is shown below.

"SSA will advise you if a name/SSN you submitted does not match our records. This does not imply that you or your employee intentionally provided incorrect information about the employee's name or SSN. It is not a basis, in and of itself, for you to take any adverse action against the employee, such as termination, suspending, firing, or discriminating against an individual who appears on the list. SSNVS should only be used to verify currently or previously employed workers. Company policy concerning the use of SSNVS should be applied consistently to all workers, e.g. if used for newly hired employees, verify all newly hired employees; if used to verify your database, verify the entire database. Any employer that uses the information SSA provides regarding name/SSN verification to justify taking adverse action against an employee may violate state or federal law and be subject to legal consequences. Moreover, this makes no statement about your employee's immigration status."

The toll-free Social Security Administration telephone number is 1-800-772-6270 and is open weekdays from 7:00 a.m. to 7:00 p.m. EST. An employer will also be asked for the company name and federal Employer Identification Number (EIN). More information is available at www.ssa.gov/employer/ssnv.htm.

Privacy and the Social Security Number

The Social Security number has been getting a great deal of attention in the media recently due to the growing problems involved in identity theft. The ability of identity thieves to obtain Social Security numbers in order to commit fraud has become a national issue (See Chapter 28 on Identity Theft). The issue of privacy and Social Security numbers is being looked at carefully in Washington DC, as well as in various states. Part of the concern expressed by privacy advocates is the proliferation of Internet websites that sell data on consumers.

For the purposes of a Safe Hiring Program, any time information is obtained by an employer or a screening firm, it is always done with the expressed consent of the applicant for the expressed purpose of employment. In addition, if a third party firm is used, such as a background screening firm, then the requirements of the Fair Credit Reporting Act kick in as well, adding additional layers of protection and privacy for the applicant.

Changes to the FCRA effective in 2004 also addressed privacy concerns and the use of the Social Security number. The FCRA requires that screening firms, upon request from a consumer, must truncate the Social Security number on a background report. When a Social Security number is truncated, only the last four digits display such as xxx-xx-1234. The reason for the truncation requirement is that, often, identity theft occurs at the consumer's mailbox, where background reports mailed to the consumer can be stolen. By truncating the SSN, the consumer has some protection if the screening report falls into the wrong hands.

At least one state, California, has already passed strong legislation to protect the confidentiality of Social Security numbers, which includes controlling the use of SSNs by employers. California Civil Code § 1798.85 places numerous limitations on the use of SSNs including restrictions on anything mailed to the consumer. There is an exception in the law for any document whereby state or federal law requires the SSN to be on the document. Another California law also requires that California residents have an opportunity to check a box so they can receive a copy of any screening report, which is typically sent by mail. They are entitled to the same report the employer receives, which includes the applicant's SSN. To comply with these various California requirements, some screening firms have taken the position that the best practice is to truncate the SSN on any report sent to a California resident, revealing only the SSN's last four digits.

Another attempt by the federal government to protect the privacy of a Social Security number is the Financial Modernization Act of 1999, also known as the "Gramm-Leach-Bliley Act" or GLB Act. The law was passed in order to protect consumers' personal financial information held by financial institutions. However, since pre-employment screening is done in a consensual matter, the GLB has not had an impact on the use of the Social Security number for safe hiring purposes, especially when screening is conducted by an outside agency under the Fair Credit Reporting Act. More information is available at the Federal Trade Commission website at www.ftc.gov/tips-advice/business-center/privacy-and-security/gramm-leach-bliley-act.

As mentioned earlier in this chapter, another post-hire tool involving the Social Security number is an E-Verify check. This search confirms the work eligibility of newly hired employees by comparing information from the employee's Form I-9 to the information in U.S. Department of Homeland Security (DHS) and Social Security Administration (SSA). This procedure is described in detail in a later chapter.

Identity Theft Near Top of FTC List of Consumer Complaints in 2015

Debt collection, identity theft, and imposter scams were the most common categories of consumer complaints received by the Federal Trade Commission (FTC) in 2015, according to the FTC's Consumer Sentinel Network Data Book for January – December 2015.

Debt collection complaints rose to the top spot among complaint categories due in large part to a data contributor collecting complaints via a mobile app. Identity theft complaints were second, increasing more than 47 percent from 2014 with a massive jump in tax identity theft complaints.

"We recognize that identity theft and unlawful debt collection practices continue to cause significant harm to many consumers," Jessica Rich, Director of the FTC's Bureau of Consumer Protection, stated in an FTC press release about the agency's annual data book.

The FTC's top ten consumer complaint categories were:

1. Debt Collection – 897,655 complaints (29 percent)
2. Identity Theft – 490,220 complaints (16 percent)

3. Imposter Scams – 353,770 complaints (11 percent)

4. Telephone and Mobile Services – 275,754 complaints (9 percent)

5. Prizes, Sweepstakes and Lotteries – 140,136 complaints (5 percent)

6. Banks and Lenders – 131,875 complaints (4 percent)

7. Shop-At-Home and Catalog Sales – 96,363 complaints (3 percent)

8. Auto-Related Complaints – 93,917 complaints (3 percent)

9. Television and Electronic Media – 47,728 complaints (2 percent)

10. Credit Bureaus, Information Furnishers, and Report Users – 43,939 complaints (1 percent)

The FTC data book is available at www.ftc.gov/reports/consumer-sentinel-network-data-book-january-december-2015.

Identity Verification Before or After the Hire

A tool that is available to employers pre-employment is the Consent Based Social Security Number Verification Service, known as CBSV (www.ssa.gov/cbsv/). CBSV can be obtained through background screening firms. However, it requires special documentation above and beyond forms applicants normally sign so here are additional administrative steps (See Chapter 17 for a discussion of this program).

There are also two post-hire processes an employer can utilize:

1. Part of the intake of a new employee is to verify that the Social Security number provided by the new employee is valid. The Social Security Administration provides several services to employers to verify the SSN. Refer to Chapter 17 for details on the Social Security Number Verification Service (SSNVS)

2. Other after the hire government programs to validate the identity and the SSN of a new employer include Form I-9 and E-Verify. These programs are examined in Chapter 16.

Employee Privacy Rights

Beth Givens, Director of the Privacy Rights Clearinghouse (www.privacyrights.org), prepared the following summary of what an employer should and must do to protect identity.

Reprinted here with permission, the original article is available at the Privacy Rights Clearinghouse website at www.privacyrights.org/ar/PreventITWorkplace.htm. For resources on responsible information handling practices, see www.privacyrights.org/ar/SDCountyIT.htm.

What Employers Can Do to Protect the Privacy Rights of Employees

By Beth Givens

Experts in identity theft report that an increasing number of cases can be traced back to dishonest employees in the workplace or computer hackers who obtain Social Security numbers (SSNs) of employees and customers, then disclose that information to individuals involved in crime rings or other identity theft schemes.

One of the keys to preventing identity theft, therefore, is to safeguard sensitive personal information *within the workplace*, whether that workplace is a government agency, private business, or nonprofit organization. Everyone must get involved in protecting personal information such as SSNs, financial account numbers, dates of birth – in other words, any information used by identity thieves to impersonate individuals in the marketplace.

Workplace Information-Handling Practices

The Privacy Rights organization makes these suggestions for the responsible handling of information. Although these recommendations are based upon California law, they comprise "best practices" for employers and institutions in all states:

- **Adopt a comprehensive privacy policy** that includes responsible information-handling practices. Appoint an individual and/or department to be responsible for the privacy policy, one who can be contacted by employees and customers with questions and complaints.

- **Store sensitive personal data in secure computer systems.** Store physical documents in secure spaces such as locked file cabinets. Data should only be available to qualified persons.

- **Dispose of documents properly**, including shredding paper with a cross-cut shredder, "wiping" electronic files, destroying computer diskettes and CD-ROMs, and so on. Comply with California's document destruction law, Civil Code 1798.80-1798.84. The FACT Act passed in 2003 also added provisions in section 628 about the proper manner to dispose of consumer reports under the FCRA. The FTC has prepared regulations at www.ftc.gov/tips-advice/business-center/guidance/disposing-consumer-report-information-rule-tells-how.

- **Build document destruction capabilities into the office infrastructure**. Place shredders around the office, near printers and fax machines, and near waste baskets. Make sure dumpsters are locked and inaccessible to the public.

- **Conduct regular staff training**, including new employees, temporary employees, and contractors.

- **Conduct privacy "walk-throughs"** and make spot checks on proper information handling. Reward employees and departments for maintaining "best practices."

- **Put limits on data collection to the minimum information needed.** For example, is SSN really required? Is complete date of birth needed, or would year and month be sufficient?

- **Put limits on data display and disclosure of SSN.** Do not print full SSNs on paychecks, parking permits, staff badges, time sheets, training program rosters, lists of who got promoted, on monthly account statements, on customer reports, etc. Unless allowed by law, do not print SSN on mailed documents or require that it be transmitted via the internet. In compliance with California law, do not use SSN as customer number, employee ID number, health insurance ID card, etc. Comply with California Civil Code 1798.85-86 and 1786.6.

- **Restrict data access to staff with a legitimate need to know.** Implement electronic audit trail procedures to monitor who is accessing what. Enforce strict penalties for illegitimate browsing and access.

- **Conduct employee background checks**, especially for individuals who have access to sensitive personal information. Screen cleaning services, temp services, contractors, etc.

- **Safeguard mobile computers**, laptops, PDAs that contain files with sensitive personal data.

- **Notify customers and/or employees of computer security breaches** involving sensitive personal information, in compliance with California law Civil Code 1798.29 and 1798.82-1798.84, including security breaches involving paper records.

You Need To Know

Other Suggestions for Employers

It should be noted that ID thieves now have even more of an opportunity for identity theft. With the adoption of so many mobile devices and increasing technology, theft of sensitive data can occur more often. Internet access can even be stolen from wireless systems with readily available equipment that can be purchased at retail stores. Targets for identity thieves include SSNs, driver's license numbers, financial account numbers, PINs, passcodes, and dates of birth.

Other helpful suggestions include:

- Implement a written Identity Theft Prevention Program to detect the warning signs – or "red flags" – of identity theft. A "how-to" guide for companies that are considered a "low risk" for identity theft is provided by the Federal Trade Commission.
- Encrypt! And make sure your wireless network is protected with the proper security settings.
- Use cross-cut (confetti) shredders rather than strip-shredders.
- Keep in mind amendment to federal Fair Credit Reporting Act (FCRA) has a provision on document disposal (Sec. 216. Disposal of consumer report information and records.).
- More than 30 states have adopted security breach notice laws. Also notify individuals when security breaches involve paper records, outside the scope of most laws. Develop a crisis management plan to be used if sensitive employee or customer data is lost, stolen, or acquired electronically. The plan should include instructions to prevent identity theft if SSNs and/or financial account numbers are obtained illegitimately.
- Regularly audit compliance with all information-handling practices and privacy policies.

Privacy and Data Protection in Background Check Screening Reports

Because background reports and background release forms contain sensitive and confidential information, efforts must be made to keep the contents private and confidential and only available to decision-makers directly involved in the hiring process.

The Report itself, along with the Release and Authorization forms signed by the applicant, should be maintained separately from the employee's personnel file. They should be kept in a relatively secured area, in the same fashion that medical files or sensitive employee matters are kept. These reports should definitely not be made available to supervisors or managers other than those in the hiring approval process. For example, during periodic performance appraisals, an employer would not want a supervisor to have access to a non-performance-related confidential background report.

For screening firms with advanced internet systems, there is no need to physically download the report. It is available online. However, an employer needs to be assured that the screening firm has appropriate internet and data security, and the employer needs to maintain a system of strong password protections. It is important that authorized users do not share passwords with those not authorized, nor reveal the password in any manner. Some screening firms require the user to change passwords periodically as a security measure and to sign security agreements.

Typically, reports are returned to either Human Resources or Security Departments. Reports are reviewed for any negative information. If the report is clear, then the hiring manager is notified, and the hiring proceeds. If there is a red flag or derogatory information, then the information itself is shared with the appropriate decision-makers. The physical report, however, should normally stay with HR or Security. This protects against confidential information wrongfully being made known generally within the company if reports are transmitted between departments either by means of a paper copy or electronically.

The question arises as to how long records and documents should be maintained after separation. Unlike Canada where privacy laws encourage the destruction of confidential data when no longer needed, there are no U.S. requirements that materials related to background screening be destroyed. In fact, there are a number of state and federal laws that control document retention, and labor attorneys will typically advise employers on how long various documents must be retained. However, for purposes involving safe hiring and background screening, the recommendation by ESR is six years. The FCRAÂ was amended in 2003 to lengthen the statute of limitations under the act to as long as five years. In addition, state laws often allow a one-year period to file and serve a lawsuit. As a workable general rule, a six-year retention period should serve employers, with the six years running from the termination of employment or, if not hired, from the time the decision was made not to hire the applicant.

Many screening firms now store reports indefinitely, and if the applicant used an online system, the consent and disclosure can also be retained indefinably. However, if an employer downloads any data, or used a paper-based consent and disclosure, then consider six years as the minimum. Although technically there is no maximum period under federal law, it is still a best practice to periodically purge old data in order to minimize the amount of Personal and Identifiable Information (PII) that is available in the work environment. After all, most identity theft occurs in the workplace.

If disposing of any information in a consumer report, it is important to follow regulations set out by the FTC pursuant to FCRA Section 628. Paper or electronic reports must be destroyed, pulverized, or erased so it cannot be read or reconstructed. An employer must show due diligence when a shredding firm is hired.

Also, review the best practice the recommendations from the Privacy Rights Clearinghouse described in the previous section.

Trend Towards Mandated Privacy and Data Protection – Massachusetts Regulations Require Businesses to Have Information Security Program to Protect Personal Information

The increased emphasis on data and information protections can be demonstrated by strict new privacy rules put in place by Massachusetts, described as the toughest data protection and privacy rules in the nation. The Massachusetts Offices of Consumer Affairs and Business Regulations (OCABR) passed regulations that went into effect March 1, 2010, and are aimed at safeguarding the personal information of Massachusetts residents by requiring a business to have a Written Information Security Program (WISP) to protect personal information.

The new rules cover any business that "receives, stores, maintains, processes, or otherwise has access to personal information in connection with the provision of goods or services or in connection with employment."

The rules define personal information as a Massachusetts resident's name combined with a Social Security number, driver's license number or state-issued ID card, or a financial account number or credit/debit card number. The regulations also apply to third parties and require that there be contracts to ensure that the regulations are implemented and maintained, although the contracts did not need to be updated before March 1, 2012. It appears that Massachusetts takes the position that the rules apply to out of state firms that handle personal information as well.

A business that is regulated by these rules must have and implement a comprehensive WISP. The rules do not specify exact policies but provides minimum requirements and indicate that a business should take a certain number of factors into account such as the kind of records it maintains and the risk of identity theft.

Some of the things a business must do include a review of foreseeable internal and external risks, evaluation and improvement of safeguards, policies for employee access outside of the business, implementing security measures such as password control and up to date firewall, employee training, ensuring that terminated employees cannot access confidential data as well as disciplinary measures for violations of the regulations.

A text of the new regulations 201 CMR 17.00: STANDARDS FOR THE PROTECTION OF PERSONAL INFORMATION OF RESIDENTS OF THE COMMONWEALTH can be viewed at www.mass.gov/ocabr/docs/idtheft/201cmr1700reg.pdf.

You Need To Know

NAPBS Executive Director Explains How Removing Birthdate from Court Records May Have Unintended Consequences

With many courts considering the removal of identifiers such as date of birth (DOB) from public records to protect citizens from identity theft, Melissa Sorenson, Executive Director of the National Association of Professional Background Screeners (NAPBS), has written a guest column for The Gazette entitled 'Removing birthdate from Iowa court records could have unintended consequences' that explains how doing this may negatively impact people seeking employment or housing.

In the opinion piece from April 2016, Sorenson shows how the Iowa State Court Administration's consideration of redacting, or "masking," the DOB from court records could prevent background screeners hired by employers, landlords, and volunteer organizations from obtaining the information necessary to make accurate hiring and leasing decisions. Sorensen explains that "having an individual's full DOB is a critical identifier in public record data as it helps ensure the correct data is matched to an individual."

Sorenson writes: *With thousands of people sharing the same name, full date of birth is critical in determining if a record belongs to an applicant. Furthermore, NAPBS members are trained to properly handle potentially identifying information and are subject to strict regulations under the Fair Credit Reporting Act and the Fair and Accurate Credit Transactions Act of 2003. Our members are also regulated by a patchwork of federal, state and local rules pertaining to data security and privacy laws.*

As a result of not having a DOB in a court record, Sorenson warns that "background screening reports cannot be as complete and thus cannot help promote safety in our communities." Screeners would have to pick between "a long list of criminal records based on the limited identifiers available and risk that most of the records will not apply to the applicant, or they can choose not to include any of the records with limited information—even though that record may very well belong to the applicant."

While Sorenson agrees that protecting the people of Iowa from identity theft is a shared goal of NAPBS and the Iowa State Court Administration, "the removal of common identifiers from court records negatively impacts the accuracy of background reports making it more difficult for Iowans to be placed for work and find housing." She also urges courts in Iowa "to examine the unintended consequences that could arise from an otherwise well intended proposition." The column is at www.thegazette.com/subject/opinion/guest-columnists/removing-birthdate-from-iowa-court-records-could-have-unintended-consequences-20160411.

Melissa Sorenson is the first dedicated Executive Director of the NAPBS. She holds a law degree from William Mitchell College of Law and is admitted to the Minnesota bar. The NAPBS – "The Voice of Screening Professionals" – represents over 730 members performing pre-employment and tenant screening across the United States and is dedicated to providing the public with safe places to live and work. For more information about the NAPBS, please visit www.napbs.com.

FTC Report on Protecting Consumer Privacy Recommends Businesses Adopt Best Privacy Practices

In March 2012, the Federal Trade Commission (FTC) issued a report – *'Protecting Consumer Privacy in an Era of Rapid Change: Recommendations For Businesses and Policymakers'* – outlining best practices for businesses to protect the privacy of American consumers and give them greater control over the collection and use of their personal data, according to an FTC press release. The FTC also recommended that Congress consider enacting general privacy legislation, data security and breach notification legislation, and data broker legislation.

The FTC report also called on businesses handling consumer data to implement recommendations for protecting privacy that include:

- **Privacy by Design** – Businesses should build in privacy protections for consumers at every stage in developing their products, including reasonable security for consumer data, limited collection and retention of consumer data, and reasonable procedures to promote data accuracy;
- **Simplified Choice for Businesses and Consumers** – Businesses should give consumers the option to decide what information is shared about them, and with whom, and should include a 'Do-Not-Track' mechanism to provide a simple and easy way for consumers to control the tracking of their online activities.
- **Greater Transparency** – Businesses should disclose details about their collection and use of personal information of consumers and provide consumers access to the data collected about them.

As the nation's chief privacy policy and enforcement agency, the FTC urges individual business to accelerate the adoption of the principles contained in the privacy framework. The FTC has indicated it will encourage consumer privacy protections by focusing on the following five action items:

- **Do-Not-Track** – The FTC commends the progress made by browser vendors that have developed tools to allow consumers to limit data collection about them, and will work with these groups to complete implementation of an easy-to-use, persistent, and effective Do Not Track system.
- **Mobile** – The FTC urges companies offering mobile services to work toward improved privacy protections, including disclosures, and will host a workshop on May 30, 2012, to address how mobile privacy disclosures can be short, effective, and accessible to consumers on small screens.
- **Data Brokers** – The FTC calls on data brokers to make their operations more transparent by creating a centralized website to identify themselves, to disclose how they collect and use consumer data, and to detail the choices that data brokers provide consumers about their own information.
- **Large Platform Providers** – The FTC cited heightened privacy concerns about the extent to which platforms, such as Internet Service Providers, operating systems, browsers and social media companies, seek to comprehensively track the online activity of consumers. The FTC will host a public workshop in the second half of 2012 to explore issues related to comprehensive tracking.
- **Promoting Enforceable Self-Regulatory Codes** – The FTC will work with the Department of Commerce to develop industry-specific codes of privacy conduct, and when companies adhere to these codes, the FTC will take

that into account in its law enforcement efforts. If companies do not honor the codes they sign up for, they could be subject to FTC enforcement actions.

Recognizing the potential burden on small businesses, the report concludes that the privacy framework should not apply to businesses that collect and do not transfer only non-sensitive data from fewer than 5,000 consumers a year. The FTC report, *'Protecting Consumer Privacy in an Era of Rapid Change: Recommendations For Businesses and Policymakers,'* is available at: www.ftc.gov/os/2012/03/120326privacyreport.pdf.

In a Dissenting Statement released along with the report, FTC Commissioner Thomas Rosch dissented from the issuance of the Final Privacy Report and voiced his concerns with the proposed reforms. Rosch warned the reforms, which were approved by a vote of 3-1, would install "Big Brother" as the watchdog over online and offline privacy practices and go "well beyond what Congress has permitted the commission to do." The Dissenting Statement is available at www.ftc.gov/speeches/rosch/120326privacyreport.pdf.

Data Breaches Can Cost Businesses Millions

Information security is critical in today's digital world. A data breach can cost a company millions of dollars as well as the trust of their customers and embarrassment due to bad publicity. Below are two examples of well-known companies that suffered expensive data breaches that can harm a company's reputation and bottom line.

Home Depot to Pay $19.5 Million for Massive Data Breach

In March of 2016, Home Depot Inc. agreed to pay **$19.5 million** – $13 million to settle class action lawsuits and $6.5 million for identity protection services – to compensate approximately 40 to 50 million consumers affected by a massive data breach in 2014, according to a report from Reuters.

Home Depot will set up a $13 million settlement fund to reimburse consumers affected by the data breach for out-of-pocket losses. In addition, the home improvement retailer will spend $6.5 million for 18 months of free identity protection services for data breach victims.

Home Depot – which did not admit wrongdoing or liability in the settlement – agreed to improve information security over a period of two years. The data breach affected consumers using payment cards in U.S. and Canadian stores between April 2014 and September 2014.

The Reuters report is available at www.reuters.com/article/us-home-depot-breach-settlement-idUSKCN0WA24Z.

Sony Data Breach Lawsuit Settlement Gets Final Approval

In April 2016, a federal judge in Los Angeles gave final approval to a multimillion-dollar settlement that finally ended a class action lawsuit against Sony Pictures stemming from a massive data breach suffered by the studio in November 2014 that exposed the personal data of thousands of employees online, Deadline Hollywood reports.

The settlement approved for 435,000 certified class action members included a maximum of $10,000 per individual plus $1,000-$3,000 to the group of initial plaintiffs, making the total price to Sony Pictures for the data breach **approximately $15 million**.

The settlement requires Sony Pictures to provide identity theft protection until the end of 2017 and a fund to compensate members who paid to protect themselves after the data breach. The ongoing identity theft protection for the data breach could see Sony Pictures paying out over $4 million.

Two former Sony employees had filed a class action lawsuit against Sony in December 2014 claiming that the company did not take adequate measures to prevent a "massive" data breach that compromised the personal data of thousands of current and former Sony employees.

According to the complaint, Sony Pictures "failed to secure its computer systems, servers, and databases despite weaknesses it has known about for years." The lawsuit also claimed sensitive data including Social Security numbers, employment files, and medical information was leaked to the public in the data breach.

The story is at http://deadline.com/2016/04/sony-hack-lawsuit-settlement-approved-class-action-1201732882/.

Massive Yahoo Data Breach Could Affect 500 Million Users

In September of 2016, technology company Yahoo confirmed user account information that may have included names, email addresses, phone numbers, dates of birth, passwords, and security questions was stolen from 500 million Yahoo user accounts by "a state-sponsored actor" in a massive data breach in late 2014.

A message from Yahoo about user security indicated an ongoing investigation found the stolen information did not include unprotected passwords, payment card data, or bank account information. The message stated that Yahoo would continue to strive to stay ahead of ever-evolving online threats and keep users and platforms secure with "strategic proactive detection initiatives and active response to unauthorized access of accounts." Yahoo is also asking users to follow these security recommendations:

- Change passwords and security questions and answers for any other accounts which use the same or similar information used for the Yahoo account.

- Review accounts for suspicious activity.

- Be cautious of any unsolicited communications that ask for personal information or refer users to a web page asking for personal information.

- Avoid clicking on links or downloading attachments from suspicious emails.

The message is at https://yahoo.tumblr.com/post/150781911849/an-important-message-about-yahoo-user-security.

Government Background Check Data Breach Affects 21.5 Million People

In July 2015, the U.S. Office of Personnel Management (OPM) announced that sensitive information including Social Security Numbers (SSNs) for 21.5 million people was compromised in a database breach involving the background check records of current, former, and prospective Federal employees and contractors.

The OPM concluded that the sensitive information stolen from the background check databases includes 19.7 million individuals who applied for a background check and 1.8 million non-applicants who are primarily spouses or cohabitants of the applicants. Some records include interview findings while approximately 1.1 million include fingerprints. Usernames and passwords used by applicants to fill out background check forms were also stolen.

The OPM warned people who underwent a background check investigation through OPM in 2000 or afterward for either a new investigation or a reinvestigation that it is "highly likely" that they are impacted by the background check data breach. Those who underwent a background check investigation prior to 2000 may be impacted although it is "less likely." The types of information involved in the background check data breach incident may include:

- Social Security Numbers (SSNs).
- Residency and educational history.
- Employment history.
- Information about immediate family and personal and business acquaintances.
- Health, criminal, and financial history that would have been provided as part of a background check investigation.

Those people affected by the background check data breach incident received a notice in the mail from the OPM containing details on the services available to them at no cost for at least three years. These services supplied by the OPM will include identity restoration support and victim recovery assistance, identity theft insurance, identity monitoring for minor children, continuous credit monitoring, and fraud monitoring services.

This background check data breach is the second of two separate but related cyber-security incidents recently discovered by the OPM that have impacted the data of Federal government employees and contractors. In April 2015, the OPM found that the personal data of 4.2 million current and former Federal government employees had been stolen. While investigating this incident, the OPM discovered that additional information of 21.5 million people had been compromised in June 2015.

Information about the OPM background check database incident is at www.opm.gov/cybersecurity/.

Government Establishes NBIB to Modernize Background Checks

In January 2016, the United States Federal Government announced a series of changes including the establishment of the National Background Investigations Bureau (NBIB) to modernize and strengthen the way Federal background checks are conducted and sensitive data protected for Federal employees and contractors.

The NBIB will absorb the U.S. Office of Personnel Management's (OPM) existing Federal Investigative Services (FIS) and be headquartered in Washington, D.C. The Department of Defense (DoD) will assume responsibility for the design, development, security, and operation of Information Technology (IT) systems for the NBIB.

The NBIB will be housed within the OPM with a mission to provide secure background checks for the Federal Government. Steps the Federal Government is taking to improve the security clearance and background investigation processes for Federal employees and contractors will include:

- Establishing a new federal entity – the NBIB – to strengthen how the government performs background checks.
- Leveraging expertise at DoD for processing background checks and protecting against security threats.
- Updating responsibilities established by Executive Order 13467 to clarify existing roles and assign new responsibilities where gaps may exist.
- Build on the security measures implemented in response to the cyber security incidents at the OPM in 2015.
- Establish an NBIB transition team transition the management of FIS IT systems to DoD and migrate the existing functions, personnel, and support structure of OPM FIS to NBIB.
- Drive continuous performance improvement to address evolving threats to ensure NBIB is successful in its critical mission to provide secure background checks.

A Fact Sheet about changes to Federal background checks also posted on the White House website is available at www.whitehouse.gov/blog/2016/01/22/modernizing-strengthening-security-effectiveness-federal-background-investigations

Job Seeker Questions and Concerns about Background Checks

Introduction

Chapter 23 is written from the point of view of a Job Applicant. Why is this information contained in a book written for employers?

- First, job applicants often have questions about the procedures. It is in the interest of both employers and applicants that these questions be answered.
- Second, while many applicants shrug off background checks as just another part of the process, employers do not want to discourage otherwise good applicants just because an applicant may be unaware of the details of the procedures or their rights in the process.
- Third, with the advent of what has been called Web 2.0, the web has become more interactive and is now a primary source of recruiting. An essential element for successful recruitment of the best talent is employer branding. In order to have a successful online brand for recruiting purposes, employers need to be aware of the applicant experience since that can impact the success of a firm's recruiting efforts. Part of that online branding extends to the applicant experience when it comes to background checks.

For job seekers, it is critical to understand that employers are increasingly turning to background screenings of job applicants as a way of minimizing legal and financial risk. Concerns about negligent hiring lawsuits, workplace violence, wrongful termination, and other problems are leading many employers to be more careful about who is hired in the first place. In many cases, a background check is considered a prerequisite for eligibility in the application process. Many applicants understand, in this post-9/11 world, that background checking is a new fact of life. Of course, a background screening is not a full-fledged FBI-type investigation. Screening companies are typically looking for red flags indicating potential problems or resumes that are not factual or omit important information.

Job Applicants Have Protection

However, for some applicants, background screening can create an uneasy feeling of mistrust from the start—or *Big Brother is watching*. The fact is, however, that applicants have a great deal of protection regarding background checks. Such checks are normally conducted by third party background firms. If an employer utilizes a third party service, the Fair Credit Reporting Act (FCRA) requires an employer to obtain the applicant's express written consent to perform a background or reference check, and the employer is also required to give certain legal disclosures.

The fact is, background screenings of job applicants benefit employees and employers alike, and with the recent changes to the Fair Credit Reporting Act (FCRA), job applicants now have greater legal protections. In fact, it can be argued that the pendulum has clearly swung in favor of job applicants given the protections afforded under the FCRA.

For applicants, the advantages of working for a company that requires screening shows efforts have been made to ensure that co-workers have the qualifications and credentials they say they have. Who wants to work in a situation where someone with a fake employment or education history is making the same salary but got the job by cheating? Or, who wants to work in an unsafe environment? In addition, employers typically screen out those people with criminal records, especially records involving violence or dishonesty, who are not suitable for the job.

The following questions and answers cover most concerns an applicant might have regarding a pre-employment background check so they can understand the importance of this process and how their rights are protected.

What Will Job Applicants Learn in this Chapter?

To help consumers, this chapter will cover a number of areas that can be of concern when seeking employment including:

1. A job seekers guide to background checks
2. What can I do to prepare for a background check?
3. What steps can I take if I have an expunged criminal record to make sure it does not follow me around and hurt my employment chances?
4. Why do employers obtain credit reports, how does it impact me and what are my rights?
5. Ten critical steps for ex-offenders to get back into the workforce,
6. Dealing with and protecting against identity theft.

A Job Seeker's Guide to Background Checks

Why is a background check necessary?

A background check is more than keeping the employer out of trouble. Employers who screen their employees demonstrate a commitment to keeping employees safe on the job. In addition to the safety and well-being of their employees, employers are held responsible for the safety of their customers and anyone who may be affected or harmed by the actions or negligence of an on-duty employee.

It doesn't stop there. Employers can be held liable for damages if a court determines the employer should have known an employee posed a potential risk to people or property. Failing to make sure an employee is "safe" can land an employer in 'hot water' as well as put innocent people at risk.

Are background checks legal?

It is legal for an employer to perform a background check on an employee or job applicant. An employer has the right to select the most qualified applicant for a position, providing the employer is basing the decision on non-discriminatory factors that are valid predictors of job performance.

However, the employer must follow the guidelines set in the Federal Fair Credit Reporting Act (FCRA). Under the FCRA, when an employer uses a background screening company to prepare a report, several steps must occur:

- The employer must clearly disclose to the applicant that a report is being prepared. This disclosure must be a separate, stand-alone document and cannot be buried in the fine print of an application form.
- The employer must obtain the applicant's express written consent in order to obtain records such as criminal convictions or pending criminal cases, driving records, credit reports, past employment data, or educational credentials.
- An additional notice is required when a background firm checks references, such as asking previous employers about job performance.
- If an employer intends to deny employment based on information in the report, the job applicant must receive a copy of the report and a notice of his or her legal rights.
- If the decision to deny employment is made final, an applicant is entitled to some additional information.

Employers are strictly bound by any state and local laws governing background checks. These laws vary from state to state and may place additional limits or requirements on the background checking process.

BBB Warns Job Seekers about Background Check Scams for Employment

In April 2013, the Better Business Bureau (BBB) warned that job seekers in the St. Louis, Missouri area said they had been scammed by thieves claiming to represent a company performing biohazard cleanup work. All victims claimed the thieves cut off communications after collecting the $89 fee job seekers paid for a supposed pre-employment criminal background check using prepaid cash cards.

The BBB urges job seekers to be "extremely skeptical of any business demanding upfront payments via prepaid cash cards or electronic wire transfer systems like Western Union or MoneyGram." In the St. Louis cases, the victims were instructed to load $89 onto a Green Dot MoneyPak card to pay for a pre-employment criminal background check. After the thieves emptied the money from the card for the background check, they stopped communications. The BBB also offered the following tips to job seekers:

- Beware of unfamiliar companies making contact through online job boards. Some of these so-called businesses may be set up to scam job seekers.

- Be cautious about paying any fees upfront for pre-employment background checks or drug tests.

- If at all possible, visit the company's office to determine that they are located where they say they are.

- Get references for the company and contact them.

- Check for a BBB Business Review at www.bbb.org or by calling 314-645-3300.

The full article is available at http://stlouis.bbb.org/article/BBB-Warns-Bio-Advocate-Pro-Steals-Money-From-Job-Seekers-40989.

BBB Warns About Background Check Email Scam

In February 2015, the BBB warned consumers in a post titled, "Someone Ordered Your Background Check? It's a Scam!" to be on the lookout for a background check email scam containing fake messages claiming someone ordered a background check on the email recipients to get them to click an infected link.

The BBB explained the background check scam sends consumers an email with the subject line, "Someone recently viewed your background information." The message claims to be an automatically generated notification that someone "has just recently ordered the results of your background check." Consumers are told to "find out more about this new-scan" with a link at the bottom of the message.

However, although consumers may be curious, the BBB warns them not to click the link. This email is a background check scam and the link will download malware to computers. The BBB also suggests consumers should not to click on links that come in "unsolicited" emails. The BBB background check scam warning also includes ways consumers can spot malicious emails not caught by spam filters:

- The email claims to have information about consumers that they never signed up for. Scams often pretend to be personalized for individuals, but they are actually 'email blasts.' If consumers never signed up for custom email alerts, they should not be receiving them.

- Check out the 'From' field to look for email addresses that do not match the brand used in the email message. Scammers have the ability to mask email addresses to make the message appear to come from a legitimate source but do not always use it.

- Watch for typos, strange phrasing, and poor grammar in the email. For example, strange hyphens in "background-information" and "new-scan" (when "background information" and "new scam" are obviously the proper phrases to use) are telltale signs of a scam.

- Hover over URLs in the email to reveal their true destination that may contain malware. Typically, the hyperlinked text will say one thing but the link will point to fake websites or hack into third-party sites and use them to host malware.

For more information on finding a job and to check the reliability of any company, visit the Better Business Bureau website at www.bbb.org.

The article is available at www.bbb.org/pittsburgh/news-events/bbb-scam-alerts/2015/02/someone-ordered-your-background-check-its-a-scam/.

Why do the same laws apply to credit reports and background checks?

Even though the name of the Fair Credit Reporting Act (FCRA) uses the term "credit," this is actually misleading because the FCRA applies to much more than just credit applications. A credit report is just one type of consumer report governed by the FCRA. The FCRA defines a consumer report as any written, oral, or other communication of any information by a consumer reporting agency bearing on a consumer's "credit worthiness, credit standing, credit capacity, character, general reputation, personal characteristics, or mode of living which is used or expected to be used or collected in whole or in part" for various listed purposes, including credit, employment, or the underwriting of insurance.

Any employer or organization obtaining an applicant's driving records, employment records, or criminal records directly from a third party assembling this information into a consumer report is subject to the FCRA. A professional third party background screening firm that gathers and assembles this information is called a Consumer Reporting Agency (CRA). Employers who fail to comply with the FCRA may be liable for damages or be subject to other penalties.

Author Tip ⟩ **FTC and EEOC Guides to Employment Background Checks**

In November 2014, the Federal Trade Commission (FTC)—the nation's consumer protection agency—issued information about **"Employment Background Checks"** that explains the legal rights that consumers have under federal and state law when employers perform background checks on them. The information from the FTC is available at www.consumer.ftc.gov/articles/0157-employment-background-checks.

In February 2014, the Equal Employment Opportunity Commission (EEOC) and the Federal Trade Commission (FTC) released a joint publication titled, **"Background Checks: What Job Applicants and Employees Should Know."** The FTC enforces a federal law that regulates background reports for employment, and the EEOC enforces federal laws against employment discrimination. This publication explains these laws, and how to contact the FTC and EEOC if you think an employer has broken the law. The publication is available at www.consumer.ftc.gov/articles/pdf-0143-background-checks-what-job-applicants-employees-need-know.pdf.

What information gets checked, and where does it come from?

A background check is not a full-scale investigation into someone's private life. Instead, the process is used to confirm the information provided on an application and that all relevant licenses, certifications, and degrees are in good standing. Previous employers and colleagues may also be contacted to confirm past employment and education. Employers and other references may be asked about job performance as well. A search may be conducted for criminal conviction records that may indicate if a person is unsuitable for a particular job. For example, if a person has a history of violent behavior, this tendency could possibly put employees, customers, or the business at risk. An applicant with a conviction for theft or fraud may not be suitable for a job that requires handling money or assets.

Some employers may attempt to collect this information themselves. Employers may contact past employers or schools. However, in order to access much of the information needed by employers, specialized search skills, knowledge, and resources are required. For that reason, many employers seek screening assistance from Consumer Reporting Agencies (CRA).

For the most part, background checks collect and verify information from state and federal agencies, credit bureaus, private institutions, and businesses. This information falls into two categories—public records checks and references/verifications.

Public Records Checks

- Social Security Number (SSN) Trace is a check of names and addresses that are associated with a Social Security number found in the databases maintained by the national credit bureaus. These checks may also include a check of other databases as well.
- Criminal record checks search for pending criminal cases or records of criminal convictions. Under federal law, the check for a conviction has no age limit, although some states do put a limit on how far back a screening firm may search. Criminal records are typically obtained from the relevant courthouse where the cases are held, and records must be manually retrieved by a researcher or clerk. Although there are some "canned" databases of criminal records available from vendors, records directly from the source are the most accurate and up-to-date.
- Driving records are typically accessed for up to three years of history and cover accident history and driver's license status. The driving records obtained for employment purposes come from the databases of individual states' Department of Motor Vehicles. Additionally, some trucking and transportation agencies will provide information about driver accidents.
- Workers' Compensation claims can provide details about past injuries, and Workers' Compensation claims filed by an individual. When an employee's claim goes through a state system or a Workers' Compensation Appeals Board (WCAB), the case becomes public record. An employer may only use this information for hiring purposes if an injury might interfere with one's ability to perform required duties AFTER there has been a conditional job offer. This rule is under the Americans with Disabilities Act (ADA) and many similar state laws.
- Credit reports retrieve a seven-year credit history, including high-low balances, trade lines, loans, mortgages, liens, bankruptcies, judgments, collections, and summaries of the individual's payment patterns. Credit checks can reveal information such as fraudulent use of a Social Security number or general credit history, as well as provide current and previous addresses. (More information about credit reports is found later in this chapter).

References and Verifications

- Employment verifications confirm dates of employment, title, salary, and eligibility for rehire with each employer listed on the application. The information is verified with a supervisor or payroll/HR representative within the company.
- Education or degree verifications confirm dates of enrollment, programs of study, and degrees held. Generally, the information comes directly from the school attended or a licensed third-party records service, usually National Student Loan Clearinghouse. Some information, such as GED records, must be obtained from state agencies.

What can my former employer say about me?

Potential employers often contact an applicant's past employers for qualitative references. Contrary to popular misconception, employers are at liberty to provide information about a previous employee's performance and ability, provided the information is truthful, job-related, and accurate. However, in this litigious society, most employers have opted to implement a policy to only confirm dates of employment, job title, and in some cases, salary. Many employers are concerned that if they give information beyond name, rank, and serial number, they could potentially be sued for defamation. Many large employers, in fact, have deposited past employment information on a telephone service, limiting new employers to hearing a computerized voice verifying only employment dates and job title.

About Past Employer References

The reluctance of employers to give information may actually work to the detriment of an applicant, making it more difficult to get a letter of recommendation. Applicants still have many avenues available to communicate about their past successes to new employers, even if past employers will not give a reference. The key is to plan ahead and to remember the importance of promoting your own career by obtaining the materials necessary to market yourself successfully:

- When leaving a job, clarify the past employer's policy on references and try to determine what will be said if a new employer calls.

- Before leaving a job, try to obtain personal letters of recommendation. Even if the firm does not give references, a supervisor or co-worker may be willing to write a favorable letter on the theory that it is a personal recommendation.

- Seek a letter of recommendation from someone who is no longer at the firm, and who can verify your job performance.

- Keep copies of outstanding performance appraisals, or keep an example of your work to show at an interview, provided it was proper to retain it; for example, if your work is not protected as a trade secret or by a non-disclosure agreement.

- Try to have references give specific examples. General statements, such as "great team player," are not nearly as strong as actual examples of your performance or behavior in specific situations.

- Retain pay stubs and other documents as a means of verifying past employment. When firms merge, go out of business, or move, it can be difficult to confirm past employment.

- If the previous employment involved a contract with an outside agency or was through an employee-leasing firm, the actual workplace may not have your records on-site.

- It is also very important to accurately summarize the job duties and titles for previous jobs on your resume. Although everyone wants a resume to shine, a resume that over-reaches can raise questions about your honesty.

In many states, employees have a right to review their own personnel files and make copies of documents they have signed. The personnel files of state or federal employees are protected under various state laws or the federal Privacy Act of 1974, and can only be disclosed under limited circumstances.

Most jobs involving the freight and transportation industries are regulated by the federal Department of Transportation. Employers are required to accurately respond to any inquiry from a prospective employer about whether an employee took a drug test, refused a drug test, or tested positive in a drug test while employed with the former or current employer.

What if the information is wrong?

Despite the best efforts of record keepers and modern information storage systems, mistakes can occasionally occur. Out of the millions of background checks done yearly, it would appear the error rate is extremely low. However, that is of little consolation for the applicant (also called the consumer) who is the subject of an error. However, the good news is that applicants who genuinely are the victims of mistaken identity or bureaucratic errors are given the opportunity to know what is being said about them and to dispute errors or discrepancies that might otherwise unfairly deny them the opportunity or eligibility for a position. Because of the rise of identity theft crimes, some applicants receive a very unpleasant surprise when a background check is conducted—they may discover that someone using their identity has a criminal record. If a person is arrested and uses your name, you become a double victim when a warrant for your arrest is issued after the arrested person fails to show up in court. Of course, since you—the applicant—was not the one arrested, you have no idea a warrant for your arrest is outstanding. There are even cases where the criminal stealing the identity pled guilty to a criminal charge using the stolen identity, creating a criminal conviction record for some unsuspecting identity theft victim. At that point, a job applicant must somehow correct the mess left by the identity thief. For more information on identity theft, see Chapter 28.

Other sources of errors can be the courts that do not update their files to show that an offense had been set aside, or a past employer's records are incorrect. Many applicants discover these issues for the first time when a background check is performed and are able to correct the underlying issue so it does not happen again.

Unfortunately, errors can sometimes be caused due to the failure of a background firm to exercise best practices and maintain accurate records under the Fair Credit Reporting Act (FCRA). A discussion of the accuracy obligations of a background firm is found in Chapter 3. However, if a background firm chooses to take shortcuts, such as using dates instead of the most current and up-to-date information, errors can occur.

Fortunately, there is an escape valve so applicants have the right to find out if there are errors, and a procedure to correct them. Under federal law, an employer intending to use information from the consumer report for an adverse action—such as denial of a job or promotion or terminating the employee—must take the steps outlined below:

1. Before the adverse action is taken, the employer must give the applicant a "pre-adverse action disclosure," including a copy of the report and an explanation of the applicant's rights under the FCRA.

2. After the adverse action is taken, the individual must be given an "adverse action notice." This document must contain 1) the name, address, and phone number of the employment screening company, 2) a statement that the employer, not the background screening company, is responsible for making the adverse decision, and 3) a notice that the individual has the right to dispute the accuracy or completeness of any of the information in the report.

3. A background checking company is required to remove or correct inaccurate or unverified information, usually within thirty days of notification.

Data Brokers, Correcting and Updating Criminal Databases & What Consumers Should Do after a Court Expungement

The majority of private background screening firms DO NOT gather, assemble, or maintain a permanent criminal record database. For a typical Consumer Reporting Agency (CRA), each report is a one-time use only. A report is generated pursuant only to prior written consent, and all records obtained are to be reviewed to determine its current state. In practice, a researcher should see that the record has been expunged and the CRA should not report it. An expunged record is one that is legally destroyed, no longer exists, and is no longer reportable. Therefore, it should not be included in current databases and should not be reported.

However, as discussed in Chapter 9, there are **data brokers** who assemble so-called *national criminal databases* using information from a variety of sources. Data brokers do, in fact, maintain ongoing lists that they the try to sell as often as possible. Unfortunately, many of these data brokers do not update their lists of convictions when a consumer has received an expungement or a conviction has been judicially set aside.

For consumers trying to get old records removed from a database, a good approach may be to reach out to the data brokers who are the ones that keep old and unreportable criminal matters in circulation. The key for job applicants is to get these data brokers to change the information in their databases. Privacy Rights Clearinghouse has assembled a list of data brokers that may be the primary source aggregators (or collectors) of private criminal record databases on their website at www.privacyrights.org/criminal-data-broker-websites.

In addition, many screening firms routinely receive letters from consumers who have gone to court and received a judicial set aside or expungement, and then contact every screening firm they can locate in order to ensure the screening firms have updated their records. A list of screening firms, as well as suggested templates and other materials, can be found at www.theexpungedrecord.com.

It takes a great deal of time and effort to send these letters. Unfortunately, it may not be a very effective approach since most screening firms do not keep or maintain their own criminal database. A screening firm that is doing its job properly should find out when performing a background report if a criminal matter has been expunged or set aside when it seeks information from the courthouse.

Another avenue is to contact the data brokers listed on the Privacy Rights website link on the Criminal Data Broker Websites noted above. If a screening firm or a website does report information that was expunged or set aside, there is a high probability it came from a data broker. Getting the data changed at the underlying source can be a critical step for a consumer.

Expungements

So what should consumers do if they get a court expungement? Just writing to every screening firm to tell them about the expungement may not be that helpful and can be very time consuming. Check to see if the state where the expungement occurred offers a "proof of expungement" for consumer reporting agencies to update their records.

Expunged criminal records of job applicants removed from government databases can still appear in some background checks performed by private screening companies. However, these expunged records should not appear if the information is verified at the primary source.

The federal Fair Credit Reporting Act (FCRA) requires screening companies to "follow reasonable procedures to assure maximum possible accuracy" of the information contained in background check reports. Professional screening firms should verify any potentially negative or derogatory information at the primary source to protect consumers from reporting matters that should not be reportable during background checks, including expunged records.

These types of issues are created where background screening firms are selling database information directly to the end user and do not go to the courthouse to verify the current status of a matter at the primary sources. Firms that provide a professional background check service would never report a criminal matter from a database search without first verifying the underlying facts from current court records.

Concerned CRAs, a group of more than 200 Consumer Reporting Agencies (CRAs)—CRAs being the technical term for background screening firms—have adopted a strict standard that no criminal information is reported from databases, and screening firms must verify data at the primary source before reporting it to end users. To learn more, visit www.concernedcras.com.

What can I do to prepare?

Applicants who anticipate changing jobs in the near term can take several steps to ensure the information to be gathered is correct, and all precautions have been taken in the event contradictory information surfaces, or records cannot be located. The following tips on *'Preparing for a Background Check'* are excerpted with permission from a Privacy Rights Clearinghouse consumer guide entitled *'Employment Background Checks: A Jobseeker's Guide,'* that is available at www.privacyrights.org/consumer-guides/employment-background-checks-jobseekers-guide.

Privacy Rights Clearinghouse –
Employment Background Checks: A Jobseeker's Guide

10. Preparing for a Background Check

When you know you are going to be on the job market, take the following steps to reduce the chances that you and/or the potential employer will be "surprised" by information found in the background check process:

- **Order a copy of your credit report.** If there is something you do not recognize or that you disagree with, dispute the information with the creditor and/or credit bureau before you have to explain it to the interviewer. Another individual's name may appear on your credit report. This happens when someone mistakenly writes down the wrong Social Security number on a credit application causing that name to appear on your file. Or you might be a victim of identity theft. The FTC's website explains how you can order your free credit reports each year. (See, www.consumer.ftc.gov/articles/0155-free-credit-reports.)

- **Check court records.** If you have an arrest record or have been involved in court cases, go to the county where this took place and inspect the files. Make sure the information is correct and up to date. Reporting agencies often report felony convictions when the consumer truly believes the crime was reduced to a misdemeanor, or that it was reported as a misdemeanor conviction when the consumer thought the charge was reduced to an infraction. Court records are not always updated correctly. For example, a signature that was needed to reduce the charges might not have been obtained or recorded by the court. Don't rely on what someone else may have told you. If you think the conviction was expunged or dismissed, get a certified copy of your report from the court. It is always a good idea to keep certified copies of any papers or documents that have been filed in court, especially the judge's order or other document that disposes of the case. If you later learn the court record is inaccurate but do not have a certified copy, first contact the clerk of the court where the matter was heard. If you cannot correct the problem at this level, it may be necessary to petition the court yourself or hire an attorney to act on your behalf.

- **Check DMV records.** Request a copy of your driving record from the Department of Motor Vehicles, especially if you are applying for a job that involves driving. Many employers ask on their application if you were ever convicted of a crime. Or they might word the question to ask whether you have ever been convicted of a felony or misdemeanor. Typically, the application says you do not have to divulge a case that was expunged or dismissed, or that was a minor traffic violation. Don't be confused. A DUI (driving under the influence) or DWI (driving while intoxicated) conviction is not considered a minor traffic infraction. Applicants with a DUI or DWI who have not checked "yes" on a job application may be denied employment for falsifying the form -- even when the incident occurred only once or happened many years before. The employer perceives this as dishonesty, even though the applicant might only have been confused by the question.

- **Do your own background check.** If you want to see what an employer's background check might uncover, hire a background screening company that specializes in such reports to conduct one for you. That way, you can discover if the databases of information vendors contain erroneous or misleading information.

- **Ask to see a copy of your personnel file from your current or former job.** Even if you do not work there anymore, state law might enable you to see your file. Under California law, you can access your file until at least a year from the last date of employment. And you are allowed to make copies of documents in your file that have your signature on them. (California Labor Code §432.) You may also want to ask if your former employer has a policy about the release of personnel records. Many companies limit the amount of information they disclose.

- **Read the fine print carefully.** When you sign a job application, you will be asked to sign a consent form if a background check is conducted. Read this statement carefully and ask questions if the authorization statement is not clear. Unfortunately, job seekers are in an awkward position, since refusing to authorize a background check may jeopardize the chances of getting the job.

- **Tell neighbors and work colleagues**, past and present, that they might be asked to provide information about you. This helps avoid suspicion, and alerts you to possible problems. In addition, their prior knowledge gives them permission to disclose information to the investigator. Forewarning others speeds up the process and helps you get the job faster.

- **Clean up your "digital dirt."** Conduct a search on your name -- in quotation marks -- in the major search engines such as Google. If you find unflattering references, contact the Web site to learn if and how you can remove them. You can monitor the web for new mentions of your name by setting up a Google Alert. Google Alert will send you email updates of the latest Google results mentioning your name. (See www.google.com/alerts.) If you have created profiles in popular social networking sites such as Facebook, review, and if necessary, edit what you have posted to make sure that an employer would not be offended. Some employers are turning to third-party screening companies to monitor and report on a potential employee's social networking activity. Understand that if employers *themselves* monitor your Internet activity, you do not have rights under the Fair Credit Reporting Act. Do you blog? Re-read your entries from the perspective of a potential employer. Remove or edit postings that could harm your job seeking efforts. But don't necessarily remove web content that shines a light on your positive achievements. A personal web site or blog that highlights your good deeds could benefit you.

- **Request previous background check reports.** If you have been the subject of a background check covered by the FCRA, you may be entitled to receive a copy of your "file" from the employment screening company. If you do not know the name of the screening company, ask the employer who requested the check.

Source: www.privacyrights.org/consumer-guides/employment-background-checks-jobseekers-guide#preparing background check

Copyright © 1994-2016 | Privacy Rights Clearinghouse | Posted: Dec 01 1994 | Revised: Sep 23 2016

Job Applicants and Credit Reports

The following is the complete text of the White Paper *The Use of Credit Reports in Employment Background Screening— An Overview for Job Applicants*. The paper was researched and written by Kerstin Bagus and Lester Rosen.

The Use of Credit Reports in Employment Background Screening – An Overview for Job Applicants

If you are looking for a job today, there is a good chance a background check will be conducted before or shortly after you are hired. Employers and volunteer organizations conduct background checks to verify the information provided on an application and to conduct due diligence. These background checks protect the employer and volunteer organization in many ways, primarily by making sure the information they were given on the job application is accurate and that the organization is not hiring someone who is inappropriate for the position. This protects the organization as well as their workers, customers, and sometimes the general public.

Most often this background check will review criminal record history. Other commonly checked areas are identification information, education, professional license, and employment history provided by the applicant. If driving is involved, driver's license status and history are often verified. Some employers will also check a person's credit history during the application process.

The use of credit reports in the job application process has been in the news lately. Concern has been raised that when credit reports are part of a background check, the information on the credit report may be used unfairly against the job applicant. The following information is intended to assist job applicants in understanding the role that a credit report may play in a background check and to explain the differences between a credit report used in the job application process versus a credit report a lender may see.

The first thing to know is that there are different types of credit reports depending on the purpose of the report. A credit report viewed by an employer or volunteer agency is called an Employment Credit Report and does not contain the same information as is found on a credit report available to lenders or even the credit report you get when you exercise your rights to view your own credit report from a credit bureau. The employment version of a credit report does provide information about your credit and payment history, just like other versions of a credit report. However, there are many things that are different in this version of a credit report:

- A credit score is not available to employers. It is recognized by credit bureaus, credit scoring companies, and background screening companies that a credit score has no relationship to job performance and is simply not provided to employers. Unlike the copy of the credit report available to you, the employer cannot even pay extra to see a credit score.

- Account numbers are not listed on the Employment Credit Report. The source and type of credit is listed, such as the store name or loan holder. But specific account numbers are not on the employment version of a credit report.

- Your age is not listed nor is your year of birth.

- The Inquiry is different and is not calculated in a credit score. An Inquiry is the listing of who requested your credit report. This must be listed on every person's credit history and is one of the things used in determining a person's credit score. There are different types of Inquiries and they have different impact on a credit report and a credit score. When an employer or volunteer agency orders an Employment Credit Report, a special type of Inquiry is listed on the person's credit history that is not used in the credit scoring process. In some cases, this Employment Inquiry may not be visible to other organizations who request your credit report – it may only be visible to you and the credit bureau. (This may not be the case for all Employment Credit Reports and depends on how the specific credit bureau treats these Employment Inquiries.)

Second, employers are not running credit reports in order to find ways to deny jobs to applicants. Background checks cost employers money and time. Employers run background checks, including credit reports, **AFTER** they have gone through the time, cost and effort to find the right candidates, usually from a large field of applicants. An employer does not invest money in a background report just to find ways not to hire. When an employer orders a background check, it is because the employer is interested in hiring the applicant and is conducting due diligence to make sure there is no business-related reason not to hire that person.

Third, employers have obligations they must follow before deciding not to hire someone as a result of any part of a background check obtained from a Consumer Reporting Agency (a company that provides these types of background checks), including a credit report. Employers and the background screening firms that provide these reports do not take these obligations lightly. There are serious penalties if employers fail to follow through with their obligations. (See the FTC's website at www.ftc.gov for more information.) More on how this affects you as a job applicant is below.

What should a job applicant do regarding credit reports and job hunting?

First, understand that if you get to the point where an employer is running a background check, that is great news. It means you made it through the preliminary stages of the hiring process so that you are most likely one of the final candidates being considered for the job.

Secondly, if you are concerned that a background check may include a credit report, do not be the last to know what your credit report may say. As a consumer (that is the term used to identify a person whose credit report is being viewed), you are entitled to a free credit report every 12 months from each of the credit bureaus, and more often in some states and under certain circumstances. Go to https://www.annualcreditreport.com/cra/index.jsp for information on how to get your free credit report. If you see some sort of error, it would be a good idea to get that corrected as soon as possible. There is a well-established procedure for contacting the credit bureaus to bring an error to their attention and request it be corrected. The FTC has excellent information about the use of credit reports and credit on their website at www.ftc.gov/bcp/menus/consumer/credit.shtm.

Third, if you are concerned that your credit history may reflect negatively, have a discussion ahead of time with the hiring manager or Human Resources about your credit reports. As most experienced Human

Resources professionals can tell you, information honestly disclosed by an applicant has much less impact than information employers discover for themselves.

Also keep in mind that hiring professionals understand that people have to deal with the realities of life. For example, if a person was undergoing economic stress due to the recession and relied on credit cards, or there was a medical issue that caused bills, let Human Resources or the hiring manager know. Also keep in mind that the only reason you are having this discussion is that the firm is seriously considering hiring you, and has gone through a great deal of time and effort to make that decision, including reviewing numerous other resumes.

Fourth, applicants need to keep in mind that they have rights. Under the federal Fair Credit Reporting Act (FCRA), a credit report is obtained only after the applicant has given consent and after a legally required disclosure on a stand-alone document has been given. Before the employer utilizes the credit report in any way not to hire, an applicant is entitled to a copy of the credit report in what is known as a pre-adverse action notice. You are also required to receive a document called a Statement of Rights which will list your rights as well as information on how to correct information on the report.

The bottom-line: If an employer feels a credit report is job-related, keep in mind that the employer has made you a finalist, and therefore has an interest in hiring you. You were evaluated without the employer having any idea of what was in the credit report. Protect your credit history. Think of it as one piece of your reputation. Know what is in your credit report and correct errors. If there are negative entries, be prepared to share them before the credit report is run.

Consumer Resources:

www.ftc.gov
www.ftc.gov/bcp/menus/consumer/credit.shtm
www.annualcreditreport.com/cra/index.jsp

Study Finds Ex-Offenders Can Be Good Workers

A study released in 2016 called, **"Does a Criminal Past Predict Worker Performance? Evidence from America's Largest Employer,"** assessed the performance of ex-offenders with past criminal records in the workplace and found that employers could be missing out on good workers by avoiding job applicants with criminal pasts when hiring.

The study co-authored by Harvard sociologist Devah Pager with Jennifer Lundquist and Eiko Strader from UMass Amherst, one of the first to assess the performance of ex-offenders in the workplace, used U.S. military data for 1.3 million soldiers—both ex-offenders and non-offenders—who enlisted between 2002 and 2009.

The study evaluated the work performance of ex-offenders re-entering the job market and found ex-offenders were no more likely than other enlistees to be discharged for negative reasons such as misconduct or poor performance. These ex-offenders were also promoted at a slightly higher rate and to higher ranks than non-offenders with no criminal record.

The results of the study may be related to the additional review ex-offenders undergo for criminal military waivers that assess the nature of the crime, time since conviction, and other factors that can result in selecting above average recruits. Also, ex-offenders receiving a second chance may be more committed to work and promotions.

According to the U.S. Bureau of Justice Statistics, the U.S. incarcerated population in 2014 was approximately four-and-a-half times larger than in 1980, and more than 2.2 million people in the United States were held in federal and state prisons and county jails.

Source:
https://paa.confex.com/paa/2016/mediafile/ExtendedAbstract/Paper2871/ASRDraft012 22016.pdf

National Reentry Week Part of DOJ Mission to Help Ex-Offenders

To help reformed ex-offenders contribute to their communities upon release from prison, the U.S. Department of Justice (DOJ) designated the week of April 24-30, 2016, as **National Reentry Week** and asked the Bureau of Prisons to coordinate reentry events such as job fairs, practice interviews, and mentorship programs at their facilities across the country. To learn more, visit www.justice.gov/reentry/reentry-week.

Ten Critical Steps for Ex-Offenders to Get Back Into the Workforce

Employers have multiple reasons for becoming increasingly concerned about knowing if an applicant has a criminal history. As a result, more employers are conducting pre-employment background checks to minimize the risk of a bad hire. One reason for their concern is that employers have been the subject of large jury verdicts for negligent hiring—a situation where a person with a criminal record is hired and then harms others—that could have been avoided by a criminal record check. Employers feel they are susceptible to these lawsuits because they have a legal duty to exercise due diligence in the hiring process, and that legal duty can be violated if an employer hires someone that they either knew or should have known in the exercise of reasonable care was dangerous or unfit for a job. The concern from the employer's point of view is that a person with a criminal past may have a propensity to re-offend in the future.

On the other hand, society also has a vested interest in helping people with a criminal record obtain and maintain employment. It is difficult for an ex-offender to become a law abiding, tax-paying citizen without a job. Unless society wants to continue to spend its tax dollars on building more and more jails and prisons, ex-offenders need the opportunity to rejoin the workforce. Getting ex-offenders back into the workforce is a win-win for everyone.

For an ex-offender, a job search can become a frustrating "Catch-22" situation. Unless prohibited by law, many employment applications may ask in some fashion if a person has a criminal record. If not on the application form, a job applicant may well be asked about a criminal record at or after an interview. If a person lies, then they are always at risk of being terminated if the criminal record is discovered later. If a person is honest and admits the past misconduct, there is a substantial risk of not even getting a chance to compete for the job. The fear is that upon learning about a past criminal conviction, the employer will simply toss the employment application in the trash can or stop considering the applicant at all.

The bottom line is that many ex-offenders seeking to rebuild their lives and get back into the mainstream, face significant challenges. Ex-offenders seeking a second chance may run into a wall where an employer will not even consider their application in the first place. That can occur when an employer has pre-judged applicants based upon their status as ex-offenders without even knowing anything about the ability of the applicant to successfully do the job. Ex-offenders may well feel there is a prejudice against them since the root of the word prejudice is "Pre-judgment." In other words, ex-offenders face the prospect of being judged by their status as an ex-offender instead of as an individual who may, in fact, be a great candidate for the job.

There is no perfect answer. A person with a criminal record is going to face greater challenges in getting employment. That is a fact of modern life. In addition, there are certain jobs where an employer will justifiably not hire an ex-offender. In fact, there are positions where, by law, an employer may be prohibited from hiring an ex-offender. This can occur, for example, if there is a government mandate licensing rule where the law specifies that certain offenses makes a person ineligible.

However, **challenging is not the same as impossible**. The key is the right attitude and getting and keeping that first job, so that as time goes by, a person has developed a successful job history that outweighs past problems. Here are ten (10) approaches a person with a past criminal record can consider when seeking employment (NOTE: More details about each step are available in the complimentary whitepaper "Ten Critical Steps for Ex-Offenders to Get Back Into the Workforce" available at www.esrcheck.com/Whitepapers/Ten-Steps-for-Ex-Offenders-to-Get-Back-in-Workforce/):

1. See an attorney to explore if you are eligible to get your conviction sealed, expunged, or judicially set aside.

This is the critical first step. Ask an attorney if the criminal record can be expunged or set aside by going back to court, or whether it is even the type of offense that an employer may legally ask about or consider. Each state has different rules, but in all states there is a mechanism for going back to court to try to seal or expunge certain offenses. This is an area of law where there are constantly new developments. In Ohio, for example, there is a procedure to apply for a "Certification of Qualification for Employment," which can assist an ex-offender in getting a job and also gives the employer some legal protection against an allegation of negligence.

The main point? Make sure you have explored your options. The attorney who represented you, the local Public Defender, Probation Office, Legal Aid or groups dedicated to helping ex-offenders should be able to assist.

The best bet is to make sure you understand the impact a criminal conviction may have on your employment chances at the time the case is in court. This is sometimes referred to as the "collateral consequences" of a guilty plea or a finding of guilt. Court cases can be complicated and going through the court system can be very stressful. As a result, some people do not always understand how a criminal conviction may impact their chances of employment or what rights they may have later on to try to go back to court and try to obtain legal protection when job hunting. You can never ask your attorney too many questions about this important topic.

Author Tip ⟩ **National Reentry Week Part of DOJ Mission to Help Ex-Offenders**

If you are able to get your criminal record sealed, expunged, or set aside under state law, see the section above on how to try to erase the record from databases kept by data brokers so an old criminal matter from the past does not haunt you in the future.

---

2. You may have the Legal Right to say NO on an application or interview if asked about a criminal record.

Assuming a criminal record cannot be set aside judicially, the next step then is to understand your rights. There are instances where an applicant can legally and ethically answer NO on a question about a past offense. For example, in many states there is no obligation to report arrests not resulting in a conviction or that are not currently pending in court. Some states have a pre-trial diversion, delayed entry of judgment, or some other type of program where a person may be able to avoid a criminal conviction by successfully completing some sort of court-mandated program. In some counties, a person may be eligible to participate in a drug court program and, if successful, avoid having a criminal record. These types of programs can result in a case that a background firm cannot report and an employer cannot consider.

If any of these situations apply to you, you may then have the right to answer NO when asked about a criminal record. However, it is important to keep in mind that for state court convictions, every state has its own laws, rules, and procedures which can vary from county by county. In order to avoid any misunderstanding or making a mistake, it can be helpful to consult a criminal attorney with experience in the county where the offense occurred.

3. Does Ban-the-Box apply to you?

A new national movement called ban-the-box seeks to prohibit public and private employers that are covered by the laws, from asking about criminal records at the beginning of the employment process. More than 100 cities, counties, and states have in some fashion made it easier for ex-offenders to apply for jobs in the first place by not forcing them to reveal upfront a past criminal matter before they even have the chance to demonstrate their merits and qualifications. A number of private employers including some large national employers, have voluntarily adopted a ban-the-box approach, and the federal Equal Employment Opportunity commission (EEOC), the federal agency that enforces anti-discrimination laws, recommended that employers utilize that approach in its 2012 Guidance on the use of criminal records.

The idea is that if a person is forced to reveal a criminal record too soon in the employment process, then they may be subject to an 'early knock-out punch', regardless of their qualifications. Ex-offenders may believe that revealing their past conviction on an employment application can mean potential employers will stick it in the trash can without even giving them a chance. As a result, an ex-offender could be chilled or deterred from even trying to apply in the first place. Given the value of getting everyone a job, the ban-the-box movement aims to pass laws to let everyone start the process on an even playing field regardless of a past criminal history. The box referred to in the name ban-the-box is the 'yes' or 'no' box often contained in an employment application that follows a question about past criminal conduct.

According to the National Employment Law Project (NELP), more than 100 million Americans—roughly one-third of the U.S. population—live in a jurisdiction with a ban-the-box hiring policy. In addition, there are an increasing number of private employers who are adopting ban-the-box even if not legally required. If you are in a ban-the-box jurisdiction then you may not be required to reveal a criminal record until during or after an interview.

4. You have certain procedural rights under the Fair Credit Reporting Act (FCRA) if there is a background check and your criminal record is being used against you.

If you are under final consideration for a job, an employer may then proceed to perform a background check. There is an important federal law called the Fair Credit Reporting Act (FCRA) that controls how background checks are done. That law includes a number of procedures that must be followed to ensure a job applicant consents to the background checks and is given certain disclosures about the process. It requires a background screening firm to use reasonable procedures to obtain maximum possible accuracy and there are special accuracy rules regarding criminal records. Some states have their own rules as well.

The important point for a job applicant is that there cannot be any "secret" background checks. You must specifically consent to it, and certain disclosures must be made to you.

Here is the good news: Employers do not spend time and money ordering a background check unless they are seriously interested in hiring you. The background check comes at the very end of the hiring process, and is used only for a person who is potentially a finalist. Employers simply do not spend time or money to check all applicants, but just the ones who have made it through the selection process to the point where the employer is seriously considering offering a job. An employer's goal is to make sure the right person is hired for the right job.

You Need To Know ▷ **Your Rights Under the FCRA**

One critical rule under the FCRA is your right to be notified if the background report is being used against you. The FCRA mandates certain protections for consumers to provide a safeguard against errors or mistakes. If something adverse or negative is reported in your background check and it impacts your chances, no matter how slightly, you have a right to know about that before a final decision is made, and to have the background firm re-investigate anything you feel is incorrect or incomplete. Under the adverse action rules, the employer MUST send you a "pre-adverse" action letter that includes a copy of the background report, as well as a document prepared by the Consumer Financial Protection Board (CFPB) called **"A Summary of Your Rights Under the Fair Credit Reporting Act" ("Un resumen de sus derechos en virtud de la Ley de Informe Justo de Crédito" in Spanish)** so you have a meaningful opportunity to review, reflect, and react to the report. Generally speaking, employers will wait 5 to 10 business days for you to respond. The employer then needs to send a second "adverse action" letter to you (which may include another copy of the report and another copy of your rights) informing you if the decision is final. The forms are available in English and Spanish at http://files.consumerfinance.gov/f/201504_cfpb_summary_your-rights-under-fcra.pdf & http://files.consumerfinance.gov/f/201504_cfpb_summary_your-rights-under-fcra_es.pdf

---

5. If a background report is not 100% correct and accurate, immediately contact the background screening firm and the employer.

A background screening firm has an absolute legal duty to investigate any and all objections a consumer has to a background report, and generally must do it within 30 days. The law is very detailed about consumers rights under the FCRA. In fact, the federal government has even prepared a document called, "A Summary of Your Rights Under the Fair Credit Reporting Act," that must be provided to an applicant if an employer intends to use any part of a background check in any way that is adverse to the consumer. See: www.esrcheck.com/file/CFPB-Summary-of-Rights-Under-FCRA-2015.pdf.

It is absolutely critical for consumers to contact the screening firm as soon as possible if they find anything they either do not understand or feel is not 100% accurate or portrayed fairly. They should not feel discouraged or defeated if something comes up that is not correct. If they do not speak up, the matter cannot ever be corrected. In fact, a professional screening firm that understands the law and their legal obligations wants to hear from you. Professional background firms are just as anxious as consumers are to ensure that all information is correct and accurate. The vast majority of screening firms take that responsibility very seriously.

6. Insist upon an Individualized Assessment of your situation.

A big boost for ex-offenders seeking a second chance arrived on April 25, 2012 when the Equal Employment Opportunity Commission (EEOC), the federal agency charged with enforcement of the federal Civil rights Act, produced a new and updated, 'Enforcement Guidance on the Consideration of Arrest and Conviction Records in Employment Decisions Under Title VII of the Civil Rights Act of 1964.' (See, www.eeoc.gov/laws/guidance/arrest_conviction.cfm)

The EEOC also suggested, although indicated it was not required, that employers consider the use of an "Individualized Assessment" in cases where an applicant is rejected due to a criminal record. An "Individualized Assessment" basically means that an employer should inform you that you were excluded due to past criminal conduct, and the employer should provide you an opportunity to make your case to the employer that either the criminal matter is incomplete or incorrect OR, even if you do have a criminal conviction, that they are reasons you should still be hired. The EEOC Guidance describes the process as follows:

Individualized assessment generally means that an employer informs the individual that he may be excluded because of past criminal conduct; provides an opportunity to the individual to demonstrate that the exclusion does not properly apply to him; and considers whether the individual's additional information shows that the policy as applied is not job related and consistent with business necessity.

An important consideration is that once the employer notifies you of your opportunity, it is your responsibility to follow up with the employer. The employer does not need to pursue you to set up a meeting. In other words, the ball is in the applicant's court once the employer sends out the notice.

The important walk away point: Be proactive and make your case if you are in the situation where you made it to the interview and then you are eliminated due to a criminal record.

7. Seek professional assistance and talk to people experiencing the same challenges.

There are also organizations that assist past offenders. Some of these organizations have relationships with employers who are willing to give an ex-offender a chance. In addition, these organizations can help job applicants prepare a resume and practice interview techniques that deal honestly with the past offense, and help job applicants put their best foot forward by explaining why they can perform the job and why the employer should hire them. Various re-entry or training programs will help ex-offenders develop new skills, or teach job search techniques.

In addition, some people have found it very helpful to network and obtain support from others experiencing the same challenges. Veteran groups, second chance organizations, faith-based organizations, and community groups may be great places to hear about experiences of others and learn about approaches that have worked well for others. You may also learn about employers that are more open to providing a second chance to people who are motivated to work hard. Ex-offenders may discover not only that are they not alone but there is light at the end of the tunnel.

8. Honesty is the best policy.

In applying for a job, honestly is always the best policy. A criminal matter honestly explained during an interview may have a much less negative impact than hiding it and having an employer discover it later. If an employer discovers an applicant was dishonest, the denial of a job could be based upon a lack of honesty, regardless of the nature of the offense. However, a person who has made a mistake and is now motivated to do well at a job may be of great interest to some employers. Sometimes a person may answer a question wrong because they are honestly mistaken about what charges they pled to, or what their rights were. This goes back to the earlier point that it is critical to make sure you understand the essential details of your criminal case.

9.   Start to rebuild your résumé one step at a time, even if it is not the "perfect" job.

All employers know that the best indicator of future job performance is past job performance. If a person with a criminal record can obtain whatever job they can, hold that job and do well, the next job becomes much easier. It is the building block approach—one block at a time.

It is critical to seek to rebuild your resume by finding any employment you can to rebuild your resume. You should first seek employment with people you know. Ask everyone who likes you if they know someone who might be willing to hire you. Yes, mention your conviction, but stress your strengths and how much you learned from your past. Someone who knows you personally is more likely than a stranger to give you a chance.

If that does not work, consider starting at the bottom. A few months of good work in an entry-level position can yield a good reference, which can start your career upward. Be the best worker you can be by showing a positive, can-do attitude, getting to work on time (or even early), and making yourself indispensable.

Eventually, what a new employer sees is a person with great recommendations and an excellent job history. As the criminal conviction gets older, and the job history becomes stronger, a person who has made mistakes in the past will eventually find that the criminal record is less of an issue. It cannot be stressed enough that the best way to get a great job in the future is to get any job you can right now, and perform well.

10. Take the long-term view.

This is the most difficult and must important advice to follow. An ex-offender is anxious to get back into the workforce to start making a living. They may also be anxious to have their old life back. Yet the deck may well be stacked against a person with a criminal record. The jobs that are available may not be the ones that you want. You may be qualified for something a great deal better. Doors may slam in your face, and you may very well be subject to unfair assumptions. The frustration level could easily build with each disappointment encountered.

What it comes down to is that an ex-offender needs to take the long view and have the faith and patience that the criminal matter will eventually be put behind them. As frustrating as it is, the basic rule still applies—a person must rebuild their résumé over time. And as time goes by, the criminal offense becomes less of a factor in a person's life. But it is going to take time.

Look at it this way. Even if it takes five years to rebuild your resume and get the job you want, five years will still go by. Five years later, what would you rather have—a new life with a good job or still be living in frustration because you couldn't get what you wanted right away?

> **You Need To Know** ▷ **Advice from A Career Coach**
>
> According to career coach, Marty Nemko, an entry level job can be a launch pad and a foot in the door. Do a great job, build relationships with higher ups, express interest in moving up, and before long, you many find yourself promoted. And if you take an entry-level job in order to rebuild your résumé, be sure it's one in which people with the power to promote you can observe the quality of your work. Avoid taking a job off-site or in a remote location. If you enjoy working for the organization, ask questions and let them know you are interested in moving up.
>
> Mr. Nemko also gives the following advice: "If you take an entry-level job in order to rebuild your resume, be sure it is one in which people with the power to promote you can observe the quality of your work. Avoid taking a job off-site or in a remote location. If you enjoy working for the organization, then ask questions, learn skills, and let them know you are interested in moving up."

Case Studies of Ex-Offenders Seeking Employment

It cannot be stressed enough—the best way to get a great job in the future is to get any job you can right now and perform well. Here are three case studies to consider:

- **Case Study One:** A schoolteacher was convicted of a misdemeanor offense that disqualified her from teaching. The person had dedicated her life to teaching, and suddenly it was no longer an option. She was very depressed and upset that she could no longer do what she loved and knew how to do so well. In order to qualify for a work-furlough program, she obtained a job with a friend in a retail store. It turned out she had a talent for the new job, became very successful and happy with it, and found a new and satisfying career.

- **Case Study Two:** A medical professional committed an offense that disqualified him from practicing his profession. He could not imagine not being employed in medicine. His career in medicine had been the most important aspect of his life and defined who he was. Over a long period of adjustment, he was very depressed and unhappy about how unfair it was he could not do what he did best. Out of necessity, he found a job in construction. It turned out he had a talent for this temporary job. He loved the hours and the freedom the job gave him. He also realized the pressures he had put himself under were the root cause of the criminal conduct. A few years later, when he would have been eligible to attempt to regain his license, he decided he enjoyed his new life and did not want to go back into medicine.

- **Case Study Three:** A young woman became involved with the wrong crowd at an early age. She was convicted of drug offenses and spent time in prison. In prison, she obtained her GED. Upon release, she found a job in a fast food place. It was not the best job, but she worked hard and made herself the best worker there. She was always on time, cared about her job, respected her co-workers and supervisors, and she showed a real interest in succeeding. Since employers need that kind of worker, she was eventually promoted to the management trainee program. She then turned for assistance to a program that helped women get jobs, and was able to find a well-paying administrative job in a growing firm. It took time, but she did everything right.

These case studies have one critical element in common—the individuals could not have been more depressed and frustrated with their situations. By being patient, taking the long view, and believing things could improve, their lives eventually went in new and better directions.

Author Tip > **Whitepaper on Steps for Ex-Offenders to Get Back Into the Workforce**

Employment Screening Resources® (ESR) has released a whitepaper entitled **"Ten Critical Steps for Ex-Offenders to Get Back into the Workforce"** written by ESR founder and CEO, Attorney Lester Rosen, to help job applicants with criminal records avoid the frustrating "Catch 22" situation where they risk not finding employment whether they lie or tell the truth about their pasts.

As Rosen explains in the whitepaper: *The bottom line is that many ex-offenders seeking to rebuild their lives and get back into the mainstream face significant challenges. An ex-offender seeking a second chance may run into a wall where an employer will not even consider their application in the first place... However, challenging is not the same as impossible. The key is the right attitude and getting and keeping that first job, so that as time goes by, a person has developed a successful job history that outweighs past problems. The goal of this paper is to provide helpful insights and suggestions to help ex-offenders get back into the workforce.*

The free whitepaper is available at www.esrcheck.com/Whitepapers/Ten-Steps-for-Ex-Offenders-to-Get-Back-in-Workforce/.

Background Check Mobile Phone Apps and Instant Background Check Web Sites: Fast and Easy, But Are They Accurate?

Job seekers should be warned that a <u>real</u> "self" background check should <u>not</u> consist solely of using a cheap and instant online database search through "apps" (applications) and websites.

According to a 2011 white paper – *'Background Check Mobile Phone Apps and Instant Background Check Web Sites: Fast and Easy, But Are They Accurate?'* – co-authored by Lester Rosen and Kerstin Bagus, users of mobile phone apps and Web sites offering so-called "instant" background checks should be aware that while these services are cheap and easy to use, they may not provide entirely accurate information.

The white paper examines background check apps and sites that allow users to perform instant background checks on anyone anytime from their mobile phones and computers by searching publicly available records and checking social networking sites such as Facebook, YouTube, Twitter, and LinkedIn. While this kind of information is viewed as a lead source for further review by professional investigators or researchers, in the hands of the average person, the data can lead to hasty and dangerous conclusions. Some of the dangers of using instant background checks offered by mobile phone apps and websites include:

- Reporting inaccurate information that can include outdated results or can show no criminal history when one actually does exist.
- Returning information for the wrong person with the same name since these services do not generally require identifiers such as dates of birth.
- Creating a false sense of security when a "clear" background check result assumes the person being searched has no criminal record.
- Privacy issues for the person being checked since the average person is not knowledgeable about proper usage of public records and there are no privacy controls in place.
- Reputational injuries to the individual being searched if the information is not correct.
- Misuse of information for employment purposes since employers who use results from these sites can find themselves in a legal and financial nightmare due to intense legal regulation surrounding the use of information for employment purposes from the FCRA as well as numerous state laws.

The white paper notes that unsuspecting users of background check apps or websites might not understand that it is not easy to get a complete picture of an individual's background, particularly their criminal history, due to the following considerations:

- No nationwide criminal record database exists that contains all criminal record convictions in the United States.
- If criminal information is found on an individual, it does not mean that the information is current, or the criminal record resulted in a conviction, or the information belongs to the person being searched.
- If no criminal record is found, it does not mean the person being searched does not have a record since the app or Web site can easily miss a criminal record.
- Some of the information returned is based on a "data dump" of billions of public records.
- The information pulled from social networking sites can be wildly inaccurate.

The white paper also discusses how to select apps, social networking data, criminal record databases, and special issues for employers and volunteer agencies. The complimentary white paper *'Background Check Mobile Phone Apps and Instant Background Check Web Sites: Fast and Easy, But Are They Accurate?'* is available at: www.esrcheck.com/Download/.

Author Tip > *Self* **Background Checks**

Since many job seekers will probably undergo some form of background check to gain employment, it would be in their best interest to make sure the information found during the background check is accurate, up-to-date, and complete. As a result, some job seekers are taking matters into their own hands by proactively conducting "self" background checks on themselves to verify the accuracy of their public information.

By conducting self background checks similar to those conducted by professional and accredited background screening companies, job seekers may discover that they have fallen victim to some of the following situations that have popped up during real background checks, situations that could hinder their attempts to find employment:

- A job seeker is the victim of identity theft.
- Someone with the same name as a job seeker has committed a crime.
- Some minor or old criminal matter that the job seeker thought was judicially set aside or was too old to matter still pops up.
- Some past employer or school does not have the job seeker's record under the proper name so that a background check may be inaccurate.
- A school may have a job seeker under a different name or may not have officially given the job seeker the degree due to not paying a final bill.
- A driving record check may reveal an old ticket that the job seeker thought was taken care of but went to a warrant for failure to appear.

What Job Seekers Can Do about Identity Theft

So far, identity and identify theft have been discussed from the point of view of the employer. Because identity theft can have an impact on background checks, Chapter 23 revisits identity theft, but from the perspective of the consumer.

The Extent of the Identity Theft Problem

An overview of the *2016 Identity Fraud Report: Fraud Hits an Inflection Point* report from Javelin Strategy & Research outlines the change in fraud as EMV (which stands for Europay, MasterCard, and Visa and is a global standard for credit cards that uses computer chips to authenticate and secure chip-card transactions) becomes more widely used:

"On its face, fraud in 2015 appears not to have changed substantially. The total number of victims remained steady at 13.1 million, and the total fraud amount fell slightly to $15 billion. However, that stability masks major changes in fraud in the U.S. As EMV becomes more ubiquitous, fraud at physical storefronts becomes very different – driving a movement from counterfeit card fraud to new account fraud. With growing online retail volume comes greater opportunity for criminals – pushing fraud to card-not-present channels. The stakes are high for both financial institutions and merchants, since poorly handled fraud undermines financial relationships and can even result in victims being less willing to take necessary steps to protect themselves.

The 2016 Identity Fraud Study found four significant trends:

- More identity fraud victims, less stolen – The number of identity fraud victims was at its second highest level in six years, but the amount stolen was at its lowest point in the past six years. Identity fraud is a serious issue as fraudsters have stolen $112 billion in the past six years. That equals $35,600 stolen per minute, or enough to pay for four years of college in just four minutes.
- EMV drives a doubling of new account fraud – In 2015 the U.S. switched to EMV, which is designed to reduce in-person fraud and the profitability of counterfeit card operations. Fraudsters have reacted by

moving away from existing card fraud to focus on new account fraud. This drove a 113 percent increase in incidence of new account fraud, which now accounts for 20 percent of all fraud losses.

- Consumer choices negatively impact fraud detection – The study found that those consumers who do not trust their financial institutions and do not take advantage of the services offered, are setting the stage for more damage if they become fraud victims. The study found consumers who do not trust their financial institutions are less likely to use transaction monitoring, email alerts, credit freezes and black market monitoring. This results in their information being used for 75 percent longer by fraudsters and incurring a 185 percent greater mean consumer expense than those victims who that have high trust in their financial institutions.

- U.S. consumer data being used for fraud internationally – Identity fraud is a global issue. The study found that 18 percent of the identity fraud using U.S. credit cards, or $2.4 billion, was conducted outside the U.S. There was an average of $1,585 per incident, although for most consumers there was no out of pocket cost as the major issuers offer $0 liability. Issuers are doing a good job of quickly detecting this type of fraud. They are proactively detecting 69 percent of these cases."

The 2016 Identity Fraud Report from Javelin Strategy & Research is available at www.javelinstrategy.com/coverage-area/2016-identity-fraud-fraud-hits-inflection-point.

Rights for Identity Theft Victims

The Consumer Financial Protection Bureau (CFPB) also offers a summary of rights for victims of identity theft called **"Remedying the Effects of Identity Theft"** **("Remediando los efectos del robo de identidad" in Spanish)**. The forms are at:

http://files.consumerfinance.gov/f/201410_cfpb_summary_remedying-the-effects-of-id-theft-fcra.pdf (English)

http://files.consumerfinance.gov/f/201410_cfpb_summary_remedying-the-effects-of-id-theft-fcra_es.pdf (Spanish)

More Proof of Identity Theft on the Rise

Additional proof of identity theft is also evident when figures from recent surveys, such as the 2012 Fraud Report from Javelin, are compared with surveys from the past decade. According to 'The Federal Trade Commission – 2006 Identity Theft Survey Report,' results of the survey suggested that approximately 8.3 million U.S. adults discovered that they were victims of some form of identity theft in 2005. The survey is available at www.ftc.gov/os/2007/11/SynovateFinalReportIDTheft2006.pdf

Along with the large human toll, there is a financial toll as well, as victims try to dig out from underneath the economic damage. Repairing identity theft can take months of frustrating calls to police, merchants, financial institutions, and credit bureaus. Although technology has made this process quicker, the FTC's '2003 Identity Theft Survey Report' available at www.ftc.gov/os/2003/09/synovatereport.pdf found:

> "Victims of ID Theft also spend a considerable amount of their own time resolving the various problems that occurred because of the misuse of their personal information. On average, victims reported that they spent 30 hours resolving their problems. On average, victims of the "New Accounts and Other Frauds" from of ID Theft spent 60 hours resolving their problems. This suggests that Americans spent almost 300 million hours resolving problems related to ID Theft in the past year, with almost two-thirds of this time – 194 million hours – spent by victims of "New Accounts and Other Frauds" ID Theft."

The damage caused by identity theft has multiple dangers to employers. A business loses productivity when one of its employees is sidetracked by serious personal financial worries. A business also faces liability if it is adjudged as the cause of the identity theft. Businesses have obligations not only to their customers but also their employees in terms of safeguarding the confidentiality of private information.

Most studies have found that early detection is the key to lessening the impact of identity theft. The economic losses are much smaller and the damage to individuals in both out-of-pocket costs and time spent resolving the problem are substantially smaller the sooner the victim discovers the theft.

GAO Report Reveals Huge Jump in Tax-Related Identity Theft Incidents Identified by IRS

The United States Government Accountability Office (GAO) issued a report in May 2011 titled, *'TAXES AND IDENTITY THEFT – Status of IRS Initiatives to Help Victimized Taxpayers'* that revealed a huge jump in the number of tax-related identity theft incidents identified by the Internal Revenue Service (IRS). Primarily refund or employment fraud attempts, the IRS identified 248,357 tax-related identity theft incidents in 2010, nearly five times the amount of such incidents reported in 2008.

The GAO report found that identity theft harmed innocent taxpayers through employment and refund fraud and that both the IRS and taxpayers may not discover refund or employment fraud until after legitimate tax returns are filed. The report also showed that the number of tax-related identity theft incidents identified by the IRS, such as refund or employment fraud, has grown rapidly in the past three years:

- 51,702 tax-related identity theft incidents in 2008.

- 169,087 tax-related identity theft incidents in 2009.

- 248,357 tax-related identity theft incidents in 2010.

In **refund fraud**, an identity thief uses a taxpayer's name and Social Security number (SSN) to file for a tax refund, which the IRS discovers after the legitimate taxpayer files. Refund fraud delays the refunds to innocent taxpayers.

In **employment fraud**, an identity thief uses a taxpayer's name and SSN to obtain a job. When the thief's employer reports income to the IRS, the taxpayer appears to have unreported income on his or her return. Employment fraud exposes innocent taxpayers to enforcement actions for unreported income.

The report, *'TAXES AND IDENTITY THEFT – Status of IRS Initiatives to Help Victimized Taxpayers'* from GAO – known as "the investigative arm of Congress" and "the congressional watchdog" – is at www.gao.gov/new.items/d11674t.pdf.

What is Identity Theft?

According to the 'About Identity Theft' section of the Federal Trade Commission (FTC) Identity Theft website at www.ftc.gov/bcp/edu/microsites/idtheft/:

"Identity theft occurs when someone uses your personally identifying information, like your name, Social Security number, or credit card number, without your permission, to commit fraud or other crimes.

The FTC estimates that as many as 9 million Americans have their identities stolen each year. In fact, you or someone you know may have experienced some form of identity theft. The crime takes many forms. Identity thieves may rent an apartment, obtain a credit card, or establish a telephone account in your name. You may not find out about the theft until you review your credit report or a credit card statement and notice charges you didn't make—or until you're contacted by a debt collector.

Identity theft is serious. While some identity theft victims can resolve their problems quickly, others spend hundreds of dollars and many days repairing damage to their good name and credit record. Some consumers victimized by identity theft may lose out on job opportunities or be denied loans for education, housing or cars because of negative information on their credit reports. In rare cases, they may even be arrested for crimes they did not commit."

How do Identity Thieves Steal an Identity?

The FTC Identity Theft website describes a variety of methods skilled identity thieves may use to get hold of your personally identifying information (PII) such as name, Social Security number, credit card numbers, or other financial account information:

1. **Dumpster Diving.** Identity thieves rummage through trash looking for bills or other paper with your personal information on it.
2. **Skimming.** Identity thieves steal credit/debit card numbers by using a special storage device when processing your card.
3. **Phishing.** Identity thieves pretend to be financial institutions or companies and send spam or pop-up messages to get you to reveal your personal information.
4. **Changing Your Address.** Identity thieves divert your billing statements to another location by completing a change of address form.
5. **Old-Fashioned Stealing**. Identity thieves steal wallets and purses; mail, including bank and credit card statements; pre-approved credit offers; and new checks or tax information. They steal personnel records or bribe employees who have access.
6. **Pretexting.** Identity thieves use false pretenses to obtain your personal information from financial institutions, telephone companies, and other sources.

Types of Identity Theft

Fundamentally, identity theft occurs when someone passes himself or herself off as someone else in order to gain a fraudulent advantage. Identity theft typically occurs when the thief gains access to another person's personal information, such as Social Security number, bank or credit card account numbers, then uses the information to commit fraud or theft. Here are three examples of identity theft:

1. The first type is **account takeover.** This occurs when a criminal literally takes over another person's existing accounts and makes purchases using a victim's credit cards.
2. The second type is what experts refer to as **true name fraud** or **application fraud.** This involves a thief creating brand new accounts using someone else's personal information such as the Social Security number. For example, a criminal may use the data to open a new American Express account.
3. A third type of identity theft is **impersonation,** where an identity thief takes over another person's identity. By utilizing the victim's identification, identity thieves obtain documents to enable them to pass themselves off as the victim. If the ruse is successful, the ID thief has the ability to commit more sophisticated "application fraud," ranging from getting a job under the false name to creating a whole life using someone else's identity. Another variation is "criminal identity theft" where a person who has stolen an identity is arrested and even convicted under the false identity. The victim of identity theft now has a criminal record in his or her name!

Identity Theft Tops Federal Trade Commission List of Complaints for 2011

For the 12th year in a row, identity theft topped the list of consumer complaints released by the Federal Trade Commission (FTC) for 2011. Of more than 1.8 million complaints filed in 2011,

279,156 – or 15 percent – were identity theft complaints, and nearly 25 percent of those identity theft complaints were tax- or wage-related fraud.

The FTC – the government agency working for consumers to prevent fraudulent, deceptive, and unfair business practices – enters complaints into the Consumer Sentinel Network (CSN), a secure online database of millions of consumer complaints available to more than 2,000 civil and criminal law enforcement agencies in the United States and abroad. In addition to storing complaints received by the FTC, the CSN also includes complaints filed with federal, state, and non-governmental organizations.

The CSN report includes complaint data on a state-by-state basis and also includes data about the 50 metropolitan areas reporting the highest per capita incidence of fraud and other complaints. In addition, the 50 metropolitan areas reporting the highest incidence of identity theft are noted. According to the FTC, the top ten complaint categories for 2011 were:

- Identity Theft: 279,156 Complaints (15 percent)
- Debt Collection: 180,928 Complaints (10 percent)
- Prizes, Sweepstakes, and Lotteries: 100,208 Complaints (6 percent)
- Shop-at-Home and Catalog Sales: 98,306 Complaints (5 percent)
- Banks and Lenders: 89,341 Complaints (5 percent)
- Internet Services: 81,805 Complaints (5 percent)
- Auto Related: 77,435 Complaints (4 percent)
- Imposter Scams: 73,281 Complaints (4 percent)
- Telephone and Mobile Services: 70,024 Complaints (4 percent)
- Advance-Fee Loans and Credit Protection/Repair: 47,414 Complaints (3 percent)

Begun in 1997 to collect fraud and identity theft complaints, the CSN now has more than 7 million complaints, including those about credit reports, debt collection, mortgages, and lending, among other subjects. Between January and December 2011, the the Consumer Sentinel Network (CSN) received more than 1.8 million consumer complaints which the FTC has sorted into 30 complaint categories.

For more information about the Consumer Sentinel Network (CSN), visit www.FTC.gov/sentinel. For more information about the FTC's Top Complaint Categories for 2011, visit: www.ftc.gov/opa/2012/02/2011complaints.shtm.

Criminal identity theft is especially worrisome. There have been numerous horror stories of innocent, law-abiding citizens arrested and tossed into jail for no apparent reason, only to find they have been the victims of identity theft. Someone who stole their identity committed some act resulting in a criminal charge or warrant, and gave the stolen name and information—your name, your information.

Report on Child Identity Theft Reveals 1 in 10 Children Targeted by Identity Thieves

It may be hard for most parents to imagine that their children could have homes in foreclosure or huge bills in collection before they are even old enough to apply for student loans for college, but a new report released by Carnegie Mellon University's CyLab – *'Child Identity Theft: New Evidence Indicates Identity Thieves are Targeting Children for Unused Social Security Numbers'* – reveals that one in ten children scanned for the report had someone else using their Social Security number (SSN) to commit identity theft and fraud.

Based on scans of over 42,000 U.S. child IDs by an identity theft protection company, the report found that 4,311 of the children in the report – or 10.2 percent – had someone else using their Social Security number to purchase homes and automobiles, open credit card accounts, secure employment, and obtain drivers' licenses. Other key findings include:

- The largest identity theft fraud ($725,000) was committed against a 16-year-old girl.
- 303 identity theft victims were under the age of five years.
- The youngest victim of identity theft was five months old.

The report offers glimpses into the real life threat of identity theft to the financial security of families, articulates vital concerns, and raises public awareness about identity theft. For more information and to download the full report, visit www.cyblog.cylab.cmu.edu/2011/03/child-identity-theft.html.

Consumer Advice From the FTC

In January 2012, the Federal Trade Commission (FTC), the nation's consumer protection agency, prepared a Guide – *Taking Charge: What To Do If Your Identity Is Stolen* – to help consumers repair the damage that identity theft can cause and reduce the risk of identity theft happening to them. The Guide has tips, worksheets, blank forms, and sample letters to guide consumers through the recovery process. The content below is taken from this Guide which is located at www.ftc.gov/bcp/edu/pubs/consumer/idtheft/idt04.pdf. The FTC's Identity Theft website is located at www.FTC.gov/idtheft.

How can identity theft victims tell that someone has stolen their information?

- They see unexplained withdrawals from bank accounts.
- They don't get bills or other mail.
- Merchants refuse their checks.
- Debt collectors call about debts that are not theirs.
- They find unfamiliar accounts or charges on their credit reports.
- Medical providers bill them for services they did not use.
- Their health plan rejects legitimate medical claims because records show they reached benefit limits.
- The Internal Revenue Service (IRS) notifies them that more than one tax return was filed in their name or they have income from an employer they did not work for.
- They get a notice that their information was compromised by a data breach at a company where they do business or have an account.
- They are arrested for a crime someone else allegedly committed in their name

What steps should consumers take if they are a victim of identity theft?

If a consumer's wallet, Social Security card, or other personal, financial, or account information is lost or stolen, the immediate steps should include:

- Contact the credit reporting companies and place an initial fraud alert on credit file.
- Check bank and other account statements for unusual activity.
- Exercise legal right to a free copy of credit report.

- Check for other rights under state law.
- Create an Identity Theft report

Another useful FTC document is its annual publication titled, *ID Theft: When Bad Things Happen to Your Good Name.* Here is an excerpt from that document.

How Identity Thieves Use Your Personal Information

- They call your credit card issuer and, pretending to be you, ask to change the mailing address on your credit card account. The imposter then runs up charges on your account. Because your bills are being sent to the new address, it may take some time before you realize there is a problem.
- They open a new credit card account using your name, date of birth, and Social Security Number. When they use the credit card and don't pay the bills, the delinquent account is reported on your credit report.
- They establish telephone or wireless service in your name.
- They open a bank account in your name and write bad checks on that account.
- They file for bankruptcy under your name to avoid paying debts they've incurred under your name, or to avoid eviction.
- They counterfeit checks or debit cards and drain your bank account.
- They buy vehicles by taking out auto loans in your name.
- They give your name to the police during an arrest. If they are released from police custody, but do not show up for their court date, then an arrest warrant is issued in your name.

How to Protect Yourself and What to Do If You Are a Victim

The immediate economic damages to a victim of identity theft are generally limited. A victim may not be liable for any amount greater than the first $50.00, if that. However, the damage can go further. Debit card users have less protection against fraud since their checking accounts have been wiped out and they could be liable for the total amount of the loss depending on how quickly they report the loss to the financial institution. (Electronic Funds Transfer Act, 15 USC sec. 1693) For more about credit card and debit card laws, read the Federal Reserve's Consumer Handbook, www.federalreserve.gov/pubs/consumerhdbk.

The text below is an excerpt from the Privacy Rights Clearinghouse website entitled *'How to Reduce Your Risk of Identity Theft.'* This document, which provides excellent advice on how consumers can reduce their risk of fraud, is available at www.privacyrights.org/consumer-guides/how-reduce-your-risk-identity-theft.

How to Reduce Your Risk of Identity Theft

1. The crime of identity theft

Using a variety of methods, criminals steal Social Security numbers (SSNs), drivers' licenses, credit and debit card numbers, and other pieces of individuals' identities such as dates of birth. They use this information to impersonate their victims, spending as much money as they can in as short a time as possible before moving on to another person's name and identifying information.

There are two types of identity theft:

- "**Existing account fraud**" or "**account takeover fraud**" occurs when a thief acquires your credit or debit card information and purchases products and services using either the actual card or the account number and expiration date. Victims may not learn of account takeover until they receive their monthly account statement.
- "**New account fraud**" or "**application fraud**" occurs when a thief uses your SSN and other identifying information to open new accounts in your name. Victims are not likely to learn of application fraud for some time because the monthly account statements are mailed to an address used by the imposter.

This guide discusses strategies for reducing the risk of both types of fraud.

Generally, victims of **credit card** fraud are liable for no more than the first $50 of the loss. In most cases, the victim will not be required to pay any part of the loss. But **debit card** users have less protection against fraud. Not only are individuals' checking accounts wiped out, debit card users could be liable for the total amount of the loss depending on how quickly they report the loss to the financial institution.

Even though victims are usually not saddled with paying their imposters' bills, they are often left with a bad credit report and must spend months and even years regaining their financial health. In the meantime, they have difficulty getting credit, obtaining loans, renting apartments, and even getting hired. Victims of identity theft find little help from the authorities as they attempt to untangle the web of deception that has allowed another person to impersonate them.

Identity thieves obtain SSNs, drivers' licenses, credit card numbers and other pieces of identification through a variety of means:

- "Dumpster diving" in trash bins for intact credit card and loan applications and documents containing SSNs.
- Stealing wallets and purses.
- Stealing mail from unlocked mailboxes to obtain newly issued credit cards, bank and credit card statements, pre-approved credit offers, investment reports, insurance statements, benefits documents, or tax information.
- Accessing your credit report fraudulently, for example, by posing as an employer, loan officer, or landlord.
- Obtaining names and SSNs from personnel or customer files in the workplace.
- "Shoulder surfing" at ATM machines in order to capture PIN numbers.
- "Skimming" your credit or debit card information at a point of sale terminal or ATM machine.
- Finding identifying information on Internet sources, via public records sites and fee-based data broker sites.
- Sending email messages that look like they are from your bank, asking you to visit a web site that looks like the bank's in order to confirm account information. This is called "phishing."
- Hacking into unsecured and unencrypted data files of financial institutions, retailers, and credit card transaction processing companies.
- Accessing unsecured web sites that contain sensitive personal information such as Social Security numbers and financial account numbers.

2. Take these steps to reduce your risk of becoming a victim of identity theft:

You cannot prevent identity theft. But you can reduce your risk of fraud by following the tips in this guide.

a. Credit cards, debit cards, and credit reports

1. Reduce the number of credit and debit cards you carry in your wallet. **We recommend that you do not use debit cards** because of the potential for losses to your checking account. Instead, carry one or two credit cards and your ATM card in your wallet. Nonetheless, debit cards are popular. If you do use them, take advantage of online access to your bank account to monitor account activity frequently. Report evidence of fraud to your financial institution immediately. Learn more about the risks associated with debit cards.

2. When using your credit and debit cards at restaurants and stores, pay close attention to how the magnetic stripe information is swiped by the waiter or clerk. Dishonest employees have been known to use small hand-held devices

called skimmers to quickly swipe the card and then later download the account number data onto a personal computer. The thief uses the account data for Internet shopping and/or the creation of counterfeit cards. Likewise, examine point of sale devices and ATM machines for tampering.

3. Do not use debit cards at all when shopping online. Use a credit card because you are better protected in case of fraud. See our online shopping guide (www.privacyrights.org/consumer-guides/online-shopping-tips).

4. Keep a list or photocopies of all your credit cards, debit cards, bank accounts, and investments -- the account numbers, expiration dates and telephone numbers of the customer service and fraud departments -- in a secure place (not your wallet or purse) so you can quickly contact these companies in case your credit cards have been stolen or accounts are being used fraudulently.

5. Never give out your SSN, credit or debit card number or other personal information over the phone, by mail, or on the Internet unless you have a trusted business relationship with the company and you have initiated the call.

6. Always take credit card receipts with you. Never toss them in a public trash container. When shopping, put receipts in your wallet rather than in the shopping bag.

7. Never permit your credit card number to be written onto your checks. It's a violation of California law (Cal. Civ. Code § 1725) and laws in many other states, and puts you at risk for fraud.

8. Watch the mail when you expect a new or reissued credit card to arrive. Contact the issuer if the card does not arrive.

9. Order your credit report at least once a year. Federal law gives you the right to one free credit report each year from the three credit bureaus: Equifax, Experian, and TransUnion. If you are a victim of identity theft, your credit report will contain the tell-tale signs – inquiries that were not generated by you, as well as credit accounts that you did not open. The earlier you detect fraud, the easier and quicker it will be to clean up your credit files and regain your financial health. We recommend that you stagger your requests and obtain one report each four months. That way, you can monitor your credit reports on an ongoing basis. But if you are in the market for credit or are a victim of identity theft, order all three at one time. For more information on your free credit reports, visit the Federal Trade Commission website (www.ftc.gov/bcp/edu/microsites/freereports/index.shtml). How to order your free annual credit report: By telephone: (877) 322-8228. Online: www.annualcreditreport.com. By mail. Print out the order form here (www.consumer.ftc.gov/articles/pdf-0093-annual-report-request-form.pdf).

10. Residents of seven states can obtain additional free annual credit reports under state law. These states are: Colorado, Maine, Massachusetts, Maryland, New Jersey, Vermont, and Georgia (two free reports per year in Georgia). If you live in one of these states, be sure to order both your free reports under federal law as well as state law each year – enabling you to even more effectively monitor your credit files on an ongoing basis.

11. Individuals nationwide are able to "freeze" their credit reports with Equifax, Experian, and TransUnion. By freezing your credit reports, you can prevent credit issuers from accessing your credit files except when you give permission. This effectively prevents thieves from opening up new credit card and loan accounts. In most states, security freezes are available at no charge to identity theft victims and for a relatively small fee for non-victims. The California Department of Justice's Privacy Enforcement and Protection Unit provides a guide on security freezes for Californians (www.oag.ca.gov/idtheft/facts/freeze-your-credit). For other states, see Consumer Action's resources (www.consumer-action.org/english/articles/freeze_your_credit_file#Topic_04). Brian Krebs' post, *How I Learned to Stop Worrying and Embrace the Security Freeze*, is a primer on what you can do to avoid becoming a victim of identity theft (http://krebsonsecurity.com/2015/06/how-i-learned-to-stop-worrying-and-embrace-the-security-freeze/). While a security freeze may be the best available deterrent to new account fraud, it may not be the best solution for everyone. It can be cumbersome for individuals who frequently apply for credit, are contemplating a new mortgage, or who plan to change jobs. On the other hand, a security freeze is particularly well-suited for seniors who are no longer in the market for new credit. Consumer's Union (www.consumersunion.org/pdf/SecurityFreeze-Consider.pdf) and Consumer Reports (www.consumerreports.org/cro/news/2014/02/should-you-put-a-security-freeze-on-the-credit-file/index.htm) provide more complete discussions of the pros and cons of security freezes.

12. Many companies, including the three credit bureaus, offer credit monitoring services for an annual or monthly fee. They will notify you when there is any activity on your credit report, thus alerting you to possible fraud. We do not endorse credit monitoring services because we believe that individuals should not have to pay a fee to track their credit. If you decide to subscribe, be sure to choose a service that monitors all three credit reports on an ongoing basis. You can create your own credit monitoring strategy at no cost by ordering one of your free credit reports every four months. For more information, read PRC's guide on monitoring services.

13. There are many identity theft insurance products available to consumers. We do not recommend them unless they are available as a free or low-cost rider on an existing insurance policy.

b. Passwords and PINS

1. When creating passwords and PINs (personal identification numbers), do not use the last four digits of your Social Security number, mother's maiden name, your birth date, middle name, pet's name, consecutive numbers or anything else that could easily be discovered by thieves. It's best to create passwords that combine upper and lower case letters, special characters and numbers.

2. Ask your financial institutions to add extra security protection to your account. Many will allow you to use an additional code or password (a number or word) when accessing your account. Do not use your mother's maiden name, SSN, or date or birth, as these are easily obtained by identity thieves. If asked to create a reminder question, do not use one that is easily answered by others.

3. Memorize all your passwords. Don't record them on anything in your wallet.

4. Shield your hand when using a bank ATM machine or retail point of sale terminal. "Shoulder surfers" may be nearby or a pinhole video camera could be recording your keystrokes.

c. Social Security numbers

1. Protect your Social Security number (SSN). Release it only when absolutely necessary (like tax forms, employment records, most banking, stock and property transactions). The SSN is the key to your credit and banking accounts and is the prime target of criminals. If a business requests your SSN, ask if it has an alternative number that can be used instead. Speak to a manager or supervisor if your request is not honored. Ask to see the company's written policy on SSNs. If necessary, take your business elsewhere. If the SSN is requested by a government agency, look for the Privacy Act notice. This will tell you if your SSN is required, what will be done with it, and what happens if you refuse to provide it. If your state uses your SSN as your driver's license number, ask to substitute another number. If possible, do not provide the SSN on job applications. Offer to provide it when you are interviewed or when a background check is conducted. Read PRC Fact Sheet 10 on SSNs (www.privacyrights.org/consumer-guides/my-social-security-number-how-secure-it) and Fact Sheet 25 on online job seeking tips.

2. Do not have your SSN or driver's license number printed on your checks. Don't let merchants write your SSN onto your checks because of the risk of fraud.

3. Do not say your SSN out loud when you are in a public place. And do not let merchants, health care providers, or others say your SSN out loud. Whisper or write it down on a piece of paper instead. Be sure to retrieve and shred that paper.

4. Do not carry your SSN card in your wallet except for situations when it is required, the first day on the job, for example. If possible, do not carry wallet cards that display the SSN, such as insurance cards, except when needed to receive healthcare services. A California law places restrictions on the display and transmission of SSNs by companies. For more information, read the California Department of Justice's Privacy Enforcement and Protection Unit guide on SSN "recommended practices." (https://oag.ca.gov/sites/all/files/agweb/pdfs/privacy/protecting_ssns.pdf?.) If you feel you must carry your health

insurance or Medicare card with you at all times, try this. Photocopy the card and cut it down to wallet size. Then remove or cut out the last four digits of the SSN. Carry that with you rather than the actual card. But be sure to carry your original Medicare card with you the first time you visit your healthcare provider who will likely want to make a photocopy of it for their files.

5. It is a violation of federal law for state motor vehicles departments to use the Social Security number as the driver's license (DL) number. (Intelligence Reform and Terrorism Prevention Act of 2004, implemented December 17, 2005). If you are carrying an older driver's license containing your SSN that is not yet ready for renewal, contact the motor vehicles agency in your state and request to have your DL replaced before the actual renewal date. This way, you are not carrying a document in your wallet that contains your SSN.

d. Internet and computer safeguards

1. Install a firewall on your home computer to prevent hackers from obtaining personal identifying and financial data from your hard drive. PRC's guide to securing your computer contains more information (www.privacyrights.org/consumer-guides/securing-your-computer-maintain-your-privacy#firewall).

2. Install and update virus and malware protection software to prevent a worm or virus from causing your computer to send out files or other stored information. PRC's guide to securing your computer contains more information. (www.privacyrights.org/consumer-guides/securing-your-computer-maintain-your-privacy#firewall).

3. Password-protect files that contain sensitive personal data, such as financial account information. Create passwords that combine numbers, special characters and letters, upper and lower case. In addition, encrypt sensitive files.

4. When shopping online, do business with companies that provide transaction security protection, and have strong privacy and security policies. For more online shopping tips, read PRC's guide to online shopping (www.privacyrights.org/consumer-guides/online-shopping-tips).

5. Before disposing of your computer, remove data by using a strong "wipe" utility program. Do not rely on the "delete" function to remove files containing sensitive information. Read more about this in PRC's guide to securing your computer. (www.privacyrights.org/consumer-guides/securing-your-computer-maintain-your-privacy#firewall).

6. Never respond to "phishing" email messages. These may appear to be from your bank, eBay, or PayPal. They instruct you to visit their web site, which looks just like the real thing. There, you are told to confirm your account information, provide your SSN, date of birth and other personal information. Legitimate financial companies never email their customers with such requests. These messages are the work of fraudsters attempting to obtain personal information in order to commit identity theft.

7. Be aware that file-sharing and file-swapping programs expose your computer to illegitimate access by hackers and fraudsters. If you use such programs, make sure you comply with the law and know what you are doing. Install and update strong firewall and virus protection. Many file-sharing programs are downloaded by children without the knowledge of their parents. There are software programs available that identify file sharing software and locate shared files on home computers.

e. Reducing access to your personal data

1. To minimize the amount of information a thief can steal, do not carry extra credit cards, debit cards, your Social Security card, birth certificate or passport in your wallet or purse, except when needed. At work, store your wallet in a safe place.

2. If possible, do not carry other cards in your wallet that contain the Social Security number (SSN), including your Medicare card, except on days when you need them.

3. To reduce the amount of personal information that is "out there," take these steps: Remove your name from the marketing lists of the three credit reporting bureaus -- Equifax, Experian, and TransUnion. Call 888-5OPTOUT or

go online to www.optoutprescreen.com. This will limit the number of pre-approved offers of credit that you receive. These, when tossed into the garbage, are a potential target of identity thieves who use them to order credit cards in your name. Sign up for the Federal Trade Commission's National Do Not Call Registry (www.donotcall.gov). You may also need to register for your state's "do not call" list, if it has one. Sign up for the Direct Marketing Association's Mail Preference Service (https://dmachoice.thedma.org/register.php). You can also register by mail ($1.00 fee applies). Your name is added to name deletion lists used by nationwide marketers. Have your name and address removed from the phone book and reverse directories.

4. Install a locked mailbox at your residence to deter mail theft. Or use a post office box or a commercial mailbox service. When you are away from home for an extended time, have your mail held at the Post Office, or ask a trusted neighbor to pick it up.

5. When ordering new checks, pick them up at the bank. Don't have them mailed to your home.

6. When you pay bills by mail, do not leave the envelopes containing your checks at your mailbox for the postal carrier to pick up, or in open boxes at the receptionist's desk in your workplace. If stolen, your checks can be altered and then cashed by the imposter. It is best to mail bills and other sensitive items at the drop boxes inside the post office rather than neighborhood drop boxes. If you use a neighborhood drop box, always deposit the mail right before the last pick-up of the day.

f. Responsible information handling

1. Each month, carefully review your credit card, bank and phone statements, including cellular phone bills, for unauthorized use.

2. Convert as much bill-paying as you can to electronic payments by using the Internet for banking and paying bills. With fewer account statements and bills mailed to your home, you will reduce the risk of mail theft and identity theft.

3. Do not toss pre-approved credit offers in your trash or recycling bin without first tearing them into very small pieces or shredding them with a cross-cut shredder. They can be used by "dumpster divers" to order credit cards in your name and mail them to their address. Do the same with other sensitive information such as credit card receipts, phone bills, bank account statements, investment account reports, and so on.

4. Use a gel pen for writing checks. Experts say that gel ink contains tiny particles of color that are trapped in the paper, making check washing more difficult.

5. Demand that financial institutions adequately safeguard your data. Discourage your bank from using the last four digits of the SSN as the PIN number they assign to customers. If you have been given the last four SSN digits as a default PIN, change it to something else.

6. When you fill out loan or credit applications, find out how the company disposes of them. If you are not convinced that they store them in locked files and/or shred them, take your business elsewhere. Some auto dealerships, department stores, car rental agencies, and video stores have been known to be careless with customer applications.

7. Store checks in a safe place. In the wrong hands, they could reveal a lot of information about you, including the account number, your phone number and driver's license number.

8. Store personal information securely in your home, especially if you have roommates, employ outside help, or have service work done in your home. Use a locking file cabinet or safe.

9. Any entity that handles personal information should train all its employees, from top to bottom, on responsible information-handling practices. Persuade the companies, government agencies, and nonprofit agencies with which you are associated to adopt privacy policies and conduct privacy training.

10. If your wallet or your Social Security number has been lost or stolen, place fraud alerts on your three credit reports right away.

3. Resources

Credit Reporting Agencies

Equifax

(888) 766-0008

http://www.equifax.com

Experian

(888) EXPERIAN (397-3742)

http://www.experian.com

TransUnion

(800) 680-7289

http://www.transunion.com

Federal Trade Commission

Phone: (877) IDTHEFT (877-438-4338)

Online: www.consumer.ftc.gov/features/feature-0014-identity-theft

FTC's comprehensive identity theft guide "Taking Charge: What To Do if Your Identity is Stolen."

FTC's interactive identity theft guide. www.identitytheft.gov

Identity Theft Resource Center

Phone: (888) 400-5530

Web: http://www.idtheftcenter.org

Additional resources:

FBI Internet Fraud Complaint Center. Report cases involving online fraud and phishing. www.ic3.gov

For tips on online safety, visit www.onguardonline.gov

The President's Identity Theft Task Force, www.idtheft.gov

CalPIRG"s report, Still @ Risk: New Technology & Identity Theft Trends in California (June 2012) discusses the crime of identity theft, prevention techniques, and ways to recover from identity theft. www.calpirg.org/sites/pirg/files/resources/CalPIRG%20ID%20Theft%20Rpt.pdf

U.S. PIRG, Why You Should Get Security Freezes Before Your Information Is Stolen (October 2015). www.calpirg.org/sites/pirg/files/resources/CalPIRG%20ID%20Theft%20Rpt.pdf

To download a PDF of this guide, visit www.privacyrights.org/printpdf/67549

Source: www.privacyrights.org/consumer-guides/how-reduce-your-risk-identity-theft

Check Your Own Credit Report Periodically

The best defense against suspected identity fraud is to obtain and review your credit report on a regular basis. The reports from all "Big Three" credit bureaus – Equifax, Experian, and TransUnion – should be reviewed each year. Consumers can contact all three bureaus and request reports. The contact numbers are listed at the end of this chapter.

The three credit bureaus have also created a centralized service for consumers called AnnualCreditReport.com at www.annualcreditreport.com. AnnualCreditReport.com provides consumers with the secure means to request and obtain a free credit report once every 12 months from each of the three nationwide consumer credit reporting companies in accordance with the Fair and Accurate Credit Transactions Act (FACT Act).

In addition, a consumer is entitled to a free credit report if he or she is a victim of identity theft, has been denied credit, receives welfare benefits, or is unemployed.

Businesses Must Protect Against Identity Theft

A substantial source of stolen personal data used for identity theft is information taken from businesses. Employers should help safeguard data concerning their employees and clients by adhering to responsible information handling practices.

How to Repair the Damage

If a person is the victim of identity theft, there can be a tremendous amount of work to unravel the damage. The topic of how to respond can be a book in itself. A number of websites give detailed advice on what to do. Some of these websites are listed as resources at the end of this chapter.

- Report the theft to the three major credit bureaus immediately. Obtain a copy of your credit report and, if necessary, place a fraud alert in your files.
- Report the theft to the police immediately. Depending upon the state where a consumer lives, there may be helpful things the police can do. At a minimum, make a police report and get a copy of the report.
- Review your credit report and credit card statements carefully for signs of fraudulent activity.
- Get complete details on any fraudulent new account or any fraudulent use of an existing account.
- If an identification document is stolen, contact the issuing agency immediately. For example, if your driver's license is stolen or lost, go to your state Department of Motor Vehicles. If your mail is stolen, report it to the office of the U.S. Postal Inspector. If your passport is stolen, check with the State Department at the address at the end of this chapter.
- If you are wrongly accused of a crime because a thief used your identity, check to see what program or procedures are available in your state to set the record straight. In California, for example, there is a special statewide repository where identity theft victims can register. You may need to contact your local police departments and courts to find out how to have any records corrected. Correcting the problem may involve having your fingerprints taken so that you can be eliminated as a suspect in a pending case.
- If a bill collector contacts you, indicate you are a victim of identity theft and the debt is not yours. However, do not stop there. Write letters to bill collectors and creditors immediately—no later than 30 days—with all of the relevant information. Include as much documentation as possible in the letter, including your police report and identity theft affidavit. You have rights under federal law to stop a bill collector from bothering you.

Additional Resources

Credit Reporting Companies

- **Equifax:**
  - Main Website: www.equifax.com
  - 1-888-766-0008 (Fraud Alerts)
  - 1-866-349-5191 (Disputes)
  - Mailing address for dispute requests: P.O. Box 740256 Atlanta, GA 30348
- **Experian:**
  - Main Website: www.experian.com
  - Phone: 1-888-397-3742 (1-888-EXPERIAN)
  - Mailing address for dispute requests: P.O. Box 4500 Allen, TX 75013

- **TransUnion:**
  - Main Website: www.transunion.com
  - Phone: 1-800-916-8800
  - Mailing address for dispute requests: P.O. Box 2000 Chester, PA 19016

Federal Government

- **Federal Communications Commission (FCC)**
  - Consumer and Governmental Affairs Bureau: www.fcc.gov/consumer-governmental-affairs
  - 1-888-225-5322
  - 1-888-835-5322 (TTY)
- **Federal Trade Commission (FTC)**
  - IdentityTheft.gov: www.identitytheft.gov
  - 1-877-438-4338
  - 1-866-653-4261 (TTY)
  - Taking Charge: What To Do If Your ID Is Stolen: www.consumer.ftc.gov/articles/pdf-0009-taking-charge.pdf
- **Federal Financial Institutions Examination Council (FFIEC)**
  - To locate the agency that regulates a bank or credit union: www.ffiec.gov/consumercenter
- **Internal Revenue Service**
  - To report identity theft: www.irs.gov/identitytheft
  - 1-800-908-4490
- **Legal Services Programs**
  - To locate a legal services provider: www.lsc.gov/grants-grantee-resources/our-grantees
- **Social Security Administration (SSA)**
  - To report fraud, waste, or abuse: https://oig.ssa.gov/report
  - 1-800-269-0271
  - 1-866-501-2101 (TTY)
- **U.S. Department of Education (DOE)**
  - To report fraud: www.ed.gov/about/offices/list/oig/hotline.html
- **U.S. Department of Justice (DOJ)**
  - To report suspected bankruptcy fraud: www.justice.gov/ust/report-suspected-bankruptcy-fraud
  - Or send email to USTP.Bankruptcy.Fraud@usdoj.gov
- **U.S. Postal Inspection Service**

- To file a complaint: https://postalinspectors.uspis.gov/contactus/filecomplaint.aspx
- 1-800-ASK-USPS (1-800-275-8777)
- **U.S. Securities and Exchange Commission**
  - To report fraud: www.sec.gov/complaint/tipscomplaint.shtml
- **U.S. Department of State**
  - Passports: https://travel.state.gov/content/passports/en/passports.html
  - 1-877-487-2778
  - 1-888-874-7793 (TDD/TTY)

Other Resources

- **American Bar Association (ABA)**
  - To locate state and local bar associations: www.americanbar.org/portals/solo_home/state-and-local-bar-association-resources.html
- **AnnualCreditReport.com**
  - To order a free annual credit report: www.annualcreditreport.com
- **Certegy**
  - To ask about a declined check: www.askcertegy.com
- **ChexSystems**
  - To report checking accounts opened in your name: www.consumerdebit.com
  - 1-800-428-9623
- **Identity Theft Resource Center (ITRC)**
  - www.idtheftcenter.org
  - 1-888-400-5530
- **Identity Theft Survival Kit**
  - www.identitytheft.org
- **National Association of Attorneys General**
  - To find a State Attorney General: www.naag.org
  - 1-202-326-6000 (Not a toll-free number)
  - feedback@naag.org
- **Opt Out**
  - To opt out of prescreened offers of credit or insurance: www.optoutprescreen.com
- **Privacy Rights Clearinghouse**
  - www.privacyrights.org
- **TeleCheck Services, Inc.**
  - To report check fraud: www.firstdata.com/telecheck
  - 1-800-710-9898

ADDENDUM

About the Addendum

The following information material is provided as additional material to discussions contained in the designated chapters. Chapters 4, 8, 11, 12, 15, and 19 through 23 do not have material in the Addendum.

From Chapter 1
- More Information about Negligent Hiring and Case Law Examples
- Sample Policies and Procedures to Implement a Safe Hiring Program Using the S.A.F.E. System Turnover Cost Calculator Form

From Chapter 2
- From Griggs to SEPTA: The EEOC's Focus on Employment Screening
- Legal Reference and Case Law Examples
- More information about California SB 909

From Chapter 3
- Preliminary Telephone Screen

From Chapter 5
- Fair Credit Reporting Act (FCRA) Mandated Forms for Background Screening Compliance
- Fair Credit Reporting Act (FCRA) Contents

From Chapter 6
- California Background Checks: Different from the Rest of the United States
- States Laws that Create Employer Immunity

From Chapter 7
- General Introduction on Selecting a Background Screening Firm
- Introduction to the National Association of Professional Background Screeners (NAPBS))
- More about the Background Screening Industry
- Sample Request for Proposal (RFP) for Background Screening Services)
- The 58 Clauses of the Background Screening Agency Accreditation Program (BSAAP)

From Chapter 9
- 21 Shortcuts and Traps that Can Lead to Inaccurate Criminal Records
- Repetition of Criminal Incident Violates FCRA
- State Criminal Record Repositories Article

From Chapter 10
- EEOC Enforcement Guidance for the Use of Criminal Records by Employers
- Studies Cited by EEOC Concerning Recidivism and Statistics
- Use of Criminal Records and the EEOC Guidance – An Attorney's View

From Chapter 13
- Highlights of General Accounting Office (GAO) Report "SEX OFFENDER REGISTRATION AND NOTIFICATION ACT"
- Sex Offender Registration and Notification Act (SORNA)

From Chapter 14
- Can Employers Demand to See Employees' and Applicants' Facebook Pages?
- Research Shows How Many Employers Use the Internet for Screening
- Senators and Facebook Warn about Dangers of Using Social Media Sites to Screen

From Chapter 16
- E-Verify History and Milestones
- Importance of Reviewing EPLI Policy

From Chapter 17
- EU-U.S. Privacy Shield Article
- Selecting an International Screening Provider

From Chapter 18
- FBI Fingerprinting vs. Name Checks
- Special Issues For Staffing Companies

More Information about Negligent Hiring and Case Law Examples

Avoiding a Negligent Hiring Lawsuit

What must an employer do to AVOID negligence in hiring? This is the million-dollar question. The answer is—it depends. What does it depend upon? Those topics will be discussed in the next several pages.

Non-Regulated Private Employers — A Moving Target

Some employers have obligations or standards created by law. However, for the vast majority of private employers, liability depends upon the jury's view of the facts in each particular case. Generally, due diligence is a moving target. Unless an employer is governed by federal or state statutes, there is no one thing an employer can do to makes itself 100% immune from being sued. In other words, with some limited exceptions discussed below, there is not a national standard of care that, if followed, ensures an employer is not negligent as a matter of law.

Generally speaking, the employer's duty of care is commensurate with the reasonably anticipated risk to third parties. That is where a Safe Hiring Program comes in. The SHP consists of a number of overlapping tools and procedures that, when combined, create an ample defense against a negligent hiring lawsuit.

Public Employers Also Must be Concerned

Public entities, ranging from local school districts, counties, states, and the federal government, also hire employees. Although governmental entities enjoy immunity from being sued, there are tort claim acts that allow lawsuits in certain situations. For example, the Federal Tort Claims Act (FTCA) allows a person to bring a lawsuit against the U.S. government for personal injury, wrongful death, or property damage under the following four conditions:

- The injury must have been caused by a U.S. government employee acting negligently or wrongfully (but not intentionally).
- The employee must have been acting within the scope of his office or employment.
- The injured party must comply with the claims procedures, which include submitting a claim to the appropriate federal agency within two years from the date of injury.
- A lawsuit can only be filed if the agency either denies the claim or six months pass with no action, whichever comes first.

The federal law also excludes a number of possible causes of action such as injuries caused by a government contractor, or caused by government employees acting in accordance with the law or carrying out discretionary duties.

Although some protections and some procedural barriers exist when it comes to a public employer getting sued for negligent hiring, public employers need to exercise due diligence in their hiring as well.

Mandated Background Checks

Some private employers have obligations created by state or federal law to perform background checks or not hire individuals with certain criminal matters in their past. When determining what is proper due diligence, an employer must be aware of any rules or regulations affecting its particular industry. For example, every state has a myriad of laws requiring a criminal record background check before someone can be hired within a certain industry (heath care, child care, etc.), or be licensed by a state licensing board (nurse, private investigator, etc.).

Employers and boards regulated by a federal or state law will likely already be aware of that obligation by virtue of being in that industry. Many public positions also require background checks. It is beyond the scope of this book to attempt to summarize the vast number of specific state laws that require background checks. However, it is clear that any private or public employers who violate the rules on mandatory checks can be sued if their failure results in harm to a co-worker or third party.

Abiding by State Laws and Industry Standards

There can also be standards which encourage employers to practice due diligence. The legislatures in several states have created standards that provide strong incentives to use background checks as a means to avoid negligent hiring. Below are two examples.

- In accordance with **Fla. Stat. Ann**. § 768.096, a Florida employer who conducts a background investigation of an employee, including utilization of the Florida Crime Information Center system through the Florida Department of Law Enforcement (FDLE), is presumed not to have been negligent in the hiring of an employee. The election by an employer not to conduct an investigation under § 768.096 does not raise a presumption that an employer failed to use reasonable care in hiring an employee.
- A similar law went into effect in **Texas** in 2003. This law created an incentive for "in-home service" or "residential delivery" companies to perform background checks on their employees. If an employer runs a background check using the Texas online database and the report comes back clear, then the employer has the protection of a rebuttable presumption that the company did not act negligently. Texas Department of Public Safety (DPS) has established an internet site for criminal records, registered sex offenders, and deferred adjudications at http://records.txdps.state.tx.us.

About Legal Presumption and Rebuttable Presumption

A legal presumption is a fact the law assumes to be true. However, once a fact is assumed true, the other party can then offer evidence to "rebut" or disprove the presumption. The advantage to an employer when there is a "rebuttable presumption" of acting with due diligence is the employer starts off not having to prove anything. The suing party has the obligation of presenting evidence to disprove the employer's due diligence.

In addition, employers should consider general industry standards and guidelines, even if they are not mandatory. For example, in Chapter 22 on Terrorism, there is a discussion of certain rules the federal government has strongly suggested, but not mandated, for the food industry. Employers should also consider if a member of its industry has been sued for negligence in connection with hiring, and the outcome. Not only can an employer learn from what has happened to other firms, but a verdict can create an industry standard that other employers may be held to as well.

Some States Offer Protections for Employers Hiring Job Applicants with Criminal Records

Several states have passed laws that offer protections for employers that hire job applicants with criminal records. Here are a few examples:

- On April 27, 2016, **Georgia** Governor Nathan Deal signed into law Senate Bill 367 (SB 367) to advance comprehensive reform for offenders entering, proceeding through, and leaving the criminal justice system to promote their successful reentry into society, benefit the public, and enact reforms recommended by the Georgia Council on Criminal Justice Reform. See: www.legis.ga.gov/legislation/en-US/Display/20152016/SB/367. In

2014, Gov. Deal signed Senate Bill 365 (SB 365) to help rehabilitated offenders successfully re-enter society by removing barriers to employment and making it easier for employers to hire ex-offenders, reduce recidivism and create jobs. The text of SB 365, which also offers protection for employers hiring ex-offenders, is at http://gov.georgia.gov/documents/sb-365.

- Effective January 1, 2015, **Michigan** Public Acts 359, 360, and 361 offer protection for employers in the state that hire ex-offenders by issuing a "certificate of employability" to certain prisoners before their release. Under the new law, these certificates may be used as evidence to show duty of care by employers when hiring or retaining ex-offenders. See: www.legislature.mi.gov/documents/2013-2014/billanalysis/Senate/pdf/2013-SFA-5216-F.pdf.

- **Texas** H.B. 1188, signed by Governor Rick Perry on June 14, 2013, amended the Texas Civil Practice and Remedies Code so that "a cause of action may not be brought against an employer, general contractor, premises owner, or other third party solely for negligently hiring or failing to adequately supervise an employee, based on evidence that the employee has been convicted of an offense." H.B. 1188 took effect September 1, 2013. See: www.legis.state.tx.us/BillLookup/History.aspx?LegSess=83R&Bill=HB1188.

- **Ohio** Senate Bill 337 that offers protections for employers hiring job applicants with criminal records which took effect September 28, 2012. The law is an extensive reform of the collateral sanctions that impose employment restrictions and limitations on over two million Ohioans with misdemeanor and felony convictions. With SB 337, Ohio offers protections for employers from tort liability for negligent hiring and retention claims. See: http://archives.legislature.state.oh.us/BillText129/129_SB_337_EN_N.html.

The states listed above have joined other states such as Colorado, Florida, Illinois, Massachusetts, New York, North Carolina, and Tennessee in offering protections for employers that hire and employ rehabilitated ex-offenders.

Proving Negligent Hiring

To prove negligent hiring, an injured party (or the surviving family members suing for a wrongful death claim in the event the victim died) must prove the following:

- **Injury.**
- **Existence of a duty of care owed toward the plaintiff.**
- **The employer breaches the duty of care.**
- **Causation between the negligent hiring and the injury.**

The following are detailed breakdowns about each of these four points proving negligent hiring.

1. Injury

For a lawsuit to be brought, the plaintiff must allege there is an injury. The injury can include injuries that are physical (assault, murder, sexual offenses), emotional or psychological (infliction of emotional distress), property loss or damage (theft, destruction), or even identity theft.

Examples of injuries in negligent hiring cases include:

- The plaintiff, Welsh Manufacturing, brought suit against the security guard company it hired, Pinkerton's, Inc. As a result of three major thefts resulting in losses in excess of $200,000, a security guard was found to have been a co-conspirator in connection with those thefts. *Welsh Mfg., Div. of Textron, Inc. v. Pinkerton's, Inc., 474 A.2d 436 (R.I. 1984).*
- The plaintiff, an industrial contractor, brought suit against the company it hired to perform janitorial services. A janitor stole cash from a desk on subsequent nights and burned down the building in order to cover up the theft. *Lou-Con, Inc. v. Gulf Building Services, Inc., 287 So.2d 192 (La.App. 4th Cir. 1973).*

- The plaintiff, a hitchhiker, brought suit against an employer of a truck driver. A rape was committed by the truck driver after he offered the plaintiff a ride in his truck. *Malorey v. B & L Motor Freight, Inc., 146 Ill. App. 3d 265 (1986).*

- The plaintiffs, the parents of a disabled minor daughter, brought suit against a home health care agency. A substitute home health aide provided by the agency injected the daughter with a large unauthorized insulin dose, causing a seizure. *Interim Healthcare of Fort Wayne, Inc. v Moyer ex rel. Moyer, 746 N.E.2d 429 (Ind. App. 2001).*

- The plaintiffs, parents of a murder victim, brought suit against their daughter's employer. A co-worker at her office murdered her at her own apartment after gaining access to her address at work. *Gaines v. Monsanto Co., 655 S.W.2d 568 (Mo.App. 1983).*

- The plaintiff, a female employee, brought suit against her employer. A co-employee harassed her using cruel practical jokes, obscene comments, behavior of a sexual nature, unwanted touching of employee's person, and veiled threats to her personal safety. *Watson v. Dixon, 502 S.E.2d 15 (N.C.App. 1998).*

- The plaintiff, a female former deputy sheriff, brought suit against the county. Another officer showed and sent to others a doctored photo of the deputy with her breasts exposed resulting in claims of defamation and invasion of privacy. *Kiesau v. Bantz, 686 N.W.2d 164 (Iowa 2004).*

An Example of Large Award Negligent Hiring Case

In November 2011, the family of a truck driver killed in a 2008 accident in Arkansas was awarded $7 million in damages in a wrongful death lawsuit brought against a timber company and its truck driver in an Arkansas Federal Court. Lawyers serving as counsel for the family of the man killed in the accident argued that the timber company had negligently hired the truck driver who caused the accident without conducting a basic background search that would have quickly revealed a history of unsafe driving that included having his license revoked twice. The case involved the timber company truck driver's qualifications to drive a commercial vehicle and the timber company's failure to appropriately screen its drivers. Evidence was introduced at the trial that the timber company truck driver never should have been permitted to drive a tractor trailer since he had lied on his application and had received two license revocations, previous infractions that the timber company could have easily discovered with a simple background search that took only 15 minutes and cost $15. The deadly crash occurred only 19 days after the truck driver was negligently hired by the timber company for the driving job. The jury returned a unanimous verdict that awarded $7 million to the victim's family and found the timber company 75 percent liable and its driver 25 percent liable.

Source: *'Langdon & Emison obtains $7 million in truck accident verdict'* 11/10/2011 *http://pressreleases.kcstar.com/?q=node/70015).*

---

2. Existence of a Duty of Care Owed Toward the Plaintiff

The injured party must show there is some connection or relationship between itself and the employer, so the employer owes a **duty of care**. This can occur in numerous situations, such as a co-worker on the job, a member of the public in a location where customers are expected to have contact with employees, tenants in an apartment building injured by a maintenance worker, and other situations where the victim and the dangerous employee are expected to come into contact. In other words, an employer breaches a duty of care if it creates a situation where a third party is expected to be brought into contact with the employee who causes the injury, under conditions for which there is an opportunity for an injury to occur. It does not matter that the particular injury was foreseeable, just that any injury was foreseeable.

Certain employers have a **higher duty of care** because of the unique situations of the job. **An employer's duty of care will increase with the degree of risk involved with the position.** For example, consider the nature of the authority and position of trust a security guard holds. Many courts impose an even higher standard of care on a security guard business than other types of employers since there is a greater likelihood of harm to third parties. *Welsh Mfg., Div. of Textron, Inc.*

v. Pinkerton's, Inc., 474 A.2d 436 (R.I. 1984). In other words, when the job enables a person to act under some color of authority, a greater risk is involved because a person can potentially abuse that authority.

Similarly, courts have held employers who send workers into people's homes to a higher standard. This is on the theory that when an employer hires an employee who is given a unique opportunity to commit a crime, the employer has a higher duty of care. Examples are firms that clean carpets, deliver or fix appliances, or perform pest control services in a home. An example is a homeowner who brought suit against the exterminating service she hired when one of its employees raped her in her home. *Smith v. Orkin Exterminating Co., Inc., 540 So.2d 363 (La.App. 1st Cir. 1989).*

Other examples of higher duties of care can be medical professionals, home health care agencies or childcare workers that serve a vulnerable population particularly at risk. An example is a prisoner whose estate brought suit against the prison for failure, as custodians, to take reasonable action to protect prisoners against the risk of self-inflicted physical harm. *Thomas v. County Com'rs of Shawnee County, 198 P.3d 182 (Kan.App. 2008).*

Another example is a worker hired in a call center who has access to sensitive financial information such as credit card numbers, or personal information such as SSNs. An example is an investor, who brought suit against a broker company when a dealer breached the duty of care it owed and used the investor's funds in a Ponzi scheme. *Dolin v Contemporary Financial Solutions, Inc., 622 F.Supp.2d 1077 (D.Colo. 2009).*

Examples Where Employers May Have an Increased Duty of Care

In deciding how extensively to perform background screening, employers need to consider the risks involved. Here are some examples:

- The workers have contact or responsibilities with groups at risk, such as the young, infirmed, the challenged, or the elderly.
- Jobs such as a security guard, where a person acts under a "color of authority." A person who wears a uniform is even a higher risk since a person may assume they have authority and may let their guard down.
- Jobs with special responsibilities such as an apartment manager who has the master key to all of the apartments.
- Jobs where a worker has access to sensitive consumer information, such as credit card numbers or Social Security numbers (SSNs).
- Jobs by statute where there is particular sensitivity, i.e. workers with safety sensitive positions at nuclear plants. Sarbanes-Oxley compliance is another area that may create a higher duty of care.
- Jobs where workers enter homes, or where other unique risks exist. A person in their own home can be extremely vulnerable since they are shielded from the public and cannot obtain help easily. In fact, as mentioned at the beginning of the book, an organization called the Sue Weaver CAUSE advocates greater due diligence where workers enter homes: www.sueweavercause.org.
- Jobs where a person is elected to a position of authority or management, where they possess power and control over a subordinate employee which in some circumstances may even be anticipated to extend to relationships or interactions outside of work.

---

3. The Employer Breaches the Duty of Care

The employer breaches or violates the duty of care when an employer has either actual knowledge of the employee's unfitness or, in the exercise of reasonable care, would have knowledge the employee was dangerous, unfit, or not qualified. In other words, if the employer does not perform a reasonable background check, a jury could find the duty of care has been breached.

- In a case against the Episcopal Diocese of Pittsburgh, a court found the jury could find that defendants breached their duty to properly hire, train, and supervise a priest because they failed to discover he was not sufficiently trained and experienced in counseling, he had problems with alcohol and his personal life, and he had a propensity to engage in dual relationships with female communicants. *Podolinski v. Episcopal Diocese of Pittsburgh, 23 Pa. D. & C.4th 385, (Pa.Com.Pl. 1995).*

- In a Wisconsin case, a court held it is foreseeable that failing to properly train or supervise a loss prevention associate would subject shoppers to unreasonable risk, injury, or damage. If the defendant fails to properly hire, train, or supervise its employees, then it breaches its duty to shoppers at its store. The jury determined the defendant negligently hired, trained, or supervised its employees and therefore breached its duty to its patrons. *Miller v. Wal-Mart Stores, Inc., 580 N.W.2d 233 (Wis. 1998).*

- In a case involving a nightclub bouncer punching a patron, a court held that by the very nature of the job, a bouncer has significant interaction with the public and is routinely placed in confrontational situations with patrons. Therefore, hiring a bouncer who is known to have violent propensities would likely be a breach of the duty. *Hall v. SSF, Inc., 930 P.2d 94 (Nev. 1996).*

- In a Georgia case, a court held that a jury could find that a security company breached a duty when it failed to conduct a background check which would have revealed that a salesman had been convicted of burglary and kidnapping. *Underberg v. Southern Alarm, Inc., 643 S.E.2d 374 (Ga.App. 2007).*

The level of the duty of care an employer must use is determined by the mythical "reasonable person standard." No one has yet located that person, although many lawyers have spent considerable time looking for the "reasonable person." The following is how one leading legal textbook describes the degree of care an employer must exercise.

You Need To Know ▷

Employer's Duty of Care Explained in Legalese

"As a general rule it may be stated that the degree of care required to be exercised by an employer in selecting or retaining an employee is the degree of care that a person of ordinary prudence would use in view of the nature of the employment and the consequences of the employment of an incompetent person. Such degree of care should be commensurate with the nature and danger of the business and the grade of service for which the employee is intended, as well as to the hazard to which other employees would be exposed from the employment of a careless or incompetent person."

Source: *29 Am. Jur. Trials 267, §9 Duty owed plaintiff by employer – Employer's knowledge of employee's incompetence (1982).*

---

4. Causation Between the Negligent Hiring and the Injury or Proximate Cause

The plaintiff must show the negligence was the proximate cause of the injury. That means the injuries were a logical consequence of the employer's misconduct or incompetence. If an employee attacks a victim and causes injuries, there is no question the attack was the actual or physical cause of the injury. However, depending upon the circumstances, there can be an argument that it was not the legal cause. For example, what if the attack occurred long after the attacker was employed? See discussion below for a defense based upon a lack of causation.

Defenses against Negligent Hiring Lawsuits

There are defenses an employer can raise in a lawsuit for negligent hiring. In the real world, an employer cannot count on a defense being successful. It is much better not to get sued in the first place. When an injury occurs and a lawsuit is initiated, most employers would have paid anything to avoid it.

Some of the defenses listed below are intertwined and could be used in more than one category.

Investigation Would Not Have Revealed Anything Negative

Even with more investigation, the employer would not have discovered anything that was relevant to the injury. A New York court held that a grade school principal's failure to perform a background check on a person recommended as a volunteer art teacher before permitting him to work with students, including a student he later molested, could not serve as a basis for a cause of action for negligent hiring, in absence of any evidence the volunteer had a criminal history and where a routine background check would not have revealed his propensity to molest minors. *Koran I. v. New York City Board of Education, 683 N.Y.S.2d 228 (1998).*

A New York court held that there was no evidence that negative information would have been disclosed through an adequate background check of a nurse who allegedly sexually assaulted a patient while sedated. *Travis v. United Health Services Hospitals, Inc., 23 A.D.3d. 884 (2005).*

A Texas court held that, even though a nightclub did not discover a security guard's past violations of the peace officer manual and a prior reprimand for the use of profanity to a member of the public, the information would not have been enough to put the club on notice that hiring the security guard posed a risk of harm to the public. *Fifth Club, Inc. v. Ramirez, 196 S.W.3d 788 (Tex. 2006).*

Lack of Foreseeability

The most successful defense has been the injury that occurred was not foreseeable, and therefore the employer's breach of a reasonable duty of care was not the "proximate cause" of the injury. Depending upon the state, these types of related defenses may be characterized as a lack of foreseeability, lack of causation, or there was a supervening or intervening cause. Some courts discuss the defense in terms of the employer's conduct being "too attenuated" to be related to the harm.

A successful foreseeability defense is based on the argument that the knowledge gained through a proper background check in light of the hazards of the job would not indicate a given injury would occur. For example, information that a school bus driver had been terminated from his former position for tardiness did not demonstrate the subsequent employer should have known the driver posed a risk of engaging in sexual misconduct with children. *Giraldi by Giraldi v. Community Consol. School Dist. No. 62, 279 Ill.App.3d 679 (1996).*

In a California case, the owner of a beauty school hired an employee to manage and supervise student training. The employee met a minor who was the son of a student at the school. As a result of meeting the minor through the school, the employee met the minor outside of the school and engaged in an illegal sexual encounter. The employee had previously been convicted of sexual offenses against children. The court held that the beauty school was not liable because even if they did a background check, nothing would have been revealed related to managing a beauty school. The past offenses did not involve students or customers of a hairdressing establishment and there was no indication the employee posed a threat to minors he may encounter in the course of his work. The court further held that an employer is not responsible for guaranteeing the safety of everyone an employee may incidentally meet while on the job. *Federico v. Superior Court, 59 Cal. App. 4th 1207 (1997).*

In an Indiana case, a corporation that supplies traffic controllers to contractors hired an employee to flag traffic at a construction site. The employee left the job site during the middle of his shift without permission, got into his personal vehicle, drove several miles, broke into a private residence, and murdered two people. The court held that, because his job did not put him into personal contact with citizens, it did not provide access to people's homes or property, and it authorized the employee to do nothing more than stand on the street and control the flow of traffic, the victims and the harm that befell them was not reasonably foreseeable. *Clark v. Aris, Inc., 890 N.E.2d. 750 (Ind.App. 2008).*

Lack of Causation

A related defense is based upon a lack of causation. An employer can argue there was no causal or factual connection between the failure to investigate and the injury. For a victim to sue, he or she must show "but for" the employer's act or omission, she would not have been injured. For example, in one case the plaintiff was injured when he was struck by a car driven by an intoxicated employee of a car repossession firm hired to repossess the car. The plaintiff alleged the firm was negligent in hiring the employee without a repossessor license. The court determined that not being licensed to repossess was insufficient to establish the employee's unfitness as a repossessor. Additionally, there was no evidence that being unlicensed to repossess cars caused the accident. *Jones v. Beker, 260 Ill.App.3d 481 (1994).*

In another case involving the issue of causation, a court held that a construction company was not liable to a plaintiff employee on theories of negligent hiring and supervision, where another employee of the construction company shot the plaintiff off the job site as a result of an altercation the previous night. Even though there was evidence the employee who did the shooting was aggressive and used drugs, the plaintiff failed to show the construction firm did anything more than hire the two employees to work at the same time so hence they knew each other. The plaintiff failed to show the defendant's alleged negligent hiring and supervision actually caused the shooting. *Escobar v. Madsen Constr. Co., 226 Ill App 3d 92 (1992).*

In a Texas case involving a vehicle that collided with a gravel truck, plaintiffs sought to introduce evidence that the driver had made misrepresentations about his immigration status to obtain his commercial driver's license and employment. The court held that the driver's immigration status did not cause the collision, and was not relevant to the negligent hiring claim. Even if the employer's failure to screen, and thus its failure to discover the driver's inability to work in the United States made the accident possible, the driver's status as an illegal alien or his use of a fake Social Security number to obtain a commercial driver's license did not create a foreseeable risk that he would negligently drive a gravel truck. *TXI Transportation Company, v. Hughes, 306 S.W.3d 230 (Tex. 2010).*

Superseding or Intervening Cause

Related to the causation and foreseeability issue is the issue of proximate cause. An employer can argue that its negligence in hiring was not the legal or "proximate" cause of the injury because there was a superseding or intervening cause that was unexpected or was not reasonably foreseeable. An employer may have started a chain of events that led to an injury by making a bad hire, but some courts have held that the result was so unexpected that the employer cannot be held liable. Even if the injury would not have occurred "but for" the acts of the employer, an employer may not be liable.

For example, in a case in New Mexico, the employee delivered a television to the victim's apartment. Three nights later the employee returned, entered the apartment without permission and raped the victim. Even though the employee would not have meet the victim "but for" being hired to deliver a television, the court ruled that at the time of the crime the employee was on his own time, was not acting within the scope of his employment, was not in the employer's business vehicle, and had no authority from the employer to enter the apartment. In addition, he did not enter the victim's apartment to repair an appliance and the offense did not occur in or near the business. The employer knew the employee had a prior criminal record and that a purse belonging to a rape victim had been found near its place of business. However, on those facts, the court held that the act of the employee was independent of the employer and too attenuated to be attributed to the employers. *F & T Co. v. Woods, 92 N.M. 697 (1979).*

However, employers should not assume that they avoid liability just because their employee acted on his or her own or committed an intentional act. The "superseding cause" defense is determined on a case-by-case basis and other courts have found employers liable for acts committed by employees where the employer should have known about the employee's dangerous propensities. In another New Mexico case, a hotel was found liable for the sexual assault of a minor guest by an employee on the hotel premises while the employee was working. The employee had consumed alcoholic beverages during working hours.

According to the court:

> "There was evidence from which a jury might find that defendant was aware or should have been aware that [the employee] had a drinking problem and a propensity for violence. Two incidents had occurred on hotel property shortly before the assault that gave rise to this lawsuit. [The employee] was terminated from his job as dishwasher for drinking prior to the incident that gave rise to this lawsuit. Shortly after that termination, [the

employee] went to defendant's place of business to inquire about re-instatement. He was drunk, interfered with the kitchen's operation, and became violent when he was asked to leave the premises. He was forcibly subdued by defendant's security personnel and he left under threat of criminal prosecution. Further, defendant later rehired [the employee] as a steward. [the employee's] position as a steward required him to help in the preparation of banquets. He had some contact with customers and other invitees in this connection. He was not closely supervised and had access to alcoholic beverages, which he consumed with some regularity while on duty. Other employees were aware of [the employee's] behavior in this regard."

The court held the employer was on notice of the dangerous propensities and the behavior was foreseeable. *Pittard v. Four Seasons Motor Inn, Inc. 101 N.M. 723, 730-31 (Ct.App. 1984).*

In a Georgia case, two 14-year-old girls sued a landlord for hiring a manager who abused them. The landlord argued that anything the manager did was on the manager's own time. However, the court held the girls would not have met the manager in the first place if the landlord had not initially hired the manager. It was alleged that the landlord was on notice that the manager had dangerous tendencies, and that the landlord could be sued for creating an opportunity for abuse. *Harvey Freeman & Sons, Inc. v. Stanley, 378 S.E.2d 857 (Ga. 1989).*

In another case, a nine-year-old girl was raped at a city playground by a city employee with a background of violent criminal behavior. He had been assigned to the children's playground generally alone and unsupervised. The City tried to defend on the basis the employee was not acting in the scope of employment, but the rape was an intervening and superseding cause breaking the chain of causation. The appellate court ruled the sole issue was in fact whether the city was negligent by allowing the employee access to the playground, and there was sufficient evidence for a jury to find that a violent assault was foreseeable when a violent employee was knowingly assigned to a children's park. *Haddock v. City of New York, 140 A.D.2d 91, 532 N.Y.S.2d 379 (1988).*

The guardian of a mentally handicapped store employee brought suit against the company that provided janitorial services to the store for a sexual assault committed on the store employee by a janitor. The janitor had no prior criminal history and had not received complaints of sexual harassment. The court found that the assault resulted from the janitor's independent criminal actions which were not reasonably foreseeable under the circumstances, and that his actions were an intervening superseding act relieving the janitorial company of liability. *Wood v. Safeway, Inc. 121 P.3d 1026 (Nev. 2005).*

An employee's mother brought suit on behalf of her son who was shot during a restaurant robbery to which a manager was connected. The court found that because neither of the manager's prior convictions (selling cocaine and nonpayment of child support) involved violence or theft, or indicated a propensity for violence the manager's participation in a robbery was not foreseeable. The court held that the manager's own criminal behavior, and that of his cohorts, was a superseding cause that precluded the employer's liability for the crimes. *Barton v Whataburger, Inc. 276 S.W.3d 456 (Tex.App. – Houston [1st Dist.] 2008).*

In reviewing these cases, the courts consider a number of factors such as the vulnerability of the victims, the existence of a special relationship or duty of care between the employer and the victim, what the employer either knew or reasonably should have known about the employee, the connection of the injury to the employer's businesses, and the foreseeability the employee may harm someone in a way that has some connection to the employer.

Industry Standard

Employers have asserted that when their background check follows industry practice or state procedure they cannot be liable for negligent hiring. However, neither compliance with an industry standard nor with state law alone insulates an employer from potential liability for negligent hiring. For example, in an Illinois case, the defendant was an investigative agency that responded to claims of insufficient background checks by asserting that it followed the industry standard. The court stated that compliance with what other firms do was no indication it had met its pre-employment screening obligations. It was inadequate to claim the defendant followed the industry standard because it is possible a whole industry could be reckless in performing background checks. *Easley v. Apollo Detective Agency, Inc., 69 Ill.App.3d 920 (1979).*

Cost

Although cost can be a consideration in a claim of negligence, it is unlikely to prevail as a defense to negligent hiring given the relatively low cost of a background check. In one case, an applicant for a truck driver position gave negative answers on his application to questions about criminal convictions and vehicular offenses. Later, a seventeen-year-old hitchhiker was raped and beaten by the truck driver. The employer had only verified the response to the questions about vehicular crimes. A criminal records check would have revealed convictions for violent sex crimes and an arrest for attacking two teenage hitchhikers. The employer asserted a defense that imposing the requirement of doing criminal background checks was too costly a burden to place on employers. The court dismissed this defense because it considered the cost minor when compared to the possible harm not performing the check could cause. *Malorney v. B & L Motor Freight, Inc., 146 Ill.App.3d 265 (1986).* Even small employers cannot claim that cost prevented them from exercising due diligence. As outlined in Chapter 26, small business are well able to implement due diligence at very little cost.

Worker was an Independent Contractor

An employer may try to contest liability by claiming the worker was an independent contractor. That would be an uphill battle. First, a court may well look at the real nature of the relationship, not what an employer chooses to label it. The fact that an employer classifies a worker as an independent contractor and issues a 1099 form at the end of the year instead of a W-2 is probably irrelevant. The IRS has published guidelines on how to differentiate between independent contractors and employees. The real issue of whether the worker was, in fact, an independent contractor or an employee is the degree of control the business can exercise over the worker. For more information, visit www.irs.gov/businesses/small/article/0,,id=99921,00.html or see additional discussion in Chapter 27.

Even if the individual was, in fact, an independent contractor, courts have found an employer may be liable for the negligent hiring of an independent contractor when the employer knew or should have known the independent contractor was not competent. A firm risks being sued for negligence for its own independent failure to adequately investigate the firm it hired, or to require that its contractor hire safely. If the task involved some peculiar risk of harm, the lawsuit may allege a failure to adequately supervise or train the contractor.

Courts have even found that a business can be held liable for negligent hiring when it hires an independent contractor that in turn negligently hires someone who causes an injury. In an Iowa case, a victim brought an action against both a cable television company and its independent contractor who employed a cable installer who raped her. The cable company argued it was not liable since the rapist worked for the contractor and was not employed by the cable company. The court held that both the cable company and its independent contractor could be held liable for the negligent hiring of the rapist. The independent contractor who employed the rapist could be liable under a general allegation of negligent hiring. The cable company had an independent duty towards its customers, and could not abandon that duty simply by hiring a contractor. *D.R.R. v. English Enterprises, 356 N.W.2d 580 (Iowa App. 1984).* For additional information about the responsibility of employers and independent contractors, see Chapter 27.

Due Diligence After Hiring

Liability does not end with the hiring process. In fact, employers can be sued for failure to exercise due diligence in retention, supervision, or promotion as well.

Negligent Retention

An employer may be liable for negligent retention when during the course of employment, the employer becomes aware or should have become aware of problems with an employee who indicated his unfitness, and the employer fails to take further action to prevent such conduct such as investigation, discharge, or reassignment. In a Minnesota case, the court ruled a church could be sued for negligent retention if the church knew or should have known about the propensity of a church pastor to engage in sexual misconduct with persons who sought spiritual or religious advice from him. *Olson v. First Church of Nazarene, 661 N.W.2d 254 (Minn.App. 2003).* In an action a co-employee brought after being assaulted, evidence that an employee had been fired previously after lunging with clenched fists at a supervisor was enough for a jury's conclusion the employer should have known of the employee's propensity to react violently when angry. Therefore, when the employee was rehired after he threatened to bring a racial discrimination claim, the defendant was liable for negligent rehiring and retention. *Tecumseh Products Co., Inc. v. Rigdon, 552 S.E.2d 910 (Ga. App. 2001).*

A customer who contracted for the installation of air-conditioning units brought a negligent retention action against an air-conditioning installation company after the employee stopped working on the installation several months into the project. The company had learned that the employee had, on two previous occasions, contracted side jobs in violation of company policy and never completed the projects. Upon discovering this, the company reprimanded the employee, but continued to employ him in the same service position. The court found that the company owed potential and existing customers a legal duty to protect them from the employee's conduct and that the customer's injury was a foreseeable consequence of the company's retention of the employee. *CoTemp, Inc. v. Houston West Corp. 222 S.W.3d 487 (Tex.App. – Houston [14th Dist.] 2007).*

Negligent Supervision

Under this theory, employers are subject to direct liability for the negligent supervision of employees when third parties are injured as a result of the tortious acts of employees. The employer's liability rests upon proof the employer knew or, through the exercise of ordinary care, should have known the employee's conduct would subject third parties to an unreasonable risk of harm. Before the employer is held liable, there must be facts or occurrences that put the employer on notice that the supervised person poses a danger to third parties. In an Arkansas case helpful to employers, a retailer was sued for invasion of privacy and outrageous conduct when a store security officer conducted an investigation of theft from the store. The court found there was no evidence that put the employer on notice that the employee would be overzealous or aggressive in an investigation and the allegation was dismissed. *Addington v. Wal-Mart Stores, Inc., 105 S.W.3d 369 (Ark.App. 2003).*

In a South Dakota case, an underage employee was given unsupervised and unrestricted access to alcoholic beverages during his shifts as a drink runner at a racetrack and was not prevented from becoming intoxicated while at work. The court held that the employer had a duty to supervise its employees as to be aware of any problems with the free access to alcohol and that it was foreseeable that an unsupervised, underage employee afforded free reign to consume alcohol could lead to abuse, leaving work premises unfit to drive, and possibly injure a member of the public. *McGuire v Curry, 766 N.W.2d 501 (S.D. 2009).*

A New York employee brought an action against her employer alleging that it negligently supervised another employee allowing harassment to take place. The court held that anything that occurred prior to when the plaintiff complained about the other employee could not form the basis of a negligent supervision claim because the employer was not on notice about the employee's predatory behavior until specific enough complaints were brought to the employer's attention as to alert the employer of the employee's misbehavior. *Tainsky v. Clarins USA, Inc. 363 F.Supp.2d 578 (S.D.N.Y. 2005).*

Negligent Promotion

For someone to successfully recover damages, it must be proven the employer knew or should have known the employee was incompetent or unfit to perform the job to which he was promoted. As a matter of law it was not negligence for a garage owner to promote an employee to the position of night garage manager without making a detailed investigation at that time of his possible criminal past, because at the commencement of his employment more than three years earlier the employee was successfully bonded, his previous job checked out satisfactorily, and during the interim period of employment he performed exemplary service for the employer. *Abraham v. S. E. Onorato Garages, 50 Haw. 628 (1968).*

Negligent Failure to Warn

The duty of care can even extend to a duty to warn consumers that a former dangerous employee was terminated and no longer works for the employer. An electronics services company terminated an employee who the employer either knew or should have reasonably known had a propensity towards violence. The employee had entered the victim's home on various occasions for business reasons. After the employee was terminated, he gained entry into the victim's home by pretending he was there for business purposes and raped the victim. The court held that because the employee had been to the victim's home in the past on the employer's behalf, a special relationship had developed between the victim and the employer, and the employer had a duty to warn the victim the employee was no longer employed. *Coath v. Jones, 277 Pa.Super. 479 (1980).*

In a case helpful to employers, a Minnesota court held that a reference check is not a "special relationship" that would evoke an affirmative duty to warn of an employee's propensities. Even though a former employer would possess direct knowledge about its past employed not available to a prospective employer, the new employer is not deprived of normal opportunities of self-protection if the former employer refuses to disclose information about the employee's prior bad acts. *Grozdanich v. Leisure Hills Health Center, Inc., 25 F.Supp.2d 953 (D.Minn. 1998).*

Employer Unaware of Past Conduct or Employee Hides It

Claiming that an employer had no duty to conduct a background check because the employer was not aware of a criminal record, or that the applicant hid it or lied about it, was rejected in a case decided by the Fourth Circuit Court of Appeals in 2004. The Court held that a janitorial service that did not check backgrounds could be sued for negligent hiring when an employee attacked a college student, and a background check may have shown prior physical assault on a woman. The court rejected the defense that there was no duty to check since the applicant denied a criminal conviction on a previous application and there was nothing to put the employer on actual notice of a prior criminal history.

The janitorial firm was hired by a college on the condition that background checks were to be performed. The janitorial service failed to conduct a background check despite having employed the attacker on several different occasions before the attack. A lower court agreed with the janitorial service that the case should be dismissed because the employee had previously indicated no criminal record on an application and the janitorial service had no reason to suspect a criminal record.

The Appellate court reversed, and determined there was sufficient basis for the case to proceed to a jury trial. The Appellate Court, citing an earlier court decision, determined an employer can be liable for the acts of an employee on a theory of negligence when:

> "an employer in placing a person with known propensities, or propensities which should have been
> discovered by reasonable investigation, in an employment position in which, because of the circumstances of
> the employment, it should have been foreseeable that the hired individual posed a threat of injury to others."
> *Blair v. Defender Services, Inc., 386 F.3d 623, 629 (4th Cir. 2004)*

According to the Court, it was a jury issue if a background check may have revealed a criminal complaint filed in a neighboring county by a woman that the employee had previously attacked.

Increased Need for Employer Due Diligence

One impact of the recent recession is the greater likelihood of job applicant fraud, which means there is an increased need for employer due diligence. Fraudulent educational claims, or worthless diplomas from degree mills, are already familiar problem for employers, recruiters and HR professionals. However, resume fraud has taken on an added urgency with the advent of services that would actually create fake employment references from fake companies. The service apparently even included a phone number that an employer could call in order to reach a service that in fact would verify the fake employment. So it appears that some job applicants have been willing to resort to these extreme and dishonest measures to gain an advantage in the job market. In the long run, worthless diplomas bought over the internet or scams to create manufactured past employment will probably be unsuccessful for the most part, provided that employers exercise some due diligence. For fake education, a competent background firm will typically verify first if a school is legitimate. If the school does not appear on accepted lists of accredited institution, then a screening firm can review lists of known diploma mills and scams. Screening firms will also verify if the accreditation agency is for real since fake schools have resorted to creating fake accreditation agencies.

Additional Examples of Negligent Hiring Cases

Here are some additional examples of negligent hiring cases that involved employers and former employees:

Difference Between Negligent Hiring and Direct Employer Vicarious Liability

A case decided by the California Supreme Court on June 23, 2011, graphically demonstrates the difference between allegations of negligent hiring as opposed to **"vicarious" liability** where an employer has direct responsibility for the acts of an employee.

In that case, the plaintiff was injured in a car accident when another driver tried to pass a truck in the middle lane. The driver ended up getting back into the middle lane but hit the truck, causing the car to spin and fly over the divider and hit the plaintiff's SUV. The plaintiff (the injured party) sued both drivers, including the truck driver on the theory that the truck driver should have been in the slow lane, should not have sped up to prevent passing, and should have avoided the collision by being aware of a car trying to pass. The trucking firm employing the truck driver was also sued under a theory of vicarious liability, which means the employer is liable for the acts of its employees committed in the scope and course of the employment. In the alternative, the plaintiff ALSO sued for negligent hiring and retention.

The basis of the negligent hiring and retention lawsuit was that the truck driver had two previous accidents, one of which he was at fault and sued and the other occurring 16 days before the events in this case. In addition, the driver was in the country illegally, had used a phony social security number, and was fired from or quit without good reason three of his last four driving jobs. Also, the only evaluation received by the truck driver's current employer was negative. In order to avoid such prejudicial evidence, the trucking firm offered to admit that it was vicariously liable for any negligent driving by its employee. Vicarious liability is based on a legal concept called "respondent superior," which means that an employer is liable for the act of its employees committed in the scope of employment. Such an admission would mean that a plaintiff would not have to prove that the employer was negligent in hiring or retaining. Just showing the employee was negligent while working for the employer is sufficient.

The trial court, however, allowed the plaintiff to introduce the evidence relating to negligent hiring and retention and the jury heard about the prior accidents and the apparent lack of due diligence in the selection process. As a result, the jury found the truck driver negligent and the trucking company was also negligent in hiring and retaining the driver.

The trucking company appealed on the basis that evidence of negligent hiring should not have been admitted where the trucking company was willing to accept liability vicariously for the acts of its employee, and that the admission of such unnecessary evidence was prejudicial. Furthermore, under California's complicated laws concerning allocation of fault between defendants, the trucking company argued that it was held liable for a larger portion of the damages than it otherwise would have.

The California Supreme Court ruled for the trucking firm, indicating that once an employer is willing to accept responsibility for an employee's act, the only issue is whether the employee was negligent. It is no longer relevant if, in addition, the employer was also negligent in hiring and/or retaining the worker. Adding evidence pertaining to negligent hiring and retention is prejudicial and in this case may well have altered the allocation of responsibility.

The case is Diaz vs. Carcamo, 253 P.3d 535 (Cal. 2011). The case underscored the difference between negligent hiring and direct vicarious liability. The case Diaz vs. Carcamo is available at http://scholar.google.com/scholar_case?case=6787332853309228079&q=Diaz+vs.+Carcamo&hl=en&as_sdt=2,5.

Case Demonstrates Outer Limits to Negligent Hiring Exposure

This case involved a plumber that was hired in 1999, even though the plumbing company knew the person had been convicted of domestic violence and/or arson involving the plumber's ex-wife. Four years later, in 2003, the plumber performed a service call at the victim's home. The plumber and the victim started a relationship that eventually turned romantic in nature. About a month after the service call with the victim, the plumber was terminated for misuse of a company vehicle, drug and alcohol use, and an allegation of threatening a co-worker. By 2005, the victim apparently had enough and ended the relationship and applied for a restraining order against the plumber. The plumber shot and killed her and was convicted of her murder. The victim's daughter brought a lawsuit for negligent hiring against the plumbing company. The case was dismissed by the trial court on a motion for summary judgment, and it was appealed. The Appeals court upheld the dismissal, for two reasons:

- First, the court ruled that an employer no longer has liability for negligent hiring after terminating and the end of the employer-employee relationship.
- As an additional ground, the Court also ruled that there was insufficient causation between the employer hiring the plumber and the murder of the victim, so that the employer's hiring was not the proximate or legal cause of the murder.

In reaching its ruling, the court reviewed California law on negligent hiring. Essentially, an employer can be held liable when it hires someone that causes harm where the employer either knew, or reasonably should have known, that the person was dangerous or unfit, it was foreseeable that harm could occur, and the injury to victim was caused by the employer's act. In this case, the court determined that the duty of care does NOT extend to acts committed by a former employee AFTER terminating. The logic was that a reasonable person could not foresee that an ex-employee would injure a party two years after termination. The California Court found that:

> "Because the employer-employee relationship ends on termination of an employee's employment, we conclude an employer does not owe a plaintiff a duty of care in a negligent hiring and retention action for an injury or harm inflicted by a former employee on the plaintiff even though that former employee, as in this case, initially met the plaintiff while employed by the employer."

As additional support for its decision, the Court also relied on a lack of causation. The court noted that there must be some "nexus or causal connection between" the employer's negligence and the harm suffered. Without sufficient connection, there is a lack of proximate or legal cause, and therefore the employer would not be liable. The Court noted that the plumbing firm could not be the guarantor of the safety of all customers or other persons whom the employee incidentally meet while performing plumbing work, especially given that the relationship began outside of the plumber's duties, and the romantic relationship did not even start until AFTER the plumber was terminated.

However employers may not want to assume this case announces a firm rule that essentially creates immunity from negligent hiring lawsuits every time a bad hire is terminated. As the Court noted, the existence of a legal duty of care has to be analyzed in the particular factual situation in question. A different argument could be made for example if the employer had hired someone for a position where it was foreseeable that a work related relationship would continue even after termination. This could occur where the job entailed working with vulnerable patients. For example, where there is a higher duty of care it is foreseeable that once the introduction is made, ongoing relationships that are work related could be established. The case is *Phillips v. TLC Plumbing, Inc. (2009)172 Cal.App.4th 1133, 1144.*

About Defenses That Do and Do Not Work in Negligent Hiring Cases

If an employer is sued for negligent hiring on the basis that they hired someone that they either knew or – in the exercise of reasonable care – should have known was dangerous, unqualified, unfit or dishonest, and it was reasonably foreseeable that some of harm could occur, an employer can be sued for negligent hiring. That is the opposite of due diligence. If the subject of a legal action, employers do have some potential defenses in a court case, but they are far from a sure thing.

The Best Defense

The best defense is that the employer did in fact exercise due diligence and reasonable care, but despite those best efforts, a bad hire fell through the cracks. An employer would have to show they took a number of steps designed to avoid bad hires. An employer can review the adequacy of their hiring efforts by taking the Safe Hiring Audit (see the last chapter.)

Another defense that had been successful is that the crime or injury was too remote or unconnected from the employer's negligence or was not foreseeable. An example is the California case mentioned earlier where a plumber with a criminal record was hired, met a woman on the job that he started dating, was terminated by the employer, and then murdered the girlfriend two years later. The victim's family argued that but for the negligent hiring, the two would not have met in the first place and the murder would not have occurred. The court found that the murder two years later and long after termination was not sufficiently connected to the hiring to hold employer legally responsible.

Another defense is that a background check would have not have revealed anything anyway, so the employer's failure to conduct an adequate pre-screening was not the cause of the injury. As the old adage goes, "every dog has its first bite." If there was nothing for a background check to locate that was a potential a "Red Flag," that is also a defense.

Defenses that Do Not Work

Employers have not been very successful in defending lawsuits on the basis that due diligence and background checks cost too much, especially considering how inexpensive it is to screen. Another argument that may not go far with a jury is that the employer did what every other employer did in their industry. The fact that all employers in an industry engage in the same practice does not mean that the employer has meet the legal duty of due diligence, since a "standard practice" is not the same as a "standard of care." The least successful defense is the argument that the employer is also the victim as well, or they were victimized by an applicant lying. An employer who claims they too were the victim may not find a sympathetic jury where the victim has suffered some grave injury, or perhaps even death.

When a negligent hiring case goes to a jury, an employer does not have a jury of their peers in the sense that there are not twelve Human Resources or Security Directors in the jury box. More likely, most if not all of the jury members are also employees or retired employees. As a practical matter, a jury may well assume that the employer had the resources, duty, and opportunity to exercise due care. After all, the victim of a case involving negligent hiring probably had no say in who was hired. At the end of the day, when there are serious allegations of harm against an employer, the employer is going to have some explaining to do. The bottom line: stay out of the situation in the first place through due diligence.

In Conclusion

When an employer fails to conduct due diligence on an employee, and someone is harmed in a situation where damage was foreseeable, the employer cannot escape liability because it did not know about the hire's past criminal conduct. The fact that an applicant denies a criminal record or the employer does not know about it is not an excuse. To avoid liability, employers should be proactive in conducting background checks. Exercising due diligence in hiring and conducting background checks is a small price to pay to avoid the "Parade of Horribles" that can befall an employer that makes bad hiring decisions.

Sample Policies and Procedures to Implement a Safe Hiring Program

Introduction: Example of a Safe Hiring Program Using the S.A.F.E. System

Here is a series of sample internal policy and procedure documents from a fictitious firm called the ABC Company. These documents cover the basics of their Safe Hiring Program and provide a hands-on example of how a S.A.F.E. System is implemented. Employers should consider utilizing the services of a labor attorney or Human Resources consultant to draft a policy that is tailored for their firm. The following material is not given or intended to be used as legal advice and is for educational purposes only. Not every sample applies to every employer and does not contain all matters that an employer may wish to consider.

The first example is a General Policy Statement (called **The Safe Hiring Statement**) which summarizes the big picture.

This Safe Hiring Statement assumes the ABC Company is outsourcing the employment screening aspect of the Safe Hiring Program to a third party background screening firm. However, if a company intends to perform those functions in-house, then the memo must be adjusted accordingly. Later in this chapter is a separate policy statement that an employer can utilize in their employee manual. In succeeding chapters, details of each element of the Safe Hiring Program are discussed.

Sample # 1 – Safe Hiring Policy Statement

ABC Company Memo: Safe Hiring Policy Statement

<u>Policy and Purpose</u>

To ensure that individuals who join this firm are well qualified and have a strong potential to be productive and successful, and to further ensure that this firm maintains a safe and productive work environment that is free from any form of violence, harassment, or misconduct, it is the policy of this company to exercise appropriate practices to conduct due diligence on job applicants to identify individuals whose employment would be inconsistent with this policy.

In addition, if an employee changes positions in the Company, any additional required background checks for that position which have not previously been performed will be performed.

It is also the position of the company that all hiring practices be conducted in strict conformity with all applicable laws and regulations and that specifically, the company will not permit any hiring practices that result in any discriminatory treatment of any applicant or employee.

To the extent possible and where permitted by law, these same policies also apply to non-employees engaged by the company, such as workers from staffing firms, independent contractors or vendors.

<u>General Statement</u>

1. The employer maintains a Safe Hiring Program. This program includes certain procedures that occur prior to an offer being made, including but not limited to the Application Review, Interview, and Reference checking process. In addition, this firm will perform pre-employment screening and credentials verification on applicants including criminal background checks.

2. A pre-employment background check is a sound business practice that benefits everyone. The fact that a candidate is subject to a pre-employment screening is not a reflection on any particular applicant and is not a sign of mistrust or suspicion. All finalists are subject to this procedure. The success of our firm depends upon our people, and although we operate in an environment of trust, our firm still must verify that all employees are both qualified and safe. All finalists for any position at this firm are subject to the same policy.

3. All offers of employment are conditioned upon the firm's receipt of a pre-employment background screening investigation that is acceptable to the firm at the firm's sole discretion.

4. This firm relies upon the accuracy of information contained in the employment application as well as the accuracy of other data presented throughout the hiring process and employment, including any oral interviews. Any misrepresentations, falsifications, or material omissions in any of the information or data, no matter when discovered, may result in the firm's exclusion of the individual from further consideration for employment or, if the person has been hired, termination of employment. Applicants also are expected to provide references from their former employers as well as educational reference information that can be used to verify academic accomplishments and records. Background checks may include verification of information provided on the completed application for employment, the applicant's resume, or on other forms used in the hiring process. Information to be verified includes, but is not limited to, Social Security Number and previous addresses. An employer may also conduct a reference check and verify the applicant's education and employment background as stated on the employment application or other documents listed above.

5. The background check may also include a criminal record check. If a conviction is discovered, then the employer will closely scrutinize the conviction in view of our policy of ensuring a safe and profitable workplace. A criminal conviction does not automatically bar an applicant from employment. Before an employment decision is made, a determination will be made whether the conviction is job related and/or an exclusion is consistent with business necessity or present a safety or security risks, taking into account the nature and gravity of the act, the nature of the position, and the age of the conviction, in the manner set forth in the most current EEOC Guidance in effect on the proper use of a criminal record. Additional checks, such as a driving record or a credit report, may be made on applicants for particular job categories if appropriate and job-related. Employment screening assessments to determine an applicant's job fit may also be required of all applicants for employment. Skills tests related to the demands of the job may also be required.

6. All procedures will be reviewed by legal counsel to ensure they are in strict conformity with the Federal Fair Credit Reporting Act, the Americans with Disabilities Act, state and federal anti-discrimination laws, privacy laws, and all other applicable federal and state laws.

   [**NOTE**: Additionally, the disclosure should include language about the impact of state laws if the employer operates in more than one state. Also, the impact of any union contract should also be considered.]

7. If a criminal record is to be used as a basis to disqualify an applicant from employment, the employer's policy is to provide an opportunity for an individualized assessment for those candidates identified by criminal background checks to determine if the policy as applied to an applicant is job related and consistent with business necessity.

8. All pre-employment background screenings are conducted by a third party to ensure privacy. All reports are kept strictly confidential and are only viewed by individuals in this firm who have direct responsibility in the hiring process. All screening reports are kept and maintained separately from employee personnel files. Under the Fair Credit Reporting Act (FCRA), all background screenings are done only after a person has signed a release and received a disclosure. Additionally, the disclosure should include language about the impact of state laws if the employer operates in more than one state. Also, the impact of any union contract

should also be considered. The specific components of a candidate's background check will depend on the job to be performed including the job duties, the essential functions of the job, and the circumstances and environment under which the job is to be performed.

9. Different jobs may be subject to a greater degree of screening deriving upon the risk factors and responsibilities associated with each job. However, it is the policy of this firm to treat similarly situated individuals in a similar fashion and, as a result, all final candidates for each job or job category will be screened in a consistent fashion.

10. It is the policy of the employer not to ask about criminal records in the initial application process. However, the employer will advise all applicants that before any employment is made final, there will be a background check including criminal records in accordance with this policy. This enables all applicants to have a full and fair understanding of the hiring process. However, any inquiry about criminal history will be asked in a way reasonable designed not deter or chill applicants with criminal histories from applying. In addition, at such time that an applicant is asked about a criminal record, the employer will undertake measures to reasonably limit any inquiries taking into account job relatedness and business necessity.

[**NOTE:** Above is optional depending upon how an employer intends to comply with the new EEOC Guidance reviewed in Chapter 10 and ban-the-box laws.]

11. It is the duty of all persons with decision-making responsibilities for hiring to understand and carry out the firm's policies regarding the Safe Hiring Program and the commitment that all law and regulation be followed, including federal, state, and local discrimination laws.

Disclaimers

It is not the purpose of this Policy to provide detailed information or descriptions of each individual pre-employment background check that can be performed. It is not the purpose of this Policy to provide detailed information on how to make a final decision regarding the results of a pre-employment background check. Every case must be decided on its own merits subject to the Company requirement that all candidates be treated equally and consistently. It is also not the purpose of this Policy to provide detailed information of all applicable law. Questions about these subjects should be directed to the Human Resources or Legal Departments.

This Policy does not limit ABC Company's right to hire, discipline or terminate. This Policy does not create a contract of employment. All employment is at will unless contract or law applies to the contrary.

Sample # 2 – Overall Practices to Carry out Employer's Safe Hiring Program

In addition to having a Safe Hiring Policy Statement, the firm's actual practices need to be documented. (As noted elsewhere in this chapter, the EEOC 2012 Guidance on the use of criminal records and ban-the-box laws may require some of the following to be altered by employers.)

The Safe Hiring Program for ABC Company

- The Safe Hiring Program will be coordinated by either the Human Resources Department or Security Department, hereinafter referred to as the Program Administrator.

- The Program Administrator is responsible for implementation of procedures to ensure that all steps in the Safe Hiring Program are documented.

- The Program Administrator is also in charge of implementing, training all managers with hiring responsibility, and auditing adherence to this program, including periodic assessments to measure and evaluate the effectiveness of the program, review potential improvements, and to ensure continuing legal compliance. The Program Administrator is also responsible for full documentation of the program and maintaining ongoing documentation of the program's operation, as well as all training. The Program

Administrator will oversee training, keeping a record of who participated, dates of attendance, the training material, as well as monitoring of the effectiveness of the training.

- The Program Administrator is also responsible for maintaining the confidentiality of any material containing Personally Identifiable Information (PII) or anything else of a confidential nature such as criminal records, and to ensure that any information collected on an applicant is only used for purposes of employment decisions.

- The Program Administrator is also responsible for maintaining and updating his or her knowledge of the legal and practical aspects of safe hiring and background checks.

- The Program Administrator will also maintain a record of consultations and research considered in crafting the policy and procedures, as well as any justifications for the policies and procedures.

Sample # 3 – Statement Implementing the Application, Interview & Reference Checking (AIR) Process

An important part of the Safe Hiring Program is what is called the **AIR Process – an acronym for the Application, Interview, and Reference Checking Process.** (Chapters 3 and 4 examine these processes in detail.) The memo below outlines how the ABC Company acknowledges and implements these important functions.

Statement of Best Practices

The ABC Company will utilize the application, interview, and reference checking stages of the hiring process. The Program Administrator is responsible for developing procedures for the implementation of these practices. These duties include:

- Developing forms that must be completed and placed in each applicant's file before the employment decision is made final.

- Training all persons with hiring responsibility in these procedures and document the training.

- Institute and document procedures to ensure these practices are being followed.

Sample # 4 – The Application Process

Application Stage – Use and Carefully Review Application Forms

[**NOTE:** The subject of ascertaining and utilizing criminal records in the hiring process is covered later in Sample # 10 – Criminal History Information.]

1. Use an application form, not just resumes:

- Use of an employment application form including the use of electronic forms is considered a best practice. Resumes are not always complete or clear. Applications ensure uniformity, include all needed information that is obtained, prevent employers from having impermissible information, and provide employers with a place for applicants to sign certain necessary statements.

- The application will include a statement that lack of truthfulness or material omissions are grounds to terminate the hiring process or employment no matter when they are discovered. Candidates are expected to provide full, accurate, and complete information as part of the hiring process.

- The application will include additional statements that must be approved by the Human Resource department and legal counsel. These can include statements that employment is "at will," and "we are an equal opportunity employer, and our firm has an arbitration policy when it comes to disputes concerning employment, such as employment is at-will."

Optional (Required if using a third party background screening firm.)

2. Require a release for a background check in the application process.

- Each job applicant must execute a consent form for a background check including a check for criminal records, past employment, and education. Under the Federal Fair Credit Reporting Act, before a background check is requested from a Consumer Reporting Agency. In addition, there must be a disclosure form on a separate stand-alone document compliant with applicable state and federal law. Such forms may be executed on a paper form or by an electronic signature on electronic forms.

3. The employer will review the application carefully for "red flags" that may indicate a need for further review, including but not limited to:

- Applicant does not sign application.
- Applicant does not sign consent to background screening.
- Applicant leaves criminal questions blank (Note: Only applies if an employer requests criminal information on the initial application form.)
- Applicant self-reports a criminal violation (taking into account that applicants can self-report matters incorrectly). (Note: See the discussion on Ban the Box in Chapter 10)
- Applicant fails to explain why he or she left past jobs.
- Applicant fails to explain gaps in employment history.
- Applicant gives an explanation for an employment gap or for the reason leaving a previous job that does not make sense.
- Applicant uses excessive cross-outs and changes, as though making it up as they go along.
- Applicant fails to give complete information, i.e. insufficient information to identify a past employer, leaves out salary, etc.
- Applicant fails to indicate or cannot recall the name of a former supervisor.
- The application form is not internally consistent or conflicts with other information obtained about the applicant.

Sample # 5 – The Interview Process

The key here is to include the six questions that should always be asked during the "housekeeping stage" of the interview.

ABC Company Interview Stage

These six questions are to be asked at every interview. These questions give a candidate the opportunity to clarify any matter in their application form. The six questions are:

1. We do background checks on everyone to whom we make an offer. Do you have any concerns you would like to discuss? Good applicants will shrug off this question.

2. We also check for criminal convictions for all finalists consistent with all rules, law, and regulations concerning the legal and appropriate use of criminal records and discrimination. Are you aware of that? (By this point, the candidate has already been invited for an interview, and an employer may decide that the process is far enough along that a question about relevant past criminal conduct can now be asked consistent with the EEOC Guidance of 2012, discussed in Chapter 10. However, the EEOC advises against open ended criminal questions. An employer may choose in view of the new EEOC Guidance, to only advise the applicant that a criminal check will be conducted on finalists.)

3. We contact all past employers. What do you think they will say?

4. Will a past employer tell us that you were tardy, did not perform well, etc.?

5. Also, use the interview to ask questions about any unexplained employment gaps and ask the applicant to confirm everything on the application.

6. Is everything in the application and everything you told us in the hiring process true, correct, and complete?

Sample # 6 – The Reference Checking Stage

ABC Company Reference Checking Standards

Check References and Look for Unexplained Employment Gaps

- All past employers for a period of 7-10 years must be contacted. All efforts to contact past employers as well as the results of any conversations must be noted and documented. Even if a past employer will not provide qualitative information about the applicant's potential performance, it is critical to verify, at a minimum, his or her start date, end date, and job titles.

- The Program Administrator will create forms that are to be used to assist in the process. These will include a call history to document who was called and when, as well as the results of the call.

- The Program Administrator will also ensure there is proper training on legal and illegal reference questions. The Hiring Manager will make the decision necessary to determine if a candidate should be offered a position. However, Human Resources or a third-party screening firm will call past employers to confirm dates of employment and job titles in order to ensure that all finalists have been subject to the same process and that no one is hired unless the firm has made reasonable efforts to confirm past employment.

- The firm will not contact the current employer without an authorization but reserves the right to call the current employer after the applicant has begun employment or to ask the applicant for a copy of their paycheck stub to confirm current employment.

Verifying past employment is one of the single most important tools an employer has. It is as important as doing criminal checks. Why? Past job performance can be an important predictor of future success. Some employers make a costly mistake by not checking past employment because they believe past employers may not give detailed information. However, even verifying dates of employment and job titles are critical because an employer must be concerned about unexplained gaps in the employment history. Although there can be many reasons for a gap in employment, if an applicant cannot account for the past seven to ten years, that can be a red flag.

In addition, documenting the fact that an effort was made will demonstrate due diligence.

It is also critical to know where a person has been because of the way criminal records are maintained in the United States. There are over 10,000 courthouses in America. If an employer knows where an applicant has been as a result of past employment checks, it increases the accuracy of a criminal search and decreases the possibility an applicant has served time for a serious offense.

Sample # 7 – The Pre-employment Screening Process

This next sample outlines the pre-employment process, including standards that the ABC Company has put into place.

ABC Company Pre-Employment Screening Process

All pre-employment screening will be conducted through a third party Consumer Reporting Agency (CRA). The Program Administrator will:

- Administer and coordinate the pre-employment screening program.

- Approve all forms utilized in the process and ensure that all forms are utilized consistently.

- To the extent deemed necessary, have the employer's legal department or outside counsel approve all forms and procedures for compliance with all applicable federal, state, and local law and regulations.

- Submit names and background requests to the CRA.

- Receive reports from the CRA.

- Contact the CRA as necessary to review the report or receive additional information.

- Review all reports, and in the case of negative or derogatory information, take appropriate action by contacting the hiring manager.

- Ensure that in the event an adverse decision is intended, the firm will take appropriate measures under the Fair Credit Reporting Act. That includes providing an applicant with a copy of the Consumer Report and statement of rights prior to the adverse action. If the adverse action is final, then the Program Administrator shall also cause a second notice, required by the FCRA, to be sent. The Program Administrator may delegate these duties to the CRA.

- When an exception is made to hire an applicant despite negative or derogatory information, the administrator will ensure the file properly documents the reasons for the decision.

- Maintain the background reports in complete privacy and confidence ensure only individuals with hiring authority are made aware of report contents, and further ensure that all reports are only ordered and utilized for screening purposes.

- Supervise the storage of all release forms and screening reports in a secure area, separate from employee personnel files.

- Select a CRA to perform pre-employment screening services through a Request for Proposal (RFP) process, and approve all billing submitted by the CRA.

- Ensure the program is administered uniformly and consistently and in compliance with all applicable laws including the Fair Credit Reporting Act, state and federal discrimination laws, ban-the-box laws, privacy and data protection laws and best practices, and laws regulating the gathering and use of information in the employment process.

- No information shall be requested, obtained, or utilized that would be in violation of any state or federal law, rule, or regulation.

- Perform such other tasks and duties in order to carry out the aims and purposes of the pre-employment screening policy.

Mechanics of the Screening Program

- All applicants for employment prior to onboarding will undergo a pre-employment background check by a qualified Consumer Reporting Agency. The applicant will receive legally compliant forms either in a paper format or in an electronic format to facilitate the background check, including forms to allow the applicant to give consent and appropriate FCRA disclosure.

- All offers of employment are conditional upon receipt of a background report that is satisfactory to the firm. In a situation where an offer is made prior to the receipt of the background report, the offer letter shall state, in writing—

  "This offer of employment is conditional upon the employer's receipt of a pre-employment background screening investigation that is acceptable to the employer at the employer's sole discretion."

- No employment will commence prior to the completion of the background report unless the Program Administrator and department head/Vice-President determines there is an exceptional circumstance. In that case, the employment will be conditional on a satisfactory report, as indicated above.

Sample # 8 – Standards for Screening

ABC Company Standards for Screening

The Program Administrator shall determine for each position, in consultation as necessary with the hiring manager, what level of pre-employment screening is required, taking into account the nature of the position, including duties and responsibilities, the essential functions of the position, the duties to be performed, and the environment in which the job is to be performed. [**NOTE:** The following factors are given as example and are not necessarily a complete statement of all factors an employer will take into account.]

- What are the essential functions of the job?
- What are the job duties?
- What are the circumstances under which the job is to be performed?
- What is the environment in which the job is to be performed (e.g. an office, a private home, etc.?)
- Does the position have access to money or assets?
- Does the position carry significant authority or fiduciary responsibility?
- Does the position carry access to trade secrets, confidential information, personal information of others, or any other information that can be considered confidential or private?
- Does the position have access to members of the public or co-workers so that any propensity to violence or dishonesty could foreseeably cause harm?
- What level of supervision does an employee have in the manner their job is to be performed?
- Would the position be difficult to replace in terms of recruitment, hiring, and training?
- Would a new hire's falsification of skills, experience, or background put the firm at risk or lower the firm's productivity?
- Would a bad hire expose the firm to litigation or financial claims from the applicant, co-workers, customers, or the public, or other risks?
- Is there a statutory, licensing, or legal requirement for certain positions to be screened?
- Does the position involve driving?
- Does the new position involve unique or peculiar risk, such as access to children, the aged or the infirmed, work inside of a home or some other environment out of public view, or hold a position of authority?

Levels of Screening

The Program Administrator will designate which positions shall be screened at which level. Additional screening may be requested as necessary for a particular position by a hiring manager or the Program Administrator. All screenings will be done consistently and uniformly. Once it has been determined that a particular position requires a particular level of pre-employment screening, all finalists for that particular position will be screened at the same level.

[**Author's Note**: The four levels listed below are examples of screening that can be utilized. Each employer needs to evaluate the screening that is appropriate for the risks the employer faces.]

1. **Individual** — For casual or temporary labor. Recommended search: County criminal search in local county or county of residence and other individual reports such as a Social Security trace and driving record.

2. **Basic** — For entry-level employees, retail or manufacturing, or positions where the employer has internally checked references and education. Recommended search: A full seven-year on-site criminal records check for felonies and misdemeanors, Credit Report or Social Security and identity check, and driver's license check.

3. **Standard** — For more responsible positions and permanent hire. Recommended search: The Basic search above plus verification of the last three employers (and references if available) and highest post high school education.

4. **Extended** — For positions involving increased responsibility or supervision of others. Recommended search: The Basic and Standard search above plus checking Superior Court civil cases in the last two relevant counties for litigation matters that may be job related.

[**Author's Note**: The Program Administrator may review other available tools such as a sexual offender or a criminal database search as long as it is used as a supplemental, and not a primary, source of information.]

Sample # 9 – Analysis of Information

ABC Company - Analysis of the Background Screen

General:

When a background check report is returned with derogatory or potentially negative information that would reasonably impact a hiring decision, the Program Administrator will contact the hiring manager or other appropriate person to review the information. The Program Administrator will normally provide a verbal summary rather than the actual written report in order to limit confidential material from circulating within the company. The Program Administrator will only convey the information that is necessary for the company to engage in a decision making process in order to maintain confidentially.

The following are general guidelines as to what information is considered potentially negative or derogatory. This list is not intended to be exhaustive or exclusive. There may be other factors which are appropriate for the position or the applicant under consideration. The decision to hire or not hire is not based upon any rigid matrix or pre-determined formula but is based upon a consideration of the totality of the circumstances. The same guidelines may also apply to decision impacting retention, promotion or reassignment. General guidelines include:

- In the event of a criminal record, in addition to any factors listed below, the employer will conduct an analysis pursuant to its Criminal History Information Policy. (See Sample #10 below.)

- The derogatory information is inconsistent with the nature of the job, taking into account the risk factors listed above under "Standards for Screening." (See Sample #8 above.)

- The applicant or employee is found to have engaged in dishonest, misleading, or untruthful conduct, including but not limited to misrepresentations or omission of material facts during the selection process. This can include but is not limited to discrepancies or falsehoods in self-reporting criminal records as well as past employment, education, and credentials, or in identification of the applicant.

- The applicant or employee is found to have engaged in violence, wrongdoing, or other conduct inappropriate in the workplace.

- The applicant is found to not have the necessary knowledge, skills, abilities, experience aptitude, or qualifications to successfully fulfill the job requirements.

- The information demonstrates that the applicant or employee has engaged in conduct that that may preclude an applicant from effectively performing his or her job duties or may create a security or safety issue in the workplace.

- The derogatory information makes the applicant unable or ineligible to perform the essential job functions or creates a potential legal liability for the firm. For example, the applicant must drive a vehicle as part of the job responsibility and does not have a valid license or a clear driving record.

Process:

If the hiring manager, the Program Administrator, or management believes the information will form the basis of an adverse action or termination based upon the application of the guidelines reviewed above, then the Program Administrator will document the basis for the decision, including specifically the job-related basis for the adverse action or termination.

In the event of an intended adverse action or termination based upon a background check by a background screening firm, , the Program Administrator will also initiate the adverse action notification procedures required by the Fair Credit Reporting Act If the decision is based in whole or in part on a criminal matter, the Program Administrator will follow the steps outlined by the EEOC in its 2012 Guidance including but not limited to providing the applicant with an opportunity for an Individualized Assessment (See Chapter 10 on the EEOC).

If the hiring manager believes the negative information should not preclude employment or promotion, the hiring manager will seek approval from the respective department head or Vice-President who will decide the issue in consultation with the Program Administrator and legal counsel, if appropriate. If the decision is to offer the position despite negative information, then the reasons for the decision shall be appropriately documented in writing and provided to the Program Administrator. The purpose is to protect the firm by showing the negative information was considered in light of all available information about the candidate and the position, and the firm exercised discretion only after a due diligence inquiry. The documentation is needed in the event the decision is challenged in the future. For example, an applicant with negative information may object to not being hired because a previous candidate with similar negative information did get hired. The previous candidate who was hired may have had excellent references or past work history that justified hiring despite negative information. In addition, if a person with adverse information is hired and that person commits an act resulting in harm to the firm or causes litigation, the fact the person was hired only after a screening process in which all facts were carefully considered would tend to establish due diligence.

In reviewing the background report or other material forming the basis of not hiring, retaining, promoting or reassigning a consumer, the Program Administrator will make all reasonable effort to protect the privacy of the consumer and the confidentiality of the information, including such processes as a not widely distributing the entire background checks, making the information only available to decision makers and only release information that is reasonably needed by decision makers.

Sample # 10 – Criminal History Information

(**NOTE:** The exact policy will depend upon how an employer chooses to comply with the EEOC Enforcement Guidance (see Chapter 10). This is presented only as an example of how an employer may prepare a policy).

Criminal Convictions: As part of the employer's policy of maintaining a safe and productive workplace, an employer will also conduct a screening of criminal records for any individual prior to or at the time of employment. However, it is also this firm's policy that a criminal conviction does not automatically preclude a person from being hired. In the event this firm confirms the applicant has a criminal record, the hiring decision will be based upon a careful consideration of the factors outlined in the current EEOC Guidance in effect. The employer will, among other things, carefully review and balance the nature of the position in question, the nature and gravity of the offense, and the amount of time that has passed since the conviction, as set forth in the EEOC Guidance, to determine whether there is a job related business justification for not hiring the applicant. For these reasons, the firm will closely scrutinize the application of any candidate with such a criminal conviction or who is currently on probation or parole, consistent with the firm's policy of not automatically excluding any applicant with a criminal record consistent with the current EEOC Guidance in effect.

- A check for criminal records is conducted to determine whether a person is fit for a particular job. The firm recognizes that society has a vested interest in giving ex-offenders a chance to obtain gainful employment. However, the firm is under a due diligence obligation to make efforts to determine if a person is reasonably fit for a particular position.

- If a criminal record is found, then the firm will first determine if there is a business reason not to hire the person as set forth in the EEOC Enforcement Guidance.

- The firm will not consider any arrest that did not result in a conviction. However, if permitted by applicable state law, the firm may consider the underlying behavior associated with the arrest if it can be determined, and will also consider any explanation offered by the applicant. However, if an applicant has a pending or current charge that has not been resolved, the firm reserves the right to request that the applicant first obtain a disposition of the matter before progressing further with the application process.

- The firm will also take into account applicable state laws that place limitations on the use or consideration of criminal conduct, such as expungement of criminal records.

- The firm's employment application will not ask about criminal convictions. It will, however, include a criminal record check advisement that a criminal record check will be conducted at an appropriate time, pursuant to all federal and state rules and regulations including discrimination rules and guidance from the EEOC. The application will also state that a criminal record will not automatically disqualify an applicant. The advisement is not intended to chill or deter applicants with criminal records from applying but is only intended to fairly and accurately disclose the nature of the firm's hiring processes. This is important for EEOC compliance.

- The firm reserves the right to inquire of any applicant if he or she has a criminal record, either during an interview, post-interview or before making an offer. The firm will request that an applicant fully complete a form specifying if the applicant has a criminal record and relevant details about it.

- The firm will make reasonable efforts to limit any inquiry about past criminal conduct in a way reasonably designed to avoid requiring the revelation of information that is old or irrelevant.

- In the event a criminal matter is revealed by the applicant, the firm will not automatically act on such information without first going through the following process:

  1. The employer will first determine whether such criminal matter is relevant to the job. If the firm determines it is not relevant, then the inquiry will end.

  2. If the firm determines the inquiry is relevant to the job, the employer will then analyze the information in light of the job utilizing the three part test as set forth by the EEOC in its most recent Guidance.

  3. In the event that an analysis of the criminal record of an applicant pursuant to the three part test leads the firm to conclude that there is a job related business justification to not consider the applicant further, the firm will send out appropriate pre- and adverse action notices pursuant to the Fair Credit Reporting Act.

4.   As part of the Adverse Action process, the firm's Program Administrator will also provide the applicant with an opportunity for an **Individualized Assessment** of the applicant pursuant to the 2012 EEOC Guidance on criminal records.

In a situation where an applicant makes a materially false statement or a material omission about a past criminal record, and the firm determines that such falsehood or omission was intentional and reflects an act of deceit or dishonesty, then the firm may make a decision not to proceed with the application process on that basis since honesty and integrity are always an essential function of any position in this company.

> **Author Tip** **Best Practices Report on Use of Criminal Records by Employers**
>
> A complete copy of the report *"Best Practice Standards: The Proper Use of Criminal Records in Hiring"* is available at www.esrcheck.com/file/Best-Practice-Standards-Criminal-Records.pdf.

Sample Policies and the Matrix of Criminal Record Use

The sample internal policy does not contain a matrix for the use of criminal records in the sense of outlining certain crimes or types of crimes that would eliminate a candidate from consideration. These are sometimes referred to variously as an Adjudication or Decision Making Matrix. Such a matrix contains an employer's criteria for who they will or will not hire. A screening firm applies the employer's criteria to information found. These matrixes can go beyond criminal searches and include past employment, credit reports, driving records, and other searches. A number of attorneys, background firms, or employers have developed such matrixes or guidelines. For example, a criminal offense matrix could list the various crimes that would make an applicant ineligible for employment. These are typically organized around a red light, orange light, and green light system. A red light means the person is not eligible based upon the nature of the offense. A green light means the applicant is clear, and the orange light means that the offense has not been included in the matrix or additional matters need consideration.

Even prior to the issuance of the EEOC Guidance on April 25, 2012, a criminal record matrix was generally considered a source of potential liability. The use of a matrix could lead to allegations of automated disqualification which would potentially run counter to the EEOC's position that each candidate with a criminal record be considered on their individual merits rather than the make a decision solely on their status as an ex-offender. This is the precise problem that the EEOC has dealt with historically and was a critical factor for part of this new Guidance.

Because of the emphasis in the new Guidance on employers only asking criminal questions relevant to a job, as opposed to broad and opened ended questions, the use of a "relevancy" matrix now may be a tool that employers need to consider. A relevancy matrix can assist in the development of the level of granular questions needed to only ask about relevant criminal matters. However, there is a critical difference between an exclusionary "red, yellow or green light" decision matrix and a relevancy matrix developed for EEOC compliance.

A relevancy matrix for EEOC compliance does not represent a final decision. There are two potential uses for a matrix in terms of compliance with the EEOC Guidance,

First, as outlined in Chapter 10, a matrix is only a tool to permit analysis as to which crimes are relevant to which jobs in the first place. A relevancy matrix can help employers decide how to design and limit questions about past criminal conduct so that questions are not overly broad, and can be more closely tailored to h job.

Second, as part of EEOC compliance program, if an applicant admits to a criminal record, it does not lead to automatic exclusions. Rather, by use of a relevancy matrix, an employer can determine if the criminal matter is relevant or not. If not relevant, the inquiry ends. If the criminal matter is relevant, then the employer moves onto the next step of the analysis, which is the application of the three-part "Green" factors. Even if the three part test leads to a conclusion that the criminal matter is job related and that exclusion is a business necessity, the applicant under the EEOC Guidance would still be entitled to an "Individualized Assessment."

It should also be noted that in the event an employer wishes to engage is such a matrix in order to comply with the EEOC requirements, a background screening firm is only applying an employer's criteria to the data found. In other words, the screening firm is administering a clerical task (although it can also be done by intelligent software) by applying the employer's criteria and is not making an independent judgment. More information about a relevancy matrix is contained in Chapter 10 dealing with EEOC guidance.

Language About Background Screening in the Employee Manual

Not every employer refers to pre-employment screening in their Employee Manuals. Even when employers screen current employees for purposes of promotion, reassignment, or retention, there are no legal requirements that compel employers to refer to "screening" in their handbooks. However, there is also no reason not to include screening in the employee handbook.

An Employee Manual is one of the most effective ways to communicate general policies and procedures to employees. A well-written manual helps avoid misunderstandings about policies or benefits, helps avoid lawsuits, and thereby enhances morale. Manuals also promote consistency of treatment and reduce the risk of charges of discrimination being made.

Using the Manual for Supplemental Background Checks

There are situations where an employer may need to perform a supplemental background check after a person is hired.

1. After the employee has been hired, an employer may need to conduct additional background checks to determine eligibility for promotion, re-assignment, or retention in the same manner as described above.
2. An employer may have to deal with specific job requirements imposed by a client, such as a background check of current employees assigned to the position. (See discussion in Chapter 16 on screening current employees.)
3. An employer may decide for due diligence reasons to conduct "on going" checks as part of a retention program (See discussion in Chapter 16 on screening current employees).
4. An employer may discover some sort of workplace misconduct or wrongdoing. Under the FACT Act, an employer can do background checks in such a situation without first obtaining a written authorization or providing a disclosure (See Chapter 5 on the Fair Credit Reporting Act).
5. An employer may have a policy requiring employees to advise an employer if they are arrested. If so, an employer many need to investigate the behavior underlying the arrest (See Chapters 15 and 16 concerning arrest records).
6. A firm may be acquired or merged with another firm, and the new owners want background checks of existing employees (See discussion in Chapter 16 on screening current employees).

The sample policy on employment screening below is suggested language for an Employee Manual. The text can be modified as appropriate for firms that choose to include their employment screening policy in the employee handbook for current employees if there is post-hiring screening. Because no one handbook applies to all businesses or all situations, this language is a general suggestion.

Sample # 11 – Sample Policy to be Placed in Employee Manual

Sample Policy on Employment Background Screening

To ensure that individuals who join this firm are well qualified and have a strong potential to be productive and successful —and to further ensure that this firm maintains a safe and productive work environment free of any form of violence, harassment, or misconduct — it is the policy of this company to perform pre-employment screening and credentials verification on applicants who are offered and accept an offer of employment. A pre-employment background check is a sound business practice that benefits everyone. It is not a reflection on a particular job applicant.

Offers of employment are conditional upon the firm's receipt of a pre-employment background screening investigation that is acceptable to the firm at the firm's sole discretion. Any applicant who refuses to sign a background screening release form will not be eligible for employment.

[**Optional:** The firm also may conduct background checks as appropriate for purposes of retention, promotion, or re-assignment. All of the same rule and policies apply.]

To ensure privacy, all pre-employment background screenings are conducted by a third party. All screenings are conducted in strict conformity with the Federal Fair Credit Reporting Act (FCRA), the Americans with Disabilities Act (ADA), and all applicable state and federal laws including anti-discrimination and privacy laws. All reports are kept strictly confidential and are only viewed by individuals in this firm who have direct responsibility in the hiring process. All screening reports are kept and maintained separately from your personnel file. Under the Fair Credit Reporting Act, all background screenings are done only after a person has received a disclosure and has signed a release. In addition, you have certain legal rights to discover and to dispute or explain any information prepared by the third party background screening agency. If the employer intends to deny employment wholly or partly because of information obtained in a pre-employment check conducted by the company's consumer reporting agency, then the applicant will first be provided with a copy of the background report, a statement of rights, and the name, address, and phone number of the consumer reporting agency to contact about the results of the check or to dispute its accuracy.

The firm also reserves the right to conduct a background screening any time after the employee has been hired to determine eligibility for promotion, re-assignment, or retention in the same manner as described above.

Applicants also are expected to provide references from their former employers as well as educational reference information that can be used to verify academic accomplishments and records. Background checks may include verification of information provided on the completed application for employment, the applicant's resume, or on other forms used in the hiring process. Information to be verified includes, but is not limited to, Social Security Number and previous addresses. An employer may also conduct a reference check and verify the applicant's education and employment background as stated on the employment application or other documents listed above.

The background check may also include a criminal record check. If a conviction is discovered, then the employer will closely scrutinize the conviction in view of our policy of ensuring a safe and profitable workplace. A criminal conviction does not necessarily automatically bar an applicant from employment. Before an employment decision is made, a determination will be made whether the conviction is related to the position for which the individual is applying or would present safety or security risks, taking into account the nature and gravity of the act, the nature of the position, and the age of the conviction, as well as the most current EEOC Guidance in effect on the proper use of a criminal record. Prior to making a final decision, the employer will afford an applicant the opportunity to present additional information and to request an "Individualized Assessment" as outlined in the 2012 EEOC Guidance.

Additional checks such as a driving record or a credit report may be made on applicants for particular job categories if appropriate and job-related. Employment screening assessments to determine an applicant's job fit may also be required of all applicants. Skills tests related to the demands of the job may also be required.

This firm relies upon the accuracy of information contained in the employment application as well as the accuracy of other data presented throughout the hiring process and employment, including any oral interviews.

Any misrepresentations, falsifications, or material omissions in any of the information or data, no matter when discovered, may result in the firm's exclusion of the individual from further consideration for employment or, if the person has been hired, termination of employment.

Sample # 12 – Duty to Self-Report an Arrest or Conviction

Some employers have a policy that requires current employees to "self-report" an arrest or conviction. Before implementing this policy, employers should contact their legal counsel concerning the laws in their state. It is important to note that the employer should not take action due to the mere fact of the arrest. That could violate the EEOC policy. The employer needs to base any decision on the underlying facts of the arrest or on the conviction. If, as a result of an arrest, a person is incarcerated, the inability to come to work may give grounds for an employer to terminate employment.

Duty to Self-Report an Arrest or Conviction

In addition, in order to ensure a safe and profitable workplace, all employees are required to report to their supervisor if they are arrested, charged, or convicted for any criminal offense, with the exception of minor traffic offenses unless the employee is in driving position (driving position is any position where the employee drives on company time or for the benefit of the company.)

If an employee is arrested, charged, or convicted for any offense, then the employee must report the matter to their direct supervisor and submit a police report or other documentation concerning the arrest and/or charges. The report must occur within two (2) business days of the arrest.

The employer will review the underlying facts of the matter. The employer will not take any adverse action based only upon the fact of an arrest. Any action will be based upon the underlying facts of the arrest. Any action will be considered on a case-by-case basis taking into account the underlying facts and the totality of all the circumstances and in conformity with EEOC policies on the consideration of criminal records as well as applicable state and federal laws. The employer's actions may range from no action, to leave with or without pay, to termination. In all cases, an employee will have the right to an individualized assessment including the opportunity to present any information the employee deems relevant to the decision making process.

Noncompliance with the above stated requirement constitutes grounds for termination. Furthermore, misrepresentation of the circumstances of the events can serve as grounds for termination. Employees that are unavailable to report for work due to incarceration are subject to suspension or termination in accordance with the terms of the employee manual."

Safe Hiring Checklist: Procedures for Implementing Your Safe Hiring Program

After formulating a general policy and outlining the practices the employer will utilize, the final step is to create the implementation procedures. A checklist such as the one below can be a handy tool to ensure that the practices are actually being followed and implemented. Each firm that implements a Safe Hiring Program will undoubtedly customize the procedural details to accommodate its particular needs. However, employers, at a minimum, should address the issues raised in this chapter. The last portion of the Safe Hiring Checklist is to be used to document the actual procedures used in the Safe Hiring Program.

The ABC Company Safe Hiring Checklist

To be completed for every new applicant before being hired.

Applicant: _____

Position: _____

Hiring Manager _____

Task	Yes/No/ NA	Date/ Initials	Notes/Follow-up
Application Process			
Did applicant sign the consent form?			
Is application complete?			
Did applicant sign and date application?			
Did applicant indicate a criminal record after the interview?			
Did applicant explain why left past jobs?			
Did applicant explain gaps in job history?			
Any excessive cross-outs or changes seen?			
Is the application internally consistent and consistent with other information in the employer's possessions?			
Interview Process			
Did applicant explain any excessive cross-outs/changes?			
Leaving past jobs: Did applicant explain?			
Leaving past jobs: Was verbal reason consistent with reason on written app?			
Employment Gaps: Did applicant explain?			
Employment Gaps: Are verbal explanations consistent with written app?			
Security Question. 1 – "Our firm has a standard policy of background checks and drug tests on all			Answer:

applicants. Do you have any concerns you would like to share with me about our procedures?"			
Security Question 2 – "We also do criminal background checks on finalists pursuant to all applicable rules and regulations including EEOC Guidance. Are you aware of that?"			Answer:
Security Question 3 – "If I were to contact past employers pursuant to the release you have signed, what do you think they would tell us about you?"			Answer:
Security Question 4 – "If I were to contact past employers pursuant to the release you have signed, would any of them tell us you were terminated or were disciplined?"			Answer:
Security Question 5 – "Please explain any gaps in employment."			Answer:
Security Question 6 – "Is everything in the application and everything you told us in the hiring process true, correct, and complete?"			Answer:
Reference Checks (performed by employer or by a third party)			
Have references been checked for at least last 5-10 years, regardless of whether past employers will give details?			
Have efforts been documented?			

Discrepancies between information located and what applicant reported in application:
  a. dates/title salary/job title
  b. reason for leaving			

Background Check			
Submitted for background check?			
Check completed?			
Background check reviewed for discrepancies/issues?			
If not CLEAR or SATISFACTORY, what action is taken per policy and procedures?			Describe:

Notes: Use back if necessary. Sign and date all entries

Turnover Cost Calculator Form

TURNOVER COSTS	AMOUNT
Separation Costs	
Cost of time required to terminate the employee	$
Cost of exit interviewer's time	$
Employee's separation/severance pay	$
Increase on unemployment taxes	$
Termination-related administrative costs	$
Vacancy Costs	
Cost of overtime required of workers covering the vacancy	$
Cost of any directly-hired temporary help in covering the vacancy	$
Cost of any agency-based temporary help (agency costs and contracts)	$
Replacement Costs	
Pre-employment administrative expenses	$
Cost of attracting applicants (recruitment advertising)	$
Cost of entrance interviews	$
Screening/testing (aptitude/skills test, drug screens, background/reference checks)	$
Hiring-related travel expenses	$
Moving or relocation expenses	$
Post-employment medical exams	$
Post-employment information gathering and dissemination costs (payroll, benefits, policies and procedures, time required to enter the individual into all relevant systems/programs, etc.)	$

Turnover Cost Calculator Form (Page 2)

Training Costs	
Costs of informational literature (manual, employee handbook, brochures, policies)	$
Formal training costs (classroom, instructor or specialty trainer)	$
Informal training costs (supervisor, on-the-job training)	$
Any overtime required by employee as s/he learns the job	$
Additional overtime required of co-workers as new employee learns the job	$
Opportunity Costs	
Cost of difference in productivity between former employee and replacement	$
Anticipated learning curve (time at which productivity returns to former standard)	$
Cost of any customers or accounts lost in conjunction with loss of employee	$
Supervisor and Staff Costs	
Cost of first-line supervisors addressing turnover (problem solving, mentoring, troubleshooting)	$
Total Cost →	

From Griggs to SEPTA: The EEOC's Focus on Employment Screening

From Griggs to SEPTA: The EEOC's Focus on Employment Screening

By Rod M. Fliegel and Jennifer L. Mora, Attorneys At Law

Littler Mendelson, P.C.

There has been a flurry of activity at the U.S. Equal Employment Opportunity Commission ("EEOC") over the past couple of years in which the EEOC's "systemic discrimination" unit has been investigating employer policies and/or practices that screen job applicants for employment based on criminal or credit records. In addition, plaintiffs' counsel have been filing lawsuits challenging employer practices in which African-American and/or Hispanic applicants are disqualified for employment based on criminal or credit records. Now more than ever, employers need to understand the EEOC's efforts in addressing the use of credit and criminal records for employment purposes and take proactive steps to ensure that, if challenged, their hiring policies will withstand scrutiny by the EEOC and the plaintiffs' bar.

Title VII of the Civil Rights Act of 1964 prohibits employers from discriminating against individuals because of, among other things, race, color or national origin. Title VII does not expressly prohibit employers from using criminal background reports for employment purposes. However, in developing regulatory guidance and pursuing litigation against employers based on their employment screening practices, the EEOC relies on Section 703(k) of Title VII, which states that if an otherwise neutral employment policy or practice has a "disparate impact" on a protected classification, the policy or practice violates Title VII. Disparate impact discrimination occurs when a uniformly applied neutral selection procedure disproportionately excludes people on the basis of a protected trait and the procedure is not "job related... and consistent with business necessity," or when the employer's business goals can be served in a less discriminatory way. 42 U.S.C. § 2000e-2(k)(1)(A)(i).

The Supreme Court's decision in *Griggs v. Duke Power Company*, 401 U.S. 424 (1971), was one of the first decisions to consider the legality of an employer's hiring practices under Title VII. In *Griggs*, the employer required applicants to have a high school diploma or pass a standardized general education test for employment purposes. The class action suit claimed that such a requirement had a disparate impact on African American workers. In concluding that the employer's hiring requirements violated Title VII, the Supreme Court held that in order to pass muster under Title VII, the practice must be "related to business necessity and/or job performance." The Supreme Court agreed that the employer violated Title VII's prohibition against unlawful disparate impact because the employer did not prove that its hiring requirements had any connection to the jobs at issue.

Thereafter, on February 4, 1987, the EEOC issued its first "Policy Statement on Conviction Records" ("1987 Policy Statement"). According to the 1987 Policy Statement, if an employer's policy or practice of excluding individuals from employment on the basis of their conviction records has an adverse impact on African Americans or Hispanics, the policy or practice is unlawful "in the absence of a justifying business necessity." In determining whether a policy is justified by business necessity, the 1987 Policy Statement stated that the employer must prove that it considers the following factors: the nature and gravity of the offense or offenses; the time that has passed since the conviction and/or completion of the sentence; and the nature of the job held or sought based on a conviction policy or practice.

The EEOC issued an additional policy statement on July 29, 1987, referred to as its "Policy Statement on the use of statistics in charges involving the exclusion of individuals with conviction records from employment." This supplemental policy statement reiterated its position that "an employer's policy or practice of excluding individuals from employment on the basis of their conviction records has an adverse impact on Blacks and Hispanics in light of statistics showing that they are convicted at a rate disproportionately greater than their representation in the population." However, the policy statement carved out an exception to its general rule, concluding that a "no cause" determination would be "appropriate" in circumstances where: (1) "the employer can present more narrowly drawn statistics showing either that Blacks and Hispanics are not convicted at a disproportionately greater rate;" or (2) "there is no adverse impact in its own hiring process resulting from the convictions policy."

Several years later, the EEOC issued its September 7, 1990 "Guidance Dealing With Arrest Records" ("1990 Guidance"). The 1990 Guidance discussed the extent to which the use of arrest records for employment purposes has an adverse impact on African Americans and Hispanics. According to the 1990 Guidance: "Since using arrests as a disqualifying criteria can only be justified where it appears that the applicant actually engaged in the conduct for which he/she was arrested and that conduct is job related, the Commission further concludes that an employer will seldom be able to justify making broad general inquiries about an employee's or applicant's arrests." The 1990 Guidance explains that an employer must focus on the conduct, not the arrest or conviction per se in relation to the job sought, to demonstrate unfitness for the position. Again, the EEOC underscored the importance of employers considering the three factors outlined in its 1987 Policy Statement and suggested that employers also consider whether "the alleged conduct was actually committed."

The EEOC has yet to update the 1987 Policy Statement or the 1990 Guidance. In the past few years, however, the EEOC has reaffirmed its long-standing position that, upon a preliminary showing of disparate impact, employers must be able to justify their conviction-based screening policies under Title VII's business necessity standard. In addition, the EEOC revisited the issue of criminal records during separate public meetings held on May 17, 2007 (focusing on employment testing and screening) and November 20, 2008 (focusing on arrest and conviction records).

The EEOC's interest in Title VII protections for job applicants with a criminal record was sparked at least in part by the Third Circuit Court of Appeals' opinion in *El v. Southeastern Pennsylvania Transportation Authority (SEPTA)*, 479 F.3d 232 (3d Cir. 2007). In El, the plaintiff was rejected for a job as a paratransit driver based on his 40-year old homicide conviction. The court of appeals affirmed judgment as a matter of law for SEPTA but ruled that, if an employer's conviction-based screening policy in fact causes a disparate impact, the employer must produce "empirical evidence" justifying its screening policy in order to establish business necessity. The court of appeals ruled that an employer must show specifically that its screening policy "accurately" distinguishes between job applicants posing an "unacceptable level of risk" and those who do not. The court of appeals seemed very skeptical of testimony from SEPTA's expert – leading criminologist Dr. Alfred Blumstein – that the plaintiff actually posed a greater crime-risk than a non-offender job applicant even though the plaintiff's conviction was from the 1960s, but explained that it had to rule for SEPTA because the plaintiff failed to offer any evidence to refute Dr. Blumstein's testimony. The court of appeals noted that, if the plaintiff had provided such evidence, it would have been a "different case."

The Third Circuit's analysis is markedly different from, and in fact criticized, the EEOC's historical enforcement guidance. As mentioned above, the EEOC has taken the position in its 1987 Policy Statement that, if an employer's conviction-based screening policy causes a disparate impact, the employer must show that it considered: (1) the "nature and gravity" of the applicant's offense; (2) the "time that has passed since the conviction and/or completion of sentence;" and (3) the "nature of the job held or sought." The distinction between the EEOC's historical enforcement guidance and *El* is material because the Third Circuit looked beyond the elements of SEPTA's screening policy to whether the results of SEPTA's screening process could be squared with the recidivism statistics and particularly with the statistics suggesting that the risk of recidivism declines as the time "clean" since release from incarceration increases.

In July 2011, the EEOC held another public meeting on the topic of protections for job applicants with arrest and conviction records under Title VII. Despite the fact that one of the Commissioners referenced at the hearing the Third Circuit's criticism of the EEOC's 1987 Policy, the EEOC did not reveal at the meeting whether it will update the 1987 Policy.

In its first post-July 2011 meeting advisory opinion letter, the EEOC's Office of Legal Counsel provided some insight into the Commission's current enforcement position. The advisory opinion letter was written in response to a request for comments from the Peace Corps about its proposed application for volunteer positions with its international service programs. The EEOC staff attorney noted at the outset that a pre-employment *inquiry* concerning criminal records "does not in itself violate Title VII because Title VII does not regulate inquiries by employers." However, the EEOC staff attorney further commented that the use of criminal record information as part of its screening process may violate Title VII if the employer intentionally and selectively enforces its screening policy against protected class members. The EEOC staff attorney further remarked that, *if* the employer's screening policy in fact has a disparate impact on protected class members, the policy must be "job related and consistent with business necessity." It is this statement by the EEOC staff attorney, which presupposes that proof of disparate impact is *required* rather than *presumed*, that suggests the Commission may not be prepared to adopt a presumption of disparate impact.

According to the advisory opinion letter, in order to exclude an applicant based on a criminal conviction, the criminal conduct should be "recent enough" and "sufficiently job-related to be predictive of performance in the position sought, given its duties and responsibilities." Given this framework, which implicitly incorporates the Third Circuit's analysis in *El*, the EEOC staff attorney was troubled by the Peace Corps' application because it asked about "all convictions regardless of when they occurred." Thus, the EEOC staff attorney recommended that the employer narrow its criminal history inquiry to focus on "convictions that are related to the specific positions in question, and that have taken place in the past seven years, consistent with the proposed provisions of the federal government's general employment application form." (In June 2011, the same EEOC staff attorney made a similar suggestion in an advisory opinion letter to the U.S. Census Bureau.)

Next, the EEOC staff attorney analyzed the employer's request that the applicant provide information about criminal arrests, noting: "[a]rrest records, by their nature, should be treated differently from conviction records." The EEOC staff attorney explained that, because the criminal justice system requires the highest degree of proof for a conviction (i.e., "beyond a reasonable doubt"), a conviction record can serve as a sufficient indication that the person in fact committed the offense. On the other hand, the EEOC staff attorney stated, arrest records are unreliable indicators of guilt because: (1) individuals are presumed innocent until proven guilty or charges may be dismissed and, therefore, an arrest record is not persuasive evidence that the person actually engaged in the conduct alleged; (2) an applicant's criminal history information may be incomplete and may not reflect that his or her arrest charges have been modified or dropped because some state criminal record repositories fail to report the final disposition of an arrest; and (3) arrest records may be inaccurate due to a variety of other factors (e.g., confusion regarding names and personal identifying information, misspellings, clerical errors, or because the individual provided inaccurate information at the time of arrest).

With this framework in mind, the EEOC staff attorney advised the employer to "consider whether its questions about arrests and charges will serve a useful purpose in screening applicants" and, if so, she recommended that the employer only ask about arrests and charges for offenses that are related to the position in question. In order to ensure that the employer relies on accurate arrest-related information when considering an individual for a volunteer position, the EEOC staff attorney recommended that the employer also give the applicant a reasonable opportunity to dispute the validity of any information showing that the applicant has an arrest record. (This varies somewhat from prior and impractical EEOC Guidance suggesting that an employer should make an effort to try to independently confirm whether the applicant in fact was guilty.)

In addition to the EEOC's Policy Statement, Guidance, and public meetings focusing on the use of criminal records for employment purposes, a handful of significant lawsuits have been initiated by the EEOC. On September 28, 2008, in *EEOC v. Peoplemark, Inc.*, the EEOC sued Peoplemark, Inc., alleging that Peoplemark's purported policy prohibiting the hiring of any person with a criminal record violated Title VII because it had a disparate impact on African American applicants. Based on certain procedural failures by the EEOC (i.e., the failure to timely identify an expert statistician) and most likely other concerns, the EEOC agreed to dismiss the case after 18 months of vigorous litigation. On March 31, 2011, the district court concluded that the EEOC's lawsuit against Peoplemark was frivolous and, therefore, ordered the EEOC to pay more than $750,000 in attorney's fees and expert costs. *EEOC v. Peoplemark, Inc.*, 2011 U.S. Dist. LEXIS 38696 (W.D. Mich., March 31, 2011) [Alternative citation: 112 FEP Cases 158 (W.D. Mich. 2011).].

The more recent case of *EEOC v. Freeman*, Case No. RWT 09cv2573 [Alternative citation: 2010 WL 1728847 (D. Md. Apr. 26, 2010).], filed in federal district court in Maryland on September 30, 2009, alleged that an African American individual applied for a position with Freeman in August 2007, and was informed that she would be hired, contingent on passing a drug, criminal, and credit background check. Shortly thereafter, Freeman informed the applicant that she would not be offered a position. In the complaint, the EEOC alleged that Freeman's hiring practices had a significant disparate impact against the protected groups and were not job related or justified by business necessity. The EEOC further asserted that there were appropriate, less-discriminatory alternative selection procedures available to Freeman.

The district court granted Freeman's motion for summary judgment, explaining, "[t]he story of the present action has been that of a theory in search of facts to support it." The district court's opinion primarily concentrated on the reasons the EEOC's expert opinion was inadmissible and thus insufficient to demonstrate disparate impact. The court felt it had "no choice" but to disregard the experts' disparate impact analysis, stating that "there appear to be such a plethora of errors and analytical fallacies underlying [the expert's] conclusions to render them completely unreliable, and insufficient to support a finding of disparate impact." The court explained that the expert's analysis was flawed because (1) it was not based on a random sample of accurate data from the relevant applicant pool and time period; (2) it did not cover the time period identified in the EEOC's claims, but instead represented a distorted fraction of the time period relevant in the case; (3) the expert used "meaningless, skewed statistics" and data generated under the company's old credit check policy to enhance his disparate impact results; (4) the expert's database omitted data from half of the company's branch offices, with no apparent explanation; and (5) the expert's database was "rife with material errors and unexplained discrepancies."

The court also opined that the national statistics cited in the experts' reports were not enough to show disparate impact. The experts relied on general population statistics to create an inference of disparate impact, even though the general population pool was not representative of the relevant applicant pool. The court went on to state that even if the expert reports were admissible, the EEOC nevertheless failed to identify any policies causing the alleged disparate impact. The company's background investigation policies consisted of multiple elements that involved different types of checks depending on the particular job an applicant sought, consideration of both subjective and objective criteria, and examination of several factors. The court explained that the EEOC made no effort to break down the company's multi-faceted policy and identify which parts were responsible for creating a disparate impact on certain classes.

The Fourth Circuit did not reach the merits of the case regarding the EEOC's challenge to the employer's use of criminal and credit checks. Rather, the Fourth Circuit affirmed the district court's grant of summary judgment "solely on the basis that the district court did not abuse its discretion in excluding the EEOC's expert reports as unreliable under [the Federal Rules of Evidence]." The court noted: "We emphasize that by our disposition we express no opinion on the merits of the EEOC's claims."

Finally, in December 2010, the EEOC filed a lawsuit against Kaplan Higher Education Corp. in the federal district of Ohio, *EEOC v. Kaplan Higher Education Corp.,* (Case No. 1:10 CV 2882) [Alternative citation: 2011 WL 2115878 (N.D. Ohio May 27, 2011).], alleging that the company engaged in a pattern of discrimination against African American workers. Specifically, the lawsuit claimed that Kaplan's use of credit history for employment purposes was neither job-related nor justified by any business necessity. Kaplan, on the other hand, publicly defended its hiring practices and denied that its use of credit history for employment purposes had any disparate impact on applicants.

On January 28, 2013, the district court judge in granted Kaplan's motion to dismiss the case without a trial, holding the EEOC failed to meet its threshold burden as the plaintiff to prove that Kaplan's screening practices disproportionately excluded protected class members (i.e., had the requisite "disparate impact").

These lawsuits show the EEOC's willingness to file lawsuits against some employers in order to promote its policy objectives. Not shown in the public filings, however, is the concerted effort by the EEOC's systemic discrimination unit to broadly investigate the use of criminal and credit information by employers in many different industries (e.g., transportation, information technology, retail, etc.). It seems evident that, likely as a result of the $750,000 award against the EEOC in the Peoplemark case, the EEOC is using its sweeping investigatory powers to try to line up lawsuits before filing them (or seeking conciliation). This, too, is not shown by the small number of active lawsuits, but is clear from the number of employers who have been, and are, responding to onerous and costly demands for documents and information from the EEOC.

All of this being said, in April 2012, the EEOC issued its long-awaited "Enforcement Guidance on the Consideration of Arrest and Criminal Conviction Records in Employment Decisions Under Title VII of the Civil Rights Act, which outlines in detail the EEOC's current concerns regarding use of criminal history in the hiring process and factors that employers are expected to consider prior to excluding any applicant based on criminal history.*

In the meantime, it is prudent for employers to assess their background check programs with an eye towards the dynamic legal landscape, including not only the activity by the EEOC, but in the state legislatures and under related laws, such as the federal Fair Credit Reporting Act (where there has been a surge in class action lawsuits against employers).

* For a comprehensive review of the EEOC's updated guidance and related legal concerns, including applicable state law compliance issues, see Barry Hartstein, Rod Fliegel, Jennifer Mora and Marcy McGovern, Criminal Background Checks: Evolution of the EEOC's Updated Guidance and Implications for the Employer Community, Littler Report (May 17, 2012) at www.littler.com/criminal-background-checks-evolution-eeocs-updated-guidance-and-implications-employer-community.

Legal Reference and Case Law Examples

Privacy

NASA Case Limits Privacy Rights of Workers in Employment Background Checks

In a case pitting individual privacy rights of citizens against national security concerns of a country, the U.S. Supreme Court unanimously overturned a ruling limiting government inquiries about contract workers at a National Aeronautics and Space Administration (NASA) laboratory and ruled the federal government can ask employees about their drug treatment, medical conditions, or other personal matters during background checks and that the questions did not violate the constitutional privacy rights of employees. The case – *NASA v. Nelson, 131 S.Ct. 746 (2011)* – concerned contract workers who challenged the extensive background checks required at a NASA jet propulsion laboratory in Pasadena, CA as overly intrusive. The Supreme Court ruling overturned a federal appeals court ruling that said the government went too far in asking contract workers questions about drug treatment and suitability for employment and gave the government broad latitude to ask personal questions during backgrounds checks of contractors at government facilities. Federal employees have undergone standard background checks since 1953, and the government began background checks of contract employees in 2005 as part of the policies developed after the terrorist attacks of September 11, 2001. Supreme Court Justice Samuel Alito wrote for the court stating that: "The challenged portions of the forms consist of reasonable inquiries in an employment background check." However, the Court did not announce broad rules or a test for interpreting what questions were permissible, and according to some legal observers, future litigation is still possible. The Court did cite several factors that made these inquiries permissible:

- Citizen employees (and citizen contractors) of the government fall under the hand of the government more than citizens not working for the Government.

- The questions are reasonable and sufficiently employment-related.

- Private employers as well as the government have long used background checks.

Information gathered in background checks would be confidential due to the federal Privacy Act on dissemination of employee and contractor information.

The U.S. Supreme Court recognized the value of background checks in the NASA privacy case. The Government has a legitimate interest in conducting basic employment background checks. Reasonable investigations of applicants and employees aid the Government in ensuring the security of its facilities and in employing a competent, reliable workforce. In the context of the case, it appears the same rule applies to private employers since the Court cited how private employers do similar searches.

The case *NASA v. Nelson* - 131 S.Ct. 746 (2011) is available at: http://supreme.justia.com/cases/federal/us/562/09-530/.

As recently as 2015, lower courts have followed the Supreme Court's holding in NASA—supporting the ability of the government to reasonably seek and collect personal info where distribution is not an issue. *See* Lavender v. Koenig, 2015 U.S. Dist. LEXIS 34141.

Hill v. National Collegiate Athletic Association

California has led the nation in issues involving employee privacy. A leading case is *Hill v. National Collegiate Athletic Association, 7 Cal.4th 1 (1994)*. The *Hill* case provides an excellent framework to analyze privacy claims. In the *Hill* case, the issue was whether a college athletic association could require student athletes to sign consent forms for drug testing. The California Supreme Court ruled that the drug testing requirement was an invasion of privacy because drug testing required an intrusion into bodily integrity. The court further held that the benefits did not outweigh the intrusion of rights, there were less intrusive means to accomplish the goal, and the NCAA failed to show the particular program it proposed furthered the intended goal. In its discussion, the Court in *Hill* discussed various privacy rights and wrote that: "A 'reasonable' expectation of privacy is an objective entitlement founded on broadly based and widely accepted community norms."

Privacy claims are typically a balancing test with different competing interests being examined and weighed. In analyzing an invasion of privacy claim in an employment context, courts will first look to see if the employer seriously invaded an employee's or applicant's legally protected privacy interests based upon whether there was a reasonable expectation of privacy under the circumstances. If the employer's action did intrude upon a zone of privacy, then the court will examine:

- Did the employer's action further a legitimate and socially beneficial aim?
- If so, did the purposes to be achieved outweigh any resulting invasion of privacy?
- Was there a less intrusive alternative that could have accomplished the same aim without invading privacy?

Hill is widely considered a landmark case in California. The California Supreme Court has repeatedly affirmed Hill's method of analyzing constitutional privacy claims in cases such as Hernandez v. Hillsides, Inc., 47 Cal. 4th 272 (Cal. 2009). California cases have used the test as recently as June 21, 2016. In re M.H., 2016 Cal. App. LEXIS 592 (Cal. App. 4th Dist. June 21, 2016)

There are other privacy matters that are not a matter of balance but have been made illegal directly by statute. For example, in 1988, the U.S. Congress enacted the Employee Polygraph Protection Act (29 U.S.C. §§ 2001-2009) This act severely limits the ability of most private employers from using a polygraph or lie detector test for job applicants or current employees who are being investigated. Although there are some narrow exceptions, as a practical matter this law ended the use of lie detectors.

California Disclosure Law - PII of Consumers Sent Off-Shore

More information about California Senate Bill 909 (SB 909) which became the first law in the nation to address the issue of Personally Identifiable Information (PII) of consumers who are the subjects of background checks being sent "offshore" (i.e. outside the United States or its territories and beyond the protection of U.S. privacy and identity theft laws) is contained in ADDENDUM - CHAPTER 2. Employers in California – and employers doing business in California – need to be aware of this new law which changed the way employers conduct background checks in the state.

More information about California SB 909

California Senate Bill 909 (SB 909)

On September 29, 2010, Governor Arnold Schwarzenegger signed into law **California Senate Bill 909 (SB 909)**, which became the first law in the nation that addresses the issue of Personally Identifiable Information (PII) of consumers who are the subjects of background checks being sent "offshore" (i.e. outside the United States or its territories and beyond the protection of U.S. privacy and identity theft laws). Employers in California – and employers doing business in California – need to be aware of this new law which changed the way employers conduct background checks in the state.

Authored by State Senator Rod Wright (D – Inglewood), SB 909 amended the California Investigative Consumer Reporting Agencies Act (ICRA) that regulates background checks in California. SB 909 requires a new disclosure and additions to a Consumer Reporting Agency's privacy policy to be made to consumers before their personally information such as Social Security Numbers (SSN) is sent offshore overseas and outside of the United States. SB 909 is NOT a regulatory bill since the bill does not regulate or prohibit offshoring. **It is a disclosure bill** – meaning consumers must be made aware of the background screening agency's privacy practices, including whether the consumer's PII will be sent outside of the country. Below is a synopsis of SB 909. (Note: The author worked with Senator Wright's office in drafting language for SB 909.)

Notification to Consumers

CA SB 909 added language to Civil Code 1786.16 that requires a consumer must be notified as part of a disclosure before the background check of the web address where that consumer "may find information about the investigative reporting agency's privacy practices, including whether the consumer's personal information will be sent outside the United States or its territories." If a background screening firm does not have a website, then the background screening firm must provide the consumer with a phone number where the consumer can obtain the same information.

Language 1786.16

(vi) Notifies the consumer of the Internet Web site address of the investigative consumer reporting agency identified in clause (iv), or, if the agency has no Internet Web site address, the telephone number of the agency, where the consumer may find information about the investigative reporting agency's privacy practices, including whether the consumer's personal information will be sent outside the United States or its territories and information that complies with subdivision (d) of Section 1786.20. This clause shall become operative on January 1, 2012.

CRA Privacy Practices on Web Site

Effective January 1, 2012, SB 909 additionally requires an investigative Consumer Reporting Agency (CRA) to "conspicuously post" on its primary Internet Web site information describing its privacy practices with respect to its preparation and processing of investigative consumer reports. If CRA does not have an Internet Web site, the CRA has to mail a written copy of the privacy statement to consumers upon request.

CRA Privacy Policies Online

The CRA's privacy policy must contain "information describing its privacy practices with respect to its preparation and processing of investigative consumer reports." Specifically, background screening firms in California (and firms that do business in California) must have a statement in their privacy policy entitled "Personal Information Disclosure: United States or Overseas" that indicates whether the personal information will be transferred to third parties outside the United States or its territories.

Conspicuously Post

The term **conspicuously post** is defined in California Business and Professions Code Section 22577:

(b) The term "conspicuously post" with respect to a privacy policy shall include posting the privacy policy through any of the following:

(1) A Web page on which the actual privacy policy is posted if the Web page is the homepage or first significant page after entering the Web site.

(2) An icon that hyperlinks to a Web page on which the actual privacy policy is posted, if the icon is located on the homepage or the first significant page after entering the Web site, and if the icon contains the word "privacy." The icon shall also use a color that contrasts with the background color of the Web page or is otherwise distinguishable.

(3) A text link that hyperlinks to a Web page on which the actual privacy policy is posted, if the text link is located on the homepage or first significant page after entering the Web site, and if the text link does one of the following:

(A) Includes the word "privacy."

(B) Is written in capital letters equal to or greater in size than the surrounding text.

(C) Is written in larger type than the surrounding text, or in contrasting type, font, or color to the surrounding text of the same size, or set off from the surrounding text of the same size by symbols or other marks that call attention to the language.

(4) Any other functional hyperlink that is so displayed that a reasonable person would notice it.

Third Parties

SB 909 defines third parties as including, but not being limited to:

A contractor,
Foreign affiliate,
Wholly owned entity, or
An employee of the investigative consumer reporting agency.

Separate Section on Privacy Policy

SB 909 also requires a "separate section that includes the name, mailing address, e-mail address, and telephone number of the investigative consumer reporting agency representatives who can assist a consumer with additional information regarding the investigative consumer reporting agency's privacy practices or policies in the event of a compromise of his or her information."

Damages

In the event a consumer is harmed by virtue of a background screening firm negligently preparing or processing data outside of the U.S., SB 909 provides for damages to the consumer in an amount equal to the sum of:

Any actual damages sustained by the consumer as a result of the unauthorized access, AND the costs of the successful legal action together with reasonable attorney's fees, as determined by the court.

Language From 1786.20

1786.20(d) (1) An investigative consumer reporting agency doing business in [California] shall conspicuously post, as defined in subdivision (b) of Section 22577 of the Business and Professions Code, on its primary Internet Web site information describing its privacy practices with respect to its preparation and processing of investigative consumer reports. If the investigative consumer reporting agency does not have an Internet Web site, it shall, upon request, mail a written copy of the privacy statement to consumers. The privacy statement shall conspicuously include, but not be limited to, both of the following:

(A) A statement entitled "Personal Information Disclosure: United States or Overseas," that indicates whether the personal information will be transferred to third parties outside the United States or its territories.

(B) A separate section that includes the name, mailing address, e-mail address, and telephone number of the investigative consumer reporting agency representatives who can assist a consumer with additional information regarding the investigative consumer reporting agency's privacy practices or policies in the event of a compromise of his or her information.

Summary

By January 1, 2012, employers should have added the URL (Uniform Resource Locator) link to their privacy policy to their online forms (or comply with the provision for firms without websites). Employers should have added the required information to their online privacy policy and the front page of their website (or have material to mail to an applicant upon request). Note there is a civil liability of $10,000 per applicant for non-compliance by an employer or CRA, so it is important to make sure to be in compliance.

See www.leginfo.ca.gov/pub/09-10/bill/sen/sb_0901-0950/sb_909_bill_20100929_chaptered.pdf

Preliminary Telephone Screen

#1 - Telephone Interview Form

For uniformity of treatment, all applicants should be asked the same questions, and the form filled out.

Applicant:

Date/Time called:

Caller:

Telephone Script—

Hello I am calling about a resume in sent us in response to our ad in the (*name of newspaper*) for (*job title*). Do you have a few minutes to talk on the phone?

1. Can you tell me why you applied for this position and what interests you about it?
2. May I ask you why you are looking for new employment?
3. Can you describe your best five[1] skills?
4. We are located in (*your town or city*) — is that convenient for you and can you get here?
    May I ask you what your salary history is in your current position?

#2 - Phone Interview Form

1. What hours are you available to work?
2. May I ask you what your salary history is in your current position?
3. If we would like to go into more detail and schedule an interview, what would be the best time and date for you?

If the person sounds acceptable, schedule an interview for as soon as possible.

If the person does not appear to be a good fit, but further discussion with them may be an option, say—

> Thank you for your time. We need to review this information with the hiring manager, and if it looks like this is a match, we will call you back.

(*It is okay to give your phone number if the person requests it, but stress that* "we will call them.")

Interview Rating and Impressions—

__ Excellent potential for position — *Interview is a priority*

__ Could be a good candidate — *Interview would be helpful*

__ *No further action necessary*

---

[1] Number of skills asked for can vary.

ADDENDUM - CHAPTER 5

Fair Credit Reporting Act (FCRA) Contents

Below is the Table of Contents for the **Fair Credit Reporting Act (FCRA), 15 U.S.C. § 1681 et seq.**, on the Federal Trade Commission (FTC) website at www.consumer.ftc.gov/sites/default/files/articles/pdf/pdf-0111-fair-credit-reporting-act.pdf:

Contents

FCRA Mandated Forms for Background Screening Compliance

Three Forms from Consumer Financial Protection Bureau (CFPB) Needed for FCRA Compliance

In 2012, the **Consumer Financial Protection Bureau (CFPB)** — www.consumerfinance.gov — modified the following three essential Fair Credit Reporting Act (FCRA) mandated forms used for employment background checks.

Mandated use of these three forms began on January 1, 2013:

1. **"A Summary of Your Rights Under the Fair Credit Reporting Act"** – The FCRA mandates that a background screening firm must provide this notice to an employer and employers in turn must provide the notice to applicants in different situations (This notice is available in English and Spanish at www.consumerfinance.gov/learnmore/).

2. **"NOTICE TO USERS OF CONSUMER REPORTS: OBLIGATIONS OF USERS UNDER THE FCRA"** - The FCRA also mandates that a background screening firm (known as a Consumer Reporting Agency or "CRA") must provide each user of its services the "Notice to Users of Consumer Reports of their Obligations under the FCRA."

3. **"NOTICE TO FURNISHERS OF INFORMATION: OBLIGATIONS OF FURNISHERS UNDER THE FCRA"** - This notice is aimed at certain furnishers of information to CRAs and must be provided in prescribed situations such as a re-investigation where the consumer disputes the report or in a situation involving identity theft.

These three forms are reprinted on the pages to follow.

Para información en español, visite www.consumerfinance.gov/learnmore o escribe a la
Consumer Financial Protection Bureau, 1700 G Street N.W., Washington, DC 20552.

A Summary of Your Rights Under the Fair Credit Reporting Act

The federal Fair Credit Reporting Act (FCRA) promotes the accuracy, fairness, and privacy of information in the files of consumer reporting agencies. There are many types of consumer reporting agencies, including credit bureaus and specialty agencies (such as agencies that sell information about check writing histories, medical records, and rental history records). Here is a summary of your major rights under the FCRA. **For more information, including information about additional rights, go to www.consumerfinance.gov/learnmore or write to: Consumer Financial Protection Bureau, 1700 G Street N.W., Washington, DC 20552.**

- **You must be told if information in your file has been used against you.** Anyone who uses a credit report or another type of consumer report to deny your application for credit, insurance, or employment – or to take another adverse action against you – must tell you, and must give you the name, address, and phone number of the agency that provided the information.

- **You have the right to know what is in your file.** You may request and obtain all the information about you in the files of a consumer reporting agency (your "file disclosure"). You will be required to provide proper identification, which may include your Social Security number. In many cases, the disclosure will be free. You are entitled to a free file disclosure if:

  - a person has taken adverse action against you because of information in your credit report;
  - you are the victim of identity theft and place a fraud alert in your file;
  - your file contains inaccurate information as a result of fraud;
  - you are on public assistance;
  - you are unemployed but expect to apply for employment within 60 days.

  In addition, all consumers are entitled to one free disclosure every 12 months upon request from each nationwide credit bureau and from nationwide specialty consumer reporting agencies. See www.consumerfinance.gov/learnmore for additional information.

- **You have the right to ask for a credit score.** Credit scores are numerical summaries of your credit-worthiness based on information from credit bureaus. You may request a credit score from consumer reporting agencies that create scores or distribute scores used in residential real property loans, but you will have to pay for it. In some mortgage transactions, you will receive credit score information for free from the mortgage lender.

- **You have the right to dispute incomplete or inaccurate information.** If you identify information in your file that is incomplete or inaccurate and report it to the consumer reporting agency, the agency must investigate unless your dispute is frivolous. See www.consumerfinance.gov/learnmore for an explanation of dispute procedures.

- **Consumer reporting agencies must correct or delete inaccurate, incomplete, or unverifiable information.** Inaccurate, incomplete or unverifiable information must be removed or corrected, usually within 30 days. However, a consumer reporting agency may continue to report information it has verified as accurate.

- **Consumer reporting agencies may not report outdated negative information.** In most cases, a consumer reporting agency may not report negative information that is more than seven years old, or bankruptcies that are more than 10 years old.

- **Access to your file is limited.** A consumer reporting agency may provide information about you only to people with a valid need – usually to consider an application with a creditor, insurer, employer, landlord, or other business. The FCRA specifies those with a valid need for access.

- **You must give your consent for reports to be provided to employers.** A consumer reporting agency may not give out information about you to your employer, or a potential employer, without your written consent given to the employer. Written consent generally is not required in the trucking industry. For more information, go to www.consumerfinance.gov/learnmore.

- **You may limit "prescreened" offers of credit and insurance you get based on information in your credit report.** Unsolicited "prescreened" offers for credit and insurance must include a toll-free phone number you can call if you choose to remove your name and address from the lists these offers are based on. You may opt-out with the nationwide credit bureaus at 1-888-5-OPTOUT (1-888-567-8688).

- **You may seek damages from violators.** If a consumer reporting agency, or, in some cases, a user of consumer reports or a furnisher of information to a consumer reporting agency violates the FCRA, you may be able to sue in state or federal court.

- **Identity Theft victims and active duty military personnel have additional rights.** For more information, visit www.consumerfinance.gov/learnmore.

States may enforce the FCRA, and many states have their own consumer reporting laws. In some cases, you may have more rights under state law. For more information, contact your state or local consumer protection agency or your state Attorney General. For more information about your federal rights, contact:

TYPE OF BUSINESS:	CONTACT:
1.a. Banks, savings associations, and credit unions with total assets of over $10 billion and their affiliates.	**a. Consumer Financial Protection Bureau** **1700 G Street, N.W.** **Washington, DC 20552**
b. Such affiliations that are not banks, savings associations, or credit unions also should list, in addition to the CFPB:	**b. Federal Trade Commission: Consumer Response Center - FCRA** **Washington, DC 20580** **(877) 382-4357**
2. To the extent not included in item 1 above: **a. National banks, federal savings associations, and federal branches and federal agencies of foreign banks.**	**a. Office of the Comptroller of the Currency** **Customer Assistance Group** **1301 McKinney Street, Suite 3450** **Houston, TX 77010-9050**
b. State member banks, branches and agencies of foreign banks (other than federal branches, federal agencies, and Insured State Branches of Foreign Banks), commercial lending companies owned or controlled by foreign banks, and organizations operating under section 25 or 25A of the Federal Reserve Act.	**b. Federal Reserve Consumer Help Center** **P.O. Box 1200** **Minneapolis, MN 55480**
c. Nonmember Insured Banks, Insured State Branches of Foreign Banks, and insured state savings associations.	**c. FDIC Consumer Response Center** **1100 Walnut Street, Box #11** **Kansas City, MO 64106**

TYPE OF BUSINESS:	CONTACT:
d. Federal Credit Unions	d. National Credit Union Administration Office of Consumer Protection (OCP) Division of Consumer Compliance and Outreach (DCCO) 1775 Duke Street Alexandria, VA 22314
3. Air carriers	Asst. General Counsel for Aviation Enforcement & Proceedings Aviation Consumer Protection Division Department of Transportation 1200 New Jersey Avenue, S.E. Washington, DC 20590
4. Creditors Subject to Surface Transportation Board	Office of Proceedings, Surface Transportation Board Department of Transportation 395 E Street, S.W. Washington, DC 20423
5. Creditors Subject to Packers and Stockyards Act, 1921	Nearest Packers and Stockyards Administration area supervisor
6. Small Business Investment Companies	Associate Deputy Administrator for Capital Access United States Small Business Administration 409 Third Street, SW, 8th Floor Washington, DC 20416
7. Brokers and Dealers	Securities and Exchange Commission 100 F Street, N.E. Washington, DC 20549
8. Federal Land Banks, Federal Lank Bank Associations, Federal Intermediate Credit Banks, and Production Credit Associations	Farm Credit Administration 1501 Farm Credit Drive McLean, VA 22102-5090
9. Retailers, Finance Companies, and All Other Creditors Not Listed Above	FTC Regional Office for region in which the creditor operates or Federal Trade Commission: Consumer Response Center – FCRA Washington, DC 20580 (877) 382-4357

All users of consumer reports must comply with all applicable regulations. Information about applicable regulations currently in effect can be found at the Consumer Financial Protection Bureau's website, www.consumerfinance.gov/learnmore.

NOTICE TO USERS OF CONSUMER REPORTS:
OBLIGATIONS OF USERS UNDER THE FCRA

The Fair Credit Reporting Act (FCRA), 15 U.S.C. 1681-1681y, requires that this notice be provided to inform users of consumer reports of their legal obligations. State law may impose additional requirements. The text of the FCRA is set forth in full at the Consumer Financial Protection Bureau's (CFPB) website at www.consumerfinance.gov/learnmore. At the end of this document is a list of United States Code citations for the FCRA. Other information about user duties is also available at the CFPB's website. **Users must consult the relevant provisions of the FCRA for details about their obligations under the FCRA.**

This first section of this summary sets forth the responsibilities imposed by the FCRA on all users of consumer reports. The subsequent sections discuss the duties of users of reports that contain specific types of information, or that are used for certain purposes, and the legal consequences of violations. If you are a furnisher of information to a consumer reporting agency (CRA), you have additional obligations and will receive a separate notice from the CRA describing your duties as a furnisher.

I. OBLIGATIONS OF ALL USERS OF CONSUMER REPORTS

A. Users Must Have a Permissible Purpose

Congress has limited the use of consumer reports to protect consumers' privacy. All users must have a permissible purpose under the FCRA to obtain a consumer report. Section 604 of the FCRA contains a list of the permissible purposes under the law. These are:

- As ordered by a court or a federal grand jury subpoena. *Section 604(a)(1)*
- As instructed by the consumer in writing. *Section 604(a)(2)*
- For the extension of credit as a result of an application from a consumer, or the review or collection of a consumer's account. *Section 604(a)(3)(A)*
- For employment purposes, including hiring and promotion decisions, where the consumer has given written permission. *Sections 604(a)(3)(B) and 604(b)*
- For the underwriting of insurance as a result of an application from a consumer. *Section 604(a)(3)(C)*
- When there is a legitimate business need, in connection with a business transaction that is <u>initiated</u> by the consumer. *Section 604(a)(3)(F)(i)*
- To review a consumer's account to determine whether the consumer continues to meet the terms of the account. *Section 604(a)(3)(F)(ii)*
- To determine a consumer's eligibility for a license or other benefit granted by a governmental instrumentality required by law to consider an applicant's financial responsibility or status. <u>Section 604(a)(3)(D)</u>
- For use by a potential investor or servicer, or current insurer, in a valuation or assessment of the credit or prepayment risks associated with an existing credit obligation. <u>Section 604(a)(3)(E)</u>

- For use by state and local officials in connection with the determination of child support payments, or modifications and enforcement thereof. Sections 604(a)(4) and 604(a)(5)

In addition, creditors and insurers may obtain certain consumer report information for the purpose of making "prescreened" unsolicited offers of credit or insurance. Section 604(c). The particular obligations of users of "prescreened" information are described in Section VII below.

B. Users Must Provide Certifications

Section 604(f) prohibits any person from obtaining a consumer report from a consumer reporting agency (CRA) unless the person has certified to the CRA the permissible purpose(s) for which the report is being obtained and certifies that the report will not be used for any other purpose.

C. Users Must Notify Consumers When Adverse Actions Are Taken

The term "adverse action" is defined very broadly by Section 603. "Adverse actions" include all business, credit, and employment actions affecting consumers that can be considered to have a negative impact as defined by Section 603(k) of the FCRA – such as denying or canceling credit or insurance, or denying employment or promotion. No adverse action occurs in a credit transaction where the creditor makes a counteroffer that is accepted by the consumer.

1. Adverse Actions Based on Information Obtained From a CRA

If a user takes any type of adverse action as defined by the FCRA that is based at least in part on information contained in a consumer report, Section 615(a) requires the user to notify the consumer. The notification may be done in writing, orally, or by electronic means. It must include the following:

- The name, address, and telephone number of the CRA (including a toll-free telephone number, if it is a nationwide CRA) that provided the report.
- A statement that the CRA did not make the adverse decision and is not able to explain why the decision was made.
- A statement setting forth the consumer's right to obtain a free disclosure of the consumer's file from the CRA if the consumer makes a request within 60 days.
- A statement setting forth the consumer's right to dispute directly with the CRA the accuracy or completeness of any information provided by the CRA.

2. Adverse Actions Based on Information Obtained From Third Parties Who Are Not Consumer Reporting Agencies

If a person denies (or increases the charge for) credit for personal, family, or household purposes based either wholly or partly upon information from a person other than a CRA, and the information is the type of consumer information covered by the FCRA, Section 615(b)(1) requires that the user clearly and accurately disclose to the consumer his or her right to be told the nature of the information that was relied upon if the consumer makes a written request within 60 days of notification. The user must provide the disclosure within a reasonable period of time following the consumer's written request.

3. Adverse Actions Based on Information Obtained From Affiliates

If a person takes an adverse action involving insurance, employment, or a credit transaction initiated by the consumer, based on information of the type covered by the FCRA, and this information was obtained from an entity affiliated with the user of the information by common ownership or control, Section 615(b)(2) requires the user to notify the consumer of the adverse action. The notice must inform the consumer that he or she may obtain a disclosure of the nature of the information relied upon by making a written request within 60 days of receiving the adverse action notice. If the consumer makes such a request, the user must disclose the nature of the information not later than 30 days after receiving the request. If consumer report information is shared among affiliates and then used for an adverse action, the user must make an adverse action disclosure as set forth in I.C.1 above.

D. Users have Obligations When Fraud and Active Duty Military Alerts are in Files

When a consumer has placed a fraud alert, including one relating to identity theft, or an active duty military alert with a nationwide consumer reporting agency as defined in Section 603(p) and resellers, 605A(h) imposes limitations on users of reports obtained from the consumer reporting agency in certain circumstances, including the establishment of a new credit plan and the issuance of additional credit cards. For the initial fraud alerts and active duty alerts, the user must have reasonable policies and procedures in place to form a belief that the user knows the identity of the applicant or contact the consumer at a telephone number specified by the consumer; in the case of extended fraud alerts, the user must contact the consumer in accordance with the contact information provided in the consumer's alert.

E. Users Have Obligations When Notified of an Address Discrepancy

Section 605(h) requires nationwide CRAs, as defined in Section 603(p), to notify users that request reports when the address for a consumer provided by the user in requesting the report is substantially different from the addresses in the consumer's file. When this occurs, users must comply with regulations specifying the procedures to be followed. Federal regulations are available at www.consumerfinance.gov/learnmore.

F. Users Have Obligations When Disposing of Records

Section 628 requires that all users of consumer report information have in place procedures to properly dispose of records containing this information. Federal regulations are available at www.consumerfinance.gov/learnmore.

II. CREDITORS MUST MAKE ADDITIONAL DISCLOSURES

If a person uses a consumer report in connection with an application for, or a grant, extension, or provision of, credit to a consumer on material terms that are materially less favorable than the most favorable terms available to a substantial proportion of consumers from or through that person, based in whole or in part on a consumer report, the person must provide a risk-based pricing notice to the consumer in accordance with regulations prescribed by the CFPB.

Section 609(g) requires a disclosure by all persons that make or arrange loans secured by residential real property (one to four units) and that use credit scores. These persons must provide credit scores and other information about credit scores to applicants, including the disclosure set forth in section 609(g)(1)(D) ("Notice to the Home Loan Applicant").

III. OBLIGATIONS OF USERS WHEN CONSUMER REPORTS ARE OBTAINED FOR EMPLOYMENT PURPOSES

A. Employment Other Than in the Trucking Industry

If information from a CRA is used for employment purposes, the user has specific duties, which are set forth in FCRA Section 604(b). The user must:

- Make a clear and conspicuous written disclosure to the consumer before the report is obtained, in a document that consists solely of the disclosure, that a consumer report may be obtained.

- Obtain from the consumer prior written authorization. Authorization to access reports during the term of employment may be obtained at the time of employment.

- Certify to the CRA that the above steps have been followed, that the information being obtained will not be used in violation of any federal or state equal opportunity law or regulation, and that, if any adverse action is to be taken based on the consumer report, a copy of the report and a summary of the consumer's rights will be provided to the consumer.

- **Before** taking an adverse action, the user must provide a copy of the report to the consumer as well as the summary of the consumer's rights. (The user should receive this summary from the CRA.) A Section 615(a) adverse action notice should be sent after the adverse action is taken.

An adverse action notice also is required in employment situations if credit information (other than transactions and experience data) obtained from an affiliate is used to deny employment. Section 615(b)(2).

The procedures for investigative consumer reports and employee misconduct investigations are set forth below.

B. Employment in the Trucking Industry

Special rules apply for truck drivers where the only interaction between the consumer and the potential employer is by mail, telephone, or computer. In this case, the consumer may provide consent orally or electronically, and an adverse action may be made orally, in writing, or electronically. The consumer may obtain a copy of any report relied upon by the trucking company by contacting the company.

IV. OBLIGATIONS WHEN INVESTIGATIVE CONSUMER REPORTS ARE USED

Investigative consumer reports are a special type of consumer report in which information about a consumer's character, general reputation, personal characteristics, and mode of living is obtained through personal interviews by an entity or person that is a consumer reporting agency. Consumers who are the subjects of such reports are given special rights under the FCRA. If a user intends to obtain an investigative consumer report, Section 606 requires the following:

- The user must disclose to the consumer that an investigative consumer report may be obtained. This must be done in a written disclosure that is mailed, or otherwise delivered, to the consumer at some time before or not later than three days after the date on which the report was first requested. The disclosure must include a statement informing the consumer of his or her right to request additional disclosures of the nature and scope of the investigation as described below, and the summary of consumer rights required by Section 609 of the FCRA. (The summary of consumer rights will be provided by the CRA that conducts the investigation.)

- The user must certify to the CRA that the disclosures set forth above have been made and that the user will make the disclosure described below.

- Upon the written request of a consumer made within a reasonable period of time after the disclosures required above, the user must make a complete disclosure of the nature and scope of the investigation. This must be made in a written statement that is mailed, or otherwise delivered, to the consumer no later than five days after the date on which the request was received from the consumer or the report was first requested, whichever is later in time.

V. SPECIAL PROCEDURES FOR EMPLOYEE INVESTIGATIONS

Section 603(x) provides special procedures for investigations of suspected misconduct by an employee or for compliance with Federal, state or local laws and regulations or the rules of a self-regulatory organization, and compliance with written policies of the employer. These investigations are not treated as consumer reports so long as the employer or its agent complies with the procedures set forth in Section 603(x), and a summary describing the nature and scope of the inquiry is made to the employee if an adverse action is taken based on the investigation.

VI. OBLIGATIONS OF USERS OF MEDICAL INFORMATION

Section 604(g) limits the use of medical information obtained from consumer reporting agencies (other than payment information that appears in a coded form that does not identify the medical provider). If the report is to be used for an insurance transaction, the consumer must give consent to the user of the report or the information must be coded. If the report is to be used for employment purposes – or in connection with a credit transaction (except as provided in federal regulations) – the consumer must provide specific written consent and the medical information must be relevant. Any user who receives medical information shall not disclose the information to any other person (except where necessary to carry out the purpose for which the information was disclosed, or as permitted by statute, regulation, or order.)

VII. OBLIGATIONS OF USERS OF "PRESCREENED LISTS"

The FCRA permits creditors and insurers to obtain limited consumer report information for use in connection with unsolicited offers of credit or insurance under certain circumstances. Sections 603(l), 604(c), 604(e), and 615(d). This practice is known as "prescreening" and typically involves obtaining from a CRA a list of consumers who meet certain preestablished criteria. If any person intends to use prescreened lists, that person must (1) before the offer is made, establish the criteria that will be relied upon to make the offer and to grant credit or insurance, and (2) maintain such criteria on file for a three-year period beginning on the date on which the offer is made to each consumer. In addition, any user must provide with each written solicitation a clear and conspicuous statement that:

- Information contained in a consumer's CRA file was used in connection with the transaction.
- The consumer received the offer because he or she satisfied the criteria for credit worthiness or insurability used to screen for the offer.
- Credit or insurance may not be extended if, after the consumer responds, it is determined that the consumer does not meet the criteria used for screening or any applicable criteria bearing on credit worthiness or insurability, or the consumer does not furnish required collateral.
- The consumer may prohibit the use of information in his or her file in connection with future prescreened offers of credit or insurance by contacting the notification system established by the CRA that provided the report. The statement must include the address and the toll-free telephone number of the appropriate notification system.

In addition, the CFPB has established the format, type size, and manner of the disclosure required by Section 615(d), with which users must comply. The relevant regulation 12 CFR 1022.54.

VIII. OBLIGATIONS OF RESELLERS

A. Disclosure and Certification Requirements

Section 607(e) of the FCRA requires any person who obtains a consumer report for resale to take the following steps:

- Disclose the identity of the end-user to the source CRA.
- Identify to the source CRA each permissible purpose for which the report will be furnished to the end-user.
- Establish and follow reasonable procedures to ensure that reports are resold only for permissible purposes, including procedures to obtain:
  1) the identity of all end-users;
  2) certifications from all users of each purpose for which reports will be used; and
  3) certifications that reports will not be used for any purpose other than the purpose(s) specified to the reseller. Resellers must make reasonable efforts to verify this information before selling the report.

B. Reinvestigations by Resellers

Under Section 611(f), if a consumer disputes the accuracy or completeness of information in a report prepared by a reseller, the reseller must determine whether this is a result of an action or omission on its part and, if so, correct or delete the information. If not, the reseller must send the dispute to the source CRA for reinvestigation. When any CRA notifies the reseller of the results of an investigation, the reseller must immediately convey the information to the consumer.

C. Fraud Alerts and Resellers

Section 605(f) requires resellers who receive fraud alerts or active duty alerts from another consumer reporting agency to include these in their reports.

IX. LIABILITY FOR VIOLATIONS OF THE FCRA

Failure to comply with the FCRA can result in state government or federal government enforcement actions, as well as private lawsuits. Sections 616, 617, and 621. In addition, any person who knowingly and willfully obtains a consumer report under false pretenses may face criminal prosecution. Section 619.

The CFPB's website, www.consumerfinance.gov/learnmore, has more information about the FCRA, including publications for businesses and the full text of the FCRA.

Citations for FCRA sections in the U.S. Code, 15 U.S.C. § 1681 et seq.:

Section 602	15 U.S.C. 1681	Section 615	15 U.S.C. 1681m
Section 603	15 U.S.C. 1681a	Section 616	15 U.S.C. 1681n
Section 604	15 U.S.C. 1681b	Section 617	15 U.S.C. 1681o
Section 605	15 U.S.C. 1681c	Section 618	15 U.S.C. 1681p
Section 605A	15 U.S.C. 1681cA	Section 619	15 U.S.C. 1681q
Section 605B	15 U.S.C. 1681cB	Section 620	15 U.S.C. 1681r
Section 606	15 U.S.C. 1681d	Section 621	15 U.S.C. 1681s
Section 607	15 U.S.C. 1681e	Section 622	15 U.S.C. 1681s-1
Section 608	15 U.S.C. 1681f	Section 623	15 U.S.C. 1681s-2
Section 609	15 U.S.C. 1681g	Section 624	15 U.S.C. 1681t
Section 610	15 U.S.C. 1681h	Section 625	15 U.S.C. 1681u
Section 611	15 U.S.C. 1681i	Section 626	15 U.S.C. 1681v
Section 612	15 U.S.C. 1681j	Section 627	15 U.S.C. 1681w
Section 613	15 U.S.C. 1681k	Section 628	15 U.S.C. 1681x
Section 614	15 U.S.C. 1681l	Section 629	15 U.S.C. 1681y

All furnishers of information to consumer reporting agencies must comply with all applicable regulations. Information about applicable regulations currently in effect can be found at the Consumer Financial Protection Bureau's website, www.consumerfinance.gov/learnmore.

NOTICE TO FURNISHERS OF INFORMATION:
OBLIGATIONS OF FURNISHERS UNDER THE FCRA

The federal Fair Credit Reporting Act (FCRA), 15 U.S.C. 1681-1681y, imposes responsibilities on all persons who furnish information to consumer reporting agencies (CRAs). These responsibilities are found in Section 623 of the FCRA, 15 U.S.C. 1681s-2. State law may impose additional requirements on furnishers. All furnishers of information to CRAs should become familiar with the applicable laws and may want to consult with their counsel to ensure that they are in compliance. The text of the FCRA is available at the website of the Consumer Financial Protection Bureau (CFPB): www.consumerfinance.gov/learnmore. A list of the sections of the FCRA cross-referenced to the U.S. Code is at the end of this document.

Section 623 imposes the following duties upon furnishers:

Accuracy Guidelines

The FCRA requires furnishers to comply with federal guidelines and regulations dealing with the accuracy of information provided to CRAs by furnishers. Federal regulations and guidelines are available at www.consumerfinance.gov/learnmore. Sections 623(e).

General Prohibition on Reporting Inaccurate Information

The FCRA prohibits information furnishers from providing information to a CRA that they know or have reasonable cause to believe is inaccurate. However, the furnisher is not subject to this general prohibition if it clearly and conspicuously specifies an address to which consumers may write to notify the furnisher that certain information is inaccurate. Sections 623(a)(1)(A) and (a)(1)(C).

Duty to Correct and Update Information

If at any time a person who regularly and in the ordinary course of business furnishes information to one or more CRAs determines that the information provided is not complete or accurate, the furnisher must promptly provide complete and accurate information to the CRA. In addition, the furnisher must notify all CRAs that received the information of any corrections, and must thereafter report only the complete and accurate information. Section 623(a)(2).

Duties After Notice of Dispute from Consumer

If a consumer notifies a furnisher, at an address specified by the furnisher for such notices, that specific information is inaccurate, and the information is, in fact, inaccurate, the furnisher must thereafter report the correct information to CRAs. Section 623(a)(1)(B).

If a consumer notifies a furnisher that the consumer disputes the completeness or accuracy of any information reported by the furnisher, the furnisher may not subsequently report that information to a CRA without providing notice of the dispute. Section 623(a)(3).

Furnishers must comply with federal regulations that identify when an information furnisher must investigate a dispute made directly to the furnisher by a consumer. Under these regulations, furnishers must complete an investigation within 30 days (or 45 days, if the consumer later provides relevant additional information) unless the disputer is frivolous or irrelevant or comes from a "credit repair organization." Section 623(a)(8). Federal regulations are available at www.consumerfinance.gov/learnmore. Section 623(a)(8).

Duties After Notice of Dispute from Consumer Reporting Agency

If a CRA notifies a furnisher that a consumer disputes the completeness or accuracy of information provided by the furnisher, the furnisher has a duty to follow certain procedures. The furnisher must:

- Conduct an investigation and review all relevant information provided by the CRA, including information given to the CRA by the consumer. Sections 623(b)(1)(A) and (b)(1)(B).

- Report the results to the CRA that referred the dispute, and, if the investigation establishes that the information was, in fact, incomplete or inaccurate, report the results to all CRAs to which the furnisher provided the information that compile and maintain files on a nationwide basis. Sections 623(b)(1)(C) and (b)(1)(D).

- Complete the above steps within 30 days from the date the CRA receives the dispute (or 45 days, if the consumer later provides relevant additional information to the CRA). Section 623(b)(2).

- Promptly modify or delete the information, or block its reporting. Section 623(b)(1)(E).

Duty to Report Voluntary Closing of Credit Accounts

If a consumer voluntarily closes a credit account, any person who regularly and in the ordinary course of business furnishes information to one or more CRAs must report this fact when it provides information to CRAs for the time period in which the account was closed. Section 623(a)(4).

Duty to Report Dates of Delinquencies

If a furnisher reports information concerning a delinquent account placed for collection, charged to profit or loss, or subject to any similar action, the furnisher must, within 90 days after reporting the information, provide the CRA with the month and the year of the commencement of the delinquency that immediately preceded the action, so that the agency will know how long to keep the information in the consumer's file. Section 623(a)(5).

Any person, such as a debt collector, that has acquired or is responsible for collecting delinquent accounts and that reports information to CRAs may comply with the requirements of Section 623(a)(5) (until there is a consumer dispute) by reporting the same delinquency date previously reported by the creditor. If the creditor did not report this date, they may comply with the FCRA by establishing reasonable procedures to obtain and report delinquency dates, or, if a delinquency date cannot be reasonably obtained, by following reasonable procedures to ensure that the date reported precedes the date when the account was place for collection, charged to profit or loss, or subject to any similar action. Section 623(a)(5).

Duty of Financial Institutions When Reporting Negative Information

Financial Institutions that furnish information to "nationwide" consumer reporting agencies, as defined in Section 603(p), must notify consumers in writing if they may furnish or have furnished negative information to a CRA. Section 623(a)(7). The CFPB has prescribed model disclosures, 12 CFR Part 222, App. B.

Duty When Furnishing Medical Information

A furnisher whose primary business is providing medical services, products, or devices (and such furnisher's agents or assignees) is a medical information furnisher for the purposes of the FCRA and must notify all CRAs to which it reports of this fact. Section 623(a)(9). This notice will enable CRAs to comply with their duties under Section 604(g) when reporting medical information.

Duties When ID Theft Occurs

All furnishers must have in place reasonable procedures to respond to notifications from CRAs that information furnished is the result of identity theft, and to prevent refurnishing the information in the future. A furnisher may not furnish information that a consumer has identified as resulting from identity theft unless the furnisher subsequently knows or is informed by the consumer that the information is correct. Section 623(a)(6). If a furnisher learns that it has furnished inaccurate information due to identity theft, it must notify each CRA of the correct information and must thereafter report only complete and accurate information. Section 623(a)(2). When any furnisher of information is notified pursuant to the procedures set forth in section 605B that a debt has resulted from identity theft, the furnisher may not sell, transfer, or place for collection the debt except in certain limited circumstances. Section 615(f).

The CFPB's website, www.consumerfinance.gov/learnmore, has more information about the FCRA, including publications for businesses and the full text of the FCRA.

Citations for FCRA sections in the U.S. Code, 15 U.S.C. § 1681 et seq.:

Section 602	15 U.S.C. 1681	Section 615	15 U.S.C. 1681m
Section 603	15 U.S.C. 1681a	Section 616	15 U.S.C. 1681n
Section 604	15 U.S.C. 1681b	Section 617	15 U.S.C. 1681o
Section 605	15 U.S.C. 1681c	Section 618	15 U.S.C. 1681p
Section 605A	15 U.S.C. 1681cA	Section 619	15 U.S.C. 1681q
Section 605B	15 U.S.C. 1681cB	Section 620	15 U.S.C. 1681r
Section 606	15 U.S.C. 1681d	Section 621	15 U.S.C. 1681s
Section 607	15 U.S.C. 1681e	Section 622	15 U.S.C. 1681s-1
Section 608	15 U.S.C. 1681f	Section 623	15 U.S.C. 1681s-2
Section 609	15 U.S.C. 1681g	Section 624	15 U.S.C. 1681t
Section 610	15 U.S.C. 1681h	Section 625	15 U.S.C. 1681u
Section 611	15 U.S.C. 1681i	Section 626	15 U.S.C. 1681v
Section 612	15 U.S.C. 1681j	Section 627	15 U.S.C. 1681w
Section 613	15 U.S.C. 1681k	Section 628	15 U.S.C. 1681x
Section 614	15 U.S.C. 1681l	Section 629	15 U.S.C. 1681y

California Background Checks: Different from the Rest of the United States

Introduction

California has unique rules for background checks that go beyond those of the other 49 states and the federal Fair Credit Reporting Act (FCRA), which regulates background checks in the United States. While California employers always need to follow the FCRA, there are additional rules and requirements in the state when it comes to background checks for employment purposes.

California employers must follow these rules to the letter since applicants can sue for up to $10,000 for any violation regardless of damages. Employers in California, and employers doing business in California, need to be aware of these laws:

The San Francisco Fair Chance Ordinance

Also known as the Ban the Box Ordinance, this Ordinance took effect August 13, 2014. Ban the Box requires employers with San Francisco City or County offices and worksites who have 20 or more employees to follow strict rules about inquiring into and using criminal record history of job applicants and employees.

The Ordinance amends Article 49 of the San Francisco Police Code that outlines procedures for considering arrests, convictions, and related information in making employment decisions. With regard to hiring, the Ordinance prohibits employers from inquiring into an applicant's criminal history in an employment application or first live interview.

Employers must post a notice informing applicants and employees of their rights under the Ordinance in a conspicuous place at every workplace. In addition, job postings must state that the employer will consider qualified applicants with criminal histories in a manner consistent with the requirements of the Ordinance.

Senate Bill No. 530—Expunged Cases

Senate Bill No. 530 (SB 530) took effect January 1, 2014 and provides significant new protection to ex-offenders who committed crimes, including felonies, when it comes to job hunting and what employers can legally discover or use.

The new law prohibits an employer from asking about, seeking, or utilizing criminal convictions that have been judicially set aside. Employers violating the new prohibitions can face civil penalties and even misdemeanor criminal charges if done intentionally. It also allows a convicted person to get a case expunged sooner.

Assembly Bill 218—Public Ban-the-Box

Assembly Bill 218 (AB 218) was signed into law in October 2013 to reduce unnecessary barriers for adult Californians with arrest or conviction records, who are seeking employment. AB 218 requires the state, counties, cities, and special districts to remove the conviction history question from their job applications and wait to ask the question when the applicant at least meets "minimum employment qualifications." Employers such as law enforcement and school districts and job positions, subject to a criminal background check by occupational or licensing law, are exempt.

Senate Bill 909—Offshoring

Senate Bill 909 (SB 909) took effect January 1, 2012 and relates to offshoring of Personally Identifiable Information (PII) of consumers who are the subjects of background checks outside of the United States and beyond the protection of U.S. privacy laws.

SB 909 requires that consumers are to be notified as part of a disclosure before the background check of the web address; where they may find information about the investigative reporting agency's privacy practices, and whether personal information will be sent outside the United States. SB 909 also requires background check firms to conspicuously post their privacy policy on websites with a statement that indicates whether the personal information will be transferred to third parties outside the U.S. In the event consumers are harmed by a background check firm negligently sending data outside of the U.S., SB 909 provides for damages to consumers.

Assembly Bill 22—Restrictions on Credit Checks

Assembly Bill 22 (AB 22) took effect January 1, 2012 and regulates the use of credit report checks of job applicants and current employees by employers for employment purposes. AB 22 prohibits employers or prospective employers—with the exception of certain financial institutions—from obtaining a consumer credit report for employment purposes unless the position of the person, for whom the report is sought, is specified under the law. In addition, AB 22 requires the written notice informing the person, for whom a consumer credit report is sought, for employment purposes to also inform that person of the specific reason for obtaining the report.

Other Considerations

In addition to these laws, California has many existing rules for background checks in the state. Employers must understand the California Investigative Consumer Reporting Agencies Act (ICRAA), CA Labor Code, and the Regulations for the California Department for Fair Employment and Housing Act (FEHA). In California, all background checks are Investigative Consumer Reports (ICR), a different terminology than the FCRA, and employers face substantial civil exposure up to $10,000 for failure to follow the special rules for background checks that include the following:

- Special CA Check the box rule for free report (similar to MN and OK).
- Second checkbox if employer obtains public records directly.
- Special CA rules for the Consent and Disclosure including name, address and phone of CRA and right to obtain additional information.
- Special language on first page of each report about accuracy.
- Consent before each ICR.

Special additional statements include:

- Special rule for employer certification-employer needs to certify additional matters above and beyond FCRA certifications.
- Spanish language form if applicant requests more information.
- 7-year limit on criminal records (unless governmental requirement) but math is tricky.
- Strong argument that California seven year rule is pre-empted by FCRA but no court has ruled to date.
- California is a "No Arrest" state (but a pending case can be reported).
- Limitation on reporting diversion programs or arrest (with exception for certain hospitals).

However, California law is complicated by additional factors.

First, even though California has a "seven year rule" when it comes to criminal record for applicants reasonably expected to earn $75,000 a year or less, there is a strong argument that the federal Fair Credit Reporting Act (FCRA) has pre-empted the California rule, meaning there is, in fact, no seven-year restriction in California.

Second, as of the publication of this book, there are cases that have declared California Civil Code Section 1786, the law that regulates background checks, to be unconstitutionally vague. A string of cases have declared that the California

Investigative Consumer Reporting Agencies Act (ICRAA) is unconstitutional because it is vague by conflicting with another law that regulates credit reports. However, one appellate court has ruled that the law is constitutional and that case has gone on appeal to the California Supreme Court.

Since those matters are still on appeal, most employers and screening firms still generally abide by the current California law. However, that situation may change as more court decisions are rendered.

Conclusion

Despite all of the laws and special rules in California, due diligence through background checks is still mission critical for employers in the Golden State. Employees are typically a firm's greatest investment and largest cost, and each hire also represents a large potential risk. Every employer has the obligation to exercise due diligence in hiring since an employer that hires someone it either knew—or should have known through reasonable screening—was dangerous, unfit, or unqualified for the work can be sued for negligent hiring. The bottom line: California employers must maintain compliance with a whole different set of rules than the rest of the country when conducting due diligence background checks.

NOTE: The information is provided for illustrative purposes only and should not be construed as legal advice.

Source: www.esrcheck.com/Articles/Background-Checks-in-California-Means-Compliance-with-a-Whole-Different-Set-of-Rules-than-Rest-of-US/168/.

States Laws that Create Employer Immunity

A Summary of Trends in Negligent Hiring Reform

Recidivism is problem exacerbated by the daunting job prospects ex-offenders face when they leave incarceration. To solve this problem, there is a growing trend among states to offer degrees of immunity from negligent hiring lawsuits to employers who hire ex-offenders.

States have different methods to accomplish this goal. Most states offer some sort of liability protection to an employer where the employee's record has been expunged or sealed, by making the records inadmissible, or by granting the employer immunity. As an example, Alabama and Minnesota both do this. However, there tend to be three basic categories of methods that states use when going above and beyond simple expungement:

    (1) Granting a certificate to an employee that grants the employer protection,
    (2) Requiring the employer to undertake some sort of affirmative action, and/or
    (3) A variety of evidentiary restrictions on the use of employee's criminal records.

The first method involves a state's judicial system granting the ex-offender a certificate establishing the individual's rehabilitation. Actually getting these certificates varies in difficulty, and often requires the help of legal counsel. The certificates can also vary slightly in function. For instance, in Michigan, Tennessee, and Ohio, the certificate can be introduced as evidence against negligent hiring. In Georgia, the certificate creates a presumption against negligent hiring. This presumption then needs to be overcome by the plaintiff. Finally, if a potential employee has a certificate, Illinois grants an employer immunity unless the employer's lack of due care in hiring was willfully or wanton.

The second method involves some sort of employer action, which then grants the employer some liability protection. Again, the action required and the breadth of protection varies from state to state. For instance, Florida grants a presumption against negligent hiring if the employer performs a background investigation in accordance with Florida law. Massachusetts grants liability protection if employers rely on its state database (called CORI) for their background investigation. The District of Columbia makes an employee's criminal record inadmissible if the employer made a reasonable hiring decision under a 7 factor test.

Finally, many states use some sort of evidentiary restriction to protect employers. For instance, Louisiana and Texas bar negligent hiring lawsuits where the employee's criminal record is the only evidence of negligent hiring. This requires a plaintiff to demonstrate an employer was negligent in hiring an employee for reasons beyond a simple criminal record, such as the employee actually being unsuitable for the job. On the other hand, Colorado just makes an employee's criminal record inadmissible unless there is a direct relationship to the injury a plaintiff suffered.

Below is a list of some sample states with explanations of the statutory scheme they use to grant employers negligent hiring liability protection when hiring ex-offenders. Some states use multiple methods. For instance, the District of Columbia requires employer action (a reasonable hiring decision) and then grants an evidentiary restriction (the criminal record is inadmissible).

Alabama – April 2nd, 2014 – Ala. Code § 15-27-16

Alabama provides protection to employers who hire ex-offenders whose criminal records have been expunged. "Enacted statute Ala. Code § 15-27-16 provides immunity from liability for employers that hire, employ, contract with or otherwise do business with persons who have expunged criminal records for damages caused by such persons if: the expunged criminal records relate to charges for felonies, misdemeanors or violations; employers are unaware that such records exist; and employers' conduct is not unreasonable, malicious, willful or intentional."

Colorado – 2010 – HB 10-1023

Colorado HB 1023 prevents an employee or former employee's criminal history from being introduced as evidence of employer negligence in four cases. First, a criminal history cannot be introduced unless it bears a direct relationship to the facts underlying the cause of action against the employer. Second, the history would be barred if the employee received a pardon, or if the court sealed the records of the case. Third, arrests or charges that did not result in convictions are not admissible. Fourth and finally, if the employee's judgment was deferred, and that deferred judgment was not revoked, it is inadmissible against the employer.

Connecticut – October 1st, 2014 – Public Act 14-27

In Connecticut, Public Act 14-27 does two things. First, an employer has some liability protection if they hire an employee who has obtained a provisional pardon (or certificate or rehabilitation) . Second, an employer cannot refuse to hire an applicant with a certificate or rehabilitation solely on the basis of a past conviction.

This provisional pardon creates a presumption that the ex-offender is rehabilitated. In order to prove employer negligence in hiring the employee, a plaintiff must show "(1) the nature of the crime and its relationship to the job; (2) information pertaining to the person's rehabilitation; and (3) the time elapsed since the conviction or release."

District of Columbia – 2012 – B19-889

The District of Columbia's bill B19-889 "provides that criminal history information may not be used as evidence in a civil suit if an employer made a reasonable hiring decision in light of specified considerations." The bill provides a seven factor test to determine if employers have made a "reasonable, good faith determination." The factors are (1) the duties of the position, (2) the bearing the criminal background will have on those duties, (3) the time since the offense, (4) the age of the person at the time of the offense, (5) the frequency and seriousness of the offense, (6) information of rehabilitation and good conduct, and (7) that public policy favors employment of people with criminal records.

Florida – October 1st, 1999 – Florida Statute 768.096

In Florida, an employer has a presumption against negligence if they conduct a background investigation in accordance with Florida Statute 768.096. If the investigation does "not reveal any information that reasonably demonstrated the unsuitability of the prospective employee for the particular work to be performed or for the employment in general," then the employer has a presumption against negligent hiring.

The investigation must include: (1) obtaining a criminal background check and verifying it with the Florida Department of Law Enforcement, (2) making a reasonable effort to contact references and former employers, (3) requiring the employee to complete a job application form that asks about past convictions and civil suits, and (4) interview the employee.

Georgia – April 13, 2014 – SB 365

Georgia's SB 365, as ESR previously wrote, limits employer liability if the ex-offender earns a "Program and Treatment Completion Certificate." Once the offender completes the required treatment plan and vocational training, they can earn the certificate. This certificate then creates "a presumption of due care in hiring, retaining, licensing, leasing to, admitting to a school or program, or otherwise engaging in activity" with the ex-offender. However, this presumption may be rebutted by introducing evidence beyond the scope of the certificate which was known, or should have been known by the employer at the time of hiring.

Illinois – January 1st, 2010 – 730 ILCS 5/5-5.5-25

In Illinois, if an ex-offender has no more than two non-violent felony convictions, they are eligible to apply for a certificate of relief from disabilities (called certificates of rehabilitation and certificates of good conduct). For employers, the code states that "An employer is not civilly or criminally liable for an act or omission by an employee who has been issued a certificate of good conduct, except for a willful or wanton act by the employer in hiring the employee who has been issued a certificate of good conduct."

Louisiana – May 30th, 2014 – HB 505

In Louisiana, House Bill 505 states "any employer . . . shall not be subject to a cause of action for negligent hiring of or failing to adequately supervise an employee or independent contractor . . . solely because that employee or independent contractor has been previously convicted of a criminal offense."

Massachusetts – 2010 – SB 2583

Massachusetts takes a slightly different approach. It has its own background check system called CORI. "Massachusetts SB 2583 (2010) shields employers from liability if they used the state's background check system (CORI) to conduct the initial background check on the employee. Conversely, the employer is not shielded from liability if it used a commercial background check provider, because CORI provides safeguards and includes limitations that commercial systems do not." The bill provides that "No employer or person relying on volunteers shall be liable for negligent hiring practices by reason of relying solely on criminal offender record information received from [CORI]"

Michigan – December 16th, 2014 – Public Acts, 359, 360, and 361

Michigan implemented three laws: Public Acts 359, 360, and 361. Under these laws, ex-offenders can obtain a certificate of employability. In addition to the benefits these certificates confer directly to ex-offenders, they grant a measure of employer immunity as well. They serve as evidence an employer fulfilled their duty of care when hiring an employee with a criminal record. However, the employer loses this protection if the employer retains the ex-offender employee after the employee subsequently (1) demonstrates he or she is a danger to individuals or property, or (2) is convicted of or pleads guilty to a felony.

Minnesota – May 14th, 2014 – HF 2576

Minnesota's bill HF 2576 "makes an employee's expunged criminal history inadmissible as evidence in a civil case against an employer or landlord." The bill entered into force on January 1st, 2015.

New York – February 1st, 2009

In New York, employers can qualify for a rebuttable presumption in favor of excluding evidence of prior employee criminal records. Employers can gain this presumption by making a good faith evaluation of (1) if there is a direction relationship between the ex-offender's offense and the duties of the job sought, and (2) whether employment of the ex-offender would cause unreasonable risk to persons or property.

Ohio – September 28th, 2012 – SB 337

In Ohio, Senate Bill 337 offers some protections for employers. Ex-offenders may apply for a Certificate of Qualification for Employment. An employer that hires an employee with such a certificate gains protection from negligent hiring lawsuits under certain circumstances. First, the employer must know of the certificate at the time of employment. Second, the employer cannot later gain actual knowledge of an employee's danger and still retain them. These certificates can be used as evidence that the employer exercised due care in hiring the employee.

Texas – June 14th, 2013 – HB 1188

As ESR previously wrote, Texas's HB 1188 prevents causes of action against employers based solely on the evidence that an employee has been convicted of a previous offense. However, there are three types of offenses where this employer immunity is not applicable. First, there is no immunity where the employee's offense is substantially similar to the duties the employee is expected to perform. Second, if the employee's offense was a sexually violent offense. Third, the offense is one listed in Section 3g, Article 42.12" of the Texas Code of Criminal Procedure.

Tennessee – May 16th, 2014 – T.C.A. § 40-29-107

Tennessee passed SB 276 in 2014, which allows ex-offenders to apply for a certificate of employability. This gives two benefits to employers. First, an employer receives immunity from negligent hiring lawsuits if the employer knew about the certificate at the time of hiring. Second, other judicial and administrative proceedings, the employer may introduce the certificate as evidence the employer exercised due care in hiring or retaining the employee.

Like other such certificates, however, employers lose that immunity if they become aware of facts that show the employee is actually a danger to other persons or property.

General Introduction on Selecting a Background Screening Firm

Selecting a Background Screening Firm

In corporate America, pre-employment background checks of new hires have become a standard risk-management tool. It is no longer a matter of whether a firm should screen applicants, but how to accomplish it.

The first decision that an employer faces is whether to perform the screening in-house or to outsource. There are some tasks an employer could certainly perform in-house, such as local criminal record checks; however, a growing trend among profitable and efficient organizations is outsourcing services that, although vital, do not represent the company's core strength. Many firms are finding it is an inefficient use of their time and energy to attempt to perform background check services that a third-party specialist can provide efficiently and cost-effectively. Furthermore, the employer would have to learn the many complicated state and federal laws governing what information they can and cannot access, and acquire specialized software and information sources.

The cost of outsourcing is also a consideration. An employer would need to devote staff time and resources to the physical management of the process, including computers and implementing a software solution to manage and track all applicants being screened. On the other hand, a typical report from a screening firm should cost less than the first day's salary paid to the new employee -- called the "Less than One Day's Pay Rule." Considering the cost of a bad hire, this is a very minimal investment. Some firms do more in-depth screening for higher-paying positions; however, even if the position is paid more, the relative cost of the increased screening compared to the higher salary remains the same. Unless an employer is so large that incurring the additional administrative overhead of an internal background checking unit pencils out, most employers outsource this task.

How to Choose a Background Screening Firm

Since there are scores of companies that offer employment pre-screening services, some cautionary advice is in order with respect to making a choice. First, an employer should look for a professional partner and not just an information vendor selling data at the lowest price. Second, an employer should apply the same criteria that it would use in selecting any other provider of critical professional services. For example, if an employer were choosing a law firm for legal representation, it would not simply choose the cheapest law firm. Although cost is always a consideration, the employer would clearly want to know it is selecting a law firm that is competent, experienced and knowledgeable, reputable and reasonably priced. Above all, an employer would want to know that it is dealing with a firm with integrity. The same criteria should be used for selecting any provider of a professional service. A screening service must have the proven ability and knowledge to provide this professional service. A review of the company's Web site and materials as well as contacting the firm's current clients for a professional reference should be helpful in establishing the firm's qualifications.

An employer should verify if a firm has joined the National Association of Professional Background Screeners (NAPBS®). Membership in NAPBS demonstrates a commitment to professionalism and an industry-wide code of conduct. More important is to ascertain if a screening firm has been accredited by the accreditation program sponsored by the NAPBS. Many employers now have a policy that they will only work with accredited firms since that is the only way to have some degree of confidence in the capability of a background firm.

The following specific suggestions are offered for any organization that chooses to use a pre-employment screening firm. Use these suggestions with the sample Request for Proposal (RFP) at www.esrcheck.com/Resource-Center/Background-Screening-RFP/index.php.

Legal Compliance and Subject Expertise

It is imperative that a screening service understands the laws surrounding pre-employment screening and hiring, and they make a commitment to provide an employer with only the information the employer may legally possess.

The federal Fair Credit Reporting Act (FCRA) governs background screening in the U.S. It defines a background screening company as a Consumer Reporting Agency (CRA). A CRA must have a deep understanding of the FCRA and applicable state laws that control everything from the forms needed and what is legal to report, to how to respond to a consumer inquiry or complaint.

- Does the CRA have 50-state legal knowledge, since state laws are as critical as federal law?
- Does the CRA keep its clients updated on legal and regulatory changes and developments?
- Does the CRA make any effort to review specific reports or data before handing them over to the employer?
- Does the firm understand that a so-called "national criminal" database search is only a secondary screening tool and cannot be relied upon generally as a primary source of information?
- Does the CRA demonstrate an understanding that the use of criminal records are subject to EEOC concerns and discrimination law?
- Does the CRA have an understanding of ban-the-box laws?

Customer Service, Consulting, and Training

Since pre-employment screening is much more than just providing raw data, an employer should determine how a CRA provides customer service. An internal trouble ticket system, for example, is a best practice to make sure nothing falls through the cracks. Having a specific account manager that knows an employer's need is a better option than calling into a general customer service pool. A service provider should also be able to work directly with the security or Human Resources department to provide whatever training and orientation is necessary.

It is also important to choose a firm that is familiar with any special needs of your industry. For example, the health care industry has special concerns and requirements—unique licensing standards and disciplinary actions.

Pricing

Although it is important to obtain competitive pricing, it is usually not advisable to choose the lowest cost provider. As the old saying goes, you get what you pay for. Although some firms are can reduce some costs through efficiency and technology, one of the biggest areas where a screening firm can cut costs in order to lower pricing is by hiring fewer and cheaper employees. Since screening is a knowledge-based profession that is heavily regulated, key criteria for selecting a firm should be the knowledge, training, and experience of the staff member serving your account.

Performance Criteria for Information Providers

Does the CRA make it clear how they obtain data, and what processes are used in-house to ensure accuracy and quick turn-around time? There may be times when there are delays that are out of the CRA's control; however, it is critical that an employer have accurate real-time status reports.

Inquire about the CRA's Internal Quality Assurance processes. This should also include how a CRA trains and updates its own staff. It's also critical to understand how a screening firm ensures accuracy. One good way to discover how well a firm performs is to ask how many requests it receives for re-investigation of reports by consumers challenging the accuracy and completeness of reports.

Software and Internet Options

A service provider should also be able to provide technology solutions that fit into employers' hiring practices. Most providers have online systems and many options are available for online consent and seamless B2B integrations with Applicant Tracking Systems (ATS) and human resources systems.

Data Security and Privacy; References

The information in a background report is sensitive and confidential. The reports must be restricted to those individuals who are directly involved in the hiring process. A screening firm should have policies and procedures in place to ensure confidentiality. It should be able to provide a privacy and data protection statement. The best indication of whether a screening firm has state of the art security and privacy protection is to look for a firm that has a Service Organization Control SOC 2® Privacy designation issued in accordance with the American Institute of Certified Public Accountants (AICPA), as well as a "Privacy Shield" designation.

Another critical quality and privacy issue is whether a screening firm is really a screening expert or just a data service. For example, some screening firms offshore all of the work to call centers in India or the Philippines. , or use home workers. Or a firm that is in the Human Resources space may offer screening as an adjunct service. There are some firms that are just data vendors who view the screening industry has a way to make a fast buck. Considering how complex the screening environment become, none of these are good options for employers.

As with any provider of a professional service, an employer would want to check the provider's references. Just as a screening company should advise an employer to carefully screen each applicant before he or she is hired, an employer should exercise the same due diligence when retaining a screening company.

The source for this article is www.esrcheck.com/Articles/Selecting-A-Background-Screening-Firm/184/.

More about the Background Screening Industry

Introduction

Many employers outsource their background screening needs to professional background screening service providers. A background screening company is a private enterprise firm and, as emphasized throughout this publication, is classified as a Consumer Reporting Agency per the Fair Credit Reporting Act (FCRA). This chapter provides an overview of this industry.

Background Screening is a Multi-Billion Dollar Industry

With the advances in technology spurring widespread data availability, the pre-employment background screening industry has grown substantially in the past 30 years. The size of the employment background screening industry is currently estimated to be anywhere between two to five billion dollars.

Although there is no exact count of the number of firms that provide employment screening services, industry observers estimate there are literally thousands of firms involved in some level of background screening. Firms range from large, publicly held companies to retired police officers and other one-person services. Using an Internet search engine to look up the keyword "employment screening" or "background checks" will take an employer to literally thousands of web pages. Of course, many firms are in adjacent industries, such as security, human resources, drug or psychological testing, or payroll, and offer screening as a secondary service.

The Different Sizes of Screening Firms

The firms in the industry can be roughly broken down into four tiers distinguished in terms of revenues and assets:

1. **Tier One:** These are the biggest firms, with annual revenues of usually 50 million dollars or more. Many tier one firms have a substantial advantage in terms of technology, branding, breadth of services, resources, and the ability to provide large-scale, cost-effective solutions for large employers.

2. **Tier Two:** While substantial in size and revenue, tier twos are not as large as the tier one players. Tier two firms can roughly be placed in the 10 million to 50 million dollar sales range. Tier two firms are also characterized by large investments in technology and deep resources, and like the tier ones, tier twos have the ability to service large employers.

> ### Sign of the Times
>
> In a previous edition of *The Safe Hiring Manual*, the tier one firms were identified. Since hen, there has been a dramatic change in that list. Due to acquisitions and consolidation in the industry, and since most firms are privately held which means revenue information is not public, it is difficult to accurately identify all the current members of tiers one and two.

3. **Tier Three:** These are smaller firms with revenues roughly in the 2 million to 10 million dollar range. Typically, tier three firms have strong regional footprints as well as some national presence. Sometimes considered "boutique" firms, tier threes can compete in the screening marketplace by virtue of some niche service or a high level of customer service particularly within their geographical footprint. Many tier threes have begun offering technology solutions like their tier one and tier two competitors. A tier three's emphasis is less on being a low cost "data vendor" and more on customer service. With a tier 3 firm, an employer is more likely to have an account executive they become familiar with that can help to provide a professional service.

4. **Tier Four:** These are very small firms or sole practitioners that primarily serve a small local area. Tier four firms are typically private investigators, retired law enforcement, franchisees or agents of larger firms, or one and two person offices. Challenges for these firms include keeping up with advancing technology and staying on top of legal compliance issues.

The Functionality Issues Screening Companies Face

When providing background reports, screening firms do not work in an *inappropriate* manner to prevent employment for applicants with minor violations or misdemeanors unrelated to the work to be performed. As part of the hiring process, applicants have the opportunity up front to disclose minor violations and provide an explanation about such incidents.

The screening process ultimately works to *appropriately* prevent employment in those cases where:
- Someone lies on an employment application or during the interview process,
- The applicant or employee has criminal violations that may have serious consequences with respect to the integrity of job performance, or
- Does not have the claimed credentials needed for the position sought.

The Government Data Source Issues Screening Companies Face

It is critical for employers, legislators, the courts, and public officials to understand that background screening is not in the same category as "data miners" and other entities who are "data profiteers."

Unreasonable restrictions on screening firms have only served to harm employers and taxpaying citizens seeking employment. When a public record-holder deletes dates of birth from files and the public index, they have inadvertently removed the primary identification – the date of birth – used by a screening firm to make a determination if a record belongs to a particular applicant. Although it is understandable that courts would desire to protect Social Security Numbers, masking a date of birth does not promote privacy or consumer protection, but only serves to delay employment decisions. This delay can ultimately hurt the very consumer who has signed a consent form and wants the potential employer to have the information. Other government restrictions and impediments that serve to hurt employers and job applicants are lengthy delays in providing access to public records and excessive court fees.

Public officials need to understand:

- Background checks by a CRA are normally only conducted when a consumer has received (or is about to receive) a job offer, and the consumer has authorized the background check in writing. Both the applicant and the employer want the report completed to the extent possible within 72 hours, which is the industry standard.
- Any delay in a CRA's ability to complete reports in a timely manner works to the determent of consumers. Consumers want a CRA to have fast access to criminal records.
- A CRA can only access criminal records with the express written authorization of a job applicant pursuant to the federal Fair Credit Reporting Act (FCRA) and applicable state laws.
- The researchers who go to courthouses across the U.S. for background screening firms do NOT make any decision as to what is or is not reportable. One of the services provided by a CRA is that they filter out any information that is non-reportable with reference to applicable federal and state rules.
- Background screening is an intensely regulated task, subject to not only to the FCRA and state laws, but also other laws including civil rights laws and privacy laws. In addition, background screening is subject to regulation by the Federal Trade Commission (FTC) and the Equal Employment Opportunity Commission (EEOC). There is also a substantial body of case law on subjects such as accuracy in reporting criminal records.
- Unless expressly authorized by an act of Congress or a state legislature, a private employer cannot utilize the Federal Bureau of Investigation (FBI) database or state criminal database for a "LiveScan" background check. The vast majority of private employers need to utilize the services of a background screening firm to perform a background check

Some courts and public officials have attempted in recent years to limit screening firms' access to public records in the mistaken belief that such restrictions protect privacy and serve the public good. Nothing could be less accurate.

Author Tip ⟩ **Screening Companies Typically Are Not Data Aggregators**

A traditional background screening firm will typically acquire data for a one-time use only, and does not maintain a database of consumer data that is used again in the future.

Conclusion

Employers depend upon pre-employment reports to make safe hiring decisions and to show due diligence to avoid litigation. Unreasonable restrictions to access public records (pursuant to the signed consent and authorization of an applicant) only work to the benefit of criminals, terrorists, and cheaters, and to the detriment of employers, employees, honest citizens, and taxpayers.

How the Background Check Industry has Changed Since 2000

The background check industry has changed much in recent years since the beginning of the 21st century. Below are comparisons of the industry from 2000 and 2016 in six critical areas that have changed in the industry:

1. Number of Employers Performing Background Checks:

- **2000:** An estimated 50 percent of companies conduct background checks on their employees according to the 1996 Society for Human Resource Management (SHRM) Workplace Violence Survey.
- **2016:** A series of surveys from SHRM in 2010 reveals that approximately three out of four U.S. businesses perform some type of background check as part of their pre-employment screening programs, with 76 percent conducting reference background checks and 73 percent conducting criminal background checks.

2. Industry Standards for Background Checks:

- **2000:** There is no national trade association, industry standards, or definitive publications on background screening.
- **2016:** The industry now has a non-profit trade association, the National Association of Professional Background Screeners (NAPBS), representing the interests of background check companies. In 2004, the first comprehensive book on employment screening (the first edition of this book) is published - *The Safe Hiring Manual – The Complete Guide to Keeping Criminals, Terrorists, and Imposters Out of Your Workplace*' by Lester Rosen. In 2010 the Background Screening Credentialing Council (BSCC) of NAPBS launches the Background Screening Agency Accreditation Program (BSAAP) for a singular background check industry standard representing a background check company's commitment to excellence, accountability, and professionalism.

3. Sources for Background Check Information:

- **2000:** Background check information is primarily limited to traditional sources such as criminal records, driving records, verifications, and reference checks.
- **2016:** With the advent of new Internet technology – and new media such as blogs, videos on YouTube, and social networking sites like Facebook, LinkedIn, and Twitter in particular – there are many more potential outlets from which employers may gather information about job applicants. There is also widespread availability of database searches such as government sanctions, terrorist lists, and other records.

4. The Need for International Background Checks:

- **2000:** Before the rise of outsourcing, much of the workforce is perceived to have lived, worked, and been educated inside of the United States, so the idea of international background checks for job applicants seems expensive and unnecessary to most companies. There are also limited resources available for such background checks.
- **2016:** According to recent U.S. government statistics, there are 38.5 million foreign-born U.S. residents representing 12.5 percent of the population, more than 1.1 million persons became Legal Permanent Residents (LPRs) of the United States in 2009, and the unauthorized immigrant population living in the U.S. reached an estimated 10.8 million in January 2009 and grew 27 percent between 2000 and 2009. Given these facts, U.S. companies must be prepared to perform international background checks on job applicants with global backgrounds. Numerous resources are now available for background screening firms to conduct international background checks, as well as resources concerning international privacy and data protection.

5. Compliance Issues Concerning Background Checks:

- **2000:** Background check companies must comply with the federal Fair Credit Reporting Act (FCRA), originally passed in 1970, that regulates the collection, dissemination, and use of consumer information and is enforced by the Federal Trade Commission (FTC).
- **2016:** Background screening has become an intensely legally regulated endeavor. Background check companies must comply with a myriad of industry regulations in addition to FCRA requirements such as the Fair And Accurate Credit Transaction Act (FACT Act) of 2003 (which amended the FCRA), Sarbanes-Oxley, the Patriot Act, E-Verify employment eligibility verification, Equal Employment Opportunity Commission (EEOC) discrimination issues against protected classes pertaining to the use of criminal records, Ban-the-Box laws and credit reports for employment purposes. There are also numerous new consumer data privacy protections

regulations both domestically and internationally such as "Privacy Shield" and privacy laws that protect the Personally Identifiable Information (PII) of consumers. There are now an abundance of state laws regulating credit reports and criminal records. California, for example, completely revamped its background screening laws in 2002 and added new requirements in 2010 for when PII is sent offshore beyond the protection of U.S. privacy laws. Many states have their own version of the FCRA.

6. Technology Used in Background Screening:

- **2000:** Most employers are required to fax orders to a background check firm. The idea of entering orders into an online system or making information available in online in real time as to the status of a report is only in the beginning stages.
- **2016:** Technology in the background check industry increased substantially with the use of online processes to not only enter orders, but also with paperless systems with electronic signatures. An applicant can enter their own information, along with integrations into Applicant Tracking Systems (ATS) so background checks can be ordered with the click of a mouse. With the advent of Web 2.0, employers may expect to see more advances in the technology for the background screening process. Firms are able to build in legal compliance into the software programs. The downside, however, is that Internet entrepreneurs have seized upon background checks as a way to make quick money and in some instances are playing off the fears of Americans by offering cheap and instant checks based upon using databases never intended to be a substitute for a background check.

Much has changed in the background check industry in the years spanning 2000 to 2016, and many more changes are sure to come in the years ahead. Both background screeners and the employers they serve need to keep pace with advancements in the many changes regarding background screening.

The Role of the Pre-Employment Screening Industry in Today's Economy

The background screening industry provides a number of services to U.S. employers. The screening industry:

- Helps employers comply with the legal hiring standards set by state and federal law.
- Plays a critical part in helping public and private employers to mitigate risk and avoid legal exposure for negligent hiring.
- Educates employers about their legal obligations, such as compliance with the FCRA and discrimination laws
- Makes a safer workplace for customers and employees and helps employers avoid the nightmares associated with workplace violence, theft, hiring based upon fraudulent credentials, or hiring terrorists.
- Plays a critical part in the homeland security effort by acting as a private sector version of law enforcement but highly regulated by federal and state laws.
- Helps protect consumer's rights and helps consumers if there is a dispute about information or the need to perform a re-investigation.
- Improves both the profitability and productivity of American business by helping employers make better hiring decisions and lowering the high cost associated with employee turnover.
- Helps to keep data protected and confidential in order to prevent identity theft

The screening process ultimately is designed to work to appropriately to help employers make intelligent hiring decisions and to minimize risk in cases such as:

- Someone lies on an employment application or during the interview process,
- The applicant is not qualified, or does not have the credentials or past employment claimed,
- The applicant or employee has criminal violations that may have serious consequences with respect to the integrity of job performance, if it is job related or contrary to business necessity,
- Does not have the claimed credentials needed for the position sought.

This helps the U.S. economy and makes the U.S. a safe place to work. Employers depend upon pre-employment reports to make safe hiring decisions and to show due diligence to avoid litigation. Screening firms provide a crucial public function in a highly-regulated environment where consumers have a full array of rights and remedies.

It should be noted that pre-employment screening is just as beneficial to job applicants as employers. No consumer wants to work in an unsafe environment, or work next to or get the same pay as someone who got the job through phony credentials for fabrication of past employment or education. Background firms will often educate their employer clients for example on the proper and fair use of criminal records. In addition, a good background firm also considers a consumer to be their client as well as the employer. A good background firm is just as concerned about accuracy and completeness as the job applicant. A CRA has a number of legal obligations to consumers. If an applicant has a concern about a report, a background firm has an obligation to conduct a re-investigation to ensure the report is accurate   and complete. Background firms play a critical role in helping consumers get jobs by providing accurate reports as quickly as possible and being available to answer questions.

Introduction to the National Association of Professional Background Screeners

NAPBS – The Background Screening Industry Trade Association

One of the most exciting developments in the pre-employment screening industry was the emergence of the first industry non-profit trade association in 2003. Called the **National Association of Professional Background Screeners**, or **NAPBS,** the new association attracted nearly 300 of the nation's leading pre-employment screening companies. The association's website is found at www.NAPBS.com.

A Brief History of NAPBS

The NAPBS began through the efforts of many people. Steve Brownstein, the editor of *The Background Investigator* (www.search4crime.com), a newspaper devoted to the screening industry, held the nation's first screening industry conference in Long Beach, CA in April, 2002. Brownstein encouraged the attendees to think in terms of a national association in order to promote and protect the screening industry. Sandra Burns agreed to head a committee to look into the possibility of forming an association. In November, 2002, Brownstein and *The Background Investigator* sponsored a large national conference in Tampa, Florida, attended by over 175 screening professionals. At this meeting, there was widespread support for the formation of an association. Michael Sankey of BRB Publications joined Sandra Burns as a member of the interim board along with Bill Brudenell, Charlotte O'Neill, Jack Wallace, Les Rosen, and Mike Cool.

Les Rosen (author of this book) was designated chairperson of the steering committee that formed NAPBS. The interim board, along with other interested members of the screening industry, met in Arizona in January, 2003 and again in Washington D.C. in April, 2003. The interim Membership and Ethics committee met in Dallas, Texas in the Spring of 2003.

A membership drive was held in the last half of 2003, resulting in over 200 members. In order to provide seed money for the group, in early 2003, several screening firms stepped forward and generously donated the necessary funds to launch the association and to retain the services of a professional management firm and were designated as "Founding Members."

First NAPBS Board of Directors

The NAPBS began its first full year of operations with an elected Board of Directors in 2004. There are now over 500 NAPBS members. The first elected NAPBS Board of Directors consisted of the following people:

- Les Rosen, Co-chairman
- David Hein, Co-chairman
- Jason B. Morris, Co-chair elect
- Mary Poquette, Co-chair elect
- Katherine Bryant, Secretary
- Barry Nadell, Co-treasurer
- Catherine Aldrich, Co-treasurer
- Kevin G. Connell
- Ann Lane
- Larry Henry
- Michael Sankey

The original operating, standing committees included:

- Ethics/Accreditation
- Finance
- Membership
- Provider Advisory
- Best Practices and Compliance
- Government Relations
- Public Awareness and Communications
- Resources Library

The First NAPBS Conference

The first NAPBS conference was held in Scottsdale, Arizona in 2004. Below is a press release announcement according to the NAPBS website:

> Scottsdale, AZ, March 30, 2004 — On March 29 and 30 more than 225 individuals representing over 175 companies converged on Scottsdale, AZ for the inaugural Annual Conference of the National Association of Professional Background Screeners (NAPBS).
>
> NAPBS was formed to promote a greater awareness among employers nationwide of the growing importance of conducting background and reference checks. According to David Hein, NAPBS Board Co-chair, "It is estimated that fewer than 35% of employers are currently screening their applicants. Yet every day headlines across the country highlight the sometimes dire consequences that may result when prospective employees' backgrounds aren't thoroughly checked."
>
> The Association's members are companies from across the country who provide pre-employment/background screening, court records research, and tenant screening services. Employers can be assured they are dealing with a screening firm that subscribes to the organization's goals and standards if the NAPBS logo appears in the screening firms collateral or on their website.
>
> Among its many missions, NAPBS will help develop and coordinate training and other relevant programs to enable its members to better serve their clients, to promote and maintain the highest standards of excellence and ethics in the background screening industry, to ensure compliance with the Fair Credit Reporting Act, and to foster awareness of issues related to consumer protection and privacy rights within the industry.

Joining the Association requires prospective members to abide by a Code of Ethics. Additionally, NAPBS is developing membership accreditation criteria to further insure member companies meet the high standards the Association has established.

Starting with the first conference in Scottsdale, AZ in 2004, the NAPBS has held an annual industry conference every year in different cities around the United States. Attendance has grown every year, with the 2016 Conference attracting more than 70 attendees, according to the NAPBS press release below. The 2017 Annual Conference will be in Orlando, FL.

Record Breaking Attendance at 2016 NAPBS Annual Conference

Palm Desert, CA, September 27, 2016 — The National Association of Professional Background Screeners (NAPBS) is pleased to announce the success of the 2016 NAPBS Annual Conference held Sept. 18-20, 2016.

In Palm Desert, Calif., a record-breaking 763 background screening professionals gathered for three days of educational programming focused around the theme, "Leading the Way." The sold-out Exhibit Showcase featured 57 companies that supply products or services to the background screening profession.

NAPBS Chair Dawn Standerwick said, "NAPBS is committed to leading the way in excellence in the screening profession and we were excited to welcome so many members and industry partners who are also committed to excellence in our profession."

NAPBS presented for its members a very robust conference with 24 educational sessions presented on a variety of topics affecting the industry including international screening, legislative issues, compliance guidelines and employment discrimination, to name just a few. New for 2016, NAPBS introduced educational tracks to assist attendees wishing to focus on a topic for intensive study.

Source: www.prlog.org/12590227-record-breaking-attendance-at-2016-napbs-annual-conference.html

Here is a list of the **past Chairs of the Board of Directors** for the NAPBS. For the first three years, NAPBS had co-chairs:

- Lester Rosen and David Hein, co-chairs
- Mary Poquette and Jason Morris, co-chairs
- Robert Capwell and Barry Nadell, co-chairs
- Art Cohen
- Larry Lambeth
- Dan Shoemaker
- Laura Randazzo
- Theresa Preg
- Fred Giles
- Judy Gootkind
- Christine Cunneen
- Julie Hakman
- Dawn Standerwick

Author Tip

NAPBS Elects Dawn Standerwick Chair of Board of Directors

Dawn Standerwick, Vice President of Strategic Growth at Employment Screening Resources (ESR) has been elected Chair of the Board of Directors of the National Association of Professional Background Screeners (NAPBS®) for the 2016-17 term.

A seasoned background screening industry professional, Standerwick is a long time member of the Board of Directors for the NAPBS. She is actively involved on the NAPBS government relations committee and regularly participates in legislative advocacy efforts on behalf of the Association.

The author of this book served as chair of the committee that founded the NAPBS and as the first co-chair.

To read more, visit www.esrcheck.com/wordpress/2016/09/09/napbs-elects-dawn-standerwick-of-employment-screening-resources-chair-of-board-of-directors/.

You Need To Know

Summary of NAPBS Conferences Available Online

To find out more about the NAPBS and past NAPBS conferences, visit the web page at www.bergconsultinggroup.com/ConferenceReports.html for yearly conference reports authored by Bruce Berg, a pioneer and innovator in the screening industry, and an acknowledged industry expert and consultant.

The NAPBS Accreditation Program

The Need for Increased Emphasis on Professionalism in Background Screening Industry

When the National Association of Professional Background Screeners (NAPBS®) was formed in 2003, the idea of an accreditation process was simply an idea, but an idea that was a central driving force in order to demonstrate that background screening was a professional endeavor. Every profession has to have standards, and NAPBS accreditation represents the standards for the screening industry.

Before the NAPBS accreditation program, employers were largely on their own when selecting a background screening firm. Background screening is a critical function subject to intense legal regulation, and so the stakes are high. With hundreds upon hundreds of background screening firms to choose from, employers faced a confusing landscape of competing screening providers that made it hard to distinguish one background screening provider from another. Some background screening firms had ISO (International Organization for Standardization) certification while others had commercial rankings published by private for-profit publications, which only added to the confusion.

Background of Accreditation Program

In April 2009, in conjunction with its Annual Conference, the NAPBS launched the Background Screening Agency Accreditation Program (BSAAP) to serve as the industry's primary vehicle for quality assurance, self-regulation, and public accountability. The NAPBS also formed a governing body for its new accreditation program – the Background Screening Credentialing Council (BSCC) – to ensure firms seeking accreditation would meet a measurable standard of competence. The BSAAP advances professionalism in the background screening industry through the promotion of best practices, awareness of legal compliance, and development of standards that protect consumers.

Over the years, it took a lot of hard work from many very dedicated people who put the NAPBS accreditation program together on their own time, and the screening industry owes a debt of gratitude to all of those people who made the accreditation program a reality.

Currently, NAPBS accreditation is quickly becoming a requirement of many employers when considering a background screening provider since it is the only practical means of third party verification of the professionalism and competency of a particular screening firm.

How the Accreditation Program Works

Governed by a set of 58 clauses divided into six sections, the BSAAP recognizes a screening company's commitment to excellence, accountability, professional standards, and continued institutional improvement. Accreditation has become a widely recognized "seal of approval" that brings national recognition to background screening organizations. To become accredited, background screening firms must pass a rigorous audit of policies and procedures related to six critical areas:

- Consumer protection;
- Legal compliance;
- Client education;
- Product standards;
- Service standards; and
- General business practices.

The BSCC oversees the application process and ensures all organizations seeking accreditation meet or exceed a measurable standard of competence in these six areas. The accreditation program is open to any U.S.-based background screening company, and the process takes approximately six months from submission to completion. Companies are accredited for five years, and the program also includes an interim surveillance audit after three years. A copy of the Standards list is presented in the Addendum to Chapter 7.

Benefits & Challenges of Accreditation Program

The benefits of NAPBS accreditation are two fold, both external and internal.

Externally, accreditation is proof positive to an employer that a background screening firm meets the accreditation guidelines. Also it is very important for this industry to show it is self-regulating before government agencies seek to over control the industry. Accreditation is a big part of demonstrating the industry can police itself.

Internally, the accreditation process reinforces the standards needed to document policies, practices, and procedures for the auditor. Once a background screening firm makes the commitment of time and energy to undergo a third party audit though NAPBS accreditation, it is actually a very exciting process to review each standard and document compliance. It's also a tremendous training opportunity for the company to educate all employees.

Author Tip

Third Party Consultants for NAPBS Accreditation

Accreditation is a goal that is within reach of any background firm that feels it is important to demonstrate their professionalism and competency. There are even third party expert consultants that can assist a background firm in achieving accreditation, such as www.CRAzoom.com headed by Derek Hinton, a background screening industry veteran.

While every business has a number of pressing shorter term priorities, it is critical to think long term and strategically about what the future holds. In the background screening industry, the "writing is on the wall" so to speak that accreditation will be nothing less than a business necessity for a professional screening company competing in the current economic environment.

NAPBS Accredited Member Spotlight:

Employment Screening Resources (ESR)

Attorney Lester Rosen, Founder and CEO of Employment Screening Resources (ESR), who also served as chairperson of the steering committee that founded NAPBS and served as its first co-chair, recently shared his thoughts on the accreditation process.

Choice to Become Accredited

In ESR's view, NAPBS accreditation will become a requisite by a great number of employers when considering a screening provider, as it's the only practical means of third party verification as to the professionalism and competency of a particular firm. Without the accreditation program, employers have no real way of differentiating between providers of screening services. With accreditation as a baseline requirement, employers have a level of assurance that a background screening firm meets the stringent accreditation standards. It is just a matter of time before most employers will only want to deal with accredited screening firms.

Benefits of Accreditation

The benefits of NAPBS accreditation are two fold, both external and internal. Externally, accreditation is proof positive to an employer that a background screening firm meets the accreditation guidelines. Internally, our going through the accreditation process was educational and reinforced the standards that ESR already upheld. Also, since the NAPBS mission relates to professionalism in the screening industry, and with most other professions having some sort of accreditation or licensing process, it is very important for our industry to show that we are self-regulating before government agencies seek to over control the industry – accreditation is a big part of demonstrating that we police ourselves.

Challenges of Accreditation

The main challenge of accreditation is that it requires a real commitment to spend the time needed to document your policies, practices, and procedures for the auditor. However, once a background screening firm makes the commitment of time and energy to undergo a third party audit though NAPBS accreditation, it is actually a very exciting process to review each standard and document compliance. It's also a tremendous training opportunity for all members of the team.

Auditor Experience

The auditor who conducted both the 'desk review' and 'onsite audit' was extremely professional and very pleasant to work with. Even though the amount of ESR's accreditation material made Tolstoy's novel "War and Pace" look like a short story, the auditor was obviously familiar with the material and all of the details giving us confidence as we went through the process.

Accreditation Advice

Every business has a number of pressing shorter term priorities, and in addition to performing against these, it is critical to think strategically about what the future holds. In the background screening industry, ESR thinks the "writing is on the wall" so to speak that accreditation will be nothing less than a business necessity for a professional screening company competing in the current economic environment. Also, keep in mind that there is nothing about the accreditation process or standards that would prevent a professional firm from achieving accreditation. It may be a lot of work, but it's very doable for any size firm. There are even consulting firms that will now help a background screening firm through the process.

Other Thoughts

When the NAPBS was founded back in 2002 and 2003, the idea of an accreditation process was a central driving force in order to demonstrate that background screening was a professional endeavor. The thought was that as an industry we needed to create standards, or risk outside regulation. Every profession has to have standards, and NAPBS accreditation represents the standards for our industry. Over the years, it took a lot of hard work from many very dedicated people who put the accreditation program together on their own time, and the results have been nothing short of tremendous. The screening industry owes a debt of gratitude to all of those people who made the accreditation program a reality.

Originally Published in NAPBS® JOURNAL for November-December 2011

Sample Request for Proposal (RFP) for Background Screening Services

Introduction

This is a sample RFP provided by Employment Screening Resources® (ESR) to assist employers, Human Resources, and Security Professionals in selecting a provider for employment screening services.

Sample RFP for Background Screening Services

Dear Service Provider,

You are invited to submit a proposal for providing our firm with pre-employment background screening services. Please submit all responses directly to the following address: (Place your contact person, company name, company address and telephone number here). Please note the following:

- All proposals must be received by the followings date: (Add date)
- All bids must be submitted in writing. Faxes are not accepted.
- Employer reserves the right to accept or reject any bid in its sole discretion and is not obligated to choose to lowest bid.
- Proposals must remain valid for a period of 180 days.
- Please direct all questions and comments to the person indicated above only.
- Communication with any other individual may be considered grounds for disqualification.
- The bid will be evaluated based upon the following criteria:
  - Price
  - Proven Ability to meet needs
  - Turnaround time commitment
  - Customer service
  - Supplier Personal
  - Understanding of legal requirements
  - Infrastructure, including the system for tracking and reporting
  - Ease of reading screening reports
  - Additional services provided
  - Quality and completeness of product provided
  - Knowledge of the process involved

I. Services Offered

- Indicate if you provide following services, describe them and your methodologies: County felony and misdemeanor records
  - o Credit Reports
  - o Social Security traces
  - o Driving records
  - o Federal Records
  - o Employment verification
  - o Education verification
  - o Professional license
  - o Sexual Offender search
  - o Terrorist databases
  - o International criminal searches
  - o International employment and education verification
  - o Others
- Do you utilize the services of any subcontractors to fulfill criminal record searches, or any other search? If so, identify the methods used including quality control procedures.
- Do you use databases for any searches? If so, please describe:
  - o The nature of the database
  - o Any limitations on the usage of the database
  - o Any legal compliance issues, such as FCRA Section 613
- Please describe any quality control procedures you follow to ensure accuracy in your reporting of results.
- Please describe your dispute rate from consumers, your dispute process, and how that information is used for quality control.
- Does your firm have national capabilities? Describe.
- Does your firm have international capabilities? Describe.
- Describe your quality control procedures.

II. Turnaround Time

- What is your turnaround time for each of the services above?
- Describe your methodology to ensure turnaround time of reports.
- Are you able to generate turnaround time reports for each order that is placed and for each search conducted?
- Do you notify employers if there is a delay and how long?
- Is there a performance guarantee?

III. Reporting Format and Technology

- Describe the software or online system utilized by your firm.
- How does an employer send an order to your firm?
- How is an employer informed of results?
- How is an employer kept advised of status?
- What protection do you provide to keep customers limited to their candidate's data only.
- Please describe your ability to integrate with Applicant Tracking Systems or HR Information Systems.
- Please describe your ability to accept online candidate consents.
- Please provide a sample report.

IV. Legal Compliance

- Describe your understanding of the laws that govern pre-employment screening and your methodology for compliance with those laws.

- How does your firm keep updated on applicable federal and state laws affecting employment screening?
- Do you maintain a guide to applicable laws in all 50 states?
- Describe what assistance you will give us, if any, in legal compliance.
- Describe how you keep your clients updated on important legal changes.
- If there is a criminal case found, who determines if it is reportable and describe the methodology used to determine whether it is reportable.

V. Privacy and Security

- Does your firm have a Privacy and Data Security policy? If so, please provide.
- Describe your security and data protection practices, including any third party certifications.
- Does your firm send Personal and Identifiable Information (PII) outside of the United States for either for domestic or international screening? If so, please describe in detail.
- How do you vet new clients to ensure your services are in compliance with the FCRA? Does your firm utilize any home based workers who have access to (PII) about an applicant? If so, describe the process and describe how personal and identifiable applicant information is protected.
- Does your firm utilize home operators to complete employment and education verifications? If so, describe the process and describe how personal and identifiable applicant information is protected.
- Does your firm have a Service Organization Control SOC 2 Privacy designation issued in accordance with the American Institute of Certified Public Accountants (AICPA)?
- Is your firm aware of the EU-U.S. Privacy Shield Framework launched by the Department of Commerce and European Commission in 2016 to comply with European Union (EU) data protection requirements and how it will affect screenings of applicants from the EU?
- Has your firm received notification from the U.S. Department of Commerce's International Trade Administration (ITA) that its self-certification of adherence to the EU-U.S. Privacy Shield Framework is approved and effective?

VI. Customer Service

- Do you provide any customer training or continuing education? If so, please describe.
- Do you provide an account executive that will handle our account?
- Do you have an internal trouble ticket system? If so, describe how it works.
- If there is not a trouble ticket system, describe your internal methodology to ensure that customer service issues are addressed in a timely manner and that there is follow-through.
- Describe your problem escalation procedures in the event of a service issue.

VII. About Your Firm

- Please describe the background and experience of your firm.
- Please provide a short biography of the principals of your firm.
- Do you require a contract?
- Describe your account set-up procedures.
- Are there set-up fees?
- Can we set up a customized screening program?
- How do you handle billing an employer with multiple locations, or different departments?
- Do you have errors and omissions issuance? Describe.
- Please list representative clients.
- Please list three references. To the extent possible, choose references that have needs similar to our firm. Please provide full contact information.
- Is your firm a member of the trade association for background firms, the National Association of Professional Background Screeners (NAPBS)? If not a member, do you certify that you adopt and agree with their goals and standards?

- Has your firm been accredited by the NAPBS Background Screening Credentialing Council (BSCC) for proving compliance with the Background Screening Agency Accreditation Program (BSAAP)? If not, are you currently in the process of obtaining an NAPBS accreditation?
- If your firm is not accredited by NAPBS, is your firm in compliance with the NAPBS Accreditation guidelines? If not, please indicate in detail the steps being taken to be in compliance with NAPBS accreditation.
- Describe how you train your employees.
- Describe how you keep your employees updated on legal issues effecting screening.

VIII. Pricing

- Please provide pricing for each item listed above.
- Do you have any package plans? Please describe.
- Are there any other costs or expenses we should know about?

IX. Other Advantages

- Are there any other advantages in selecting your firm to provide pre-employment background screening services?
- There are many firms that provide this service. Why should we choose you?

Source: www.esrcheck.com/Resource-Center/Background-Screening-RFP/.

The 58 Clauses of the Background Screening Agency Accreditation Program

Here is a list of the 58 individual clauses of the National Association of Professional Background Screeners (NAPBS®) Background Screening Agency Accreditation Program (BSAAP) that every NAPBS Accredited Consumer Reporting Agency (CRA) must adhere to in order to remain in compliance. These standards can be modified. For the most current version, visit www.napbs.com/accreditation/.

Section 1 - Consumer Protection

1.1 Information Security Policy
CRA shall have a Written Information Security Policy (WISP). CRA shall designate one or more individuals within the organization who are responsible for implementing, managing and enforcing the information security policy.

1.2 Data Security
CRA shall have procedures in place to protect consumer information under the control of the CRA from internal and external unauthorized access. These procedures shall include specifications for the securing of information in both hard copy and electronic form, including information stored on portable and/or removable electronic devices

1.3 Intrusion and Data Security
CRA shall have procedures in place to reasonably detect, investigate and respond to an information system intrusion, including consumer notification where warranted.

1.4 Stored Data Security
CRA shall have procedures in place to reasonably ensure backup data is stored in an encrypted or otherwise protected manner.

1.5 Password Protocol

CRA shall require strong password protocol pursuant to current security best practices.

1.6 Electronic Access Control
CRA shall have procedures in place to control access to all electronic information systems and electronic media that contain consumer information. CRA shall have procedures in place to administer access rights. Users shall only be given the access necessary to perform their required functions. Access rights shall be updated based on personnel or system changes.

1.7 Physical Security
CRA shall have procedures in place to control physical access to all areas of CRA facilities that contain consumer information.

1.8 Consumer Information Privacy Policy
CRA shall have a Consumer Information Privacy Policy detailing the purpose of the collection of consumer information, the intended use, and how the information will be shared, stored and destroyed. The CRA shall post this policy on its Web site, if it has one, and will make said policy available to clients and/or consumers upon request in at least one other format.

1.9 Unauthorized Browsing
CRA shall have a policy that prohibits workers from searching files and databases unless they have a bona fide business necessity.

1.10 Record Destruction
When records are to be destroyed or disposed of, CRA shall follow FTC regulations and take measures to ensure that all such records and data are destroyed and unrecoverable.

1.11 Consumer Disputes
CRA shall have procedures in place for handling and documenting a consumer dispute that comply with the federal FCRA

1.12 Sensitive Data Masking
CRA shall have a procedure to suppress or truncate Social Security numbers and other sensitive data elements as required by law.

1.13 Database Criminal Records
When reporting potentially adverse criminal record information derived from a non-government owned or non-government sponsored/supported database pursuant to the federal FCRA, the CRA shall either: A) verify the information directly with the venue that maintains the official record for that jurisdiction prior to reporting the adverse information to the client; or B) send notice to the consumer at the time information is reported.

Section 2 - Legal Compliance

2.1 Designated Compliance Person(s)
The CRA shall designate an individual(s) or position(s) within the organization responsible for CRA's compliance with all sections of the federal FCRA that pertain to the consumer reports provided by the CRA for employment purposes.

2.2 State Consumer Reporting Laws
The CRA shall designate an individual(s) or position(s) within the organization responsible for compliance with all state consumer reporting laws that pertain to the consumer reports provided by the CRA for employment purposes.

2.3 Driver Privacy Protection Act (DPPA)
The CRA shall designate an individual(s) or position(s) within the organization responsible for compliance with the DPPA that pertain to the consumer reports provided by the CRA for employment purposes, if the CRA furnishes

consumer reports that contain information subject to the DPPA.

2.4 State Implemented DPPA Compliance

If the CRA furnishes consumer reports that contain information subject to the DPPA-implementing statutes in a particular state(s), the CRA shall designate an individual(s) or position(s) within the organization responsible for compliance with state implementations of the DPPA that pertain to the products and services provided by the CRA for employment purposes.

2.5 Integrity

CRA shall not engage in bribery or any other fraudulent activity to obtain preferential treatment from a public official.

2.6 Prescribed Notices

CRA shall provide client all federal FCRA-required, FTC-prescribed documents which the federal FCRA mandates be provided to client by the CRA (NOTE: CFPB now prescribes certain FCRA mandated notices)

2.7 Agreement from Client

Before providing consumer reports to clients, CRA shall obtain a signed agreement from client (referred to as "user" in federal FCRA) in which client agrees to meet the requirements of the federal FCRA, and applicable state and federal laws.

Section 3 - Client Education

3.1 Client Legal Responsibilities

CRA shall have procedures in place to inform client that they have legal responsibilities when using consumer reports for employment purposes. CRA shall recommend that client consult their legal counsel regarding their specific legal responsibilities.

3.2 Client Required Documents

CRA shall provide sample documents or inform client of specific documents which are needed to meet legal requirements regarding employer's procurement and use of consumer reports.

3.3 Truth in Advertising

CRA shall communicate to clients the nature of the original source, limitations, variables affecting the information available and scope of information provided by each consumer reporting product offered by the CRA.

3.4 Adverse Action

CRA shall inform client that there are legal requirements imposed by the federal FCRA and, in some instances, state consumer reporting laws, regarding taking adverse action against a consumer based on a consumer report. CRA shall recommend to client that they consult with counsel to develop a legally compliant adverse action policy.

3.5 Legal Counsel

CRA shall communicate to client that they are not acting as legal counsel and cannot provide legal advice. CRA shall communicate to client the importance of working with counsel to develop an employment screening program specific to their needs. CRA shall also communicate to client the necessity to work with counsel to ensure that client's policies and procedures related to the use of CRA-provided information is in compliance with applicable state and federal laws.

3.6 Understanding Consumer Reports

CRA shall provide guidance to client on how to order, retrieve, read and understand the information provided in consumer reports provided by the CRA.

3.7 Information Protection

CRA shall provide information to client regarding (1) the sensitive nature of consumer reports, (2) the need to protect such information and (3) the consumer report retention and destruction practices as outlined in the federal FCRA and the DPPA.

Section 4 - Product Standards

4.1 Public Record Researcher Agreement

CRA shall require a signed agreement from all non-employee public record researchers. The agreement shall clearly outline the scope of services agreed to by CRA and researcher, including jurisdictions covered, search methodology, depth of search, disclosure of findings, methodology and time frame for communication and completion of requests, methodology for confirming identity of subject of record(s), confidentiality requirements, and reinvestigation requirements.

4.2 Vetting Requirement

CRA shall have procedures in place to vet or qualify new public record researchers.

4.3 Public Record Researcher Certification

CRA shall require public record researcher to certify in writing that they will conduct research in compliance with all applicable local, state and federal laws, as well as in the manner prescribed by the jurisdiction which maintains the official record of the court; never obtain information through illegal or unethical means; and utilize document disposal and/or destruction methods pursuant to the federal FCRA.

4.4 Errors and Omissions Coverage (E&O)

CRA shall obtain proof of public record researcher's Errors and Omissions Insurance. If public record researcher is unable to provide proof of insurance, CRA shall maintain coverage for uninsured and/or underinsured public record researcher.

4.5 Information Security

CRA shall provide a secure means by which public record researcher will receive orders and return search results.

4.6 Auditing Procedures

CRA shall maintain auditing procedures for quality assurance in regard to their active public record researchers.

4.7 Identification Confirmation

CRA shall follow reasonable procedures to assure maximum possible accuracy when determining the identity of a consumer who is the subject of a record prior to reporting the information. CRA shall have procedures in place to notify client of any adverse information that is reported based on a name match only.

4.8 Jurisdictional Knowledge

The CRA shall designate a qualified individual(s) or position(s) within the organization responsible for understanding court terminology, as well as the various jurisdictional court differences if CRA reports court records.

Section 5 - Service Standards

5.1 Verification Accuracy

CRA shall maintain reasonable procedures to assure maximum possible accuracy when obtaining, recording and reporting verification information.

5.2 Current Employment

CRA shall have procedures in place to contact consumer's current employer directly only when authorized by client and/or consumer.

5.3 Diploma Mills

When attempting educational verifications from known or suspected diploma mills, CRA shall have reasonable procedures in place to advise client of such.

5.4 Procedural Disclosures

CRA shall provide full disclosure to clients about general business practices regarding number of attempts to verify information, what constitutes an "attempt," locate fees, fees charged by the employer or service provider and standard question formats prior to providing such services.

5.5 Verification Databases

If CRA compiles and stores employment or education verification information for sale, CRA shall have procedures in place to ensure that data is accurate at the time information is provided to end user and have procedures in place for handling consumer disputes.

5.6 Use of Stored Data

If CRA provides investigative consumer reports from stored data, CRA shall have procedures in place to ensure the CRA does not provide previously reported adverse information unless it has been re-verified within the past three months, or for a shorter time if required by state or local law.

5.7 Documentation of Verification Attempts

CRA shall have procedures in place to document all verification attempts made and the result of each attempt, in completing all verification services.

5.8 Outsourced Verification Services

CRA shall require a signed agreement from all providers of outsourced verification services. The agreement shall clearly outline the scope of services to be provided, verification methodology, documentation of verification efforts, disclosure of findings, time frame for communication and completion of requests, confidentiality requirements, reinvestigation requirements and other obligations as furnishers of information under the federal FCRA.

5.9 Conflicting Data

Should CRA receive information from the verification source subsequent to the delivery of the consumer report, and as a direct result of the initial inquiry, that conflicts with originally reported information, and that new information is received within 120 days of the initial report, (or as may be required by law), CRA shall have procedures in place to notify client of such information.

5.10 Professional Conduct

CRA shall train all employees engaged in verification work on procedures for completing verifications in a professional manner.

5.11 Authorized Recipient

If CRA is requesting verification by phone, fax, email or mail, CRA shall have procedures in place to confirm that verification request is directed to an authorized recipient.

Section 6 - General Business Practices

6.1 Character

Owners, officers, principals and employees charged with the enforcement of company policy must consent to undergo a criminal records check and be found free of convictions for any crimes involving dishonesty, fraud or moral turpitude.

6.2 Insurance

CRA shall maintain errors and omissions insurance. If CRA does not maintain errors and omission insurance, CRA must self-insure in a manner compliant with its state's insurance requirements.

6.3 Client Authentication

CRA shall have a procedure to identify and authenticate all clients prior to disclosing consumer reports or other consumer information. The procedure shall require the CRA to maintain written records regarding the qualification of each client who receives consumer reports or other consumer information.

6.4 Vendor Authentication

CRA shall have a procedure to identify and authenticate all vendors prior to disclosing consumer information. The procedure shall require the CRA to maintain written records regarding the qualification of each vendor who receives consumer information.

6.5 Consumer Authentication

CRA shall develop and implement requirements for what information consumers shall provide as proof of identity prior to providing file disclosure to the consumer. The CRA shall maintain procedures to document the information used to identify each consumer to whom file disclosure is provided.

6.6 Document Management

CRA shall have a written record retention and destruction policy pursuant to the federal FCRA.

6.7 Employee Certification

CRA shall require all workers to certify they will adhere to the confidentiality, security and legal compliance practices of the CRA.

6.8 Worker Training

CRA shall provide training to all workers on confidentiality, security and legal compliance practices of the CRA.

6.9 Visitor Security

CRA shall utilize a visitor security program to ensure visitors do not have access to consumer information.

6.10 Employee Criminal History

CRA shall conduct a criminal records check on all employees with access to consumer information when such searches can be conducted without violating state or federal law. These searches shall be conducted at least once every two years for the duration of their employment. Criminal offenses shall be evaluated to determine initial or continued employment based upon their access to consumer information and state and federal laws.

6.11 Quality Assurance

CRA shall have procedures in place to reasonably ensure the accuracy and quality of all work product.

6.12 Responsible Party

CRA shall have on staff one person designated to oversee and administer the certification process and future compliance by the CRA, including enforcement of the standard by all concerned. This person shall be vested with the responsibilities and authority attendant to this task, and shall be the CRA contact for the auditor and certification related matters for NAPBS®.

21 Shortcuts and Traps that Can Lead to Inaccurate Criminal Records

The following is summary of 21 ways that screening firms could potential take short cuts that may undermine the accuracy of criminal records data provided to an employer leading to either a false positive or a false negative.

21 Shortcuts and Traps that Can Lead to Inaccurate Criminal Records

Unfortunately, because there are so many moving parts when searching criminal records, there are numerous ways to cut corners. A screening firm may appear to be doing a complete job and yet take shortcuts under the hood that may allow them to advertise faster turnaround times, or to lower their internal costs and increase profits. But the real question is whether employers and job applicants are well served.

The problem for decision makers is that it can very difficult to know if a background screening firm is taking shortcuts or not. It requires a deep dive into a screening firm's back office practices. Unless an employer or Human Resources (HR) professional really understands how to take a look "under the hood," it can be very difficult know if a screening firm is taking the right steps to obtain accurate and complete information. To borrow an old expression, it can be difficult to understand how the sausage is made if you are not a sausage maker.

However, the following is a summary of 21 shortcuts that can be taken by firms providing criminal record information to employers that are not necessarily to the employer's advantage.

1. **Using a so-called national criminal database:** So-called national criminal databases offered by private firms are a source of confusion and potential mistakes. Although these databases are comprised of millions of records sourced from public records information from all 50 states, the depth, breadth, and accuracy varies widely.

   Because the information can be so hit and miss, it's a complete misnomer to call it a "national" criminal search. It's merely a large data dump of publically available court records that can be screen scraped, purchased in bulk, or obtained from some courts. In states that do not provide access to bulk-criminal records data, such as California, these databases are nearly useless.

   While such privately assembled databases can be useful to screening firms as an internal research tool, employers need to be aware that these databases are not a "real" standalone background check. When a screening firm is sued for providing inaccurate data, the use of an unconfirmed database record is often the source of the issue. For example, if a consumer obtains an expungement or there has been some other post-disposition change in status, there is little guarantee that private databases will be updated with that information. Employers need to ensure that any criminal provider is taking steps to ensure that impermissible information such as expungements are not being reported. The only way for a screening firm to ensure the information from such a database is accurate and actionable is to check the courthouse file to determine if the information is complete, accurate, and up to date.

2. **Using incomplete statewide system:** Some screening firms may try to save time and money by using statewide databases to avoid the cost and trouble of performing county court searches. However, state websites often have a disclaimer that the database has limitations, is subject to errors, and is not intended for commercial use. A limited number of states have a statewide records system that is the equivalent of courthouse searches, such as those

maintained by Washington, Oregon, and New York. A recent study by BRB Publications Inc. noted that some statewide criminal record repositories have inaccuracies that make the completeness, consistency, and accuracy of these records suspect. See: www.esrcheck.com/wordpress/2016/07/07/new-study-reveals-inaccuracies-in-state-criminal-record-repositories/.

3. **Screen Scraping & B2B automation:** Problems can be created if a screening firm tries to speed up turnaround time on criminal record searches by using automated computerized "connections" to various court websites by "scraping" information off screens or performing an automated connection routine. The problem is that a screening firm may be electronically obtaining information that is incomplete, old, or incorrect. Just because a court's criminal data is online does not mean it is accurate. A screening firm needs to demonstrate it went through a vetting process and is only using electronic access to courts that provides the same information they would get if they sent someone to the physical courthouse. If the electronic connection is not the functional equivalent of going to the physical courthouse, then the employer is not getting a real background check.

4. **Instant Searches:** The words "instant" and "criminal checks" simply do not belong together in the same sentence. An employer is well advised to avoid any screening service that advertises itself as providing "instant" criminal records. First of all, it is a potential violation of the accuracy requirements contained in the Fair Credit Reporting Act (FCRA), the federal law that regulates employment purpose background checks, when a screening firm provides database information with instant results. If there is any type of potential match, a professional screening firm will need to go through steps to verify that the record is, in fact, related to the applicant, and that the record is accurate and up to date as well as reportable, meaning there was no expungement and does not fall under any legal prohibition on reporting. A record that meets all of the above is considered is reliable and actionable. In addition, there are numerous counties in the U.S. where there is no electronic access or the access is not a real search because the electronic records are not complete and accurate. Any screening firm offering instant reports is offering potential litigation risk to both itself and its clients.

5. **Seven-year search shortcut:** Some firms sell a standard "seven-year" criminal search. Why seven years? Prior to the 1998 revision of FCRA, a Consumer Reporting Agency (CRA) was prohibited from reporting a criminal conviction that was older by more than seven years. There are some states that still enforce a seven-year reporting limitation based upon certain income limits, even though some of these state rules are likely pre-empted by the federal FCRA. But this limit is not always seven calendar years from the verdict. The seven-year limit was measured under federal law and remains measured under state law, from the date of disposition, release, or parole which may be much later than the date of the verdict, thereby making the information relevant and reportable. For example, if a person was convicted 12 years ago and was just released from custody 5 years ago, that would still be reportable. The seven-year limitation generally means being out of jail for seven years, not the age of the offense. If a screening firm is only looking for convictions occurring in the past seven years that can be a shortcut that only benefits the screening firm and can harm the employer. In addition, a good screening firm will also have measures in place to protect against revealing civil suits and judgments along with similar potentially adverse information that antedate the report by more than 7 years.

6. **Using substandard past address information to get less potential places to search:** When a screening firm provides a seven-year search that it represents to include all relevant addresses, the source of the past addresses is critical. A screening firm doing a real background check will use a source of information that provides as many addresses as possible, including addresses where the subject has worked or gone to school. However, a screening firm that wants to cut corners can choose to utilize just the subset of addresses contained in a credit report header, which normally provides fewer addresses to search, thereby reducing the cost to the CRA. That is another area where there a potential conflict of interest between the employer and the screening provider. The best practice is for a criminal records search to be based upon a past address reporting tool that gives the most addresses.

7. **Ignoring highly-related alias names:** Another potential trap for an unwary employer is whether a screening firm is only running the criminal record search based upon the provided name even if other logically valid "alias" names are known or developed as part of the screening. A screening firm cutting corners can choose to

intentionally wear blinders and ignore other names it is provided or discovered as part of developing past addresses to search. A screening firm may also purposely not request previously used names just to avoid having to do more searches. This is particularly troublesome if a screening firm is offering a flat price so that there is an incentive to run less searches in order to make more profit.

Employment Screening Resources® (ESR) uses its proprietary "Highly Related Alias Name Technology" to achieve a thorough name search taking into account, for example, when the name was changed so that appropriate counties are searched. The most common instance of former name(s) involves a female applicant who has changed her last name as a result of marriage. Although less common, both male and female applicants may have obtained a legal name change for other reasons through a civil court proceeding. Because of these possibilities, an employment application or screening form should ask for previous legal names and the dates of use.

8. **Claiming Alias Names are included at the same price:** A related issue is if a screening firm claims that all alias names that are located are included in the search provided no additional cost. This can be a danger signal that the screening firm is not doing a real criminal search but instead is relying upon the use of the so-called "national" criminal database discussed above. A real criminal search that includes an alias name requires that each name be searched separately. From the point of view of court records, searching for a John Smith versus a John Jones is two separate searches. That means each search is separate and independent. If a screening firm claims they are doing it all at once at no additional cost, the only unfortunate explanation is that they are using a databases or some sort of short cut and are not providing employers with a real criminal search.

9. **Ignoring other available information such as past employment when establishing search parameters:** Since county criminal searches are based upon where an applicant has lived, worked, or studied, past employment addresses can be very relevant. If a screening firm goes out of it way to avoid obtaining past employment locations or does not take those addresses into account, that is another example of a subtle shortcut that potentially puts an employer at risk.

10. **Ignoring Middle Names:** There are times when middle names can be used to either identify a record as belonging to a candidate, or eliminating the record from consideration. For example, if the record contains full middle name or initial different than the applicant's middle name or initial, a screening firm is on notice that more research is needed. However, there are limits to the use of middle name logic. A court record may not even have a middle name at all. A good screening firm will utilize algorithms that also address middle names or initials. There have also been instances where consumers used different middle initials on purpose in order to thwart a background check. The walk away point is that middle name matches or middle initial matches are an additional element to review, but they are not always the determining factor.

11. **Using call centers offshore or home based remote workers to access courthouse computers:** Another area of risk is offshore business processing centers in locations such as India or the Philippines to take advantage of cheaper labor to perform manual access of courthouse websites. A similar issue can be found if a screening firm uses home-based remote workers. One problem, of course, is the offshoring of Personal Identifiable Information (PII) of consumers outside of the privacy protections of U.S. laws that can arguably put job applicants at risk for offshore identity theft. At least one state, California, has a set of disclosure rules concerning offshoring of data that a background screening firm must also follow. Sending confidential data to homeworkers can also create security and data protection issues. Another potential issue is whether offshore or home workers have the necessary training and qualifications to navigate U.S. court systems and understand the records being viewed. There is no prohibition against using offshore or home-based workers, but employer may find that they want to ask questions to determine if such a practice meets their needs.

12. **Using untrained personnel to evaluate criminal records:** Related to offshore centers is whether a screening firm is using untrained personnel who are not native English speakers to make very complex decisions about criminal records. Since there are 50 states, each with their own rules and processes, it requires trained and knowledgeable people to understand what can and cannot be reported to an employer. Where it gets more complicated is that each case must be analyzed to determine if it is reportable. For example, a person may have

been charged with a felony but only plead guilty to a misdemeanor. It would be erroneous to report the case as a felony. Or a consumer may have been charged with several criminal counts but only found guilty of one count, with the remaining counts dismissed. Unless a screening firm employed skilled and experienced personnel who know how to read records of court proceedings, a screening firm may inaccurately report dismissed counts.

A competent background screening firm generally operates on the principle that it will not report information an employer cannot use. Although a screening firm does not provide legal advice, a competent firm will review the reportability of the record based upon generally accepted industry standards. Competent, experienced, and trained professionals need to determine if the record is accurate and actionable. If foreign workers are used, it can raise significant issues about the process. A firm such as ESR will only use native English speakers located in the U.S. that are highly trained and experienced to review the reportability of criminal records.

13. **Failure to have internal process or procedures to analyze if a criminal matter is reportable:** A related matter is to have internal processes and training material to help a screening firm make decisions on what criminal matters are reportable. It is critical for a CRA to have written policies and procedures for each state to fully understand what is or is not reportable. ESR compares all dispositions to its database of non-reportable and/or non-conviction state based restrictions so the client sees what is permitted under the circumstances.

14. **Reselling without quality control or knowledge of complex criminal reporting requirements:** Another trap to avoid in using a screening firm that is a reseller of criminal data provided by other firms and does not perform its own quality control to ensure that the criminal information supplied by their researchers is accurate and reliable. A credible screening firm will impose stringent quality control measures—including audits—to ensure accuracy and not just choose the cheapest supplier of data in order to increase its own profits. One common control is the use of a salting program to ensure that criminal researchers are performing their jobs properly.

15. **Ignoring consumer complaints that can lead to discovering errors in a background firm's process:** Another warning sign that a screening firm may not have processes in place to promote accuracy is the failure to examine its own complaints from consumers to determine if there is a pattern or practice that is leading to errors in reporting criminal records. The federal Consumer Financial Protection Bureau (CFPB) has made it clear that it expects a screening firm to review their own consumer complaint files in order to engage in process improvement for criminal record reporting.

16. **Relying on a "613" letter to correct any errors:** Background firms have a generalized duty of accuracy for all matters reported to an employer. Under the FCRA section 607(b), a background screening firm must "follow reasonable procedures to assure maximum possible accuracy of the information concerning the individual about whom the report relates." When a criminal result is reported that is likely to impact employment, that duty is even greater. Under FCRA section 613, a screening firm must either maintain "strict procedures" to ensure the information reported is complete or up to date or, as an alternative, can send a letter to the consumer that a criminal matter is being reported.

It is problematic if a screening firm interprets the "letter" process liberally to mean that as long as they send a letter to the consumer, the screening firm is absolved of all responsibility for accuracy. The problem, however, is that the so-called "letter" option does not relieve a screening firm of the legal duty to comply with the general duty to use "reasonable procedures for maximum possible accuracy." That means if a screening firm either knows, or reasonably should know, that they are reporting junk data from databases, just sending a 613 letter notice to a consumer does not mean the screening firm can forget about taking precautions. Even with sending a letter to the applicant, there is always an underlying duty of accuracy.

As a result, employers are advised to carefully consider if they want the liability and potential legal entanglements that can result if they use screening firms that utilize a letter to the consumer as a substitute for taking real steps to ensure accuracy. Just relying on a letter does not provide an employer with assurance that the screening firm is performing real background checks. Some firms, like ESR are now giving consumers an extra level of protection by both maintaining strict procedures for accuracy of criminal records as well as sending out a letter to the consumer.

17. **Using artificial limits on how many matters reported:** An employer needs to ensure that their screening firm has not decided to artificially limit the number of criminal cases where a consumer appears to have a large number of records. The logic appears to be to save time and money for the background firm since after a certain number of records, an employer may not need additional information. There are a number of problems with this approach. First, an inexperienced researcher may not know which criminal records are relevant and which ones should not even be reported. Secondly, a firm may report less serious matters and not report a case that is relevant to the position. Third, other than saving the screening firm time and money, there is no advantage to the employer.

18. **Searching only the Primary County in a ZIP code:** Many screening firms use zip codes as a basis for determining which counties to search. One big problem is that many zip codes cover more than one county, and a standard zip code database may only report the primary county in the zip code. That means unless a screening firm has researched this issue and has formulated a way to avoid missing counties, critical and relevant counties can be missed. This can result in a "false negative" in a background screening report.

19. **Not revealing search may be limited to the central Court only:** A related issue is that many counties in the U.S. have more than one court. Typically, a county may have lower courts, such as municipal or justice of the peace courts where more minor cases are heard. There are also counties where there may be multiple branches of the higher court where serious cases are handled. Here is the problem. When a background firm researcher looks for county criminal records, the search is conducted at the "central" court. The central court may or may not have records from other courts located the same county. It is important for a screening firm to clearly alert employers that only the central court is typically being searched, or an employer can have a false sense of security thinking every court in the county is being searched for criminal reports, which in many counties is not practical and would drive up the cost of a criminal search substantially. The important point is the employers understand there may be limits to what is available.

20. **Failure to advise employer about Ban the Box or Individualized Assessment rules:** Another area of potential liability for employer and screening firms is providing criminal information without advising employers on the limits on using criminal records under applicable "Ban the Box" rules and discrimination rules. Numerous states, counties, and cities have passed forms of Ban the Box rules that places limitations on when and what an employer can ask about past criminal records, and in some instances will limit an employer's use of certain records. In addition, employers need to be aware that automatic elimination of a person with a criminal record can result in an allegation of discrimination. The EEOC Guidance on the use of criminal records issued in April of 2012 examines in depth the fair and non-discriminatory use of criminal records in hiring, and also urges employers to utilize an "Individualized Assessment" approach to criminal records. To learn more, read the complimentary ESR whitepaper "Practical Steps Employers Can Take to Comply with EEOC Record Guidance" by visiting www.esrcheck.com/Whitepapers/.

21. **Reporting arrests or non-convictions:** This is an area that can get employers and background firms sued. Reporting records that have been expunged or judicially set aside or arrests not resulting in convocations can be forbidden under state law.

21 Suggested Questions for Your Current Background Screening Provider

In order to avoid receiving criminal information that is incomplete, incorrect, or not actionable, employers may want to ask their background screening providers the following 21 questions.

1. Does your firm use a so-called national criminal database? If so:
   a. Please describe how it is used.
   b. Please describe your understanding of the accuracy and value of the data in such a database.
   c. Please describe steps you take to ensure accuracy before information is reported to the employer.
2. Does your firm provider use any statewide systems? If so:

    a.   Please describe how it is used.

    b.   Please describe your understanding of the accuracy and value of the data in such a database.

    c.   Please describe steps you take to ensure accuracy before information is reported to the employer.

3.   Does your firm use screen scraping and B2B automation to obtain information directly from courts? If so:

    a.   Please describe how it is used.

    b.   Please describe your understanding of the accuracy and value of the data in such a database.

    c.   Please describe steps you take to ensure accuracy before information is reported to the employer.

4.   Does your firm provide "instant" criminal checks? If so:

    a.   Please describe how it is used.

    b.   Please describe your understanding of the accuracy and value of the data in such a database.

    c.   Please describe steps you take to ensure accuracy before information is reported to the employer.

5.   Does your firm use a seven-year rule for reporting? If so:

    a.   Please describe and give example of how the seven year period is calculated.

6.   How does your firm obtain past address information? If so:

7.   Does your firm utilize highly-related alias names in determining where to search? If so:

    a.   Please describe your policies and procedures.

8.   Does your firm include alias names are as part of the same price? If so:

    a.   Please describe how alias names are searched.

    b.   Please describe tools used to ensure accuracy.

    c.   Are alias names searched only by use of a database?

9.   Does your firm utilize other available information such as past employment when establishing criminal search parameters? If so, please describe.

10. Does your firm consider middle names or initial in determining if a record is reportable? If so, please describe your processes and procedures.

11. Does your firm utilize using offshore or remote to access courthouse computers? If so, please describe processes utilized to ensure accuracy.

12. Who does your firm use to evaluate if a criminal record is accurate and reportable? If so, describe educational and training process for anyone with that responsibility.

13. Does your firm have an internal process or procedures to analyze if a criminal matter is reportable? If so, please describe.

14. Describe your firm's quality control and knowledge of complex criminal reporting requirements? If using another firm to provide criminal records, describe how you ensure accuracy and compliance from third party sources.

15. Does your firm systematically review consumer or requests for re-investigation of criminal records? If so, please describe.

16. Does your firm utilize a 613 letter sent to consumers? If so, please describe your process and procedures surrounding the sending of 613 letters.

17. Does your firm report all available criminal records that can be reported?

18. How does your firm utilize ZIP codes in determining where to search for criminal records?

19. Where a county has more than one court, which court do you search and is that policy published anywhere online or in your client contract?

20. Does your firm stay current on Ban the Box and EEOC compliance issues and how do you communicate such information to your clients?

21. How does your firm guard against reporting non-convictions or offenses that have been expunged or otherwise set aside?

Repetition of Criminal Incident Violates FCRA

The case described below further underscores that background screening is far from being a data driven endeavor where employers are just given data. It is a professional endeavor that is heavily legally regulated and can be unbelievably complex. It requires the services of background firms that have a great deal of ability and knowledge when it comes to federal and state legal compliance.

Federal Court Rules Unnecessary Repetition of Single Criminal Incident can be Misleading and be the Basis of an Allegation for Punitive Damages Against Background Screening Firm

A case decided by a Federal District Court demonstrates the need for background screening firms to exercise reasonable procedures for maximum possible accuracy in order to avoid lawsuits for punitive damages.

In this case, the plaintiff alleged among other things that his background report unnecessarily repeated information about a single criminal incident multiple times, causing the criminal record to appear much more serious than it was. The case was brought on behalf of not only the plaintiff, but also on behalf of "the thousands of employment applicants throughout the country who have purportedly been the subject of prejudicial, misleading and inaccurate background reports performed by Defendant and sold to employers."

The plaintiff complained that the repeated reference to a single incident was inaccurate under the federal Fair Credit Reporting Act (FCRA) because it was misleading in such a way and to such an extent that it could be expected to affect employment decisions.

The plaintiff contended this constituted a violation of FCRA section 607(b) which states:

> *(b) Accuracy of report. Whenever a consumer reporting agency prepares a consumer report it shall follow reasonable procedures to assure maximum possible accuracy of the information concerning the individual about whom the report relates.*

The background firm brought a motion to dismiss on the basis the plaintiff did not state a claim upon which relief could be granted. In reviewing this motion, the Court did not make any factual determination, but instead assumed the plaintiff's allegations were true for purposes of the motion. The Court then determined that if all the factors are assumed to be true, if there is a basis for a judgment in favor of the plaintiff.

The plaintiff also asked for punitive damages. The background firm requested that claim be dismissed.

The Court ruled the prevailing national rule is a claim can be made where the plaintiff alleges sufficient facts in the legal pleadings to demonstrate even an accurate report can be misleading if it presents information in such a way it is misleading or it creates a materially misleading impression. (Although the 6th Circuit has adopted a more limited rule that looks at the technical accuracy of the report, the Court noted the majority of courts have agreed on a broader definition that would include misleading information.)

It is important to note, however, that while it was still a factual issue for the trier of fact (such as jury or a judge in the case of a Court trial) as to whether the information was misleading, the mere fact that a background report may be incorrect or misleading does not prove that a background firm did not utilize reasonable procedures. In some circumstances, the error can be so egregious that the error itself demonstrates a lack of reasonable procedures. The background firm however, still has the opportunity to present evidence that even though there was an error, the firm uses reasonable procedures, and the error was not a usual occurrence.

To prevail in a claim for an erroneous, inaccurate or misleading background report, a plaintiff must generally prove that:

- There was inaccurate or misleading information in a report;

- The report was inaccurate because a screening firm failed to exercise reasonable care;
- There was harm to the consumer; and
- The harm was caused by the background firm.

The case also discussed the punitive damages allegation which the background screening firm sought to dismiss. The background firm argued, among other things, that any alleged error in the report did not rise to the level of willful recklessness under Supreme Court case of *Safeco Ins Co. v. Burr, 551 U.S. 47 (2001)*. That case arguably lowered the threshold for punitive damages against a background screening firm. Here, the background firm argued that the allegations made against it did not meet to the standards in the Safeco case. However, the court held that the "statutory text at issue here …has a plain and clearly ascertainable meaning." Since the allegations in case were that the background firm's conduct under FCRA section 607(b) could be found to be an objectively unreasonable interpretation of the statute, the plaintiff had the right to request punitive damages.

It should be noted that the actual case is much more detailed and contains other issues. In addition, it is critical to note that the motion was decided at the stage where the court only had legal pleadings and allegations, and there have been no actual facts determined.

However, the case does have some walkway points for background screening firms:

- Unnecessary reporting of a single criminal event multiple times in a background report where the impact is arguably to mislead an employer into believing that the consumer's background is more serious than it really is can be the basis for a claim of inaccuracy.
- Given the presence of punitive damages, it is even more critical for screening firms to pay close attention to their legal obligations. Errors made in such a way that is arguably objectively unreasonable under the plain meaning of the FCRA or in violation of clearly stated authority, can raise the stakes in any litigation.

The case is at www.paed.uscourts.gov/documents/opinions/10d0473p.pdf.

State Criminal Record Repositories Article

The following is an article from BRB Publications, Inc. (www.brbpublications.com) about State Criminal Record Repositories posted on June 16, 2016, that is available at www.brbpublications.com/documents/crimrepos.pdf.

New Facts About the Currency and Accuracy of Criminal Records at State Criminal Record Repositories

Employers and state occupation licensing boards often depend on states' criminal record repositories as primary resources when performing a criminal record background check. However, these entities may not realize that a search of these record repositories may not be as accurate and complete as assumed, regardless if fingerprints are submitted.

There are three key reasons why the completeness, consistency, and accuracy of state criminal record repositories could be suspect—

1. Timeliness of Receiving Arrest and Disposition Data
2. Timeliness of Entering Arrest and Disposition Data into the Repository
3. Inability to Match Dispositions with Existing Arrest Records

The basis for these concerns is supported by documented facts provided by the U.S. Department of Justice (DOJ). Every two years the DOJ's Bureau of Justice Statistics releases an extensive *Survey of State Criminal Record Repositories*. The latest survey, released December 2015 and based on statistics compiled as of Dec 31, 2014, is a 117-page document with 36 data tables. The survey is available at www.ncjrs.gov/pdffiles1/bjs/grants/249799.pdf.

Below are some eye-catching facts reflected from the current *Survey*:

- 8 states report 25% or more of all dispositions received could NOT be linked to the arrest/charge information in the state criminal record database. 14 states don't know how many dispositions they have that cannot be linked. (Table 8a)
- 20 states have over 3 million unprocessed or partially processed court dispositions, ranging from 200 in Michigan and North Dakota to over 1 million in Nevada. (Table 14)
- 11 states report at least a 50 day backlog between the time when a felony case is decided and when the record is entered in that state's criminal history database. 18 states do not know how long the delay is. (Table 14)

The statistics below are taken directly from this *Survey*.

State	% of Arrests in last 5 years that have final case dispositions recorded (Table 1)	Percentage of all dispositions received that could NOT be linked to a specific arrest record.	Average # of Days between occurrence of final felony court disposition and receipt of data by repository	Average # of Days between receipt of final felony court disposition and entry in state criminal database
AL	20%	unknown	1	nr
AK	91%	unknown	23	35
AR	79%	1%	21	1
AZ	66%	16%	16	2
CA	na	8%	nr	60
CO	34%	44%	0	0
CT	98%	15%	1	1
DE	96%	0%	1	1
DC	43%	nr	nr	nr
FL	66%	28%	28	1
GA	85%	0%	30	2
HI	89%	22%	9	0
IA	88%	2%	7	7
ID	39%	nr	1	1
IL	37%	3%	30	32
IN	43%	40%	nr	1
KS	41%	nr	nr	nr
KY	19%	18%	90	90
LA	na%	14%	na	60
MA	na	nr	nr	nr
MD	95%	26%	10	0
ME	65%	unknown	15	0
MI	75%	11%	248	2,233
MN	nr	nr	<1	1
MO	70%	17%	507	2
MS	11%	nr	nr	2
MT	53%	5%	16	32
NC	72%	0%	12	0

State	% of Arrests in last 5 years that have final case dispositions recorded (Table 1)	Percentage of all dispositions received that could NOT be linked to a specific arrest record.	Average # of Days between occurrence of final felony court disposition and receipt of data by repository	Average # of Days between receipt of final felony court disposition and entry in state criminal database
ND	81%	nr	nr	0
NE	75%	0%	1	1
NH	83%	41%	nr	nr
NJ	83%	19%	nr	7
NM	20%	nr	nr	nr
NV	55%	44%	nr	nr
NY	88%	8%	1	1
OH	40%	47%	na	na
OK	34%	nr	30	30
OR	78%	12%	na	100
PA	62%	26%	nr	1
RI	na	0%	5	5
SC	na	unknown	16	1
SD	na	nr	nr	nr
TN	75%	2%	30	nr
TX	92%	2%	30	1
UT	72%	19%	0	0
VA	89%	21%	14	14
VT	88%	5%	60	60
WA	94%	3%	7	5
WI	83%	8%	nr	nr
WV	na	2%	nr	nr
WY	82%	3%	60	2

Editor's Note: This information should not be confused with criminal record data obtained from centralized state judicial court systems.

Studies Cited by EEOC Concerning Recidivism and Statistics

The Studies Cited by the EEOC Concerning Recidivism

The following chapter summarizes two important areas for employers dealing with criminal records:

1. Studies cited by the **U.S. Equal Employment Opportunity Commission (EEOC)** in the 2012 Guidance on criminal records concerning the time period that criminal records are relevant.
2. Statistics from the **Bureau of Justice Statistics (BJS)** on recidivism in the U.S.

The reason this is relevant for employers is because of the need to determine an appropriate "look back" period for criminal records. That literally means how far back an employer can go in looking at criminal matters, or to put it another way, how old is too old when it comes to criminal records.

If employers go too far back, there is a concern a consumer will be denied employment unfairly if the criminal matter is too old to be relevant. On the other hand, if there is an artificial cut-off date that is unreasonably short, employers may be denied important information.

Studies cited by the EEOC in the 2012 Guidance on Criminal Records

Review of Carnegie Mellon Study on Redemption for Purposes of Employment

One study cited by the U.S. Equal Employment Opportunity Commission (EEOC) in its guidance is a 2009 study released by researchers from Carnegie Mellon University. The study attempted to devise a model to quantify what most people assume intuitively – that the relevance of a criminal record for employment recedes over time when a person is not re-arrested. The study looks to develop a methodology to measure how much time must pass before an applicant with a criminal record is no greater risk than an applicant without a criminal record. (Blumstein, A. and Nakamura, K. *"Redemption in the Presence of Widespread Criminal Background Checks,"* Criminology, Volume 47, Issue 2, pp 327-359 (May 2009)).

The study focused on the problems faced by ex-offenders in obtaining employment due to the perception that once a person has offended in the past, they are more likely to do so in the future. The study sought to explore empirically when a past criminal act was no longer relevant so a person could be considered to be "redeemed" for purposes of seeking employment.

The study was based upon data from the state of New York for individuals first arrested within New York State at ages 16, 18, and 20 for three specific crimes: robbery, burglary, and aggravated assault. The study was seeking to establish two values. First, the study was aimed at determining how many years must pass before the risk of re-offending was no greater than for other individuals of the same age. The second value was how many years must pass before the chance of re-offending was no greater than that of the general population that never offended.

The study found that with time, a person with a criminal record was no greater threat than persons without a criminal record. Depending upon the offenses included in the study and the age at which the offenses were committed, the study suggested that after approximately 4½ to 8 years without further arrests, an offender had a minimal risk of re-offending. Of course, the more violent the offense, the longer the time would be required before a person could be considered "redeemed." Serious crimes such as murder, rape, or child molestation were not part of this particular study, but presumably more serious crimes would have a different result.

Although there is a temptation for the press to take "sound bites" from the findings, the authors were clear that much more study was needed, and there are substantial issues still to be addressed. The authors' characterization that the study represents a "significant step forward in area where so little is known empirically" is well-taken.

The study does not have nearly enough data to reach conclusions from which policy recommendations can be effectively made, and has a number of drawbacks that can affect its reliability. Many of these limitations were acknowledged by the authors.

- First, the study was based only on records from New York State. Records maintained by federal law enforcement were not available, and it is clear from the study that the authors wanted to examine federal records and those of other states as well.
- Second, the study notes a number of issues that the researchers indicated needed further consideration. For example, the researchers were unable to determine whether offenders re-offended out of state. Without access to that data, it is certain the study was not totally accurate in terms of how many re-offended, which would have skewed the result in favor of ex-offenders.

Another very critical issue raised by the researchers is that further study is needed to differentiate between arrests only and those cases that ended up with a conviction. This is most critical since overall it would appear cases resulting in a conviction would be more serious than an arrest only. Including individuals who were never convicted could significantly skew the time required for a criminal record to lose relevance to a number that is artificially low.

In addition, arrests not resulting in convictions are not generally as relevant to employment decisions, since the FCRA limits the reporting of arrests to seven years and many states prohibit reporting arrests without convictions at all. Even if arrests are considered, the EEOC cautions employers to give the arrest no weight unless the employer can ascertain the underlying facts.

Another critical area the authors indicate needs to be taken into account in further studies is the amount of time an individual spent in custody. If someone committed a serious crime five years ago and just got out of custody, it is doubtful the person could be considered "redeemed" for purposes of all types of employment.

Yet another issue is the fact more studies are needed to research a much wider range of offenses before coming to conclusions that can be used as the basis for policy recommendations.

In reviewing the study, it appears there are two unstated assumptions that need to be folded into the analysis as well. First is the apparent assumption that criminals in 1980 are the same as criminals in 2009. The problem with this assumption is there has arguably been an explosion in streets gangs, drug sales, new potent drugs, and gun violence in the past few decades. Before utilizing a study for policy changes, this question should be explored.

The second assumption is just because a person was not re-arrested that consequently he or she has stayed clean and is closer to a point of redemption. This overlooks the fact there are large numbers of unsolved crimes, and not everyone is arrested for every crime that he or she commits. It is entirely possible these individuals committed new crimes for which they were not caught. Of course, it is also possible that people with no criminal records may have committed crimes where they were never arrested as well, but one cannot assume without additional study that both groups get away with crimes at the same rate.

The bottom-line is these drawbacks suggest it is entirely possible that the actual point of redemption may well turn out to be substantially longer than suggested in this initial study. This underlines, once again, it is extremely premature to draw policy conclusions from this one study.

The study did recite in general terms why employers were concerned about hiring individual with criminal records, but perhaps not to the degree needed. When bad hiring decisions are made, horrendous harm can be done. The Parade of Horribles resulting from hiring an unsuitable candidate can range from workplace violence that results in death, grave harm, or other serious matters, to lawsuits that could ruin a business.

Although alluded to in the study, attention should be directed to the fact there are a substantial number of state laws which in fact protect applicants from the unfair use of past criminal records. The study reports correctly that the availability of past convictions has risen dramatically due to computerization as well as the number of background checks demanded. It is equally important to emphasize the tremendous growth in state laws that limit the use of criminal records, as well as laws that prohibit the use of criminal data not resulting in convictions or cases that were judicially set aside under state law.

Ironically, the use of a mathematical approach taking into account the type of crime and age when first committed could result in discrimination. The EEOC clearly discourages automated decision-making regarding the use of criminal records. As stated earlier, the EEOC Guidance suggests employers should not automatically reject an applicant on the basis of a conviction, but should consider whether there is a business justification by taking into account the nature and gravity of the crime, the nature of the job, and the time that has passed. Assigning a numerical value to a person based upon a mathematical formula and treating that person accordingly may not be an improvement over the current system and in fact may be a step backwards.

The study also notes that the time period can be affected by the risk that an employer is willing to tolerate. What that appears to be driving at is the notion that risk is related to the nature of the job, which is one of the EEOC factors. Jobs with higher risk may well require a greater period of time. For example, a petty theft committed three years ago would logically have little to do with a job on a refrigerator manufacturing line. It may however affect if a person should handle a cash register. In other words, the amount of time required for the point of redemption also relates to the risks associated with the job. The problem with this general area of research is that there is a lack of attention paid to studying how to assign the risk associated with all of the various jobs available in the U.S. Further research on risk factors would appear to be a requirement before policy can rationally be changed.

If anything, this study demonstrates that trying to predict a future "lack of dangerousness" is just as difficult as predicting future "dangerousness." This study is critical since this entire area of research is at an embryonic state. Much more study is needed before a broad general rule can be articulated across all situations and all jobs that after a certain time, a past criminal conviction is statistically not relevant.

The bottom line is that is it premature to contemplate policy changes based upon one study where the meaning of the data is not fully understood and where a great deal more work needs to be done. There are some policy recommendations in the study, which are consistent with a number of recommendations commonly discussed concerning this issue. However, this study is not an appropriate vehicle at this point for policy recommendations.

The policy recommendations are also rendered less effective due to an apparent lack of appreciation by the study as to how certain things actually work in "the real world." For example, the study discusses that certain sealed or expunged records that occur earlier in time and are no longer relevant need to be removed. In fact, a large number of states already prohibit the use of such records, and they are removed by background screening firms from reports. The authors discuss issues related to problems with setting aside convictions and the problems related to concealment of records. They do not appear to understand that in reality, public records are rarely physically destroyed. The records are still generally available even if there is a pardon or some other judicial set aside.

The current protections afforded to applicants are laws that either prohibit screening firms from reporting the record or prohibit employer from using them. For the most part, it is the background screening industry that protects applicants by filtering out records that are not reportable. A number of states already have some sort of seven-year rule, and there are numerous restrictions as to what employers can consider. These issues underscore the need for an interdisciplinary approach which includes experts in background screening and public records to be included in these discussions.

It should be noted that most background screeners take great effort to educate employers that criminal records cannot be used automatically to prevent employment, and the screening industry's trade association has in fact donated money to programs to assist ex-offenders to re-enter society. No one denies that everyone needs a job to be a taxpaying, law-abiding citizen and that as a society, it is better to build more schools and hospitals than prisons. However, not every applicant is suited to every job, and the role of the screening industry is to advise employers of the facts so they can make intelligent selection decisions.

The study *Redemption in the Presence of Widespread Criminal Background Checks* is available at www.heinz.cmu.edu/research/233full.pdf.

Other Recidivism Studies Cited in the EEOC Guidance

The following recidivism studies were cited in the updated EEOC Guidance for the use of arrest and conviction records in employment decisions. As one study notes, "these findings are but a first look at this important question. To further understand patterns of desistance, we encourage further inquiry into this issue." These studies are, at best, a first step towards creating the necessary information for informed discussion about the relative risks of offending presented by individuals with past criminal records.

These studies tend to confirm the comments made in the Carnegie Mellon University study that this is an area where very little is known empirically. As in the Carnegie Mellon University study, there are issues as to the size of the sample, whether the sample is representative, as well as unstated assumptions such as a lack of a subsequent arrest or conviction means the subject was crime free during a relevant period. At the end of the day, the best that one could rationally conclude is that depending upon the nature of the offense, the age and frequency of the offense or offenses, and the time lapse between any new offenses, that over time, in some circumstances and for some people, the relevancy of past criminal conduct in term of employment decisions diminishes. This is likely a proposition that most reasonable employers would normally accept, even in the absence of academic studies.

The real issue however is that in the real-world, employers that create the jobs that are responsible for the economy of the county need to make real decisions about real individuals, in a legal environment where even one mistake will lead to a lawsuit for negligent hiring, not to mention the legal and financial nightmare associated with a bad hiring decision. A theoretical academic construct that over time for some people in some circumstances that past criminal records may be less relevant is not very helpful. The following studies, although extremely interesting and critically important, have hardly matured to a level of scientifically tested empirical evidence upon which social policies can be decided much less serve as the basis for hiring decisions.

- *'The Predictive Value of Criminal Background Checks: Do Age and Criminal History Affect Time to Redemption?'* by Shawn D. Bushway, Paul Nieuwbeerta, and Arjan Blokland
    - Published in Criminology, Volume 49, Issue 1, pp. 27-60 ©2011 American Society of Criminology.
    - The study is available online (limited access) at http://dx.doi.org/10.1111/j.1745-9125.2010.00217.x or on the website of the Netherlands Institute for the Study of Crime and Law Enforcement (NSCR), a research institute of the Netherlands Organization for Scientific Research, at www.nscr.nl/index.php?option=com_content&view=article&id=239%3Ahoe-lang-behouden-strafbladen-hun-voorspellende-waarde-publicatie&catid=47%3Apublicaties&Itemid=123&lang=en.
    - Email coauthor Arjan Blokland at ablokland@nscr.nl to receive a copy.
- *'The Risk of Offending: When do Ex-Offenders Become Like Non-Offenders?'* by Keith Soothill & Brian Francis

- o Available at www.docstoc.com/docs/36215747/WHEN-DO-EX-OFFENDERS-BECOME-LIKE
- *'Enduring Risk? Old Criminal Records and Short-Term Predictions of Criminal Involvement'* by Megan C. Kurlychek, University of South Carolina, Robert Brame, University of South Carolina, and Shawn D. Bushway, University of Maryland
    - o Available at http://blogs.law.columbia.edu/4cs/files/2008/11/crime-and-delinquency-racine.pdf
- *'Scarlet Letters and Recidivism: Does an Old Criminal Record Predict Future Offending?'* by Megan C. Kurlychek, Robert Brame, and Shawn D. Bushway.
    - o Available at: www.jjay.cuny.edu/centersinstitutes/pri/events/032406Desistance/ScarletLetter.pdf

Repeat Offenders and Recidivism

The other relevant statistics when considering an appropriate "look back" period for the relevancy of criminal record concern recidivism. There is voluminous material on the topic but the report below provides a good summary of the subject.

In April 2014, the Bureau of Justice Statistics (BJS) released a report titled *Recidivism of Prisoners Released in 30 States in 2005: Patterns from 2005 to 2010 (NCJ 244205)* written by Alexia D. Cooper, Ph.D., Matthew R. Durose, and Howard N. Snyder, Ph.D. The report examined the 5-year post-release offending patterns of persons released from state prisons in 2005 by offender characteristics, prior criminal history, and commitment offense and provided estimates on the number and types of crimes former inmates commit both prior to their imprisonment and after release.

A core portion of the report tracked a sample of former inmates from 30 states for five years following their release from prison in 2005 and the findings are based on prisoner records obtained from the state departments of corrections through the National Corrections Reporting Program (NCRP) and criminal history records obtained through requests to the FBI's Interstate Identification Index (III) and state repositories via the International Justice and Public Safety Network (Nlets). Highlights show that among the 404,638 state prisoners released in 30 states in 2005 are below.

- About two-thirds (67.8%) of released prisoners were arrested for a new crime within 3 years, and three-quarters (76.6%) were arrested within 5 years.
- Within 5 years of release, 82.1% of property offenders were arrested for a new crime, compared to 76.9% of drug offenders, 73.6% of public order offenders, and 71.3% of violent offenders.
- More than a third (36.8%) of all prisoners who were arrested within 5 years of release were arrested within the first 6 months after release, with more than half (56.7%) arrested by the end of the first year.
- Two in five (42.3%) released prisoners were either not arrested or arrested once in the 5 years after their release.
- A sixth (16.1%) of released prisoners were responsible for almost half (48.4%) of the nearly 1.2 million arrests that occurred in the 5-year follow-up period.
- An estimated 10.9% of released prisoners were arrested in a state other than the one that released them during the 5-year follow-up period
- Within 5 years of release, 84.1% of inmates who were age 24 or younger at release were arrested, compared to 78.6% of inmates ages 25 to 39 and 69.2% of those age 40 or older.

Additional findings mentioned in the report include:

- Among prisoners released in 2005 in 23 states with available data on inmates returned to prison, about half (50 percent) had either a parole or probation violation or an arrest for a new crime within three years that led to imprisonment, and more than half (55 percent) had a parole or probation violation or an arrest within five years that led to imprisonment.
- The longer released prisoners went without being arrested, the less likely they were to be arrested at all during the follow-up period. For example, 43 percent of released prisoners were arrested within one year of release,

compared to 13 percent of those not arrested by the end of year four who were arrested in the fifth year after release.

- Released prisoners who were incarcerated for a violent, property or drug crime were more likely than other released inmates to be arrested for a similar type of crime. Regardless of the incarceration offense, the majority (58 percent) of released prisoners were arrested for a public order offense within five years of release. An estimated 39 percent of released prisoners were arrested within five years for a drug offense, 38 percent for a property offense and 29 percent for a violent offense.

- Recidivism was highest among males, blacks and young adults. By the end of the fifth year after release, more than three-quarters (78 percent) of males and two-thirds (68 percent) of females were arrested, a 10 percentage point difference that remained relatively stable during the entire 5-year follow-up period.

- Five years after release from prison, black offenders had the highest recidivism rate (81 percent), compared to Hispanic (75 percent) and white (73 percent) offenders.

- Recidivism rates declined with age. Within five years of release, 84 percent of inmates who were age 24 or younger at release were arrested for a new offense, compared to 79 percent of inmates ages 25 to 39 and 69 percent of those at age 40 or older.

- The arrest of former prisoners after release increased with the extent of their criminal history. Within five years of release, 61 percent of released inmates with four or fewer arrests in their prior criminal history were arrested, compared to 86 percent of those who had 10 or more prior arrests.

- Many inmates had multi-state criminal history records. About a tenth (11 percent) of prisoners had an arrest within five years of release in a state other than the one that released them, and nearly a quarter (25 percent) of the released prisoners had a prior out-of-state arrest.

The entire report can be found on the BJS website at www.bjs.gov/content/pub/pdf/rprts05p0510.pdf.

Conclusion about EEOC Cited Studies and Recidivism Statistics

In reviewing various studies cited by the EEOC and the recidivism statistics provided by the BJS, what emerges is that when evaluating the time period where an ex-offender is no more likely to re-offend than a non-offender, several things stand out:

1. The statistics and studies are not likely at a point where social scientists, much less legislators, can set certain time periods for the "look back" period, meaning how far back an employer should be able look at a criminal offense. Presumably, anything beyond the look back period is considered old or irrelevant, but employers should consider the number of moving parts involved in determining if the use of a criminal record is fair, recent, and relevant.

2. There is an argument to be made that an employer should really be considering a whole host of factors that would absolutely run contrary to state and federal discrimination rules. For example information that is extremely useful may be matters such as the age of the first offense, the type and nature of past offenses and time on the street between offenses. Other facets affecting social stability may also have an influence, such as marital status or children. Yet, an attempt to inquire into any one of these areas of inquiry would run afoul of state and federal discrimination rules. For example the EEOC has made it clear that asking an open ended and non-job related questions about a person's entire criminal history from the beginning may be discriminatory. That of course, denies the critical information needed according to various studies. Asking about age (to determine age at time of past offenses), marital status, or children could also be problematic in many states. The end result, ironically, may be to deny employers the very information that may be most relevant to accomplish the EEOC's objectives.

Use of Criminal Records and the EEOC Guidance
– An Attorney's View

The following article was written by Ms. Pamela Q. Devata from the law firm of Seyfarth Shaw shortly after the EEOC Guidance was made public and has been updated by Ms. Devata and Ms. Courtney Stieber of Seyfarth Shaw. Ms. Devata and Ms. Stieber are widely respected authorities regarding the FCRA, EEOC, and the use of criminal records. The author sincerely wishes to thank them both for permitting the inclusion of their article within this publication.

How Should Employers Use Criminal History in Employment Now That The EEOC Has Issued Enforcement Guidance?

By Pamela Q. Devata, Seyfarth Shaw

Introduction

Criminal history information can be a crucial tool in the employment decision process. During the past few years, federal agencies and state governments have been limiting, employers' use of criminal history information in the employment process through regulation, litigation, and legislation. In 2012, the Equal Employment Opportunity Commission ("EEOC") issued detailed guidance in an effort to limit employers' options with respect to their use of this tool. The EEOC's Enforcement Guidance on Consideration of Arrest and Conviction Records in Employment Decisions Under Title VII of the Civil Rights Act of 1964 (the "Guidance") passed on April 25, 2012 by a 4-1 vote of the EEOC's Commissioners. See www.eeoc.gov/eeoc/newsroom/release/4-25-12.cfm.

The 2012 Guidance's roots can be traced back to the Unites States Supreme Court's 1971 opinion in *Griggs v. Duke Power Company* and the EEOC E-RACE (Eradicating Racism and Colorism in Employment) Initiative, which seeks, among other things, to address "21st century manifestations of discrimination" under Title VII of the Civil Rights Act of 1964. According to the EEOC, studies reveal that people of certain races, colors, and national origins are arrested more frequently than others outside of those groups. In 2011 alone, 50,060 charges of discrimination alleging race/color/national origin-based discrimination were filed with the EEOC, which accounted for 50% of the charges filed that year. See www.eeoc.gov/eeoc/statistics/enforcement/charges.cfm. The Guidance also supports its reasoning by citing studies finding that criminal history information is often incomplete and inaccurate.

The EEOC's Unilateral Move

The EEOC did not release a draft of this Guidance for public notice and comment before finalizing it. Based on this unilateral move, many industry groups have protested against the issuance of the Guidance. These protests, however, were ineffective in stopping new charges of discrimination and lawsuits from being lodged based on the Guidance. Indeed, now that it has been over four years since the Guidance was released, most employers have already changed their hiring practices to comply with the letter and the spirit of the EEOC's publication.

Some additional employer tips were gleaned during a March 2012 conference where EEOC Commissioner Victoria Lipnic cautioned employers to avoid blanket policies on their use criminal history information (e.g., policies that prohibit individuals who have committed certain crimes from even being considered for employment). According to Commissioner Lipnic, employers with blanket policies will be targeted by the EEOC for investigation and even litigation. This statement was confirmed in the EEOC Guidance. Although not every EEOC investigation results in a lawsuit, an investigation alone can exhaust an employer's time, energy, and finances. This is especially true given that Commissioner Ishimaru stated in his remarks at the public meeting that the EEOC was currently investigating hundreds of cases where employers illegally used criminal history information in employment decisions.

The EEOC's History Of Enforcement

Because the EEOC did not allow for public comment, it is unclear whether or not the EEOC's Guidance will be upheld by the courts. Unlike Congress, the EEOC does not have the authority to create statutes or issue non-procedural regulations under Title VII. Regardless, however, the EEOC can make it difficult and costly for employers that choose not to follow this Guidance through its investigations, enforcement actions and subsequent litigation. Either employers will face substantial costs in following the Guidance or fighting it in court. At the very least, if any of the non-legal challenges are upheld, employers now have the EEOC's "playbook" to investigations involving the use of criminal history. As part of its E-RACE Initiative, the EEOC has already filed several lawsuits against companies it believes use criminal history information in a manner that creates a disparate impact on race, color, or national origin. For example:

- In January 2012, the EEOC entered into a conciliation agreement with a beverage company for $3.13 million based on allegations that the company racially discriminated against African American applicants based on their criminal history information. According to its press release, the EEOC stated that its investigation revealed that the Company had a policy of not hiring applicants with pending criminal charges that had not resulted in convictions; and failed to hire applicants with arrests or minor conviction records.

- In September 2009, the EEOC filed a complaint against Freeman Companies (Case No. 09-CV-2573) in the District of Maryland alleging that the company's use of credit histories and criminal backgrounds as selection criteria has a "significant disparate impact on [African American] applicants and that [the company's] use of criminal history information has an adverse impact on Hispanic and male applicants." In an August 9, 2013 ruling by Judge Titus of the U.S District Court for the District of Maryland, the Court granted summary judgment for Freeman, dismissing the EEOC's complaint in its entirety. In short, the Court found that the EEOC's case relied upon "laughable" and "unreliable" expert analysis. This decision was affirmed by the Fourth Circuit on February 20, 2015.

- In September 2008, the EEOC filed a complaint against Peoplemark, Inc. (Case No. 08-CV-0907) in the Western District of Michigan alleging that the company maintained a blanket no-hire policy that denied hiring or employment to any person with a criminal record and that such policy had a disparate impact on African American applicants. This was a nationwide class action lawsuit under Title VII. After many months of expensive discovery, it became clear that the EEOC did not have a statistical expert to rebut Peoplemark, Inc.'s expert, so the case was voluntarily dismissed in March 2010, and thereafter, sanctions were imposed against the EEOC. In October 2013, the Sixth Circuit affirmed sanctions against the EEOC of more than $750,000.

- The EEOC also brought suit against Kaplan Higher Education Corp. for using credit checks in its hiring process claiming that the practice had a disparate impact on African Americans. On January 28, 2013, Judge Patricia A. Gaughan of the U.S. District Court for the Northern District of Ohio granted summary judgment in favor of Kaplan, finding that the EEOC's statistical evidence of disparate impact was not reliable and not representative of Kaplan's applicant pool as a whole. The Sixth Circuit affirmed on April 9, 2014 and found no abuse of discretion. The EEOC's "homemade" methodology for determining race – by asking its "race raters" to label photographs – was, in the Sixth Circuit's words, "crafted by a witness with no particular expertise to craft it, administered by persons with no particular expertise to administer it, tested by no one, and accepted only by the witness himself." While there is no official separate guidance by the EEOC on the use of credit information, the EEOC's view as to an employer's use of credit information generally tracks that as it relates to criminal history.

- In June 2013, the EEOC filed suit against a BMW manufacturing facility in South Carolina, arguing that its background check practices violated Title VII of the Civil Rights Act by disproportionately screening out African Americans from jobs, and that its policy was not job related nor consistent with business necessity. In September 2015, BMW agreed to resolve the matter for $1.6 million and further agreed to provide job opportunities to the discharged workers and up to 90 African American applicants who had been screened out.

- In June 2013, the EEOC also filed suit against Dollar General, alleging that it, too, violated Title VII by disproportionately screening out African American candidates through background checks. This matter remains ongoing.

State And Local Laws Addressing Criminal History Information

Many states have their own laws concerning "job relatedness" requirements for an employer's use of criminal history information, including Hawaii, Kansas, Missouri, New York, Pennsylvania, and Wisconsin. Other states do not even permit employers to inquire about criminal history information on the initial written application form, subject to a couple of narrow exceptions. Although most of these states apply this prohibition to public employers or state agencies, many also cover private employers. Some 60 cities and counties in California, Connecticut, Delaware, the District of Columbia, Florida, Georgia, Illinois, Indiana, Kentucky, Maryland, Massachusetts, Michigan, Minnesota, Missouri, New Jersey, New York, North Carolina, Ohio, Oregon, Pennsylvania, Rhode Island, Tennessee, Texas, Virginia, Washington, and Wisconsin also have this prohibition. Many of these state and local laws, such as New York City, Baltimore, MD, Columbia, MO, Hawaii and others also prohibit employers from inquiring about an applicant's criminal history information until after a conditional offer of employment is made. Additional states, cities, and counties have similar legislation currently pending.

The EEOC Guidance

The EEOC's Guidance consolidates and supersedes the EEOC's 1987 and 1990 policy statements concerning employers' use of criminal history information. The following are the key highlights of the new Guidance.

What An Employer Can Ask

The EEOC recommends as a best practice that employers not ask about criminal history on applications. As such, employers should evaluate if asking such a question later in the process may mitigate their risk. According to the EEOC, inquiries about criminal history, if made, should be limited only to those that are job-related. Many employers currently ask about convictions in a blanket fashion or with minimal exclusions required by state or local laws. Per the Guidance, employers should review their job applications and pre-employment inquiries. Even when considering convictions to determine job-relatedness, however, it is very difficult for an employer to establish whether a given conviction is job-related, and employers may need to rely on outside experts to make such an analysis. Employers may also want to consider the scope of their criminal history question as it relates to time of conviction or release from incarceration or specific types of crimes. Additionally, as discussed above, there are now a myriad of state and local ban the box laws that restrict or limit what and when an employer can ask as it relates to an applicant's criminal history. Additionally, as discussed above, there are now a myriad of state and local ban the box laws that restrict or limit what and when an employer can ask as it relates to an applicant's criminal history.[2]

Arrest Records

The Guidance makes clear that use of arrest records "is not job related and consistent with business necessity," but goes on, however, to state that an employer may make a decision on the underlying conduct if the conduct makes the individual unfit for a position. Such an analysis will require additional investigation and at the very least will

---

[2] As of late 2016, they following states and localities had ban the box restrictions for private employers: Connecticut, Hawaii, Illinois, Massachusetts, Minnesota, New Jersey, Oregon, Rhode Island, Vermont, Washington, DC, San Francisco, CA, Chicago, IL, Baltimore, MD, Montgomery County and Prince Georges County, MD, Columbia, MO, Buffalo, NY, New York, NY, Rochester, NY, Philadelphia, PA, Portland, OR, Austin, TX, and Seattle, WA.

require a credibility determination by the employer. As such, employers should consider how, if at all, they want to use arrest records. The Guidance does not specifically discuss whether pending records are different from arrests, which may cause additional difficulty for employers. The Guidance does state person can be placed on an unpaid administrative leave while an employer investigates the underlying facts.

Factors To Consider When Evaluating Criminal History Information

It is no surprise that the EEOC reinforced its earlier guidance that bright line policies relating to the use of criminal history information will be unlawful. The good news is that the Guidance does not contain any rule specifically limiting how far back in time an employer may consider recent criminal history information, or only a specified list of offenses—which many thought would be contained in the Guidance. Rather, the Guidance gives more insight into the factors that were originally set forth in the EEOC Policy Statement on the Issue of Conviction Records Under Title VII, www.eeoc.gov/policy/docs/convict1.html, as well as adding some additional factors to be considered. Based on the Guidance, employers should consider the following factors when evaluating criminal history information and making an individualized assessment to determine:

- The nature and gravity of the offense or offenses (which the EEOC explains may be evaluating the harm caused, the legal elements of the crime, and the classification, i.e., misdemeanor or felony);

- The time that has passed since the conviction and/or completion of the sentence (which the EEOC explains as looking at particular facts and circumstances and evaluating studies of recidivism); and

- The nature of the job held or sought (which the EEOC explains requires more than examining just the job title, but also specific duties, essential functions, and environment).

Individualized Assessment

One of the biggest areas of change in the Guidance is that the EEOC recommends that an "individualized assessment" can help employers avoid Title VII liability. Reading between the lines, although the Guidance states that "Title VII does not necessarily require individualized assessment in all circumstances," employers may be challenged by the EEOC or private litigants if they do not do so. But, according to Commissioner Lipnic's opening statement at the public meeting, there may be instances "when particular criminal history will be so manifestly relevant to the position in question that an employer can lawfully screen out an applicant without further inquiry. A day care center need not ask an applicant to "explain" a conviction of violence against a child, nor does a pharmacy have to bend over backward to justify why it excludes convicted drug dealers from working in the pharmacy lab."

The EEOC sets forth a number of individual pieces of evidence that an employer should review when making an individualized determination including:

- The facts or circumstances surrounding the offense or conduct;

- The number of offenses for which the individual was convicted;

- Age at the time of conviction, or release from prison;

- Evidence that the individual performed the same type of work, post-conviction with the same or a different employer, with no known incidents of criminal conduct;

- The length and consistency of employment history before and after the offense or conduct;

- Rehabilitation efforts, e.g., education/training;

- Employment or character references and any other information regarding fitness for the particular position; and

- Whether the individual is bonded under a federal, state, or local bonding program.

This is perhaps the most concerning area of the Guidance. Clearly, this list is extremely burdensome and will cause employers to spend time and resources in evaluating criminal history information. One saving grace is the Guidance indicates if the applicant does not respond to the employer's attempt to gather data, the employer can make the determination without the additional information. Employers will need to evaluate if there are any criminal offenses that have a "demonstrably tight nexus to the position in question" such that an individualized assessment may be circumvented. These will likely be in rare instances. In all other cases, employers should consider both when and how to provide an applicant the opportunity to respond to criminal history and when to conduct the individualized assessment.

Compliance With Other Laws

The Guidance acknowledges that compliance with "federal laws and regulations" disqualifying convicted individuals from certain occupations is a defense to charges of discrimination. For example, convictions of theft and fraud that disqualify in the financial services industry. Also recognized as a defense in the Guidance: denying employment based on failure to obtain a federal security clearance—if the clearance is required for the job. However, the EEOC opines that compliance with state and local laws and regulations will not shield employers from Title VII liability due to Title VII pre-emption of state and local laws. Employers should therefore evaluate whether other laws on which they may be relying as a defense to run specific criminal history or eliminate an applicant/employee are preempted by Title VII.

Next Steps For Employers

Based on the Guidance, employers should evaluate their pre-employment and hiring practices. Because the EEOC will be enforcing Title VII with this Guidance in mind, employers are well advised to consider adjusting their use of criminal history information in accordance with it. Whether or not the EEOC prevails in any of its enforcement actions or lawsuits, the employers in these actions will be forced to spend substantial financial resources to defend and resolve them. The new Guidance itself sets forth a few employer "best practices:"

- Employers should eliminate policies or practices that exclude people from employment based on any criminal record.

- Employers should train managers, hiring officials, and decision-makers about Title VII and its prohibition on employment discrimination.

- Employers should develop a narrowly tailored written policy and procedures for screening for criminal history information. The policy should: (i) identify essential job requirements and the actual circumstances under which the jobs are performed; (ii) determine the specific offenses that may demonstrate unfitness for performing such jobs (i.e., identify the criminal offenses based on all available evidence); (iii) determine the duration of exclusions for criminal conduct based on all available evidence (i.e., include an individualized assessment); (iv) record the justification for the policy and procedures; and (v) note and keep a record of consultations and research considered in crafting the policy and procedures.

- Employers should train managers, hiring officials, and decision-makers on how to implement the policy and procedures consistent with Title VII.

- When asking questions about criminal history information, employers should limit inquiries to records for which exclusion would be job related for the position in question and consistent with business necessity.

- Employers should keep information about applicants' and employees' criminal history information confidential and only use it for the purpose for which it was intended.

ADDENDUM - CHAPTER 13

Sex Offender Registration and Notification Act

Introduction

In February 2013, the General Accounting Office (GAO) issued the report *"SEX OFFENDER REGISTRATION AND NOTIFICATION ACT: Jurisdictions Face Challenges to Implementing the Act, and Stakeholders Report Positive and Negative Effects."* Here are highlights of the report available at www.gao.gov/assets/660/652032.pdf:

SEX OFFENDER REGISTRATION AND NOTIFICATION ACT

Jurisdictions Face Challenges to Implementing the Act, and Stakeholders Report Positive and Negative Effects

Highlights of GAO-13-211 (www.gao.gov/products/GAO-13-211), a report to the Subcommittee on Crime, Terrorism, and Homeland Security, Committee on the Judiciary, House of Representatives.

Why GAO Did This Study

Studies estimate that about 1 in every 5 girls and 1 in every 7 to 10 boys are sexually abused. In 2006, Congress passed SORNA, which introduced new sex offender registration standards for all 50 states, 5 U.S. territories (American Samoa, Guam, the Northern Mariana Islands, Puerto Rico, and the U.S. Virgin Islands), the District of Columbia, and certain Indian tribes. SORNA established the SMART Office to determine if these jurisdictions have "substantially implemented" the law, and to assist them in doing so. The deadline to implement SORNA was July 2009; given that none of the jurisdictions met this deadline, DOJ authorized two 1-year extensions. This report addresses: (1) To what extent has the SMART Office determined that jurisdictions have substantially implemented SORNA, and what challenges, if any, have jurisdictions faced? (2) For jurisdictions that have substantially implemented SORNA, what are the reported effects that the act has had on public safety, criminal justice stakeholders, and registered sex offenders?

GAO analyzed SMART Office implementation status reports from September 2009 through September 2012. To identify any challenges, GAO surveyed officials in the 50 states, 5 U.S. territories, and the District of Columbia; GAO received responses from 93 percent (52 of 56) of them. The survey results can be viewed at GAO-13-234SP (www.gao.gov/products/GAO-13-234SP). GAO visited or interviewed criminal justice officials in five jurisdictions that have substantially implemented SORNA, chosen to represent a range in the number of registered sex offenders per 100,000 residents. Their perspectives are not generalizable, but provided insights.

View GAO-13-211 (www.gao.gov/products/GAO-13-211).

What GAO Found

The Office of Sex Offender Sentencing, Monitoring, Apprehending, Registering, and Tracking (SMART Office) within the Department of Justice (DOJ) has determined that 19 of the 37 jurisdictions that have submitted packages for review have substantially implemented the Sex Offender Registration and Notification Act (SORNA). Although the SMART Office has determined that 17 of the jurisdictions that submitted packages have not yet substantially implemented SORNA, the office concluded that 15 of these 17 jurisdictions have implemented at least half of the SORNA requirements; the office has not yet made a determination for 1 jurisdiction that submitted a package. A majority of nonimplemented jurisdictions reported that generating the political will to incorporate the necessary changes to their state laws and related policies or reconciling legal conflicts are among the greatest challenges to implementation. For example, officials from 27 nonimplemented jurisdictions reported reconciling conflicts between SORNA and state laws—such as which offenses should require registration—as a challenge to implementing SORNA. Officials from 5 of 18 jurisdictions that responded to a survey question asking how DOJ could help address these challenges reported that the SMART Office could provide greater flexibilities; however, SMART Office officials said they have offered as many flexibilities as possible and further changes would take legislative action.

A few studies have been conducted on the effects of certain SORNA requirements on jurisdictions and registered sex offenders, but GAO did not find any that evaluated the effects on public safety following SORNA implementation; stakeholders reported both positive and negative effects as a result of implementing the law. Officials from 4 of 12 implementing jurisdictions who responded to the survey reported that one benefit was improved monitoring of registered sex offenders. Stakeholders also reported that SORNA resulted in enhanced information sharing on registered sex offenders between criminal justice components, in part through the use of certain databases that enable jurisdictions to share information with one another. Stakeholders and survey respondents also identified negative or unintended consequences of implementing SORNA. For example, officials from three of five state agencies and all eight of the local law enforcement agencies GAO interviewed stated that their workload has increased, in part because of the increased frequency at which sex offenders must update their registration information as a result of the act. Officials from a majority of the public defender and probation offices also said that SORNA implementation has made it more difficult for registered sex offenders to obtain housing and employment, which can negatively affect their ability to reintegrate into their communities. The National Institute of Justice (NIJ) is statutorily required to study SORNA's effectiveness in increasing compliance with requirements and the effect of these requirements on increasing public safety. As of December 2012, DOJ had not requested the funding to conduct this study and the funding had not been appropriated. NIJ officials stated that NIJ does not proactively request funding for specific studies, but waits for Congress to decide when to appropriate the funding. Neither DOJ nor the Administrative Office of the United States Courts provided written comments on this report.

Sex Offender Registration and Notification Act (SORNA)

Introduction

The following information about the Office of Sex Offender Sentencing, Monitoring, Apprehending, Registering, and Tracking (SMART) is from www.smart.gov/about.htm:

The SMART Office was authorized by the Adam Walsh Child Protection and Safety Act of 2006 to:

- *Administer the standards for the Sex Offender Registration and Notification Program (SORNA) set forth in Title 1 of the Adam Walsh Act;*
- *Administer grant programs relating to sex offender registration and notification authorized by the Adam Walsh Act and other grant programs authorized by the Adam Walsh Act as directed by the Attorney General;*
- *Cooperate with and provide technical assistance to states, the District of Columbia, principal U.S. territories, units of local government, tribal governments, and other public and private entities involved in activities related to sex offender registration or notification or to other measures for the protection of children or other members of the public from sexual abuse or exploitation; and*
- *Perform such other functions as the Attorney General may delegate.*

The SMART Mission is to protect the public by supporting the national implementation of a comprehensive sex offender registration and notification system.

Sex Offender Registration and Notification Act (SORNA)

The following information about the Sex Offender Registration and Notification Act (SORNA) is from www.smart.gov/sorna.htm:

SORNA refers to the Sex Offender Registration and Notification Act which is Title I of the Adam Walsh Child Protection and Safety Act of 2006 (Public Law 109-248). SORNA provides a comprehensive set of minimum standards for sex offender registration and notification in the United States. SORNA aims to close potential gaps and loopholes that existed under prior law and generally strengthens the nationwide network of sex offender registration and notification programs. Additionally, SORNA:

- *Extends the jurisdictions in which registration is required beyond the 50 states, the District of Columbia, and the principal U.S. territories, to include also federally recognized Indian tribes.*
- *Incorporates a more comprehensive group of sex offenders and sex offenses for which registration is required.*
- *Requires registered sex offenders to register and keep their registration current in each jurisdiction in which they reside, work, or go to school.*
- *Requires sex offenders to provide more extensive registration information.*
- *Requires sex offenders to make periodic in-person appearances to verify and update their registration information.*
- *Expands the amount of information available to the public regarding registered sex offenders.*
- *Makes changes in the required minimum duration of registration for sex offenders.*

For more information about the implementation status of the state/U.S. territory and Indian tribe registration and notification systems that have been found to have substantially implemented SORNA, use the map at www.smart.gov/sorna.htm.

More Information about SORNA

The following information is also available at www.smart.gov/sorna.htm:

Federal role in the administration of SORNA

The Federal Government is working to assist with the implementation of SORNA and protect the public from sexual abuse and exploitation through:

- *Stepped-up federal investigation and prosecution efforts to assist jurisdictions in enforcing sex offender registration requirements;*
- *New statutory provisions for the FBI's National Sex Offender Registry (part of the National Crime Information Center) and the Dru Sjodin National Sex Offender Public Website that compile information obtained from registration programs across the country and make it readily available to law enforcement or the public;*
- *Federal development of software tools, which jurisdictions will be able to use to facilitate the operation of their registration and notification programs in conformity with the SORNA standards; and*
- *Establishment of the SMART Office to administer the national standards for sex offender registration and notification and to assist jurisdictions in their implementation efforts.*

The SMART Office

SORNA established the Office of Sex Offender Sentencing, Monitoring, Apprehending, Registering, and Tracking (SMART Office), a component of the Office of Justice Programs within the U.S. Department of Justice. The SMART Office is authorized by law to administer the standards for sex offender registration and notification that are set forth in SORNA. It is further authorized to cooperate with and provide assistance to states, local governments, tribal governments, and other public and private entities in relation to sex offender registration and notification and other measures for the protection of the public from sexual abuse or exploitation. The SMART Office is a key federal partner and resource for jurisdictions as they continue to develop and strengthen their sex offender registration and notification programs.

SORNA Final Guidelines

The Final Guidelines provide all jurisdictions with guidance, explanation and advice regarding the administration and implementation of SORNA. The Attorney General has issued these Guidelines to promote and assist in the implementation of the SORNA standards.

See: www.smart.gov/guidelines.htm

Jurisdictions included under SORNA

The 50 States, the District of Columbia, the five principal U.S. territories, and federally recognized Indian tribes that elect to function as registration jurisdictions are all defined as "jurisdictions" under SORNA. "Jurisdiction", as used by SORNA, does not include counties, cities, towns, or other political subdivisions located within states, tribes or territories. However, this definition does not limit the ability of states, tribes or territories to carry out these functions through their political subdivisions or other entities within the jurisdiction.

SORNA Applicability

SORNA refers to the persons required to register under its standards as "sex offenders," and SORNA defines "sex offender" to mean "an individual who was convicted of a sex offense."

Sex offenses under SORNA

The convictions for which SORNA requires registration include convictions for sex offenses by any U.S. jurisdiction, including convictions for sex offenses under federal, military, state, territorial, tribal or local law. Foreign convictions are also covered if certain conditions are satisfied.

Generally speaking, the following are considered sex offenses under SORNA:

- *SEXUAL ACTS AND SEXUAL CONTACT OFFENSES. These include criminal offenses that have an element involving a sexual act or sexual contact with another. The offenses covered include all sexual offenses whose elements involve: (i) any type or degree of genital, oral, or anal penetration, or (ii) any sexual touching of or contact with a person's body, either directly or through the clothing.*
- *SPECIFIED OFFENSES AGAINST MINORS. A criminal offense against a minor that involves any of the following:*
  - *Non-Parental Kidnapping*
  - *Non-Parental false imprisonment*
  - *Solicitation to engage in sexual conduct*
  - *Use in a sexual performance*
  - *Solicitation to practice prostitution*
  - *Video voyeurism*
  - *Possession, production, or distribution of child pornography*
  - *Criminal sexual conduct involving a minor*
  - *Use of the internet to facilitate criminal sexual conduct involving a minor*
  - *Any conduct that by its nature is a sex offense against a minor*
- *SPECIFIED FEDERAL OFFENSES. These include the following specific offenses: ○18 U.S.C. §1591 (Sex Trafficking of Children)*
  - *18 U.S.C. §2241 (Aggravated Sexual Abuse)*
  - *18 U.S.C. §2242 (Sexual Abuse)*
  - *18 U.S.C. §2243 (Sexual Abuse of a Minor or Ward)*
  - *18 U.S.C. §2244 (Abusive Sexual Contact)*
  - *18 U.S.C. §2245 (Offenses Resulting in Death)*
  - *18 U.S.C. §2251 (Sexual Exploitation of Children)*
  - *18 U.S.C. §2251A (Selling or Buying of Children)*
  - *18 U.S.C. §2252 (Material Involving the Sexual Exploitation of Minors)*
  - *18 U.S.C. §2252A (Material Containing Child Pornography)*
  - *18 U.S.C. §2252B (Misleading Domain Names on the Internet)*
  - *18 U.S.C. §2252C (Misleading Words or Digital Images on the Internet)*

- o   *18 U.S.C. §2260 (Production of Sexually Explicit Depictions of a Minor for Import in to the United States)*
- o   *18 U.S.C. §2421 (Transportation of a Minor for Illegal Sexual Activity)*
- o   *18 U.S.C. §2422 (Coercion and Enticement of a Minor for Illegal Sexual Activity*
- o   *18 U.S.C. §2423 (Transportation of Minors for Illegal Sexual Activity, Travel With the Intent to Engage in Illicit Sexual Conduct with a Minor, Engaging in Illicit Sexual Conduct in Foreign Places))*
- o   *18 U.S.C. §2424 (Failure to File Factual Statement about an Alien Individual)*
- o   *18 U.S.C. §2425 (Transmitting Information about a Minor to further Criminal Sexual Conduct)*
- *SPECIFIED MILITARY OFFENSES. These include sex offenses under the Uniform Code of Military Justice, as specified by the Secretary of Defense. These offenses are primarily located at 28 C.F.R. §571.72(b).*
- *ATTEMPTS AND CONSPIRACIES. These include attempts and conspiracies to commit offenses that are otherwise covered by the definition of "sex offenses."*

See Part IV.A-D of the Final Guidelines for more detail.

Offenses that involve consensual sexual conduct

SORNA section 111(5)(C) addresses the minimum standards for requiring sex offender registration for consensual sexual conduct under the Adam Walsh Act. SORNA does NOT require registration in the following situations: 1) If both participants are adults, and neither is under the custodial authority of the other (e.g., inmate/prison guard) and the conduct was consensual, then this conduct does not constitute a registerable sex offense for purposes of the Adam Walsh Act. 2) With respect acts involving at least one minor (person under 18) who engages in consensual sexual conduct, the following minimum standards apply: Where both participants are at least 13 years old and neither participant is more than 4 years older than the other, a sex offense conviction based on consensual sexual conduct does not require registration under the Adam Walsh Act. In all situations, jurisdictions have discretion to exceed the minimum standards of SORNA and require registration upon convictions based on consensual sexual conduct.

Convictions under SORNA

A sex offender is "convicted" for SORNA purposes if the sex offender has been subject to penal consequences based on the conviction, however it may be styled. Likewise, the sealing of a criminal record or other action that limits the publicity or availability of conviction information, but does not deprive the conviction of continuing legal validity, does not change its status as a "conviction" for purposes of SORNA.

*"Convictions" for SORNA purposes include convictions of juveniles who are prosecuted as adults. It does not include juvenile delinquency adjudications, **except** under the circumstances specified in 42 U.S.C. §16911(8), which stipulate juvenile registration only if the juvenile was at least 14 years old at the time of the offense and was adjudicated delinquent for committing (or attempting or conspiring to commit) a sexual act with another by force, by the threat of serious violence, or by rendering unconscious or drugging the victim.*

See Part IV.A of the Final Guidelines for more detail.

CLASSES OF SEX OFFENDERS

Section 111(2)-(4) of SORNA defines three "tiers" of sex offenders. The tier classifications have implications in three areas: (i) under section 115, the required duration of registration depends primarily on the tier; (ii) under section 116, the required frequency of in person appearances by sex offenders to verify registration information depends on the tier; and (iii) under section 118(c)(1), information about tier I sex offenders convicted of offenses other than specified offenses against a minor may be exempted from website disclosure.

The use of the "tier" classifications in SORNA relates to substance, not form or terminology. Thus, to implement the SORNA requirements, jurisdictions do not have to label their sex offenders as "tier I," "tier II," and "tier III," and do not have to adopt any other particular approach to labeling or categorization of sex offenders. Rather, the SORNA requirements are met so long as sex offenders who satisfy the SORNA criteria for placement in a particular tier are consistently subject to at least the duration of registration, frequency of in person appearances for verification, and extent of website disclosure that SORNA requires for that tier. (See: www.smart.gov/pdfs/final_sornaguidelines.pdf.

Other SORNA Resources:

- *SORNA Tools*
  - *www.smart.gov/sorna_tools.htm*
- *Submitting Substantial Implementation Materials to the SMART Office*
  - *www.smart.gov/sorna_tools_materials.htm*

International Tracking of Sex Offenders

When the Sex Offender Registration and Notification Act (SORNA) was enacted and its Final Guidelines were published, the U.S. Department of Justice was tasked with creating a tracking system for sex offenders who depart and reenter the United States. To that end, the SMART Office created the International Tracking of Sex Offenders Working Group in 2008, which has been working to enable appropriate information sharing about sex offenders who either intend to travel or are traveling internationally. This proposed system is outlined in a white paper made available to Congress in December 2010.

See www.smart.gov/pdfs/InternationalTrackingofSexOffendersWorkingGroup.pdf.

Supplemental Guidelines for Sex Offender Registration and Notification

On January 11, 2011, the Department of Justice released supplemental guidelines for SORNA. The SORNA Supplemental Guidelines address, among other things, public notification of juveniles adjudicated delinquent for serious sex crimes, the posting of sex offender information, such as email addresses and other Internet identifiers, and reporting of international travel requirements. Other issues addressed in the Supplemental Guidelines include on-going review of SORNA implementation, the sharing of information across jurisdictions, and the application of SORNA to newly federally-recognized Indian tribes. The final Supplemental Guidelines can be found at www.smart.gov/pdfs/SORNAFinalSuppGuidelines01_11_11.pdf.

SORNA Retroactive Rule Finalized

The Department of Justice finalized an interim rule specifying that the requirements of the Sex Offender Registration and Notification Act, title I of Public Law 109-248, apply to all sex offenders, including sex offenders convicted of the offense for which registration is required before the enactment of that Act. The final rule can be found at www.smart.gov/pdfs/FinalRule2010-32719.pdf.

GAO Report on SORNA

A report released by the United States Government Accountability Office (GAO) in February 2013 entitled '*SEX OFFENDER REGISTRATION AND NOTIFICATION ACT – Jurisdictions Face Challenges to Implementing the Act, and Stakeholders Report Positive and Negative Effects*' shed light on the state of sex offender databases. An excerpt from the report is below (See: www.gao.gov/assets/660/652032.pdf).

SEX OFFENDER REGISTRATION AND NOTIFICATION ACT – Jurisdictions Face Challenges to Implementing the Act, and Stakeholders Report Positive and Negative Effects (February 2013)

United States Government Accountability Office (GAO)

Why GAO Did This Study

Studies estimate that about 1 in every 5 girls and 1 in every 7 to 10 boys are sexually abused. In 2006, Congress passed SORNA, which introduced new sex offender registration standards for all 50 states, 5 U.S. territories (American Samoa, Guam, the Northern Mariana Islands, Puerto Rico, and the U.S. Virgin Islands), the District of Columbia, and certain Indian tribes. SORNA established the SMART Office to determine if these jurisdictions have "substantially implemented" the law, and to assist them in doing so. The deadline to implement SORNA was July 2009; given that none of the jurisdictions met this deadline, DOJ authorized two 1-year extensions. This report addresses: (1) To what extent has the SMART Office determined that jurisdictions have substantially implemented SORNA, and what challenges, if any, have jurisdictions faced? (2) For jurisdictions that have substantially implemented SORNA, what are the reported effects that the act has had on public safety, criminal justice stakeholders, and registered sex offenders?

GAO analyzed SMART Office implementation status reports from September 2009 through September 2012. To identify any challenges, GAO surveyed officials in the 50 states, 5 U.S. territories, and the District of Columbia; GAO received responses from 93 percent (52 of 56) of them.

What GAO Found

The Office of Sex Offender Sentencing, Monitoring, Apprehending, Registering, and Tracking (SMART Office) within the Department of Justice (DOJ) has determined that 19 of the 37 jurisdictions that have submitted packages for review have substantially implemented the Sex Offender Registration and Notification Act (SORNA). Although the SMART Office has determined that 17 of the jurisdictions that submitted packages have not yet substantially implemented SORNA, the office concluded that 15 of these 17 jurisdictions have implemented at least half of the SORNA requirements; the office has not yet made a determination for 1 jurisdiction that submitted a package. A majority of nonimplemented jurisdictions reported that generating the political will to incorporate the necessary changes to their state laws and related policies or reconciling legal conflicts are among the greatest challenges to implementation. For example, officials from 27 nonimplemented jurisdictions reported reconciling conflicts between SORNA and state laws—such as which offenses should require registration—as a challenge to implementing SORNA. Officials from 5 of 18 jurisdictions that responded to a survey question asking how DOJ could help address these challenges reported that the SMART Office could provide greater flexibilities; however, SMART Office officials said they have offered as many flexibilities as possible and further changes would take legislative action.

A few studies have been conducted on the effects of certain SORNA requirements on jurisdictions and registered sex offenders, but GAO did not find any that evaluated the effects on public safety following SORNA implementation; stakeholders reported both positive and negative effects as a result of implementing the law. Officials from 4 of 12 implementing jurisdictions who responded to the survey reported that one benefit was improved monitoring of registered sex offenders. Stakeholders also reported that SORNA resulted in enhanced information sharing on registered sex offenders between criminal justice components, in part through the use of certain databases that enable jurisdictions to share information with one another. Stakeholders and survey respondents also identified negative or unintended consequences of implementing SORNA. For example, officials from three of five state agencies and all eight of the local law enforcement agencies GAO interviewed stated that their workload has increased, in part because of the increased frequency at which sex offenders must update their registration information as a result of the act. Officials from a majority of the public defender and probation offices also said that SORNA implementation has made it more difficult for registered sex offenders to obtain housing and employment, which can negatively affect their ability to reintegrate into their communities. The National Institute of Justice (NIJ) is statutorily required to study SORNA's effectiveness in increasing compliance with requirements and the effect of these requirements on increasing public safety. As of December 2012, DOJ had not requested the funding to conduct this study and the funding had not been appropriated. NIJ officials stated that NIJ does not proactively request funding for specific studies, but waits for Congress to decide when to appropriate the funding. Neither DOJ nor the Administrative Office of the United States Courts provided written comments on this report.

Source: www.gao.gov/assets/660/652032.pdf

Can Employers Demand to See Employees' and Applicants' Facebook Pages?

Can Employers Demand to See Employees' and Applicants' Facebook Pages?

By Stephen J. Hirschfeld, Curiale Hirschfeld Kraemer LLP, CEO Employment Law Alliance &

Kristin L. Oliveira, Curiale Hirschfeld Kraemer LLP

It has been reported that some employers are requiring job applicants to disclose their login information and passwords in order to access Facebook and other private information housed on social media. Interviewers commonly troll the Internet to obtain publicly-available information about a candidate as part of a background check. But now, as more people are making their social media profiles private, employers are requesting login information from prospective candidates in order to see their profiles. Some hiring managers are directing candidates to access their private accounts on the employer's computer and then "shoulder-surfing" the candidate's photographs, posts, and "tweets." This practice is now illegal in nearly half of the states.

Motivations for Accessing Private Social Media Accounts

Why do some employers resort to reviewing social media sites or searching the Internet as part of their background check on applicants?

Most employers today are reluctant to provide meaningful references for fear of being sued for defamation. For example, California prohibits employers from intentionally interfering with former employees' attempts to find jobs by giving false or misleading references. While the law in most states permits an applicant to sue for defamation if the statements made by his or her former employer as part of a job reference are false and contributed to the candidate not receiving the position, the reality is that very few such lawsuits have been filed. Nonetheless, many employers resort to providing only 'name, rank and serial number' for former employees or simply say "no comment," in response to a reference request. Consequently, future employers have little meaningful data about a prospective employee's performance or workplace demeanor to make an informed hiring decision.

Second, many employers are concerned about being held liable for failing to conduct a full and complete background check out of fear that one of their applicants – who had a history of misconduct that wasn't uncovered during the background check – repeats that conduct once again after being hired. These "negligent hiring" lawsuits are still relatively rare. The theory behind these claims is based upon the notion that had the employer conducted a sufficient background check, it could have prevented later harm by never hiring the applicant in the first place.

The question of whether an employer could actually be held liable for failing to insist upon reviewing password-protected social media accounts is far from settled leaving many with legitimate concerns.

Finally, the sad reality is that resume fraud appears to be on the rise. Many employers have come to realize that applicants whom they have already hired have either fabricated work experience or education or greatly exaggerated and embellished credentials. Employers are seeking new ways to combat this trend.

The Legal Consequences of Requiring Access to Private Social Media Accounts

Numerous legal issues are triggered when employers require applicants to provide access to this information. Discrimination claims are one of the biggest concerns. For example, an employer might learn information about an applicant (such as their marital status, religion, sexual orientation or ethnicity) which might later allow that individual, if they are not hired, to contend said information is the reason why they weren't ultimately chosen for the job. Learning that a candidate either recently became pregnant or is planning to – whether held against that individual or not – can form the basis of a discrimination claim. Once the employer is on notice of a trait or characteristic discovered from social media, they subject themselves to the very same claim that would be brought if identical information had been learned during an interview. The major difference – one that could be viewed very differently by a trier of fact – is that this information will have been obtained involuntarily by requiring Facebook credentials as opposed to perhaps voluntarily disclosed by the candidate.

Employers also subject themselves to claims that the applicant's right of privacy was invaded. California, for example, affords a constitutional right of privacy that applies to private entities. A California applicant may have a viable claim that requiring the disclosure of a confidential password – which allows access to private, personal information – constitutes an invasion of privacy. Other states may allow such a claim to proceed based upon some type of common law invasion of privacy cause of action. Regardless of the type of claim, a court will first look at whether the applicant had a reasonable expectation of privacy. Clearly, if the applicant or employee does not restrict his social media such that postings are publicly available, then there is no reasonable expectation of privacy.

In addition, some states have laws that prohibit employers from making adverse decisions based on off-duty lawful conduct. For instance, under New York law, employers cannot refuse to hire an individual based on his off-duty recreational activities, certain political activities, and the use of legal consumable products. A handful of states protect employees from discrimination based on their political views or affiliation, and thus disciplining an employee for a political posting that endorses a candidate or cause could be illegal. While there does not appear to be a court decision directly on this point, it is feasible that an applicant may pursue a claim under these types of statutes.

An employer's request for access to personal electronic accounts clearly violates the law in several states. As of July 2016, twenty-five states and Guam have enacted laws preventing employers from requesting passwords for, or accessing password protected, social media accounts. For example, California Labor Code section 980 prohibits an employer from requiring or requesting an employee or applicant disclose a username or password for the purpose of accessing personal social media, nor may the employer insist that the employee or applicant access the personal social media in the employer's presence. Employers cannot retaliate against an employee or applicant if they fail to give access as prohibited by this statute. In addition, employers in California cannot require or ask an employee or applicant to divulge the content of any personal social media (such as their own or coworkers' social media postings). There is an exception to this particular ban if the employer reasonably believes the social media is relevant to an "investigation of allegations of employee misconduct" or employee violation of any "applicable laws or regulations."

Even for states that lack specific laws prohibiting access to personal social media, there is legal authority for the proposition that coercing employees to divulge passwords violates an existing federal statute – the Stored Communications Act (SCA). The SCA is violated when one intentionally accesses electronic information without authorization. Federal courts have found that an employee had a cognizable legal claim under the SCA when his employer accessed a secure website that contained criticisms of management using someone else's login information. *Pietrylo v. Hillstone Restaurant Group d/b/a Houston's,* 2009 U.S. Dist. LEXIS 88702 (D.N.J., September 25, 2009). The SCA does not apply when someone is authorized to access electronic communications; however, authorization does not exist if it is coerced or provided under pressure. *Ehling v. Monmouth-Ocean Hosp.*

Corp. 961 F.Supp. 2d 659 (D.N.J., August 20, 2013). Arguably, an employee or applicant could argue that providing user login and password information is "under pressure" given certain circumstances.

State and Federal Legislative Actions To Watch

Several other states are considering passing similar laws prohibiting employers from requesting, requiring, suggesting, or causing employees or potential employees to grant access to personal social media. Illinois, Alaska, Massachusetts, and Missouri are just a number of several states with pending legislation.

For the last three years, Congress has attempted to take federal action on the issue by introducing "The Password Protection Act". The House of Representatives presented this bill in 2012, 2013 and 2015. The most recent version of The Password Protection Act amends the federal Computer Fraud and Abuse Act and has been referred to the House Committee on the Judiciary. As written, the 2015 bill prohibits employers from:

- Knowingly and intentionally compelling or coercing any person to authorize access, such as by providing a password or similar information through which a computer may be accessed, to a protected computer that is not the employer's computer;
- Discharging, disciplining, or discriminating against in any manner or threatening to take any such action against any person because they refuse to provide access to a password-protected account or have filed a complaint related to these provisions; and
- Engaging in an adverse employment action as a consequence of an employee's failure to provide access to his/her own private accounts.

Practical Considerations and Conclusion

Employers have legitimate concerns as to whether they are obtaining the information they need to make a fully informed decision about candidates they are interested in hiring. At the same time, they need to be mindful that there are legal risks if they attempt to obtain information from password protected social media sites. Beyond this, employers need to seriously consider what these actions say about their corporate culture. Given the proliferation of social media usage and in light of how important the new entrants into the workforce feel about their ability to communicate and express themselves online, an employer may be hindering its ability to attract the best and brightest applicants by using these methods.

Employers need to decide if the existing procedures for conducting extensive, legal background checks are sufficient methods for obtaining needed information to perform due diligence in hiring and maintaining your workforce, or if more aggressive means need to be employed.

Stephen J. Hirschfeld is a founding partner at Hirschfeld Kraemer LLP and the CEO of the San Francisco-based Employment Law Alliance – a network of more than 3,000 labor and employment attorneys worldwide. He can be reached at shirschfeld@hkemploymentlaw.com or www.hkemploymentlaw.com.

Kristin Oliveira is Of Counsel at Hirschfeld Kraemer. She can be reached at koliveira@hkemploymentlaw.com

Research Shows How Many Employers Use Social Media for Screening

Introduction

There is no question that employers and recruiters have dramatically increased the use of social media for recruiting and hiring. A number of surveys on the topic are shown below.

CareerBuilder Social Media Study

Use of Social Media Background Checks Increased 500 Percent in Past Decade

The number of employers using social media background checks to screen job candidates increased 500 percent over the past decade, according to the annual CareerBuilder social media recruitment survey released in April 2016, with 60 percent of employers using social media to research job candidates in 2016, up significantly from 52 percent in 2015, 22 percent in 2008, and 11 percent in 2006, when the survey was first conducted.

"Tools such as Facebook and Twitter enable employers to get a glimpse of who candidates are outside the confines of a resume or cover letter," Rosemary Haefner, chief human resources officer of CareerBuilder, stated in a press release about the survey. "And with more and more people using social media, it's not unusual to see the usage for recruitment to grow as well."

The CareerBuilder social media recruitment survey revealed that of the 59 percent of hiring managers who used search engines to research candidates, nearly half of them – 49 percent – found information available through social media that caused them not to hire a job candidate. The following are the top five types of social media content that had a negative effect on potential employers:

- Provocative or inappropriate photographs, videos, or information – 46 percent
- Information about candidate drinking or using drugs – 43 percent
- Discriminatory comments related to race, religion, gender, etc. – 33 percent
- Candidate bad-mouthed previous company or fellow employee – 31 percent
- Poor communication skills – 29 percent

However, the survey also found that nearly one-third of employers who screened candidates through social media – 32 percent – found information that caused them to hire a candidate, including:

- Candidate's background information supported job qualifications – 44 percent
- Candidate's site conveyed a professional image – 44 percent
- Candidate's personality came across as a good fit with company culture – 43 percent
- Candidate was well-rounded, showed a wide range of interests – 40 percent
- Candidate had great communication skills – 36 percent

In addition, the survey found that employers did not just screen potential employees through social media, as 41 percent of employers used social networking sites to research current employees, nearly a third – 32 percent – used search engines to check up on current employees, and more than one in four – 26 percent – found content online that caused them to reprimand or even fire an employee.

The national survey was conducted online by Harris Poll on behalf of CareerBuilder between February 10, 2016, and March 17, 2016, and included a representative sample of 2,186 hiring managers and human resource professionals and 3,031 full-time U.S. workers in the private sector across industries and company sizes.

Source:
www.careerbuilder.com/share/aboutus/pressreleasesdetail.aspx?sd=4%2f28%2f2016&siteid=cbpr&sc_cmp1=cb_pr945_&id=pr945&ed=12%2f31%2f2016

Microsoft Study

On Data Privacy Day in January 2010, Microsoft released a commissioned research study that outlined the ways human resources professionals worldwide used personal, yet publicly available, online information when screening job candidates. Twelve hundred interviews were conducted for the study in the United States, United Kingdom (U.K.), Germany, and France. Some of the results raised eyebrows.

For example, 79 percent of HR professionals surveyed in the U.S. reported reviewing the information found on the Internet when examining job candidates. In addition, 84 percent of the HR professionals surveyed in the U.S. categorized online reputation information as one of the top two factors they considered when reviewing a comprehensive set of candidate information.

The Microsoft study also found that employers were not only reviewing the information, they were acting on it, as 70 percent of those surveyed in the U.S. had rejected a candidate based on online information, with the top factor for rejection being unsuitable photos and videos online. The study revealed that HR professionals are regularly using information about candidates found on the Internet, which could have significant repercussions.

SHRM Survey Finds Employers Wary of Using Social Media Background Checks

An August 2011 survey from the Society for Human Resource Management (SHRM) – *'SHRM Survey Findings: The Use of Social Networking Websites and Online Search Engines in Screening Job Candidates'* – found that, contrary to popular belief, only roughly one-quarter (26 percent) of organizations indicated they used online search engines such as Google to screen job candidates during the hiring process while even fewer organizations (18 percent) used social networking sites like Facebook for that purpose.

Conversely, the SHRM survey found that close to two-thirds (64 percent) of organizations had never used online search engines to screen job candidates or used them in the past but no longer did so, while more than two-thirds (71 percent) of organizations had never used social networking websites to screen job candidates or used them in the past but no longer did so. The reasons why some organizations did not use social networking websites to screen job candidates included the following:

- Two-thirds (66 percent) of organizations indicated they did not use social networking websites due to concerns about the legal risks/discovering information about protected characteristics such as age, race, gender, and religious affiliation.
- Nearly one-half (48 percent) of organizations did not use these sites because they could not verify with confidence the information from the social networking website pages of job candidates.
- Another 45 percent of organizations indicated that the information found on the social networking sites may not be relevant to a job candidate's work-related potential or performance.

The survey also revealed a significant increase in the prevalence of formal or informal policies regarding the use of social networking websites to screen candidates over the past three years. While 72 percent of organizations had no formal or informal policies regarding the use of social networking websites for job screening in 2008, this figure has dropped to 56 percent in the more recent survey. In addition, 29 percent of organizations plan to implement a formal policy in the next 12 months, up from 11 percent in 2008.

As for how many organizations disqualified candidates based on information found by online search engines or social networking websites, of the small percentage of organizations that used such information only 15 percent of this group indicated that they used online search engine information to disqualify job candidates while 30 percent indicated they used social networking information to disqualify job candidates.

The SHRM survey 'The Use of Social Networking Websites and Online Search Engines in Screening' is at: www.shrm.org/research/surveyfindings/articles/pages/theuseofsocialnetworkingwebsitesandonlinesearchenginesinscreeni ngjobcandidates.aspx.

Using Social Media for Talent Acquisition – Recruitment and Screening

In January of 2016, the Society of Human Resource Management (SHRM) released research on *'Using Social Media for Talent Acquisition—Recruitment and Screening.'* SHRM surveyed HR professionals to learn about use of social media for talent acquisition and the recruitment and screening of job candidates. Key findings include:

- Two-thirds of organizations (66%) have taken steps to leverage mobile recruiting—to target smartphone users.
- Recruiting via social media is growing with 84% of organizations using it currently and 9% planning to use it.
- Recruiting passive job candidates (82%) continues to be the top reason that organizations use social media for recruitment.
- Overall, 43% of organizations said they use social media or online search engines to screen job candidates, an increase from 2013, while 44% of HR professionals said a job candidate's public social media profile can provide information about work-related performance.
- Over one-third, (36%) of organizations have disqualified a job candidate in the past year because of concerning information found on a public social media profile or through an online search.

The full results of the survey are available at www.shrm.org/hr-today/trends-and-forecasting/research-and-surveys/Documents/SHRM-Social-Media-Recruiting-Screening-2015.pdf.

Senators and Facebook Warn about Dangers of Using Social Media to Screen

Introduction

In September 2011, the dangers of using social networking sites was recognized by two members of the United States Senate – Senator Richard Blumenthal (D-Connecticut) and Senator Al Franken (D-Minnesota) – in a letter sent to a background screening firm that specializes in reviewing and storing social networking data for employment background checks.

Senators Blumenthal and Franken requested information about the business practices of the company as they relate to personal privacy and were concerned that the company's collection of online and social media information about job applicants and distribution of that information to potential employers. Their letter addressed concerns if the firm's services could contain inaccurate information, invade consumers' right to privacy online, violate the terms of service agreements of the websites from which the company culls data, and infringe upon intellectual property rights.

The Senators were also concerned that there are numerous scenarios under which a job applicant could be unfairly harmed by the information the company provides to an employer.

The questions the Senators asked in their letter are shown below. They provide an excellent set of criteria for employers to consider.

Accuracy of Information

1. How does your company determine the accuracy of the information it provides to employers?
2. Does your company have procedures in place for applicants to dispute information contained in the reports your company produces? If so, what are these procedures?
3. Is your company able to differentiate among applicants with common names? How?
4. Is your company able to determine whether information it finds on a website is parody, defamatory, or otherwise false? How?
5. Does your company accord less weight to certain sources of information that may be inaccurate, such as community-edited websites like Wikipedia?
6. Search engines like Google often provide archived versions of websites; these cached web pages may contain false information that was later updated. Search engines also provide "mirrors" of websites, like Wikipedia or blog articles; these mirrored pages may be archives of inaccurate information that has since been corrected. Is your company able to determine whether information it is providing is derived from an archived version of an inaccurate website? How?

Consumers' Right to Online Privacy

1. Does your company require the consent of a job applicant before conducting a background check on the applicant? If so, who requests the applicant's consent: your company, or the potential employer? Based on your experience with employers, does an applicant's refusal to consent to a background check by your company damage his or her eligibility for a job?
2. Does your company specify to employers and/or job applicants where it searches for information—e.g., Facebook, Google, Twitter?
3. Is the information that your company collects from social media websites like Facebook limited to information that can be seen by everyone, or does your company endeavor to access restricted information, for example by creating a Facebook profile with the same city and/or alma mater of an applicant, in an attempt to see information restricted by geographical or university network? Has your company ever endeavored to access a user's restricted information by joining the user's network of "friends" on sites like Facebook?
4. Companies like Google and Facebook have faced scrutiny in the past for making public portions of their users' information that the users had set as private, often without the consent of users. This has resulted in previously private information, such as pictures, being made publicly available against the wishes of the users. Users are then required to opt out of sharing information they had previously thought to be private. Does your company include such information in its reports?
5. If your company conducts multiple background checks on an applicant, to what extent does it reuse information it has collected in previous checks? If your company were to gain access to private information in a manner contemplated in the previous question, and found that it no longer had access to such information in a subsequent search, would it include the previously accessed information in subsequent reports?

Terms of Service and Intellectual Property Violations

1. The reports that your company prepares for employers contain screenshots of the sources of the information your company compiles. One publicly available report contains pictures of a user's Facebook profile, LinkedIn profile, blog posts for a previous employer, and personal websites. These websites are typically governed by terms of service agreements that prohibit the collection, dissemination, or sale of users' content without the consent of the user and/or the website. LinkedIn's user agreement, for example, states that one may not "rent, lease, loan, trade, sell/re-sell access to LinkedIn or any information therein, or the equivalent, in whole or in part." Your company's business model seems to necessitate violating these agreements. Does your company operate in compliance with the agreements found on sites whose content your company compiles and sells? If so, how?

2. More troubling than the apparent disregard of these websites' terms of service are what appear to be significant violations of users' intellectual property rights to control the use of the content that your company collects and sells. Your company includes pictures in its background reports; example reports have included a picture depicting the subject holding a gun to illustrate alleged "potentially violent behavior." These pictures, taken from sites like Flickr and Picasa, are often licensed by the owner for a narrow set of uses, such as non-commercial use only or a prohibition on derivative works. Does your company obtain permission from the owners of these pictures to use, sell, or modify them?"

The full text of the letter is available at: www.blumenthal.senate.gov/newsroom/press/release/blumenthal-franken-call-on-social-intelligence-corp-to-clarify-privacy-practice

Facebook Warns Employers Asking Job Applicants for Social Media Passwords
May Expose Businesses to Legal Liability

Responding to an increase in reports of employers seeking to gain inappropriate access to social network profiles of job applicants, online social media giant Facebook issued a warning to employers in a recent blog posted on the company website – 'Protecting Your Passwords and Your Privacy' – that the practice of asking job applicants for their social media passwords "undermines the privacy expectations and the security of both the user and the user's friends" and could potentially expose businesses to "unanticipated legal liability."

In a blog dated March 23, 2012, Erin Egan, Facebook's Chief Privacy Officer, responded to recent news reports of employers "seeking to gain inappropriate access" to the social media profiles of job applicants and employees. She also said that Facebook would "take action to protect the privacy and security" of users and consider "initiating legal action" where appropriate. The entire blog is below:

> **"Protecting Your Passwords and Your Privacy**
>
> In recent months, we've seen a distressing increase in reports of employers or others seeking to gain inappropriate access to people's Facebook profiles or private information. This practice undermines the privacy expectations and the security of both the user and the user's friends. It also potentially exposes the employer who seeks this access to unanticipated legal liability.
>
> The most alarming of these practices is the reported incidences of employers asking prospective or actual employees to reveal their passwords. If you are a Facebook user, you should never have to share your password, let anyone access your account, or do anything that might jeopardize the security of your account or violate the privacy of your friends. We have worked really hard at Facebook to give you the tools to control who sees your information.
>
> As a user, you shouldn't be forced to share your private information and communications just to get a job. And as the friend of a user, you shouldn't have to worry that your private information or communications will be revealed to someone you don't know and didn't intend to share with just because that user is looking for a job. That's why we've made it a violation of Facebook's Statement of Rights and Responsibilities to share or solicit a Facebook password.
>
> We don't think employers should be asking prospective employees to provide their passwords because we don't think it's right the thing to do. But it also may cause problems for the employers that they are not anticipating. For example, if an employer sees on Facebook that someone is a

member of a protected group (e.g. over a certain age, etc.) that employer may open themselves up to claims of discrimination if they don't hire that person.

Employers also may not have the proper policies and training for reviewers to handle private information. If they don't—and actually, even if they do–the employer may assume liability for the protection of the information they have seen or for knowing what responsibilities may arise based on different types of information (e.g. if the information suggests the commission of a crime).

Facebook takes your privacy seriously. We'll take action to protect the privacy and security of our users, whether by engaging policymakers or, where appropriate, by initiating legal action, including by shutting down applications that abuse their privileges.

While we will continue to do our part, it is important that everyone on Facebook understands they have a right to keep their password to themselves, and we will do our best to protect that right.

– Erin Egan, Chief Privacy Officer, Policy"

The blog is available at: www.facebook.com/notes/facebook-and-privacy/protecting-your-passwords-and-your-privacy/326598317390057.

ADDENDUM - CHAPTER 16

E-Verify History and Milestones

Descriptions of E-Verify History and Milestones

Here is a chronological summary of important milestones of the E-Verify Program taken from the 'History and Milestones' page of the USCIS website at www.uscis.gov/e-verify/about-program/history-and-milestones.

Year	Description of E-Verify History and Milestone	Number of Participating Employers
1986	**The Immigration Reform and Control Act of 1986 (IRCA) Enacted:** The Immigration Reform and Control Act (IRCA) of 1986 required employers to examine documentation from each newly hired employee to prove his or her identity and eligibility to work in the United States. This act led to the Form I-9, Employment Eligibility Verification, requiring employees to attest to their work eligibility, and employers to certify that the documents presented reasonably appear (on their face) to be genuine and to relate to the individual.	
1996	**Illegal Immigration Reform and Immigrant Responsibility Act of 1996 (IIRIRA) Enacted:** The Illegal Immigration Reform and Immigrant Responsibility Act (IIRIRA) of 1996 required the then Immigration and Naturalization Service (INS) – which became part of the U.S. Department of Homeland Security in 2003 – to conduct three distinct pilot programs: Basic Pilot, the Citizen Attestation Pilot, and the Machine-Readable Document Pilot. These pilots were used to determine the best method of verifying an employee's employment verification.	
1997	**Basic Pilot Program Launched:** The INS, in conjunction with the Social Security Administration (SSA), implemented the Basic Pilot Program in California, Florida, Illinois, Nebraska, New York and Texas. The Basic Pilot Program was voluntary and allowed employers to confirm the work eligibility of their newly hired employees. The Basic Pilot Program used information from the employee's Form I-9 and compared it to the information in INS and SSA records. To verify information with SSA, employers were required to call SSA. Once the SSA information was confirmed by phone, the employer entered I-9 data into a computer program which transmitted the data to INS via a modem connection.	
1999	**Designated Agent Basic Pilot Launched:** INS, in conjunction with the Social Security Administration (SSA), implemented the Designated Agent Basic Pilot Program. The Designated Agent Basic Pilot Program was voluntary and allowed employers to use a third-party agent to confirm the work eligibility of their newly hired employees.	
2001	**Basic Pilot Program Reauthorized:** Congress reauthorized and extended the Basic Pilot program until 2003.	**1,064 employers enrolled in E-Verify**

Year	Description of E-Verify History and Milestone	Number of Participating Employers
2003	**Basic Pilot Program Extension and Expansion Act of 2003 Enacted:** Congress enacted the Basic Pilot Program Extension and Expansion Act of 2003. This extended the Basic Pilot Program to November 2008. The new law also required the expansion of the Basic Pilot Program to all 50 states no later than December 1, 2004.	**2,144 employers enrolled in E-Verify**
2004	**Basic Pilot Program Access Expanded to World Wide Web:** The Basic Pilot Program implemented a new Web-based access method to confirm employment eligibility. The new Web-based access method allowed users to access Basic Pilot through any Internet-capable computer. Other features of the Internet version include online enrollment, reporting capability for users, and availability of the web interface 23 hours a day.	**3,478 employers enrolled in E-Verify**
2007	**Basic Pilot Improved and Renamed E-Verify:** The Basic Pilot Program was renamed E-Verify. Along with the new name, the program added more features including an automatic flagging system that prompts employers to double-check the data entered into the web interface for those cases that are about to result in a mismatch. This change reduced data entry errors and initial mismatches by approximately 30 percent. The launch of E-Verify also marked the addition of photo matching. Photo matching is the first step in incorporating biometric data into the web interface. Photo matching was developed for employees presenting a Permanent Resident Card or Employment Authorization Document, and allows the employer to match the photo on an employee's document with the photo in USCIS records. State workforce agencies were encouraged to use E-Verify to confirm the employment eligibility of any worker referred to an employer in response to an H-2A job order.	**24,463 employers enrolled in E-Verify**
2009	**Congress authorizes a three year extension of E-Verify until the end of September 2012 & Federal Contractor Regulation Goes into Effect:** On September 8, 2009, the "Federal Contractor Regulation" went into effect. The new rule implements Executive Order 12989, as amended on June 6, 2008. Executive Order 12989 directs federal agencies to require many federal contractors entering into new contracts to use E-Verify on all new employees, and on existing employees working on covered federal contracts.	**156,659 employers enrolled in E-Verify**
2011	**Self-Check Goes Nationwide & USCIS Launches Spanish E-Verify:** E-Verify Self-Check ("Self Check"), a voluntary, fast, free and simple service that allows individuals to check their employment eligibility in the United States, launched and expanded to residents of 21 states. In May 2011, USCIS launched Spanish E-Verify, which contains important information for both employees and employers in Spanish. USCIS plans to expand the E-Verify Spanish web pages with additional sections on an ongoing basis.	**292,624 employers enrolled in E-Verify**
2012	**Self Check Expands Nationwide:** In February, USCIS announced the nationwide expansion of Self Check allowing workers anywhere in the U.S. to check their own work eligibility. This expansion is also available in Washington D.C., Puerto Rico, Guam, the U.S. Virgin Islands, and the Commonwealth of the Northern Mariana Islands. In March, USCIS redesigned the Self Check Webpages.	**404,295 employers enrolled in E-Verify**
2013	**Fraud Alert:** On November 18, 2013, Verification deployed a process to lock Social Security numbers (SSNs) suspected of fraudulent use in E-Verify. This enhancement helps combat identity fraud by identifying and deterring fraudulent	**482,694 employers enrolled in E-**

Year	Description of E-Verify History and Milestone	Number of Participating Employers
	use of SSNs for employment eligibility verification. There is no change to the E-Verify process for employers as a result of this enhancement.	Verify
2014	**E-Verify's 500,000th Employer:** On January 3, 2014, more than 500,000 employers were enrolled in E-Verify. FRONTLINE Selling, LLC, of Alpharetta, Georgia, was the 500,000th employer to enroll in E-Verify.	**553,626 employers enrolled in E-Verify**
2015	**myE-Verify Expands:** On April 12, 2015, myE-Verify became available nationwide.	**602,621* employers enrolled in E-Verify *As of 5/15/2015**

Importance of Reviewing EPLI Policy

The article below, *"Importance of Reviewing EPLI Policy,"* by Attorney Scott M. Paler, Partner, Chair of Labor and Employment Practice Group, DeWitt Ross & Stevens S.C., explains how Employment Practices Liability Insurance (EPLI) coverage is not *created equal*.

Importance of Reviewing EPLI Policy

By Attorney Scott M. Paler,
Partner, Chair of Labor and Employment Practice Group, DeWitt Ross & Stevens S.C.

It has become commonplace for employers to obtain Employment Practices Liability Insurance (EPLI) to provide protection from employment-related claims, including potential background screening claims. Although such EPLI coverage can indeed provide protection from background screening lawsuits, not all EPLI coverage is "created equal."

Employers are well advised to make sure that they understand the details of their prospective or actual EPLI coverage to ensure that they are not surprised later. Below are some questions to consider before signing on or renewing an EPLI policy.

1. Does the policy contain an "exclusion" for "Privacy," "Consumer Protection," or "FCRA" claims?

Because background screening claims have been increasing in number, and because the damage awards and settlements associated with background screening claims have been surprisingly high, many insurers are now taking steps to exclude background screening claims from EPLI coverage. Often, such exclusions take one of three forms: a "privacy claim" exclusion, a "consumer protection claim" exclusion, or a "Fair Credit Reporting Act (FCRA)" exclusion. Some, but not all insurers, are willing to add coverage for these types of claims for an additional fee. Employers that want to make sure that they have EPLI coverage for background screening claims should either carefully review their policy or work with an experienced attorney to do so.

2. Does the policy contain an "exclusion" for "intentional or willful acts"?

Insurance policies typically exclude coverage for any claim based upon an "intentionally dishonest or fraudulent act or omission" or "willful violation of any statute, rule, or law." However, some policies appear to suggest that a simple allegation of intentional or fraudulent conduct may lead to coverage denial, while others provide coverage up until a judge or jury says that the defendant acted in an intentional or willful manner. Since most background screening lawsuits allege willfulness, this policy language distinction can be meaningful. Ideally, a policy would provide coverage for alleged intentional or willful conduct unless and until a "final adjudication" determined such conduct was willful or intentional.

3. Does the policy contain an "exclusion" for class action lawsuits?

Not all insurance policies cover class action lawsuits. Some do. Some don't. It is important to realize that background screening class action lawsuits are sharply increasing in number. If an employer has EPLI coverage, but such coverage excludes class actions, an employer may lack insurance coverage for the most concerning background screening claims.

4. Does the policy contain an "exclusion" for "fines or penalties"?

Many EPLI policies exclude coverage for any "fine" or "penalty" assessed against the employer. This is important because most background screening class action lawsuits seek only "statutory damages" of $100 to $1000 per violation under the FCRA, and some insurers have taken the position that "statutory damages" are excluded "penalties." As of this printing, at least one insurer has lost on this argument, but there are certain to be more coverage challenges using this theory. Employers may wish to take this issue into account as they weigh EPLI options. For example, they may wish to seek confirmation from their insurance carrier that "statutory damages" are not excluded "penalties."

5. Does the policy have a cap on coverage at a million dollars or lower?

Although a million dollars of coverage typically exceeds the amount of potential damages in a single-plaintiff background screening case, it may fall well short of possible damages in a class action lawsuit. It is not unusual to see background screening class actions involving hundreds or thousands of applicants or employees, which naturally drives up the amount in dispute. Although experienced observers would remind employers that there is much to consider in deciding the appropriate amount of coverage, employers are well advised to thoughtfully consider this issue.

6. Does the policy have a deductible below $10,000 or over $75,000?

The "deductible" refers to the amount an employer will pay on its own in connection with a new lawsuit before reimbursements "kick in." EPLI deductibles range widely. It is not unusual to see deductibles as low as $2,500 or as high as $100,000. The amount of the deductible profoundly impacts the extent to which the policy will provide meaningful coverage as well as the cost of the policy. For example, a deductible of $100,000 will mean that an employer will often have no coverage for single- plaintiff suits since single-plaintiff suits typically involve attorneys' fees and resolutions falling below $100,000. Smart employers will think strategically about the deductible to ensure that they are getting helpful coverage without "overpaying." Many employers find that deductibles in the $20,000 range are "just right," but the "best" deductible varies from employer to employer.

ADDENDUM - CHAPTER 17

EU-U.S. Privacy Shield Article

The following is an article containing detailed analysis of the EU-U.S. Privacy Shield submitted for this book by attorney Kevin L. Coy, Partner, Arnall Golden Gregory LLP, entitled 'EU/US Privacy Shield Program Replaces Safe Harbor as an Additional Data Transfer Mechanism from the EU to the United States.'

EU/US Privacy Shield Program Replaces Safe Harbor as an Additional Data Transfer Mechanism from the EU to the United States

On August 1, 2016 the U.S. Department of Commerce began accepting self-certifications from eligible U.S. organizations for participation in the EU-US Privacy Shield program ("Privacy Shield").[3] Privacy Shield can be used by eligible participating U.S. organizations to facilitate the transfer of personal data from the 28 European Union Member States as well as Norway, Iceland, and Liechtenstein to the United States.[4] The European Union approved an adequacy decision for the Privacy Shield on July 12th,[5] deeming the program to be an adequate basis for transferring personal data from the European Union to the United States. The Privacy Shield replaces the EU-US Safe Harbor Program ("Safe Harbor") which effectively was struck down as a valid transfer mechanism in October 2015, when the European Court of Justice ("ECJ") invalidated the European Commission adequacy finding for that program.

Participation in Privacy Shield is voluntary. The new Privacy Shield builds upon and "enhances" the requirements of the old Safe Harbor. Participation in the Privacy Shield, like Safe Harbor before it, will be limited to organizations subject to the investigatory and enforcement authority of the Federal Trade Commission ("FTC"), including background screeners, or the Department of Transportation (other US enforcement agencies may be added later). Privacy Shield registration fees are based on the revenue of the participating company and ranged from $250 to $3250.[6]

Like the Safe Harbor program that preceded it, the Privacy Shield is organized around seven primary principles: Notice; Choice; Accountability for Onward Transfer; Security; Data Integrity and Purpose Limitation; Access; and Recourse, Enforcement and Liability.[7] The Privacy Shield also includes a series of sixteen "supplemental principles" which replace the "Frequently Asked Questions" that were used in the Safe Harbor program.[8]

---

[3] *See www.privacyshield.gov*

[4] It is anticipated that the United States and Switzerland will replace the US/Swiss Safe Harbor program with a program similar to the Privacy Shield. Transfers of personal data from the United Kingdom to the United States were covered by the Privacy Shield when the program launched because the United Kingdom was still a member of the European Union. The longer term applicability of the Privacy Shield to transfers from the UK as a result of the anticipated departure of the United Kingdom from the EU (the so-called "Brexit") remains to be determined.

[5] "Commission Implementing Decision of 12.7.2016 pursuant to Directive 95/46/EC of the European Parliament and of the Council on the adequacy of the protection provided by the EU-U.S. Privacy Shield" C(2016) 4176 (available online at: http://ec.europa.eu/justice/data-protection/files/privacy-shield-adequacy-decision_en.pdf).

[6] An additional, yet to be announced, levy on participants is expected for support of the Privacy Shield's arbitration program.

[7] The text of the seven Privacy Shield Principles follow this article.

[8] The Supplemental Principles address: Access; Sensitive Data; Journalistic Exceptions; Secondary Liability; Performing Due Diligence and Conducting Audits; The Role of the Data Protection Authorities; Self-Certification; Verification; Human Resources Data; Obligatory Contracts for Onward Transfers; Dispute Resolution and Enforcement; Choice -- Timing of Opt-Out; Travel Information; Pharmaceutical and Medical Products; Public Record and

Privacy Shield involves obligations under each of the seven principles, including, for example:

- **Notice.** Participating organizations will be required to address 13 points laid out in the enhanced notice principle, including information about its participation in the Privacy Shield, its information practices, and information about how the organization's promises can be enforced and the organization's potential liability for failures to comply.
- **Choice.** As was the case under Safe Harbor, Privacy Shield participating organizations will be required to provide individuals with choice as to whether their personal information is disclosed to third parties (other than service providers) or used for purposes other than those for which the information was originally collected.
- **Accountability for Onward Transfer**. The Privacy Shield includes significant enhancements to the Safe Harbor's Onward Transfer Principle, which governs how the personal information may be transferred by a Privacy Shield participating organization to other parties.
  - Contracts will be required for transfers of personal information by a Privacy Shield participant to third-party controllers.
  - In the case of transfers to service providers (referred to as third-party agents in the Privacy Shield documents) contracts will be required and participating companies will be required to take reasonable and appropriate steps to ensure that their agents effectively process the data transferred. Participating companies also will be required to take steps to address unauthorized processing by third-party agents and provide the Department of Commerce, upon request, with a summary or representative copy of the privacy provisions of its contracts with its third-party agents.
  - Organizations that self-certify for participation in the Privacy Shield within two months of its effective date were given up to nine months from the date they certify to bring existing relationships with third parties into compliance.
  - In addition, a participating organization will remain liable under the Principles if its agent processes personal information in a manner inconsistent with the Principles, unless the organization proves that it is not responsible for the event giving rise to the damage.
- **Security.** Participating organizations must take reasonable and appropriate measures to protect personal information from loss, misuse and unauthorized access, disclosure, alteration and destruction, taking into due account the risks involved in the processing and the nature of the personal data.
- **Data Integrity and Purpose Limitation**. As was the case under Safe Harbor, personal data generally must be relevant to the purposes for which it is being processed. Processing must be compatible with the purposes for which it was originally collected or subsequently authorized by the individual and participating organizations must take reasonable steps to ensure that personal data is reliable for its intended use, accurate, complete, and current. Privacy Shield also includes a new data retention limitation which provides, with certain exceptions, that personal data may only be retained for as long as it serves a purpose of processing compatible with the purposes for which it was originally collected or for which processing was subsequently authorized by the individual.
- **Access**. As was the case under Safe Harbor, individuals have a right to access personal information about them that a participating organization holds and be able to correct, amend, or delete that information where it is inaccurate, or has been processed in violation of the Principles, except where the burden or expense of providing access would be disproportionate to the risks to the individual's privacy in the case in question, or where the rights of persons other than the individual would be violated.
- **Recourse, Enforcement and Liability**.
  - The expectation is that if an individual objects to the manner in which the participating organization is processing data about the individual, then the individual will take that complaint to the participating organization.

Publicly Available Information; and Access Requests by Public Authorities. The text of the Supplemental Principles is available at www.privacyshield.gov.

- Participating organizations must select an independent third party dispute mechanism for resolution of disputes that the company cannot resolve directly with the individual. The participating organization can choose which available mechanism it will use, as was the case under Safe Harbor. The exception is human resources data, which is subject to mandatory cooperation with a panel of EU data protection authorities (DPAs) for dispute resolution.
- The FTC has committed to giving priority to Privacy Shield Complaints from the DPAs, third-party independent dispute mechanisms, and the Department of Commerce.
- Participating organizations also must provide information relating to the Privacy Shield when requested by the Department of Commerce and organizations must respond expeditiously to complaints regarding their compliance that are referred through the Department by the DPAs.
- Under the Privacy Shield, an individual has a new right to initiate arbitration as a "residual" remedy if other dispute resolution mechanisms fail to resolve the issue.
  - The limited purposes of the arbitration are: (a) to determine whether the company has violated its obligations under the principles; and (b) whether any such violation remains fully or partially unresolved.
  - The arbitration panel is not authorized to impose monetary relief, but has the authority to impose only individual-specific non-monetary equitable relief.
  - Prior to initiating arbitration, an individual is required to file an internal complaint with the implicated participating organization, seek recourse through an independent recourse mechanism (other than arbitration), and file a complaint through the DPAs.
  - The ultimate arbitration decision is binding—barring claims for monetary damages otherwise available in the courts. Either party may seek to set aside or enforce the award pursuant to the Federal Arbitration Act. The venue for such action would be in the Federal District Court where the primary place of business of the company is located.
  - The Department of Commerce and the European Commission will develop a list of at least 20 arbitrators. The arbitrators must be independent and qualified U.S. lawyers with experience in privacy law. The arbitral rules will be developed by the Department of Commerce and the European Commission based on an existing set of rules (such as AAA or JAMS). The rules must provide that: (1) the individual exhausted his remedies prior to initiating arbitration, (2) there is no duplication of remedies and procedures; (3) FTC action may proceed in parallel; (4) governmental bodies cannot participate in the arbitrations; (5) the location will be in the U.S. but the individual may participate by video or telephone; (6) language of arbitration will be English but a free translation may be available to the individual; (7) arbitration will be confidential; (8) discovery may be available; and (8) arbitration should be completed within 90 days of the notice.
  - The cost of arbitration will be covered from a fund financed by contributions from the companies participating in the Privacy Shield. Attorney's fees are not covered by the fund. The amount of contributions will be based on the size of the company and determined annually by the Department of Commerce and the Commission. The arbitration fee is expected to be announced in late 2016 or early 2017.

The Department of Commerce will have an enhanced role in administering the Privacy Shield program. Including:
- Verifying information provided as part of the self-certification process;
- Verifying participation in a third party dispute resolution mechanism;
- Expanding follow-up efforts with organizations that cease to participate in the Privacy Shield;
- Searching for and address false claims of participation in the Privacy Shield;
- Conducting periodic compliance reviews and assessments of the program;
- Tailoring its Privacy Shield website for different audiences (EU citizens; EU businesses, and US businesses);
- Increasing cooperation with the DPAs;
- Facilitating resolution of complaints received from the DPAs;

- Establishing the arbitration program (discussed above); and
- Participating in annual reviews of the Privacy Shield with EU officials.

While not likely to be relevant to the typical commercial organization participating in Privacy Shield, the Program also addresses mechanisms for handling complaints from EU citizens about the practices of the National Security Agency and other agencies, including an Ombudsman at the State Department to address complaints from EU citizens that are submitted by EU officials.

Companies that chose to self-certify for participation in the Privacy Shield program are expected, with one limited-time exception, to be in full compliance at the time they self-certify. Companies that self-certified for Privacy Shield during the first two months (i.e. by September 30, 2016) were given additional time (not to exceed nine months from the organization's self-certification date) to bring their commercial contracts involving the onward transfer of personal information to third parties into compliance with the new Privacy Shield requirements. During this transition period, however, certain interim steps are required, such as ensuring that contractors provide at least the same level of protection as required by the Privacy Shield Principles.

Companies considering participation in the Privacy Shield program should consider when to join the new program. For some organizations, the additional time to bring partner contracts into compliance with the new onward transfer requirements may have been a significant incentive to sign up early for the new program. Other organizations may prefer to wait to see if the new program survives the expected legal challenges in the EU, although it may take several years for such challenges to work their way to the ECJ, which was the court that effectively struck down Safe Harbor. The Privacy Shield also is subject to an annual review by EU and US officials, which means that the program's requirements could be much more dynamic than was the case under the Safe Harbor program, which was not significantly revised between its adoption in 2000 and the invalidation of the program's adequacy decision in 2015.

Privacy Shield Principles

NOTICE

a. An organization must inform individuals about:
  i. its participation in the Privacy Shield and provide a link to, or the web address for, the Privacy Shield List,
  ii. the types of personal data collected and, where applicable, the entities or subsidiaries of the organization also adhering to the Principles,
  iii. its commitment to subject to the Principles all personal data received from the EU in reliance on the Privacy Shield,
  iv. the purposes for which it collects and uses personal information about them,
  v. how to contact the organization with any inquiries or complaints, including any relevant establishment in the EU that can respond to such inquiries or complaints,
  vi. the type or identity of third parties to which it discloses personal information, and the purposes for which it does so,
  vii. the right of individuals to access their personal data,
  viii. the choices and means the organization offers individuals for limiting the use and disclosure of their personal data,
  ix. the independent dispute resolution body designated to address complaints and provide appropriate recourse free of charge to the individual, and whether it is: (1) the panel established by DPAs, (2) an alternative dispute resolution provider based in the EU, or (3) an alternative dispute resolution provider based in the United States,
  x. being subject to the investigatory and enforcement powers of the FTC, the Department of Transportation or any other U.S. authorized statutory body,
  xi. the possibility, under certain conditions, for the individual to invoke binding arbitration,

    xii. the requirement to disclose personal information in response to lawful requests by public authorities, including to meet national security or law enforcement requirements, and

    xiii. its liability in cases of onward transfers to third parties.

b.   This notice must be provided in clear and conspicuous language when individuals are first asked to provide personal information to the organization or as soon thereafter as is practicable, but in any event before the organization uses such information for a purpose other than that for which it was originally collected or processed by the transferring organization or discloses it for the first time to a third party.

CHOICE

a.   An organization must offer individuals the opportunity to choose (opt out) whether their personal information is (i) to be disclosed to a third party or (ii) to be used for a purpose that is materially different from the purpose(s) for which it was originally collected or subsequently authorized by the individuals. Individuals must be provided with clear, conspicuous, and readily   available   mechanisms   to   exercise   choice.

b.   By derogation to the previous paragraph, it is not necessary to provide choice when disclosure is made to a third party that is acting as an agent to perform task(s) on behalf of and under the instructions of the organization. However, an organization shall always enter into a contract with the agent.

c.   For sensitive information (i.e., personal information specifying medical or health conditions, racial or ethnic origin, political opinions, religious or philosophical beliefs, trade union membership or information specifying the sex life of the individual), organizations must obtain affirmative express consent (opt in) from individuals if such information is to be (i) disclosed to a third party or (ii) used for a purpose other than those for which it was originally collected or subsequently authorized by the individuals through the exercise of opt-in choice. In addition, an organization should treat as sensitive any personal information received from a third party where the third party identifies and treats it as sensitive.

ACCOUNTABILITY FOR ONWARD TRANSFER

a.   To transfer personal information to a third party acting as a controller, organizations must comply with the Notice and Choice Principles. Organizations must also enter into a contract with the third-party controller that provides that such data may only be processed for limited and specified purposes consistent with the consent provided by the individual and that the recipient will provide the same level of protection as the Principles and will notify the organization if it makes a determination that it can no longer meet this obligation. The contract shall provide that when such a determination is made the third party controller   ceases   processing   or   takes   other   reasonable   and   appropriate   steps   to   remediate.

b.   To transfer personal data to a third party acting as an agent, organizations must: (i) transfer such data only for limited and specified purposes; (ii) ascertain that the agent is obligated to provide at least the same level of privacy protection as is required by the Principles; (iii) take reasonable and appropriate steps to ensure that the agent effectively processes the personal information transferred in a manner consistent with the organization's obligations under the Principles; (iv) require the agent to notify the organization if it makes a determination that it can no longer meet its obligation to provide the same level of protection as is required by the Principles; (v) upon notice, including under (iv), take reasonable and appropriate steps to stop and remediate unauthorized processing; and (vi) provide a summary or a representative copy of the relevant privacy provisions of its contract with that agent to the Department upon request.

SECURITY

a.   Organizations creating, maintaining, using or disseminating personal information must take reasonable and appropriate measures to protect it from loss, misuse and unauthorized access, disclosure, alteration and destruction, taking into due account the risks involved in the processing and the nature of the personal data.

DATA INTEGRITY AND PURPOSE LIMITATION

a.   Consistent with the Principles, personal information must be limited to the information that is relevant for the purposes of processing.[9] An organization may not process personal information in a way that is incompatible with the purposes for which it has been collected or subsequently authorized by the individual. To the extent necessary for those purposes, an organization must take reasonable steps to ensure that personal data is reliable for its intended use, accurate, complete, and current. An organization   must   adhere   to   the   Principles   for   as   long   as   it   retains   such   information.
b.   Information may be retained in a form identifying or making identifiable[10] the individual only for as long as it serves a purpose of processing within the meaning of 5a. This obligation does not prevent organizations from processing personal information for longer periods for the time and to the extent such processing reasonably serves the purposes of archiving in the public interest, journalism, literature and art, scientific or historical research, and statistical analysis. In these cases, such processing shall be subject to the other Principles and provisions of the Framework. Organizations should take reasonable and appropriate measures in complying with this provision.

ACCESS

a.   Individuals must have access to personal information about them that an organization holds and be able to correct, amend, or delete that information where it is inaccurate, or has been processed in violation of the Principles, except where the burden or expense of providing access would be disproportionate to the risks to the individual's privacy in the case in question, or where the rights of persons other than the individual would be violated.

RECOURSE ENFORCEMENT AND LIABILITY

a.   Effective privacy protection must include robust mechanisms for assuring compliance with the Principles, recourse for individuals who are affected by non-compliance with the Principles, and consequences for the organization when the Principles are not followed. At a minimum such mechanisms must include:

    i.   readily available independent recourse mechanisms by which each individual's complaints and disputes are investigated and expeditiously resolved at no cost to the individual and by reference to the Principles, and damages awarded where the applicable law or private-sector initiatives so provide;

    ii.   follow-up procedures for verifying that the attestations and assertions organizations make about their privacy practices are true and that privacy practices have been implemented as presented and, in particular, with regard to cases of non-compliance; and

    iii.   obligations to remedy problems arising out of failure to comply with the Principles by organizations announcing their adherence to them and consequences for such organizations. Sanctions must be sufficiently rigorous to ensure compliance by organizations.

b.   Organizations and their selected independent recourse mechanisms will respond promptly to inquiries and requests by the Department for information relating to the Privacy Shield. All organizations must respond expeditiously to complaints regarding compliance with the Principles referred by EU Member State authorities through the Department. Organizations that have chosen to cooperate with DPAs, including organizations that process human resources data, must respond directly to such authorities with regard to the investigation and resolution of complaints.

---

[9] Depending on the circumstances, examples of compatible processing purposes may include those that reasonably serve customer relations, compliance and legal considerations, auditing, security and fraud prevention, preserving or defending the organization's legal rights, or other purposes consistent with the expectations of a reasonable person given the context of the collection.

[10] In this context, if, given the means of identification reasonably likely to be used (considering, among other things, the costs of and the amount of time required for identification and the available technology at the time of the processing) and the form in which the data is retained, an individual could reasonably be identified by the organization, or a third party if it would have access to the data, then the individual is "identifiable."

c.   Organizations are obligated to arbitrate claims and follow the terms as set forth in Annex I, provided that an individual has invoked binding arbitration by delivering notice to the organization at issue and following the procedures and subject to conditions set forth in Annex I.

d.   In the context of an onward transfer, a Privacy Shield organization has responsibility for the processing of personal information it receives under the Privacy Shield and subsequently transfers to a third party acting as an agent on its behalf. The Privacy Shield organization shall remain liable under the Principles if its agent processes such personal information in a manner inconsistent with the Principles, unless the organization proves that it is not responsible for the event giving rise to the damage.

e.   When an organization becomes subject to an FTC or court order based on non-compliance, the organization shall make public any relevant Privacy Shield-related sections of any compliance or assessment report submitted to the FTC, to the extent consistent with confidentiality requirements. The Department has established a dedicated point of contact for DPAs for any problems of compliance by Privacy Shield organizations. The FTC will give priority consideration to referrals of non-compliance with the Principles from the Department and EU Member State authorities, and will exchange information regarding referrals with the referring state authorities on a timely basis, subject to existing confidentiality restrictions.

Selecting an International Screening Provider

The following article is by Kerstin Bagus, Director of Global Initiatives, ClearStar, and Andy Hellman, Managing Director, International & Strategic Initiatives, ClearStar.

Selecting an International Screening Provider

As you have seen from this chapter, conducting international background screening is very complex. It is possible for an employer to process some searches without outside assistance but an in-depth screen will require the help of a third party. There are literally hundreds, if not thousands, of companies and individuals around the world who provide screening services. How do you go about selecting a screening provider?

A good place to start is with the National Association of Professional Background Screeners (NAPBS). The website, www.napbs.com, has an employer oriented page11 with support documents for selecting a background screener. Members of NAPBS, especially those who are active in the Association and Committees, are dedicated to the industry and the quality of the results for employers and candidates. This is an international group, with members across the globe. The home page contains a directory which can be used to filter members by country and services. Large employers may want to consider membership in NAPBS if they are running a background screening unit in-house.

If you want to use a third party, you will need to decide if you need one global provider or multiple providers. Smaller companies may find a single provider to be the most helpful since managing multiple vendors is difficult when the volume is low. For larger companies, especially multi-nationals, the decision is more complex. A single provider brings the hope of a unified method of processing searches in all countries. Unfortunately, there are very few, true global providers. And, as we have seen in previous discussions, there are local and cultural aspects to consider. One size will not fit all. On the other hand, a network of all local providers can mean a hodge podge of standards, since each provider will have their own set of processes. Something as simple as an employment verification, if not standardized, can cause great variances. One provider makes one phone call and closes the search as unable to verify, where another provider may call 10 times in 15 days in an attempt to get a result. Managing large numbers of vendors is an expense for a company and increases risk, since the vendor's information

---

11   www.napbs.com/resources/for-employers-end-users/

security, data protection, and bribery risks must all be assessed. Plus, spreading work among multiple vendors causes a company to lose the economy of scale in pricing.

Here are some high-level things to look for when selecting a global background screener. These are not only good review points for global providers but can also help with domestic provider selection.

- **How do they select their service partners?** All background screeners must rely on service partners at some level. Even if background checks are only obtained from the United States, no screener has coverage in every U.S. courthouse with their own staff. Magnify this by all of the world's countries and potential services and you can see why a third party network is required. Ask the screener how they select their service partners. Screeners should have Service Agreements in place with their service partners, at a minimum. The Service Agreement should go beyond pricing and include data protection, security, and anti-bribery requirements. Look for a process that goes beyond just the signing of a contract.

- **How do they identify which background searches to offer?** Obtaining data is the easy part. It can be bought on the black market as well as in a legitimate setting. Look for a screener that has a process for evaluating what background searches to offer. Be cautious of any screener that indicates they offer searches just because their vendor network offers them.

- **Look for an understanding of global regulations.** The screening company should have a basic understanding of the global privacy regulations such as those in the EU, Canada, and Asia. Ask the company how they meet the basic global data protection regulations. Look for someone who understands, at least at a high level, the requirements of notice, consent, data minimization, accuracy, and subject access rights. With over 100 privacy regulations to keep track of, it's ok if the provider needs to rely on resources to know the specifics of a country's privacy regulation. What is of concern is if the provider has no understanding at all of global requirements.

- **Ask about the company's information security.** Without security you cannot meet data protection requirements. This is true outside of the U.S. and in the U.S.

- **Have them describe their version of the various global background searches.** A screener handling global work should understand the difference between a criminal record check and an Adverse Media check. Pick a few countries and ask them to describe the criminal record check process in those countries. In high corruption risk countries such as India, are they doing court checks or police checks? Why did they choose the type of search for that country? Here you are looking for an understanding of the risks of each process and how they mitigate those risks.

- **Ask about the process.** How does the screener get you the requirements for ordering the global background check? Is it available on a website or in the ordering portal? Ask to see an example to make sure the process is functional for your environment. How will the screener handle missing information? The requirement for additional information once a background check has been requested is ongoing. Even when the ordering requirements have been outlined and followed in minute detail, there will always be some source that will want something different. How does the screener communicate with the requestor to obtain this missing information? Does this process work within your environment?

- **Experience matters in global screening.** This is not to say that the only good global background screener is one that has been around for years. Many new companies are established by industry veterans, and many industry veterans work in the global supply chain to help new background screening companies. In such a complex environment, it is important to have access to experienced global screeners. A background check provider may not have this experience in-house but they may have a resource network to provide it. Ask how the screener gets their global support. Don't shy away from a young company just because they are new. But be cautious of any company who thinks they have all of the answers.

- **Knowledge of vendor in that particular region.** Nobody can be a specialist everywhere. Some vendors have more experience and knowledge in certain areas and regions than others. This can be due to where they have office locations, where their customers are located, where their staff has worked before, or what language capabilities the employees have. If a particular country or region is important for your company, it is important to ensure that your background screening provider has good support capabilities in that area. They should be able provide you with some information on local laws and regulations[12], what common practice is and what the local flavors are for each search.

- **Local language abilities.** For some searches, local language capabilities are not always important. However, for many searches, language skills can be critical to conducting a quality check. For example, when conducting verifications, some providers will always attempt a first call in English, while others may always try to use the local language. Depending on your needs, either one could be appropriate. A vendor doing calls in English might be sufficient if all you are trying to do is confirm that the person did graduate, or that they worked at the company. However, if you are concerned with verifying critical skills or experience, ensuring that nothing is 'lost in translation' can be very important. In this case, a vendor conducting calls in the local language might be very important.

You've Selected Your Global Provider; Now What?

Once you have selected a provider, have reasonable expectations. Background screening providers are experts in the area of background screening. They know where to get the information and have systems to allow for the order and delivery of the product. They are not law firms. A screening firm should have some information about the ability to obtain and use background checks in a country but they will be unable to provide detailed legal advice on the use in a specific country for a specific position.

Spend time with the provider to map out the searches you want and the countries from which you want them. Understand how the ordering requirements are provided, and follow them as closely as possible. Remember, providing the information required for the search when the order is placed is a key tool for a successful and quick search.

---

[12] Keep in mind that a background screening company is not a law firm and will not be able to provide legal advice.

FBI Fingerprinting vs. Name Checks

The Big Controversy over FBI Fingerprinting vs. Name Checks

The following materials that discuss the pros and cons of **Federal Bureau of Investigation (FBI) fingerprinting vs. name checks by professional screening companies** includes information and reports from the National Association of Professional Background Screeners (NAPBS), the National Employment Law Project (NELP), the Government Accountability Office (GAO), and the National Recreation and Park Association (NRPA).

Many FBI Criminal Background Checks for Employment Contain Inaccurate Information

An infographic released by the **National Association of Professional Background Screeners (NAPBS)** in April 2015 'A Comparison of Background Screening: PROFESSIONAL BACKGROUND SCREENING VS. FBI FINGERPRINT CHECKS' showed that fingerprint-based searches of the FBI database return an FBI Identification Record that is "a listing of information taken from fingerprint submissions in connection with arrests and, in some instances, federal employment, naturalization, or military service." Also:

- "A screening performed through the FBI database can only be done if the employer has legal authority under statute.
- A fingerprint search is not investigative; it only reflects information received by the FBI from states and municipalities.
- If a state or county fails to report arrest records or a court disposition then that data will not appear on the FBI Identification Record. This reliance on arrest and court records, coupled with the passive collection system can lead to a large number of incomplete files.
- FBI results are contingent upon the consumer having his/her prints taken by an approved vendor as well as FBI processing times.
- There is no single government database containing complete and up-to-date records regarding a person's criminal history."

Another section of the NAPBS infographic called 'How Professional Background Screening and Fingerprint-Based Searches Compare' revealed the following differences.

"Professional Background Screening:

- Pushed by market forces to maintain high levels of accuracy to remain competitive.
- Pushed by market forces to return results—both positive and negative—in a timely manner.
- Applicant's identity can be confirmed through alternate means such as middle name, DOB, address and other unique identifiers.
- Encourages review of sources other than databases to verify completeness of records.
- Screening allows supplementation of database records with the complete record and disposition information obtained directly from the source.
- Collection of information performed as part of an investigative process.
- Collected data gathered, investigated, analyzed, and checked for accuracy by a professional screener.

- Screening is tailored to provide a more complete picture of an applicant and may include education verification, employment verification, references, driving records, etc…based on the nature of the position and the employer's needs.
- Applicant in screening process protected by the Fair Credit Reporting Act.
- Applicant in screening process protected by state privacy laws.
- Screening performed by "ensuring maximum possible accuracy" of reported information.
- Can include information from sources within the United States and globally.
- Results returned within 48 – 72 hours."

The article also mentioned this about Professional Background Screening and Fingerprint-Based Searches:

- "Used to screen out potential threats to vulnerable populations and certain regulated industries.
- Incorrect information may be disputed by an applicant."
- Applicants required to submit fingerprints and are identified solely by existence of a fingerprint—no fingerprint, no information.
- Can only be performed when granted access by state or federal statute.
- Screening reliant solely on completeness of records in a database."

Source: http://pubs.napbs.com/pub.cfm?id=0BADA47F-070C-90D0-2115-7F00FC321FAD.

There's No Such Thing as a National Database for Background Checks

An article released in April 2013 by current NAPBS Executive Director Melissa Sorenson called "There's No Such Thing as a National Database for Background Checks" explains that "there currently is no such thing as a single national database that contains all criminal records in the United States." Instead, Sorenson explains that "there are actually many different databases used to conduct background checks on individuals." While the FBI database is considered the "gold standard," Sorenson says that it "is actually not one single database but a collection of different systems organized under the National Criminal Information Center (NCIC).

While these multi-jurisdictional databases may seem to be useful and serve a valid purpose for employment background screening, Sorenson warns employers to keep some key points in mind:

- *"National" Is A Misnomer. While multi-jurisdictional databases contain millions of records, there exists no single national database.*
- *Data Cannot be Counted on to be 100% Accurate and Complete. The data is only as accurate as the person adding it into the database at the time of record origination.*
- *Data Structures Within the Database are Not Always Reliable. When combining several different databases into one, the methods used to structure the data will impact search results.*
- *Use of any Data in an Employment Decision Must be FCRA-Compliant. Use of national criminal databases through third parties requires careful consideration and compliance with the FCRA.*

Source: http://pubs.napbs.com/pub.cfm?id=08D04294-ACC2-75D4-9A68-3749DAE8673B.

Many FBI Criminal Background Checks for Employment Contain Inaccurate Information

The National Employment Law Project (NELP) released a report in July 2013 – 'Wanted: Accurate FBI Background Checks for Employment' – that estimates 1.8 million workers a year are subjected to Federal Bureau of Investigation (FBI) background checks that contain "faulty or incomplete information" and that as many as 600,000 of those workers "may be prejudiced in their job search" because of inaccurate FBI records. The complete report is available at http://nelp.3cdn.net/bd23dee1b42cff073c_8im6va8d2.pdf.

The report from NELP — a national advocacy organization for the employment rights of lower-wage and unemployed workers — spotlights the failure of the FBI "to ensure that its records are accurate and complete." While arrests are recorded, the final disposition of cases often is not, which is a critical defect since NELP estimates that "one-third of felony arrests are ultimately dismissed and charges are frequently reduced." Other key findings of the 51-page report include:

- The use of FBI background checks for employment is rapidly increasing. Roughly 17 million FBI background checks were conducted for employment and licensing purposes in 2012, which is six times the number conducted a decade ago.
- Despite clear federal mandates that require the background reports to be complete and accurate, 50 percent of the FBI's records fail to include information on the final disposition of the case.
- African Americans are especially disadvantaged by the faulty records because people of color are consistently arrested at rates greater than their representation in the general population, and large numbers of those arrests never lead to conviction.

Two important points about the National Crime Information Center (NCIC) – the formal name for the automated database of criminal justice records maintained by the FBI – are:

- The NCIC is not nearly as complete as portrayed in the movies. Because of the chain of events that must happen in multiple jurisdictions in order for a crime to appear in NCIC, many records of crime do not make it into the system.
- The information the NCIC does have is predominantly arrest-related. The disposition of most crimes in NCIC must be obtained by searching at the adjudicating jurisdiction. Dispositions are important issue for employers.

GAO Report on Criminal History Records

The Government Accountability Office (GAO) – the "congressional watchdog" investigating how the federal government spends taxpayer dollars – released a report in March 2015 on the use of criminal background checks titled 'Criminal History Records: Additional Actions Could Enhance the Completeness of Records Used For Employment-Related Background Checks (GAO-15-162).' The complete report from the GAO is available at www.esrcheck.com/file/GAO-Criminal-History-Records-Report.pdf.

According to a 'GAO Highlights' document about the report, authorized employers use information from Federal Bureau Investigation (FBI) criminal history record checks to assess a person's suitability for employment or to obtain a license. States create criminal records and the FBI facilitates access to these records by other states for nationwide background checks. The GAO was asked to assess efforts to address concerns about incomplete records.

The GAO analyzed laws and regulations used to conduct criminal record checks and assessed the completeness of records; conducted a nationwide survey, which generated responses from 47 states and the District of Columbia; and interviewed officials that manage checks from the FBI and 4 states (California, Florida, Idaho, and Washington) selected based on geographic location and other factors.

The GAO report addresses to what extent:

- States conduct FBI record checks for selected employment sectors and face any challenges;
- States have improved the completeness of records, and remaining challenges that federal agencies can help mitigate; and
- Private companies conduct criminal record checks, the benefits those checks provide to employers, and any related challenges.

The GAO's nationwide survey found most states conducted FBI criminal history record checks for individuals working with vulnerable populations such as children and the elderly. The GAO report found that some states did not conduct FBI record checks because those states lacked a designated agency to review check results. The employment sectors that most used FBI criminal history record checks were:

- Job or license to be a teacher in schools;
- Youth development positions (e.g. Boys and Girls Club);

- Volunteers serving the elderly or individuals with disabilities; and
- National Service Program participants (e.g. AmeriCorps).

The GAO report also found that states improved the completeness of criminal history records used for FBI checks with more records containing both the arrest and final disposition (such as a conviction). Twenty states reported that more than 75 percent of their arrest records had dispositions in 2012, up from 16 states in 2006. However, there are still gaps such as incomplete records that can delay criminal record checks and affect applicants seeking employment.

Although the Department of Justice (DOJ) helped states improve the completeness of records, challenges remain. A Disposition Task Force created by the FBI's Advisory Policy Board in 2009 to address issues regarding disposition reporting has taken actions to better measure the completeness of state records and identify state requirements for reporting disposition information. However, the task force does not have plans with time frames for completing remaining goals. The GAO recommends that the FBI establish plans with time frames for these remaining goals and the DOJ concurred.

NRPA Compares Fingerprints vs. Social Security Trace

The following Q&As were taken from a **National Recreation and Park Association (NRPA)** web page article titled "NRPA Has Set the Bar for Background Checks."

"After ten years of surveys, focus groups, staff research, debate, and study, NRPA created the Recommended Guidelines for Credentialing outlining the best practices in conducting a comprehensive national criminal background check for park, recreation, and conservation agencies."

"Q. **Our current background check policy is to run fingerprints. The NRPA Recommended Guidelines for Credentialing uses Social Security numbers. Why?**

A. The primary goal of the NRPA Recommended Guidelines for Credentialing is to implement a consistent approach to screening among all parks, recreation, and conservation professionals in every state. And, to ensure staff and volunteers are validated as respectable, law abiding people with nothing in their background anywhere in any state that would pose a threat or present a risk.

Without verification of identity, to continue the process is futile. To conduct a proper, due diligent background check the FIRST step must be to verify the person is in fact who they claim to be. There are only two primary and court tested methods of verifying an applicant's identity for the purpose of employment screening: **collecting fingerprints and tracing social security numbers.** While the common assumption is that fingerprinting is the fail safe method, after exhaustive study of both methods, the NRPA concludes that the best outcome for this industry is through the social security trace with added steps that would maximize effectiveness and reduce errors.

Q. It has been a long standing practice that we have relied on fingerprints alone to determine identity because no two people have the same set. Why would social security numbers be better?

A. It would be inaccurate to say one method of identity verification is "better" than the other. Again, there are only two methods to verify identity and restricting the option to only one limit the agency's ability to take full advantage of both methods and to apply the most appropriate method to meet the specific needs of the agency.

Q. Isn't it a fact that by using the fingerprint method we will obtain everything we need to know about a person's background?

A. Fingerprinting gives only a partial story behind someone's background. There are a number of serious misdemeanors and other disqualifying offenses that result in many police jurisdictions issuing only a citation to appear in court to address the charges. **Because the offender was not jailed, no fingerprints were taken!** However, utilizing a social security number trace coupled with a county courthouse search (non fingerprint) reveals these offenses and case outcomes including charges, court dispositions, and sentencing. All this information is essential to determine if the individual qualifies to be appointed as paid or unpaid staff.

Q. When looking at both methods of identity verification specifically for conducting background checks on volunteers serving parks, recreation, and conservation what are some considerations that were given to recommend the social security trace over fingerprinting?

A. The primary considerations given to the social security trace method over fingerprinting include:

- The cost - State and federal fees over and above equipment and manpower

- The inconvenience, intrusiveness and is intimidating to many volunteers

- The impracticality – In many cases it can take weeks to obtain results

- The access – The NCIC (FBI) database is not available to Parks and Recreation agencies in every state

- The imperfection - 1 in 7 criminal records never make it to the NCIC database

- The inadequacy of information - May provide arrest numbers only with no details on crime or disposition – I.e. person matching fingerprint arrested 2 times – prompting a complete criminal records check with additional costs to be conducted to obtain the necessary information to qualify or disqualify this person

Q. In your research did you look at California LiveScan before deciding on using Social Security numbers?

A. Yes and the California LiveScan system came up short in our definition of "comprehensive" only revealing records associated with:

1. Crimes relating to child abuse or elder abuse

2. Sex Offenders within the State - Not Sex Offenders outside of the State

3. Convictions or incarcerations only in the last 10 years as a result of committing theft, robbery, burglary, or any felony only in the State of California

And, not revealing other potential disqualifying offenses like assault, battery, domestic violence, drug possession, indecent exposure, and lewd conduct just to name a few.

Source: www.nrpa.org/uploadedFiles/nrpaorg/Membership/Endorsed_Business_Provider/Fingerprints-Vs-Social-Security-Trace.pdf

Special Issues For Staffing Companies

The following article, **"Special Issues For Staffing Companies,"** is written by Scott Paler, Partner, Chair of Labor and Employment Practice Group, DeWitt Ross & Stevens S.C.. Mr. Paler also contributed another article "Importance of Reviewing EPLI Policy" in Chapter 20.

Special Issues For Staffing Companies

By Attorney Scott M. Paler,
Partner, Chair of Labor and Employment Practice Group, DeWitt Ross & Stevens S.C.

Background checks in the staffing context tend to give rise to additional complications and risks. Given the surge in background screening lawsuits, such issues should not be ignored. Below are example issues for staffing companies to think through.

1. **Should A Staffing Company's Client Be Permitted To View A Potential Worker's Background Screening Report?**

Many staffing companies provide their clients with a copy of a potential worker's background screening report to "prove" that the candidate does not have any red flags. Although this practice is understandable, it also carries some risk.

First, providing a report copy to the client may not be permitted under the staffing company's contract with the background screening agency. Many (and perhaps most) background screening contracts state that an end-user cannot share the report with any third-party.

Second, an entity cannot receive a copy of a background screening report unless it has obtained written consent from the applicant to do so. Often times staffing companies may share a copy of the report without the candidate ever providing written consent for another third-party to receive it, creating risks for both the staffing company and client.

Third, once a staffing company's client gains access to a report, it arguably becomes responsible for satisfying other legal obligations that it may not be aware of, such as adverse action obligations.

Fourth, a shared review of the background screening report may contribute to a finding that the staffing company and client are "joint employers." One or both parties may not be comfortable with this determination, as it can create additional legal obligations and consequences for the parties.

For all of these reasons, a decision as to whether to share the background screening report with the client deserves careful consideration. It should not be viewed as a "given."

2. Should A Staffing Contract Include Promises To Exclude Applicants With Certain Criminal Backgrounds?

Written contracts in the staffing space often contain promises to exclude potential workers with certain criminal backgrounds. For example, a contract may contain language confirming that "no felons shall be staffed" or "no individuals with criminal convictions shall be referred" or "no individuals with violent crimes or drug offenses shall be directed to client site."

Although this practice is popular, it may unwittingly expose both the staffing company and client to risk. An increasing number of states and municipalities have enacted laws limiting the types of criminal history that employers may consider. For example, California prohibits employers from considering certain marijuana convictions. Massachusetts bars employers from considering certain misdemeanors. And New York City requires employers to weigh a number of factors before excluding someone based on a criminal conviction. By inserting "black and white" contractual language confirming certain candidates with criminal histories will be automatically rejected, the staffing company may be providing a prospective plaintiff's attorney with strong evidence of discrimination or illegal employment practices. Therefore, staffing companies should carefully consider any contractual language pertaining to background checks.

3. Should A Staffing Company Honor A Request To Exclude A Candidate Based Upon Certain Criminal History Or Credit Information?

A staffing company obviously cannot force a client to accept a worker that it does not want. However, the risks associated with honoring any and all client requests to exclude workers with certain criminal or credit histories have escalated. Many staffing companies have begun efforts to try to lower some of these new risks. Such efforts include:

• Increased Client Education.

Some clients simply do not realize that the "no felons allowed" policies of yesteryear are now subject to attacks in ways that they never were in the 1980s or 1990s. Many clients also do not realize that under "joint employment" theories they may be held partially culpable for an unwise hiring decision. To address these information gaps, some staffing companies are conducting seminars to educate their clients. Others are simply alerting clients to issues when the need arises.

• Indemnification Agreements.

As background screening risks increase so too do the number of staffing companies asking for indemnification promises from their clients. Under an indemnification agreement, a client may promise to defend a staffing company if it is sued because of the client's strict background screening requirements. For business and client relationship reasons, however, not all staffing companies feel comfortable making such a request.

• Alternative Employment Opportunities.

Many staffing companies have redoubled efforts to find alternative employment opportunities for candidates rejected by a client due to rigid background screening policies. Even if a client will not budge on their criminal history or credit information requirements, the staffing company can often reduce risks by helping an applicant find another job before his or her frustration mounts.

The Index

About the Author Lester S. Rosen

Attorney at Law Lester S. Rosen is Founder and CEO of **Employment Screening Resources® (ESR)** – www.ESRcheck.com – a nationwide accredited background screening company located in Novato, California. He is the author of "The Safe Hiring Manual," the first comprehensive guide to background checks, and "The Safe Hiring Audit." A recognized background check expert, his speaking appearances have included numerous national and regional conferences, as well as international conferences. See: www.esrcheck.com/Stay-Updated/ESR-Speaks/. He has been quoted in websites, newspapers, and trade journals across the United States and the world.

In 1997, Mr. Rosen founded Employment Screening Resources with a mission to promote safe workplaces for employers, employees, and the public as well as to protect the rights of consumers. ESR – 'The Background Check Authority®' – provides accurate and actionable information, empowering clients to make informed safe hiring decisions. ESR is accredited by the National Association of Professional Background Screeners (NAPBS®) Background Screening Credentialing Council (BSCC) for successfully proving compliance with the Background Screening Agency Accreditation Program (BSAAP). ESR also completes annual SOC 2® audit reports to confirm the organization meets high standards set by the American Institute of Certified Public Accountants (AICPA) for protecting the privacy, security, and confidentiality of consumer information used for background checks.

Mr. Rosen was the chairperson of the steering committee that founded the NAPBS, the professional trade organization for the background screening industry, and also served as the first co-chairman. He has served as an expert witness and has testified on issues surrounding employment screening, safe hiring, due diligence.

Mr. Rosen has practiced civil litigation, is a former deputy District Attorney and as a criminal defense attorney represented numerous individuals accused of crimes in both state and federal court He has taught criminal law and criminal procedure at the University of California Hastings College of the Law. He was also an instructor at the Hastings College of Trial Advocacy. His jury trials have included murder, death penalty, and federal cases. He graduated UCLA with Phi Beta Kappa honors and received a J.D. degree from the University of California at Davis, serving on the Law Review. He holds the highest attorney rating of A.V. in the national Martindale-Hubbell listing of U.S. Attorneys.

To contact Mr. Rosen for a speaking engagement, story information, or professional consultation, please email lsr@esrcheck.com.

Regarding Updates and Changes to the Content

Updates to this book and important new information can be found online at www.esrcheck.com/The-Safe-Hiring-Manual/Updates.

There is no charge for this service.